Writers'
& Artists'
YEARBOOK
2024

Other Writers' and Artists' titles

Writers' & Artists' Guides to ...

Self-publishing
Writing for Children and YA by Linda Strachan
Getting Published by Alysoun Owen
How to Hook an Agent by James Rennoldson
How to Write by William Ryan

The Organised Writer: How to stay on top of all your projects and never miss a deadline by Antony Johnston

The Right Word: A Writer's Toolkit of Grammar, Vocabulary and Literary Terms

A Writer's Journal Workbook: Creating space for writers to be inspired by Lucy van Smit

Writers on Writing: A Book of Quotations

Writers' & Artists' Poetry Writers' Handbook by Sophia Blackwell

NEW in July 2023
Children's Writers' & Artists' Yearbook 2024
'A one-stop welcome to the world of publishing ... worth its weight in gold.'
Smriti Halls

You can buy copies of all these titles from your local bookseller or online at www.writersandartists.co.uk/shop

Writers' & Artists' YEARBOOK 2024

ONE HUNDRED AND SEVENTEETH EDITION

THE ESSENTIAL GUIDE TO THE MEDIA AND PUBLISHING INDUSTRIES

The perfect companion for writers of fiction and non-fiction,
poets, playwrights, journalists, and commercial artists

BLOOMSBURY YEARBOOKS
LONDON · OXFORD · NEW YORK · NEW DELHI · SYDNEY

BLOOMSBURY YEARBOOKS
Bloomsbury Publishing Plc
50 Bedford Square, London, WC1B 3DP, UK
29 Earlsfort Terrace, Dublin 2, Ireland

BLOOMSBURY YEARBOOKS, WRITERS' & ARTISTS' and the Diana logo are trademarks of
Bloomsbury Publishing Plc

First published in Great Britain 1906
This edition published 2023

A catalogue record for this book is available from the British Library

ISBN: PB: 978-1-3994-0889-9; eBook: 978-1-3994-0890-5

2 4 6 8 10 9 7 5 3 1

Typeset by DLxml, a division of RefineCatch Limited, Bungay, Suffolk
Printed and bound in Great Britain by CPI Group (UK) Ltd, Croydon, CRO 4YY

To find out more about our authors and books visit www.bloomsbury.com and sign up for our
newsletters.

Writers' & Artists' team
Editor Alysoun Owen
Assistant editor Eden Phillips Harrington
Articles copy-editor Virginia Klein
Listings editors Lisa Carden, Rebecca Collins, Lauren MacGowan
Editorial assistance Brooke James; Sophia Blackwell (poetry)
Production controller Rachel Murphy

A note from the Editor

This latest edition of the *Yearbook* does what it claims to do: it provides impartial, expert knowledge and information on all aspects of the writing and publishing processes. As such, it is useful for all types of writers – those starting out and those who have already made their work available to readers or viewers or theatre-goers. The content in this hefty tome is equally relevant to traditionally published (via a publisher and a literary agent) and self-published or indie authors, and indeed for who those who seek to do both. There is advice for writers *and* artists, as Claire Fuller's *Foreword* on page xiii makes clear; she is a perfect example of a writer who has changed creative lanes during the course of her career. Tom Tivnan, who reports for *The Bookseller*, the industry's main source of news, gives a roundup of the successes and the challenges from the last year, providing a succinct context for readers on the publishing landscape (see *The publishing year: news, views and trends* on page 102).

In addition to the enticements to get creative and find a home for your writing and illustration, the *Yearbook* provides up-to-date practical support on *all* aspects of being a writer. This includes the not-so-glamorous bits about money, legal matters and keeping body and soul together. In a time of inflation and economic restraint, the how-tos of living a writing life become even more acute. The *Yearbook* has long been respected for the breadth and depth of the advice it gives. Don't just take my word for it, look at the quotes from bestselling authors who have consulted these pages in the past, pages viii-ix.

New articles this year, on legal, financial and practical topics, in particular for indie authors, include *Protecting your content: piracy and IP* on page 714, *Paid-for publishing services: Is it a steal?* on page 605, *Understanding book design* by Catherine Lutman on page 608 and *Editing: what the professional writer needs to know* from Dea Parkin (on page 637). In addition, we have a new entry in the ever-expanding Literary agents section from Rebecca Carter: *Your non-fiction proposal for agents and publishers* (see page 403).

If you think your talents and ambitions lie in writing for magazines and newspapers, consult *How to write features for the national and regional press* by journalist Georgina Fuller (on page 6), as well as *The hidden art of B2B journalism* by Blake Evans-Pritchard (on page 10), who extols the benefits of writing for the trade press. Both pieces highlight the money that might be made (or not!) by writing for such publications and how to approach editors with your pitch.

We have new pieces to encourage the writer and the presenter in you, with articles from novelists Paula Hawkins (author of the international bestseller *The Girl on the Train*; read her *Writing thrilling fiction* on page 254) and Annie Garthwaite, whose *Reigniting the past: writing historical fiction* appears on page 268. Sam Delaney invites you to get to know your community in *Guerrilla podcasting* on page 348. Poet-publisher Aaron Kent makes a passionate case for 'degentrifying' the publishing industry, in *Being a poet and a publisher* on page 314, by encouraging poets to 'build a community and engage as part of one'. The range of opportunities for the budding poet are also explored by performance poet, lecturer and editor, Sophia Blackwell in her article *The portfolio poet* (on page 309).

Whatever your ambitions as a writer (or performer) and illustrator, I hope the articles and the contact details in this *Yearbook* set you firmly on the path to creative success.

Alysoun Owen
Editor

All articles, listings and other material in this *Yearbook* are reviewed and updated every year in consultation with the bodies, organisations, companies and individuals that we select for inclusion. To the best of our knowledge the websites, emails and other contact details are correct at the time of going to press.

Short story competition

The annual *Writers' & Artists' Yearbook* Short Story Competition offers published and aspiring writers the chance to win a place on an Arvon Residential Writing Week (worth £850). In addition, the winner's story will be published on the Writers & Artists website.

   To enter the competition, submit a short story (for adults) of no more than 2,000 words, on the theme of 'risk' by 12 February 2024 to waybcompetitions@bloomsbury.com. For full details, terms and conditions, and to find out more about how to submit your entry, visit www.writersandartists.co.uk/competitions.

ARVON hosts residential creative writing courses in three rural writing houses in the UK. With the opportunity to live and work with professional writers, participants transform their writing through workshops, one-to-one tutorials, time and space to write. Five-day courses and shorter courses are available in a wide range of genres and have provided inspiration to thousands of people at all stages of their writing lives. An online programme of writing courses, masterclasses and live readings also runs year-round. Find out more and book a course online at www.arvon.org.

More than a book

The Writers & Artists **website** (www.writersandartists.co.uk) offers more free content and resources to compliment the *Yearbook*.

Here you will find hundreds of **articles** on the writing and publishing process, regular **writing competitions**, and a **community** space to share your work or ask questions about the entire creative process. Brand new features, such as being able to annotate and bookmark pages, can be accessed by creating your **free user account.** As a registered member of the *Writers' & Artists'* community, you will receive – straight to your dashboard – exclusive discounts on books, events and editing services and regular content to match your particular interests.

You can also find details of our range of **editing services**, **writing courses** and **masterclass evenings**. A selection of bursaries are available as well as payment installment plans.

Our **Listings subscription** provides access to the entire database of contacts in the latest edition of this *Yearbook*, plus hundreds of additional online-only entries.

Whatever your needs, we hope that *Writers' & Artists'* resources, whether delivered in an ebook, print, online or at our events, will provide you with the information, advice and inspiration you are looking for.

Writers&Artists

A FREE WRITING PLATFORM TO CALL YOUR OWN

- Share your writing
- Build reward points
- Free writing advice articles
- Publishing guidance
- Save margin notes
- Exclusive discounts

REGISTER NOW
WWW.WRITERSANDARTISTS.CO.UK

Praise for the *Yearbook*

'The one-and-only, indispensable guide to the world of writing.'
William Boyd

'So much of interest, and so much that the budding writer needs explained.'
Martina Cole

'I went out and bought myself a copy of the *Writers' & Artists' Yearbook* ... I talked to editors about ideas for stories. Pretty soon I found myself hired to do interviews and articles.'
Neil Gaiman

'A lifeline ... it set my feet on the publishing path.'
Joanne Harris

'The writers' Bible.'
Susan Hill

'Read this book very carefully. Treasure it. Keep it beside you.'
Rachel Joyce

'An indispensable companion for anyone seriously committed to the profession of author.'
David Lodge

'Full of information that all writers need to know.'
Deborah Levy

'Essential reading ... the A-Z of how to survive in publishing.'
Kate Mosse

'Practical, no-nonsense, supportive and encouraging – quite simply the best friend an aspiring writer can have.'
Julie Myerson

Praise for the *Yearbook*

'When you're looking to get published, it's your bible.'
Patrick Ness

'Everything you need to know about the business of being a writer.'
Lawrence Norfolk

'Even established writers can feel as though they're climbing a mountain. Think of the *Writers' & Artists' Yearbook* as your sherpa.'
Ian Rankin

'Full of useful stuff.'
J.K. Rowling

'... buy a copy of the current *Writers' & Artists' Yearbook* and get yourself out there.'
Donal Ryan

'Get a copy of the *Yearbook*. It's the key that will help you unlock the world of publishing.'
Samantha Shannon

'A must for established and aspiring authors.'
Society of Authors

'The wealth of information is staggering.'
The Times

'Every writer can remember her first copy of the *Writers' & Artists' Yearbook*.'
Rose Tremain

'... the book which magically contains all other books ... an entrance ticket to the world you long for.'
Fay Weldon

'the definitive resource'
Writing Magazine

Contents

Foreword

Claire Fuller

How good are your juggling skills? Can you keep three balls in the air, or four, or more? Most writers and artists have many demands on their time: caring for children, parents or others, full-time jobs, running a household, other hobbies or activities. Creative work often has to be squeezed into the spaces in between. And that doesn't include time for 'filling up the well', so that your brain has something to use when you can finally sit down and work. But creative endeavour *can* sometimes be done in those tiny gaps of time and, even if that isn't possible, you might be able to think about the work while you're doing other tasks, so that the ideas flow more easily when you do find a few minutes to sit at your desk. For some people, however, those other roles are simply too demanding to allow any time to create; sometimes you might have to wait years until your circumstances have changed. And although that can be frustrating, sometimes the waiting – or rather, the getting on with living your life – can lead to outcomes you've never imagined.

The first time I thumbed through the *Writers' & Artists' Yearbook* must have been in the summer of 1989, when I was 22. I was probably sitting at one of the long communal desks in my local reference library (long since sold off and turned into flats), with the light streaming in through the high windows. I'd recently graduated with a degree in Fine Art and, luckily for me, I wasn't required to do any juggling – I could spend my time making art and looking for representation. I sent photographs of my work through the post, with a covering letter and a stamped addressed envelope for their safe return – though usually didn't even get my pictures back, let alone a rejection letter. Even so, I thought that, somehow, I would make art my life. But of course, commitments and the need for money got in the way. I moved out of the squat I was living in and, although I was warmer and probably cleaner, I had rent to pay and less space to create. I got a 'proper' job and only made art occasionally.

Skip forward about 25 years and I was looking for representation again, but this time as a writer with my first novel. My local library had been renamed the Discovery Centre and had more areas given over to gallery space and computers than to desks or shelves with books, but they still had a copy of the *Writers' & Artists' Yearbook*. I'd had a long career in marketing and had fallen into writing via some public art projects I'd been doing. Without intending to be a writer, I wrote a short story, and then a novel. By then I had children, a full-time job, and I was studying for an MA in Creative Writing. I was doing some serious juggling and, without doubt, I dropped some balls along away. I wrote that novel, *Our Endless Numbered Days* (Penguin 2015) in the time between getting my two teenagers out of the house and off to school and when I had to leave for work – often about ten minutes; and then after work, dinner, washing up, and any other family commitments were completed – maybe half an hour, if I was lucky. But still the novel got finished. I didn't know anyone in publishing and I didn't know any published authors, so lists of agents were vital in selecting who I should send my manuscript to.

No one was more surprised than me to find myself at 48 with a literary agent, a book published by Penguin and around the world, and able to give up the marketing job and take the financial risk of becoming a full-time writer. You might think that 25 years is a long time to take to come to writing – to creative work that satisfies me and that I seem to have some success with. Although that's true, I don't see all that time as wasted. In those years I was still producing work, albeit not things which looked like books – but more importantly, I was raising children, working and living. I see that time as a kind of composting of material, taking note of my experiences and letting them settle.

If you're juggling or waiting for a moment when you can focus on creating, try not to be too frustrated; I promise that everything you see, feel, hear or imagine in that hiatus will blend and break down and add a richness to whatever you create in the future.

Claire Fuller is the author of five novels, published by Penguin. Her latest, *The Memory of Animals* was published in April 2023. Her previous novel, *Unsettled Ground* (2021), won the Costa Novel Award 2021 and was shortlisted for the Women's Prize for Fiction. Her first, *Our Endless Numbered Days* (2015) won the 2015 Desmond Elliott Prize; her second, *Swimming Lessons* (2017) was shortlisted for the Encore Prize; and her third, *Bitter Orange* (2018) was on the International Dublin Literary Award longlist. Her books have been translated into more than 20 languages. Claire also writes flash fiction and short stories. Many have been published, and she has won the BBC Opening Lines short story competition, and the Royal Academy/Pindrop Short Story Award. You can find more about Claire at www.clairefuller.co.uk or follow her on Instagram @writerclairefuller.

Newspapers and magazines

Getting started

Most of the titles included in the newspapers and magazines section of this *Yearbook* offer opportunities to the writer. To help you get started, see the guidelines below.

Study the market

• It is an editor's job to know what readers want and to see that they get it. Thus, freelance contributions must be tailored to fit a specific market; subject, theme, treatment and length must meet the editor's requirements.

• Before sending in a pitch, an article or feature, always look at the editorial requirements of the magazine: the subjects covered by the publication as well as the approach, treatment, style and typical length of pieces.

Check with the editor first

• Before submitting material to any newspaper or magazine it is advisable to first contact the relevant editor. A quick telephone call or email will establish the name of the relevant commissioning editor.

• It is not advisable to send illustrations 'on spec'; check with the editor first.

Understand how the market works

• It is worth considering using an agent to syndicate material. Most agents operate on an international basis and are aware of current market requirements. See page 97.

• The larger newspapers and magazines buy many of their stories, and the smaller papers buy general articles, through well-known syndicates.

• For the supply of news, most of the larger UK and overseas newspapers depend on their own staff and press agencies. The most important overseas newspapers have permanent representatives in the UK who keep them supplied with news and articles. While many overseas newspapers and magazines have a London office, it is usual for freelance contributions to be submitted to the headquarters' editorial office overseas.

Payment

• Many newspapers and magazines are reluctant to state a standard rate, since the value of a contribution may be dependent not upon length but upon the standing of the writer or the information supplied. Many other periodicals prefer to state 'by negotiation' or 'by arrangement', rather than giving precise payment information.

Life's a pitch: how to get your ideas into print

Mike Unwin has lots of valuable advice for would-be freelance writers keen to see their work in print, and explains what magazine and newspaper editors are looking for in a pitch.

Dear Editor

I'm desperate to write for you. Please let me. I'm not yet sure what to write – and I hesitate to share my ideas, in case you don't like them. But if you could just explain what you're looking for I'm sure I could do the job. I know you've never heard of me, but I'm a great writer – all my friends say so – and I could certainly match what you usually publish. Other editors haven't yet recognised my talent but you can change all that. Commission me and you won't regret it.
What do you say?

Kind regards
A.D. Luded-Freelance

How does an aspiring freelance get into print? The answer, short of blackmail or nepotism, is via the 'pitch'. This is a written proposal to a commissioning editor. Get it right and it can bag you a commission, complete with brief, fee and deadline. Get it wrong, and the first impression you make may well be your last.

Pitching is a notoriously tricky art. With editors' inboxes already groaning, the odds are stacked against freelances, especially first-timers. The example above may be ridiculous, but it nonetheless expresses the frustration felt by many freelances. How on earth do you break through?

Every freelance has a subjective take on this dilemma, depending on their field. Mine is travel and wildlife, so my advice is drawn from experience in this particular part of the industry. But the challenges are likely to be pretty similar whatever you write about. If there is a foolproof formula for success, I've yet to find it. What follows reflects over 20 years of trial and error.

'Some pitches are good, most are OK, but many are dire,' says freelance commissioning editor Sue Bryant. You may never learn why your pitch succeeds or fails, but you *can* ensure that it always falls into the first of those three categories. The rest may just come down to luck.

Do your homework

First, before you write a word, familiarise yourself with your target publication. Trawl the website – or splash out on a paper copy. Establish how often it comes out: pitching a story about an imminent one-off event to a quarterly whose next edition won't appear for three months is wasting the editor's time. And check that nothing similar has already appeared. 'My bugbear is when people pitch something we've recently covered,' says Andrew Purvis, commissioning editor at *Telegraph Travel*.

Second, consider the readership. 'This is where people most often go wrong,' says Lyn Hughes, publisher of magazine *Wanderlust*. 'It's vitally important that you understand who the readers are and what interests them.' You don't need demographics: the ads and letters pages speak volumes. Hughes describes how *Wanderlust* has received pitches for articles on golf – utterly irrelevant to readers interested in adventure travel and the natural world. Ignorance shows. 'You can always tell if they've not thought about the magazine and the target audience,' confirms Laura Griffiths-Jones of *Travel Africa* magazine, who would never entrust a fact-finding commission to a writer who can't even be bothered to research the magazine.

Don't cut corners. An all-purpose pitch to several publications simultaneously may save you time but will seldom get past the editor, who has a nose for the mail shot. Mistakes can be excruciating. 'We see a lot of cut-and-pasting,' says Hughes. 'The giveaway is the different font.'

Finally, address your pitch to the right person. Larger publications may have different commissioning editors for different sections, including their website, and a misdirected pitch may disappear without trace. Heed protocol: copying in the commissioning editors of rival publications in your address line – a common mistake, according to Griffiths-Jones – will *not* endear you to the editor you're addressing. And don't pull rank. 'Never go over the editor's head and talk to the publisher,' warns Bryant. 'That used to make me furious.'

Most commissioning editors would rather not receive a pitch by phone: it can feel confrontational – and they will, in any case, seldom be able to say yes or no without investigating further. Social media is also seen by many as too throw-away for the initial pitch – although, if you establish a relationship, it may become useful further down the line.

Get to the point

Once you've worked out where to direct your pitch, your challenge is to make it stand out from all the others. First comes the subject line, which must convey the gist in as few words as possible. 'You've almost got to put in as much effort on the subject line as in the pitch,' stresses Hughes. Bear in mind that longer lines may half disappear on the screen of a smartphone. Thus 'New snow leopard safari to Ladakh' is more effective than 'Proposal to write a travel feature about visiting the Himalayas in search of snow leopards'.

If the editor takes the bait, the pitch that follows must flesh out that subject line succinctly. 'Ideally one paragraph, explaining what the story is,' recommends Griffiths-Jones. I aim for one paragraph of no more than 100 words, sometimes adding a few brief supplementary details (see example overleaf). It can help to think of your pitch as being like a 'standfirst': the introductory paragraph that a magazine often places above an article.

Your 'angle' is critical. In travel journalism this might be a new means of experiencing an old destination or a topical hook, such as a forthcoming movie. In reality, your angle may not be very original – in travel, as elsewhere, subjects are revisited and dusted down on rotation – but your job is to make it sound novel and convince the editor that you are the one to write it. 'If I think: "So what? I could write that from my desk," then it's a non-starter,' warns Bryant.

A scattergun approach suggests lack of focus, so don't cram too many ideas into one story and certainly don't bundle several stories into one pitch. Settling on one idea can be difficult: in travel writing, almost any trip could yield multiple stories, but it can be risky to cram all your eggs into one basket. But editors are commissioning a story, not a destination. If torn, one compromise is to lead with a main angle but allow a little room for manoeuvre by including two or three brief subsidiary points that might suggest other angles should the main idea not appeal. Here's an example:

New snow leopard safari to Ladakh
In January I join a new tour to Ladakh, India, in search of snow leopards. This endangered big cat recently starred on BBC's *Planet Earth* and is one of the world's most sought-after wildlife sightings. Confined to the high Himalayas, it has long been off the tourist agenda. This pioneering venture (www.snowleopardsafaris.com) now offers snow leopard tracking for the first time. Accommodation is in community home-stays, from where expert local trackers guide small groups in to the mountains. Tourism revenue helps fund community-based conservation. Highlights include:
– Tracking snow leopards
– Wolves, ibex, eagles and other wildlife
– Trekking in the high Himalayas
– The ancient Ladakh capital of Leh (3,500m)
– Buddhist culture: monasteries, festivals, village home-stays
– Snow leopard conservation project
Peak season Jan–April; could file story from end January.

If the editor doesn't know you, some brief credentials might help: a simple sentence at the end explaining who you are, plus a sample or two of your work. Keep any attached files small: the editor won't want PDFs clogging up their inbox. Any weblinks should be to articles relevant to your pitch. 'Don't just say "visit my website",' warns Bryant. 'It sounds really arrogant and I haven't got time.'

Mind your language
Even the most perfectly structured pitch can founder on the detail. Typos happen, but this is one place where they mustn't. Hughes describes how *Wanderlust* regularly receives pitches for stories about 'Equador' and 'Columbia'. Remember, you are trying to persuade an editor to trust your ability with words. What will they think if you stumble at the first hurdle? Editors work to tight budgets and schedules, so the last thing they want is more work. 'If it's riddled with errors, and they can't construct a sentence or a paragraph correctly,' asks Purvis, 'why would I waste all that time – and budget – sorting it out?'

So double-check your pitch before sending. If in doubt, print it out: research shows that we all spot errors more easily on the printed page. To guard against embarrassing disasters, never insert the recipient's address in your email until you're ready to press 'Send'.

Style is important too. In general, less is more: the pitch is not a place for purple prose. And try to avoid journalistic faux pas, such as opening with long subordinate clauses or overusing the passive voice. And avoid cluttering your pitch with clichés: 'land of contrasts' and 'best-kept secret' are travel industry horrors that spring to mind. Editors are writers too. It doesn't take much for them to sniff out a weakness.

Me, me, me ...
Perhaps the worst error in pitching your story is to make yourself its subject. 'Don't make the pitch about you,' insists Bryant, 'unless you're really famous or really funny.' A travel editor is not generally looking for a Bruce Chatwin or Bill Bryson; they have no use for your hilarious anecdotes or journey of discovery. They want your writing to sell an

experience that their readers can go out and buy. 'We're not interested in you,' confirms Hughes. 'We're interested in our readers.' That's why any travel article will have at the end a fact box 'call to action', with all the details that the reader will need in order to replicate your experience.

Any hint of neediness is an instant deterrent. Your needs are not important, so don't suggest that by publishing your work the editor will be helping launch your career. A particular bugbear for travel editors is 'blagging': securing a commission in order to get yourself a free trip. 'I was recently offered a place on an Amazon River trip, but couldn't find a sponsor for the flights to Lima,' began one pitch that Bryant instantly rejected. Whilst a commission is a part of the equation that enables freelance travel writers to travel, the publication in question does not generally want to be caught up in the mechanics. You're a freelance; that's *your* lookout.

And beware how you present yourself. Editors talk to one another and reputations are quickly acquired. Social media can be a minefield: Bryant recalls discovering a long rant on Twitter from a writer she was considering commissioning that threatened to have a PR fired because the writer had not received a flight upgrade. 'When you're on the road on a commission,' she stresses, 'you are representing the publication and our advertisers.'

Editor empathies

If in doubt, try placing yourself in the shoes of the commissioning editor. Invariably they will be overburdened, against deadline and quite possibly battling some cost-cutting edict from on high. The last thing they're looking for, usually, is unsolicited pitches from writers that they've never heard of. 'Editors can be lazy,' admits Bryant. 'They don't like surprises.'

What's more, an editor's job is not to showcase your writing but to publish material that trumps the competition. Ultimately all editorial decisions are commercial. 'You're going to be held accountable for spending the money,' points out Purvis. Your job is to make their life easier by offering something that meets their needs.

Remember, too, that it was you who made the approach. An editor is under no obligation to justify their decision. Indeed – common courtesy aside – they are not even obliged to reply. The frustrating reality for freelances is that responses may be very slow and, at times, non-existent. Your pitch may never reach the front of the queue.

If you don't hear back, do send a gentle reminder. I usually leave it a couple of weeks and if I still hear nothing after that, I drop it. But never express your frustration; swallow it and look elsewhere. Who knows? Your name or idea may have struck a chord. The editor may get back to you months later, when you least expect it. It has happened to me. Don't burn your bridges.

And never give up. Somewhere out there is an article with your byline on it.

Mike Unwin is a freelance writer, editor and photographer who specialises in travel and wildlife. He worked for 14 years in book publishing before leaving to pursue a freelance career. Today he writes for a variety of newspapers and magazines, including the *Telegraph*, the *Independent*, *BBC Wildlife*, *Wanderlust* and *Travel Africa*. Among his 40 published books for both adults and children are *Migration* (Bloomsbury 2018), *The Enigma of the Owl* (Yale 2016), *Swaziland* (Bradt Travel Guides 2012) and *Endangered Species* (Aladdin Books 2000). His latest book is *Around the World in 80 Birds* (Laurence King Publishing 2022). His awards include BBC Wildlife Nature Travel Writer of the Year 2000, the British Guild of Travel Writers' UK Travel Writer of the Year 2013 and Latin American Travel's Newspaper Feature of the Year 2018. He was a finalist in the 2020 GTMA Global Travel Writer Award.

How to write features for the national and regional press

Freelance journalist Georgina Fuller describes the appeal and variety of feature-writing, as well as the financial and commissioning challenges that make determination, flexibility and resilience essential attributes for a freelancer. She gives valuable tips on how to get started and how to pitch your piece to an editor for the best chance of success.

If you have ever watched an episode of the HBO hit show 'Sex and the City', you might think that freelance journalists spend their days going to glitzy parties, chain-smoking their way through work deadlines, and wearing fabulous shoes. Well, I've been freelance for almost 15 years now and I'm here to tell you, it's more grit than glam – more frantic pitching, existential dread and chasing invoices than Manolo's, brunch and cocktails. Having said that, there is still little else I would rather do. 'Writing is the only thing that, when I do it, I don't feel I should be doing something else,' as the great Gloria Steinem once said.

Over the years, I have written for everyone from *Tatler* to *Take a Break*, but the process itself – pitching, writing, editing – is much the same, regardless of the publication you are writing for. The digital age has changed the face of journalism in many ways over the last decade or so. Topical news stories are published on a digital-first basis now and many publications pay less for online articles than they do for print pieces (see **Money matters** below). This is probably partly due to the ever-changing news cycle, the many-headed Hydra that is social media, and the fact that journalism has become increasingly focused on clickbait rather than long reads. That's not to say the job of a freelance journalist has changed greatly. The skills required are still much the same – thinking of a different angle on a topical story, sourcing case studies, turning clean copy around quickly – though now it's also essential to have a basic understanding of SEO (search engine optimisation) and to know how to insert a few hyperlinks.

When I first went freelance, in about 2008, any publication I pitched to usually had a decent-sized editorial team – with a sub-editor, a picture desk, staff writers and an editorial assistant, as well as various editors handling news, features, art and so on. Nowadays, many publications have had their budgets slashed as the cost-of-living crisis bites and are running on a skeleton staff. This means, essentially, that freelancers are expected to do more for less – to source pictures, write headlines and sub their own work. It has also made it harder and harder to get commissions and generate work, as staff writers who are already on the payroll are cheaper than freelancers.

So what options are available to aspiring freelance journalists today? The good news is that newspapers and magazines are always looking for fresh voices, opinion pieces and a new take on a topical issue. The bad news is it's become harder and harder to make a living from freelance journalism. This is partly because there are a growing number of bloggers, influencers and chancers who will write for free, but also because – around the early 2000s or even the late '90s – freelance rates crashed and burned.

Starting out

Some publications seem to take the 'free' in 'freelance' quite literally and think that they can get away without paying a writer for their work. I would avoid doing this at all costs if you are looking to make a career out of it. Making a living as a freelancer is hard. If you are starting from scratch, it is pretty much essential that you have another form of income; this could be something related to freelance journalism, such as corporate communications, PR or blogging. Unless of course you have a trust fund or a famous surname (and the two, naturally, often go hand in hand). Not only is the pay lousy, it's also very precarious; many titles run on a pay-on-publication basis or they over-commission and then offer a paltry 'kill fee' (the term they use when a piece gets scrapped or doesn't make the cut) that is less than the rate you were commissioned to write the piece for. Furthermore, many magazines now expect you to sign away all your 'rights' to a piece, which means they can syndicate it out to other titles in their publishing group without paying you for the privilege. For those reasons, I would always advise anyone starting out on a freelance career to build on or capitalise on a niche area because, whatever it is – beekeeping, gong baths, white-water rafting – there will be a magazine for it. If you can write, and there's something you know a bit about – a quirky subject or hobby, or something 'zeitgeisty' such as the world of dating apps – that is a potential source of income.

My background was in business magazines and HR, so that was my main source of income when I started out as a freelancer. I then moved into writing more for consumer titles on family, parenting and, subsequently, mid-life (I've written about everything from *Peppa Pig* to the gentrification of the Cotswolds and how Black fathers are under-represented in the media). Some freelancers start out in the regional press, although that too has seen some seismic changes in recent years. In 2020, the *Press Gazette* estimated that at least 265 local newspapers had closed since 2005[1] the advent of social media, decline in advertising revenues and an evolving younger population of readers are all contributing factors. Many local newspapers offer work experience, though, so that could be a great way of getting your foot in the door. Having local knowledge isn't always essential, but having a good eye for a story, a flexible attitude and a dogged determination *is*.

Bitching pitching: how to place a piece in a national newspaper

OK ... you've had a brilliant idea for an article. How do you place it in a national newspaper or magazine? Firstly, you need to find the right editor to pitch it to, so do your research, know your stuff and the publications you'd like to write for. If you can pitch it for a specific page or slot, that's even better. Don't expect any favours! Here are some important rules to follow:

• **Hone it down.** Be sure to hone your pitch down to four or five sentences or points so that it's concise and easy to understand. You should be able to sum up your story in a single sentence. Think about the 'who, what, where, when and why,' and make sure you cover the basics.

• **Make it relevant.** Check that your pitch passes the 'so what' test. Remember, editors don't owe you anything and just because something is of interest to you, it may not be to them. So make it relevant, timely and interesting. Think of the headline, 'sell' and crux of the article.

[1] https://pressgazette.co.uk/news/uk-local-newspaper-closures-at-least-265-local-newspaper-titles-gone-since-2005-but-pace-of-decline-has-slowed

• **Show a topical link.** Tag your pitch to a recent news story, survey or topic to give it extra currency, and make it as easy and succinct as possible so that the editor 'gets it'. Pre-empt any questions with relevant stats, figures and reports.

• **Include pictures.** Always include suitable pictures, ideally hi-res landscape pics (which are better for print) in jpeg format. If you have interviewed any case studies, it's almost essential to include headshots.

• **Follow up.** Editors get hundreds of emails a day, so make sure you follow up at least once, to check if they have read it. If it's a No, ask them what else they might be interested in receiving pitches on.

Money matters

Jon Harris, chairman of the National Association of Press Agencies and managing director of Manchester-based news agency Cavendish Press, wrote in the *Press Gazette* in 2022 that the UK's national newspapers were in a 'time warp' when it came to fees. 'Even my own daughter once made more money doing a night's babysitting than I did covering a murder trial,' he said.

Payment rates[2] can vary hugely depending on the title and, sadly, some have hardly gone up since I first started freelancing in 2010. The benchmark set by the National Union of Journalists (NUJ; see page 515) used to be £250 per 1,000 words for features, but the focus on digital-first journalism has eclipsed this on many national newspapers. National newspapers typically pay between 25p and 50p a word, although many offer a standard rate for either a one-page or double-page spread (DPS). This can vary according to which section of the newspaper the article will appear in; the *Daily Mail*, for example, might pay £1,000 for a double-page spread for its *Femail* magazine, while its health pages pay £600–900. *Grazia* magazine paid £450 for a 900-word print feature in 2020, while *Grazia Daily* paid £200 for an 800-word feature in 2023. The *Daily Telegraph* have a lower rate – 35p a word and a higher rate of 45p a word for established journalists. The *Guardian* pay 34.5p a word across the paper, but a colleague who writes for *The Times* recently told me they were down to just 25p a word. Regional newspapers can pay an abysmal £60 per 1000-word feature or up to £120 a day.

Day rates for shifts at regional papers can vary significantly from £90 to £120, with stories ranging from £30 to £60 a feature. Standard day rates on the nationals for news are even lower. *The Times* paid £120 for a page lead and £58.50 for a shorter story in 2023, while the *Sun* paid £110–150 and the *Daily Express* £100–150 for day rate/page lead. One freelance colleague who writes regularly for women's weekly magazines pointed out that the rate had gone down considerably – from £500 for a DPS in 2019 to around £300 in 2023: 'Nothing ever seems to go up and, if you make a fuss, it's suggested that there is always someone else willing to do it for less,' she said.

And finally...

If all of that hasn't put you off, I am here to tell you that being a freelance journalist can be the most rewarding, fun and varied job you will ever have. It's a job that has taken me from interviewing ex-offenders in the most deprived part of Glasgow to interviewing celebrities on their houseboats in Chelsea and stately houses in the Home Counties. While

[2] Sources: NUJ, *Freelancing for Journalists* podcast (https://podcasts.apple.com/gb/podcast/freelancing-for-journalists/id1511920418) and my fellow journalists.

the pay might be abysmal, the perks (travel, press do's, freebies) can be great fun. But you do have to be tenacious, resilient and, of course, an excellent writer; the competition is fierce and you have to learn not to take it personally if your pitch isn't picked up. It's not all strutting around the streets of New York in a tutu (although I once did that with a clipboard and microphone in Covent Garden ...).

Good luck!

Georgina Fuller is a freelance journalist, editor and media consultant with over 20 years' experience, who has had bylines in the *Daily Telegraph, Guardian, The Times, Daily Mail, Observer, i Paper, Daily Express, Red, Tatler, Marie Claire, Grazia, Prima, Good Housekeeping, Woman, Woman's Own* and *Take a Break* magazine. She also writes a column for her local paper, the *Stratford Herald*. Georgina has lectured on journalism at several well-known universities, and she offers 1:1 or team media consultancy and training to small businesses. See her website www.georginafuller.co.uk for more information. Follow her on Twitter @GeorgieR30.

The hidden art of B2B journalism

Blake Evans-Pritchard describes how writing for the specialist trade press can be both intellectually stimulating and highly lucrative. He sheds light on B2B and its place in the market, with essential advice and top tips on how to establish yourself in this doubly rewarding field.

The collapse of Archegos, a US hedge fund, in 2021 was one of the biggest financial scandals of the past ten years. In just two days, South Korean-born Bill Hwang managed to lose a staggering 20 billion US dollars. Few individuals in history have blown through so much cash in such a short period of time. The incident left a number of prominent investment banks reeling. Financial journalists were all over the story. But some of the best reporting lay not within the pages of mainstream newspapers; it was the trade press that had the technical expertise and the resources to understand what was really going on. Within weeks of the Archegos collapse, I was pleasantly surprised to spot, right on the front page of the *Financial Times*, a story that came directly from the B2B magazine I was writing for. The *Financial Times* was even good enough to credit us as the source.

Admittedly, I can't really take credit for this particular story. I was working in Hong Kong at the time and, although Bill Hwang was originally from Asia, the most exciting action was taking place in the USA and Europe. I think that, out of the 135 articles about Archegos that we eventually published, I was able to contribute just one. Still, it was hugely satisfying to be at the centre of such a significant story, and to be one of those few journalists who had the close contacts and technical nous to really get to the heart of what was going on. This is what writing for the trade press is all about – having the knowledge and understanding that more mainstream journalists simply don't have the time, inclination or opportunity to match. Done well, this kind of journalism can be hugely lucrative too.

What is the B2B trade press – and why write for it?

B2B stands for 'business-to-business'. Put simply, B2B journalism is about writing specifically for businesses, so that they can take more informed and better decisions in the work that they do. This is different from business-to-consumer (B2C) journalism, which sees the public as the target audience. Let's illustrate this distinction with an example. Travel magazines such as *Condé Nast Traveller* or *Wanderlust*, which you can purchase in most British supermarkets, have as their core focus the individual traveller. Their articles do not dwell on how the travel industry works, but on how readers can get the most out of their travel experiences. These would be classed as B2C magazines.

Contrast this to *Travel Weekly* or *Travel Bulletin*. Each of these publications exist to serve the needs of the travel industry itself, preferring articles about the latest big tour company merger rather than a first-hand account of trekking in Antarctica. This would be B2B journalism. My background is in financial journalism, but B2B journalism is not just limited to this area. Healthcare periodicals for the medical profession, agricultural journals for farmers, fashion magazines for the clothing sector – all of these would also be considered B2B.

There are two main reasons why you might want to look to the B2B sector as an outlet for your writing. The first is cerebral. It can be hugely rewarding to be one of an elite group of journalists who understand the minute intricacies of a niche – though hugely important

– story. I have attended many media receptions organised by banks where some of the most important people at the event have migrated towards my corner of the room, simply because they know they will be able to have a more informed and interesting discussion about a subject they are really passionate about. The second reason for considering this avenue of writing is financial. In all my years of professional writing, both for mainstream and trade publications, I have always been able to earn more as a B2B journalist. Now that I am a freelancer, I find myself using my B2B earnings to supplement the other writing that I want to pursue but which invariably does not pay as much. We'll get on to the specifics of financials in a bit, but the logic is clear: B2B publications tend to pay more than less-specialist media because the readers that they serve are using the knowledge they find within articles to advance their business or their career. This provides a very important clue as to how to succeed in the B2B world.

Starting out

One of the most important pieces of advice for any aspiring journalist is: 'Know your readers'. This is doubly important when it comes to writing for B2B publications. Readers of B2B publications are prepared to fork out hefty subscription fees in the belief that they will get access to information they simply can't find elsewhere. As a B2B writer, you need to be able to provide that information. But how do you set about acquiring the knowledge base you need to market yourself convincingly as an industry expert? There are no quick-and-easy short cuts, unfortunately – but persistence, good preparation and a decent contact book can take you a long way.

Many years ago, before I had carved out a niche for myself as a B2B writer, I approached a British pensions magazine to ask if they would be interested in me writing for them. I had never written about the pensions industry before, but I had spotted an opportunity: a lot of news was emerging from the European Union, but no one was systematically covering its impact on the pensions industry. My optimistic approach resulted in a monthly column and a lasting freelance relationship with the publication. Understanding what readers want to learn about, and therefore what might interest potential editors, is crucial. It's simple enough to get this information – just go out there and ask them. One of the great things about B2B journalism is that many of the consumers of articles are often also the sources of such stories. Every single B2B interview I have these days ends with the question: 'So what else do you want to know about?'. This invariably leads to at least one or two good story ideas that I can work on at a later date.

Start by choosing your niche, based on what interests you and what magazines are available on the market. *Writers' & Artists' Yearbook* is a good starting place, but there are other ways of researching the sector too. Type 'trade magazines' into Google (avoid 'B2B publications' as a search term, as this can be confused with other uses of the word). When you feel confident enough in your chosen subject, approach an editor you want to work for and ask whether they ever take freelance contributions. At this stage, it is a good idea to suggest a few articles that you could start work on. The best way to catch the editor's eye is with an idea for an in-depth feature on something topical. The daily news churn will most likely be handled in-house.

In your pitches, be as specific as possible. A good tip is to try and focus on how companies are responding to a particular trend or development in the market. For example, an investment publication might be interested in an in-depth story on at how asset managers are reassessing their China strategy in a post-Covid world – with the promise that you would be able to speak to a handful of them. The editor might be less interested in a more general pitch about how much money is flowing into and out of the country (readers can gain this insight from the less specialist publications that they also regularly read). As long as you have been suitably convincing in your introductory letter, and have presented yourself as something of an authority on a particular industry, there is a good chance that the editor will be interested. There is a shortage of good B2B journalists out there, and most specialist publications are only too happy to take good freelance copy.

The relationship with the commissioning editor is key. In every approach, make sure that you display a high level of professionalism and knowledge of the market. Trade publications have a highly symbiotic relationship with readers. The last thing that an editor wants is an uninformed hack speaking to subscribers. If you have the enthusiasm and interest to pursue this, the trade press should not be overlooked. Once you have established a solid relationship as an expert in the field, editors should be chasing you to work for them, rather than the other way round. Remember: you do not have to become a top expert in your chosen field; you just have to acquire enough knowledge to convince your sources (and your editor) that you are.

Let's talk financials

So how much can a B2B journalist expect to earn for a particular article? Well, as with all forms of writing, the answer is: it depends. However, as you gain more confidence and experience within the B2B space, you will learn that you can command a much higher rate than when you first started out and can quickly leave behind those publications that are not prepared to pay top dollar. These days I find myself being much choosier than I used to be about who I write for.

I am generally happy to accept 75p per word. This means that, for a 2,000-word article, I would be able to charge around £1,500. Such a piece would typically take me around three days of total work, including interviews, to put together. Of course, not all publications pay so generously, and I sometimes accept 0.35p per word. The rate paid often depends on how specialist the writing has to be, and on how many others are capable of producing such copy. I would rarely accept less than 0.35p per word. The important thing is to feel your way around the market; as you gain confidence, you can start pushing for higher remuneration. If you're good and consistently deliver meaningful value to your readers, you'll be able to get it.

Top tips for B2B journalism:

• Study the market carefully before settling on your niche. Is this a sector in which you will be able to develop a lasting interest? What publications currently serve this industry? Is there enough scope within the sector for you to develop a regular income stream?
• Speak to readers and sources as much as you possibly can. They are usually only too happy to talk about a subject they are passionate about, and you need to learn from them.
• Remember to end every interview with the question: 'So, what else do you want to know about?'
• Make sure you demonstrate a high level of expertise at all times, both when communicating with your editor and when interviewing sources.
• Avoid asking uninformed questions. Sources will quickly tire of a lazy journalist who hasn't done their homework properly and displays a lack of understanding (or care) about the industry that they work for.

• Don't expect official spokespeople to understand the subject matter as well as you or your sources do. Spokespeople, especially within large organisations, regularly prioritise the mainstream press over trade publications. It can take skill and tact – and sometimes the helping hand of an inside source – to overcome this hurdle.

• Spend time cultivating a personal relationship with the editor(s) you want to write for. Once you have established a solid relationship as an expert in the field, editors should be chasing you to work for them rather than the other way round.

• And, finally, make sure that you enjoy the work. It will show in your copy. Industry leaders are passionate about what they do. You need to be too.

Blake Evans-Pritchard is a freelance journalist based in Barcelona, Spain. He was previously Hong Kong bureau chief for Risk.net, a global publication covering the derivatives markets and risk management within financial institutions. He has also served as Editor-in-Chief of *InsuranceAsia News*, another B2B publication. He currently freelances for publications all over the world, including for a number of B2B titles. For more information see https://blakerig.wordpress.com and follow him on Twitter @blakerig.

Setting up and editing a new magazine

Ed Needham shares his experience and outlines the essential steps, decisions and realities involved in publishing a new magazine as a solo operation, and gives practical advice on how to turn your concept into a successful venture in today's changing digital industry.

I have spent much of my adult life working as a journalist and editor in magazines. I edited *FHM* in its million-selling heyday in the '90s, and launched and edited that magazine in the United States. Also in the USA, I was the managing editor at *Rolling Stone* and editor-in-chief at *Maxim*, then the biggest men's magazine in the world. I've established a successful online publishing and marketing company, and developed magazines for other companies. But, over the last decade or so, the magazine as a fact of life – a glossy, portable, affordable luxury, object of desire and trusted source of guidance – has fallen badly out of fashion, evicted from so many of the gaps it used to fill in people's lives by the mobile phone. That one gadget has changed the fortunes of the industry calamitously. Readers and advertising have wandered off. Titles have closed. And by 2017 I found myself looking for a job, in a market where positions for top editors had become reserved for candidates with far more modest salary expectations than mine.

But a couple of interesting developments also emerged from the magazine industry's change of life: 1) many of the special skills and physical processes that used to require an army of talent had been replaced by affordable software; 2) while legacy magazine publishers were struggling for sustenance at a diminishing waterhole, there was still plenty of margin for people operating in niche markets and who didn't have a heavy payroll or central London floorspace to maintain. Perhaps I could publish my own magazine? And to keep the costs really low, perhaps I could do the whole thing on my own?

I found an envelope and did a few sums on the back of it. I produced a dummy – a trial issue – to see whether one person could write and edit an entire magazine (and then another one in short order – the revelation that Issue Two comes hard on the heels of Issue One routinely comes as a shock to people 'having a go' at magazines). I had it printed to see what it would look like, liked it, and in 2018 launched *Strong Words*, a magazine about books. It appears six times a year, and each issue has reviews of over 100 titles, as well as interviews and features that send readers into an ecstasy of book-buying, trying authors, genres and categories of books they wouldn't previously have dreamt of dabbling in. And it does so entertainingly – people like to be informed and amused by reviews, not lectured gravely on how important something is. There is no sad head-shaking nor acts of critical violence; if I find a book disappointing, I don't cover it, but I think the days of the snooty, disdainful review to showcase the critic's cleverness are nearly over. *Strong Words* is for people who want to read more, not less. So why waste valuable space urging people not to buy a book? Even though it requires my attention all seven days of the week, I've proved it can be done. At time of writing, I've just sent Issue 43 to the printer. And here are some of the things I've learned, if you'd like to have a go yourself.

1. Do some initial thought experiments

I was taught that the first question to ask when embarking on a new magazine project was 'Who's it for?' But the people asking that question used to be big magazine companies whose starting point was identifying which market to shove themselves into next. Now I think you need to answer two different questions first: 1) 'Why am I doing it?' and 2) 'Where's the money coming from?' If you can answer those two questions honestly, rather than as a delusional pipe dream, you'll have sketched a foundation for your project. My answer to 1) was that I needed to earn a living – but with a view to eventually also applying my model to established magazines that might benefit from my approach to costs. My answer to 2) was initially the Bank of Ed Needham and then through subscriptions. Not advertising – at first, that's another cost. But until you can answer those questions with confidence, you can't go to the next square.

2. Who's it for?

Identify your market. Why does anyone need your magazine? Bear in mind that the younger consumers can easily imagine reaching the end of their lives without ever once touching one. I chose a print product because I understand them, and they have a credibility that online doesn't; it's like the difference between a house and a picture of a house. Neither did I have the time to do print *and* online to an acceptable standard. I chose to write about books because the UK is the world's bookiest nation (no other country publishes as many books per capita), yet there is no consistently reliable source for book buyers to find out what's new.

There are the highbrow journals and the broadsheets, but all too often they make books feel like homework, whereas most people buy books for pleasure. The internet is a formidable marketing machine, but it rarely leaves a person thinking, 'That's the book for me.' If anyone is going to appreciate the special magic of ink on paper, it's book buyers. Books are a great untapped reservoir of the new and the useful, the funny and the gossipy, endless revelation about just how dysfunctional our planet and its population is. And that is the stuff of life – something people have a gluttonous appetite for.

3. The practicalities

If you haven't made a magazine before, familiarise yourself with InDesign, the universal page-making software from Adobe, for which you pay a license fee. Work out how many pages you want – it should be a multiple of eight, plus four more for the cover. Make a flatplan, i.e. decide, before you start, what is going on every page and in what order. The only bit of the process I can't do is design, so my original concept for *Strong Words* was to pay a designer friend to establish a template, which I could re-use with different content each issue, thus keeping design costs low. But I do still need a designer for a couple of weeks each issue.

You're going to need content, which – unless you know people keen to work for nothing – you either have to produce yourself or pay for. And you're going to need pictures, which you also either have to produce yourself or pay for. Helping yourself from the internet is not advisable. You might get away with it, or you might end up in court. I get my stock pictures from Shutterstock (www.shutterstock.com), more specific images such as archive news images from Alamy (www.alamy.com), and I use press-approved images from the books I write about, where possible.

As for copy, I produce it all myself – it amounts to reading the equivalent of *War and Peace* each week (about 1,500 pages) and writing the equivalent of *The Great Gatsby* each issue (about 45,000 words). I cut the copy to fit, write the headlines, write the display copy (the various other bits, like captions) check the spellings and punctuation and prices. You need a cover – traditionally known as the most important page in a magazine. If you're selling your publication in shops, you need a bar code; these are easy to buy (see www.axicon.com), but before that you need an ISSN number … If I can get one, you can.

You may want to trademark your name; do it yourself at www.gov.uk/how-to-register-a-trade-mark (apply in class 09 for digital, class 16 for print). Don't pay a third party. And ignore the avalanche of scam letters that follow straight after.

4. Print it

I'd always thought this was the big barrier to a solo operation. You used to have to order the paper, and well in advance. If you wanted special paper, even more in advance. You usually had to buy quite a lot of it. It required middlemen. Now you can print a single copy. This was where I began to see what was possible: someone mentioned a business called Newspaper Club (www.newspaperclub.com) who print on newsprint, and so the first three issues of *Strong Words* came as a newspaper. You just upload your files, choose your paper quality, and pay.

My original marketing plan was to print loads and give them away … then everyone would faint with delight and subscribe on the spot. When I discovered that news-stands couldn't cope with a tabloid newsprint magazine, because it didn't fit their racks, I switched to a conventional A4 format, and used a company called Mixam (https://mixam.co.uk). Note: if you're sending your magazine out by post, you need to know how much it's going to weigh before you print it. Postage costs are brutal, so you want to keep them down but still ensure a decent paper stock. Printers' websites enable you to calculate the weight of an issue. This is a nasty shock to any budget (… keep smelling salts handy). And don't forget to factor in the weight of the envelope. Mixam provided great quality, but I needed specific delivery dates; I use The Magazine Printing Company (www.magprint.co.uk), who also give stunning quality and invaluable customer service. Upload the files, approve them, send. It is mind-blowingly easy.

5. Distribution

I thought this would be a big barrier too, but no. I use a third-party company called Webscribe (www.webscribe.co.uk) to run the subscription fulfilment, so they take the money and send the issues out – I don't have to handle credit cards and customer data, all that tricky stuff. If you want to sell in shops, third-party companies will look after that too; I used one called MMS (www.mmslondon.co.uk) and sold in independents and in WHSmith travel outlets at railways and airports (you have to pay an annual fee per outlet). When travel fell out of favour during lockdown, I switched to subscription only, and the poor Smith's staff weren't always sure where to rack *Strong Words*, so I'd sometimes find it shoved somewhere inappropriate like gardening, so I'm not sure I'd go back.

And now for some difficult news. Congratulations for getting this far, but you have only reached the foot of the mountain, because the biggest challenge is …

6. Marketing

I think you can divide people into two groups: people who make things and people who sell things. Few excel at both. Persuading someone to buy your product is not a skill that emerges naturally from learning how to produce magazines. This is the main reason why people have business partners – to overcome this skill set schism. But those magazines aren't going to sell themselves and, having made such a thing of beauty, it's heartbreaking to see them not find new homes.

I wish I could reveal the golden key to marketing serenity, but it hasn't been revealed to me yet. This is what I think I know. There are two steps: 1) make people aware of the magazine; 2) persuade them to subscribe. The tools at your disposal are: social media; conventional media (I find the former better for step one, the latter for step two); newsletters, podcasts, events, influential people (someone once recommended focusing on your 1,000 most influential customers first, rather than scatter-gunning your efforts in a frantic marketing orgy). Make sure everyone you have ever met knows what you are doing. Somehow make yourself a topic of conversation. Explain how your product helps people. Trade favours. Most of all, get on with it and find out what works for you, and spend as much time on selling as on making.

Your project may be an act of supreme folly or it may transform the media landscape, but if you don't give it your everything, it WILL fail, and you will never find out. Looking forward to seeing you all on my subscription list soon. Good luck.

Ed Needham is an editor and journalist, and publisher of *Strong Words* magazine which he launched in 2018, published by his own company De Pentonville Media Ltd. His former roles include Editor, then Editor-in-Chief, of *FHM* in the UK and USA, 1997–2002, Managing Editor of *Rolling Stone*, 2002–04, Editor-in-Chief of *Maxim*, 2004–06, and founder and Editor-in-Chief of *Coach* magazine, 2015–16. For more information see www.strong-words.co.uk. Follow Strong Words on Twitter @StrongWordsMag.

National newspapers UK and Ireland

This section includes listings for national newspapers available in print, in both print and online, and as online-only news websites.

BBC News

email haveyoursay@bbc.co.uk
website www.bbc.co.uk/news
Facebook www.facebook.com/bbcnews
Twitter @BBCNews
Ceo of BBC News Deborah Turness

Online only. The website contains international and regional news coverage as well as entertainment, sport, science and political news. Founded 1997.

Business Post

2nd Floor, Block B, The Merrion Centre,
Merrion Road, Dublin D04 H2H4,
Republic of Ireland
tel +353 (0)16 026000
email editor@businesspost.ie
website www.businesspost.ie
Facebook www.facebook.com/businessposthq
Twitter @businessposthq
Editor Daniel McConnell
Sun €4.20

Features on financial, economic and political topics; also lifestyle, media and science articles. Illustrations: colour and b&w photos, graphics, cartoons. Payment: by negotiation. Founded 1989.
Deputy & Health Editor Susan Mitchell
Head of Podcasting & Editor Nadine O'Regan
Managing Editor Gillian Neilis
Political Editor Michael Brennan

City AM Ltd

3rd Floor, Fountain House, 130 Fenchurch Street,
London EC3M 5DJ
tel 020-3201 8900
website www.cityam.com
Facebook www.facebook.com/cityam
Twitter @cityam
Editor Andy Silvester
Mon–Fri Free

Financial and business newspaper. Covers the latest economic, political and business news as well as comment, sport and lifestyle features. Founded 2006.
Comment & Features Editor Sascha O'Sullivan
Life & Style Editor Steve Dinneen
Sports Editor Frank Dalleres

The Conversation

Shropshire House (4th Floor), 11–20 Capper Street,
London WC1E 6JA
email uk-editorial@theconversation.com
website https://theconversation.com/uk/
Facebook www.facebook.com/ConversationUK
Twitter @ConversationUK
Editor Jo Adetunji

An online-only independent source of news and views, sourced from the academic and research community and delivered direct to the public. Founded 2011.
Cities, Education & Young People Editor Grace Allen
Deputy Editor Steven Vass
Environment & Energy Editor Jack Marley
Health & Medicine Editor Clint Witchalls
Investigations Affairs Editor Jonathan Este
Politics Editor Laura Hood
Science Editor Miriam Frankel
Senior Arts & Cultural Editor Anna Walker
Special Projects Editor Holly Squire

Daily Express

One Canada Square, Canary Wharf, London E14 5AP
tel 020-7293 3000
email news.desk@express.co.uk
website www.express.co.uk
Facebook www.facebook.com/DailyExpress
Twitter @Daily_Express
Editor-in-Chief Gary Jones
Daily Mon–Fri £1.20, Sat £1.75
Supplements **Daily Express Saturday**

Exclusive news; striking photos. Leader page articles (600 words); facts preferred to opinions. Payment: according to value. Founded 1900.
Environment Editor Steph Spyro
Head of Lifestyle, Travel & Personal Finance Lauren O'Callaghan
News Editor Geoff Maynard
Political Editor Sam Lister
Science Editor Callum Hoare
Senior Digital Sports Editor Mikael McKenzie
Travel Editor Nigel Thompson

Daily Express Saturday Magazine
Free with paper

Daily Mail

Northcliffe House, 2 Derry Street, London W8 5TT
tel 020-7938 6000
email news@dailymail.co.uk
website www.dailymail.co.uk
Facebook www.facebook.com/DailyMail
Twitter @MailOnline
Editor Ted Verity
Daily Mon–Fri 90p, Sat £1.40
Supplements **Weekend**

Founded 1896.

City Editor Alex Brummer
Executive Editor of Features Dominic Midgley
Literary Editor Sandra Parsons
Moneymail Editor Lee Boyce
News Editor Neville Dean
Political Editor Jason Groves
Social Editor Richard Eden
Sports Editor Martin Samuel
Travel & Property Editor Mark Palmer

MailOnline

tel 020-7938 6000
email tips@dailymail.com
Editor Danny Groom

The online platform for the *Daily Mail*.
Founded 2003.

Daily Mirror

One Canada Square, Canary Wharf, London E14 5AP
tel 020-293 2411
email mirrornews@mirror.co.uk
website www.mirror.co.uk
Facebook www.facebook.com/DailyMirror
Twitter @DailyMirror
Editor Alison Phillips
Daily Mon–Fri £1.0, Sat £1.90
Supplements **We Love TV**

Top payment for exclusive news and news pictures.
Freelance articles used and ideas bought: send
synopsis only. Unusual pictures and those giving a
new angle on the news are welcomed; also cartoons.
Founded 1903.

Business Editor Graham Hiscott
Mirror Online Editorial Director Ben Rankin
News Editor Dominic Herbert
Political Editor John Stevens
Sports Editor David Walker

Daily Record

1 Central Quay, Glasgow G3 8DA
tel 0141 309 3000
email reporters@dailyrecord.co.uk
website www.dailyrecord.co.uk
Facebook www.facebook.com/
TheScottishDailyRecord
Twitter @Daily_Record
Editor David Dick
Daily Mon–Fri £1.20 Sat £1.80
Supplements **Saturday, Seven Days, Living, TV
Record, Road Record, Recruitment Record, The
Brief**

Topical articles, from 300–700 words; exclusive
stories of Scottish interest and exclusive colour
photos. Founded 1895.

Assistant Editor & Head of News Kevin Mansi
Assistant Editor & Head of Sports Austin Barrett
Digital Editor Graeme Thomson
Health & Education Editor Vivienne Aitken
Political Editor Paul Hutcheon

Saturday
Free with paper
Lifestyle magazine and entertainment guide. Reviews,
travel features, shopping, personalities, colour
illustrations. Payment: by arrangement.

Daily Star

One Canada Square, London E14 5AP
tel 020-7293 3000
email news@dailystar.co.uk
website www.dailystar.co.uk
Facebook www.facebook.com/thedailystar
Twitter @DailyStar
Editor Jon Clark
Daily Mon–Fri 80p, Sat £1.30
Supplements **Hot TV, Seriously Football**

Hard news exclusives, commanding substantial
payment. Major interviews with big-star personalities;
short features; series based on people rather than
things; picture features. Illustrations: line, half-tone.
Payment: by negotiation. Founded 1978.

Daily Star Online Editor Jon Livesey
Deputy Online Sports Editor Dan Gibbs
Senior Lifestyle & Travel Editor Samantha Bartlett
News Editor Steve Hughes

Daily Star Sunday

Express Newspapers, The Northern & Shell Building,
10 Lower Thames Street, London EC3R 6EN
tel 020-7293 3000
website www.dailystar.co.uk/sunday
Editor Denis Mann
Sun £1.60
Supplements **OK! Extra**

Opportunities for freelancers. Founded 2002.

Daily Telegraph

111 Buckingham Palace Road, London SW1W 0DT
tel 020-7931 2000
email dtnews@telegraph.co.uk
website www.telegraph.co.uk
Facebook www.facebook.com/telegraph.co.uk
Twitter @Telegraph
Editor Chris Evans
Daily Mon–Fri £2.80, Sat £3.50
Supplements **Gardening, Cars, Property, Culture,
Sport, Telegraph Magazine, Travel, Your Money**

Articles on a wide range of subjects of topical interest
considered. Preliminary letter and synopsis required.
Length: 700–1,000 words. Payment: by arrangement.
Founded 1855.

Associate Editor Gordon Rayner
Fashion Editor Lisa Armstrong
Health Editor Laura Donnelly
Home News Editor Bill Gardner
News Editor Mark Hughes

Telegraph Magazine
Free with Sat paper
Short profiles (about 1,600 words); articles of topical

interest. Preliminary study of the magazine essential. Illustrations: all types. Payment: by arrangement. Founded 1964.

Telegraph Online
email dtnews@telegraph.co.uk
website www.telegraph.co.uk

Readers need to set up a monthly subscription after 30 days free access to view full articles. Founded 1994.
   Managing Director Will Lewis

Financial Times
Bracken House, 1 Friday Street, London EC4M 9BT
tel 020-7873 3000
email ean@ft.com
website www.ft.com
Facebook www.facebook.com/financialtimes
Twitter @FinancialTimes
Editor Roula Khalaf
Daily Mon–Fri £3.50, Sat £4.80
Supplements **Companies, FTfm, FT Special Reports, FT Executive Appointments, FT Weekend Magazine, House and Home, FT Money, How To Spend It, FT Wealth, Life & Arts**

One of the world's leading business news organisations, the *FT* provides news, commentary and analysis. Founded 1888.
   Deputy Editor Patrick Jenkins
   Chief Economics Commentator Martin Wolf
   FT Weekend Editor Janine Gibson
   House & Home Editor Nathan Brooker
   International Business Editor Peggy Hollinger
   Managing Editor Peter Spiegel
   Markets Editor Katie Martin
   News Editor Matthew Garrahan
   Political Editor Sebastian Payne
   UK Editor-at-Large Robert Shrimsley

Guardian
Kings Place, 90 York Way, London N1 9GU
tel 020-3353 2000
email national@theguardian.com
website www.theguardian.com
Facebook www.facebook.com/theguardian
Twitter @guardian
Editor Katharine Viner
Daily Mon–Fri £2.50, Sat £3.50
Supplements **Sport, G2, Film & Music, The Guide, Weekend, Review, Money, Work & Careers, Travel, Family, Cook**

Few articles are taken from outside contributors except on feature and specialist pages. Illustrations: news and features photos. Payment: apply for rates. See contributors guidelines on website. Founded 1821.
   Books Editor Charlotte Northedge
   Business Editor John Collingridge
   City Editor Anna Isaac
   Deputy Editor Owen Gibson
   Economics Editor Larry Elliott

   Education Editor Richard Adams
   Fashion Editor Jess Cartner-Morley
   Head of National News Fay Schlesinger
   Head of Travel Andy Pietrasik
   Health Editor Andrew Gregory
   Music Editor (acting) Laura Snapes
   Political Editor Pippa Crerar

Weekend
Free with Sat paper

Features on world affairs, major profiles, food and drink, home life, the arts, travel and leisure. Also good reportage on social and political subjects. Illustrations: photos, line drawings and cartoons. Payment: apply for rates.

theguardian.com/uk
website www.theguardian.com/uk

Free website where the *Guardian* and the *Observer* publish all their current and archived content. Currently gives access to over three million stories. Although the service is free, readers are invited to make a donation. There are also US and Australian editions of the website. Founded 2013.

Herald
Herald & Times Group, 125 Fullarton Drive, Glasgow East Investment Park, Glasgow G32 8FG
tel 0141 302 7002
email news@theherald.co.uk
website www.heraldscotland.com
Facebook www.facebook.com/heraldscotland
Twitter @heraldscotland
Editor Catherine Salmond
Mon–Fri £2.00, Sat £2.40

News and stories about Scotland, the UK and the world. Opportunities for freelancers with quality contacts. Founded 1783.
   Arts Editor Keith Bruce
   Deputy Editor Garry Scott
   Foreign Affairs Editor David Pratt
   Group Business Editor Ian McConnell
   Head of Digital News Gregor Kyle
   News Editor Alan Simpson
   Scottish Political Editor Tom Gordon

Herald on Sunday
Herald & Times Group, 125 Fullarton Drive, Glasgow East Investment Park, Glasgow G32 8FG
tel 0141 302 7000
email news@theherald.co.uk
website www.heraldscotland.com
Editor Catherine Salmond
Sun £2.40
Supplements **Sport, Scottish Life Magazine**

News and stories about Scotland, the UK and the world. Opportunities for freelancers with quality contacts. Founded 2018.

i

Northcote House, 2 Derry Street, London W8 5TT
tel 020-3615 0000
email i@inews.co.uk
website https://inews.co.uk/
Facebook www.facebook.com/theipaper
Twitter @theipaper
Editor Oly Duff
Mon–Fri 80p

Originally sister paper to the *Independent* which is now online only. Founded 2010.
  Arts Editor Sarah Carson
  Breaking News Editor Hatty Collier
  Deputy Editor & Editorial Director Amy Iggulden
  Economics Editor David Parsley
  Foreign Editor Emma Reynolds
  Head of News Mark Davies
  Managing Editor Tal Gottesman
  National Editor Lewis Smith
  Picture Editor Sophie Batterbury
  Scotland Editor Chris Green
  Sports Editor Ally McKay

i Weekend

Northcote House, 2 Derry Street, London W8 5TT
tel 020-3615 0000
email i@inews.co.uk
website https://inews.co.uk/
Editor Hanna Tavner
Sat £1.50

Weekend newspaper of the weekly i. Founded 2012.

Independent

Northcliffe House, 2 Derry Street, London W8 5HF
tel 020-7005 2000
email newsdesk@independent.co.uk
website www.independent.co.uk
Facebook www.facebook.com/TheIndependentOnline
Twitter @independent
Editor Geordie Greig

Online only. Occasional freelance contributions; preliminary letter advisable. Payment: by arrangement. Founded 1986.
  Culture Editor Patrick Smith
  Executive Editor Chloe Hubbard
  Lifestyle Editor Harriet Hall
  Sports Editor Ben Burrows
  Travel Editor Helen Coffey

Irish Examiner

Linn Dubh, Assumption Road, Blackpool, Cork T23 RCH6, Republic of Ireland (Cork)
tel +353 (0)21 4272722 (newsroom)
email news@examiner.ie
4th Floor – Irish Times Building, 24–28 Tara Street, Dublin 2 D02 CX89, Republic of Ireland (Dublin)
website www.irishexaminer.com
Facebook www.facebook.com/IrishExaminer
Twitter @irishexaminer

Editor Tom Fitzpatrick
Daily Mon–Fri €2.40, Sat €3.60

Features. Material mostly commissioned. Length: 1,000 words. Payment: by arrangement. Founded 1841.
  Editor for Digital Products & Projects Dolan O'Hagan
  News Editor Deirdre O'Shaughnessy
  Sports Editor Tony Leen

Irish Independent

Independent House, 27–32 Talbot Street, Dublin D01 X2E1, Republic of Ireland
tel +353 (0)17 055333
email info@independent.ie
website www.independent.ie
Facebook www.facebook.com/independent.ie
Twitter @Independent_ie
Editor Cormac Bourke
Daily Mon–Fri €2.20, Sat €3

Special articles on topical or general subjects. Length: 700–1,000 words. Payment: editor's estimate of value. Founded 1905.
  Business Editor Donal O'Donovan
  Group Head of News Kevin Doyle
  Sports Editor Patrick Keane

The Irish Times

The Irish Times Building, PO Box 74, 24–28 Tara Street, Dublin D02 CX89, Republic of Ireland
tel +353 (0)16 758000
email newsdesk@irishtimes.com
website www.irishtimes.com
Facebook www.facebook.com/irishtimes
Twitter @IrishTimes
Editor Ruadhán Mac Cormaic
Daily Mon–Fri €2.40, Sat €3.70
Supplements **The Irish Times Magazine, The Ticket (Sat), Health + Family (Tue), Business (Daily), Sport (Mon, Wed, Sat)**

Mainly staff-written. Specialist contributions (800–2,000 words) by commission on basis of ideas submitted. Illustrations: photos and line drawings. Payment: at editor's valuation. Founded 1859.
  Arts & Culture Editor Hugh Linehan
  Business Editor Ciaran Hancock
  Digital Editor Paddy Logue
  Education Editor Carl O'Brien
  Foreign Editor Chris Dooley
  Literary Editor Martin Doyle
  News Editor Mark Hennessy
  Opinion Editor John McManus
  Political Editor Pat Leahy
  Sports Editor Malachy Logan

BreakingNews.ie

website www.breakingnews.ie
Editor Michael McAleer
Online platform for news for *The Irish Times*.

Mail on Sunday

Northcliffe House, 2 Derry Street, London W8 5TT
tel 020-7938 6000
email news@mailonsunday.co.uk
website www.mailonsunday.co.uk
Editor Ted Verity
Sun £2
Supplements **You, EVENT**

Articles. Illustrations: line, half-tone; cartoons. Payment: by arrangement. Founded 1982.
  Arts Editor Gordon Smith
  Business Editor Neil Craven
  Literary Editor Susanna Gross
  Political Editor Glen Owen
  Sports Editor Alison Kervin

Financial Mail on Sunday

tel 020-7938 6984
Part of main paper

City, industry, business and personal finance. News stories up to 1,500 words. Full-colour illustrations and photography commissioned. Payment: by arrangement.

EVENT

Free with paper

Fresh and exclusive take on celebrity, film, music, TV and radio, books, theatre, comedy, food, technology and cars. Founded 2013.

You

Editor Jackie Annesley
Free with paper

Women's interest features. Length: 500–2,500 words. Illustrations: full colour and b&w drawings commissioned; also colour photos. Payment: by arrangement.

Metro

Northcote House, 2 Derry Street, London W8 5TT
tel 020-3615 0600
email news.london@ukmetro.co.uk
website https://metro.co.uk/
Facebook www.facebook.com/metroUK
Twitter @metroUK
Editor Deborah Arthurs
Mon–Fri Free

Sister paper to the *Daily Mail* (page 18). Distributed freely on mainline trains, Tube trains and buses and in hospitals and stations in and around selected locations in the UK. Founded 1999.
  Communities Editor Claire Wilson
  Lifestyle Editor Rachel Moss
  Opinions Editor Jess Austin
  Technology/Science Editor Jeff Parsons

Morning Star

People's Press Printing Society Ltd, Ruskin House, 23 Coombe Road, Croydon CR0 1BDS
tel 020-8510 0815
email enquiries@peoples-press.com
website www.morningstaronline.co.uk
Editor Ben Chacko
Daily Mon–Fri £1.30, Sat–Sun £1.70

Newspaper for the Labour movement. Articles of general interest. Illustrations: photos, cartoons, drawings. Founded 1930.
  News Editor Will Stone

The National

125 Fullarton Drive, Glasgow G32 8FG
tel 0141 302 7007
email reporters@thenational.scot
website www.thenational.scot
Facebook www.facebook.com/
thenationalnewspaperscotland
Twitter @ScotNational
Editor Laura Webster
Mon–Sat £1.20, Sun £2.40

Scottish daily newspaper owned by Newsquest and the first daily newspaper in Scotland to support Scottish independence. Founded 2014.
  Community Editor Shona Craven
  Foreign Affairs Editor Davi Pratt
  Political Reporter Hamish Morrison

The New European

22 Highbury Grove, Islington, London N5 2EF
tel 020-8959 1175
email contactus@tnepublishing.com
website www.theneweuropean.co.uk
Facebook www.facebook.com/theneweuropean
Twitter @TheNewEuropean
Editor Steve Anglesey
Weekly Thurs £3.95

A pro-EU weekly newspaper. Writers include Alastair Campbell, Michael White, Bonnie Greer, Hardeep Singh-Kohli, Yasmin Alibhai-Brown and A.C. Grayling. Founded 2016.

The Observer

Kings Place, 90 York Way, London N1 9GU
tel 020-3353 2000
email observer.news@observer.co.uk
website www.theguardian.com/observer
Editor Paul Webster
Sun £3.50
Supplements **Observer Magazine, New Review, Sport, Observer Food Monthly**

Some articles and illustrations commissioned. Payment: by arrangement. Founded 1791.
  Assistant Editor & Comment Editor Robert Yates
  Arts Editor Sarah Donaldson
  Books Editor Ursula Kenny
  Fashion Editor Jo Jones
  New Review Editor Jane Ferguson
  Observer Food Monthly Editor Allan Jenkins
  Political Editor Toby Helm
  Readers' Editor Elisabeth Ribbans

Observer Magazine
tel 020-3353 2000
email magazine@observer.co.uk
Editor Harriet Green
Free with paper

Commissioned features. Length: 2,000–3,000 words.
Illustrations: first-class colour and b&w photos.
Payment: NUJ rates; see website for details.

The Poke

email info@thepoke.co.uk
website www.thepoke.co.uk
Facebook www.facebook.com/PokeHQ
Twitter @ThePoke

Online only. A satirical and topical news source.
Founded 2002.

politics.co.uk

Senate Media Ltd, 4 Croxted Mews, Croxted Road,
London SE24 9DA
tel 020-3758 9407
email editorial@politics.co.uk
website www.politics.co.uk
Facebook www.facebook.com/politicscoukofficial
Twitter @politics_co_uk
Editor John Plunkett

Online only. See website for details on how to submit
articles or drawings and animations.

Scotland on Sunday

80 George Street, Edinburgh EH2 3BU
tel 0131 311 7311
email reception@scotsman.com
website www.scotsman.com
Editor Catherine Salmond
Sun £2.50

Features on all subjects, not necessarily Scottish.
Payment: varies. Founded 1988.
   Politics Editor Alistair Grant
   Sports Editor Mark Atkinson

Spectrum Magazine
Editor Claire Trodden
Free with paper

Scotsman

80 George Street, Edinburgh EH2 3BU
tel 0131 311 7311
email reception@scotsman.com
website www.scotsman.com
Facebook www.facebook.com/
TheScotsmanNewspaper
Twitter @TheScotsman
Editor Neil McIntosh
Daily Mon–Fri £2, Sat £2.50
Supplements **Saturday Magazine, Critique, Property,
Motoring, Recruitment**

Considers articles on political, economic and general
themes which add substantially to current

information. Prepared to commission topical and
controversial series from proved authorities. Length:
800–1,000 words. Illustrations: outstanding news
pictures, cartoons. Payment: by arrangement.
Founded 1817.
   Arts & Books Editor Roger Cox
   Head of Content Alan Young
   Political Editor Alistair Grant
   Sports Editor Mark Atkinson

Scottish Sun

Guildhall, 57 Queen Street, Glasgow G1 3EN
tel 0141 420 5200
email scottishsunletters@the-sun.co.uk
website www.thescottishsun.co.uk
Facebook www.facebook.com/thescottishsun
Twitter @ScottishSun
Editor Gill Smith
Daily Mon–Fri 70p, Sat £1.10, Sun £1.40
Supplements **Fabulous**

Scottish edition of the *Sun*. Illustrations:
transparencies, colour and b&w prints, colour
cartoons. Payment: by arrangement. Founded 1985.

Socialist Worker

PO Box 74955, London E16 9EJ
tel 020-7840 5600
email reports@socialistworker.co.uk
website https://socialistworker.co.uk/
Facebook www.facebook.com/SocialistWorkerBritain
Twitter @socialistworker
Editor Charlie Kimber
Weekly £1

A revolutionary socialist newspaper produced by the
Socialist Workers Party. Founded 1968.

Sun

1 London Bridge Place, London SE1 9GF
tel 020-7782 4100
email exclusive@the-sun.co.uk
website www.thesun.co.uk
Facebook www.facebook.com/thesun
Twitter @TheSun
Editor Victoria Newton
Daily Mon–Fri 80p, Sat £1.10
Supplements **Cashflow, TV Magazine**

Takes freelance material, including cartoons.
Payment: by negotiation. Founded 1969.
   Deputy Editor James Slack
   Bizarre Editor Simon Boyle
   Business Editor Ashley Armstrong
   Political Editor Harry Cole
   Showbiz Editor Amy Brookbanks
   Head of Sport Content Mike Anstead
   Travel Editor Lisa Minot
   TV Editor Andy Halls

Sun on Sunday

1 London Bridge Place, London SE1 9GF
tel 020-7782 4100

email exclusive@the-sun.co.uk
website www.thesun.co.uk
Editor Victoria Newton
Sun £1.40
Supplements **Fabulous**

Takes freelance material. Founded 2012.

Sunday Express
Northern & Shell Building, 10 Lower Thames Street,
London EC4R 6EN
tel 020-8612 7000
email sundaynews@express.co.uk
website www.express.co.uk/news/sunday
Editor David Wooding
Sun £2.20
Supplements **'S', Property, Review, Sport, Travel,
Finance**

Exclusive news stories, photos, personality profiles
and features of controversial or lively interest. Length:
800–1,000 words. Payment: top rates. Founded 1918.
 Business & Finance Editor Geoff Ho
 Health Editor Lucy Johnston
 Literary Editor Charlotte Heathcote
 Political Editor David Maddox
 Sports Editor Scott Wilson
 Television Editor David Stephenson

'S'
tel 020-8612 7257
email sundaymag@express.co.uk
Free with paper

Sunday Independent
27–32 Talbot Street, Dublin D01 X2E1,
Republic of Ireland
tel +353 (0)17 055333
email info@independent.ie
website www.independent.ie
Editor Alan English
Sun €4

Special articles. Length: according to subject.
Illustrations: topical or general interest, cartoons.
Payment: at editor's valuation. Founded 1905.

Sunday Mail
1 Central Quay, Glasgow G3 8DA
tel 0141 309 3232
email reporters@sundaymail.co.uk
London office One Canada Square, Canary Wharf,
London E14 5AP
website www.dailyrecord.co.uk
Editor Brendan McGinty
Sun £2.50
Supplements **Entertainment, Fun on Sunday,
Jobsplus!, 7-Days, Right at Home**

Exclusive stories and pictures of national and Scottish
interest; also cartoons. Payment: above average.
Founded 1982.

Sunday Mirror
One Canada Square, Canary Wharf, London E14 5AP
tel 020-7293 3000
email scoops@sundaymirror.co.uk
website www.mirror.co.uk
Editor Gemma Aldridge
Sun £2.20
Supplements **Notebook, Holidays & Getaways**

Concentrates on human interest news features, social
documentaries, dramatic news and feature photos.
Ideas, as well as articles, bought. Payment: high,
especially for exclusives. Founded 1963.
 News Editor Mark Wood
 Political Editor Nigel Nelson
 Sports Editor David Walker

Sunday National
125 Fullarton Drive, Glasgow G32 8FG
tel 0141 302 7007
email reporters@thenational.scot
website www.thenational.scot
Facebook www.facebook.com/
thenationalnewspaperscotland
Twitter @ScotNational
Editor Laura Webster
Sun £2.40

Scottish Sunday newspaper owned by Newsquest.
Replaced the *Sunday Herald*. Sister paper of *The
National*, the first daily newspaper in Scotland to
support Scottish independence. Founded 2018.

Sunday People
One Canada Square, Canary Wharf, London E14 5AP
tel 020-7293 3842
email feedback@people.co.uk
website www.mirror.co.uk/all-about/sunday-people
Editor Gemma Aldridge
Sun £2.20
Supplements **Take it Easy**

Exclusive news and feature stories needed.
Investigative and campaigning issues. Features and
human interest stories as speciality. Strong sports
following. Payment: rates high, even for tips that lead
to published news stories. Founded 1881.

Take it Easy
Editor Samantha Cope
Free with paper

Sunday Post
Spiers View, 50 High Craighall Road,
Glasgow G4 9UD
tel (01382) 223131
email news@sundaypost.com
website www.sundaypost.com
Editor Jim Wilson
Sun £2.30
Supplements **Travel & Homes, TV & Entertainment**

Human interest, topical, domestic and humorous articles, and exclusive news. Payment: on acceptance. Founded 1914.

P.S.
tel (01382) 223131
Editor Jayne Savva
Monthly Free with paper
General interest articles. Length: 1,000–2,000 words. Illustrations: colour transparencies. Payment: varies. Founded 2019.

Sunday Telegraph
111 Buckingham Palace Road, London SW1W 0DT
tel 020-7931 2000
email stnews@telegraph.co.uk
website www.telegraph.co.uk
Editor Allister Heath
Sun £3
Supplements **Business Reporter, Life, It's Your Money, Sport, Stella, Discover**

Occasional freelance material accepted. Founded 1961.

The Sunday Times
The News Building, 1 London Bridge Place, London SE1 9GF
tel 020-7782 5000
email newsdesk@sunday-times.co.uk
website www.thetimes.co.uk
Facebook www.facebook.com/timesandsundaytimes
Twitter @thesundaytimes
Editor Ben Taylor
Sun £3.50
Supplements **Appointments, Business, Culture, Driving, Home, Money, News Review, Sport, Style, The Sunday Times Magazine, Travel**

Special articles by authoritative writers on politics, literature, art, drama, music, finance, science and topical matters. Payment: top rate for exclusive features. Founded 1822.
 Economics Editor David Smith
 Literary Editor Robin Millen
 Political Editor Tim Shipman
 Social Affairs Editor Emily Dugan
 Sports Editor Tom Clarke

The Sunday Times Magazine
tel 020-7782 5000
Free with paper
Articles and pictures. Illustrations: colour and b&w photos. Payment: by negotiation.

Tes (The Times Educational Supplement)
70 Gray's Inn Road, London WC1X 8NH
tel 020-3194 3000
email newsdesk@tes.com
email features@tes.com
website www.tes.com
Twitter @tes

Editor Jon Severs
Daily £15 per quarter

Education magazine publishing daily online. The latest news, analysis and teaching and learning research for those who work in schools. Specialist knowledge required and ideas should be emailed to the relevant sector editor. Payment: by arrangement. Founded 1910.

Tess (The Times Educational Supplement Scotland)
70 Gray's Inn Road, London WC1X 8NH
email henry.hepburn@tes.com
website www.tes.com/magazine/hub/scotland
Twitter @TesScotland
Scotland Editor Henry Hepburn
Updated daily; see website for subscription options

Online education magazine. Articles on education, preferably 500–600 words, written with special knowledge or experience. News items about Scottish educational affairs, especially those affecting schools. Payment: by arrangement. Founded 1965.

THE (Times Higher Education)
26 Red Lion Square, London WC1R 4HQ
email john.gill@timeshighereducation.com
website www.timeshighereducation.co.uk
Facebook www.facebook.com/timeshighereducation
Twitter @timeshighered
Editor John Gill
Weekly £4.50

Articles on higher education written with special knowledge or experience, or articles dealing with academic topics. Also news items. Illustrations: suitable photos and drawings of educational interest. Payment: by arrangement. Founded 1971.

The Times
1 London Bridge Place, London SE1 9GF
tel 020-7782 5000
email home.news@thetimes.co.uk
website www.thetimes.co.uk
Facebook www.facebook.com/timesandsundaytimes
Twitter @thetimes
Editor Tony Gallagher
Daily Mon–Fri £2.50, Sat £3
Supplements **Books, Crème, Football Handbook, The Game, The Knowledge, Money, Times 2, Times Law, The Times Magazine, Times Sport, Travel, Arts and Entertainment, Fashion, Saturday Review, Technology, Weekend**

Outside contributions considered from experts in subjects of current interest and writers who can make first-hand experience or reflection come readably alive. Phone appropriate section editor. Length: up to 1,200 words. Founded 1785.
 Business Editor Richard Fletcher
 Education Editor Sian Griffiths
 Foreign Editor Roland Watson

Health Editor Kat Lay
Literary Editor Robbie Millen
Political Editor Steven Swinford
Head of Sport Tom Cotterell
Travel Editor Duncan Craig

The Times Magazine
Free with Sat paper
Features. Illustrated.

Timesonline
website www.thetimes.co.uk
Editor Alan Hunter

Subscription website containing news from *The Times* and *The Sunday Times*. Founded 1999.

TLS (The Times Literary Supplement)
The News Building, 1 London Bridge Street,
London SE1 9GF
tel 020-7782 6000
email queries@the-tls.co.uk
website www.the-tls.co.uk
Editor Martin Ivens
Weekly £4.50

Will consider poems for publication, literary discoveries and articles on literary and cultural affairs. Payment: by arrangement. Founded 1902.

Tortoise
website www.tortoisemedia.com
Facebook www.facebook.com/agathathetortoise
Twitter @tortoise
Editor & Founder James Harding

Online-only British news service dedicated to being selective and deliberative in the news it reports. Founded 2019.

The Voice
Unit 1, Bricklayers Arms, Mandela Way,
London SE1 5SR
tel 020-7510 0340
email newsdesk@thevoicemediagroup.co.uk
website www.voice-online.co.uk
Facebook www.facebook.com/voicenews
Twitter @TheVoiceNews
Editor Lester Holloway
Weekly £2.50

Weekly newspaper for Black Britons. Includes news, features, arts, sport and a comprehensive jobs and business section. Illustrations: colour and b&w photos. Open to ideas for news and features on sports, business, community events and the arts. Founded 1982.

Lifestyle, Arts & Entertainment Editor Joel Campbell
News Editor Vic Motune
Sports & Features Editor Rodney Hinds

Wales on Sunday
6 Park Street, Cardiff CF10 1XR
tel 029-2024 3604
email newsdesk@walesonline.co.uk
website www.walesonline.co.uk
Facebook www.facebook.com/WalesOnline
Twitter @walesonline
Editor Steffan Rhys
Sun £2.10
Supplements **Life on Sunday, Sport on Sunday**

National Sunday newspaper of Wales offering comprehensive news, features and entertainment coverage at the weekend, with a particular focus on events in Wales. Accepts general interest articles, preferably with a Welsh connection. Founded 1989.
Political Editor David Williamson
Head of Sport Paul Abbandonato

Weekly Gleaner
Unit 1, Bricklayers Arms, Mandela Way,
London SE1 5SR
tel 020-7510 0366
email george.ruddock@gvmedia.co.uk
website www.jamaica-gleaner.com
Facebook www.facebook.com/GleanerJamaica
Twitter @JamaicaGleaner
Editor George Ruddock
Weekly Thurs £1.20

Offshoot of the *Daily Gleaner*, the oldest operating newspaper in the English-speaking Caribbean. Newspaper for the UK Black British/Caribbean community, available in most of the major cities, including London, Birmingham, Manchester, Liverpool, Nottingham, Leicester, Bristol and Leeds. Content covers news, analytical viewpoints, art, entertainment, sports and various lifestyle feature supplements. Founded 1951.

Regional newspapers UK and Ireland

Regional newspapers are listed in alphabetical order under region. The list is not exhaustive. Over recent years, it has become increasingly difficult for freelance writers to have pitches accepted or commissions requested by regional news companies. The below listing includes those papers that may still be accepting work from freelance writers. Some will accept and pay for brief fillers and gossip paragraphs, as well as puzzles and quizzes.

BELFAST

Belfast Telegraph
Belfast Telegraph House, 33 Clarendon Road, Clarendon Dock, Belfast BT1 3BG
tel 028-9026 4000
email newseditor@belfasttelegraph.co.uk
website www.belfasttelegraph.co.uk
Facebook www.facebook.com/belfasttelegraph
Twitter @beltel
Editor Eoin Brannigan
Daily Mon–Sat £1.20

An independent news and media publication. Any material relating to Northern Ireland. Payment: by negotiation. Founded 1870.

Irish News
113–117 Donegall Street, Belfast BT1 2GE
tel 028-9032 2226
email newsdesk@irishnews.com
website www.irishnews.com
Facebook www.facebook.com/IrishNewsLtd
Twitter @irish_news
Editor Noel Doran
Daily Mon–Sat £1.40

Founded 1855.

News Letter
Suites 302–303, Glandore, Arthur House, 41 Arthur Street, Belfast BT1 4GB
tel 028-3839 5577
email newsdesk@newsletter.co.uk
website www.newsletter.co.uk/news
Facebook www.facebook.com/belfastnewsletter
Twitter @News_Letter
Editor Ben Lowry
Daily Mon–Fri £1.60, Sat £2.20

Pro-Union. Founded 1737.

Sunday Life
Belfast Telegraph House, 33 Clarendon Road, Clarendon Dock, Belfast BT1 3BG
tel 028-9026 4000
email sinews@sundaylife.co.uk
website www.belfasttelegraph.co.uk/sunday-life
Editor Eoin Brannigan
Sun £2.10

Items of interest to Northern Ireland Sunday tabloid readers. Illustrations: colour and b&w pictures and graphics. Payment: by arrangement. Founded 1988.

CHANNEL ISLANDS

Jersey Evening Post
PO Box 582, Five Oaks, St Saviour, Jersey JE4 8XQ
tel (01534) 611611
email news@jerseyeveningpost.com
website https://jerseyeveningpost.com/
Facebook www.facebook.com/jerseyeveningpost
Twitter @jepnews
Editor Andy Sibcy
Daily Mon–Sat £1

News and features with a Channel Islands angle. Length: 1,000 words (articles/features), 300 words (news). Illustrations: colour and b&w. Founded 1890.

CORK

Evening Echo
Linn Dubh, Assumption Road, Blackpool, Cork T23 RCH6, Republic of Ireland
tel +353 (0)21 4272722
email news@eecho.ie
website www.eveningecho.ie
Facebook www.facebook.com/echolivecork
Twitter @echolivecork
Editor Maurice Gubbins
Daily Mon–Sat €1.90

Articles, features and news for the area. Illustrations: colour prints. Founded 1892.

DUBLIN

Dublin Gazette
Suite 15, The Cube, Sandyford, Dublin 18, Republic of Ireland
website https://dublingazette.com/
Facebook www.facebook.com/dublingazettenewspapers
Twitter @dublingazette
Editor P.J. Cunningham
Weekly Thursday Free

Publishes City, Fingal, West, and South editions. Founded 1689.

EAST ANGLIA

Cambridge Independent

Iliffe Media Ltd, Winship Road, Milton,
Cambridge CB24 6PP
tel (01223) 320320
email newsdesk@iliffemedia.co.uk
website www.cambridgeindependent.co.uk
Facebook www.facebook.com/cambridgeindependent
Twitter @cambridgeindy
Editor Paul Brackley
Weekly Wed £1.70

News from Cambridge and surrounding area. Founded 1815.

Cambridge News

Winship Road, Milton, Cambridge CB4 6PP
tel (01223) 632293
email newsdesk@cambridge-news.co.uk
website www.cambridge-news.co.uk
Facebook www.facebook.com/cambridgeshirelive
Twitter @CambsLive
Editor Charlotte Page
Daily Mon–Sat £1.55

The voice of the Cambridge region – news, views and sport. Illustrations: colour prints, b&w and colour graphics. Payment: by negotiation. Founded 1888.

East Anglian Daily Times

1 Bath Street, Ipswich IP2 8SD
tel (01473) 230023
email newsroom@archant.co.uk
website www.eadt.co.uk
Facebook www.facebook.com/eadt24
Twitter @eadt24
Editor Liz Nice
Daily Mon–Fri £1.05, Sat £2

Features of East Anglian interest, preferably with pictures. Length: 500 words. Illustrations: NUJ rates. Payment: negotiable. Founded 1874.

Eastern Daily Press

Prospect House, Rouen Road, Norwich NR1 1RE
tel (01603) 628311
website www.edp24.co.uk
Facebook www.facebook.com/edp24
Twitter @edp24
Editor Richard Porritt
Daily Mon–Fri £1.20, Saturday £2.20

Limited market for articles of East Anglian interest not exceeding 650 words. Founded 1870.

Ipswich Star

1 Bath Street, Ipswich IP2 8SD
tel (01473) 230023
website www.ipswichstar.co.uk
Facebook www.facebook.com/ipswichstar24
Twitter @ipswichstar24
Editor Liz Nice
Daily Mon–Fri 90p

Founded 1885.

Norwich Evening News

Prospect House, Rouen Road, Norwich NR1 1RE
tel (01603) 628311
website www.eveningnews24.co.uk
Facebook www.facebook.com/NorwichEveningNews
Twitter @EveningNews
Editor Richard Porritt
Daily Mon–Sat 90p

Interested in local news-based features. Length: up to 650 words. Payment: agreed rates. Founded 1882.

EAST MIDLANDS

Burton Mail

Unit 1–2 ,Milton House, Worthington Way,
Burton upon Trent, Staffs. DE14 1BQ
tel (01283) 510075
email editorial@burtonmail.co.uk
website www.burtonmail.co.uk
Facebook www.facebook.com/BurtonNews
Twitter @BurtonMailNews
Editor Julie Crouch
Daily Mon–Sat £1.40

Features, news and articles of interest to Burton and south Derbyshire readers. Length: 400–500 words. Illustrations: colour and b&w. Payment: by negotiation. Founded 1898.

Chronicle & Echo, Northampton

Northamptonshire Newspapers Ltd,
400 Pavilion Drive, Northampton NN4 7PA
tel (01604) 467032
email editor@northantsnews.co.uk
website www.northamptonchron.co.uk
Facebook www.facebook.com/northamptonchron
Twitter @ChronandEcho
Editor David Summers
Weekly Thurs £1.80

Articles, features and news – mostly commissioned – of interest to the Northampton area. Length: varies. Payment: by negotiation. Founded 1931.

Derby Telegraph

2 Siddals Road, Derby DE1 2PB
tel (01332) 411888
website www.derbytelegraph.co.uk
Facebook www.facebook.com/derbyshirelive
Twitter @Derbyshire_live
Editor Sam Dimmer
Daily Mon–Fri £1.30, Sat £1.35

Articles and news of local interest. Payment: by negotiation. Founded 1879.

Newspapers and magazines

Leicester Mercury
c/o 3rd floor, City Gate, Tollhouse Hill,
Nottingham NG1 5FS
tel 03444 060910
website www.leicestermercury.co.uk
Facebook www.facebook.com/leicestershirelive
Twitter @LeicsLive
Editor Adam Moss
Daily Mon–Sat £1.40

Occasional articles, features and news; submit ideas
to editor first. Length/payment: by negotiation.
Founded 1874.

Nottingham Post
3rd Floor, City Gate, Tollhouse Hill,
Nottingham NG1 5FS
tel 0115 948 2000
email newsdesk@nottinghampostgroup.co.uk
website www.nottinghampost.com
Facebook www.facebook.com/Nottinghamshirelive
Twitter @NottsLive
Editor Natalie Fahy
Daily Mon–Sat £1.45

Material on local issues considered. Founded 1878.

Peterborough Telegraph
c/o Brightfields Business Hub, Bakewell Road,
Peterborough PE2 6XU
tel (01733) 555111
email news@peterboroughtoday.co.uk
website www.peterboroughtoday.co.uk
Facebook www.facebook.com/peterboroughtoday
Twitter @peterboroughtel
Editor David Summers
Weekly Thurs £1.70

Founded 1948.

LONDON

London Evening Standard
Alphabeta, 14–18 Finsbury Square,
London EC2A 1AH
email news@standard.co.uk
website www.standard.co.uk
Facebook www.facebook.com/eveningstandard
Twitter @standardnews
Acting Editor Jack Lefley
Daily Mon–Fri Free

Founded 1827.

ES-Magazine
Editor Laura Weir
Twice weekly Thurs, Fri Free with paper
Feature ideas, exclusively about London. Illustrations:
all types. Payment: by negotiation.

Homes & Property
email homesandproperty@standard.co.uk
Editor Prudence Ivey

Weekly Wed Free with paper
UK property. Payment: by negotiation.

This Is London
website www.standard.co.uk
Online news website for *London Evening Standard*.

NORTH EAST

Berwick Advertiser
North East Head Office,
North East Business & Innovation Centre (BIC),
Warfield Enterprise Park East, Sunderland SR5 2TA
tel (01289) 334686
email Berwick.advertiser@nationalworld.com
website www.northumberlandgazette.co.uk
Facebook www.facebook.com/BAdvertiser
Twitter @BAdvertiser
Editor Amanda Bourn
Weekly Thurs £1.60

News, sport and features. Founded 1808.

The Chronicle
2nd Floor, Eldon Court, Percy Street,
Newcastle upon Tyne NE1 7JB
tel 0191 232 7500
email ec.news@ncjmedia.co.uk
website www.chroniclelive.co.uk
Facebook www.facebook.com/NewcastleChronicle
Twitter @ChronicleLive
Editor Helen Dalby
Daily Mon–Fri £1.35, Sat £2.20

News, photos and features covering almost every
subject of interest to readers in Tyne & Wear,
Northumberland and Durham. Payment: by prior
arrangement. Founded 1858.

Darlington and Stockton Times
PO Box 14, Priestgate, Darlington DL1 1NF
tel (01325) 381313
email newsdesk@nne.co.uk
website www.darlingtonandstocktontimes.co.uk
Facebook www.facebook.com/
darlingtonstocktontimes
Twitter @DAndSTimes
Editor Hannah Chapman
Weekly Fri £1.60

Founded 1847.

Durham Advertiser
PO Box 14, Priestgate, Darlington DL1 1NF
tel 0191 384 4600
email newsdesk@nne.co.uk
website www.thenorthernecho.co.uk/news/local/
northdurham/durham
Facebook www.facebook.com/durhamadvertiser
Editor Gavin Foster
Weekly Fri 80p

Founded 1814.

The Gazette

Ground Floor, Hudson Quay, The Halyard,
Middlehaven, Middlesbrough TS3 6RT
tel (01642) 245401
email news@gazettemedia.co.uk
website www.gazettelive.co.uk
Facebook www.facebook.com/Teessidelive
Twitter @TeessideLive
Editor Ian McNeal
Daily Mon–Sat 95p

News, topical and lifestyle features. Length: 600–800
words. Illustrations: line, half-tone, colour, graphics,
cartoons. Payment: scale rate or by agreement for
illustrations. Founded 1869.

Hartlepool Mail

New Clarence House, Wesley Square,
Hartlepool TS24 8BX
tel (01429) 225644
email mail.news@northeast-press.co.uk
website www.hartlepoolmail.co.uk
Facebook www.facebook.com/hartlepoolmailnews
Twitter @HPoolMail
Editor Gavin Ledwith
Daily Mon–Sat £1.30

Features of local interest. Length: 500 words.
Illustrations: colour, b&w photos, line. Payment: by
negotiation. Founded 1877.

The Journal

Eldon Court, Percy Street,
Newcastle upon Tyne NE1 7JB
tel 0191 201 6446
email ec.news@ncjmedia.co.uk
website www.chroniclelive.co.uk
Facebook www.facebook.com/NewcastleChronicle
Twitter @TheJournalNews
Editor Graeme Whitfield
Daily Mon–Sat £1

News, sport items and features of topical interest
considered. Payment: by arrangement.

The Northern Echo

Suite 10, 2nd Floor, Coniscliffe House,
5-7 Coniscliffe Road, Darlington,
County Durham DL3 7EE
tel (01325) 381313
email newsdesk@nee.co.uk
website www.thenorthernecho.co.uk
Facebook www.facebook.com/thenorthernecho
Twitter @TheNorthernEcho
Editor Gavin Foster
Daily Mon–Fri £1, Sat £1.50

Articles of interest to the north east and North
Yorkshire; all material commissioned. Preliminary
study of newspaper advisable. Length: 800–1,000
words. Illustrations: line, half-tone, colour – mostly
commissioned. Payment: by negotiation.
Founded 1870.

The Shields Gazette

North East Business and Innovation Centre,
Wearfield, Enterprise Park East, Sunderland SR5 2TA
tel 0191 501 7326
website www.shieldsgazette.com
Facebook www.facebook.com/shieldsgazette
Twitter @shieldsgazette
Editor Liam Kennedy
Daily Mon–Sat £1

Founded 1855.

Sunday Sun

Eldon Court, Percy Street,
Newcastle upon Tyne NE1 7JB
tel 0191 201 6201
email scoop.sundaysun@ncjmedia.co.uk
website www.chroniclelive.co.uk/all-about/sunday-sun
Editor Matt McKenzie
Weekly Sun £2.20

Looking for topical and human interest articles on
current problems. Particularly welcomed are features
of family appeal and news stories of special interest to
the North of England. Length: 200–700 words.
Illustrations: photos. Payment: normal lineage rates,
or by arrangement. Founded 1919.

Sunderland Echo

JPI Media, 1st Floor, North East BIC, Wearfield,
Enterprise Park East, Sunderland SR5 2TA
tel 0191 501 5800
email echo.news@northeast-press.co.uk
website www.sunderlandecho.com
Facebook www.facebook.com/sunderlandechoonline
Twitter @SunderlandEcho
Editorial Director Gary Oliver
Daily Mon–Sat £1

Local news, features and articles. Length: 500 words.
Illustrations: colour and b&w photos, line, cartoons.
Payment: by negotiation. Founded 1875.

NORTH WEST

Blackpool Gazette

Stuart House, 89 Caxton Road, Fulwood,
Preston PR2 9ZB
tel (01253) 400888
email editorial@blackpoolgazette.co.uk
website www.blackpoolgazette.co.uk
Facebook www.facebook.com/blackpoolgazette
Twitter @the_gazette
Editor Nicola Adam
Daily Mon–Sat £1.20

Local news and articles of general interest, with
photos if appropriate. Length: varies. Payment: on
merit. Founded 1929.

Bolton News

Suite A, 1st Floor, Knowsley House, Knowsley Street,
Bolton BL1 2AH
tel (01204) 522345
email newsdesk@nqw.co.uk
website www.theboltonnews.co.uk
Facebook www.facebook.com/theboltonnews
Twitter @TheBoltonNews
Editor Ian Savage
Daily Mon–Sat 85p

Founded 1867.

The Chester Chronicle

Maple House, Park West, Sealand Road,
Chester CH1 4RN
tel (01244) 606455
email newsroom@cheshirenews.co.uk
website www.chesterchronicle.co.uk
Facebook www.facebook.com/CheshireLive
Twitter @CheshireLive
Editor Frances Barrett
Weekly Thurs £2.10

Local news and features. Founded 1775.

Lancashire Post

Stuart House, 89 Caxton Road, Fulwood,
Preston PR2 9ZB
tel (01772) 838134
email lep.newsdesk@lep.co.uk
website www.lep.co.uk
Facebook www.facebook.com/lancashireeveningpost
Twitter @leponline
Editor Nicola Adam
Daily Mon–Sat £1.10

Topical articles on all subjects. Area of interest:
Wigan to Lake District, Lancs. and coast. Length:
600–900 words. Illustrations: colour and b&w
photos, cartoons. Payment: by arrangement.
Founded 1886.

Lancashire Telegraph

Suite 6c, Freckleton Business Centre,
Freckleton Street, Blackburn BB2 2AL
tel (01254) 678678
email lancsnews@nqnw.co.uk
website www.lancashiretelegraph.co.uk
Facebook www.facebook.com/lancashiretelegraph
Twitter @lancstelegraph
Editor Richard Duggan
Daily Mon–Sat 80p

Will consider general news items from east
Lancashire. Payment: by arrangement. Founded 1886.

Liverpool Echo

5 St Paul's Square, Liverpool LS3 9SJ
tel 0151 472 2453
website www.liverpoolecho.co.uk
Facebook www.facebook.com/theliverpoolecho
Twitter @LivEchonews
Editor Maria Breslin

Daily Mon–Fri, Sun £1.40, Sat £1.80

Articles of up to 600–800 words of local or topical
interest; also cartoons. Payment: according to merit;
special rates for exceptional material. Connected
with, but independent of, the *Liverpool Post*: articles
not interchangeable. Founded 1879.

The Mail

Newspaper House, 1 Wainwrights Yard,
Kendal LA9 4DP
tel (01229) 840150
email news.em@newsquest.co.uk
website www.nwemail.co.uk
Facebook www.facebook.com/northwesteveningmail
Editor Joy Yates
Daily Mon–Fri 90p, Sat £1

Articles, features and news. Length: 500 words.
Covering the whole of south Cumbria.
Illustrations: colour photos and occasional artwork.
Founded 1898.

Manchester Evening News

Mitchell Henry House, Hollinwood Avenue,
Chadderton, Oldham OL9 8EF
tel 0161 832 7200 (editorial)
email newsdesk@men-news.co.uk
website www.manchestereveningnews.co.uk
Facebook www.facebook.com/
ManchesterEveningNews
Twitter @MENNewsdesk
Editor Sarah Lester
Daily Mon–Fri £1.40, Sat £1.70, Sun £1.20

Feature articles of up to 1,000 words, topical or
general interest and illustrated where appropriate,
should be addressed to the Features Editor. Payment:
on acceptance. Founded 1868.

News and Star (Carlisle)

CN Group, Newspaper House, Dalston Road,
Carlisle CA2 5UA
tel (01228) 612617
website www.newsandstar.co.uk
Facebook www.facebook.com/newsandstar
Twitter @newsandstar
Editor Joy Yates
Daily Mon–Sat 90p

Founded 1910.

Southport Reporter

4A Post Office Avenue, Southport PR9 0US
tel 08463 244195
email news24@southportreporter.com
website www.southportreporter.com
Facebook www.facebook.com/SouthportReporter
Twitter @SouthportReport
Editor Patrick Trollope

Online only. An independent news and information
online newspaper. Founded 1999.

SCOTLAND

The Courier

D.C. Thomson & Co. Ltd, 2 Albert Square,
Dundee DD1 1DD
tel (01382) 575291
London office 185 Fleet Street, London EC4A 2HS
tel 020-7400 1030
website www.thecourier.co.uk
Facebook www.facebook.com/thecourieruk
Twitter @thecourieruk
Editor David Clegg
Daily Mon–Fri £1.55, Sat £1.80
Supplements **Motoring, House & Home, What's On,
Menu, Weekend, Beautiful Homes, Perfect
Weddings, Farming, Business, Sport**

One of Britain's biggest regional morning newspapers
and an established title in east central Scotland.
Publishes three daily editions and covers local news
for Perthshire, Fife, Angus and Dundee.
Founded 1810.

Dundee Evening Telegraph

D.C. Thomson & Co. Ltd, 2 Albert Square,
Dundee DD1 1DD
tel (01382) 575452
email newsdesk@eveningtelegraph.co.uk
website www.thecourier.co.uk
Facebook www.facebook.com/eveningtele
Twitter @Evening_Tele
Editor Dave Lord
Daily Mon–Sat 90p

Founded 1877.

Evening Express (Aberdeen)

Aberdeen Journals Ltd, 1 Marischal Square,
Broad Street, Aberdeen AB10 1BL
tel (01224) 343033
email ee.news@ajl.co.uk
website www.pressandjournal.co.uk
Facebook www.facebook.com/
EveningExpressAberdeen
Twitter @eveningexpress
Editor Frank O'Donnell
Daily Mon–Sat 90p

Evening paper. Illustrations: colour and b&w.
Payment: by arrangement. Founded 1879.

Evening News (Edinburgh)

80 George Street, Edinburgh EH2 3BU
tel 0131 311 7311
email reception@scotsman.com
website www.edinburghnews.scotsman.com
Facebook www.facebook.com/
edinburgh.evening.news
Twitter @edinburghpaper
Editor Euan McGrory
Daily Mon–Sat £1.10

Features on current affairs, preferably in relation to
the circulation area. Women's talking points; local
historical articles; subjects of general interest; health,
beauty and fashion. Founded 1873.

Glasgow Evening Times

Herald & Times Group, 125 Fullarton Drive,
Glasgow East Investment Park, Glasgow G32 8FG
tel 0141 302 7000
website www.glasgowtimes.co.uk
Facebook www.facebook.com/glasgowtimes
Twitter @TheEveningTimes
Editor Callum Baird
Daily Mon–Sat 85p

Founded 1876.

Greenock Telegraph

2 Crawfurd Street, Greenock PA15 1LH
tel (01475) 558904
email editorial@greenocktelegraph.co.uk
website www.greenocktelegraph.co.uk
Facebook www.facebook.com/greenocktelegraph
Twitter @greenocktele
Editor Brian Hossack
Daily Mon–Sat 75p

News and features from the area in and around
Greenock. Founded 1857.

Inverness Courier

Suite 3.04, Moray House, 16–18 Bank Street,
Inverness IV1 1QY
tel (01463) 246575
email newsdesk@hnmedia.co.uk
website www.inverness-courier.co.uk
Facebook www.facebook.com/invernesscourier
Twitter @InvCourier
Editor Andrew Dixon
Bi-weekly Tues, Fri £1.60

Articles of Highland interest only. Unsolicited
material accepted. Illustrations: colour and b&w
photos. Payment: by arrangement. Founded 1817.

Paisley Daily Express

One Central Quay, Glasgow G3 8DA
tel 0141 309 3555
email pde@reachplc.com
website www.dailyrecord.co.uk/all-about/paisley
Facebook www.facebook.com/paisleydailyexpress
Twitter @PDEofficial
Editor Cheryl McEvoy
Daily Mon–Sat £1

Articles of Paisley interest only. Considers unsolicited
material. Founded 1874.

Press and Journal

5th Floor, 1 Marischal Square, Broad Street,
Aberdeen AB10 1BL
tel (01224) 343311

email pj.newsdesk@ajl.co.uk
website www.pressandjournal.co.uk
Facebook www.facebook.com/ThePressandJournal
Twitter @pressjournal
Editor Frank O'Donnell
Daily Mon–Fri £1.65, Sat £2.30

Contributions of Scottish interest. Illustrations: half-tone. Payment: by arrangement. Founded 1747.

SOUTH EAST

The Argus

33 Bond Street, Brighton, East Sussex BN1 1RD
tel (01273) 021400
email editor@theargus.co.uk
website www.theargus.co.uk
Facebook www.facebook.com/brightonargus
Twitter @brightonargus
Editor Aaron Hendy
Daily Mon–Fri £1, Sat £1.10

Founded 1880.

Banbury Guardian

c/o Regus Milton Keynes, Atterbury Lakes,
Fairburn Drive, Milton Keynes MK10 9RG
tel 07803 506319
email editorial@banburyguardian.co.uk
website www.banburyguardian.co.uk
Facebook www.facebook.com/banburyguardian
Twitter @banburynews
Editor Phil Hubble
Daily Mon–Sat £1.50

Local news and features. Founded 1838.

Echo

Echo House, Howard Chase, Basildon SS14 3BE
tel (01268) 522792
email echonews@nqe.com
website www.echo-news.co.uk
Facebook www.facebook.com/echo.essex
Twitter @Essex_Echo
Editor Michael Adkins
Daily Mon–Fri 90p

Mostly staff-written. Only interested in local material. Payment: by arrangement. Founded 1969.

Essex Chronicle

Kestrel House, Hedgerows Business Park,
Chelmsford CM2 5PF
tel (01245) 602730
email newsdesk@essexlive.news
website www.essexlive.news/news
Twitter @essexlive
Editor Katrina Chilver
Weekly Thurs £1.90

Local news and features for Essex. Founded 1764.

Hampshire Chronicle

5 Upper Brook St, Winchester SO23 8AL
tel (01962) 860836
email news@hampshirechronicle.co.uk
website www.hampshirechronicle.co.uk
Facebook www.facebook.com/hampshire.chronicle
Twitter @hantschronicle
Editor Kimberley Barber
Weekly Thurs £1.50

Founded 1772.

Isle of Wight County Press

Brannon House, 123 Pyle Street, Newport,
Isle of Wight PO30 1ST
tel (01983) 259003
email editor@iwcp.co.uk
website www.countypress.co.uk
Facebook www.facebook.com/iwcponline
Twitter @iwcponline
Editors Lori Little, Lucy Morgan
Weekly Fri £1.30

Articles and news of local interest. Founded 1884.

Kent and Sussex Courier

Courier House, 80–84 Calverley Road,
Tunbridge Wells TN1 2UN
tel (01892) 239042
email kentlivenewsdesk@reachplc.com
website www.kentlive.news
Facebook www.facebook.com/kentlivenews
Twitter @kentlivenews
Editor Luke Jacobs
Weekly Fri £2.20

Local news, articles and features. Founded 1872.

Medway Messenger

Medway House, Ginsbury Close,
Sir Thomas Longley Road, Medway City Estate,
Strood, Kent ME2 4DU
tel (01634) 227800
email medwaymessenger@thekmgroup.co.uk
website www.kentonline.co.uk
Facebook www.facebook.com/MedwayMessenger
Twitter @MedwayMessenger
Editor Matt Ramsden
Weekly Thurs £1.80

Emphasis on news and sport from the Medway Towns. Illustrations: line, half-tone. Founded 1855.

The News, Portsmouth

100 Lakeside, North Harbour, Portsmouth PO6 3EN
tel 023-9262 2118
email newsdesk@thenews.co.uk
website www.portsmouth.co.uk
Facebook www.facebook.com/portsmouthnews
Twitter @portsmouthnews
Editor Mark Waldron
Daily Mon–Sat £1.10

Articles of relevance to south east Hampshire and West Sussex. Payment: by arrangement. Founded 1873.

Oxford Mail

5 King's Meadow, Ferry Hinksey Road, Osney Mead, Oxford OX2 0DP
tel (01865) 425262
email news@nqo.com
website www.oxfordmail.co.uk
Facebook www.facebook.com/oxfordmail
Twitter @TheOxfordMail
Editor Andrew Colley
Daily 90p

Founded 1928.

The Oxford Times

5 King's Meadow, Ferry Hinksey Road, Osney Mead, Oxford OX2 0DP
tel (01865) 425262
email news@nqo.com
website www.oxfordtimes.co.uk
Facebook www.facebook.com/TheOxfordTimes
Twitter @oxfordtimes
Editor Andrew Colley
Weekly Thurs £1.70

Local weekly newspaper for Oxford. The team is also responsible for the daily *Oxford Mail* and weeklies *Bicester Advertiser*, *Witney Gazette* and the *Herald* series. Founded 1862.

Reading Chronicle

2–10 Bridge Street, Reading RG1 2LU
tel 0118 955 3333
email news@readingchronicle.co.uk
website www.readingchronicle.co.uk
Facebook www.facebook.com/readingchronicle
Twitter @rdgchronicle
Acting Editor Naomi Herring
Weekly Thurs £1.10

Southern Daily Echo

The Quay, 30 Channel Way, Southampton, Hants SO14 9JX
tel 023-8042 4777
email newsdesk@dailyecho.co.uk
website www.dailyecho.co.uk
Facebook www.facebook.com/dailyecho
Twitter @dailyecho
Editor Ben Fishwick
Daily Mon–Fri 55p, Sat £1

News, articles, features, sport. Length: varies. Illustrations: line, half-tone, colour, cartoons. Payment: NUJ rates. Founded 1888.

Stratford Herald

Guild House, Guild Street, Statford-upon-Avon, Warwickshire CV37 6RP
tel (01789) 266261
email news@stratford-herald.com
website www.stratford-herald.com
Facebook www.facebook.com/stratfordherald
Twitter @heraldnewspaper
Editor Andy Veale
Weekly Thurs £1

Local news and features. See website for details. Founded 1860.

Swindon Advertiser

Richmond House, Unit 1 and 2, Edison Park, Swindon SN3 3RB
tel (01793) 528144
email newsdesk@swindonadvertiser.co.uk
website www.swindonadvertiser.co.uk
Facebook www.facebook.com/swindonadvertiser
Twitter @swindonadver
Editor Daniel Chipperfield
Daily Mon–Sat 85p

News and information relating to Swindon and Wiltshire only. Considers unsolicited material. Founded 1854.

SOUTH WEST

Bournemouth Echo

2nd/3rd Floors, The Echo Building, 18 Albert Road, Bournemouth, Dorset BH1 1BZ
tel (01202) 554601
email newsdesk@bournemouthecho.co.uk
website www.bournemouthecho.co.uk
Facebook www.facebook.com/bournemouthdailyecho
Twitter @bournemouthecho
Editor Diarmuid MacDonagh
Daily Mon–Fri 95p, Sat £1

Founded 1900.

Bristol Post

Temple Way, Bristol BS2 0BU
tel 0117 934 3000
email bristolpostnews@localworld.co.uk
website www.bristolpost.co.uk
Facebook www.facebook.com/bristolpost
Twitter @BristolLive
Editor Pete Gavan
Daily Mon–Thurs £1.50, Fri £1.90

Takes freelance news and articles. Payment: by arrangement. Founded 1932.

Cornish Guardian

1st Floor, Princess Court, 23 Princess Street, Plymouth PL1 2EX
tel (01872) 271451
email jeff.reines@reachplc.com
website www.cornwalllive.com
Facebook www.facebook.com/cornwalllivenews
Twitter @CornwallLive

Editor Jeff Reines
Weekly Wed £1.60

Items of interest for Cornwall. Founded 1901.

Cornishman

1st Floor, Princess Court, 23 Princess Street,
Plymouth PL1 2EX
tel (01872) 271451
email jeff.reines@reachplc.com
website www.cornwalllive.com
Facebook www.facebook.com/cornwalllivenews
Twitter @cornishmanpaper
Editor Jeff Reines
Weekly Thurs £1.80

Local news and features. Founded 1878.

Dorset Echo

Fleet House, Hampshire Road, Weymouth DT4 9XD
tel (01305) 830930
email newsdesk@dorsetecho.co.uk
website www.dorsetecho.co.uk
Facebook www.facebook.com/dorsetecho
Twitter @Dorsetecho
Editor Diarmuid MacDonagh
Daily Mon–Fri 70p, Sat 75p

News and occasional features, length: 1,000–2,000
words. Illustrations: b&w photos. Payment: by
negotiation. Founded 1921.

Express & Echo

1st Floor, Princess Court, 23 Princess Street,
Plymouth PL1 2EX
tel (01392) 346763
email newsdesk@devonlive.co.uk
website www.devonlive.com
Facebook www.facebook.com/devonlivenews
Twitter @DevonLiveNews
Editor Alex Richards
Weekly Thurs £1.90

Features and news of local interest. Length: 500–800
words (features), up to 400 words (news).
Illustrations: colour. Payment: lineage rates;
illustrations: by negotiation. Founded 1904.

Gloucester Citizen

Reach PLC, Suite 121C, 1st Floor, Gloucester Quays,
St Ann Way, Gloucester GL1 5SH
tel (01452) 689320
email gloslivenews@reachplc.com
website www.gloucestershirelive.co.uk
Facebook www.facebook.com/GlosLiveOnline
Twitter @GlosLiveOnline
Editor Jenni Phillips
Weekly Thurs £2.20

Local news, business, entertainment, property,
motors and sport for Gloucester, Stroud and the
Forest of Dean. Founded 1876.

Gloucestershire Echo

Reach PLC, Suite 121C, 1st Floor, Gloucester Quays,
St Ann Way, Gloucester GL1 5SH
tel (01242) 689320
email gloslivenews@reachplc.com
website www.gloucestershirelive.co.uk
Facebook www.facebook.com/GlosLiveOnline
Twitter @GlosLiveOnline
Editor Jenni Phillips
Weekly Thurs £1.80

Local news, business, entertainment, property,
motors and sport for Cheltenham, Cotswolds and
Tewkesbury. Founded 1873.

The Herald/Plymouth Live

1st Floor, Princess Court, 23 Princess Street,
Plymouth PL1 2EX
tel (01752) 765500
email news@plymouthherald.co.uk
website www.plymouthlive.com
Facebook www.facebook.com/plymouthlive
Twitter @plymouth_live
Editor Clare Ainsworth (Herald), Edd Moore
(PlymouthLive)
Daily Mon–Fri £1.35, Sat £1.45

Local news, articles and features. Will consider
unsolicited material. Welcomes ideas for articles and
features. Illustrations: colour and b&w prints.
Founded 1895.

Herald Express

Harmsworth House, Barton Hill Road, Torquay,
Devon TQ2 8JN
tel (01752) 293084
website www.devonlive.com
Editor Andy Phelan
Weekly Thurs £1.80

Founded 1925.

Hereford Times

Stirling House, Unit 23, 1st Floor, Centenary Park,
Skylon Central, Hereford HR2 6FJ
tel (01432) 274413
email news@herefordtimes.com
website www.herefordtimes.com
Facebook www.facebook.com/herefordtimes
Twitter @HerefordTimes
Editor John Wilson
Weekly Thurs £1.60

Local news and sports. Correspondence by email
only. No phone calls or postal submissions.
Founded 1832.

Voice

Independent Media, Indy House, Lighterage Hill,
Truro, Cornwall TR1 2XR
tel 0333 305 3000
email news@indyonline.co.uk
website https://indyonline.co.uk/
Wed £1.50

Weekly newspapers available in print and digital format published across Cornwall: *Bodmin Voice, Newquay Voice, Penzance Voice, Saltash Voice, St Austell Voice, Truro Voice*. Founded 2001.

Western Daily Press

Yeovil Innovation Centre, Barracks Close, Copse Road, Yeovil BA22 8RN
tel (01935) 709735
website www.somersetlive.co.uk
Facebook www.facebook.com/WesternDaily
Twitter @SomersetLive
Editor David Shepherd
Daily Mon–Fri £1.60, Sat £2.60

National, international or west country topics for features or news items, from established journalists, with or without illustrations. Payment: by negotiation. Founded 1858.

Western Morning News

1st Floor, Princess Court, 23 Princess Street, Plymouth PL1 2EX
tel (01392) 346763
website www.devonlive.com
Facebook www.facebook.com/devonlivenews
Twitter @Devonlivenews
Editor Emma Slee
Daily Mon–Fri £1.55, Sat £2.65

Articles with illustrations considered on west country subjects. Founded 1860.

WALES

Cambrian News

7 Cefn Llan Science Park, Aberystwyth SY23 3AH
tel (01970) 615000
email edit@cambrian-news.co.uk
website www.cambrian-news.co.uk
Facebook www.facebook.com/CambrianNews
Twitter @CambrianNews
Editor Mick O'Reilly
Weekly Wed £1.50

Payment for freelance articles and pictures by arrangement. Founded 1860.

Daily Post

Bryn Eirias, Colwyn Bay LL29 8BF
tel (01492) 584321
email welshnews@dailypost.co.uk
website www.dailypost.co.uk
Facebook www.facebook.com/northwaleslive/
Twitter @northwaleslive
Editor Dion Jones
Daily Mon–Fri £1.40, Sat £1.80

Founded 1855.

The Leader

NWN Media Ltd, Mold Business Park, Wrexham Road, Mold CH7 1XY
tel (01352) 707707
website www.leaderlive.co.uk
Facebook www.facebook.com/LeaderLive
Twitter @leaderlive
Editor Susan Perry
Mon–Fri 85p

Founded 1973.

South Wales Argus

1st Floor, Chartist Tower, Upper Dock Street, Newport NP20 1DW
tel (01633) 810000
email newsdesk@gwent-wales.co.uk
website www.southwalesargus.co.uk
Facebook www.facebook.com/southwalesargus
Twitter @southwalesargus
Editor Gavin Thompson
Daily Mon–Sat 85p

News and features of relevance to Gwent. Length: 500–600 words (features); 350 words (news). Illustrations: colour prints and transparencies. Founded 1892.

South Wales Echo

6 Park Street, Cardiff CF10 1XR
tel 029-2024 3600
email newsdesk@walesonline.co.uk
website www.walesonline.co.uk
Twitter @walesonline
Editor Tryst Williams
Daily Mon–Fri £1.45, Sat £1.75

Evening paper: news, sport, features, showbiz, news features, personality interviews. Length: up to 700 words. Illustrations: photos, cartoons. Payment: by negotiation. Founded 1884.

South Wales Evening Post

Urban Village, High Street, Swansea SA1 1NW
tel (01792) 555520
email postnews@mediawales.co.uk
website www.walesonline.co.uk
Twitter @WalesOnline
Editor Jonathan Roberts
Daily Mon–Sat £1.35

Founded 1893.

WEST MIDLANDS

The Asian Today

6A Olton Wharf, Richmond Road, Solihull B92 7RN
tel 0121 314 2892
email editorial@theasiantoday.com
website www.theasiantoday.com
Facebook www.facebook.com/theasiantoday
Twitter @theasiantoday
Editor Zakia Yousaf

A free fortnightly community newspaper for the Midlands providing the region's south-Asian community access to important news stories and current events; encourages community interaction and dialogue, debate and discussion. Founded 2002.

Coventry Telegraph
c/o 60 Church Street, 8th Floor, Birmingham B3 2DJ
tel 024-7663 3633
email news@coventrytelegraph.net
website www.coventrytelegraph.net
Facebook www.facebook.com/livecoventry
Twitter @live_coventry
Editor Adam Moss
Daily Mon–Sat £1.45

Topical, illustrated articles with a Coventry or Warwickshire interest. Length: up to 600 words. Payment: by arrangement. Founded 1891.

Express & Star
51–53 Queen Street, Wolverhampton WV1 1ES
tel (01902) 313131
email newsdesk@expressandstar.co.uk
website www.expressandstar.com
Facebook www.facebook.com/expressandstar
Twitter @expressandstar
Editor-in-Chief Martin Wright
Daily Mon–Fri 85p, Sat £1

Founded 1874.

Sentinel
Staffordshire Sentinel News & Media Ltd,
Sentinel House, Bethesda Street, Hanley,
Stoke-on-Trent ST1 3GN
tel (01782) 864100
email newsdesk@thesentinel.co.uk
website www.stokesentinel.co.uk
Facebook www.facebook.com/stokeontrentlive
Twitter @SotLive
Editor Marc Waddington
Daily Mon–Fri £1.30, Sat £1.40

Articles and features of topical interest to the north Staffordshire and south Cheshire area. Illustrations: colour and b&w. Payment: by arrangement. Founded 1873.

Shropshire Star
2 Bellstone, Shrewsbury, Shrops. SY1 1HX
tel (01952) 242424
website www.shropshirestar.com
Facebook www.facebook.com/ShropshireStar
Twitter @ShropshireStar
Editor Martin Wright
Daily Mon–Fri 85p, Sat £1

News and features. No unsolicited material; write to Features Editor with outline of ideas. Payment: by arrangement. Founded 1964.

The Shuttle
2nd Floor, Copthall House, 1 New Road,
Stourbridge DY8 1PH
tel (01384) 358050
website www.kidderminstershuttle.co.uk
Facebook www.facebook.com/kidderminstershuttle
Twitter @ksshuttle
Editor Stephanie Preece
Weekly Thurs 90p

Formerly the *Kidderminster Shuttle*, a free weekly newspaper available in the Wyre Forest area in Worcestershire. Founded 1870.

Sunday Mercury
Weaman Street, Birmingham B4 6AY
tel 0121 234 5567
website www.birminghamlive.co.uk
Print Editor David Brookes
Sun £2.10

News specials or features of Midland interest. Illustrations: colour, b&w. Payment varies. Founded 1918.

Worcester News
Rear 1st Floor Office, Redhill House,
227 London Road, Worcester WR5 2JG
tel (01905) 748200
website www.worcesternews.co.uk
Facebook www.facebook.com/theworcesternews
Twitter @worcesternews
Editor Stephanie Preece
Daily Mon–Sat 85p

Local and national news, sport and features. Will consider unsolicited material. Welcomes ideas for articles and features. Length: 800 words (features), 300 words (news). Illustrations: colour jpg files. Payment: by negotiation. Founded 1935.

YORKSHIRE/HUMBERSIDE

Grimsby Telegraph
80 Cleethorpe Road, Grimsby DN31 3EH
tel 020-7293 3000
email newsdesk@grimsbytelegraph.co.uk
website www.thisisgrimsby.co.uk
Facebook www.facebook.com/grimsbylive
Twitter @GrimsbyLive
Editor Jamie Macaskill
Daily Mon–Sat £1.35

Considers general interest articles. Illustrations: line, half-tone, colour, cartoons. Payment: by arrangement. Founded 1897.

Halifax Courier
The Fire Station, Dean Clough Mills,
Halifax HX3 5AX
tel (01422) 260208
email editor@halifaxcourier.co.uk
website www.halifaxcourier.co.uk
Facebook www.facebook.com/HalifaxCourier
Twitter @HXCourier

Editor Chris Lever
Weekly Fri £1.80

Huddersfield Daily Examiner

PO Box A26, Queen's Street South,
Huddersfield HD1 2TD
tel (01484) 430000
email editorial@examiner.co.uk
website www.examinerlive.co.uk
Twitter @YorkshireLive
Editor Wayne Ankers
Mon–Fri £1.50, Sat £1.90

No contributions required at present. Founded 1851.

Hull Daily Mail

Blundell's Corner, Beverley Road, Hull HU3 1XS
tel (01482) 315016
email news@hulldailymail.co.uk
website www.hulldailymail.co.uk
Facebook www.facebook.com/hulllive
Twitter @hulllive
Editor Neil Hodgkinson
Daily Mon–Sat 90p

Founded 1885.

Lincolnshire Echo

Ground Floor, Witham Wharf, Brayford Wharf East,
Lincoln LN5 7AY
tel (01522) 804300
website www.lincolnshirelive.co.uk
Facebook www.facebook.com/LincsLive
Twitter @LincsLive
Editor Natalie Fahy
Weekly Thurs £1.80

The Press

Newsquest York, PO Box 29, 84–86 Walmgate,
York YO1 9YN
tel (01904) 567131
email newsdesk@thepress.co.uk
website www.yorkpress.co.uk
Facebook www.facebook.com/thepressyork
Twitter @yorkpress
Editor Nigel Burton
Daily Mon–Fri 85p, Sat £1

Articles of North and the East Riding of Yorkshire
interest. Length: 500–1,000 words. Illustrations: line,
half-tone. Payment: by arrangement. Founded 1882.

The Scarborough News

Woodend Creative Centre, The Crescent,
Scarborough YO11 2PW
tel (01723) 860161
email newsdesk@jpress.co.uk
website www.thescarboroughnews.co.uk
Facebook www.facebook.com/thescarboroughnews
Twitter @TheScarboroNews
Editor Steve Bambridge
Weekly £1.80

Also publishes daily news on website. Founded 1882.

Scunthorpe Telegraph

4–5 Park Square, Scunthorpe DN15 6JH
tel (01724) 709067
email newsdesk@scunthorpetelegraph.co.uk
website www.scunthorpetelegraph.co.uk
Facebook www.facebook.com/scunthorpelive
Twitter @ScunthorpeLive
Editor Jamie Macaskill
Weekly Thurs £2.10

Local news and features. Founded 1937.

Telegraph & Argus

The West Wing, New Hall Way, Bradford,
West Yorkshire BD5 8FF
tel (01274) 729511
email newsdesk@telegraphandargus.co.uk
website www.thetelegraphandargus.co.uk
Facebook www.facebook.com/telegraphandargus
Twitter @Bradford_TandA
Editor Nigel Barton
Daily Mon–Fri 85p, Sat £1

Daily paper: news, articles and features relevant to or
about the people of West Yorkshire. Length: up to
1,000 words. Illustrations: line, half-tone, colour.
Payment by negotiation. Founded 1868.

Yorkshire Post

No1 Leeds, 26 Whitehall Road, Leeds LS12 1BE
tel 0113 243 2701
website www.yorkshirepost.co.uk
Facebook www.facebook.com/
yorkshirepost.newspaper
Twitter @yorkshirepost
Editor James Mitchinson
Daily Mon–Fri £1.60, Sat £3

Authoritative and well-written articles on topical
subjects of general, literary or industrial interests.
Founded 1754.

Magazines UK and Ireland

Listings for regional newspapers start on page 27 and for national newspapers on page 18. For quick reference, magazines are listed by subject area starting on page 742. If you do have a piece placed with a magazine or journal, read any contract or licence agreement carefully: retaining copyright over your own writing is important and you should understand what you are agreeing to.

Abridged

email abridged@ymail.com
website www.abridged.zone
Facebook www.facebook.com/people/Abridged/
Twitter @Abridged030
Curatorial Editor/Project Coordinator Gregory McCartney, *Project Editor* Susanna Galbraith
Free

Literary magazine specialising in contemporary or experimental poetry. Themed issues: see Facebook and Twitter feeds for information about upcoming themes prior to submitting. Payment: none. Founded 2004.

Accountancy Age

Contentive, Scale Space, 58 Wood Lane, London W12 7RZ
website www.accountancyage.com
Twitter @AccountancyAge
Editor Aaran Fronda
Online

Articles of accounting, financial and business interest. Freelance assignments commissioned. Payment: by arrangement. Founded 1969.

Accountancy Daily

Croner-i, 240 Blackfriars Road, London SE1 8BU
tel 020-3965 2410
email sara.white@croneri.co.uk
email max.austin@croneri.co.uk
website www.accountancydaily.co/
Editor Sara White, *Reporter* Max Austin
Daily online news service; free for registered readers

Articles on accounting, taxation, audit, financial, tax law and regulatory compliance targeted at accountants, tax advisers and finance professionals in practice or industry. All feature ideas to be submitted by email in the form of a brief synopsis. Founded 1889.

Accounting & Business

Association of Chartered Certified Accountants, The Adelphi, 1–11 John Adam Street, London WC2N 6AU
tel 020-7059 5000
email info@accaglobal.com
website https://abmagazine.accaglobal.com/uk/en.html
Editor-in-Chief Jo Malvern
Online Free

Journal of the Association of Chartered Certified Accountants. Features accountancy, finance and business topics of relevance to accountants and finance directors. Illustrated. Founded 1998.

Acumen Literary Journal

4 Thornhill Bridge Wharf, Caledonian Wharf, London N1 0RU
email acumeneditor@gmail.com
email info@acumen-poetry.co.uk
website www.acumen-poetry.co.uk
Editor Danielle Hope
3 p.a. £5.50 or £15.50 p.a.

Poetry, literary and critical articles, reviews, literary memoirs, etc. Send sae with submissions; online submissions also accepted (see website for guidelines). Please send books for review to Andrew Geary, 25 Southbrook Drive, Cheshunt EN8 0QJ; email acumenreviews@gmail.com. Payment: none. Founded 1985.

Aeroplane Monthly

Key Publishing Group, Units 1–4, Gwash Way Industrial Estate, Ryhall Road, Stamford, Lincs. PE9 1XP
email ben.dunnell@keypublishing.com
website www.key.aero/aeroplanemonthly
Editor Ben Dunnell
Monthly £5.70

Articles and photos relating to historical aviation and aircraft preservation. Length: up to 5,000 words. Illustrations: line, colour. Payment: £60 per 1,000 words, payable on publication (open to negotiation); photos £25 or more depending on size. Founded 1973.

Aesthetica Magazine

21 New Street, York YO1 8RA
email info@aestheticamagazine.com
website www.aestheticamagazine.com
Twitter @AestheticaMag
Instagram @aestheticamag
Editor Cherie Federico
Bi-monthly £6.95

Spans visual art, design and photography. Distributed nationally and internationally. Also produces a number of awards, exhibitions and events focused on talent development in art, photography, literature and film. These comprise the Aesthetica Short Film Festival, the Art Prize, the Future Now Symposium and the Creative Writing Award. Founded 2002.

Africa: St Patrick's Missions

St Patrick's Missionary Society, Kiltegan, Co. Wicklow W91 Y022, Republic of Ireland
tel +353 (0)59 6473600
email africa@spms.ie
website www.spms.org
Facebook www.facebook.com/AfricaMagazineKiltegan
Editor Rev. Seán Deegan
7 p.a. €15 p.a.

Articles of missionary and topical religious interest. Length: up to 1,000 words. Illustrations: colour.

Africa Confidential

37 John's Mews, London WC1N 2NS
email andrew@africa-confidential.com
website www.africa-confidential.com
Twitter @Africa_Conf
Deputy Editor Andrew Weir
Fortnightly £952 p.a. (print and online), £818 p.a. (online only)

News and analysis of political and economic developments in Africa. Unsolicited contributions welcomed, but must be exclusive and not published elsewhere. Length: 1,200-word features, 500-word pointers. No illustrations. Payment: from £300 per 1,000 words. Founded 1960.

African Business

IC Publications Ltd, 7 Coldbath Square, London EC1R 4LQ
tel 020-7841 3210
email info@icpublications.com
website www.africanbusiness.com
Monthly From £56 p.a.

Articles on business, economic and financial topics of interest to business professionals, ministers and officials concerned with African affairs. Length: 1,000–1,400 words; shorter coverage 500 words. Illustrations: by arrangement. Payment: by arrangement for both words and illustrations. Founded 1978.

Agenda

c/o School of English, Castle House, The Scores, St Andrews KY16 9AL
email submissions@agendapoetry.co.uk
website www.agendapoetry.co.uk
Twitter @agendapoetry
Editor John Burnside
£28 p.a. (individuals), £22 p.a. (concessions), £35 p.a. libraries and institutions

Poetry and criticism. Potential contributors are advised to study the journal and visit the website for

submission details before submitting via email. Younger poets and artists (from age 15 to mid/late 30s) are invited to submit work for the online publication *Broadsheet*. Detailed criticism of poems available to subscribers. International issues, general anthology issues and special issues (focusing on an undeservedly neglected poet). Known, lesser known and new voices.

AIR International

Key Publishing Ltd, PO Box 100, Stamford, Lincs. PE9 1XQ
tel (01780) 755131
email airint@keypublishing.com
website www.airinternational.com
Monthly £64.99 p.a. (as part of Key Aero)

Technical articles on aircraft; features on topical aviation subjects – civil and military. Length: up to 3,000 words. Illustrations: by arrangement. Payment: by arrangement. Founded 1971.

Allegro Poetry

email allegropoetry@gmail.com
website www.allegropoetry.org
Editor Sally Long
2 p.a. Free

Online journal of contemporary poetry. Published twice a year, in March (general issue) and September (themed issue) respectively. See website for information on forthcoming submission windows and full details. Previously published work is not accepted. Payment: none.

Amateur Gardening

Future Publishing Ltd, Unit 415, Winnersh Triangle, Eskdale Road, Winnersh RG41 5TP
tel 0330 390 3722
email amateurgardening@futurenet.com
website www.amateurgardening.com
Editor Garry Coward-Williams
Weekly £2.10

Does not accept any form of unsolicited material. Founded 1884.

Amateur Photographer

(incorporating Photo Technique)
Kelsey Publishing Ltd, The Granary, Downs Court, Yalding Hill, Yalding, Maidstone, Kent ME18 6AL
email ap.ed@kelsey.co.uk
website www.amateurphotographer.co.uk
Facebook www.facebook.com/amateur.photographer.magazine
Twitter @AP_Magazine
Group Editor Nigel Atherton
Weekly £120 p.a.

Unsolicited editorial submissions are not encouraged. Founded 1884.

Angling Times

Bauer Media Group, Media House, Lynch Wood, Peterborough Business Park, Peterborough PE2 6EA
tel (01733) 395097
email newsdesk@anglingtimes.co.uk
website www.anglingtimes.co.uk
Facebook www.facebook.com/anglingtimes/
Twitter @angling_times
News Editor Freddie Sandford
Weekly £2.60

Articles, pictures, news stories, on all forms of angling. Illustrations: line, half-tone, colour. Payment: by arrangement. Founded 1953.

Apollo

22 Old Queen Street, London SW1H 9HP
tel 020-7961 0150
email ed@apollomag.com
website www.apollo-magazine.com
Editor Edward Behrens
Monthly £7.95

Scholarly and topical articles of c. 2,000–3,000 words on art, architecture, ceramics, photography, furniture, armour, glass, sculpture and any subject connected with art, museums and collecting. Interviews with collectors, leading international artists and cultural leaders. Exhibition and book reviews, articles on current developments in the culture sector, regular columns on the art market. Illustrations: colour. Payment: by arrangement. Founded 1925.

The Architects' Journal

emap Publishing Ltd, 4th Floor, Harmsworth House, 15 Bouverie Street, London EC4Y 8DP
tel 020-3953 2600
email emily.booth@emap.com
website www.architectsjournal.co.uk
Twitter @ArchitectsJrnal
Editor Emily Booth
Monthly From £248 p.a.

Articles (mainly technical) on architecture, planning and building, accepted only with prior agreement of synopsis. Illustrations: photos and drawings. Payment: by arrangement. Founded 1895.

Architectural Design

John Wiley & Sons, 25 John Street, London WC1N 2BS
tel 020-8326 3800
website https://onlinelibrary.wiley.com/journal/15542769
6 issues p.a. £151 p.a. (print, individual; other rates available)

International architectural publication comprising an extensively illustrated thematic profile and magazine back section, *AD Plus*. Uncommissioned articles not accepted. Each issue has a guest editor. Payment: by arrangement. Founded 1930.

The Architectural Review

emap Publishing Ltd, 4th Floor, Harmsworth House, 15 Bouverie Street, London EC4Y 8DP
tel 020-3033 2741
email editorial@architectural-review.com
website www.architectural-review.com
Editor Manon Mollard
Monthly £17.50

Articles on architecture and the allied arts (urbanism, design, theory, history, technology). Writers must be thoroughly qualified. Length: up to 3,000 words. Illustrations: photos, drawings, etc. Payment: by arrangement. Founded 1896.

Architecture Today

Built Environment and Architecture Media, 2–6 Boundary Row, London SE1 8HP
tel 020-3714 4240
email editorial@architecturetoday.co.uk
website www.architecturetoday.co.uk
Twitter @Arch_Today
Editor Isabel Allen
10 p.a. Circulated free of charge to architects; subscription options available

Mostly commissioned articles and features on contemporary European architecture. Length: 200–800 words. Illustrations: colour. Payment: by negotiation. Founded 1989.

Art + Framing Today

Unit 2, Wye House, 6 Enterprise Way, London SW18 1FZ
tel 020-7381 6616
email lynn@fineart.co.uk
website www.fineart.co.uk/art_and_framing_today.aspx
Managing Editor Lynn Jones
5 p.a. From £39.90 p.a.

Distributed to the fine art and framing industry. Covers essential information on new products and technology, artist and gallery news, market trends and business analysis. Length: 800–1,600 words. Illustrations: colour photos, cartoons. Payment: by arrangement. Founded 1905.

Art Monthly

Peveril Garden Studios, 140 Great Dover Street, London SE1 4GW
tel 020-7240 0389
email info@artmonthly.co.uk
website www.artmonthly.co.uk
Twitter @ArtMonthly
Editor Patricia Bickers
10 p.a. From £35 p.a.

Features on modern and contemporary visual artists and art history, art theory and art-related issues; exhibition and book reviews. All material commissioned. Length: 750–1,500 words.

Illustrations: by arrangement. Payment: by arrangement; none for photos. Founded 1976.

The Art Newspaper

17 Hanover Square, London W1S 1BN
tel 020-3586 8054
email info@theartnewspaper.com
website www.theartnewspaper.com
Editor Alison Cole
11 p.a. From £12 per quarter

International coverage of visual art, news, politics, law, exhibitions with some feature pages. Length: 200–1,000 words. Illustrations: by arrangement. Payment: by arrangement. Founded 1990.

Art Quarterly

Art Fund, 2 Granary Square, London N1C 4BH
tel 020-7225 4800
email artquarterly@artfund.org
website www.artfund.org
Editor Helen Sumpter
Quarterly Free to Art Fund members with National Art Pass

Magazine of Art Fund, the national charity for art, which supports museums and galleries across the UK. Features information about what's on in UK galleries and museums. Also includes in-depth features, interviews and conversations about art and artists, exhibition previews and reviews, opinion by writers, critics, commentators and experts in the field, and updates on the impact of Art Fund's charitable programme.

ArtReview and ArtReview Asia

1 Honduras Street, London EC1Y 0TH
tel 020-7490 8138
email office@artreview.com
website www.artreview.com
Facebook www.facebook.com/ArtReview.Magazine
Twitter @ArtReview_
Editor Mark Rappolt
ArtReview 9 p.a. £35 p.a. (print and online); ArtReviewAsia 4 p.a. £24 p.a. (print and online)

Contemporary art features and reviews. Proposals welcome. Illustrations: colour. Payment: £350 per 1,000 words. Founded 1949.

ARTEMISpoetry

3 Springfield Close, East Preston,
West Sussex BN16 2SZ
email admin@secondlightlive.co.uk
website www.secondlightlive.co.uk/artemis.shtml
Contact Dilys Wood
2 p.a. £7, £12 p.a. + p&p, £5 as pdf, or free to members of Second Light Network

Bi-annual journal of women's poetry and writing about poetry. Published in May and November each year by the Second Light, membership of which is open to female poets over the age of 40 (associate membership if under 40). Submissions should be hitherto unpublished work by women authors. See website for full details and specific information on forthcoming issues.

The Artist

Warners Group Publications Plc., The Maltings, West Street, Bourne, Lincs. PE10 9PH
email admin@tapc.co.uk
website www.painters-online.co.uk
Facebook www.facebook.com/paintersonline
Twitter @artpublishing
Editor Sally Bulgin
13 p.a. (issues published every four weeks) £5.25

Practical, instructional articles on painting for all amateur and professional artists. Illustrations: line, half-tone, colour. Payment: by arrangement. Founded 1931.

Artists & Illustrators

Jubilee House, 2 Jubilee Place, London SW3 3TQ
tel 020-7349 3700
email info@artistsandillustrators.co.uk
website www.artistsandillustrators.co.uk
Twitter @AandImagazine
Editor Niki Browes
13 p.a. From £39.95 p.a.

Practical and inspirational articles for amateur and semi-professional artists. Length: 500–1,500 words. Illustrations: hi-res digital images, hand-drawn illustrations. Payment: by arrangement. Founded 1986.

Astronomy Now

Pole Star Publications, PO Box 175, Tonbridge, Kent TN10 4ZY
tel (01732) 446110
email editorial2023@astronomynow.com
website https://astronomynow.com/
Facebook www.facebook.com/astronomynow
Twitter @astronomynow
Editor Keith Cooper
Monthly £5.99

Specialises in translating exciting astronomy research into articles for the lay reader. Also covers amateur astronomy with equipment reviews and observing notes. Submit article pitches to the email address above. Length: 800–2,000 words. Payment: 15p per word; from £10 per photo. Founded 1987.

Asylum

c/o PCCS Books, Wyastone Business Park, Wyastone Leys, Monmouth NP25 3SR
tel (01600) 891509
email editors@asylummagazine.org
website https://asylummagazine.org/
Twitter @AsylumMagUK
Editor H. Spandler
Quarterly From £16 p.a.

Forum for debate about critical, radical and alternative perspectives on mental health, psychiatry and related professions. Especially welcomes contributions from service users, ex-users or survivors, carers, activists and frontline psychiatric or mental health workers. Founded 1986.

Atrium

email atriumpoetrysubmissions@gmail.com
website https://atriumpoetry.com
Facebook www.facebook.com/AtriumPoetry
Twitter @Atrium_Poetry
Editors Holly Magill, Claire Walker

Worcestershire-based poetry webzine. Poems published on Tuesdays and Fridays each week. Up to three poems of up to 50 lines may be submitted at once; see website for full details. Payment: none. Founded 2017.

Attitude

Stream Publishing Limited, The Cowshed, Ladycross Farm, Hollow Lane, Dormansland, Surrey RH7 6PB
email attitude@attitude.co.uk
website www.attitude.co.uk
Twitter @AttitudeMag
Editor-in-Chief Cliff Joannou
13 p.a. £5.50

Men's style magazine aimed primarily, but not exclusively, at gay men. Covers style/fashion, interviews, reviews, celebrities, humour. Illustrations: by arrangement. Payment: by arrangement. Founded 1994.

The Author

24 Bedford Row, London WC1R 4EH
tel 020-7373 6642
email theauthor@societyofauthors.org
website https://societyofauthors.org/News/The-Author
Editor James McConnachie
Quarterly Membership publication

Commissioned articles from 800–1,500 words on any subject related to the craft, legal, commercial or technical side of authorship. Little scope for the freelance writer: preliminary email advisable. Artwork and illustrations: by arrangement. Payment: by arrangement. Founded 1890.

Auto Express

Autovia Publishing, 48 Charlotte Street, London W1T 2NS
tel 020-3900 1901
email editorial@autoexpress.co.uk
website www.autoexpress.co.uk
Twitter @AutoExpress
Editor-in-Chief Steve Fowler
Weekly £3.99

News stories and general interest features about drivers as well as cars. Illustrations: colour photos. Payment: varies. Founded 1988.

Aviation News

Key Publishing Group, Units 1–4, Gwash Way Industrial Estate, Ryhall Road, Stamford, Lincs. PE9 1XP
tel (01780) 755131
email martin.needham@keypublishing.com
website www.aviation-news.co.uk
Twitter @AvNewsMag
Editor Martin Needham
Monthly £5.20

Covers all aspects of aviation. Many articles commissioned. Payment: by arrangement.

AW (Athletics Weekly)

Wildfire Sport Ltd, The Barn, Calcot Mount, Calcot Lane, Curdridge, Hants SO32 2BN
email euan.crumley@athleticsweekly.com
website www.athleticsweekly.com
Facebook www.facebook.com/athleticsweekly
Twitter @athleticsweekly
Instagram @athletics.weekly
Editorial Director Euan Crumley
Monthly £5.95

News and features on track and field athletics, road running, cross country, fell running and race walking. Material mostly commissioned. Length: 300–1,500 words. Illustrations: by arrangement. Payment: varies. Founded 1945.

BackTrack

Pendragon Publishing, PO Box 3, Easingwold, York YO61 3YS
tel (01347) 824397
email pendragonpublishing@btinternet.com
website www.pendragonpublishing.co.uk
Editor Michael Blakemore
Monthly £5.50

British railway history from 1820s to 1980s. Welcomes ideas from writers and photographers. Articles must be well researched, authoritative and accompanied by illustrations. Length: 3,000–5,000 words (main features), 500–3,000 words (articles). Illustrations: colour and b&w. Payment: £30 per 1,000 words, £18.50 colour, £10 b&w. Founded 1986.

bandit.

email banditfiction@gmail.com
website https://banditfiction.com
Facebook www.facebook.com/bandit.fic/
Twitter @BanditFiction
Instagram @BanditFiction
Editor-in-Chief Alisdair Hodgson

Online literary journal. Actively looking for: flash fiction (500 to 1,000 words); short stories (1,000 to 2,500 words). Submissions accepted during recurring submission periods via website.

The Banker

FT Specialist, Bracken House, 1 Friday Street,
London EC4M 9BT
tel 020-7873 3000
email joy.macknight@ft.com
website www.thebanker.com
Editor Joy MacKnight
Monthly From £95 per month

Global coverage of retail banking, corporate banking, banking technology, transaction services, investment banking and capital markets, regulation, sustainable finance and Top 1000 World Bank rankings.

Baptist Times

129 Broadway, Didcot, Oxon OX11 8RT
tel (01235) 517677
email editor@baptisttimes.co.uk
website www.baptisttimes.co.uk
Twitter @baptisttimes
Editor Paul Hobson
Online

Religious or social affairs, news, features and reviews. Founded 1855.

BBC Countryfile Magazine

Our Media Ltd, Eagle House, Colston Avenue,
Bristol BS1 1EN
tel 0117 927 9009
email editor@countryfile.com
website www.countryfile.com
Twitter @BBCCountryfile
Editor Fergus Collins
Monthly £5.50

Articles and features on making the most of the UK's countryside, and the lives of its rural communities.

BBC Gardeners' World Magazine

Immediate Media Co. Ltd, Vineyard House,
44 Brook Green, London W6 7BT
tel 020-7150 5770
email magazine@gardenersworld.com
website www.gardenersworld.com
Twitter @GWmag
Head of Content Kevin Smith, *Features Editor* Adam Duxbury
Monthly £5.99

Advice, support and features for gardeners of all levels of expertise. Fully illustrated. Does not accept speculative features.

BBC Good Food

Immediate Media Co. Ltd, Vineyard House,
44 Brook Green, London W6 7BT
email enquiries@bbcgoodfoodmagazine.com
website www.bbcgoodfood.com
Twitter @bbcgoodfood
Editor-in-Chief Christine Hayes
Monthly £5.99

Inspiration for everyday, weekend and seasonal cooking for cooks of all levels. Features recipes from many BBC TV chefs as well as other leading food writers, along with an extensive range of hints, tips and features.

BBC History Magazine

Immediate Media Co. Ltd, Eagle House,
Colston Avenue, Bristol BS1 1EN
email historymagazine@historyextra.com
website www.historyextra.com
Facebook www.facebook.com/historyextra
Twitter @historyextra
Editor Rob Attar
Monthly £5.99

Popular history writing on a wide range of topics, from Ancient Egypt to the Second World War. Contents include feature spreads, book reviews, opinion and news. Contributors include Mary Beard, Tracy Borman, Dan Snow and Michael Wood. Illustrated. Founded 2000.

BBC Music Magazine

Our Media Ltd, Eagle House, Colston Avenue,
Bristol BS1 1EN
email music@classical-music.com
website www.classical-music.com
Twitter @MusicMagazine
Acting Editor Jeremy Pound
Monthly £6.99

Reviews and articles on all aspects of classical music. Also interviews with leading practitioners, information on technical equipment and forthcoming tours. Free CD with every issue.

BBC Science Focus

Immediate Media Co. Ltd, Eagle House,
Colston Avenue, Bristol BS1 1EN
tel 0117 314 8779
email daniel.bennett@immediate.co.uk
website www.sciencefocus.com
Twitter @sciencefocus
Editor Daniel Bennett
Monthly £5.50

Science and technology magazine featuring articles from popular scientists and leading academics, as well as news. Submissions accepted for articles only from experienced and previously published science writers: send 2–8pp overview along with feature pitch form provided on the website to jason.goodyer@immediate.co.uk. Photography and illustration submissions also accepted: see website for full specifications.

BBC Sky at Night Magazine

Our Media Ltd, Eagle House, Bristol BS1 1EN
email contactus@skyatnightmagazine.com
website www.skyatnightmagazine.com
Twitter @skyatnightmag

Editor Chris Bramley
Monthly £5.99

Aimed at both experienced amateur astronomers and those new to the subject. The magazine's main focus is on practical astronomy, both visual and photographic: the best sights to observe and image in the night sky each month; the telescopes, cameras and accessories to do that with; and how to put these to best use. Also covers news in all branches of space science, in particular cosmology and exoplanets; dark skies travel, both in the UK and internationally; and the history of astronomy. Founded 2005.

BBC Top Gear

BBC Broadcast Centre, 201 Wood Lane, London W12 7TQ
email editor@bbctopgearmagazine.com
website www.topgear.com
Twitter @BBC_TopGear
Editor Jack Rix
13 p.a. £5.50

Articles and photographic features on motoring, lifestyle and cars.

BBC Wildlife Magazine

Our Media Ltd, Eagle House, Colston Avenue, Bristol BS1 1EN
email wildlifemagazine@ourmedia.co.uk
website www.discoverwildlife.com
Twitter @WildlifeMag
Editor Paul McGuinness
Monthly £5.50

Consumer natural history magazine. Expert-written articles and features, along with award-winning photography.

Bella

Bauer Media, The Lantern, 75 Hampstead Road, London NW1 2PL
tel 020-7241 8000
email bella.mag@bauermedia.co.uk
website www.bellamagazine.co.uk
Weekly £1.50

Women's magazine with celebrity interviews, exclusive photos, real-life stories, high-street fashion, diet advice, health, food and travel. Payment: by arrangement. Founded 1987.

Best

Hearst UK, House of Hearst, 30 Panton Street, London SW1Y 4AJ
tel 020-7339 4500
email siobhan.wykes@hearst.co.uk
Twitter @BestMagOfficial
Editor-in-Chief Siobhan Wykes
Weekly £1.99

Unsolicited work not accepted, but always willing to look at ideas/outlines. Payment: by agreement. Founded 1987.

BFS Horizons

The British Fantasy Society, The Apex, 2 Sheriffs Orchard, Coventry CV1 3PP
email bfshorizons@britishfantasysociety.org
email poetry@britishfantasysociety.org
website www.britishfantasysociety.org
Fiction Editor Pete W. Sutton, *Poetry Editor* Ian Hunter

Official publication of the British Fantasy Society, focusing on fiction and poetry across a broad fantasy genre, including weird fiction, horror and science fiction. Length: stories of up to 5,000 words (ideally); poems of no more than 36 lines. See website for full guidelines and house style guide. Payment: £20 per story (flat rate).

BFS Journal

The British Fantasy Society, The Apex, 2 Sheriffs Orchard, Coventry CV1 3PP
email bfsjournal@britishfantasysociety.org
website www.britishfantasysociety.org/bfs-journal/

Official publication of the British Fantasy Society, focusing on features, non-fiction and academic articles, including interviews, opinion pieces and biographies. Contact editor with outline first. Length: preferably 2,500-6,000 words. Payment: none.

The Big Issue

43 Bath Street, Glasgow G2 1HW (editorial office)
tel 0141 352 7260
email editorial@thebigissue.com
website www.bigissue.com
Editor Paul McNamee
Weekly £4

Features, current affairs, reviews, interviews – of general interest and on social issues. Length: 1,000 words (features). No short stories or poetry. Illustrations: colour and b&w photos and line. Payment: £160 per 1,000 words. Founded 1991.

Bike

Bauer Media Group, Media House, Lynch Wood, Peterborough Business Park, Peterborough PE2 6EA
tel (01733) 468099
email bike@bauermedia.co.uk
website www.bikemagazine.co.uk
Editor Mike Armitage
Monthly £5.49

Motorcycle magazine. Interested in articles, features, news. Length: articles/features 1,000–3,000 words. Illustrations: colour and b&w photos. Payment: £140 per 1,000 words; photos per size/position. Founded 1971.

Bird Watching

Bauer Media Group, Media House, Lynch Wood, Peterborough Business Park, Peterborough PE2 6EA
tel (01733) 468201

email birdwatching@bauermedia.co.uk
website www.birdwatching.co.uk
Twitter @BirdWatchingMag
Editor Matt Merritt
13 p.a. £4.99

Broad range of bird-related features and photography, particularly looking at bird behaviour, bird news, reviews and UK birdwatching sites. Limited number of overseas features. Emphasis on providing accurate information in entertaining ways. Send synopsis first. Length: up to 1,200 words. Illustrations: by arrangement. Payment: by negotiation. Founded 1986.

Birdwatch

The Maltings, West Street, Bourne PE10 9PH
tel 020-8881 0550
email editorial@birdwatch.co.uk
website www.birdguides.com
Editor Josh Jones
Monthly £5.99

Topical articles on all aspects of British and Irish birds and birding, including conservation, identification, sites and habitats and equipment, as well as overseas destinations. Length: 700–1,500 words. Illustrations: hi-res jpgs (300 dpi at 1,500 pixels min. width) of wild British and European birds considered; submit on CD/DVD or full size via email or file-sharing site. Artwork: by negotiation. Payment: by arrangement. Founded 1991.

Black Beauty & Hair

Hawker Publications, Lombard Business Park, 12 Deer Park Road, Wimbledon, London SW19 3TL
tel 020-3746 2626
email info@blackbeautyandhair.com
website www.blackbeautyandhair.com
Twitter @BlackBeautyMag
Instagram @blackbeautymag
Editor-in-Chief Irene Shelley
Bi-monthly £5

Beauty and style articles relating specifically to women of colour; celebrity features. True-life stories and salon features. Length: approx. 1,000 words. Illustrations: by arrangement. Payment: by arrangement. Founded 1982.

Blithe Spirit

email bhsjournal@fastmail.org
website http://britishhaikusociety.org.uk/journal/
Editor Iiyana Stoyanova
Quarterly Free to members

Journal of the British Haiku Society: c. 90pp. Includes original poems (from Society members only), articles and reviews. Four submission windows (see website for up-to-date details); poems must not have appeared, or be under consideration, elsewhere.

Boat International

41–47 Hartfield Road, London SW19 3RQ
tel 020-8545 9330
email support@boatinternational.com
website www.boatinternational.com
Twitter @boatint
Editor-in-Chief Stewart Campbell
12 p.a. From £46 p.a.

News and features on superyachts and the lifestyles of those who own them. Also yacht listings in a brokerage section and reviews.

The Book Collector

(incorporating Bibliographical Notes and Queries)
PO Box 1163, St Albans AL1 9WS
email editor@thebookcollector.co.uk
website www.thebookcollector.co.uk
Facebook www.facebook.com/TheBookCollectorUK/
Instagram @thebookcollectoruk
Online £60 p.a. (UK), €70 (Europe), US$80 (RoW)

Articles, biographical and bibliographical, on the collection and study of printed books and MSS. Payment: for reviews only. Founded 1952.

Books Ireland

Unit 9, 78 Furze Road, Dublin D18 C6V6, Republic of Ireland
tel +353 (0)1 2933568
email ruth@wordwell.ie
website www.booksirelandmagazine.com
Twitter @booksirelandmag
Editor Ruth McKee
Online

Reviews of Irish-interest and Irish-author books, as well as articles of interest to librarians, booksellers and readers. Length: 800–1,400 words. Founded 1976 (print); fully digital as of 2019.

The Bookseller

The Stage Media Company Ltd, 47 Bermondsey Street, London SE1 3XT
tel 020-3403 1818
email tom.tivnan@thebookseller.com
website www.thebookseller.com
Twitter @thebookseller
Editor Philip Jones, *Deputy Editor* Benedicte Page, *Managing Editor* Tom Tivnan
Weekly £5.95

Long-established magazine of the UK book industry magazine, featuring news, analysis, bestseller charts, interviews, previews of forthcoming titles and jobs in the industry, as well as in-depth coverage of international book fairs including Frankfurt, Bologna and Beijing. While outside contributions are welcomed, most of the journal's contents are commissioned. Length: c. 1,000–1,500 words. Payment: by arrangement. Founded 1858.

Bowls International
Key Publishing Ltd, PO BOX 100, Stamford,
Lincs. PE9 1XQ
email editor@bowlsinternational.com
website http://www.bowlsinternational.keypublishing.com
Facebook www.facebook.com/BowlsInternational
Twitter @BowlsInt
Editor-at-Large Ceris Hewlings, *Associate Editor* Matt Wordingham
12 p.a. £5.20

Sport and news items and features; occasional, bowls-oriented short stories. Illustrations: colour transparencies, b&w photos, occasional line, cartoons. Payment: by arrangement. Founded 1981.

Breathe
GMC Publications Ltd, 86 High Street,
Lewes BN7 1XN
tel (01273) 477374
email hello@breathemagazine.com
website www.breathemagazine.com/submissions
Publisher Jonathan Grogan
9 p.a. £6.99

Mindfulness magazine aiming to help readers achieve a healthier life across five key areas: wellbeing, living, creativity, mindfulness and escape. Submissions welcomed from experienced or new writers, and from illustrators. See website above for specific requirements for each type of potential contributor.

British Birds
email editor@britishbirds.co.uk
website www.britishbirds.co.uk
Facebook www.facebook.com/britishbirdsmagazine/?ref=br_rs
Twitter @britishbirds
Editor Stephen Menzie
Monthly From £40 p.a.

Publishes major papers on bird identification, behaviour, conservation, distribution, ecology, movements, status and taxonomy with official reports on: rare breeding birds, scarce migrants and rare birds in Britain. Payment: token. Founded 1907.

British Chess Magazine
Albany House, Shute End, Wokingham,
Berks. RG40 1BJ
email support@britishchessmagazine.co.uk
website www.britishchessmagazine.co.uk
Monthly £5.50

Authoritative reports and commentary on the UK and overseas chess world. Payment: by arrangement. Founded 1881.

British Journal of Photography
The Green House, Ethical Building,
244–254 Cambridge Heath Road, London E2 9DA
email editorial@bjphoto.co.uk
website www.1854.photography/journal
Editor Izabela Radwanska Zhang
6 p.a. £20

Focus on all aspects of contemporary photography: articles on fine art, commercial, fashion, documentary and editorial, alongside trend reports and technical reviews. Founded 1854.

British Journalism Review
SAGE Publications, 1 Oliver's Yard, 55 City Road, London EC1Y 1SP
tel 020-7324 8500
email editor@bjr.org.uk
website www.bjr.org.uk
Twitter @TheBJReview
Editor Kim Fletcher
Quarterly £56 p.a. for individuals (print only; institutional rates also available)

Comment, criticism and review of matters published by, or of interest to, the media. Length: 1,500–3,000 words. Illustrations: b&w photos. Payment: by arrangement. Founded 1989.

British Medical Journal
BMJ Publishing Group, BMA House,
Tavistock Square, London WC1H 9JR
tel 020-7387 4410
email editor@bmj.com
website www.bmj.com
Editor-in-Chief Dr Kamran Abbasi
Weekly Free to members of BMA; see website for subscription details

Medical and related articles. Payment: by arrangement. Founded 1840.

Broadcast
Media Business Insight, 12 Essex Street,
London WC2R 3AA
tel 020-8102 0900
email chris.curtis@broadcastnow.co.uk
website www.broadcastnow.co.uk
Editor Chris Curtis
Weekly From £341 p.a.

For people working or interested in the UK and international broadcast industry. News, features, analysis and opinions across a variety of platforms. Covers the latest developments in programming, commissioning, digital, technology and post-production.

Building
Assemble Media Group, 64 High St, Wanstead,
London E11 2RJ
email chloe.mcculloch@building.co.uk
website www.building.co.uk
Editorial Director Chloë McCulloch
49 p.a. From £199 p.a.

Covers all aspects of the construction industry and built environment, from architecture to property development. Sectors include housing, commercial property, education and health buildings, and infrastructure. Will consider articles on the built environment in the UK and abroad; including news, comment, analysis and photos. Payment: by arrangement. Founded 1843.

Building Design

Assemble Media Group, 64 High St, London E11 2RJ
website www.bdonline.co.uk
Facebook www.facebook.com/BDmagazine
Twitter @BDonline
Editorial Director Chloë McCulloch, *Architectural Editor* Ben Flatman
Annual subscriptions from £99 p.a.

Daily online newspaper and magazine. News and features on all aspects of architecture and urban design. Plus annual *World Architecture (WA) 100* printed magazine, the authoritative survey of world's largest architects. Founded 1970.

The Burlington Magazine

14–16 Duke's Road, London WC1H 9SZ
tel 020-7388 8157
email editorial@burlington.org.uk
website www.burlington.org.uk
Editor Michael Hall
12 p.a. £25

Academic journal dealing with the history and criticism of art; book and exhibition reviews; publishes free-access online journal on contemporary art, *Burlington Contemporary*, with reviews of exhibitions and books. Submissions must offer new research; potential contributors must have specialist knowledge of the subjects treated. Length: 500–5,000 words. Illustrations: colour images. Payment: by arrangement. Founded 1903.

Buses

Key Publishing Ltd, Foundry Road, Stamford, Lincs. PE9 2PP
tel (01780) 755131
Consultant Editor Alan Millar, PO Box 14644, Leven KY9 1WX
tel (01333) 340637
email alan.millar@keypublishing.com
website www.keybuses.com
Monthly £5.50

Articles of interest to both road passenger transport operators and bus enthusiasts. Preliminary enquiry essential. Illustrations: digital (first preference), colour transparencies, half-tone, line maps. Payment: on application. Founded 1949.

Business Traveller

tel 020-7821 2700
email editorial@businesstraveller.com
website www.businesstraveller.com

Editor Tamsin Cocks
10 p.a. £4.99

Articles, features and news on consumer travel aimed at individual frequent international business travellers. Submit ideas with recent clippings/links and a CV. Length: varies. Illustrations: colour for destinations features. Payment: on application. Founded 1976.

Butcher's Dog

1 Jackson Street, North Shields NE30 2JA
email editor@butchersdogmagazine.co.uk
website www.butchersdogmagazine.co.uk
Facebook www.facebook.com/butchersdogmagazine/
Twitter @ButchersDogMag
Instagram @butchersdogmag
Managing Editor Dr Jo Clement
2 p.a. £6.99

Bi-annual poetry magazine founded and published in North-East England. Aims to print outstanding poems by diverse writers with distinctive voices from across the UK and ROI, regardless of their career stage. Submissions accepted during open calls digitally via the homepage. Unpublished and original work only, although translations are welcome as long as the author has granted permission in advance. Payment: none, but contributors receive free copies. Tip-jar option. Founded 2012.

Campaign

Haymarket Ltd, Bridge House, 69 London Road, Twickenham TW1 3SP
tel 020-8267 8032
email maisie.mccabe@haymarket.com
website www.campaignlive.co.uk
UK Editor Maisie McCabe
Monthly From £45 per month

News and articles covering the whole of the mass communications field, particularly advertising in all its forms, marketing and the media. Features should not exceed 2,000 words. News items also welcome. Payment: by arrangement.

Candis

Newhall Publications Ltd, Newhall Lane, Hoylake, Wirral CH47 4BQ
tel 0151 632 3232
email helen@candis.co.uk
website www.candis.co.uk
Twitter @candismagazine
Monthly Subscription only

Commissions one 2,500-word short story each month by a well-known published author. Unsolicited material is no longer received and will be returned unread. Writers willing to share a personal life story or experience for real lives feature may send a synopsis to the email address above. Also covers health, news, celebrity interviews, family issues, fashion and beauty.

Car

Bauer Media Group, Media House, Lynch Wood,
Peterborough Business Park, Peterborough PE2 6EA
tel (01733) 468379
email car@bauermedia.co.uk
website www.carmagazine.co.uk
Editor-in-Chief Phil McNamara, *Editor* Ben Miller
Monthly From £49.99 p.a.

Top-grade journalistic features on car driving, car
people and cars. Length: 1,000–2,500 words.
Illustrations: b&w and colour photos to professional
standards. Payment: minimum £350 per 1,000 words.
Founded 1962.

Car Mechanics

Kelsey Publishing Ltd., The Granary, Downs Court,
Yalding Hill, Yalding, Maidstone, Kent ME18 6AL
email cm.ed@kelsey.co.uk
website www.carmechanicsmag.co.uk
Facebook www.facebook.com/Car-Mechanics-
123672554385156/
Twitter @CarMechanics
Monthly £4.70

Practical articles on maintaining, repairing and
uprating modern cars for DIY plus the motor trade.
Always interested in finding new talent for this rather
specialised market, but study a recent copy before
submitting ideas or features. Email outlining feature
recommended. Illustrations: line drawings, colour
prints, digital images. Supply package of text and
pictures. Payment: by arrangement. Founded 1958.

Caravan Magazine

Warners Group Publications Plc, The Maltings,
West Street, Bourne, Lincs. PE10 9PH
tel (01778) 391000
email caravan@warnersgroup.co.uk
Facebook www.facebook.com/Caravanmag/
Editor Clare Kelly
Monthly £5.75

Lively articles based on real experience of touring
caravanning, especially if well illustrated by photos
provided by the author or from regional Tourist
Boards, attractions etc. Payment: by arrangement.
Founded 1933.

The Caterer

Jacobs Media Group, 52 Grosvenor Gardens,
London SW1W 0AU
tel 020-7881 4803
email info@caterer.com
website www.thecaterer.com
Editor James Stagg, *Assistant Editor* Emma Lake, *News
Editor* Sophie Witts
Weekly From £61.78 p.a. (some content remains free)

Multimedia brand for the UK hospitality industry. In
print and online, offers content, job news and a
digital platform for hotel, restaurant, food service,
and pub and bar operators across the country. Article
length: up to 1,500 words. Illustrations: by
arrangement. Payment: by arrangement.
Founded 1878.

The Catholic Herald

Herald House, Lamb's Passage, Bunhill Row,
London EC1Y 8TQ
tel 020-7448 3603
email magazine@catholicherald.co.uk
website www.catholicherald.co.uk
Facebook www.facebook.com/
CatholicHeraldMagazine/
Twitter @CatholicHerald
Editor William Cash
Weekly From £37.99 p.a.

Independent magazine covering national and
international affairs from a Catholic/Christian
viewpoint as well as church news. Length: articles
800–1,200 words. Illustrations: photos of Catholic
and Christian interest. Payment: by arrangement.

Catholic Pictorial

3 & 4 Pacific Chambers, 11–13 Victoria Street,
Liverpool L2 5QQ
tel 0151 522 1007
email p.heneghan@rcaol.co.uk
website www.catholicpic.co.uk
Editor Peter Heneghan
Monthly Free

News and photo features (maximum 450 words plus
illustration) on Merseyside, regional and national
Catholic interest only. Payment: by arrangement.
Founded 1961.

Ceramic Review

63 Great Russell Street, London WC1B 3BF
tel 020-7183 5583
email editorial@ceramicreview.com
website www.ceramicreview.com/
Facebook www.facebook.com/ceramicreview
Twitter @ceramicreview
Instagram @ceramicreview
YouTube @CeramicReviewmagazine
Editor Karen Bray, *Assistant Editor* Jessica Browne
6 p.a. £9.90

International magazine containing critical features,
reviews and practical information on all forms of
ceramics and clay art and craft. It also looks at the
role of ceramics within contemporary culture.
Welcomes article proposals – critical, profile,
technical, historical or experiential. Feature articles
run from 800 to 1,500 words and must include large,
hi-res images. Payment: offered at current rates on
publication.

Chat

Future Publishing Ltd, 121–141 Westbourne Terrace,
London W2 6JR
tel 020-3148 5000

email kate.williams@futurenet.com
website www.lifedeathprizes.com
Facebook www.facebook.com/ChatMagazine
Twitter @ChatMagazine
Editor Kate Williams
Weekly £1.20

Tabloid for women. Includes readers' letters, tips and true-life features. Payment: by arrangement. Founded 1985.

Church of England Newspaper

Religious Intelligence Ltd, 14 Great College Street, London SW1P 3RX
tel 020-7878 1001
email cen@churchnewspaper.com
website www.churchnewspaper.com
Twitter @churchnewspaper
Weekly £75 p.a. (print and digital)

Anglican news and articles relating the Christian faith to everyday life. Evangelical basis; almost exclusively commissioned articles. Prior study of paper desirable. Length: up to 1,000 words. Illustrations: by arrangement. Payment: by arrangement. Founded 1828.

Church Times

3rd Floor, Invicta House, 108–114 Golden Lane, London EC1Y 0TG
tel 020-7776 1060
email editor@churchtimes.co.uk
website www.churchtimes.co.uk
Twitter @ChurchTimes
Editor Paul Handley
Weekly £3.10

Articles on religious topics are considered. No verse or fiction. Length: up to 1,000 words. Illustrations: news photos, sent promptly. Payment: £100 per 1,000 words. Negotiated rates for illustrations. Founded 1863.

Classic Boat Magazine

The Chelsea Magazine Company, Jubilee House, 2 Jubilee Place, London SW3 3TQ
tel 020-7349 3755
email cb@chelseamagazines.com
website www.classicboat.co.uk
Contact Steffan Meyric Hughes
Monthly £4.95

Cruising and technical features, restorations, events, new boat reviews, practical guides, maritime history and news. Study of magazine essential: read three to four back issues and send for contributors' guidelines. Length: 500–2,000 words. Illustrations: colour and b&w photos; line drawings of hulls. Payment: £75–£100 per published page. Founded 1987.

Classic Cars

H. Bauer Publishing, Media House, Lynch Wood, Peterborough Business Park, Peterborough PE2 6EA

tel (01733) 468000
email classic.cars@bauermedia.co.uk
website www.classiccarsmagazine.co.uk
Facebook www.facebook.com/classiccarsmagazine
Editor Phil Bell
Monthly £5.99

Specialist articles on older cars and related events. Length: from 150–4,000 words (subject to prior contract). Photography: classic car event photography on spec; feature photography on commission basis. Payment: by negotiation. Founded 1973.

Classical Music

St Jude's Church, Dulwich Road, London SE24 0PB
tel 020-7338 5454
email florence.lockheart@classical-music.uk
website www.classical-music.uk
Twitter @ClassicalMusic_
Editor Florence Lockheart
Quarterly From £55 p.a.

News, opinion, features on the classical music business. All material commissioned. Illustrations: colour photos and line; colour covers. Payment: minimum £130 per 1,000 words. Founded 1976.

Climber

email info@climber.co.uk
website www.climber.co.uk
Twitter @climbermagazine
Instagram @climbermag
6 p.a. £5.99, or from £30 p.a.

Articles on all aspects of rock climbing/mountaineering in Great Britain and abroad, and on related subjects. Study of magazine essential. Length: 1,300–3,000 words. Illustrations: colour transparencies. Payment: by arrangement. Founded 1962.

Closer

Bauer Media, The Lantern, 75 Hampstead Road, London NW1 2PL
email closer@closermag.co.uk
website www.closeronline.co.uk
Editor Lisa Burrow
Weekly £1.99

Women's celebrity magazine with real-life stories, lifestyle, fashion, beauty and TV entertainment and listings sections. Payment: by negotiation.

Coin News

Token Publishing Ltd, 8 Oaktree Place, Manaton Close, Matford Business Park, Exeter, Devon EX2 8WA
tel (01404) 46972
email info@tokenpublishing.com
website www.tokenpublishing.com
Editor John W. Mussell
Monthly £4.75

Articles of high standard on coins, tokens, paper money. Send text in digital form. Length: up to 2,000 words. Payment: by arrangement. Founded 1983.

Commercial Motor
6th Floor, Chancery House, St Nicholas Way, Sutton, Surrey SM1 1JB
tel 020-8912 2163
email george.barrow@roadtransport.com
website www.commercialmotor.com
Twitter @Comm_Motor
Editor George Barrow
Weekly From £148.50 p.a.

Technical and road transport articles only. Length: up to 1,500 words. Illustrations: drawings and photos. Payment: by arrangement. Founded 1905.

Community Care
St Jude's Church, Dulwich Road, Herne Hill, London SE24 0PB
tel 020-3915 9444
email communitycare@markallengroup.com
website www.communitycare.co.uk
Editor Mithran Samuel

Online magazine site with articles, features and news covering the Social Services sector.

Computer Weekly
9th Floor (West), 10 Exchange Square, London EC2A 2BR
email cw-news@computerweekly.com
website www.computerweekly.com
Facebook www.facebook.com/computerweekly
Twitter @computerweekly
Editor Bryan Glick
Weekly Free to registered subscribers

Feature articles on IT-related topics for business/industry users. Length: 1,200 words. Illustrations: colour photos. Payment: £250 per 1,000 words. Founded 1966.

Computeractive
Future Publishing Ltd, Quay House, The Ambury, Bath BA1 1UA
Facebook www.facebook.com/computeractive
Group Editor Daniel Booth
Fortnightly £2.80

Computing magazine offering plain-English advice for PCs, tablets, phones and the internet, as well as product reviews and technology news.

Condé Nast Traveller
The Condé Nast Publications Ltd, Vogue House, 1–2 Hanover Square, London W1S 1JU
cntraveller@condenast.co.uk
website www.cntraveller.com
Features Editor Lydia Bell
Monthly £4.99

Lavishly photographed articles on all aspects of travel, featuring exotic destinations and those close to home. Specialist pieces include food and wine, motoring, health, foreign correspondents, travel news, hotels. Illustrations: colour. Payment: by arrangement. Founded 1997.

Cosmopolitan
Hearst UK, House of Hearst, 30 Panton Street, London SW1Y 4AJ
tel 020-7439 5000
website www.cosmopolitan.co.uk
Twitter @CosmopolitanUK
Editor-in-Chief Claire Hodgson, *Features Editor* Jennifer Savin
Monthly £2.99

Commissioned material only. Payment: by arrangement. Illustrated. Founded 1972.

Cotswold Life
Redhill House, 227 London Road, Worcester WR5 2JG
tel 07834 104843
email candia.mckormack@newsquest.co.uk
website www.cotswoldlife.co.uk
Facebook www.facebook.com/cotswoldlife/
Twitter @cotswoldlife
Instagram @cotswoldlife
Editor Candia McKormack
Monthly £4.50

Articles on the Cotswolds, including places of interest, high-profile personalities, local events, arts, history, interiors, fashion and food. Founded 1967.

Country Homes and Interiors
Future Publishing Ltd, 161 Marsh Wall, London E14 9AP
tel 020-3148 5000
email countryhomes@futurenet.com
website www.homesandgardens.com/country
Facebook www.facebook.com/countryhomesandinteriors
Twitter @countryhomesmag
Editor Andrea Childs
Monthly £5.50

Articles on country homes and gardens, interiors, food, lifestyle. Payment: from £250 per 1,000 words. Founded 1986.

Country Life
Future Publishing Ltd, Unit 415, Eskdale Road, Winnersh Triangle RG41 5RA
tel 0330 390 6591
email paula.lester@futurenet.com
website www.countrylife.co.uk
Twitter @Countrylifemag
Editor Mark Hedges, *Deputy Editor* Kate Green, *Managing/Features Editor* Paula Lester
Weekly £4.50

Illustrated journal chiefly concerned with British country life, social history, architecture and the fine arts, natural history, agriculture, gardening and sport. Length: about 1,000 or 1,300 words (articles). Illustrations: mainly colour photos. Payment: according to merit. Print editorial team can be contacted via the email address above. Founded 1897.

Country Living

Hearst UK, House of Hearst, 30 Panton Street, London SW1Y 4AJ
tel 020-7439 5000
email country.living@hearst.co.uk
website www.countryliving.co.uk
Twitter @countrylivinguk
Editor-in-Chief Louise Pearce
Monthly £5.99

Up-market home-interest magazine with a country lifestyle theme, covering interiors, gardens, crafts, food, wildlife, rural and green issues. Unsolicited material not accepted. Illustrations: line, half-tone, colour. Payment: by arrangement. Founded 1985.

Country Walking

Bauer Consumer Media, Media House, Lynch Wood, Peterborough Business Park, Peterborough PE2 6EA
tel (01733) 468205
email country.walking@bauermedia.co.uk
Editor Guy Procter
13 p.a. £5.80

Features. Length: 1,000 words on average. Illustrations: digital images. Payment: by arrangement. Founded 1987.

The Countryman

Dalesman Publishing, The Gatehouse, Skipton Castle, Skipton, North Yorkshire BD23 1AL
tel (01756) 701381
email editorial@thecountryman.co.uk
website www.countrymanmagazine.co.uk
Twitter @Countrymaned
Editor Lorraine Connolly
Monthly £3.99

Features rural life, wildlife and natural history, country people, farming, traditions, crafts, covering whole of UK. Positive view of countryside and rural issues. Non-political, and no bloodsports. Unusual or quirky topics welcomed. Copy must be well written and accurate, for well-informed readership who are generally 40+ with strong affection for countryside. Articles between 600–1,000 words. Illustrations: good-quality digital images. Study magazine before submitting ideas. Send detailed outline first. Payment: by arrangement. Founded 1927.

Crafts Magazine

44A Pentonville Road, London N1 9BY
tel 020-7806 2538
email crafts@craftscouncil.org.uk
website www.craftsmagazine.org.uk
Bi-annual From £20

Magazine for contemporary art, craft and design, published by the Crafts Council and The River Group. Its content spans specialist features, craft news and reviews, covering a global range of makers, artists and designers. Submissions for review should include pictures.

Crannóg

email editor@crannogmagazine.com
website www.crannogmagazine.com/submit
Editors Sandra Bunting, Tony O'Dwyer, Ger Burke, Jarlath Fahy
2 p.a. €8.00

Literary magazine bringing together the best poetry and fiction from Irish and international contributors, plus interviews with authors on their writing life. Published bi-annually in March and September: submission windows are the month of November for the March issue and the month of May for the September issue. See website for further information. Contributor's fee paid. Founded 2002.

The Critic

Carlyle House, 235–237 Vauxhall Bridge Road, London SW1V 1EJ
email editorial@thecritic.co.uk
website https://thecritic.co.uk
Twitter @thecriticmag
Editor Christopher Montgomery
10 p.a. (monthly, with July/August and January/February double issues) £6.95

Essays, non-fiction, reportage, reviews and arts reflections. Pitch ideas before submitting and study magazine before pitching. Poetry and cartoon submissions welcome. Length: dependent on type of piece; individual pieces range from 800–4,500 words. Payment: by arrangement. Founded 2019.

Critical Quarterly

email cs-journals@wiley.com
website https://onlinelibrary.wiley.com/journal/14678705
Editor Colin MacCabe
Quarterly From £41 p.a.

Fiction, poems, literary criticism. Length: 2,000–5,000 words. Study magazine before submitting MSS. Payment: by arrangement. Founded 1959.

Crystal Magazine

3 Bowness Avenue, Prenton, Birkenhead CH43 0SD
tel 0151 608 9736
email christinecrystal@hotmail.com
website www.christinecrystal.blogspot.com
Editor Christine Carr
6 p.a. £3.50, £21 p.a. (UK), £25 p.a. (overseas)

A4, spiral-bound with colour images. Stories, poems, articles. Wordsmithing, Letters, News. Surprise Competitions open to all: £1.23, small surprise gift. Sample editions are available for £2. Subscribers (Crystallites) receive six issues a year and occasional free gifts.

Cumbria and Lake District Magazine
Dalesman Publications Ltd, The Gatehouse, Skipton Castle, Skipton, North Yorkshire BD23 1AL
tel (01756) 701381
email Mick@dalesman.co.uk
website www.cumbriamagazine.co.uk
Twitter @CumbriaMagazine
Editor Mick Smith
Monthly £3.30

Articles of rural interest concerning the people and landscapes of the Lake District and surrounding county of Cumbria. Short length preferred; articles should be of a journalistic nature and no more than 1,200 words. Illustrations: first-class photos, illustrations. Payment: £70 per 1,000 words. Pictures extra. Founded 1947, New Series 1951.

Custom Car
Assignment Media, PO Box 8632, Burton on Trent DE14 9PR
tel (01283) 742970
email enquiries@assignment-media.co.uk
Facebook www.facebook.com/CustomCarMagazine/?locale=en_GB
Four-weekly £4.99

Hot rods, customs and drag racing. Length: by arrangement. Payment: by arrangement. Founded 1970.

Cycling Weekly
Future Publishing Ltd, Quay House, The Ambury, Bath BA1 1UA
tel (01225) 442244
email cycling@futurenet.com
website www.cyclingweekly.com
Facebook www.facebook.com/CyclingWeekly
Twitter @cyclingweekly
Editor Simon Richardson
Weekly £3.25

Racing, fitness, features and technical reviews. Illustrations: topical cycling racing photos considered; cartoons. Length: not exceeding 2,000 words. Payment: by arrangement. Founded 1891.

Cyphers
3 Selskar Terrace, Ranelagh, Dublin D06 DW66, Republic of Ireland
tel +353 (0)1 4978866
website www.cyphers.ie
Editor Eiléan Ní Chuilleanáin
2 p.a. €16 p.a. See website for international rates.

Poems, fiction, translations. Submissions cannot be returned unless accompanied by postage (Irish stamps). Email submissions are not accepted. Payment: €35 to 50 per page. Founded 1975.

Darts World
email info@dartsworld.com
website www.dartsworld.com/
Twitter @Darts_World
Managing Editor C.J. Harris-Hulme, *Lead Writer* Paul Woodage
Monthly £4

Articles and stories with darts theme. Illustrations: half-tone, cartoons. Payment: negotiable per 1,000 words; illustrations by arrangement. Founded 1972.

The Dawntreader
24 Forest Houses, Cookworthy Moor, Halwill, Beaworthy, Devon EX21 5UU
email dawnidp@indigodreams.co.uk
website www.indigodreamspublishing.com
Facebook www.facebook.com/ronniegoodyeridp
Twitter @IndigoDreamsPub
Editor Dawn Bauling
Quarterly £4.50, £17 p.a.

Poetry, short stories and articles up to 1,000 words encompassing themes of the mystic, myth, legend, landscape, nature and love. New writers welcome. Lively feedback pages. No payment. Email submission preferred. Founded 2007.

Decanter
Future Publishing Ltd, 121–141 Westbourne Terrace, London W2 6JR
email editor@decanter.com
website www.decanter.com
Editor-in-Chief Chris Maillard, *Magazine Editor* Amy Wislocki, *Editor, Decanter.com* Lisa Riley, *Editor, Decanter Premium* Georgie Hindle
Monthly £6.49

Articles and features on wines, wine travel and food-related topics. Welcomes ideas for articles and features. Length: 1,000–1,800 words. Illustrations: colour. Payment: £300 per 1,000 words. Founded 1975.

delicious.
10 Kennington Park Place, London SE11 4AS
email info@deliciousmagazine.co.uk
website www.deliciousmagazine.co.uk
Facebook www.facebook.com/deliciousmagazineuk/
Twitter @deliciousmag
Instagram @deliciousmag
Editorial Director Karen Barnes, *Feature Writer and Co-ordinator* Phoebe Stone
Monthly £5.99

Articles on food, recipes, skills, trends, chefs, sustainability, food waste, producers, food issues, humour, wine and ingredients. Founded 2003.

Derbyshire Life

tel 07725 829565
email nathan.fearn@newsquest.co.uk
website www.greatbritishlife.co.uk
Editor Nathan Fearn
Monthly £4.50

Articles, preferably illustrated, about Derbyshire life, people, places and history. Length: up to 1,200 words. Some short stories set in Derbyshire accepted; no verse. Illustrations: photos of Derbyshire subjects. Payment: according to nature and quality of contribution. Founded 1931.

Descent

Stalactite Publishing, PO Box 297, Kendal LA9 9GQ
email editor@descentmagazine.co.uk
website www.descentmagazine.co.uk
Facebook www.facebook.com/
DescentCavingMagazine
Twitter @CavingMagazine
Instagram @descentcavingmagazine
Editor Chris Scaife
Bi-monthly £7.25

Articles, features and news on all aspects of cave and mine sport exploration, including history (coalmines, active mining or showcaves are not included). Submissions must match magazine style. Length: up to 2,500 words (articles/features), up to 1,000 words (news). Illustrations: colour. Payment: on consideration of material based on area filled. Founded 1969.

Devon Life

email catherine.courtenay@newsquest.co.uk
website www.devonlifemagazine.co.uk
Editor Catherine Courtenay
Monthly £4.50

Articles on all aspects of Devon, including inspiring people, places, walks, local events, arts, history and food. Unsolicited ideas welcome: 'ideal' features of 1,200 words, with a selection of eight to ten good-quality, high-resolution images. Founded 1963.

The Dickensian

The Dickens Fellowship,
The Charles Dickens Museum, 48 Doughty Street, London WC1N 2LX
email E.J.L.Bell@leeds.ac.uk
website www.dickensfellowship.org/dickensian
Editor Dr Emily Bell, 9.2.10 Cavendish Road, School of English, University of Leeds, Leeds LS2 9JT
3 p.a. £14 p.a. (online access), £19 p.a. (UK individuals, print and online), £29 p.a. (UK institutions); £21 p.a. (overseas individuals, print and online), £32 p.a. (overseas institutions); reduced rate for Dickens Fellowship members

Welcomes articles (max. 5,000 words) on all aspects of Dickens's life, works and character. Send contributions by email attachment to the Editor. See website for house-style conventions and specifications for any photographic material. Payment: none.

Digital Camera

Future Publishing Ltd, Quay House, The Ambury, Bath BA1 1UA
tel (01225) 442244
email digitalcamera@futurenet.com
website www.digitalcameraworld.com
Editor Niall Hampton
Monthly £7.99

Leading digital photography magazine. Practical guide to creating best-ever photographs. Each issue contains inspirational images, expert techniques and essential tips for capturing great photos, plus how to perfect them on a computer. Also includes reviews of the latest cameras, accessories and image-editing software.

Diva

Twin Media Group, Room 32, Spectrum House, 32–34 Gordon House Road, London NW5 1LP
tel 020-3735 7873
email editorial@divamag.co.uk
website www.divamag.co.uk
Editor-in-Chief Roxie Bourdillon
Monthly £4.95

Lesbian and bisexual women's lifestyle and culture: articles and features. Length: 200–2,000 words. Illustrations: colour. Payment: by arrangement. Founded 1994.

Dogs Today

The Old Print House, 62 High Street, Chobham, Surrey GU24 8AA
tel (01276) 858880
email enquiries@dogstodaymagazine.co.uk
website www.dogstodaymagazine.co.uk
Twitter @Dogs_Today
Monthly £5.99

Study of magazine essential before submitting ideas. Interested in human interest dog stories, celebrity interviews, holiday features and anything unusual – all must be entertaining and informative and accompanied by illustrations. Length: 800–1,200 words. Illustrations: colour, preferably digital. Payment: negotiable. Founded 1990.

Dorset Life – The Dorset Magazine

3 Rempstone Barns, Corfe Castle, Wareham, Dorset BH20 5DT
tel (01929) 551264
email editor@dorsetlife.co.uk
website www.dorsetlife.co.uk
Editor Lindsay Harrad
Monthly £2.95

Articles (c. 1,000 or 1,500 words), photos (colour) with a specifically Dorset theme. Payment: for text, on publication and by agreement with the editor; for photos, dependent on size used. Founded 1968.

Drapers

4th Floor, Harmsworth House, 15 Bouverie Street,
London EC4Y 8DP
tel 020-3033 2770
email Jill.geoghegan@emap.com
website www.drapersonline.com
Facebook www.facebook.com/Drapersonline
Twitter @Drapers
Editor Jill Geoghan
From £247 p.a.

Online only. Business editorial aimed at fashion
retailers, large and small, and all who supply them.
Illustrations: colour and b&w photos. Payment: by
negotiation. Founded 1887.

Dream Catcher

Stairwell Books, 161 Lowther Street, York YO31 7LZ
tel (01904) 733767
email hannah@stairwellbooks.com
website www.dreamcatchermagazine.co.uk
Facebook www.facebook.com/
DreamCatcherLiteraryArtsMag/
Twitter @literaryartsmag
Editor Hannah Stone
2 p.a. £8, £15 p.a.

International literary and arts journal. Welcomes
poetry, short stories (optimum length of 2,000
words), artwork, interviews and reviews. Each issue
features a selected artist whose work is reproduced on
the cover and inside. Promotes reading and
workshops across the UK. Founded 1996 by Paul
Sutherland.

The Dublin Review

PO Box 7948, Dublin 1, Republic of Ireland
tel +353 (0)1 6788627
email enquiry@thedublinreview.com
website www.thedublinreview.com
Editor Brendan Barrington
Quarterly €11.25 (UK)

Essays, memoir, reportage and fiction for the
intelligent general reader. Payment: by arrangement.
Founded 2000.

Early Music

Faculty of Music, University of Cambridge,
11 West Road, Cambridge CB3 9DP
email earlymusic@oxfordjournals.org
website https://em.oxfordjournals.org/
Twitter @EarlyMus
Editors Alan Howard, Elizabeth Eva Leach, Stephen
Rose
Quarterly £95 p.a. (individual, print)

Lively, informative and scholarly articles on aspects of
medieval, renaissance, baroque and classical music.
Payment: £20 per 1,000 words. Illustrations: line,
half-tone, colour. Founded 1973.

East Lothian Life

The Lighthouse, Unit 2, Heugh Road,
North Berwick EH39 5PX
tel 07878 822395
email info@eastlothianlife.co.uk
website www.eastlothianlife.co.uk
Twitter @eastlothianlife
Founder Pauline Jaffray, *Editor* Kim Williams
Quarterly £5

Articles and features with an East Lothian slant.
Length: up to 1,000 words. Illustrations: b&w photos,
line. Payment: negotiable. Founded 1989.

Economica

STICERD, London School of Economics,
Houghton Street, London WC2A 2AE
tel 020-7955 7855
website https://onlinelibrary.wiley.com/journal/
14680335
Editors Timothy Besley, Wouter den Haan, Maitreesh
Ghatak, Daniel Gottlieb and Henry Overman
Quarterly From £60 p.a. (other subscription rates on
application)

Learned journal covering the fields of economics,
economic history and statistics. Payment: none.
Founded 1921; New series 1934.

The Economist

1–11 John Adam Street, London WC2N 6HT
tel 020-7576 8000
website www.economist.com
Facebook www.facebook.com/TheEconomist
Twitter @TheEconomist
Editor-in-Chief Zanny Minton Beddoes
Weekly £7.99

Staff-written articles. Founded 1843.

Educate

National Education Union, Hamilton House,
Mabledon Place, London WC1H 9BD
tel 020-7380 4708
email educate@neu.org.uk
website https://neu.org.uk/educate
Editor Max Watson
6 p.a. Free to NEU members

Articles, features and news of interest to all those
involved in the education sector. Email outline in the
first instance. Length: 500 words (single page), 1,000
(double page). Payment: NUJ rates to NUJ members.

Electrical Review

SJP Business Media Ltd, 2nd Floor,
123 Cannon Street, London EC4N 5AU
tel 020-7062 2526
email jordano@sjpbusinessmedia.com
website www.electricalreview.co.uk
Twitter @elecreviewmag
Editor Jordan O'Brien
Monthly Free (restricted qualification; see website for
details) or £232 p.a. (print and digital subscription)

Technical and business articles on electrical and control engineering; outside contributions considered. Good-quality imagery an advantage. Electrical news welcomed. Payment: according to merit. Founded 1872.

ELLE (UK)

Hearst UK, House of Hearst, 30 Panton Street, London SW1Y 4AJ
tel 020-7150 7000
website www.elleuk.com
Facebook www.facebook.com/Ellemagazine
Twitter @Ellemagazine
Editor-in-Chief Kenya Hunt
Monthly £4.99

Commissioned material only. Illustrations: colour. Payment: by arrangement. Founded 1985.

Embroidery magazine

The Embroiderers' Guild,
c/o Bucks County Museum, Church Street, Aylesbury, Bucks. HP20 2QP
email embroideryeditorial@warnersgroup.co.uk
website https://embroiderymagazine.co.uk/writing-for-embroidery/
Editor Claire Waring
6 p.a. £6.75

News and illustrated features on all aspects of embroidery and contemporary textiles in art, design, craft, illustration, fashion, interiors and world textiles. Features on internationally renowned artists, makers and designers working with modern textiles, stitch and embroidery. News covering exhibitions, books and products, plus event listings, book and exhibition reviews and opportunities. Contributors should familiarise themselves with the publication before contacting the editor with ideas. Max length: 1,000 words features; 500 words reviews. See for forthcoming deadlines. Published every two months from January each year. Founded 1932.

Empire

Endeavour House, 189 Shaftesbury Avenue, London WC2H 8JG
tel 020-7295 6700
website www.empireonline.com
Facebook www.facebook.com/empiremagazine
Twitter @empiremagazine
Editor Nick de Semlyen
13 p.a. £5.50

Guide to film on all its platforms: articles, features, news. Length: various. Illustrations: colour and b&w photos. Payment: approx. £300 per 1,000 words; varies for illustrations. Founded 1989.

Energy Engineering

Media Culture Ltd, Pure Offices, Plato Close, Leamington Spa, Warks. CV34 6WE
tel (01926) 671338
email info@energyengineering.co.uk
website https://energyengineering.co.uk
Managing Editor Steve Welch
6 p.a. From £65 p.a.

Features and news for those engaged in technology, manufacturing and management. Contributions considered on all aspects of engineering. Illustrations: colour. Founded 1866.

The Engineer

Mark Allen Group, St Jude's Church, Dulwich Road, London SE24 0PB
tel 020-7970 4437
email jon.excell@markallengroup.com
website www.theengineer.co.uk
Twitter @TheEngineerUK
Editor Jon Excell
Monthly Price on application (free in some instances)

Features and news on innovation and technology, including profiles, analysis. Length: up to 800 words (news), 1,000 words (features). Illustrations: colour transparencies or prints, artwork, line diagrams, graphs. Payment: by negotiation. Founded 1856.

Engineering in Miniature

Warners Group Publications Plc, The Maltings, West Street, Bourne, Lincs. PE10 9PH
tel (01778) 391000
website www.world-of-railways.co.uk
Publisher (Railways) Steve Cole
Monthly £4.50

Articles containing descriptions and information on all aspects of model engineering. Articles welcome but technical articles preferred. Payment dependent on pages published. Founded 1979.

The English Garden

Jubilee House, 2 Jubilee Place, London SW3 3TQ
tel 020-7349 3700
email theenglishgarden@chelseamagazines.com
website www.theenglishgarden.co.uk
Facebook www.facebook.com/theenglishgardenmagazine
Twitter @TEGmagazine
Editor Clare Foggett
13 p.a. £5.50

Features on gardens in the UK and Ireland, plants, practical gardening advice and garden design. Length: 800–1,200 words. Illustrations: colour photos and botanical artwork. Payment: variable. Founded 1997.

Erotic Review

email info@ermagazine.org
website https://ermagazine.com/
Twitter @EroticReviewMag
Instagram @eroticreview
Editor Lucy Roeber
3 p.a.

Relaunching in 2023 as a tri-annual literary and art journal in print. Publishing longer, considered pieces that explore desire. Essays, fiction, long reviews, poetry and art collections. Not accepting submissions at present, but updates can be found online, including plans for an annual literary prize. Founded 1995.

Esquire

Hearst UK, House of Hearst, 30 Panton Street, London SW1Y 4AJ
tel 020-7439 5601
website www.esquire.com/uk
Editor-in-Chief Alex Bilmes
4 p.a. £7

Quality men's general interest magazine – articles, features, short stories. Length: various. Illustrations: colour and b&w photos, line. Payment: by arrangement. Founded 1991.

Essex Life

tel 07785 616244
email hannah.gildart@newsquest.co.uk
website www.greatbritishlife.co.uk/
Editor Hannah Gildart
Monthly £4.50

No unsolicited material. Founded 1952.

The Face

email hello@theface.com
website https://theface.com
Twitter @TheFaceMagazine
Instagram @thefacemagazine
Editor Matthew Whitehouse
Quarterly £9.95

Iconic magazine in a new guise, covering style, music, culture and society. Founded 1980; relaunched 2019.

Family Law journal

LexisNexis, 30 Farringdon Street, London EC4A 4HH
tel 0330 161 1234
email elsa.booth.1@lexisnexis.co.uk
email editor@familylaw.co.uk
website www.familylaw.co.uk
Facebook www.facebook.com/JordansFamilyLaw
Twitter @JPFamilyLaw
Contact Lucinda Stokes
Monthly £510 p.a.

Practitioner journal, aimed at helping family law professionals keep abreast of latest developments in the field and their impact. Each issue includes news on legislative change, case reports, articles and news items. Length between 2,000 and 3,000 words, no illustrations. Founded 1971.

Family Tree

Warners Group Publications Plc, The Maltings, West Street, Bourne, Lincs. PE10 9PH
tel (01778) 395050
email editorial@family-tree.co.uk
website www.family-tree.co.uk
Facebook www.facebook.com/familytreemaguk
Twitter @familytreemaguk
Editor Helen Tovey
Monthly £5.99

Features on family history, genealogy and related topics. Payment: by arrangement. Founded 1984.

Farmers Weekly

Quadrant House, The Quadrant, Sutton, Surrey SM2 5AS
tel 020-8057 8500
email farmersweekly@markallengroup.com
website www.fwi.co.uk
Editor Andrew Meredith
Weekly From £40 quarterly

Commissions freelance contributors to write articles; willing to consider pitches. Office move likely during 2023. Founded 1934.

Feminist Review

SAGE Publications Ltd, 1 Oliver's Yard, 55 City Road, London EC1Y 1SP
tel 020-7324 8517
website https://uk.sagepub.com/en-gb/eur/feminist-review/journal203522
Twitter @FeministReview_
Edited by a Collective
3 p.a. Subscriptions from £59 p.a. (digital) and £64 p.a. (print)

Peer-reviewed, interdisciplinary journal that aims to set new agendas for feminism. Invites critical reflection on the relationship between materiality and representation, theory and practice, subjectivity and communities, contemporary and historical formations. Publishes academic articles, experimental pieces, visual and textual media and political interventions, including, for example, interviews, short stories, poems and photographic essays. Founded 1979.

Fenland Poetry Journal

PO Box 234, Wisbech PE14 4EZ
email fenlandpoetryjournal@gmail.com
website www.fenlandpoetryjournal.co.uk
Facebook www.facebook.com/fenlandpoetryjournal/
Twitter @FenlandJ
Editor Elisabeth Sennitt Clough
Bi-annual £6 per issue, or £10 p.a.

Poetry and art magazine. Accepts new and previously published work as well as simultaneous submissions, but see website for full details. Poets with a connection to the Fenland area are encouraged to submit their work, but contributions from other areas, national and international, are welcomed too. Payment: none, but contributors will receive a free copy of the edition featuring their work.

The Field

Future Publishing Ltd, 121–141 Westbourne Terrace, Paddington, London W2 6JR
tel 0330 3906609
email field.secretary@futurenet.com
website www.thefield.co.uk
Facebook www.facebook.com/TheFieldMagazine
Twitter @TheFieldmag
Instagram @thefieldmagazine
Editor Alexandra Henton
Monthly £5.99

Specific, topical and informed features on the British countryside and country pursuits, including natural history, field sports, gardening and rural conservation. Overseas subjects considered but opportunities for such articles are limited. No fiction or children's material. Articles of 800–2,000 words by outside contributors considered; also topical 'shorts' of 200–300 words on all countryside matters. Illustrations: colour photos of a high standard. Payment: by arrangement. Founded 1853.

Financial Adviser

Financial Times Business, 1 Southwark Bridge, London SE1 9HL
tel 020-7775 3000
email simoney.kyriakou@ft.com
website www.ftadviser.com
Editor Simoney Kyriakou
Online Free (after registering)

Topical personal finance news and features. Length: variable. Payment: by arrangement. Founded 1987.

FIRE

Blue Sky Offices, 25 Cecil Pashley Way, Shoreham-by-Sea BN43 5FF
tel (01273) 434943
email andrew.lynch@fireknowledge.co.uk
website www.fire-magazine.com
Editor and Publisher Andrew Lynch
Monthly £86.50 p.a.

Articles on firefighting and fire prevention from acknowledged experts only. Length: 1,500 words. No unsolicited contributions. Illustrations: dramatic firefighting or fire brigade rescue colour photos. Payment: by arrangement. Founded 1908.

Firewords

email info@firewords.co.uk
website https://firewords.co.uk
Twitter @FirewordsMag
Editors Dan Burgess, Jen Scott
2 p.a. £9 inc. delivery

Literary magazine with high design and production standards. Accepts submissions for fiction, short stories and poetry: issues are (loosely) themed, so check website for forthcoming themes and specifications. Original work preferred, but previously published pieces may be considered:

prospective authors should indicate if their material has appeared elsewhere. Payment: none. Founded 2014.

fish: A literary celebration of scale and fin

Warners Group Publications Plc, The Maltings, West Street, Bourne, Lincs. PE10 9PH
tel (01778) 391194
website www.practicalfishkeeping.co.uk
Instagram @fish_the_literary_magazine
Editor Nathan Hill
2 p.a. £14.99

Natural history, conservation, art, recipes, fiction, poetry, personal accounts, biology, trivia, all pertaining to fish and/or marine life. Personal artworks and photography considered. Payment: by arrangement. Founded 2021.

Fishing News

Kelsey Publishing Ltd, The Granary, Downs Court, Yalding Hill, Yalding, Maidstone, Kent ME18 6AL
tel (01959) 543747
email fishingnews.ed@kelsey.co.uk
website www.fishingnews.co.uk
Twitter @YourFishingNews
Editor Andy Read
Weekly £3.30

News and features on all aspects of the commercial fishing industry. Length: up to 1,000 words (features), up to 500 words (news). Illustrations: colour and b&w photos. Payment: negotiable. Founded 1913.

Flash: The International Short-Short Story Magazine

Department of English, University of Chester, Parkgate Road, Chester CH1 4BJ
tel (01244) 513 152
email flash.magazine@chester.ac.uk
website www1.chester.ac.uk/flash-magazine
Editors Dr Peter Blair, Dr Ashley Chantler
Bi-annual £6, £11 p.a. Subscription includes membership of International Flash Fiction Association (IFFA)

Quality stories of up to 360 words (title included); see website for submission guidelines. Suggestions for reviews and articles considered. Payment: complimentary copy. Founded 2008.

Flora

4–5 Kinnerton Place South, Belgravia, London SW1X 8EH
tel 020-7235 6235
email editor@judithblacklock.com
website www.flora-magazine.co.uk
Editor Judith Blackstock
Bi-monthly £4.75

Magazine for flower arranging and floristry; also features flower-related crafts and flower arrangers' gardens. Unsolicited enquiries and suggestions welcome on any of these subjects. Send brief synopsis together with sample illustrations. Payment: by arrangement. Founded 1974.

Fly Fishing & Fly Tying
Rolling River Publications, The Locus Centre, The Square, Aberfeldy, Perthshire PH15 2DD
tel (01887) 829868
email MarkB.ffft@btinternet.com
website www.flyfishing-and-flytying.co.uk
Facebook www.facebook.com/Fly-Fishing-Fly-Tying-Magazine-117880628246068/
Twitter @FFFTmag
Instagram @flyfishingandflytyingmagazine
Editor Mark Bowler
12 p.a. £4.75

Fly-fishing and fly-tying articles, fishery features, limited short stories, fishing travel. Length: by arrangement. Illustrations: colour photos. Payment: by arrangement. Founded 1990.

Fortean Times
Diamond Publishing, 2nd Floor, Saunders House, 52-53 The Mall, Ealing Broadway, London W5 3TA
tel 020-3890 3890
email drsutton@forteantimes.com
website www.forteantimes.com
Facebook www.facebook.com/ForteanTimes
Twitter @forteantimes
Editor David Sutton
13 p.a. £4.95

Journal of strange phenomena, experiences, related subjects and philosophies. Includes articles, features, news, reviews. Length: 500–5,000 words; longer by arrangement. Illustrations: colour photos, line and tone art, cartoons. Payment: by negotiation. Founded 1973.

The Fortnightly Review
email info@fortnightlyreview.co.uk
website https://fortnightlyreview.co.uk/
Twitter @TheFortnightly
Co-editors Denis Boyles, Alan Macfarlane, *Poetry Editor* Peter Riley

Online. Cultural criticism, commentary, perspective. Poetry submissions are accepted via email: query first or send direct, pasted into the body of an email. Payment: minimal.

Forty20
tel 0113 225 9797
email editorial@forty-20.com
Facebook www.facebook.com/forty20magazine
Twitter @forty20magazine
Monthly £4.25

Independent illustrated rugby league magazine, available nationally. Features interviews and articles on rugby league both in the UK and overseas and at a variety of levels. Articles and images welcome; email on address above.

FourFourTwo
Future Publishing Ltd, 121–141 Westbourne Terrace, London W2 6JR
email fourfourtwo@futurenet.com
website www.fourfourtwo.com
Editor James Andrew
13 p.a. £5.99

Football magazine with interviews, in-depth features, issues pieces, odd and witty material. Length: 2,000–3,000 (features), 100–1,500 words (Up Front pieces). Illustrations: colour transparencies and artwork, b&w prints. Payment: £200 per 1,000 words. Founded 1994.

fourteen poems
email hello@14poems.com
website www.fourteenpoems.com
Twitter @fourteenpoems
Instagram @14poems
3 p.a. £7.50, £25 p.a.

London-based poetry journal, featuring 14 LGBTQIA+ poets per issue. Rolling submissions window but check website for any forthcoming deadlines. Up to five poems may be submitted at any one time in a single Word document or pdf. Payment: £25 per poem published.

France
France Media Ltd, Spaces, 2nd & 3rd Floors, Northgate House, Upper Borough Walls, Bath BA1 1RG
tel (01225) 463752
email info@francemedia.com
website www.completefrance.com
Monthly £4.99

Informed quality features and articles on the real France, ranging from cuisine to culture to holidays exploring hidden France. Length: 800–2,000 words. Payment: by arrangement. Founded 1989.

The Friend
173 Euston Road, London NW1 2BJ
tel 020-7663 1010
email editorial@thefriend.org
website www.thefriend.org
Editor Joseph Jones
Weekly From £77 p.a.

Material of interest to Quakers and like-minded people; spiritual, political, social, economic, environmental or cultural, considered from outside contributors. Length: up to 1,200 words. Illustrations: b&w or colour photographs and line drawings by email preferred. Payment: not usually but will negotiate a small fee with professional writers. Founded 1843.

Frieze

1 Surrey Street, London WC2R 2ND
tel 020-3372 6111
email editors@frieze.com
website www.frieze.com
8 p.a. £9.95 (back issues £15)

Magazine of European contemporary art and culture including essays, reviews, columns and listings. Frieze Art Fair is held every October in Regent's Park, London, featuring over 150 of the most exciting contemporary art galleries in the world. Founded 1991.

The Frogmore Papers

21 Mildmay Road, Lewes, East Sussex BN7 1PJ
email frogmorepress@gmail.com
website www.frogmorepress.co.uk/submission-guidelines/
Editor Jeremy Page
2 p.a. £5

Long-established poetry and prose magazine. Two submission windows per year: 1–31 October for the March issue and 1–30 April for the September issue. Submissions from UK-based writers should be made by post to the address above, but overseas writers may contribute via email. Send no more than four to six poems at one time; short stories should be no more than 2,000 words. Familiarity with the magazine advised; also see website for further guidance.

The Furrow

St Patrick's College, Maynooth,
Co. Kildare W23 TW77, Republic of Ireland
tel +353 (0)1 7083741
email editor.furrow@spcm.ie
website www.thefurrow.ie
Editor Rev. Pádraig Corkery
Monthly €4.50

Religious, pastoral, theological and social articles. Length: up to 3,500 words. Articles are available through JSTOR and from the Secretary at *The Furrow* office. Illustrations: line, half-tone. Payment: average €20 per page (450 words). Founded 1950.

Garden Answers

Bauer Media Group, Media House, Lynch Wood, Peterborough Business Park, Peterborough PE2 6EA
tel (01733) 468000
email gardenanswers@bauermedia.co.uk
website www.gardenanswersmagazine.co.uk
Twitter @GardenAnswers
Editor Melissa Mabbitt
Monthly £5.20

Some commissioned features and articles on all aspects of gardening. Reader garden photo and

interview packages considered. Study of magazine essential. Approach by email with examples of published work. Length: approx. 750 words. Illustrations: digital images and artwork. Payment: by negotiation. Founded 1982.

Garden News

Bauer Media Group, Media House, Lynch Wood, Peterborough Business Park, Peterborough PE2 6EA
tel (01733) 468000
email gn.letters@bauermedia.co.uk
website www.gardennewsmagazine.co.uk
Facebook www.facebook.com/GardenNewsOfficial
Twitter @GardenNewsMag
Instagram @gardennewsmagazine
Weekly £2.30

Up-to-date information on everything to do with plants, growing and gardening. Payment: by negotiation. Founded 1958.

Gay Times

Room 2.03, 133 Whitechapel High Street, London E1 7QA
tel 020-7424 7400
email editorial@gaytimes.co.uk
website www.gaytimes.co.uk
Twitter @gaytimesmag
Instagram @gaytimesmag
Editorial Director Lewis Corner
Monthly £8.95

Digital magazine featuring diverse LGBTQIA+ talent. Includes features and interviews on celebrity, gay lifestyle, health, parenting, music, film, technology, current affairs, opinion, culture, art, style and grooming. Length: up to 2,000 words. Payment: by arrangement. Founded 1984.

Geographical

Unit 3, Boleyn Business Suite,
Hever Castle Golf Club, Hever Road, Edenbridge, Kent TN8 7NP
email katie@geographical.co.uk
website www.geographical.co.uk
Facebook www.facebook.com/GeographicalMagazine
Twitter @Geographicalmag
Editor Katie Burton
Monthly From £39.99 p.a.

Magazine of the Royal Geographical Society (with the Institute of British Geographers). Covers culture, wildlife, environment, science and travel. Illustrations: top-quality hi-res digital files, vintage material. Payment: by negotiation. Founded 1935.

The Geographical Journal

Royal Geographical Society (with the Institute of British Geographers), 1 Kensington Gore, London SW7 2AR
tel 020-7591 3026

email journals@rgs.org
website https://rgs-ibg.onlinelibrary.wiley.com/journal/14754959
Editors Darren Smith, Ben Anderson, Parvati Raghuram and Rob Wilby
4 p.a. Subscriptions from £303 p.a. (institutional rate available only)

Papers range across the entire subject of geography, with particular reference to public debates, policy-oriented agendas and notions of 'relevance'. Illustrations: photos, maps, diagrams. Founded 1893.

Gibbons Stamp Monthly
Stanley Gibbons Ltd, 7 Parkside, Ringwood, Hants BH24 3SH
tel (01425) 481042
email dshepherd@stanleygibbons.co.uk
website www.stanleygibbons.com/publishing/gibbons-stamp-monthly
Twitter @GSM_Magazine
Editor Dean Shepherd
Monthly £5.35

Articles on philatelic topics. Contact the Editor first. Length: 500–2,500 words. Illustrations: photos, line, stamps or covers. Payment: by arrangement.

Glamour
The Condé Nast Publications Ltd, The Adelphi, 1–11 John Adam Street, London WC2N 6HT
email glamoureditorialmagazine@condenast.co.uk
website www.glamourmagazine.co.uk
European Editorial Director Deborah Joseph
Principally online but occasional print editions £2

Lifestyle magazine containing fashion, beauty, real-life features and celebrity news aimed at women aged 18–34. Feature ideas welcome; approach with brief outline. Length: 500–800 words. Payment: by arrangement. Founded 2001.

Golf Monthly
Future Publishing Ltd, Unit 2, Eelmore Road, Farnborough, Hants GU14 7QN
tel (01225) 442244
email nick.bonfield@futurenet.com
website www.golfmonthly.com/features/the-game/want-to-write-for-golf-monthly-207655
Editor Michael Harris, *Content Editor* Nick Bonfield
Monthly £5.50

Original articles on golf considered (not reports), golf clinics, handy hints. Illustrations: half-tone, colour, cartoons. Payment: by arrangement. Founded 1911.

Good Housekeeping
Hearst UK, House of Hearst, 30 Panton Street, London SW1Y 4AJ
email goodh.mail@hearst.co.uk
website www.goodhousekeeping.com/uk
Editor-in-Chief Gaby Huddart
Monthly £5.99

Articles on topics of interest to women. No unsolicited features or stories accepted. Homes, fashion, beauty and food covered by staff writers. Illustrations: commissioned. Payment: magazine standards. Founded 1922.

Governance and Compliance
The Chartered Governance Institute UK & Ireland, Saffron House, 6–10 Kirby Street, London EC1N 8TS
tel 020-7580 4741
website www.govcompmag.com
Editor Holly Benson
Monthly £150 + VAT p.a. (full rate; free to members)

Published by The Chartered Governance Institute UK & Ireland. Offers news, views and practical advice on the latest developments in governance and compliance.

GQ
The Condé Nast Publications, The Adelphi, 1–11 John Adam Street, London WC2N 6HT
tel 020-7851 1800
website www.gq-magazine.co.uk
Twitter @BritishGQ
Head of Editorial Content Adam Baidawi
Monthly £3.99

Style, fashion and general interest magazine for men. Illustrations: b&w and colour photos, line drawings, cartoons. Payment: by arrangement. Founded 1988.

Granta
12 Addison Avenue, London W11 4QR
tel 020-7605 1360
email editorial@granta.com
website www.granta.com
website https://granta.submittable.com/submit
Twitter @GrantaMag
Editor Thomas Meaney
Quarterly £14.99

Original literary fiction, poetry, non-fiction, memoir, reportage and photography. Study magazine before submitting work. No academic essays or reviews. Note that submissions are accepted only via online submissions system (see above). Length: determined by content. Illustrations: photos and original artwork. Payment: by arrangement. Founded 1889; reconceived 1979.

Grazia
Bauer Media, The Lantern, 75 Hampstead Road, London NW1 2PL
email anna.silverman@graziamagazine.co.uk
website https://graziadaily.co.uk/
Twitter @graziauk
Editor-in-Chief Hattie Brett, *Features Editor* Anna Silverman
Fortnightly £3.25

Women's magazine with the latest trends, gossip, fashion and news in bite-size pieces.

Greetings Today

(formerly Greetings Magazine)
Lema Publishing, 1 Churchgates, The Wilderness,
Berkhamsted, Herts. HP4 2AZ
tel (01442) 289930
email tracey@lemapublishing.co.uk
website www.greetingstoday.media/
Monthly Controlled circulation

Trade magazine with articles, features and news
related to the greeting card industry. Mainly written
in-house; some material taken from outside. Length:
varies. Illustrations: line, colour and b&w photos.
Payment: by arrangement.

The Grocer

William Reed Publishing Ltd, Broadfield Park,
Crawley, West Sussex RH11 9RT
tel (01293) 613400
website www.thegrocer.co.uk
Facebook www.facebook.com/TheGrocer
Twitter @TheGrocer
Editor-in-Chief Adam Leyland
Weekly From £290 p.a. (digital; other rates are
available)

Trade journal: articles, news or illustrations of general
interest to the grocery and provision trades. Payment:
by arrangement. Founded 1861.

Grow Your Own

25 Phoenix Court, Hawkins Road,
Colchester CO2 8JY
tel (01206) 505979
email laura.hillier@aceville.co.uk
website www.growfruitandveg.co.uk
Editor Laura Hillier
Monthly £6.99

Magazine for kitchen gardeners of all levels of
expertise. Will consider unsolicited material.
Welcomes ideas for articles and features. Length:
1,000 words (articles), 1,500 words (features), 200
words (news). Illustrations: transparencies, colour
prints and digital images. Payment: varies.

Guitarist

Future Publishing Ltd, Quay House, The Ambury,
Bath BA1 1UA
tel (01225) 442244
website www.musicradar.com/guitarist
Editor Jamie Dickson
13 p.a. £7.49

Aims to improve readers' knowledge of the
instrument, help them make the right buying choices
and assist them in becoming a better player. Ideas for
articles welcome. Founded 1984.

Gutter

0/2, 258 Kenmure Street, Glasgow G41 2QY
email contactguttermagazine@gmail.com
website www.guttermag.co.uk
Twitter @Gutter_Magazine
Instagram @Gutter_Magazine
Managing Editor Kate MacLeary
Bi-annual From £14 p.a.

Award-winning print journal featuring new Scottish
and international poetry and prose. Invites
submissions of up to 3,000 words of fiction or 120
lines of poetry, and seeks provocative work that
challenges, reimagines or undermines the individual
or collective status quo. See website for more
information. No longer offering editorial review.

H&E naturist

Hawk Editorial Ltd, PO Box 545, Hull HU9 9JF
tel (01482) 342000
email editor@henaturist.net
website www.henaturist.net
Editor Paul Rouse
Monthly £5.50

Articles on naturist travel, clubs, beaches and naturist
lifestyle experiences from the UK and beyond.
Length: 800–1,200 words. Illustrations: digital images
featuring naturists in natural settings; also photos,
letters and features with naturist theme. Payment: by
negotiation but guidelines for contributors and basic
payment rates available on request.

Harper's Bazaar

Hearst UK, House of Hearst, 30 Panton Street,
London SW1Y 4AJ
tel 020-7439 5000
website www.harpersbazaar.co.uk
Editor-in-Chief Lydia Slater
Monthly £5.25

Features, fashion, beauty, art, theatre, films, travel,
interior decoration – some commissioned.
Founded 1867.

HCM

Leisure Media Company Ltd, Portmill House,
Portmill Lane, Hitchin, Herts. SG5 1DJ
tel (01462) 431385
email lizterry@leisuremedia.com
website www.healthclubmanagement.co.uk
Editor Liz Terry
11 p.a. From £67 p.a.

Europe's leading publication for the health and
fitness industry, covering the latest news, interviews,
new openings and trends across the public and
private health and fitness sectors. Print and digital
editions of the magazine are available, as is *Health
Club Management Handbook*, an annual reference
book for buyers and decision-makers in the health
and fitness sector. Founded 1995 as *Health Club
Management*.

Heat

Bauer Media, The Lantern, 75 Hampstead Road,
London NW1 2PL

email heatEd@heatmag.com
website www.heatworld.com
Editor-in-Chief Julia Davis
Weekly £2.60

Features and news on entertainment and popular media. Founded 1999.

hedgerow: a journal of small poems

email hedgerowsubmission@gmail.com
website https://hedgerowhaiku.com
Editor Caroline Skanne
Quarterly £11 inc. postage (UK and US), £14 inc. postage (Europe and Canada), £17 (RoW)

Short-poetry journal dedicated to publishing an eclectic mix of new and established voices across the spectrum of the short poem, with particular attention to the constantly evolving forms of English-language haiku and related works. Includes original poems, photographs and artwork. Four submission windows (see website for up-to-date details).

Two sections are available to read for free online: hedgerow: young voices (haiku and related short poems by poets under the age of 16); hedgerow: vines (collaborative poems, sequences, linked forms & articles).

Hello!

Wellington House, 69–71 Upper Ground, London SE1 9PQ
tel 020-7667 8700
email holly.nesbitt-larking@hellomagazine.com
website www.hellomagazine.com
Twitter @hellomag
Weekly £2.95

News-based features – showbusiness, celebrity, royalty; exclusive interviews. Illustrated. Payment: by arrangement. Founded 1988.

Here Comes Everyone

email raef@hcemagazine.com
website www.hcemagazine.com
Facebook www.facebook.com/HCEmagazine
Twitter @HereComesEvery1
Editor Raef Boylan
3 p.a. £5

Original prose, poetry, non-fiction and art written to fit a theme. Submissions are accepted via online submissions form on the website (see above; submissions guidelines available here too). Current and past issues can be purchased in print and digital forms, and an archive of older issues can also be previewed online.

Hi-Fi News

AVTech Media Ltd, Enterprise House, Enterprise Way, Edenbridge, Kent TN8 6HF
tel 0844 8488822
email paul.miller@hifinews.com
website www.hifinews.com

Editor Paul Miller
Monthly £5.99

Articles on all aspects of high-quality sound recording and reproduction; also extensive record review section and supporting musical feature articles. Audio matter is essentially technical, but should be presented in a manner suitable for music lovers interested in the nature of sound. Length: 2,000–3,000 words. Illustrations: line, half-tone. Payment: by arrangement. Founded 1956.

High Life

Cedar Communications Ltd, 9th Floor, Bankside 3, 90–100 Southwark Street, London SE1 0SW
tel 020-7550 8000
email high.life@cedarcom.co.uk
website https://bahighlife.com/
Online Editor Florence Derrick
Bi-monthly

Online consumer magazine for British Airways passengers. Articles on entertainment, travel, fashion, business, sport and lifestyle. Founded 1973.

History Today

9/10 Staple Inn, London WC1V 7QH
tel 020-3219 7810
email admin@historytoday.com
website www.historytoday.com
Editors Rhys Griffiths, Kate Wiles
Monthly £6.50

History in the widest sense – political, economic, social, biography, relating past to present; world history as well as British. Length: 3,500–4,000 words (feature articles); 1,300–2,200 words (mid-length features); 600–1,000 words (news/views). Do not send original material until publication is agreed. Accepts freelance contributions dealing with genuinely new historical and archaeological research. Payment: by arrangement. Founded 1951.

Homes & Gardens

Future Publishing Ltd, 121–141 Westbourne Terrace, London W2 6JR
tel 020-3148 5000
email HomesAndGardens@futurenet.com
website www.homesandgardens.com
Twitter @homesandgardens
Editorial Director Sarah Spiteri
Monthly £5.99

Articles on home interest or design, particularly well-designed British interiors (snapshots should be submitted). Length: 900–1,000 words (articles). Illustrations: all types. Payment: generous, but exceptional work required; varies. Founded 1919.

Horse & Hound

Future Publishing Ltd, Unit 415, Winnersh Triangle, Eskdale Road, Winnersh RG41 5TU
email pippa.roome@futurenet.com
website www.horseandhound.co.uk

Editor-in-Chief Sarah Jenkins, *Magazine Editor* Pippa
Roome, *Website Editor* Carol Phillips
Weekly £3.25

News, reports, features and opinion, covering all
areas of equestrianism, particularly the Olympic
disciplines of eventing, showjumping and dressage,
plus showing and hunting. Payment: by arrangement.

Horse & Rider

DJ Murphy Publishers Ltd, Olive Studio,
Grange Road, Tilford, Farnham, Surrey GU10 2DQ
tel (01428) 601020
email editor@djmurphy.co.uk
website www.horseandrideruk.com
Twitter @HorseandRiderUK
Editor-in-Chief Louise Kittle
Monthly £4.49

Covers all forms of equestrian activity at home and
abroad. Good writing and technical accuracy
essential. Length: 1,500–2,000 words. Illustrations:
photos and drawings, the latter usually
commissioned. Payment: by arrangement.
Founded 1959.

Hortus

Upland Mansion, Upland Arms,
Carmarthen SA32 8DZ
tel (01544) 260001 (editorial), *tel* 07943 724726
(sales/subs)
email d.a.wheeler@hotmail.com (editorial)
email all@hortus.co.uk (sales)
website www.hortus.co.uk
Editor David Wheeler
Quarterly £42 plus postage

Articles on decorative horticulture: plants, gardens,
history, design, literature, people; book reviews.
Length: 1,500–5,000 words, longer by arrangement.
Illustrations: line, half-tone and wood-engravings.
Payment: by arrangement. Founded 1987.

Hot Press

100 Capel Street, Dublin 1, Republic of Ireland
tel +353 (0)1 2411500
email editorial@hotpress.ie
website www.hotpress.com
Twitter @hotpress
Editor Niall Stokes
Fortnightly €5.95

High-quality, investigative stories, or punchily
written offbeat pieces, of interest to 16–39 year-olds,
including politics, music, sport, sex, and religion.
Length: varies. Illustrations: colour with some b&w.
Payment: by arrangement. Founded 1977.

House & Garden

The Condé Nast Publications Ltd, Vogue House,
Hanover Square, London W1S 1JU
email houseandgarden@condenast.co.uk
website www.houseandgarden.co.uk

Editor Hatta Byng
Monthly £4.99

Articles (always commissioned), on subjects relating
to domestic architecture, interior decorating,
furnishing, gardens and gardening, exhibitions, travel,
food and wine.

House Beautiful

Hearst UK, House of Hearst, 30 Panton Street,
London SW1Y 4AJ
tel 020-7439 5000
email house.beautiful@hearst.co.uk
website www.housebeautiful.com/uk/
Executive Editor Terry Barbrook
Monthly £5.99

Specialist features for the homes of today. Unsolicited
submissions are not accepted. Illustrated.
Founded 1989.

Housebuilder

27 Broadwall, London SE1 9PL
tel 020-7960 1630
email info@house-builder.co.uk
website www.house-builder.co.uk
Twitter @housebuildermag
Publishing Director Ben Roskrow
10 p.a. Free to read online

Official journal of the Home Builders Federation
published in association with the National House-
Building Council. Technical articles on design,
construction and equipment of dwellings, estate
planning and development, and technical aspects of
house-building, aimed at those engaged in house and
flat construction and the development of housing
estates. Preliminary letter advisable. Length: articles
from 500 words, preferably with illustrations.
Illustrations: photos, plans, construction details,
cartoons. Payment: by arrangement.

Icon Magazine

Media 10, Crown House, 151 High Road, Loughton,
Essex IG10 4LF
tel 020-3235 5200
email submissions@icon-magazine.co.uk
website www.iconeye.com
Facebook www.facebook.com/iconeye/
Twitter @iconeye
Instagram @iconeye
Editor Jessica-Christin Hametner
Monthly From £27.99 p.a.

Articles on architecture and design culture, including
projects and practitioners. Founded 2003.

Ideal Home

Future Publishing Ltd, 121–141 Westbourne Terrace,
London W2 6JR
tel 020-3148 5000
email ideal_home@futurenet.com
website www.idealhome.co.uk
Twitter @idealhome

Editor Heather Young
Monthly £5.99

Lifestyle magazine, articles usually commissioned. Contributors advised to study editorial content before submitting material. Illustrations: usually commissioned. Payment: according to material. Founded 1920.

The Idler

Great Western Studios, 65 Alfred Road, London W2 5EU
tel 020-3176 7907
email mail@idler.co.uk
email art@idler.co.uk
website www.idler.co.uk
Founder Tom Hodgkinson
Bi-monthly £9

Magazine dedicated to 'the art of living'. Includes a range of features and articles on topics from film to music, business and eating out, as well as readers' letters and diary pieces. Also runs online courses and stages live events in London. Unsolicited material rarely commissioned, but ideas may be emailed to the Editor. Illustrators may send their portfolio to the Art Director via the second email address given above.

Improve Your Coarse Fishing

Bauer Media Group, Media House, Lynch Wood, Peterborough Business Park, Peterborough PE2 6EA
tel (01733) 395104
email iycf@bauermedia.co.uk
Facebook www.facebook.com/iycfmag/
Editor James Furness
13 p.a. £4.60

Articles on technique and equipment, the best venues, news and features. Ideas welcome by email. Founded 1991.

The Independent Publishing Magazine

website www.theindependentpublishingmagazine.com
Facebook www.facebook.com/TheIndependentPublishingMagazine
Twitter @theindiepubmag
Editor-in-Chief Mick Rooney

Online magazine for writers and publishers with a focus on providing essential information, news, resources, reviews of publishing service providers and an overview of the changing landscape of the publishing industry. Provides a regularly updated publishing service index. Guest posts welcome, but see website for full guidelines. Founded 2007.

Index on Censorship

3rd Floor, 86–90 Paul Street, London EC2A 4NE
email info@indexoncensorship.org
website www.indexoncensorship.org
Twitter @IndexCensorship
Editor-in-Chief Jemimah Steinfeld
Quarterly £7.99

Articles of up to 3,000 words dealing with all aspects of free speech and political censorship. Illustrations: b&w, cartoons. Payment: £200 per 1,000 words. Founded 1972.

Ink Sweat & Tears

email enquiries@inksweatandtears.co.uk
website https://inksweatandtears.co.uk/
Facebook https://en-gb.facebook.com/InkSweatandTears/
Twitter @InkSweatTears
Instagram @insta.inksweatandtears
Editor Helen Ivory, *Publisher* Kate Birch
Online

Poetry, short prose, word and image and film poem webzine. Accepts previously unpublished submissions of up to 750 words. Publishes something new every day. Has a paid editing internship programme for writers from the Black, Asian, Latinx and other global majority communities and a 'Pick of the Month' feature voted for by readers.

Publishes both new and more established writers and welcomes submissions of well-written reviews. The IS&T Commission Competition is an occasional project to write a pamphlet of poems published by IS&T Press.

Inside Soap

Hearst UK, House of Hearst, 30 Panton Street, London SW1Y 4AJ
tel 020-7439 5000
email editor@insidesoap.co.uk
website www.insidesoap.co.uk
Facebook www.facebook.com/insidesoap
Twitter @InsideSoapMag
Executive Editor Gary Gillatt
Weekly £2.99

Gossip and celebrity interviews with soap and popular TV characters on terrestrial and satellite channels. Submit ideas by email in first instance. Payment: by arrangement.

Inspire Magazine

FSJ Ltd, Room 51, BizSpace, Courtwick Lane, Littlehampton, West Sussex BN17 7TL
tel (01903) 604343
email editor@inspiremagazine.org.uk
website www.inspiremagazine.org.uk
Twitter @inspirestories
Editor Russ Bravo
Online

Digital portal with 'good news' stories of Christian faith in action and personal testimonies. Length: 400–700 words (features). Freelance articles used rarely. Payment: by arrangement.

Insurance Age

InfoPro Digital Services, 133 Houndsditch, London EC3A 7BX

tel 020-7316 9458
email lauren.graham@infopro-digital.com
email emmanuel.kenning@infopro-digital.com
website www.insuranceage.co.uk
Editor Lauren Graham, *News Editor* Emmanuel Kenning
10 p.a. £550 p.a. for FCA registered brokers

News, features, research and rankings on general insurance and the regional broker market covering commercial lines, personal lines, regulation, people, opinion and technology. Payment: by arrangement. Founded 1979.

Insurance Post

InfoPro Digital Services, 133 Houndsditch, London EC3A 7BX
tel 020-7316 9000
email postonline@infropro-digital.com
website www.postonline.co.uk
Editor Emma Ann Hughes
Weekly From £1,365 p.a.

Commissioned specialist articles on topics of interest to insurance professionals in the UK, Europe and Asia; news. Illustrations: colour photos and illustrations, colour cartoons and line drawings. Payment: by arrangement. Founded 1840.

InterMedia

InterMedia International Institute of Communications, Suite 107, 143 Kingston Road, London SW19 1LJ
email enquiries@iicom.org
website www.iicom.org
Editor Russell Seekins
Quarterly Free to IIC members

International journal concerned with policies, events, trends and research in the field of communications, broadcasting, telecommunications and associated issues, particularly cultural and social. Founded 1970.

International Affairs

The Royal Institute of International Affairs, Chatham House, 10 St James's Square, London SW1Y 4LE
tel 020-7957 5728
email kcsortea@chathamhouse.org
website www.chathamhouse.org/publications/ia
website https://academic.oup.com/ia
Twitter @ChathamHouse
Editor Professor Andrew Dorman
6 issues p.a. From £104 p.a. (individuals), or from £692 p.a. (institutions)

Peer-reviewed academic articles on international affairs; up to 40 books reviewed in each issue. Unsolicited articles welcome; submissions on ScholarOne: mc.manuscriptcentral.com/inta. Article length: 7,000–10,000 words. Illustrations: none. Payment: by arrangement. Founded 1922.

Investors' Chronicle

Bracken House, 1 Friday Street, London EC4M 9BT
tel 020-7873 3000
website www.investorschronicle.co.uk
Editor Rosie Carr
Weekly £5.99

Journal covering investment and personal finance. Occasional outside contributions for features are accepted. Payment: by arrangement.

Ireland's Own

Channing House, Upper Rowe Street, Wexford Y35 TH2A, Republic of Ireland
tel +353 (0)53 9140140
email info@irelandsown.ie
email submissions@irelandsown.ie
website www.irelandsown.ie
Editor Seán Nolan, *Editor Monthly Editions* Shea Tomkins
Weekly €2, Monthly specials €3.20

Short stories: non-experimental, traditional with an Irish orientation (1,800–2,000 words); articles of interest to Irish readers at home and abroad (750–800 words); general and literary articles (750–800 words). Monthly special bumper editions, each devoted to a particular seasonal topic. Suggestions for new features considered. Payment: varies according to quality and length. Founded 1902.

Irish Arts Review

Tower 3, Fumbally Court, Fumbally Lane, Dublin DO8 TXY8, Republic of Ireland
tel +353 (0)1 6766711
email news@irishartsreview.com
website www.irishartsreview.com
Twitter @IrishArtsReview
Editor Brigid Mulcahy
Quarterly €75 p.a. (UK and Europe), €90 p.a. (US), €110 p.a. (RoW)

Magazine committed to promoting Irish art and heritage around the world with reviews of Irish painting, design, heritage, sculpture, architecture, photography and decorative arts. To submit info on Irish Art Exhibitions overseas, email: production@irishartsreview.com

Irish Farmers Journal

Irish Farm Centre, Bluebell, Dublin D12 YXW5, Republic of Ireland
tel +353 (0)1 4199530
email edit@farmersjournal.ie
website www.farmersjournal.ie
Interim Editor Jack Kennedy
Weekly From €9.99 per month

Readable, technical articles on any aspect of farming. Length: 700–1,000 words. Payment: £100–£150 per article. Illustrated. Founded 1948.

Irish Journal of Medical Science

Royal Academy of Medicine in Ireland,
Setanta House, 2nd Floor, Setanta Place, Dublin 2,
Republic of Ireland
tel +353 (0)1 6334820
email preethi.prasad@springernature.com
website www.springer.com/journal/11845
Editor William P. Tormey
Bi-monthly

Official publication of the Royal Academy of
Medicine in Ireland. Original contributions in
medicine, surgery, midwifery, public health, etc;
reviews of professional books, reports of medical
societies, etc. Illustrations: line, half-tone, colour.

Irish Medical Times

Corville Road, Roscrea, Co. Tipperary, E53 H224,
Republic of Ireland
tel +353 (0)1 8176300
email editor@imt.ie
website www.imt.ie
Editor Terence Cosgrave
Weekly Free to medical professionals, otherwise
€298 p.a. (Republic of Ireland), €434 p.a. (UK)

Medical articles. Opinion column length: 850–1,000
words.

Irish Pages: A Journal of Contemporary Writing

129 Ormeau Road, Belfast BT7 1SH
tel 028-9043 4800
email editor@irishpages.org
website www.irishpages.org
Twitter @irishpages
Editor Chris Agee, *Irish Language Editor* Cathal Ó
Searcaigh, *Scottish Editor* Kathleen Jamie, *Scottish
Gaeilge Editor* Meg Bateman, *Managing Editor*
Jennifer Kerr
Bi-annual €22

Poetry, fiction, essays, creative non-fiction, memoir,
essay reviews, nature writing, translated work, literary
journalism, and other autobiographical, historical
and scientific writing of literary distinction. Publishes
in equal measure writing from Ireland and abroad.
Accepts unsolicited submissions by post only.
Payment: pays only for certain commissions and
occasional serial rights. Founded 2002.

The Irish Post

88 Fenchurch Street, London EC3M 4BY
tel 020-8900 4137
email editor@irishpost.co.uk
website www.irishpost.co.uk
Twitter @theirishpost
Editor Mal Rogers
Weekly £1.50

Coverage of all political, social and sporting events
relevant to the Irish community in Britain. Also
contains a guide to Irish entertainment in Britain.
Annual events include *The Irish Post* Awards. In
addition, *The Post* also has links to some of the
biggest Irish festivals and events in Britain, including
the Mayor of London St Patrick's Day Festival and
the GAA All-Britain Competition. Annual magazines
include *Building Britain*, which promotes the Irish
construction industry; *Companies100*, a guide to the
top 100 Irish companies in Britain; and *In Business*,
an informative list of Irish business leaders across
Britain. Founded 1970.

Irish Tatler

Business Post Media Group, Merrion Road,
Dublin 4, Republic of Ireland
email info@businesspost.ie
website www.irishtatler.com
Twitter @irishtatler
Editor Jessie Collins, *Assistant Editor* Amy Heffernan
Monthly Free with *Business Post* (subscription offers
apply)

General interest women's magazine: fashion, beauty,
interiors, cookery, current affairs, reportage and
celebrity interviews. Length: 2,000–4,000 words.
Payment: by arrangement.

Jane's Defence Weekly

Sentinel House, 163 Brighton Road, Coulsdon,
Surrey CR5 2YH
tel 020-3253 2100
website www.janes.com
Weekly From £544 p.a.

International defence news; military equipment;
budget analysis, industry, military technology,
business, political, defence market intelligence.
Illustrations: colour. Payment: minimum £200 per
1,000 words used. Founded 1984.

Jewish Chronicle

915 High Road, London N12 8QJ
tel 020-7415 1500
email editor@thejc.com
website www.thejc.com
Twitter @JewishChron
Editor Jake Wallis Simons
Weekly £3.20

Authentic and exclusive news stories and articles of
Jewish interest from 500–1,500 words are considered.
Includes a lively arts and leisure section and regular
travel pages. Illustrations: of Jewish interest, either
topical or feature. Payment: by arrangement.
Founded 1841.

Jewish Telegraph

Telegraph House, 11 Park Hill, Bury Old Road,
Prestwich, Manchester M25 0HH
tel 0161 740 9321
email manchester@jewishtelegraph.com
The Galehouse Business Centre, Chapel Allerton,
Leeds LS7 4RF

tel 0113 295 6000
email leeds@jewishtelegraph.com
120 Childwall Road, Liverpool L15 6WU
tel 0151 475 6666
email liverpool@jewishtelegraph.com
May Terrace, Giffnock, Glasgow G46 6LD
tel 0141 621 4422
email glasgow@jewishtelegraph.com
website www.jewishtelegraph.com
Facebook www.facebook.com/jewishtelegraph/
Twitter @JewishTelegraph
Editor Paul Harris
Weekly Price varies per location

Non-fiction articles of Jewish interest, especially
humour. Exclusive Jewish news stories and pictures,
international, national and local. Length: 1,000–1,500
words. Illustrations: line, half-tone, cartoons.
Payment: by arrangement. Founded 1950.

Kent Life

The Editor, Newsquest Media Group Limited,
1st Floor, Chartist Tower, Upper Dock Street,
Newport NP20 1DW
tel 07809 551221
email anna.lambert@newsquest.co.uk
website www.greatbritishlife.co.uk/magazines/kent
Facebook www.facebook.com/kentlife
Twitter @kentlife
Instagram @kentlifemag
Group Editor Katy Pearson, *Chief Features Writer*
Anna Lambert
Monthly £3.99

Local lifestyle magazine, celebrating the best of
county life. Features local people, entertainment,
Kent towns, walks, history and heritage. Welcomes
ideas for articles and features. Length: 1,000 words.
Illustrations: hi-res jpgs. Payment: contact editor.
Founded 1962.

Kerrang!

Wasted Talent, 14 Charles II Street,
London SW1Y 4QU
email feedback@kerrang.com
website www.kerrang.com
Twitter @KerrangMagazine
Editor Luke Morton
Weekly £3.50

News, reviews and interviews; music with attitude. All
material commissioned. Illustrations: colour.
Payment: by arrangement. Founded 1981.

Kitchen Garden

Mortons Media Group Ltd, Media Centre,
Morton Way, Horncastle, Lincs. LN9 6JR
tel (01507) 529396
email SOtt@mortons.co.uk
website www.kitchengarden.co.uk
Editor Steve Ott
Monthly £6.50

Magazine for people with a passion for growing their
own vegetables, fruit and herbs. Includes practical
tips and inspirational ideas. Specially commissions
most material but welcomes ideas for articles and
features. Length: 700–2,000 (articles/features).
Illustrations: all commissioned. Payment: varies.
Founded 1997.

The Lady

The Kinetic Business Centre, Theobald Street,
Borehamwood WD6 4PJ
tel 020-7379 4717
email editors@lady.co.uk
website www.lady.co.uk
Facebook www.facebook.com/TheLadyMagazine
Twitter @TheLadyMagazine
Acting Editor Helen Robinson
Fortnightly £5.75

Features, interviews, comment, columns, arts and
book reviews, fashion, beauty, interiors, cookery,
health, travel and pets. Plus classified ads, holiday
cottages and pages of puzzles. Brief pitches by email
preferably. Founded 1885.

The Lake

email info@thelakepoetry.co.uk
website www.thelakepoetry.co.uk
Twitter @thelakepoetry

Online poetry magazine. Contributors may submit
up to five poems within the body of an email or
attach one Word document with 'Poetry Submission'
in the subject line; a short third-person biography (50
words max) should also be included. Accepts some
previously published poems and is open to
simultaneous submissions under certain conditions;
see the website for details.

The Lancet

125 London Wall, London EC2Y 5AS
tel 020-7424 4922
email editorial@lancet.com
website www.thelancet.com
Twitter @TheLancet
Editor-in-Chief Dr Richard Horton
Weekly From £204 p.a.

Research papers, review articles, editorials,
correspondence and commentaries on international
medicine, medical research and policy. Material may
be submitted directly through a dedicated online
system. Founded 1823.

LandScape Magazine

Bauer Media, Media House, Lynch Wood,
Peterborough PE2 6EA
tel (01733) 468000
email landscape@bauermedia.co.uk
website www.landscapemagazine.co.uk
Editor Rachel Hawkins
Monthly £5.20

Seasonal content covering gardening, cookery, history and heritage, craft, travel, walks and country matters.

Law.com International
18 King William St, Candlewick, London EC4N 7BP
tel 020-3875 0662
website www.law.com/international-edition/region/uk-legal-week/
Editor-in-Chief Paul Hodkinson
Online From £455

News and features aimed at business lawyers. Length: 750–1,000 words (features), 300 words (news). Considers unsolicited material and welcomes ideas for articles and features. Founded 1999.

The Lawyer
79 Wells Street, London W1T 3QN
tel 020-7970 4000
email editorial@thelawyer.com
website www.thelawyer.com
Editor Catrin Griffiths
Weekly From £550 p.a.

News, articles, features and views relevant to the legal profession. Length: 600–900 words. Illustrations: as agreed. Payment: by arrangement. Founded 1987.

Leisure Painter
Leisure Painter, Warners Group Publications plc, West Street, Bourne, Lincs. PE10 9PH
tel (01778) 391000
email leisurepainterletters@tapc.co.uk
website www.painters-online.co.uk
Editor Ingrid Lyon
12 p.a. £5.25

Instructional articles on painting and fine art. Payment: £75 per 1,000 words. Illustrations: high-resolution digital images only. Founded 1967.

LGC (Local Government Chronicle)
4th Floor, Harmsworth House, 15 Bouverie Street, London EC4Y 8DP
email lgcnews@emap.com
website www.lgcplus.com
Editor Sarah Calkin
Weekly From £336 p.a.

Aimed at senior managers in local government. Covers politics, management issues, social services, education, regeneration, industrial relations and personnel, plus public sector finance and Scottish and Welsh local government. Length: 1,000 words (features). Illustrations: b&w and colour, cartoons. Payment: by arrangement. Founded 1855.

Life and Work: The Magazine of the Church of Scotland
121 George Street, Edinburgh EH2 4YN
tel 0131 225 5722
email magazine@lifeandwork.org
website www.lifeandwork.org

Editor Lynne McNeil
Monthly £3.50 (print), £1.99 (digital download)

Articles not exceeding 1,200 words and news; occasional stories and poetry. Study the magazine and contact the Editor first. Illustrations: photos and colour illustrations. Payment: by arrangement.

Lighthouse Literary Journal
130 Silver Road, Norwich NR3 4TG
email subs.lighthouse@gmail.com
website https://storymachines.co.uk/portfolio/lighthouse
Poetry Editors Julia Webb, Jo Surzyn, *Prose Editors* Anna De Vaul, Helen Rye, *Art Editor* Natty Peterkin
3 p.a. £6 plus postage

Publishes poetry, short fiction and artwork from new writers/artists from within the UK and beyond. Submissions by email only; see website for details. Payment: none at present, but all published receive a free copy of the journal and are able to purchase more at a discounted rate. Now an imprint of Story Machine. Founded 2012.

Lincolnshire Life
County House, 9 Checkpoint Court, Sadler Road, Lincoln LN6 3PW
tel (01522) 527127
email studio@lincolnshirelife.co.uk
website www.lincolnshirelife.co.uk
Monthly £3.95

Articles and news of county interest. Approach in writing. Length: up to 1,500 words. Illustrations: colour photos and line drawings. Payment: varies. Founded 1961.

The Linguist
The Chartered Institute of Linguists, 7th Floor, 167 Fleet Street, London EC4A 2EA
tel 020-7940 3100
email linguist.editor@ciol.org.uk
website www.ciol.org.uk
Twitter @Linguist_CIOL
Editor Miranda Moore
Bi-monthly Free online to CIOL members; other subscription options are available

Articles of interest to professional linguists in translating, interpreting and teaching fields. Most contributors have special knowledge of the subjects with which they deal. Articles usually contributed, but payment by arrangement. Length: 800–2,000 words.

Literary Review
44 Lexington Street, London W1F 0LW
tel 020-7437 9392
email editorial@literaryreview.co.uk
website www.literaryreview.co.uk
Facebook www.facebook.com/LiteraryReviewLondon
Twitter @lit_review

Editor Nancy Sladek
Monthly (double issue December/January) £5.50

Reviews, articles of cultural interest, interviews and profiles. Material mostly commissioned. Length: articles and reviews 800–1,500 words. Illustrations: by arrangement. Payment: by arrangement; none for illustrations. Founded 1979.

Litro

180 Piccadilly, London W1J 9HF
email info@litro.co.uk
website www.litromagazine.com
Twitter @LitroMagazine
Publisher and Editor-in-Chief Eric Akoto FRSA
Quarterly £44 p.a.

Print and online literary magazine featuring fiction, non-fiction, reviews, articles of cultural interest, interviews, profiles and a monthly short story competition. Length: short stories, 2,500 words; articles and reviews, 800–1,500 words. Illustrations: line and b&w photos. Founded 2006.

Little White Lies

TCO London, Unit 2H, Zetland House,
109-123 Clifton Street, London EC2A 4LD
tel 020-7729 3675
email hello@tcolondon.com
website https://lwlies.com/
Editor David Jenkins
5 p.a. From £28 p.a.

Independent movie magazine that features cutting-edge writing, illustration and photography to get under the skin of cinema. Also explores the worlds of music, art, politics and pop culture as part of its mission to reshape the debate across the movie landscape. Length: various. Illustrations and photography. Payment: varies for illustration, articles and reviews. Founded 2005.

Living Plantfully

email editor@livingplantfully.co.uk
website www.livingplantfully.co.uk
Facebook www.facebook.com/livemoreplantfully
Twitter @LivePlantfully
Editor Lindsey Harrad

Online magazine embracing food, nutrition, health and wellness, growing and gardening, sustainability and eco issues, focusing on a holistic plant-centred lifestyle. Guest contributions and collaborations are welcome; contact the editor for guidelines.

London Grip

email editor@londongrip.co.uk
email poetry@londongrip.co.uk
website http://londongrip.co.uk/
Facebook www.facebook.com/londongrip
Twitter @LondonGrip
Instagram @londongrip

Founder Patricia Morris, *Editor* Stephen McGrath (reviews and articles), *Poetry Editor* Michael Bartholomew-Biggs

International online cultural magazine. The usual submission windows for poetry are December–January, March–April, June–July and September–October; reviews may be submitted at any time. Founded 2007.

The London Magazine: A Review of Literature and the Arts

Administration 11 Queen's Gate, London SW7 5EL
email info@thelondonmagazine.org
website www.thelondonmagazine.org
Editor Steven O'Brien, *Managing Editor* Lucy Binnersley
Bi-monthly £6.95

The UK's oldest literary magazine. Poems, stories (2,000–5,000 words), memoirs, critical articles, features on art, photography, theatre, music, architecture, etc. Submission guidelines available online. Founded 1732.

London Review of Books

28 Little Russell Street, London WC1A 2HN
tel 020-7209 1101
email edit@lrb.co.uk
website www.lrb.co.uk
Twitter @LRB
Editors Jean McNicol and Alice Spawls, *Consulting Editor* Mary-Kay Wilmers
Fortnightly £5.45

Features, essays, poems. Payment: by arrangement.

Long Poem Magazine

20 Spencer Rise, London NW5 1AP
email longpoemmagazine@gmail.com
website www.longpoemmagazine.org.uk
Facebook www.facebook.com/groups/longpoemmagazine
Twitter @LongPoemMag
Editor Linda Black, *Deputy Editor* Claire Crowther
2 p.a. £10.50 (UK, inc. p&p), £18 (RoW, inc. p&p)

Published in May and October each year. Offers a wide range of poetry, including sequences and translations, plus one essay per issue on an aspect of the long poem. Also publishes online reviews and essays on the poetic practice, by invitation. See website for up-to-date details of current submission windows. Send no more than two original, unpublished poems of at least 75 lines each inside the dates indicated, by email only. Simultaneous submissions not accepted. Contributors should familiarise themselves with the magazine before sending in material. Founded 2008.

Lothian Life

4/8 Downfield Place, Edinburgh EH11 2EW
tel 07905 614402

email office@lothianlife.co.uk
website www.lothianlife.co.uk
Twitter @LothianLife
Editor Anne Hamilton
Online

Articles, profiles, etc with a Lothians angle. Length: 500–2,000 words. Payment terms can be found on the website. Founded 1995.

Magma Poetry

23 Pine Walk, Carshalton SM5 4ES
email info@magmapoetry.com
website https://magmapoetry.com
website https://magmapoetry.submittable.com/submit
Twitter @magmapoetry
Chair Lisa Kelly
3 p.a. £8.50 (inc. p&p), £22 p.a. (inc. p&p)

Magazine of contemporary poetry and writing about poetry including reviews, each issue of which has a different editor and theme (see website for details). Features new and established writers: recent contributors include Simon Armitage, Jackie Kay, Mona Arshi, Leo Boix, Jen Hadfield, Kathryn Maris and Andrew McMillan. Previously unpublished poems are welcome via Submittable (see above) or (from UK writers only) by post, but potential contributors should check the website first for calls for submission and any specific requirements.

Management Today

Bridge House, 69 London Road, Twickenham, TW1 3SP
email kate.magee@haymarket.com
website www.managementtoday.co.uk
Editor Kate Magee
4 p.a. plus digital content From £25 per month

Company profiles and analysis, features up to 3,000 words. Payment: £350 per 1,000 words. Founded 1966.

Maritime Journal

Mercator Media Ltd, Spinnaker House, Waterside Gardens, Fareham, Hants PO16 8SD
tel (01329) 825335
email editor@maritimejournal.com
website www.maritimejournal.com
Editor Debbie Mason
Monthly Three-month free trial; subscription options thereafter

Industry information and news for the European commercial marine business. Also reviews products and services. Founded 1987.

Marketing Week

Floor M, 10 York Road, London SE1 7ND
tel 020-7970 4000
email lucy.tesseras@xeim.com
website www.marketingweek.co.uk
Editor-in-Chief Russell Parsons,

Managing Editor Lucy Tesseras
Weekly From £455 p.a.

Aimed at marketing management. Accepts occasional features and analysis, but no bylined pieces. Length: 1,000–2,000 words. Payment: by arrangement. Founded 1978.

MBUK (Mountain Biking UK)

Our Media Ltd, 1st Floor, Eagle House, Colston Avenue, Bristol BS1 1EN
tel 0117 927 9009
email mbuk@ourmedia.co.uk
website www.mbuk.com
Editor James Costley-White
Every 4 weeks From £44.99 p.a.

Magazine for mountain bike enthusiasts with features, reviews, news and world and domestic racing coverage.

MCN (Motor Cycle News)

Bauer Media Group, Media House, Lynch Wood, Peterborough Business Park, Peterborough PE2 6EA
tel (01733) 468000
email mcn@motorcyclenews.com
website www.motorcyclenews.com
Editor Richard Newland
Weekly From £9.50 per month

Leading authority on all things motorbike – both in print and online – from riding the latest models to in-depth news investigations, up-to-the-minute sports news and insight. Adheres to strict modern journalism standards, with full fact-checking and unique angles on all stories sourced and developed through an extensive network of industry contacts and biking community relationships. Founded 1955.

Medal News

Token Publishing Ltd, 8 Oaktree Place, Manaton Close, Matford Business Park, Exeter, Devon EX2 8WA
tel (01404) 46972
email info@tokenpublishing.com
website www.tokenpublishing.com
Group Managing Editor John Mussell
10 p.a. £4.75

Well-researched articles on military history with a bias towards medals. Send text in digital form. Length: up to 2,000 words. Illustrations: if possible. Payment: by arrangement; none for illustrations. Founded 1989.

Men's Health

Hearst UK, House of Hearst, 30 Panton Street, London SW1Y 4AJ
email contact@menshealth.co.uk
website www.menshealth.co.uk
Editor-in-Chief Toby Wiseman
10 p.a. £4.99

Active pursuits, grooming, fitness, fashion, sex, career

and general men's interest issues. Length 1,000–4,000 words. Ideas welcome. No unsolicited MSS. Payment: by arrangement. Founded 1994.

Methodist Recorder

1 Merchant Street, London E3 4LY
tel 020-7793 0033
email editorial@methodistrecorder.co.uk
website www.methodistrecorder.co.uk
Twitter @MethRecorder
Weekly £4.20

Methodist newspaper; ecumenically involved. Limited opportunities for freelance contributors. Preliminary contact advised. Founded 1861.

MMM (The Motorhomers' Magazine)

Warners Group Publications Plc, The Maltings, West Street, Bourne, Lincs. PE10 9PH
tel (01778) 391000
email danielattwood@warnersgroup.co.uk
website www.outandaboutlive.co.uk
Head of Content, Outdoor Leisure Daniel Attwood
Every four weeks £6.99

Articles including motorcaravan travel, owner reports and DIY. Length: up to 2,500 words. Illustrations: line, half-tone, colour prints and transparencies, high-quality digital. Payment: by arrangement. Founded 1966 as Motor Caravan and Camping.

Model Boats

Mortons Media Group Ltd, Media Centre, Mortons Way, Horncastle, Lincs LN9 6JR
email editor@modelboats.co.uk
website www.modelboats.co.uk
Editor Lindsey Amrani
Monthly £6.20

Founded 1964.

Model Engineer

Mortons Media Group Ltd, Media Centre, Morton Way, Horncastle, Lincs. LN9 6JR
tel (01507) 529589
email MEeditor@mortons.co.uk
website www.model-engineer.co.uk
Editor Martin Evans
Fortnightly £4.95

Detailed description of the construction of engineering models, small workshop equipment, machine tools and small electrical and mechanical devices; articles on small power engineering, mechanics, electricity, workshop methods, clocks and experiments. Relevant event reporting and visits. Illustrations: line, half-tone, colour. Payment: up to £50 per page. Founded 1898.

Modern Language Review

Modern Humanities Research Association, Salisbury House, Station Road, Cambridge CB1 2LA
email mail@mhra.org.uk
email l.e.o'meara@kent.ac.uk
website www.mhra.org.uk/journals/MLR
General Editor Dr Lucy O'Meara
Quarterly

Articles and reviews of a scholarly or specialist character on English, American, French, Hispanic, Italian, Germanic and Slavonic languages, literatures and cultures, as well as comparative pieces within these areas. Payment: none, but electronic offprints are given. Founded 1905.

Modern Poetry in Translation

The Queen's College, Oxford OX1 4AW
email editor@mptmagazine.com
website www.modernpoetryintranslation.com
Twitter @mptmagazine
Editor Khairani Barokka
3 p.a. £23 p.a.

Features the work of established and emerging poets and translators from around the world. Welcomes translated work that has not been published previously; contemporary pieces preferred. Up to six poems may be submitted. Potential contributors should familiarise themselves with the magazine before sending their work. See website to submit, for full guidelines and to keep up to date with open calls.

Mojo

Bauer Media, The Lantern, 75 Hampstead Road, London NW1 2PL
email mojo@bauermedia.co.uk
email danny.eccleston@bauermedia.co.uk
website www.mojo4music.com
Editor-in-Chief John Mulvey, Senior Editor Danny Eccleston
Monthly £6.50

Serious rock music magazine: interviews, news and reviews of books, live shows and albums. Send pitches to the senior editor. Length: up to 10,000 words. Illustrations: photos and caricatures by arrangement. Payment: by arrangement. Founded 1993.

MoneyWeek

121–141 Westbourne Terrace, London W2 6JR
tel 020-3890 4060
email editor@moneyweek.com
website https://moneyweek.com/
Twitter @MoneyWeek
Editor Andrew Van Sickle
Weekly £4.50

Economic analysis, investment recommendations and market tips, as well as in-depth looks at national and international politics. Founded 2000.

Motor Boat and Yachting

Future Publishing Ltd, Quay House, The Ambury, Bath BA1 1UA
email hugo.andreae@futurenet.com
website www.mby.com

Editor Hugo Andreae
Monthly £5.50

General interest as well as specialist motor boating material welcomed. Features up to 2,000 words considered on all sea-going aspects. Payment: varies. Illustrations: hi-res photos. Founded 1904.

The Motorship

Mercator Media Ltd, Spinnaker House, Waterside Gardens, Fareham, Hants PO16 8SD
tel (01329) 825335
email editor@motorship.com
website www.motorship.com
Twitter @Motorship
Editor Nick Edstrom
11 p.a. Free three-month trial; subscription options thereafter

News, information and insight for marine technology professionals.

Mslexia

PO Box 656, Newcastle upon Tyne NE99 1PZ
tel 0191 204 8860
email postbag@mslexia.co.uk
website www.mslexia.co.uk
Twitter @Mslexia
Editorial Director Debbie Taylor
Quarterly £8.95

Magazine for women writers which combines features and advice about writing with new fiction and poetry by women. Considers unsolicited material within specific submission slots. Length: up to two short stories of no more than 2,200 words, up to four poems of no more than 40 lines each, in any style, or up to two short scripts of no more than 1,000 words, which must relate to current themes (or adhere to poetry or short story competition rules). Also accepts submissions for other areas of the magazine, including Mslexia Moths, Bedtime Stories, Poet Laureate, etc., variously themed and unthemed. Articles/features by negotiation. Illustrations: by commission only; email submissions welcome. Payment: by negotiation. Founded 1998.

Music Teacher

MA Education, St Jude's Church, Dulwich Road, London SE24 0PB
email phil.croydon@markallengroup.com
website https://musicteachermagazine.co.uk/
Twitter @MusicTeacherMag
Editor Phil Croydon
Monthly From £67 p.a.

Information and articles for classroom music teachers and private/peripatetic instrumental teachers, including reviews of books, music, software and other music education resources. Articles and illustrations must both have a teaching, as well as a musical, interest. Length: articles 400–2,000 words. Payment: by arrangement. Founded 1908.

Music Week

Future Publishing Ltd, 1–10 Praed Mews, Paddington, London W2 1QY
tel 0330 390 6751
email ben.homewood@futurenet.com
website www.musicweek.com
Head of Content George Garner, *Features Editor* Ben Homewood
Monthly £11.99

News and features on all aspects of producing, manufacturing, marketing and retailing music, plus the live music business and all other aspects of the music industry. Payment: by negotiation. Founded 1959.

Musical Opinion

1 Exford Road, London SE12 9HD
tel 020-8857 1582
email musicalopinion@hotmail.co.uk
website www.musicalopinion.com
Editor Robert Matthew-Walker
Bi-monthly £32 p.a.

Suggestions for contributions of musical interest, scholastic, educational, anniversaries and ethnic. DVD, CD, opera, festival, book, music reviews. Illustrations: by arrangement. Founded 1877.

Musical Times

7 Brunswick Mews, Hove, East Sussex BN3 1HD
email mted@gotadsl.co.uk
website http://themusicaltimes.blogspot.co.uk
Editor Antony Bye
4 p.a. £10

Musical articles, reviews, 500–6,000 words. All material commissioned; no unsolicited material. Check website to see if submissions are being considered. Illustrations: music. Founded 1844.

My Weekly

D.C. Thomson & Co. Ltd, 2 Albert Square, Dundee DD1 1DD
tel (01382) 223131
email myweekly@dcthomson.co.uk
website www.myweekly.co.uk
Twitter @My_Weekly
Editor Susan Watson
Weekly £1.75

Modern women's magazine aimed at 50+ age group. No unsolicited MSS considered. Send ideas or pitches to editor. Illustrations: colour. Payment by negotiation. Founded 1910.

The National Trust Magazine

The National Trust, Heelis, Kemble Drive, Swindon SN2 2NA
tel (01793) 817716
email magazine@nationaltrust.org.uk
website www.nationaltrust.org.uk

Editor Sally Palmer
3 p.a. Free to members or £4.95

Lifestyle title with focus on the National Trust, encompassing interiors, gardens, food, UK travel, wildlife, environment, topical features and celebrity content. No unsolicited articles. Length: 1,000 words (features), 200 words (news). Illustrations: colour transparencies and artwork. Payment: by arrangement; picture library rates. Founded 1932.

Nature

Springer Nature, The Macmillan Building,
4 Crinan Street, London N1 9XW
tel 020-7833 4000
email nature@nature.com
website www.nature.com/nature
Editor-in-Chief Dr Magdalena Skipper
Weekly £199 p.a.

Devoted to scientific matters and to their bearing upon public affairs. All contributors of articles have specialised knowledge of the subjects with which they deal. Illustrations: full colour. Founded 1869.

NB Magazine

c/o Agile Ideas, Studio 10, Glove Factory Studios,
Brook Lane, Holt, Wilts. BA14 6RL
tel (01225) 302266
email madeleine@nbmagazine.co.uk
website https://nbmagazine.co.uk
Managing Director Alistair Giles, *Editor* Madeleine Knowles, *Managing Editor* Jade Craddock
4 p.a. from £34.99 (UK, including p&p)

Literary magazine aimed at avid readers and book groups. Includes a variety of features about authors, publishers, book prizes and bookshops, as well as author interviews and a selection of book reviews. A diverse range of genres are covered within the magazine, and readers' voices and opinions are represented. Bespoke book subscription packages are also available alongside the basic magazine subscription.

Neon

email info@neonmagazine.co.uk
website www.neonmagazine.co.uk
Twitter @Neon_Lit_Mag
Editor Krishan Coupland
Bi-annual £8

Independent literary magazine publishing fiction, poetry, comics and photography. Print and digital editions. Slight speculative/sci-fi leanings. Prose: 400–5,000 words. Poetry: 10–60 lines. Illustrations: photographs. Payment: 2p/word for prose, 20p/line for poetry, £5 per image or comic page. Submissions are welcomed, but see website for up-to-date guidelines, as issues are themed. Supporters of the magazine receive personalised feedback on submissions.

New Humanist

The Green House, 244–254 Cambridge Heath Road,
London E2 9DA
tel 020-3633 4633
email editor@newhumanist.org.uk
website https://newhumanist.org.uk
Editor Niki Seth-Smith
Quarterly £27 p.a. (print), £10 p.a. (digital)

Articles on current affairs, philosophy, science, the arts, literature, religion and humanism. Length: 750–4,000 words. Illustrations: colour photos. Payment: 10–20p per word. Founded 1885.

New Internationalist

The Old Music Hall, 106–108 Cowley Road,
Oxford OX4 1JE
tel (01865) 403345
email amy.hall@newint.org
website https://newint.org
Twitter @newint
Contact Amy Hall
Bi-monthly From £7.85 per quarter

World issues, ranging from food to feminism to peace and the environment; one subject examined in each issue. Length: up to 2,000 words. Illustrations: by arrangement. Payment: £250 per 1,000 words. Founded 1973.

New Law Journal

LexisNexis, Quadrant House, The Quadrant,
Brighton Road, Sutton SM2 5AS
tel 0330 161 1234
email jan.miller@lexisnexis.co.uk
website www.newlawjournal.co.uk
Twitter @newlawjournal
Editor Jan Miller
48 p.a. £525 p.a.

Articles and news on all aspects of civil litigation and dispute resolution. Length: up to 1,900 words. Payment: by arrangement.

New Scientist

25 Bedford Street, London WC2E 9ES
tel 020-7611 1202
email abby.beall@newscientist.com
email alison.flood@newscientist.com
website www.newscientist.com
Editor-in-Chief Emily Wilson, *Physics and Tech Features Editor* Abby Beall, *Comment and Culture Editor* Alison Flood
Weekly £6.95

Authoritative articles of topical importance on all aspects of science and technology. Pitches, ideas and reviews welcomed (see email addresses above). Potential contributors should study recent copies of the magazine. Illustrations: by arrangement.

New Statesman

(formerly New Statesman & Society)
12–13 Essex Street, London WC2R 3AA

tel 020-7936 6400
email editorial@newstatesman.co.uk
website www.newstatesman.co.uk
Editor-in-Chief Jason Cowley
Weekly £5.50

Interested in news, reportage and analysis of current political and social issues at home and overseas, plus book reviews, general articles and coverage of the arts, environment and science seen from the perspective of the British Left but written in a stylish, witty and unpredictable way. Length: strictly according to the value of the piece. Illustrations: commissioned for specific articles, although artists' samples considered for future reference; occasional cartoons. Payment: by agreement. Founded 1913.

New Theatre Quarterly

email m.shevtsova@gold.ac.uk
website www.cambridge.org/core/journals/new-theatre-quarterly
Editors Professor Maria Shevtsova, Dr Philippa Burt
Quarterly £283 p.a.

Articles, interviews, documentation, reference material covering all aspects of live theatre. An informed, factual and serious approach essential. Preliminary discussion and synopsis desirable. Payment: by arrangement. Founded 1985; as *Theatre Quarterly* 1971.

New Welsh Reader

(formerly New Welsh Review)
PO Box 170, Aberystwyth, Ceredigion SY23 1WZ
tel (01970) 628410
email editor@newwelshreview.com
website www.newwelshreview.com
Editor Gwen Davies
3 p.a. From £14.99 p.a.

Literary magazine featuring critical articles, creative non-fiction, short stories, poems, book reviews and profiles. Especially, but not exclusively, concerned with Welsh writing in English. Length: up to 3,000 words (articles). Send by email or hard copy with a sae for return of material. Decisions within three months of submission. See website for information on New Welsh Writing Awards and *New Welsh Rarebyte* (books). Illustrations: colour. Payment: by arrangement. Founded 1988.

NME (New Musical Express)

(incorporating Melody Maker)
email editors@nme.com
website www.nme.com
Facebook www.facebook.com/nmemagazine
Twitter @nme
Online only

Music news, features and album reviews. Length: by arrangement. Illustrations: hi-res images. Payment: by arrangement. Founded 1952.

The North

Campo House, 54 Campo Lane, Sheffield S1 2EG
email office@poetrybusiness.co.uk
website https://poetrybusiness.co.uk/the-north-magazine
Twitter @poetrybusiness
Editors Ann Sansom, Peter Sansom
2 p.a. £10

Contemporary poetry from new and established writers, as well as book reviews, critical articles and a range of features. Up to six poems may be submitted online only; full information on submission windows given on the website.

Nursery World

MA Education, St Jude's Church, Dulwich Road, London SE24 0PB
tel 020-8501 6693
email karen.faux@markallengroup.com
website www.nurseryworld.co.uk
Editor Karen Faux
Fortnightly From £11 per month

For all grades of primary school, nursery and childcare staff, nannies, foster parents and all those concerned with the care of expectant mothers, babies and young children. Authoritative and informative articles, 800 or 1,300 words, and photos on all aspects of child welfare and early education, from 0–8 years, in the UK. Practical ideas, policy news and career advice. No short stories. Illustrations: by arrangement. Payment: by arrangement.

Nursing Times

emap Publishing Limited, 4th Floor, Harmsworth House, 15 Bouverie Street, London EC4Y 8DP
tel 020-3953 2707
email steve.ford@emap.com
website www.nursingtimes.net
Twitter @nursingtimes
Twitter @nursingtimesed
Editor Steve Ford
Monthly From £29 per quarter

Articles of clinical interest, nursing education and nursing policy. Illustrated articles not longer than 2,000 words. Press day: first or last Friday of the month. Illustrations: photos, line. Payment: NUJ rates; by arrangement for illustrations. Founded 1905.

OK!

Reach plc, Northern & Shell Building, 10 Lower Thames Street, London EC3R 6EN
website www.ok.co.uk/home
Editor-in-Chief Caroline Waterston
Weekly £3.40

Exclusive celebrity interviews and photographs. Submit ideas in writing. Length: 1,000 words. Illustrations: colour. Payment: £150–£200 per feature. Founded 1993.

The Oldie

Moray House, 23–31 Great Titchfield Street,
London W1W 7PA
tel 020-7436 8801
email editorial@theoldie.co.uk
website www.theoldie.co.uk
Editor Harry Mount
Monthly £4.75

General interest magazine reflecting attitudes of older
people but aimed at a wider audience. Features
(600–1,000 words) on all subjects, as well as articles
for specific sections. Potential contributors should
familiarise themselves with the magazine prior to
submitting work. See website for further guidelines.
Enclose sae for reply/return of MSS. No poetry.
Illustrations: welcomes b&w and colour cartoons.
Payment: approx. £250 per 850 words; £100 for
cartoons. Founded 1992.

Olive

Immediate Media Co. Ltd, Vineyard House,
44 Brook Green, London W6 7BT
tel 020-7150 5000
email alex.crossley@immediate.co.uk
website www.olivemagazine.com
Facebook www.facebook.com/olivemagazine/
Twitter @olivemagazine
Digital Editor Alex Crossley, *Reviews Editor* Lucy
Roxburgh
Monthly £5.99

Upmarket food magazine which aims to encourage
readers to cook, eat and explore. Each edition
includes a range of recipes for both everyday and
weekend cooking, as well as information on
techniques, trends and tips; restaurant
recommendations across the UK; and foodie-inspired
travel ideas from around the world.

Opera

36 Black Lion Lane, London W6 9BE
tel 020-8563 8893
email editor@opera.co.uk
website www.opera.co.uk
Editor John Allison
13 p.a. £6.95

Reviews of opera from the UK and around the world,
including profiles of opera's greatest performers and
a comprehensive calendar of productions and events.
Length: up to 2,000 words. Illustrations: photos.
Payment: by arrangement.

Opera Now

Mark Allen Group, St Jude's Church, Dulwich Road,
London SE24 0PB
tel 020-7333 1701
email opera.now@markallengroup.com
website www.rhinegold.co.uk/rhinegold-publishing/
magazines/opera-now/
Editor-in-Chief Ashutosh Khandekar
Monthly From £76 p.a.

Articles, news, reviews on opera. All material
commissioned only. Length: 150–1,500 words.
Illustrations: by arrangement. Founded 1989.

Orbis International Literary Journal

17 Greenhow Avenue, West Kirby, Wirral CH48 5EL
tel 0151 625 1446
email carolebaldock@hotmail.com
website www.orbisjournal.com
Editor Carole Baldock
Quarterly £6.50, £20 p.a. (UK), £42 p.a. (RoW).
Introductory offer: 4 issues as pdfs, plus one print
back copy of magazine for £12 (UK).

Literary magazine; provides feedback with proofs.
Publishes poetry, fiction (1,000 words maximum),
flash fiction, non-fiction, and translations. UK
submissions: four poems; include C5-sized sae.
Overseas: two submissions via email. Readers' Award:
£50, plus £50 split between four runners-up.
Subscribers also receive the Xtra Kudos Newsletter.
Founded 1969.

Our Dogs

Unit 1.01 Boat Shed, 12 Exchange Quay,
Salford M5 3EQ
tel 0161 709 4550
email editor@ourdogs.co.uk
website www.ourdogs.co.uk
Facebook www.facebook.com/www.ourdogs.co.uk/
Twitter @OURDOGSNEWS
Editor Alison Smith
Weekly From £2.95

Articles and news on the breeding and showing of
pedigree dogs worldwide. Unsolicited material not
accepted. Founded 1895.

Oxford Poetry

c/o Partus Press Ltd, 266 Banbury Road,
Oxford OX2 7DL
email editors@oxfordpoetry.co.uk
website www.oxfordpoetry.com
Twitter @OxfordPoetry
Editor-in-Chief Luke Allan, *Managing Editor* Vala
Thorodds
2 p.a. £23.23 (inc. p&p)

Previously unpublished poems (in English) and
translations, both unsolicited and commissioned; also
interviews, articles and reviews. Submissions via the
website only. Founded 1910.

Panorama: The Journal of Travel, Place and Nature

email enquiries@panoramajournal.org
website https://panoramajournal.org/submissions
Twitter @Panorama_J
Instagram @panorama_journal
Director Matthew Webb, *Editor* Troy Onyango
Online 3 p.a.

Online literary journal featuring literary-themed contemporary works of non-fiction, fiction and poetry about travel and the world; illustrations, photo essays and film stills also welcomed. Accepts submissions from experienced writers and emerging voices, with a special interest in global perspectives. See website above for submission notes; calls for themes also appear online and on social media. Payment: none. Founded 2016.

PC Pro

Future Publishing Ltd, Quay House, The Ambury, Bath BA1 1UA
email editor@pcpro.co.uk
Facebook www.facebook.com/pcpro
Twitter @pcpro
Editor-in-Chief Tim Danton
Monthly £4.99

Expert advice and insights from IT professionals, plus in-depth reviews and group tests, aimed at IT pros and enthusiasts. Email feature pitches to editor@pcpro.co.uk but only after reading the magazine first. Founded 1994.

Peace News

5 Caledonian Road, London N1 9DY
tel 020-7278 3344
email editorial@peacenews.info
website www.peacenews.info
Editor Milan Rai
6 p.a. From £12 p.a.

Political articles based on nonviolence in every aspect of human life. Illustrations: line, half-tone. No payment. Founded 1936.

People Management

Haymarket Ltd, Bridge House, 69 London Road, Twickenham TW1 3SP
tel 020-8267 5013
email pmeditorial@haymarket.com
website www.peoplemanagement.co.uk
Twitter @PeopleMgt
Acting Editor Abbie Dawson
10 p.a. Free to CIPD members

Magazine of the Chartered Institute of Personnel and Development. News items and feature articles on recruitment and selection, training and development; pay and performance management; industrial psychology; employee relations; employment law; working practices and new practical ideas in personnel management in industry and commerce. Length: up to 2,500 words. Illustrations: contact art editor. Payment: by arrangement.

The People's Friend

D.C. Thomson & Co. Ltd, 2 Albert Square, Dundee DD1 1DD
tel (01382) 223131
email peoplesfriend@dcthomson.co.uk
website www.thepeoplesfriend.co.uk
Facebook www.facebook.com/PeoplesFriendMagazine
Twitter @TheFriendMag
Editor Angela Gilchrist
Weekly £1.85

Fiction magazine for women of all ages. Serials (60,000–70,000 words) and complete stories (1,000–4,000 words) of strong romantic and emotional appeal. Includes knitting and cookery. No preliminary letter required; send material for the attention of the Editor. Illustrations: colour. Payment: on acceptance. Founded 1869.

Period Living

Future Publishing Ltd, Quay House, The Ambury, Bath BA1 1UA
email period.living@futurenet.com
website www.homesandgardens.com/period-living
Twitter @PeriodLivingMag
Acting Editor Rachel Crow
Monthly £4.75

Articles and features on decoration, furnishings, renovation of period homes; gardens, crafts, decorating in a period style. Illustrated. Payment: varies, according to work required. Founded 1990.

The Photographer

BIPP, The Artistry House, 16 Winckley Square, Preston PR1 3JJ
tel (01772) 367 968
email editor@bipp.com
website www.bipp.com
Editor and Communications Manager Joel Hansen
Quarterly free to all members of British Institute of Professional Photography or £7.50

Journal of the British Institute of Professional Photography. Authoritative reviews, news, views and high-quality photographs.

Picture Postcard Collecting

16 Heron Road, Twickenham TW1 1PQ
tel 07715 054609
email picturepostcardcollecting@gmail.com
website www.picturepostcardcollectingmagazine.com
Editor Michael Goldsmith
10 p.a. £7 (inc. p&p), £54 p.a. (inc. p&p)

Lively illustrated magazine for collectors of picture postcards. Regular news and features on e-Bay prices, postcard fairs, auctions, clubs and national postcard activity. Topics covered in recent editions include: Steve Bloomer – England's Greatest Footballer, Airship Disaster over Hull, Henry Corn – Cardiff Photographer or Spy?, The Battle of The Boyne, Barnard Castle, Belgian Art Nouveau, England's Railway King. Founded 2020.

Planet: The Welsh Internationalist

PO Box 44, Aberystwyth, Ceredigion SY23 3ZZ
tel (01970) 611255

email planet.enquiries@planetmagazine.org.uk
website www.planetmagazine.org.uk
Twitter @Planet_TWI
Editor Emily Trahair
Quarterly From £22 p.a.

Articles on culture, society, Welsh current affairs and international politics, as well as short fiction, poetry, photo essays and review articles. Article length: 1,500–2,500 words. Payment: £45 per 1,000 words, £30 per poem. Submissions by post or email, preferably by email. For articles, email enquiry in first instance. Founded 1970.

PN Review

(formerly Poetry Nation)
Carcanet Press Ltd, 4th Floor, Alliance House, 30 Cross Street, Manchester M2 7AQ
tel 0161 834 8730
email PNRsubmissions@carcanet.co.uk
website www.pnreview.co.uk
Editors Michael Schmidt, John McAuliffe, Andrew Latimer
6 p.a. From £45 p.a.

Poems, essays, reviews, translations. Submissions by e-mail (subscribers); otherwise by post only. Payment: by arrangement. Founded 1973

Poetry Ireland Review/Iris Éigse Éireann

11 Parnell Square East, Dublin 1 D01 ND60, Republic of Ireland
tel +353 (0)1 6789815
email publications@poetryireland.ie
website www.poetryireland.ie
Editor Colm Keegan, *Irish-language Editor* Aifric Mac Aodha
3 p.a. €12, €38 p.a. (Republic of Ireland and Northern Ireland), €43 p.a. (RoW)

Poetry. Features and articles by arrangement. Payment: €50 minimum per contribution; €100 minimum for reviews. Founded 1981.

Poetry London

Goldsmiths, University of London, New Cross, London SE14 6NW
tel 020-7919 7171
email admin@poetrylondon.co.uk
website www.poetrylondon.co.uk
Facebook www.facebook.com/poetrylondon
Twitter @Poetry_London
Editors André Naffis-Sahely (poetry), *Reviews Editor* Isabelle Baafi
3 p.a. + digital access £30 p.a.

Poems of the highest standard, articles/reviews on any aspect of contemporary poetry. Contributors must be knowledgeable about contemporary poetry. Payment: £30 minimum. Founded 1988.

The Poetry Review

The Poetry Society, 22 Betterton Street, London WC2H 9BX

tel 020-7420 9880
email poetryreview@poetrysociety.org.uk
website https://poetrysociety.org.uk/publications-section/the-poetry-review/submissions-guidelines/
Editor Wayne Hollway-Smith
Quarterly From £24.99 p.a.

Poems, features and reviews. Send no more than six poems with sae. Preliminary study of magazine essential. Payment: £50+ per poem.

Poetry Wales

Suite 6, 4 Derwen Road, Bridgend CF31 1LH
tel (01656) 663018
email info@poetrywales.co.uk
website www.poetrywales.co.uk
Editor Zoë Brigley
3 p.a. From £27 p.a. (or from £20 p.a./£2 per month for students/readers on a low income)

National poetry magazine of Wales, publishing contemporary poetry, features and reviews. Payment: £20/page for poems. Founded 1965.

The Police Journal: Theory, Practice and Principles

SAGE Publications, 1 Oliver's Yard, 55 City Road, London EC1Y 1SP
tel 020-7324 8500
website https://uk.sagepub.com/en-gb/eur/journal/police-journal
Editor-in-Chief Jason Roach
Quarterly From £78 p.a. for individual print issues; see website for further details

Articles of technical or professional interest to the Police Service throughout the world. Illustrations: line drawings. Payment: none. Founded 1928.

The Political Quarterly

Wiley-Blackwell, 9600 Garsington Road, Oxford OX4 2DQ
tel (01865) 776868
website www.politicalquarterly.org.uk
Twitter @po_qu
Editors Deborah Mabbett, Ben Jackson, Anna Killick
4 p.a. From £11 p.a. for personal online subscription; see website for full list

Topical aspects of national and international politics and public administration; takes a progressive, but not a party, point of view. See website for submissions information. Length: average 5,000 words. Payment: by arrangement. Founded 1930.

Popshot Quarterly

Jubilee House, 2 Jubilee Place, London SW3 3TQ
tel 020-7349 3700
email hello@popshotpopshot.com
website www.popshotpopshot.com
Twitter @popshotmag
Editor Matilda Battersby
4 p.a. £6

Original short stories, flash fiction and poetry paired with bespoke illustrations. Study magazine before submitting work. Each issue is themed and submissions should be tailored accordingly: see the website for latest details. Length: maximum 3,000 words, shorter is preferable. Illustrations: send portfolios to illustration@popshotpopshot.com. Founded 2009.

Poultry World

Postbus 4, 7000 BA Doetinchem, The Netherlands
website www.poultryworld.net/UK
Twitter @PoultryWorld
Editor-in-Chief Fabian Brockötter
10 p.a. From €10 per month

Articles on poultry breeding, production, marketing and packaging. News of international poultry interest. Payment: by arrangement.

PR Week

Haymarket Ltd, Bridge House, 69 London Road, Twickenham TW1 3SP
tel 020-8267 5000
email john.harrington@haymarket.com
website www.prweek.com
Twitter @prweekuknews
UK Editor John Harrington
Bi-monthly From £31.50 per month

News and features on public relations. Length: approx. 800–3,000 words. Payment: by arrangement. Send pitches to the news editor. Founded 1984.

Practical Boat Owner

Future Publishing Ltd, Quay House, The Ambury, Bath BA1 1UA
tel 0330 390 6467
email pbo@futurenet.com
website www.pbo.co.uk
Facebook www.facebook.com/practicalboatownermag
Twitter @p_b_o
Editor Katy Stickland
Monthly £4.99

Boating magazine: sail and power. Hints, tips and practical articles for cruising skippers. Send full text and high-res images: see pbo.co.uk/submission_guide for details. Illustrations: photos or drawings. Payment: by negotiation. Founded 1967.

Practical Caravan

Future Publishing Ltd, Quay House, The Ambury, Bath BA1 1UA
email practical.caravan@futurenet.com
website www.practicalcaravan.com
Twitter @pcaravan
Editor-in-Chief Sarah Wakely
Every four weeks £5.99

Caravan-related travelogues, caravan site reviews; travel writing for existing regular series; technical and DIY matters. Illustrations: colour. Payment negotiable. Founded 1967.

Practical Fishkeeping

Warners Group Publications Plc, The Maltings, West Street, Bourne, Lincs. PE10 9PH
tel (01778) 391194
website www.practicalfishkeeping.co.uk
Twitter @PFKmagazine
12 p.a. £5.25

Practical fishkeeping in tropical and coldwater aquaria and ponds. Heavy emphasis on inspiration and involvement. Good colour photography always needed, and used. No verse or humour, no personal biographical accounts of fishkeeping unless practical. Payment: by worth. Founded 1966.

Practical Wireless

Warners Group Publications Plc, The Maltings, West Street, Bourne, Lincs. PE10 9PH
tel (01778) 391000
email practicalwireless@warnersgroup.co.uk
website www.radioenthusiast.co.uk
Twitter @REnthusiasts
Editor Don Field
Monthly £5.99

Articles on the practical and theoretical aspects of amateur radio and communications. Constructional projects. Telephone or email for advice and essential *PW* author's guide. Illustrations: by arrangement. Payment: by arrangement. Founded 1932.

The Practising Midwife

Saturn House, Mercury Rise, Altham Industrial Park, Altham, Lancs. BB5 5BY
email jayne@all4maternity.com
website www.all4maternity.com/about-us/tpm-writing-for-us/
Twitter @TPM_Journal
Editor-in-Chief Alys Einion, *Managing Editor* Jayne Purdy
Monthly

Disseminates evidence-based material to a wide professional audience. Research and review papers, viewpoints and news items pertaining to midwifery, maternity care, women's health and neonatal health with both a national and an international perspective. All articles submitted are peer-reviewed anonymously. See website for full submissions details. Illustrations: hi-res digital images. Payment: by arrangement. Founded 1997.

Press Gazette

40 Hatton Garden, London EC1N 8EB
tel 020-7936 6433
email pged@pressgazette.co.uk
website https://pressgazette.co.uk
Twitter @pressgazette
Editor-in-Chief Dominic Ponsford
Weekly Online only

News and features of interest to journalists and others working in the media. Length: 1,200 words (features),

300 words (news). Payment: by arrangement. Founded 1965.

Pride

1 Garratt Lane, London SW18 4AQ
tel 020-8870 3755
email editor@pridemagazine.com
website https://pridemagazine.com
Twitter @Pridemag
Publisher CJ Cushnie, *Fashion and Beauty Editor* Shevelle Rhule
Monthly £3

Lifestyle magazine incorporating fashion and beauty, travel, food and entertaining articles for the woman of colour. Length: 1,000–3,000 words. Illustrations: by arrangement. Payment: by arrangement. Founded 1991; relaunched 1997.

Prima

Hearst UK, House of Hearst, 30 Panton Street, London SW1Y 4AJ
tel 020-7312 3815
email prima@hearst.co.uk
website www.prima.co.uk
Facebook www.facebook.com/primamagazine
Twitter @Primauk
Instagram @primamag
Editor Jo Checkley
Monthly £4.99

Articles on fashion, home, crafts, health and beauty, cookery; features. Founded 1986.

Private Eye

6 Carlisle Street, London W1D 3BN
tel 020-7437 4017
email strobes@private-eye.co.uk
website www.private-eye.co.uk
Twitter @PrivateEyeNews
Editor Ian Hislop
Fortnightly £2.99

News and current affairs. Satire. Illustrations and cartoons: colour or b&w. Payment: by arrangement. Founded 1961.

Prole

email submissionspoetry@prolebooks.co.uk
email submissionsprose@prolebooks.co.uk
website https://prolebooks.co.uk
Facebook www.facebook.com/people/Prole/100041257775797/
Twitter @Prolebooks
Editors Brett Evans, Phil Robertson
2 p.a. (June/December) £6.82

Submissions of poetry, short fiction and creative non-fiction (7,500 words max) and photographic cover art welcome (see website for submission guidelines). Annual poetry competition. Payment: profit share. Founded 2010.

Prospect Magazine

2 Queen Anne's Gate, London, SW1H 9AA
tel 020-7255 1344
email editorial@prospect-magazine.co.uk
email webdesk@prospect-magazine.co.uk
website www.prospectmagazine.co.uk
Twitter @prospect_uk
Editor Alan Rusbridger
Monthly £5.95

Political and cultural magazine. Essays, features, special reports, reviews, short stories, opinions/analysis. Length: 3,000–6,000 words (essays, special reports, short stories), 1,000 words (opinions). Illustrations: by arrangement. Payment: by negotiation. See website for full submission information. Founded 1995.

Psychologies

Kelsey Publishing Ltd, The Granary, Downs Court, Yalding Hill, Yalding, Maidstone, Kent ME18 6AL
tel (01959) 541444
email sally.saunders@kelsey.co.uk
website www.psychologies.co.uk
Editor-in-Chief Sally Saunders
Monthly £4.99

Women's magazine with a focus on how to flourish, improving mental health and helping readers create the life they want on their terms. Features cover relationships, family and parenting, personality behaviour, health, wellbeing, beauty, society and social trends, travel, spirituality and sex. Welcomes new ideas by email which fit into one of these areas, and suggestions should offer a combination of psychological insight and practical advice.

Pulse

Cogora, 1 Giltspur Street, London EC1A 9DD
email jaimiekaffash@cogora.com
website www.pulsetoday.co.uk
Twitter @pulsetoday
Editor Jaimie Kaffash
Online

Articles and photos of direct interest to GPs. Purely clinical material can be accepted only from medically qualified authors. Length: 600–1,200 words. Illustrations: b&w and colour photos. Payment: by arrangement. Founded 1959.

Pushing Out the Boat

email info@pushingouttheboat.co.uk
website www.pushingouttheboat.co.uk
Facebook www.facebook.com/pushingouttheboat
Twitter @POTBmag
Biennial See website for pricing details

North-East Scotland's magazine of new writing and visual arts. Features new prose, poetry and art from both the local area and the wider world, all selected (anonymously) from online submissions. Next edition will be published in 2025. The full-colour A4 print magazine (also available to view online) is run as a not-for-profit charity by volunteers. POTB's costs are met by sales revenue, plus events.

RA Magazine

Royal Academy of Arts, Burlington House, Piccadilly, London W1J 0BD
tel 020-7300 5820
email ramagazine@royalacademy.org.uk
website www.royalacademy.org.uk/ra-magazine
Twitter @RA_Mag
Editor Sam Phillips
Quarterly £6.95, £28 p.a.

Visual arts and culture articles relating to the Royal Academy of Arts and the wider British and international arts scene. Length: 150–2,500 words. Illustrations: consult the Editor. Payment: average £350 per 1,000 words; illustrations by negotiation. Founded 1983.

Racing Post

Floor 7, Vivo Building, South Bank Central, 30 Stamford Street, London SE1 9LS
email editor@racingpost.co.uk
website www.racingpost.com
Editor Tom Kerr
Daily £4.50, Weekender edition £5.20

News on horseracing, greyhound racing and sports betting. Founded 1986.

Radio Times

Immediate Media Co. Ltd, Vineyard House, 44 Brook Green, London W6 7BT
tel 020-7150 5429
email editor@radiotimes.com
website www.radiotimes.com
Editors Tom Loxley, Shem Law
Weekly £4

Articles and interviews that preview the week's programmes on British TV and radio as well as on-demand programming. All articles are specially commissioned – ideas and synopses are welcomed but not unsolicited MSS. Length: 600–2,500 words. Illustrations: mostly in colour; photos, graphic designs or drawings. Payment: by arrangement.

RAIL

Bauer Media Group, Media House, Lynch Wood, Peterborough Business Park, Peterborough PE2 6EA
tel (01733) 468000
email rail@bauermedia.co.uk
website www.railmagazine.com
Facebook www.facebook.com/Railmagazine
Twitter @RAIL
Managing Editor Nigel Harris
Fortnightly From £99 p.a.

News and in-depth features on current UK railway operations. Length: 1,000–3,000 words (features), 250–400 words (news). Illustrations: colour and b&w photos and artwork. Payment: by arrangement. Founded 1981.

Railway Gazette International

1st Floor, Chancery House, St Nicholas Way, Sutton, Surrey SM1 4JB
tel 020-8652 5200
email editor@railwaygazette.com
website www.railwaygazette.com
Twitter @railwaygazette
Executive Editor Nick Kingsley
Monthly £130 p.a.

Covers management, engineering, operation and finance of railway, metro and light rail transport worldwide. Articles of business interest on these subjects are considered and paid for if accepted. No 'enthusiast'- or heritage-oriented articles. Phone or email to discuss proposals. Illustrated articles, of 1,000–2,000 words, are preferred.

The Railway Magazine

Media Centre, Morton Way, Horncastle, Lincs. LN9 6JR
tel (01507) 529589
email railway@mortons.co.uk
website www.railwaymagazine.co.uk
Editor Paul Bickerdyke, *Deputy Editor* Gareth Evans
Monthly £5.25

Illustrated magazine dealing with all railway subjects; no fiction or verse. Articles from 1,000–3,000 words accompanied by photos. Preliminary email or letter desirable. Illustrations: digital; b&w and colour scans. Payment: by arrangement. Founded 1897.

Reach Poetry

Indigo Dreams Publishing Ltd, 24 Forest Houses, Halwill, Beaworthy, Devon EX21 5UU
email publishing@indigodreams.co.uk
website www.indigodreamspublishing.com
Twitter @IndigoDreamsPub
Editor Ronnie Goodyer
Monthly £5.50, £55.00 p.a.

Unpublished and original poetry. Magazine subscribers submit up to two poems per month for consideration by post (include sae for reply) or email (preferred). New poets encouraged. Features lively subscribers' letters and votes pages. No payment, but competition winners have their subscriptions increased through a readers' vote. Founded 1998.

Reader's Digest

Warners Group Publications, The Maltings, West Street, Bourne, Lincs. PE10 9PH
email eva.mackevic@readersdigest.co.uk
website www.readersdigest.co.uk
Facebook www.facebook.com/readersdigestuk
Twitter @readersdigestUK
Instagram @readersdigest_UK
Editor-in-Chief Eva Mackevic

Monthly From £19.99 p.a.

Original anecdotes, short stories, letters to the editor and jokes may be submitted online for consideration. Founded 1922.

Reality

St Joseph's Monastery, St Alphonsus Road, Dundalk, Co. Louth A91 F3FC, Republic of Ireland
tel +353 (0)1 492248
email info@redcoms.org
website www.redcoms.org
Monthly €2.50

Illustrated magazine for Christian living. Articles on all aspects of modern life, including family, youth, religion, leisure. Length: 1,000–1,500 words. Payment: by arrangement. Founded 1936.

Record Collector

Diamond Publishing, 2nd Floor, Saunders House, 52–53 The Mall, Ealing, London W5 3AT
email paul.lester@metropolis.co.uk
website www.recordcollectormag.com
Twitter @RecCollMag
Editor Paul Lester
Monthly £7.25

Covers all areas of music, with the focus on collectable releases and the reissues market. Specially commissions most material but will consider unsolicited material. Welcomes ideas for articles and features. Length: 2,000 words for articles/features; 200 words for news. Illustrations: all commissioned. Payment: negotiable. Founded 1980.

Red

House of Hearst, 30 Panton Street, Leicester Square, London SW1Y 4AJ
tel 020-7150 7600
email red@redmagazine.co.uk
website www.redonline.co.uk
Twitter @RedMagDaily
Executive Editor Sarah Tomczak
Monthly £5.99

High-quality articles on topics of interest to women aged 25–45: humour, memoirs, interviews and well-researched investigative features. Approach with ideas in writing in first instance. Length: 900 words upwards. Illustrations: by arrangement. Payment: by arrangement. Founded 1998.

Red Pepper

44–48 Shepherdess Walk, London N1 7JP
website www.redpepper.org.uk/get-involved/write-for-us/
Facebook www.facebook.com/redpeppermagazine
Twitter @redpeppermag
Instagram @redpeppermagazine
Edited by A collective
4 p.a. Subscribers may choose how much to pay

Independent radical magazine run by an editorial collective: news and features and debates on politics, culture and everyday life, written by and of interest to the feminist, green and international radical Left. Material for inclusion in print mostly commissioned. Length: online 650-1200 words; print 500–2,000 words. Illustrations: by arrangement. Payment: £62 flat fee for online; up to £90 for print for investigations, otherwise only exceptionally. See website for full information for editorial contact and pitching details, which vary per subject/topic. Founded 1994.

Reform

(published by United Reformed Church)
86 Tavistock Place, London WC1H 9RT
tel 020-7916 8630
email reform@urc.org.uk
website www.reform-magazine.co.uk
Twitter @Reform_Mag
Editor Stephen Tomkins
10 p.a. From £18 p.a.

Explores theology, ethics, personal spirituality and Christian perspectives on social and current affairs. Offers articles about Christian ideas from a range of viewpoints, as well as interviews and reviews. Published by the United Reformed Church but has readers from all Christian denominations, as well as readers from other faiths and from no faith tradition. Illustrations: graphic artists/illustrators. Payment: by arrangement. Founded 1972.

Resurgence & Ecologist

The Resurgence Trust, The Resurgence Centre, Fore Street, Hartland, Bideford, Devon EX39 6AB
tel (01237) 441293
email editorial@resurgence.org
website www.resurgence.org
Editor Susan Clark
6 p.a. £6.95

Interested in environment and social justice investigations and features, green living advice and ideas, grassroots activism projects, artist profiles and reviews. Proposal first in most cases. Payment: various. See website for further guidance.

Retail Week

William Reed Ltd, Broadfield Park, Crawley RH11 9RT
email content@retail-week.com
website www.retail-week.com
Twitter @retailweek
Editor-in-Chief Charlotte Hardie, *Executive Editor* George MacDonald, *Features Editor* Ellis Hawthorne
Weekly From £499 p.a.

Features and news stories on all aspects of retail management. Length: up to 1,400 words. Illustrations: colour photos. Payment: by arrangement. Founded 1988.

The Rialto

c/o 74 Britannia Road, Norwich NR1 4HS
email info@therialto.co.uk
website www.therialto.co.uk
Editors Michael Mackmin, Degna Stone, Edward
Doegar, Will Harris
3 p.a. £9, From £25 p.a.

62pp A4 magazine, mainly poetry but with occasional
prose pieces. Prose is commissioned, poetry
submissions are very welcome: up to six poems may
be submitted either by post (sae essential) or online
via Submittable. See website for details of submission
windows. Payment: by arrangement. Founded 1984.

Riptide Journal

The Editors, Riptide Journal,
The Department of English,
The University of Exeter, Queen's Building,
Queen's Drive, Exeter EX4 6QH
email editors@riptidejournal.co.uk
website www.riptidejournal.co.uk
Twitter @RiptideJournal
Editors Dr Virginia Baily, Dr Sally Flint
1 short-story collection p.a. as well as other
publications; price varies

Anthologies of short fiction by established and
emerging writers. Also accepts poetry occasionally.
Submissions should be original, unpublished work.
See website for information on submission windows
and deadlines for forthcoming editions. Fiction pieces
should typically be no more than 3,000 words and
poems no longer than 40 lines. All submissions
should be accompanied by a biographical note of 50
words max.

Royal National Institute of Blind People (RNIB)

105 Judd Street, London WC1H 9NE
tel 0303 123 9999
email helpline@rnib.org.uk
website www.rnib.org.uk
Twitter @RNIB

Publishes a variety of titles in a range of formats
(including audio, large print, braille and DAISY) for
adults and young people who have sight loss.

Rugby World

Future Publishing Ltd, Future Publishing Ltd,
Unit 415, Winnersh Triangle, Eskdale Road,
Winnersh RG41 5TU
tel 0330 390 6479
email alan.dymock@futurenet.com
website www.rugbyworld.com
Twitter @Rugbyworldmag
Editor Sarah Mockford, *Features Editor* Alan Dymock
Monthly £5.50

Features and exclusive news stories on rugby. Length:
approx. 1,200 words. Illustrations: by arrangement.
Payment: by arrangement. Founded 1960.

Runner's World

Hearst UK, House of Hearst, 30 Panton Street,
London SW1Y 4AJ
tel 020-7339 4400
email editor@runnersworld.co.uk
website www.runnersworld.com/uk
Facebook www.facebook.com/runnersworlduk
Twitter @runnersworlduk
Editor-in-Chief Andy Dixon, *Deputy Editor* Joe
Mackie
Monthly £5.99

Articles on running, health and fitness, and nutrition.
Payment: by arrangement. Founded 1979.

RUSI Journal

Whitehall, London SW1A 2ET
tel 020-7747 2600
email EmmaD@rusi.org
website https://rusi.org/publication/rusi-journal
Editor Emma De Angelis
Bi-monthly; available as part of RUSI membership
(see website for full list; concessions available) or a
subscription in conjunction with RUSI Whitehall
Papers.

Journal of the Royal United Services Institute for
Defence and Security Studies. Articles on
international security, military science, defence
technology and procurement, and military history;
also book reviews and correspondence. Length:
3,000–3,500 words. Illustrations: colour photos, maps
and diagrams.

Saga Magazine

Saga Publishing Ltd, The Saga Building,
Enbrook Park, Sandgate, Folkestone, Kent CT20 3SE
tel (01303) 771523
email editor@saga.co.uk
website www.saga.co.uk/magazine
Commissioning Editor Dominic Connolly
Monthly From £29.95 p.a.

General interest magazine aimed at the intelligent,
literate 50+ reader. Wide range of articles from
human interest, real-life stories, intriguing overseas
interest (not travel), some natural history, celebrity
interviews, photographic book extracts – all subjects
are considered in this general interest title. Articles
mostly commissioned or written in-house, but
genuine exclusives welcome. Illustrations: colour,
digital media; mainly commissioned but top-quality
photo feature suggestions sometimes accepted.
Payment: competitive rate, by negotiation.
Founded 1984.

Sailing Today with Yachts & Yachting

The Chelsea Magazine Company, Jubilee House,
2 Jubilee Place, London SW3 3TQ
email georgie.corlett-pitt@chelseamagazines.com
website www.yachtsandyachting.co.uk
Editor Georgie Corlett-Pitt

Monthly £4.95

Technical sailing and related lifestyle articles. Illustrations: line, half-tone, colour. Payment: by arrangement. Founded 1947.

Sainsbury's magazine

SevenC3, WeWork, 145 City Road, London EC1V 1AZ
tel 020-3995 4082
email feedback@sainsburysmagazine.co.uk
website www.sainsburysmagazine.co.uk
website www.seven.co.uk/
Editor-in-Chief Helena Lang, *Associate Editor (Lifestyle)* Sarah Maber
Monthly £3

Features: food and drink, health, travel; all material commissioned; no unsolicited material. Length: up to 1,500 words. Illustrations: colour and b&w photos and line illustrations. Payment: varies. Founded 1993.

Sarasvati

24 Forest Houses, Cookworthy Moor, Halwill, Beaworthy, Devon EX21 5UU
email dawnidp@indigodreams.co.uk
website www.indigodreamspublishing.com
Facebook www.facebook.com/ronniegoodyeridp
Twitter @IndigoDreamsPub
Editor Dawn Bauling
Quarterly £4.50, £17 for 4 issues

International poetry and short story magazine. New writers/poets encouraged. Lively feedback pages. Several pages given to each subscriber. Prose length: 1,000 words or under. Email submissions only. Founded 2008.

The School Librarian

School Library Association, 1 Pine Court, Kembrey Park, Swindon SN2 8AD
tel (01793) 401154
email tsl@sla.org.uk
website www.sla.org.uk
Quarterly Free to SLA members, £125 p.a. to others

Official journal of the School Library Association. Articles on news, best practice, education developments, school library management, literacy, publishing, developing reading, research skills and information literacy. Reviews of books, websites and other library resources from preschool to adult. Length: 1,200–1,800 words (articles). Payment: by arrangement. Founded 1937.

School Libraries in View

School Libraries Group,
CILIP: The Library and Information Association, 7 Ridgmount Street, London WC1E 7AE
email info@barbaraband.com
website www.cilip.org.uk

Articles on school librarianship, library management, information and digital skills, authors and illustrators, literacy and reading. News about books, education and resources.

Scientific Computing World

4 Signet Court, Cambridge CB5 8LA
tel (01223) 275464
email editor.scw@europascience.com
website www.scientific-computing.com
Editor Robert Roe
6 p.a. Free to qualifying subscribers, other subscription rates apply (see website)

Features on hardware and software developments for the scientific community, plus news articles and reviews. Length: 800–2,000 words. Illustrations: colour transparencies, photos, electronic graphics. Payment: by negotiation. Founded 1994.

The Scots Magazine

D.C. Thomson & Co. Ltd, 2 Albert Square, Dundee DD1 1DD
tel (01382) 223131
email mail@scotsmagazine.com
website www.scotsmagazine.com
Twitter @ScotsMagazine
Editor-in-Chief Robert Wight
Monthly £4.50

Articles on all subjects of Scottish interest, but authors must also be Scottish. Illustrations: colour and b&w photos. Unsolicited material considered but preliminary enquiries advised. Payment: on acceptance. Founded 1739.

The Scottish Farmer

Newsquest Scotland, 125 Fullerton Drive, Glasgow G32 8FG
tel 0141 302 7732 , *tel* 07803 970225
email ken.fletcher@thescottishfarmer.co.uk
website www.thescottishfarmer.co.uk
Editor Ken Fletcher
Weekly From £48 p.a.

Articles on agricultural subjects. Length: 1,000–1,500 words. Illustrations: line, half-tone, colour. Payment: £90 per 1,000 words. Founded 1893.

Scottish Field

Fettes Park, 496 Ferry Road, Edinburgh EH5 2DL
tel 0131 551 1000
email editor@scottishfield.co.uk
website www.scottishfield.co.uk
Facebook www.facebook.com/scottishfield/
Twitter @scottishfield
Editor Richard Bath
Monthly £4.95

Scottish lifestyle magazine: interiors, food, travel, wildlife, heritage, general lifestyle. Length of article accepted: 1,200 words. Founded 1903.

Screen Daily

Media Business Insight, Essex Street, London WC2R 3AA

tel 020-8102 0900
email matt.mueller@screendaily.com
website www.screendaily.com
Editor Matt Mueller
Monthly From £175 p.a.

News and features on the international film business.
No unsolicited material. Length: variable. Payment:
by arrangement.

Sea Angler

Kelsey Publishing Ltd, The Granary, Downs Court,
Yalding Hill, Yalding, Maidstone, Kent ME18 6AL
website www.seaangler.co.uk
Facebook www.facebook.com/seaanglermag/
Twitter @TheSeaAngler
13 p.a. £4.50

Topical articles on all aspects of sea-fishing around
the British Isles. Illustrations: colour. Payment: by
arrangement. Founded 1972.

Sea Breezes

The Office, Strenaby Farm,
Lonan Church Road Laxey, Isle of Man IM4 7JX
tel (01624) 863672
website www.seabreezes.co.im
Editor Captain Peter Corrin
Monthly £6.70

Factual articles on ships and the sea past and present,
preferably illustrated. Length: up to 4,000 words.
Illustrations: by arrangement. Payment: by
arrangement. Founded 1919.

Seen and Heard

Nagalro, PO Box 264, Esher, Surrey KT10 0WA
tel (01372) 818504
email mail@rodneynoon.co.uk
website www.nagalro.com/seen-and-heard-journal/
seen-and-heard.aspx
Editor Rodney Noon
Quarterly £35 p.a.

Professional journal of Nagalro, the professional
association of children's guardians, family court
advisers and independent social workers. Publishes
high-quality articles and academic papers on issues
relating to the professional practice of child-
protection social workers, child abuse and protection,
adoption and the law relating to children. Potential
contributors are advised to contact the editor initially
with proposals. Payment: on publication, ranging
from £50 to £100.

The Sewing Directory

1 Pound Terrace, Wellington, Somerset TA21 8BY
tel (01823) 978137
email julie@thesewingdirectory.net
website www.thesewingdirectory.co.uk
Facebook www.facebook.com/thesewingdirectory
Twitter @sewingdirectory
Instagram @sewingdirectory

Content Editor Julie Briggs

Online directory of UK sewing business – sewing
courses, fabric shops and sewing groups. Plus free
sewing projects and technique guides. Payment: by
arrangement. Founded 2010.

SFX Magazine

Future Publishing Ltd, Quay House, The Ambury,
Bath BA1 1UA
tel (01225) 442244
email sfx@futurenet.com
website www.gamesradar.com/sfx
Facebook www.facebook.com/SFXmagazine
Twitter @SFXmagazine
13 p.a. £5.50

Sci-fi and fantasy magazine covering TV, films,
DVDs, books, comics, games and collectables.
Founded 1995.

Ships Monthly

Kelsey Publishing Ltd, The Granary, Downs Court,
Yalding Hill, Yalding, Maidstone, Kent ME18 6AL
tel (01959) 541444
email ships.monthly@btinternet.com
website www.shipsmonthly.com
Editor Nicholas Leach
Monthly £4.99

Illustrated articles of shipping and maritime interest –
both mercantile and naval, preferably of 20th- and
21st-century ships. Well-researched, factual material
only. No short stories or poetry. 'Notes for
contributors' available. Mainly commissioned
material; preliminary letter or email essential.
Illustrations: half-tone and line, colour
transparencies, prints and digital images via email,
DVD or CD. Payment: by arrangement.
Founded 1966.

Shooter Literary Magazine

98 Muswell Hill Road, London N10 3JR
email shooterlitmag@gmail.com
website www.shooterlitmag.com
Facebook www.facebook.com/
ShooterLiteraryMagazine
Twitter @ShooterLitMag
Instagram @ShooterLitMag
Editor Melanie White
2 p.a. £19.99 p.a.

Submissions of short fiction and non-fiction
(2,000–6,000 words) and poetry welcome. Annual
story and poetry competitions. Rolling monthly flash
fiction/non-fiction competition. Editing services
available. Please visit the website for guidelines,
current theme and deadline information. Payment:
£25 for prose, £5 for poetry, plus complimentary
issue. Founded 2015.

Shooting Times and Country Magazine

Future Publishing Ltd, 121–141 Westbourne Terrace,
London W2 6JR

email patrick.galbraith@futurenet.com
website www.shootingtimes.co.uk
Twitter @ShootingTimes
Editor Patrick Galbraith
Weekly £2.99

Articles on fieldsports, especially shooting, and on related natural history and countryside topics. Unsolicited MSS not encouraged. Length: up to 1,400 words. Illustrations: photos, drawings, colour transparencies. Payment: by arrangement. Founded 1882.

Shoreline of Infinity

email contact@shorelineofinfinity.com
website www.shorelineofinfinity.com
Twitter @shoreinf
Co-founder, Editor-in-Chief, Editor Emeritus Noel Chidwick
2 p.a. £8.50 (print)

Science fiction and fantasy science fiction stories, poetry, author interviews, articles and reviews. Based in Edinburgh, Scotland, but with a worldwide readership and contributor base. Invites submissions of short stories and poetry, both originals and translations into English, specifically: original and previously unpublished fiction of up to 6,000 words; up to six original and previously unpublished poems per issue. Contributors should indicate any translation rights issues in their cover note. Payment: 5p/word for stories and articles. Copies for contributors; any additional copies at discount rates. Check website for submission window openings. Founded 2014; additional funding for 2022 received from Creative Scotland.

Sight and Sound

BFI, 21 Stephen Street, London W1T 1LN
tel 020-7255 1444
email isabel.stevens@bfi.org.uk
website www.bfi.org.uk/sightandsound
Twitter @SightSoundmag
Editor-in-Chief Mike Williams, *Managing Editor* Isabel Stevens, *Features Editor* James Bell, *Reviews Editor* Katie McCabe
Monthly £6.50

Topical and critical articles on world cinema; reviews of every film theatrically released in the UK; book reviews; DVD reviews; festival reports. Length: 1,000–5,000 words. Contact Managing Editor in the first instance. Illustrations: by arrangement. Payment: by arrangement. Founded 1932.

Skier and Snowboarder Magazine

15 Knowsley Way, Hildenborough, Kent TN11 9LG
tel 07768 670158
email frank.baldwin@skierandsnowboarder.co.uk
website www.skierandsnowboarder.com
Editor Frank Baldwin
Print and online issues throughout the year 5 p.a. Free

Ski features, based around a good story. Length: 800–1,000 words. Illustrations: colour action ski photos. Payment: by negotiation. Founded 1940.

Slightly Foxed

53 Hoxton Square, London N1 6PB
tel 020-7033 0258
email office@foxedquarterly.com
website www.foxedquarterly.com
Facebook www.facebook.com/foxedquarterly
Twitter @foxedquarterly
Instagram @foxedquarterly
Publisher/Co-editor Gail Pirkis
Quarterly Single issue £14.50 (UK and Republic of Ireland), £16.50 (RoW); annual subscription £56 p.a. (UK and Ireland), £64 p.a. (Overseas)

Independent-minded quarterly magazine that introduces its readers to books that are no longer new and fashionable but have enduring appeal. Each issue contains 96pp of recommendations for books of lasting interest, old and new, both fiction and non-fiction. Unsolicited submissions are welcome; see website for guidelines.

Slimming World Magazine

Clover Nook Road, Alfreton, Derbyshire DE55 4SW
tel (01773) 546071
email editorial@slimmingworld.com
website www.slimmingworld.co.uk/magazine
Editor Sara Ward
7 p.a. £3.45

Magazine about healthy eating, fitness and feeling good with real-life stories of how Slimming World members have changed their lives, as well as recipes and menu plans, health advice, beauty and fitness tips, features, competitions and fashion.

Snowflake Magazine

tel 0115 648 9573
email info@snowflakeculture.com
website www.snowflakeculture.com/submit-guidelines
Twitter @SnowflakeMag
Instagram @Snowflake_Magazine
4 p.a. £9.99 (print), £2.99 (digital)

Quarterly literary and arts magazine that focuses on providing up-and-coming LGBTQIA+ creators an entrance to, or boost within, the artistic community through a professional publication. Accepts submissions of fiction, poetry, art, essays, interviews, photographs, and more from anyone who identifies as LGBTQIA+. Ecological focus: magazine and shipping materials are made using predominantly recycled paper and soy-based inks. See website for full guidelines, submission windows, current themes and prompts.

The Songwriter

International Songwriters Association, PO Box 46, Limerick City, Republic of Ireland

tel +353 (0)61 228837
email internationalsongwriters@gmail.com
website www.songwriter.co.uk
Editor James D. Liddane
Quarterly

Articles on songwriting and interviews with songwriters, music publishers and recording company executives. Length: 1,000–10,000 words. Illustrations: photos. Payment: by arrangement. Founded 1967.

Songwriting and Composing

30 Brantwood, Chester le Street,
Co. Durham DH2 2UL
tel 0330 2020 760
email gisc@songwriters-guild.co.uk
website www.songwriters-guild.co.uk
Editor Colin Eade
Quarterly Free to members

Magazine of the Guild of International Songwriters and Composers. Profiles/stories, articles, contacts relating to songwriting, music publishing, recording and the music industry. Illustrations: collaboration register. Payment: £65 per year. Founded 1986.

SOUTH Poetry Magazine

PO Box 9338, Wimborne BH21 9JA
email south@southpoetry.org
website www.southpoetry.org
Facebook www.facebook.com/SOUTHpoetry
2 p.a. £7.50, £12 p.a.

Poetry magazine featuring previously unpublished poems written in English. Poems featured in the magazine are chosen by a selection panel which changes for every issue. Up to three poems (two copies required) may be submitted for each issue, but see website for full details, including annual deadlines. Potential contributors are advised to study the magazine prior to sending in their work.

Spear's Magazine

John Carpenter House, John Carpenter Street,
London EC4Y 0AN
tel 020-7936 6445
email edwin.smith@spearwms.com
website www.spearsmagazine.com
Twitter @SpearsMagazine
Editor Edwin Smith
4 p.a. From £14.99 p.a.

Guide to wealth management, business and culture. Topics covered include wealth management, the law, art, philanthropy, luxury, food and wine and global affairs. Readership includes ultra-high-net-worths, private bankers, top lawyers, philanthropists etc. Standard length of articles 850–1,300 words (features). Illustrations: colour and b&w. Payment: by arrangement. Founded 2003.

The Spectator

22 Old Queen Street, London SW1H 9HP
tel 020-7961 0200
email editor@spectator.co.uk
website www.spectator.co.uk
Editor Fraser Nelson
Weekly £5.75

Articles on current affairs, politics, the arts; book reviews. Illustrations: colour and b&w, cartoons. Payment: on merit. Founded 1828.

Square Mile

Threadneedle Media, 60 Gracechurch Street,
London EC3V 0HR
tel 020-3970 0330
website https://squaremile.com
Twitter @SQUAREMILE_COM
Editorial Director Mark Hedley
Monthly Free

Luxury lifestyle magazine aimed at men working and living in the City of London.

The Stage

Stage House, 47 Bermondsey Street, London SE1 3XT
tel 020-7403 1818
email alistair@thestage.co.uk
website www.thestage.co.uk
Editor Alistair Smith, *Features Editor* Georgia Snow
Weekly £3.50

Original and interesting articles on the theatre and performing arts industry may be sent for the Editor's consideration. Features range in length from 800 to 3,000 words. Payment: £100 per 1,000 words. Founded 1880.

Stamp Magazine

David Hall Publishing, 1st Floor, Nene House,
Sopwith Way, Daventry NN11 8EA
email Guy.Thomas@dhpub.co.uk
website www.stampmagazine.co.uk
Editor Guy Thomas
13 p.a. £4.99

Informative articles and exclusive news items on stamp collecting and postal history. Preliminary letter. Payment: by arrangement. Illustrations: by arrangement. Founded 1934.

Stand Magazine

School of English, University of Leeds, Leeds LS2 9JT
tel 0113 233 4794
email engstand@leeds.ac.uk
website www.standmagazine.org
Managing Editor John Whale, *Editors* Hannah Copley, Kathryn Jenner, Ian Fairley
4 p.a. From £16 p.a. (online), £32 p.a. (print)

Poetry, short stories, translations, literary criticism. Submissions should be made via email. Will consider only original, previously unpublished material;

potential contributors should familiarise themselves with the magazine first. Poetry submissions should be of four to six poems max; fiction should be no more than 3,000 words. Founded 1952.

The Stinging Fly

PO Box 6016, Dublin 1, Republic of Ireland
email info@stingingfly.org
website https://stingingfly.org/submissions/
Facebook www.facebook.com/StingingFly
Twitter @stingingfly
Editor Lisa McInerney
2 p.a. €6

Publishes and promotes the best new Irish and international writing. Submissions of new, previously unpublished fiction, non-fiction and poetry welcomed: see website for guidelines, forthcoming submissions windows and payment information. Founded 1997.

The Strad

Newsquest Media Group, 4th Floor, Queens House. 55–56 Lincoln's Inn Fields, London WC2A 3LJ
tel 020-7618 3095
email thestrad@thestrad.com
website www.thestrad.com
Facebook www.facebook.com/thestrad
Twitter @TheStradMag
Instagram @the_strad_
Editor Emma Baker
12 p.a. plus occasional supplements £5.95

Features, news and reviews for stringed instrument players, teachers, makers and enthusiasts – both professional and amateur. Specially commissions most material but will consider unsolicited material. Welcomes ideas for articles and features. Length: 1,000–2,250 (articles/features), 100–150 (news). Illustrations: by arrangement. Payment: £150–£350 (articles/features), varies for news. Founded 1890.

Strong Words

email info@strong-words.co.uk
website www.strong-words.co.uk
Twitter @strongwordsmag
Instagram @strongwordsmag
Editor Ed Needham
9 p.a. £60 p.a.

Book reviews, author interviews and features on new books, trends, backlist titles and tips on how to write in various genres. Very limited options for outside contributions, but any pitches and information about new books for possible review can be sent via the email address. No academic essays or reviews. For a sample of an issue, see website.

Structo

email editor@structomagazine.co.uk
website www.structomagazine.co.uk
Twitter @structomagazine

Instagram @structopress
Editor Euan Monaghan
2 p.a. £7

Fiction, poetry, interviews and essays. Nominally based in the UK, but with a worldwide staff, readership and contributor base. Invites submissions of short stories and poetry, both originals and translations into English, specifically: original and previously unpublished fiction of up to 4,000 words; up to three original and previously unpublished poems per issue. Payment: £25 plus contributor copy. Published by Structo Press. Founded 2008.

Stuff

Kelsey Media, The Granary, Downs Court, Yalding Hill, Yalding, Kent ME18 6AL
email stuff.ed@kelsey.co.uk
website www.stuff.tv
Twitter @StuffTV
Editor-in-Chief Dan Grabham
Monthly £5.25

Articles on technology, games, films, lifestyle. Features and reviews. Payment by negotiation. Founded 1996.

Style at Home

Future Publishing Ltd, 121–141 Westbourne Terrace, London W2 6JR
email styleathome@futurenet.com
website www.housetohome.co.uk/styleathome
Facebook www.facebook.com/StyleAtHomeMag
Twitter @styleathomemag
Editor Heather Young
Monthly £2.99

Interiors magazine aimed at woman interested in updating, styling and decorating their home. With an emphasis on achievable, affordable home make-overs, the magazine has regular articles showing transformed rooms as well as step-by-step projects, shopping ideas and a recipe section for keen cooks.

Stylist

D.C. Thomson & Co. Ltd, 185 Fleet Street, London EC4A 2HS
tel 020-7611 9700
email stories@stylist.co.uk
website www.stylist.co.uk
Twitter @StylistMagazine
Editor-in-Chief Lisa Smosarski
12 p.a. From £2.99 per month

Women's interest magazine that covers topics from fashion and beauty to books, travel, money and women in the news. Email synopses of feature ideas to the address above. Also extensive online presence.

Suffolk Norfolk Life

Today Magazines Ltd, The Publishing House, Station Road, Framlingham, Suffolk IP13 9EE
tel (01728) 622030

email editor@suffolknorfolklife.com
website www.suffolknorfolklife.com
Editor Kevin Davis
Monthly £3.50

Articles relevant to Suffolk and Norfolk – current topics plus historical items, art, leisure, etc. Considers unsolicited material and welcomes ideas for articles and features. Send via email. Length: 900–1,500 words. Illustrations: transparencies, digital colour and b&w prints, b&w artwork and cartoons. Payment: £60–£80 per article. Founded 1989.

The Tablet

1 King Street Cloisters, Clifton Walk,
London W6 0GY
tel 020-8748 8484
email thetablet@thetablet.co.uk
website www.thetablet.co.uk
Twitter @The_Tablet
Editor Brendan Walsh
Weekly £4.50

Catholic weekly: religion, philosophy, politics, society, books and arts. International coverage. Freelance work commissioned: do not send unsolicited material. Length: various. Illustrations: cartoons and photos. Payment: by arrangement. Founded 1840.

Take a Break

Bauer Media, The Lantern, 75 Hampstead Road,
London NW1 2PL
tel 020-7241 8000
email tab.features@bauer.co.uk
website www.takeabreak.co.uk
Weekly £1.20

Lively, illustrated tabloid women's weekly. True-life features, health and beauty, family; lots of puzzles. Payment: by arrangement. Founded 1990.

Take a Break's Take a Puzzle

Bauer Media, The Lantern, 75 Hampstead Road,
London NW1 2PL
email take.puzzle@bauer.co.uk
website www.puzzlemagazines.co.uk/takeapuzzle
Monthly £3.10

Puzzles. Fresh ideas always welcome. Illustrations: colour transparencies and b&w prints and artwork. Payment: from £25 per puzzle, £30–£90 for picture puzzles and for illustrations not an integral part of a puzzle. Founded 1991.

Tate Etc

Tate, Millbank, London SW1P 4RG
tel 020-7887 8724
email enrico.tassi@tate.org.uk
email figgy.guyver@tate.org.uk
website www.tate.org.uk/tate-etc
Twitter @TateEtcMag
Deputy Editor Enrico Tassi,

Assistant Editor Figgy Guyver
3 p.a. £23 p.a. (UK)

Independent visual arts magazine: features, interviews, previews and opinion pieces. Length: up to 3,000 words but always commissioned. Illustrations: colour and b&w photos. Payment: negotiable.

Tatler

The Condé Nast Publications Ltd, Vogue House,
1 Hanover Square, London W1S 1JU
website www.tatler.com
Twitter @Tatlermagazine
Editor Richard Dennen
Monthly £4.95

Smart society magazine favouring sharp articles, profiles, fashion and the arts. Illustrations: colour, b&w, but all commissioned. Founded 1709.

Taxation

Quadrant House, The Quadrant, Sutton SM2 5AS
tel 020-8212 1949
email taxation@lexisnexis.co.uk
website www.taxation.co.uk
Twitter @Taxation
Editor-in-Chief Andrew Hubbard
48 issues p.a. £531 p.a.

Updating and advice concerning UK tax law and practice for accountants and tax experts. All articles written by professionals. Founded 1927.

Tears in the Fence

Flats, Durweston Mill, Mill Lane, Durweston,
Blandford Forum, Dorset DT11 0QD
email tearsinthefence@gmail.com
website https://tearsinthefence.com
Twitter @TearsInTheFence
Editor David Caddy
Bi-annual £12 per issue, or £30 for three issues/£50
for six issues

Socially aware literary magazine with an international outlook and author base. Includes regular columnists as well as critical reviews of recent books and essays on English and American poets, flash fiction, translations and interviews. See website for up-to-date information on forthcoming submission windows. Submissions of original, unpublished work should be made by email to the address above in the body of the message and as an attachment.

Television

RTS, 3 Dorset Rise, London EC4Y 8EH
tel 020-7822 2810
email publications@rts.org.uk
website www.rts.org.uk
Editor Steve Clarke
Monthly

Articles on all aspects of TV and related content sectors including the people, programmes, politics and media policy. Coverage of RTS events. Payment: by arrangement. Founded 1928.

Tempo

Cambridge University Press,
The Edinburgh Building, Shaftesbury Road,
Cambridge CB2 8RU
email tempoeditor@cambridge.org
website https://www.cambridge.org/core/journals/tempo
Editor Professor Christopher Fox
Quarterly From £193 p.a.

Authoritative articles on contemporary music.
Length: 2,000–4,000 words. Illustrations: music type,
occasional photographic or musical supplements.
Payment: by arrangement.

TGO (The Great Outdoors) Magazine

Kelsey Publishing Ltd, The Granary, Downs Court,
Yalding Hill, Yalding, Maidstone, Kent ME18 6AL
tel (01959) 541444
email carey.davies@kelsey.co.uk
website www.tgomagazine.co.uk
Twitter @TGOmagazine
Editor Carey Davies
13 p.a. £3.90

Articles on walking or lightweight camping in specific
areas, mainly in the UK, preferably illustrated with
photography. Apply for guidelines. Length: 700–2,000
words. Illustrations: colour. Payment: by
arrangement. Founded 1978.

that's life!

Bauer Media, The Lantern, 75 Hampstead Road,
London NW1 2PL
tel 020-7241 8000
email stories@thatslife.co.uk
website www.thatslife.co.uk
Group Head of Content and Commissioning Sophie
Hearsey
Weekly 85p

Dramatic true-life stories about women. Length:
average 1,000 words. Illustrations: colour photos and
cartoons. Payment: up to £2,000. Founded 1995.

This England

185 Fleet Street, London EC4A 2HS
tel 020-7400 1083
email editor@thisengland.co.uk
website www.thisengland.co.uk
Quarterly £5.95

Articles about England's traditions, customs and
places of interest. Regular features on towns, villages,
the English countryside, notable men and women,
and readers' recollections. Length 250–3,000 words.
Illustrations: digital images accepted when
accompanying articles. Payment: by arrangement.
Founded 1968.

Time Out London

email hello@timeout.com
website www.timeout.com/london
Facebook www.facebook.com/TimeOutLondon/
Twitter @timeoutlondon
Instagram @timeoutlondon
Online

Digital curated content – written by professional
journalists – covers the best food, drink, culture,
entertainment and travel across 327 cities in 58
countries. Founded 1968.

Today's Golfer

Bauer Media Group, Media House, Lynch Wood,
Peterborough Business Park, Peterborough PE2 6EA
tel (01733) 468000
email chris.jones@bauermedia.co.uk
website www.todaysgolfer.co.uk
Facebook https://en-gb.facebook.com/
TodaysGolferBauer/
Twitter @TheTodaysGolfer
Editor Chris Jones
13 p.a. From £3.00 per month

Specialist features and articles on golf instruction,
equipment and courses. Founded 1988.

Top Santé

Kelsey Publishing Ltd, The Granary, Downs Court,
Yalding Hill, Yalding, Maidstone, Kent ME18 6AL
tel (01959) 541444
website www.topsante.co.uk
Twitter @topsanteuk
Editor Katy Sunnassee
13 p.a. £4.50

Features and news on all aspects of health, wellbeing,
fitness and beauty. Ideas welcome. Founded 1993.

Total Film

Future Publishing Ltd, 121–141 Westbourne Terrace,
London W2 6JR
tel 020-7042 4831
email jane.crowther@futurenet.com
website www.gamesradar.com/totalfilm
Monthly £6.50

Movie magazine covering all aspects of film. Email
ideas before submitting material. Length: 400 words
(news items); 1,000 words (funny features). Payment:
20p per word. Founded 1996.

Trail

Bauer Consumer Media, Media House,
Lynch Wood, Peterborough Business Park,
Peterborough PE2 6EA
tel (01733) 468363
website www.trailmagazine.com
Editor Oli Reed
Monthly £5.20

Outdoor activity magazine focusing mainly on high –

level walking with some scrambling and climbing. Some opportunities for freelancers; ideas welcome.

Trout & Salmon

Bauer Consumer Media, Media House, Lynch Wood, Peterborough Business Park, Peterborough PE2 6EA
tel (01733) 468000
email troutandsalmon@bauermedia.co.uk
website www.troutandsalmon.com
Editor Andrew Flitcroft
13 p.a. From £58 p.a.

Articles of good quality with strong trout or salmon angling interest. Length: 400–2,000 words, accompanied if possible by good quality colour photographs. Illustrations: line, colour transparencies and prints, cartoons. Payment: by arrangement. Founded 1955.

Truck & Driver

DVV Media International Ltd, Road Transport Media Ltd, First Floor, Chancery House, St Nicholas Way, Sutton, Surrey SM1 1JB
tel 020-8912 2131
email dougie.rankine@roadtransport.com
website www.truckanddriver.co.uk
Twitter @TRUCKNDRIVER
Editor Dougie Rankine
Monthly From £57 p.a.

News, articles on trucks, personalities and features of interest to truck drivers. Words and picture packages preferred. Preferred feature length: 500-1,500 words. Payment: negotiable. Founded 1984.

Trucking

Kelsey Publishing Ltd, The Granary, Downs Court, Yalding Hill, Yalding, Maidstone, Kent ME18 6AL
tel (01733) 347559
email trucking.ed@kelsey.co.uk
website www.truckingmag.co.uk
Twitter @truckingmag
Editor Andy Stewart
Monthly £4.50

For truck drivers, owner–drivers and operators: news, articles, features and technical advice. Length: 750–2,500 words. Illustrations: mostly 35mm digital. Payment: by negotiation. Founded 1983.

TV Times Magazine

Future Publishing Ltd, 121–141 Westbourne Terrace, London W2 6JR
tel 020-3148 5615
website www.whatsontv.co.uk/tv-times
Twitter @tvtimesmagazine
Weekly £2.60

Features with an affinity to ITV, BBC1, BBC2, Channels 4 and 5, satellite and digital channels, as well as radio personalities and TV generally. Length:

by arrangement. Photographs: commissioned only. Payment: by arrangement.

25 Beautiful Homes

Future Publishing Ltd, 121–141 Westbourne Terrace, London W2 6JR
email 25beautifulhomes@futurenet.com
website www.idealhome.co.uk/25-beautiful-homes
Twitter @25BHomesMag
Instagram @25beautifulhomesmagazine
Monthly £4.99

Interiors magazine aiming to inspire affluent readers in their love for their homes. Each edition shows a selection of properties in the UK and Europe that have been renovated or built to a high standard. The magazine also features a selection of best buys in decorative accessories to help make beautiful homes achievable.

Vanity Fair

The Condé Nast Publications Ltd, The Adelphi, 1–11 John Adam Street, London WC2N 6HT
tel 020-7851 1800
website www.vanityfair.com
Twitter @VanityFair
Editor-in-Chief Radhika Jones
Monthly £4.99

Media, glamour and politics for grown-up readers. No unsolicited material. Payment: by arrangement. Illustrated.

The Vegan

The Vegan Society, Donald Watson House, 21 Hylton Street, Birmingham B18 6HJ
tel 0121 523 1730
email editor@vegansociety.com
website www.vegansociety.com
Editor Elena Orde
Quarterly £3, free to members

Articles on health, nutrition, cookery, vegan lifestyles, land use, climate change, animal rights. Length: approx. 1,000 words. Illustrations: photos, foods, animals, livestock systems, crops, people, events; colour for cover. Payment: £150–£500 per piece. Founded 1944.

Vegan Food & Living

Anthem Publishing, Suite 6, Piccadilly House, London Road, Bath BA1 6PL
tel (01225) 489984
email sally.fitzgerald@anthem.co.uk
website www.veganfoodandliving.com/contact
Facebook www.facebook.com/veganfoodandliving
Twitter @veganfoodliving
Instagram @veganfoodandliving/
Publisher Sally Fitzgerald
Monthly £5.25

Plant-based recipes (75 per month), along with features on new trends and cooking techniques. Also nutrition advice, and guides for gourmet travellers. Founded 2015.

Viz

Diamond Publishing Ltd, 7th Floor, Vantage, London, Great West Road, Brentford TW8 9AG
email viz@viz.co.uk
website www.viz.co.uk
Twitter @vizcomic
10 p.a. £3.99

Cartoons, spoof tabloid articles, spoof advertisements. Illustrations: half-tone, line, cartoons. Payment: by arrangement. Founded 1979.

Vogue

The Condé Nast Publications Ltd, The Adelphi, 1–11 John Adam Street, London WC2N 6HT
website www.vogue.co.uk
Twitter @BritishVogue
Editor Edward Enninful
Monthly £3.99

Fashion, beauty, health, decorating, art, theatre, films, literature, music, travel, food and wine. Length: articles from 1,000 words. Illustrated.

Waitrose Food

Dentsu Creative, 10 Triton Street, Regents Place, London NW1 3BF
tel 020-7565 3236
email waitrose.food@dentsu.com
Editor Jessica Gunn
Monthly £3 (free to MyWaitrose members)

In-house magazine of the Waitrose Group. Features seasonal recipes, menu ideas, interviews, lifestyle and travel.

walk

The Ramblers, 3rd Floor, Clink Street, London SE1 9DG
tel 020-3961 3141
email walkmag@ramblers.org.uk
website www.ramblers.org.uk/news/walk-magazine
Twitter @WalkMagazine
Quarterly Free to members

Magazine of the Ramblers, Britain's walking charity. Articles on walking, access to countryside and related issues, and interviews. Material mostly commissioned. Length: up to 1,500 words. Illustrations: colour photos, preferably hi-res, digitally supplied. Payment: by agreement. Founded 1935.

Wallpaper*

Future Publishing Ltd, 121–141 Westbourne Terrace, London W2 6JR
website www.wallpaper.com
Twitter @wallpapermag
Instagram @wallpapermag
Editor-in-Chief Sarah Douglas
12 p.a. £10

International media brand covering architecture, design, art, travel, entertaining, beauty and grooming, transport, technology, fashion, and watches and jewellery. Brand extensions include an in-house creative agency, an interior design service, and a digital learning programme in collaboration with Parsons School of Design. Founded 1996.

Wanderlust

Capital House, 25 Chapel Street, London NW1 5DH
email submissions@wanderlust.co.uk
website www.wanderlust.co.uk
Editor-in-Chief George Kipouros
8 p.a. £5.95

Features on independent, adventure and special-interest travel. See website for contributor guidelines. Length: up to 2,500 words. Illustrations: hi-res digital. Payment: by arrangement. Founded 1993.

The War Cry

The Salvation Army, 101 Newington Causeway, London SE1 6BN
tel 020-7367 4900
email warcry@salvationarmy.org.uk
website www.salvationarmy.org.uk/warcry
Facebook www.facebook.com/TheWarCryUK
Twitter @TheWarCryUK
Editor Andrew Stone
Weekly 50p

Voluntary contributions: human interest stories of personal Christian faith. Founded 1879.

Wasafiri

School of English and Drama, Queen Mary University of London, Mile End Road, London E1 4NS
email wasafiri@qmul.ac.uk
website www.wasafiri.org
Editor and Publishing Director Emily Mercer
4 p.a. £11, from £38 p.a.

International contemporary literature. Accepts submissions for fiction, poetry, articles and interviews; see website for details. Founded 1984.

Waterways World

Waterways World Ltd, 151 Station Street, Burton-on-Trent DE14 1BG
tel (01283) 742950
email editorial@waterwaysworld.com
website www.waterwaysworld.com
Twitter @waterwaysworld
Editor Bobby Cowling
Monthly £4.99

Feature articles on all aspects of inland waterways in Britain and abroad, including historical material; factual and technical articles preferred. No short stories or poetry. See website for notes for potential contributors (under the contact section). Illustrations: by arrangement. Payment: by arrangement. Founded 1972.

The Week

Future Publishing Ltd, Quay House, The Ambury, Bath BA1 1UA
email editorialadmin@theweek.co.uk
website www.theweek.co.uk
Weekly From £51 p.a. (special offers may be available)

Magazine that distils the best from the British and foreign press into 44pp, including news, art, science, business, property and leisure. Founded 1995.

Wet Grain

18/3 Marchmont Road, Edinburgh EH9 1HZ
email wetgrainpoetry@protonmail.com
website www.wetgrainpoetry.com
Facebook www.facebook.com/WetGrain
Twitter @WetGrainPoetry
Editors Patrick Romero McCafferty, Christian Lemay; also Guest Editors
1 p.a. £7

Annual print poetry magazine based in Edinburgh. See website for information on current guest editors and for submission window dates. Potential contributors may submit up to four poems in a Word document via email (names should not be included); familiarity with the magazine encouraged. Simultaneous submission welcomed. Founded 2019.

What Car?

Haymarket Motoring Magazines Ltd, Bridge House, 69 London Road, Twickenham TW1 3SP
tel 020-8267 5688
email editorial@whatcar.com
website www.whatcar.com
Editor Steve Huntingford
Monthly £6.99

Road tests, buying guide, consumer stories and used car features. No unsolicited material. Illustrations: by arrangement. Payment: by negotiation. Founded 1973.

What's On TV

Future Publishing Ltd, 121–141 Westbourne Terrace, London W2 6JR
tel 020-3148 5573
email kim.palfrey@futurenet.com
website www.whattowatch.com
Facebook www.facebook.com/whatsontvuk/
Weekly 79p

Features on TV programmes and personalities. All material commissioned. Length: up to 250 words. Illustrations: colour and b&w photos. Payment: by agreement. Founded 1991.

The White Review

A.104 Fuel Tank, 8–12 Creekside, London SE8 3DX
email submissions@thewhitereview.org
website www.thewhitereview.org
Twitter @TheWhiteReview
Instagram @thewhitereview
Editors Rosanna Mclaughlin, Izabella Scott, Skye Arundhati Thomas
Quarterly £12.99

Contemporary arts and literature journal. Welcomes submissions of fiction, poetry, essays and interviews. See website for full submission details, but briefly: all fiction and non-fiction submissions should be in English, not have been published elsewhere and (poetry excepted) be at least 1,500 words long. Interview pitches also accepted, but see previous editions for style and tone. Email no more than three poems to poetry@thewhitereview.org; all other submissions should be sent to the email address above. Founded 2011.

WI Life

(formerly WI Home & Country)
104 New King's Road, London SW6 4LY
tel 020-7731 5777
email WILife.Editor@nfwi.org.uk
website www.thewi.org.uk/wienterprises/look-inside
Twitter @WILifemagazine
Editor Sarah Drew Jones
8 p.a. as part of the WI subscription

Journal of the National Federation of Women's Institutes for England and Wales. Publishes material related to the Federation's and members' activities with articles of interest to active women engaged in their communities and campaigns, mainly written in-house and by WI members but some freelance opportunities. Illustrations: colour photos. Payment: all commissions are paid; rates on request.

Woman

Future Publishing Ltd, 121–141 Westbourne Terrace, London W2 6JR
tel 020-3148 5000
email woman@futurenet.com
website www.womanmagazine.co.uk
Group Editor Hannah Fernando
Weekly £1.60

News, celebrity and real-life features, of no more than 1,000 words. Particular interest in celebrity and diet exclusives. Digital images only. Read magazine prior to submission. Fiction not published. Payment: by negotiation. Founded 1937.

Woman Alive

(formerly Christian Woman)
Premier Christian Communications Ltd, Unit 6, April Court, Sybron Way, Crowborough TN6 3DZ
email womanalive@premier.org.uk
website www.womanalive.co.uk
Facebook www.facebook.com/womanalivemagazine
Twitter @WomanAliveUK
Instagram @WomanAliveUK
Editor Tola-Doll Fisher
Monthly £45 p.a.

Aimed at women aged 35 upwards. Celebrity interviews, topical features. Explores modern issues facing women within the context of Christian faith, profiles of women in interesting occupations, Christian testimonies and real-life stories, fashion, beauty, travel, health, crafts. Length: 500–1200 words. Payment £50–£150. Founded 1982.

woman&home

Future Publishing Ltd, 121–141 Westbourne Terrace, London W2 6JR
email sharon.sweeney@futurenet.com
website www.womanandhome.com
Group Editor Hannah Fernando, *Features Editor* Sharon Sweeney
Monthly £5.50

Centres on the personal and home interests of the lively minded mature, modern woman. Articles dealing with fashion, beauty, leisure pursuits, gardening, home style; features on topical issues, people and places. Fiction: complete stories from 3,000–4,500 words in length. Illustrations: by arrangement. Non-commissioned work is not accepted and cannot be returned. Founded 1926.

Woman's Own

Future Publishing Ltd, 121–141 Westbourne Terrace, London W2 6JR
tel 020-3148 5000
email womansown@futurenet.com
website www.womansown.co.uk
Editor Kira Agass
Weekly £1.60

Modern women's magazine aimed at the 35–50 age group. No unsolicited features. Address work to relevant department editor. Payment: by arrangement.

Woman's Way

Harmonia Ltd, Rosemount House, Dundrum Road, Dublin D14 P924, Republic of Ireland
tel +353 (0)1 2405318
email womansway@harmonia.ie
website www.womansway.ie
Twitter @Womans_Way
Editor Norah Casey
Weekly €3.50

Human interest, personality interviews, features on fashion, beauty, celebrities and investigations. Founded 1963.

Woman's Weekly

Future Publishing Ltd, 121–141 Westbourne Terrace, London W2 6JR
tel 020-3148 5000
email geoffrey.palmer@futurenet.com
website www.womansweekly.com
Facebook www.facebook.com/WomansWeekly
Editor Geoffrey Palmer
Weekly £1.70

Lively family-interest magazine. Unsolicited short stories currently not accepted. Celebrity and strong human interest features, health, finance and consumer features, plus beauty, diet, travel, homes, craft, knitting, gardening and cookery; also inspirational and entertaining personal stories. Illustrations: full-colour fiction illustrations, small sketches and photos. Payment: by arrangement. Founded 1911.

The Woodworker

MyTime Media Ltd, Eden House, Enterprise Way, Edenbridge, Kent TN8 6HF
tel 0844 848 8822
website www.thewoodworkermag.com
Editor Tegan Foley
Monthly £4.99

For the craft and professional woodworker. Practical illustrated articles on cabinet work, carpentry, polishing, wood turning, wood carving, rural crafts, craft history, antique and period furniture; also wooden toys and models, musical instruments; timber procurement, conditioning, seasoning; tools, machinery and equipment reviews. Illustrations: line drawings and digital photos. Payment: by arrangement. Founded 1901.

World Fishing & Aquaculture

Spinnaker House, Waterside Gardens, Fareham PO16 8SD
tel (01329) 825335
email jholland@mercatormedia.com
website www.worldfishing.net
Editor Jason Holland
10 p.a. Three-month free trial; subscription options thereafter

International journal of commercial fishing. Technical and management emphasis on catching, processing and marketing of fish and related products; fishery operations and vessels covered worldwide. Length: 500–1,500 words. Illustrations: photos and diagrams for litho reproduction. Payment: by arrangement. Founded 1952.

The World of Interiors

The Condé Nast Publications Ltd, The Adelphi, 1–11 John Adam Street, London WC2N 6HT
tel 020-7851 1800
email ariadne.fletcher@condenast.co.uk
website www.worldofinteriors.co.uk
Twitter @wofinteriors
Editor-in-Chief Hamish Bowles
Monthly £4.99

All material commissioned: send photographs/synopsis for article ideas. Length: 1,000–1,500 words. Illustrations: by arrangement. Founded 1981.

World Soccer

Kelsey Publishing Ltd, The Granary, Downs Court, Yalding Hill, Yalding, Maidstone, Kent ME18 6AL

tel (01959) 541444
email WOS.ed@kelsey.co.uk
website www.worldsoccer.com
Editor Stephen Fishlock
Monthly £5.99

Articles, features, news concerning football, its
personalities and worldwide development. Length:
600–2,000 words. Payment: by arrangement.
Founded 1960.

The World Today

Chatham House, 10 St James's Square,
London SW1Y 4LE
tel 020-7957 5712
email REscobales@chathamhouse.org
website www.chathamhouse.org/publications/the-
world-today
Editor Roxanne Escobales
6 p.a. From £43 p.a. (student rate £34)

Analysis of international issues and current events by
journalists, diplomats, politicians and academics.
Length: 1,200–1,500 words. Payment: nominal.
Founded 1945.

Writing Magazine

Warners Group Publications Plc, 5th Floor,
31–32 Park Row, Leeds LS1 5JD
tel 0113 200 2929
email tjackson@warnersgroup.co.uk
website www.writers-online.co.uk
Facebook www.facebook.com/writingmagazine
Twitter @writingmagazine
Content Editor Tina Jackson
Monthly £5.25

Articles on all aspects of writing. Length: 800–2,000
words. Payment: by arrangement. Founded 1992. In
addition, Writers' News (now part of Writing
Magazine) features news, competitions and market
information. Length: up to 350 words. Payment: by
arrangement. Founded 1989.

Yachting Monthly

Future Publishing Ltd, Quay House, The Ambury,
Bath BA1 1UA
tel 0330 390 3933
email yachtingmonthly@futurenet.com
website www.yachtingmonthly.com
Editor Theo Stocker
Monthly £4.99

Articles on all aspects of seamanship, navigation, the
handling of sailing craft, and their design,
construction and equipment. Well-written narrative
accounts of cruises in yachts. Please read the
magazine to understand where your submission
might fit before contacting the editorial team, who
can advise on what any requirements will be.
Illustrations: colour photos. Payment: quoted on
acceptance. Founded 1906.

Yachting World

Future Publishing Ltd, Quay House, The Ambury,
Bath BA1 1UA
tel (01225) 442244
email yachting.world@futurenet.com
website www.yachtingworld.com
Editor Helen Fretter
Monthly £5.50

Practical and inspirational articles of an original
nature, dealing with sailing yachts, both cruising and
racing, for the experienced and knowledgeable sailor/
owner. Length: 1,500–2,000 words. Illustrations:
digital files, drawings, cartoons. Payment: varies.
Founded 1894.

The Yorkshire Dalesman

Country Publications Limited, The Gatehouse,
Skipton Castle, Skipton, North Yorkshire, BD23 1AL
tel (01756) 693479
email mick@dalesman.co.uk
website www.dalesman.co.uk
Facebook www.facebook.com/yorkshire.dalesman
Twitter @The_Dalesman
Editor Mick Smith
Monthly £3.40

Articles and stories of genuine interest concerning
Yorkshire (1,000 to 1,200 words). Payment: £70 per
1,000 words plus extra for usable photos/illustrations.
Founded 1939.

Yorkshire Life

email kathryn.armstrong@newsquest.co.uk
website www.greatbritishlife.co.uk
Editor Kathryn Armstrong
Monthly £4.50

Articles on Yorkshire, including places of interest,
high-profile personalities, local events, arts, history
and food. Unsolicited ideas welcome. Founded 1946.

Your Cat Magazine

Warners Group Publications Plc, The Maltings,
West Street, Bourne, Lincs. PE10 9PH
email editorial@yourcat.co.uk
website www.yourcat.co.uk
Facebook www.facebook.com/yourcatmagazine
Editor Michael Hallam
Monthly £4.99

Practical advice on the care of cats and kittens,
general interest items and news on cats, and true-life
tales and fiction (commission ideas welcome).
Length: 800–1,500 words (articles), 200–300 words
(news), up to 1,000 words (short stories).
Illustrations: hi-res digital, colour transparencies and
prints. Founded 1994.

Your Dog Magazine

Warners Group Publications Plc, The Maltings,
West Street, Bourne, Lincs. PE10 9PH

email editorial@yourdog.co.uk
website www.yourdog.co.uk
Facebook www.facebook.com/yourdogmagazine
Twitter @yourdog
Monthly £4.99

Articles and information of interest to dog lovers; features on all aspects of pet dogs. Length: approx. 800–1,500 words. Payment: £140 per 1,000 words. Founded 1994.

Your Horse Magazine

Kelsey Media Ltd, The Granary, Downs Court, Yalding Hill, Yalding, Maidstone, Kent ME18 6AL
email yh.ed@kelsey.co.uk
website www.yourhorse.co.uk
Facebook www.facebook.com/YourHorse
Magazine Editor Julie Harding, *Digital Editor* Aimi Clark
13 issues p.a. £4.75

Practical horse care, riding advice and inspirational interviews, features and real-life articles for riders, owners and horse lovers to enjoy. Send feature ideas with examples of previous published writing. Welcomes ideas for articles and features. Length: 1,500 words. Payment: (approx.) £130 per 1,000 words. Founded 1983.

Yours

Bauer Media, Media House, Lynch Wood, Peterborough Business Park, Peterborough PE2 6EA
tel (01733) 468000
email yours@bauermedia.co.uk
website www.yours.co.uk
Facebook www.facebook.com/Yoursmagazine
Twitter @yoursmagazine
Editor Sharon Reid
Fortnightly £1.85

Features and news about and/or of interest to the over-50s age group, including nostalgia and short stories. Study of magazine essential. Length: articles up to 300 words, short stories up to 1,200 words. Payment: by arrangement. Founded 1973.

Syndicates, news and press agencies

Before submitting material, you are strongly advised to make preliminary enquiries and to ascertain terms of work. Strictly speaking, syndication is the selling and reselling of previously published work although some news and press agencies handle original material.

Neil Bradley Studio

tel 07814 526808
email enquire@neilbradleystudio.co.uk
Director Neil Bradley

Supplies cartoons to national and regional press; emphasis placed on variety and topicality with work based on current media listings. Daily single frame and strip cartoons. Founded 1981.

Brainwarp

23 Chatsworth Avenue, Culcheth, Warrington, Cheshire WA3 4LD
tel (01925) 765878
email sarah@brainwarp.com
website www.brainwarp.com
Contacts Trixie Roberts, Tony Roberts, Sarah Simmons

Writes and supplies original crosswords, brainteasers, wordsearches, quizzes and word games to editors for the printed page. Does not accept work from external sources. Standard fees for syndicated puzzles. Customised work negotiable. Founded 1987.

Bulls Presstjänst AB

Augustendalsvägen 51, 131 52 Nacka Strand, Sweden
tel +46 8-55520600
email info@bulls.se
website www.bullspress.com

Market: newspapers, magazines, weeklies and advertising agencies across Northern Europe. Syndicates human-interest picture stories; topical and well-illustrated background articles and series; photographic features dealing with science, people, personalities, glamour; genre pictures for advertising; condensations and serialisations of bestselling fiction and non-fiction; cartoons, comic strips, film and TV rights, merchandising and newspaper graphics online.

DMG Media Licensing

Northcliffe House, 9 Derry Street, London W8 5HY
tel 020-7566 0360
website www.solosyndication.co.uk
Director of Licensing & Syndication William Gardiner

Worldwide syndication of newspaper features, photos, cartoons, puzzles and strips. Represents the international syndication of Associated Newspapers Ltd (*Daily Mail*, *Mail on Sunday*, the *i* newspaper, Mail Online, *Metro*), New Scientist, Andrews McMeel Syndication (US) and Creators Syndicate (US) in Great Britain and Ireland, Africa and the Middle East. Formerly Solo Syndication.

Europress Features (UK)

18 St Chad's Road, Didsbury, Nr Manchester M20 4WH
tel 0161 445 2945
email europressmedia@yahoo.com

Representation of newspapers and magazines in Europe, Australia and the US. Syndication of top-flight features with exclusive illustrations – human interest stories – showbusiness personalities. 30–35% commission on sales of material successfully accepted; 40% on exclusive illustrations.

Foresight News

Centaur Media Plc, 10 York Road, London SE1 7ND
tel 020-7970 4299
email enquiries@foresightnews.co.uk
website www.foresightnews.com
Twitter @ForesightNewsUK
Publisher Nicole Wilkins

Offers a vast, fully searchable database featuring thousands of forthcoming events and news from across the UK and around the world, spanning a variety of sectors including politics, business, crime and home affairs, health, entertainment and sport.

Guardian Licensing

Kings Place, 90 York Way, London N1 9GU
tel 020-3353 2539
email licensing@theguardian.com
website https://licensing.theguardian.com/
Head of Licensing Ross Paterson

International syndication services of news and features from the *Guardian*, the *Observer* and theguardian.com. Unable to syndicate content which has not been published in its own titles. All permission requests to be submitted via online form.

Hayters Teamwork

47 Dean Street, London W1D 5BE
tel 020-7183 6727
email sport@hayters.com
website www.hayters.com
Instagram @haytersTV
Contacts Nick Callow, Gerry Cox

Sports news, features and data supplied to all branches of the media. Commission: negotiable according to merit. Founded 1955.

Headliners

200A Pentonville Road, London N1 9JP
email enquiries@headliners.org
website www.headliners.org
Twitter @HeadlinersUK

Chief Executive James Hunt

UK-wide journalism and multi-media charity. Offers young people aged 8–18 the opportunity to write on issues of importance to them for newspapers, radio and TV. Founded 1995.

Independent Radio News (IRN)

The Harley Buidling, 77–79 New Cavendish Street, London W1W 6XB
tel 020-7485 9800
email news@irn.co.uk
website www.irn.co.uk
Twitter @IRNRadioNews
Managing Director Tim Molloy

National and international news.

Knight Features Ltd

Trident Business Centre, 89 Bickersteth Road, London SW17 9SH
tel 020-3051 5650
email info@knightfeatures.co.uk
website www.knightfeatures.com
Contacts Gaby Martin, Andrew Knight, Sam Ferris

Worldwide selling of puzzles, strip cartoons, crosswords, horoscopes and serialisations for print and digital media. Agent in the UK and Republic of Ireland for Creators Syndicate, Tribune Content Agency. Founded 1985.

New Blitz Literary and Editorial TV Agency

Via del Fossaccio, 19, 01010 Marta, Italy
email blitzgacs@inwind.it
Manager Giovanni A.S. Congiu

Syndicates worldwide: cartoons, comic strips, humorous books with drawings, feature material, topical. Average rates of commission 60/40%, monthly report of sales, payment 60 days after the date of sale.

PA Media

37 N Wharf Road, London W2 1AF
website https://pa.media/
Facebook www.facebook.com/PAMediaGroupUK/
Twitter @PA
Chief Executive Clive Marshall

Provider of multimedia content and services, and the national news agency for the UK and Ireland. Has offices in several key locations (see website). Customers include major national, regional and international media and digital brands, as well as businesses and public sector organisations. Services include: news wire and digital ready-to-publish articles, pictures; video; data APIs; hosted live blogs; graphics; listings pages; social media curation; and page production. Part of the PA Media Group of specialist media companies. Founded 1868.

The Puzzle House

Ivy Cottage, Battlesea Green, Stradbroke, Suffolk IP21 5NE
tel (01379) 384656
email enquiries@thepuzzlehouse.co.uk
website www.thepuzzlehouse.co.uk
Partners Roy Preston & Sue Preston

Supply original crosswords, quizzes and puzzles of all types. Commissions taken on any topic, with all age ranges catered for. Wide selection of puzzles available for one-off usage. Founded 1988.

Rann Media

120 Molesworth Street, North Adelaide, SA 5006 Australia
tel +61 (0)4 1883 2512
website www.rann.com.au
Managing Director Chris Rann

Professional PR, press releases, special newsletters, commercial and political intelligence, media monitoring. Welcomes approaches from organisations requiring PR representation or press release distribution. Founded 1982.

Sirius Media Services Ltd

37 Lower Brook Street, Ipswich IP4 1AQ
tel (01449) 833834
email info@siriusmedia.co.uk
website www.siriusmedia.co.uk

Crosswords, puzzles and quizzes, and Zygolex.

The Telegraph – Content Licensing & Syndication

Telegraph Media Group,
111 Buckingham Palace Road, London SW1W 0DT
email syndication@telegraph.co.uk
website www.telegraph.co.uk/syndication/

Digital platforms, data aggregation, newswire services. News, features, photography and graphics, video, worldwide distribution and representation. Content licensing packages available for both print and all other media platforms.

WENN

78 York Street, London W1H 1DP
tel 020-7607 2757
email enquiries@wenn.com
website www.wenn.com

Provides the world's media with up-to-the-minute entertainment news and photos. Founded 1989.

Wessex News, Features and Photos Agency

Little Mead, Lower Green, Inkpen, Berks. RG17 9DW
tel (01488) 668308
email news@britishnews.co.uk
website www.britishnews.co.uk
Editor Jim Hardy

Freelance press agency with a network of writers and photographers across the UK. Providing real-life news stories and features for national and international newspapers and magazines. Founded 1981.

Books
How to get published

The combined wisdom of the writers of the articles in this *Yearbook* provide some of the best practical advice you will need to negotiate your way through the world of publishing. Whether you opt for the traditional route via an agent or the self-publishing model, there are key things it would be useful to consider before you begin.

How can you give yourself the best chance of success whichever route you take?

1. Know your market
• Is there a readership for your book? Explore the intended market so you are sure that your publishing idea is of potential interest to an agent, publisher or reader.
• Know your competition and keep up to date with the latest publishing trends: look in bookshops, at ebook stores, at online book sites, take an interest in publishing stories in the media and, above all, *read*.

2. Agent, publisher or self-publishing?
• First decide if you want to try and get signed by a literary agent and be published by an established publisher. Self-publishing in print and digital can be a viable alternative to the traditional approach.
• If you opt for the agent/publisher route, note that many publishers, particularly of fiction, will only consider material submitted through a literary agent. See *What a debut novelist should expect from an agent* on page 395 and *Advice from an 'accidental' agent* on page 407
• For information about self-publishing, consult the Self-publishing and indie authors section of the *Yearbook* starting on page 605.

3. Choose the right publisher, agent or self-publishing provider
• Study the entries in this *Yearbook*, examine publishers' lists and their websites, and look in the relevant sections in libraries and bookshops for the names of publishers which might be interested in your material.
• Consult the *Children's Writers' & Artists' Yearbook 2024* (Bloomsbury 2023) for in-depth coverage of writing and publishing for the children's and young adult markets.
• Familiarise yourself with the diagram on the next page that outlines the different stages that make up the publishing process.
• Authors should not pay publishers for the publication of their work. There are many companies that can help you self-publish your book but you will need to make sure you know what it is the company will actually do and agree any fees in advance.
• Crowdfunding is becoming a viable option for some (see pages 114 and 191).

4. Prepare your material well
• Presentation is important. If your material is submitted in the most appropriate electronic format an agent or publisher will be more inclined to give it attention.

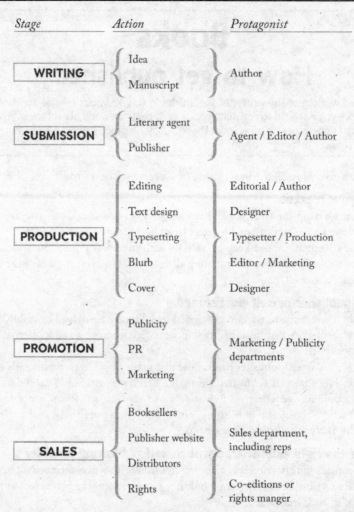

Stage	Action	Protagonist
WRITING	Idea / Manuscript	Author
SUBMISSION	Literary agent / Publisher	Agent / Editor / Author
PRODUCTION	Editing	Editorial / Author
	Text design	Designer
	Typesetting	Typesetter / Production
	Blurb	Editor / Marketing
	Cover	Designer
PROMOTION	Publicity / PR / Marketing	Marketing / Publicity departments
SALES	Booksellers	Sales department, including reps
	Publisher website	
	Distributors	
	Rights	Co-editions or rights manger

Typical stages in the publishing process

• It is understandable that writers, in their eagerness to get their work published, will send their manuscript out in a raw state. Do not send your manuscript to a literary agent or publisher and do not self-publish your script until it is *ready* to be seen. Wait until you are confident that your work is as good as it can be. Have as your mantra: edit, review, revise and then edit again.

5. Approach a publisher or literary agent in the way they prefer

• Submit your work to the right person within the publishing company or literary agency. Look at the listings in this *Yearbook* for more details. See listings starting on page 124 and page 422. Most agents will expect to see a synopsis and up to three sample chapters or the complete manuscript. Most publishers' and literary agents' websites give guidance on how to submit material.

• Always keep a copy of your manuscript. Whilst reasonable care will be taken of material in the possession of a publisher or agent, responsibility cannot be accepted if material is lost or damaged.

6. Write a convincing cover letter or email

• It will be your first contact with an agent or publisher and needs to make them take notice of your book for the right reasons.

• What is the USP (unique selling point) of the material you are submitting? You may have an original authorial 'voice', or you may have come up with an amazingly brilliant idea for a series. If, after checking out the marketplace, you think you have something truly original to offer, be confident in what you have written and be convincing when you offer it around.

7. Network

• Talk to others who write in the same genre or share a similar readership. You can meet them at literature festivals, conferences and book or writers' groups. Consider doing a course – see *Writers' retreats and creative writing courses* on page 683.

• Go to a festival and be inspired. There are numerous literature festivals held throughout the year at which authors appear (see *Festival fun* on page 491).

• Join one of the numerous online communities, book review and manuscript share sites; see *Book sites, blogs and podcasts* on page 696.

8. Don't give up!

• Be prepared to wait for a decision on your work. Editors and agents are very busy people so be patient when waiting for a response. Don't pester them too soon.

• Publishing is big business and it is more competitive than ever. Even after an editor has read your work, there are many other people involved before a manuscript is acquired for publication. People from the sales, marketing, publicity, rights and other departments all have to be convinced that the book is right for their list and will sell.

• The harsh reality of submitting a manuscript to a publisher or literary agent is that you have to be prepared for rejection. But many successful authors have received such rejections at some time so you are in good company.

• Have patience and persevere. If the conventional route doesn't produce the results you were hoping for, consider the self-publishing route as a viable alternative.

   Good luck!

Books

The publishing year: news, views and trends

Tom Tivnan casts his eye back over the last publishing year, which saw healthy sales and continuing boom in comics and graphic novel sales as well as LGBTQ+ titles, boosted by the TikTok phenomenon, but now faces worrying inflationary costs and supply chain challenges, negatively affecting consumer confidence. He looks at the industry's responses, plus the vexed issue of costly lawsuits being brought against publishers and authors.

Question: the British book trade has come out of the first restrictions-free year since the pandemic in fine fettle, setting a near-record with domestic sales of £1.8bn as bookshops (particularly independents) were largely firing on all cylinders. How should you feel about the months ahead? A) optimistic and buoyant; B) pessimistic and full of soul-crushing angst?

If you answered 'A' you are eminently sensible but probably don't work in books; most people in the industry are decidedly in the 'B' camp, for the trade is ever Eeyore-ish. My magazine, *The Bookseller*, has covered the industry since 1858 and much of our archives are a litany of doom and gloom from publishers, retailers and agents, often running counter to the evidence at hand … which continues to this day. Take a piece we ran at the tail end of 2022 on bigwigs' thoughts about the previous 12 months, with predictions for the coming year: Joanna Prior, the new boss of Pan Macmillan, called 2022 'unsettling and convulsive' (Pan Mac's 2022 was its third-best return in the company's 180 years of trading); Bloomsbury chief executive Nigel Newton highlighted the current climate's 'deep economic challenges' (on the very day I am writing this Bloomsbury has released a trading update saying it will shatter its record for turnover and profit); Bonnier head honcho Perminder Mann noted the 'tough landscape' (in 2022, Bonnier had its best-ever year for both home market and export sales).

To be fair, this time around the glass-half-empty view might be wise. There are huge difficulties that threaten to hit the trade hard, many stemming from out-of-their-hands geopolitical issues: the energy crisis, the ongoing effects of Brexit, the ripples from the Ukraine war, the cost-of-living crisis, and on and on. Ultimately, costs are rising while consumer confidence is plummeting and you don't need a Harvard MBA to glean that this is not ideal. The challenges are perhaps most acute in the ongoing supply chain crisis, as the outlay for freight, shipping, energy, print and paper is spiking. For example, sending a shipping container from China (where many UK books, particularly illustrated and children's titles, are still printed) to Britain is at this writing is about treble the pre-pandemic cost. This may be fine if your company produces small, high-priced products such as smartphones, but not so great if you trade in relatively big, bulky and low-cost books.

You may have already felt the pinch at the tills. The average recommended retail price of fiction titles for the first quarter of 2023 was £9.97; in the same period of the year before the pandemic it was £9.27. Meanwhile, fiction's average selling price – what book buyers actually pay after discounting – rose 73p to £7.61. Outrageous, you might say. But that is an 11% jump for books when the UK's inflation rate has risen 17% in the last three years. Therefore, books remain – to use a publishing buzz phrase – 'a good-value proposition', i.e. a relatively cheap form of entertainment. The real concern is what happens if a recession bites and consumers have to ditch most forms of entertainment. Will they choose to continue to buy books or to keep the Disney+ subscription?

Less is more?

One of the consequences of rising costs will not be welcome to new or emerging writers hungry for a book deal: publishers are releasing fewer titles. This is true on a macro scale, as in 2022 there were a little over 158,000 new books published in the UK (technically, that's the number of new ISBNs registered), which represents a 15-year low. This includes self-published and academic titles which balloon the figures (scholarly monographs alone account for about 60% of all books published in a given year), but the reduction is true almost across the board for general publishers, too. And this does not look like some cost-of-living crisis/pandemic-era blip, as the mantra now is 'publish fewer but better'.

The less-is-more formula seems to work for conglomerates and independents alike. Simon & Schuster had by far its best-ever year through industry sales monitor Nielsen BookScan, shifting £52.4m and beating its previous record by a whopping 21%. Yet it released its fewest new titles over a calendar year in a decade. Indie stalwart Canongate cut back on new books to among its lowest level this century, yet posted record revenues and profits. Yes, it helped that S&S is the main publisher for a number of TikTok-boosted superstars such as Colleen Hoover (the UK's bestselling author in 2022 not named Julia Donaldson), Taylor Jenkins Reid and Elena Armas; and that Canongate has Matt Haig (fun fact: Britain's top-selling author not published by a conglomerate) and Ruth Ozeki, whose *The Book of Form and Emptiness* (2021) won the 2022 Women's Prize for Fiction. But I am in no way cherry-picking – reining back and more careful 'curation' of lists is the order of the day. This might benefit many writers, as it may mean more marketing and publicity welly for *all*, rather than just the concentration on the big brands. It could also mean that publishers become more invested in the long-term prospects of authors, rather than dumping them if the first or second books don't quite take off. That point of entry, though, your first book deal, may now be a little bit harder to secure.

La-La Land comes to London

In agenting, the past year saw rather more than the usual crop rotation of people moves and smaller firms getting hoovered up by larger players. The shake-the-foundations deal was the UK's second-biggest agency, Curtis Brown, being bought by Hollywood power-house United Talent Agency in summer 2022. News that the UK's most prominent agency (United Agents is larger than Curtis Brown by revenue but its model is more behind-the-scenes) was on the block had long been a hot rumour, but it was still eyebrow-raising when the sale came to pass. UTA's bitter Tinsel Town rival, Creative Artists Agency (CAA), had been tipped as the Curtis Brown suitor; instead, CAA decided to step up its own British footprint by going on a hiring spree for its London office (heretofore a small concern, with few UK-originated deals). This included poaching one of Curtis Brown's stars, Karolina Sutton, the 2020 Agent of the Year at the British Book Awards. Meanwhile, the film studio Lionsgate – which holds a special place in my heart for bringing out the John Wick films – took a minority share in Soho-based 42MP whose authors include Hanna Jameson, S.K. Tremayne and Lucy Jago.

So, what do the movers and shakers of the Dream Factory want with literary London? At the time of the Curtis Brown buy, UTA's David Kramer said the move 'is about the vanishing borders of the global entertainment business and our united determination to ensure artists and creators remain at the heart of the opportunities ahead'. Sorry … you may not speak press release guff-ese, so I'll translate: 'We want heaps of intellectual property (IP) to extend and adapt into as many formats as possible'.

Book adaptations are nothing new, of course, but unquestionably the streaming-services-led boom of recent years is what makes a British literary agency all the more attractive to Hollywood. There was a point even a couple years ago, as streamers seemed to be acquiring every book under the sun, when many in publishing wondered how long it would be until the bubble burst. It hasn't happened yet, though agents report the fever pitch has reduced to somewhat more 'considered' commissioning (during the pandemic the competition for IP was so fierce, Netflix *et al* would even bid on early manuscript drafts). But arguably there has been no better time in history for authors to get their work adapted for the screen. This ranges from unknowns – as Alice Oseman was when her *Heartstopper* graphic novels series was optioned – to massive concerns, such as the Roald Dahl Story Company which was acquired by Netflix in a deal reportedly worth over £500m.

Perfect comic timing

Oseman is a good author to explore, as she is at the confluence of a few trends. The adaptation of her gay coming-of-age romance *Heartstopper* titles was one of the Netflix's biggest hits of 2022, and the sensitive treatment of the subject matter is one of the best examples of book-to-screen in recent years. But *Heartstopper* is also IP extension par excellence: it began life as a Tumblr webcomic and has also been spun out into audio, games, stationery, T-shirts, key chains and almost every other bit of merch you can think of. The only thing missing seems to be theme-park rides.

The *Heartstopper* series was also in the fore of the comics boom of the last few years. Graphic novel sales in the UK had their biggest year ever in 2022, with over £70m shifted across adult and children's categories, while Alice Oseman posted the all-time best 12 months of any graphic novelist, selling £6.6m (she also shifted an additional £3.3m in non-graphic Young Adult books). *Heartstopper Volume One* (Hachette Children's Group 2019) is now the bestselling graphic novel since records began, with Alan Moore and Dave Gibbons' classic *Watchmen* (DC Comics 1987) in second place. But it is not just Oseman, as a number of comics author/illustrators have broken through, including Jamie Smart and his *Bunny vs Monkey* series (David Fickling Books). Smart had been publishing comics and picture books since the start of the millennium, but he sold more in 2022 (£1.9m) than he did in the previous 20 years combined.

But manga was the main driver of the comics surge, accounting for a little over £1 in every £2 spent on a graphic novel in 2022. This has made household names (for certain members, most likely the teenage ones, of your household) of the likes of Hajime Isayama, Kohei Horikoshi and Junji Ito. Interestingly, the manga model runs counter to other fiction genres, with no huge bestsellers, relying almost completely on backlist, author loyalty and booksellers willing to stock all 32 volumes of Horikoshi's *My Hero Academia* (Viz). The upshot of the manga and general graphic novel craze is that it has probably never been a better time for comics creators, as publishers are greedily searching for 'the next Oseman'.

Tokking about a revolution

The hunt for the next Oseman does not just refer to graphic novels, but also to titles with LGBTQ+ themes. Books with queer subject matter have obviously been published since time immemorial. The shift now is that LGBTQ+ is a badge (dare I say 'brand'?) to be celebrated, that the publishing is out and proud. One of the main news threads of *The Bookseller* is covering the industry's hot book deals; at this writing, running a search on our rights database for the last 12 months including the terms 'LGBTQ', 'gay', 'lesbian' or 'queer' brings up 72 news stories. Doing that same search for 2019 comes up with just seven results. This is not publishers being particularly brave or 'woke' (though this commissioning accords with the 'diversity and inclusion' push of recent years), but that these titles can sell shedloads. Oseman, Casey McQuiston, Samantha Shannon, Madeline Miller and Adam Silvera are among the many authors with monster LGBTQ+-themed hits over the last couple of years.

A commonality of the writers in the above sentence is that they are beloved by TikTok. I wrote about the 'BookTok' phenomenon in the *Writers' & Artists' Yearbook 2023* but it bears reiterating, as it has again been one of the biggest driving forces for book sales in the past 12 months. TikTok's main effect is that of making a few genres mainstream that have often been sniffed at: graphic novels, romance, science fiction and fantasy. And it has helped create some new categories, including 'romantasy' – the blend of romance and fantasy – led by Sarah J. Maas' *A Court of Thorns and Roses* (Bloomsbury 2015) series. Being embraced by BookTokkers can be transformational for an author. Take Colleen Hoover: she has long been published in the UK and her native USA, selling well in America but never troubling the bestseller lists in Blighty. In 2019, the year prior to her being taken to TikTok's bosom, Hoover's titles sold £32,000 worth in the UK; in 2022 it was £15.9m, almost all of which came from books originally released before 2019.

The SLAPPs heard round the world

If you said 'slap' to most people recently, their minds would undoubtedly drift to the Will Smith and Chris Rock bust-up at the 2022 Oscars and the millions of memes and thousands of hot takes it spawned. Say that word to many a publisher or author, however, and they may immediately think of their legal teams' billable hours, for 'SLAPPs' (Strategic Lawsuits against Public Participation) have become a huge talking point and a troubling industry issue. SLAPPs, or 'lawfare' as they are also known, are broadly often spurious defamation and libel suits brought against publishers and authors by wealthy individuals – most often in the investigative non-fiction and history space – in order to quash publication, seek monetary damages or both. It is quite simply censorship through the courts, helped by the British claimant-friendly system which has long made the UK a destination for 'libel tourists'. The issue came to a head in 2022 when HarperCollins division William Collins successfully fought off a number of suits from Russian oligarchs and corporations against two books, Tom Burgis' *Kleptopia* (William Collins 2020) and Catherine Belton's *Putin's People* (William Collins 2021).

A triumph for free speech, then? Well, not a full triumph and certainly not 'free': William Collins publishing director Arabella Pike revealed it cost £1.5m just to get to the preliminary hearings. Had it lost, the publisher would have been £10m in the hole. And Pike has spoken of the ongoing 'fear factor' that is preventing good investigative work getting out. William Collins has had difficulty selling translation rights of Burgis and Belton's books, as publishers across the globe were leery of lawsuits in their own countries. Plus, there are only a handful of British publishers that have the resources of HarperCollins to wage lengthy legal battles of this type, so many houses are passing on such books in the first place. A silver lining: the immediate consequence of the Burgis and Belton cases was that some limited anti-SLAPPs measures have been put in place in England and Wales, though trade bodies like the Publishers Association and Society of Authors are lobbying government for deeper reforms.

I end on this because free speech is becoming a somewhat partisan issue in our culture-war climate. People across the political spectrum are often free-speech purists until they come up against something that counters their own views. And publishing is often accused of being too woke, at least by right-leaning news outlets. Although I disagree, I can appreciate where that view comes from. But it is worth noting that authors and the book industry are often the ones putting their necks on the line to further free speech … and that should be celebrated.

Tom Tivnan is Managing Editor of *The Bookseller*. Tom was a freelance writer and his work has appeared in the *Glasgow Herald*, the *Independent*, the *Daily Telegraph* and the *Times Literary Supplement*. Before joining *The Bookseller* in 2007 he worked as a bookseller for Blackwell's in the UK and for Barnes & Noble in the USA. He wrote the text for *Tattoed by the Family Business* (Pavilion 2010) and his debut novel is *The Esquimaux* (Silvertail 2017). Follow him on Twitter @tomtivnan.

The mathematics of publishing

Scott Pack reveals the numbers underlying the publishing business and spells out the important, surprising and sobering figures – for publisher and author alike – to be considered when publishing a book, even a bestseller.

When you think about the world of writing and publishing you probably picture an industry built upon words. And rightly so. The book world would be nothing without the written word. But numbers play a crucial part too, and some of the numbers that crunch away behind the scenes of publishing may surprise you.

How many copies does a book need to sell to become a bestseller?

100,000? 50,000? 10,000? Each week the *Sunday Times* publishes four separate book charts: top tens in Hardback Fiction, Hardback Non-fiction, Paperback Fiction and Paperback Non-fiction. For a book to be able to feature the three magic words '*Sunday Times* Bestseller' on the cover, it needs to have appeared in one of these charts for at least one week.

To sit at the top of these charts, especially Paperback Fiction, you generally need to sell thousands of copies. But pick a quiet time of year, perhaps February or March, and you could sneak in at number 10 in the Hardback Non-Fiction chart by selling around 500 copies, a somewhat less daunting figure.

Let's put that in perspective. There are close to 5,000 book outlets in the UK. A book could sell one copy in just 10% of these locations in any given week and hit the bestseller chart. 90% of shops wouldn't need to have sold any at all, and you'd still have a bestseller on your hands – assuming your book is on a non-fiction subject and is published in hardback, of course.

Things are very different at the top of the charts. The bestselling paperback novel in the UK would typically have to sell well into five figures, although that could be anywhere between 10,000 and 90,000 depending on the time of year and what books are out that week.

And things get more interesting when you start to delve into the chart data a bit more. The *Sunday Times* top tens are taken from a much larger sales report generated by Nielsen Bookscan. They create a Top 5,000 chart each week that is distributed widely within the book trade, with retailers and publishers poring over the figures in some detail.

Let's say the bestselling book in the country sold 25,000 copies in a week. That's a lot of books, but not many titles can deliver that level of sales. In the same week it is likely that the tenth bestselling book sold around 7,000 copies – still a lot, but quite a drop-off. The book at number 100 in the charts will have sold 1,500 or so. The book at 500 may actually have sold 500 copies, and you can often get into the bottom regions of the Top 5,000 by selling 50 or so copies in a week.

So how does this pan out across an entire year? In a very good year, the bestselling book in the UK can sell close to a million copies, but it would more often be about half that number. The tenth bestseller may have sold half that again. The book at number 500 might have sold around 50,000, and you could have the 5,000th bestselling book of the year by selling 5,000 copies – or just one copy in every bookshop in the land across a year.

It is important to stress that with the many tens of thousands of books published every year, and the hundreds of thousands already in circulation, the vast majority of books never even get close to the top 5,000 at all.

How much does it cost to publish a book?

These sales figures are all well and good, and may prove fascinating, but you cannot sell a single book until it is printed and distributed to shops, and that can prove to be a costly exercise.

Different types of books have different budgets – a big, illustrated, coffee-table book will usually cost several times more to produce than a fairly straightforward paperback – but for this example we are going to look at the costs for a standard novel with no fancy design elements or illustrations.

To get the manuscript ready for publication, with a developmental edit, copy edit, typesetting and proofread, you are rarely going to have much change from £4,000. A designer might charge around £750 to create a cover. Printing costs vary depending on the size of the print run, but 75p per copy is not untypical. So, to produce and print 3,000 copies of a paperback novel will cost a publisher in the region of £6,700. Of course, the major publishing houses manage a lot of these services in-house, and that can save costs, but most medium- and small-sized publishers will be paying freelancers to do much of this work.

And that £6,700 is without spending any money on warehousing, distribution, sales, marketing or publicity, the combined costs of which could easily bring the total outlay to more than £10,000.

Example P&L

Sales
Book RRP
£7.99

Book sales
3,000

Retailer discount
55%
NET BOOK SALES £10,787

Production costs
Editorial
£2,500

Typesetting
£750

Cover design
£750

Printing costs
Print costs
£2,700

Sales and marketing costs
Sales and distribution
£2,500

Marketing and publicity
£1,500
TOTAL COSTS £10,700

Other deductions
Returns @ 20%
£2,157

Royalties
@ 7.5% £1,800
Total costs + deductions £14,657

TOTAL PROFIT: -£3,870

How much money does a publisher make from a book?

So, a publisher has spent £10,000 to produce, sell, distribute and promote 3,000 copies of a new novel. Let's assume all 3,000 copies sell to bookshops, a rare feat but one that makes our maths a little easier, and that it has an RRP (recommended retail price) of £7.99.

Book retailers receive discount from publishers which can be anywhere from 30% to 70%, depending on the size of the retailer, how many copies they are ordering and whether or not the book goes into a big promotion – but let's use 55% as an average. That means that for every copy sold to bookshops the publisher receives just over £3.59. Across 3,000 copies that comes to £10,787 of revenue.

Cast your eye back a few paragraphs and you'll be reminded that it cost just over £10,000 to produce these books in the first place, so even by selling the whole of the first print run, the publisher is only just breaking even. But wait! We forgot returns. In the UK, most books are sold to retailers on a sale-or-return basis, meaning shops can return unsold stock and typically 15-20% of all books sold to retailers are sent back. So that £10,787 revenue mentioned above may end up being more like £8,630 once the returns are accounted for, and that means the publisher makes a loss, even after selling 3,000 books.

So how do publishers make any money from their books? Well, the truth is that many do not. They are often reliant on one or two books selling in excess of 10,000 copies, and ideally lots more than that, in order to generate the income needed to fund the other books on the list that sell below 3,000. Over time, they can build up a backlist of older titles that tick over, generating ongoing revenue. And ebooks can help too; they are cheaper to sell, as there are no warehouse costs and no returns, and many a book these days moves into profit on the back of healthy digital sales.

And how much money can an author make?

You probably know the score when it comes to royalties: for every copy of a book that sells, the author receives a percentage of the revenue. There are many variations on the basic deal but, if we continue with our example of a paperback novel, typically an author will receive 7.5% of the RRP for each copy that sells. On our £7.99 paperback that would be just under 60p – but I am feeling generous so will round it up.

Again, sticking with our example, if we sell 3,000 copies, the author will have made just 154under £1,800 in royalties. Hardly a life-changing amount, but not to be sniffed at either.

But let's not focus on such tiny numbers. Instead, let's be ambitious and bold and go back to the bestsellers that we discussed earlier. Remember that bestselling book that sold 25,000 copies in a week, taking it to the top of the charts? Assuming it was a £7.99 paperback, that book will have earned its author £15,000 in just one week. The book at number 10, selling 7,000, will have generated £4,200. And even the number 500 book will have made £300, which isn't bad for one week's work. Although don't forget that the agent will take 15% of that!

What does this all add up to?

It is important that authors understand the numbers behind the publishing world. If a book becomes a bestseller, then it is possible for both author and publisher to make a lot of money, and even a moderate seller can, over time, generate some decent income. However, the majority of books published will only make a small amount of money for their authors.

For most of us, this is not a get-rich-quick industry. Does that matter? Only you can answer that, but if you have decided to write a book in order to make your fortune, you are probably going to be disappointed. If, however, you are writing a book because you want to share your story, and you value a connection with readers above all else, then great fortune may await – it just may not be a financial one.

Scott Pack is a writer, editor and publisher. He was formerly head of buying for Waterstones and spent many years at HarperCollins. These days he works as a freelance editor and helps authors get their submission packages ready for agents and publishers. He also gives workshops and classes on writing and publishing and is one of the specialist subject question setters for the BBC quiz show *Mastermind*. He is the author of *Tips From a Publisher: A Guide to Writing, Editing, Submitting and Publishing Your Book* (Eye Books 2020). He can be contacted at helloscott@hey.com.

Books

Books

Getting books to market: how books are sold

David Wightman, of Global Book Sales, describes the various parts, people and processes, skills and systems within the world of book sales that interlink to bring a book from publisher to customer, and what makes this a fascinating, challenging and satisfying area of work.

I've always been excited about sales and wanted to set up a company where the focus is on maximising the sales of every book that we represent. My company, Global Book Sales, has the distribution network in place to be able to supply books to any customer in the world, and we have skilled and passionate sales teams persuading booksellers that they should stock our publishers' books.

Who sells to whom, how and where?

Selling a book globally is a complicated process, but most publishers have excellent systems in place to ensure they maximise the sales of each book in every country. The process starts

Definitions

• Distribution

All publishers of print books have a distribution facility. This is a **warehouse** where the publisher stores the books they have published. From this warehouse, the books are sent out to customers. The distributor is also responsible for invoicing the customer for their book order and collecting the money. An example of a large book distributor in the UK is Macmillan Distribution (MDL). They distribute their own books published by Macmillan imprints, as well as distributing for third parties such as Bloomsbury and many other publishers.

• Key accounts

These are the main customers for books, including chain booksellers, wholesalers, online retailers and supermarkets. UK examples of key accounts are WHSmith, Waterstones, Blackwell, Gardners, Amazon and Tesco. Key accounts generally expect to buy new books six to nine months prior to publication.

• Sales rep/representative

A sales representative is a member of the publisher's sales team. They visit independent bookshops and other accounts, such as museums and galleries, to sell new titles. Reps tend to sell a book three to five months prior to publication. In most cases, they sell a large selection of different new titles across a range of genres. They sell to customers using either AIs (advance information sheets), printed catalogues, or glossy brochures known as *blads*.

• Stock control/inventory management

Bookshops want to have stock of a selection of books that they think they can sell during a given time period, and many bookshops have automated systems that generate re-orders when a book is sold. Distributors and wholesalers have developed sophisticated warehouse and delivery systems that enable them to process orders and get books out to shops very quickly; this reduces the need for a bookshop to hold significant levels of stock of any one title.

• Wholesaler

A wholesaler is similar to a distributor but it handles books from lots of different publishers. Gardners is the biggest wholesaler in the UK and they claim to have over 500,000 different titles in stock at any one time. The benefit of a wholesaler is that any bookshop or retailer that wants to sell books can easily source all the titles it needs from one place, rather than having to contact a variety of different distributors. This obviously cuts out a lot of administration and is more efficient for the customer.

with setting up *metadata* for a new title; this includes information such as ISBN, title, author, format, price, publication date, number of pages, etc. This metadata is then added to databases owned by bibliographic agencies, such as Nielsen in the UK, who are then responsible for disseminating that information to customers globally.

Once the metadata is available, the publisher's sales teams kick into action. Key account managers and sales representatives (**Definitions** box on page 110) will pre-sell new titles to their customers three to nine months prior to publication. This is a long *sell-in* period, but during that time the distributor will be recording any orders that come in for each book. These orders are known in the UK as *dues* and in the USA as *backorders*. The number of dues a new title has will help to determine how many copies the publisher will print in the initial run.

The aim of the publisher's sales team is to make sure the book is available for the consumer to buy on the date the book is published. This may mean that there are copies in stock at an independent bookshop or a branch of Waterstones, or that it is available to order easily through an online bookseller. When the book is published (or in the run-up to publication) then a publisher's publicity team and the author take over, to alert the consumer that the book is available to buy and persuade them that it's worth reading.

Day-to-day activity of a sales manager
Working with sales partners, distributors and agents

Global Book Sales has partnerships in place for book distribution with Macmillan Distribution (MDL) in the UK and Ingram Publishers Services LLC in the USA. Stock of our publishers' books are stored in both locations and this gives us the capability of supplying any customer quickly and cost-efficiently with any book they want to order, wherever they are located across the world.

We also have a network of sales agents across the world that sells new titles to customers in different countries. Each territory may have a slightly different way of working but the principles of the 'sell in' remain the same. To successfully sell a book in advance, the sales agent or representative needs accurate metadata, strong visual sales material, good information on what the book is about and who its audience is, and finally to know why this book stands out above the many thousands of other books that will publish at the same time.

The opportunities

The traditional high-street book trade is still important for book sales, but it has declined in recent years, with some independent bookshops closing down and smaller bookshop chains either closing or being swallowed up by larger rivals. However, there is now a huge range of online booksellers, museums, galleries, gift shops, clothes retailers, music shops and toy shops that all want to sell books as part of their range. Publishers are becoming very strategic in what they publish, and they are increasingly expanding into non-book items such as games and toys to increase their overall customer base.

These opportunities to sell outside of the traditional bookshops are also evident in a number of export markets. Concept stores in Scandinavia are now selling many books and this is also happening in China, Hong Kong, Singapore, Korea and Taiwan where demand for quality books, particularly in areas such as art, photography and design, are very strong. Marketing and publicising new books using social media is now both easy and relatively

Books

cheap to do. Authors who have a large number of followers on Twitter can alert potential readers that their book is now available to buy. This can have a huge impact on book sales.

The challenges

One of the biggest challenges publishers face at the moment is shipping books between countries quickly and cost-efficiently. The pandemic has significantly reduced the number of commercial flights, and this has driven up the price of moving books by air, almost to the point that it's not profitable to do so anymore. Shipping times for sea-freight have also increased. The UK leaving the European Union has added to the cost of sending books to Europe and the price of paper is also increasing, which puts further pressure on publisher's margins.

Finances, margins, discounting and terms

In the UK, books are mostly sold at a trade discount off the RRP (recommended retail price). Each publisher will set its own discount in agreement with their customers. The range of trade discounts can vary significantly, from around 25% to 60%, depending on the type of book. Academic and education books tend to be sold at lower discounts than more consumer, mass-market titles. The average discount for more general titles would be from 45% to 50%.

Sale-or-return, and how it works

In the UK, books are sold on a sale-or-return basis. This means that any trade customer (not individuals) can buy books from a publisher and return them if they don't sell them. This means that the risk of publishing and paying to print a book rests with the publisher. For export markets, books are still sold on a sale-or-return basis but, in practice, returns are low from export customers. These customers tend to buy in a less speculative way because they are also responsible for paying the cost of shipping these books from the UK, plus any additional import taxes and duties. Publishers will often have return allowances for export customers but this allowance is rarely fully used.

In the UK, the book and publishing industry have agreed some rules which means that a customer cannot return a book within three months of buying it and not after 15 months. The books should also be returned in a saleable condition. These restrictions don't apply in other countries, in particular the USA, where there are no such restrictions.

EPOS

EPOS (electronic point of sale) is system that allows bookshops to keep track of the books they sell. It's linked to their tills and will automatically generate a stock replenishment report suggesting to the buyer which books they should re-order.

How do publishers know how well their books are selling?

Publishers can subscribe to Nielsen BookScan (https://online.nielsenbookscan.net) which records sales of books through the tills of a range of UK booksellers. Alternatively, a publisher can check to see on a daily basis how many copies of a book are being sent out by their warehouse. With these sales figures, you do need to factor in any potential returns – whereas the Nielsen figures record firm sales.

Working with marketing

Marketing departments are responsible for providing the sales team with what they need to sell a book to a buyer. They also provide regular updates of any marketing and publicity that may be happening to promote a particular title. This information can then be passed on by the sales team to their individual buyers.

Marketing departments produce *AIs* (advance information sheets) for individual new books; some will produce six-monthly catalogues featuring the publisher's spring and autumn new books, and for lead titles they often provide bound proofs and *blads* (promotional samples). The typical 'lead time' for a book is five to six months; it takes this time for the various sales teams around the world to be briefed about the book, provided with the information to sell the book, and then to contact their customers in order to sell the book to them.

The pleasure of sales

I still get a thrill from seeing a book selling a lot of copies or from discovering a new customer for books. A recent example was when a Korean website that was selling Scandinavian-designed furniture was persuaded to add a range of books with a Scandinavian interest – something that resulted in some significant sales for one of our publishers.

David Wightman is Managing Director of Global Book Sales (www.globalbooksales.co.uk), an independent sales and distribution company that works with publishers to sell their titles across the world. He was previously Group International Sales Director at Bloomsbury Publishing, Sales, Marketing and Rights Director at A&C Black Publishers, and UK Academic Sales Manager at Oxford University Press.

See also...
● *Getting your book stocked in a high-street bookshop,* page 617

Books

Crowdfunding your novel

Alice Jolly discusses why she turned to crowdfunding to publish her memoir and subsequent novels, how the system works, its place as an alternative to mainstream and self-publishing, and the pros and cons of this new publication option.

It is April 2014. I am in a bar in Soho, talking to John Mitchinson, one of the founders of the crowdfunding publisher Unbound. He is interested in publishing a memoir I have written called *Dead Babies and Seaside Towns*. Our conversations about the book itself are straightforward but the wider purpose of our meeting is more problematic. He is thinking – *she is not the ideal person to crowdfund a book*. And I would have to agree with his unspoken assessment.

I'm a country mum, a quiet, academic type, who doesn't attend literary events. I have never used social media. On top of that, mainstream publishers have already told me that, no matter how good my memoir is, there is simply no market for it. Yet, despite these inauspicious omens, John has already decided he wants the book. And I agree to the crowdfunding idea because I am absolutely determined to get my memoir published.

Cut to June 2016 and I'm standing on a platform being awarded the Pen/Ackerley prize for that same memoir. John is in the audience and I catch his eye. Neither of us need to say – *well, that's stuck it to them!* It turns out that my book *did* need to be published … and that crowdfunding was as good a way to publish it as any other.

On the basis of this experience, you might assume that I am something of an expert on crowdfunded publishing and that I would unreservedly recommend it to other writers. But the reality is more complicated. Although I have subsequently crowdfunded another two books with Unbound (both novels), I only really know about what *I* have done – and not much more; and although crowdfunding has been a good choice for me, that does not mean I would suggest every other writer should go down the same road.

The crowdfunding process

So how does a writer decide if crowdfunding might be a good choice for them? First, let me give a quick summary of how it works. The process starts with the writer submitting his or her idea (or book) to a crowdfunder. Unbound are 'curated' crowdfunders and so (like any mainstream gate-keeping publisher) they decide whether or not they want that book. The important difference from a mainstream publisher is that the company is run by three people who are writers themselves. If one of them wants to publish a certain book, then it will happen. This means that you won't be told: *'The editors loved your book but unfortunately the Sales and Marketing team just couldn't …'*

If Unbound agree to work with you, then they help you to put together a page on their website which will include a biography and an extract from your book. A short film will also be made which explains the book. This web page then becomes the tool which you will use to bring in pledges or – to put it more simply – to pre-sell copies of the book. This idea is far from new. It is actually the same as 'publishing by subscription', which was how many books were published in the 19th century.

If you chose Unbound's digital option, then you might need to raise £3,000 or £4,000. If you are going to be producing a hard-copy book, then the cost rises to £10,000 or £12,000, depending on length, illustrations, etc. The budget is something you discuss with Unbound and it can be adjusted. Once all of this has been agreed, then you have to bring in the pledges. Unbound have a well-developed social media presence and a huge mailing list, so that helps spread the word but, fundamentally, it is down to you, as the writer, to raise that money. That process is tough – very tough. You need thick skin, persistence and confidence in what you are doing. You will suffer many dark moments – but you will also regularly be amazed by the random generosity of people you have never even met.

Writers have a hundred different crowdfunding strategies. Some authors are highly professional and imaginative; others, like me, shamble through the whole thing, relying on the support of family and friends, slowly and painfully spreading the word by doing readings, and events and workshops.

Once the money is raised, Unbound operate in just the same way as any other publisher. They do the editing, proofreading, cover design, publicity and distribution. When the book is published, the writer does not get royalties as such but they receive a profit share of 50% (obviously much higher than the usual 10% royalty). Unbound have a distribution agreement with independent sales force PGUK.

From my own experience, I know that Unbound can publicise and distribute a book widely. But, of course, the experience of one writer may be wildly different from that of another. How often have you actually heard a writer say how pleased they were by the publicity for their new book? More or less never, I would bet. As a breed, we tend to be naturally ungrateful and disappointed, even when we don't really have a reason to be so. All the same, we know that it is not the case that big publisher equals big publicity and small publisher equals small publicity. It all depends on the type of book, the timing, the status of the author, and the personnel in the publicity department. A junior and inexperienced book publicist in a small publishing house can sometimes achieve great things if they have a passion for a particular title.

Comparisons with self-publishing

Of course, I am regularly asked – why don't you self-publish? I know that the potential financial gains are much greater. Those who do self-publish also tell me that the Unbound £10,000 budget is too high. But I've looked into it (comparing the cost with quality self-publishing) and I rather doubt that. If you want a beautiful book then the process is long, slow and expensive. Book production values are a matter of personal choice but, as ever, if you want quality you have to pay for it. Personally I don't necessarily expect my books to sell thousands of copies but I would be desperately disappointed if they looked shoddy.

Although I know that self-publishing has worked well for some genre writers, there is little evidence that it works for more literary books. There is also the intractable question of time. I don't have IT or marketing skills and I don't particularly want to acquire them. I struggle to find time for my writing – there is no chance that I'd manage to be a publisher as well. At a more fundamental level, I also want to be part of a collaborative process. Writing is a horribly lonely business. I need some people to celebrate with when it goes well, and to down a consoling glass with when it does not. Mainstream publishers, in general, seem to take a 'divide and rule' attitude to writers (. . . *For God's sake don't get more than two of them in a room together or they'll whinge incessantly*). Unbound, by contrast, have created an online forum for their authors. There are some challenging discussions, but there is also a huge amount of camaraderie, consolation and support, plus many examples of writers clubbing together to promote each other's books and organise readings and events.

A developing role for crowdfunding

I've described my experience with Unbound, but what other crowdfunding options are available? There are many online organisations who offer crowdfunding to novelists, although none (as far as I know) are 'curated' crowdfunders. Kickstarter is a platform which anyone can use to raise money, but that still leaves the writer with all the book production work. Might this approach be the worst of both worlds? I'm not qualified to judge. But do remember – publishing is not the same as printing.

So far Unbound have done well – their books have won major prizes, reached the bestseller lists and, perhaps most importantly, fuelled important debate, meaning that there are real benefits to being published by them. For me personally, being published by Unbound has continued to be a great success, with my novel *Mary Ann Sate, Imbecile* being runner up for the Rathbones Folio Prize 2019 plus being longlisted for the Ondaatje Prize and becoming a Walter Scott recommended novel for 2019.

But what are the limits of this approach? Well, sadly, I don't think it can do much to improve diversity in publishing. It does return more money to the author than the mainstream model. And that's important given that the median earnings for a professional writer is approximately £10,500 (according to ALCS figures from 2017), far below the £17,900 which the Joseph Rowntree Foundation suggests is needed for a single person to reach the minimum income standard.

In addition, Unbound bravely publish anthologies which look at issues of social justice (notably *Common People: An Anthology of Working Class Writers*, edited by Kit de Waal, 2019, *The Good Immigrant*, edited by Nikesh Shukla, 2016 and *Trans Britain*, edited by Christine Burns, 2018). However, the crowdfunding model itself will tend to favour those who already have a name, a reputation, a network.

Although a 2017 Arts Council report (*Literature in the 21st Century: Understanding Models of Support for Literary Fiction*) suggests that crowdfunding may be able to play a role in addressing the difficulties in publishing literary fiction, despite my own successes, I remain less than certain how much can be achieved. But the reality is that, if a book is going to be hard to sell, it will usually to be hard to crowdfund as well.

Unbound have made it possible for some of those challenging, difficult, eccentric books to be published which would otherwise languish in a box under a writer's bed. That matters to me. I passionately believe in a world where all the voices are heard, a world we need now more than ever. I've always preferred the 'out-crowd' to the in-crowd.

Novelist and playwright **Alice Jolly's** memoir *Dead Babies and Seaside Towns* (Unbound 2015) won the 2015 Pen/Ackerley Prize. Her short story *Ray the Rottweiler* won the V.S. Pritchett Memorial Prize in 2014. Her novel *Mary Ann Sate, Imbecile* (Unbound 2018) was runner-up for the Rathbones Folio Prize, was longlisted for the Ondaatje Prize and was a Walter Scott Prize recommended novel in 2019. Her most recent novel is *Between the Regions of Kindness* (Unbound 2019). Her collection of short stories, *From Far Around They Saw Us Burn*, will be published by Unbound in spring 2023. Alice teaches Creative Writing at Oxford University and Goldsmiths (University of London). Her website is http://alicejolly.com/wp. Follow her on Twitter @JollyAlice.

Managing a successful writing career

Tony Bradman shares the five guiding principles that have helped him successfully sustain the writing career he has always wanted and worked to achieve, stressing the importance of bolstering talent with market knowledge, all-round professionalism and some much-needed resilience.

I was probably about 15 when I decided I wanted to be a writer. Like most writers, I had become an obsessive bookworm at an early age and, after years of spending all my pocket money on books as well as borrowing them from the local library, I had begun to think it would be marvellous to write some of my own. Imagine having your name on the cover of a book you had written yourself! I couldn't think of anything more amazing, and from that moment on I never seriously considered any other kind of career.

Of course, I had a sneaking feeling it might not be all that easy to get published. But I was convinced I would manage it and that, once I'd written a few books, everything would fall into place. As I explained to my girlfriend at university ('She Who Is Now My Wife'), apparently there were these payments called *royalties*. Each book I published would keep earning money, so that after a while we could just sit back and watch the cash roll in.

I wasn't entirely stupid. I did realise that my writing (which mostly consisted of a few notebooks crammed with unfinished and very mediocre poems) might not be all that attractive to publishers – not yet, anyway. So I applied for jobs in journalism, with the idea that my employer would help me improve my writing and pay me into the bargain – I never doubted that I had talent. The plan seemed to work, too. I was employed by several magazines, and after a while I even began to do a bit of freelancing on the side.

Eventually I found myself working for *Parents*, a magazine about young family life. By then I was a parent myself, and I was surprised the magazine didn't review children's books, even though we were sent lots of review copies. I therefore persuaded the editor to let me write about them, and I started a regular column. Pretty soon I got to know the publicity people at most of the children's book publishers, and I also began to meet editors at book launches and other events. By then I was starting to think that I wanted to write for children myself, so when an editor asked me if I had any ideas for a children's book I seized the opportunity and sent her some rhymes I'd written for my daughters.

Those rhymes became the basis for my first picture book, and the rest, as they say, is history. More commissions followed, and my books sold well in the UK and abroad (this was the mid-1980s, the heyday of 'co-editions' in children's books). The royalties really did flow, and before long I was able to give up my job and become a full-time freelancer. That was over 30 years ago, and I've managed to make a pretty good living as a writer ever since. It turned out not to be quite as easy as I had expected – far from it, in fact. But it can be done, and I offer you here the five principles on which I've based my career.

1. Cultivate your talent

I believe there is such a thing as talent. Some people are just better at certain things; you can see that in any artistic pursuit – writing, music, art, acting. And, to be brutal, if you haven't got talent then you're unlikely ever to achieve a career as a professional in any of those fields. Yes, I know from time to time we all read books, or watch plays or TV shows or films, that appear to have been written by someone with no talent whatsoever. But trust me, it would be very hard to sustain a long-term career without any talent at all.

Books

So let's assume you have talent. The question is, what kind of talent do you have? I could have spent years trying to write poetry for grown-ups and not got anywhere at all. In my mid-20s I began to realise I wasn't ever going to be the next Seamus Heaney or Ted Hughes, but by then I'd also started to get interested in children's books. I wrote verse for my daughters, then picture book texts (which often depend on a poet-like ability to use language creatively). After that I steadily moved up the age range with my children, and discovered I had a talent for writing well-plotted stories that kept readers gripped.

I didn't leave it there though. I thought about what I was doing and tried to build on the things that worked, my aim being simply to get better. Back in the 1980s there weren't anywhere near as many creative writing courses, but there were plenty of books about the art and craft of writing, and I read as many as I could. I listened to my editors too, and tried to learn from them, and from anyone else who might give me insight into what makes good writing. I edited anthologies of short stories, which meant I often had to tell writers exactly why I didn't think their stories worked – and that was invaluable experience.

I believe this approach is the foundation of any writing career. Understanding your talent will help to make you a good writer. But you can always make yourself into a better one.

2. Know the market

This is the section of my piece that will be anathema to the purists, those who believe that writing shouldn't ever be about 'satisfying the needs of the market'. Some people believe that great writers simply write what they need to and that it will find its own way to a readership or an audience. Well, good luck with that if you want to make a living as a writer. Of course, your 1,000-page surrealist fantasy written without using the letter 'e' might well become a runaway bestseller and make you a fortune. But what if it doesn't?

I think it's perfectly possible to combine Art and Commerce as a writer; satisfying the needs of the market doesn't mean 'selling out'. If you want a good example, what about the greatest writer of all time – Shakespeare himself? It's clear from his plays that he wrote very consciously for 'the market' in theatre as it was then. But he also managed to produce the most sublime literary art. Awareness of what the market is interested in can often be very stimulating creatively – it may well give you plenty of ideas on what to write.

So how do you study the market? That's easy and fun. Simply read widely, or watch plays, films and TV shows in the areas you find interesting. Find out as much about them as possible – who's hot in your chosen field, and what's doing well. The more you know, the better. Networking is part of this, especially if you see it as something that will help you learn about the business of being a writer. Go on courses, join writing groups; editors and agents sometimes give talks at these, and they're the people you want to meet. Keep it up after you get published – opportunities will usually arise from the contacts you make. You will also be a better prospect for agents and editors if they feel you know the market.

3. Be professional (part one)

… or to put it another way, 'Don't Be Desperate or Grateful'. Begging for a commission won't get you anywhere and, if you are offered an opportunity, there's no need to be thankful. You should always be professional – and that means thinking of what you're doing as a job, the way you earn your living. It's the person who is commissioning you or buying your work who should be grateful. Your editor almost certainly has a target, a number of books to publish in a year, and you're the means of getting that done. *You* are the solution.

Being professional also means making sure you always keep up a high standard as far as your performance is concerned. You should follow the brief, hit the word count, and deliver a clean manuscript that's as good as you can make it, by the deadline you've been given. If you can't deliver on time for whatever reason (it had better be a good one!), you should let your editor know, and agree a revised delivery date. If you're asked to do edits or revisions (and they're an essential part of being a writer), you should take it as positive criticism that aims to help make your writing better. If you disagree, say so – but be courteous.

The purpose is to present yourself as someone who is good to work with, 'a safe pair of hands' who can be trusted. With that kind of reputation, you will always get work.

4. Be professional (part two)

Being professional also means taking care of business, and that's something you should make a priority. The hard truth is that few writers earn a great deal from their writing, but if you want to make sure you can make a living, then you need to think about money. I've always thought of myself as the owner of a small business, so right from the beginning I took on an accountant, made sure I kept scrupulous records, and paid my taxes.

I've also always tried to think strategically in the way that good businesses have to. I keep track of what I'm earning and think about cashflow, as well as what I'm likely to earn over the next year (for a freelance it's hard to look much further than that). I then make judgements about what kind of work I'm going to do: if it's looking like a good year, I might think about doing something more speculative, maybe that story I've always wanted to write … if it's not looking good, then I start trying to drum up new commissions before I run out of money. I do a variety of things too – books, editing, reviews, bits of consultancy and teaching, school visits and festivals – the 'Many-Eggs-In-Many-Baskets' approach.

Having an agent helps, and the commission is tax-deductible. If your books are likely to be in libraries, you should sign up for Public Lending Right (PLR; see page 655), which will pay you for loans of your books. You should also become a member of the Authors' Licensing and Collecting Society (ALCS; see page 618), which collects money for secondary uses of our work such as photocopying, foreign PLR, cable re-transmission and so on. It all adds up, and even a small payment can come at a very useful time. You should also join a union, such as the Writers' Guild of Great Britain (WGGB; page 498), or the Society of Authors (page 495). They're great sources of support, information and networking for writers - you'll find details of all these organisations elsewhere in this excellent book – itself an essential tool for the professional.

5. Be resilient

Last but not least – you should bear in mind that there will be times when everything goes wrong. Books will be rejected or sell poorly, commissions will be hard to come by, favourite editors will move on, your particular area of experience will become unfashionable, royalties that once seemed secure will dry up. I've been through all of those things, and I've had my share of struggles with the usual demons we writers have to deal with – self-doubt, worry, periods of real stress.

But I kept going, through the bad times and the good, and I have my natural resilience (my 'bounce-back-ability') to thank for that. I might get knocked down, but I get up again, and if you don't think you can manage that, well, the life of a professional writer isn't for you. But if you do, and you're prepared to work hard, and have some talent to offer, you'll be fine.

I wish you the best of luck.

Tony Bradman has written for children of all ages, from babies to teenagers and is probably best known for his historical fiction such as *Viking Boy*. His most recent book is *Operation Banana* (Walker Books 2022). He has edited many anthologies of short stories and poetry, and has reviewed for the *Times Educational Supplement*, the *Daily Telegraph* and the *Guardian*. Tony was Chair of the Authors' Licensing and Collecting Society (ALCS) between 2016 and 2022.

See also...
- *Public Lending Right*, page 655
- *Society of Authors*, page 495
- *WGGB (Writers' Guild of Great Britain)*, page 498
- *Authors' Licensing and Collecting Society*, page 718

On mentoring

Bestselling author Jill Dawson explains just how valuable personal mentoring from a successful author can be in bringing out the best from a new or aspiring writer. She provides information and advice on current mentoring schemes.

In the early '90s, when writing my first novel, *Trick of the Light* (Sceptre 1996), I longed to have some feedback. Popular wisdom is that writing workshops or writers' groups are the way new writers learn. So I tried a couple of workshops at the City Lit and immediately discovered they weren't for me. I was shy. I hated groups. And I have a sort of permeable self, which – though very useful in a novelist – means I take in *everything* from everybody else and can't fend it off. Even more problematically, I realised belatedly that the very reason I *wanted* to write was to connect with this self more securely: how could I do this when inundated by the cacophony of critical voices and jostling egos of the other writers in the group?

Writing fiction was a negotiation between the joys of being hidden and the potential disaster of never being found. I do understand that writing groups and courses are the way forward for many people who want to write – please don't think I'm dismissing their value. I've taught many over the years and I try to make them a space where individual voices can be heard and where a group consensus doesn't develop. But I also know I'm not alone in finding workshops too exposing and agitating to be helpful.

What I needed was *one* trusted person, someone whose writing I admired, someone who knew what they were doing and would somehow know what I was trying to do and help me to do it better (my fantasy was Margaret Atwood, but how on earth to get hold of Margaret Atwood or ask her to read my novel?).

At that point in my life I'd never met any published writers. I was on the dole, a single parent of a toddler and living in a council flat in Hackney. What I longed for was an opportunity to meet and learn from those I thought of as 'real' writers: published authors with a body of work, and to discover if I could count myself among them. There seemed to be no way to find that, so I signed up for an MA in writing anyway, aware that a novelist I admired (Jane Rogers) ran it, and hoping for her input, or that of the esteemed poet who also taught on the course, E.A. Markham. I wasn't aware of it, but I think I was trying to see if a writer was *someone like me*. Could I imagine myself into their shoes?

It sounds obvious, but for those of us who don't have the luck of Martin Amis – to grow up in a home where books, writing, and intellectual questions were discussed at the kitchen table, and publishers and agents and other writers were real people who lived upstairs or came for dinner – it's hard to downplay how audacious it felt, to try to imagine myself a writer. Jane Rogers helped with that, with her quiet, affirming manner. She helped me too with a crucial question: what was the hook in my novel; why would a reader want to read on? In response to my uncertainty about the early chapters of my novel – should they be in another tense? should I change to the third person? – she read the extract I'd submitted and simply said: 'No, leave it as it is. The first person present tense is working fine.'

I felt that the MA didn't offer me nearly enough of Jane's time and input and I would have paid the entire fee of the course (£4,000 sterling back then) to have her all to myself.

I have to be frank and say I found the group workshop element as hard to manage as ever. However, as guests, the course had other writers (Pat Barker, James Kelman) and, thrillingly, I got to hear them talk about their work. The diagram Jane drew of how she'd structured the seven voices in her novel *Mr Wroe's Virgins* (Overlook Press 1999) provided the most extraordinary insight into how a successful novelist tackles structure. So meeting writers was part of the answer, but also receiving the detailed insider discussion of process and practice that I couldn't get from listening to workshop members who, like me, hadn't really done it yet.

That's how I dreamed up the idea of Gold Dust Mentoring. Gold Dust offers 16 hours of input from an established author of at least five books, often many more, who has taught or been a professor or course director on one of the best writing courses and won, been shortlisted for or judged major prizes, such as the Booker, Costa, Women's Prize, etc. It's a selective scheme and the applicant has to submit a sample of their writing, which is read by the writer they hope might be their mentor. The mentoring usually takes the form of eight meetings spread over eight months to a year, plus eight hours of the mentor reading the work in progress. Gold Dust has had lots of successes so far, despite being small. On our website (www.gold-dust.org.uk) we name with pride some of those who have gone on to publish or to win prizes: Guinevere Glasfurd, Harriet Tyce, Stephanie Scott, Sally-Anne Martyn, Kathleen Whyman, Sarah Aspinall and many more.

During lockdown, the mentoring was all done via Zoom – the need for another, more experienced writer to offer guidance, support and encouragement felt more essential than ever. As well as providing feedback on the work in progress, a mentor is well placed to offer the professional advice that most new writers crave. Approaching an agent can be a bewildering task and a mentor can demystify that world. Sarah Dunnakey, author of *The Companion* (Orion 2017) said: 'Towards the end of my time on Gold Dust, Jill helped me to draw up a list of prospective agents using her knowledge of what type of submissions they wanted. She was happy for me to mention that she recommended my writing to them. This helped to make the process far less daunting.' (We also used the good old *Writers' & Artists' Yearbook*, of course).

A high profile scheme like Gold Dust can help you be taken seriously by the publishing world once you start approaching agents and editors. Something else to consider when choosing a mentoring scheme. Not all schemes are equal and some have more influence in the publishing world. Mentoring is now offered by The Literary Consultancy (https://literaryconsultancy.co.uk) or the high-profile Rathbones Folio Mentorships (see www.rathbonesfolioprize.com/mentorship). Word Factory offers mentoring for short story writers (https://thewordfactory.tv) and there are others which might be closer to you, such as the Oxford Literary Consultancy (www.oxfordwriters.com), Adventures in Fiction (http://adventuresinfiction.co.uk) and the National Centre for Writing (https://nationalcentreforwriting.org.uk), as well as the service offered by Writers & Artists (www.writersandartists.co.uk/editing-services/bespoke-mentoring).

Formal schemes aren't the only way to find a mentor. You might be lucky enough to know a writer you could ask for feedback or professional advice. But beware: published writers get asked an awful lot to read the novels of aspiring writers, friends, and sometimes sons, daughters and brothers-in-law of friends. Authors also get sent books to review and requests for quotes for book jackets on a weekly basis. Then they have their writer friends who have just published, and perhaps their student's work to read, and that's before we even mention reading for research or pleasure! So that casual question, 'Would you mind just reading my novel?' is perhaps a bigger ask than many realise and should be approached with caution (... or you could wait to be invited).

Mentoring can be beneficial at any point in a writing career – not just the early years (although once published, of course, we have an agent and editor and meet other writers at festivals and book events, so are probably not at such a loss to find insider industry advice). Many of us remain grateful to those who have helped us in our writing lives. I know that Andrew Miller credits Angela Carter with tutoring him on an Arvon course (see page 683), and Ian McEwan says that his time on the University of East Anglia's Creative Writing MA (see page 691) mainly consisted of him discussing his work with Malcolm Bradbury, as McEwan was the only student that first year.

There has always been informal mentoring in the past – some of it rather hidden: Virginia Woolf had Anne Thackeray (although she wouldn't have admitted it); George Eliot was having salons with Henry James; Gertrude Stein took lots of male writers under her wing. Perhaps there is a danger of influence, or of the 'mentee' developing too great a dependence on the mentor, but with formal schemes like the ones mentioned above there are clear boundaries and usually a signed contract which helps to guard against this. It's satisfying to have dreamed up and created the scheme I wanted to find myself, years ago. No need to go it alone in an attic then ... unless of course you really want to. But for many of us, as Emerson put it, 'Our chief want in life is somebody who will make us do what we can.'

Jill Dawson has won awards for poetry, fiction and short stories. Described by Philip Hoare as 'our most consummate historical novelist' she is the author of 11 novels, editor of six anthologies and the founder of Gold Dust Mentoring Scheme (www.gold-dust.org.uk). Her books, all published by Sceptre, include *The Crime Writer* (2016), winner of the East Anglian Book of the Year, and *Fred and Edie* (2000), shortlisted for the Orange Prize and the Whitbread. Her latest novel is *The Bewitching* (2022), the true story of a 16th-century witch trial in England. For more information visit https://jilldawson.co.uk.

See also...
• *Managing a successful writing career*, page 117

Book publishers UK and Ireland

There are changes to listings in this section every year. We aim to provide a comprehensive list of publishing imprints, the name or brand under which a specific set of titles are sold by a publisher. Any one publisher might have several imprints; for example Bloomsbury publishes cookery books under the Absolute Press imprint and nautical books under Adlard Coles. The imprint usually appears on the spine of a book. Imprints are included either under a publisher's main entry or in some cases as entries themselves. Information is provided in a way that is of most use to a reader. The subject indexes, which start on page 742, list publishers and imprints for different genres and forms of writing. The listings that follow are updated by the *Writers' & Artists'* editors based on information supplied by those listed. Increasingly, some legitimate publishers are offering paid-for editorial services in addition to their standard publishing model; please check carefully what they offer. Our section on Self-publishing, notably the publishing services for independent authors on page 626 provides advice on this.

*Member of the Publishers Association or Publishing Scotland
†Member of the Irish Book Publishers' Association
‡Member of the Independent Publishers Guild
sae = self-addressed envelope
MS = manuscript (MSS = manuscripts)

AA Publishing
AA Media Ltd, Fanum House, Basing View, Basingstoke, Hants. RG21 4EA
tel (01256) 491524
email aapublish@theaa.com
website www.theaa.com/books
Twitter @theaa_lifestyle

Atlases, maps, leisure interests, travel including City Packs and AA Guides. Founded 1910.

Abacus – see Little, Brown Book Group

Acair Books*
An Tosgan, 54 Seaforth Road, Stornoway, Isle of Lewis HS1 2SD
email info@acairbooks.com
website https://acairbooks.com/
Facebook www.facebook.com/acairbooks
Twitter @acairbooks

Publishes Scottish Gaelic children's books and a wide range of titles in Scottish Gaelic and English. Founded 1977.

ACC Art Books Ltd
Sandy Lane, Old Martlesham, Woodbridge, Suffolk IP12 4SD
tel (01394) 389950
email uksales@accartbooks.com
website www.accartbooks.com/uk
Facebook www.facebook.com/ACCArtBooks
Twitter @ACCArtBooks
Instagram @accartbooks
Publisher James Smith

Publisher and distributor of books on art, photography, decorative arts, fashion, gardening, design and architecture. Founded 1966.

Ad Hoc Fiction
6 Old Tarnwell, Stanton Drew, Bristol BS39 4EA
email jude@adhocfiction.com
website www.adhocfiction.com
Director Jude Higgins

Award-winning small independent publisher specialising in short-short fiction. Closely associated with the Bath Flash Fiction Award (page 545). Publishes anthologies of flash fiction from the thrice-yearly Bath Flash Fiction Award and anthologies from the Bath Short Story Award. Also produces novellas-in-flash from the yearly Bath Novella-in-Flash Award. Publishes single author collections of flash fictions, guidebooks on writing flash fiction and anthologies of stories from participants at the Flash Fiction Festival. Founded 2015.

Ad Lib Publishers
email info@adlibpublishers.com
website www.adlibpublishers.com
Facebook www.facebook.com/adlibpublishers
Twitter @adlibpublishers
Publishers John Blake, Duncan Proudfoot

Non-fiction publisher of true crime and celebrity memoir. Founded 2020.

Mardle Books
email jo@mardlebooks.com
Contact Jo Sollis
Commercial, mass-market books for adults.

Agenda Publishing*‡
PO Box 185, Newcastle upon Tyne NE20 2DH
tel (0191) 4957330
email enquiries@agendapub.com
website www.agendapub.com
Facebook www.facebook.com/agendapub
Twitter @agendapub

Independent publisher of books and journals in economics and political economy for students and lecturers in institutions of education worldwide. Founded 2016.

J.A. Allen – see The Crowood Press

Allison & Busby Ltd‡
11 Wardour Mews, London W1F 8AN
tel 020-3950 7834
email susie@allisonandbusby.com
website www.allisonandbusby.com
Facebook www.facebook.com/allisonandbusbybooks
Twitter @allisonandbusby
Publishing Director Susie Dunlop, *Publishing Manager* Lesley Crooks, *Head of Sales* Daniel Scott

Fiction, general non-fiction, YA and preschool. No unsolicited MSS. Founded 1967.

Alma Books
Thornton House, Thornton Road,
London SW19 4NG
tel 020-8405 6406
website www.almabooks.com, www.almaclassics.com
Directors Alessandro Gallenzi, Elisabetta Minervini

Contemporary literary fiction, non-fiction, European classics, poetry, drama, art, literary, music and social criticism, biography and autobiography, essays, humanities and social sciences. No unsolicited MSS. Series include: *Alma Classics, Overture Opera Guides, Calder Publications.* Around 40% English-language originals, 60% translations. Founded 2005.

Amazon Publishing
1 Principal Place, Worship Street, London EC2A 2FA
tel 0843 504 0495
email amazonpublishing-pr@amazon.com
website https://amazonpublishing.amazon.com/
Head of Publishing Worldwide Mikyla Bruder

Amazon Publishing is the full-service publishing arm of Amazon. Please see website for editorial contacts for each imprint and to see what each imprint specialises in. Imprints: Amazon Crossing, Amazon Crossing Kids, AmazonEncore, Amazon Original Stories, Amazon Publishing, 47North, Grand Harbor Press, Jet City Comics, Lake Union Publishing, Little A, Mindy's Book Studio, Montlake, Skyscape, Thomas & Mercer, TOPPLE Books, Two Lions, Waterfall Press. Also publishes ebooks via its Kindle Direct Publishing platform (page 630). Currently not accepting unsolicited MSS. Founded 2009.

Amber Books Ltd‡
United House, North Road, London N7 9DP
tel 020-7520 7600
email enquiries@amberbooks.co.uk
website www.amberbooks.co.uk
Facebook www.facebook.com/amberbooks
Twitter @amberbooks
Instagram @amberbooksltd
Chairman Stasz Gnych, *Managing Director* Sara McKie, *Editorial Director* Charles Catton

Illustrated non-fiction publisher for adults and children. Subjects include photography, travel, gift books, military technology, military history, general history, humour, music, survival, natural history and family reference. Works include encyclopedias and highly illustrated reference. Opportunities for freelancers. Founded 1989.

Amberley Publishing‡
The Hill, Stroud, Glos. GL5 4EP
tel (01453) 847800
email info@amberley-books.com
website www.amberley-books.com
Facebook www.facebook.com/amberleybooks
Twitter @amberleybooks
Ceo Nick Hayward

General history/non-fiction and local interest; specialisations include transport (railways, road transport, canals, maritime), industry, sport, biography and military history. Owns Quiller Publishing (page 175) and Icon Books (page 155). Founded 2008.

Amgueddfa Cymru – National Museum Wales‡
Cathays Park, Cardiff CF10 3NP
tel 029-2057 3235
email post@museumwales.ac.uk
website www.museumwales.ac.uk
Twitter @AmgueddfaBooks
Head of Publishing Mari Gordon

Books based on the collections and research of Amgueddfa Cymru for adults, schools and children, in both Welsh and English. Founded 1907.

And Other Stories*
Central Library, Surrey Street, Sheffield S1 1XZ
email info@andotherstories.org
website www.andotherstories.org
Facebook www.facebook.com/AndOtherStoriesBooks
Twitter @andothertweets
Publisher Stefan Tobler

Contemporary literary fiction and non-fiction from around the world. Has an open submissions policy, but strict submissions guidelines: www.andotherstories.org/submissions. Submissions not complying with these guidelines will be disregarded. Founded 2011.

Books

Andersen Press Ltd*

20 Vauxhall Bridge Road, London SW1V 2SA
tel 020-7840 8703 (editorial) / 020-7840 8701
(general)
email andersenedtorial@penguinrandomhouse.co.uk
website www.andersenpress.co.uk
Managing Director Mark Hendle, *Publisher* Klaus
Flugge

Children's books: picture books, fiction for 5–8 and
9–12 years and YA fiction. Founded 1976.

Angry Robot Books

Unit 11, Shepperton House, 89 Shepperton Road,
London N1 3DF
tel 020-3813 6940
email incoming@angryrobots.com
website www.angryrobotbooks.com
Facebook www.facebook.com/angryrobotbooks
Twitter @angryrobotbooks
Directors Etan Ilfeld, Vicky Hartle

Publishers of modern adult sci-fi and fantasy with a
speculative slant. Part of Watkins Media (page 189).
Crime fiction imprint: Datura Books. Founded 2009.

Anness Publishing

email info@anness.com
website www.annesspublishing.com
Managing Director Paul Anness, *Publisher* Joanna
Lorenz

Practical illustrated books on lifestyle, cookery, crafts,
reference, gardening, health and children's non-
fiction. Imprints include: Armadillo, Lorenz Books,
Peony Press and Practical Pictures and Southwater.
Founded 1988.

Apa Publications

7 Bell Yard, London WC2A 2JR
tel 020-7403 0284
website www.insightguides.com,
www.roughguides.com, www.berlitzpublishing.com
Facebook www.facebook.com/InsightGuides,
www.facebook.com/RoughGuides
Twitter @InsightGuides, @RoughGuides
Instagram @InsightGuides, @RoughGuides
Managing Director Agnieszka Mizak, *Publishing
Director* Sarah Clark

Publishers of Rough Guides, Insight Guides and
Berlitz products for travel and language, and related
digital content. Founded 1970.

Appletree Press Ltd†

164 Malone Road, Belfast BT9 5LL
tel 028-9024 3074
email editorial@appletree.ie
website www.appletree.ie

Gift books, guidebooks, history, Irish interest,
Scottish interest, photography, sport, travel.
Founded 1974.

Arachne Press

email cherry@arachnepress.com
website https://arachnepress.com/
Director Cherry Potts

Small, independent publisher of award-winning short
fiction, poetry and select non-fiction, for adults and
children. Founded 2012.

Arc Publications

Nanholme Mill, Shaw Wood Road,
Todmorden OL14 6DA
tel (01706) 812338
email info@arcpublications.co.uk
website www.arcpublications.co.uk
Facebook www.facebook.com/arcpublications
Twitter @arc_poetry
Founder & Managing Editor Tony Ward, *Publisher &
Editor of Arc Music* Angela Jarman; *Editors* James
Byrne, Jean Boase-Beier, Tony Ward

Specialises in contemporary poetry and neglected
work from the past: poetry from the UK and Ireland;
world poetry in English; bilingual translations mainly
from the smaller languages (individual poets and
anthologies); and occasional books on music and
musicians. Imprints: Arc Publications and Arc Music.
Refer to website for current publication list/catalogue
and submissions policy. Founded 1969.

Arena Books‡

82A James Carter Road, Mildenhall, Suffolk IP28 7D
tel (01284) 754123
email arenabooks.bse@gmail.com
website www.arenabooks.co.uk
Director James Farrell

Publishers of quality fiction, travel, history and
current affairs, also of specialised social science,
politics, philosophy and academic dissertations
suitable for transcribing into book format. New
authors welcome. Founded 1890.

Arkbound*

Rogart Street Campus, 4 Rogart Street,
Glasgow G40 2AA
tel (0117) 290 0386 / 0871 268 9869
email hello@arkbound.com
website https://arkbound.com/

Publishes a range of fiction and non-fiction,
principally focused on works that cover important
social or environmental issues. Aims to support
authors from disadvantaged and diverse
backgrounds. Also enables people and other
publishers to publish books through its dedicated
crowdpublishing website, Crowdbound (page 138).
Based in England and Scotland, operating on behalf
of the Arkbound Foundation charity. Founded as a
social enterprise with the support of the Princes'
Trust. Founded 2015.

Ashmolean Museum Publications

Beaumont Street, Oxford OX1 2PH
tel (01865) 288070
email dec.mccarthy@ashmus.ox.ac.uk
website www.ashmolean.org
Contact Declan McCarthy

Publisher of exhibition catalogues, fine and applied art of Europe and Asia, archaeology, history, numismatics. Photographic archive and picture library. Museum founded 1683.

Atlantic Books*‡

Ormond House, 26–27 Boswell Street,
London WC1N 3JZ
tel 020-7269 1610
email enquiries@atlantic-books.co.uk
website https://atlantic-books.co.uk/
Managing Director & Publisher Will Atkinson

Literary fiction, thrillers, history, current affairs, politics, sport, biography and memoir. Strictly no unsolicited submissions or proposals. In 2014 the Australian publisher Allen & Unwin became the majority owner of Atlantic Books. Founded 2000.

Atrium and Attic Press – see Cork University Press

Aureus Publishing Ltd

Castle Court, Castle-upon-Alun, St Bride's Major,
Vale of Glamorgan CF32 0TN
tel (01656) 880033
email info@aureus.co.uk
website www.aureus.co.uk
Director Meuryn Hughes

Rock and pop, autobiography, biography, sport. Founded 1993.

Aurora Metro‡

80 Hill Rise, Richmond TW10 6UB
tel 020-8948 1427
email submissions@aurorametro.com
website www.aurorametro.com
Facebook www.facebook.com/AuroraMetroBooks
Twitter @aurorametro
Managing Director Cheryl Robson

Adult fiction, YA fiction, biography, drama (including plays for young people), non-fiction, theatre, cookery and translation. Submissions: send synopsis and three chapters. Runs a biennial competition for women novelists (odd years): Virginia Prize for Fiction. Entry fee for submission of either adult or YA novel. Imprints include Aurora Metro Books and Supernova Books. Founded 1996.

Authentic Media Ltd

PO Box 6326, Bletchley, Milton Keynes MK1 9GG
tel (01908) 268500
email info@authenticmedia.co.uk
website www.authenticmedia.co.uk
Facebook www.facebook.com/authenticmedia

Twitter @authenticmedia
General Manager Donna Harris

Biblical studies, Christian theology, ethics, history, mission, commentaries, Christian biographies, devotionals, children's books and Bibles. Imprints: Paternoster, Authentic. Founded 2001.

The Authority Guides

Studio 6, 9 Marsh Street, Bristol BS1 4AA
tel 0117 422 5540
email info@therightbookcompany.com
website www.rightbookpress.com
Director Sue Richardson

Pocket-sized business books for entrepreneurs and business professionals. Concise and practical, titles range across business subjects from finance to leadership, sales and marketing to personal development. Submissions welcomed, email for guidelines. Founded 2017.

Avon – see HarperCollins Publishers

Award Publications Ltd

The Old Riding School, The Welbeck Estate,
Worksop, Notts. S80 3LR
tel (01909) 478170
email info@awardpublications.co.uk
Facebook www.facebook.com/awardpublications
Twitter @award_books
Instagram @award.books

Picture story books, fiction, early learning, information and activity books for 0–12 years. No unsolicited material. Refer to social media sites for details of submission windows. Founded 1972.

Ayebia Clarke Publishing Ltd

7 Syringa Walk, Banbury, Oxon OX16 1FR
email ayebia@ayebia.co.uk
website www.ayebia.co.uk
Managing Director Nana Ayebia Clarke

An award-winning independent publisher of specialist African and Caribbean writing. Publishes both fiction and non-fiction, including novels, poetry, short stories, biographies, autobiographies, literary criticism and books on important subjects such the immigrant condition in the world. Founded 2003.

Bernard Babani (publishing) Ltd

The Grampians, Shepherds Bush Road,
London W6 7NF
tel 020-7603 2581
email enquiries@babanibooks.com
website www.babanibooks.com
Director M.H. Babani

Practical handbooks on radio, electronics and computing. Founded 1942.

Books

Bad Betty Press

Cobden Place, Unit 5, Cobden Chambers,
Pelham Street, Nottingham NG1 3ED
tel 07850 430117
email info@badbettypress.com
website www.badbettypress.com
Facebook www.facebook.com/badbettypress
Twitter @badbettypress
Instagram @badbettypress
Founding Editor Amy Acre, *Founding Producer* Jake
Wild Hall, *Pamphlet Editors* Gboyega Odubanjo, Anja
Konig

Award-winning independent publisher of new
poetry, and curator of live literature events across the
UK. Founded 2017.

Bad Press Ink‡

The Studio, High Turney Shield, Hexham NE47 8AW
tel (01434) 345529
website www.badpress.ink
Directors & Commissioning Editors Pat Blayney, Iain
Parke

Independent publisher of alternative, cult and niche
lifestyle fiction. Run by authors for authors,
interested in edgy fiction with a distinctive voice
including crime, horror and urban subjects. Actively
looking for new and unpublished talent. Submissions
test available at: https://badpress.ink/submissions/.
Founded 2018.

Banshee Press Ltd†

email bansheelit@gmail.com
website www.bansheelit.com
Facebook www.facebook.com/bansheelit
Twitter @bansheelit
Instagram @banshee.lit
Directors Laura Cassidy, Claire Hennessy, Eimear
Ryan

Small independent Irish publisher of a print literary
journal *Banshee*, as well as a select list of books.
Publishes contemporary writing in all forms. Open to
enquiries and proposals from contributors to the
journal, particularly those who have not yet
published a book-length work. Occasionally opens
for unsolicited submissions, check website for details.
Founded 2014.

Barbican Press Ltd‡

tel 07507 554731
email martin@barbicanpress.com
website https://barbicanpress.com/
Twitter @barbicanpress1
Instagram @barbicanpress
Directors Martin Goodman, James Thornton

An independent micro-publisher. The list includes
poetry, drama, writing for children, translations and
compelling non-fiction, including issues-driven
memoir and vivid tales of maritime communities.
LGBTQI+ friendly. Founded 2009.

Barrington Stoke*

18 Walker Street, Edinburgh EH3 7LP
tel 0131 225 4113
email info@barringtonstoke.co.uk
website www.barringtonstoke.co.uk

Short fiction for children, specially adapted and
presented for reluctant, struggling and dyslexic
readers, including picture books up to YA fiction. No
unsolicited submissions. Acquired by HarperCollins
Publishers (page 151) in 2023. Founded 1998.

BBC Books – see Ebury Publishing

Bearded Badger Publishing Ltd

33 High Street, Belper, Derbyshire DE56 1GF
tel 07470 458761
email paulh@beardedbadgerpublishing.com
website www.beardedbadgerpublishing.com
Facebook www.facebook.com/
beardedbadgerpublishing
Twitter @beardedbadgerpc
Instagram @bearded_badger_publishing
Managing Director Paul Handley

Independent publishing company based in
Derbyshire, with a mission to publish high-quality
literature across all genres, with an initial focus on
publishing writers with a link to the often-overlooked
East Midlands region. Founded 2020.

Bedford Square Publishers‡

14 Bedford Square, London WC1B 3JA
email info@bedfordsquarepublishers.co.uk
Facebook www.facebook.com/bedfordsq.publishers
Twitter @bedsqpublishers
Managing Director & Publisher Jamie Hodder-
Williams, *Commercial Director* Laura Fletcher

An independent publisher of fiction and non-fiction.
Subjects include wellness and literary fiction.
Founded 2022.

No Exit Press

Crime and thrillers.

Bedtime Books†

20 Victoria Road, Dublin D06 DRO2,
Republic of Ireland
contact@betimesbooks.com
website www.bedtimebooks.com
Directors Tanja Slijepčević, John Sheil, Maria Tirelli

Not-for-profit literary press based in Dublin.
Founded 2020.

Bennion Kearny Ltd‡

6 Woodside, Churnet View Road, Oakamoor,
Staffs. ST10 3AE
tel (01538) 703591
email info@BennionKearny.com
website www.BennionKearny.com
Publisher James Lumsden-Cook

Non-fiction: academic, professional, popular, niche and practical titles; all subjects considered. See website for submission details. Publishes titles both nationally and internationally. Imprints include: Bennion Kearny, Dark River, Hawksmoor Publishing, and Oakamoor Publishing. Founded 2008.

BFI Publishing*‡
Bloomsbury Publishing Plc, 50 Bedford Square, London WC1B 3DP
tel 020-7631 5600
email academic@bloomsbury.com
website www.bloomsbury.com
Publisher Rebecca Barden

Film, TV and media studies; general, academic and educational resources on moving image culture. BFI books and resources are published in partnership with Bloomsbury Publishing Plc (page 130). Founded 1982.

Birlinn Ltd*‡
West Newington House, 10 Newington Road, Edinburgh EH9 1QS
tel 0131 668 4371
email info@birlinn.co.uk
website www.birlinn.co.uk
Directors Hugh Andrew, Jan Rutherford, Andrew Simmons, Laura Poynton, Joanne Macleod

Founded 1992.

Arena Sport
Subjects include football, rugby, golf, running and cycling.

BC Books
Children's imprint providing quality illustrated books for young readers.

Birlinn
Genres include Scottish history, local interest/history, Scottish humour, guides, military, adventure, history, archaeology, sport, general non-fiction.

John Donald
Publishes academic history books and biographies.

Polygon
Imprint of classic and modern literary fiction, poetry, music and film titles.

Bitter Lemon Press‡
47 Wilmington Square, London WC1X 0ET
email books@bitterlemonpress.com
website www.bitterlemonpress.com
Facebook www.facebook.com/bitterlemonpress
Twitter @bitterlemonpub

Publishes crime fiction that exposes the darker side of countries such as Argentina, Cuba, Mexico, Belgium, France, Germany, Italy, Netherlands, Poland, Spain, Switzerland, Turkey, India, Iraq, New Zealand, Australia and the USA. Founded 2015.

Wilmington Press
Culture and society.

Black & White Publishing Ltd*‡
Nautical House, 104 Commercial Street, Edinburgh EH6 6NF
tel 0131 625 4500
email mail@blackandwhitepublishing.com
website www.blackandwhitepublishing.com
Executive Publisher Campbell Brown, *Publishing Director* Alison McBride

Non-fiction: general, sport, cookery, lifestyle, biography, humour, crime. Fiction: women's fiction, contemporary, historical, psychological thrillers, crime. Also publisher of *Itchy Coo*. See website for latest submission guidelines. Acquired by Bonnier Books (page 131) 2021. Founded 1999.

Ink Road
YA fiction.

Black Bee Books‡
Bryn Heulog, Talley, Llandeilo, Wales SA19 7YH
email info@blackbeebooks.wales
website www.blackbeebooks.wales
Twitter @BlackBeeBooks

Fiction and non-fiction, YA and adult, from under-represented voices, including LGBTQIA2S+ authors. Currently looking to work with authors that reflect the wide range of communities in Wales, especially under-represented voices. Publishes titles that will resonate with a diverse readership. See website for details. Founded 2020.

Black Dog Press
The Maple Building, 39–51 Highgate Road, London NW5 1RT
tel 020-8371 4000
email office@blackdogonline.com
website www.blackdogonline.com
Twitter @blackdogpress
Instagram @blackdogpress

Contemporary art, design, photography, music. Founded 1995.

Blackstaff Press Ltd†
Colourpoint House, Jubilee Business Park, 21 Jubilee Road, Newtownards, Co. Down BT23 4YH
tel 028-9182 0505 (within the UK) / +353 (0)48 91826339 (Republic of Ireland)
email info@blackstaffpress.com
website www.blackstaffpress.com
Facebook www.facebook.com/Blackstaffpressni
Twitter @BlackstaffNI
Managing Editor Patsy Horton

Local interest titles, particularly memoir, history and humour. See website for submission guidelines before sending material. Acquired by Colourpoint Creative Ltd (page 136) in 2017. Founded 1971.

John Blake Publishing*

Victoria House, Bloomsbury Squre,
London WC1B 4DA
tel 020-3770 8888
email hello@bonnierboos.co.uk
website www.bonnierbooks.co.uk
Twitter @jblakebooks
Instagram @johnblakebooks
Publisher Matthew Phillips

A commercial non-fiction imprint that publishes a
mix of real-life stories, biographies, true crime,
alternative histories and gift and humour. An imprint
of Bonnier Books UK (page 131). Founded 1991.

Blink Publishing*

Victoria House, Bloomsbury Square,
London WC1B 4DA
tel 020-3770 8888
email hello@bonnierbooks.co.uk
website www.bonnierbooks.co.uk
Twitter @blinkpublishing
Instagram @blinkpublishing
Publisher Matthew Phillips, *Editorial Director*
Susannah Otter, *Senior Editor* Joe Hallsworth

Publishes commercial adult non-fiction. Blink
Publishing is an imprint of Bonnier Books UK
(page 131). Founded 2014.

Bloodaxe Books Ltd

Eastburn, South Park, Hexham,
Northumberland NE46 1BS
tel (01434) 611581
email editor@bloodaxebooks.com
website www.bloodaxebooks.com
Editor Neil Astley

Poetry. Check submissions guidelines on website and
send sample of up to a dozen poems with sae only if
the submission fits the guidelines. No email
submissions or correspondence. Founded 1978.

Bloodhound Books Ltd‡

9 Hills Road, Cambridge CB2 1GE
email info@bloodhoundbooks.com
website www.bloodhoundbooks.com
Facebook www.facebook.com/BloodhoundBooks
Twitter @BloodhoundBook
Founders Fred Freeman, Betsy Reavley

A digital-focused publisher of commercial and
literary fiction, with a focus on psychological,
thrillers, crime, historical, romance and women's
fiction. Accepts unsolicited MSS. Acquired by US-
based marketing tech company Open Road Media
(OR/M) in 2021. Founded 2014.

Bloomsbury Publishing Plc*‡

50 Bedford Square, London WC1B 3DP
tel 020-7631 5600
website www.bloomsbury.com
Founder & Chief Executive Nigel Newton

A leading independent publishing house with authors
who have won the Nobel, Pulitzer and Booker prizes.
Bloomsbury has offices in London, New York
(page 205), New Delhi, Oxford and Sydney
(page 192). MSS must normally be channelled
through literary agents, with the exception of
academic and professional titles. Founded 1986.

BLOOMSBURY CONSUMER DIVISION

Managing Director Ian Hudson

Imprints include: Absolute Press, Bloomsbury
Children's Books, Bloomsbury Circus, Bloomsbury
Press, Raven Books, Bloomsbury Tonic (wellbeing),
Head of Zeus (page 153).

Bloomsbury Adult Trade Publishing

Adult Editor-in-Chief Paul Baggaley, *Head of Trade
Division* Alexis Kirschbaum (non-fiction, literary
fiction & poetry); *Publishing Directors* Ian Marshall,
Emma Herdman, Katy Follain (general: commercial
fiction & non-fiction, crime & sci-fi/fantasy), Alison
Hennessey (Raven Books), Rowan Yapp (Bloomsbury
Lifestyle, including illustrated & cookery), *Poetry
Editor* Kayo Chingonyi

Fiction authors include: Isabel Allende, Madeline
Miller and Ann Patchett. Non-fiction authors
include: Reni Eddo-Lodge, William Dalrymple, Peter
Frankopan, Hugh Fearnley-Whittingstall and Paul
Hollywood.

Bloomsbury Children's Books

Publishing Director & International Editor-in-Chief
Rebecca McNally

Authors include J.K. Rowling, Louis Sachar, Neil
Gaiman, Sarah J. Maas, Sarah Crossan, Brian
Conaghan. No unsolicited MSS.

Bloomsbury Education

Head of Education Helen Diamond, *Editorial Director*
Hannah Rolls (educational fiction & poetry), *Senior
Commissioning Editor* Joanna Ramsay (early years &
CPD), *Commissioning Editor* Emily Badger (primary
& CPD)

Publishes around 75 print titles per year: educational
fiction, children's poetry, teacher resource books and
CPD titles. Imprints include ABC-CLIO (page 203),
Andrew Brodie, Featherstone Education.

BLOOMSBURY ACADEMIC AND PROFESSIONAL DIVISION

website www.bloomsburyprofessional.com,
www.bloomsbury.com/academic
Managing Director Jenny Ridout

Specialises in scholarly and educational content in the
arts, humanities and social sciences, law, business and
management, and study skills. Imprints include: The
Arden Shakespeare, Bloomsbury Visual Arts,
Fairchild Books, Hart Publishing (page 152), I.B.
Tauris (page 184), Oberon Books, Red Globe Press,
Zed Books (page 191), Methuen Drama, T&T Clark
and BFI Publishing (as publishing partner, page 129).

Bloomsbury Digital Resources
Managing Director Kathryn Earle
Award-winning digital platforms across the humanities and social sciences, including Drama Online, Bloomsbury Collections, the Churchill Archive, Bloomsbury Fashion Central.

Bloomsbury Special Interest
Publishes a wide variety of non-fiction including politics, history, business, sport and wellbeing, popular science, philosophy and religion, as well as reference works. Imprints include: Adlard Coles, Bloomsbury Continuum, Bloomsbury Wildlife, Green Tree, Christopher Helm, Herbert Press, Osprey Games, Osprey Publishing (page 169), Sigma, UIT Cambridge, and Philip Wilson Publishers (page 190).

Blue Diode Publishing
email bluedioderob@gmail.com
website www.bluediode.co.uk
Facebook www.facebook.com/bluediodepress
Twitter @DiodeBlue
Founder Rob A. Mackenzie

A publisher of anthologies and poetry, based in Leith, Scotland. Publishes poetry collections. Founded 2018.

Blue Guides Ltd
Unit 2, Old Brewery Road, Wiveliscombe TA4 2PW
tel 020-8144 3509
email editorial@blueguides.com
website www.blueguides.com
Facebook www.facebook.com/blueguides
Twitter @blueguides

Publishes *Blue Guides* and *Blue Guide Travel Companions,* detailed guidebooks with a focus on history, art and architecture for the independent traveller. Founded 1918.

Bluemoose Books*
25 Sackville Street, Hebden Bridge HX7 7DJ
email kevin@bluemoosebooks.com
website www.bluemoosebooks.com
Twitter @ofmooseandmen
Publisher Kevin Duffy

Publisher of literary fiction. No children's, YA or poetry. Founded 2006.

Bodleian Library Publishing‡
Broad Street, Oxford OX1 3BG
tel (01865) 283850
email publishing@bodleian.ox.ac.uk
website www.bodleianshop.co.uk
Facebook www.facebook.com/bodleianlibraries
Twitter @BodPublishing
Instagram @BodleianLibraryPublishing
Head of Publishing Samuel Fanous

Helps to bring some of the riches of Oxford's libraries to readers around the world through a range of beautiful and authoritative books. Bodleian Library founded 1602.

The Bodley Head – see Vintage

Boldwood Books‡
23 Bowerdean Street, London SW6 3TN
email info@boldwoodbooks.com
website www.boldwoodbooks.com
Facebook www.facebook.com/bookandtonic
Twitter @BoldwoodBooks
Instagram @BookandTonic
Ceo & Founder Amanda Ridout, *Publishing / Sales & Marketing Director* Nia Beynon, *Publishing Director* Sarah Ritherdon

Publishes fiction: crime, mystery, historical fiction, thrillers, women's fiction, romance and suspense. Founded 2019.

Bonnier Books UK*
Victoria House, Bloomsbury Square, London WC1B 4DA
tel 020-3770 8888
email hello@bonnierbooks.co.uk
website www.bonnierbooks.co.uk
Ceo Perminder Mann

Publishes across a wide variety of genres for different ages. From crime to reading group fiction; memoir to self-help; activity to reference. Publishers of a number of imprints. Adult trade: Black & White Publishing, John Blake (page 130), Blink (page 130), Echo Publishing (page 193), Embla Books, Eriu, Heligo Books, Ithaka, Lagom, Manilla Press (page 163), Nine Eight Books, Twelve, Point Audio, Zaffre (page 190). Children's trade: Autumn Publishing, Big Picture Press, Hot Key Books (page 155), Igloo Books, Piccadilly Press (page 173), Studio Press (page 183), Templar (page 184). Founded 2015.

The Book Guild Ltd
Unit E2 Airfield Busines Park, Harrison Road, Market Harborough, Leics. LE16 7UL
tel 0800 999 2982
email info@bookguild.co.uk
website www.bookguild.co.uk
Facebook www.facebook.com/thebookguild
Twitter @BookGuild
Managing Director Jeremy Thompson

Offers traditional and partnership publishing arrangements, with all titles published being funded or co-funded by The Book Guild Ltd (does not offer self-publishing). MSS accepted in fiction, children's and non-fiction genres, see the website for details. The Book Guild is part of Troubador Publishing Ltd. Founded 1996.

Bookouture*
Carmelite House, 50 Victoria Embankment, London EC4Y 0DZ

Books

email pitch@bookouture.com
website www.bookouture.com
Facebook www.facebook.com/bookouture
Twitter @bookouture
Instagram @bookouture
Managing Director Jenny Geras, *Publisher* Ruth Tross

A digital imprint publishing commercial fiction across all genres including sci-fi and fantasy. Welcomes submissions via the website. Part of Hachette UK (page 150). Founded 2012.

Thread
website www.thread-books.com
Facebook www.facebook.com/threadbooks
Twitter @threadbooks
Instagram @threadbooks
Publisher Claire Bond

Publishes books by leading experts across a range of non-fiction topics including self-development, personal finance, parenting, nutrition and fitness, popular psychology and inspirational memoir.

Boom House Books[‡]
8 Chapel Street, Derby DE56 1AR
email hello@boomhousebooks.co.uk
website https://boomhousebooks.co.uk/
Facebook www.facebook.com/boomhousebooks
Founders Jo Leigh, Sascha Landskron, Zoe McCullagh-George

Children's fiction and non-fiction publisher with a focus on the local area, health, diversity and sustainability. Also publishes books for adults on parenting. Founded 2021.

Marion Boyars Publishers Ltd/Prospect Books
26 Parke Road, London SW13 9NG
email catheryn@marionboyars.com
website www.marionboyars.co.uk,
www.prospectbooks.co.uk
Directors Catheryn Kilgarriff, Ella Kilgarriff, Tessa Kilgarriff, *Editor* Tom Jaine

Prospect Books accepts submissions in food history. Marion Boyars Publishers has an active backlist including literary fiction, film, cultural studies and modern music; it is not accepting submissions. Founded 1975.

Boydell & Brewer Ltd
Bridge Farm Business Park, Top Street, Martlesham IP12 4RB
tel (01394) 610600
email editorial@boydell.co.uk
website www.boydellandbrewer.com
Ceo James Powell

Medieval studies, early modern and modern history, maritime history, literature, archaeology, art history, music, Hispanic studies. No unsolicited MSS. See website for submission guidelines. Founded 1969.

James Currey
website www.jamescurrey.com
Academic studies of Africa and developing economies.

Bradt Travel Guides Ltd[‡]
31A High Street, Chesham, Bucks. HP5 1BW
tel (01753) 893444
email info@bradtguides.com
website www.bradtguides.com
Twitter @BradtGuides
Managing Director Adrian Phillips, *Commissioning Editor* Claire Strange

Travel and wildlife guides with emphasis on unusual destinations and ethical/positive travel. Travel narratives and anthologies of travel writing. Submission guidelines: bradtguides.com/write-for-us. Contract publishing imprint: Journey Books (page 629). Founded 1974.

Breakdown Press
1 Berwick Street, Soho, London W1F 0DR
email editors@breakdownpress.com
website www.breakdownpress.com
Twitter @breakdownpress
Instagram @breakdownpress
Publishers Simon Hacking, Josh Palmano, Tom Oldham

Publishes contemporary comics. For submission guidelines see website. Founded 2012.

Nicholas Brealey – see John Murray Press

The Bright Press
18 Circus Street, Brighton BN2 9QF
tel (01273) 727268
website www.quartoknows.com/Bright-Press

Illustrated books on science, lifestyle, culture, craft and adult activity. Part of the Quarto Group (page 175). Founded 2018.

Brilliant Publications Ltd[*‡]
Unit 10, Sparrow Hall Farm, Edlesborough, Dunstable LU6 2ES
tel (01525) 222292
email info@brilliantpublications.co.uk
website www.brilliantpublications.co.uk
Facebook www.facebook.com/Brilliant.Publications
Twitter @Brilliantpub, @BrillCreative
Managing Director Priscilla Hannaford

Publishes easy-to-use educational resources, featuring engaging approaches to learning, across a wide range of curriculum areas, including English, foreign languages, maths, art and design, thinking skills and PSHE. No children's picture books, non-fiction books or one-off fiction books. See guidelines on website before sending proposal. Founded 1993.

Bristol University Press/Policy Press*‡
University of Bristol, 1–9 Old Park Hill, Clifton,
Bristol BS2 8BB
tel 0117 374 6645
email bup-info@bristol.ac.uk
website www.policypress.co.uk,
www.bristoluniversitypress.co.uk
Facebook www.facebook.com/PolicyPress
Twitter @policypress, @BrisUniPress
Ceo Alison Shaw, *Journals Director* Julia Mortimer,
Sales & Marketing Director Jo Greig, *Editorial Director*
Victoria Pittman

Bristol University Press specialises in politics and
international relations, sociology, human geography,
business and management, economics and law. Policy
Press specialises in social and public policy,
criminology, social work and social welfare. Bristol
University Press founded 2016, Policy Press founded
1996.

British Library Publishing*
Publishing Office, The British Library,
96 Euston Road, London NW1 2DB
tel 020-7412 7294
email publishing_editorial@bl.uk
website www.bl.uk/aboutus/publishing

Publishes around 50 books a year: classic crime, sci-fi,
weird fiction and women's fiction, art, maps,
manuscripts, history, literature and facsimiles.
Founded 1979.

The British Museum Press
Great Russell Street, London WC1B 3DG
tel 020-7323 8000
email publicity@britishmuseum.org
website www.britishmuseum.org/publishing
Head of Publishing Claudia Bloch

Publishes illustrated books for general readers,
families, academics and students, inspired by the
collections of the British Museum. Titles range across
the fine and decorative arts, history, archaeology and
world cultures. Division of The British Museum
Company Ltd. Founded 1973.

Broken Sleep Books
email aaron@brokensleepbooks.com
website www.brokensleepbooks.com
Facebook www.facebook.com/brokensleepbooks
Twitter @brokensleep
Director Aaron Kent

A working-class indie publisher working towards
greater access to the arts and degentrification of
publishing. Publishes pamphlets and collections from
a diverse range of writers. Founded 2018.

Brown, Son & Ferguson Ltd*
Unit 1A, 426 Drumoyne Road, Glasgow G51 4DA
tel 0141 883 0141

email info@skipper.co.uk
website www.skipper.co.uk
Editorial Directors Richard Brown, Wendy Brown

Nautical books, ships stationery and plays.
Founded 1832.

Bryntirion Press
Waterton Cross Business Park, South Road,
Bridgend CF31 3UL
tel (01656) 655886
email office@emw.org.uk
website www.emw.org.uk/bryntirion
Publications Officer Stefan Job

Formerly Evangelical Press of Wales. Theology and
religion (in English and Welsh). Founded 1955.

Burning Chair Publishing*
61 Bridge Street, Kington HR5 3DJ
email info@burningchairpublishing.com
website www.burningchairpublishing.com
Facebook www.facebook.com/
BurningChairPublishing
Twitter @Burning_Chair
Directors Simon Finnie, Peter Oxley

Welcomes unsolicited fiction submissions (from
authors direct as well as through agents) in the
following genres: mystery, thriller, suspense, crime,
action and adventure, sci-fi, fantasy (including urban
fantasy and YA), paranormal, horror, historical
fiction. Completed MSS of novel-length only (at least
60,000 words). A synopsis is required (no more than
two pages) plus the completed MS. Email and postal
submissions not accepted. Submissions only accepted
through the online portal at:
www.burningchairpublishing.com/submissions.
Founded 2018.

Burning Eye Books
email infodata@burningeye.co.uk
website https://burningeyebooks.wordpress.com/
Facebook www.facebook.com/burningeyebooks
Twitter @burningeyebooks
Founder Clive Birnie

An independent publisher publishing work from
spoken word artists. Founded 2011.

Buster Books – see Michael O'Mara Books Ltd

Cambridge University Press & Assessment*‡
University Printing House, Shaftesbury Road,
Cambridge CB2 8BS
tel (01223) 358331
email directcs@cambridge.org
website www.cambridge.org
Facebook www.facebook.com/
CambridgeUniversityPress
Twitter @CambridgeUP

Chief Executive Peter Phillips; *Managing Directors* Mandy Hill (academic), Jill Duffy (UK education), Rod Smith (international education)

Academic: anthropology and archaeology, art history, astronomy, biological sciences, classical studies, computer science, dictionaries, earth sciences, economics, engineering, history, language and literature, law, mathematics, medical sciences, music, philosophy, physical sciences, politics, psychology, reference, technology, social sciences, theology, religion. Education: ELT, educational (primary, secondary, tertiary), e-learning products. Journals: humanities, social sciences, science, technical and medical. Also publishes The Bible and Prayer Book. Founded 1534.

Campbell – see Pan Macmillan

Canbury Press Ltd‡
14 Beresford Road, Kingston upon Thames, Surrey KT2 6LR
email info@canburypress.com
website www.canburypress.com
Facebook www.facebook.com/canburypress
Twitter @canburypress
Instagram @canburypress
Director Martin Hickman

Modern non-fiction books. Politics, philosophy, health, environment, biography and technology. Non-fiction submissions (synopsis and two chapters) welcome by email to submissions@canburypress.com. Strictly no fiction. Founded 2013.

Candy Jar Books
Mackintosh House, 136 Newport Road, Cardiff CF24 1DJ
tel 029-2115 7202
email submissions@candyjarbooks.co.uk
website www.candy-jar.co.uk/books
Facebook www.facebook.com/CandyJarLimited
Twitter @Candy_Jar
Head of Publishing Shaun Russell

Publishes children's, YA, cult media, biography, general non-fiction, military history and fantasy. Publishes about 30 titles per year. Unsolicited material welcome; submissions form on website. No children's picture books. Partner imprint of Jelly Bean Self-Publishing. Founded 2010.

Canelo Digital Publishing Ltd
Unit 9, 5th Floor, Cargo Works, 1–2 Hatfields, London SE1 9PG
email hello@canelo.co
website www.canelo.co
Facebook www.facebook.com/canelobooks
Twitter @canelo_co
Managing Director Iain Millar, *Publishing Directors* Michael Bhaskar, Louise Cullen

Publishes commercial fiction and a small amount of select non-fiction. Acquired Hera Books in 2021.

Imprints include: Canelo, CaneloAction, CaneloAdventure, CaneloCrime, CaneloSaga, CaneloEscape, CaneloHistory, Hera Books (page 153). Founded 2015.

Canongate Books Ltd*‡
14 High Street, Edinburgh EH1 1TE
tel 0131 557 5111
email info@canongate.co.uk
Alternative address Eardley House, 4 Uxbridge Street, London W8 7SY
website www.canongate.co.uk
Ceo Jamie Byng

Adult general non-fiction and fiction, literary fiction, translated fiction, memoir, politics, popular science, humour, travel, popular culture, history and biography. Founded 1973.

Canongate Audio
Head of Audio Joanna Lord, *Senior Audio & Online Executive* Gaia Poggiogalli

Publishes Canongate Books in audio. Acquired CSA Word, a list of modern and contemporary classics in audio.

Canterbury Press – see Hymns Ancient and Modern Ltd

Jonathan Cape – see Vintage

Capuchin Classics – see Stacey Publishing Ltd

Carcanet Press Ltd*‡
4th Floor, Alliance House, 30 Cross Street, Manchester M2 7AQ
tel 0161 834 8730
email info@carcanet.co.uk
website www.carcanet.co.uk
Managing Director Michael Schmidt

Poetry, translations. Imprints include Carcanet Poetry, Carcanet Classics, Lives and Letters, Anvil Press Poetry, Northern House. Founded 1969.

Cassava Republic Press‡
9 Eri Studio C11, Mainyard Studios, 94 Wallis Road, London E9 5LN
email info@cassavarepublic.biz
website https://cassavarepublic.biz/
Facebook www.facebook.com/CassavaRepublic
Twitter @cassavarepublic
Instagram @cassavarepublicpress
Publishing Director Bibi Bakare-Yusuf

Publishes contemporary Black and African writing. Aims to bring high-quality fiction and non-fiction for adults and children to a global audience. Has offices in Abuja and London. Founded 2006.

Caterpillar Books – see Little Tiger Group

Catholic Truth Society[‡]
42–46 Harleyford Road, London SE11 5AY
tel 020-7640 0042
email p.finaldi@ctsbooks.org
website www.ctsbooks.org
Ceo & Publisher Pierpaolo Finaldi

General books of Roman Catholic and Christian interest, liturgical books, missals, bibles, prayer books, children's books and booklets of doctrinal, historical, devotional or social interest. MSS of 10,000–20,000 words with up to six illustrations considered for publication as booklets. Founded 1868.

Cengage Learning*
Cheriton House, Andover SP10 5BE
tel (01264) 332424
email emeahepublishing@cengage.com
website www.cengage.co.uk

Actively commissioning print and digital content for further education and higher education courses in the following disciplines: IT, computer science and computer applications; accounting, finance and economics; marketing; international business; human resource management; operations management; strategic management; organisational behaviour; business information systems; quantitative methods; psychology; hairdressing and beauty therapy. Submit content-writing interest either by email or post. Founded 2007.

Century – see Cornerstone

CGI Publishing Ltd[‡]
Saffron House, 6–10 Kirby Street, London EC1N 8TS
tel 020-7612 4741
email publishing@cgi.org.uk
website www.cgi.org.uk/shop
Publisher Saqib Lal Saleem

Publishing company of CGIUKI: The Chartered Governance Institute UK & Ireland, specialising in professional books, study texts for qualifications and online technical content for the governance and compliance market. Founded 1981.

Chapman Publishing
4 Broughton Place, Edinburgh EH1 3RX
tel 0131 557 2207
email chapman-pub@blueyonder.co.uk
website www.chapman-pub.co.uk
Editor Dr Joy Hendry

Includes the Chapman New Writing and the Chapman Wild Women series, poetry and drama. No unsolicited MS. Founded 1986.

Charco Press*
Office 59, 44–46 Morningside Road,
Edinburgh EH10 4BF

email info@charcopress.com
website https://charcopress.com/
Facebook www.facebook.com/CharcoPress
Twitter @CharcoPress

Focuses on finding contemporary Latin American literature and bringing it to new readers in the English-speaking world. Founded 2017.

Chatto & Windus/Hogarth – see Vintage

Chicken House
2 Palmer Street, Frome, Somerset BA11 1DS
tel (01373) 454488
email hello@chickenhousebooks.com
website www.chickenhousebooks.com
Twitter @chickenhsebooks
Instagram @chickenhousebooks
Managing Director & Publisher Barry Cunningham,
Deputy Managing Director Rachel Hickman

Fiction for 7+ years and YA. No unsolicited MSS. See website for details of *Times*/Chicken House Children's Fiction Competition for unpublished writers. Part of Scholastic Ltd (page 178). Founded 2000.

Child's Play (International) Ltd
Ashworth Road, Bridgemead, Swindon,
Wilts. SN5 7YD
tel (01793) 616286
email office@childs-play.com
website www.childs-play.com
Facebook www.facebook.com/ChildsPlayBooks
Twitter @ChildsPlayBooks
Chairman Adriana Twinn, *Publisher* Neil Burden

Children's educational books: board, picture, activity and play books; fiction and non-fiction. Founded 1972.

Choc Lit – see Joffe Books

Christian Education
5/6 Imperial Court, 12 Sovereign Road,
Birmingham B30 3FH
tel 0121 472 4242
email sales@christianeducation.org.uk
website https://shop.christianeducation.org.uk/,
www.retoday.org.uk
Facebook www.facebook.com/RETodayServices
Twitter @IBRAbibleread

Incorporating RE Today Services and International Bible Reading Association. Publications and services for teachers and other professionals in religious education including *REtoday* magazine, curriculum booklets and classroom resources. Also publishes bible reading materials. Founded 2001.

Churchwarden Publications Ltd
PO Box 420, Warminster, Wilts. BA12 9XB
tel (01985) 840189

email enquiries@churchwardenbooks.co.uk
website www.churchwardenbooks.co.uk
Directors J.N.G. Stidolph, S.A. Stidolph

Publisher of *The Churchwarden's Yearbook*. Publishes on the topics of care and administration of churches and parishes. Founded 1986.

Cicada Books*

Unit 9, 6 Cliff Road, Cliff Road Studios,
London NW1 9AN
email info@cicadabooks.co.uk
website www.cicadabooks.co.uk
Twitter @cicadabooks
Instagram @cicadabooks

Independent publisher specialising in highly illustrated books for children. Publishes between 10 and 12 titles a year. Founded 2009.

Cicerone Press‡

Juniper House, Murley Moss Business Village,
Oxenholme Road, Kendal, Cumbria LA9 7RL
tel (01539) 562069
email info@cicerone.co.uk
website www.cicerone.co.uk
Managing Director Jonathan Williams

Guidebooks: walking, trekking, mountaineering, climbing, cycling in Britain, Europe and worldwide. Founded 1969.

Cico Books – see Ryland Peters & Small

Cinnamon Press

Office 49019, PO Box 15113 Birmingham B2 2NJ
email info@cinnamonpress.com
website https://cinnamonpress.com/

A small, independent family-based publisher. Publishes books of poetry, fiction and creative non-fiction. Founded 2005.

Cipher Press

website www.cipherpress.co.uk
Twitter @cipherpress
Publishers Jack Thompson, Ellis K.

An independent publishing house with a focus on amplifying the work of LGBTQIA2S+ writers from the UK and beyond. Publishes books by queer writers and are especially interested in literary fiction and creative non-fiction. Founded 2020.

Claret Press‡

51 Iveley Road, London SW4 0EN
tel 020-7622 0436
email contact@claretpress.com
website www.claretpress.com
Facebook www.facebook.com/ClaretPublisher
Twitter @Claret_Press
Founder & Editor-in-Chief Katie Isbester

Publishing fiction and creative non-fiction. Flexible about genre, favouring deeply interesting and engaging narratives, often with a political edge. Founded 2015.

James Clarke & Co. Ltd‡

PO Box 60, Cambridge CB1 2NT
tel (01223) 350865
email publishing@jamesclarke.co.uk
website www.jamesclarke.co
Facebook www.facebook.com/JamesClarkeandCo
Twitter @JamesClarkeLtd
Managing Director Adrian Brink

Published the religious magazine *Christian World*. Now publishes books and ebooks on: academic theology, philosophy, history and biography, biblical studies and reference books. Sister imprint The Lutterworth Press is one of the oldest independent publishing houses in the UK (see page 162). Founded 1859.

Cló Iar-Chonnacht Teo†

Indreabhán, Co. Galway H91 CHO1,
Republic of Ireland
tel +353 (0)91 593307
email eolas@cic.ie
website www.cic.ie

Irish-language: novels, short stories, plays, poetry, songs, history; audio (writers reading from their works in Irish and English), downloads and bilingual books. Promotes the translation of contemporary Irish fiction and poetry into other languages. Founded 1985.

Cloud Lodge Books Ltd

Niddry Lodge, 51 Holland Street, London W8 7JB
tel 020-7225 1623
email info@cloudlodgebooks.co.uk
website www.cloudlodgebooks.com
Facebook www.facebook.com/cloudlodgebooks
Twitter @CLBPressUK
Managing Director William Campos, *Fiction Editor* Oliver Walton, *Science Fiction Editor* Alexander Hernandez

Publisher of daring literary fiction, crime fiction and sci-fi. Publishes up to four original titles per year, in print, digital and audio formats. Features writers (and characters) of every race, religion, nationality, gender and sexual orientation. Founded 2016.

Colourpoint Creative Ltd†

Colourpoint House, Jubilee Business Park,
21 Jubilee Road, Newtownards, Co. Down BT23 4YH
tel 028-9182 6339 (within UK) / +353 (0)48 91846339 (Republic of Ireland)
email sales@colourpoint.co.uk
website www.colourpoint.co.uk
Twitter @colourpoint
Publisher Malcolm Johnston, *Head of Educational Publishing* Wesley Johnston

Irish, Ulster-Scots and general interest including local history; transport (covering the whole of the British

Isles), railways, buses, road, aviation; educational textbooks and resources. Full submission by email only including details of proposal, sample chapter/ section, qualification/experience in the topic, full contact details. Imprints: Colourpoint Educational, Blackstaff Press Ltd (page 129). Founded 1993.

Columba Books†

Unit 3B, Block 3, Bracken Business Park, Bracken Road, Sandyford, Dublin D18 K277, Republic of Ireland
tel +353 (0)16 874096
email info@columba.ie
website www.columbabooks.com
Facebook www.facebook.com/columbabooks
Twitter @columbabooks
Publisher & Managing Director Garry O'Sullivan

Religion (Roman Catholic and Anglican) including pastoral handbooks, spirituality, theology, liturgy and prayer; counselling and self-help. Founded 1984.

Comma Press*

Studio 510A, 5th Floor, Hope Mill,
113 Pollard Street, Manchester M4 7JA
email info@commapress.co.uk
website https://commapress.co.uk/
Facebook www.facebook.com/CommaPressMcr
Twitter @commapress
Founder & Ceo Ra Page

A not-for-profit publishing initiative dedicated to promoting new writing with an emphasis on the short story and translated fiction. One of the Arts Council's new National Portfolio Organisations (NPOs) since 2012. For submissions see 'resources' section of the website: https://commapress.co.uk/resources/submissions/. Founded 2002.

Concord Theatricals

Aldwych House, 71–91 Aldwych,
London WC2B 4HN
tel 020-7054 7200
email customerservices@concordtheatricals.co.uk
website www.concordtheatricals.co.uk
Facebook www.facebook.com/concordukshows
Twitter @concordukshows
Instagram @concordukshows

A licensing, publishing, recording and producing company comprising R&H Theatricals, Samuel French Ltd and Tams-Witmark. As well as licensing shows to perform, sells an extensive range of scripts and theatre books both online and at the Samuel French Bookshop at the Royal Court Theatre, Sloane Square, London SW1W 8AS. Email the bookshop at bookshop@royalcourttheatre.com or call 020 7565 5024. More information on play and musical submissions can be found on the website. Founded 1830.

Cōnfingō Publishing

249 Burton Road, Didsbury, Manchester M20 2WA
email tim@confingopublishing.uk
website www.confingopublishing.uk
Facebook www.facebook.com/confingopublishing
Twitter @confingo

An independent publishing house specialising in creating beautiful editions of new fiction, poetry and works of art in all forms. Twice a year, the company produces a unique collection of previously unpublished works. Founded 2014.

Constable & Robinson Ltd – see Little, Brown Book Group

Cork University Press†

Boole Library, University College Cork,
College Road, Cork T12 ND89, Republic of Ireland
tel +353 (0)21 490 2980
website www.corkuniversitypress.com
Editor Maria O'Donavan

Irish literature, history, cultural studies, landscape studies, medieval studies, English literature, musicology, poetry, translations. Founded 1925.

Atrium and Attic Press
email corkuniversitypress@ucc.ie
Books by and about women in the areas of social and political comment, women's studies. Cookery, psychology, biography and Irish cultural studies (trade).

Cornerstone*

20 Vauxhall Bridge Road, London SW1V 2SA
tel 020-7840 8400
website www.penguin.co.uk/company/publishers/cornerstone
Managing Director Venetia Butterfield, *Director of Publicity & Media Relations* Charlotte Bush, *Associate Publisher* Nigel Wilcockson (non-fiction)

Part of Penguin Random House UK (page 172). No unsolicited MSS accepted.

Century
tel 020-7840 8394
Publisher Selina Walker, *Publishing Directors* Ben Brusey (non-fiction), Emily Griffin (fiction)
Commercial hardcover and paperback fiction and non-fiction.

Cornerstone Press
tel 020-7840 8793
Publisher Helen Conford, *Editorial Director* Anna Argenio
Non-fiction: business, economics, smart thinking, psychology and self-development.

Del Rey
tel 020-7139 3690
Publishing Director Ben Brusey, *Editorial Director* Sam Bradbury
Adult and YA crossover sci-fi, fantasy and horror.

Hutchinson Heinemann
tel 020-7139 8384
Publisher Helen Conford, *Publishing Directors* Ailah Ahmed, Charlotte Cray (fiction), *Editorial Director* Rowan Borchers, *Senior Commissioning Editor* Ansa Khan Khattack

Literary and book-club fiction, as well as a broader range of non-fiction encompassing the following: history, politics, popular science, polemic, memoir, and biography.

#Merky Books
tel 020-7840 8454
Publisher Helen Conford, *Senior Commissioning Editor* Lemara Lindsay-Prince, *Assistant Editor* Tallulah Lyons

Fiction: literary fiction, commercial fiction, genre fiction, poetry. Non-fiction: current affairs, narrative non-fiction, politics, memoir.

Council for British Archaeology
92 Micklegate, York YO1 6JX
tel (01904) 671417
email info@archaeologyuk.org
website www.archaeologyuk.org
Facebook www.facebook.com/Archaeologyuk
Twitter @archaeologyuk
Director Mike Heyworth

British archaeology – academic; practical handbooks; general interest archaeology. Publishes *British Archaeology* magazine. Founded 1944.

Country Books
38 Pulla Hill Drive, Storrington, West Sussex RH20 3LS
tel 07889 234964
email jonathan@spiralpublishing.com
website www.countrybooks.biz, www.sussexbooks.co.uk

Part of Spiral Publishing Ltd and incorporating Ashridge Press. Local history (new and facsimile reprints), family history, autobiography, general non-fiction, novels, customs and folklore. Books for the National Trust, Chatsworth House, Peak District NPA, Derbyshire County Council. Founded 1985.

Countryside Books‡
35A Kingfisher Court, Hambridge Road, Newbury, Berks. RG14 5SJ
tel (01635) 43816
website www.countrysidebooks.co.uk
Partners Nicholas Battle, Suzanne Battle, Alex Batho

Publishes books of local or regional interest, usually on a county basis: walking, outdoor activities, also heritage, aviation, railways and architecture. Founded 1976.

Cranthorpe Millner Publishers
9 Hills Road, Cambridge CB2 1GE
tel 020-3441 9212
email kirsty.jackson@cranthorpemillner.com
website www.cranthorpemillner.com
Facebook facebook.com/CranthorpeMillner
Twitter @CranthorpeBooks
Instagram @CranthorpeMillner
Managing Director Kirsty Jackson

Titles include fiction and non-fiction: memoir, celeb autobiographies, history, sci-fi, YA, historical fiction, crime/thriller, literary fiction. Founded 2018.

CRC Press – see Taylor & Francis Group

Crescent Moon Publishing
PO Box 393, Maidstone, Kent ME14 5XU
tel (01622) 729593
email cresmopub@yahoo.co.uk
website www.crmoon.com
Director Jeremy Robinson; *Editors* C. Hughes, B.D. Barnacle

Literature, poetry, arts, cultural studies, media, cinema, feminism. Submit sample chapters or six poems plus sae, not complete MSS. Founded 1988.

Cressrelles Publishing Co. Ltd
10 Station Road Industrial Estate, Colwall, Malvern, Herefordshire WR13 6RN
tel (01684) 540154
email simon@cressrelles.co.uk
website https://cressrelles.co.uk/
Directors Leslie Smith, Simon Smith

General publishing. Founded 1973.

J. Garnet Miller
Plays and theatre textbooks.

Kenyon-Deane
Plays and drama textbooks for amateur dramatic societies. Plays for women.

New Playwrights' Network
Plays for amateur dramatic societies (page 126).

Crowdbound
4 Rogart Street, Glasgow G40 2AA
tel (01415) 724602
email info@crowdbound.org
website www.crowdbound.org
Facebook www.facebook.com/ArkboundFoundation
Twitter @ArkboundUK
Contact Zoe McClellan

A crowdpublishing platform that enables authors and other publishers to raise funds to launch their books, with match funding opportunities and addition of Gift Aid also available. Seeks to support books and projects that cover social and/or environmental themes. Anyone can apply and if eligible a campaign can be started there for free, with no cost at any stage of the process. It is run under the ambit of the Arkbound Foundation (page 126), a literature charity based in Bristol and Glasgow. Founded 2022.

Books

Crown House Publishing Ltd*‡

Crown Buildings, Bancyfelin, Carmarthen SA33 5ND
tel (01267) 211345
email books@crownhouse.co.uk
website www.crownhouse.co.uk
Facebook www.facebook.com/CrownHousePub
Twitter @CrownHousePub
Instagram @crownhousepub
Directors David Bowman, Karen Bowman

Award-winning independent publisher specialising in the areas of education, coaching, business training and development, leadership, NLP, hypnotherapy, psychotherapy, self-help, personal growth and children's books. Founded 1998.

Independent Thinking Press

email books@independentthinkingpress.com
website www.independentthinkingpress.com
Publishes CPD books and resources for teachers and school leaders, including business, training and development, coaching, health and wellbeing, NLP, hypnosis, counselling and psychotherapy. Publishes a range of children's books.

The Crowood Press

The Stable Block, Ramsbury, Marlborough, Wilts. SN8 2HR
tel (01672) 520320
email enquiries@crowood.com
website www.crowood.com
Director Mollie Broadhead

Art, architecture, craft, general interest and hobbies, home and garden, military history, sport, performing arts, motoring and transport. Imprints include: Airlife Publishing (aviation, technical and general, military, military history), J.A. Allen (equestrian), N.A.G. Press (horology and gemology) and Black Horse Westerns. Robert Hale (general non-fiction) now owned by Joffe Books (page 157). Founded 1982.

Crux Publishing

34 Holford Road, Guildford, Surrey GU1 2QF
tel 020-8871 0594
email hello@cruxpublishing.co.uk
website www.cruxpublishing.co.uk
Boutique publisher offering to produce, distribute and market selected high-quality non-fiction titles. Operates an open submissions policy for new authors and digitally republishes backlist titles for existing authors. Works with individual authors to create and execute a unique marketing plan that drives sales. Founded 2011.

Dahlia Books

108 Spencefield Lane, Leicester LE5 6HF
email f.shaikh@dahliapublishing.co.uk
website www.dahliapublishing.co.uk
Twitter @dahliabooks

Independent publisher of original, contemporary short story collections. Particularly interested in working with first-time writers. Champions of regional and diverse voices. Founded in 2010

Darf Publishers Ltd

277 West End Lane, London NW6 1QS
tel 020-7431 7009
email enquiry@darfpublishers.co.uk
website www.darfpublishers.co.uk
Facebook www.facebook.com/DarfPublishers
Twitter @DarfPublishers
Director Ghassan Fergiani, *Editor* Ghazi Gheblawi

Focuses on diversity and inclusion. Publishes and reprints historical, geographic and classical works in English about the Middle East, North Africa and the UK. Also focuses on contemporary works of fiction, non-fiction and children's books from other languages into English, introducing new authors to the British market and the wider English-speaking world. Recent published works from Arabic (Libya, Yemen, Sudan, Eritrea), Italian, German, and Japanese with plans to widen to include writers from other European countries, South America, Asia and Africa. Founded 1981.

Darton, Longman and Todd Ltd

1 Spencer Court, 140–142 Wandsworth High Street, London SW18 4JJ
tel 020-8875 0155
email editorial@darton-longman-todd.co.uk
website www.darton-longman-todd.co.uk
Editorial Director David Moloney

Spirituality, prayer and meditation; books for the heart, mind and soul; self-help and personal growth; biography; political, environmental and social issues. Founded 1959.

Daunt Books

207–209, Kentish Town Road, London NW5 2JU
email publishing@dauntbooks.co.uk
website www.dauntbookspublishing.co.uk
Twitter @dauntbookspub
Publisher Marigold Atkey

An independent publisher of new writing in English and in translation: literary fiction (novels and short stories), narrative non-fiction (essays, memoir). Also publishes modern classics. Not currently accepting unsolicited submissions, check website for details. Founded 2010.

David & Charles Ltd‡

Tourism House, Pynes Hill, Exeter EX2 5WS
tel (01392) 790650
website www.davidandcharles.com
Managing Director James Woollam

Special interest publisher of books for hobbyists with a focus on craft and creative categories. Founded 1960.

DB Publishing

29 Clarence Road, Nottingham NG9 5HY
tel 07914 647382
email steve.caron@dbpublishing.co.uk
website www.dbpublishing.co.uk
Managing Director Steve Caron

An imprint of JMD Media Ltd. Primarily: football, sport, local history, heritage. Currently considering all topics including fiction. Unsolicited MSS welcome. Preliminary letter essential. Founded 2009.

Dead Ink Books

Northern Lights, 5 Mann Street, Liverpool L8 5AF
email nathan@deadinkbooks.com
website https://deadinkbooks.com/
Director Nathan Connolly

Literary publisher supported by Arts Council England. Published books have three times made the shortlist for the Saboteur Awards, the longlists for both the *Guardian*'s First Book Award and Not the Booker Prize, and the longlist for the Edge Hill Short Story Award. Founded 2017.

Dedalus Ltd*

24 St Judith's Lane, Sawtry, Cambs. PE28 5XE
tel (01487) 832382
email info@dedalusbooks.com
website www.dedalusbooks.com
Chairman Margaret Jull Costa, *Publisher* Eric Lane, *Editorial* Timothy Lane

Original fiction in English and in translation; 12–14 titles a year. Imprints include: Original English Language Fiction in Paperback, Dedalus European Classics, Dedalus Euro Shorts, Dedalus Europe Contemporary Fiction, Dedalus Africa, Dedalus Concept books, Young Dedalus, City Noir, Dark Masters Literary Biography. Founded 1983.

Dedalus Press

13 Moyclare Road, Baldoyle, Dublin D13 K1C2, Republic of Ireland
email editor@dedaluspress.com
website www.dedaluspress.com
Facebook www.facebook.com/DedalusPressPoetry
Twitter @dedaluspress
Directors Raffaela Tranchino, Pat Boran

Publishes contemporary Irish poetry and poetry from around the world in translation. Also publishes occasional prose titles by poets, or books which survey or explore aspects of the world of poetry. Founded 1985.

Richard Dennis Publications

The New Chapel, Shepton Beauchamp, Ilminster, Somerset TA19 0JT
tel (01460) 240044
email books@richarddennispublications.com
website www.richarddennispublications.com

Books for collectors specialising in ceramics, glass, illustration, sculpture and facsimile editions of early catalogues. Founded 2008.

André Deutsch – see Welbeck Publishing Group

Dialogue Books*

Carmelite House, 50 Victoria Embankment, London EC4Y 0DZ
website www.dialoguebooks.co.uk
Facebook www.facebook.com/dialoguebooks
Twitter @dialoguebooks
Publisher Sharmaine Lovegrove

Established first as an English language bookshop in Berlin in 2009, Dialogue Books was reignited as part of the Little, Brown Book Group in July 2017. In 2023, Dialogue Books became a division within the Hachette UK Group (page 150). Publishes within LGBTQI+, disabled, working-class and Black, Asian and marginalised communities, across fiction, non-fiction, literary and commercial. Founded 2017.

Discovery Walking Guides Ltd

10 Tennyson Close, Northampton NN15 7HJ
tel (01604) 244869
email ask.discovery@ntlworld.com
website www.dwgwalking.co.uk
Chairman Rosamund C. Brawn

Publishes *Walk!* walking guidebooks for UK and European destinations; *Tour & Trail Super-Durable* large-scale maps for outdoor adventures; *Bus & Touring* maps; and *Drive* touring maps. Premium content provider to 3G phone/tablet gps apps for digital mapping and hiking adventures. Publishing in conventional book/map format along with digital platforms. Welcomes project proposals from technologically (gps) proficient walking writers. Founded 1994.

DK*

One Embassy Gardens, 8 Viaduct Gardens, London SW11 7BW
tel 020-7139 2000
website www.dk.com
Ceo Carston Coefeld

A member of the Penguin Random House (page 172) division of Bertelsmann, publishing illustrated books for adults and children: travel, licensing, reference, education, gardening, food and drink. Founded 1974.

Do Book Company‡

Hackney Downs Studios, 1.2, 17 Amhurst Terrace, London E8 2BT
tel 07957 597540
email info@thedobook.co
website www.dobook.co
Facebook www.facebook.com/dobookco
Twitter @dobookco

Instagram @dobookco
Founder & Publisher Miranda West, *Rights Manager* Anya Glazer, *Editorial Assistant* Jess Fry

Publishes concise guides across business, design, wellbeing and sustainable living to help creative entrepreneurs, makers and doers work smarter and create positive change. Founded 2013.

Dodo Ink

email sam@dodoink.com
website www.dodoink.com
Facebook www.facebook.com/Dodo-Ink-775175252560383
Twitter @DodoInk
Managing Director Sam Mills, *Editorial Director* Thom Cuell

An independent press dedicated to publishing daring and difficult literary fiction. Publishes two to three novels a year. No unsolicited MSS by post; see the website for submission guidelines. Founded 2015.

Dogberry Ltd

13 The Rafters, Nottingham NG7 7FG
email contact@memoirist.org
website www.dogberrybooks.com
Publisher Auriel Roe

English-language publisher of humorous literary fiction, YA fiction and memoir. Founded 2020.

Dorling Kindersley – see DK

The Dovecote Press Ltd

Stanbridge, Wimborne Minster, Dorset BH21 4JD
tel (01258) 840549
email online@dovecotepress.com
website www.dovecotepress.com
Editorial Director David Burnett, *Office* Lynn Orchard

Books of local interest: natural history, architecture, history. Founded 1974.

Dref Wen

28 Church Road, Whitchurch, Cardiff CF14 2EA
tel 029-2061 7860
website www.drefwen.com
Directors Roger Boore, Anne Boore, Gwilym Boore, Alun Boore, Rhys Boore

Welsh-language publisher. Original Welsh-language novels for children and adult learners. Original, adaptations and translations of foreign and English-language full-colour picture story books for children. Educational material for primary/secondary school children in Wales and England. Founded 1970.

University College Dublin Press[†]

Room H103, Humanities Institute, Belfield, Dublin 4, Republic of Ireland
tel +353 (0)1 7164680
email ucdpress@ucd.ie
website www.ucdpress.ie
Twitter @UCDPress
Executive Editor Noelle Moran

North American representation: University of Chicago Press. Academic trade: humanities, Irish studies, history and politics, literary studies, social sciences, sociology, music and food science. Recently expanded to include architecture, ecology and environmental studies. Founded 1995.

Duckworth Books Ltd[‡]

1 Golden Court, Richmond TW9 1EU
email info@duckworthbooks.com
website www.duckworthbooks.co.uk
Twitter @Duckbooks
Managing Director Peter Duncan

Publishers of non-fiction: biography and memoir, popular science, popular history, popular psychology, nature and travel writing. Fiction: (Duckworth) historical fiction, (Farrago) ebook-first, series-led humorous fiction, humorous mystery and cosy crime, social comedy and satire, sci-fi and fantasy. Also represents The School of Life Press to the trade for sales. Imprints: Duckworth, Farrago. Founded 1898.

Dunedin Academic Press*

Hudson House, 8 Albany Street, Edinburgh EH1 3QB
tel 0131 473 2397
email mail@dunedinacademicpress.co.uk
website www.dunedinacademicpress.co.uk
Director Anthony Kinahan

Earth and environmental sciences. See website for submission guidelines. Founded 2000.

Dynasty Press

c/o Lucraft, Hodgson & Dawes LLP, 19 New Road, Brighton BN1 1UF
tel 020-8675 3435
email david@dynastypresslondon.co.uk
website www.dynastypress.co.uk
Contact David Hornsby

A boutique publishing house specialising in works connected to royalty, dynasties and people of influence. Committed to the freedom of the press to allow authentic voices and important stories to be made available to the public. Usually publishes titles which reveal and analyse the lives of those placed in the upper echelons of society. Founded 2008.

Ebury Publishing*

20 Vauxhall Bridge Road, London SW1V 2SA
tel 020-7840 8400
website www.penguin.co.uk/company/publishers/ebury
Managing Director Joel Rickett, *Publishing Director* Andrew Goodfellow

Non-fiction publisher. Part of Penguin Random House UK (page 172). Founded 1961.

BBC Books
Publishing Director Albert DePetrillo

Non-fiction with a BBC connection from history, natural history and science to cookery, lifestyle and pop culture.

Ebury Entertainment
Publishing Director Charlotte Hardman, *Senior Editorial Director* Lorna Russell

Imprint: Ebury Spotlight. Publishes autobiography, memoir, TV, sport and popular culture books.

Ebury Lifestyle & Food
Deputy Publisher Lizzy Gray, *Publishing Director* Laura Higginson

Imprints: Ebury Press, Pop Press. Cookery, wellbeing and lifestyle guides. Pop Press is Ebury's gift publishing, creating affordable, trend-led books for all occasions and all audiences.

Ebury Partnerships
Publishing Director Elizabeth Bond

Gift books, branded and bespoke books across food/drink, health/lifestyle, museums/galleries, and entrepreneurs/business pioneers.

Ebury Self
Publishing Director Olivia Morris

Imprints: Rider, Vermilion, Happy Place Books. Rider publishes 'books with soul' across popular psychology, philosophy, inspirational memoir, spirituality and wellbeing. Vermilion publishes personal development, popular psychology, health, diet, relationships and parenting titles written by experts with influence. Happy Place Books champions wellbeing talent and exciting new voices to share positive stories and practical ideas for physical and mental happiness.

Ebury Smart
Deputy Publisher Drummond Moir, *Editorial Director & Head of WH Allen* Jamie Joseph

Imprints: WH Allen, Ebury Edge, Ebury Press, Witness Books. Memoir, history, politics, current affairs, science, technology and business.

Edinburgh University Press*‡
The Tun – Holyrood Road, 12 Jackson's Entry, Edinburgh EH8 8PJ
tel 0131 650 4218
email editorial@eup.ac.uk
website www.edinburghuniversitypress.com, www.euppublishing.com
Facebook www.facebook.com/EdinburghUP
Twitter @EdinburghUP
Head of Editorial Tom Dark

Academic publishers of scholarly books and journals: American studies, classics and ancient history, film, media and cultural studies, history, Islamic and Middle Eastern studies, languages, law, linguistics, literary studies, philosophy, politics, religious studies and Scottish studies. Trade: literature and culture, Scottish history and politics. Founded 1949.

The Educational Company of Ireland
Ballymount Road, Walkinstown, Dublin D12 R25C, Republic of Ireland
tel +353 (0)14 500611
email info@edco.ie
website www.edco.ie

Educational MSS on all subjects in English or Irish language. A member of the Smurfit Kappa Group plc. Founded 1910.

Eland Publishing Ltd
61 Exmouth Market, London EC1R 4QL
tel 020-7833 0762
email info@travelbooks.co.uk
website www.travelbooks.co.uk
Directors Rose Baring, John Hatt, Barnaby Rogerson

Classic travel literature. No unsolicited MSS. Email in first instance. Founded 1982.

Electric Monkey – see HarperCollins Publishers

Edward Elgar Publishing Ltd‡
The Lypiatts, 15 Lansdown Road, Cheltenham, Glos. GL50 2JA
tel (01242) 226934
email info@e-elgar.co.uk
website www.e-elgar.com
Managing Director Tim Williams

Economics, business, law, public and social policy. Founded 1986.

Elliott & Thompson‡
2 John Street, London WC1N 2ES
tel 020-3405 0310
email pippa@eandtbooks.com
website www.eandtbooks.com
Twitter @eandtbooks
Chairman Lorne Forsyth, *Executive Publisher* Robin Harvie, *Publishing Director* Sarah Rigby

Publisher of narrative non-fiction, history, nature writing, politics, popular science, gift, economics, smart thinking and selective fiction. Founded 2009.

Elsevier Ltd*
The Boulevard, Langford Lane, Kidlington, Oxford OX5 1GB
tel (01865) 843000
website www.elsevier.com
Twitter @ElsevierConnect
Ceo Kumsal Bayazit

Academic and professional reference books; scientific, technical and medical products and services (books, journals, electronic information). No unsolicited MSS, but synopses and project proposals welcome. Imprints: Academic Press, Architectural Press,

Bailliere Tindall, Butterworth-Heinemann, Churchill Livingstone, Digital Press, Elsevier, Elsevier Advanced Technology, Focal Press, Gulf Professional Press, JAI, Made Simple Books, Morgan Kauffman, Mosby, Newnes, North-Holland, Pergamon, Saunders, Woodhead Publishing. Division of RELX Corp., Amsterdam. Founded 1986.

Elsewhen Press

Alnpete Limited, PO Box 757, Dartford, Kent DA2 7TQ
tel 07956 237041
email info@elsewhen.co.uk
website https://elsewhen.press
Facebook www.facebook.com/ElsewhenPress
Twitter @elsewhenpress
Instagram @elsewhenpress
Managing Director Alison Buck, *Editorial Director* Peter Buck

Small independent publisher, delivering new talents in speculative fiction (including sci-fi, fantasy, paranormal, horror, alternative history), for ages YA upwards. Digital first publisher. For submission guidelines see website. Founded 2011.

The Emma Press Ltd‡

Jewellery Quarter, Birmingham B18 6HQ
email hello@theemmapress.com
website https://theemmapress.com/
Facebook www.facebook.com/TheEmmaPress
Twitter @TheEmmaPress
Director Emma Dai'an Wright

Publishes single-author books and pamphlets in poetry and prose – including short stories, essays and translations. Their children's chapter books and poetry collections include CLiPPA Award-winning titles. Does not consider unsolicited MSS but runs regular calls for poetry and prose. Check website for details. Founded 2012.

Encyclopaedia Britannica (UK) Ltd

2nd Floor, Unity Wharf, 13 Mill Street, London SE1 2BH
tel 020-7500 7800
email enqbol@britannica.co.uk
website www.britannica.co.uk

Global digital educational publisher of instructional products used in schools, universities, homes, libraries and in the workplace. Founded 1999.

Enitharmon Editions

tel 020-7430 0844
email info@enitharmon.co.uk
website www.enitharmon.co.uk
Directors Stephen Stuart-Smith, Isabel Brittain

Artists' books and prints, poetry, including fine editions. Some literary criticism, fiction, translations. No unsolicited MSS. No freelance editors or proofreaders required. Founded 1967.

Everyman's Library

50 Albemarle Street, London W1S 4BD
tel 020-7493 4361
email books@everyman.uk.com
email guides@everyman.uk.com
website www.everymanslibrary.co.uk
Facebook www.facebook.com/everymanslibrary
Twitter @EverymansLib
Publisher David Campbell

Everyman's Library (clothbound reprints of the classics); *Everyman Pocket Classics*; *Everyman's Library Children's Classics*; *Everyman's Library Pocket Poets*; *Everyman Guides*; P.G. Wodehouse. No unsolicited submissions. Imprint of Knopf Doubleday Publishing Group. Founded 1905.

Everything with Words Ltd

16 Limekiln Place, London SE19 2RE
tel 020-8771 2974
email info@everythingwithwords.com
website www.everythingwithwords.com
Managing Director & Publisher Mikka Bott

Children's fiction for 5 years to YA and adult fiction. Accepts unsolicited MSS. Founded 2016.

University of Exeter Press

Reed Hall, Streatham Drive, Exeter EX4 4QR
tel 0845 468 0415
email info@exeterpress.co.uk
website www.exeterpress.co.uk
Facebook www.facebook.com/UniversityofExeterPress
Twitter @UExeterPress
Publisher Nigel Massen

Academic and scholarly books on international relations, film history, performance studies, linguistics, folklore and local history (Exeter and the South West). Founded 1958.

Helen Exley

16 Chalk Hill, Watford, Herts. WD19 4BG
tel (01923) 474480
website www.helenexleygiftbooks.com
Facebook www.facebook.com/helenexleylondon
Twitter @helen_exley
Ceo Helen Exley

Popular colour gift books for an international market. No unsolicited MSS. Founded 1976.

Eye Books & Lightning Books

29A Barrow Street, Much Wenlock, Shrops. TF13 6EN
tel 020-3239 3027
email dan@eye-books.com
website www.eye-books.com
Twitter @EyeAndLightning
Publisher Dan Hiscocks

Commercial narrative non-fiction with particular emphasis on business, travel and 'ordinary people doing extraordinary things'. Founded 1996.

Lightning Books

Literary and commercial fiction, particularly interested in writers under-represented by traditional publishers. Founded 2015.

Faber & Faber Ltd*‡

Bloomsbury House, 74–77 Great Russell Street, London WC1B 3DA
tel 020-7927 3800
website www.faber.co.uk
Facebook www.facebook.com/FaberBooks
Twitter @FaberBooks
Publishers Alex Bowler (adult), Leah Thaxton (children's)

Award-winning, independent publisher of high-quality picture books, fiction, middle grade, YA, non-fiction and poetry. Publishes books to support teachers, libraries and book clubs with relevant, inclusive and necessary stories. Authors include Emma Carroll, Jason Reynolds, Kieran Larwood, Swapna Haddow, Marissa Meyer, Kacen Callender, Kate Saunders, Bonnie-Sue Hitchcock and Natasha Farrant. Founded in 1929.

Fabian Society

61 Petty France, London SW1H 9EU
tel 020-7227 4900
email info@fabians.org.uk
website www.fabians.org.uk
Facebook www.facebook.com/fabiansociety
Twitter @thefabians
Editorial contacts Kate Murray, Iggy Wood

Current affairs, political thought, economics, education, environment, foreign affairs, social policy. Founded 1884.

Fahrenheit Press

85–97 Bayham Street, London NW1 0AG
website www.fahrenheit-press.com
Facebook www.facebook.com/FahrenheitPress
Twitter @fahrenheitpress
Founder Chris McVeigh

An independent publisher specialising in crime fiction. Publishes around 50 books per year in both ebook and paperback. Has an open submissions policy to give new writing talent the opportunity to get their work seen. Publishes three imprints. Fahrenheit Press publishes a blend of traditional crime fiction from established and debut novelists. Fahrenheit 13 produces a collection of hard-boiled noir and experimental crime fiction. Fahrenheit Editions publishes limited edition hardbacks. Founded 2015.

Fairchild Books – see Bloomsbury Publishing Plc

Fairlight Books Ltd‡

Summertown Pavilion, 18–24 Middle Way, Oxford OX2 7LG
email submissions@fairlightbooks.com
website www.fairlightbooks.co.uk
Facebook www.facebook.com/FairlightBooks
Twitter @fairlightbooks
Instagram @fairlightbooks

Specialises in literary fiction, particularly novellas (the Fairlight Moderns) and online short stories. Founded in 2017.

CJ Fallon

Ground Floor, Block B, Liffey Valley Office Campus, Dublin D22 X0Y3, Republic of Ireland
tel +353 (0)16 166400
email editorial@cjfallon.ie
website www.cjfallon.ie
Executive Director Brian Gilsenan

Educational textbooks. Founded 1927.

Farshore Books – see HarperCollins Publishers

David Fickling Books‡

31 Beaumont Street, Oxford OX1 2NP
tel (01865) 339000
website www.davidficklingbooks.com
Publisher David Fickling, *Publishing Director* Liz Cross

Independent publisher of picture books, novels and non-fiction for all ages, as well as graphic novels. Currently not accepting unsolicited MSS. Founded 1999.

Fig Tree – see Penguin General

Fighting High‡

23 Hitchin Road, Stotfold, Hitchin, Herts. SG5 4HP
tel 07936 415843
email fightinghigh@btinternet.com
website www.fightinghigh.com
Facebook www.facebook.com/groups/24337176057
Twitter @FightingHigh
Founder Steve Darlow

Publishes non-fiction books that focus on human endeavour, particularly in a historical military setting. For submission guidelines see website. Founded 2009.

Fincham Press*

University of Roehampton, School of Humanities, Fincham Building, Roehampton Lane, London SW15 5PH
email finchampress@roehampton.ac.uk
website https://fincham.press/
Facebook www.facebook.com/finchampress
Twitter @finchampress

Based at the University of Roehampton. Titles are commissioned, edited and published by a team based in English and creative writing, part of the School of Humanities and Social Sciences. Publishes creative writing anthologies, a journalism anthology, a book on representations of the professor in children's literature and a book on YA writing by a pre-eminent practitioner of the form. Founded 2014.

Findhorn Press

email sabine@findhornpress.com
website www.innertraditions.com/imprints/findhorn-press

Mind, body & spirit; spirituality, holistic health, self-help, nature. Founded 1971.

Fircone Books Ltd‡

The Holme, Church Road, Eardisley, Herefordshire HR3 6NJ
tel (01544) 327182
email info@firconebooks.com
website www.firconebooks.com
Facebook www.facebook.com/firconebooks
Twitter @firconebooks
Directors Richard Wheeler, Su Wheeler

Illustrated books on church art and architecture. Welcomes submission of ideas: send synopsis first. Founded 2009.

Firefly Press Ltd*‡

Britannia House, Caerphilly Business Park, Van Road, Caerphilly CF83 3GG
email hello@fireflypress.co.uk
website www.fireflypress.co.uk
Facebook www.facebook.com/FireflyPress
Twitter @fireflypress
Publisher Penny Thomas, *Editor* Janet Thomas

Award-winning publisher of fiction for 5–19 years. Founded 2013.

Fisherton Press

email general@fishertonpress.co.uk
website www.fishertonpress.co.uk
Facebook www.facebook.com/FishertonPress
Twitter @fishertonpress
Director Ellie Levenson

A small, independent publisher producing picture books for children under 7 years. Not currently accepting proposals but illustrators are welcome to send links to a portfolio. Founded 2013.

Fitzcarraldo Editions

A103 Fuel Tank, 8–12 Creekside, London SE8 3DX
email info@fitzcarraldoeditions.com
website www.fitzcarraldoeditions.com
Twitter @FitzcarraldoEds
Instagram @FitzcarraldoEds

An independent publisher specialising in contemporary fiction and long-form essays. It focuses on ambitious, imaginative and innovative writing, both in translation and in the English language. Publishes, among other authors, 2015 and 2018 Nobel Prize in Literature laureates Svetlana Alexievich and Olga Tokarczuk. Founded 2014.

5mBooks‡

Lings, Great Easton, Essex CM6 2HH
email hello@5mbooks.com
website www.5mbooks.com
Managing Director Jeremy Toynbee

Independent publisher publishing books for professionals, students and the general reader in veterinary medicine, companion animals, aquaculture and agriculture/smallholding. Founded 2020.

Flame Tree Publishing‡

6 Melbray Mews, Fulham, London SW6 3NS
tel 020-7751 9650
email info@flametreepublishing.com
website www.flametreepublishing.com, www.flametreepress.com
Publisher & Founder Nick Wells, *Executive Editor* Don D'Auria

Art, music, lifestyle and fiction. Accepts unsolicited MSS for fiction imprint Flame Tree Press, horror and suspense, sci-fi and fantasy. No YA titles. Look out for the short story submission windows for our thematic anthologies. Founded 1992.

Flapjack Books

Faircote House West Green, Pocklington, York YO42 2NH
email mail@flapjackpress.co.uk
website https://flapjackpress.co.uk
Facebook www.facebook.com/groups/296992752366
Twitter @FlapjackPress
Director Paul Wilson

Publishes poetry, poetry-theatre, plays and art collections for adults and children. Founded 2017.

Fleming Publications

9/2 Fleming House, 134 Renfrew Street, Glasgow G3 6ST
tel 0141 328 1935
email info@ettadunn.com
website www.flemingpublications.com
Managing Editor Etta Dunn

Fiction, non-fiction, poetry, history, biography, photography and self-help. Founded 2012.

Flipped Eye Publishing‡

email books@flippedeye.net
website https://flippedeye.net
Facebook www.facebook.com/flipped.eye.publishing
Twitter @flippedeye
Instagram @flippedeye
Directors Nii Ayikwei Parkes (director & senior editor), Mitchell Albert (editorial director, fiction & non-fiction), Jacob Sam-La Rose (senior editor, poetry), Niall O'Sullivan (senior editor, poetry)

Publishes an eclectic catalogue of fiction, non-fiction and poetry. Founded 2001.

Books

Books

Floris Books*

Canal Court, 40 Craiglockhart Avenue,
Edinburgh EH14 1LT
email floris@florisbooks.co.uk
website www.florisbooks.co.uk
Facebook www.facebook.com/FlorisBooks
Twitter @FlorisBooks
Commissioning Editors Sally Polson, Eleanor Collins

Religion; philosophy; holistic health; organics; mind,
body & spirit; crafts; parenting. Children's books:
board books, picture books, story anthologies. See
website for submission details. Founded 1976.

Kelpies

website www.discoverkelpies.co.uk
Contemporary Scottish fiction – board books (1–3
years), picture books (3–6 years), young readers series
(6–8 years) and novels (8–15 years). Annual Kelpies
Prize, see website.

Flying Eye Books Ltd*

27 Westgate Street, London E8 3RL
tel 020-7033 4430
email info@nobrow.net
website www.flyingeyebooks.com
Twitter @flyingeyebooks

Publishes picture books, illustrated fiction and non-
fiction and graphic novels. Founded 2013.

Imprint 27

Celebrates experimental writing in fiction and non-
fiction.

Nobrow

email info@nobrow.net
website www.nobrow.net
Twitter @NobrowPress

Comics and graphic novel imprint. Fiction and non-
fiction. Founded 2008.

Flyleaf Press

19 Balally Avenue, Dundrum D16 Y274,
Republic of Ireland
tel +353 (0)4 429014
email info@ancestornetwork.ie
website www.ancestornetwork.ie

Imprint of Ancestor Network. Irish family history.
Founded 1988.

Fly on the Wall Press

56 High Lea Road, New Mills, Derbyshire SK22 3DP
email flyonthewallpress@hotmail.com
website www.flyonthewallpress.co.uk
Facebook www.facebook.com/flyonthewallpress
Twitter @fly_press
Instagram @flyonthewallpress
Managing Director Isabelle Kenyon

Publisher of politically engaged fiction, poetry and
cross-genre anthologies. Titles showcase international
talent, focusing on under-represented stories. Cross-
genre anthologies generate discussion around social
issues and fundraise for chosen charities.
Founded 2018.

Folens Publishers

Hibernian Industrial Estate, Greenhills Road,
Tallaght, Dublin D24 DH05, Republic of Ireland
tel +353 (0)14 137200
email info@folens.ie
website www.folens.ie
Facebook www.facebook.com/FolensIreland
Twitter @FolensIreland
Chairman David Moffitt

Educational (primary, secondary). Founded 1958.

Fonthill Media Ltd

Millview House, Toadsmoor Road, Stroud,
Glos. GL5 2TB
tel (01453) 886959
email office@fonthillmedia.com
website www.fonthillmedia.com
Facebook www.facebook.com/fonthillmedia
Twitter @fonthillmedia
Publisher & Ceo Alan Sutton

General history. Specialisations include biography,
military history, aviation history, naval and maritime
history, regional and local history, transport (railway,
canal, road) history, social history, sports history,
ancient history and archaeology. Also publishes
widely in the USA with American regional, local,
military and transport history under the imprints of
Fonthill, America Through Time and American
History House. Founded 2011.

W. Foulsham & Co. Ltd

The Old Barrel Store, Brewery Courtyard,
Draymans Lane, Marlow, Bucks. SL7 2FF
tel (01628) 400631
email annemarie.howe@foulsham.com
website www.foulsham.com
Contact Annemarie Howe

Publishes in print: life issues; mind, body & spirit;
health; therapies; lifestyle; popular philosophy;
practical psychology; food and drink; parenting.
Publishes in digital: content management systems
and data; iGuides travel; nutrition; self-help;
gardening; cookery. Founded c.1800.

Quantum

Mind, body & spirit; popular philosophy and
practical psychology.

Four Courts Press

7 Malpas Street, Dublin D08 YD81,
Republic of Ireland
tel +353 (0)14 534668
email info@fourcourtspress.ie
website www.fourcourtspress.ie

Publisher Martin Fanning, *Senior Editor* Sam Tranum

Academic books in the humanities, especially history, Celtic and medieval studies, art, theology. Founded 1970.

404 Ink*

Summit House, 4–5 Mitchell Street,
Edinburgh EH6 7BD
email hello@404Ink.com
website www.404ink.com
Facebook www.facebook.com/404Ink
Twitter @404Ink
Directors Heather McDaid, Laura Jones

An independent publisher specialising in confronting, powerful fiction and social issue-based non-fiction and poetry. The main list and non-fiction pocket-book series Inklings welcome submissions during specific windows which are announced on the website. Founded 2016.

4th Estate – see HarperCollins Publishers

Free Association Books

1 Angel Cottages, Milespit Hill, London NW7 1RD
email contact@freeassociationpublishing.com
website www.freeassociationpublishing.com
Twitter @Fab_Publishing
Director Trevor E. Brown, *Publishing Director* Alice Solomons, *Marketing & Editorial Consultant* Lisa Findley

Social sciences, psychoanalysis, psychotherapy, counselling, cultural studies, social welfare, addiction studies, child and adolescent studies, mental health, parenting, health studies. No poetry, fiction or memoir. Founded 1984.

Gaia Books – see Octopus Publishing Group

The Gallery Press

Loughcrew, Oldcastle, Co. Meath A82 N225, Republic of Ireland
tel +353 (0)49 8541779
email books@gallerypress.com
website www.gallerypress.com
Directors Peter Fallon, Jean Fallon

Publishes the work of writers who are Irish by birth, residence or citizenship (or who have applied for citizenship). See website for submission guidelines. Only accepts postal submissions. Founded 1970.

Galley Beggar Press

email info@galleybeggar.co.uk
website www.galleybeggar.co.uk
Twitter @GalleyBeggars
Co-directors Eloise Millar, Sam Jordison

Independent publisher based in Norwich. Looks for authors whose writing shows great ambition and literary merit in their chosen genre. When submitting a MS authors must provide proof that they have read

another book that Galley Beggar Press has published. Prefers completed MS; email as pdf or Word document. One submission per author. Considers a wide range of genres including fiction, non-fiction, quality sci-fi, novels and short stories. No poetry or children's. Founded 2011.

Gallic Books‡

12 Eccleston Street, London SW1W 9LT
tel 020-7259 9336
email info@gallicbooks.com
website www.gallicbooks.com
Facebook www.facebook.com/gallicbooks
Twitter @BelgraviaB
Managing Director Joe Harper

Independent publisher with focus on French writing in translation. Publishes fiction, fiction in translation, historical fiction, crime and noir, biography and memoir. Accepts submissions from agents and foreign publishers. Part of the Belgravia Books Collective. Founded 2007.

J. Garnet Miller – see Cressrelles Publishing Co. Ltd

Garnet Publishing Ltd*‡

8 Southern Court, South Street, Reading RG1 4QS
tel 0118 959 7847
email info@garnetpublishing.co.uk
website www.garnetpublishing.co.uk

Comprises three imprints. Founded 1991.

Garnet Publishing

website www.garnetpublishing.co.uk
Trade non-fiction pertaining to the Middle East (art and architecture, cookery, culture, current affairs, history, photography, political and social issues, religion, travel and general). Accepts unsolicited material.

Ithaca Press

website www.ithacapress.co.uk
Leading publisher of academic books with a focus on Middle Eastern studies. Accepts unsolicited material.

Periscope

website www.periscopebooks.co.uk
Literary fiction and trade non-fiction from around the world: biography, crime fiction, current affairs, historical fiction, literary translations, memoir, political and social issues, popular history, popular science, reportage, general literary fiction and general trade non-fiction. Accepts unsolicited material.

Geddes & Grosset

31 Six Harmony Row, Glasgow G51 3BA
tel 0141 375 1998
email info@geddesandgrosset.co.uk
website www.geddesandgrosset.com
Publishers Ron Grosset, Liz Small

Books

An imprint of The Gresham Publishing Company Ltd (page 149). Mass market reference *Word Power* – English language learning and health and wellbeing. Associated imprint: Waverley Books. Founded 1988.

Gibson Square‡

tel 020-7096 1100
email info@gibsonsquare.com
website www.gibsonsquare.com
Facebook www.facebook.com/gibson.square
Publisher Martin Rynja

Non-fiction: general non-fiction, biography, current affairs, philosophy, politics, cultural criticism, psychology, history, travel, art history. Some fiction. See website for guidelines or email to receive an automated response. Authors include Alexander Litvinenko, Melanie Phillips, Bernard-Henri Lévy, Diana Mitford, Anthony Grayling, John McCain, Naomi Klein, Niall Ferguson. Founded 2001.

Gill†

Hume Avenue, Park West, Dublin D12 YV96, Republic of Ireland
tel +353 (0)15 009500
email sales@gill.ie
website www.gill.ie
Managing Director Ruth Gill

An independent publisher and distributor in Dublin. In partnership with the Macmillan Group in London, Gill & Macmillan was formed in 1968. Now fully owned by the Gill family following the buyout of the Macmillan interest in 2013. Founded 1856.

Gill Books

website www.gillbooks.ie
Facebook www.facebook.com/gillbooks
Twitter @gillbooks

Trade publishing. Irish interest: biography, cookery, children's, wellness, history, politics, current affairs, reference, lifestyle and fiction. Publisher of established authors and champion of new voices.

Gill Education

website www.gilleducation.ie, www.gillexplore.ie
Primary and post-primary publisher. Working with educators to create books and resources, tailored to the Irish market. Also supplies Irish schools with a range of literacy and numeracy resources.

Gingko

4 Molasses Row, London SW11 3UX
tel 020-3637 9730
email gingko@gingkolibrary.com
website www.gingko.org.uk
Publisher Barbara Schwepcke

Works with scholars of diverse backgrounds and research interests to increase understanding of the Middle East, West Asia and North Africa through conferences, public events and cultural programmes as well as publications. Founded 2014.

Godsfield Press – see Octopus Publishing Group

Goldsmiths Press

Room 108, Deptford Town Hall, New Cross, London SE14 6NW
tel 020-7919 7258
email goldsmithspress@gold.ac.uk
website www.gold.ac.uk/goldsmiths-press
Twitter @goldsmithspress
Director Sarah Kember

Publishes print and digital media across disciplinary boundaries and between theory, practice and fiction, aims to create a culture around inventive academic-knowledge practices. Goldsmiths Press is an Open Access monograph publisher, combining Open Access with a fair pricing model for print books. Founded 2016.

Graffeg

24 Stradey Park Business Centre, Mwrwg Road, Llangennech, Llanelli SA14 8YP
tel (01554) 824000
email croeso@graffeg.com
website https://graffeg.com/
Facebook www.facebook.com/graffegbooks
Twitter @graffeg_books
Founder Peter Gill

Publishes non-fiction illustrated books about food, art, music, culture and heritage, architecture, gardens, photography, sport and lifestyle, and illustrated fiction for children. Founded 2003.

Granta Books‡

12 Addison Avenue, London W11 4QR
tel 020-7605 1360
website www.granta.com
Twitter @GrantaBooks
Publisher Sigrid Rausing, *Managing Director* Bella Lacey, *Deputy Publishing Director* Laura Barber

Literary fiction, memoir, nature writing, cultural criticism and travel. No submissions except via a reputable literary agent. An imprint of Granta Publications. Founded 1982.

Green Print – see Merlin Press Ltd

Gresham Books Ltd

The Carriage House, Ningwood Manor, Ningwood, Isle of Wight PO30 4NJ
tel (01983) 761389
email info@gresham-books.co.uk
website www.gresham-books.co.uk
Managing Director Nicholas Oulton

Hymn books, prayer books, service books, school histories and other bespoke publications. Founded 1979.

The Gresham Publishing Company Ltd
31 Six Harmony Row, Glasgow G51 3BA
tel 0141 375 1996
email info@waverley-books.co.uk
website www.waverley-books.co.uk,
www.geddesandgrosset.com
Facebook www.facebook.com/WaverleyBooks
Twitter @WaverleyBooks
Publishers Ron Grosset, Liz Small

Books for the general trade and Scottish interest books. Imprints: Geddes & Grosset (page 147) and Waverley Books. Founded 2013.

Grub Street Publishing‡
4 Rainham Close, London SW11 6SS
tel 020-7924 3966 / 020-7738 1008
email post@grubstreet.co.uk
website www.grubstreet.co.uk
Principals John B. Davies, Anne Dolamore

Adult non-fiction: military, aviation history, cookery. Founded 1992.

Guild of Master Craftsman Publications Ltd*
166 High Street, Lewes, East Sussex BN7 1XU
tel (01273) 477374
email jonathanb@thegmcgroup.com
website www.gmcbooks.com
Twitter @GMCbooks
Instagram @gmcpublications
Managing Director Jonathan Phillips, *Publisher* Jonathan Bailey

Publisher of leisure and hobby project books, with a focus on all types of woodworking; from carving and turning to routing. Craft subjects include needlecraft, paper crafts, forest schooling and jewellery-making. The books are aimed at craftspeople of all skill levels. Founded 1979.

Ammonite Press
website www.ammonitepress.com
Twitter @AmmonitePress
Publisher Jonathan Bailey
Publishes highly illustrated non-fiction for the international market including mindfulness journals, escape puzzle books and other gift books featuring illustration, infographics and photography on pop culture, pop reference, biography and history. Practical photography titles written by professional photographers provide authoritative guides to technique and equipment.

Button Books
website www.buttonbooks.co.uk
Publishes design-led children's books, which includes award-winning non-fiction, round-cornered board books, wipe-clean flash cards, hardbacks with poster jackets, activity books with stickers and picture books with pop-out animals to make. Combining beautiful illustration, from retro to modern, with high production values and innovative ideas.

Guinness World Records
Ground Floor, The Rookery, 2 Dyott Street, London WC1A 1DE
tel 020-7891 4567
website www.guinnessworldrecords.com
Editor-in-Chief Craig Glenday

Guinness World Records, *GWR Gamer's Edition*, TV and brand licensing, records processing. No unsolicited MSS. A Jim Pattison Group company. Founded 1954.

Guppy Publishing Ltd*‡
Bracken Hill, Cotswold Road, Oxford OX2 9JG
tel 07884 068983
email bella@guppybooks.co.uk
website www.guppybooks.co.uk
Facebook www.facebook.com/guppybooks
Twitter @guppybooks
Instagram @guppypublishing
Director Bella Pearson

Publishing children's and YA fiction for 5–18 years. Illustrated books for newly emerging readers, fiction for middle-grade readers and novels for YA. Poetry, prose, graphic novels. No unsolicited submissions outside the Guppy Open Submission Competition (run annually in May). Founded 2019.

Hachette Audio
Little, Brown Audio from May 2023
Carmelite House, 50 Victoria Embankment, London EC4Y 0DZ
email sarah.shrubb@littlebrown.co.uk
website www.littlebrown.co.uk
Twitter @HachetteAudioUK
Audio Publisher Sarah Shrubb

Audiobook list that focuses on unabridged titles from Little, Brown's bestselling authors such as Robert Galbraith, Delia Owens, Ann Leckie and Mark Billingham, as well as classics including Joseph Heller's *Catch-22* and Erich Maria Remarque's *All Quiet on the Western Front*. Publishes approx. 400 audiobooks per year. Founded 2003.

Hachette Children's Group*
Carmelite House, 50 Victoria Embankment, London EC4Y 0DZ
email editorial@hachettechildrens.co.uk
website www.hachettechildrens.co.uk
Facebook www.facebook.com/hachettechildrens
Twitter @HachetteKids
Instagram @Hachettechildrens

Hachette Children's Group is one of the largest children's publishers in the UK, publishing baby and preschool books, picture books, illustrated gift, fiction, non-fiction, series fiction, books for the school and library market and licensed publishing.

Books

Comprising of imprints Hodder Children's Books, Laurence King Children's Books, Little, Brown Books for Young Readers, Orchard Books, Orion Children's Books, Quercus Children's Books, Pat-a-Cake, Wren & Rook, Franklin Watts and Wayland Books and Welbeck Children's Books and is the owner of Enid Blyton Entertainment. Generally only accepts submissions sent via an agent. Occasionally holds periods of open submissions for a limited time or a specific genre. See social media channels for details. Founded 1986.

Hachette UK*

Carmelite House, 50 Victoria Embankment, London EC4Y 0DZ
tel 020-3122 6000
website www.hachette.co.uk
Ceo David Shelley

Part of Hachette Livre SA since 2004. Hachette UK group companies: Bookouture (page 131); Dialogue Books (page 140); Little, Brown Audio (see Hachette Audio page 149), Hachette Book Publishing India Private Ltd; Hachette Children's Group (page 149); Hachette Australia (page 193); Hachette Ireland; Hachette New Zealand (page 200); Headline Publishing Group (page 153); Hodder Education (page 154); Hodder & Stoughton (page 154); Little, Brown Book Group (page 160); John Murray Press (page 164); Octopus Publishing Group (page 167); Orion Publishing Group (page 169); Quercus Publishing Plc (page 175), Welbeck Publishing Group (page 189). Founded 1986.

Hadean Press Ltd‡

Unit 30, Mantra House, South Street, Keighley, West Yorks. BD21 1SX
email info@hadeanpress.com
website www.hadeanpress.com
Facebook www.facebook.com/hadeanpress
Instagram @hadeanpress
Managing & Editorial Director Erzebet Barthold

A small press producing titles in modern occultism, publishing academic and independent scholarship in the areas of folklore, folk magic and spellbooks. Founded 2008.

Halban Publishers‡

176 Goldhurst Terrace, London NW6 3HN
tel 020-7692 5541
email books@halbanpublishers.com
website www.halbanpublishers.com
Facebook www.facebook.com/HalbanPublishers
Twitter @Halban_publishers
Instagram @Halban_Publishers
Directors Martine Halban, Peter Halban

General fiction and non-fiction; history and biography; Jewish subjects and Middle East. No unsolicited MSS considered; preliminary letter or email essential. Founded 1986.

Halcyon Publishing*

64 Kingsbarns Drive, Glasgow G44 4SL
website https://halcyonpublishing.co.uk/
Twitter @HalcyonPublish1
Founders Rob MacDonald, Adam Bushby

Publisher of books that tell real stories about real football. Founded 2020.

Robert Hale Ltd – see Joffe Books

Halsgrove Publishing

Halsgrove House, Ryelands Business Park, Bagley Road, Wellington, Somerset TA21 9PZ
tel (01823) 653777
email sales@halsgrove.com
website www.halsgrove.com
Facebook www.facebook.com/Halsgrove.Publishing
Twitter @Halsgrove
Directors Julian Davidson, Steven Pugsley, *Associate Publisher* Simon Butler

Regional books for local-interest readers in the UK. Also illustrated books on individual artists. Founded 1986.

Hamish Hamilton – see Penguin General

Hamlyn – see Octopus Publishing Group

Happy Yak

1 Triptych Place, London SE1 9SH
tel 020-7000 8084
website www.quartoknows.com/happy-yak

A children's imprint of the Quarto Group, Inc. (page 175). Publishes preschool, picture books and illustrated non-fiction for children from birth upwards, with a focus on fun, accessible content and contemporary illustration. Founded 2021.

Hardie Grant UK‡

5th and 6th Floors, Pentagon House, 52–54 Southwark Street, London SE1 1UN
tel 020-7601 7500
email info@hardiegrant.co.uk
website www.hardiegrant.com/uk
Founders Sandy Grant, Fiona Hardie

Non-fiction, categories include: food and drink, gift and humour, craft, gardening; wellness, interiors and pop culture. Founded 1994.

Harlequin (UK) Ltd*

HarperCollins Publishers Ltd, 1 London Bridge Street, London SE1 9EF
tel 0844 844 1351
website www.millsandboon.co.uk
Facebook www.facebook.com/millsandboon
Twitter @MillsandBoon
Executive Publisher of Mills & Boon UK Lisa Milton, *Executive Editor of Harlequin/Mills & Boon Series* Bryony Green

Part of HarperCollins Publishers. Founded 1908.

Mills & Boon Historical
Senior Editor Carly Byrne

Historical romance fiction.

Mills & Boon Medical
Senior Editor Sheila Hodgson

Contemporary romance fiction in a medical setting.

Mills & Boon Modern Romance
Senior Editor Flo Nicoll

Contemporary romances – luxury and passion.

Mills & Boon True Love
Senior Editor Sheila Hodgson

Contemporary romances – emotion and escapism.

HarperCollins Publishers*
The News Building, 1 London Bridge Street,
London SE1 9GF
tel 020-8741 7070
Alternative address Westerhill Road, Bishopbriggs,
Glasgow G64 2QT
tel 0141 772 3200
website www.harpercollins.co.uk
Ceo Charlie Redmayne, *Managing Director* Kate
Elton, *Executive Publishers* Sarah Emsley, Kimberly
Young

All fiction and trade non-fiction must be submitted
through an agent. Owned by News Corporation.
Founded 1817.

Avon
Managing Director Kate Elton, *Publisher* Helen
Huthwaite

General fiction, crime and thrillers, women's fiction.

The Borough Press
Executive Publisher Kimberly Young, *Publishing
Director* Suzie Dooré

Literary fiction and non-fiction.

William Collins
Executive Publisher David Roth-Ey, *Publishing
Directors* Arabella Pike (history, politics, current
affairs, biography), Myles Archibald (natural history,
science)

Science, history, art, politics and current affairs,
biography, religion and natural history.

Collins
website www.collins.co.uk
Managing Director Alex Beecroft

Reference publishing, including dictionaries and
atlases, as well as the National Trust and *The Times*
lists. Collins is also an education publisher for UK
and international school curriculums, and publishes
extensive revision and home learning support for
parents and children.

Farshore Books
website www.farshore.com
Executive Publisher Cally Poplak, *Publishing Directors*
Lindsey Heaven, Melissa Fairley, John Packard

Children's fiction, YA (Electric Monkey), picture
books, non-fiction (Red Shed), film/TV, toy and
gaming. Previously known as Egmont UK.

4th Estate
Executive Publisher David Roth-Ey, *Publishing
Directors* Louise Haines (cookery, art, music, popular
science, biography), Michelle Kane (fiction, memoir,
popular culture, self-improvement), Kishani
Widyaratna (literary fiction, memoir, essays)

Fiction, literary fiction, current affairs, popular
science, biography, humour, travel, cookery, art,
music, memoir, popular culture, self-improvement,
essays.

HarperCollins Audio
Group Technology & Digital Director Joanna Surman,
Audio Publishing Director Fionnuala Barrett

Publishes various audio formats. Leading publisher of
trade fiction and non-fiction audiobooks for children
and adults, as well as standalone audio projects.
Publishes in excess of 75,000 audiobooks each year.

HarperCollins Children's Books
Executive Publisher Cally Poplak; *Publishers* Nick
Lake, Juliet Matthews

Children's fiction (5–8, 9–12 years), YA fiction and
series fiction; film/TV tie-in brands.

HarperCollins Ireland
Managing Director Kate Elton, *Publishing Director*
Conor Nagle

Promotes authors who are either Irish by birth or
living and working in Ireland. Fiction, non-fiction
and children's books.

HarperFiction
Executive Publisher Kimberley Young, *Publishers*
David Brawn, Lynne Drew, Julia Wisdom

General, historical fiction, crime and thrillers,
women's fiction.

Harper NonFiction
Executive Publisher Sarah Emsley, *Publisher* Adam
Humphrey; *Publishing Directors* Joel Simons, Kelly
Ellis, Katya Shipster, Rose Sandy, Ajda Vucicevic,
Lydia Good

Autobiographies, entertainment, sport, cookery,
lifestyle and culture. Includes the imprints Element,
Mudlark and Thorsons.

HarperNorth
Executive Publisher Sarah Emsley, *Publishing Director*
Genevieve Pegg

Fiction: general, historical, crime and thrillers. Non-
fiction: autobiographies, memoir, politics, history,
sport, nature writing, smart-thinking.

Books

Harper360

This imprint aims to have all books for which the company has rights, in all markets around the world, in all formats, available for sale in the UK.

Harper Voyager

Executive Publisher Kimberley Young, *Publishing Director* Natasha Bardon

Publishes fantasy and sci-fi.

HQ

Executive Publisher Lisa Milton, *Fiction Publishers* Kate Mills, Manpreet Grewal, *Non-fiction Editorial Director* Louise McKeever

For fiction: commercial fiction, crime and thrillers, women's fiction, historical and book club. For non-fiction: memoir, cookery, self-help and wellbeing, and smart thinking.

HQ Digital

Editorial Director Abigail Fenton

Digital-first commercial fiction list, general, crime and thrillers, women's fiction, psychological thrillers, saga.

Mills & Boon

Executive Editor (Series) Bryony Green, *Commissioning Editor (Trade)* Rebecca Slorach

One More Chapter

Executive Publisher Kimberley Young, *Publisher* Charlotte Ledger

Digital-first commercial fiction.

Pavilion Books

website www.pavilionbooks.com
Publishing Director Stephanie Milner

Food and drink, craft, hobbies, health and wellbeing, and gift. Imprints include: Collins & Brown, Pavilion, Portico and Robson. Formerly Anova Books Group. Founded 2013.

Times Books

Publishes a range of *The Times* puzzle books.

Harriman House[‡]

3 Viceroy Court, Bedford Road, Petersfield, Hants GU32 3LJ
tel (01730) 233870
email contact@harriman-house.com
email commissioning@harriman-house.com
website www.harriman.house

Boutique press specialising in practical non-fiction books: smart thinking, business and finance, lifestyle and more. Publishes in UK and US simultaneously. For submission guidelines see website. Founded 1992.

Hart Publishing[*‡]

Kemp House, Chawley Park, Cumnor Hill, Oxford OX2 9PH
tel (01865) 598648

email mail@hartpub.co.uk
website www.bloomsbury.com
Facebook www.facebook.com/HartPublishing2
Twitter @hartpublishing
Editorial Director Sinéad Moloney

Legal academic texts for law students, scholars and practitioners. Covers all aspects of law (UK domestic, European and international). An imprint of Bloomsbury Publishing (page 130). Founded 1996.

Harvill Secker – see Vintage

Hashtag Press[*‡]

10 Bankfields, Headcorn, Kent TN27 9RA
email submissions@hashtagpress.co.uk
website www.hashtagpress.co.uk
Facebook www.facebook.com/hashtagbooks
Twitter @hastag_press
Founders Abiola Bello, Helen Lewis

A female-led independent publishing house specialising in diverse and inclusive stories and writers, led by bestselling author Abiola Bello and award-winning book publicist Helen Lewis. Publishes children's, YA, non-fiction and some commercial fiction. Founded 2017.

Hashtag BLAK

email info@hashtagblak.co.uk
website www.hashtagblak.co.uk

Supported by Arts Council England. An imprint that celebrates love stories written by under-represented writers.

Haunt Publishing[*]

90 Letham Way, Dalgety Bay, Dunfermline, Fife, Scotland, KY11 9FT
email boo@hauntpublishing.com
Facebook www.facebook.com/HauntPublish
Twitter @HauntPublishing
Director & Managing Editor Rebecca Wojturska

An independent publisher of Gothic, horror and dark fiction in all formats. Founded 2018.

Haus Publishing Ltd

4 Cinnamon Row, Plantation Wharf, London SW11 3TW
tel 020-3637 9729
email haus@hauspublishing.com
website https://hauspublishing.com/
Twitter @HausPublishing
Editor Ella Carr

Publishes history, literary fiction in translation, biography, memoir and current affairs. Founded 2003.

Hawthorn Press[*‡]

1 Lansdown Lane, Stroud, Glos. GL5 1BJ
tel (01453) 757040

email info@hawthornpress.com
website www.hawthornpress.com
Director Martin Large

Publishes books and ebooks. Series include *Early Years*, *Steiner/Waldorf Education*, *Crafts*, *Storytelling* and *Parenting*. Founded 1981.

Hay House Publishers‡

The Sixth Floor, Watson House, 54 Baker Street, London W1U 7BU
tel 020-3927 7290
email info@hayhouse.co.uk
website www.hayhouse.co.uk
Facebook www.facebook.com/HayHouse
Twitter @HayHouseUK
Managing Director & Publisher Michelle Pilley

Publishers of mind, body & spirit; self-help; personal development; health; spirituality and wellness. Head office in San Diego, California. For submissions use website only. Acquired by Renard Press Ltd 2022 (page 176). Founded 1984.

Haynes Publishing

Sparkford, Yeovil, Somerset BA22 7JJ
tel (01963) 440635
website www.haynes.co.uk
Chairman Eddie Bell, *Chief Executive* J. Haynes

Practical lifestyle manuals for the home, motorsport, space, military, aviation, entertainment and leisure activities. Founded 1960.

Hazel Press

website https://hazelpress.co.uk/
Publisher & Editor Daphne Astor

An independent publisher based in East Anglia. Specifically publishes poetry, books and essays with a subject focus on the environment, the realities of climate change, feminism and the arts. Contact can be made via website. Founded 2020.

Head of Zeus*‡

Clerkenwell House, 5–8 Hardwick Street, London EC1R 4RG
tel 020-7253 5557
email hello@headofzeus.com
website www.headofzeus.com
Facebook www.facebook.com/headofzeus/
Twitter @HoZ_Books
Ceo Nicholas Cheetham

General and literary fiction, genre fiction and non-fiction. Imprint of Bloomsbury Publishing plc (page 130). Founded 2012.

Zephyr
Children's imprint.

Headline Publishing Group*

Carmelite House, 50 Victoria Embankment, London EC4Y 0DZ
tel 020-3122 7222
email enquiries@hachette.co.uk
website www.headline.co.uk
Twitter @headlinepg
Managing Director Mari Evans

Commercial and literary fiction (hardback, paperback and ebook) and popular non-fiction including autobiography, biography, food and wine, gardening, history, popular science, sport, TV tie-ins. Publishes under Headline (page 150), Headline Review, Tinder Press, Headline Eternal, Wildfire, Headline Home. Founded 1993.

Henley Hall Press

Woofferton Grange, Brimfield, Ludlow, Shrops. SY8 4NP
tel 07984 585861
email susanne@henleyhallpress.co.uk
website www.henleyhallpress.co.uk
Twitter @HenleyHallPress
Contact Susanne Lumsden

An independent non-fiction publisher. Categories include farming, topical affairs, gardening, history and biography. Launch title *On Plan & Proportion* by award-winning garden designer George Carter. Founded 2019.

Hera Books

email submissions@herabooks.com
website www.herabooks.com
Publishing Director Keshini Naidoo

Independent commercial fiction publisher. Publishes crime and thriller, romance, saga and general fiction. Send a one-page synopsis and the whole MS in Word format to submissions email. Part of Canelo Digital Publishing Ltd (page 134). Founded 2018.

Nick Hern Books Ltd‡

The Glasshouse, 49A Goldhawk Road, London W12 8QP
tel 020-8749 4953
email info@nickhernbooks.co.uk
website www.nickhernbooks.co.uk
Facebook www.facebook.com/NickHernBooks
Twitter @NickHernBooks
Publisher Nick Hern, *Managing Director* Matt Applewhite

Theatre and performing arts books, professionally produced plays, performing rights. Initial letter required. Founded 1988.

Hesperus Press Ltd

13 Staines Road, Hounslow TW4 5DJ
tel 020-7436 0943
email publishing@hesperus.press
website https://hesperus.press/
Facebook www.facebook.com/hesperuspress
Twitter @HesperusPress

Under three imprints, publishes over 300 books. Hesperus Classics introduces older works of

Books

literature, Hesperus Nova showcases contemporary literature and Hesperus Minor publishes well-loved children's books from the past. Founded 2001.

Hippopotamus Press
22 Whitewell Road, Frome, Somerset BA11 4EL
tel (01373) 466653
email rjhippopress@aol.com
email mphippopress@aol.com
Editor Roland John

Poetry, essays, criticism. Submissions from new writers welcome. Founded 1974.

The History Press Ltd‡
97 St Georges Place, Cheltenham, Glos. GL50 3QB
tel (01242) 895310
website www.thehistorypress.co.uk
Managing Director Gareth Swain, *Publishing Director* Laura Perehinec

Founded 2008.

The History Press
History and biography, general non-fiction.

Flint Books
Non-fiction books.

Hobeck Books‡
24 Brookside Business Park, Stone, Staffs. ST15 0RZ
email hobeckbooks@gmail.com
website www.hobeck.net
Facebook www.facebook.com/Hobeckbooks10
Twitter @hobeckbooks
Instagram @hobeckbooks
Directors Rebecca Collins, Adrian Hobart

Publishes crime, thrillers, mystery and suspense. Titles have been shortlisted for Bloody Scotland and the CWA Daggers. For submission guidelines see website. Also hosts a weekly podcast called the Hobcast Book Show (https://adrianhobart.podbean. com/) for writers and lovers of the crime fiction genre. Runs the four-times-a-year Henshaw Press Short-Story Competition and publishes the biannual charity anthology of winning short stories. See www.henshawpress.co.uk for details on how to enter. Founded 2019.

Hodder & Stoughton*
Carmelite House, 50 Victoria Embankment, London EC4Y 0DZ
tel 020-3122 6777
website www.hodder.co.uk
Ceo Katie Espiner, *Managing Director* Oliver Malcolm, *Fiction Executive Publisher* Jo Dickinson, *Hodderscape Publisher* Molly Powell, *Sceptre Executive Publisher* Federico Andornino, *Non-fiction Publisher* Kirty Topiwala, *Hodder Lifestyle & Yellow Kite Publisher* Liz Gough, *Coronet Publisher* Hannah Black

Commercial and literary fiction; biography; autobiography; history; humour; mind, body & spirit;
travel; lifestyle and cookery; other general interest non-fiction; audio. No unsolicited MSS or synopses. Publishes under Hodder & Stoughton, Hodderscape, Sceptre, Coronet, Yellow Kite. Part of Hachette UK (see page 150). Founded 1960.

Hodder & Stoughton Audio
Audio Publisher Dominic Gribben
Specialist audiobook team publishing fiction and non-fiction audiobooks from within the Hodder group by authors including Stephen King, John Grisham, Jodi Picoult, Graham Norton, John Connolly and David Mitchell. The team also commissions and publishes original audiobook content and podcasts.

Hodder Education*
Carmelite House, 50 Victoria Embankment, London EC4Y 0DZ
tel (01235) 827720
website www.hoddereducation.co.uk,
www.galorepark.co.uk, www.risingstars-uk.com
Managing Director Seshni Jacobs

School and college publishing. Includes Rising Stars, RS Assessment, Hodder Education and Galore Park. Part of Hachette UK (page 150). Founded 1960.

Hodder Gibson*
50 Frederick Street, Edinburgh EH2 1EX
email hoddergibson@hodder.co.uk
website www.hoddergibson.co.uk
Managing Director Paul Cherry

Educational books specifically for Scotland. Part of Hachette UK (see page 150). Founded 1960.

Honno Ltd (Welsh Women's Press)‡
D41 Hugh Owen Building, Penglais Campus, Aberystwyth University, Aberystwyth SY23 3DY
tel (01970) 623150
email post@honno.co.uk
website www.honno.co.uk
Facebook www.facebook.com/honnopress
Twitter @honno

Literature written by women born or living in Wales or women with a significant Welsh connection. All subjects considered – fiction, non-fiction, autobiographies. No poetry or works for children. Honno is a community cooperative. Founded 1986.

HopeRoad‡
PO Box 55544, Exhibition Road, London SW7 2DB
email rosemarie@hoperoadpublishing.com
website www.hoperoadpublishing.com
Facebook www.facebook.com/HopeRoadPublishing
Twitter @hoperoadpublish
Instagram @hoperoadpublishing
Director & Publisher Rosemarie Hudson

Publishes a wide range of fiction for adults and YA from and about Africa, Asia and the Caribbean. Founded 2010.

Small Axes

Small Axes focuses on republishing out-of-print postcolonial classics. Founded 2019.

Hopscotch

St Jude's Church, Dulwich Road, London SE24 0PB
tel 020-7501 6736
email orders@hopscotchbooks.com
website www.hopscotchbooks.com
Associate Publisher Angela Morano Shaw

A division of MA Education. Teaching resources for primary school teachers. Founded 1997.

Practical Pre-School Books

Early years teaching resources.

Hot Key Books*

Victoria House, Bloomsbury Square, London WC1B 4DA
tel 020-3770 8888
email hello@bonnierbooks.co.uk
website www.hotkeybooks.com,
www.bonnierbooks.co.uk
Twitter @HotKeyBooksYA
Executive Publisher Emma Matthewson

Publishes original and thought-provoking teen and YA fiction, some books also suitable for an adult audience. An imprint of Bonnier Books UK (page 131). Founded 2012.

House of Lochar

Isle of Colonsay, Argyll PA61 7YR
tel (01951) 200320
email sales@houseoflochar.com
website www.houseoflochar.com

Scottish history, transport, Scottish literature. Founded 1995.

Howgate Publishing Ltd‡

Station House, North Street, Havant, Hants. PO9 1QU
email info@howgatepublishing.com
website www.howgatepublishing.com
Twitter @kirstin_howgate
Publisher & Director Kirstin Howgate

Publishes military training, education, and narrative books. Shortlisted for the 2023 Independent Publisher Awards – Nick Robinson Newcomer Award. Submission guidelines and bookshop available on website. Founded 2019.

John Hunt Publishing Ltd*‡

Unit 11, Shepperton House, 89 Shepperton Road, London N1 3DF
email office@jhpbooks.com
website www.johnhuntpublishing.com
Directors Etan Ilfeld, Vicky Hartley

Publishes a range of non-fiction and fiction genres including culture, politics, spirituality, Christianity,

history and fiction titles for adults and children. See the website for submission procedure. Imprints include O-Books, Business Books, Essentia Books, Iff Books, Changemakers Books, Christian Alternative Books, Chronos Books, Cosmic Egg Books, Roundfire Books, Top Hat Books, Lodestone Books, Moon Books and Zer0 Books. Founded 2001.

Hutchinson Heinemann – see Cornerstone

Hymns Ancient and Modern Ltd*‡

Third Floor, Invicta House, 108–114 Golden Lane, London EC1Y 0TG
tel 020-7776 7551
website www.hymnsam.co.uk
Publishing Director Christine Smith

Theological books with special emphasis on text and reference books and contemporary theology for both students and clergy. Founded 1929.

Canterbury Press

Norwich Books and Music, 13A Hellesdon Park Road, Norwich NR6 5DR
tel (01603) 785925
website www.canterburypress.co.uk
Twitter @canterburypress

Hymnals, popular religious writing, spirituality and liturgy.

Church House Publishing
website www.chpublishing.co.uk
Twitter @CHPublishingUK

Publisher of the Church of England – church resources, stationery and Common Worship.

The Revised English Hymnal

Imprint for the publication of a completely new and updated edition of the English Hymnal.

Saint Andrew Press
website www.standrewpress.hymns.co.uk
Twitter @standrewpress

Publisher of the Church of Scotland.

SCM Press
website www.scmpress.co.uk
Twitter @SCM_Press
Associate Publisher David Shervington

Academic theology.

Icon Books Ltd‡

The Omnibus Business Centre, 39–41 North Road, London N7 9DP
tel 020-7697 9695
email info@iconbooks.com
website www.iconbooks.com
Ceo Nick Hayward, *Editor* Clare Bullock

Popular, upmarket non-fiction: literature, history, philosophy, politics, psychology, sociology, sport, humour, science, current affairs, music, economics. Will consider unsolicited MSS (adult non-fiction

Books

only). Now owned by Amberly Publishing (page 125). Founded 1991.

Igloo Books Ltd
Cottage Farm, Mears Ashby Road, Sywell, Northants. NN6 0BJ
tel (01604) 741116
email customerservices@igloobooks.com
website www.igloobooks.com
Twitter @igloo_books

Children's books: licensed books, novelty, board, picture, activity, education. Adult books: cookery, lifestyle, gift, trivia and non-fiction. Not currently accepting submissions. Founded 2005.

Imagine That Publishing Ltd
Marine House, Tide Mill Way, Woodbridge, Suffolk IP12 1AP
tel (01394) 386651
email customerservice@imaginethat.com
website www.imaginethat.com
Facebook www.facebook.com/ImagineThatPublishing
Twitter @imaginethatbook
Instagram @imaginethatbook
Chairman Barrie Henderson, *Managing Director* David Henderson

Children's activity books, novelty books, picture books, reference, character, gift books and early learning books. Founded 1999.

Imprint Academic Ltd
PO Box 200, Exeter, Devon EX5 5YX
tel (01392) 851550
email graham@imprint.co.uk
website www.imprint.co.uk
Publisher Keith Sutherland, *Managing Editor* Graham Horswell

Books and journals in politics, society, philosophy and psychology for both academic and general readers. Book series include *St Andrews Studies in Philosophy and Public Affairs*, *British Idealist Studies*, *Societas* (essays in political and cultural criticism) and the *Library of Scottish Philosophy*. Also publishes under Amphora Press (biography and general historical interest titles). Unsolicited MSS, synopses and ideas welcome by email to the managing editor or with sae only. Founded 1980.

Indigo Dreams Publishing Ltd‡
24 Forest Houses, Halwill, Beaworthy, Devon EX21 5UU
email indigodreamspublishing@gmail.com
website www.indigodreamspublishing.com
Twitter @IndigoDreamsPub
Editors Ronnie Goodyer, Dawn Bauling

Main subject areas: (poetry) anthologies, collections, pamphlets, competitions, one monthly poetry magazine, two quarterly poetry and prose magazines. New and experienced writers welcome. Founded 2010.

Infinite Ideas
20 Stratfield Road, Oxford OX2 7BQ
tel 07802 443957
email info@infideas.com
website www.infideas.com
Managing Director Richard Burton

Publishes titles in wine (*Classic Wine Library*) and business. Founded 2003.

Influx Press
The Greenhouse, 49 Green Lanes, London N16 9BU
email hello@influxpress.com
website www.influxpress.com
Twitter @InfluxPress
Instagram @influxpress
Directors Gary Budden, Kit Caless

Award-winning and boundary pushing literary and experimental fiction. Imprint: New Ruins. Established 2012.

Inkandescent Ltd
Flat 4, 60 Cambridge Gardens, London W10 6HR
tel 020-8962 0063
email admin@inkandescent.co.uk
website www.inkandescent.co.uk
Facebook www.facebook.com/InkandescentPublishing
Twitter @inkandescentUK
Instagram @inkandescentUK
Publisher Justin David, *Editor* Nathan Evans

Focuses on writers underrepresented in mainstream publishing. Publishes fiction, non-fiction and poetry. Also produces a monthly podcast and a quarterly Queer Poetry Soirée. Founded 2016.

Institute of Public Administration†
57–61 Lansdowne Road, Ballsbridge, Dublin D04 TC62, Republic of Ireland
tel +353 (0)12 403600
email information@ipa.ie
website www.ipa.ie
Managing Editor John Paul Owens

Government, economics, politics, law, public management, health, education, social policy and administrative history. Founded 1957.

Integrity Media Ltd
The London Office,
85 Great Portland Street (1st Floor),
London W1W 7LT
email enquiries@integrity-media.co.uk
website www.integrity-media.co.uk
Facebook www.facebook.com/IntegrityMediaUK
Contact Grant Budge

A boutique publishing company with offices in London and Yorkshire. Publishes multi-genre fiction and non-fiction. Especially interested in autobiographies and memoirs dealing with significant life challenges. Welcomes approaches from agents and authors, including first-time authors of original material. All submission in a first instance should include a cover letter, synopsis and first three chapters. Founded 2020.

IOP Publishing*‡

No. 2, The Distillery Glassfields, Avon Street, Bristol BS2 0GR
tel 0117 929 7481
email customerservices@ioppublishing.org
website https://ioppublishing.org/
Twitter @IOPPublishing

A subsidiary of the Institute of Physics. Its portfolio includes more than 85 journals, a books programme, conference proceedings, magazines and science news websites. It focuses on physics, materials science, biosciences, astronomy and astrophysics, environmental sciences, mathematics and education. Also publishes on behalf of other scientific organisations and represents their needs and those of their members. Founded 1874.

Irish Academic Press Ltd†

Merrion Press, Tuckmill House, 10 George's Street, Newbridge, Co. Kildare W12 PX39, Republic of Ireland
tel +353 (0)45 432497
email info@merrionpress.ie
website www.merrionpress.ie
Publisher Conor Graham, *Commissioning Editor* Patrick O'Donoghue, *Production Manager* Wendy Logue, *Marketing Manager* Maeve Convery

General and non-fiction publisher with a focus on Irish history, politics, biography, memoir, current affairs, literature, culture, arts and heritage. Imprints: Irish Academic Press, founded 1974; Merrion Press, founded 2012.

The Irish Pages Press/Cló An Mhíl Bhuí

129 Ormeau Road, Belfast BT7 1SH
tel 028 9043 4800
email editor@irishpages.org
website https://irishpages.org/
Editor Chris Agee

Publishes poetry, essays, memoir and other forms of non-fiction (including the graphic novel form), in both English and Irish. Founded 2002.

ISF Publishing

8 Belmont, Lansdown Road, Bath BA1 5DZ
email info@idriesshahfoundation.org
website www.idriesshahfoundation.org
Facebook www.facebook.com/idriesshah
Twitter @idriesshah

Dedicated to releasing new editions of the work of Idries Shah, who devoted his life to collecting, selecting and translating key works of Eastern Sufi classical literature, adapting them to the needs of the West and disseminating them in the Occident. Founded 2014.

Ithaca Press – see Garnet Publishing Ltd

IWM (Imperial War Museums) Publishing

Lambeth Road, London SE1 6HZ
tel 020-7416 5000
email publishing@iwm.org.uk
website www.iwm.org.uk
Facebook www.facebook.com/iwm.london
Twitter @I_W_M

IWM tells the stories of people who have lived, fought and died in conflicts involving Britain and the Commonwealth since 1914. Produces a range of books, drawing on the expertise and archives of the museum. Books are produced both in-house and in partnership with other publishers. Founded 1917.

Jacaranda Books Ltd*‡

27 Old Gloucester Street, London WC1N 3AX
tel 020-8133 4841
email office@jacarandabooksartmusic.co.uk
website www.jacarandabooksartmusic.co.uk
Facebook www.facebook.com/jacarandabooks
Twitter @jacarandabooks
Founder & Publisher Valerie Brandes

Black-owned, diversity-led independent publisher of literary and genre fiction and non-fiction. Dedicated to promoting and celebrating brilliant diverse literature. Aims to directly address the ongoing lack of diversity in the industry and has an interest in Caribbean, African and diaspora writing. Founded 2012.

Jane's

163 Brighton Road, Coulsdon, Surrey CR5 2YH
tel 020-3159 3255
email communications@janes.com
website www.janes.com

Jane's delivers defence and security insight using open-source intelligence and powerful analytical tools. Jane's solutions and their publications cover key areas including: military platforms, systems and weapons; threat intelligence; defence markets, forecasts and budgets; sustainment and procurement. Founded 1898.

Joffe Books‡

111 Shoreditch High Street, Hackney, London E1 6JN
email office@joffebooks.com
website www.joffebooks.com
Facebook www.facebook.com/joffebooks
Twitter @joffebooks
Publisher Jasper Joffe

A leading independent publisher of digital and print fiction, specializing in top-quality crime thrillers, mysteries, historical, rom-com, saga and psychological fiction. Accepts submissions from authors and agents, see website for guidelines.

Books

Encourages submissions from under-represented backgrounds. Offers the largest prize in Britain for new crime writers of colour. Bestselling authors include Joy Ellis, Faith Martin and Helen H. Durrant. Shortlisted for Independent Publisher of the Year 2020, 2021 and 2022 at the British Book Awards. Shortlisted for The Alison Morrison Diversity and Inclusivity Award. Imprints: Choc Lit (romance), Robert Hale (general non-fiction), Lume Books (fiction and non-fiction), Ostara Classics. Founded 2014.

Jordan Publishing Ltd
21 St Thomas Street, Bristol BS1 6JS
website www.lexisnexis.co.uk/products/jordan-publishing.html

Produces practical information, online and in print, for practising lawyers and other professionals. Publishes textbooks, looseleafs, journals, court reference works and news services and also supplies software to law firms in the form of digital service PracticePlus, which combines step-by-step workflows, practice notes, automated court forms and links to core reference works. The company works with partners in key areas, such as the APIL series of guides, and also publishes around 40 new books and editions annually across a wide range of practice areas. Now owned by LexisNexis (page 159). Founded 1863.

Kelpies – see Floris Books

Kenilworth Press – see Quiller Publishing Ltd

Laurence King Publishing Ltd*
Carmelite House, 50 Victoria Embankment, London EC4Y 0DZ
tel 020-3122 6000
email commissioning@laurenceking.com
website www.laurenceking.com
Publishing Directors Elen Jones, Philip Contos

Publishes over 120 titles each year in the illustrated mainstream, children's and gifting markets, on topics including architecture, art, design, fashion, film, photography and popular culture. Imprint of Quercus Publishing Plc (page 175). Founded 1976.

Jessica Kingsley Publishers – see John Murray Press

Kitchen Press*
1 Windsor Place, Dundee DD2 1BG
tel 07951 451571
website www.kitchenpress.co.uk
Facebook www.facebook.com/kitchenpress
Twitter @Kitchen_Press
Instagram @kitchenpress

Independent publisher specialising in food writing, particularly restaurant cookery. Established 2011.

Knight Errant Press*
45 Kelvin Street, Grangemouth FK3 8EX
email knighterrantpress@outlook.com
website www.knighterrantpress.com
Twitter @knightserrantpub
Publisher Nathaniel Kunitsky

Publishes stories written by and about LGBTQIA2S+, working-class people, people with disabilities as well as migrants and the displaced. Acts as the bridge for these narratives from cultures and languages beyond the Anglophone sphere of influence by supporting translators and publishing works and authors in translation. Publishes fiction, poetry, flash fiction, non-fiction, graphic novels and comics. Founded 2017.

Kogan Page Ltd*‡
2nd Floor, 45 Gee Street, London EC1V 3RS
tel 020-7278 0433
website www.koganpage.com
Chairman Phillip Kogan, *Managing Director* Helen Kogan, *Editorial Director* Chris Cudmore

Leading independent global publisher of business books, digital solutions and content with over 1,000 titles in print. Key subject areas: accounting, finance and banking; business and management; digital and technology; human resources, learning and development; marketing and communications; risk and compliance; skills, careers and employability; and logistics, supply chain and operations. Founded 1967.

Korero Press‡
tel 07906 314098
email contact@koreropress.com
website www.koreropress.com
Facebook www.facebook.com/koreropress
Twitter @KoreroPress
Instagram @koreropress

A London-based publisher of art and design books. The list is mainly made up of titles related to illustration, pop culture and comic books. Founded 2013.

Kube Publishing Ltd
Markfield Conference Centre, Ratby Lane, Markfield, Leics. LE67 9SY
tel (01530) 249230
email info@kubepublishing.com
website www.kubepublishing.com
Managing Director Haris Ahmad

Publishes books of a Muslim interest. Founded 2006.

Kyle Books
Carmelite House, 50 Victoria Embankment, London EC4Y 0DZ
tel 020-3122 6000
email general.enquiries@kylebooks.co.uk
website www.kylebooks.co.uk
Twitter @Kyle_Books

Publisher Joanna Copestick

Food and drink; health; beauty; gardening; reference; style; design; mind, body & spirit. Part of Octopus Publishing Group (page 167). Founded 1990.

Peter Lang Ltd‡
John Eccles House, Science Park,
Robert Robinson Ave, Littlemore, Oxford OX4 4GP
tel (01865) 502124
email oxford@peterlang.com
website www.peterlang.com
Facebook www.facebook.com/PeterLangPublishers
Twitter @PeterLangOxford
Ceo, Peter Lang Publishing Group Arnaud Béglé,
Global Publishing Director Lucy Melville, *Senior Commissioning Editors* Tony Mason, Laurel Plapp

Part of the international Peter Lang Publishing Group, publishes across the humanities and social sciences, producing texts in print and digital formats and Open Access publications. All forms of scholarly research as well as textbooks, readers, student guides. Welcomes submissions from prospective authors. Blog: peterlangoxford.wordpress.com. Founded 2006.

Lantana Publishing
Clavier House, 21 Fifth Road, Newbury RG14 6DN
email info@lantanapublishing.com
website https://lantanapublishing.com/
Facebook www.facebook.com/lantanapublishing
Twitter @lantanapub
Instagram @lantana_publishing
Ceo Alice Curry, *Commissioning Editors* Holly Tonks, Katrina Gutierrez

An award-winning children's book publisher and social enterprise publishing inclusive books by authors from under-represented groups. Looking for inclusive picture books for babies and toddlers, and fiction for 5–8 years and 9–12 years. Authors should send full MS, illustrators their portfolio and link to their website and author-illustrators a complete book dummy. See submissions page on website for how to submit. Founded 2014.

Lawrence & Wishart Ltd
Central Books Building, Freshwater Road,
Chadwell Heath RM8 1RX
tel 020-8597 0090
email lw@lwbooks.co.uk
website www.lwbooks.co.uk
Book Editor Jumanah Younis

Cultural studies, current affairs, history, socialism and Marxism, political philosophy, politics, popular culture. Founded 1936.

Leamington Books*
32 Leamington Terrace, Edinburgh EH10 4JL
email peter@leamingtonbooks.com
website https://leamingtonbooks.com/
Facebook www.facebook.com/leamingtonbooks
Twitter @leamingtonbooks
Instagram @leamingtonbooks
Managing Editor Peter Burnett

A Scottish social enterprise working under the ethos of 'transformative publishing'. Publishes approx. 14 titles every year across multiple genres, including fiction, non-fiction, crime, anthology and poetry. TikTok and Pintrest: @leamingtonbooks. Imprints include: Leamington Books, Garrison, The Magic Road, Gothic World Literature Editions, Pierpoint and a poetry imprint. Founded 2020.

Legend Press Ltd‡
51 Gower Street, London WC1E 6HJ
tel 020-8127 0793
email info@legendtimesgroup.co.uk
website www.legendpress.co.uk
Twitter @legend_times
Managing Director Tom Chalmers

Focused predominantly on publishing mainstream literary and commercial fiction. Imprints: Legend Originals, Legend Thrillers and Legend Classics. Submissions can be sent to submissions@legendtimesgroup..co.uk. Works closely with South African publisher Blackbird Books (page 201), with the aim of helping bring more African literary voices to a wider global audience. Founded 2005.

LexisNexis
Lexis House, 30 Farringdon Street,
London EC4A 4HH
tel 0330 1611234
email customer.services@lexisnexis.co.uk
website www.lexisnexis.co.uk

Formerly LexisNexis Butterworths. Division of Reed Elsevier (UK) Ltd. Founded 1974.

Lexus Ltd
47 Broad Street, Glasgow G40 2QW
tel 0141 556 0440
email peterterrell@lexusforlanguages.co.uk
website www.lexusforlanguages.co.uk
Director P.M. Terrell

Publisher of language books. Publishes *Lexus Travelmate* series and *Chinese Classroom* series; *Insider China*; and *UK4U*. Also dual-language books: *Cross Over into Gaelic* series; *Scottish Folk Tales in English and French*; *Scottish Folk Tales in English and Spanish*; and *ScotlandSpeak*. For children: dual-language books for young children. Founded 1980.

The Lilliput Press Ltd†
62–63 Sitric Road, Arbour Hill, Dublin D07 AE27,
Republic of Ireland
tel +353 (0)16 711647
email publicity@lilliputpress.ie
website www.lilliputpress.ie
Facebook www.facebook.com/Lilliput-Press
Twitter @LilliputPress

Books

Managing Director Antony T. Farrell

General and Irish literature: essays, memoir, biography/autobiography, fiction, criticism; Irish history; philosophy; Joycean contemporary culture; nature and environment. Founded 1984.

Frances Lincoln

The Old Brewery, 6 Blundell Street, London N7 9BH
tel 020-7700 6700
email philip.cooper@quarto.com
website www.quarto.com/Frances-Lincoln
Publisher Philip Cooper

Illustrated, international co-editions: gardening, architecture, environment, interiors, photography, art, walking and climbing, design and landscape, gift, children's books. Imprint of The Quarto Group (page 175). Founded 1977.

Lion Hudson Ltd‡

Prama House, 267 Banbury Road, Summertown, Oxford OX2 7HT
tel (01865) 302750
email info@lionhudson.com
website www.lionhudson.com
Managing Director Suzanne Wilson-Higgins

Books for children and adults. Christian spirituality, reference, biography, history, contemporary issues, inspiration and fiction from authors with a Christian worldview. Also specialises in children's bibles and prayer collections, as well as picture storybooks and illustrated non-fiction. Adult submissions: via website, by email or hardcopy with sae if return required. Children's submissions: hardcopy only with sae if return required. Part of the SPCK Group (page 181). Founded 1971.

Little, Brown Book Group*

50 Victoria Embankment, London EC4Y 0DZ
tel 020-3122 7000
email info@littlebrown.co.uk
website www.littlebrown.co.uk
Twitter @LittleBrownUK
Managing Director Charlie King, *Deputy Managing Director* Cath Burke

Hardback and paperback fiction and general non-fiction. No unsolicited MSS. Part of Hachette UK (page 150). Founded 1988.

Abacus

Publisher Richard Beswick (Abacus Non-Fiction), *Executive Publisher* Clare Smith (Abacus Fiction)

Literary fiction, politics, biography, crime fiction, general fiction.

Atom

website www.atombooks.co.uk
Deputy Publisher (Atom & Corsair) Sarah Castleton

Teen fiction with a fantastical edge.

Blackfriars

website www.blackfriarsbooks.com
Executive Publisher Clare Smith (literary fiction)

Digital imprint.

The Bridge Street Press

Publisher Sameer Rahim

A boutique literary non-fiction imprint.

Constable & Robinson Ltd

Publishing Directors Andreas Campomar (Constable Non-Fiction), Krystyna Green (Constable Fiction)

Fiction, non-fiction, psychology, humour, brief histories and how-to books.

Corsair

Twitter @CorsairBooks
Publisher James Gurbutt

Pioneers of literary fiction from groundbreaking debuts to established authors.

Fleet

Publisher Ursula Doyle

Literary imprint, which publishes six to eight titles a year, both literary fiction and narrative non-fiction.

Little, Brown Audio

Publisher Sarah Shrubb

CDs, downloads and ebooks. See Hachette Audio (page 149).

Orbit

website www.orbitbooks.com
Publisher Anna Jackson

Sci-fi and fantasy.

Piatkus Constable & Robinson

website www.piatkus.co.uk
Executive Publisher Zoe Bohm (PCR Non-Fiction), *Publisher* Anna Boatman (PCR Fiction)

Fiction and general non-fiction.

Sphere

Executive Publisher Lucy Malagoni (Sphere Fiction), *Publisher* Emily Barrett (Sphere Non-Fiction)

Hardbacks and paperbacks: original fiction and non-fiction.

Virago

website www.virago.co.uk
Publisher Sarah Savitt

Women's literary fiction and non-fiction.

Little Tiger Group*

1 Coda Studios, 189 Munster Road, London SW6 6AW
tel 020-7385 6333
email contact@littletiger.co.uk
website www.littletiger.co.uk
Group Publishing Director Thomas Truong, *Publisher* Jude Evans

Children's books: board, picture books, activity books. See website for submission details. Owned by Penguin Random House (page 214). Founded 1987.

Caterpillar Books
website www.littletiger.co.uk/imprint/caterpillar-books
Editorial Director Pat Hegarty
Books for children, including novelty board and picture books.

Little Tiger Press
website www.littletiger.co.uk
Editorial Director Eleanor Farmer
Children's picture books, board books and novelty books for preschool–7 years. See website for submissions guidelines.

Stripes
website www.littletiger.co.uk/imprint/stripes-publishing
Editorial Director Lauren Ace
Fiction for children 6–12 years and YA. Quality standalone titles and series publishing in all age groups. Will consider new material from authors and illustrators; see website for guidelines.

360 Degrees
website www.littletiger.co.uk/special/360degrees
Editorial Director Pat Hegarty
Non-fiction novelty for children aged 5–12 years.

Little Toller Books*
2 Church Street, Beaminster, Dorset DT8 3AZ
email adrian@littletoller.co.uk
website www.littletoller.co.uk
Facebook www.facebook.com/littletoller
Twitter @littletoller

A family-run publishing company that specialises in non-fiction about place, nature and culture. Publisher of the *Nature Classics* series and writers including Dara McAnulty, Jeff Young, Tim Dee, Jay Griffiths and John Burnside. Also publishes the online journal *The Clearing*. Founded 2008.

Liverpool University Press‡
4 Cambridge Street, Liverpool L69 7ZU
tel 0151 794 2233
email lup@liv.ac.uk
website www.liverpooluniversitypress.co.uk
Twitter @LivUniPress
Managing Director Anthony Cond

LUP is the UK's third-oldest university press, with a distinguished history of publishing exceptional research since its foundation, including the work of Nobel Prize winners. Rapidly expanded in recent years and now publishes approximately 150 books a year and 34 journals, specialising in literature, modern languages, history and visual culture. Founded 1899.

Logaston Press
The Holme, Church Road, Eardisley, Herefordshire HR3 6NJ
tel (01544) 327182
email info@logastonpress.co.uk
website www.logastonpress.co.uk
Twitter @LogastonPress
Proprietors Richard Wheeler, Su Wheeler

History, social history, archaeology and guides to Herefordshire, Worcestershire, Shropshire, rural West Midlands and Mid-Wales. Welcomes submission of ideas relevant to this geographical area: send synopsis first. Founded 1985.

LOM ART
16 Lion Yard, Tremadoc Road, London SW4 7NQ
tel 020-7720 8643
email enquiries@mombooks.com
website www.mombooks.com/lom
Facebook www.facebook.com/MichaelOMaraBooks
Twitter @OMaraBooks
Managing Director Lesley O'Mara

Illustrated non-fiction for children and adults. Publishes approx. ten titles a year. Unable to guarantee a reply to every submission received, but the inclusion of an sae is necessary for submissions to be returned by post. Imprint of Michael O'Mara Books Ltd (page 168). Founded 2015.

Lonely Planet Publications Ltd
240 Blackfriars Road, London SE1 8NW
tel 020-3771 5100
email recruiting_contributors@lonelyplanet.com
website www.lonelyplanet.com
Ceo Luis Cabrera

A travel media company. Publishes 900 titles in 14 different languages and products in over 150 countries. The company's ecosystem also includes mobile apps, magazines, ebooks, a website and a dedicated traveller community. Offices in USA, UK, Australia, Ireland, India and China. Founded 1973.

Longman – see Pearson UK

Luath Press Ltd*‡
543/2 Castlehill, The Royal Mile, Edinburgh EH1 2ND
tel 0131 225 4326
email gavin.macdougall@luath.co.uk
website www.luath.co.uk
Facebook www.facebook.com/LuathPress
Twitter @LuathPress
Director Gavin MacDougall

Committed to publishing well-written books worth reading – modern fiction, history, travel guides, art, poetry, politics, humour and more in English, Scots and Scottish Gaelic. Over 800 titles in print, mostly with a Scottish connection, but many not. Founded 1981.

Lume Books – see Joffe Books

Luna Press Publishing*

149/4 Morrison Street, Edinburgh EH3 8AG
email lunapress@outlook.com
website www.lunapresspublishing.com
Founder & Owner Francesca T. Barbini

Fantasy, dark fantasy and sci-fi (no children's) in fiction and academia. Fiction: publishes novels, novellas, graphic novels, collections, anthologies. Academia Lunare is the non-fiction, academic branch, dealing with sci-fi and fantasy and non-genre: academic papers, proceedings, calls for papers, PhDs. Now running regular open submission days – check website for details. Submissions email: submissionsluna@outlook.com. Founded 2015.

Lund Humphries‡

email info@lundhumphries.com
website www.lundhumphries.com
Facebook www.facebook.com/LHArtBooks
Twitter @LHArtBooks
Instagram @lhartbooks
Managing Director Lucy Myers

Independent publishing imprint of quality art and architecture books. Founded 1895.

The Lutterworth Press

PO Box 60, Cambridge CB1 2NT
tel (01223) 350865
email publishing@lutterworth.com
website www.lutterworth.com,
www.lutterworthpress.wordpress.com
Facebook www.facebook.com/JamesClarkeandCo
Twitter @LuttPress
Managing Director Adrian Brink

A long-established independent publishing house. Originally founded as the Religious Tract Society and publisher of *The Boy's Own Paper* and *The Girl's Own Paper*. Now a publisher of educational and adult non-fiction including books and ebooks on: history, biography, literature and criticism, science, philosophy, art and art history, biblical studies, theology, mission, religious studies and collecting. Imprints: James Clarke & Co, Acorn Editions, Patrick Hardy Books. Founded 1995.

Mabecron Books Ltd

3 Briston Orchard, St Mellion, Saltash,
Cornwall PL12 6RQ
tel (01579) 350885
email ronjohns@mabecronbooks.co.uk
website www.mabecronbooks.co.uk
Twitter @mabecronbooks

Award-winning publisher. Produces children's picture books and books with a Cornish or west country subject. Linked to bookshops in Falmouth, St Ives and Padstow. Founded 1998.

McGraw-Hill Education*

8th Floor, 338 Euston Road, London NW1 3BH
tel 020-3429 3400
email emea_schools_intl@mheducation.com
website www.mheducation.co.uk
Facebook www.facebook.com/mheducationemea
Twitter @mhe_emea

McGraw Hill is an educational publisher and digital solution provider for primary and secondary education in English language arts, maths, science, and other subject areas, including intervention and learning support. Founded 1988.

Macmillan Education – see Springer Nature Group Ltd

McNidder & Grace

21 Bridge Street, Carmarthen SA31 3JS
tel 07788 219370
website https://mcnidderandgrace.com/
Publishing Director Caroline Peden Smith, *Publisher* Andrew Peden Smith

Specialises in non-fiction and fiction titles for adults. With a particular emphasis on popular culture, the non-fiction list includes books on photography, art, music, biography, history, country pursuits and, more recently, health and wellbeing in partnership with BBC Radio 2's Janey Lee Grace. Publishes the *Railway Journeys in Art Poster to Poster* series, a nine-volume set of illustrated railway travel books in collaboration with the National Railway Museum and Swann Galleries, New York. Fiction list concentrates primarily on crime and thrillers to include the bestselling *Torquil MacLeod Malmö* series. Founded 2011.

Management Books 2000 Ltd

36 Western Road, Oxford OX1 4LG
tel (01865) 600738
website www.mb2000.com
Directors N. Dale-Harris, R. Hartman

Practical books for working managers and business professionals: management, business and lifeskills, and sponsored titles. Unsolicited MSS, synopses and ideas for books welcome. Founded 1993.

Manchester University Press‡

176 Waterloo Place, The University of Manchester, Oxford Road, Manchester M13 9GP
email mup@manchester.ac.uk
website www.manchesteruniversitypress.co.uk
Chief Executive Simon Ross

Trade publishers with intelligent non-fiction programme: history, literary criticism, popular culture, politics, global affairs, economics and art history. Works of academic scholarship: anthropology, archaeology and heritage, art, architecture and visual culture, economics and business, film, media and music, history, human geography, international relations, law, literature and theatre, methods and guides, philosophy and critical theory, politics, religion and sociology. Textbooks and monographs. Subscription and Open Access journals. Founded 1904.

Mandrake of Oxford
PO Box 250, Oxford OX1 1AP
tel (01865) 243671
email mandrake@mandrake.uk.net
website www.mandrake.uk.net
Director Mogg Morgan

Art, biography, classic crime studies, fiction, Indology, magic, witchcraft, philosophy, religion. Query letters only. Founded 1986.

Mango Books
18 Soho Square, London W1D 3QL
tel 020-7060 4142
email adam@mangobooks.co.uk
website www.mangobooks.co.uk

Publishes non-fiction books for lovers of crime, detection and mystery. Imprints: Blue Lamp Books and Little Wing. Founded 2017.

Manilla Press*
Victoria House, Bloomsbury Square,
London WC1B 4DA
tel 020-3770 8888
email hello@zaffrebooks.co.uk
email hello@bonnierbooks.co.uk
website www.bonnierbooks.co.uk
Publisher Margaret Stead

Boutique literary imprint of fiction and non-fiction. The imprint is named after Nedre Manilla: the Bonnier family home on the outskirts of Stockholm. An imprint of Bonnier Books UK (page 131).

Mantra Lingua Ltd
Global House, 303 Ballards Lane, London N12 8NP
tel 020-8445 5123
email info@mantralingua.com
website https://uk.mantralingua.com/
Facebook www.facebook.com/Mantralingua
Twitter @mantralingua
Managing Director R. Dutta

Publishes bilingual picture books and educational resources for UK, US, Swedish and German audiences. Looking for illustrators with ability to draw diverse racial faces and authors and storytellers with ability to interpret or imagine modern city lives. Commission and royalty based relationships with print runs covering between 10 and 15 language editions. Translators and audio narrators, tel: 0845 600 1361. Founded 2002.

Maverick House†
Unit 33, The Business Centre,
Stadium Business Park, Ballycoolin Road,
Dublin D11 HY40, Republic of Ireland
email info@maverickhouse.com
website www.maverickhouse.com
Facebook www.facebook.com/maverickhouse
Twitter @maverickhouse
Managing Director Jean Harrington

Publishes socially and politically relevant non-fiction books. Publishes books on true-crime, terrorism, sport, memoirs, biographies and environmental issues. Founded 2002.

Kevin Mayhew Ltd
Fengate Farm, Rattlesden, Suffolk IP30 0SZ
tel (01284) 374495
email info@kevinmayhew.com
website www.kevinmayhew.com
Director Barbara Mayhew

Christianity: prayer and spirituality, pastoral care, preaching, liturgy worship, children's, youth work, drama, instant art, educational. Music: hymns, organ and choral, contemporary worship, piano and instrumental, tutors. Read submissions section on website before sending MSS/synopses. Founded 1976.

Mensch Publishing
51 Northchurch Road, London N1 4EE
tel 07793 264455
website www.menschpublishing.com
Publisher Richard Charkin

Books for the general reader. Founded 2018.

Mentor Books
43 Furze Road, Sandyford Industrial Estate,
Dublin D18 PN30, Republic of Ireland
tel +353 (0)12 952112
email admin@mentorbooks.ie
website www.mentorbooks.ie

General: non-fiction, humour, biographies, politics, crime, history, guidebooks. Educational (secondary): languages, history, geography, business, maths, sciences. No unsolicited MSS. Founded 1979.

The Mercier Press†
email info@mercierpress.ie
website www.mercierpress.ie
General Manager Mary Feehan

Irish literature; folklore; history; politics; humour; academic; current affairs; health; mind, body & spirit; general non-fiction; children's. Founded 1944.

Merlin Press Ltd
Central Books Building, Freshwater Road,
London RM8 1RX
tel 020-8590 9700 / 020-8590 9700
email info@merlinpress.co.uk
website www.merlinpress.co.uk
Managing Director Anthony Zurbrugg

Radical history and social studies. Letters/synopses only. Founded 1957.

Green Print
Green politics and the environment.

Merrell Publishers Ltd

70 Cowcross Street, London EC1M 6EJ
email hugh.merrell@merrellpublishers.com
website www.merrellpublishers.com
Publisher Hugh Merrell

Illustrated books on all aspects of visual culture, including art, architecture, photography, garden design, interior design, product design and books specially developed for institutions, foundations, corporations and private collectors. Unsolicited carefully prepared proposals welcomed via email. Founded 1989.

Methuen & Co Ltd

Orchard House, Railway Street, Slingsby,
York YO62 4AN
tel (01653) 628152 / 628195
email editorial@methuen.co.uk
website www.methuen.co.uk
Managing Director Peter Tummons, *Editorial Director* Naomi Tummons, *Sales* Peter Newsom, *Editor-at-Large* Dr Jonathan Tummons

Literary fiction and non-fiction: biography, autobiography, travel, history, sport, humour, film, children's, performing arts. No unsolicited MSS. Founded 1998.

Metro Publications Ltd

tel 020-8533 7777
email info@metropublications.com
website www.metropublications.com
Twitter @metrolondon

Produces well-researched and beautifully designed guidebooks on many aspects of London life. Founded 2007.

Mills & Boon – see Harlequin (UK) Ltd

Milo Books Ltd

14 Ash Grove, Wrea Green, Preston, Lancs. PR4 2NY
tel (01772) 672900
email info@milobooks.com
website www.milobooks.com
Publisher Peter Walsh

True crime, sport, current affairs. Founded 1997.

Mirror Books‡

One Canada Square, Canary Wharf, London E14 5AP
tel 020-7293 3740
email mirrorbooks@reachplc.com
website www.mirrorbooks.co.uk
Twitter @themirrorbooks
Managing Director Steve Hanrahan

The imprint focus is non-fiction real-life (memoir, crime, nostalgia, personalities and celebrities). Accepts submissions online: mirrorbooks.co.uk/pages/submissions. Founded 2016.

Mitchell Beazley – see Octopus Publishing Group

Moonflower Press*‡

Unit 303, The Pill Box, 115 Coventry Road,
London E2 6GH
tel 0208-054 8111
email hello@moonflowerbooks.co.uk
website www.moonflowerbooks.co.uk
Twitter @moonflowerbooks
Instagram @moonflower_books
Publisher Jack Jewers, *Editorial Director* Christi Daugherty, *Head of Communications* Emma Waring, *Head of Digital* Jasmine Poole

Independent publisher of commercial fiction. Publishes both adult and YA fiction, including crime, women's fiction, historical, coming of age, fantasy, and thrillers: commercial, but slightly out of the mainstream. For submissions guidelines see website. Founded 2020.

Morrigan Book Company

Killala, Co. Mayo, Republic of Ireland
tel +353 (0)96 32555
email morriganbooks@gmail.com
website http://conankennedy.com/About.html
Publishers Gerry Kennedy, Hilary Kennedy

Non-fiction: general Irish interest, biography, history, local history, folklore and mythology. Founded 1979.

Mud Pie

Leckford Road, Oxford OX2 6HY
tel 07985 935320
email info@mudpiebooks.com
website www.mudpiebooks.com
Facebook www.facebook.com/Mud-Pie-Books-665982096919314
Twitter @mudpiebooks
Founder & Director Tony Morris

Buddhist books and books for Buddhists. An independent specialist online publisher, dedicated to showcasing the best in Buddhist writing. Founded 2016.

Murdoch Books‡

Ormond House, 26–27 Boswell Street,
London WC1N 3JZ
tel 020-8785 5995
email info@murdochbooks.co.uk
website www.murdochbooks.co.uk

Non-fiction: cookery, homes and interiors, gardening, self-help, environment, physical and mental wellbeing. Owned by Australian publisher Allen & Unwin Pty Ltd. Founded 1991.

John Murray Press*

Carmelite House, 50 Victoria Embankment,
London EC4Y 0DZ
tel 020-3122 6777

website www.johnmurraypress.co.uk
Facebook www.facebook.com/johnmurraybooks
Twitter @johnmurraypress
Managing Editor Nick Davies

No unsolicited MSS without preliminary letter. Part of Hachette UK (page 150). Founded 1768.

Basic Books
Publishing Director Sarah Caro
History, biography, science, philosophy and economics.

Nicholas Brealey Publishing
Publishing Director Iain Campbell
Coaching and leadership, personal development and popular psychology, smart thinking, business, finance and economics.

Jessica Kingsley Publishers
Managing Director Sanphy Thomas
Autism and neurodiversity, gender diversity, inclusive teaching and learning, mental health, counselling and other therapies, social care and health professions. The Singing Dragon imprint includes books on alternative health, Chinese medicine and wellbeing.

John Murray
Executive Publisher Jocasta Hamilton (John Murray, Baskerville, Two Roads)
Quality literary fiction and non-fiction: science, business, travel, history, reference, biography and memoir. The J M Originals imprint publishes distinctive new voices.

John Murray Learning
Publishing Directors Sarah Cole (languages), Iain Campbell (learning)
Professional and personal development. Home to learning brands including Teach Yourself, Michel Thomas language courses, and Brewers and Chambers reference.

Sheldon Press
Senior Editor Victoria Roddam
Imprint of John Murray Learning. Physical and mental health, parenting, psychology, emotional wellbeing.

Two Roads
Publishing Director Kate Hewson
Commercial and non-fiction: biography and memoir, social history, personal development, popular culture, gift and humour.

Muswell Press‡
72 Cromwell Avenue, London N6 5HQ
email team@muswell-press.co.uk
website www.muswell-press.co.uk
Facebook www.facebook.com/MuswellPress/
Twitter @MuswellPress
Directors Kate Beal, Sarah Beal, *Editor-at-Large* Matt Bates

Independent publisher publishing an eclectic mix with the emphasis on contemporary fiction, crime, biography and travel. The queer list republishes forgotten gay classics. Imprint publishes queer writing. Founded 2008.

Myriad Editions‡
New Internationalist Publications,
The Old Music Hall, 106–108 Cowley Road,
Oxford OX4 1JE
tel (01865) 403345
email info@myriadeditions.com
website www.myriadeditions.com
Twitter @MyriadEditions
Publishing Director Candida Lacey

Independent publisher of literary fiction, crime written by women, graphic novels and feminist non-fiction. Merged with New Internationalist in 2017 as part of a joint plan to expand and embrace diversity. Founded 1993.

Natural History Museum Publishing
Cromwell Road, London SW7 5BD
tel 020-7942 5336
email publishing@nhm.ac.uk
website www.nhm.ac.uk/publishing
Head of Publishing Colin Ziegler

Natural history, life sciences, earth sciences, wildlife photography, art of natural history, books for children. Founded 1881.

Neem Tree Press*‡
95A Ridgmount Gardens, London WC1E 7AZ
tel 020-7993 5581
website www.neemtreepress.com
Facebook www.facebook.com/neemtreepress
Twitter @neemtreepress
Ceo & Publisher Archna Sharma, *Head of Marketing & PR* Divia Kainth, *Project Manager & Creative Lead* Lisa Cohen, *Marketing Executive* Jade McGrath

Award-winning fiction, non-fiction and children's/YA books including translation and short stories. Diverse and inclusive with the aim to inspire, inform and provoke. See website for submission guidelines. Founded 2013.

New Island Books†
10 Richview Office Park, Clonskeagh,
Dublin 14 D14 V8C4, Republic of Ireland
tel +353 (0)12 784225
email info@newisland.ie
website www.newisland.ie
Facebook www.facebook.com/NewIslandBooks
Twitter @NewIslandBooks
Director Edwin Higel, *Commissioning Editor* Aoife K. Walsh

Fiction, poetry, drama, humour, biography, current affairs, history, memoir/personal essay. Unsolicited submissions during open call only via publisher's

Books

website, www.newisland.ie/submissions. See publisher's social media platforms for notice of open submission call. Founded 1992.

New Playwrights' Network

10 Station Road Industrial Estate, Colwall, Malvern, Herefordshire WR13 6RN
tel (01684) 540154
email simon@cressrelles.co.uk
website www.cressrelles.co.uk
Publishing Director Leslie Smith

General plays for the amateur, one-act and full length.

New Welsh Rarebyte

PO Box 170, Aberystwyth, Ceredigion SY23 1WZ
tel (01970) 628410
website www.newwelshreview.com
Facebook www.facebook.com/NewWelshReview
Twitter @newwelshreview
Instagram @newwelshreview
Editor Gwen Davies

Publish prize-winners from the annual New Welsh Writing Awards, the writer development initiative run by New Welsh Review since 2015, which seeks prose works of 5,000–30,000 words on a different theme each year. See New Welsh Reader (page 75) or website for more information.

Nine Arches Press

Unit 14, Frank Whittle Business Centre,
Great Central Way, Rugby, Warks. CV21 3XH
tel (01788) 226005
email mail@ninearchespress.com
website www.ninearchespress.com
Facebook www.facebook.com/NineArchesPress
Twitter @NineArchesPress
Editorial Director Jane Commane

Independent publisher of poetry based in the Midlands. Founded 2008.

Nobrow – see Flying Eye Books Ltd

No Exit Press – see Bedford Square Publishers

Nordisk Books Ltd

81 Harbour Street, Whitstable CT5 1AE
tel 07437 202582
email info@nordiskbooks.com
website www.nordiskbooks.com
Facebook www.facebook.com/nordiskbooks
Twitter @nordiskbooks
Instagram @nordisk_books
Director Duncan J. Lewis

Modern and contemporary fiction from the Nordic countries. Publishing a wide range of exciting literary titles from across the Scandinavian peninsular and beyond. No crime. Founded 2016.

Northcote House Publishers Ltd

Horndon House, Mary Tavy, Tavistock PL19 9NQ
tel (01822) 810066
email northcotepublishers@gmail.com
website www.liverpooluniversitypress.co.uk

Imprint of Liverpool University Press (page 161). Education and education management, educational dance and drama, literary criticism (*Writers and their Work*). Founded 1985.

Northodox Press

email submissions@northodox.co.uk
website www.northodox.co.uk
Facebook www.facebook.com/northodoxpress
Twitter @northodoxpress
Contacts Tom Copeland, Ted O'Connor, James Keane

Represents authentic Northern voices and caters to readers of quality crime fiction. Founded 2020.

W.W. Norton & Company‡

15 Carlisle Street, London W1D 3BS
tel 020-7323 1579
email crusselli@wwnorton.co.uk
website www.wwnorton.co.uk
Facebook www.facebook.com/WW-Norton-UK
Twitter @wwnortonuk
Managing Director John Donovan

English and American literature, economics, music, psychology, science. Founded 1980.

Nosy Crow*‡

Wheat Wharf, 27A Shad Thames, London SE1 2XZ
tel 020-7089 7575
email hello@nosycrow.com
website www.nosycrow.com
Group Ceo Kate Wilson, *Publishing Directors* Kirsty Stanfield (fiction), Louise Bolongaro (picture books), Rachel Kellehar (non-fiction, preschool & activity)

Independent children's publisher. Publishes child-focused, parent-friendly children's books. Also children's publisher for The National Trust and The British Museum. Founded 2010.

Nourish Books

Unit 11, Shepperton House, 89 Shepperton Road, London N1 3DF
tel 020-3813 6940
email enquiries@watkinspublishing.com
website https://nourishbooks.com/
Facebook www.facebook.com/nourishbooks
Twitter @nourishbooks

A modern cookery list which focuses on feel-good food. Part of Watkins Media (page 189).

Oak Tree Press†

NSC Campus, Mahon, Cork T12 XY2N, Republic of Ireland

tel +353 (0)21 230 7021
email info@oaktreepress.com
website https://oaktreepress.eu/
Directors Axel Neefs, Pierre Delroisse; Publisher Brian
O'Kane

Business management, enterprise, accountancy and
finance, law. Special emphasis on titles for small
business owner/managers. Now part of Corporate
Group. Founded 1991.

Nubooks
Ebooks.

Oberon Books – see Bloomsbury Publishing Plc

The O'Brien Press Ltd†
12 Terenure Road East, Rathgar, Dublin D06 HD27,
Republic of Ireland
tel +353 (0)1 4923333
email books@obrien.ie
website obrien.ie
Directors Ivan O'Brien, Kunak McGann

Adult non-fiction: biography, politics, history, travel,
food, drink, sport, humour, reference. No poetry or
academic. Children: picture books; fiction for all ages;
illustrated fiction for ages 3+, 5+, 6+, 8+ years, novels
(10+ and YA): contemporary, historical, fantasy.
Non-fiction. Unsolicited MSS (sample chapters only),
synopses and ideas for books welcome, submissions
will not be returned. Further information on website.
Founded 1974.

Octopus Publishing Group*
Carmelite House, 50 Victoria Embankment,
London EC4Y 0DZ
tel 020-3122 6000
email info@octopusbooks.co.uk
email publisher@octopusbooks.co.uk (submissions)
website www.octopusbooks.co.uk
Managing Director Anna Bond

Part of Hachette UK (page 150). Founded 1998.

Aster
Publisher Stephanie Jackson
Food, drink, wellness and lifestyle.

Brazen
Publishing Director Romily Morgan
Non-fiction and fiction.

Cassell
Publisher Trevor Davies
Popular culture, music, reference.

Conran Octopus
Publisher Alison Starling
Illustrated books, particularly lifestyle, cookery,
gardening.

Gaia Books
Publisher Stephanie Jackson
The environment, natural living and health.

Godsfield Press
email publisher@godsfieldpress.com
Publisher Stephane Jackson
Mind, body & spirit with an emphasis on practical
application.

Hamlyn
Publisher Stephanie Jackson
Food, drink, home, garden, health and parenting.

Ilex
Publisher Alison Starling
Illustrated books on practical art, photography, craft
and books exploring visual culture.

Kyle Books
Publisher Joanna Copestick
Quality cookery, lifestyle and craft books (page 158).

Mitchell Beazley
Publisher Alison Starling
Quality illustrated books on food and drink, home
and garden, the outdoors, fashion and music.

Monoray
Publisher Jake Lingwood
Memoir, current affairs, music, modern history,
health and big ideas.

Philip's
email publisher@philips-maps.co.uk
Publishing Director Sarah Bailey
Atlases, maps and astronomy.

Pyramid
email bountybooksinfo-bp@bountybooks.co.uk
Publisher Lucy Pessell
Mind, body & spirit; gift and humour; cookery; craft
and reference.

Radar
Publisher Briony Gowlett
Popular culture.

Short Books
Publisher Joanna Copestick
Popular non-fiction.

Summersdale
Managing Director Alastair Williams
Gift, humour, travel and health (page 183).

Offord Books
email offordbooks@gmail.com
website www.offordroadbooks.co.uk
Facebook www.facebook.com/offordbooks
Twitter @offordbooks
Editor Martha Sprackland

Publishers of poetry books and pamphlets that have
won or been shortlisted for accolades including the
Ledbury Forte Award, the Forward Prize for Best

First Collection and the T.S. Eliot Prize. Founded 2017.

Old Barn Books*‡
Warren Barn, Bedham Lane, Fittleworth,
West Sussex RH20 1JW
tel (01798) 865010
email ruth@oldbarnbooks.com
website www.oldbarnbooks.com
Facebook www.facebook.com/oldbarnbooks
Twitter @oldbarnbooks
Instagram @oldbarnbooks

Independent publisher of picture books and fiction for children up to 14 years and the occasional gift book for adults. Interested in the natural world and promoting empathy. Not currently accepting unsolicited submissions. Founded 2015.

Old Pond Publishing
20–22 Wenlock Road, London N1 7GU
email info@foxchapelpublishing.co.uk
website www.foxchapelpublishing.co.uk
Publisher Richard Dodman

A leading specialist publisher of agriculture, trucking, machinery and practical farming books. Owned by Fox Chapel Publishers International. Founded 1997.

The Oleander Press
16 Orchard Street, Cambridge CB1 1JT
tel (01638) 500784
website www.oleanderpress.com
Managing Director Dr Jane Doyle

Travel, language, Libya, Arabia and Middle East, Cambridgeshire, history, reference, classics. No unsolicited MSS. Founded 1960.

Michael O'Mara Books Ltd*
9 Lion Yard, Tremadoc Road, London SW4 7NQ
tel 020-7720 8643
email enquiries@mombooks.com
email publicity@mombooks.com
website www.mombooks.com
Facebook www.facebook.com/MichaelOMaraBooks/
Twitter @OMaraBooks
Chairman Michael O'Mara, *Managing Director* Lesley O'Mara

General non-fiction: biography, autobiography, history, lifestyle, humour. See website for submission guidelines. Founded 1985.

Buster Books
website www.mombooks.com/buster
Facebook www.facebook.com/BusterBooks
Twitter @BusterBooks
Instagram @Buster_Books

Activity, novelty, picture books, fiction and non-fiction for children.

LOM ART
website www.mombooks.com/lom
Activity, arts & crafts, reference, picture books for children (page 161).

Omnibus Press/Wise Music Group
14–15 Berners Street, London W1T 3LJ
tel 020-612 7400
email omniinfo@wisemusic.com
website www.omnibuspress.com
Chief Editor David Barraclough

Music biographies, autobiographies, illustrated books, books about music. Founded 1976.

On Stream Publications
Currabaha, Cloghroe, Blarney, Cork T23 EW08, Republic of Ireland
tel +353 (0)21 4385798
email info@onstream.ie
website www.onstream.ie
Owner Rosalind Crowley

Cookery, wine, travel, human interest non-fiction, local history, academic and practical books. Contract publishing. Founded 1986.

Oneworld Publications*‡
10 Bloomsbury Street, London WC1B 3SR
tel 020-7307 8900
email info@oneworld-publications.com
website www.oneworld-publications.com
Facebook www.facebook.com/oneworldpublications
Twitter @OneworldNews
Directors & Publishers Juliet Mabey, Novin Dootstdar

Fiction and general non-fiction: current affairs, politics, history, Middle East, business, popular science, philosophy, psychology, green issues, world religions and Islamic studies; literary and commercial fiction with a focus on diverse voices and great stories; children and YA fiction and upmarket crime/suspense novels, as well as fiction in translation. No unsolicited MSS; email or send non-fiction proposals via website. Founded 1986.

Onwe Press
71–75 Shelton Street, London WC2H 9JQ
email info@onwepress.com
website https://www.onwe.co/
Twitter @weareonwe

Publishes monthly short stories from under-represented writers. These stories feature on the website, the monthly newsletter going out to thousands and on social media pages. Stories welcome from all genres but they need to centre bespoke cultures, diverse voices or come from under-represented writers. Payment: £50 for up to 5,000 words. Also publishes fiction and non-fiction from children to adult. Founded 2019.

Open University Press – see McGraw-Hill Professional

Orbit – see Little, Brown Book Group

Orenda Books
16 Carson Road, West Dulwich, London SE21 8HU
tel 020-8355 4643
email info@orendabooks.co.uk
website www.orendabooks,co.uk
Facebook www.facebook.com/orendabooks
Twitter @OrendaBooks
Instagram @orendabooks
Publisher Karen Sullivan, *Editorial Director* West
Camel, *Digital & Marketing Manager* Cole Sullivan,
Marketing Assistant Chloe Murphy

An independent publisher specialising in literary
fiction, with a heavy emphasis on crime thrillers,
about half in translation. Shortlisted for IPG Best
Newcomer Award 2015 and 2016. Winner of the
CWA Dagger for Best Crime & Mystery Publisher of
2020. British Book Awards: Regional Finalist for
Small Press of the Year 2021. Founded 2014.

The Orion Publishing Group Ltd*
Carmelite House, 50 Victoria Embankment,
London EC4Y 0DZ
tel 020-3122 6444
website www.orionbooks.co.uk
Managing Director Anna Valentine

No unsolicited MSS; approach in writing in first
instance. Part of Hachette UK (page 150).
Founded 1992.

Gollancz
Sci-fi, fantasy and horror.

Laurence King
One of the world's leading publishers of books and
gifts on creative arts.

Orion Audio
Senior Audio Manager Paul Stark
Adult fiction and non-fiction. Authors include Ian
Rankin, Ben Aaronovitch, Candice Carty-Williams
and Meg Mason.

Orion Fiction
Trade and mass market fiction.

Orion Spring
Wellbeing, health and lifestyle non-fiction.

Seven Dials
Trade and mass market: cookery, memoir and
autobiography, gift and humour, personal
development and parenting, lifestyle, diet and fitness.

Trapeze
Trade and mass market fiction: reading group, crime
and thriller, women's fiction; trade and mass market
non-fiction: memoir and autobiography, lifestyle, gift
and humour, popular psychology and entertainment.

Weidenfeld & Nicholson
Literary fiction, translated fiction; non-fiction:
history, memoir, ideas-driven books, popular science,
biography, sport, business, diaries and narrative non-
fiction.

White Rabbit
Music: memoir, history, fiction, limited editions.

Ortac Press‡
1 Cumberland Gardens, London WC1X 9AF
email hello@ortacpress.com
website www.ortacpress.com
Twitter @ortacpress
Instagram @ortacpress
Managing Director & Publisher Henry Rowley

Publishes non-fiction and novels with a focus on art,
culture music and social science. See website for
information on submissions. Founded 2021.

Osprey Publishing Ltd*‡
Kemp House, Chawley Park, Cumnor Hill,
Oxford OX2 9PH
tel 020-7631 5600
email info@ospreypublishing.com
website https://ospreypublishing.com/
Editorial Director Marcus Cowper

Military history with 3,000 titles in print on a wide
range of military history subjects from ancient times
to the modern day. Owned by Bloomsbury
Publishing Plc (page 130). Founded 1968.

Out-Spoken Press
Unit 39, Containerville, 1 Emma Street,
London E2 9FP
email press@outspokenldn.com
website www.outspokenldn.com
Twitter @outspoken_press
Instagram @out_spoken_press
Editor Anthony Anaxagorou

Independent publisher of poetry and critical writing.
Provides a platform for compelling writing from
voices under-represented in mainstream publishing.
Founded 2015.

Oversteps Books Ltd
6 Halwell House, South Pool, Nr Kingsbridge,
Devon TQ7 2RX
tel (01548) 531969
email alwynmarriage@overstepsbooks.com
website www.overstepsbooks.com
Director/Managing Editor Alwyn Marriage

Poetry. Check the submissions information on
website to ascertain whether accepting submissions at
any time. If the submissions window is open, you
may email six poems that have either won major
competitions or been published, giving details of the
competitions or magazines in which they appeared,
the dates or issue numbers and the email addresses of
the editors. Founded 1992.

Books

170 Books

Peter Owen Publishers

c/o Pushkin Press, Somerset House, Strand,
London WC2R 1L
tel 020-8350 1775
email kirsten@pushkinpress.com
website www.peterowen.com
Facebook www.facebook.com/peter.owen.publishers
Twitter @PeterOwenPubs
Contact Kristen Chapman

Backlist includes 10 Nobel Prize winners. Arts, belles
lettres, biography and memoir, literary fiction,
general non-fiction, history, theatre, philosophy and
entertainment. Owned by Pushkin Press (page 174).
Founded 1951.

Oxford University Press*

Great Clarendon Street, Oxford OX2 6DP
tel (01865) 556767
email enquiry@oup.com
website www.oup.com
Ceo Nigel Portwood

Archaeology, architecture, art, belles lettres, bibles,
bibliography, children's books (fiction, non-fiction,
picture), commerce, current affairs, dictionaries,
drama, economics, educational (foundation, primary,
secondary, technical, university), encyclopedias, ELT,
electronic publishing, essays, foreign language
learning, general history, hymn and service books,
journals, law, medical, music, oriental, philosophy,
political economy, prayer books, reference, science,
sociology, theology and religion; educational
software; *Grove Dictionaries of Music & Art*. Trade
paperbacks published under the imprint of Oxford
Paperbacks. Founded 1478.

P8tech

6 Woodside, Churnet View Road, Oakamoor,
Staffs. ST10 3AE
tel (01538) 703591
email info@P8tech.com
website www.P8tech.com

IT and computer-related titles, including books on
video games and artificial intelligence. Specialises in
Oracle and Java-related titles. Founded 2012.

Palgrave Macmillan – see Springer Nature Group Ltd

Pan Macmillan*

6 Briset Street, Farringdon, London EC1M 5NR
tel 020-7038 5000
email publicity@macmillan.com
website www.panmacmillan.com
Ceo Joanna Prior

Novels, literary, crime, thrillers, romance, sci-fi,
fantasy and horror, autobiography, biography,
business, gift books, health and beauty, history,
humour, natural history, travel, philosophy, politics,
world affairs, theatre, film, gardening, cookery,
popular reference. Founded 1843.

Bluebird & Oneboat

A non-fiction imprint for books. Subjects include
personal development, environment, inspirational
memoir, parenting, cookery, feminism, creativity and
more.

Campbell

Early learning, pop-up, novelty, board books for the
preschool market.

Kingfisher

Illustrated non-fiction books for children.

Macmillan

Hardback imprint of fiction and non-fiction.

Macmillan Children's Books

Imprint for Macmillan Children's Books.

Macmillan Collector's Library

Publishes classics in high-quality binding, from Jane
Austen to Charles Dickens, from Sir Arthur Conan
Doyle to F. Scott Fitzgerald. Also non-fiction, poetry,
short stories and children's books.

Mantle

Genres include: crime, thriller, general and literary
fiction to narrative non-fiction and memoir.

Pan

Commercial fiction and non-fiction.

Picador

Literary international fiction, non-fiction and poetry
published in hardback and paperback. Founded 1972.

Tor

Sci-fi and fantasy published in hardback and
paperback.

Two Hoots

Illustrated children's books.

Parthian Books

The Old Surgery, Napier Street, Cardigan SA43 1ED
email info@parthianbooks.com
website www.parthianbooks.com
Facebook www.facebook.com/parthianbooks/
Twitter @parthianbooks
Publishing Editor Susie Wildsmith

Independent publisher of poetry, literary fiction,
creative non-fiction and translations that reflect a
diverse and contemporary Wales and wider world.
See website for submission opportunities and
guidelines on how to submit MSS. Founded 1993.

Pavilion Books – see HarperCollins Publishers

Pavilion Poetry

Liverpool University Press, 4 Cambridge Street,
Liverpool L69 7ZU

email lup@liverpool.ac.uk
website https://www.liverpooluniversitypress.co.uk/
topic/imprints/pavilion-poetry/
Twitter @PavilionPoetry

An imprint of the Liverpool University Press, an award-winning academic and researcher publisher. Publishes contemporary poetry from both British and international poets. Founded 2014.

Pearson UK*

Edinburgh Gate, Harlow, Essex CM20 2JE
tel 0845 313 6666
email schools@longman.co.uk
website www.pearsoned.co.uk
Ceo Andy Bird

Consists of five divisions: Virtual Learning, Higher Education, English Language Learning, Workforce Skills and Assessment and Qualifications. Imprints include: Addison-Wesley Professional, Adobe Press, Allyn & Bacon, BBC Active, Benjamin Cummings, Causeway Press, Cisco Press, Edexcel, Exam Cram, FT Press (formerly FT Prentice Hall), Ginn & Company, Edwin Ginn, Harvester Wheatsheaf, IBM Press, InformIT, LifeBound, Macromedia Press, Maths Champs, MySQL Press, New Riders, Novell Press, Oliver & Boyd, Payne Galway, Peachpit, Pearson Custom Publishing, Pearson Longman (formerly Longman), Penguin Books, Pi Press, Pitman, Prentice Hall, Propero, Puffin, Que Publishing, Rigby, SAMS Publishing, VangoBooks, Wharton School Publishing and York Notes. Founded 1998.

Peepal Tree Press*

17 King's Ave, Burley, Leeds LS6 1QS
tel 0113 245 1703
email contact@peepaltreepress.com
website www.peepaltreepress.com
Facebook www.facebook.com/peepaltreepress
Twitter @peepaltreepress
Founder & Managing Editor Jeremy Poynting

Leading independent publisher of BAME, in particular Caribbean and Black British writing, publishing around 20 books a year. Has published over 300 titles, and are committed to keeping most of them in print. The list features new writers and established voices. In 2009 the *Caribbean Modern Classics* series was launched, which restores to print essential books from the past with new introductions. Founded 1985.

Pelagic Publishing‡

20–22 Wenlock Road, London N1 7GU
tel 0845 468 0415
email info@pelagicpublishing.com
website www.pelagicpublishing.com
Facebook www.facebook.com/pelagicpublishing
Twitter @pelagicpublish
Instagram @pelagicpublishing

Publisher Nigel Massen

Academic and trade books on natural history, ecology, conservation, data analysis and environmental science. Founded 2010.

Pen & Sword Books Ltd

47 Church Street, Barnsley, South Yorkshire S70 2AS
tel (01226) 734555 / (01226) 734222
email editorialoffice@pen-and-sword.co.uk
website www.pen-and-sword.co.uk
Managing Director Charles Hewitt, *Publisher* Jonathan Wright, *Commissioning Editors* Henry Wilson, Phil Sidnell, Sarah-Beth Watkins, Michael Leventhal, Julian Mannering, Rob Gardiner, Martin Mace, Tara Moran

Military history, aviation history, naval and maritime, general history, local history, family history, transport, social history, archaeology, health and lifestyle, natural history, gardening, space, science, sports, hobbies, retro video games, movie history, biographies, crafts. Imprints: Leo Cooper, Frontline Books, White Owl, Pen & Sword Aviation, Pen & Sword Naval & Maritime, Remember When, Frontline, Seaforth, Pen & Sword Digital, Pen & Sword Transport, Pen & Sword Discovery, Pen & Sword Social History, Pen & Sword Archaeology. Founded 1990.

Penguin General*

20 Vauxhall Bridge Road, London SW1V 2SA
tel 020-7010 3000
Managing Director Preena Gadher

No unsolicited MSS or synopses. Part of Penguin Random House UK (page 172). Penguin Books founded 1855.

Penguin Business
Publishing Director Martina O'Sullivan

Fig Tree
Publishing Director Helen Garnons-Williams
Fiction and general non-fiction.

Hamish Hamilton
Publishing Director Simon Prosser
Fiction, biography and memoirs, current affairs, history, literature, politics, travel.

Penguin Life
Publishing Director Emily Robertson
Health, lifestyle, wellbeing, trends.

Viking
Publishing Director Daniel Crewe, *Publisher* Harriet Bourton, *Editorial Director* Isabel Wall
Fiction, biography and memoirs, current affairs, popular culture, sport, history, literature, politics, travel.

Penguin Michael Joseph*

One Embassy Gardens, 8 Viaduct Gardens, London SW11 7AY

tel 020-7010 3000
website www.penguin.co.uk/company/publishers/
penguin-michael-joseph
Managing Director Louise Moore

Part of Penguin Random House UK. Founded 1935.

Penguin Press*

20 Vauxhall Bridge Road, London SW1V 2SA
tel 020-7010 3000
website www.penguin.co.uk/company/publishers/
penguin-press.html
Managing Director Stefan McGrath

Incorporates the non-fiction imprint Allen Lane, the
innovative Particular Books, the newly revitalised
Pelican imprint, new poetry and the world of
Penguin Classics. No unsolicited MSS. Founded 1997.

Allen Lane

Non-fiction: history, science, politics, economics,
philosophy, psychology, language and current affairs.

Particular Books

Non-fiction: history, science, politics, travel,
biography and memoirs, current affairs and
photograph.

Pelican

Non-fiction: history, science, politics, economics and
finance, philosophy, psychology, language and
current affairs.

Penguin Classics

Classic literature, poetry, drama, biography and
memoir.

Penguin Random House Children's UK*

One Embassy Gardens, 8 Viaduct Gardens,
London SW11 7AY
tel 020-7139 3000
website www.penguin.co.uk/company/publishers/
penguin-random-house-children-s
Managing Director Francesca Dow

Part of Penguin Random House UK (see below).
Children's paperback and hardback books: wide
range of picture books, board books, gift books and
novelties; fiction; non-fiction, popular culture, digital
and audio. Preschool illustrated developmental books
for 0–6 years; licensed brands; children's classic
publishing and merchandising properties. No
unsolicited MSS or original artwork or text. Imprints:
Ladybird, Puffin, Penguin. Founded 2013.

Penguin Random House UK*

One Embassy Gardens, 8 Viaduct Gardens,
London SW11 7BW
tel 020-7139 3000
website www.penguin.co.uk
Ceo Tom Weldon

Penguin Random House UK publishing divisions:
Cornerstone (page 137), Ebury Press (page 142),
Penguin General (page 171), Penguin Michael Joseph
(page 171), Penguin Press, Penguin Random House
Children's UK, Penguin Random House UK Audio
(all this page), Transworld (page 185) and Vintage
(page 188). Founded 2013.

Penguin Random House UK Audio

Penguin Studios, One Embassy Gardens,
Nine Elms Lane, London SW8 5BL
website www.penguinrandomhouse.co.uk
Head of Audio Content Hannah Cawse, *Executive
Producer* Roy McMillan, *Head of Audio Production*
Chris Thompson, *Producer & Composer* Kate
MacDonald, *Senior Producer* Michael Pender,
Producer Charlotte Davey

Includes classic and contemporary fiction and non-
fiction, autobiography, poetry and drama. Authors
include Jo Nesbø, Lee Child, Kathy Reichs, Claire
Tomalin, Zadie Smith and Paula Hawkins.
Founded 2013.

Persephone Books

8 Edgar Buildings, Bath BA1 2EE
tel (01225) 425050
email info@persephonebooks.co.uk
website www.persephonebooks.co.uk
Managing Director Nicola Beauman

Reprints of neglected fiction and non-fiction, mostly
by women writers and mostly mid-20th century, in
elegant grey matching editions. Founded 1999.

Phaidon Press Ltd

2 Cooperage Yard, London E15 2GR
tel 020-7843 1000
email enquiries@phaidon.com
website www.phaidon.com
Editorial Director Tracey Smith, *Vice-President &
Publisher* Deborah Aaronson, *Associate Publisher,
Children's Books* Maya Gartner.

Visual arts, lifestyle, culture and food. Founded 1923.

Philip's – see Octopus Publishing Group

Phoenix Publishing House Ltd

62 Bucknell Road, Bicester, Oxon OX26 2DS
tel 020-8442 1376
email hello@firingthemind.com
website www.firingthemind.com
Facebook www.facebook.com/firingthemind
Twitter @firingthemind
Instagram @firingthemind
Publisher Kate Pearce, *Publishing Assistant* Sophie-Jo
Gavin

Independent specialists in mental health publishing
for professionals. For submission guidelines see
website. Founded 2018.

Piatkus Constable & Robinson – see Little,
Brown Book Group

Piccadilly Press*

Victoria House, Bloomsbury Square,
London WC1B 4DA
tel 020-3770 8888
email hello@bonnierbooks.co.uk
website www.bonnierbooks.co.uk
Twitter @PiccadillyPress
Managing Director Helen Wicks

Publishes books primarily for readers 5 to 12 years
old. Titles can be standalone stories or part of a series.
Imprint of Bonnier Books UK (page 131).
Founded 1983.

Pimlico – see Vintage

Pimpernel Press Ltd‡

22 Marylands Road, London W9 2DY
tel 07775 917202, 07976 047767
email info@pimpernelpress.com
website www.pimpernelpress.com
Facebook www.facebook.com/pimpernelpress
Twitter @PimpernelPress
Instagram @Pimpernel_Press
Publisher Jo Christian, *Managing Director* Gail Lynch,
Commissioning Editor Anna Sanderson

Independent publisher of books on gardens and
gardening; art; design; architecture and places;
practical books on arts and crafts; gift books and
stationery. Founded 2015.

The Playwrights Publishing Company

70 Nottingham Road, Burton Joyce,
Notts. NG14 5AL
email playwrightspublishingco@yahoo.com
website www.playwrightspublishing.com
Proprietors Liz Breeze, Tony Breeze

Looking for previously performed one-act and full-
length dramas to be published on the net; serious
pieces or comedies, mixed cast or single sex (no
musicals). Reading fee charged; email for submission
guidelines. Founded 1990.

Plexus Publishing Ltd

26 Dafforne Road, London SW17 8TZ
tel 020-767 7126
email editorialassistant@plexusbooks.com
website www.plexusbooks.com
Editorial Director Sandra Wake

Film, music, biography, popular culture, fashion, gift.
Imprint: Eel Pie. Founded 1973.

Pluto Press‡

New Wing, Somerset House, Strand,
London WC2R 1LA
tel 020-8348 2724
email pluto@plutobooks.com
website www.plutobooks.com
Twitter @plutopress
Editorial Director David Castle, *Senior Commissioning
Editor* David Shulman, *Executive Editor* Neda Tehrani

An independent, political publisher of radical non-
fiction. Politics, economics, history, race, Black
studies, gender and sexuality, international relations.
Founded 1969.

Policy Press – see Bristol University Press/
Policy Press

Polity Press‡

65 Bridge Street, Cambridge CB2 1UR
tel (01223) 324315
website www.politybooks.com

Social and political theory, politics, sociology, history,
media and cultural studies, philosophy, literary
studies, feminism, geography, anthropology.
Founded 1983.

Poolbeg Press Ltd

123 Grange Hill, Baldoyle, Dublin D13 N529,
Republic of Ireland
tel +353 (0)18 063825
email info@poolbeg.com
website www.poolbeg.com
Directors Kieran Devlin, Barbara Devlin

Popular fiction, non-fiction, current affairs. Imprint:
Poolbeg. Founded 1976.

Portland Press Ltd*

email editorial@portlandpress.com
website www.portlandpress.com
Twitter @PPPublishing

Owned by the Biochemical Society, embedded in the
global scientific community and dedicated to
promoting and sharing research for the advancement
of science. Founded 1990.

Prestel Publishing Ltd

16–18 Berners Street, London W1T 3LN
tel 020-7323 5004
email ahansen@prestel-uk.co.uk
website www.prestel.com
Facebook www.facebook.com/PrestelPublishing
Twitter @Prestel_pub
Instagram @prestel_publishing
Vice-President Andrew Hansen

Pop culture, major exhibition catalogues and artist
retrospectives. Publishes in the following genres: art,
architecture, photography, fashion, lifestyle, design
and children's books. Book submissions:
submissions@prestel-uk.co.uk. Press enquiries:
publicity@prestel-uk.co.uk. Founded 1924.

Princeton University Press – Europe*‡

99 Banbury Road, Oxford OX2 6JX
tel (01993) 814500
email claire_williams@press.princeton.edu
website www.press.princeton.edu
Facebook www.facebook.com/
PrincetonUniversityPress

Books

Twitter @PrincetonUPress
Editor for Humanities Ben Tate, *Publisher for Sciences*
Ingrid Gnerlich, *Senior Editor for Social Science*
Rebecca Brennan, *Associate Editor for Economics &*
Political Science Hannah Paul

Academic publishing for the social sciences,
humanities and sciences. The European office of
Princeton University Press. Founded 1999.

Profile Books Ltd*‡

29 Cloth Fair, London EC1A 7JQ
tel 020-7841 6300
email info@profilebooks.com
website www.profilebooks.com
Managing Director Rebecca Gray, *Publishing Director*
Cecily Gayford, *Editorial Directors* Izzy Everington,
Nick Humphrey

General non-fiction: history, biography, current
affairs, popular science, politics, business,
management, humour. Also publishers of *The
Economist* books. No unsolicited MSS. Founded 1996.

Profile Editions
Publisher Peter Jones

Custom arts, heritage and company histories. No
unsolicited MSS.

Serpent's Tail
email info@serpentstail.com
website www.serpentstail.com
Publisher Hannah Westland

Fiction and non-fiction; literary and non-mainstream
work and work in translation. No unsolicited MSS.
Founded 1986.

Souvenir Press
Publisher Rebecca Gray

Non-fiction, especially practical and expert advice,
spiritual, gift, memoir. No unsolicited MSS.

Tuskar Rock
Publisher Peter Straus

Fiction and non-fiction. No unsolicited MSS.

Psychology Press – see Taylor & Francis Group.

Puffin – see Penguin Random House Children's UK

Pure Indigo Ltd

Publishing Department, 17 The Herons, Cottenham,
Cambridge CB24 8XX
tel 07981 395258
email ashley.martin@pureindigo.co.uk
website www.pureindigo.co.uk/publishing
Commissioning Editor Ashley Martin

Currently closed to submissions. Children's books:
develops innovative junior series fiction. Also
develops software products that complement the
product range. The junior series fiction titles are
developed in-house and on occasion authors and
illustrators are commissioned to complete project-
based work. Founded 2005.

Pushkin Press*

New Wing, Somerset House, Strand,
London WC2R 1LA
email books@pushkinpress.com
website www.pushkinpress.com
Facebook www.facebook.com/PushkinPress
Twitter @pushkinpress
Publisher Adam Freudenheim, *Deputy Publisher*
Laura Macaulay, *Commissioning Editor* Daniel Seton

Publishes European classics of the 20th century and
novels, essays, memoirs, children's books (Pushkin's
Children's Books). Imprints: Pushkin Press, Pushkin
Children's Books, Pushkin Vertigo, ONE.
Founded 1997.

Pyramid – see Octopus Publishing Group

Quadrant Books

Suite 2, 7 Dyer Street, Cirencester, Gloucs. GL7 2PF
tel 020-3290 0290
email info@quadrant-books.com
website www.quadrant-books.com
Twitter @BooksQuadrant
Publisher Antonia Tingle, *Editor-in-Chief* Peter Jacobs
Publicist Grace Pilkington

Publishes contemporary fiction, crime, mystery,
historical, romance, speculative fiction and non-
fiction. Founded 2020.

Quadrille

5th and 6th Floors, Pentagon House,
52–54 Southwark Street, London SE1 1UN
tel 020-7601 7500
email enquiries@quadrille.co.uk
website www.hardiegrant.com/quadrille
Marketing Director Sarah Lavelle

Non-fiction, categories include: food and drink, gift
and humour, craft, wellness, lifestyle and pop culture.
Imprint of Hardie Grant UK (page 150).
Founded 1994.

Quantum – see W. Foulsham & Co. Ltd

Quartet Books

27 Goodge Street, London W1T 2LD
tel 020-7636 3992
email info@quartetbooks.co.uk
website www.quartetbooks.co.uk

Independent publisher with a tradition of pursuing
an alternative to mainstream. Books by women in the
areas of literary and crime fiction, biography and
autobiography, health, culture, politics, handbooks,
literary criticism, psychology and self-help, the arts.
Accepting submissions; see website for guidelines.
Founded 1978.

The Quarto Group, Inc.

The Quarto Group, Inc., 1 Triptych Place,
Second Floor, London SE1 9SH
tel 020-7700 9000 / 020-7700 8066
email dan.rosenberg@quarto.com
website www.quarto.com
Chairman Peter Read, *Group Ceo* Alison Goff

Composed of three publishing divisions: Quarto
International Co-editions Group, Quarto Publishing
Group USA and Quarto Publishing Group UK
(below). The division includes: Quarto Publishing,
Quarto Children's Books, Happy Yak (page 150),
Qu:id, Quintessence, Quintet Publishing, QED,
RotoVision, Marshall Editions, Marshall Editions
Children's Books, Harvard Common Press, Small
World Creations, Fine Wine Editions, Apple Press,
Global Book Publishing, Iqon Editions Ltd, Ivy Press
and Quantum Publishing. Book categories: practical
art and crafts, graphic arts, lifestyle, reference, food
and drink, gardening, popular culture.
Founded 1976.

Quarto Group Publishing UK‡

The Quarto Group, Inc., 1 Triptych Place,
Second Floor, London SE1 9SH
tel 020-7700 9000
website www.quarto.com
Ceo Alison Goff

General adult non-fiction, illustrated and non-
illustrated: history, sport, entertainment, biography,
autobiography, military, gardening, architecture,
environment, interiors, photography, art, walking
and climbing, design and landscape, gift, interiors,
food and drink, lifestyle and craft. Children's picture
books and general children's non-fiction.
Founded 1976.

Quercus Publishing Plc*

Carmelite House, 50 Victoria Embankment,
London EC4Y 0DZ
website www.quercusbooks.co.uk
Managing Director Jon Butler

Fiction and non-fiction. Imprints: Arcadia
Publishing, Jo Fletcher Books, Greenfinch, Laurence
King (page 158), MacLehose Press, Quercus, Quercus
Non-Fiction and riverrun. Part of the Hachette
Group (page 150). Founded 2005.

Quiller Publishing Ltd‡

12 The Hill, Merrywalks, Stroud, Glous. GL5 4EP
tel (01453) 847800
email info@quillerbooks.com
website www.quillerpublishing.com
Ceo Nick Hayward

Owned by Amberley Publishing (page 125).
Founded 2001.

Kenilworth Press

Equestrian (riding, training, dressage, eventing, show
jumping, driving, polo). Publisher of BHS official

publications and exclusive distributor for *The Pony
Club*.

Quiller

Biographies, history, food and drink, sport, art and
photography, humour and gift books and specialist
practical books on country pursuits including dog
training, fishing, shooting, stalking, gamekeeping,
deer, falconry, natural history and gardening.

Radio Society of Great Britain*

3 Abbey Court, Fraser Road, Priory Business Park,
Bedford MK44 3WH
website https://rsgb.org/
Facebook www.facebook.com/theresgb
Twitter @thersgb

Publishes books for the amateur radio community.
Founded 1913.

Ransom Publishing Ltd*‡

Unit 7, Brocklands Farm, West Meon GU32 1JN
tel (01730) 829091
email ransom@ransom.co.uk
website www.ransom.co.uk
Managing Director Jenny Ertle, *Creative Director* Steve
Rickard

Children's fiction and non-fiction, phonics and
school reading programmes, and books for children
and adults who are reluctant or struggling readers.
Range covers high interest age/low reading age titles,
quick reads and reading schemes. Currently not
accepting any unsolicited submissions.
Founded 1995.

Raven Books

Publishes fiction and non-fiction for children 8–14
years.

Rat's Tales Ltd

Burnt House Farm, Old Fosse Road, Bath BA2 2SS
tel 07838 460905
email enquiries@ratstales.co.uk
website www.ratstales.co.uk
Facebook www.facebook.com/ratstalespublishing
Twitter @rats_tales

Publishes illustrated crime and thrillers that don't
conform to genre standards. Founded 2016.

Reaktion Books

Unit 32 Waterside, 44–48 Wharf Road,
London N1 7UX
tel 020-7253 4965
email info@reaktionbooks.co.uk
website www.reaktionbooks.co.uk
Facebook www.facebook.com/ReaktionBooks
Twitter @reaktionbooks
Instagram @reaktionbooks
Publisher Michael R. Leaman

Non-fiction publisher. Publishes around 100 new
titles each year in fields including art, architecture,

Books

design and photography, popular science, food, history, nature, film, music, philosophy, economics and politics. Founded 1985.

Red Dog Press‡

email hello@reddogpress.co.uk
website www.reddogpress.co.uk
Facebook www.facebook.com/reddogpressuk
Twitter @reddogtweets
Director Sean Coleman

Independent publishers of crime and thrillers. Founded 2018.

Red Planet Books

Dove House, Tregoniggie Industrial Estate, Falmouth, Cornwall TR11 4SN
email info@redplanetbooks.co.uk
website https://redplanetmusicbooks.com/
Facebook www.facebook.com/RedPlanetBooks
Twitter @RedPlanetZone
Founder Mark Neeter

An independent publishing company that specialises in books about music. Founded 2017.

Renard Press Ltd‡

Kemp House, 124 City Road, London EC1V 2NX
tel 020-8050 2928
email info@renardpress.com
website www.renardpress.com
Facebook www.facebook.com/therenardpress
Twitter @renardpress
Instagram @renardpress
Publisher Will Dady

Predominantly publishes classics, supplemented by a list of contemporary literary fiction, non-fiction, poetry and theatre titles. Founded 2020.

Repeater Books

email enquiries@repeaterbooks.com
website https://repeaterbooks.com/
Facebook www.facebook.com/repeaterbooks
Twitter @RepeaterBooks
Publisher Tariq Goddard

Publishes books expressing new and radical ideas: counter-culture fiction and non-fiction, politics, music, popular culture and current affairs. Part of Watkins Media (page 189). Founded 2014.

Revenge Ink

6D Lowick Close, Hazel Grove, Stockport SK7 5ED
email amita@revengeink.com
website www.revengeink.com
Director Amita Mukerjee, *Editor* Gopal Mukerjee

Publishes adult fiction (all kinds) and prefers unsolicited, first-time novelists or established writers seeking a new outlet for edgier material. Considers poetry if presented in an original, creative manner. Currently publishes approx. seven titles a year. Does not publish children's fiction or non-fiction titles

such as cookery, gardens and how-to books. The company is aiming to create a non-fiction imprint for new research in philosophy, history, critical theory and political analysis. Submission guidelines can be found on the website. By email, preferably, send short sample and query first. Founded 2007.

Rider – see Ebury Publishing

George Ronald

3 Rosecroft Lane, Oaklands, Welwyn, Herts. AL6 0UB
tel (01438) 716062
email sales@grbooks.com
website www.grbooks.com
Managers E. Leith, M. Hofman

Religion, specialising in the Bahá'í Faith. Founded 1939.

Route

PO Box 167, Pontefract, West Yorks. WF8 4WW
tel (01977) 793442
email info@route-online.com
website www.route-online.com
Twitter @Route_News
Contacts Ian Daley, Isabel Galán

Memoir, cultural non-fiction and biography, with a strong interest in music books. Occasional fiction. Unsolicited MSS discouraged, book proposals in first instance. Founded 2000.

Routledge – see Taylor & Francis Group

Rowman & Littlefield‡

86–90 Paul Street, London EC2A 4NE
tel 020-3111 1080
email info@rowmaninternational.com
website www.rowmaninternational.com
Facebook www.facebook.com/
RowmanLittlefieldInternational
Twitter @rowmaninternat
Directors James Lyons, Oliver Gadsby, Michael Lippenholz

The London office of an independent publisher specialising in both academic publishing in the humanities and social sciences and trade non-fiction publishing. Founded 2013.

Royal Collection Trust

Stable Yard House, St James's Palace, London SW1A 1JR
tel 020-7839 1377
website www.rct.uk/about/publishing
Head of Publishing Kate Owen, *Publishing Editor* Polly Fellows

Creates trade books, exhibition catalogues, guides and children's books to celebrate the royal residences and works of art found within them. Also produces scholarly catalogues raisonnés, which demonstrate the highest standards of academic research. Worldwide distribution by University of Chicago Press in the USA and Canada, and by Thames & Hudson Ltd throughout the rest of the world. Contact details on website. Founded 1993.

Royal National Institute of Blind People (RNIB)*‡

Midgate House, Midgate, Peterborough, Cambs. PE1 1TN
tel 0303 123 9999
email helpline@rnib.org.uk
website www.rnib.org.uk

Magazines, catalogues and books for blind and partially sighted people, to support daily living, leisure, learning and employment reading needs. Includes the charity's flagship Talking Books service, providing more than 30,000 fiction and non-fiction titles to borrow free of charge for adults and children with sight loss and commercial audio production services. Produced in braille, audio, large/clear print and email. Founded 1868.

Ruby Tuesday Books Ltd‡

6 Newlands Road, Tunbridge Wells, Kent TN4 9AT
tel (01892) 557767
email shan@rubytuesdaybooks.com
website www.rubytuesdaybooks.com
Twitter @RubyTuesdaybk
Publisher & Author Ruth Owen

Publishes children's books. Founded 2008.

Ryland Peters & Small‡

20–21 Jockey's Fields, London WC1R 4BW
tel 020-7025 2200
email info@rylandpeters.com
website https://rylandpeters.com/
Managing Director David Peters

Illustrated books: food, drink, home and garden, babies and children, gift. Founded 1995.

Cico Books

Lifestyle and interiors; crafts; mind, body & spirit; health. Founded 1999.

Saffron Books

PO Box 13666, London SW14 8WF
tel 020-8392 1122
email saffronbooks@eapgroup.com
website www.saffronbooks.com, www.sajidrizvi.net, www.eapgroup.com
Twitter @saffronbooks, @Safnetoffers, @sajidrizvi, @eapgroupnews
Instagram @EAPGROUP
Founding Publisher & Editor-in-Chief Sajid Rizvi

Art criticism and art history, history, African and Asian architecture, African and Asian art and archaeology, Central Asian studies, East Asia journal monographs, African and Asian linguistics including the *Saffron Korean Linguistics* Series, general non-fiction and fiction including the *Absolute Fiction* series. Also publishes European Crossroads Monographs. Founded 1989.

SAGE Publishing*‡

1 Oliver's Yard, 55 City Road, London EC1Y 1SP
tel 020-7324 8500
email info@sagepub.co.uk
website www.sagepublishing.com
Facebook www.facebook.com/SAGEPublishing
Twitter @SAGE_Publishing
Instagram @sage_publishing

Journals, books and library products for the educational, scholarly and professional markets. Founded 1965.

St David's Press

PO Box 733, Cardiff CF14 7ZY
tel 029-2021 8187
email post@st-davids-press.wales
website www.st-davids-press.wales
Facebook www.facebook.com/StDavidsPress
Twitter @StDavidsPress
Instagram @StDavidsPress

Sport and popular culture, including rugby, football, cricket, boxing, horse racing, cycling, athletics, walking, music. Also general titles of a Welsh and/or Celtic interest. Founded 2002.

St Pauls Publishing

St Pauls, Westminster Cathedral, Morpeth Terrace, Victoria, London SW1P 1EP
tel 020-7828 5582
email editor@stpauls.org.uk
website www.stpauls.org.uk

Theology, ethics, spirituality, biography, education, general books of Roman Catholic and Christian interest. Founded 1948.

Salmon Poetry

The Salmon Bookshop & Literary Centre, 9 Parliament Street, Ennistymon, County Clare, Republic of Ireland
tel +353 (0)65 7071856
email info@salmonpoetry.com
website www.salmonpoetry.com

Publishes alternative voices in Irish literature, specialises in the promotion of new poets, particularly women poets. Has published over 600 volumes. Founded 1981.

Salt Publishing‡

12 Norwich Road, Cromer, Norfolk NR27 0AX
email sales@saltpublishing.com
website www.saltpublishing.com
Twitter @saltpublishing
Publishing Directors Christopher Hamilton-Emery, Jennifer Hamilton-Emery

Books

Award-winning independent publisher of fiction and poetry. Home of the annual Best British Short Story anthology. Founded 1999.

Sandstone Press Ltd*‡

PO Box 41, Muir of Ord, Highland IV6 7YX
tel (01463) 567080
email info@sandstonepress.com
website www.sandstonepress.com
Facebook www.facebook.com/SandstonePress
Twitter @sandstonepress
Instagram @sandstonepress
Directors Robert Davidson, Moira Forsyth, Eric Macleod

Publishers of quality fiction and non-fiction for adults. Literary fiction, speculative fiction, crime novels and thrillers. Literary biography, memoir, sport, natural world, outdoor and Scottish interest, other general narrative non-fiction. For up to date information on submissions, full guidelines are available at https://sandstonepress.com/contact/submissions. Founded 2002.

Sapere Books‡

24 Trafalgar Road, Ilkley LS29 8HH
website www.saperebooks.com
Facebook www.facebook.com/saperebooks
Twitter @SapereBooks
Instagram @SapereBooks
Editorial Director Amy Durant

A digital-first publisher, specialising in historical fiction (including crime, mysteries, thrillers and sagas), action and adventure (military, naval and aviation fiction), crime fiction, mysteries, thrillers and history. Not currently open for submissions but remains open to publishing backlist books that may have gone out of print. Founded 2018.

Saqi Books*‡

Gable House, 18–24 Turnham Green Terrace, London W4 1QP
tel 020-7221 9347
email lynn@saqibooks.com
website www.saqibooks.com
Facebook www.facebook.com/SaqiBooks
Twitter @SaqiBooks
Instagram @SaqiBooks
Publisher Lynn Gaspard, *Associate Publisher* Simon Liebesney, *Editorial Director* Elizabeth Briggs

Independent publisher of global trade and academic books on the Middle East and North Africa. Successes include *The Crusades through Arab Eyes* by Amin Maalouf, *Beyond the Veil* by Fatema Mernissi, *Black Britain: A Photographic History* by Paul Gilroy and *The White Family* by Maggie Gee. Also translates new and classic Arabic literature, including works by Naguib Mahfouz, Mahmoud Darwish, Adonis and Nawal El Saadawi. Founded 1978.

Westbourne Press

Publishes alternative and progressive non-fiction works.

Telegram

Publishes new and classic international writing.

Saraband*‡

email hermes@saraband.net
website www.saraband.net
Facebook www.facebook.com/sarabandbks
Twitter @sarabandbooks
Instagram @sarabandbooks

Publishes nature and environmental writing, memoir, history and local interest non-fiction (especially on Scotland and the north of England), as well as literary and historical fiction, occasionally in translation. Under the Contraband imprint, publishes literary noir and dark fiction. Founded 1994.

Schofield & Sims Ltd*

7 Mariner Cour, Wakefield, West Yorks. WF4 3FL
tel (01484) 607080
email editorial@schofieldandsims.co.uk
website www.schofieldandsims.co.uk

Educational: nursery, infants, primary; posters. Founded 1901.

Scholastic Ltd*

Euston House, 24 Eversholt Street, London NW1 1DB
tel 020-7756 7756
website www.scholastic.co.uk
President & Ceo Peter Warwick

Children's fiction, non-fiction and picture books, education resources for primary schools. Owned by Scholastic Inc. Founded 1964.

Chicken House

See page 135.

Scholastic Children's Books

tel 020-7756 7761
email submissions@scholastic.co.uk
website www.scholastic.co.uk
Twitter @scholasticuk
Fiction Publisher Lauren Fortune, *Non-Fiction Publisher & Licensing* Elizabeth Scoggins, *Editorial Director, Illustrated Books* Felicity Osborne

Activity books, novelty books, picture books, fiction for 5–12 years, teenage fiction, series fiction and film/TV tie-ins. Imprints: Scholastic, Alison Green Books, Klutz. No unsolicited MSS. Unsolicited illustrations are accepted, but do not send any original artwork as it will not be returned.

Scholastic Educational Resources

Book End, Range Road, Witney, Oxon OX29 0YD
tel (01993) 893456
Publishing Director Robin Hunt

Professional books, classroom materials, home learning books and online resources for primary teachers, and GCSE support material.

Science Museum Group

Publishing Department, Enterprises, Exhibition Road, London SW7 2DD
tel 0870 870 4771
website www.sciencemuseumgroup.org.uk

Science, technology, engineering, medicine and mathematics. Adult science non-fiction and children's science non-fiction (licensed). Museum guides. Founded 1857.

SCM Press – see Hymns Ancient and Modern Ltd

Scorpius Books

10 Erle Havard Road, West Bergholt, Essex CO6 3LH
website www.scorpiusbooks.com
Facebook www.facebook.com/scorpiusbooks.com
Instagram @scorpiusbooks
Publisher & Founder Jacqueline Kibby

Publishes fantasy, horror, paranormal and general fiction. Produces dyslexic-friendly editions of adult titles – the first in the UK to do so. See website for submission guidelines. Founded 2020.

Scotland Street Press*

email info@scotlandstreetpress.com
website www.scotlandstreetpress.com
Facebook www.facebook.com/ScotStreetPress
Twitter @scotstreetpress
Instagram @scotstreetpress
Founder & Ceo Jean Fraser

Publishes biography, literary fiction and poetry Submissions window in February. Allow three to six months for a response. Founded 2014.

Scottish Mountaineering Press

5 South Charlotte Street, Edinburgh EH2 4AN
email mail@scottishmountaineeringpress.com
website https://scottishmountaineeringpress.com/
Facebook www.facebook.com/
scottishmountaineeringpress
Director Susan Jensen

Publisher of guidebooks, fiction and non-fiction about Scottish nature. Subsidiary of the Scottish Mountaineering Trust, a charity. All profits are channelled into the Trust. Founded 1990.

Scribe*

2 John Street, London WC1N 2ES
tel 020-3405 4218
email info@scribepub.co.uk
website https://scribepublications.co.uk/
Facebook www.facebook.com/ScribePublicationsUk
Twitter @scribeukbooks
Instagram @scribe_uk

An award-winning independent publisher, with offices in Australia, the UK and the USA. Publishes a range of fiction and non-fiction for the general reader, and has a picture books imprint called Scribble. In the UK, it is a member of the Independent Alliance. Does not accept submissions. Founded 1976.

Scripture Union

Trinity House, Opal Court, Fox Milne,
Milton Keynes MK15 0DF
tel (01908) 856000
email hello@scriptureunion.org.uk
website www.scriptureunion.org.uk
Director of Ministry Development (Publishing) Terry Clutterham

Christian books and bible reading materials for people of all ages; educational and worship resources for churches; children's fiction and non-fiction; adult non-fiction. Founded 1867.

Search Press Ltd‡

Wellwood, North Farm Road, Tunbridge Wells, Kent TN2 3DR
tel (01892) 510850
email searchpress@searchpress.com
website www.searchpress.com,
www.bookmarkedhub.com
Facebook www.facebook.com/SearchPress
Instagram @SearchPress
Managing Director Martin de la Bédoyère, *Publisher* Samantha Warrington

An independent, multi award-winning, family owned art and craft book publisher. Founded 1970.

SelfMadeHero

139 Pancras Road, London NW1 1UN
email info@selfmadehero.com
website www.selfmadehero.com
Facebook www.facebook.com/selfmadehero
Twitter @selfmadehero
Instagram @selfmadehero
Managing Director & Publisher Emma Hayley

The UK's leading independent publisher of graphic novels and visual narratives. The list of award-winning fiction and non-fiction graphic novels spans literary fiction, biography, classic adaptation, sci-fi, horror, crime and humour. Founded 2007.

September Publishing‡

tel 020-3637 0116
email info@septemberpublishing.org
website www.septemberpublishing.org
Facebook www.facebook.com/SeptemberPublishing
Twitter @septemberbooks
Instagram @septemberpublishing
Publisher Hannah MacDonald

Non-fiction publishers of illustrated and narrative adult books, including memoir and biography, travel, humour, art, politics. Founded 2013.

Books

Seren[‡]

Suite 6, 4 Derwen Road, Bridgend CF31 1LH
tel (01656) 663018
email seren@serenbooks.com
website www.serenbooks.com
Publisher Mick Felton

Poetry, fiction, literary criticism, biography, art –
mostly with relevance to Wales. Founded 1981.

Severn House

Eardley House, 4 Uxbridge Street, London W8 7SY
tel 020-3011 0525
email info@severnhouse.com
website www.severnhouse.com
Facebook www.facebook.com/severnhouse
Twitter @severnhouse
Instagram @severnhouseimprint
Publisher Joanne Grant

Hardback, paperback, ebook and large print adult
genres for the library market: mysteries, thrillers,
detective, horror, romance, sci-fi, fantasy. Imprint of
Canongate (page 134) Founded 1974.

Shearsman Books[‡]

PO Box 4239, Swindon SN3 9FN
tel 0330 1136514
email editor@shearsman.com
website www.shearsman.com
Facebook www.facebook.com/Shearsman-Books-
272720625528
Twitter @ShearsmanBooks
Editor & Publisher Tony Frazer

Contemporary poetry in English and in translation.
Founded 2003.

Sheldon Press – see John Murray Press

Sheldrake Press

PO Box 74852, London SW12 2DX
tel 020-8675 1767
email enquiries@sheldrakepress.co.uk
website www.sheldrakepress.co.uk,
www.sheldrakepress.com
Twitter @SheldrakePress
Publisher J.S. Rigge

History and art, travel, architecture, cookery, music;
humour; stationery. Founded 1979.

Shepheard-Walwyn (Publishers) Ltd[‡]

107 Parkway House, Sheen Lane, London SW14 8LS
tel 020-8241 5927
email books@shepheardwalwyn.com
website www.shepheardwalwyn.com,
www.ethicaleconomics.org.uk
Facebook www.facebook.com/
ShepheardWalwynPublishers
Twitter @SWPublishing
Instagram @swpublishers
Director M. Lombardo, *Marketing Manager* T.
Kerrigan, *Production Manager* K. Toth

Publishes authoritative and thought-provoking titles,
specialisms include history, biography, political
economy, perennial philosophy, women's studies,
social, environmental and climate issues. Publishing
partner of The School of Philosophy and Economic
Science, London. Hosts a podcast: https://
shepheardwalwyn.podbean.com. Founded 1971.

Short Books – see Octopus Publishing Group

Sigma Press

Stobart House, Pontyclerc, Penybanc Road,
Ammanford, Carmarthenshire SA18 3HP
tel (01269) 593100
email info@sigmapress.co.uk
website www.sigmapress.co.uk
Directors Nigel Evans, Jane Evans

Leisure: country walking, cycling, regional heritage,
ecology, folklore; biographies. Founded 1979.

Silvertail Books

email editor@silvertailbooks.com
website www.silvertailbooks.com
Twitter @silvertailbooks
Publisher Humfrey Hunter

Independent publisher which specialises in
commercial fiction and non-fiction. Especially likes
publishing newsworthy non-fiction and fiction which
tells captivating stories well. No children's books.
Founded 2012.

Simon & Schuster UK Ltd*

222 Gray's Inn Road, London WC1X 8HB
tel 020-7316 1900
email enquiries@simonandschuster.co.uk
website www.simonandschuster.co.uk
Facebook www.facebook.com/simonschusterUK
Twitter @simonschusteruk
Directors Ian Chapman (Ceo), Suzanne Baboneau
(managing director, adult), Clare Hey (publishing
director, adult), Katherine Armstrong (deputy
publishing director, adult), Holly Harris (publishing
director, non-fiction), Kris Doyle (deputy publishing
director, non-fiction), Sophie Missing (publishing
director, Scribner), Rachel Denwood (managing
director, children's), Ali Dougal (publishing director,
children's)

Adult non-fiction (history, biography, current affairs,
science, self-help, political, popular culture, sports
books, memoirs and illustrated titles). Adult fiction
(mass-market, literary fiction, historical fiction,
commercial women's fiction, general fiction).
Children's and YA fiction, picture books, novelty,
pop-up and licensed character. Simon & Schuster
Audioworks Fiction, non-fiction and business.
Founded 1986.

Simon & Schuster Audio

website www.simonandschuster.co.uk/audio
Publisher Dominic Brendon

Fiction, children's, YA and non-fiction audiobooks. Authors include Graham Swift, Philippa Gregory, Bruce Springsteen and Anita Anand.

Siri Scientific Press

Arrow Mill, Queensway, Castleton, Rochdale OL11 2YW
tel 07770 796913
email books@siriscientificpress.co.uk
website www.siriscientificpress.co.uk
Facebook www.facebook.com/Siri-Scientific-Press-134567006626977
Publishing Consultant David Penney

Publisher of specialist natural history books including academic monographs, compiled edited volumes, photographic atlases, field guides and more general works. Specialise in works on entomology, arachnology and palaeontology, but will also consider other topics. Happy to hear directly from potential new authors. Founded 2008.

Skein Press†

Talbot Mews, Vernon Grove, Rathgar Dublin 6, Republic of Ireland
email info@skeinpress.com
website www.skeinpress.com
Twitter @skeinpress
Editor Gráinne O'Toole

Publishes traditionally under-represented voices in Irish literature. Founded 2017.

Smokestack Books

1 Lake Terrace, Grewelthorpe, Ripon HG4 3BU
tel (01765) 658917
email info@smokestack-books.co.uk
website https://smokestack-books.co.uk/
Contact Andy Croft

An independent publisher of radical and unconventional poetry. Founded 2014.

Colin Smythe Ltd

38 Mill Lane, Gerrards Cross, Bucks. SL9 8BA
tel (01753) 886000
email info@colinsmythe.co.uk
website www.colinsmythe.co.uk
Director Colin Smythe

Irish biography, phaleristics, heraldry, Irish literature and literary criticism, Irish history. Other imprints: Dolmen Press, Van Duren Publishers. Founded 1966.

Snowbooks Ltd

55 North Street, Thame, Oxon OX9 3BH
email emma@snowbooks.com
website www.snowbooks.com
Directors Emma Barnes (managing), Rob Jones

Genre fiction: steampunk, fantasy, sci-fi and horror. General non-fiction. See website for submission guidelines. No postal submissions or calls. Founded 2003.

Society for Promoting Christian Knowledge‡

36 Causton Street, London SW1P 4ST
tel 020-7592 3900
email spck@spck.org.uk
website www.spckpublishing.co.uk
Ceo Sam Richardson

Founded 1698.

IVP

Theology and academic, commentaries, biblical studies, contemporary culture.

Marylebone House

Commercial and literary fiction.

SPCK

Theology, bibles, history, contemporary culture, children's picture books and fiction, biography, liturgy, prayer, spirituality, biblical studies, educational resources, social and ethical issues, mission, gospel and culture. Imprint: Form.

Society of Genealogists

356 Holloway Road, London N7 6PA
tel 020-7251 8799
email sales@sog.org.uk
website www.sog.org.uk
Contact Else Churchill

Local and family history books, software and magazines plus extensive library facilities. Founded 1911.

Somerville Press Ltd

Dromore, Bantry, Co. Cork P75 NY22, Republic of Ireland
tel +353 (0)28 32873
email somervillepress@gmail.com
website www.somervillepress.com
Directors Andrew Russell, Jane Russell

Irish interest: fiction and non-fiction. Founded 2008.

Southwater – see Anness Publishing

Sparsile Books*

PO Box 2861, Glasgow G61 9ED
tel 07938 864485
email enquiries@sparsilebooks.com
website www.sparsilebooks.com
Facebook www.facebook.com/sparsilebooks
Twitter @sparsileb
Publisher James Campbell

Small independent publisher based in Scotland. Publishes books that stand out from the crowd rather than genre-specific. Contemporary fiction and non-fiction, literary fiction, biography, history, general science, memoir. Open periodically for submissions, check website for details. Founded 2018.

Books

SPCK – see Society for Promoting Christian Knowledge

Sphere – see Little, Brown Book Group

Springer Nature Group Ltd*
4 Crinan Street, London N1 9XW
tel 020-7833 4000
website www.springernature.com
Chief Publishing Officer Harsh Jegadeesan

Global and progressive research, health, educational and professional publisher, home to a number of trusted brands, including Springer, Nature Portfolio, BMC, Scientific American and Palgrave Macmillan. Committed to advancing discovery through innovative products and service. Founded 1842.

BMC
website www.biomedcentral.com
Global scientific, technical and medical portfolio, providing researchers in academia, scientific institutions and corporate R&D departments with content through innovative information, products and services.

Macmillan Education
email info@macmillaneducation.com
website www.macmillaneducation.com
Language Learning division focuses mainly on ELT content but also produces resources in Spanish and Chinese for certain regions. The Schools Curriculum Division creates materials to fit with the curricula of countries around the world and the Higher Education division publishes content at university level across a wide range of subject areas.

Palgrave Macmillan
website www.palgrave.com
Publisher of books and journals with more than 175 years experience in the humanities and social sciences. Publishes award-winning research – monographs and journals – which changes the world across the humanities, social sciences and business for academics, professionals and librarians.

SRL Publishing Ltd*
email admin@srlpublishing.co.uk
website www.srlpublishing.co.uk
Facebook www.facebook.com/srlpublishing
Twitter @srlpublishing
Instagram @srlpublishing

A climate-positive publisher. Titles range from YA, new adult, contemporary fiction and crime/thriller to non-fiction. Founded 2014.

Stacey Publishing Ltd
14 Great College Street, London SW1P 3RX
tel 020-7221 7166
email info@stacey-international.co.uk
website www.stacey-international.co.uk
Founder Tom Stacey

Topical issues for *Independent Minds* series, encyclopedic books on regions and countries, Islamic and Arab subjects, world affairs, children's books, art, travel, belles lettres, biography. Imprints: Capuchin Classics, Gorilla Guides. Founded 1974.

Capuchin Classics
email info@capuchin-classics.co.uk
website www.capuchin-classics.co.uk
Enduring literary fiction, mostly 19th and 20th century. Founded 2008.

Stainer & Bell Ltd
PO Box 110, Victoria House, 23 Gruneisen Road, London N3 1DZ
tel 020-8343 3303
email post@stainer.co.uk
website www.stainer.co.uk

Books on music, religious communication. Founded 1907.

Stairwell Books
161 Lowther Street, York YO31 7LZ
website www.stairwellbooks.co.uk
Twitter @StairwellBooks
Founder Rose Drew

Small press of literary fiction and poetry. Founded 2005.

Stenlake Publishing Ltd
54–58 Mill Square, Catrine, Ayrshire KA5 6RD
tel (01290) 552233
email sales@stenlake.co.uk
website www.stenlake.co.uk
Managing Director Richard Stenlake

Local history, Scottish language and literature especially Robert Burns, studio pottery, beekeeping, railways, transport, aviation, canals and mining covering Wales, Scotland, England, Northern Ireland, Isle of Man, Republic of Ireland and Zambia. Founded 1987.

Alloway Publishing
website www.allowaypublishing.co.uk
Publishes work by ploughman poet, Robert Burns.

Oakwood Press
Specialising in railway and transport books. Founded 1931.

Stewed Rhubarb Press
email charlie@stewedrhubarb.org
website https://stewedrhubarb.org/
Facebook www.facebook.com/stewedrhubarb
Twitter @stewedbooks
Director Duncan Lockerbie, *Head of Publishing Programme* Charlie Roy

Publisher of poetry anthologies, special collections and pamphlets. Founded 2018.

Stonewood Press
email stonewoodpress@gmail.com
website www.stonewoodpress.co.uk
Facebook www.facebook.com/stonewoodpress
Twitter @stonewoodpress
Publisher & Production Editor Martin Parker

A small independent publisher dedicated to promoting new writing with an emphasis on contemporary short stories and poetry. Aims to publish challenging and high-quality writing in English without the pressures associated with mainstream publishing. See website for up-to-date submission guidelines and submission window. Founded 2011.

Storm Publishing
Stafford House, Loudwater Heights, Rickmansworth, Herts. WD3 4AX
email hello@stormpublishing.co
website https://stormpublishing.co/
Facebook www.facebook.com/stormpublishingco
Twitter @stormbooks_co
Managing Director Oliver Rhodes, *Editorial Director* Emily Gowers

Digital-first publisher of crimes, thrillers, mysteries, romance, sci-fi and historical fiction. Founded 2022.

Stripes – see Little Tiger Group

Studio Press*
Victoria House, Bloomsbury Square, London WC1B 4DA
tel 020-3770 8888
email hello@bonnierbooks.co.uk
website www.bonnierbooks.co.uk
Twitter @StudioPress
Executive Director Helen Wicks

Publishes a diverse range of books for all ages. Subjects include: pop culture trends and health, well-being and environmental issues. Publishing partner to major brands including Disney, Marvel and Harry Potter. An imprint of Bonnier Books UK (page 131). Founded 2015.

Summersdale Publishers Ltd
46 West Street, Chichester, West Sussex PO19 1RP
tel (01243) 771107
email submissions@summersdale.com
website www.summersdale.com

Popular non-fiction, humour and gift books, travel writing and health and wellbeing. See website for guidelines. Imprints include Summersdale and Vie. Owned by Octopus Publishing Group (page 167). Founded 1990.

Sunflower Books
PO Box 36160, London SW7 3WS
tel 020-7589 2377

email info@sunflowerbooks.co.uk
website www.sunflowerbooks.co.uk
Director P.A. Underwood

Travel guidebooks. Founded 1973.

Sweet Cherry Publishing*‡
Unit 4u18, The Book Brothers Business Park, Tolwell Road, Leicester LE4 1BR
tel 0116 253 6796
email info@sweetcherrypublishing.com
website www.sweetcherrypublishing.com
Facebook www.facebook.com/sweetcherrypublishing
Twitter @sweetcherrypub
Director A. Thadha

Award-winning specialist in children's fiction series. Children's picture books, novelty books, gift books, board books, educational books and fiction series for all ages. Also welcomes YA novels and series. See website for submission guidelines. Imprints include Clock Tower and Cherry Stone. Clock Tower aims to champion marginalised voices and values diversity, inclusivity and representation. Founded 2011.

Swift Press Ltd‡
43 Drewstead Road, London SW16 1LY
tel 020-8265 2062
email info@swiftpress.com
website www.swiftpress.com
Facebook www.facebook.com/SwiftPressBooks
Twitter @_swiftpress
Instagram @_swiftpress
Managing Director Diana Broccardo, *Publisher* Mark Richards

An independent publishing company, part of the Independent Alliance, publishes fiction and a wide range of non-fiction. Founded 2020.

Tangerine Press
Unit 18, Wimbledon Stadium Business Centre, Riverside Road, London SW17 0BA
email info@thetangerinepress.com
website https://thetangerinepress.com
Twitter @tangerinepress
Instagram @tangerine_press
Publisher Michael Curran

Publishes new, neglected and innovative writing in handbound, hardcover limited editions, often in tandem with more readily available paperbacks. Also releases chapbooks, broadsides, vinyl records, artwork, screen prints, posters, ephemera. Founded 2006.

Tango Books Ltd
PO Box 32595, London W4 5YD
tel 020-8996 9970
email sales@tangobooks.co.uk
website www.tangobooks.co.uk
Directors Sheri Safran, David Fielder

Books

Children's fiction and non-fiction novelty books, including pop-up, touch-and-feel and cloth books. No unsolicited MSS. Founded 2004.

Tarquin Publications
Suite 74, 17 Holywell Hill, St Albans AL1 1DT
tel (01727) 833866
email info@tarquinbooks.com
website www.tarquinbooks.com

Mathematics and mathematical models, puzzles, codes and logic; paper cutting, paper engineering and pop-up books for children. No unsolicited MSS; send suggestion or synopsis in first instance. Founded 1970.

Taschen UK Ltd
Suite 1, Blandel Bridge House, 56 Sloane Square, London SW1W 8AX
tel 020-7845 8585
email contact-uk@taschen.com
website www.taschen.com

Publishers of art, anthropology and aphrodisia. Founded 1980.

Tate Enterprises Ltd*
The Lodge, Millbank, London SW1P 4RG
tel 020-7887 8869
email publishing.press@tate.org.uk
website www.tate.org.uk/about-us/tate-publishing
Publishing Director Tom Avery, *Merchandise Director* Rosey Blackmore, *Sales & Marketing Manager* Maxx Lundie

Publishers for Tate in London, Liverpool and St Ives. Exhibition catalogues, art books, children's books and merchandise. Also product development, picture library and licensing. Founded 1911.

I.B. Tauris*‡
50 Bedford Square, London WC1B 3DP
tel 020-7631 5600
website www.bloomsbury.com/uk/academic/middle-east
Twitter @ibtauris
Editorial Director David Avital

An imprint of Bloomsbury Publishing Plc (page 130). Middle East studies. Founded 1983.

Taylor & Francis Group*
4 Park Square, Milton Park, Abingdon, Oxon OX14 4RN
tel 020-7017 6000
email enquiries@taylorandfrancis.com
website https://taylorandfrancis.com/
Ceo Annie Callanan, *Managing Director* Jeremy North (Taylor & Francis, Academic Learning)

Academic and reference books. Founded 1798.

CRC Press
Science: physics, mathematics, chemistry, electronics, natural history, pharmacology and drug metabolism,

toxicology, technology, history of science, ergonomics, production engineering, remote sensing, geographic information systems, engineering.

Routledge
website www.routledge.com

Addiction, anthropology, animation, archaeology, architecture, art history, Asian studies, audio, business, behavioural science, civil engineering, classical studies, construction, counselling, criminology, development and environment, dictionaries, economics, education, film, gaming, geography, health, history, Japanese studies, law, leisure and recreation management, library science, language, linguistics, literary studies, media and culture, music, nursing, performance studies, philosophy, photography, politics, psychiatry, psychology, reference, social administration, social studies/sociology, social work, sports science, theatre and women's studies. Also directories, international relations, reference and yearbooks.

Templar Books*
Victoria House, Bloomsbury Square, London WC1B 4DA
tel 020-3770 8888
email hello@bonnierbooks.co.uk
website www.bonnierbooks.co.uk
Twitter @templarbooks
Publisher Sophie Hallam

Children's imprint. Series include the *Ology* series, *Jonny Duddle's Gigantosaurus* titles and the *Amazing Baby* range of board and novelty books. Imprint of Bonnier Books UK (page 131). Founded 1978.

Templar Poetry
58 Dale Road, Matloc, Derbyshire DE4 3NB
tel 07582 219078
email info@templarpoetry.com
website www.templarpoetry.com
Facebook www.facebook.com/templarpoetry
Twitter @templarpoetry

An independent publisher originally based in Scotland and now located in Derbyshire. Publishes poetry and fiction. Founded 2005.

Thames & Hudson Ltd*‡
181A High Holborn, London WC1V 7QX
tel 020-7845 5000
email submissions@thameshudson.co.uk
website www.thamesandhudson.com
Facebook www.facebook.com/thamesandhudson
Twitter @thamesandhudson
Instagram @thamesandhudson
Ceo & Publisher Sophy Thompson

Illustrated non-fiction for an international audience (adults and children), specialising in art and art history, architecture, photography, design, fashion, popular culture, history and archaeology. For submission guidelines see website. Founded 1949.

Think Books

20 Mortimer Street, London W1T 3JW
tel 020-3771 7200
email info@thinkpublishing.co.uk
website www.thinkpublishing.co.uk
Founder & Chairman Ian McAuliffe, *Director* Tilly McAuliffe

Specialises in books on the outdoors, gardening and wildlife. Publishes with the Wildlife Trusts, the Royal Horticultural Society and the Campaign to Protect Rural England and others. Founded 2005.

Thinkwell Books

7 Winsford Crescent, Little Bispham,
Thornton-Cleveleys, Lancs. FY5 1PS
tel 07940 933159
email thinkwellbooksuk@gmail.com
website https://thinkwellbooks.org/
Managing Editors Jeff Weston, Patricia Khan

Literary fiction, political and social works, sports journalism and commercial fiction. New authors and unsolicited MSS welcome. See website for details regarding submissions. References must be Vancouver style using Word superscript and not footnotes or endnotes. Founded 2019.

Thistle Publishing

36 Great Smith Street, London SW1P 3BU
tel 020-7222 7574
email david@thistlepublishing.co.uk
website www.thistlepublishing.co.uk
Facebook www.facebook.com/ThistlePublishing
Twitter @ThistleBooks
Publishers David Haviland, Andrew Lownie

Trade publisher of quality fiction and non-fiction. Accepts unsolicited submissions, send three chapters and a synopsis by email. Founded 1996.

Thomson Reuters – Round Hall*

Third Floor, 12/13 Exchange Place,
International Financial Services Centre, Dublin 1,
Republic of Ireland
tel 0345 600 9355
website www.sweetandmaxwell.co.uk/roundhall
Directors M. Keen, M. McCann

Formerly The Roundhall Press. Acquired by Sweet & Maxwell in 1995. Publishes law. Now part of Thomson Reuters. Founded 1980.

Tilted Axis Press*

639 High Road, London N17 8AA
email info@tiltedaxispress.com
website www.tiltedaxispress.com
Facebook www.facebook.com/tiltedaxispress
Twitter @tiltedaxispress

Publishes mainly work by Asian and African writers, translated into a variety of Englishes. Founded 2015.

Tiny Owl Publishing Ltd

6 Hatfield road, London W4 1AF
email info@tinyowl.co.uk
website www.tinyowl.co.uk
Facebook www.facebook.com/tinyowlpublishing
Twitter @TinyOwl_Books
Publisher Delaram Ghanimifard

An independent publisher of global children's literature. Publishes high-quality picture books for children 3–11 years. Aims to promote diversity and human rights values. Founded 2015.

Titan Books

144 Southwark Street, London SE1 0UP
tel 020-7620 0200
website www.titanbooks.com
Divisional Head Laura Price

Publisher of original fiction under the genres of sci-fi, fantasy, horror, crime and YA crossover. Licensed fiction and non-fiction covering TV, film, gaming and popular culture. No children's proposals or middle grade. All fiction submissions must come from an agent. Division of Titan Publishing Group Ltd. Founded 1981.

Tramp Press*

email info@tramppress.com
email submissions@tramppress.com
website www.tramppress.com
Facebook www.facebook.com/tramppress
Twitter @TrampPress
Founding Publishers Lisa Coen, Sarah Davis-Goff

Publishes award-winning fiction and narrative non-fiction. Tramp Press is a feminist press. Founded 2014.

Transworld*

Penguin Random House, One Embassy Gardens,
8 Viaduct Gardens, London SW11 7BW
tel 020-7840 8400
website www.penguin.co.uk/transworld
Publisher Bill Scott-Kerr (Transworld), *Publisher* Sarah Adams (fiction & brand), *Publisher* Frankie Gray (Bantom UK), *Publishing Director* Susanna Wadeson (non-fiction), *Publishing Director* Kirsty Dunseath (Doubleday, UK)

Imprints include: Bantam (UK), Doubleday (UK), Torva, Penguin. Part of Penguin Random House UK (page 172). No unsolicited MSS accepted. Non-fiction: autobiography, biography, business, current affairs, crime, health and diet, history, humour, memoir, military, music, natural history, personal development and self-help, science, travel and adventure. Fiction (commercial): crime, thrillers, contemporary, historical and saga fiction; sci-fi, horror and fantasy; literary and book club fiction. Founded 1950.

Books

Troika*

Troika Books Ltd, Well House, Green Lane, Ardleigh, Colchester, Essex CO7 7PD
email info@troikabooks.com
website www.troikabooks.com
Publisher Martin West, *Publicity, Marketing & Editorial* Roy Johnson

Publishes picture books, poetry and fiction for all ages, with an emphasis on quality, accessibility and diversity. Founded 2012.

TSO (The Stationery Office)

St Crispins, Duke Street, Norwich NR3 1PD
tel (01603) 696876
email customer.services@tso.co.uk
website www.tsoshop.co.uk

Publishing and information management services: business, directories, pharmaceutical, professional, reference, *Learning to Drive*. Founded 1996.

Turas Press†

6–9 Trinity Street, Dublin 2, D02 EYA7, Republic of Ireland
email admin@turaspress.ie
website https://turaspress.ie/
Twitter @TurasPress
Founder Liz McSkeane

Independent publisher of poetry and fiction. Founded 2017.

Two Rivers Press Ltd‡

7 Denmark Road, Reading, Berks. RG1 5PA
tel 0118 987 1452
email tworiverspress@gmail.com
website www.tworiverspress.com
Facebook www.facebook.com/tworiverspress
Twitter @TwoRiversPress
Publisher Anne Nolan, *Editorial Director, Botanical Art Portfolios* Sally Mortimore, *Poetry Editor* Peter Robinson, *Creative Director* Nadja Guggi, *Design & Illustration* Sally Castle, Martin Andrews, *Contracts* Karen Mosman

Champions Reading and surrounding area's heritage and culture through contemporary and classic poetry, art and local interest books. Publishes an international *Botanical Art Portfolios* series. Founded 1994.

UCLan Publishing

Victoria Street, Preston PR1 2HE
email uclanpublishing@uclan.ac.uk
website https://uclanpublishing.com/
Facebook www.facebook.com/uclanpublishing
Twitter @publishinguclan
Publisher Hazel Holmes

Supporting students at the University of Central Lancashire, not-for-profit publishers of early years, middle grade, teen and YA fiction. Currently closed to submissions. Founded 2010.

UCL Press*

University College London (UCL), Gower Street, London WC1E 6BT
email uclpresspublishing@ucl.ac.uk
website www.uclpress.co.uk
Twitter @UCLPress
Commissioning Editors Chris Penfold, Pat Gordon Smith

Publishes scholarly monographs, edited collections, textbooks, journals and other research outputs. Founded 2015.

Ulric Publishing

PO Box 55, Church Stretton, Shrops. SY6 6WR
tel (01694) 781354
email info@ulricpublishing.com
website www.ulricpublishing.com
Directors Ulric Woodhams, Elizabeth Oakes

Non-fiction military and motoring history. Licensing, bespoke bindings and publishing services. No unsolicited MSS. Visitors by appointment. Founded 1992.

Ulverscroft Ltd

The Green, Bradgate Road, Anstey, Leicester LE7 7FU
tel 0116 236 4325
email customersupport@ulverscroft.co.uk
website www.ulverscroft.co.uk
Facebook www.facebook.com/ulverscroft
Twitter @UlverscroftLt

Offers a wide variety of large print and unabridged audiobooks, many of which are written by the world's favourite authors and includes award-winning titles. eAudio is also available to libraries and their patrons via the uLibrary app. Founded 1964.

Unbound‡

Runway East, 20 St Thomas Street, London SE1 9RS
tel 020-3997 6790
email hello@unbound.co.uk
website www.unbound.co.uk
Facebook www.facebook.com/unbound
Twitter @unbounders

The world's first crowdfunding publisher. Considers submissions from literary agents and direct from writers. Includes an audio and podcasting arm, Unbound Audio. Writers should submit projects using the website submission page: unbound.co.uk/authors. Founded 2011.

Unicorn Publishing Group‡

Charleston Studio, 1 Meadow Business Centre, Lewes BN8 5RW
tel (01273) 812066
email ian@unicornpublishing.org
website www.unicornpublishing.org
Twitter @UnicornPubGroup
Directors Lord Strathcarron, Lucy Duckworth, Simon Perks, Ryan Gearing, David Breuer

A leading independent publisher with four imprints: Unicorn, the visual arts and cultural history imprint; Uniform, specialising in military history; Universe, an historical fiction imprint; and Unify, which publishes health and philosophy titles. Submissions welcomed, see website for guidance. Founded 1985.

Merlin Unwin Books Ltd*‡
Palmers House, 7 Corve Street, Ludlow, Shrops. SY8 1DB
tel (01584) 877456
email books@merlinunwin.co.uk
website www.merlinunwin.co.uk
Chairman Merlin Unwin, *Managing Director* Karen McCall

Countryside books. Founded 1990.

Usborne Publishing Ltd‡
Usborne House, 83–85 Saffron Hill, London EC1N 8RT
tel 020-7430 2800
email mail@usborne.co.uk
website www.usborne.com
Ceo Peter Usborne, *Directors* Nicola Usborne, Jenny Tyler (editorial), Andrea Parsons

An independent, family publisher of books for children of all ages, including baby, preschool, novelty, activity, non-fiction and fiction. Looking for high-quality imaginative children's fiction. No unsolicited MSS. Founded 1973.

Vallentine Mitchell‡
Catalyst House, 720 Centennial Court, Centennial Park, Elstree WD6 3SY
tel 020-8292 5637
email info@vmbooks.com (general)
email editor@vmbooks.com (submissions)
website www.vmbooks.com
Directors Stewart Cass, A.E. Cass, H.J. Cass

International publisher of books of Jewish interest, both for the scholar and general reader. Subjects published include Jewish history, culture and heritage, modern Jewish thought, Holocaust studies, Middle East studies, biography and reference. Founded 1949.

Valley Press
Woodend, The Crescent, Scarborough YO11 2PW
email hello@valleypressuk.com
website www.valleypressuk.com
Facebook www.facebook.com/valleypress
Twitter @valleypress
Publisher Jamie McGarry

Publishes poetry (collections, pamphlets and anthologies); fiction (novels and short stories); graphic novels; and non-fiction (memoirs, travel writing, journalism, music, art and more). Founded 2008.

Velocity Press
16 Long Meadow Close, West Wickham BR4 0EQ
tel 07595 823298
email info@velocitypress.uk
website https://velocitypress.uk/
Facebook www.facebook.com/velocitypressbooks
Twitter @PressVelocity
Director Colin Steven

Publishes electronic music and club culture non-fiction and fiction. It aims to create a catalogue that feels like a trusted record label in its integrity and vision and deliver exciting stories to serious electronic music fans who enjoy good literature. Founded 2019.

Veritas Publications†
Veritas House, 7–8 Lower Abbey Street, Dublin D01 W2C2, Republic of Ireland
tel +353 (0)18 788177
email publications@veritas.ie
website www.veritas.ie

Liturgical and church resources, religious school books for primary and post-primary levels, biographies, academic studies, and general books on religious, moral and social issues. Founded 1983.

Vermilion – see Ebury Publishing

Verso Ltd‡
6 Meard Street, London W1F 0EG
tel 020-7437 3546
email enquiries@verso.co.uk
website www.versobooks.com
Managing Director Jacob Stevens

Current affairs, politics, sociology, economics, history, philosophy, cultural studies. Founded 1970.

Vertebrate Publishing‡
Omega Court, 352 Cemetery Road, Sheffield S11 8FT
email info@adventurebooks.com
website www.adventurebooks.com
Facebook www.facebook.com/vertebratepublishing
Twitter @VertebratePub
Founder Jon Barton

Publishes books inspired by the outdoors. Based in the Peak District, subjects covered include mountain biking, cycling, climbing, walking, running, wildlife and photography. Also publishes fiction inspired by the outdoors. Founded 2004.

Verve Poetry Press
tel 07713 236205
email mail@vervepoetrypress.com
website https://vervepoetrypress.com/
Twitter @VervePoetryPress
Instagram @verve.publisherofpoetry
Co-founders Stuart Bartholomew, Amerah Saleh

Birmingham-based publisher; predominantly promotes and publishes poets who are from Birmingham and the Midlands. Founded 2018.

Books

Viking – see Penguin General

Vintage*

One Embassy Gardens, 8 Viaduct Gardens,
London SW11 7BW
tel 020-7840 8602
website www.penguin.co.uk/vintage
Managing Director Hannah Telfer, *Deputy Managing Director* Faye Brewster

Part of Penguin Random House UK (page 172).
Quality fiction and non-fiction. No unsolicited MSS.
Founded 1954.

The Bodley Head
tel 020-7139 3824
Publishing Director Stuart Williams, *Deputy Publishing Director* Will Hammond, *Editorial Director* Jorg Hensgen, *Paperback Editor* Alice Johnstone, *Assistant Editor* Laura Reeves

Non-fiction: natural history, science, history, current affairs, politics, tech, big ideas, economics, autobiography, how to live.

Jonathan Cape
tel 020-7139 3264
Publishing Director Hannah Westland, *Associate Publisher* Dan Franklin (graphic novels), *Associate Publisher* Robin Robertson (poetry), *Deputy Publishing Director* Bea Hemming, *Editorial Director* Željka Marošević, *Editorial Director* David Milner, *Senior Commissioning Editor* Alex Russell, *Editorial Assistant* Jane Link

Biography and memoirs, current affairs, fiction, history, poetry, travel, politics, graphic novels.

Chatto & Windus/Hogarth
tel 020-7139 3695
Editorial Director Rose Tomaszewska, *Senior Editor* Victoria Murray-Browne, *Commissioning Editor* Kaiya Shang, *Assistant Editor* Rosanna Hildyard, *Editorial Assistant* Asia Choudhry

Non-fiction, fiction and poetry. No unsolicited MSS.

Classics and Paperbacks
tel 020-8231 6604
Publishing Director Beth Coates, *Editorial Director* Nicholas Skidmore, *Senior Editors* Victoria Murray-Browne, Charlotte Knight, Alex Russell, *Assistant Editors* Anna Nightingale, Alice Johnstone, Dredheza Maloku

Harvill Secker
tel 020-7840 8394
Publishing Director Liz Foley; *Deputy Publishing Directors* Katie Ellis-Brown (crime & crossover), Kate Harvey (Harvill Secker); *Senior Editor* Ellie Steel, *Editor* Mikaela Pedlow, *Assistant Editor* Sania Riaz

English literature, crime and crossover fiction and world literature in translation. Non-fiction (history, current affairs, literary essays, music). No unsolicited MSS.

Pimlico
tel 020-7840 8836
History, biography, literature. Exclusively in paperback. No unsolicited MSS.

Square Peg
tel 020-7139 3664
Publishing Director Marianne Tatepo, *Assistant Editor* Emily Martin

Commercial and literary non-fiction across narrative and memoir, food and drink, activism and pop culture, nature and wellbeing. Unsolicited MSS with sae.

Yellow Jersey Press
tel 020-7840 8438
Senior Editorial Joe Pickering

Literary and prize-winning sports writing of all kinds. No unsolicited MSS.

Virtue Books Ltd

Edward House, Tenter Street, Rotherham S60 1LB
tel (01709) 365005
email info@virtue.co.uk
Directors Peter E. Russum, Margaret H. Russum

Books for the professional chef: catering and drink.
Founded 1949.

University of Wales Press‡

University Registry, King Edward VII Avenue,
Cardiff CF10 3NS
tel 029-2037 6999
email press@press.wales.ac.uk
website www.uwp.co.uk,
www.gwasgprifysgolcymru.org
Director Natalie Williams

Academic, educational and trade non-fiction publisher (Welsh and English). Specialises in the humanities and social sciences across a broad range of subjects: Welsh studies, European studies, literary criticism, history, Celtic and Medieval studies, political philosophy. Founded 1922.

Calon
Focuses on trade non-fiction rooted in Wales. Currently open to submissions from both agents and authors for non-fiction books aimed at a general readership, with a link to Wales and/or Welsh history and culture. Does not only publish books focused solely on Wales and welcomes submissions from authors of all nationalities and backgrounds.

Walker Books Ltd*‡

87 Vauxhall Walk, London SE11 5HJ
tel 020-7793 0909
website www.walker.co.uk
Facebook www.facebook.com/walkerbooks
Twitter @walkerbooksuk
Instagram @walkerbooksuk
Editors Karen Lotz, Jane Winterbotham, Denise Johnstone-Burt, Annalie Grainger

Children's: activity books, novelty books, picture books, fiction for 5–8 years and 9–12 years, YA fiction, series fiction, film/TV tie-ins, plays, poetry, digital and audio. Imprints: Walker Books, Walker Studio, MIT Kids Press, MITeen Press and Walker Entertainment. Founded 1980.

Watkins Media*

Unit 11, Shepperton House, 89 Shepperton Road, London N1 3DF
tel 020-3813 6940
email enquiries@watkinsmedia.org
website www.watkinsmedia.org
Owner Etan Ilfeld

Media company that incorporates magazine publishing and retail activities, as well as book publishing. Imprints: Angry Robot (sci-fi and fantasy – page 126), Datura (crime fiction), Nourish Books (health and wellbeing, food and drink – page 166), Repeater (counter-culture fiction and non-fiction, including politics and current affairs – page 176), Watkins Publishing (self-help, personal development; mind, body & spirit – page 189). Founded 1893.

Watkins Publishing‡

Unit 11, Shepperton House, 89 Shepperton Road, London N1 3DF
tel 020-3813 6940
email enquiries@watkinspublishing.com
website www.watkinspublishing.com
Facebook www.facebook.com/WatkinsPublishing
Twitter @WatkinsWisdom

Publishers of wellbeing, personal development and esoteric books. Works in partnership with authors and aims to produce authoritative, innovative titles, both illustrated and non-illustrated. Part of Watkins Media. Founded 1893.

The Waywiser Press

Christmas Cottage, Church Enstone, Chipping Norton, Oxon OX7 4NN
tel (01608) 677492
website https://waywiser-press.com/
Facebook www.facebook.com/thewaywiserpress
Twitter @Waywiserpress
Editor-in-Chief Philip Hoy

Small independent publisher, with its main office in the UK, and a subsidiary in the USA. A literary press, with a special interest in modern poetry and fiction. Sometimes publishes memoir, criticism, history. Founded 2001.

Josef Weinberger Plays Ltd

12–14 Mortimer Street, London W1T 3JJ
tel 020-7580 2827
email shows@jwmail.co.uk
website www.josef-weinberger.com

Stage plays only, in both acting and trade editions. Preliminary letter essential. Founded 1936.

Welbeck Publishing Group*

20 Mortimer Street, London W1T 3JW
tel 020-7612 0400
email enquiries@welbeckpublishing.com
website www.welbeckpublishing.com

No unsolicited MSS; synopses and ideas welcome, but no fiction or poetry. Acquired by Hachette UK (page 150) 2022. Founded 2019.

André Deutsch

Sci-fi, fantasy, crime and classic reissues.

Mortimer

Children's entertainment, licensing and gaming.

Mountain Leopard Press

Editor Christopher MacLehose
Literary and books-in-translation.

OH! Orange Hippo

Humour, nostalgia, gift, lifestyle, food and drink, art and photography, interiors.

Welbeck Childrens

General children's non-fiction, narrative and illustrated, all ages excluding preschool.

Welbeck Balance

Wellbeing, personal development and mind, body & spirit.

Welbeck Editions

Illustrated non-fiction.

Welbeck Fiction

Women's, thriller, crime, historical, saga, romance, reading group.

Welbeck Flame

Associate Publisher Felicity Alexander
Children's fiction.

Welbeck Non-Fiction

Narrative and illustrated non-fiction: smart thinking, history, memoir and biography, popular science and psychology, soft business, true crime, sport, music and film, military, puzzles and games, lifestyle.

Welsh Academic Press

PO Box 733, Cardiff CF14 7ZY
tel 029-2021 8187
email post@welsh-academic-press.wales
website www.welsh-academic-press.wales
Facebook www.facebook.com/WelshAcademicPress
Twitter @WelshAcadPress
Instagram @WelshAcademicPress

History, political studies, public affairs, education, medieval Welsh and Celtic studies, Scandinavian and Baltic studies. Founded 1994.

Whittet Books Ltd

1 St John's Lane, Stansted, Essex CM24 8JU
tel (01279) 815871
email mail@whittetbooks.com
website www.whittetbooks.com
Director George J. Papa, *Publisher* Shirley Greenall

Natural history, wildlife, countryside, poultry, livestock, horses, donkeys. Publishing proposals considered for the above lists. Send outline by email. Founded 1976.

Wide Eyed Editions

The Old Brewery, 6 Blundell Street, London N7 9BH
tel 020-7700 6700
website www.quartoknows.com/Wide-Eyed-Editions
Publisher Georgia Amison-Bradshaw

Imprint of the Quarto Group, Inc. (page 175). Creates original non-fiction for children. Founded 2014.

Wild Things Publishing

Freshford, Bath BA2 7WG
tel 07761 375717
email hello@wildthingspublishing.com
website www.wildthingspublishing.com
Facebook www.facebook.com/wildthingspublishing
Twitter @wildswimming
Instagram @wildswimming
Founders Daniel Start, Tania Pascoe

Publishes books (and apps) that get people out, experiencing and enjoying nature. Founded 2011.

John Wiley & Sons Ltd

The Atrium, Southern Gate, Chichester,
West Sussex PO19 8SQ
tel (01243) 779777
email customer@wiley.com
Alternative address 9600 Garsington Road, Oxford OX4 2DQ
tel (01865) 776868
website www.wiley.com
Ceo Brian A. Napack

Wiley's core businesses publish scientific, technical, medical and scholarly journals, encyclopedias, books and online products and services; professional/trade books, subscription products, training materials and online applications and websites; and educational materials for undergraduate and graduate students and lifelong learners. Global headquarters in Hoboken, New Jersey, with operations in the USA, Europe, Asia, Canada and Australia. Founded 1807.

Philip Wilson Publishers*‡

50 Bedford Square, London WC1B 3DP
email ContactPWP@bloomsbury.com
website www.bloomsbury.com/uk/discover/superpages/non-fiction/philip-wilson-publishers
Publisher Jayne Parsons

An imprint of Bloomsbury Publishing Plc (page 130). Fine and applied art, architecture, photography, collecting, museums. Founded 1975.

Wooden Books

The Lawn, Walsham-le-Willows, Bury St Edmunds, Suffolk IP31 3AW
email woodenbooksoffice@gmail.com
Alternative address Red Brick Building, Glastonbury BA6 9FT
website www.woodenbooks.com
Ceo John Martineau

Liberal arts, modern and ancient arts and sciences. Founded 1996.

Wrecking Ball Press

5 Theatre Mews, Egginton Street, Hull HU2 8DL
email editor@wreckingballpress.com
website www.wreckingballpress.com
Facebook www.facebook.com/wreckingballpress
Twitter @wbphull
Editor Shane Rhodes

Independent publisher of contemporary cutting-edge literature. Founded 1997.

Y Lolfa Cyf

Talybont, Ceredigion SY24 5HE
tel (01970) 832304
email ylolfa@ylolfa.com
website www.ylolfa.com
Director Garmon Gruffudd, *Editor* Lefi Gruffudd

Welsh language and English books of Welsh/Celtic interest, biographies and sport. Founded 1967.

Yale University Press London‡

47 Bedford Square, London WC1B 3DP
tel 020-7079 4900
website www.yalebooks.co.uk
Twitter @YaleBooks
Managing Director Heather McCallum, *Sales & Marketing Director* David Brand, *Editorial Directors* Mark Eastment (art & architecture), Julian Loose (trade & academic), *Production Director* Stuart Weir, *Finance & Operations Director* Emma Arnolda

Art, architecture, history, economics, political science, religion, history of science, biography, current affairs and music. Founded 1961.

Yellow Jersey Press – see Vintage

Zaffre Publishing Group*

Victoria House, Bloomsbury Squre,
London WC1B 4DA
tel 020-3770 8888
email hello@zaffrebooks.co.uk
website www.zaffrebooks.co.uk, www.bonnierbooks.co.uk
Twitter @zaffrebooks
Publisher Margaret Stead, *Publishing Director* Sarah Benton, *Editorial Director* Sophie Orme

Commercial fiction including crime, thrillers, saga, women's and reading group fiction. Publishes established authors focusing on a wide range of crime, thrillers, women's and reading-group fiction. Imprint of Bonnier Books UK (page 131). Founded 2014.

Zambezi Publishing Ltd
22 Second Avenue, Camels Head, Plymouth PL2 2EQ
tel (01752) 367300
email info@zampub.com
website www.zampub.com
Contacts Sasha Fenton, Jan Budkowski

Mind, body & spirit. Founded 1998.

Zed Books Ltd*‡
50 Bedford Square, London WC1B 3DP
website www.bloomsbury.com
Twitter @ZedBooks
Editor Editorial Director David Avital

African studies. Owned by Bloomsbury Publishing Plc (page 130). Founded 1976.

ZigZag Education
Unit 3, Greenway Business Centre, Doncaster Road, Bristol BS10 5PY
tel 0117 950 3199
email submissions@publishmenow.co.uk
website www.zigzageducation.co.uk, www.publishmenow.co.uk
Development Director John-Lloyd Hagger, *Strategy Director* Mike Stephens

Secondary school teaching resources: English, maths, ICT, geography, history, science, business, politics, P.E., media studies. Founded 1998.

CROWDFUNDED PUBLISHING

Crowdfunding, the raising of small investments from a wide pool of individuals to fund a project, can be a viable option for writers wishing to publish their work. Publishers and platforms that use crowdfunding as a way to raise funds include the following:

And Other Stories (page 125)
Crowdbound (page 138)

Inkshares (page 210)
Unbound (page 186)

Indiegogo
website www.indiegogo.com

Acts as a 'launchpad' for creative ideas.

Kickstarter
website www.kickstarter.com

Helps artists, musicians, filmmakers and designers find resources and support needed for a project.

Publishizer
website https://publishizer.com/

Books only. Authors submit a proposal and launch a pre-orders campaign. Publishers receive proposals based on targets. If a publisher signals interest, an exchange is initiated between author and publisher. Alternatively approach a crowdfunding publisher to help raise finances with you. The publisher will critically assess your work before presenting it for funding opportunities and will publish and distribute the book. Some publishers seek investment from readers across their operation and not for a specific title.

SOCIAL ENTERPRISE PUBLISHING

Organisations with social enterprise at their heart offer publishing support – expertise and funding – to those who might not otherwise be published. These initiatives, many not-for-profit charitable operations, are motivated by social, community and environmental objectives rather than by money. There are an increasing number of social enterprise publishers in operation now, including the following:

Acair Books (page 124)
Arkbound (page 126)
Bedtime Books (page 129)
Comma Press (page 137)
Dead Ink Books (page 140)
Fly on the Wall Press (page 146)
Honno Ltd (Welsh Women's Press) (page 154)
Lantana Publishing (page 159)
Leamington Books (page 159)
Scottish Mountaineering Press (page 179)
UCLan Publishing (page 186)

Books

Book publishers overseas

Listings are given for book publishers in Australia (below), Canada (page 195), New Zealand (page 199), South Africa (page 201) and the USA (page 203).

sae = self-addressed envelope

AUSTRALIA

Member of the Australian Publishers Association

ACER Press*

19 Prospect Hill Road, Private Bag 55, Camberwell, VIC 3124
tel +61 (0)3 9277 5555
email proposals@acer.org
website www.acer.org/au

Publisher of the Australian Council for Educational Research. Produces a range of books and assessments including professional resources for teachers, psychologists and special educational needs professionals. Founded 1930.

Affirm Press*

28 Thistlethwaite Street, South Melbourne, VIC 3205
tel +61 (0)3 8695 9623
email info@affirmpress.com.au
website https://affirmpress.com.au/
Facebook www.facebook.com/affirmpress
Twitter @affirmpress
Ceo & Publishing Director Martin Hughes

Non-fiction, fiction and young fiction. Founded 2010.

Allen & Unwin Pty Ltd*

83 Alexander Street, Crows Nest, NSW 2065
Postal address PO Box 8500, St Leonards, NSW 1590
tel +61 (0)2 8425 0100
website www.allenandunwin.com
Chairman Patrick Gallagher, *Ceo* Robert Gorman, *Publishing Directors* Jane Morrow (Murdock Books), Eva Mills (children & YA), Cate Paterson (Atlantic Books)

General trade, including fiction and children's books, and broad-ranging non-fiction. Imprints include: Allen & Unwin, Albert Street Books, Atlantic Books, Inspired Living, Crows Nest, House of Books, Murdoch Books, Pier 9. Submission guidelines: will consider unsolicited MSS. Will only accept MSS through electronic Friday Pitch system. Founded 1990.

Bad Apple Press*

Sydney: 33 Blacks Road, Arcadia, NSW 2159
email enquiry@badapplepress.com.au
website https://badapplepress.com.au/bad-apples/
Facebook www.facebook.com/ApplePressPublisher

Twitter @PressApple
Co-founder & Publishing Manager Samantha Miles

Independent publisher of fiction and non-fiction. Founded 2018.

Bloomsbury Publishing Pty Ltd*

Level 6, 387 George Street, Sydney, NSW 2000
tel +61 (0)2 8820 4900
email au@bloomsbury.com
website www.bloomsbury.com/au
Facebook www.facebook.com/bloomsburypublishingaustralia
Twitter @BloomsburySyd
Managing Director Cristina Cappelluto

Supports the worldwide publishing activities of Bloomsbury Publishing: caters for the Australia and New Zealand territories. See Bloomsbury Publishing Plc (page 130). Bloomsbury Publishing Plc founded 1986.

Bonnier Publishing Australia*

Level 6, 534 Church Street, Richmond, VIC 3121
tel +61 (0)3 9421 3800
email info@bonnierpublishing.com.au
Twitter @bonnierpubau

Based in Melbourne. The company represents UK sister-company imprints across the ANZ markets. Bonnier Publishing Australia is a division of international publishing group, Bonnier Publishing. Imprint: Echo Publishing (page 193). Founded 1979.

Cambridge University Press & Assessment Education Australia*

477 Williamstown Road, Private Bag 31, Port Melbourne, VIC 3207
tel +61 (0)3 8671 1400
email enquiries@cambridge.edu.au
website www.cambridge.edu.au/education
Executive Director Mark O'Neill

Academic, educational, reference, ESL. Founded 1534.

Cengage Learning Australia*

Level 7, 80 Dorcas Street, South Melbourne, VIC 3205
tel +61 (0)3 9685 4111
website www.cengage.com.au

Educational books. Founded 2007.

Cordite Books*

email cordite@cordite.org.au
website https://corditebooks.org.au/

Facebook www.facebook.com/corditepublishing
Twitter @corditepoetry

Not-for-profit poetry publisher. Founded 1997.

Echo Publishing*
Level 45, World Square, 680 George Street, Sydney, NSW 2000
website https://www.echopublishing.com.au/
Facebook www.facebook.com/echopublishingaustralia
Twitter @echo_publishing
Publisher & Managing Director Juliet Rogers

Publishers of adult commercial fiction (all genres except sci-fi) and non-fiction. Open to submissions for fiction on the first Friday of every month and non-fiction on the third Friday of every month. See website for details. Part of Bonnier Books Australia (page 192). Founded 1991.

ELK Publishing
PO Box 2828, Toowoomba, QLD 4350
tel +61 (0)4 0030 1675 / +61 (0)4 7592 3670
email contactus@elk-publishing.com
website www.elk-publishing.com
Facebook www.facebook.com/elkpublishing
Twitter @elkpublish
Instagram @elkpublishing
Founder & Ceo Selina Kucks

An Australian-grown, independent publishing house of children's and educational literature. Established in Korea, the company is presently based in Queensland, Australia. ELK Publishing creates children's and educational books, provides opportunities for unknown artists and illustrators to collaborate with in-house authors and offers internships to university students who are presently engaged in literary scholarship. Founded in Seoul, Korea 2009.

Elsevier Australia*
Level 1, Tower 2, 475 Victoria Avenue, Chatswood NSW 2067
tel +61 (0)2 9422 8500
email customerserviceau@elsevier.com
website www.elsevierhealth.com.au

Science, medical and technical books. Imprints: Academic Press, Butterworth-Heinemann, Churchill Livingstone, Endeavour, Excerpta Medica, Focal Press, The Lancet, MacLennan and Petty, MD Consult, Morgan Kauffman, Mosby, Saunders, Science Direct, Syngress. Founded 1972.

Exisle Publishing*
Unit 11, 201 Main Street, Gosford, NSW 2250
website www.exislepublishing.com
Facebook www.facebook.com/ExislePublishing
Twitter @exislebooks
Instagram @exislepublishing
Ceo Gareth St John Thomas

Independent publisher with passion and purpose. Publishes non-fiction for adults, and both fiction and non-fiction for children under the imprint EK Books. Founded in 1991.

Freemantle Press
PO Box 158, North Fremantle, WA 6159
tel +61 (0)8 9430 6331
email admin@fremantlepress.com.au
website https://fremantlepress.com.au/
Facebook www.facebook.com/FremantlePress
Twitter @FremantlePress

A not-for-profit team of publishers, authors and artists who bring uniquely Australian stories to the world. Publishes fiction, non-fiction, poetry and children's literature. Founded 1976.

Hachette Australia Pty Ltd*
Level 17, 207 Kent Street, Sydney, NSW 2000
tel +61 (0)2 8248 0800
email auspub@hachette.com.au
website www.hachette.com.au
Ceo Louise Stark

General, children's. Accepts MSS via website. Founded 1971.

HarperCollins Publishers (Australia) Pty Ltd Group*
Postal address PO Box A565, Sydney South, NSW 1235
tel +61 (0)2 9952 5000
website www.harpercollins.com.au
Children's Publishing Director Michelle Weisz,
Department Heads Ana Vivas (children's), Catherine Milne (fiction), Helen Littleton (non-fiction)

Literary fiction and non-fiction, popular fiction, children's, reference, biography, autobiography, current affairs, sport, lifestyle, health/self-help, humour, true crime, travel, Australiana, history, business, gift, religion. Founded 1989.

Lawbook Co.
Level 6, 16 Harris Street, Pyrmont, NSW 2009
tel +61 (0)2 8587 7980
website www.thomsonreuters.com.au

Law. Part of Thomson Reuters. Founded 1985.

LexisNexis Butterworths Australia*
Tower 2, 475–495 Victoria Avenue, Chatswood, NSW 2067
tel +61 (0)2 9422 2174
Postal address Level 9, Locked Bag 2222, Chatswood Delivery Centre, Chatswood, NSW 2067
website www.lexisnexis.com.au

Accounting, business, legal, tax and commercial. Founded 1970.

McGraw-Hill Australia Pty Ltd*
Level 2, 82 Waterloo Road, North Ryde, NSW 2113
Postal address Private Bag 2233, Business Centre, North Ryde, NSW 1670

Books

tel +61 (0)2 9900 1800
website www.mcgraw-hill.com.au
Facebook www.facebook.com/MHEducationANZ
Twitter @MHeducationAU

Educational publisher: higher education, primary education and professional (including medical, general and reference). Division of the McGraw-Hill Companies. Founded 1964.

Major Street Publishing*

Suite 5, Level 2, 22 Horne Street, Elsternwick, VIC 3185
email info@majorstreet.com.au
website https://majorstreet.com.au/
Facebook www.facebookk.com/MajorStreetPublishing
Twitter @MajorStreetPub
Publisher Lesley Williams

Publishes market books in leadership, business, entrepreneurship, career development, personal finance, personal development, share market and property investing, self-care, personal growth and motivation genres. Founded 2009.

Melbourne University Press*

Level 1, 715 Swanston Street, Carlton, VIC 3053
tel +61 (0)3 9035 3333
email mup-contact@unimelb.edu.au
website www.mup.com.au
Ceo & Publisher Nathan Hollier

Trade, academic, history and society; non-fiction. Imprints: Miegunyah Press, Melbourne University Press, *Meanjin* journal. Founded 1922.

New Holland Publishers (UK) Ltd

Level 1, 178 Fox Valley Road, Wahroonga, NSW 2076
tel +61 (0)2 8986 4700
email orders@newholland.com.au
website https://au.newhollandpublishers.com/

Illustrated non-fiction books on natural history, sports and hobbies, animals and pets, travel pictorial, reference, gardening, health and fitness, practical art, DIY, food and drink, outdoor pursuits, craft, humour, gift books. New proposals accepted, send CV, synopsis and sample chapters in first instance; sae essential. Founded 1955.

Pan Macmillan Australia Pty Ltd*

Level 25, 1 Market Street, Sydney, NSW 2000
tel +61 (0)2 9285 9100
email pan.reception@macmillan.com.au
website www.panmacmillan.com.au
Directors Ingrid Ohlsson (publishing)

Commercial and literary fiction; children's and YA fiction; non-fiction and character products; general non-fiction; sport; cooking and lifestyle. Founded 1843.

Penguin Random House Australia Pty Ltd*

Sydney office Level 3, 100 Pacific Highway, North Sydney, NSW 2060
tel +61 (0)2 9954 9966
email information@penguinrandomhouse.com.au
Melbourne office 707 Collins Street, Melbourne, VIC 3008
website www.penguinrandomhouse.com.au
Ceo Julie Burland, *Publishing Directors* Holly Toohey, Laura Harris (Penguin Young Readers), Karen Reid (Launch Title)

General fiction and non-fiction; children's, illustrated. MS submissions for non-fiction accepted, unbound in hard copy addressed to Submissions Editor. Fiction submissions are only accepted from previously published authors, or authors represented by an agent or accompanied by a report from an accredited assessment service. Imprints: Arrow, Bantam, Ebury, Hamish Hamilton, Knopf, Michael Joseph, Penguin, Viking, Vintage and William Heinemann. Subsidiary of Bertelsmann AG. Founded 2013.

University of Queensland Press*

PO Box 6042, St Lucia, QLD 4067
tel +61 (0)7 3365 7244
email reception@uqp.com.au
website www.uqp.com.au

Publishes books of high quality and cultural significance. It has launched the careers of Australian writers such as David Malouf, Peter Carey, Kate Grenville, Doris Pilkington and Nick Earls. Originally founded as a traditional university press, the company has since branched into publishing books for general readers in the areas of fiction, non-fiction, poetry, Indigenous writing and youth literature. Books and authors have received national and international recognition through literary prizes, rights sales and writers' festivals. Founded 1948.

Rhiza Edge

PO Box 302, Chinchilla, QLD 4413
tel +61 (0)7 3245 1938
email editor@rhizaedge.com.au
website www.rhizaedge.com.au
Facebook www.facebook.com/rhizaedge
Commissioning Editor Emily Lighezzolo

Publishes issue-based stories for YA readers. Imprint of Wombat Books (page 195). Founded 2018.

Scholastic Australia Pty Ltd*

76–80 Railway Crescent, Lisarow, Gosford, NSW 2250
tel +61 (0)2 4328 3555
website www.scholastic.com.au
Chairman David Peagram

Children's fiction and non-fiction. Founded 1968.

Simon & Schuster (Australia) Pty Ltd*

Office address Suite 19A, Level 1, Building C,
450 Miller Street, Cammeray, NSW 2062
Postal address PO Box 448, Cammeray, NSW 2062
tel +61 (0)2 9983 6600
email cservice@simonandschuster.com.au
website www.simonandschuster.com.au
Facebook www.facebook.com/SimonSchusterAU
Twitter @simonschusterAU
Instagram @simonschusterau
Managing Director Dan Ruffino

Part of Paramount, the company publishes and
distributes in Australia and New Zealand the
following: fiction, non-fiction and children's books.
Imprints include: Adams Media, Atria, Avid Reader
Press, Free Press, Gallery, Howard, One Signal,
Pocket, Scout Press, Scribner, Simon & Schuster,
Tiller Press and Touchstone. Also acts as the local
sales and distribution partner for 4 Ingredients,
Aconyte Books, Berbay Publishing, Big Sky
Publishing, Black Library, Brolga Publishing, Elliott &
Thompson, Fox Chapel Publishing, Gelding Street
Press, Hazelden Publishing, Inner Traditions, Insight
Editions, Noel Whittaker, Pegasus Books, Post Hill
Press, powerHouse Books, Printer's Row Publishing,
Regan Arts, Rockpool Publishing, Two Good Co,
Ventura Press, Viz Media, Waterhouse Press, Weldon
Owen, Wild Dog Books and Z2 Comics.
Founded 1987.

Spinifex Press*

PO Box 105, Mission Beach, QLD 4852
email women@spinifexpress.com.au
Postal address PO Box 5270, North Geelong, VIC
3215
website www.spinifexpress.com.au
Facebook www.facebook.com/spinifexpress
Twitter @spinifexpress
Managing Directors Susan Hawthorne, Renate Klein

Fiction, poetry, biography, autobiography, feminism,
women's studies, art, astronomy, ecology, literary
criticism, violence against women, education, lesbian,
health and nutrition, technology, travel, ebooks.
Spinifex publishes writers from every continent. No
unsolicited MSS. Founded 1991.

UNSW Press*

University of New South Wales, Sydney, NSW 2052
tel +61 (0)2 8936 1400
email enquiries@unswpress.com.au
website https://unsw.press/
Ceo Kathy Bail

Academic and general non-fiction. Politics, history,
indigenous history, popular science, environmental
studies, art and design. Founded 1962.

UWA Publishing*

University of Western Australia, M419,
35 Stirling Highway, Crawley, WA 6009

tel +61 (0)8 6488 3670
email admin-uwap@uwa.edu.au
website www.uwap.uwa.edu.au
Publishing Manager Kate Pickard

Fiction, general non-fiction, natural history,
contemporary issues. Founded 1935.

John Wiley & Sons Australia, Ltd*

Level 4, 600 Bourke Street, Melbourne, VIC 3000
tel +61 (0)8 0077 7474
email custservice@wiley.com
website www.wiley.com

Educational, technical, atlases, professional, reference,
trade journals. Imprints: John Wiley & Sons,
Jacaranda, Wiley-Blackwell, For Dummies, Jossey-
Bass, Capstone, Polity. Founded 1807.

Wilkinson Publishing*

PO Box 24135, Melbourne, VIC 3001
email enquiries@wilkinsonpublishing.com.au
website www.wilkinsonpublishing.com.au
Facebook www.facebook.com/WilkinsonPublishing
Twitter @WPBooks
Owner & Director Michael Wilkinson

A family-owned, independent publisher. Publishes
art, biography, memoir, business, finance, children's,
cookery, fiction, health, history, humour, personal
development, philosophy and religion, poetry,
politics, opinion, society, culture, sport and true
crime. Founded 2005.

Wombat Books*

PO Box 302, Chinchilla, QLD 4413
tel +61 (0)7 3245 1938
email website@wombatrhiza.com.au
website www.wombatrhiza.com.au
Facebook www.facebook.com/wombatbooks
Publisher Rochelle Manners

An independent publisher of children's picture books
and books for early readers. YA and adult imprint:
Rhiza Edge (page 194). Founded 2009.

CANADA

*Member of the Canadian Publishers' Council
†Member of the Association of Canadian Publishers

Annick Press Ltd†

388 Carlaw Avenue, Suite 200 Toronto,
ON M4M 2T4
tel +1 416-221-4802
email annickpress@annickpress.com
website www.annickpress.com
Owner & Director Rick Wilks

Preschool to YA fiction and non-fiction. Publishes
approx. 24 titles each year. Recent successes include: *I
Love My Purse* (picture book); *#NotYourPrincess*
(non-fiction); *Fire Song* (fiction, YA); *Stormy Seas*

(non-fiction). To send MS or illustration submission, visit website and view submission guidelines. Founded 1975.

Anvil Press[†]
PO Box 3008, Station Terminal, Vancouver, BC V6B 3X5
email info@anvilpress.com
website www.anvilpress.com
Facebook www.facebook.com/Anvil-Press-115437275199047
Twitter @anvilpress
Publisher Brian Kaufman

A publisher of progressive, contemporary Canadian literature with an entrenched urban sensibility. Also publishes poetry, fiction and non-fiction. Founded 1990.

Bayeux Arts[†]
119 Stratton Crescent SW, Calgary AB T3H 1T7
email ashis.bayeux@gmail.com
website www.bayeux.com
Facebook www.facebook.com/Bayeux-Arts-105201535300599
Twitter @Bayeux_Arts
Publisher Ashis Gupta

Publishes non-fiction. Imprints include Gondolier and Odd Little Books. Gondolier highlights subjects related to management and social sciences. Odd Little Books brings together visual artists, dramatists, poets, puppeteers, playwrights, musicians in a charming collection of pocket-sized gems. Founded 1994.

Between the Lines[†]
401 Richmond Street West, Studio 281, Toronto, ON M5V 3A8
tel +1 416-535-9914
email info@btlbooks.com
website https://btlbooks.com/
Facebook www.facebook.com/BTLbooks
Twitter @BTLbooks
Managing Editor Amanda Crocker

Publishes non-fiction books that expose and challenge oppression in society. Aims to amplify the struggles of Black, Indigenous and racialised communities; migrants; women; queer folks and working-class people. Founded 1977.

Breakwater Books[†]
PO Box 2188, St John's, NL A1C 6E6
tel +1 709-722-6680
email orders@breakwaterbooks.com
website https://breakwaterbooks.com/
Facebook www.facebook.com/breakwaterbooksltd
Twitter @breakwaterbooks
President & Publisher Rebecca Rose

Publishes award-winning writing in all literary genres: fiction, non-fiction, poetry, drama, art, YA and children's books, as well as cookery, guidebooks and educational resources. Founded 1973.

The Charlton Press
645 Avenue, Lepine, Dorval, QC H9P 2R2
tel +1 416-962-2665
email info@charltonpress.com
website www.charltonpress.com

Collectables, numismatics, sportscard price catalogues. Founded 1952.

Douglas & McIntyre (2013) Ltd[†]
4437 Rondeview Road, PO Box 219, Madeira Park, BC V0N 2H0
tel +1 604-883-2730
email info@douglas-mcintyre.com
website www.douglas-mcintyre.com

General list: Canadian biography, art and architecture, natural history, history, native studies, Canadian fiction. Unsolicited MSS accepted. Now owned by Harbour Publishing. Founded 1971.

Dundurn Press[†]
1382 Queen Street E, Toronto, ON M4L 1C9
tel +1 416-214-5544
email submissions@dundurn.com
website www.dundurn.com
Facebook www.facebook.com/dundumpress
Twitter @dundumpress

Canadian history, fiction, non-fiction and YA fiction, mystery fiction, popular non-fiction, translations. Founded 1972.

ECW Press Ltd[†]
665 Gerrard Street E, Toronto, ON M4M 1Y2
tel +1 416-694-3348
email info@ecwpress.com
website www.ecwpress.com
Facebook www.facebook.com/ecwpress
Twitter @ecwpress
Co-Publishers David Caron, Jack David, *Acquisitions Editors* Jen Knoch, Susan Renouf, Michael Holmes, Jennifer Smith, Jen Sookfong Lee

Popular culture, TV and film, sports, humour, general trade books, biographies, memoir, popular science, guidebooks. Founded 1979.

Fernwood Publishing[†]
2970 Oxford Street, Halifax, Nova Scotia B3L 2W4
tel +1 902-857-1388
email info@fernpub.ca
website https://fernwoodpublishing.ca/
Facebook www.facebook.com/fernwood.publishing
Twitter @fermpub

Publishes critical books that inform, enlighten and challenge. Imprint: Roseway. Founded 1992.

Fitzhenry & Whiteside Ltd
209 Wicksteed Avenue, Unit 51, East York, ON M4G 0B1
tel +1 905-477-9700

email hdoll@fitzhenry.ca
website www.fitzhenry.ca
Facebook www.facebook.com/FitzWhits
Twitter @FitzWhits
Ceo Sharon Fitzhenry

Trade, educational, children's books. Founded 1966.

Goose Lane Editions[†]
500 Beaverbrook Court, Suite 330, Fredericton,
NB E3B 5X4
tel +1 506-450-4251
email info@gooselane.com
website https://gooselane.com/
Facebook www.facebook.com/gooselaneeditions
Twitter @goose_lane
Publisher Susanne Alexander

Publishes fiction, non-fiction and poetry.
Founded 1954.

Gordon Hill Press[†]
130 Dublin Street North, Guelph, ON N1H 4N4
website www.gordonhillpress.com
Facebook www.facebook.com/gordonhillpress
Twitter @gordonhillpress
Managing Editor Shane Neilson

Publishes poetry and stylistically innovative fiction,
non-fiction, and literary criticism (especially
concerning poetry). Founded 2019.

Harlequin Enterprises Ltd*
PO Box 603, Fort Erie, ON L2A 5X3
tel +1 888-432-4879
email customer_ecare@harlequin.ca
website www.harlequin.com
Publisher Craig Swinwood

Fiction for women, romance, inspirational fiction,
African American fiction, action adventure, mystery.
Imprints include: Carina Adores, Harlequin Desire,
Harlequin Heartwarming, Harlequin Historical,
Harlequin Intrigue, Harlequin Medical Romance,
Harlequin Presents, Harlequin Romance, Harlequin
Romance Suspense, Harlequin Special Edition,
Harlequin Special Releases, Love Inspires, Love
Inspired Suspense, Love Inspired Special Releases.
Founded 1949.

HarperCollins Publishers Ltd*
22 Adelaide Street West, 41st Floor, Toronto,
ON M5H 4E3
tel +1 416-975-9334
email hcOrder@harpercollins.com
website www.harpercollins.ca

Literary fiction and non-fiction, history, politics,
biography, spiritual and children's books.
Founded 1989.

House of Anansi Press and Groundwood Books[†]
128 Sterling Road, Lower Level, Toronto,
ON M6R 2B7

tel +1 416-363-4343
email publicity@houseofanansi.com
website https://houseofanansi.com/
Facebook www.facebook.com/houseofanansi
Twitter @HouseofAnansi
Publisher Scott Griffin

House of Anansi Press is a publisher of literary
fiction. Groundwood Books publishes books for all
ages, including fiction, picture books, graphic novels
and non-fiction. Founded 1967.

Inanna Publications and Education[†]
210 Founders College, York University,
4700 Keele Street, Toronto, ON M3J 1P3
tel +1 416-736-5356
email inanna.publications@inanna.ca
website www.inanna.ca
Facebook www.facebook.com/InannaPublications
Twitter @inannapub
Interim Publisher Brenda Cranney

Publishes feminist-inspired fiction, poetry, and
creative non-fiction. Founded 1978.

Kids Can Press Ltd[†]
25 Dockside Drive, Toronto, ON M5A 0B5
tel +1 416-479-7000
email customerservice@kidscan.com
website www.kidscanpress.com
Facebook www.facebook.com/kidscanbooks
Twitter @kidscanpress
Editorial Director Yvette Ghione

Middle grade/YA books. Founded 1973.

Knopf Canada – see Penguin Random House Canada Ltd

LexisNexis Canada, Inc.*
111 Gordon Baker Road, Suite 900, Toronto,
ON M2H 3R1
tel +1 800-668-6481
email info@lexisnexis.ca
website www.lexisnexis.ca
Facebook www.facebook.com/lexisnexiscanada
Twitter @lexisnexiscan

Law and accountancy. Division of Reed Elsevier plc.
Founded 1979.

McGill-Queen's University Press[†]
1010 Sherbrooke Street West, Suite 1720, Montreal,
QC H3A 2R7
tel +1 514-398-3750
email mqup@mcgill.ca
website www.mqup.ca
Editor-in-Chief Jonathan Crago, *Senior Editor* Kyla
Madden, *Editor* Richard Ratzlaff, *UK Editor* Richard
Baggaley

Academic, non-fiction, poetry. Founded 1969.

Books

McGraw-Hill Canada*
145 Kings Street West, Suite 1501,
Toronto ON M5H 1J8
tel +1 800-565-5758
website www.mheducation.ca
Facebook www.facebook.com/mcgrawhillcanada
Twitter @mcgraw_canada

Educational and trade books. Founded 1972.

Nelson Education*
2005 Sheppard Ave E, Suite 700, Toronto,
ON M2J 5B4
tel +1 416-752-9448
website www.nelson.com
President & Ceo Steve Brown

Educational publishing. Canada's leading K–12
educational publisher, founded on equitable,
inclusive and engaging learning. Creator of Edwin, a
revolutionary digital platform. Founded 1914.

NeWest Press†
8540, 109 Street, Edmonton, AB T6G 1E6
tel +1 780-432-9427
email info@newestpress.com
website www.newestpress.com
President Leslie Vermeer

Fiction, drama, poetry and non-fiction.
Founded 1977.

Nimbus Publishing†
PO Box 9166, Halifax, NS B3K 5M8
tel +1 800-646-2879
website https://nimbus.ca/
Facebook www.facebook.com/nimbuspub
Twitter @nimbuspub

Publishes children's picture books and fiction, literary
non-fiction, social and cultural history, nature
photography, current events, biography, sports and
cultural issues. Founded 1978.

Oberon Press
203–105 Spruce Street, Ontario, Ottawa, K1R 6P1
tel +1 613-238-3275
email oberon@sympatico.ca
website www.oberonpress.ca

General fiction, short stories, poetry, some
biographies, art and children's. Only publishes
Canadian writers. Currently not accepting unsolicited
MSS. Founded 1985.

Oxford University Press, Canada*
8 Sampson Mews, Suite 204, Don Mills,
ON M3C 0H5
tel +1 416-441-2941
website www.oupcanada.com

Educational and academic. Founded 1586.

Pearson Canada*
26 Prince Andrew Place, North York, ON M3C 2T8
tel +1 800-361-6128
website www.pearson.com/ca/en.html

Academic, technical, educational, children's and
adult, trade. Founded 1998.

Penguin Random House Canada Ltd*
320 Front Street West, Suite 1400, Toronto,
ON M5V 3B6
tel +1 416-364-4449
website www.penguinrandomhouse.ca
Ceo Kristin Cochrane

Literary fiction, commercial fiction, memoir, non-
fiction (history, business, current events, sports),
adult, teen and young readers. No unsolicited MSS;
submissions via an agent only. Imprints: Allen Lane
Canada, Anchor Canada, Appetite by Random
House, Bond Street Books, Doubleday Canada,
Emblem, Hamish Hamilton Canada, Knopf Canada,
McClelland & Stewart, Penguin Canada, Penguin
Teen, Portfolio Canada, Puffin Canada, Random
House Canada, Seal Books, Signal, Strange Light,
Tundra Books, Viking Canada, Vintage Canada.
Subsidiary of Penguin Random House.
Founded 2013.

Rebel Mountain Press†
email rebelmountainpress@gmail.com
website www.rebelmountainpress.com
Facebook www.facebook.com/rebelmountainpress
Twitter @rebelmountain1
Publisher Lori Szwydky

Publishes children's and YA literature, anthologies
and poetry that feature characters and authors who
are BIPOC, LGBTQIA2S+ and/or have disabilities.
Founded 2015.

Ronsdale Press†
125A–1030 Denman Street, Vancouver, BC V6G 2M6
tel +1 604-738-4688
email ronsdale@shaw.ca
website www.ronsdalepress.com
Facebook www.facebook.com/ronsdalepress
Twitter @ronsdalepress
Director Veronica Hatch

A Canadian publisher based in Vancouver with some
290 books in print. Founded 1988.

Second Story Press†
20 Maud Street, Suite 401, Toronto, ON M5V 2M5
tel +1 416-537-7850
email info@secondstorypress.ca
website https://secondstorypress.ca/
Facebook www.facebook.com/secondstorypress
Twitter @secondstory

Publishes feminist-inspired fiction and non-fiction
for adults, children and YA. Founded 2015.

Thompson Educational Publishing†

20 Ripley Avenue, Toronto, ON M6S 3N9
tel +1 416-766-2763
email info@thompsonbooks.com
website www.thompsonbooks.com

Social sciences. Founded 1989.

University of Toronto Press

800 Bay Street, Mezzanine, Toronto, ON M5S 3A9
tel +1 416-978-2239
email publishing@utpress.utoronto.ca
website www.utorontopress.com
Facebook www.facebook.com/utpress
Twitter @utpress

Imprints include: Aevo UTP; New Jewish Press; Rotman-UTP Publishing. Publishers of non-fiction, monographs, textbooks and academic books, ESL/EFL, teacher reference, adult basic education and school texts. Founded 1901.

Tundra Books†

320 Front Street West, Suite 1400, Toronto, ON M5V 3B6
tel +1 416-364-4449
email submissions@tundrabooks.com
email art@tundrabooks.com
website www.penguinrandomhouse.ca/imprints/TU/tundra-books
Facebook www.facebook.com/tundrabooks
Twitter @TundraBooks

Publisher of high-quality children's picture books and novels, renowned for its innovations. Publishes books for children to teens. A division of Penguin Random House Canada Ltd (page 198). Founded 1967.

Whitecap Books Ltd

209–314 West Cordova Street, Vancouver, BC V6B 1E8
tel +1 800-387-9776
website www.whitecap.ca
Facebook www.facebook.com/whitecapbooks
Twitter @whitecapbooks
Ceo Sharon Fitzhenry

Diverse list features books on food, wine, gardening, health and wellbeing, regional history and regional guidebooks. Market expanded into the United States through Midpoint Books. Submissions must be sent by mail. Full details can be found on website. Founded 1977.

NEW ZEALAND

*Member of the Publishers Association of New Zealand (PANZ)

Auckland University Press*

University of Auckland, Private Bag 92019, Auckland 1142
tel +64 (0)9 373 7528
email press@auckland.ac.nz
website https://aucklanduniversitypress.co.nz
Director Sam Elworthy

Archaeology, architecture, art, biography, business, health, New Zealand history, Māori and Pacific studies, poetry, politics and law, science and natural history, social sciences. Founded 1966.

David Bateman Ltd*

Unit 2/5 Workspace Drive, Auckland 0618
tel +64 (0)9 415 7664
email info@bateman.co.nz
website www.batemanbooks.co.nz
Facebook www.facebook.com/batemanbooks
Instagram @batemanbooks

General trade publisher focusing on fiction, children's, craft, natural history, gardening, health, sport, cookery, history, travel, motoring, maritime history, business, art, humour, lifestyle for the international market. Founded 1979.

The Caxton Press

32 Lodestar Ave, Wigram, PO Box 36 411, Christchurch 8042
tel +64 (0)3 366 8516
email sales@caxton.co.nz
website www.caxton.co.nz
Managing Director Bridget Batchelor

Local history, tourist pictorial, Celtic spirituality, parent guides, book designers and printers. Founded 1935.

Cengage Learning New Zealand*

Unit 4B, Rosedale Office Park, 331 Rosedale Road, Albany, North Shore 0632
Postal address PO Box 33376, Takapuna, North Shore 0740
tel +64 (0)9 415 6850

Educational books. Founded 2007.

The Cuba Press

Level 6, 138 Wakefield Street, Te Aro, Wellington 6011
email hello@thecubapress.nz
website www.thecubapress.nz
Co-directors Mary McCallum, Sarah Bolland, *Publisher* Paul Stewart

Fiction, creative non-fiction, poetry, memoir, biography, social history, children's fiction and poetry. Founded 2018.

Dunmore Publishing Ltd

PO Box 28387, Auckland 1541
tel +64 (0)9 521 3121
email books@dunmore.co.nz
website www.dunmore.co.nz

Books

Education secondary/tertiary texts and other, New Zealand society, history, health, economics, politics, general non-fiction. Founded 1970.

Edify Ltd*

PO Box 36502, Northcote, Auckland 0748
tel +64 (0)9 972 9428
email mark@edify.co.nz
website www.edify.co.nz
Ceo Adrian Keane

A publishing, sales and marketing business providing its partners with opportunities for their products and solutions in the New Zealand educational market. Exclusive representatives of Pearson and the educational publisher, Sunshine Books. Founded 2013.

Hachette New Zealand Ltd*

PO Box 3255, Shortland Street, Auckland 1140
tel +64 (0)9 379 1480
email contact@hachette.co.nz
website www.hachette.co.nz
Facebook www.facebook.com/HachetteNZ
Ceo Louise Sherwin Stark

International fiction and non-fiction. Local publishing includes children's and fiction titles. Founded 1970.

HarperCollins Publishers (New Zealand) Ltd*

Unit D, 63 Apollo Drive, Rosedale, Auckland 0632
tel +64 (0)9 443 9400
email publicity@harpercollins.co.nz
Postal address PO Box 1, Shortland Street, Auckland 1140
website www.harpercollins.co.nz

Publishes a range of high-quality non-fiction titles each year by New Zealand authors. Submissions can be sent digitally to nz.submissions@harpercollins.co.nz. Founded 1989.

LexisNexis NZ Ltd

Level 31, 2-6 Gilmer Terrace, Wellington 6011
tel 0800 800 986
email customersupport@lexisnexis.co.nz
Postal address PO Box 472, Wellington 6140
website www.lexisnexis.co.nz
Publisher Christopher Murray

Law, business, academic. Founded 1914.

McGraw-Hill Book Company New Zealand Ltd

Level 8, 56–60 Cawley Street, Ellerslie, Auckland 1005
Postal address Private Bag 11904, Ellerslie, Auckland 1005
tel +64 (0)9 526 6200
website www.mcgraw-hill.com.au
Facebook www.facebook.com/MHEducationANZ

Twitter @MHEducationAU

Educational publisher: higher education, primary and secondary education (grades K–12) and professional (including medical, general and reference). Division of the McGraw-Hill Companies. Always looking for potential authors. Has a rapidly expanding publishing programme. See website for author's guide. Founded 1974.

Mākaro Press*

Level 6, 138 Wakefield Street, Te Aro, Wellington 6011
email kiaora@makaropressl.com
Publishers Mary McCallum, Paul Stewart

Fiction. Founded 2013.

New Zealand Council for Educational Research

Box 3237, Education House, 178–182 Willis Street, Wellington 6140
tel +64 (0)4 384 7939
email info@nzcer.org.nz
website https://www.nzcer.org.nz

Education, including educational policy and practice, early childhood education, educational achievement tests, Māori education, schooling for the future, curriculum and assessment. Founded 1934.

Otago University Press*

533 Castle Street, Dunedin 9010
tel +64 (0)3 479 8807
email university.press@otago.ac.nz
website www.otago.ac.nz/press
Publisher Sue Wootton

Non-fiction books on New Zealand and the Pacific, particularly history, natural history, Māori and Pacific; also biography/memoir, poetry, literature and the arts. Also publishes New Zealand's longest-running literary journal, *Landfall*. Founded 1958.

Penguin Random House New Zealand Ltd*

Private Bag 102 902, North Shore, Auckland 0745
tel +64 (0)9 442 7400
email publishing@penguinrandomhouse.co.nz
website www.penguin.co.nz
Facebook www.facebook.com/PenguinBooksNewZealand
Twitter @PenguinBooks_NZ
Instagram @penguinbooksnz
Head of Publishing Claire Murdoch

Adult and children's fiction and non-fiction. Imprints: Penguin, Vintage, Black Swan, Godwit, Viking, Puffin Books. Part of Penguin Random House. Founded 2013.

Te Herenga Waka University Press*

Victoria University of Wellington, PO Box 600, Wellington 6140

tel +64 (0)4 463 6580
email thwup@wgtn.ac.nz
website https://teherengawakapress.co.nz/
Publisher Fergus Barrowman, *Publicist* Tayi Tibble,
Publishing Manager Craig Gamble, *Editors* Ashleigh
Young, Kyleigh Hodgson, Jasmine Sargent

Formerly Victoria University Press. Literary fiction
and poetry; scholarly works on New Zealand history,
sociology, law; Māori language; biography, memoir
and essays. Founded 1974.

Viking Sevenseas NZ Ltd
201A Rosetta Road, Raumati Beach, Wellington 5032
tel +64 (0)4 902 8240
email vikingsevenseas@gmail.com
website www.vikingsevenseas.co.nz

Natural history books on New Zealand only.
Founded 1957.

SOUTH AFRICA

*Member of the Publishers' Association of South Africa

Ad Donker – see Jonathan Ball Publishers

Jonathan Ball Publishers*
PO Box 33977, Jeppestown 2043
tel +27 (0)11 601 8000
email annie.oliver@jonathanball.co.za
website www.jonathanball.co.za
Ceo Eugene Ashton

Specialises in South African history, politics and
current affairs. Also acts as agents for British and
American publishers, marketing and distributing
books on their behalf in southern Africa. A division
of Media24 (Pty) Ltd. Owners of Icon Books, a UK
based publishing company, since 2020.
Founded 1977.

Ad Donker
Africana, literature, history.

Jonathan Ball
General publications, current affairs, politics, history,
business, reference.

Delta Books
Military history.

Sunbird Publishers
Natural history.

Blackbird Books
email info@blackbirdbooks.africa
website https://blackbirdbooks.africa/
Twitter @blackbirdbooks
Instagram @blackbirdbooks_africa
Publisher Thabiso Mahlape

Publishes stories that cut to the core and reflect the
African experience. Founded 2015.

Burnet Media
PO Box 53557, Kenilworth, Cape Town 7745
email info@burnetmedia.co.za
website www.burnetmedia.co.za
Twitter @BurnetMedia
Publishing Manager Tim Richman

Independent publisher of the Two Dogs and Mercury
imprints, specialising in close author–publisher
relationships. Founded 2006.

Mercury
Interesting, accessible and engaging non-fiction with
broad subject matter for the South African and
international markets. Publishes a growing number
of international titles, with a particular focus on
authors with their own platforms.

Two Dogs
Innovative and irreverent non-fiction focusing on
contemporary and lifestyle subject matter for the
South African market.

Cambridge University Press & Assessment, Africa*
Unit OW3A Old Warehouse Building,
Black River Park, 2 Fir Street, Observatory,
Cape Town, 7925
tel +27 (0)21 412 7800
email cambridge-sa@cambridge.org
website www.cambridge.org
Publishing Director Johan Traut

Textbooks and literature for sub-Saharan African
countries, as well as primary reading materials in 28
African languages. Founded 1534.

Delta Books – see Jonathan Ball Publishers

Juta and Company (Pty) Ltd*
1st Floor, Sunclare Building, 21 Dreyer Street,
Claremont 7708
tel +27 (0)21 659 2300
email orders@juta.co.za
website www.juta.co.za
Facebook www.facebook.com/JutaSouthAfrica
Twitter @JutaZA
Ceo Kamal Patel

Academic, education, agencies, learning, law and
health. Publishers of print and digital print solutions.
Founded 1853.

University of KwaZulu-Natal Press*
Private Bag X01, Scottsville, Pietermaritzburg,
KwaZulu-Natal 3209
tel +27 (0)33 260 5226
email books@ukzn.ac.za
website www.ukznpress.co.za
Facebook www.facebook.com/UKZNPress

Twitter @UKZNPress
Director Phindile Dlamini

Southern African social, political and economic history, sociology, politics and political science, current affairs, literary criticism, gender studies, education, biography. Founded 1948.

Macmillan Education South Africa

4th Floor, Building G, Hertford Office Park, 90 Bekker Road, Vorna Valley, Midrand 1685
tel +27 (0)11 731 3300
Postal address Private Bag X19, Northlands 2116
website www.macmillan.co.za
Managing Director Preggy Naidoo

Educational titles for the RSA market. Founded 1843.

NB Publishers (Pty) Ltd*

12th Floor, Media24 Centre, 40 Heerengracht, Cape Town 8001
tel +27 (0)21 406 3033
email nb@nb.co.za
website www.nb.co.za

General: Afrikaans fiction, politics, children's and youth literature in all the country's languages, non-fiction. Imprints: Tafelberg, Human & Rousseau, Queillerie, Pharos, Kwela, Best Books and Lux Verbi. Founded 1950.

New Africa Books (Pty) Ltd*

Unit 13A, Athlone Industrial Park, 10 Mymoena Crescent, Cape Town 7764
tel +27 (0)21 467 5860
email info@newafricabooks.co.za
Postal address PostNet, Suite 144, Private Bag X9190, Cape Town 8000
Contacts Dušanka Stojaković, Nerina van Wyngaarden Lindhout, Cheraldine Smit

Winner of Best Children's Publisher in Africa Award 2022 (Bologna Children's Book Fair), member of IBBY and member of the UN SDG Publisher's Compact. An independent publisher of picture books publishing approx. 60 titles per year. Publishes fiction, non-fiction and comics with South African content in all South African languages. Award-winning writers and illustrators include Sindiwe Magona, Gcina Mhlophe, Richard Rive, Elinor Sisulu, Lebohang Masango, Paddy Bouma, Loyiso Mkhize, Subi Bosa, Nokuthula Mazibuko Msimang, Nicolaas Maritz, Lorato Trok and Xolisa Guzula. Founded 1971.

Oxford University Press Southern Africa*

Vasco Boulevard, N1 City, Goodwood, Cape Town 7460
tel +27 (0)21 596 2300
email oxford.za@oup.com

Postal address PO Box 12119, N1 City, Cape Town 7463
website www.oxford.co.za
Managing Director Hanri Pieterse

One of the leading educational publishers in South Africa, producing a wide range of quality educational material in print and digital format. The range includes books from Grade R to Grade 12, as well as TVET textbooks, textbooks, school literature, dictionaries and atlases. Founded 1586.

Pan Macmillan SA (Pty) Ltd*

2nd Floor, 1 Jameson Avenue, Melrose Estate, Johannesburg 2196
tel +27 (0)11 684 0400
email roshni@panmacmillan.co.za
Postal address Private Bag X19, Northlands, Johannesburg 2116
website www.panmacmillan.co.za
Facebook www.facebook.com/panmacmillansa
Twitter @panmacmillansa
Managing Director Terry Morris

Imprints: Pan Macmillan UK, Macmillan US, Pan Macmillan Australia, Walker Books, Priddy Books, Hachette Children's Books, Hinkler Books, Pan Macmillan South Africa, Pan KinderBoeke/Pan Children's Books, Guinness. Publishes titles in autobiography, biography, business, children's books, cookery and wine, crafts and hobbies, crime, environment, fiction (popular and literary), humour, inspiration, literature, business, reference, sport and stationery. Founded 1943.

Pearson South Africa*

4th Floor, Auto Atlantic, Corner Hertzog Boulevard and Herengracht, Cape Town 8001
tel +27 (0)21 532 6000
email pearsonza.enquiries@pearson.com
website https://za.pearson.com/

Pearson South Africa provides learning materials, technologies and services for use in schools, TVET colleges, higher education institutions and in home and professional environments. Founded 2010.

Penguin Random House (Pty) Ltd*

The Estuaries, No 4, Oxbow Crescent, Century Avenue, Century City 7441
email info@penguinrandomhouse.co.za
Postal address PO Box 1144, Cape Town 8000
tel +27 (0)21 460 5400
website www.penguinrandomhouse.co.za
Ceo Steve Connolly

Imprints: Penguin Random House, Struik Lifestyle, Struik Nature, Struik Travel & Heritage, Zebra Press, Penguin Non-Fiction, Penguin Fiction, Umuzi, Lapa, Romanza, Luca. Genres include general illustrated non-fiction; lifestyle; natural history; South African politics; sport; business; memoirs; contemporary fiction; literary fiction; local fiction; Afrikaans; children's books, religion. Part of Penguin Random House. Founded 2013.

Shuter and Shooter Publishers (Pty) Ltd*

110 CB Downes Road, Pietermaritzburg, KwaZulu-Natal 3201
tel +27 (0)33 846 8700
email sales@shuters.com
Postal address PO Box 61, Mkondeni, KwaZulu-Natal 3212
website www.shuters.co.za
Ceo Primi Chetty

Core curriculum-based textbooks for use at foundation, intermediate, senior and FET phases. Supplementary readers in various languages; dictionaries; reading development kits, charts. Literature titles in English, isiXhosa, Sesotho, Sepedi, Setswana, Tshivenda, Xitsonga, Ndebele, isiZulu and Siswati. Founded 1925.

Sunbird Publishers – see Jonathan Ball Publishers

Unisa Press*

University of South Africa, PO Box 392, Unisa, Mackleneuk, Pretoria 0003
tel +27 (0)12 429 3182
email pietehc@unisa.ac.za
website www.unisa.ac.za/press
Commissioning Editor Hetta Pieterse

All academic disciplines, African history, sustainable development, economics, the arts and the humanities generally. Imprint: UNISA. Email for MS submissions. Founded 1957.

Van Schaik Publishers*

PO Box 12681, Hatfield, Pretoria 0028
tel +27 (0)12 342 2765
email JRead@vanschaiknet.com
website www.vanschaiknet.com
General Manager Julia Read

Textbooks for the higher education market in southern Africa. Founded 1915.

Wits University Press*

tel +27 (0)11 717 8700/1
email corina.vanderspoel@wits.ac.za
Postal address PO Wits, Johannesburg 2050
website www.witspress.co.za

Publishes well-researched, scholarly books in print and digital formats for both academic and general readers in the following areas: art and heritage, political and social sciences, history and literary studies, playscripts and select textbooks. Founded 1922.

USA

Member of the Association of American Publishers Inc.

ABC-CLIO*

147 Castilian Drive, Santa Barbara, CA 93117
tel +1 805-968-1911
website www.abc-clio.com
Facebook www.facebook.com/ABCCLIO
Twitter @ABC_CLIO

Academic resources for secondary and middle schools, colleges and universities, libraries and professionals (librarians, media specialists, teachers). Owned by Bloomsbury Publishing USA (page 205). Founded 1955.

Abingdon Press

810 12th Ave South, Nashville, TN 37203
tel +1 800-251-3320
website www.abingdonpress.com
Facebook www.facebook.com/AbingdonPress
Twitter @AbingdonPress
President & Publisher Neil Alexander

General interest, professional, academic and reference, non-fiction and fiction, youth and children's non-fiction and Vatican Bible School; primarily directed to the religious market. Imprint of United Methodist Publishing House with tradition of crossing denominational boundaries. United Methodist Publishing House founded 1789.

Harry N. Abrams, Inc.

195 Broadway, 9th Floor, New York, NY 10007
tel +1 212-206-7715
email abrams@abramsbooks.com
website www.abramsbooks.com

Art and architecture, photography, natural sciences, performing arts, children's books. Imprints include: Abrams, Abrams Appleseed, Abrams Books for Young Readers, Abrams ComicArts, Abrams Image, Abrams Noterie, Abrams Press, Amulet Books, Amulet Paperbacks, Cernunnos, Magic Cat, The Overlook Press. Founded 1949.

Akashic Books Ltd

232 Third Street, Suite A115, Brooklyn, NY 11215
tel +1 718-643-9193
email info@akashicbooks.com
website www.akashicbooks.com
Facebook www.facebook.com/AkashicBooks
Twitter @AkashicBooks
Publisher & Editor-in-Chief Johnny Temple,
Managing Editor Johanna Ingalls

A Brooklyn-based independent company dedicated to publishing urban literary fiction and political non-fiction. Founded 1997.

The University of Alabama Press

Box 870380, Tuscaloosa, AL 35487-0380
tel +1 205-348-5180

Books

website www.uapress.ua.edu
Managing Editor Jon Berry

American and Southern history, African American studies, religion, rhetoric and communication, Judaic studies, literary criticism, anthropology and archaeology. Founded 1945.

Applause Theatre and Cinema Book Publishers

64 S. Main Street, Essex, CT 06246
tel +1 203-458-4500
email ApplauseSubmissions@rowman.com
website www.applausebooks.com
Facebook /www.facebook.com/globepequo
Twitter @ApplauseBooks
Publisher Chris Chappell

Performing arts. Part of Rowman and Littlefield. Founded 1980.

Arcade Publishing

11th Floor, 307 West 36th Street, New York, NY 10018
tel +1 212-643-6816
website www.arcadepub.com
Executive Editor Cal Barksdale

General trade, including adult hardback and paperbacks. No unsolicited MSS. Imprint of Skyhorse Publishing (page 217) since 2010. Founded 1988.

The University of Arkansas Press

McIlroy House, 105 N. McIlroy Avenue, Fayetteville, AR 72701
tel +1 479-575-7544
email info@uapress.com
website www.uapress.com
Facebook www.facebook.com/uarkpress
Twitter @uarkpress
Instagram @uark
Director & Publisher Mike Bieker

Publishing Arkansas and regional history, poetry and literature, African American studies, food studies, sports studies, art and architecture. Home of the Miller Williams Poetry Prize, awarding publication and a cash prize for a new collections of poetry, and the Etel Adnan Poetry Prize for collections of poetry by writers of Arab heritage. Founded 1980.

Astra Publishing House

19 West 21st Street, #1201, New York, NY 10010
email info@bmkbooks.com
website www.boydsmillsandkane.com
Facebook www.facebook.com/BMKbooks
Twitter @kanepress
President Leying Jiang

Fiction, non-fiction and poetry trade books for children and YA. Imprints: Astra House, Astra Young Readers, Calkins Creek, Hippo Park, Kane Press, mineditionUS, TOON Books, Word Song. Founded 1991.

Avery – see Penguin Publishing Group

Barefoot Books

23 Bradford Street, Concord, MA 01742
tel +1 617-576-0660
email help@barefootbooks.com
website www.barefootbooks.com
Facebook www.facebook.com/barefootbooks
Twitter @BarefootBooks
Editorial Director Emma Parkin

Children's picture books, activity decks and board books: diverse, inclusive and global stories that build social-emotional and literacy skills. See website for submission guidelines. Founded 1993.

Basic Books*

1290 Avenue of the Americas, 5th Floor, New York, NY 10104
tel +1 212-346-1100
email Basic.Books@hbgusa.com
website www.basicbooks.com
Facebook www.facebook.com/BasicBooks
Twitter @BasicBooks
Publisher Lara Heimert

Publishes books in history, science, natural history, sociology, psychology, biography, politics, African American studies. Basic Books is an imprint of Perseus Books, a Hachette Book Group company (page 209). Founded 1952.

Beacon Press

24 Farnsworth, Boston, MA 02110
tel +1 617-742-2110
website www.beacon.org
Director Helene Atwan

General non-fiction in fields of religion, ethics, philosophy, current affairs, gender studies, environmental concerns, African American studies, anthropology and women's studies, nature. Founded 1854.

Bella Books

PO Box 10543, Tallahassee, FL 32302
tel +1 800-729-4992
email info@bellabooks.com
website www.bellabooks.com

Lesbian fiction: mystery, romance, sci-fi. Founded 1973.

Bellevue Literary Press

90 Broad Street, Suite 2100 New York, NY 10004
website https://blpress.org/
Facebook www.facebook.com/bellevue.literary.press
Twitter @bellevuepress
Publisher & Editorial Director Erika Goldman,
Assistant Editor Laura Hart

Publishes literary fiction and non-fiction in both the arts and sciences. Founded 2007.

Berkley Books – see Penguin Publishing Group

Bloomsbury Publishing USA*

1385 Broadway, New York, NY 10018
tel +1 212-419-5300
email Contact-USA@bloomsbury.com
website www.bloomsbury.com/us
President Adrienne Vaughan, *Publishing Director*
Nancy Miller

Supports the worldwide publishing activities of
Bloomsbury Publishing Plc: caters for the US market.
For submission guidelines see website. Established in
1998 as an American subsidiary of Bloomsbury
Publishing Plc. Founded 1986.

Bold Strokes Books, Inc.

648 South Cambridge Road, Building A,
Johnsonville, NY 12094
email service@boldstrokesbooks.com
website www.boldstrokesbooks.com
Facebook www.facebook.com/BoldStrokesBooks/
Twitter @boldstrokebooks
Publisher Len Barot

Offers a diverse collection of LGBTQIA2S+ general
and genre fiction. Genres include romance, mystery/
intrigue, crime, erotica, speculative fiction (sci-fi/
fantasy/horror), general fiction, and, through the
Soliloquy imprint, YA fiction. Aims to bring quality
queer fiction to readers worldwide and to support an
international group of authors in developing their
craft and reaching an ever-growing community of
readers via print, digital and audio formats. Over
1,300 titles in print. For submission instructions see
www.boldstrokesbooks.com/submissions.
Founded 2004.

R.R. Bowker

26 Main Street, Suite 102, Chatham, NJ 07928
website www.bowker.com

Bibliographies and reference tools for the book trade
and literary and library worlds, available in hardcopy,
on microfiche, online and CD-Rom. Reference books
for music, art, business, the computer industry, cable
industry and information industry. Division of
Cambridge Information Group. Founded 1868.

George Braziller

90 Broad Street, Suite 2100, New York, NY 10004
tel +1 212-260-9256
website https://georgebraziller.squarespace.com/
Facebook www.facebook.com/george-braziller-inc
Twitter @BraziillerBooks
Publisher & Editorial Director Michael Braziller

Originally a publisher of art books, now publishes
literary fiction and poetry as well. Founded 1955.

Burford Books, Inc.

757 Warren Road, #4137, Ithaca, NY 14852
tel +1 607-319-4373

email pburford@burfordbooks.com
website www.burfordbooks.com
President Peter Burford

Outdoor activities: golf, sports, fitness, nature, travel.
Founded 1997.

Cambridge University Press & Assessment*

1 Liberty Plaza, Floor 20, New York, NY 10006
tel +1 212-337-5000
email customer_service@cambridge.org
website www.cambridge.org/gb/academic/contact-us/
united-states

Academic and professional; Cambridge Learning
(ELT, primary and secondary education).
Founded 1534.

Candlewick Press*

99 Dover Street, Somerville, MA 02144
tel +1 617-661-3330
email bigbear@candlewick.com
website www.candlewick.com
President & Publisher Karen Lotz, *Creative Director &
Associate Publisher* Chris Paul, *Executive Editorial
Director & Associate Publisher* Liz Bicknell, *Editorial
Director & Director of Editorial Operations* Mary Lee
Donovan

Books for babies through teens: board books, picture
books, novels, non-fiction, novelty books. Submit
material through a literary agent. Subsidiary of
Walker Books Ltd, UK. Founded 1991.

Candlewick Entertainment

Group Editorial Director Joan Powers
Media-related children's books, including film/TV
tie-ins.

Candlewick Studio

Group Editorial Director Karen Lotz, *Group Art
Director* Chris Paul
Books for all ages.

C&R Press

email info@crpress.org
website www.crpress.org
Facebook www.facebook.com/cr.press.lit
Twitter @CRPress
Instagram @candrpress
Publisher & Editorial Director Andrew Ibis, *Assistant
Editor* Benjamin Tyrrell

Solicited or agented queries only. Independent
publisher of literary fiction, non-fiction and poetry.
Founded 2006.

Catapult Book Group

email contact@catapult.co
website https://books.catapult.co/
Facebook www.facebook.com/catapultstory
Twitter @CatapultStory

Co-founder & Ceo Elizabeth Koch, *Editor-in-Chief* Kendall Storey

Publishes award-winning fiction and non-fiction, offers writing classes taught by acclaimed emerging and established writers, produces a daily online magazine of narrative non-fiction and fiction and hosts an open online platform where writers can showcase their own writing, find resources, and get inspired. Catapult Book Group is a collection of imprints that includes the following: Catapult, Counterpoint Press, Soft Skull Press. Founded 2015.

Center Street*

Hachette Book Group USA, 6100 Tower Cir #210, Franklin, TN 37067
email centerstreetpub@hbgusa.com
website www.centerstreet.com

Books with traditional values for readers in the US heartland. Imprint of Hachette Book Group (page 209). Founded 2005.

University of Chicago Press*

1427 East 60th Street, Chicago, IL 60637
tel +1 773-702-7700
website www.press.uchicago.edu
website www.journals.uchicago.edu

Scholarly books and monographs (humanities, social sciences and sciences); general trade books; reference books; and 80 scholarly journals. Founded 1891.

Chronicle Books*

680 Second Street, San Francisco, CA 94107
tel +1 415-537-4200
email hello@chroniclebooks.com
website www.chroniclebooks.com,
www.chroniclebooks.com/titles/kids-teens
Facebook www.facebook.com/ChronicleBooks
Twitter @ChronicleBooks
Instagram @chroniclekidsbooks
Chairman & Ceo Nion McEvoy

Publishes award-winning, innovative books. Publishing list includes illustrated books and gift products in design, art, architecture, photography, food, lifestyle, pop culture and children's titles. Founded 1967.

City Lights Publishers*

261 Columbus Avenue, San Francisco CA 94133
tel +1 415-362-1901
website http://citylights.com/publishing/
Facebook www.facebook.com/CityLightsBooks
Twitter @CityLightsBooks

Publishes cutting-edge fiction, poetry, memoirs, literary translations and books on vital social and political issues. Founded 1955.

Coffee House Press

79 13th Avenue NE, Suite 110, Minneapolis, MN 55413

tel +1 612-338-0125
email info@coffeehousepress.org
website www.coffeehousepress.org
Senior Editor Lizzie Davies

Literary fiction, essays, literature in translation, and poetry. Founded 1984.

Columbia University Press*

61 West 62nd Street, New York, NY 10023
tel +1 212-459-0600
website https://cup.columbia.edu/
Twitter @ColumbiaUP
Associate Provost & Director Jennifer Crewe, *Editorial Director* Eric Schwartz

General interest, scholarly and textbooks in the humanities, social sciences, sciences and professions; reference works in print and electronic formats. Subjects include: African American and African diaspora studies, Asian studies, business, earth science and sustainability, economics, English and comparative literature, film and media studies, global and American history, international relations, journalism, life science, Middle Eastern studies, neuroscience, palaeontology, philosophy, political science and international relations, religion, sociology and social work. Publishes Asian and Russian literature in translation. For MSS submission information see https://cup.columbia.edu/manuscript-submissions. Founded 1893.

Concordia Publishing House

3558 South Jefferson Avenue, St Louis, MO 63118
tel +1 314-268-1000
website www.cph.org
Facebook www.facebook.com/concordiapublishing
Twitter @concordiapub
Acting President & Ceo Jonathan D. Schultz

Religious books, Lutheran perspective. Few freelance MSS accepted; query first. Founded 1869.

Cornell University Press

Sagé House, 512 East State Street, Ithaca, NY 14850
tel +1 607-253-2338
email cupressinfo@cornell.edu
website www.cornellpress.cornell.edu
Director Jane Bunker

Comstock Publishing Associates, Cornell East Asia Series, ILR Press, NIU Press, SEAP Publications and Three Hills. Scholarly books. Founded 1869.

The Countryman Press

500 Fifth Avenue, New York, NY 10110
tel +1 212-354-5500
email countrymanpress@wwnorton.com
website www.countrymanpress.com
Editorial Director Ann Treistman

Cooking and lifestyle, outdoor recreation guides for anglers, hikers, cyclists, canoeists and kayakers, US travel guides, New England non-fiction, how-to books, country living books, books on nature and the environment, classic reprints and general non-fiction. No unsolicited MSS. Division of W.W. Norton & Co. (page 213), Inc. Founded 1973.

Crown Publishing Group*
1745 Broadway, New York, NY 10019
tel +1 212-366-2000
website www.randomhousebooks.com/imprint/crown
President David Drake

A publishing group, one of four within Penguin Random House, publishing across a wide range of non-fiction genres with an emphasis on politics, current affairs, social justice, personal narrative, biography, history, economics, business, cultural criticism, science, social science, and psychology. Imprints: Crown, Currency, Clarkson Potter, and Ten Speed Press (page 218). Founded 1933.

DAW Books, Inc.*
1745 Broadway, New York, NY 10019
tel +1 212-366-2096
email daw@penguinrandomhouse.com
website https://astrapublishinghouse.com/imprints/daw-books/

Sci-fi, fantasy, horror and paranormal: originals and reprints. Part of Astra Publishing, which publishes under Penguin Random House (page 214). Founded 1971.

Dover Publications, Inc.
31 East 2nd Street, Mineola, NY 11501
tel +1 516-294-7000
website https://store.doverpublications.com/
Facebook www.facebook.com/doverpublications
Twitter @doverpublications

Art, architecture, antiques, crafts, juvenile, food, history, folklore, literary classics, mystery, language, music, mathematics and science, nature, design and ready-to-use art. Founded 1941.

Dutton – see Penguin Publishing Group

Elsevier (Clinical Solutions)
1600 John F. Kennedy Boulevard, Philadelphia, PA 19103-2398
tel +1 215-239-3900
website www.elsevierhealth.co.uk
website www.elsevier.com/clinical-solutions
President Dr. John Danaher

Medical books, journals and electrical healthcare solutions. No unsolicited MSS but synopses and project proposals welcome. Imprints: Bailliere Tindall, Churchill Livingstone, Elsevier, Mosby, Pergamon, Saunders. Founded 1880.

Europa Editions
27 Union Square West, Suite 302, New York, NY 10003
email info@europaeditions.com
website www.europaeditions.com
Facebook www.facebook.com/europaeditionsNYS
Twitter @europaeditions
Editor-in-Chief Michael Reynolds

An independent publisher of literary fiction. Publishes an eclectic mix, reflecting the belief that dialogue between nations and cultures is of vital importance. Founded 2005.

Farrar, Straus and Giroux, LLC
175 Varick Street, 9th Floor, New York, NY 10014
tel +1 212-741-6900
website https://us.macmillan.com/fsg/
Facebook www.facebook.com/fsgoriginals
Twitter @FSOriginals
President & Publisher Jonathan Galassi

Founded 1946.

75 FSG
Publishes a wide variety of literary and commercial fiction and non-fiction.

FSG Originals
website www.fsgoriginals.com
Original fiction that does not fit into any obvious category.

Hill and Wang
General non-fiction, history, public affairs, graphic novels. Founded 1956.

MCD
Publishes literary fiction.

North Point Press
Literary non-fiction, with an emphasis on natural history, ecology, yoga, food writing and cultural criticism.

Feather Proof Books
website www.featherproof.com
Facebook www.facebook.com/featherproof
Twitter @featherproof
Publisher & Editor-in-Chief Jason Sommer, *Co-founder* Zach Dodson

Publishes literary fiction in the form of novels, short stories and poetry, and also non-fiction and post-, trans-, and inter-genre tragicomedy. Founded 2005.

The Feminist Press
365 Fifth Avenue, Suite 5406, New York, NY 10016
website www.feministpress.org
Facebook www.facebook.com/feministpress
Twitter @feministpress
Publisher Margot Atwell

Publishes books that ignite movements and social transformation. Publishes 12 to 15 books a year and specialises in an array of genres including cutting-edge fiction, activist non-fiction, literature in translation, hybrid memoirs and children's books. Founded 1970.

Flyaway Books

100 Witherspoon Street, Louisville, KY 40202–1396
tel +1 502-569-5000
website www.flyawaybooks.com
President & Publisher David Dobson

Children's picture books with a social justice and spiritual angle. Division of Presbyterian Publishing Corp. Founded 1938.

Fonthill Media Inc

2c Rose Lane, Charleston, SC 29403
tel +1 843-203-3432
email info@fonthillmedia.com
website www.fonthillmedia.com
Publisher & President (Charleston SC Office) Alan Sutton

General history. Specialisations include biography, military history, aviation history, naval and maritime history, regional and local history, transport history, social history, sports history, ancient history and archaeology. US imprints: Fonthill, America Through Time and American History House. Founded 2012.

Forest Avenue Press

website www.forestavenuepress.com
Facebook www.facebook.com/forestavenuepress
Twitter @forestavepress
Instagram @forestavenuepress

Based in Portland, Oregon, publishes literary fiction on a joyride and the occasional memoir. Founded 2012.

Forge – see Tor Books

Fulcrum Publishing

3970 Youngfiled Street, Wheat Ridge, CO 80033
tel +1 303-277-1623
email orders@fulcrumbooks.com
website https://fulcrum.bookstore.ipgbook.com/

Publishes a wide variety of educational non-fiction texts and children's books, also books and support materials for teachers, librarians, parents and elementary through middle school children. Subjects include: science and nature, literature and storytelling, history, multicultural studies, and Native American and Hispanic cultures. Founded 1965.

Getty Publications*

1200 Getty Center Drive, Suite 500, Los Angeles, CA 90049
tel +1 310-440-6536
email booknews@getty.edu
website www.getty.edu

Art, art history, architecture, classical art and archaeology, conservation. Founded 1983.

Gibbs Smith

570 N Sportsplex Drive, Kaysville, UT 84037
tel +1 800-835-4993
email info@gibbs-smith.com
website www.gibbs-smith.com

An employee-owned, independent, Utah-based publisher. Its book and gift division publishes home reference, cookery, non-fiction, and children's titles. The Gibbs Smith Education division is the nation's leading publisher of state history programs. All unsolicited queries, submissions and correspondence should be via email. Responds only to projects of interest. Founded 1969.

David R. Godine, Publisher, Inc.

PO Box 1682, Biddeford, ME 04005
tel +1 617-451-9600
website www.godine.com
Publisher David Alexander, *Editorial Director* Joshua Bodwell

Fiction, non-fiction, poetry, biography, children's, essays, history, photography, art, typography, architecture, nature and gardening, music, cooking, words and writing and mysteries. No unsolicited MSS. Founded 1970.

Grand Central Publishing*

1290 6th Avenue, New York, NY 10104
tel +1 212-364-1100
email grandcentralpublishing@hbgusa.com
website www.grandcentralpublishing.com
Facebook www.facebook.com/grandcentralpub
Twitter @grandcentralpub
Senior Vice-President & Publisher Ben Sevier

Previously Warner Books, Inc. Fiction and non-fiction. Imprints: Balance (wellbeing), Twelve (publishes authors with unique perspectives), Forever (romance), Forever Yours (romance) and Twelve (authors from under-represented backgrounds). Division of Hachette Book Group (page 209). Founded 1970.

Graywolf Press

212 Third Avenue North, Suite 485, Minneapolis, MN 55401
tel +1 651-641-0077
email wolves@graywolfpress.org
website www.graywolfpress.org
Twitter @graywolfpress
Director & Publisher Carmen Giménez

A not-for-profit publisher of poetry, non-fiction, literary fiction and works in translation. Founded 1974.

Grove Atlantic, Inc.

154 West 14th Street, 12 Floor, New York, NY 10011
tel +1 212-614-7850
email info@groveatlantic.com
website www.groveatlantic.com
Facebook www.facebook.com/groveatlantic

Twitter @groveatlantic
Vice-President & Editorial Director Elisabeth Schmitz

Fiction, biography, autobiography, history, current affairs, social science, belles lettres, natural history. No unsolicited MSS. Imprints: Atlantic Monthly Press, Black Cat, Mysterious Press, Grove Press. Founded 1952.

Hachette Book Group*
1290 Avenue of the Americas, New York, NY 10104
tel +1 212-364-1100
website www.hachettebookgroup.com

Publishing groups: Grand Central Publishing (page 208); Hachette Nashville; Little, Brown Audio; Little, Brown and Company (page 211); Little, Brown Books for Young Readers; Orbit; Perseus Books. Workman imprints: Grand Central: Balance; Forever; Forever Yours; Legacy Lit; Twelve; Vision. Hachette Nashville: Center Street; Ellie Claire; FaithWords; Worthy Books; WorthyKids. Little, Brown and Company: Back Bay Books; Little, Brown Spark; Mulholland Books; Voracious. Little, Brown Books for Young Readers: Christy Ottaviano Books; JIMMY Patterson; LB Kids; LBYR+; Poppy. Orbit: Redhook. Perseus Books: Avalon Travel, Basic Books; Black Dog & Leventhal; Bold Type Books; Hachette Books; Hachette Go; Moon Travel; Rick Steves; RP Studio; Running Press; Running Press Kids; PublicAffairs; Seal Press. Founded 1996.

HarperCollins Publishers*
195 Broadway, New York, NY 10007
tel +1 212-207-700
website https://corporate.harpercollins.com/us/
President & Ceo Brian Murray

Fiction, history, biography, poetry, science, travel, cookery, juvenile, educational, business, technical and religious. Founded 1817.

Harpeth Road Press
PO Box 158184, Nashville, TN 37215
website www.harpethroad.com
Facebook www.facebook.com/harpethroad
Twitter @harpethroad
Instagram @harpethroad
Founder Jenny Hale

Digital-first romantic fiction publishers. Currently accepting mainstream commercial romantic fiction (no erotica). Founded 2020.

Harvard University Press*
79 Garden Street, Cambridge, MA 02138
tel +1 617-495-2600
email contact_hup@harvard.edu
website www.hup.harvard.edu
Director George Andreou, *Editorial Director* Sharmila Sen

History, philosophy, literary criticism, politics, economics, sociology, music, science, classics, social sciences, behavioural sciences, law. Founded 1913.

Hippocrene Books, Inc.
171 Madison Avenue, New York, NY 10016
tel +1 718-454-2366
email info@hippocrenebooks.com
website www.hippocrenebooks.com

International cookery, foreign language dictionaries, travel, military history, Polonia, general trade. Founded 1971.

Holiday House, Inc.*
120 Broadway, New York, NY 10271
tel +1 212-646 5025
email info@holidayhouse.com
website www.holidayhouse.com

General children's books. Send entire MS. Only responds to projects of interest. Founded 1935.

Henry Holt and Company LLC
120 Broadway, New York, NY 10271
tel +1 646-307-5095
website https://us.macmillan.com/henryholt/

History, sports, politics, biography, memoir, novels. Imprints: Holt, Metropolitan Books, Andy Cohen Books, Holt Paperbacks. Imprint of Macmillan Publishers Inc (page 211). Founded 1866.

Johns Hopkins University Press*
2715 North Charles Street, Baltimore, MD 21218–4319
tel +1 410-516-6900
email tcl@press.jhu.edu
website www.press.jhu.edu
Director Barbara Kline Pope

History, literary studies, classics, environmental studies, biology, history of STEM, bioethics, public health and health policy, health and wellness, physics, astronomy, mathematics, education. Founded 1878.

Houghton Mifflin Harcourt
3 Park Avenue, Floor 19, New York, NY 10016
tel +1 212-598-5730
website www.hmhco.com

Educational content and solutions for K–12 teachers and students of all ages; also reference, and fiction and non-fiction for adults and young readers. Founded 1832.

Ig Publishing
PO Box 2547, New York, NY 10163
tel +1 718-797-0676
website www.igpub.com
Facebook www.facebook.com/ig-publishing
Twitter @igpublishing
Publisher Elizabeth Clementson

Publishes literary fiction and political non-fiction. Founded 2002.

Books

University of Illinois Press

1325 South Oak Street, Champaign, IL 61820
tel +1 217-333-0950
email uipress@uillinois.edu
website www.press.illinois.edu
Director Laurie Matheson

American studies (history, music, literature, religion), working-class and ethnic studies, communications, regional studies, architecture, philosophy, women's studies, film, sports history, folklore, food studies. Founded 1918.

Indiana University Press

Herman B Wells Library 350, 1320 East 10th Street, Bloomington, IN 47405–3907
tel +1 812-855-8817
email iupress@indiana.edu
website https://iupress.org/
Director Gary Dunham

Specialises in the humanities and social sciences: African, Jewish and Holocaust, Middle East, Russian and East European, and women's and gender studies; film, history, music, palaeontology, philosophy and religion. Imprint: Quarry Books (regional publishing). Red Lightning Books (trade publishing). Founded 1950.

Infobase Publishing

132 West 31st Street, New York, NY 10001
tel +1 800-322-8755
website www.infobase.com/about
Editorial Director Laurie E. Likoff

General reference books and services for colleges, libraries, schools and general public. Founded 1940.

Inkshares

95 Linden Street, Suite 6, Oakland, CA 94607
email hello@inkshares.com
website www.inkshares.com
Facebook www.facebook.com/inkshares
Twitter @Inkshares
Co-founder & Ceo Adam Gomolin, *Co-founder & Cpo* Thad Woodman, *Co-founder* Larry Levitsky

A book publisher that has readers, not agents or editors, decide what is published. Publishes books that successfully hit a pre-order threshold on the company's platform, or win a contest run in partnership with an imprint on the platform. The process is as follows: authors pitch, readers pre-order, and the company publishes. Any author can submit a proposal for a book. Once the project goes live, readers support the project by pre-ordering copies of the book. Once the 750 pre-order goal is hit, the work is published: authors are assigned an editor, a designer and the company deals with printing, distribution, marketing and publicity once the MS is finished. Founded 2013.

Inner Traditions Bear & Company

PO Box 388, Rochester, Vermont 05767
tel +1 800-246-8648
email comcustomerservice@InnerTraditions.com
website www.innertraditions.com
Editor Jon Graham

Subjects include: spirituality, the occult, ancient mysteries, new science, holistic health and natural medicine. Founded 1975.

Jolly Fish Press

2297 Waters Drive, Mendota Heights, MN 55120
tel +1 888-417-0195
email publicity@jollyfishpress.com
email submit@jollyfishpress.com
website www.jollyfishpress.com
Facebook www.facebook.com/JollyFishPress
Twitter @JollyFishPress

Dedicated to promoting exceptional, unique new voices in middle-grade fiction and jump-starting writing careers. See website above for submission guidelines. Accepts electronic submissions only. Imprint of North Star Editions, Inc. Founded 2011.

University Press of Kansas

2502 Westbrooke Circle, Lawrence, KS 66045–4444
tel +1 785-864-4154
email upress@ku.edu
website www.kansaspress.ku.edu
Interim Faculty Director Mike Haddock, *Editor-in-Chief* Joyce Harrison, *Senior Editor* David Congdon

American history (political, social, cultural, environmental), military history, American political thought, American presidency studies, law and constitutional history, political science. Founded 1946.

Knopf Doubleday Publishing Group*

1745 Broadway, New York, NY 10019
tel +1 212-782-9000
website https://knopfdoubleday.com/
President & Publisher Maya Mavjee; *Executive Vice-Presidents & Publishers* Reagan Arthur (Knopf), Bill Thomas (Doubleday), Suzanne Herz (Vintage & Anchor); *Senior Vice-President & Publisher* Lisa Lucas (Pantheon & Schoken)

A publishing group, one of four within Penguin Random House (page 214). Alfred A. Knopf was founded in 1915 and has long been known as a publisher of distinguished hardback fiction and non-fiction. Imprints: Alfred A. Knopf, Vintage Books, Anchor Books, Doubleday, Everyman's Library, Pantheon Books, Schocken Books, and Vintage Español. Founded in 2008.

Krause Publications*

5525 Joerns Drive, Suite 2, Stevens Point WI 544817
tel +1 75-445-2214
website www.krausebooks.com

Antiques and collectables: coins, stamps, automobiles, toys, trains, firearms, comics, records; sewing, ceramics, outdoors, hunting. Imprint of Penguin Random House (page 214). Founded 1952.

Little, Brown & Company

1290 Avenue of the Americas, New York, NY 10104
tel +1 212-364-1100
email lbpublicity.Generic@hbgusa.com
website www.littlebrown.com
Facebook www.facebook.com/littlebrownandcompany
Twitter @littlebrown
Senior Vice-President & Publisher Bruce Nichols

General literature, fiction, non-fiction, biography, history, trade paperbacks, children's. Founded 1837.

Back Bay Books

Fiction and non-fiction. Founded 1993.

Little, Brown Spark

Publishes books for young people and adults that spark ideas, feelings and change. Looking for authors who are experts and thought leaders in the fields of health, lifestyle, psychology and science.

Mulholland Books

Suspense and crime.

Voracious

Non-fiction: cookery, self-help, current issues and interest.

Llewellyn Worldwide

2143 Wooddale Drive, Woodbury, MN 55125
tel +1 651-291-1970
email publicity@llewellyn.com
website www.llewellyn.com
Facebook www.facebook.com/LlewellynBooks
Twitter @llewellynbooks
Publisher Bill Krause

A publisher of new age and mind, body & spirit books, including self-help, holistic health, astrology, tarot, paranormal and alternative spirituality titles. Imprints: Llewellyn, Midnight Ink, Flux. Founded 1901.

Lonely Planet

230 Franklin Road, Building 2B, Franklin, TN 37064
email pressusa@lonelyplanet.com
website www.lonelyplanet.com
Facebook www.facebook.com/lonelyplanet
Twitter @lonelyplanet
Ceo Luis Cabrera

An international travel publisher, printing over 120 million books in 11 different languages, along with guidebooks and ebooks to almost every destination on the planet. Also produces a range of gift and reference titles, a website, a magazine and a range of digital travel products and apps. Founded 1973.

The Lyons Press

246 Goose Lane, Guilford, CT 06437
tel +1 203-458-4500
website www.lyonspress.com, www.globepequot.com
Contact Stephanie Scott

Fishing, hunting, sports, outdoor skills, history, military history, reference, true crime, entertainment and non-fiction. An imprint of Globe Pequot, the trade division of Rowman & Littlefield. Founded 1978.

McGraw-Hill Professional*

1325 Avenue of the Americas, 7th Floor, New York, NY 10019
website www.mhprofessional.com
Facebook www.facebook.com/mcgrawhilleducation
Twitter @MHEducation
Associate Publisher Donya Dickerson

Divisions and imprints include: Business, Education and Test Prep, International Marine and Ragged Mountain Press, Medical, Open University Press. To find individual editorial contacts check website. Founded 1966.

Macmillan Publishers, Inc.

120 Broadway, New York, NY 10271
tel +1 646-307-5151
email press.inquiries@macmillanusa.com
website https://us.macmillan.com/

Imprints for adults: Castle Point Books, Celadon Books, Farrar, Straus & Giroux (page 207), Flatiron Books, Henry Holt & Co. (page 209), Macmillan Audio, Metropolitan Books, Minotaur Books, Picador, Quick and Dirty Tips, St Martin's Essentials, St Martin's Griffin, St Martin's Press (page 216), St Martin's Publishing Group, Tor Publishing Group, Wednesday Books. For children: FSG Books for Young Readers, Feiwel & Friends, First Second, Holt Books for Young Readers, Kingfisher, Macmillan Children's Publishing Group, Neon Squid, Odd Dot, Priddy Books, Roaring Brook, Starscape/Tor Teen, Square Fish, Swoon Reads, Young Listeners. Founded 1843.

McPherson & Company

PO Box 1126, Kingston, NY 12402
tel +1 845-331-5807
email bmcphersonco@gmail.com
website www.mcphersonco.com
Facebook www.facebook.com/McPherson-and-Company
Twitter @bookmaverick
Publisher Bruce R. McPherson

Literary fiction; non-fiction: art criticism, writings by artists, film-making; occasional general titles (e.g. anthropology). No poetry. No unsolicited MSS; query first. Imprints: Documentext, Treacle Press, Saroff Books. Founded 1974.

Books

Books

McSweeney's Books

PO Box 410987, San Francisco, CA 94141
website www.mcsweeneys.net

An independent not-for-profit publishing company based in San Francisco. As well as operating a daily humour website, they also publish an ever-growing selection of books under various imprints. Founded 1998.

The University of Massachusetts Press*

New Africa House, 180 Infirmary Way, 4th Floor, Amherst, MA 01003-9289
email info@umpress.umass.edu
website www.umass.edu/umpress
Director Mary Dougherty, *Executive Editor* Matt Becker

Scholarly books and works of general interest: American studies and history, Black and ethnic studies, women's studies, cultural criticism, architecture and environmental design, literary criticism, poetry, fiction, philosophy, political science, sociology, books of regional interest. Founded 1964.

Melville House*

46 John Street, Brooklyn, NY 11201
tel +1 718-722-9204
email info@mhpbooks.com
website www.mhpbooks.com
Co-founders Valerie Merians, Dennis Johnson

An independent publisher located in Brooklyn, New York. It was founded by sculptor Valerie Merians and fiction writer/journalist Dennis Johnson in order to publish *Poetry After 9/11*. Publishes literary fiction and thought-provoking non-fiction. Founded 2001.

The University of Michigan Press

839 Greene Street, Ann Arbor, MI 48104–3209
tel +1 734-764-4388
email um.press@umich.edu
website www.press.umich.edu
Facebook www.facebook.com/universityofmichiganpress
Twitter @UofMPress
Director Charles Watkinson

Scholarly and general interest works in literary and cultural theory, classics, history, theatre, women's studies, political science, law, American history, American studies, anthropology, economics, jazz; textbooks in English as a second language; regional trade titles. Founded 1930.

Microsoft Press Books

One Microsoft Way, Redmond, WA 98052–6399
tel +1 425-882-8080
email 4bkideas@microsoft.com
website www.microsoftpressstore.com

Computer books. Published by Pearson. Founded 1983.

Milkweed Editions

1011 Washington Avenue South, Suite 300, Minneapolis, MN 55415
tel +1 612-332-3192
website www.milkweed.org
Editors Daniel Slager, Joey McGarvey

Fiction, poetry, essays, the natural world. Founded 1979.

University of Missouri Press

113 Heinkel Building, 201 South 7th Street, Columbia, MO 65211
tel +1 573-882-7641
email upress@missouri.edu
website https://upress.missouri.edu/
Facebook www.facebook.com/umissouripress
Twitter @umissouripress
Editor-in-Chief Andrew Davidson

US history (esp. 20th-century military, African American, women, sports, political/constitutional, early Republic), journalism, political science, Missouri and regional history, and literary criticism (US and Mark Twain). Founded 1958.

The MIT Press

One Broadway, 12th Floor, Cambridge, MA 02142–1209
tel +1 617-253-5646
website https://mitpress.mit.edu/
Facebook www.facebook.com/mitpress
Twitter @mitpress

Art and architecture; cognitive sciences, philosophy, and bioethics; computer science; culture and technology; design and visual culture; education and learning; economics, finance and business, environmental studies, urbanism, and food studies; information science and communication; life sciences, neuroscience, and trade science; linguistics, new media, game studies, and digital humanities; physical sciences, mathematics, and engineering; science, technology, and society; and MIT and regional interest. Founded 1962.

Thomas Nelson Publisher*

PO Box 141000, Nashville, TN 37214
tel +1 800-251-4000
email publicity@thomasnelson.com
website www.thomasnelson.com

Bibles, religious, non-fiction and fiction general trade books for adults and children. Acquired by HarperCollins in 2012. Founded 1798.

New Directions

80 Eighth Avenue New York, NY 10011
tel +1 212-255-0230
website www.ndbooks.com
Executive Vice-President Laurie Callahan

Independent publisher of literary fiction and poetry. Founded 1936.

New Harbinger Publications

5674 Shattuck Avenue, Oakland, CA 94609
tel +1 800-748-6273
email customerservice@newharbinger.com
website www.newharbinger.com
Facebook www.facebook.com/NewHarbinger
Twitter @NewHarbinger

Publisher of books on psychology, health, spirituality and personal growth. Imprints include: New Harbinger, Instant Help, Impact Publishers, Context Press, Non-Duality Press, Reveal Press. For submission guidelines see: www.newharbinger.com/publishing-new-harbinger. Founded 1973.

University of New Mexico Press

1717 Roma NE, Albuquerque, NM 87106
tel +1 505-277-3495
email custserv@unm.edu
website www.unmpress.com
Director Stephen Hull, *Publishing Assistant* Brenton Woodward

Western history, anthropology and archaeology, Latin American studies, photography, multicultural literature, fiction, poetry. Founded 1929.

Noemi Press

website www.noemipress.org
Facebook www.facebook.com/noemi.press
Twitter @noemi_press
Publisher Carmen Giménez Smith

A literary arts publisher based in Blacksburg, Virginia, dedicated to publishing and promoting the work of emerging and established authors and artists. Founded 2002.

The University of North Carolina Press*

116 South Boundary Street, Chapel Hill, NC 27514
tel +1 919-966-3561
website https://uncpress.org/
Facebook www.facebook.com/UNCPpress
Twitter @UNC_Press

American history, American studies, Southern studies, European history, women's studies, Latin American studies, political science, anthropology and folklore, classics, regional trade. Founded 1922.

North Point Press – see Farrar, Straus and Giroux, LLC

W.W. Norton & Company, Inc.*

500 Fifth Avenue, New York, NY 10110
tel +1 212-354-5500
website www.wwnorton.com
Vice-President & Editor-in-Chief John Glusman

Narrative non-fiction and literary fiction, history, politics, science, biography, music and memoir. Founded 1923.

University of Oklahoma Press

2800 Venture Drive, Norman, OK 73069–8216
tel +1 405-325-2000
website www.oupress.com
Director Dale Bennie, *Editorial Director* Andrew Berzanskis

American West, American Indians, classics, political science. Founded 1928.

OR Books

40 Avenue C, New York, NY 10009
tel +1 212-514-6485
email info@orbooks.com
website www.orbooks.com
Facebook www.facebook.com/orbooks
Twitter @orbooks
Founders John Oakes, Colin Robinson

Publishes non-fiction, literature, history and politics, activism, society, the Internet and the Middle East. Founded 2009.

Orbit – see Little, Brown & Company

The Overlook Press

195 Broadway, 9th floor, New York, NY 10007
tel +1 212-206-7715
website www.abramsbooks.com/imprints/overlookpress
Facebook www.facebook.com/overlookpress
Twitter @overlookpress

Literary fiction, commercial fiction, fiction in translation, select drama. Imprint of Abrams. Founded 1971.

Oxford University Press

198 Madison Avenue, New York, NY 10016
tel +1 212-726-6000
website https://global.oup.com/academic/
President Niko Pfund

Academic and trade, bibles; ELT and ESL; dictionaries; higher education and science, technology, medicine and scholarly; law, medicine and music; journals; online; reference. Publishes globally for a range of audiences, across a multitude of cultures, education systems and languages. Currently publishes more than 6,000 titles a year worldwide, in a variety of formats. Many of these titles are created specifically for local markets and are published by regional publishing branches. Founded 1586.

Pelican Publishing

990 N. Corporate Drive, Suite 100, New Orleans, LA 70123
tel +1 504-684-8976
email editorial@pelicanpub.com
website www.arcadiapublishing.com
Publisher & President Scott Campbell

Books

Gulf South cookery, biography, history, paranormal, children's, holiday. Founded 1926.

Penguin Publishing Group*
1745 Broadway, New York, NY 10019
tel +1 212-366-2000
website www.penguin.com
President Allison Dobson

A publishing group, one of four within Penguin Random House. A leading adult trade book division with a wide range of imprints. Imprints include: Avery, Berkley Books, Dutton, G.P. Putnam's Sons, Optimism Press, Pamela Dorman Books, Penguin Books, Penguin Classics, Penguin Press, Plume, Portfolio, TarcherPerigee, Riverhead, Sentinel, Viking and Writer's Digest Books. Founded 1935.

Penguin Random House*
1745 Broadway, New York, NY 10019
tel +1 212-782-9000
website www.penguinrandomhouse.com
Interim Ceo Nihar Malaviya

Consists of 300 independent imprints and brands, more than 15,000 new print titles a year, and has published close to 800 million print, audio and ebooks. Committed to publishing adult and children's fiction and non-fiction print editions, and is a pioneer in digital publishing. Its book brands include storied imprints such as Doubleday, Viking and Alfred A. Knopf (US); Ebury, Hamish Hamilton and Jonathan Cape (UK); Plaza & Janés and Alfaguara (Spain); and Sudamericana (Argentina); as well as the international imprint DK. See Crown Publishing Group, Knopf Doubleday Publishing Group (page 210), Penguin Publishing Group (above), Random House Publishing Group (page 215), Penguin Young Readers (below) and Random House Children's Books (page 215). Founded 2013.

Penguin Young Readers*
1745 Broadway, New York, NY 10019
tel +1 212-366-2000
website www.penguin.com/children
Facebook www.facebook.com/penguinkidsbooks
Twitter @penguinkids
President Jen Loja

A leading children's book publisher in the USA. The company owns a wide range of imprints and trademarks including Dial Books, Dutton, Grosset & Dunlap, Kathy Dawson Books, Kokila, Nancy Paulsen Books, Penguin Workshop, Philomel, Puffin, G.P. Putnam's Sons, Razorbill, Speak, Viking and Frederick Warne. Penguin Young Readers is a division of Penguin Group LLC, a Penguin Random House company. Founded 1935.

University of Pennsylvania Press*
3905 Spruce Street, Philadelphia, PA 19104–4112
tel +1 215-898-6261

email custserv@pobox.upenn.edu
website www.pennpress.org
Editor-in-Chief Walter Biggins

American and European history, African American studies, anthropology, Atlantic studies, architecture, cultural studies, ancient studies, human rights, literature, medieval and early modern studies, Jewish studies, religious studies, current affairs, politics and public policy, urban studies and Pennsylvania regional studies. Founded 1890.

Pennsylvania State University Press*
820 North University Drive, USB1, Suite C, University Park, PA 16802
tel +1 814-865-1327
website www.psupress.org
Director Patrick Alexander, *Assistant Director & Editor-in-Chief* Kendra Boileau

Art history, literary criticism, religious studies, philosophy, political science, sociology, history, Latin American studies and medieval studies. Send proposals to: www.psupress.org/books/author_resources/proposals.html. Founded 1956.

The Permanent Press
4170 Noyac Road, Sag Harbor, NY 11963
tel +1 631-725-1101
website www.thepermanentpress.com
Facebook www.facebook.com/ThePermanentPress
Twitter @TPermanentPress
Publisher Judith Shepard

Literary fiction. Imprint: Second Chance Press. Founded 1978.

Plume – see Penguin Publishing Group

Potomac Books, Inc.
c/o Longleaf Services, Inc, 116 S Boundary Street, Chapel Hill, NC 27514
tel +1 800-848-6224
email customerservice@longleafservices.org
website www.nebraskapress.unl.edu/potomac

National and international affairs, history (military and diplomatic); reference, biography. Purchased by the University of Nebraska Press in 2013. Founded 1984.

powerHouse Books
32 Adams Street, Brooklyn, NY 11201
tel +1 718-666-3049
email madison@powerhousebooks.com
website www.powerhousebooks.com
Facebook www.facebook.com/pages/powerHouseBooksNY
Twitter @powerhousebooks
Instagram @powerhousebooks
Ceo & Publisher Daniel Power

World-renowned and critically acclaimed publisher, best known for a diverse publishing program which specialises in fine art, documentary, pop culture, fashion, and celebrity books. Check submissions page on website for submissions procedure. Founded 1995.

Press 53

560 N Trade Street, Ste 103,
Winston-Salem NC 27101
tel +1 336-770-5535
website www.press53.com
Publisher & Editor-in-Chief Kevin Morgan Watson

An independent publisher specialising in short stories and poetry, and championing voices who might not normally get heard. Founded 2005.

Princeton University Press*

Princeton, NJ 08540
tel +1 609-258-4900
Postal address 41 William Street, Princeton, NJ 08540
website www.press.princeton.edu
Director Christie Henry

Scholarly and scientific books on all subjects. Founded 1905.

Puffin – see Penguin Young Readers

Quarto Publishing Group USA

142 West 36th Street, Fourth Floor, New York, NY 10018
tel +1 212-779-4972
website www.quarto.com

Creates and publishes illustrated books in North America and sells co-editions of them internationally. Subject categories include home improvement, gardening, practical arts and crafts, licensed children's books, transport, graphic arts, food and drink, sports, military history, Americana, health and body, lifestyle, pets and music. The division comprises 15 imprints: Book Sales, Cool Springs Press, Creative Publishing International, Fair Winds Press, Motorbooks, Quarry Books, QDS, Quiver, Race Point Publishing, Rock Point, Rockport Publishers, Voyageur Press, Walter Foster Publishing, Walter Foster, Jr. and Zenith Press. Details of the imprints can be found on the website. Founded 2004.

Quirk Books*

215 Church Street, Philadelphia, PA 19106
tel +1 215-627-3581
website www.quirkbooks.com
Facebook www.facebook.com/quirkbooks
Twitter @quirkbooks
President David Borgenicht

Publishes a highly curated list of entertaining, enlightening and strikingly unconventional books for adults and children in a number of genres and categories. Founded 2002.

Rand McNally

PO Box 7600, Chicago, IL 60680
tel +1 847-329-8100
website www.randmcnally.com/publishing
Facebook www.facebook.com/randmcnally
Twitter @randmcnally

Maps, guides, atlases, educational publications, globes and children's geographical titles and atlases in print and electronic formats. Founded 1856.

Random House Children's Books*

1745 Broadway, New York, NY 10019
tel +1 212-782-9000
website www.rhcbooks.com,
www.randomhouse.com/teachers
President & Publisher Barbara Marcus

An English-language children's trade book publisher. Creates books for preschool children through YA readers, in all formats from board books to activity books to picture books, graphic novels, novels and non-fiction. Imprints: Dragonfly, Ember, Laurel-Leaf, Little Golden Books, Make Me A World, Princeton Review, Random House Books for Young Readers, Random House Graphic, Rodale Kids, Schwartz & Wade Books, Sylvan Learning, Wendy Lamb Books, Yearling Books. Part of Penguin Random House (page 214). Founded 1925.

Random House Publishing Group*

1745 Broadway, New York, NY 10019
tel +1 212-782-9000
website www.randomhousebooks.com
President & Publisher Sanyu Dillon

A publishing group, one of four within Penguin Random House. Publishes literary and commercial fiction; narrative non-fiction across genres such as history, science, politics, current affairs, biography, memoir, religion and business, as well as in preeminent culinary and lifestyle titles. Imprints: Ballantine Books, Bantam Books, Broadway Books, Convergent Books, Crown Archetype, Crown Forum, Delacorte Press, Dell, Del Rey, The Dial Press, Harmony Books, Hogarth, Hogarth Shakespeare, Ink & Willow, Lorena Jones Books, Modern Library, One World, Random House, RocLit 101, Rodale Books, SJP for Hogarth, Three Rivers Press, Tim Duggan Books, WaterBrook Multnomah and Watson-Guptill. Founded 1927.

Rare Bird Books

website https://rare-bird-books.myshopify.com/
President & Publisher Tyson Cornell

An independent publisher of approximately 50+ books each year in multiple formats, including print, ebook, audiobook, and limited edition. Founded 2010.

Razorbill – see Penguin Young Readers

Rizzoli International Publications, Inc.
300 Park Avenue South, New York, NY 10010
tel +1 212-387-3400
email publicity@rizzoliusa.com
website www.rizzoliusa.com
Publisher Charles Miers

Art, architecture, photography, fashion, gardening, design, gift books, cookery. Founded 1976.

Rodale Book Group
733 Third Avenue, New York, NY 10017
tel +1 212-573-0300
website https://crownpublishing.com/archives/imprint/rodale-books/
Ceo Maria Rodale

General health, women's health, men's health, senior health, alternative health, fitness, healthy cooking, gardening, pets, spirituality/inspiration, trade health, biography, memoir, current affairs, science, parenting, organics, lifestyle, self-help, how-to, home arts. Imprint of the Crown Publishing Group (page 207). Founded 1932.

Routledge
711 Third Avenue, New York, NY 10017
tel +1 212-216-7800
website www.routledge.com

Music, history, psychology and psychiatry, politics, business studies, philosophy, education, sociology, urban studies, religion, film, media, literary and cultural studies, reference, English language, linguistics, communication studies, journalism. Editorial office in the UK. Subsidiary of Taylor & Francis, LLC. Imprint: Routledge. Founded 1834.

Rowman & Littlefield
4501 Forbes Boulevard, Suite 200, Lanham, MD 20706
tel +1 301-459-3366
email customercare@rowman.com
website www.rowman.com
Facebook www.facebook.com/rowmanuk
Twitter @rowmanuk
President & Ceo James E. Lyons

An independent publisher specialising in both academic publishing in the humanities and social sciences and trade non-fiction publishing. Founded 1925.

Running Press Book Publishers
2300 Chestnut Street, Suite 200, Philadelphia, PA 19103
tel +1 215-567-5080
email perseus.promos@perseusbooks.com
website www.runningpress.com
Facebook www.facebook.com/runningpressbooks
Twitter @running_press

General non-fiction, TV, film, humour, history, children's fiction and non-fiction, food and wine, pop culture, lifestyle, illustrated gift books. Imprints: Running Press Adults, Running Press Kids, Running Press Minis, Running Press Studio. Member of the Perseus Books Group which is an imprint of Hachette Book Group (page 209). Founded 1972.

Rutgers University Press
106 Somerset Street, Third Floor, New Brunswick, NJ 08901
tel +1 800-848-6224
website www.rutgersuniversitypress.org
Director Micah Kleit, *Editorial Director* Kimberly Guinta

Women's studies, LGBTQIA2S+ studies, anthropology, childhood studies, Latin American and Caribbean studies, higher education, human rights, television, film and media studies, communication, sociology, public health, history of medicine, Asian American studies, African American studies, American studies, Latinx studies, Jewish studies, religious studies, regional titles. Founded 1936.

St Martin's Press, Inc.
120 Broadway, New York, NY 10271
website https://us.macmillan.com/smp/

Trade, reference, college. No unsolicited MSS. Imprints include: Minotaur Press, Wednesday's Books, St Martin's Essentials, Castle Street Books, St Martin's Griffin. Imprint of Macmillan (page 211). Founded 1952.

Santa Monica Press
PO Box 850, Solana Beach, CA 92075
tel +1 858-832-7906
email acquisitions@santamonicapress.com
website www.santamonicapress.com
Twitter @santamonicapress
Instagram @santamonicapress1
Publisher Jeffrey Goldman

Titles are sold in chain, independent, online and university bookstores around the world, as well as in retail outlets in North America and the UK. Publishes modern non-fiction titles: pop culture, film, music, humour, biography, travel and sports, as well as regional titles focused on California. YA historical fiction and YA narrative non-fiction recently added to the list. Visit website to view author guidelines. Founded 1994.

Sasquatch Books
1904 Third Avenue, Suite 710 Seattle, WA 98101
tel +1 206-467-4300
email custserv@sasquatchbooks.com
website www.sasquatchbooks.com
Facebook www.facebook.com/SasquatchBooksSeattle
Twitter @sasquatchbooks

Publishes a variety of non-fiction books, as well as children's books under the Little Bigfoot imprint. Will consider queries and proposals from authors and agents for new projects that fit into the company's West Coast regional publishing programme. Imprints: Sasquatch Adult, Little Big Foot, Spruce Books. Founded 1986.

Scholastic, Inc.*

557 Broadway, New York, NY 10012
tel +1 212-343-6100
email news@scholastic.com
website www.scholastic.com
Facebook www.facebook.com/scholastic
Twitter @scholastic

The world's largest publisher and distributor of children's books and a leader in education technology and children's media. Divisions: Scholastic Book Clubs, Scholastic Book Fairs, Scholastic Education, Scholastic International, Media, Licensing and Advertising, Scholastic Trade Publishing. Imprints include: Arthur A. Levine Books, The Blue Sky Press, Cartwheel Books, Chicken House, David Fickling Books, Graphix, Orchard Books, Point, PUSH, Scholastic en español, Scholastic Focus, Scholastic Licensed Publishing, Scholastic Nonfiction, Scholastic Paperbacks, Scholastic Press and Scholastic Reference. In addition, Scholastic Trade Books includes Klutz, a highly innovative publisher and creator of 'books plus' for children. Founded 1920.

Seal Press*

1290 Avenue of the Americas, 5th Floor, New York, NY 10104
tel +1 212-364-1100
email Basic.Books@hbgusa.com
website www.sealpress.com
Facebook www.facebook.com/sealpress
Twitter @SealPress
Instagram @sealpress

Publishes radical feminist, antiracist and LGBTQIA+ non-fiction books. Seal Press is an imprint of Basic Books (page 204), an imprint of Perseus Books, a Hachette Book Group company (page 209). Founded 1976.

Sentinel – see Penguin Publishing Group

Simon & Schuster Children's Publishing Division*

1230 Avenue of the Americas, New York, NY 10020
tel +1 212-698-7200
website www.simonandschuster.com/kids
President & Publisher Jon Anderson

Preschool to YA, fiction and non-fiction, trade, library and mass market. Imprints: Aladdin Paperbacks, Atheneum Books for Young Readers, Beach Lane Books, Little Simon, Margaret K. McElderry Books, Salaam Reads, Simon & Schuster Books for Young Readers, Simon Pulse, Simon Spotlight, Paula Wiseman Books. Division of Simon & Schuster, Inc. Founded 1924.

Simon & Schuster, Inc.*

1230 Avenue of the Americas, New York, NY 10020
tel +1 212-698-7000
website www.simonandschuster.com
President & Publisher Jonathan Karp, *Vice-President & Associate Publisher* Irene Kheradi

General fiction and non-fiction. No unsolicited MSS. Imprints: 37 Ink, Adams Media, Aladdin, Atria Books, Atheneum Books for Young Readers, Avid Reader Press, Beach Lane Books, Beyond Words, Caitlyn Dlouhy Books, Denene Millner Books, Emily Bestler Books, Folger Shakespeare Library, Free Press, Gallery Books, Gallery 13, Howard Books, Jeter Publishing, Little Simon, Marble Arch Press, Margaret K. McElderry, Paula Wiseman Books, Pocket Books, Pocket Star, Saga Press, Salaam Reads, Scout Press, Scribner, Signal Press, Simon & Schuster, Simon & Schuster Books for Young Readers, Simon Pulse, Simon Spotlight, Skybound Books, Star Trek®, Strebor Books, Threshold Editions, Tiller Press, Washington Square Press. Founded 1924.

Skyhorse Publishing

307 West 36th Street, 11th Floor, New York, NY 10018
tel +1 212-643-6816
website www.skyhorsepublishing.com
Facebook www.facebook.com/SkyhorsePublishing
Twitter @skyhorsepub
Instagram @skyhorsepub

Publishes outdoor sports, adventure, team sports, nature and country living, with a good dose of politics, true crime, history and military history, reference and humour (practical, literary and general trade). Imprints include: Sky Pony Press, Sports Publishing, Allworth Press and Arcade Publishing (page 204). Founded 2006.

Soho Press, Inc.

853 Broadway, New York, NY 10003
tel +1 212-260-1900
email soho@sohopress.com
website www.sohopress.com
Facebook www.facebook.com/SohoPress
Twitter @soho_press
Publisher Bronwen Hruska

Literary fiction, commercial fiction, mystery, memoir. Imprints: Soho Crime, Soho Press, Soho Teen. Founded 1986.

Sourcebooks, Inc.

PO Box, 4410, Naperville, IL 60567-4410
website www.sourcebooks.com
Editorial Director Todd Stocke

A leading independent publisher in a wide variety of genres including fiction, romance, children's, YA, gift/calendars and college-bound. E-commerce businesses include *Put Me In the Story*, the number one personalised books platform. Imprints include:

Cumberland House, Dawn Publications, Little Pickle Press, Poison Pen Press, Simple Truths, Sourcebooks, Sourcebooks Casablanca, Sourcebooks Fire, Sourcebooks Kids, Sourcebooks Landmarks. Founded 1987.

Sourcebooks

Publishes narrative history, science, memoirs, study aids, self-help and personal development, and topics of particular interest to women, as well as practical and prescriptive books that help readers improve their lives under our trade imprint.

Sourcebooks Casablanca

Publishes six to eight romance novels per month: contemporary, paranormal, romantic suspense and historical romance.

Sourcebooks Fire

Aims to publish books with authentic teen voices that create and validate the teen experience in all of its diversity. Bridging both the commercial and literary, publishes across genres, and is known for books that teens want to recommend to their friends.

Sourcebooks Kids

Publishes notable fiction and non-fiction projects including board books, picture books, chapter books and middle-grade works with the hope of engaging children in the pure fun of books and the wonder of learning new things.

Sourcebooks Landmarks

Publishes contemporary women's and feel-good fiction, historical fiction, speculative crossover and mysteries, thrillers and suspense – all perfect for the book club audience.

Stanford University Press*

485 Broadway, First Floor, Redwood City, CA 94063-8460
tel +1 650-723-9434
email information@www.sup.org
website www.sup.org
Facebook www.facebook.com/stanforduniversitypress
Twitter @stanfordpress

Scholarly (humanities and social sciences), professional (business, law, economics and management science), high-level textbooks. Founded 1893.

Tachyon Publications

1459 18th Street, #139, San Francisco CA 94107
tel +1 415-285-5615
email Tachyon@tachyonpublications.com
website https://tachyonpublications.com/
Facebook www.facebook.com/Tachyon-Publications
Twitter @TachyonPub
Publisher Jacob Weisman

A publisher of smart sci-fi, fantasy and horror, as well as occasional mysteries, memoirs, YA and literary fiction. Founded 1995.

Ten Speed Press*

1745 Broadway, 10th Floor, New York, NY 10019
tel +1 510-559-1600
website https://crownpublishing.com/archives/imprint/ten-speed-press
Publisher David Drake

Career/business, cooking, practical non-fiction, health, women's interest, self-help, children's. Imprints include Watson-Guptill, publisher of art, design, and photography titles, and Lorena Jones Books, publisher of cooking and lifestyle titles. *PUNCH*, the James Beard Award-winning online magazine about wine, spirits, beer, and cocktails, is published in collaboration with Ten Speed Press. Imprint of the Crown Publishing Group (page 207). Founded 1971.

University of Tennessee Press

110 Conference Center Building, Knoxville, TN 37996
tel +1 865-974-3321
website www.utpress.org
Twitter @utennpress
Director Scot Danforth

American studies: African American studies, Appalachian studies, history, religion, literature, historical archaeology, folklore, vernacular architecture, material culture. Founded 1940.

University of Texas Press*

3001 Lake Austin Blvd, 2,200 Stop E4800, Austin, TX 78703–4206
tel +1 800-252-3206
email info@utpress.utexas.edu
website https://utpress.utexas.edu/
Facebook www.facebook.com/utexaspress
Twitter @utexaspress
Editor-in-Chief Casey Kittrell

A book and journal publisher – a focal point where the life experiences, insights and specialised knowledge of writers converge to be disseminated in both print and digital format. Founded 1950.

Tor Books

120 Broadway, 22nd Floor, New York, NY 10271
tel +1 212-388-0100
email enquiries@tor.com
website www.torforgeblog.com
Facebook www.facebook.com/torbooks
Twitter @torbooks

Fiction: general, historical, western, suspense, mystery, horror, sci-fi, fantasy, humour, juvenile, classics (English language); non-fiction: adult and juvenile. Imprints: Tor, Forge. Founded 1980.

Forge

Publishes general fiction, both contemporary and historical; thrillers, mysteries and suspense novels; Westerns and Americana; military fiction and non-fiction.

Tor

Sci-fi and fantasy published in hardback and paperback.

Tupelo Press

PO Box 1767 North Adams, MA 01247
tel +1 413-664-9611
email contact@tupelopress.org
website www.tupelopress.org
Facebook www.facebook.com/tupelopress
Twitter @tupelopress
Publisher & Artistic Director Jeffrey Levine

Publishes novels, literary fiction, poetry and creative non-fiction. Founded 1999.

Tuttle Publishing/Periplus Editions

Airport Business Park, 364 Innovation Drive, North Clarendon, VT 05759
tel +1 802-773-8930
email info@tuttlepublishing.com
website www.tuttlepublishing.com
Facebook www.facebook.com/tuttlebooks
Twitter @tuttlebooks

Asian art, culture, cooking, gardening, Eastern philosophy, martial arts, health. Founded 1948.

Unnamed Press

email info@unnamedpress.com
website www.unnamedpress.com
Facebook www.facebook.com/theunnamedpress
Twitter @unnamedpress
Co-founders C.P. Heiser, Olivia Taylor Smith

A leading independent publisher of fiction and non-fiction, based in Los Angeles. Publishes a diverse list of voices that challenge conventional perspectives while appealing to a broad general audience. Puts an emphasis on debuts by women, under-represented voices and people of colour, as well as internationally focused speculative fiction and fantasy. Aims to nurture emerging talent and partner with more established authors to help their platform grow. Founded 2014.

Viking Press – see Penguin Publishing Group

Walker Books US

99 Dover Street, Somerville, MA 02144
tel +1 617-661-3330
website www.walkerbooksus.com,
www.candlewick.com
Facebook www.facebook.com/CandlewickPressBooks
Directors Susan Van Metre (editorial), Maria Middleton (art)

Walker Books US is a division of Candlewick Press. Founded 2017.

University of Washington Press

4333 Brooklyn Avenue NE, Seattle, WA 98105
Postal address Box 359570, Seattle, WA 98195-9570
tel +1 206-543-4050
website https://uwapress.uw.edu/
Editorial Director Larin McLaughlin

American studies; anthropology; art history and visual culture; Asian American studies; Asian studies; critical ethnic studies; environmental history; Native American and Indigenous studies; nature and environment; women's, gender, and sexuality studies; and Western and Pacific Northwest history. Also publishes a broad range of books about the Pacific Northwest for general readers, often in partnership with regional museums, cultural organisations, and local tribes. Founded 1920.

WaterBrook Multnomah Publishing Group*

10807 New Allegiance Drive, Suite 500, Colorado Springs, CO 80921
tel +1 719-590-4999
email info@waterbrookmultnomah.com
website www.waterbrookmultnomah.com
Facebook www.facebook.com/WaterBrookMultnomah
Twitter @WaterBrookPress

Fiction and non-fiction with a Christian perspective. No unsolicited MSS. Subsidiary of Penguin Random House (page 214). Founded 1996.

John Wiley & Sons, Inc.*

111 River Street, Hoboken, NJ 07030
tel +1 201-748-6000
email info@wiley.com
website www.wiley.com
President & Ceo Brian A. Napack

Specialises in scientific, technical, medical and scholarly journals; encyclopedias, books and online products and services; professional/trade books, subscription products, training materials and online applications and websites; and educational materials for undergraduate and graduate students and lifelong learners. Founded 1807.

Workman Publishing Company*

225 Varick Street, New York, NY 10014
tel +1 212-254-5900
email info@workman.com
website www.workman.com
Facebook www.facebook.com/workmanpublishing
Twitter @workmanpub
Publisher & Editorial Director Susan Bolotin

General non-fiction for adults and children. Calendars. Owned by Hachette Book Group (page 209). Founded 1968.

Books

Writer's Digest Books

1745 Broadway New York, NY 10019
tel +1 212-782-9000
website www.writersdigest.com/wd-books

Market directories, books and magazine for writers, photographers and songwriters. Imprint of Penguin Random House (page 214). Founded 1920.

Yale University Press*

PO Box 209040, New Haven, CT 06520-9040
tel +1 203-432-0960

UK office 47 Bedford Square, London WC1B 3DP
website www.yale.edu/yup

Scholarly, trade books and art books. Founded 1908.

Yen Press

150 W 30th Street, 19th floor, New York 10001
email yenpress@hbgusa.com
website www.yenpress.com
Facebook www.facebook.com/yenpress
Twitter @yenpress

Graphic novels and manga in all formats for all ages. Founded 2006.

Audio providers and distributors

Below are a list of suppliers who support the production of audiobooks for download and streaming. Where publishers have their own audio imprints, these are listed in their entries in the book publishers section, starting on page 124.

Audible
email partners-uk@audible.co.uk
website www.audible.co.uk
Twitter @audibleuk

Producer and seller of digital audio entertainment, including fiction and non-fiction audiobooks for adults and children. Publishers interested in exploring business opportunities with Audible may email the address above, or find out more about turning print books into audiobooks at www.acx.com. Founded 1995; acquired by Amazon 2008.

Audio Factory
Unit 8, High Jarmany Rural Workshops, Barton Saint David, Somerset TA11 6DA
email contact@audiofactory.co.uk
website www.audiofactory.co.uk
Facebook www.facebook.com/audiofactoryuk
Co-founders Dave Perry, Arran Dutton

Audiobook production company. Recommends narrators based on an author's brief, followed by an audition process at the end of which the author makes the final decision. Studio recording takes place over multiple sessions and is guided by a detailed plan created by producers with guidance and feedback from the author. The audiobook goes through editing, mixing, mastering and proofing before being delivered to the author or their chosen distributor.

Audiobook Creation Exchange (ACX)
email support-uk@acx.com
website www.acx.com/help/audiobook-publishers/200679720
Facebook www.facebook.com/goacx
Twitter @acx_com

Authors are invited to create a profile for their book, including a synopsis and a brief sample. If authors choose not to narrate for themselves, interested narrators will submit an audition tape reading from the sample; authors can then make an offer to their preferred narrator. Once the full audiobook is completed, ACX will distribute on the author's behalf to Audible, Amazon and iTunes and return monthly payments and sales reports. ACX take a percentage of earnings and narrators can be compensated either through a one-off payment or through a share of royalties.

Audiobooks.com
email acquisitions@audiobooks.com
website www.audiobooks.com
Facebook www.facebook.com/audiobookscom
Twitter @audiobooks_com

Subscription audiobook service, offering a wide range of fiction and non-fiction genres, as well as some children's titles. Publishers interested in having their titles included in the company's library may get in touch via the email address above.

Author's Republic
email info@authorsrepublic.com
website https://authorsrepublic.com, https://authorsrepublic.com/creation
Facebook www.facebook.com/authorsrepublic
Twitter @AuthorsRepublic

Global operation. Accepts completed audiobooks which are then submitted on the author's behalf to over 30 audiobook retailers, including Audible and iTunes. Does not assist with the production process, but offers hints and tips about how to create an audiobook (see above) and the quality of all submissions is tested before they are shared. All income from these retailers is combined into one monthly payment which is delivered alongside a sales report showing how many audiobooks an author is selling and where. Services cost a percentage of all audiobook profits.

BookBeat
email info@bookbeat.com
website www.bookbeat.com/uk
Twitter @BookBeatUK
Instagram @bookbeat

Digital streaming service for adult and children's audiobooks across a variety of fiction and non-fiction genres. Monthly subscription model (from £5.99). Owned by Bonnier. Founded 2017.

Creative Content Ltd
5th Floor, Watson House, 54–60 Baker Street, London W1U 7BU
tel 07771 766838
email ali@creativecontentdigital.com
website www.creativecontentdigital.com
Twitter @CCTheLowdown
Publisher Ali Muirden, *Editorial Director* Lorelei King

Publishes audio digital downloads, ebooks and print-on-demand books in the business, language improvement, self-improvement, lifestyle, crime fiction, classic fiction, sci-fi, short stories and YA genres. Founded 2008.

W.F. Howes Ltd

Unit 5, St George's House, Rearsby Business Park, Gaddesby Lane, Rearsby, Leicester LE7 4YH
tel (01664) 423000
email info@wfhowes.co.uk
website www.wfhowes.co.uk

Audiobook and large-print publisher, distributing its content through consumer and library vendors. Catalogue includes over 6,500 titles, including authors such as Danielle Steel, Val McDermid, Dan Jones, V.E. Schwab, Mark Dawson, Julia Quinn and Nicci French. UK subsidiary of RBmedia. Founded 1999.

Isis Audio

14 King's Meadow, Ferry Hinksey Road, Oxford OX2 0DP
email thereadinghouse@firstygroup.com
website https://thereadinghouse.co.uk
Facebook www.facebook.com/Isis.Soundings
Twitter @Isisaudio
Instagram @isisaudio

Complete and unabridged audiobooks: fiction, non-fiction, autobiography, biography, crime, thrillers, family sagas, mysteries, romances.

Kobo

website www.kobo.com/gb/en
Twitter @kobo

Audiobook streaming service, for a monthly fee. Offers fiction, non-fiction, adult, children's and YA titles.

Media Music Now

email support@mediamusicnow.com
website www.mediamusicnow.co.uk

Facebook www.facebook.com/mediamusicnow
Twitter @MusicMediaNow
Co-founders Lee Pritchard, Adam Barber

Audio production company. Supplies royalty-free music and sound effects as well as voice-overs and narration. For the latter, authors submit a brief indicating their preferred choice of narrator from a catalogue. Once a narrator has accepted, production will begin, with the author being given the opportunity to review and make edits to a completed proof copy. If authors have already recorded an audiobook, Media Music Now can edit and/or polish it as required. Completed audiobooks are returned to authors, who are responsible for organising distribution. Founded 2005.

Naxos AudioBooks

5 Wyllyotts Place, Potters Bar, Herts. EN6 2JD
tel (01707) 653326
email info@naxosaudiobooks.com
website www.naxosaudiobooks.com
Twitter @NaxosAudioBooks
Managing Director Anthony Anderson

Recordings of classic literature, modern fiction, non-fiction, drama and poetry. Founded 1994.

Sounded.com

Second Floor, 18–20 North Quay, Douglas, Isle of Man IM1 4LE
email info@sounded.com
website www.sounded.com
Twitter @sounded.com

Online audiobook production platform designed for both authors and publishers to use. Offers narration in over 50 languages, with more than 30,000 audiobooks, listed on its own audiobook store. Fully customisable with over 800 available narrators. Prices start at less than £100.

Book packagers

Many illustrated and reference books are created by book packagers for mainstream publishers. They often have particular skills in book design and graphic content. In-house desk editors and art editors match up the expertise of specialist writers, artists and photographers, who are usually freelance.

Aladdin Books Ltd

PO Box 53987, London SW15 2SF
tel 020-3174 3090
email sales@aladdinbooks.co.uk
website https://simonandschusterpublishing.com/aladdin/
Editorial Director Kirstin Gilson

Full design and book packaging facility specialising in children's non-fiction and reference. Part of Simon & Schuster (page 180). Founded 1980.

Nicola Baxter

16 Cathedral Street, Norwich NR1 1LX
tel (01603) 766585 / 07778 285555
email nb@nicolabaxter.co.uk
website www.nicolabaxter.co.uk
Director Nicola Baxter

Full packaging service for children's books in both traditional and digital formats. Happy to take projects from concept to finished work or supply bespoke authorial, editorial, design, project management or commissioning services. Produces both fiction and non-fiction titles in a wide range of formats, for babies to YA, and experienced in novelty books and licensed publishing. Founded 1990.

Brown Bear Books Ltd

Unit 1/D, Leroy House, 436 Essex Road, London N1 3QP
tel 020-3176 8603
website www.windmillbooks.co.uk
Children's Publisher Anne O'Daly

Specialises in high-quality illustrated reference books and multi-volume sets for trade and educational markets. Opportunities for freelancers. Imprint of Windmill Books (page 224). Founded 1967.

Canopus Publishing Ltd

8 Foxcombe Road, Bath BA1 3ED
tel 07970 153217
email robin@canopusbooks.com
website www.canopusbooks.com
Twitter @robin_rees
Directors Robin Rees, Sarah Tremlett

Packager of books on astronomy, aerospace, photography and rock music; publisher for the London Stereoscopic Company and Starmus. Founded 1999.

Diagram Visual Information Ltd

10 Athol Road, Sunderland SR2 8LW
tel 07841 043307
email info@diagramgroup.com
website www.diagramgroup.com
Director Jane Johnson

Research, writing, design and illustration of reference books, supplied as disks. Founded 1967.

Elwin Street Productions Ltd

10 Elwin Street, London E2 7BU
tel 020-7033 6706
email silvia@elwinstreet.com
website www.elwinstreet.com
website www.modern-books.com
Director Silvia Langford, *Operations Manager* Claire Anouchian

Trade imprint: Modern Books. Upmarket illustrated co-edition publisher of adult non-fiction: reference, visual arts, popular culture and science, lifestyle, food, health and nutrition, parenting, gift. Founded 2001.

Global Blended Learning Ltd

Singleton Court, Wonastow Road, Monmouth NP25 5JA
tel (01993) 706273
email hello@globalblendedlearning.com
website www.globalblendedlearning.com

Primary, secondary academic education (geography, science, modern languages) and co-editions (travel guides, gardening, cookery). Multimedia (CD-Rom programming and animations). Opportunities for freelancers. Founded 1985.

Graham-Cameron Publishing & Illustration

59 Hertford Road, Brighton BN1 7GG
tel (01273) 385890
email enquiry@gciforillustration.com
Alternative address The Art House, Uplands Park, Sheringham, Norfolk NR26 8NE
tel (01263) 821333
website www.gciforillustration.com
Partners Helen Graham-Cameron, Duncan Graham-Cameron

Educational and children's books; information publications; sponsored publications. Illustration agency with 37 artists. Do not send unsolicited MSS. Founded 1985.

Books

Heart of Albion

Syringa Cottage, Chapel Street, Orston,
Nottingham NG13 9NL
tel (01949) 850631
email albion@indigogroup.co.uk
website www.hoap.co.uk
Director Bob Trubshaw

Publishes folklore, mythology, cultural studies and local history. Founded 1989.

Ivy Press Ltd

18 Circus Steet, Brighton BN2 9QF
tel 020-77006 700
email ivypress@quarto.com
Twitter @QuartoExplores
Group Publisher Richard Green

Publishers of illustrated trade books on art, science, popular culture, design, children's non-fiction, natural history and conscious living. Opportunities for authors and freelancers. Part of the Quarto Group (page 175). Founded 1996.

Little People Books

The Home of BookBod, Knighton,
Radnorshire LD7 1UP
tel (01547) 520925
email littlepeoplebooks@thehobb.tv
website www.littlepeoplebooks.co.uk
Directors Grant Jessé (production & managing)

Packager of audio, children's educational and textbooks, digital publications. Parent company: Grant Jessé UK.

Market House Books Ltd

Kedua, Oving Road, Whitchurch, Aylesbury,
Bucks. HP22 4ER
tel (01296) 484911
email books@mhbref.com
website www.markethousebooks.com
Twitter @markethousebook
Directors Jonathan Law (editorial), Anne Kerr (production)

Book packagers with experience in producing reference books from small pocket dictionaries to large multi-volume colour encyclopedias and from specialist academic reference books to popular books for crossword enthusiasts. Deals with publishers worldwide. Services offered include: start-to-finish

project management; commissioning of writers and editors; writing and rewriting; editing and copy-editing; proofreading; checking of final pages; keyboarding; typesetting; page design and make-up; text conversion; data manipulation; database management. Founded 1970.

Orpheus Books Ltd

2 Hewlett Place, Cheltenham, Glos. GL52 6DQ
tel (01993) 774949
email info@orpheusbooks.com
website www.orpheusbooks.com, www.Q-files.com
Executive Directors Nicholas Harris, Sarah Hartley

Children's illustrated non-fiction/reference books and ebooks. Orpheus Books are the creators of Q-files.com, the online educational resource for schools and libraries. Founded 1993.

Toucan Books Ltd

128 Aldersgate Street, Suite 106, London EC1A 4AE
tel 020-7250 3388
website www.toucanbooks.co.uk

International co-editions; editorial, design and production services. Founded 1985.

Windmill Books Ltd

Unit 1/D, Leroy House, 436 Essex Road,
London N1 3QP
tel 020-3176 8603
website www.windmillbooks.co.uk
Children's Publisher Anne O'Daly

Publisher and packager of books and partworks for trade, promotional and international publishers. Opportunities for freelancers. Imprint: Brown Bear Books Ltd (page 223). Founded 2009.

Working Partners Ltd

9 Kingsway, 4th Floor, London WC2B 6XF
tel 020-7841 3939
email enquiries@workingpartnersltd.co.uk
website www.coolabi.com/books
Managing Director Chris Snowdon

Part of the Coolabi Group. Creators of children's and YA fiction. Genres include: animal fiction, fantasy, horror, historical, detective, magical, adventure. Unable to accept any submissions. Pays advance and royalty; retains copyright on all works. Selects writers based on specific brief. Founded 1995.

Becoming a bestselling author: my writing story

Peter James shares his first-hand experience of the ups and downs, false starts and challenges a writer may face along the route to success, and the value of passion and persistence – and chance moments of opportunity.

I am so pleased to have been invited to write this piece for the *Writers' & Artists' Yearbook*, not only because it was the first place I turned to when I finished my first novel in 1967, but also because I want to share with all of you all to know that a successful writing career does not come overnight. Mine had many detours but I always kept my destination in mind.

I often get asked why I became a writer. I always wanted to be one, right from the age of seven, but I had very little self-confidence and never believed I would ever actually succeed. I kept a notebook by my bed and used to write my thoughts and ideas into it. I remember the very first entry, a great pearl of wisdom: 'Life is a bowl of custard – it's all right until you fall in.' When I went to my boarding school, Charterhouse, I had one English teacher, David Summerscale, who believed in me and encouraged me. He went on to become headmaster of Westminster School and we are still in touch today. At 15 I won a school poetry prize and then at 17 I won a BBC short story competition, and these both gave my confidence a boost – but I was still a troubled, uncertain kid. My housemaster, Ted Hartwell, turned out to be absolutely bang on prophetic in his leaving report for me: 'Enigmatic and unpredictable, a literary career seems inevitable, but there may be some false starts.'

I guess it really started when my dad bought me a portable electric typewriter for my 17th birthday, along with a real battle-axe of a typing tutor, who would put sticky tabs on the keys to make them unreadable and then rap my fingers with a ruler if I looked down! I learned to touch-type within days and it has stood me in good stead ever since. Eighteen months later I set to work writing my first novel, *Ride Down A Rollercoaster*, in a garage converted into a bedsit on the Fulham Road, and when I finished I went straight out and bought *Writers' & Artists' Yearbook* so that I could send my manuscript off to literary agents. The replies I received said it was 'too American' and, instead of letting that deter me, I referred to the American section of the *Yearbook* and started sending copies to the States. After mailing countless letters, I finally received a reply from Kurt Helmer, a New York literary agent who said I showed 'real promise' and encouraged me to re-work the book and send him another draft. However, in the arrogance of youth, I insisted the second novel that I had written in the meantime, a zany sci-fi comedy, was much better. He didn't agree and asked me to return to the first book. Instead, now 21, I wrote a third. Again, he told me to go back to the first book, and again I ignored him.

During this time, I had been attending Ravensbourne Film School, after trying to get into Oxford. Although I got in on my second attempt, I turned down Oxford's offer as the idea of telling stories through film had got under my skin. However, after graduation from Ravensbourne I realised how hard it is to get your first job in film without having a contact on the inside. Nor had I managed to publish a novel yet. On the advice of my Canadian uncle, I moved to Canada and got my first job in television as a gofer on a children's show called *Polka Dot Door*. Through a twist of fate, I had the chance to write an episode and, following the success of that first episode, was asked to take on the writing three days a week. I sent a letter to Kurt Helmer, my literary agent, sharing my excitement. He replied, 'You a**hole, never do both. Don't have a job writing in the day and expect to write a novel in the night.' He told me the only way I'd ever write a good novel was if I got a job in a factory and wrote after work. This proved to have been very good advice, after I went on to work on a 'movie-gone-wrong' in Spain called *Spanish Fly* (that I had had to help finance on my own credit card during production) starring Terry-Thomas and Lesley Philips. It was described by the eminent critic Barry Norman as 'the worst British film since the Second World War and the least funny British funny film ever made'. So I joined the family business and started working in the factory of Cornelia James Glovemakers by day and writing at night. I decided to write a spy novel and wrote my first published book, *Dead Letter Drop* (W.H. Allen 1981). I would love to say this was a shining start to my career as a published author, but it was, as my teacher had predicted, a false start. *Dead Letter Drop* sold around 1,800 copies and 1,500 of those were to libraries. I remember a particularly bad press interview where the journalist asked me how I had found Namibia, a location in my second published novel, and I couldn't answer … because I had never been. I vowed then to never write about something I had not fully researched and experienced. This was reinforced by a chance meeting with the author Elizabeth Buchan who told me, 'You'll never be successful writing something you're not passionate about and can't research.' This was a real turning point for me in terms of how I approached my writing.

An unexpected lucky break came when my former wife and I were burgled after moving into a house in Brighton. Sussex Police arrived to take my statement and eagle-eyed detective, Mike Harris, noticed my books. He said that if I ever needed help with research I should let him know. This was the beginning of my long-term relationship with Sussex Police. Ever since, after years of earning their trust, I have been privileged to join officers on shifts, to go out in response and traffic patrol cars, attend raids, and some crime scenes, as well as social events and I have been able to talk to officers about their experiences. I am regularly reminded of the breadth of life a police officer sees over their career, and the extraordinary situations they experience. I have been told many times over the years that I have 'become part of the furniture' in the station! So, at this point, I knew I needed to write a crime novel, but my protagonist still eluded me. It would be a few more years before I would meet the man who would inspire Roy Grace.

Writing from what I knew and what I was passionate about took a surprisingly supernatural turn after the death of the son of good friends in a car accident, soon after the death my own father. My friends consulted a medium to try and make contact with their son, and this gave me an idea: how the intense love between a mother and her son might continue, but with dangerous consequences, from beyond the grave. The result was my supernatural thriller, *Possession* (Gollancz 1988), and for the first time I experienced a bidding war, with every major publisher in the UK vying for it. I had started to be called 'Britain's answer to Stephen King' in the press and I was encouraged by my publisher to write further horror books. But this would once again prove to be a false start, as the sales of horror books started a sharp decline in the 1990s.

Knowing I was keen to meet police officers with an interesting story to tell, my friends at Sussex Police invited me down to the station to chat with a young Detective Inspector called Dave Gaylor. I walked into his office and was surprised to see there were plastic crates all over the floor, piled with documents. When I asked if he was moving Dave explained that, in addition to being an active homicide investigator, he was also in charge of reviewing all the county's unsolved murders where there was still a perpetrator at large or someone alive who could benefit from a successful conclusion: 'I'm the last chance the victims have for justice, and I'm the last chance the families have for closure.' In talking to Dave I realised that he had the rare qualities that make a truly great homicide detective – that is to be calm, to have a high degree of emotional intelligence and empathy, and to be highly methodical yet, at the same time, open to creative, blue-sky thinking. Over the next few years, I switched from supernatural to psychological thrillers, putting policing more and more into my novels.

In 2002 Dave was promoted to Detective Chief Superintendent, and effectively became head of major crime for Sussex Police. My publishers, Pan Macmillan, approached me just and asked if I'd ever thought of creating a fictional detective as my central character. I went straight to Dave and asked him, 'Would you like to be a fictional cop?'. He loved the idea! Dave, my notebook and I spent many nights in Brighton pubs talking in detail about his life and police procedure. From this, we then worked out the plot of *Dead Simple* (Pan Macmillan 2005) together, with Dave ensuring that I was absolutely correct in my research. We've worked closely on every Roy Grace novel since and we've become great friends, with Dave being best man when my wife Lara and I married. Dave reads all my manuscripts to make sure they are entirely accurate in how I portray the way the police would approach a case. This was when I finally, and thankfully, got my writing career on the trajectory I had been hoping for. My first Roy Grace novel was published in 2005, my 18th Roy Grace novel, *Picture You Dead*, came out in September 2022, and a smash hit ITV series, *Grace*, with John Simm playing Detective Superintendent Roy Grace, first aired in 2021. In addition, there have now been five highly successful Roy Grace stage plays, the most recent, *Wish You Were Dead*.

The most important lesson I can offer – and I hope that this has come across – is never to give up. If you believe you have a story to tell, keep going. Even when I was published for the first time, it was not the end of my struggles; in fact, it was still the beginning. Another lesson that I learned the hard way is that research is paramount and frequently bizarre. For example, when a character in *Dead Simple* got buried alive, I asked a funeral parlour to nail me into a coffin so that I could understand the experience and write about it in a convincing way. Too often an author who has spent years working on their writing is called an 'overnight success', and this is hardly ever accurate. Writers are craftspeople and we need to spend time making mistakes and honing our skills. I often liken writing to being a mechanic; the best way to learn is to take things apart and put them back together in your own way. Read and reread the bestselling novels in the genre you want to write, pick apart what makes them great novels, and apply that in your own work.

Good luck, and never let a false start send you off course.

Peter James is an international bestselling author and film producer. His crime thriller series featuring Detective Superintendent Roy Grace has included 19 consecutive *Sunday Times* Number 1 bestsellers (all published by Pan Macmillan) and he has won over 40 awards, including the WHSmith Best Crime Author of All Time Award and the Crime Writers' Association Diamond Dagger. Born in Brighton, he graduated from Ravensbourne Film School, and worked as a film producer and screenwriter for some years before starting to write novels. His first book, *Dead Simple* (W.H. Allen) was published in 1981. His latest book, *Picture You Dead*, was published by Macmillan in September 2022. Peter's Roy Grace novels are now a major ITV series, *Grace*, starring John Simm and Richie Campbell. His website is www.peterjames.com; follow him on Twitter @peterjamesuk.

Books

My rocky road trip to writing success

Sarah Clarke shares the ups and downs of her journey to becoming a published author and has valuable advice on how to give yourself the greatest chance of success as a writer.

As a child I always wanted to be an author, and I showed my propensity for the thriller genre from an embarrassingly young age. My mother still has a rather chilling poem I wrote, aged about ten, about a violent criminal in our local area, and I remember sneaking thrillers – P.D. James, Frederick Forsyth, Dick Francis – off my father's bookshelf when he wasn't looking. My love for the genre has never waned and I think my skills as a thriller writer have largely developed from being a thriller reader for so long.

I started my first novel when I finished university. I remember going to my local bookshop to buy the *Writers' & Artists' Yearbook* and methodically working through it to find the right publishers to submit to (this was before agents became the main route into publishing). But, with both the arrogance and impatience of youth, I sent off my query as soon as I'd finished my first three chapters and, funnily enough, a series of rejections followed. What's even worse is that I didn't learn from my mistake. After repeating the same error with two more books, and getting the same results, I decided to 'give up' novel writing. However, I did develop a career as a copywriter, so I got to practise my craft in a different way.

Fast forward 20 years, and in 2018 my youngest child started secondary school. This gave me more spare time and the perfect opportunity to resurrect my childhood dream. But still, I hesitated – the arrogance had gone and had taken my confidence with it. I knew the odds were heavily stacked against me and getting published felt impossible without any industry contacts or a host of writing prizes under my belt. But then two things happened: an ex-work colleague secured a two-book deal, and a friend's daughter got through multiple auditions to be cast in a West End show. These events made me realise that dreams can come true, but only if you commit to them fully. So I applied and was accepted for the Faber Academy 'Writing a Novel: First 15,000 Words' online course. And, to use the analogy of a journey, Faber Academy (see page 684) taught me how to drive.

Learning to drive

The Faber Academy course required a big-time commitment and high levels of self-motivation – as I imagine all similar courses do. As well as hitting chapter deadlines and completing additional writing tasks, we were expected to review each other's work and provide advice where we could. Luckily, though, it never felt like a chore. The course taught me lots of things within two specific categories: 1) novel-writing skills and 2) industry knowledge. By the time I finished writing my book in June 2019 – which later became my debut novel *A Mother Never Lies* (HQ Digital 2021) – I also had a clear set of instructions on how to navigate my journey, including a heavily edited cover letter and synopsis.

Setting off

As part of the course, I received detailed feedback on my first 15,000 words. My tutor's comments were incredibly positive, my optimism had grown exponentially and I had started to believe my dream might actually come true. I joined Twitter and followed all the right people. I read the *Bookseller* and gleaned information from industry websites. And then I submitted my book to six agents and crossed my fingers .

Hitting traffic

I should have been more prepared for how long the first stage of my journey would take. Agents explain on their websites that a response can take 12 weeks or longer – but I found it impossible to put it out of my mind. I checked my email multiple times a day and daydreamed about a spot on Graham Norton's radio show. The first rejection made me cry. By the third, I'd learned to swear instead. It was later that someone advised me to respond to every rejection by submitting to a new agent, and I now give that advice to anyone who asks. It is both distracting and empowering (it even beats swearing) and, in total, I submitted to 29 agents over eight months.

Navigating road bumps

Two months after I started querying, I received my first full manuscript request. I can still remember reading the email (it had gone into my junk folder, so always check that!) and responding with shaking fingers, my dream feeling so much closer to coming true. Over the following six months, I received a total of six full manuscript requests – including two asking for edits and resubmission – but my manuscript was ultimately rejected by each one. After those rejections, I never quite managed to swap tears for swear-words.

Hailing a cab

One agent asked me to work with a freelance editor to iron out the problems in my manuscript. I wasn't sure, as it would cost me a few hundred pounds and still offered no guarantee of success, but eventually I decided to go for it. And, while the revisions didn't lead directly to representation, I have never regretted having input from a professional editor. We live and breathe our books and it is an impossible task to step far enough away to make fresh or objective observations. And remember, that insight doesn't have to be something you pay for – joining writing groups can provide it too.

Pitstop

As for so many other people around the world, the pandemic turned life upside down for my family, and I chose to put my writing aspirations aside so that I could focus on the day-to-day of our 'new normal'. But when the pandemic appeared to be in retreat in the autumn of 2020 (oh, how wrong we were!) I resumed my journey, with a little help from Sophie Hannah's Dream Author coaching programme (see below).

Turning left (field)

One day in late 2020, I was scrolling through Twitter when I paused on a familiar name. It was my sister-in-law's name, but it also belonged to a publishing professional. I dug a little deeper and found out that she was open to submissions from debut authors. It felt like destiny, and I quickly set about sending her my manuscript. And this is how I stumbled upon digital-first publishing.

Changing course

Initially I was excited purely because digital-first publishers accept manuscripts directly. After lots of failed attempts and oh-so-close misses, being able to circumvent agents felt like a positive step. But, as I learned more, digital-first publishing started to appeal for other reasons too. Although there is no advance, the ebook royalties are generous and, with the ebook being the first format released, the process tends to be quicker than with more traditional publishing (which appealed to my impatient side!). And, while the ebook is also the core focus for marketing activity, the book is released in paperback and audio formats too (usually coming two months after the ebook).

The final climb

I sent my manuscript to three digital-first publishers and in January 2021 I had positive responses from two. One of them was HQ Digital, an imprint of Harper Collins, which I was particularly excited about, but the commissioning editor wanted me to change one fundamental aspect of my story. So I spent the next month editing the manuscript, as well as writing synopses for two new book ideas. When I submitted at the end of February, I did so with my fingers *un*crossed; I had realised by then that luck wasn't the driving force behind these decisions.

Dream destination

Through various writing groups , such as my brilliant Faber Academy alumni group, I had heard the story many times of the author who battled through numerous rejections before finally finding representation and/or a book deal. But I never thought it would happen to me ... how could an agent or publisher possibly like my book if 29 others had not? So I feel like a fraud asking you to believe me now – but I hope that you do, because it does indeed happen. Resilience, tenacity and a confidence in your book and your writing talent are the tools you need for success.

Road trip

When I danced around my kitchen in March 2021, I thought I had arrived; I had been offered a three-book publishing deal with a brilliant publisher. But I soon realised that it was only the start of my journey. While I enjoyed the amazing high of reaching No.39 in the UK Kindle charts and reading reviews that were so lovely they brought tears to my eyes, I was also learning to cope with negative reviews, rollercoaster rankings and trying to write my second book to a tight deadline. But, of course, I wouldn't change it for the world, and I hope this road trip is going to continue for a long while yet.

Tips for submitting to agents

- Record every submission with names, dates and details of whether and when you can chase for a response.
- Research agents fully before submitting and choose 30 possible targets.
- Split these agents into three categories (dream; very good; perfectly acceptable) and send your MS to an even spread of agents in small groups, e.g. six submissions at a time.
- Be grateful for any feedback and give yourself time to consider how best to apply it (remember that agents only provide this if they think your book has potential).
- Treat agent submissions like job interviews. If one is unsuccessful, it is because that agent isn't the right fit for you.

Building a support network

Writing is a very personal experience, and it can be a lonely one, especially if you're dealing with rejections. Having a support network around you is important. As well as friends and family, I use the following support to keep me on track:

- Other authors. Before I was published, I was introduced to a local crime author. She gave me lots of useful advice and made me believe being an author was possible.
- Sophie Hannah's Dream Author coaching programme (https://dreamauthorcoaching.com). I signed up to Sophie's programme to help build my confidence after dozens of rejections and a pandemic. Sophie is an experienced thriller writer with a very positive message, and her programme made a big difference to my mindset.
- Virtual writing community. The Faber Academy alumni group plus Twitter and Facebook writer groups have all helped me feel part of a community with similar fears and hopes.

Sarah Clarke signed her first book deal in March 2021 at the age of 48, after a career as a copywriter, and has since become the bestselling author of three psychological thrillers published by HQ Digital: *A Mother Never Lies* (2021), *Every Little Secret* (2022) and *My Perfect Friend* (2022). Two more thrillers with HQ Digital are coming in 2023 and 2024. Follow Sarah on Twitter @SCWwriter.

See also...

- *Becoming a bestselling author: my writing story*, page 225
- *Becoming a successful copywriter*, page 292
- *Writers' retreats and creative writing courses*, page 683

Keeping the writing dream alive

S.J. Watson proves why no writer should give up on their dream of being published one day.

I'm writing this in late March 2020, sitting not in my office but at a table I've set up in the bay window of my sitting room. From here I have a view of the garden – I can watch the birds as they flit from branch to branch and eventually settle at the feeder outside the window; I can chart the day's progress by the changing light. But the world has changed – suddenly I can move no further than I can see, other than in an emergency or to collect provisions and, even then, I must stay a minimum of two metres from anyone I may meet. A virus is tearing through the population, threatening to overwhelm us, and it must be slowed. Collectively, we're in lockdown.

And so, unable to travel, we temporarily escape our surroundings in other ways. We reach out to our friends on social media and through meet-up apps, checking in, lifting each other up. And we turn to stories – to our books and films, our TV shows and, yes, even our plays, as theatres stream recorded performances direct to our living rooms. Through words we bond, we are entertained and amused, offered ways to escape and expand. Never before has the importance of a shared story been more apparent.

Yet it has always been so. I grew up in the Black Country, an only child, gay. My childhood was far from unhappy, but it felt … limited, confusing. I turned to books at a very early age, visited the local library weekly, taking out and reading my allotted five books without fail. They were my escape, my life raft, and it wasn't long before I began to write stories of my own. Encouraged by teachers, I dreamt of one day seeing a book of mine on a shelf in a library or bookshop, of having the power to transport people as I had been transported. When asked what I wanted to be when I grew up, I replied, 'A writer!' – without hesitation, every time.

It took me a long time (or a long time to be a *published* writer, at least; I've been a writer my whole life, and the distinction is important). Seduced by the idea that I needed a sensible career alongside my writing, I studied physics and eventually worked in the NHS. But the writing was always there. I filled notebooks, I wrote stories and poems and started novels, I pushed forward. I vowed I wouldn't stop as long as my output was improving. My dream never left me.

The publishing side of things, though? That remained a mystery. I hoovered up as much advice as I could, yet much of it was conflicting, and the path to publication remained impossibly opaque. I read somewhere that one needed an agent to be published, then read somewhere else that to get an agent one needed to have been published. 'Win a prize!', they said, 'or no one will even look at your work. Get some short stories into magazines!', though no one told me how, or which magazines.

But then, one day, in a now-vanished bookshop in North London, I lifted down from the shelf an earlier version of the book you're holding now. And my eyes were opened. Here was a guide, a clear way through what had previously been misty and unclear – not only a reference guide that listed agents, publishers and other helpful organisations along with their contact details and preferences, but also a treasure trove of invaluable and inspirational articles and guides covering every stage of the writer's journey. Here, at last, was a beacon that could guide me through the choppy waters ahead. I kept it on hand the whole time and referred to it frequently for information, inspiration or support. And when, in my late thirties and ground down by working in an overstretched health service, I decided it was time my career took a back seat to my writing ambitions, it was *this* book that gave me the courage to drop to part-time at work and really go for it.

A definitive guide, in here you'll find everything you need. It won't write your book for you, quite, but it'll demystify the whole process of getting your book into the hands of readers, however you choose to do that, as well as illuminating the 'business' side of being a writer. There can be few published writers who haven't turned to the *Writers' & Artists' Yearbook* at some stage in their development, and many use it still. All writing is an act of optimism, including this foreword – I hope that, by the time you're reading it, the world will be in a different, better place. But we'll still need stories, perhaps more than ever. We'll always need stories. They make us human. They connect us – across space, across time. The only way to learn to write is by doing it, by practising, over and over … but for every other aspect of the world of publishing, we have this book.

S.J. Watson is the award-winning author of the international bestsellers *Before I Go to Sleep* (Doubleday 2011), winner of the Crime Writers' Association Award for Best Debut Novel and the Galaxy National Book Award for Crime Thriller of the Year, and *Second Life* (Doubleday 2015). He was born in the Midlands and studied physics at Birmingham University, later working as an audiologist in the NHS, before enrolling on the first Faber Academy 'Writing a Novel' course in 2009. He now lives in Brighton. The film adaption of *Before I Go to Sleep*, directed by Rowan Joffe, starring Nicole Kidman and Colin Firth, was released in 2014. S.J. Watson's latest book, *Final Cut*, was published by Transworld in August 2020. Join his newsletter community at sjwatson.substack.com.

Foreword from *Writers' & Arists' Yearbook 2021*

Books

Reading as a writer

Cathy Rentzenbrink shares her life-long passion for reading. She shows how it can open up new worlds and possibilities, providing an invaluable learning resource for aspiring writers as well as pleasure for the reader, and how studying the lives, work and technique of other authors can drive, inform and enhance your own individual practice.

I have always loved reading more than pretty much anything else. It enables exploration and escape, gives consolation and pleasure, and fuels my desire to know the world. I don't remember learning how to do it, so it doesn't feel like a skill I had to acquire, more like a gift bestowed by a benevolent fairy godmother. 'I will make this one a reader,' she said, as she waved her wand over my crib. Perhaps it was this way for you, too, or maybe you came to reading later in life. My dad only learnt to read as an adult, and it strengthens my gratitude for books and reading to know that what is a comfort and joy for me, is not always easy for everyone. So welcome, dear reader, no matter what your journey to this page has been. My mission today is to share with you that, as well as everything else it offers, reading is probably the single best thing you can do in the service of your writing.

If reading was my first love, then writing was hard on its heels. When asked what I wanted to do when I grew up, I would announce that I wanted to be a writer or a detective (the influence of all those Enid Blytons, I'm sure) and would be told not to be silly by my teachers. Luckily my parents were encouraging and I had books where children were always striking out on adventures, solving crimes, and ruling magical kingdoms.

This, perhaps, is the first thing reading can do for us as well as offering entertainment – it opens up alternative realities. If you are struggling to find your tribe, if you are surrounded by people who care less about words and stories than you do, then look for friends in books. As a child I loved Anne Shirley as much as if she existed in my real life and I could visit her at Green Gables. I've never really stopped imagining myself into books in this way and it is a great cure for loneliness. In addition to fiction, I have always loved books about writers – both memoir and biography – and I see now that I was looking for clues as to how writing could be done. I was looking for the granular details: what time someone got up; where they wrote; how they earned money; and how they transitioned between the states of aspiration and arrival. When I had a child, I wanted to read about how authors managed their childcare, and when my first book, *The Last Act of Love* (Picador 2015), came out I wanted to read about how they dealt with attention. This is all available to you, dear reader, this mentoring via what writers say about themselves. Consider it all as you forge your own path.

And engage with the process: read a novel and then seek out what the writer says about how they made it. Go to events in bookshops, libraries and festivals (see *Festivals and conferences for writers, artists and readers* on page 593). If you can see authors in the flesh – our scruffy shoes, our bitten nails – the prospect of joining the ranks becomes less intimidating. There is a vast amount of stuff, often free, that you can access online. I have taken huge inspiration over the years from Hilary Mantel; from her books, yes, but also from her Reith Lectures and her interviews with the *Paris Review* and the *Guardian*. This is about chemistry. Maya Angelou, Maggie O'Farrell and Kit de Waal all float my boat, but your search might lead you to a different writer. Experiment. Read around. Find your soulmates. They don't have to know you for a relationship to have a significant impact and influence on your work.

Some writers send me directly to the page. And this doesn't seem to have anything to do with the subject. When I read Maggie Nelson or Elena Ferrante then I yearn to wield my own pen. One of the things that makes me happiest is when people tell me that reading my books has encouraged them in their own practice. I go forth into my day with great joy that someone out there is opening a notebook and sharpening their pencil because of me.

The most useful way to learn about technique, the nuts-and-bolts stuff, is to look at what other writers do. What point of view they have chosen? How do they handle any time shifts? How have they selected the start and end point of their story? When I get stuck on a point like this, I will look for the answer on my bookshelves. If I'm struggling with handling the dialogue when there are lots of characters present, then I'll search out dinner party scenes. At the moment I'm considering writing a novel that happens largely in flashback, but when I tried this before I found it too hard. This time I am going to reread *The Secret History* by Donna Tartt, *Rebecca* by Daphne du Maurier and *The Confessions of Frannie Langton* by Sara Collins and carefully study exactly how it is done.

And I'm always on the lookout. I read a book for pleasure first, racing through, and then, if it fits the bill, I go back and read it again with forensic attention. How did they do it? How did they capture and then hold my attention? How did they make me care so much about that really quite unpleasant character? As well as doing this with a brilliant book, it can be useful to do it when a book has fallen short. Where did the author lose your interest? Where did the pace drop? What didn't quite ring true? If you were this book's editor, what would you suggest to make it better? Would it be less confusing if there were fewer characters? Does that relentless present tense get on your nerves? Is there too much back story? If so, how could you fix this?

A word of caution, though. Don't compare your work in progress with a finished book – that's like watching the Oscars from the sofa in your pyjamas and berating yourself for not being red-carpet-ready. If a book is good, and the author has done their job; it will read as though they sat down one day and it just flowed out in the time it takes you to read it. That is the magic trick of literature; we all sign up to suspend disbelief and allow the wizard to wave their wand – but, if you are going to write as well as read, you need to know just how much work is involved in that sleight of hand. A finished book has almost always involved gargantuan effort, sometimes years of wailing and gnashing of teeth and pulling out of hair and endless drafts, and then finally – finally – the writer got an agent who made suggestions, and an editor who worked on several drafts, and then a copy-editor and a proofreader made the manuscript the best version of itself it could be. I didn't always know this – I would allow myself to be swamped with despair and I'd down tools because I didn't see how I could ever measure up. Eventually I realised how futile it is to brood on the knowledge that I will never be as good as Julian Barnes or Bernardine Evaristo. How pointless! I don't want to be trying to sound like them, I want to be putting all my time and energy into trying to sound like *myself*.

When you get deep into your work-in-progress you might want to be careful about exposing yourself to new ideas. I do press pause on certain things every so often. When I was finishing my novel *Everyone is Still Alive* (Phoenix 2021) I stopped reading new fiction and confined myself to memoirs or rereading Agatha Christie and Georgette Heyer. Then, when the novel was safely dispatched to my editor, I went on a fiction binge to make up for lost time. Another tip is an occasional week or two of complete deprivation. If you can make your manuscript the most interesting thing in your life, if you have no other sources of distraction – no email, no Netflix, no books – then you'll have to get all your entertainment from your own words. This isn't terribly compatible with living a 21st-century life, but I find it pays great dividends every so often, especially at the start of a project when the green shoots are tender and need a bit of protection, and when I'm coming towards the end of a draft; at that stage I feel like a juggler with all the colourful balls of my own story up in the air and I'm ready to commit to dedicated concentration as I bring the novel to an end with a flourish. But most of the time I am reading and think you should be too. These days, I have to carve out and protect both writing and reading time so that I am not seduced by the easy, empty pleasure of the internet. I write in the mornings, before I have looked at my email, and then, unless I have an event, I firmly shut down my computer and phone in the evening and give myself up to someone else's book.

So, read. Because it's useful. Because it's pleasurable. Because books are the best that humanity has to offer. Because your life will be enlarged when you spend as much of it as you can engaged in long-form narrative. Because you will feel better than if you toss away your time on the internet. And because you can take it all back to your own work; then one day you will know the joy of having readers of your own, as well as being a reader, and maybe someone will tell you that your book has inspired them to start writing their own and you will fill up with a sense of meaning and purpose that makes it all worthwhile.

Cathy Rentzenbrink is the author of the memoir *The Last Act of Love (2015)*, *How to Feel Better* (2017) and *Dear Reader: The Comfort and Joy of Books* (2020), all published by Picador. *Everyone is Still Alive* (Phoenix 2021) is her first novel. Her latest book is *Write It All Down: How to put your life on the page* (Pan Macmillan 2022). Cathy has worked for the Reading Agency and Waterstones and regularly contributes to the media on all aspects of books and reading. She is President of the Budleigh Salterton Literary Festival. For more information see https://cathyreadsbooks.com. Follow her on Twitter and instagram @catrentzenbrink.

See also...
● *Festival fun: your guide to how, why and what,* page 491

Alphabet alchemy: turning letters into gold

Owen Sheers reflects on the art of turning letters into words, and words into magic.

If you are holding this book, then you already have a writer's relationship with language. It's very likely that you have already experienced, to whatever degree, something of the addictive miracle and failure of trying to capture life in words. A miracle because, with the same letters of the alphabet with which we order a coffee or fire off a WhatsApp message, you have created something unique, something that has never existed before in the history of the universe – a new poem, article or short story. And a failure because – well, isn't that how we get better? By acknowledging what's worked in our writing, but also by being attuned to what hasn't. By going back to those few letters of the alphabet and trying again.

All of us have our own paths towards this experience: maybe there was a teacher who opened our minds to a certain story, a certain writer; a novel or a poem that transported us, leaving us wanting to know just how that magic happened; a film or a play that left you altered, so that you walked out a subtly, and yet also significantly, different person from the one who entered a couple of hours before.

For me, it began with words on the air, not the page ... early memories of my mother singing ballads such as 'William and Dinah' and then, one day in the car, on an anthology tape of Anglo-Welsh poetry, the poet Dannie Abse reading his poem 'In the Theatre'. It wasn't a long poem but, as the best poems can, it took me a vast distance over a short space of speech. By the time Dannie was intoning the words of a brain-surgery patient suddenly awoken mid-surgery – *Leave my soul alone, leave my soul alone* – the poem had very much done the opposite. That most elusive of poetic calibrations – a crafted weighting of music, language, imagery and rhythm – had somehow altered my internal weather and left me wanting not just more, but also to try my own hand at this strange alchemy.

Encouraged by a succession of teachers in my local schools and a clutch of placings or prizes in young people's poetry competitions, I began my own journey into the miracles and failures of writing. One of those competitions, run by an early two-tents-down-by-the-river Hay Festival, offered the prize of a week's residential course at the beautiful Ty Newydd in Llanystumdwy, North Wales. The competition had been for short stories, but the only course I could attend was poetry. One afternoon, sitting in the Ty Newydd garden, one of the tutors, Gladys Mary Coles, scribbled down a list of poetry magazine titles on the back of my poem. 'Start sending your poems out,' she told me. 'See what happens.'

On returning home, when I unpacked I found that list of titles, written in faint pencil: *Envoi, Ambit, PN Review, Poetry Wales*. I'd seen the same titles on the shelves of Ty Newydd; I'd taken some of those magazines off those shelves, opened their pages to read the poems inside, seen the shapes of the black-printed words – each poem, as Glyn Maxwell says, the mark of 'a human presence.' And all of it felt so far away ... so impossible.

But then I remembered a book I'd seen on my mother's desk: bright red with yellow writing – *Writers' & Artists' Yearbook*. I found the book and, inside, saw that the magazines in Gladys Mary's list had editors behind them, people with names and addresses. And so

I wrote to these people, sending them my poems in the way the *Yearbook* had advised me. And I waited … to see what would happen.

Which was, mostly, of course, that my poems were rejected. But nearly always politely and often with advice, suggestions – which is when I realised that the *Yearbook* hadn't just given me a way to find addresses, but also a way to find people who, like me, were in love with language and words and what they could do. The advice and suggestions some of those people gave made my poems better, and eventually some of them were printed – which in turn led me to more people, other editors and other writers, some of whom went on to guide me towards writing my first books. And at that point *Writers' & Artists' Yearbook* proved a vital resource once again – from researching agents to helping me understand the marks of a copy-editor on my manuscript.

This was all over 20 years ago now, and much has changed, of course. The internet offers myriad new ways to be published, or to find new voices and new work. But perhaps that makes a book like *Writers' & Artists' Yearbook* all the more useful, not less. In such a crowded, competitive landscape, a writer starting out on their individual journey needs a trusted map and compass more than ever. And this is what the book you're now holding offers you – a way of navigating your own path into writing, of finding the people behind those companies, web addresses and profiles who will help you on your way. It might be that, at first, these people will write back to you more often about the failures of your writing than about its miracles. But if they do, remember that such advice is no less valuable and, perhaps, even more so.

Owen Sheers is an award-winning novelist, poet and playwright. His books include *The Dust Diaries* (2005), *Resistance* (2008), *I Saw A Man* (2015) and *Pink Mist* (2013), all published by Faber & Faber. His poetry collections include *Skirrid Hill* (Faber & Faber 2005), which won a Somerset Maugham Award. In 2018 Owen was the winner of the Wilfred Owen Prize. His BBC film-poem to mark the 50th anniversary of the Aberfan disaster, *The Green Hollow*, won three BAFTA Cymru awards. His dramatic work include *Mametz* and *The Passion* for National Theatre Wales, and *The Two Worlds of Charlie F.* , winner of the Amnesty International Freedom of Expression Award at the 2021 Edinburgh Festival. A stage version of his verse drama *Pink Mist* was produced by Bristol Old Vic in 2015, and his one-man play *Unicorns, almost*, about the life and poetry of WWII poet Keith Douglas, premiered at the Hay-on-Wye Festival of Literature in 2018. His first children's book *Drew, Moo and Bunny, Too* is published by Walker Books in September 2023. Owen is Professor in Creativity at Swansea University. See his website www.owensheers.co.uk for more information and follow him on Twitter @owensheers.

Real people write books

Samantha Shannon reflects on the unknowable and untraceable mystery of the published author from the perspective of the fledgling writer. She sheds light on what finally allowed her to 'illuminate every dark corner of publishing' and become a bestselling author herself.

Some years ago, I wrote my first story. I believe I was seven or eight years old. From what little I remember of it, it was about a princess who inherited the moon. The reason I know nothing else about this piece of my juvenilia is that I only printed one copy, and I sent that copy to a publishing house (don't do this). I used spotless paper and double-checked that the ink had dried. I stapled the pages together, sealed them in an envelope, and penned the address in my very best handwriting. My grandmother walked me down the street to the postbox and, together, we sent my little story to the only publisher I could recall off the top of my head.

For a long time, I forgot about that story. I have no proof that it existed; it survives as a cobweb in the corner of my memory. Still – for a short time – it was out in the world. I imagine someone heaved a sigh when it arrived as it did, bereft of an agent to represent it or a synopsis to describe it. Perhaps a kind-hearted editor would have sent me a reply, had they known I was a child with a vivid imagination and no idea how publishing worked – but they would have hit a dead end if they'd tried. I had sent no letter to introduce myself, nor included a self-addressed envelope. I'm not confident I even thought to include my name on the cover.

Perhaps it was because I never got an answer that in my young mind a silence grew around publishing. My impression of it was all shadow and clockwork. Perhaps machines created books. Perhaps they grew on trees. Either way, it was clear that little girls like me had no place in the process. I continued to write stories, but I set aside the notion that anyone would ever find them in a bookshop. The author became an abstract concept. I glossed over the names on my favourite books, for they belonged to ethereal beings whose lives were worlds away from mine.

Then a media storm around a certain author brought her name to my attention. People weren't just talking about a book but about its creator – about her life, her dreams, and how she had conjured a universe in a café and on trains. There was fierce interest in her personal story. She was telling marvellous tales, but she was not a clockwork toy, not a shadow. Reading about her reminded me of what I must have always known – that people wrote books. Real people. From then on, I plunged back in to writing ferociously, with a luminous dream: I was going to be an author.

When I was 15, I started a full-length novel. Once it was finished, I decided to try to get it published but found myself with as little knowledge of publishing as I'd possessed when I was a child. All I had gained was a suspicion that there were many more pieces in the jigsaw than one author and one story, and I had no sense of how to fit those pieces together. I turned to the internet, where I found a local freelance editor and paid her all of my saved-up pocket money to look at a few chapters. Countless websites sang to me, promising me they could publish my book if I paid them far more money than I had ever had. I had only a tenuous understanding of what an agent was. In short, I was overwhelmed.

When I found the *Writers' & Artists' Yearbook* it was like striking a match in the dark. After someone mentioned it to me in passing, I got my hands on a copy straight away. With every page I turned, I understood more about the trade that had flummoxed me since I was a child. Soon I was armed with the knowledge I needed to begin my journey.

Writers' & Artists' Yearbook does not come with a guarantee of publication. There is no formula to publishing, no code to crack, no single 'right answer' that will launch your book onto the shelves. I don't think I've ever heard exactly the same publication story twice. All writers are wayfarers, and there are many paths we travel on ... some longer than others. That novel I wrote when I was 15 never saw the light of day. Even though I followed agency guidelines, even though I used the right font and the right line spacing – it was not to be.

You might have a book like that. You might have several. Trying to get someone to see them can sometimes feel like knocking on a door that never opens. But, if there's one thing I can tell you from the other side, it's that each minute you spend writing is worthwhile. Every story whets your craft. Every story hones your ability to see a tale through to its end. I would not have written my debut novel, *The Bone Season* (Bloomsbury 2013), without having first written the one I had to put away.

I got my book deal when I was 20. I've now been in the industry for seven years and have three bestsellers under my belt – yet there are still things I'm only just learning, things that take me by surprise. As with any vocation, getting to grips with being a writer is a lifelong process. But, by opening *Writers' & Artists' Yearbook*, you've taken your first step. This is your toolbox, your skeleton key, and the torch that will illuminate every dark corner of publishing. I wish you all the luck in the world.

Samantha Shannon is the *New York Times* and *Sunday Times* bestselling author of *The Bone Season* series: *The Bone Season* (2013), *The Mime Order* (2015), *The Song Rising* (2017) and *The Mask Falling* (2021), with three more instalments to come. Her first book outside the series was *The Priory of the Orange Tree* (2019), a finalist for the Lambda Literary Awards 2020. Samantha's work has been translated into 26 languages.

Shelf space: a debut writer's journey to claim his place

Femi Kayode looks back at how, mid-career, he turned a creative compulsion into an award-winning reality with his debut novel; he describes the specific sense of purpose that drove him to take that leap, building on previous experience and working through challenges, and explains why crime fiction was his chosen genre.

As I considered how to approach this article, Burna Boy, a Nigerian musician, won the Grammy for his album, *African Giant*. In his acceptance speech, he said something along the lines of: 'Here's to every African. You must know that no matter where you are, you can make it.' For some reason, this well-meaning but erroneous advice (placing a whole continent in the category of marginalised minorities) struck a chord. My debut novel, *Lightseekers* (Bloomsbury 2021), had just been published in a pandemic that prevented the traditional publicity circuit. At home in Windhoek, toasting with my publishers on Zoom, I felt like I was looking in on someone else's life. Even as reviews poured in from all over the English-speaking world and I received my first reader mail from New Zealand, it all seemed to be happening to someone else. Not Femi Kayode, father of two, husband, writer of soaps by night and advertising copywriter by day. 'But you said all this will happen,' my wife reminds me whenever the imposter syndrome takes over. Indeed, I remember.

After writing across mediums for almost three decades, I suffered something I had assumed was beneath me: a crisis of purpose. A lot of my works were the products of workshops, a complex and convoluted production-value chain with outcomes that bear little or no resemblance to my initial creative vision. At 45, I looked back on my life and desired something uniquely mine that I could brandish as a testament to a life of story-telling. I can admit now that I was assailed by a crushing sense of my mortality. I realised that this wish for something wholly my own was in fact worry about my legacy, and with this epiphany of sorts. A compulsive need that overtook every waking moment, spurring me into action.

I catalogued all the reasons why I couldn't write a novel (there were a lot) and all the ones why I should do it anyway. I made friends with published writers, attended writers' festivals in the region where I lived, and applied for every writing workshop I could find on the internet. I had prepared a 500-word short story that I deemed pretty good, but nobody on the selection panels of those workshops agreed. I made the decision not to write for the screen or theatre during this time, convinced that my experience in scriptwriting was impeding my ability to write The Novel. I knew I could tell a compelling story in script form, so if these competitions/workshops were rejecting my story, it had to be because I had not mastered the art of prose. This would prove to be untrue, but I digress. Despite amassing books on writing and endless YouTube tutorials, the words did not tumble out of me with the urgency I expected. Deep inside, I knew I was scared, insecure and in need of a community of peers. I decided to go back to school. It was a decision few understood. I was relatively successful in advertising, I had teenage sons whose education was more a priority and, well, I was old. The guilt I felt about this rather selfish decision was only outweighed by my conviction: I was going to write a novel and it was now or never.

The response to my application to the inaugural MA in Crime fiction at University of East Anglia went to spam and I missed my interview. I contacted the university and was told my application could only be considered in the next year. 'I will be 46, practically close to my grave!', I nearly screamed at the poor Admissions Officer over the phone. Still, I had to wait and, in that time, desperate to occupy my mind with something other than my writing ambition, I enrolled for a postgraduate programme in Futures Studies where I learned to use Systems Thinking as a storytelling tool. Perhaps afraid for my sanity based on our initial interaction, UEA did offer me a place in the Crime Writing programme the next year. I was now at the end of one postgraduate programme while starting another one. The pressure was immense, but from the first day of class at UEA, sitting with a dozen other writers – some already published – I felt a sense of purpose, as though everything I did in the past had led to this place.

'I want to debunk this myth of "African literature",' I said when asked why I was taking the course. While waiting to be accepted into a creative writing programme, I had scoured enough bookshops and attended enough festivals to notice that novels written by writers of African origin (including African Americans!), no matter the genre, were placed in the African Literature category – even the ones marked with little stickers as long/shortlisted for one prize or another. On the shelves that housed the crime authors who had entertained me in my youth – Stephen King, Sidney Sheldon, David Baldacci, – I would search for an indication that the publishing world treated all narratives as equally important, but found none.

Apart from the popularity of the genre, crime fiction is one of the most expansive forms of novel. Perhaps because no one, no class or race, is immune from the cause and effect of crime, the genre lends itself to lateral thinking and allows for the synthesis of a modern world. I wanted to write grand, complex stories with tropes reminiscent of the movies I watched and the books I read while growing up. I wanted to present a world that defied classification, stories that genre-hopped and characters that inhabited an exciting and evolving world, not one 'developing' by the standards of an amorphous rating system. Certainly not one consigned by a reductionist model to 'African literature'. As I sat in class at UEA, the only black student, struggling to make out the accents of my equally ardent classmates, I knew it was important to create a character they could relate to in the same way they did with me. I set about creating a hero with a deliberateness that employed all my experience as a psychologist-turned-advertising-practitioner. I understood the concept of branding, the importance of a consistent narrative that brands need to appeal to their target audience, and I was learning the tropes of crime fiction at one of the best creative writing programmes in the world. I was ready.

From the get-go, I planned a series. Before attending UEA, I had created several TV shows. To pitch a TV series required a sound knowledge of the target audience, the characters' back stories, the main plot arc, the world of the show, and more. I was adept at creating what the industry called 'show bibles', not least because, as an advertising practitioner, I was well versed in the elements of a document like this, and I applied the same principles to the book series I planned to write. Now I needed a story befitting of the pilot episode of such a series.

The story was always there. It was an event which left me horrified at the scale of its inhumanity: the 'necklace killing' of four undergraduates in a university town in South-eastern Nigeria. The many questions this incident raised in my mind made it the perfect case for my protagonist, an investigative psychologist who, despite being Nigerian, had lived most of his life in the States. Then self-doubt appeared abruptly. I started asking myself: who am I writing for? The more I developed the character(s), the more I became concerned that I was becoming alienated from the story. Perhaps I have taken my desire to appeal to a predominantly western audience a bit too far. I was writing through what Toni Morrison referred to as the 'white gaze'. For months, I could not write. Indeed, I *was* ready … but now was stuck. 'Write a love letter to Nigeria,' my tutor advised when I shared my challenge, and snap, everything fell into place. I realised I was apportioning blame, delivering judgment, and meting out my version of justice to victim and perpetrator from the pedestal I placed my protagonist on; my story was rebelling. To move forward, I needed to go beyond empathy to demonstrating love: love for the characters – victim, accused, witness. I had to appreciate that, as soon as the characters became living and breathing beings in *my* story, they came with *their* stories to tell. I had to give them space.

To complement the feedback from my mostly British classmates, I did what any self-respecting advertising practitioner would do – I created a focus group. I reached out to a diverse group of people in different parts of the world with two critical things in common: they were avid readers and they were all Nigerian. Their brief was simple – to tell me how my protagonist made them feel. Are there red flags of disdain and judgment in his tone? Did he come across as standoffish, patronising, warm or caring? Was he sufficiently invested in the case and in the people that the tragedy had affected? Most of all, did he exhibit an ambivalence towards Nigeria that almost every national, both in the country and the diaspora, could relate to?

The completion of the manuscript, graduation and subsequently winning the Little, Brown/UEA Award for Crime Fiction gave me the perfect subject line for my emails to agents: 'Award-winning writer seeks representation'. I got referrals from the university and from the judging panel at Little, Brown. While the award may have inspired prompt feedback from agents, I quickly saw that the genre I was writing in was not consistent with their expectation of what an African should be writing. I used this insight as a benchmark in my search for an agent, never failing to ask that critical question: 'Where do you see my book on the shelves?'

On 1 February 2020 my UK publishers sent me a congratulatory note. *Lightseekers* was reviewed as the Standout Thriller of the Month by the *Independent*. By the end of the first week of publication, *Lightseekers* had made nine Best of the Month Crime Fiction lists in the UK, including *The Times, Sunday Times, Guardian, Observer, Independent, Literary Review, Financial Times, Irish Times* and the *Herald*.

When they spot the novel at bookshops I cannot visit because of the pandemic, friends take pictures of the shelf labels and send them to me. In nearly all cases, it resides in the 'new releases' section, not in New African Writing or World Literature (we need to talk about this category, but not today). My book is placed next to the works of other writers from around the world, both known and unknown, but all storytellers. Just like me.

Burna Boy was right. No matter where you are, you can make it. First, believe. Then, do.

Femi Kayode works in advertising and has written for stage and screen. While studying for an MA in Creative Writing – Crime Fiction at the University of East Anglia, he wrote his first novel, *Lightseekers* (Bloomsbury 2021), which won the Little, Brown/UEA Award for Crime Fiction in 2018. His second novel, *Gaslight*, is published in November 2023. Femi lives in Windhoek, Namibia. Follow him on Twitter @FemiKay_Author.

The winning touch: the impact of winning an award

Ingrid Persaud traces the zigzag route, via law, art and parenting, that led to the discovery of her writing voice. She describes the powerful life-changing effect award-winning success had on her fledgling writing career, and encourages others to pursue their own writing passion at whatever stage of life.

Writing is one of the few careers that you can start at any time – and the later in life the better. But I am bound to say that, given that I took the scenic route myself. Writing is my third (and final) act. If you were born into a lower-middle-class Trinidadian family like mine, particularly one with East Indian roots, there were only three career options: a young person with academic leanings could become a doctor, a lawyer or a failure. Keen to please, I read law at the LSE with every intention of returning home to practise as a barrister, have children and die. But it didn't take long to discover that practising law wasn't for me. I was horrified, but I couldn't lie; I just preferred hanging out at university. So I stayed on at LSE, only leaving when I got a job teaching law across the Aldwych at King's College. I was living my dream.

And yet ... deep within myself I knew something was missing. I was desperate for some form of self-expression which aligned my head, heart and hands. But I couldn't articulate the unease – I took time off to reflect. That's when I stumbled across the Slade Art Foundation Course. I had no background in art, and arrived at the entrance interview with my two hands swinging. They politely asked for my portfolio. Unfazed, I said I didn't have one; I was enthusiastic though, and would that be enough? I don't know why, but they decided to take a chance on me. At the end of a few intense months of immersion in art and art history, I had decided that I wanted to be an artist. That crazy decision took me back to university – this time to Goldsmiths College as an art undergraduate, and then to Central Saint Martins for a Masters in Fine Art. Oh, and along the way I gave birth to gorgeous identical twin boys. As is my wont, I stuck around institutions of higher education, picking up bits of teaching at Saint Martins and occasionally exhibiting work.

I might have made this mix of teaching, art practice and parenting work, but my then partner decided the twin babies deserved a childhood away from the confines of city life. We had ties to Barbados, and with reluctance I packed us in boxes and shipped us there, all the while grieving for the London art scene I would no longer inhabit. Writing a weekly essay became my way of interrogating this new life on a small rock. I discovered classified ads for Boss Fix, Uncrossing and Come to Me magical oils and went to the fish market with a bar full of ballroom dancers. Somewhere during the writing of that blog, I fell in love with the act of writing. When I tried to express myself on the page, I found the logic of law meeting the play of art, and melding. What I was discovering was the beginnings of a writing voice.

When I am introduced now, people often mention that I won both the Commonwealth Short Story Prize and the BBC National Short Story Award (NSSA) for my first short story, 'The Sweet Sop'. But I'm not a genius who opened her laptop and immediately wrote an award-worthy text. 'The Sweet Sop' flowed out of years spent grappling with language, with meaning, and with finding a way to express my *self*. I felt immensely lucky and honoured to win those two awards. But in the wake of the ceremonies and celebrations, I quickly found out just how much of an impact winning awards could have on a fledgling writing career. Agents are the first gatekeepers in the publishing world and I, of course, didn't have one; but on the night I won the BBC NSSA I let slip that I wasn't yet represented. Agents who a day before would not have read my emails, much less the unfinished novel manuscript I was working on, queued up to offer their services. Add serendipity to the mix and I signed with Zoe Waldie of RCW Literary Agency, and three years on I know I've chosen well. She is a fierce critic and my loyal champion. Her integrity and expertise means I can entrust the management of my writing life to her hands.

Right this minute, if industry surveys are correct, about one million people are writing a novel. A goodly proportion will not finish what they started. But that still leaves a lot of competition. As Zoe helped me realise, the awards I had won meant that – for a moment at least – I had name recognition. If ever there was an opportunity to sell my novel manuscript, it was then. But Zoe was hampered by one slight problem – although I could hand over 20,000 words, the other 80,000 were as-yet unwritten. So I sat down at my desk and for the next three months wrote with back-breaking intensity, leaving off only for the most essential bodily needs: eating, sleeping and going to the bathroom. The work paid off. With Zoe's light editing, the MS was sent off to all the major UK-based publishing houses.

Love After Love was bought by Faber after a seven-way auction. And what a great publisher: I worked with a super-bright editor, Louisa Joyner, who took a decent manuscript and transformed it into an excellent novel. But then something happened that none of us could have predicted … Almost overnight, the world shut down. Borders closed and nations retreated as Covid-19 raged. It was in this scary, precarious atmosphere that *Love After Love* was published in April 2020. And here is where I understood the value of a small, nimble publisher like Faber: marketing and sales changed tack and pushed all their resources online; they lined up Zoom events to promote the book; and somehow, the book managed to gain visibility.

No spin can change the fact that 2020 was a ghastly year – on top of the pandemic, my long marriage was ending. Bookstores shuttered their doors just as my novel came out. I would have continued crying into my breakfast cereal except for the amazing good fortune of winning another life-changing award: the Costa First Novel Award. And let's be clear that prizes are simply what a particular panel of judges on a particular day decide about a particular book. Chance is a huge component. When I was told I'd won, it took me a good 20 minutes to speak. All the anxiety, hard work and sacrifice were vindicated. Positive reviews from publications such as the *Economist*, the *Guardian* and the *New York Times* were now independently justified. Zoe's faith as my agent and the Faber publishing team's trust had paid off. I exhaled.

My writing life post-Costa has shifted. The prize is now my calling card. Invitations to bookish events, never in short supply, now overwhelm and threaten my productivity. Commissions to write articles, short stories and essays arrive with increasing regularity. Foreign rights to *Love After Love* are being sold. The Italian iteration of the novel is being published earlier than planned to catch the wave of publicity that has accompanied the prize. Sales have increased. I can let go – because *Love After Love* has found its way in the world. But the real shifts have been internal. More than anything else, my long bouts of self-doubt have shortened. I sit a little straighter at my desk, and I am relishing this third act of my life. Not only am I doing what I love, but I'm making a modest living. Every morning I wake up ready to work. It doesn't mean I don't have unproductive, uninspired days; but I know now that I can get past these dips because I am doing what I love and I've been lucky enough to have some recognition.

In a crowded field, prizes and awards help to give our work a platform – a fighting chance of finding the readership it deserves. I hope my zigzag path and inability to qualify as a best young thing to hit the writing scene give you hope and courage. Now, get back to your desk, open that blank page and write. The muse will come, but she's often stuck in traffic. Meanwhile your passion awaits you.

Ingrid Persaud was born in Trinidad. Her debut novel, *Love After Love*, won the Costa First Novel Award 2020, the Author's Club First Novel Award 2021 and the Indie Book Award for Fiction 2021. She also won the BBC National Short Story Award in 2018 and the Commonwealth Short Story Prize in 2017. Follow her on Twitter @IngridPersaud.

The 'how to' of writing how-to books

Author Kate Harrison had published 12 novels when she made the unexpected move of writing a diet book. Here she talks through the six things you need to know to write a how-to book.

Becoming a how-to author was not part of my plan – and as for being a diet guru, my lifelong battle with the scales meant I was surely never going to be in a position to tell others how to eat. Yet here I am, the author of four books on the intermittent fasting approach to weight loss: the first, *The 5:2 Diet Book*, was turned down by my own publisher, but I published it myself and it became a bestseller, shifted more copies than my (still successful) novels and, at the last count, has been translated into 16 languages. And I'm two stone lighter than I was before this whole new world opened up ….

Maybe dieting isn't your area of expertise, but all of us have some specialist knowledge. Whether you're the go-to person for assembling flat-pack furniture, organising kids' birthday parties or training wilful puppies, there are readers out there who'd love to know how.

But how can you turn your skills into book sales? Here's the 'how to' of how-to books:

1. Know your stuff
What do you know more about than the average Joe or Joanna? Do your friends regularly ask you for help with something? Do you have a job or a hobby that gives you expertise?

Understanding a subject inside out is the key to a great how-to book. But that doesn't mean you need academic qualifications. Decades of experience in a practical skill will give you the understanding – and the short cuts and tips – that readers may prefer.

My experience: I'd spent years of my life losing and regaining weight on different regimes, yet when I tried intermittent fasting after watching the BBC's 'Horizon', I immediately sensed this could be different for me. There wasn't much practical information around, so I tried different approaches, and set up a Facebook group to share tips with friends. I was both an expert in dieting – including emotional factors and the reasons for failure – and a natural sceptic because, as a journalist, I was trained to question everything.

2. Know your readership
Often, the readership of a how-to book will be people like you, but the you *before* you went on the journey that equips you to write the book. Or they might be people you already teach in your day job or as a volunteer.

Whether you're a craftsperson with tricks that have taken you decades to learn, or a therapist who wants to help people in print as well as face to face, you need to understand the readers who might buy your book, so you can get the tone right.

My experience: I knew my ideal reader was me, six months earlier. But I did understand that, while I was fascinated by the science of fasting, not all readers would share my interest. So when I planned the book I aimed for the middle ground, interspersing real-life experiences, with more complex biology. I included a glossary, and lots of hyperlinks – particularly useful in an ebook – so that readers could easily read the research for themselves.

3. Know the question your book will answer
All how-to books answer a question or solve a problem. It's worth spending time thinking through what that question or need is, to help refine what your book will offer. One

Books

practical way to do this is to use Google or Amazon search functions. When you type in the beginning of a phrase, search engines predict what the rest of your phrase might be, based on millions of previous searches. It can be hilarious, but useful too.

For example, type 'DIY' into the Amazon books search bar, and you'll see: projects, for women, complete manual ... Or type 'vegan eating' on Google and you'll see other people have searched for 'meal plan' or 'breakfast'. Do this around lots of possible combinations and write down key words.

Once you understand what people want to know, you can structure your book around telling them, dealing with one key point or area per chapter. Use the key words in the title of the book itself: it makes it easier for readers to find your book!

Some questions or needs are very niche, which is not a problem if you're writing an ebook. Because the costs of producing the book are low, you can create shorter books – at lower prices – that address single issues and work well at the shorter length. Or bring different questions on one topic together in a 'complete' guide.

One important point: if you're writing about health, or potentially risky activities, include clear and appropriate warnings to ensure you're not putting readers in danger. If you have any doubt at all, look at the warnings in books on similar topics, or take professional advice. The last thing you want is to be sued!

My experience: 'How can I lose weight and keep it off?' is a need shared by millions of people worldwide. Discovering what worked for me was a life-changer, and I focused on explaining why the approach was different, and on practical ways to fit it into your life.

4. Know your unique story/point of view

Stories aren't just for children. We learn the three-act structure of stories – beginning, middle, end – from movies, books and even jokes. Structuring your non-fiction book around a story makes it more enjoyable. For example, a book about money or changing your job could easily follow the 'rags to riches' Cinderella storyline.

Your book doesn't have to be a fairy tale, but readers will enjoy reading your own story and/or case studies or people you've helped. Explaining your own struggles or problems, and then how you found the solution, establishes you as credible. Your story also makes your book unique. Even if you're a high-powered expert – a brain surgeon or a leading detective – talking as one person to another will make your book accessible, and help you stand out, even if there are many other books already on your topic.

My experience: as a consumer of previous 'diet books' written by scientific experts, I knew they could be patronising. I decided to be 100% honest about my struggles, interspersing research and advice with my own weight-loss diary. After the book was published, I had countless emails from other dieters saying 'it was like reading my own story' and my success, after years of failure, helped inspire them to try the plan.

5. Know how to publish your book

Writing may be a solitary activity, but publishing your book will almost certainly be a team effort!

You have two main options: look for an agent and publishing deal, or self-publish your work as an ebook and a print-on-demand title. The decision is worthy of an article in itself, but how-to books are very well suited to self-publishing. If your subject is quite niche, then it may not be worthwhile for a mainstream publisher, but if you get your title and cover right, readers can find you easily online, and will you will receive the lion's share of the profits. Agents and publishers are more likely to be interested if you're well-known in your field and already have thousands of followers on social media, and they may offer you an advance based on a proposal.

Self-publishing doesn't mean going it alone: you will need an editor/proofreader, and a cover designer who can make your cover as appealing as possible. The investment will help make your book stand out. Formatting an ebook is straightforward, but you may also want to hire someone for that, especially if it contains illustrations or photographs.

My experience: I thought my book had potential, but my publishers didn't agree. So I worked with my agent to self-publish on Amazon Kindle. It went to Number 1 in the diet charts within a few days – and later my publisher did republish an expanded version, plus we worked together on three recipe books and a self-help title, *5:2 Your Life.*

In 2020, I decided to expand the approach I outline in this article in *Pitch Power: Discover what makes your book irresistible & how to sell it.* I knew the market for this was smaller than a diet book so a mainstream publisher wouldn't be interested – so decided to publish it myself and love the fact I could pick the perfect cover and publish instantly and I can revise it whenever I wish, adding in new examples.

6. Know how to sell your book

Hooray – your book is ready! But the hard work is not over. You need to let potential readers know it exists.

If you already have a blog or a website, post there, and on Twitter or Facebook. Be generous with your knowledge and content; offering free samples of your work is far more convincing than just screaming BUY MY BOOK! Ebooks can be given away for free or at a reduced price, which can help get you early reviews, or increase your visibility by helping the book rise in the charts. But use with caution; don't undersell yourself.

Good reviews on Amazon and other sites are very important, but never post them under fake names or via family members' accounts. You will be found out. A better idea is to put a note to readers at the end of your ebook asking them to review it if they've enjoyed it.

Articles in newspapers or magazines can really boost your sales. Press releases are simple to write but do research the right format online. Offer yourself, or people you've taught, as case studies. Local media often like to feature authors, so approach your local radio station or newspaper.

My experience: I had already shared tips in a private Facebook group I'd set up with a few friends who were also fasting. The group grew massively and when I decided to write the book, I included members' experiences. This meant that, when it went on sale, they were keen to read and discuss it. The group is now 70,000 members strong, and I still use their comments to influence my books.

7. Finally, know what to do next

Whether you find a handful of readers, or many thousands, writing a how-to book can be rewarding and fun. And it can be a platform to so much more: a new book, a podcast or YouTube channel, an e-course, or offering yourself as a public speaker.

The possibilities are endless, but whatever you do, there's nothing like that first email from a reader thanking you for making something easy … or even for changing their lives.

My experience: I've hosted my own podcast, and still enjoy chatting to people about diet and health. But after eight years of fasting – and writing about it – I decided to return to my fiction writing roots, and have separate pen names for thrillers and love stories. Plus I offer tips for new writers on social media. I'm living proof we can find an audience for anything we are passionate about. Whatever your ambitions, remember that writing is a labour of love, and we can and should follow our hearts.

Kate Harrison worked at the BBC as a TV correspondent and news producer before becoming a full-time writer. Kate wrote nine adult novels, including the *Secret Shopper* series (Orion 2008-11), and a young adult thriller trilogy, *Soul Beach* (Orion 2011), before starting her non-fiction journey. She first self-published *The 5:2 Diet Book* as an ebook in 2012, followed by a print version with Orion, and six more recipe/self-help titles. Her books have been translated into more than 20 languages. She still writes fiction including thrillers for Zaffre as Kate Helm: *The Secrets You Hide* (2018) and *The House Share* (2020), and women's fiction as Eva Carter, including *How to Save a Life* (2021) and *Owner of a Lonely Heart* (2022), both published by Mantle. Read more about Kate's 7-step method for planning and writing books in *Pitch Power: discover what makes your book irresistible & how to sell it* and visit her website at https://kate-harrison.com/pitch-power-book or follow her on Twitter, Instagram and YouTube @KateWritesBooks.

Changing lanes: writing across genres and forms

Mark Illis describes the shifting path, form and shape his writing career has taken – from adult novels and short stories, through TV and radio drama to writing for teenagers – and shows how the unexpected challenges and changes writers may encounter serve to develop and refresh their work.

I started early. My first short story was published in 1984, when I was 21, and my first novel when I was 25 (it was a short novel with a young male protagonist whose experiences weren't a million miles from my own). I had another two books published by Bloomsbury before I was 30, and at that point I thought that the road ahead was clear: I wrote literary novels for adults. If the process of writing the novel got a bit stodgy around the middle, I'd pause to write a couple of short stories, send them off to magazines or competitions and return to the novel refreshed. Novels and short stories. I was pretty sure that I knew what I was going to write for the rest of my life.

I was wrong. A writer's career is seldom that straightforward. Writing novels is what I love, it's what I always return to, it's the thread that runs through my writing life, but I've stepped – or sometimes lurched, and occasionally been shoved – in other directions many times over the years.

The first time this happened was when Bloomsbury turned down my fourth novel. This was a blow after the relatively smooth road I'd travelled up to that point. I'd only ever wanted to be a writer and, amazingly, up till then I'd succeeded in being a writer. Now I had to stop and think. What could I do if no one wanted to publish me? I wrote a couple of calling card scripts for TV – one-off, one-hour dramas that gave a sense of what my writing was like. I sent them to *EastEnders* and *The Bill*. These days you might try *Doctors*, the BBC Writers' Room, its Channel 4 equivalent, or the Northern Writers' Awards. *EastEnders* and *The Bill* replied, and then I was writing for TV.

For a while I felt like I was having an affair. I was married to novels but I'd run away with this glamorous stranger. But after two or three years the first excitement of the affair began to wear off, and I started thinking about going back to my first love – to novels. However, TV is where the money is, and it sort of sidled up to me and whispered in my ear: 'Stay with me, and I'll buy you a house.' So I stayed with TV. My screen agent was happy, my book agent dropped me, and the years slipped by.

I enjoyed working in TV because it didn't just buy me a house, it introduced me to a new way of writing. This is one of the great advantages of writing across different genres and forms – your technique, your assumptions, your approach to your craft will all be challenged, shaken up and enriched. My TV journey took me on to *Peak Practice* and then to *Emmerdale*, where I stayed for over a decade. It was all new to me. Soap writing is collaborative, it loves big characters and big stories, it trades in jeopardy, high stakes and cliffhangers, and it explores the art of finding surprise in the context of the familiar. I found some of this strange at first, even alienating, but as I discovered the rhythm of soap, and got accustomed to how it worked, it became increasingly satisfying. Writing for soap deepened my understanding and appreciation of story. How do you keep people coming back for more, night after night, week after week, year after year? A soap writer is like a modern Scheherazade, spinning story to stop the fickle audience from changing channels.

I enjoyed the collaborative aspect of writing for TV. At *Emmerdale* we had a story conference every month, with about 20 writers, along with storyliners, script editors and the producer, all sitting round a table and talking story for two days – and then going out for a meal together in the evening. It was a major change in my life. Until then, writing had involved me sitting alone with my laptop. I would unpeel myself from the screen occasionally and find some pretext to leave the house, to get some fresh air and meet some humans. Writing for TV came with fellow humans included.

Diving into story was fascinating, and collaborating at story conferences was usually creative, productive and fun. Having your script edited was often like that too … but sometimes it wasn't. When you're writing a novel, you're the god of your own world for a year or so, as you write it and polish it and get it into its best possible form. Then an agent and an editor will almost certainly have suggestions and your manuscript will develop, but it's unlikely that you'll need to make radical changes. Script editing on a soap is different. It's your episode, but it's not your story. They can decide at a late stage to strip out your 'A' story and replace it with something else. They can – and probably will – tell you that your favourite scene, where you've used humour and nuance to really delve into character, has to be cut to make way for another story beat. So writing for soap was sometimes frustrating, but it's a distinct way of working; it's skilled and involving, and it produces six episodes a week watched by millions.

Still, I couldn't write exclusively for soap. It was my enjoyable, intellectually stimulating, income-generating day job, but I needed to do other writing as well. I got on to a course that the BBC was running, on writing radio plays, and over the next few years I had two and a half plays on Radio 4 (one of them was co-written). It was fascinating to explore a new medium, with new difficulties and opportunities, while in terms of collaboration it was an interesting halfway house, in that I had to get an idea accepted, and then a producer would have notes on my script, but still it was *my* script, my story. In fact, it felt a bit like writing a short story. I also wrote a screenplay, which won a prize, but it was based closely on someone else's storyline, so it wasn't fully satisfying.

The truth is, I wanted to be writing novels again. That thread I mentioned, running through my writing life, was still there, even if it was currently a bit buried under TV scripts. I'd never stopped writing short stories, because they fit nicely in between TV deadlines, and I began to notice that there were thematic and character-based links between some of these stories. I'd been reading the wonderful *Olive Kitteridge* (Random House 2008) by Elizabeth Strout around this time, which is a book of linked short stories, and I realised that I could use the same approach. So I took six months off *Emmerdale* to work on the project. I sent the collection to Salt Publishing, and *Tender* appeared in 2009. I was delighted to finally be a novelist again. My novel *The Last Word* (Salt Publishing 2011) followed, and I was starting to think that I had achieved an ideal situation, in which I could write both TV and fiction.

Then, in 2013, *Emmerdale* sacked me. As when that fourth novel was rejected back in the 1990s, it was a bit of a shock. Around that time, my children were becoming teenagers and I was reading some of the books they were reading: *The Knife of Never Letting Go* (Walker Books 2008) by Patrick Ness, *The Hunger Games* (Scholastic 2008) by Suzanne

Collins, *Maggot Moon* (Hot Key Books 2012) by Sally Gardner, *Noughts and Crosses* (Random House 2001) by Malorie Blackman. My geeky, angsty, inner teenager who loved reading and writing – and who is never very far beneath the surface – sat up. I thought, 'I'd like to write something like that; I'd like to use what I've learnt from TV, along with what I've learnt from writing novels for adults, in order to produce stories for teenagers.' So that's what I did. My novel *The Impossible* (Quercus Children's 2017) is about four teenagers navigating the tricky world of relationships and family – but there are also aliens and mutants in the mix, and there's a metaphorical (and autobiographical) layer involving the alarming changes that occur in teenagers' lives. It's influenced by John Wyndham, whom I read as a teenager, and the US science fiction series *Stranger Things*, which I watched on Netflix, and yet in some ways it's just as personal as my first novel.

So … I got a new book agent, *The Impossible* was published, a sequel came out in 2018, and a new novel for teenagers is coming out in 2024. I love writing for this age-group, and it feels exciting at my age to have entered a new field. I think it's probably very good for a writer to experience the occasional upheaval. Change refreshes your work and refreshes your brain as well. Writing novels for young people has spilled over into my TV work, as I wrote a couple of episodes of *Jamie Johnson* for CBBC, and I spent some time developing my own children's drama with Lime Pictures.

Some days I'll work on the novel in the morning and on TV in the afternoon. Some weeks it'll be all about a TV project. I do some teaching for Arvon, and for the Royal Literary Fund, I might visit a school to do a reading, a talk or a workshop, and I still squeeze in the odd short story now and then. I think the variety is helpful, but novels, I'm happy to say, are still the essential thread running down the centre of my writing life.

I hope it's clear from all the above that – like a lot of writers – I've been demoralised in the past and tempted to give up. For the most part I've been very lucky, but writing isn't easy, and rejection, compromise and outright failure are occasional or regular visitors for most of us. New genres and forms have been a lifeline for me; they've kept me writing, kept me working, kept me earning, and kept me excited about my craft. When change comes, I think we should try to welcome it, and when it doesn't come … perhaps we should seek it.

Mark Illis is a novelist, short story writer, and writer for TV, radio and film. His latest novel for teenagers, *Running Away For Beginners*, will be published by Scholastic in 2024. His first three novels, *A Chinese Summer* (1988), *The Alchemist* (1990) and *The Feather Report* (1992) were published by Bloomsbury. He has written for *EastEnders*, *The Bill*, *Peak Practice*, *Emmerdale* and *Jamie Johnson*, and has written three radio plays. Mark's other books are *Tender* (2009) and *The Last Word* (2011), published by Salt Publishing, and *The Impossible* (2017) and *The Impossible: On the Run* (2018), published by Quercus, and aimed at teenagers. *The Impossible* has been optioned for TV. Visit his website http://markillis.co.uk.

Writing thrilling fiction

Bestselling author Paula Hawkins explores the essential elements and creative process involved in the art of thriller-writing, revealing some of the key tools inside 'the crime novelist's box of tricks', and has valuable, practical tips and encouragement for aspiring crime writers.

Where to begin? With a concept, maybe? There are zombies on this runaway train! Or perhaps a devastating opening line: 'Once the queen's head is severed, he walks away'.[1] Some novelists begin at the end and work backwards, reverse-engineering their plots so that events flow neatly and inexorably to the end they started from. Others talk about beginning with a single image for which they have no context whatsoever, only the strong sense that they *must* write about it. A novel can begin anywhere.

This is how it starts for me: someone is telling a story, about something that happened to them, or to someone they know. It's usually something terrible or tragic or frightening, and I find myself grasping at some small detail of this story, latching onto it, turning it over in my mind, examining it from different angles, wondering: but *then what*? What became of the person at the heart of that terrible story? *Who* did they become?

Character

My stories start with character. But characters don't arrive in the imagination fully formed; they start off as one peculiar characteristic, one particular trait. To use an obvious example, I might know that this character drinks too much – so much, in fact, that she can't remember what she did last night, or with whom. Immediately you begin thinking about a person like that, questions arise: why is she like this? What happened to her? Did her drinking become problematic gradually, or was there one major trigger? And what does it mean for her day to day? How does she cope? Does she cope? Do her friends help her, or have they tired of her now? And what of her sense of self?

Now we're getting somewhere. But in order to really get somewhere, we need to go somewhere. What I mean by that is a character isn't enough: I need something else, some other element, to get her moving. It's usually a location: a commuter train, say, trundling through suburbia. Or a cold, black river winding its way through a village, or a neglected houseboat, half-sinking into the sludgy waters of a London canal. A character on her own is an intriguing idea, but a character plus a location is the beginning of a story.

I believe quite strongly that there are no right or wrong ways to write crime novels (or indeed any kind of novel). Moreover, I sometimes think that following too slavishly the advice of others can hinder more than it helps. But I also believe there are certain elements which are essential to a thrilling psychological suspense novel, and right up at or near the top of the list is a compelling character – hopefully, a whole cast of compelling characters. I like to write about outsiders, about people who don't quite fit. They aren't doing as they're told, they're failing somehow to live up to expectations, they struggle. They're rarely *good*, but they aren't bad either. They are frequently frustrating – indeed they are often labelled 'unlikable'. I don't care about that. I don't expect readers of crime fiction to come to my novels to make friends. What I want is for them to find people who are psychologically true, people whose actions – however ill-advised – make sense in context. So, let's

[1]. *The Mirror and the Light*, Hilary Mantel (Fourth Estate 2020)

say, in the context of this particular woman's day or week or life. We know why Rachel drinks. If we were Rachel, we might drink too.

Voice

What *you* find compelling in a protagonist might be quite different: you might focus on humour, or a good heart, someone a reader will fall in love with. You need to find characters who chime with your own unique voice.

You also need to find the characters' voices; maybe try writing them from various perspectives, to see what feels most comfortable. At times I have started off in third person and found myself, almost without noticing, switching to first. If you do that, take notice. You may not want to switch points of view, but you might want to move *closer* to a different point of view if the character demands it. First-person narratives have their detractors – and they are perhaps overused in a certain sort of psychological thriller – but there is no denying their immediacy or the fierce attraction of allowing your readers direct access to your central character's deepest, darkest, most discomforting, strange, horrifying, funny or moving thoughts and feelings. What first-person narration lacks, of course, is distance. And that can be a problem for the thriller writer. If the reader has access to a character's every thought and feeling, then there is no place to hide. And hiding things – concealing by sleight of hand certain pertinent facts – is a key tool in the crime novelist's box of tricks.

Structure

If character is the aspect of a story readers consciously cling to – the one they most clearly remember – then structure has a more subtle effect, yet it is key to what makes the experience of reading a novel satisfying. Do you need to use flashbacks, or separate out timelines? Is the narrative divided into sections, and what is the effect of this? I want to achieve a moment when it dawns upon the reader that the story is being told in this way for a very particular reason – a moment of realisation that should make them sit back and smile and think, 'Oh, I see. This is where she's taking me.'

A strong structure is invaluable to a writer: it will help you through your story; you will start to know what needs to come next, what to reveal next, because it will fit into the framework you've been building. It becomes your guide, too. There's no handbook for this, no template. Every novel is different, and each has its own requirements. For me, finding the right way to tell a story is often the trickiest bit of the writing process. In *The Girl on the Train* (Doubleday 2015), I had the gift of the commute – the perfect vehicle to give the early part of the novel a rhythm. As Rachel travelled back and forth every morning and every evening, I invited the reader onto the train to sit with her, and within a page or two they knew exactly where they were: sitting in a train carriage, running through the grubby outskirts of London, looking out of the window.

The construction of *A Slow Fire Burning* (Penguin 2022) felt quite different. I imagined the crime at the heart of this novel having the effect of a stone thrown into water, causing a ripple effect, and I tried to recreate that effect in some ways in how I told the story – in the way the characters were introduced and how they encountered each other. But it is notable that this ripple effect idea was not something I thought about at the beginning of the writing process. When I wrote the early scenes, I had no idea what the novel would end up looking like. I think it's rarely possible to visualise the shape of your novel at its outset. But whether you are a writer who plots out each chapter in detail, the sort who starts out with no idea whatsoever where they are going, or you're somewhere in between, the likelihood is that at some point during the process (for me it's generally around half way to two-thirds through) you will have to draw up some sort of schematic to help with that visualisation.

This might be as simple as a list of key points in a Word document; it might be a complicated hunt-the-serial-killer style board, complete with bits of string and photographs. When you stand back and look at this plan, it should help you notice patterns in your story, gauge the shape of your characters' arcs, and spot any imbalances there might be. Are there periods where the pace slackens? Are there sections where there is perhaps too much action? Sometimes you need to pause for a moment, allow the reader to take a breath. If your subject matter is very dark, you might want to allow some light in.

As I mentioned above, some people are planners and others are not; I think most of us are somewhere in between. Even if you are a plotter, my advice would be to leave plenty of room for manoeuvre, especially in early drafts. Give yourself space for surprises. I have always found that the best, most exciting, most joyful writing happens when I am in the thick of a novel, when my mind starts to make connections I hadn't conceived of at the outset, when twists and turns start to occur to me in a way they had not before, when suddenly the way ahead is clear and I start to understand more fully what the novel is really about. Don't plot so tightly that you do not allow yourself the freedom and excitement of a spontaneous twist in the road.

Twisting

Twists, while we're on the subject, can be overdone. Often what people describe as twists are not twists at all – they are simply shocking revelations thrown into the final third of a novel. Such revelations may have their place, but a real twist is more than just a surprise; a twist wrongfoots you; it makes you gasp and sit up and re-evaluate everything you have read up unto that point. Gillian Flynn did it in *Gone Girl* (Crown Publishing 2012), Ian McEwan did it in *Atonement* (Jonathan Cape 2001), Louise Doughty managed a killer twist on the very last page of *Apple Tree Yard* (Faber & Faber 2014). Good twists are earned: they will surprise you, but as a reader you will also have the sense that, had you been paying very careful attention, you might have been able to see this coming. A twist is not a bolt from the blue, it is a filter which changes the complexion of everything that has gone before.

A few other tips:

• **Share your work** when you're starting out – not with everyone, just with one or two select readers who share your taste in books. It's daunting to show your writing to anyone in the early stages, but I urge you to do so. Be sure to avoid what happened to me: I never progressed because I didn't seek feedback. I had no idea whether people would engage with the characters I was writing or whether they found my story intriguing – because I didn't ask. This meant that the only voice I had to listen to was the one in my head, telling me that this was no good, that it wasn't working. So I would give up on the work in progress and move on to the next: write, doubt, abandon, repeat.

• **Treat writing like a job** (even if it's not your job). There may be people who can afford to search for the ideal writer's room, who have the luxury of lounging about, waiting for the muse to appear, but I don't think many of them are working novelists. If you are serious about finishing a novel, you have to find a way to carve out time in your day (or at least your week) to write regularly. I know it's easy for a childless full-time novelist to say that, but it is the truth as I see it. Writing a novel is hard work and it takes a long time: there are no hacks and no shortcuts; it's a slog. It is also rewarding – rarely financially, admittedly, but creatively it can be enormously so.

• **Learn from the best.** By that I mean learn from what you think is best, what you love. Think for a moment about how painters learn to paint: they study the work of painters they admire, they copy it, they scrutinize it – and not just the effect but the paint itself, the brushstrokes on the canvas. Think about why you love your favourite novelists; what is it about their sentences that attracts you?

• **Beware word counts.** Writing 2,000 words a day might work for some writers, but it won't work for them all the time. A high word-count target can look dispiriting if you are struggling through a difficult point in your book. Give yourself a different goal – say, five sentences. Not five average sentences, but five brilliantly crafted sentences, the ones that bring a smile to your face when you're editing. Then maybe tomorrow you'll write 2,000 words…

• **Find your creative place** – the place where you feel most energized, where you fizz with ideas. It might be an actual place, or a time of day, or a particular group of people, or one like-minded friend. Where are you when you have your best ideas? Who are you with? What makes you feel inspired? Keep returning to that place; keep mining it for more.

• **Stay faithful to the stories in your head.** Don't allow yourself to be swayed by fashion, because fashions can change from month to month, while writing and publishing a book takes years. Big success stories, like *The Girl on the Train*, are often born out of a kind of alchemy – a combination of the right book at the right time, the right agent, editor, publisher, the right marketing strategy. Most of those things you cannot control, so focus on the things you can: your characters and your plot and your sentences on the page.

Good luck!

Paula Hawkins worked as a journalist for 15 years before turning her hand to fiction. She is the author of international bestseller *The Girl on the Train* (Doubleday 2015), which has sold 23 million copies worldwide and has been adapted into a major motion picture, and *Into the Water* (Black Swan 2018). Both books were *Sunday Times* and *New York Times* number one bestsellers. Her latest thriller, *A Slow Fire Burning*, also a *Sunday Times* number one bestseller, was published by Doubleday in 2021. Paula was born in Zimbabwe and now splits her time between London and Edinburgh. For more information see http://paulahawkinsbooks.com. Follow her on Instagram @paulahawkins2010.

Books

Writing romantic fiction

Raffaella Barker describes the lure of romantic fiction for reader and writer alike, the pleasure and challenge of creating characters real enough for the reader to fall in love with, and the importance of providing structure and the promise of a satisfying resolution as the story unfolds.

The first time I fell in love it was in a book. I was 11 and I fell in love with a boy called Dion in *Fire in the Punchbowl* (Collins 1969), a novel by Monica Edwards. I knew Dion quite well by the time I fell in love with him; he was one of the family in Edwards' series of novels set on Punchbowl Farm in Sussex, where the topography and detail of daily life, the weather, animals, journey to school, and the granular experience of their day-to-day existence made a believable world I wanted to be part of – indeed, one I really felt I *was* part of. By the time I read this penultimate novel in the series, the family I myself had grown up with was doing just that, and I, on the cusp of adolescence, stepped forward with these characters. As Dion grappled with a terrifying fire on the farm, taking a characteristically brave and tenacious part in putting out the flames, I fell for his unassuming strength, his gentle thoughtfulness and his noble motives. I could love him safely, within the confines of my imagination, rehearsing something I was not at all ready, or likely, to experience in real life at that point (11 years old, I attended a girls' school and spent the holidays riding my pony in the wild countryside of '70s rural North Norfolk, with no one my age for miles around).

From that moment, though, I never stopped falling in love in literature. After Dion came many more infatuations: older, less suitable, engaging, dashing, silent, injured, brooding, married, blind … the possibilities were endless. I read romantic fiction hungrily, always with an eye for humour and fallibility in the object of my affections. From novelists Georgette Heyer, Jilly Cooper, Elizabeth Jane Howard, Olivia Manning and Daphne du Maurier I learnt several things: writing a romance can be funny (as in Jilly Cooper's joyful early novels); it can be part of a much bigger picture (as in Olivia Manning's wonderful Balkan Trilogy); it can be epic (as in Elizabeth Jane Howard's series on the Cazelet family); and it can be an engine of fear and of what is left unsaid (as in Daphne du Maurier's *Rebecca*). Later Maggie O'Farrell and Audrey Niffenegger showed me that it can be tragic. My take on what defines romantic fiction remains broad; for me, there just needs to be someone I can fall in love with.

Romance, and the love affair in fiction, hit the spot like nothing else – unlike real-life romance which can be awkward, fleeting, and too frequently riddled with clichés and the uneasy awareness that things are not going to plan. Things may not always turn out right for the characters in romantic fiction, but the reader can take pleasure in the journey – packaged as it is within the trajectory of a novel, and with the promise of resolution.

In fiction, the reader gets to inhabit the world of the characters as an observer, no matter how close to the story. Even if the piece is written in the first person, the act of reading provides a flexible distance that keeps us outside the experience of the protagonists. Yet we have the intimacy of moving inside the characters' lives, which sometimes brings us closer to them than to anyone we live with or love. It is this, I think, that makes romantic fiction a most useful insight into human beings and the way we behave. In fiction, the reader is there with the characters, living in their altered temporal universe, as they misunderstand and make up, separate then come together, kiss, experience loss, joy, yearning and confusion – all on their way to the kingdom of happy-ever-after. Romance is wonderful to read, and it is also wonderful to write.

It can be a daunting challenge to create believable characters and set up a world in which it is impossible yet inevitable that two people (or maybe more) will fall in love. We tend to think that so many good writers have done this already, that too many instances depict the rules of love and attachment being broken just to be mended with an intoxicating embrace. The idea of romantic love as the core of a novel is wide open to the hazards of cliché and overfamiliarity. But there is nothing more interesting than the way human beings relate to one another, and romantic love manifests this in myriad forms. This is what is exciting for the writer embarking on the romantic novel. Who is it about, why is it about these people, and what will be revealed to bring something different to the genre?

In *Poppyland* (Headline 2008) I took up the challenge of how a novelist creates two people who could believably fall in love with one another, and how to make real the magnetic, hypnotic, unstoppable collision that occurs when they do. This was a volte-face from my previous novel, *A Perfect Life* (Headline 2006), which depicts a divorce. In another novel, *Hens Dancing* (Headline 1999), I had played with the romantic idea differently; my central character was unaware of the attraction and the 'rightness' of the love interest, even though the reader could see their chemistry in the scenes they appeared in together. Long before Venetia, the central character, knew she was in love with David, *we* knew it, and we were on the complex journey of discovery with our heroine, cheering her on to the finish line. Well, everyone loves a happy ending.

There are many ways of approaching the job of writing romantic fiction but, to me, it always makes sense to start with character. After all, there can be no hope of romance without two people between whom the chemistry will ignite. And here lies the first and most important decision for the author. For the purposes of satisfactory storytelling, the characters need to be very different from one another, to present apparently insurmountable clashes of temperament or timing, and to exist with a vivid and believable autonomy bringing veracity to the paradoxical notion that, while they are completely capable of having full and vivid lives without one another, they can only thrive and be the best version of themselves when they find their way together. The path of true love is never smooth, but it leads to an end at some point; the writer must lay this out clearly for the reader, if obscurely for the characters.

Given that the engine of the narrative is driven by these characters, now it's important to decide on perspective. Will the story be told from one character's perspective or both? Or will it be told by someone else observing them? Will we only ever see one of the two characters through the eyes of the other, or will we know both through an omniscient overarching voice from outside? These questions determine the structure of the novel. If they are both telling the story, for example, the urgency might be contained in two parallel narratives, one for each central character, with the energetic heart of the novel being exploited when they finally meet and spend time together. In this way the ending is lit with the possibility of a potential get-together, a state of 'happily ever after', and creates a trajectory with a pleasing arc. On the other hand, the author might opt for a third party telling the story, so that the lovers are seen from the outside, their motivation opaque, the journey of their romance filtered through the perspective of this third party, and our relationship to it similarly distanced.

Books

Perspective is one issue; the unfolding of the action is another. Misunderstandings are a vital element of romance – plenty of them. Think of *Pride and Prejudice*. The title alone suggests a constant seesawing of confusion and wrong-footedness. The author is managing both the expectations of the characters and those of the readers, so the placing of these devices must be strategic. If the difficulties the characters face are too profound, the pulse that keeps the story moving forward will cease to beat, both on the page and off. Readers are sophisticated – their interest needs to be stoked, and the way love and romance is built is crucial. The writer is best to avoid recourse to stereotypes, as in fairy tales, instead applying focus and depth to the individual characteristics of the protagonists. The more human these characteristics are, the more relatable, the more satisfying the romance.

'Satisfying' is a word I use advisedly here. It describes the task that romantic fiction is meant to fulfil. By the end of the narrative, romantic fiction is meant to deliver a fully believable love story, one that suggests a beginning of something else for the characters – they deserve it, the reader deserves it. In romantic fiction, perhaps more than any other genre, the potential of the future needs to be lit, like a touch paper, by the bright joy of the ending. It is not that the characters' future needs to be implied or discussed, more that it is plausible; its foundations have been laid. In *Pride and Prejudice* we know, when Mr Darcy and Elizabeth walk down the aisle, that their marriage will be filled with discussion, energy, amusement, and deep respect for the intelligence each has finally seen in the other. In romantic fiction, the characters focus the beam of their attention on one another, not on their circumstances. This is the intensity the reader seeks.

The love affairs we create in our writing are like the music we hear in our dreams – they exist in a dimension beyond those in which we inhabit our lives. They are, by definition, unreal yet also hyper-real. Any writer who knows the pleasure of living alongside their characters as they develop will enjoy the experience of writing a love life for them – even one that will never work out. We agree with the Romantic poet Alfred Lord Tennyson that ''Tis better to have loved and lost than to have never loved at all.' To write about people finding love, and make it real enough for a reader to follow that experience with them, is a joy – worth any amount of hard work.

Raffaella Barker is an author and journalist who published her first novel *Come and Tell Me Some Lies* with Hamish Hamilton in 1994. Her other books include *The Hook* (Bloomsbury 1996), *Hens Dancing* (1999), *Summertime* (2001), *Green Grass* (2002), *A Perfect Life* (2006) and *Poppyland* (2008), all published by Headline Review, *From A Distance* (Bloomsbury 2014), and the children's book *Phosphorescence* (Macmillan Children's 2005). Raffaella has written short stories for radio, worked at *Harpers & Queen* magazine, as a columnist for *Country Life* and has been a regular contributor to the *Sunday Times*, the *Sunday Telegraph*, *Harper's Bazaar* and the *Spectator*. She teaches Creative Writing at the University of East Anglia and the *Guardian* Novel Writing Masterclass. Her website is www.raffaellabarker.co.uk.

Ever wanted to write a saga?

Bestselling author Di Redmond (aka Daisy Styles) outlines the key elements required for a successful saga, and shares her insights into the market, character and demands of this popular genre.

Be prepared for the long haul!

A saga, by definition, is a genre of literature which chronicles the life of a family, interconnecting dramatic events over a long period of time – think *Game of Thrones*, *The Crown*, *The Archers* and *Coronation Street*. The saga as an art form is as old as the Norse myths, but more recently writers like Jeffrey Archer, Maeve Binchy, Danielle Steele, Anne Tyler and Catherine Cookson (to name but a few) have put them firmly at the top of the bestseller list. The key ingredients of any successful saga are: background content (e.g. the Napoleonic Wars, the Victorians, WW2); the pace of the writing; the accuracy to historical detail; and the strength of the core characters who hold the entire structure tightly together.

A series can run from two to six books, with each book usually having a word count of 100,000 words, roughly 40 chapters, and with a swift turnaround from the end of one book to the start of the next. The public appetite for sagas is surprisingly voracious … I know this for certain from my 'Daisy Styles' Facebook page (I had to take Daisy Styles as a nom de plume, since my real name – I'm proud to say – is often associated with writing *Bob the Builder*!). People who buy sagas (mostly women) regularly treat themselves to a new paperback whilst doing their weekly shop in any of the big supermarkets – Tesco, Asda, Sainsburys, Morrisons. They sell cheaply – usually on offer at two for £7 – thereby undercutting regular bookshop prices. With a short shelf life of about 12 weeks, the books have their popularity ratings flagged up beside the titles; these are based on the success of their sales figures and run from No. 1 Bestseller to No. 20. Believe me, these books virtually fly off the shelf! As they sell, their numbers are regularly topped up until a batch of newly published sagas arrive, immediately replacing the previous batch; it's a case of 'out with the old and in with the new' – a never-ending cycle.

Sagas follow a seasonal pattern; mine covered *Bomb Girl Brides* (Penguin 2018) and *Christmas with the Bomb Girls* (Penguin 2017), but for other seasons the sagas might have covered springtime and rationing, or summertime and evacuees. Saga readers are a dedicated fan base – hence the ever-hungry market – and their loyalty and dedication is such that they each build up their own personal library of favourite authors, and (touchingly) they're hot on ordering the next saga – the very one the author is in the process of writing – well in advance on Amazon. They also like to keep in touch with their saga author on Facebook, relishing details of work in progress, deadlines, edits, research and travel related to the forthcoming book. It's almost as if you were having a baby!

A fan base can also be very exacting; get a fact wrong, such as confusing Prime Minister Chamberlain's WW2 timeline with Prime Minister Churchill's, and you'll know about it. As they respect you, they in turn expect you to respect the territory – which is where research comes in …

The research

When I launched into my saga-writing career, I spent more time researching the period than I did writing the book. I had to back up almost every paragraph I wrote with hard facts and it nearly drove me crazy. Was I writing a history text or a novel? With the plotline rapidly unfolding in my head, and my fabulous characters champing at the bit, I was as eager to get cracking as they were, but I felt thwarted at every turn. I was constantly checking and re-checking references in my mounting pile of history books and endlessly on a search engine. When it came to googling 'how to build a bomb' for a spy plotline, a good friend advised me to always insert a date – 1941 or 1944 for example – otherwise I would have a Special Branch officer knocking on my front door!

After decorating my study walls with a printout of WW2's timeline, I decided I was going to go for it – otherwise I would never meet my deadline. Though I was nervous, I told myself that wherever I felt uncertain about a date I would leave a blank and address the problem at the end of the working day, rather than spend the entire working day thumbing through history books. I'm happy to say, it worked. As the story unrolled and my fabulous *Bomb Girls* stepped out of the woodwork, I became more and more familiar with the dreaded timeline. At the drop of a hat I could have told you when the Canadians joined the war ('God love 'em', as the nation chorused), when the Yanks bombed Pearl Harbor, how to slaughter a pig, build an air-raid shelter, read Morse code, and the price of nylons on the black market. The moral of the story is not to get bogged down by facts, which I know are very important and must be respected, but there has to come a point when you have to let the writing flow, secure in the knowledge that if you make a mistake you can go back and rectify it later.

The setting

Once you've got your timeframe, you have to establish exactly where your saga will be played out. When I was asked by my agent if I might be interested in writing a saga series, my mind immediately flew to Lancashire where I was brought up and where, as a child, I rambled for miles across the moors – sometimes coming across a crumbling ruin of a mill which locals told me had been a munitions factory. During wartime the locations of these sites were kept top secret, for fear of spies reporting their whereabouts to the Luftwaffe who would unquestionably bomb both the site and the workers to kingdom come. I'd considered writing about land girls, nurses on the front line, WRNS, Special Ops, Women's Auxiliary Air Force (WAAF) and the Auxiliary Territorial Services (ATS), but memories of that dark ruin defined my choice – I'd write about conscripted women building bombs in a former cotton mill on Pendle Moor.

The core characters

It's vital that your core group of characters can pack a punch! My *Bomb Girls* were all very different characters; the lead girl was savvy and a brilliant cook, the second shy and bookish, the third poor and bullied and the fourth sexy and a bit of a comedian, whilst the fifth girl was posh. Though vastly different in every respect, they complemented each other in rather surprising and unexpected ways, stirring up plots and complications because of their intrinsic differences. Conscription was a great leveller, bringing together the rich and the poor, forcing them to live under the same roof whether they liked it or not. Poor girls, used to an outside privy and an old water pump, couldn't believe the luxury of having hot and cold running water in their domestic lodgings and a flush toilet too, whilst the rich girls were appalled at the thought of sharing a bathroom and queueing for the toilet.

In my enthusiasm I went for five women and thereby created a problem for myself; not that the women were a problem – all of them were fantastic to write for – but five characters going off in different directions is just too many to juggle. My advice is to keep your core group down to three or four; it's a more manageable number, especially as the characters develop and become stronger than you originally anticipated (a little mouse of a girl can grow into a lion when she's building bombs to fight Hitler!). The environment in which these women worked round-the-clock shifts fed them propaganda that didn't just strengthen their muscles to do the gruelling hard work, but strengthened their mindset too. The women who entered the factory at the start of the war had changed into very different women by the time they left at the end.

Location, location ...

The setting for saga-based novels is important for both the reader and the writer. Big old industrial towns like Glasgow, Manchester, Liverpool, Leeds, Sheffield, Bristol and Birmingham bring their own history – cotton and woollen mills, docks, steelworks, shipyards and harbours. Added to which, there's a war raging, bombs are falling, men dying, telegrams arriving, sweethearts grieving, and innocent children being evacuated. It's drama upon drama; at the heart of any saga there are irrefutable facts. In every reader's family there will be someone who lived through the war and has a story to tell – a true and cherished story which they are proud to pass on to the next generation.

When it came to writing *The Wartime Midwives* (Penguin 2019), my love of the Lake District lured me further north; on visiting Grange-over-Sands, Cartmel, Kendal and the whole breathtaking sweep of Morecambe Bay and the Irish Sea I knew that it was the perfect place to set a secluded mother and baby home. For my latest series, *Engine Girls*, I chose Nottingham for my location, close to Derby and the industrial Midlands it's an area where many iconic wartime aircraft were built by conscripted women during WW2.

A word of warning

Although Catherine Cookson – queen of the saga – made a fortune from her books, it would be insincere of me to suggest you're going to get rich from this genre. You will get royalties when you've paid off your publisher's advance, but the royalty payment depends on how big your sales are and if the book goes to a reprint. The plus side is that sagas don't stop with one publication; the demand will grow, and so will your fan base, as your books become a regular feature on the supermarket shelves.

If you have an agent, approach them with an outline of your characters, location and an exact timeframe (be warned – taking on the entire six years of the war is huge, so focus on a section of the WW2 you want to work around, such as after Dunkirk, before Pearl Harbor, or during the Blitz). Your agent may ask you to write three sample chapters and then present to a number of publishers known to be on the lookout for a new saga series. If you haven't got an agent, you should do extensive research on the publishers that have a particular interest in the genre (there are a lot), then submit your outline and three sample chapters to the editor of that department.

If you love writing on a broad canvas, about a pivotal point in history with a possible cast of thousands, and you can keep a convoluted plot line running over 100,000 words, this is the one for you!

Di Redmond, under the pen name Daisy Styles, is the author of the bestselling *Bomb Girls* and *Engine Girls* series published by Penguin. Di is also a prolific writer, writing for children's television, stage and radio, and is an established celebrity ghostwriter. She has published over 120 books and is the Audio-Visual Director on ALCS's Board of Directors.

Writing Regency romances

Katy Moran uncovers the captivating character and appeal of Regency romance, its evolution and popularity as a genre, and the creative possibilities it offers a writer. She shares her recommended reading and insights for aspiring romantic novelists.

Sunlight glanced in through the window, striking the bookshelves in my parents' home office. Thrillers by James Clavell jostled with 30-year-old textbooks and *Readers' Digest* volumes passed down from my grandparents. I thought I'd long since read every book in this house, but I was wrong. It was the yellow Pan Macmillan logo that first caught my eye, followed by the battered taupe spine. I pulled out a well-thumbed paperback edition of *The Toll-Gate*, raising an eyebrow at the front cover: a red-headed woman locked in an embrace with a tall, masterful man. Georgette Heyer? I'd never heard of her. I never looked back, either – swept away by Captain Jack Staple, a bored war-hero with a twinkling sense of humour and a fine-tuned appreciation of the ridiculous. The redhead was Nell, a gloriously competent orphan left to run a crumbling estate and outwit her grasping cousin. Having so far evaded his family's best efforts to see him married off, Jack says to his mother that he doesn't mean to offer marriage to any girl who doesn't give him a leveller. Although 'If one *did*,' he added thoughtfully, 'it's Lombard Street to a China orange that you wouldn't take to her.' Heyer lays her cards on the table the moment Jack meets Nell for the first time: 'He stood as though stunned, for he had received his leveller at last.'

I came to love Heyer's books, craving her sparkling wit in times of crisis, and the satisfaction of a happy ending. Nowadays my relationship with her novels is more nuanced, complicated by instances of antisemitism and racism, or age gaps between heroes and heroines that I can no longer view as romantic – even if they do reflect a darker side of the Georgian period that it might be easier to forget. Romance as a genre can so often be dismissed, and it's my belief that critiquing Heyer's work in this way isn't to judge her unfairly by the standards of our time. She was the grand dame of Regency romance, and her work is worthy of critical discussion.

What's the appeal of the Regency, anyway? If you don't already know your curricles from your top boots, I hope my enthusiasm will be infectious. Officially, this period began in 1811 when a spoiled and complex man became de facto ruler in place of his incapacitated father. It ended in 1820 when King George III died, and the Prince Regent became George IV. Researching, I fell headlong into a compelling world of progress, discovery, glamorous ballrooms and giddy excess. It was also a time when our economy was still tied to the illegal slave trade and men could be hanged for the crime of having sex with another man. We were next door to a bloody theatre of war on the continent, a drama extended to provincial British towns when the redcoats passed by – so memorably brought to life by Jane Austen's Lydia Bennet and the scoundrel Mr Wickham.

The Regency took place against a backdrop that must have been, by turns, exhilarating and terrifying to live through. As Regency romance author Catherine Kullmann points out, during this period calls for political reform and emancipation intensify – and the fashion was wearable too. Our heroes and heroines look gorgeous in a way we can relate to: we don't have to get past ruffs or powdered wigs. But even in a Regency romcom or soothing comfort-read, brutal social mores create a backdrop of peril that doesn't exist now, with the course of many a young woman's life being dependent on success or failure in her first Season, when a single malicious rumour could condemn her to life as a disempowered unmarried daughter. A man whose heart led him to other men might find himself on the gallows. In the Regency, the dramatic stakes are anything but trivial.

Georgette Heyer ignited my fascination with the Regency; she's the reason I started scribbling plot diagrams in a notebook one day. But how on earth could I do justice to this era? Over time, I came to realise what my predecessors already understood. As bestselling historical romance author Lynne Connolly puts it, 'The Regency was a historical period, but many authors deviate from the historical reality to create their own Regencyland.' It's true – whether this Regencyland is a place of ebullient escapism, like that of Julia Quinn or tenured Shakespeare professor Eloisa James, where handsome young noblemen proliferate (with all their own teeth), or one where dragons appear as part of a glorious magical backdrop, as they do in Stephanie Burgis's glittering romcom *Scales and Sensibility* (2021).

When sketching out my own Regencyland I followed not only Heyer, and all the other Regency romance authors who had gone before me, but also the Diana Wynne Jones novels of my childhood. I took a sideways step into a history almost like our own but not quite, creating a Napoleonic alternate universe where a mutinous Cornwall echoes the previous century's Jacobite rebellion in Scotland and the French have outwitted the British navy, mounting a successful invasion. I was hurrying after a hero, Crow, Earl of Lamorna, who at first glance looked very much like Wynne Jones' mercurial Chrestomanci. Tall, dark-haired and arrogant, Crow is capable of visiting violence upon his enemies and tenderness on those he loves in (more or less) equal measure. My Cornish-island dwelling heroine, Hester Harewood, is a capable sailor and a practical young woman who is about to take Crow down by several pegs. In *Game of Hearts* (Head of Zeus 2017), Crow first meets Hester in a none too patient frame of mind. After rescuing his rebellious young brother from occupation soldiers, by ruining his captor at dice, he encounters a young woman washed up on a beach:

'You're coming back to London with me.' All Crow could do was hope she wouldn't give him any trouble.
She stared at him, incredulous. 'Am I, indeed?'
'Yes.' Crow reached for his hip flask and contented himself with a scalding shot of the 1811 Le Courvoisier, before holding the flask to Miss Harewood's lips. Somewhat to his surprise, she didn't protest against the cognac, but took a swallow and straightened herself to her full height, tall and queenly in a sodden gown, and Crow could not escape the notion that he had met his match.
'Take another drink, my lord,' said Miss Harewood. 'You look as though you need it.'[1]

Crow has received his leveller and he knows it. A fictional war throws Hester and Crow together, but it's the strict social rules of the true Regency that raise the stakes, because Hester has no female chaperone. Crow might offer Hester his protection but, alone as she is, even being in his presence is enough to ruin her. Around the time that I first drafted this scene, I was watching the first series of *Outlander*, based on Diana Gabaldon's passionate timeslip romances. I had no idea then whether the story I was writing for my own

---

[1] *From Game of Hearts* (Head of Zeus) © Katy Moran 2017

pleasure would ever be published, but I remember thinking that if it ever was, given the alternate history, it would need to be picked up by an editor with an eye for something as different as it was swashbuckling and romantic. Sure enough, the book that became *Game of Hearts* was signed by Rosie de Courcy, who years earlier bought UK rights to *Outlander* and became Diana Gabaldon's editor in the UK.

Writing the book of your heart without regard to genre and then seeing it published is only one way into Regency romance. Since Georgette Heyer published *Regency Buck* in 1935, the genre has evolved with spectacular invention. As a first port of call, I'd advise anyone interested in writing Regency romance to read it widely – including books published recently. Read Regency romances first published in the States, too, where the market is not only larger but different. UK-based authors Emily Royal, Emily Windsor and Virginia Heath have found great success across the pond with their joy-filled romances and romcoms. Vanessa Riley is from the US and writes award-winning examples of the genre with sparkling heroines, shining a light on the hidden histories of women of colour. Here in the UK, Audrey Harrison, Penny Hampson and Fenella Miller all successfully self-publish in this category. Sophie Irwin is an exciting voice in UK Regency romcom with the *Sunday Times* bestselling *A Lady's Guide to Fortune-Hunting* (HarperCollins 2022), and Jane Lark writes passionate Regency romance. Felicity George's *A Lady's Risk* is a delightful Regency romance that has a classic feel.

KJ Charles writes in a variety of periods including the Regency, and her witty, escapist, subversive and sexy m/m romances have a huge and devoted worldwide following of fans, as do those of well-loved romance author Alexis Hall, who writes sparkling and witty queer Regency romance. Jenni Fletcher's *How to Lose an Earl in Ten Weeks* (Penguin 2021) was published for the YA market but has also found a wider readership – which is no surprise given the appeal of the Regency genre, and Fletcher's uplifting take on it. Amita Murray's new Regency series is about the daughters of an English earl and his Indian mistress. This breathtaking romantic adventure opens with *Unladylike Lessons in Love*, starring a heroine who dares to break the mould. And, as Amita says, 'there's all the usual witty banter and runaway horses and suppressed passion of a Regency but in a way that allows room understand the impact of colonial history'. Another relative newcomer is Emma Orchard, with *The Second Lady Silverwood*, a passionate, romance with deeply authentic emotional weight and Heyer's wit.

So … read! Read as much in the genre as you can, and in doing so you'll understand who your own ideal readers will be. As a reader, do you enjoy on-page sex or do you find it off-putting? As a writer, do you relish exploring human chemistry to that extent or might you prefer to show the heat of attraction between your characters in smaller gestures, leaving sex behind closed doors? The more we read, the sooner we understand what we're best placed to create. Over the years I've been developing as a writer, a particular piece of wisdom from Alan Garner has come to take on deeper meaning for me: 'If the other fellow can do it, let him.' Is there a special niche within Regency romance that you can explore like no one else?

There are other questions to consider too. Do stories like yours tend to be published independently (self-published) or traditionally? If you're aiming at the traditional market, you should research which publishers and agents deal with the sort of novel that you want to write – and the book in your hands now is the perfect place to start. If you're unpublished or new to the genre, I'd strongly recommend joining the Romantic Novelists' Association (RNA; see page 539). Not only is it a great way of meeting fellow romantic novelists, but they also curate and run the New Writers' Scheme, which aims to support emerging writers. Philippa Carey spent three years refining the craft of writing Regency romance within this scheme and found success submitting to The *People's Friend* magazine. And, taking a broader look at routes to market: Catherine Tinley made an unsolicited submission to Harlequin Mills & Boon and secured a deal for *Waltzing with the Earl* (2017), which went on to win a prestigious award; Jasmina Svenna has had several pocket novels published with *My Weekly* (Jasmina advises that, at 50,000 words or fewer, pocket novels are ideal for writers who aren't sure if they can manage anything longer, and that the best submission format is three chapters and a synopsis, with the third chapter ending on a dramatic cliffhanger). Submission guidelines and all other details can be found at www.myweekly.co.uk/2022/03/09/calling-all-fiction-writers.

If you want to write Regency romance, then welcome to the ballroom. You'll be in for an exhilarating time – reading and writing books that can challenge stereotype just as much as they comfort readers in our hour of need.

After a career in publishing, **Katy Moran** began writing books for young adults. She is the author of the Regency romance trilogy for adults, published by Head of Zeus: *Game of Hearts* (2017), *Wicked by Design* (2022) and *Scandalous Alchemy* (2022). *My Lady's Secrets* (2024) is a fast-paced standalone Regency romance. You can find out more at katymoran.co.uk and follow her on Twitter @KatyjaMoran.

See also...

Books

Reigniting the past: writing historical fiction

Annie Garthwaite's debut historical novel *Cecily* (Penguin 2021) was born out of a lifelong interest in the women of the Wars of the Roses. Her greatest ambition (and most fearful challenge), she says, was to make these long-dead matriarchs live for today's readers. Here she offers some of the lessons she learned from writing their story.

'Cecily who?' This was the most common response I got when I told people I was writing a novel about Cecily Neville. I soon learnt that I needed to explain: 'Richard III's mother,' I'd say, then wait for the spark of recognition to light their faces. It usually didn't take long. Most people know something about Richard – the King in the Carpark, the hunchback tyrant, Shakespeare's villain. I'm not here to defend Richard's reputation; think of him what you will, most people know his name and have an opinion. Of Cecily, however, few have any opinion at all. And it's this very thing that, to my mind, made her a ripe subject for fiction. Cecily is one of those women – a giant in her time – who has slipped through the net of history, ignored by the (mostly male) writers who, over centuries, have curated our understanding of the civil wars that tore 15th-century England apart.

My interest in the Wars of the Roses began when I was a teenager, but it took years of reading and study for me to realise how large a part Cecily played in them. The only major protagonist to live through the wars from beginning to end, Cecily was England's most powerful lady, close to the centre of political power and driving the action much more decisively than you might imagine. By the time I was in my twenties, the desire to tell her story was burning hot within me. And that brings me to my first piece of advice: if you're setting out to write historical fiction, choose a character that you simply can't *not* write about. You're going to be spending a lot of time with them, so you have to want it badly.

Find the obsession

Historical fiction is hard, a long haul, and the depth of research required to do it well will shock you – it shocks me still. From that first spark of interest in Cecily, it took me the best part of 40 years to reach the point where I could start to write her story. Admittedly, a business career and 'life' got in the way but, even if they hadn't, the time spent in research and preparation would have been measured in years rather than months. Throughout those years – my twenties, thirties and forties – when I wasn't working I was reading constantly, attending conferences and talks, and delving deep into the controversies surrounding Cecily and her family. So, unless you're 100% committed to your character's story – obsessed by it even – stop now. This is a serious undertaking. Writing historical fiction isn't just an act of imaginative creation, it's *work*. Sign up or sign out.

The obsession thing was never hard for me. Cecily set her teeth in my flesh early and wasn't letting go. And, to be fair, the research was a joy. One of the things that has pleased me most since Cecily was published is that real historians (people who make their living by studying the past) have recognised the level of research that informs it. That means a lot to me. I've always felt a responsibility to root out the likely truth of Cecily's life from the dark soil of known fact. But here comes the next hard lesson: once you've completed that tireless preparatory research – once you understand the physical, political, religious and emotional 'scape' your character lives in and can navigate it as confidently as they can – you need to look *beyond* it. Somewhere deep within their history you'll find their story.

Find the story

For me, walking within Cecily's 'scape' meant coming to understand the complex twists and turns of the wars and the motivations of the key players. It also meant grappling with European as well as English politics, and being familiar with the role of women in medieval society – from their experiences of childbirth to their rights under the law. It meant knowing the fashions of the times in music, literature and clothes, from Burgundian waistlines to the depth and texture of Italian velvets. It meant bending my post-reformation sensibilities around the arcane practices and beliefs of the medieval catholic church, and appreciating that, within the medieval mind, religious conviction could live side by side with a belief in witchcraft, sorcery and astrology.

As I've said before, this was a work of many years. But, in the end, everything I'd learned was only – as the much-lamented Dame Hilary Mantel described such things – 'furniture': vital if you want to create a world, tedious if described in detail. Just because you know how a 15th-century door handle works, you don't need to describe it; just give us the satisfying thud as the door is slammed. The truth is, everything you will have learned in your research is 'just' history – political, social, cultural or decorative. And although that history is utterly vital, fascinating, revelatory and occasionally mind-blowing, it isn't a story. It's the *starting* point for your work, not its conclusion.

If readers want to read history, they'll read history books. They should. Your appeal is to readers who have chosen fiction, whose first hunger is for propulsive narrative and compelling characters. In the reader of historical fiction, I believe, the need for emotional engagement is at least equal to, if not greater than, intellectual curiosity. Your readers will want to walk through your character's 'scape' with you, take in its scents and sounds, and experience its dramas first-hand. E. L. Doctorow described perfectly the difference between the historian and the novelist: 'The historian,' he said, 'will tell you what happened. The novelist will tell you what it felt like.'

So I stick by my guns; your primary responsibility as a writer of historical fiction is to find your character's compelling story. It must be one that, though set within an arcane, long-ago world, will be comprehensible to today's audience. To be so, it must appeal to the human mind and heart. Let me explain through example: there are two ways to describe what *Cecily* is about. First and most obviously, it's about the matriarch of the house of York during the Wars of the Roses. Now, that's a fine description, accurate and succinct so far as it goes, but hardly revelatory. More meaningfully, my book is about how women exercise power in a world where men hold most of the power cards. It's about what a woman might do to protect her family and future. It's about what happens to a person when they reach for power rather than let themselves be destroyed by it. It's about matters that preoccupy us today but set in a world and time that lets us view those matters through a new lens. Someone interested in 15th-century history might buy the book based on the first description; someone interested in life and story will be attracted by the second. And here's a universal truth you need to grasp, because it will directly impact on your sales: there are many more people interested in life than in history.

Books

At the heart of every great story, of course, sits the protagonist – the character who drives the action and whose fate, ultimately, matters most. In my first book that's obviously Cecily. Who might it be for you? To write successfully, you'll need to know them (and everyone with whom they interact) at least as well as you know yourself. Once you've learned their story and 'scape', your next challenge is to uncover their nature – their ambition, motivation and emotional range.

Know your characters

I was given a head start in this regard by an inspiring teacher. Keith Hill taught history like it happened yesterday and, while others of his ilk were stuffing kid's heads with dates and facts, he asked the most important questions: 'So why do you think she did that?' he'd ask. 'What was in his mind when…?' My A level result wasn't that impressive; I was a bit woolly on dates – but I was very strong on character motivation!

I think this is the most important advice I have to offer any aspiring writer of historical fiction: know your history, but understand your character. History, after all, will only tell us so much. Here I must quote Hilary Mantel (what can I say? She was a genius, and her *Wolf Hall* trilogy is a landmark in historical fiction). Hilary pointed out that what we know of the past from history is incomplete; there's a great deal we're ignorant of, or that's been misrepresented or forgotten. 'History,' she says, 'is no more the past than a map is a journey.' To find your character, pick up the imperfect map and take the journey with them. Walk it in their shoes. Your hard-won knowledge of their world – from its politics to its door handles – will help you find the route, but it's the days on the road together that will unlock the secrets of their personality.

For me, Mantel's greatest achievement is that her novels are peopled with characters who live and breathe, who are simultaneously of their time and all time, who are both distant and familiar. And it's particularly impressive that she's achieved this with characters so 'famous' (quite the reverse of my own Cecily) that they've almost become caricatures: Henry the lusty and frustrated king, Anne Boleyn the vixen queen and, of course, Thomas Cromwell, the thuggish Machiavel who brought down the church for money. In Mantel's hands their personalities and their motivations stretch; they become multidimensional, sometimes contradictory – just as people are. Cromwell is ruthless enough to see his enemies hang, but takes in beggars and stray cats. He is rigorously pragmatic, but motivated by profound faith. He is at the same time arrogant and fearful; he remembers every one of his personal hurts. In short, he is utterly human, completely relatable.

To create characters of such authenticity we have to put our own sensibilities aside and adopt theirs. Sometimes I find, when I'm writing Cecily, that her dialogue spins out almost without my intervention… ('Ouch!' – I'll find myself thinking, as she lets fly some verbal barb – 'That's a terrible thing to say!'. 'I don't care,' she replies. 'I speak as I find.' I can almost see the shrug of her silk-laden shoulders.) This is when you know it's working – when dialogue falls from your pen, or when you can't help but weep at your character's disasters or grin at their triumphs. When the grief you feel at the loss of them is as fresh as if they'd died this morning.

But, before I turn whimsical, let me share with you some Cromwellian wisdom: 'Choose your prince', he advises in *Wolf Hall* (Fourth Estate 2009). And I advise: choose your characters and hitch your wagon firmly to their star. Stay with them, walk with them, lay down in the dust and weep with them if the occasion demands it. Make it your business to put flesh on their bones and breath in their lungs, by understanding the three things that shape us all: our history, our 'scape' and our nature.

Annie Garthwaite grew up in a working-class community in the north east of England. She studied English at the University of Wales before embarking on a 30-year international business career, eventually establishing her own communications consultancy. In 2017 she studied for an MA in creative writing at Warwick University and, during two years of study, wrote her debut novel *Cecily* (Penguin 2021). *Cecily* was named a 'top pick' by *The Times* and *Sunday Times* and a Best Book of 2021 by independent bookshops and Waterstones. Her second novel, *The King's Mother*, will be published in July 2024. Find more on www.anniegarthwaite.com. Follow her on Twitter @anniegarthwaite.

See also...
- *Weaving fact into fiction*, page 283
- *Writing popular history books*, page 286

Writing speculative fiction

Author Claire North considers the nature of 'speculative fiction', and the blurry nature of genres more broadly, and provides advice for writers on the boundless world-building possibilities that writers of fantastical fiction can develop to grab a reader's imagination.

You could spend as much time arguing about what 'speculative fiction' is as writing it. Magic realism? Literature with a twist? Science fiction? Hi-tech social commentary? It's worth asking this question as – although hopefully you are writing out of love for words on the page – your experience of being a published author will vary hugely, depending on where (rather arbitrarily) the world decides your speculative fiction falls.

The question of genre
Revolutions in film, TV and games now mean that science fiction and fantasy have never been more popular and accepted in the mainstream. Yet the world of literary criticism and review frequently still treats genre as if it were less worthy of note than literature, despite its potent selling power. Without making 'literature' a term of exclusions (NOT crime, NOT thriller, NOT romance) it can be hard to say what 'literary' actually means, and the inclusion of writers such as Margaret Atwood, David Mitchell, Kazuo Ishiguro and George Orwell on mainstream shelves only adds to the justified arch of your raised eyebrow.

Partly in response to this, 'speculative fiction' has grown in recent years as a term that tweaks the definition of genre into something mainstream – and therefore perhaps more acceptable. Not quite 'hard' science fiction or pure fantasy, but laced through with an element of something strange, fantastical or other, it is the land of Emily St. John Mandel, Nick Harkaway, Naomi Alderman, and – in film/TV terms – of *Black Mirror* or *Stranger Things*. Speculative fiction is, in short, an excellent corner to claim for marketing purposes, encompassing the best of so many worlds: if only you can work out what it means.

The simplest truth may be the truth of all genres, namely that the key difference between, say, hard science fiction and speculative fiction is a publisher's marketing choice. In the case of M.R. Carey's *Girl with all the Gifts* (Orbit 2014) this meant removing any reference to 'zombies' from both book and blurb, transforming an excellent apocalypse story into something sold as nuanced character-study in a difficult world. Both aspects are of course true – it is both a character study and a straight-up zombie book – but most books are more than one thing, and it could have been positioned a dozen other ways. Genre is an increasingly blurry line – a comforting tool for helping us find books that we love, as well as an imprisoning categorisation used to define what we don't read as much as what we do. What we read defines us; there is still a social pressure to be seen to read the 'right' thing. Men do not read books about shopping with Comic Sans lettering on pink covers; adults do not read Harry Potter unless they have silver embossed jackets – and so on. The world is changing, perhaps, but social pressures remain.

Does genre even matter?
Of course, appreciating the nuances of how genre is positioned in the changing world of bookshop categories and predictive algorithms may not affect what you write. Indeed, I would argue that at the early stages of writing, it shouldn't. Writing is a business, but it is also a joy, a gift. Forget market positioning, forget reviewer bias; the best book you can

possibly write is the one you loved writing the most. And if you have chosen to write speculative fiction – embrace it, enjoy it! In the future you might find yourself making artistic choices based on where a publisher seeks to sell you, but this makes *now* the moment to choose a path that you'll always love walking. That said, there are a few things to bear in mind in those earliest stages, that may help you on your quest:

1. Have confidence
Easier said than done, but this is key, especially in speculative fiction, to bringing a reader into a place where their imagination has never been before. You do not need to explain your choices; you do not need to info-dump your world. If you know every detail of it already, it will manifest in the actions of your text, in the story that you *show* rather than the information that you tell. In doing so, you have already won half the battle.

'Show, don't tell' is one of the classic rules. It is the art of revealing information through story, rather than through exposition.
- 'The witches are coming!'
- *'No – not the witches of the west!'*
- 'Yes, the very ones, who drink the blood of infants!'
- *'Oh my God – and who wear blue robes while chanting to their pagan gods?'*
- 'That's them!'

Nah, mate. Think of the tools you have available to you as a writer to help us **live** a story – third person, first person, extracted texts, second person, biased narrator, past tense, present tense, future tense, flashback. There is a tool out there that is waiting for you to **show** us your world, and to transform information into experience. It is the secret of every great medical drama. Very few people know why the CT scan matters or what the spleen does, but we all hear the truth of **feeling** beneath this language and are caught up by the emotional urgency beneath the technobabble.

Where information must be given, be succinct:
- 'The western witches in robes of blue, who drank the blood of babies and worshipped their pagan gods, came upon the town as it was sleeping.'

Job done. You have imparted data. Now move on; there's a story to tell.

2. Use story for world-building
The same 'show, don't tell' applies to speculative fiction world-building. Show us what we need to know. It is the difference between:
- 'She was one of the sisters, an ancient order of healers, who look after dying men on the battlefield.'

and
- 'The sister's robe was still caked in the blood of the men she had tended on the battlefield ...'

The immediacy of one brings us into the moment; the other is just information. Resist putting every detail of your world on the page; the story must come first, and the world will unfold as it does. A focus on story allows you to start harder, faster, and let the reader invest more in building the world for themselves.

3. Obey your own rules
It is the classic *Dr Who/Buffy the Vampire Slayer* trope: around 40 minutes into a 45-minute episode (or 250 pages into an average book), when things have got just about as bad as

they can possibly get, someone finds a giant button/a mystic spell that fixes everything. In crime, this is the unexpected witness who busts the case wide open; thrillers have the dramatic helicopter rescue. But in speculative fiction, if you try to write yourself out of that plot-hole with an unexpected *deus ex machina*, there is a danger that you will undermine a reader's immersion in what that world is. Don't be afraid of deleting your way to freedom and take time to structure your story. Especially in speculative fiction, death need not be the thing that *matters*. In thrillers in the Chris Ryan vein, soldiers live and soldiers die, but *betrayal* hurts more than actual bullets. Gout doesn't kill Falstaff; the betrayal of Prince Hal does. What matters to the story is not life or death, but what these things mean to our characters. Mount Doom erupting in Middle-Earth has nothing on Frodo succumbing to the dark side. Find what matters to your world and characters; obey your own rules.

4. Humanity is your gift

Speculative fiction is a genre that offers you so many possibilities, from the pure joy of space cowboy adventure through to tales of horror and deceit. But, more than anything, it lets you ask what humanity *is*. What is it to be human, in a world where apps and algorithms run our lives? Are we still ourselves with 30% of our brain grown from something else? 40%? 50%? Are we still ourselves, unique and true, when our clone sits opposite us? Is it human nature to build or to destroy? If we know the thoughts of others, does that elevate us or destroy the very essence of humanity? Is Kafka's twisted human cockroach still a man? Does humankind need gender? Can humans be grown in a lab?

We ask these questions, and in doing so we can tear down the barriers that are used to stratify humanity into exclusionary ideas of 'not I', such as class, race, ethnicity and sex. Fiction tells stories that catch the heart and then bring the head along after. We can do all of this, and we can have fun doing it, poking at the world while having badass, awesome adventures.

This being so, embrace the scope of humanity that is offered to you. Forget normative, oppressive ideas of women, men or culture. Speculative fiction opens up realms of boundless imagination to you; be awesome, and imagine humanity – lots and lots of it.

Claire North is the pen name of Catherine Webb, who also writes under the name Kate Griffin. Her novel, *The First Fifteen Lives of Harry August* (Orbit 2014) was shortlisted for the Arthur C. Clarke Award and was selected for the Richard and Judy Book Club, the Waterstones Book Club and the Radio 2 Book Club. Also published by Orbit, her novel *The Sudden Appearance of Hope* (2017) won the 2017 World Fantasy Award for Best Novel and *The End of the Day* (2017) was shortlisted for the *Sunday Times*/PFD Young Writer of the Year Award. Recent books under the Claire North pseudonym are *Notes from the Burning Age* (2021) and *Ithaca* (2022), the first book in a trilogy telling the story of Penelope, wife of Odysseus, all published by Orbit. Follow her on Twitter @ClaireNorth42.

Writing and publishing short stories

Paul McVeigh describes what he has learned about the world of short stories, stressing the value of performing one's work live and hearing it performed. He has tips on the practicalities, as well as the rewards and opportunities, of competitions and radio commissions catering for this demanding and alluring art form.

I had given up writing for a few years – due to a mixture of rejection and, getting older, needing the financial security of a job, especially as I was living in that beautiful, big, bank-account vampire called London. In a final attempt at the whole writing dream, I thought to kick-start the old writing engine by going along to a one-day course. The tutor mentioned she was reading a short story that night at a live event in Soho. I went along and, unexpectedly, fell in love with short stories.

Since that night, I've read stories at events, had stories read on BBC radio and even 'performed' one on TV for Sky Arts, as well as being published in newspapers, journals and anthologies. I also became involved in producing short story events such as Word Factory – described by the *Guardian* as 'the national organisation for excellence in the short story' – and co-founding the London Short Story Festival. At the same time, I became a reader for small prizes and eventually a judge for bigger ones – the Royal Society of Literature's V.S. Pritchard Short Story Prize, the Edge Hill Short Story Award and the Dylan Thomas Prize. For this article, I'll try to condense as much of what I've learned judging, performing, producing events, publishing and reading short stories as I can possibly fit in. Let's start with a short-story avenue that little has been written about. Here goes …

Live events

I know that some people, for numerous reasons, hate reading their work live. If you like the idea, or if you could push yourself, give it a go. It can be a little like the difference between traditional poetry and performance poetry – some writers love it as an art in itself, with publication as an added pleasure rather than the purpose. Some writers appear like actors or performers; at a reading there will be those who write solely to be seen and heard, while others try out ideas or hone a piece before submitting for publication. It's a small but vibrant scene that enables you to meet other writers for community support and gain potential book buyers for the future. And, in my case, it was where my agent saw and signed me. Listening to the work of others, like reading, makes you a better writer – either because you learn tricks and tools of the trade or because you learn what *not* to do.

Even if you don't continue to do live reading for its art, think of it as excellent practice for when that publishing deal happens and you're asked to read from your collection (or novel) at a literary event or festival. If you're good at reading from your work, and can engage or electrify the audience, word travels – not only will you be asked back but you'll also be asked to attend other events. The opposite can happen too, so it's worth starting in a small and supportive environment where the stakes are low.

Top tip: even if you don't want to read your work at an event, read it out loud to yourself. It's one of the best pieces of editing advice I ever received and it gives you some of the benefits that live readings provide. If you stumble in a sentence, so will your reader; you also get a real feel for rhythm. In addition, if you can bear it, get someone else to read your work to you; see where they stumble. When reading our own work, we often read what we intended to write and with the inflection we desire, whereas a new reader reads out what you have actually written – just what's on the page.

Short stories for radio

Live events provide a good arena to start thinking about writing short stories for radio. In the rush for publication, writing for radio is often forgotten, and the irony is that radio is probably the largest commissioner of short stories in the UK and Ireland. Put BBC Radio 4 Short Story in your search bar and you will find a treasure trove of recordings read by our greatest performers. You can listen to stories from some of the best short story writers the world has to offer. Don't forget, Radio 4 is also the home to the BBC National Short Story Award (see page 545), offering £15,000 for the winner, so once you've honed your style to the platform you can send a story in. On the website you'll find past winning stories and also those shortlisted, as well as specially-commissioned stories celebrating the art of the short story.

These stories, like those at live events, are also written to be read out and listened to, and there is a vocal performance (usually by professional actors and only occasionally by the author). But there aren't the visual cues we get from watching a reading. This sounds obvious, I know, but it requires a recalibration of your writing – it's a style that sits in between writing to be read and writing to be read out.

Here are some useful tips given to me by my first radio producer, Heather Larmour. Firstly, it pays to be mindful that radio slots tend to be in the afternoon (… think parents listening with children in the car on the school run). You can tackle serious issues, but don't be too bleak or depressing, and strong language wouldn't be encouraged. Consider how intimate the radio experience is – this makes your words so much more powerful and potentially shocking than they would be in written form. And using fast dialogue is fine on the page, but it can be difficult to read out and confusing to the listener; remember there will be only one reader and not a cast (you are not writing a play). Do you live or are you from a region? There are BBC studios all around the UK, each of which commission work, so you might have more of a fighting chance with your local studio than by trying to get noticed in London, say – simply due to the number of writers hoping for that spot. The great news is that you can earn up to £500 for a new story. Doesn't sound like a lot to you? Compare it to the fact that the average debut novelist gets less than £1000 for their 120,000-word opus.

Top tip: short stories for the radio are 2,100 words, give or take a word of two. This is much shorter than you'd expect; the slots are 15 minutes but, with intro and outro music, and credits, it comes in under that time. So give it a try – you might be one of those writers who is relieved by the very achievable word count (similar to the length of this article, for comparison) but it's quite a task to conjure a world, a character or three, and take the listener on a satisfying journey in such a short time. Even if it's not your thing, it's a good challenge. Which brings me to the question …

How short is a short story?

Stories for the radio slots mentioned above are the shortest example I've heard of for what is traditionally accepted as a short story. In the UK and Ireland, a lot of journals and competitions use the 3,000-word mark. Why? Market forces would be my guess. From the admin side, they are quicker to read, saving your first readers and editors (often unpaid or, at best, poorly paid) precious time; also, you can fit more of these in your magazine. And there's the much-debated argument that, these days, readers' attention is harder to keep – so-called 'swipe culture' – made worse by the amount of free content online. There are those who do take longer stories, such as the aforementioned BBC award which takes stories up to 8,000 words (although this will be heavily edited when aired), so have a look around if that's your bag.

It is worth mentioning that the US market is a different kettle of fish. In a country where everything seems super-sized, a popular magazine like *Glimmer Train* (www.glimmertrain.com) has a 'Very Short Story Competition' which is up to 3,000 words, while their magazine accepts stories up to 20,000 words! Be aware that they get approximately 40,000 story submissions a year and publish around 40. Literary journals and magazines in the UK and Ireland won't be getting this kind of submission number, but I hear that Ireland's most prestigious literary magazine, *The Stinging Fly* (https://stingingfly.org), publishes about 5% of submissions. If you're thinking of getting into short stories because it's easy to get published, then you might want to reconsider.

Some writers also think they'll write short stories because they are easy, or easier, than writing a novel. It may take you less time … but easier? Most short-story writers will tell you that a great short story takes a novel's worth of thinking. Every word counts, and so much needs to be conveyed in such a short space, that each sentence has to do a lot of work covering at least a couple of these elements: hint at back story, reveal character, further the plot, create tension … Think about the Hemingway story 'Iceberg Theory'; in the short story you are reading just the surface, the tip of the iceberg that can be seen, but nine tenths of its mass is unseen, below the surface, below the words.

Awards, competitions and prizes

I've been a reader and judge for awards, competitions and prizes. The odds are as tough as submitting for publication – sometimes worse, as there may only be one winner. If it's so tough, why try? Well, the benefits can be career-making; even being shortlisted can lead to success. A writer who was shortlisted for the *Sunday Times* Audible Short Story Award a couple of years ago landed a six-figure, multi-book deal from it. The awards themselves can be lucrative too. The *Sunday Times* prize money comes in at a whopping £30,000. Not bad for a short story, eh? Apart from these biggies, there are lots of small and mid-sized competitions that not only offer prize money but also the chance of publication, as they print the shortlisted stories in an anthology. Some are free to enter but others can ask for a fee. Though some writers get cross about this, these prizes are charities and the entrance fee goes towards the administration as well as paying the readers and judges.

Top tip: to paraphrase Stephen King, to be a good writer you have to be a good reader. Every writing class I've been to tells you the same thing: read, read, read. Anthologies are a great place to start – they can hold a large number of stories, usually in a 'best of' collection, so you also know you are reading what are considered to be prime examples by readers and the industry. You can also read free stories in the *New Yorker*; these are newly written and by the best writers in the field today. The *Paris Review* also has an interview series free online in which the greatest of modern and 'classic' writers, such as Hemingway and Fitzgerald, have discussed their craft.

Good luck!

Books

Paul McVeigh began his writing career in Belfast as a playwright, and has written comedy, short stories and flash fiction, as well as a novel, *The Good Son* (Salt Publishing 2015) which won the Polari First Book Prize and the McCrea Literary Award. His work has been performed on radio, stage and TV, and his short stories published in anthologies, newspapers and literary journals. Paul has been the judge for several international literary prizes and his work has been translated into seven languages. He co-founded the London Short Story Festival, is Associate Director at the Word Factory, and was Head of Literature for the Arts Council of Northern Ireland. You can listen to his new ten-part linked short story series *The Circus* on BBC Sounds. For more information, see his website https://paulmcveighwriter.com.

Writing a romcom

Rachel Winters defines the essential constituents of a successful romcom, offering her experience as both editor and writer.

The first short story I ever wrote was when I was eight, and it was about a serial killer. So when I say my journey to being a romcom writer hasn't exactly been straightforward, I don't exaggerate. In my defence, I was reading a lot of Point Horror at the time.

In time I moved on to writing more wholesome fantasy. My undergrad degree was in creative writing, as I'd harboured dreams of becoming the next Robin Hobb (creator of the *Assassin's Apprentice* series). Sadly, though I loved being a student (classes were four hours a week and the campus was so small most people turned up in their slippers), at the end of the course I was told I wasn't very good. I'd never had much confidence and this was the deal-breaker for me – I pretty much stopped writing altogether.

I still loved books and decided to go into publishing – which, it turned out, was fiercely competitive. Cue several years of being a personal assistant (a very bad one), a part-time Publishing MA student, an academic editor, and then, finally, landing my dream job – working at HarperVoyager. During this time, while I barely typed a sentence of fiction, I was writing. I had my own column for a cat newspaper (though I didn't own a cat) and spent five years writing entertainment reviews for an online magazine. By the time I became a commissioning editor at Gollancz, the UK's oldest and biggest science fiction and fantasy imprint, I thought that my writing days were well and truly behind me. Thankfully, I was wrong.

My job is a creative one – we get to work with incredible writers; some are debut authors, some are well established, all of them have spent years honing their craft. As editors we learn to pick apart the building blocks of narrative and examine how it all works. A key aspect of my job is to develop ideas. This involves building a book from the ground up – coming up with a concept, thinking about the readership, creating an overarching plot, characters, a grand finale. Doing this for my day job gave me the confidence I needed to start writing fiction again. I've always loved the romantic comedy genre, and I had an idea that would utilise my healthy appreciation of 90s Hugh Grant. My idea was that of a self-referential romcom, because readers are savvy and well aware of the tropes, while still being a love letter to the genre. Maybe, this time, I could silence the person's voice who'd told me I wasn't good enough – and write.

So I did (assisted by my good friends: chocolate and coffee). With the help of brilliant editors, it became *Would Like to Meet* (Trapeze 2020), which to date has sold in 15 territories and has been optioned for a major film deal. There's no set formula to writing a book, but as a debut author I found it useful to consider the following elements. It's no coincidence that these are also what I focus on as an editor:

1. Concept

The concept helps you find your audience by hooking them in and revealing the genre. It is, to use a familiar term, the 'elevator pitch' – your book's USP. It is what makes it stand out from the market, while at the same time appealing to a certain readership. Simple, eh? (Laughs forever …)

The concept of *Would Like to Meet* is this: Assistant Evie Summers has to prove romcoms are realistic, in order to convince an arrogant screenwriter to write one and save the film agency she works for. It's tricky trying to narrow a whole book down to its core idea, but it's worth it. It will help you establish your book's goal. I raised a question at the beginning of *WLTM* – one that interested me: can real love ever be like the movies? And by the end of the book I had to answer it. The concept is what you can keep coming back to when you wander from the story path that leads to your conclusion. Ask yourself: am I still honouring that initial premise? Is it working? If not, why not?

2. Plot development

Next, you can unpack the plot. I'd established the goal in *WLTM* – to save the agency, and how my main character would achieve this goal – by proving it was possible to fall in love via a romcom 'meet-cute' (the moment the two love interests meet for the first time). And, of course, she had to unexpectedly, for her at least, find love along the way. Now, every step of the plot – from the settings to the best friend characters – had to serve that story.

I'd advise outlining the plot first to give your book its best possible start. You have to lay out the playing field before you can begin the game (which is the only sports analogy I'll ever use). You might prefer to write a particular type of romcom: love-to-hate, friends-to-lovers, enemies-to-lovers, etc. There are tropes associated with these categories, which can help when plotting (whether you follow or subvert them).

Know your ending – not just who the main character ends up with, but how. With a romantic comedy, the end is likely to be at least partially predictable, and yet it must still be satisfying. It's often not so much about the ending but the journey. What are all your key plot points to get you there? What obstacles will the love interests face? Will you weave in some red herrings? What are the emotional conflicts? When planning, I used the meet-cute re-enactments as focal points which served as my plot skeleton. In practice, I had to revise most of these scenes for myriad reasons – characters will often surprise you; you'll come up with multiple new ideas as you write; you accidentally overwrite the first draft by 40,000 words, etc. It's totally ok for your book to veer from your initial outline – it was just your playing field, after all. Having laid the groundwork, now you can start moving your pieces around.

3. Characters

You might choose to have two main characters who share the narrative, as in Beth O'Leary's *The Flatshare* (Quercus 2019). *Would Like to Meet* was a first-person narrative with one main character, Evie. I have a confession: in the first draft she was (whisper it) sort of based on me. She had my sense of humour and a good dose of my social anxiety. The more I wrote, however, I realised that how I would act within the story wasn't how Evie could act (big surprise). Yes, she had to have flaws, and I wanted her to go on a journey of self-discovery as much as finding love, but she also had to be far bolder than I would be. I wouldn't spill a drink on a stranger – she would.

Ask yourself, who does your main character have to be in order to achieve what they need to within the story? Evie needed to be incredibly passionate about her job, if she was to go to such extremes for it. And she had to start out with a lack of self-belief in order to grow, eventually, to a place of self-confidence. As you plot out your story, also consider how each step along the way will grow and shape your character on their own journey.

They can be likeable, but their flaws and emotional conflicts still need to get in their way occasionally, to create tension.

As for the rest – every character should fulfil a function that the other characters don't. Parents. Friends. Bosses. Enemies. What role are they playing that's crucial to the story? How do their personalities and goals affect your main characters?

4. Love interest

As in Helen Fielding's *Bridget Jones's Diary* (Picador 1996), with Mark Darcy and Daniel Cleaver, you might choose to have more than one prospective partner for your character. What makes yours swoon-worthy? Looks help of course, but in that story it's Mark Darcy's uptight stoicism and Daniel Cleaver's rakish arrogance and wit that readers thirst for – two opposing personalities, each bringing their own emotional conflict for Bridget.

Does your love interest enter the stage fully formed, or do they have some growing to do? What is their own journey through the plot, and how does that intersect with your main character's? Do their characters complement or oppose each other? If there are two love interests, does one fit with your main character at the start, and the other the person they become by the end? Ben, the widower dad in *WLTM*, is a closed book at the start, whereas the arrogant screenwriter, Ezra, is seemingly an open one. As I progressed the plot, and Ben's and Ezra's characters, I wanted to convince readers to change their allegiances as to who they wanted Evie to choose, right up until the end.

Conflict can create sparks or drama; so can competition. What creates those essential sparks between your characters?

5. Conflict

Ah, sweet, sexy conflict. It's what drives romcoms and keeps them so ridiculously compelling. In the plot itself there will be setbacks for your character, as when other characters have goals that conflict with theirs, and conflict between the love interests.

In romcoms people expect obstacles; they want to see emotional (i.e. 'internal') conflict – something that creates enough tension that makes it all the more satisfying when the two love interests eventually do get together. External conflict – a missed plane, a dead phone battery – doesn't really have the zing romcom readers crave. Internal conflict, however, that's the good stuff – loyalty to family, or ambition to succeed in your career, whatever it takes (here's looking at you, Tom Hanks in *You've Got Mail*).

Of course, external conflict can (and should) lead to internal conflict: what if your character missed that plane when they were trying to prove they could be reliable? Or the battery dies on their phone midway through an important sentence ('I absolutely hate you[niversity]')? By the end, your love interests have to survive the conflict. It can't be insurmountable, but it does have to be satisfying, effective and believable. A classic example is Nora Ephron's script for the film *When Harry Met Sally*. The initial conflict is that Harry believes men and women can't be friends. Sally believes they can. Eventually, that conflict manifests in their friendship, until it finally resolves itself through emotional growth.

6. Pace

Romcoms tend to be fairly short, pacey books (75,000-95,000 words), with attention-keeping chapters. Write what you need to get the story out, then trim. Be brutal with yourself. Do you need that scene? Does that indulgently lengthy Christmas chapter move the story along, or can it (as in *WLTM*) be reduced to a single email? Can you halve that dialogue? Is every single sentence serving your story?

7. Comedy

Ah, the essential 'com' part of the romcom. There are all kinds of comedy you can include: slapstick, situational, observational, wordplay. Whatever works for you. Trimming will help keep it snappy. What makes other people laugh is often indefinable. My rule is, it's a romance first. After that, if it makes me laugh, it goes in (though always listen to your editors, no matter how funny you might find toilet humour).

Finally, write because you love it – it always shows – and don't let someone else's thoughtless words prevent you doing so.

Rachel Winters is the author of *Would Like to Meet* (Trapeze 2020). She has a degree in Creative Writing and an MA in Publishing. After writing freelance for local papers and online magazines, she later worked as a commissioning editor for Orion Books and is now a Lecturer in Creative Writing at Lancaster University. Follow her on Twitter @Frostycheeks.

See also...
• *Writing romantic fiction*, page 258

Weaving fact into fiction

Jo Browning Wroe tells how the story for her debut novel came into being, woven around the personal experience of those deeply affected by a true-life disaster. She describes what she learned in the process of collecting and immersing herself in historical facts to craft her fictional characters and narrative.

As a debut novelist, I only have one experience to draw on for this piece about weaving real events into fiction. I was a novice; I was conscious that I had to pay close and careful attention to what I was trying to do and how I went about it.

The idea for my novel *A Terrible Kindness* (Faber & Faber 2022) started with me reading an account, in some 50-year-old conference papers, for the annual gathering of the UK funeral industry. I was in Cambridge University Library, researching a different project. The account was written by the man who had co-ordinated the extraordinary voluntary operation carried out by embalmers from all over the UK following the Aberfan disaster of 1966, when a coal tip thundered down a mountainside burying a primary school and killing most of its children. I was floored by the heroic kindness called upon from people because of their profession, how they stood shoulder to shoulder with a community at the outer limits of human distress. I was pulled in as if by power suction and, with no agent, let alone publisher, I was soon flying to Belfast to meet the author of that account.

Breaking his silence of fifty years, he talked with me for hours about his experience. I was left wanting to honour his and his colleagues' contribution, whilst respecting the people of Aberfan. I would never have taken it upon myself to write a story from the perspective of someone from the village, but to try and crawl under the skin of someone who went to help, because they had a skill that nobody ever wants to need, felt worth a try. So this is the story of how I went about it – and the important things I've learned. My book begins and ends in Aberfan; in between are 17 years of my protagonist's life – as a boarding boy chorister in Cambridge, a trainee embalmer, and someone living with undiagnosed PTSD. I had a lot to find out, consider and apply.

I sought out people whose lived experience was relevant to my characters, I prepared questions and then, whenever possible, I travelled to where they were, or occasionally we spoke on the phone. One way or another, I interviewed them. Lots of them ... embalmers who had been in Aberfan, press photographers and news reporters, former Cambridge choristers, current-day choristers, choirmasters, therapists. I had prepared a lot of questions.

And here's the most important thing I learned early on: too many questions can seriously get in the way of the best material. Constantly pulling the conversation back to an agenda I'd drawn up when I didn't know what I didn't know could so easily close down valuable recollections and reflections. Whilst there were many particular and important things I needed to find out, I learned to leave those until the end. It became my priority to create a space in which people could talk freely about their experience in the way that came naturally to them. All sorts of things came out that I could never ever have anticipated or thought to have asked about – elements that became vital threads in my woven story. The specificity of these memories was so often the gold I was hoping for; details to surprise and move readers, pulling them into the story. I stopped thinking of these meetings as interviews and started thinking of them as *listenings*.

I have alluded already to the many specific and practical questions that really did need answering. To write about the experience of being a chorister in the 1950s, I needed to know how their days panned out, what they sang, when they sang, how they rehearsed, how they managed all the other schoolwork, what mealtimes and bedtimes were like. And what initially felt like more of a challenge was that I was writing from the point of view of an embalmer – a profession and process about which I knew little.

The men who had been to Aberfan were generous with their time, dredging up memories that couldn't have been easy to reconnect with, and I remain hugely indebted to them for the opening section of the story. When I started writing in earnest and questions quickly started stacking up, I was uncomfortable going back to bother them for more detail. They had breathed life into my imagining of the disaster from an embalmer's point of view and it felt inappropriate to pester them for practical questions. So, in order to avoid anachronisms, I found someone who had been an embalmer during the 1960s, but who hadn't attended the disaster. He was happy for me to email him questions whenever they arose and was astonishingly quick and detailed in his response.

Even before I went into the mortuary to watch this, I'd had three visits with a young, third-generation embalmer, and it was these encounters that were most responsible for me shifting my emphasis from 'interviews' to 'listenings'. He not only shared factual details with me but, unexpectedly and unasked, he talked about the emotional and psychological cost of coming into work each day to face the very thing the rest of us work so hard to ignore. He had 'looked after' two beloved family members within a short space of time; it was simply too much and resulted in time off work. This self-imposed expectation, of needing to step up and embalm loved ones, became an important part of William's story. So many of William's experiences and struggles originated in this way, from real people, which I then wove into the life of my character.

My interviews with former choristers reminded me that humans may share experiences with others, but they actually *experience* and remember them differently. I spoke with one former chorister who had entered the choir school three years later than other boys. He was talented and was fast-tracked to soloist. I asked one of his contemporaries, a gentle, kind soul, how the rest of them had felt about this. He said, as far as he could remember, they all felt it was 'jolly well done to him', that he had a marvellous voice. The chorister in question said it was awful and that he was beaten up every day for a week. The idea of a chorister arriving late to their cohort, but with prodigious talent, caught my attention and became part of William's story also.

I spent hours with another former chorister who, though likeable and hugely talented, was badly beaten at school for his bad behaviour. When I started talking to him, it was to find out the specifics of a chorister's day – but by the time I had finished I had found the character of Martin, William's best friend, who became essential to the story. A few months later, after the ten year-old Martin was well-rooted in my novel, the same man unexpectedly came to lead a rehearsal of my choir because our director was away. He was a phenomenal teacher – the atmosphere was electric. I dashed home to try and capture these moments, and decided I wanted the adult version of this character in my story too.

Clearly these listenings are the bedrock of my story – real events, memories and feelings that I wove into a fictional narrative with what I hope is emotional truth. Of course, I also read all I could, trawled the internet for articles and images and tracked down old documentaries; writers develop an insatiable hunger for their subject matter. I also listened endlessly to recordings of the music I featured. My final edit was done in a slightly feverish manner with Allegri's 'Miserere mei' playing loudly.

My experience tells me that if I find out what I need to know – the factual stuff, and the stories from the people who matter – it will sit in my unconscious ready to spark, trigger and inform my imagination as I write. It's also true that there will be things I didn't find out that would have helped, and I will have got some things wrong. But I've done my best.

And what about Aberfan? I started by saying that I didn't set out to write about the disaster per se, but about outsiders who went in to help and left again, each to deal with their own personal aftermath. But of course, I was apprehensive about entering such tender territory. I visited Aberfan several times, wandering round on my own and once escorted by someone who'd grown up there during the '60s and '70s. Later, I shared the relevant passages with this person, and they then showed it to one of the survivors, someone I never met and who asked not to be quoted. I've been asked if I ever considered making up a disaster. I didn't. What drew me to this story was completely rooted in one particular place, time and event. To have invented a situation would have diluted both the power of the story and the tribute I wanted to pay.

I'll end with the dedication from the book: *For the embalmers who went to Aberfan and for the people they went to help.*

Jo Browning Wroe teaches on the post graduate certificate in teaching creative writing at Cambridge University. She has an MA in Creative Writing from the University of East Anglia. Her debut novel, *A Terrible Kindness*, published by Faber & Faber in 2022, was a *Sunday Times* bestseller, shortlisted for the Bridport Peggy Chapman-Andrews First Novel Award, longlisted for the Prix du Roman Fnac and was a Richard and Judy Pick. Follow her on Twitter @JoBrowningWroe.

Books

Writing popular history books

On turning from fiction to non-fiction, author Tom Holland was able to re-connect fully with his childhood love of history and find a fulfilling place as a writer. He reflects on the importance of historical accuracy in popular history, and on the literary and scholarly giants whose work has combined to influence and inspire him.

When I began writing, I wanted to be Proust. No novel had ever inspired me quite as much as his *À la recherche du temps perdu* (1913–27) – and so, with the lunatic hubris of youth, I decided that I would devote my career to emulating it. Naturally, it did not turn out well. My laborious attempt to write a 'Great Novel' proved abortive. My first published work of fiction, *The Vampyre* (Little, Brown 1995), instead featured Lord Byron as a vampire. Two more in the series followed, set respectively in 1880s London and the Restoration. My final vampire novel featured Howard Carter, a deranged Fatimid caliph, and blood-sucking pharaohs. It was all a long way from madeleines dipped in tea.

Or was it? Proust's great theme was memory – the hold that it has on us, and the tricks that it can play on our minds. My mistake had been to imagine that my formative experiences, my formative passions, were best served by fiction. In truth, the emotions that lived most vividly in my memory, I came to realise, were those bred of my childhood love of history. That all my novels were set in the past was, perhaps, a desperate cry for recognition to my ego from my id. In writing historical fiction, I could now see that what really stirred me was less the fiction than the history. To invent things that had happened in the reign of Akhenaten, the heretic pharaoh who served as the central protagonist in my last vampire novel, was to gild the lily. He was quite extraordinary enough as he was, without me giving him a taste for human blood.

So I decided to turn to non-fiction. Pointedly, though, I chose as my subject the period that had given me my first ever rush of fascination with vanished empires. It was a book on the Roman army (complete with a gory cover showing one of Caesar's officers getting spitted by a Gaul) that had first persuaded me, at the age of eight, to abandon an obsession with palaeontology for one with humanity's past. Rome was the apex predator of the ancient world: like a tyrannosaur, it was lethal, glamorous, and extinct. Yet it was also a civilisation of astonishing brilliance, possessed of poets and historians who, over the course of my studies, and then into my adult life, had allowed my fascination with it to mature as I myself grew older. Rome, as a theme, was unavoidably steeped in my memories. In researching the age of Caesar and the collapse of the Roman Republic, I was exploring an aspect of my own past, as surely as if I been writing an autobiography.

Which is not to say that *Rubicon* (Little, Brown 2003), my first work of non-fiction, did not aspire to stringent accuracy and objectivity. History has always had pretensions to rank as a science. Thucydides, writing back in the 5th century BC, scorned the exaggerations of poets and the meretricious taste for fantasy of chroniclers; presenting his account of the great war between Athens and Sparta, he assured his readers that 'the conclusions I have drawn from the proofs quoted may, I believe, safely be relied upon.'

History today, as an academic discipline, is recognisably the descendant of such a methodology. Scholarship, in university history departments, ranks as a vocation. The books that result tend to be written by experts for experts, and in a style that is distinctively academic. Historians who write for the general reader cannot afford to indulge in jargon; but neither can they afford to jettison the exacting standards that serve to qualify a book published by a university press. With large readerships come large responsibilities. No less than academics, writers of popular history are dependent for their career upon a reputation for not making mistakes.

An evident aspect of history's enduring appeal beyond the groves of academe, though, is precisely the fact that it is *not* a science. Herodotus, Thucydides' great predecessor and rival, declared – in the first sentence of the first work of history ever written – that it was his ambition to ensure that 'human achievement may be spared the ravages of time'. Literally, he spoke of not allowing them to become *exitela*, a word that could be used in a technical sense to signify the fading of paint from inscriptions or works of art. To Thucydides, the colours applied by Herodotus to his history were too bright, too distracting, to qualify him as a true historian – a criticism that would see him, in due course, named the 'Father of Lies' as well as the 'Father of History'. Herodotus himself, though, might have retorted that Thucydides was too dry, too narrow, too lacking in colour. His own history was rich with the plenitude that is the mark of great literature. If his concern with the means of gathering evidence was something revolutionary, then so too was the sheer scope and range of his interests. No one before him had ever thought to write on such a heroically panoramic scale. Unlike the austere narrative of Thucydides, with its focus on politics and war, that of Herodotus might lead in an often bewildering variety of directions: to a laugh-out-loud story of a drunk man dancing on a table, perhaps, or to the chilling account of a eunuch's revenge on the man who had him castrated as a child. 'Clio,' as Isaiah Berlin once put it, 'is, after all, a muse.'

It is the mark of the direction that my career took, I now recognise, that the great literary influence on my life has turned out to be, not Proust, but Herodotus. He too, like Caesar's legions, was a part of my childhood; and ever since I first read him at the age of 12, he has been a constant companion. I translated him for Penguin Classics, and *Persian Fire* (Little, Brown 2005), the book I wrote after *Rubicon*, was in large part a refraction of his work. Much of what we know about the early 5th century BC – the Persian Empire, the Greek world, and the wars that were fought between them – is dependent upon Herodotus; and it was as a quarry full of data that I gleefully mined him for my own history of the Persian wars. Yet Herodotus – in his love of wonders, in his complex relationship to evidence, and in his style, which today can appear closer to *Tristram Shandy* than to any conventional work of history – was a great literary artist as well as a historian. To write in his shadow is, of necessity, to acknowledge that. Which is why, in academia, the study of Herodotus is as much the prerogative of literary critics as it is of historians; and it is why, to the writer of popular history, he affords quite as many opportunities to meditate upon the nature of memory and narrative as any novelist would.

'*Stat rosa pristina nomine, nomina nuda tenemus.*' So Umberto Eco ended his bestselling novel, *The Name of the Rose* (Secker & Warburg 1983). 'The rose that once was now exists just in name – for bare names are all we have.' It is given to few writers to combine scholarship with fiction to the remarkable degree that Eco did; but to write about the distant past is, perforce, to wrestle with the implications of Eco's Latin tag. Even when the sources are at their most plentiful, uncertainties and discrepancies crop up everywhere. This is the fascination of ancient history, as well as its frustration. Although to write about it is, indeed, to impose upon the past an artificial pattern, that need be no drawback. The ancients, after all, when they wrote their own histories, did the same. Rare, for instance, in the era of Caesar, was the citizen who did not fancy himself the hero of his own history. This was an attitude which did much to bring Rome to disaster, but it also gave the epic of the Republic's fall its peculiarly lurid and heroic hue. Barely a generation after it had occurred, men were already shaking their heads in wonderment, astonished that such a time, and such giants, could ever have been.

A half-century later, the panegyrist of the Emperor Tiberius, Velleius Paterculus, could exclaim that 'It seems an almost superfluous task, to draw attention to an age when men of such extraordinary character lived,' – and then promptly write it up. He knew, as all Romans knew, that it was in action, in great deeds and remarkable accomplishments, that the genius of his people had been most gloriously displayed. Accordingly, it was through narrative that this genius could best be understood.

This intersection between the reliability of ancient sources and their unreliability, between their value as a record of facts and their often incorrigibly literary character, is the furrow which, as a writer, I find I most enjoy ploughing. It has led me to various dimensions in which reality and fantasy can easily seem intermingled: to the court of Nero; to the origins of Islam; to Viking England; to the First Crusade. The pleasure I have taken in writing about all of them is the pleasure of someone who, after years of restless wandering, has finally found somewhere that feels like home. I am not Proust, nor was I meant to be. The relief of this discovery is what enabled me at last, after many false starts, to become fulfilled as a writer.

Tom Holland is the author of the prize-winning history titles *Rubicon: The Triumph and Tragedy of the Roman Republic* (2003) and *Persian Fire* (2005), as well as *Millennium: The End of the World and the Forging of Christendom* (2008), *In the Shadow of the Sword* (2012), *Dynasty* (2015), and *Dominion* (2019), all published by Little, Brown. Tom's translation of *Herodotus: The Histories* was published in 2013 and his translation of Suetonius' *The Lives of the Caesars* will be published in 2024, both by Penguin Classics. His novels include *The Vampyre* (1995), *Deliver Us From Evil* (1997) and *The Bonehunter* (Abacus 2001). His latest book, *Pax: War and Peace in Rome's Golden Age* (Abacus 2023). Tom has adapted Herodotus, Homer, Thucydides and Virgil for BBC Radio 4 and is co-host of the podcast *The Rest Is History*. He has written and presented TV documentaries on subjects ranging from religion to dinosaurs and he is a trustee of the British Library. Visit www.tom-holland.org or follow him on Twitter @holland_tom.

Ghostwriting

Gillian Stern sheds light on the invisible role of the ghostwriter, describing the often intense process involved in the art of writing another person's story in their own voice.

Everyone has a story. I learned this as a Saturday dental nurse at my father's NHS practice in Tottenham. Even the smallest details of people's lives are important, he would tell me. Listen carefully and you will hear.

His tiny surgery vibrated with life. Even before I had a chance to show a patient to the chair, they took up whatever they had been telling him during their last visit, which may have been six months or a year previously. They talked about their children, their families; they pre-emptively repeated their vow to quit eating sugary things; they gave their opinions on what Thatcher was or wasn't doing; told him how they brushed their teeth, what dental problems they were having. And as he filled their mouth with cotton wool rolls and started probing, he would take up the thread of their conversation, to which the patient would nod their head or roll their eyes, trying to make themselves understood.

As I mixed the mercury and amalgam for fillings, or held the hand of a nervous patient, I would listen. Everyone who sat in that chair had a distinctive voice; they were mostly living hard, complex lives. And I learned to hear, I learned to ask questions, and eventually I learned that sometimes what a patient *wasn't* saying was as interesting as what they were saying. My father made each and every one of his patients feel as if they mattered and how I wish now that I had written down the words that filled his surgery, in the rich and varied voices of his patients.

Maybe, then, it is no surprise that I am a ghostwriter – a writer who gives voice to other people's stories. I am paid to listen, to hear, to become someone else, to tell their story in their voice. In this, I am completely invisible, a siphon for their words, their story, their life, their soul. I do not interpret or pass judgement and though I might steer my questions in a direction I think their story should head, ultimately the book I am ghosting is entirely theirs, made up of their words.

While there are a range of ghostwriters – from those who ghost speeches to others ghosting novels – I ghost memoirs. I am a more reactive type of ghost in that I take commissions; many ghosts are more proactive, coming up with the idea of who they are going to ghost, taking responsibility for the outline, and involving themselves in all aspects of the publishing deal to writing the book itself. Ghostwriters are proper writers, often excellent writers, and in a world where we suspend our egos almost entirely, swapping recognition for invisibility, ghostwriters deserve all the accolades the industry and public are so keen not to throw our way. Going into a large, unnamed publishing house, where they were painting beautiful swirls of their author's names up and down the walls, I was completely unsurprised to see my own and other ghostly colleagues' names *not* included.

There is a peculiar snobbery and fuss out there about ghostwritten books and I can't quite work out why. There are plenty of people with book-worthy stories, from the already famous to the completely unknown, who have been busy living their lives – noisily or quietly – but who have never written a book before and are honest enough to know that writing is not one of their talents. While everyone has a story, not everyone has the ability to write that story. So, in order for their *commissioned* book to be the best possible read,

Books

they, their agent and publisher decide that it is better to employ the services of a professional writer rather than have them inflict underdeveloped, clumsy prose on their readers. I can see nothing wrong with this. The art is in how that story is told.

I came to ghosting through being a structural editor. A publisher handed me a manuscript by someone pretty famous (signing Non-Disclosure Agreements means I am not allowed to disclose who I am ghosting, before, during and after) and asked me to edit it. It was so tortuously written – so oblique and wooden – that I simply couldn't, and I requested time with the author, persuading them to let me have a go at re-working what they had written. The book went on to do extremely well and so the same publisher commissioned me to ghost another memoir. Publishing is a small world and publishers get used to reading between the lines in acknowledgements. 'A special thank you to Gillian Stern, without whom none of this would have hit the page' is a bit of a giveaway in the industry (and to my family), and so the acknowledgement, on many levels, is everything.

Often I am asked to attend what is, quaintly and oddly, still known as a 'beauty parade', where the person who needs a ghost – the author – with their agent and the publisher interview a number of potential ghosts, offering the job to the person whom the author feels best fits the profile of whatever it is they are looking for. I have walked into some such events and it is obvious immediately, or as the interview proceeds, that there is no way I fit, either because of a massive difference in outlook or voice or a complete lack of connection; I have walked into others and the connection and fit have been instant – not that that means I always then got the job. Mostly, though, because I've been around a bit, I am asked directly by a publisher to meet the author, with a view that I am the right person for the job. I am careful about what I accept; I am likely to be spending a great deal of time with the author, investing emotionally in them and their story, even 'becoming' them as I get into and develop the writing. I can only write someone's story if I can *imagine* myself in their voice. I will not accept a job if I think I will bring judgment and bias to the page.

Once I accept a commission, I either involve my agent or negotiate the contract myself. I read as much as I can about the author that already exists. Sometimes that can be just the outline on which the publisher has bought the book; in general, though, there is a body of material online, in existing books or articles and often they have diaries or letters or papers. I listen to, or watch, whatever programmes or clips I can and then spend time with the author, chatting, walking, eating (– for one author even frenetically working out with them at their gym while they talked!). I tape as much as I can and in the early stages, as I go about my day, I stick in my headphones and listen to their voice, allowing their way of talking, the patterns in their speech, to become mine too. I try it out as I shop or talk to friends. I try to understand the way they look at the world, the way they see the everyday, what it is they want to convey. I love that aspect of the job, the beginning of becoming part of someone else's life so intimately. It's a strange internal intimacy; *becoming* them – as I write and *am* them – can be overwhelming, although when I'm actually with that person, I can feel oddly detached.

Typically, the author and I have a couple of sessions where we decide how we are going to work and then we get going. I generally spend as much time as I can with them; some like me to tape everything over a number of days or weeks and get writing; others prefer to get together once a week or so, with me writing and them going over what I have written in between times. Most authors I have worked with like to pore over every word, checking that I am expressing them as they believe they express themselves, hearing the flow of the narrative, the timbre of the tone, the sound of their words. I have the world's best transcriber and I download tapes to her as soon as I get home and write from the transcripts. One thing I would strongly advise aspiring ghosts to do is to insist that your publisher or author pay for all transcribing expenses.

Once we settle on style and rhythm, I like my editor or the author's agent to see a few initial draft chapters so that there are no great surprises near to the delivery deadline. I didn't do this on the first book I ghosted, and a couple of days before delivery received 18 pages of vicious criticism from the author's agent, none of which I disagreed with.

I get emotionally attached to my authors, of course I do. I have fallen in (appropriate) love; I have wanted to be the person I am ghosting; I have been a part of the lives of people I would never have otherwise had access to and I have seen things that would fill a book I can never write. And I have learned, painfully at first, that once the script is delivered and the book goes into production, I need to get out of there. I don't own the book; I don't own the story and I have no part in the publishing process once the script is delivered. Quite often the author and I stay in touch; quite often they tell me I am the most important person in their lives, the person who 'knows them the best', but that is moonshine and after the launch, after the razzmatazz, after the sales (and even prizes), life moves on. I did ghost two memoirs for one author and she told me shocking things she had genuinely never told anyone before, which was a burden for me but one I was prepared to carry and not include in the book. But I am not in this business to make friends. Ghosting, like editing, is a job and, once a book is written, I need to write the next.

The questions I am most frequently asked are: Why don't you write your own book? and How can you write a book without your name on the front? Here are my answers: I do not have a novel in me; I do not have a story about my life or an aspect of my life that I believe would interest readers; I have no desire to see my name on the front of a book when the story belongs to someone else. I get a great deal of satisfaction bringing interesting stories to life, in capturing someone else's voice so convincingly that they hear themselves come off the page. Ghostwriting is challenging and complex and a great privilege.

These days, well into his eighties, my father is still collecting stories – be it on the streets of his neighbourhood as he goes for his daily 'ball of chalk', in the stands at White Hart Lane, or around the table with his grandchildren. And, if I had time, I would tell you his story. Or maybe, one day, I will ghost it.

Gillian Stern is a former non-fiction commissioning editor, who happily discovered a novel that went on to win prizes and become a bestseller. She then crossed over into the world of commercial and literary fiction and has since been a freelance fiction and non-fiction editor for literary agents and publishers including Bloomsbury, Picador, Hodder, Penguin Random House and Orion as well as a judge for the Lucy Cavendish Fiction Prize for the past six years. She combines this with her work as a ghostwriter. A memoir she ghosted was named as WHSmith's Non-Fiction Book of the Year and she has since ghosted a sequel for the same author, as well as several other memoirs that have been *Sunday Times* and Amazon Bestsellers. Contact her at gillybethstern@hotmail.com or follow her on Twitter @gillybethstern.

Becoming a successful copywriter

Freelance content writer Carina Martin explains the multitude of roles that fall under the banner of copywriting and offers pointers for breaking into the industry.

Copywriting is a job you can start straight out of college or something you can switch to later in life. So what do copywriters do? (clue – it has nothing to do with trademarking). Copywriters use words to attract attention and to persuade readers to behave in a certain way.

For a role that relies on clarity and simplicity, the term 'copywriter' is something of an archaic misnomer, harking back to the invention of the printing press. In those early days, newspapers would differentiate between news writers and advertising copywriters, with the latter producing factual, rational sales messages. The 1950s were a turning point. US advertising pioneer Bill Bernbach was the first to place art directors (responsible for the visual elements of an ad) and copywriters in teams of two, believing the dynamic between those disciplines would result in more creative, emotional advertising. And it did. Bernbach's humorous writing for Volkswagen and David Ogilvy's long copy for Rolls-Royce have stood the test of time and have earned their places in advertising's Hall of Fame. The team model worked then, and it still exists in agencies to this day.

Fast forward to the 2020s and copywriting has exploded in a million different directions. Sadly, the popularity of long advertising copy has, to some extent, succumbed to today's shorter attention spans, but what the copy lacks in volume is more than made up for in variety.

The many faces of copywriting

Advertising copywriting is probably the area that has experienced the least change over the years, although digital channels such as YouTube, Facebook and Instagram have brought new challenges. It remains the domain of *creative teams*, also known as *concept teams*, under the watchful eye of the creative director. The focus here is on idea generation, while the roles of art director and copywriter are sometimes blurred. These creative duos often begin agency life as paid interns, plucked from Creative Advertising degree courses at reputable universities like Bucks New or Falmouth. This is done either formally – through graduate schemes – or informally through direct approaches.

Teams may be given a single execution to work on or they may be responsible for overarching campaign ideas that are then optimised for different media. Given how much creatives are expected to learn about the client, teams are generally employed full-time by an agency, with freelancers being brought in when fresh ideas and perspectives are needed.

Beyond creative teams, brand writers tend to fall into two camps: copywriters – who use persuasive copy to influence customers to choose one product or service over another and content writers – whole output tends to be less hard-sell and more informative/entertaining to build relationships with prospective audiences. These solo operators might choose to work for an agency, a business (known as working 'in-house'), or for one or both as a freelancer. There are many different types of agency that hire copywriters, including branding, design, advertising and PR agencies, and there are many different job titles within each. If you are strongly drawn to write about a particular subject, you may prefer to take the in-house route.

In-house or freelance?

My own decision to freelance was a lifestyle choice as much as anything. I was tired of commuting and wanted to get a dog. It still suits me. I enjoy working on my own, away from distractions, and I like the variety of work I get – from agencies and businesses in equal measure. I can write a website about a medical breakthrough one day and be naming an ice lolly the next. As such, I can turn my hand to pretty much any brief.

That's not for everyone, though. Freelance life can be lonely, and the cliché about feast and famine couldn't be truer. My friends working in agencies get a buzz from being in a creative environment while enjoying the range of work coming from the agency's clients. Those who work in-house love getting to know one business thoroughly, rather than being a jack-of-all-trades. It's a personal choice, and there are pros and cons whichever route you choose.

Squiggly career paths

I discovered copywriting by accident. I was working in-house as a marketing manager and my budget had been slashed; I needed to reduce my external expenses and one way to do this was for me to write all our copy rather than outsource it. I already had experience of writing from working in PR and advertising, so it was a logical step. And it soon became clear that copywriting was my true love. I moved into full-time writing, at an editorial consultancy, and subsequently became Head of Copy at a digital agency. To broaden my skill set, I also did a Masters in Screenwriting for Film and TV. I've now been freelancing as a copywriter and screenwriter for around 15 years.

Whenever I've recruited copywriters, I've always been interested in candidates' previous lives and what those experiences can bring. For example, an account manager wanting to make the switch to copywriting might bring discipline and diplomacy. Someone with an acting background might find it easy to get into character, becoming the 'voice' of different clients. If you're thinking of a career change, just think about the transferable skills you can offer. My own experience in marketing has proved invaluable, as I understand the pressures my clients are under and am good at mediating if creative differences arise. A good command of the English language is, of course, a must – but a natural ability to write interesting, informative copy triumphs over any number of qualifications.

Day-to-day life

An entry-level copywriter may be tasked with writing product descriptions or SEO (search engine optimised) articles, which are designed to improve rankings on search engines. You'll be given a brief, with the key messages to convey, and your job is to produce copy that grabs attention and persuades the reader to buy/find out more/make an appointment, etc. You might work in the social media team, writing tweets and posts on behalf of different brands, or help the human resources team to generate attractive job ads. In a nutshell, copy requests can come from virtually anywhere and they can take many different forms. If something needs to be written well, it tends to fall to the copywriter.

A senior copywriter might help the board of a company to draft the non-financial section of its annual report or write white papers and thought-leadership articles. They may help develop businesses' manifestos, shape their brand tone of voice, or name their product ranges. The higher up the chain, the more strategic the job becomes.

Books

Books

Getting started

My advice to new copywriters is to create a portfolio website. You can do this even if you have yet to find your first role. I created mine on WordPress by following YouTube videos; you don't need to throw money at it, just time. If you're interested in becoming one half of a creative team, start writing ads now. Maybe pick a campaign and deconstruct it until you've figured out what the client's original brief was. You'll notice there are some variables between different ads, and some mandatory elements. Stick to those rules and write a better ad.

Pick up a product in a supermarket and find a great hook for it that grabs attention. It's important to make it clear on your website that your idea is independently created and not linked in any way to the agency or client. That said, if you're proud of it, it's worth sharing. Think, too, about how you might stretch that idea into other media. The more life an idea has, the more likely it is to be bought.

You can do the same as a solo copywriter. Write speculative press releases, articles, social media posts and website pages. Show an understanding of pace, prioritisation of messaging and subbing. Get into the habit of writing succinct copy – less is nearly always more. And think about your audiences; you have to wear many hats as a copywriter, and you need to be able to flex your language to appeal to the intended reader.

Try writing for business-to-business (B2B) clients as well as business-to-consumer (B2C). Target social posts at influencers and a press release to a broadsheet newspaper. The more variety you can show, the more flexible you will appear to potential employers.

Building your personal brand

It's a good idea, right from Day One, to think of yourself as a brand. As Jeff Bezos once said, 'A brand is what other people say about you when you're not in the room.' Consider how you want to be perceived and make sure you permeate that message consistently – from the way you dress in your profile picture on LinkedIn to the colours you use on your website. It is about playing to your strengths and not trying to be someone you're not.

As well as your website, which will act as your calling card, you will need a well-crafted CV and some business cards. I use shocking pink consistently on everything from my email signature to my laptop cover. It acts as an aide memoire when I leave my (shocking pink) business card behind. Another way to reinforce 'brand you' is to write opinion pieces that you can post on your social media. Write blogs, articles in local magazines, even thank-you letters. Take any excuse you can to practise writing. The more you do it, and the more you're known for it, the higher your chances of getting spotted.

Getting yourself out there

Once you've got a website (or a PDF portfolio) that you're proud of, you need to drive traffic to it. I recommend you look at other copywriters' profiles on LinkedIn and make yours as powerful as possible. Then make it work for you. Connect with potential employers, comment on creative directors' posts and be an active contributor to online debates. Set up job alerts and follow recruitment agencies that specialise in creative appointments. Join networks such as The Dots (https://the-dots.com), YunoJuno (www.yunojuno.com) and Creativepool (https://creativepool.com) where you can build a profile and apply for jobs. There's also a lot of good advice for copywriters on LinkedIn and Twitter.

It's old school, I know, but try writing some letters to clients or agencies where you believe you have a natural fit. Structure it like a compelling argument, explaining your strengths and selling your benefits. When was the last time you received a handwritten letter? I bet you opened it straight away. And remember – you'll write better copy if you're interested in the product or service you're marketing, so rather than writing to the top ten agencies, or the biggest spending clients, think how you'd *feel* writing for them (I love design, art and innovation, so I'll always jump at those briefs). Get as much experience on as many subjects as you can, then find your niche and chase your dream.

Carina Martin is a freelance content writer. Her previous experience includes roles as marketing manager at Capital Radio and Channel 4 (FilmFour), and head of copy at digital marketing agency Dare. Carina has an MA in Screenwriting for Film & TV from Royal Holloway. For more information see www.carinamartin.co.uk and her LinkedIn profile. Follow her on Instagram @carina_martin_content_writer.

The art and craft of literary translation

Jianan Qian sheds light on the challenges and intricacies of literary translation , sharing her experience and valuable advice for would-be translators on how to get started, hone your skills and get your translated works published.

Perhaps you may think that, since your Italian is good enough to get you around coffee shops and grocery stores, you could perhaps try translating some Italian poems or short stories into English. You are not alone in displaying such misplaced confidence. So before you do anything hasty, let's take a closer look at the concept of literary translation.

What is literary translation?

How do you translate 'in bocca al lupo', the Italian idiom that literally means 'in the mouth of the wolf'? The phrase originates from a theatre setting and is used to wish a performer good luck before a performance. So that's easy – you immediately come up with its English equivalent, 'break a leg'. Now let me add a bit of context: someone says 'in bocca al lupo' to his classmate before a school exam. Would you still translate it as 'break a leg'? In that case Italians might respond with that strange expression 'crepi il lupo', literally 'the wolf shall die', and you may find a perfect alternative – 'knock em' dead' or (in the USA) 'kick the exam's ass'. Very good. And now let's add even more to the previous context. In the story, it is an Italian student who uses that phrase to wish a Chinese international student good luck before an exam, and the latter doesn't seem to understand the idiom. Would you still translate the phrase as 'knock em' dead'? I would either retain the expression in Italian or use its literal translation 'in the mouth of the wolf' if the Chinese student understands what every Italian word means.

Perhaps this gives you a sense of where I am headed. Literary translation is more than Google translation plus human editing. Because every language functions differently, one of our biggest challenges as literary translators is to create something in the target language that will evoke similar feelings in the reader as the original but without deviating too far away. Then again, we translators have to carefully define what we mean by 'similar' and 'too far' in every individual case. Tone, atmosphere, character, humour, irony, metaphor and rhythm must all stay in our minds as we chew over every word choice.

If you speak a language other than English, try translating the famous opening of Shakespeare's *Richard III* – 'Now is the winter of our discontent/ Made glorious summer by this sun of York' – into that language. How would you manage to retain the political connotations within its simple and yet powerful syntax? If you are already attempting to solve any of these puzzles, welcome to our rabbit hole.

Getting started

This first glimpse into literary translation may make you wonder whether it's necessary to be an expert in both the source and target languages to translate. Ideally, a literary translator demonstrates a deep knowledge of the languages and cultures on both sides. If you deal with a more complicated text – such as Dante Alighieri's *Divine Comedy* from the 15th century or Cao Xueqin's *Dream of the Red Chamber* from the 18th century – additional knowledge is a must .

But there are practical solutions too. You can work with a co-translator if you feel the need to. In today's English-speaking world, Richard Pevear and Larissa Volokhonsky are perhaps the best-known collaborative literary translators, whose translations of Tolstoy, Dostoevsky, Chekhov and Gogol have won numerous awards and recognitions. Volokhonsky is a native speaker of Russian, whereas Pevear, a native English speaker, does not read Russian. Usually, that is how collaborative translation works. The native speaker of the source language closely studies the original text and attempts a first draft marked with her notes of the author's literary style. The English speaker then edits the draft, weighing every change with the co-translator to make sure their rendition stays true to the original and also connects to the English-speaking audience. While translating contemporary Chinese author Zhu Yue's story collections into English, I also work with a wonderful co-translator, Alyssa Asquith. Alyssa is not only a native English speaker but also a fabulous fantasy writer. Like the famous Argentine author Jorge Louis Borges, Zhu Yue mixes the real and the fantastic, fact with fiction. Working collaboratively, Alyssa and I are able to render the stories of Zhu Yue's mind-blowing stories vividly on the page. Then again, the majority of literary translators work solo and, in that case, maintaining a humble mind and doing lots of research are key to keeping mistakes in check.

Selecting your work

What to translate? Normally we don't jump into translating foreign literature overnight. Perhaps when studying Korean at university you read Ae-ran Kim's stories for a class and have been in love with them ever since? Maybe you attended a reading of another literary translator from the same language who mentioned the names of the most important literary journals in that language? The bottom line is that you must translate something that you genuinely enjoy reading. Then you can use the internet to check whether the piece or book has been previously translated. If it hasn't, find the contacts of the author to ask for permission. Some authors have their own Facebook pages or websites, others can be reached through the universities they work at or the journals they have published their works in. It's necessary to ask the authors to sign an agreement that allows you to translate and submit the works to the publishers. If you are new in your career, ask for permission to translate a single story/poem/essay first. Win trust through your good work and then your dream authors will be delighted to work with you.

As a general practice, literary works enter the public domain 70 years after the death of their authors. In that case, you do not need permission from the author or the agent. But keep in mind that many of those authors have had previous translations published. If you want to do a new translation, make sure you can persuade the publisher why your version is going to be better. You learn and grow as you translate. But it is always a good idea to prepare yourself with some handy techniques, such as how to sneak in necessary cultural contexts without complicating the sentences. Several schools offer literary translation classes; these two institutions, in particular, come with stellar recommendations:

• University of East Anglia, MA Literary Translation (www.uea.ac.uk/course/postgraduate/ma-literary-translation)

Books

• University of Iowa, MFA in Literary Translation (https://translation.uiowa.edu/; Iowa's program is fully funded, if money is a concern.)

I took translation classes at Iowa while doing an MFA in fiction there. Each of the students in the class worked from a different language. As a group, we started with the English translation and discussed the translation issues that we spotted on the page (for example, where the diction was not consistent or an expression seemed to be confusing). The translator was invited to explain the problems she had met and, in talking about how to solve those specific issues, the professor taught us both useful techniques and fundamental principles in literary translation. Taking translation classes at Iowa was a life-changing experience for me.

One particularly helpful way of learning translation skills is to study good translations vis-à-vis the original text. I pored over every small change Ken Liu makes in translating the 2016 Hugo Prize-winning story *Folding Beijing* from Chinese to English. His every choice – breaking paragraphs, converting indirect speeches to direct quotations in certain cases, clarifying the physical spaces – taught me something important.

After translation

Congratulations – you have finished the translation and revised the manuscript. But your job is not done yet. Unless you are hired by the author only to produce the translation, you must get your translated works published. Submission can be overwhelming – you will face a lot of rejection before you make things happen. But here is a wonderful tip I have received from a fiction classmate: devote half a day every week to submit your works. Try starting with the journals where your favourite authors first published their works. Although not all literary journals accept translation, it never hurts to try. Chances are that most journals accept translation, so long as the stories/poems are good. Some of the best journals that are dedicated to translations include:

• *Asymptote* (www.asymptotejournal.com)
• *Exchanges* (https://exchanges.uiowa.edu)
• *Samovar* (http://samovar.strangehorizons.com)
• *Two Lines* (www.catranslation.org/journal/#display-tile)

When you have your entire manuscript ready, then it is time to contact publishers. Translators usually find that independent presses, such as New Directions, Archipelago Books, Open Letter Books, And Other Stories and Action Books, are more friendly. Different presses have different reading times. You may want to bookmark their websites and revisit them frequently.

Making a living

Another rule of thumb is always to keep your day job. Literary authors are not well paid, and translators even worse. Besides, it is a fact that the English-speaking world does not read much literature in translation, which means the market can be small. In recent years, however, things are slowly but surely changing. The Booker Prize launched its first International Prize, for literature in translation (see page 547) in 2016, when Korean author Han Kang and her English translator Deborah Smith shared the £50,000 award. In the USA, literary translators can apply for fellowships such as the National Endowment for the Arts and PEN/Heim Translation Fund. Note: those fellowships are very competitive. The American Literary Translators Association (ALTA; https://literarytranslators.org) is arguably the largest professional community for literary translators in the USA; you should definitely check out their conferences and mentorship programs. Translators across the world also exchange information and ideas in this Facebook group: Literary Translation (www.facebook.com/groups/351836658289669).

It is very rare for translators to get royalties (except for the books in the public domain), but you must make sure you get paid for the published book. Sadly, it is still a norm that some books do not even include the translator's name on their covers. You must fight for the credit that you deserve. Money talk can be depressing for literary translators, but there is light at the end of the tunnel. More and more universities around the globe are launching literary translation programs, which means more teaching jobs. Writers may experience writers' block, but translators do not. Translators never run out of books that they can't wait to share with a bigger audience.

Literary translation also pays off in different ways. As Italian author Elena Ferrante writes (via translator Ann Goldstein) in *Incidental Inventions* (Europa 2019), 'My only heroes are translators. […] Translators transport nations into other nations. They are the first to reckon with distant modes of feelings. Even their mistakes are evidence of a positive force. Translation is our salvation. It draws us out of the well in which, entirely by chance, we are born.' Ferrante's words deeply resonate with me. Translation teaches me that sometimes I have to move away so I can get closer. The most beautiful souls I have ever met in my life are mostly literary translators. They are altruistic, compassionate, knowledgeable and deeply curious. Whenever I find myself inundated with disturbing news, and feeling hopeless about the future, their friendship inspires and guides me, reminding me of the best of humanity.

Jianan Qian is a writer and translator. She has published four books in her native language Chinese, with her latest essay collection, *A Future that I Do Not Want to Have* listed by Douban as Top 10 Chinese non-fiction in 2019. In English, her works have appeared in the *New York Times*, *Granta*, the *O. Henry Prize Stories* and elsewhere. She has translated five books from English to Chinese, the latest being a story collection by Shirley Jackson. Her English translations with co-translator Alyssa Asquith of Chinese author Zhu Yue's stories have widely appeared in American journals such as the *Washington Square Review*, the *Portland Review* and the *Margins*.

See also...
● *Putting together your submission*, page 398

Books

Writing about science for the general reader

Consultant neurologist Suzanne O'Sullivan has advice for science writers on communicating ideas clearly, without jargon and with purpose and passion, to engage and inform a general audience.

I recently happened upon a museum of barbed wire. I assure you, barbed wire is not a subject to which I had given a moment's thought before, but I have learned that it's fascinating. The museum reminded me that everything has the potential to be interesting if it is told to you in a story. The curators didn't try to draw me into the subject by giving me a dry explanation about the evolution of wire fences from single to double strand, or by describing the numerous types of twists and barbs. I know about these things now, but only because I was told them through the chronicles of cowboys, barbed wire barons and the Wild West. Yeehaa!

The principles of writing about technical subjects for a general audience are the same as those for any other sort of creative writing – it is all about telling a compelling human story, in a language to which the audience can relate. Five years ago, I started writing about my work as a neurologist. I had never written for the public before. It may have seemed to others that I had a radical change of direction in my career. That was not the case. I regard my writing as nothing more than an extension of my everyday interactions with my patients. The skills required to be a good doctor are much more closely aligned to those a writer needs than people realise. Fundamental to medicine is the ability to communicate ideas clearly to audiences of all levels – while never forgetting the person at the heart of the story.

Of course, neuroscience is more innately interesting than barbed wire – but it is also considerably more complex. I have my patients in mind in several different ways when I write about them. Ella came to my clinic in a state of high anxiety. She had had a cluster of seizures and was convinced that she was dying; another doctor had told her that her brain scan was abnormal. Ella had come to me for help. After reviewing her tests, I was able to reassure her that things weren't as bad as she thought. Her scan showed a small scar that was likely to be an anomaly present since birth. It wasn't growing or changing but it was causing epileptic seizures. There was a good chance I could treat those successfully. The scar presented no imminent threat to her life.

I could have given Ella the diagnosis in a completely different way. I could have told her she had a brain tumour – because that's technically what she has. I could have immediately labelled the 'scar' by its proper name: a *dysembryoplastic neuroepithelial tumour*. I would of course give her all that information as our conversation progressed, but first I needed to translate the diagnosis into language she could understand and, in doing so, dispel the myths that were frightening her. Things were not as bad as the scientific terminology made them sound.

My first piece of advice to any science writer would be to avoid excessive jargon and to use technical terms very carefully. Think of the audience. Lots of specialist terminology have different meanings to different people. If I told you that you had a brain tumour, what would you think? To a doctor a tumour is just a swelling; not all tumours grow unabated and not all require treatment. But to many people the word 'tumour' is synonymous with cancer … a death sentence. It is a good example of how easily misunderstandings can arise.

Communicating in plain English allows a science writer to avoid the pitfalls caused by the different ways in which specialists and the general public use terminology. Plain English doesn't mean dumbing down. In fact, I would say it is the opposite; people often use complicated terminology to appear knowledgeable, but the ability to express detailed ideas without it is a much more sophisticated skill. Then there is the question of just how technical and detailed one should get. Although science is a body of facts and truth, there are few absolutes. The scientific world is fraught with controversies and disagreements. Medical conferences are hotbeds of debate and rivalry. It would be impossible for any one book to represent every single expert view without simultaneously getting bogged down in unnecessary detail. When I am writing, I have as a constant companion an imaginary panel of angry-looking colleagues sitting on my shoulder criticising my choices. So my second piece of advice is, never forget the purpose of the book you set out to write. I quieten my critics gallery by never allowing myself to lose sight of who I am writing for, and why. Science books written for non-science audiences are not supposed to be textbooks. Textbooks are available if your reader wants to take the next step.

So far so good – you write clearly and keep the audience and the purpose of the book in mind – except, of course, that translating science into an accessible language is the easy bit; it doesn't conflict with a scientist's natural repertoire of abilities. If a reader only wanted the facts, they could read a scientific paper for that; something more is required of creative non-fiction. My next piece of advice is to take a leaf out of the Barbed Wire Museum's book and learn how to be entertaining. That is the bigger challenge, particularly for career scientists who have never been required to be entertaining before – but it's far from impossible because, when you think about it, science is intrinsically full of mystery and high stakes. Science is trying to save the planet and cure cancer and find extraterrestrials. What could be more exciting than that? Show the reader the bigger picture and give them something or someone to root for. Apply the scientific fact to a circumstance from life that people can understand. In medicine that is of course easier than in other fields of science writing.

Ella had her first seizure when she was 15. She was at breakfast with her family when she reported feeling unwell. She started to behave strangely. She became convinced that she could smell something burning. She started talking rubbish, telling her sister over and over again that she could see cartoon horses romping around the room. Her anxiety level built slowly until she abruptly lost consciousness and fell to the floor. When she woke up in hospital, her only memory of the event was eating bagels one moment and battling with paramedics the next. Like so many of my patients, Ella has taught me about resilience and humanity. But the specifics in her story also offer a lesson about how the brain works. From hallucinatory smells, to confusion and illusory visions of cartoon horses, once examined, Ella's experience provides an anatomical tour through the brain. It can be used to cast a light on hallucinations and consciousness, the brain's way of processing smell and vision. The fact that Ella has kindly allowed her story to be shared means that I can do without lists and flow charts and diagrams when talking about the brain.

There is always a story, you just have to find it. Sometimes it is the scientist's own: I was a fledgling doctor once and had many of the same misconceptions about neuroscience as anybody else; I have made lots of mistakes and learned from them; I fell in love with the work I do for a reason. I took a journey to get to where I am now and, when I write, I try to bring people on that journey with me. Scientific discoveries come from hard-fought research, from wrong turns and blind alleyways, and from errors. Sometimes I tell my patients' stories and sometimes I tell my own.

All of science explains something apparently ordinary – but actually extraordinary – in the world around us. So many breakthroughs have come from a brilliant mind observing something that the rest of us took for granted. When I think of gravity, the first thing I think of is Newton sitting under a tree. I cannot picture Archimedes anywhere but in his bath. Evolution brings to mind Darwin's travel to the Galapagos. A teacher wouldn't dream of trying to engage a child in physics or chemistry by showing them an equation. Everything can be related to something that interests people, even if they never considered it as being scientific before; did you know that, by the time a batsman or batswoman sees the ball leave the bowler's hand, they are seeing something that happened a quarter of a second in the past? That was one writer's introduction to a discussion on the speed of light.

There is something incredibly invigorating about enthusing others about your work. I suppose some science writers jump on a bandwagon, exploit the zeitgeist, but I think science writing works best when the writer is genuinely passionate about their subject. If you are not entertaining yourself, how can you expect anybody else to join you? The same applies to the act of writing.

To write a book one must love to write. I started writing in 2013 – writing, apparently out of nowhere, to people who didn't know me. In truth, though, I had had a love of writing since my school days; my greatest ambition as a child was to write a book. Being a doctor distracted me from that ambition for a long time, but I never abandoned the basic building block of writing – which is reading. It may seem obvious, but to write any book (science or otherwise) you have to love reading and you have to love writing. Writing a book is hard work: it takes a long time; there's no guarantee of success; the monetary rewards are measly; sacrifice is required. When I was *just* a doctor my evenings, weekends and holidays were largely free time to do with what I wished. I no longer have time off. I have ever-present deadlines and a constant fear that if I stop writing I'll forget how. My medical career will always be there, my writing career requires maintenance. But if you are honestly driven to write, doing so will enrich your life to such a degree that sacrifices become irrelevant.

Suzanne O'Sullivan is the author of *It's All in Your Head* (Vintage 2016), which won the Wellcome Book Prize and the Royal Society of Biology General Book Prize. She has been a consultant in neurology since 2004 and currently works as a consultant in clinical neurophysiology and neurology at the National Hospital for Neurology and Neurosurgery and for a specialist unit based at the Epilepsy Society. She is the author of *Brainstorm: Detective Stories From the World of Neurology* (Chatto & Windus 2018); her latest book, *The Sleeping Beauties*, about the social life of illness, was published in 2021 (Picador) and was shortlisted for the Royal Society Science Book Prize.

How to be a food writer

Felicity Cloake describes the diverse scope and potential offered by food writing , and gives advice on how and where to find new ideas, inspiration and opportunities, learn the trade, and hone your descriptive skills as well as your tastebuds.

So you want to be a food writer? Welcome, and congratulations – a lifetime of eating means you're already more than qualified for the role. In some specialisms you're addressing a fairly niche audience, but food is something we all have in common. Wherever you are in the world, and whatever your circumstances, you can still take pleasure in a piece of chocolate. Even the least 'foodie' person amongst us discusses the subject endlessly – from what we're having for lunch today to what happened on *Bake Off* last night. You've already got a certain amount of expertise; it's up to you where you apply it.

Reviews and recipes

One of the things I love most about my job, which – as a freelancer with her finger in as many pies as possible – includes recipes, columns, news pieces and food-focused travel books, is its incredible diversity of scope . Because food is universal, it is a topic that allows you to take it in almost any direction that interests you, from history and chemistry to sport and art. Of course, depending on your experience and circumstances, you may prefer (initially at least, like me) to keep your eggs in a number of baskets. Only a few restaurant critics, for example, make a living doing that alone. That said, when I tell people I'm a food writer they always, without fail, ask if I get to eat out for free. (Occasionally they also wonder if they might have seen me pulling faces on *Masterchef*.) But while food critics like Grace Dent and Jimi Famurewa are perhaps its most visible public face, they represent only a tiny proportion of the industry – and such is the desirability of these gigs that vacancies don't come up very often. Please don't be disheartened by this; smaller and local publications also run food reviews – to say nothing of the many websites dedicated to eating out in individual cities or regions. As so often in journalism, it pays to look in unexpected places .

I must confess that, on the odd occasion when I've been asked to fill in as a restaurant critic at the *Guardian*, I've found the role unexpectedly stressful. Not only do you have to craft, on the train home, an entertaining narrative arc from a three-course meal – whilst being fair to businesses often operating on the slimmest of profit margins – but the constant deception involved in booking under a series of fake names can lead to a faint, but lingering, sense of paranoia. Which is not to put you off restaurant criticism; after all, you get paid to eat, and then share your opinions on the experience, instead of ranting for free on TripAdvisor. But it is by no means the only form of food writing on the table. Recipes reach a far wider audience and, if you love to cook as well as write, then this might be the route for you – whether you choose to concentrate on recipe development alone or, like me, you enjoy researching companion pieces on the dish's history and cultural context .

While every food writer might secretly think they've got a cookbook in them, unless you've had a lot of practice in the recipe creation department I'd suggest learning your trade first. Writing a good recipe is a skill that goes beyond just being able to cook. Start by getting a pile of food magazines or cookbooks (the library is a good source of both) and studying how recipes are constructed; most these days follow a standard pattern, and this is what any editor will expect you to supply too. You might like to get some work experience on food magazines, just to see how they're put together or, if you have a social media presence, team up with one of the many brands that employ influencers to come up with and promote recipes using their products. Finally – and I cannot stress this enough – always test a recipe before putting it online or sending it to a client; any mistakes will soon be found out.

The business of food

Maybe you are more concerned about the business of food than cooking it – such as the politics of food production and supply, the science of nutrition, or the environmental impact of diet. Happily, the media is becoming increasingly aware of the importance of such things and waking up to the potential of food writing to be more than the usual lists of Glasgow's top ten burgers, or ideas for using up Christmas leftovers. Food lends itself to everything from serious investigative journalism and news stories to lighter or more esoteric topics. If you're interested in a particular aspect, then there's a good chance someone else will be, whether it's a deep dive into the catering at Britain's first motorway service stations or the history of human cannibalism – both of which are subjects I've written about in the past simply because I wanted to know more about them. As well as food magazines and pages, features with wide appeal may be worth pitching to a more general readership, such as glossy newspaper supplements, *Guardian* Long Reads, or places like *Country Life* or the *New Yorker*. Remember that a piece on, say, the last cheesemaker in Paris could be relevant to travel sections, airline, expat and the Eurostar magazines, as well as more obviously food-centred publications .

If you're raring to get going, but find yourself stuck on where to begin, you might be surprised how often I come up with ideas while doing the shopping – whether that's at the supermarket (… is today the day I finally decide to do that baked bean taste test?), the halal butchers up the road, which crams an astonishing selection of ingredients from around the world into its tiny premises (… is there any such thing as sustainable palm oil?) or the Sunday farmers' market (… what's the big deal about unpasteurised milk?). Restaurant menus can throw up similar questions; every time I log on to a food delivery app, I have a look at the incredible array of stuff available in my area to see what's new … and wonder if the Great British public will ever cotton on to the joys of Ethiopian cooking.

Social media is another good source of inspiration; I try to follow as diverse a range of food people as possible – from a Mumbai chef to a Cumbrian shepherd – as well as the usual big names. Equally, I keep an eye on content from around the world. American food media is particularly fascinating, bearing in mind that what's popular there often ends up here sooner or later. Always read as widely as possible – even if it's only to find out what you *don't* like – and take a note of pieces or styles you especially admire, to see if you can incorporate them in some way into your own work; even the most experienced writers have something to learn from their competitors.

Sharing the experience

Once you actually start typing, writing about food is, frankly, much like writing about anything else, but there is a sensual aspect which distinguishes some of the best stuff. Here is an exercise I find useful to develop or refresh skills in this department. Take something simple – let's say an apple – and write down, in turn: what it looks like; what it feels like (and not just the outside; explore the core and the stem too); what it smells like; what it sounds like (you might need to bite into it here); and, only lastly, what it tastes like. Approach this quite ordinary fruit as if you're assessing a fine wine or a piece of art. As will quickly become clear, describing food is not just about capturing the flavour, but also the texture, the smell, the way it looks – just as, when writing about a restaurant, your audience will expect to find out a bit about the location, the dining room and the service, as well as what you ate. Remember that your readers are not there, so your job is to share your experience with them so vividly that they enjoy it alongside you – or not, of course, if it's awful (… that's another great skill, capturing the tiny tragedy of a bad meal).

Think carefully about each word, and whether it reflects your true experience. Clichés are not only boring, but so well worn that the reader's eye slides quickly over them without taking them in, while a truly original observation will make them sit up and take notice. It's all too easy to slip into such familiar grooves as describing slow-cooked meat as 'meltingly tender' or a chocolate brownie as 'fudgy'; so stop and ponder whether the meat has broken down into silky strands rather than actually melted, or if the brownie reminds you more of the texture of dark, damp earth than a solid block of fudge. Discussing such things at the dinner table occasionally, if your nearest and dearest are game, can be very good practice.

Books and blogs

For more serious writing projects, my advice to anyone starting out without an existing portfolio of work to show to editors is to consider a blog, as old-fashioned as that may seem . Plenty of very successful authors cut their teeth in this way, from Ella Mills with *Deliciously Ella* to Kate Allinson and Kay Featherstone, the duo behind the bestselling *Pinch of Nom* series. Social media is great for getting your name out there, but it's hard to fit much into an Instagram caption or, worse still, a tweet. A blog, by contrast, will allow you to hone your writing skills, and hopefully begin to build a fanbase, in a non-pressurised space. Once you have a few posts under your belt, you can then use the blog as a

Some tips for further reading

First Bite: How We Learn to Eat (Fourth Estate 2015) by Bee Wilson – one of our best and most thoughtful food writers

Women on Food (Abrams Press 2019), ed. Charlotte Druckman – a wide-ranging collection of pieces on food, by a diverse collection of authors

Vittles (https://vittles.substack.com), ed. Jonathan Nunn – a regular food newsletter covering everything from the chippie traditions of the British Isles to the coffee supply chain

The Longthroat Memoirs: Soups, Sex and Nigerian Taste Buds (Cassava Republic Press 2017) by Yemisi Aribisala – beautiful, evocative prose that should be required reading for any aspiring food writer

Feeding Britain: Our Food Problems and How to Fix Them (Pelican 2021) by Tim Lang – an important read for anyone interested in our food system, and how to write about it in an accessible way

shop window for prospective editors to assess your work before commissioning you – or indeed, to use as sample text to send to agents, should you be thinking about a book. Bear in mind that food magazines, in particular, tend to work several months ahead of schedule; this means that Christmas ideas, for example, should be sent in early summer to ensure they're on their radar in good time, whereas daily papers and websites can be pitched for same- or next-day coverage.

Books

Whether you're writing about baking, Bangladeshi cuisine or Bronze Age diets, my advice is to embrace social media – for support with your writing as well as for inspiration. It gets a bad rap in other spheres, but the food community on social media is remarkably inclusive and welcoming. You only have to look at Nigella Lawson's feed, in which she responds to questions personally, to realise how much more democratic it has made the discourse. Follow as many editors, publications, fellow writers and cooks as you can, and make the effort to engage with them on a regular basis.

And my final piece of advice is – enjoy it. Writing about food is unlikely to make you fabulously wealthy (although you never know…), but you will certainly meet some wonderful people, and eat some truly memorable meals; bon appétit!

Felicity Cloake is a multi-award-winning freelance journalist and writer, *Guardian* and *New Statesman* columnist, and the author of seven books, including the bestselling travelogue *One More Croissant for the Road* (Mudlark 2019), which was shortlisted for a Fortnum & Mason Food Book of the Year Award and chosen as a Radio Four Book of the Week, and *Red Sauce Brown Sauce: A British Breakfast Odyssey* (Mudlark 2022). Follow her on Twitter and Instagram @FelicityCloake.

See also...
● *Life's a pitch: how to get your ideas into print*, page 2

Poetry

Poems for the page and on stage

Raymond Antrobus celebrates poetry on the page and in performance, a passion he shares with fellow poet Anthony Anaxagorou. Here he records their views on writing and reading poetry in private and in public spaces to offer comfort, particularly in times of change.

While London was in lockdown, I and my fellow poet Anthony Anaxagorou, curator of Out-Spoken and Out-Spoken Press, decided to choose four poems (by other poets) to read on Instagram live. We started this series and, as of the time of writing this article, each week we have attracted between 300 and 400 viewers. We discuss the poems and why they resonated with us in these times of uncertainty.

At first, I was unsure of how this would be received. I was anxious that at times it felt more like exploiting the moment rather than living it but, after a month of these sessions, I could see how it was sharing the moment we're living in with people – giving a sort of fly-on-the-wall perspective to the kind of private discussions Anthony and I, as peers, have been having for years about the writing and reading of poetry. We found that these discussions have helped give a wider dimension to the Audenesque anxieties of our times; the crucial element to it is that it is improvised, unrehearsed sharing.

For example, Anthony and I didn't know in advance which poems each of us was going to read; everything was revealed live, but there was often a natural relationship of some kind that happened between each of the poems. In the third episode we both happened to choose poems with animals and children in them, poems that ask questions rather than claim answers; in some there were tones of cynicism woven around sentimentality. Sometimes images even reoccured within the poems we chose, and Anthony and I delighted in these mystic synchronicities.

I asked Anthony if he missed giving readings and performances. He said no – he prefers reading poetry alone and engaging with poems on the page to reading for an audience. Watching poetry readings online, I notice that a lot of poems do sound the same in the air even though they make different sounds and shapes on the page. There is an assumed poetry voice for every poem – a kind of jolting, careful reading where, even if the content has different tones, it is still read in that same kind of stately, over-pronounced voice.

Coming from the spoken word scene, I know that part of the craft is knowing how to surprise an audience beyond just the words; the voice and body also have agency, in the same way that line breaks and line length do on the page. In performance, monotony bores audiences – you see it – but this is craft talk for poems in performance, something rarely considered by poets who only think of the readers who come to them on the page.

Anthony's preference for engaging on his own with poems on the page is significant, because both of us started out on the London 'open mic' circuit. We both co-curate poetry nights (mine were Chill Pill and Keats House Poets Forum, and his was Out-Spoken). Anthony, as well as running a live night, also runs a publishing house (Out-Spoken Press). I miss giving readings where you feel your poems connecting with audiences in real time, but I do also love quietly reading other people's poems privately on the page. I love geeking out about enjambments and voltas and how to create volume and surprise around the white space. I read poetry collections the way most people read novels; first poem to last poem fast, then going again – first poem to last poem – marking the poems that moved me.

For years Anthony has been the one person I know who has both that kind of sustained, intense relationship with poetry on the page and also comes from the stage. Polarising stage and page has always felt like a loaded issue to me, in the sense that the open mic and spoken word scene is a lot more diverse culturally than the literary scene. The dismissal of spoken word as low art, from the *Guardian* to *PN Review*, came with racial and class undertones; it's a kind of prejudice hidden in language, but it works both ways. Poets I know who also come from the spoken word scene say literary poets are too posh, that they write poems where you don't know if they're starting or finishing. I do understand that, but this is a discussion about the expectations of audience. Those poems that end quietly without declaring some kind of resolve or punch line are often expecting their audience to meet the poem halfway. This requires a different kind of listening – a kind of listening that engages subtlety with meanings that are sometimes less immediate. Often there are no digressions or statements or opinions of the poet guiding the poem; it's more of a focusing-in on smaller moments or ideas.

Now, I don't want to privilege one style over the other. To pull off a quality spoken-word performance and a good page poem takes craft and talent. But talking to Anthony about performance has highlighted to me that, as we've grown older, our taste has developed and our expectations of poetry have changed. However, there is still a fundamental integrity in what we expect from poems, and that is a kind of widening curiosity and wonder about the world and our existence – an openness. I think an easier way to put it is: heart and imagination.

Even now, I remember the slam poems from my days in Slam. 'Gay Poem' by Keith Jarrett beat me in a national Slam championship final back in 2009. The poem is a conversation between the poem and the poet: the poem comes to life to ask the poet, 'Am I gay?' In spoken word, there is a lot of space for self-affirmation because of how active the body and voice is in the way poems are received. This poem stood out because it engages with the visibility and *invisibility* of the poet.

Other memorable poems from the London spoken word scene include Ross Sutherland's poem about how the language of customer service has changed over the centuries (Ross performs his dramatic poem in the dialect of each period of history between a customer and a shopkeeper) and Kae Tempest's poem 'Ballad of a Hero' about a soldier returning from war, which they performed at a reading commemorating the poet Christopher Logue. These live experiences are an important part of my poetry history as a reader and as a listener, so I can't privilege page over stage … or vice versa. I acknowledge them as two different species of poetry that co-exist with my poetry eye and ear.

Raymond Antrobus is the author of *To Sweeten Bitter* (Out-Spoken Press 2017), *The Perseverance* (Penned in the Margins 2018) and *All The Names Given* (Picador 2021). His first children's picture book *Can Bears Ski?* was published in 2021. In 2019 Raymond was awarded the Rathbones Folio Prize for best work of literature in any genre, the first poet to receive the prize. Other accolades include the Ted Hughes Award, *Sunday Times* Young Writer of the Year Award and *Guardian* Poetry Book of the Year 2018. He has been shortlisted for the Griffin Prize, T.S. Eliot Prize and the Forward Prize. He is a fellow of The Royal Society of Literature and Cave Canem, and was awarded an MBE for his services to literature. For more information see www.raymondantrobus.com.

See also …
● *Getting your poetry out there*, page 316

The portfolio poet

Poet Sophia Blackwell explores the varied options, opportunities and combinations available to poets who are suited to the variety, creative freedom and independence of a portfolio career. She offers ideas and encouragement on the many ways to make a living and supplement your income while growing as a writer.

The idea of a poetry career is not exactly an oxymoron, but it's not straightforward either. This article might more aptly be called, 'How to make whatever money you can from poetry while doing other things you don't hate'. Poetry careers often involve a certain amount of juggling, and some people enjoy it more than others. You might be more of a portfolio poet than someone who moves linearly from one grant and project to another. Generally, portfolio poets:

• **Enjoy trying different things** and aren't daunted by the prospect of learning new skills.
• **Have a 'butterfly mind'** and jump from one task to another. They find it helpful to approach a task by doing a less urgent item on their to-do list and then returning to the original task.
• **Don't want to be tied down** to a rigorous publishing schedule – this isn't as problematic for poets as for commercial novelists, but some poets still find a strict timetable an unappealing prospect.
• **Like keeping their options open** by being able to do a variety of different things and enjoy being independent, with the creative freedoms that come with that.

There's a lot to be said for the portfolio approach in terms of future-proofing your career. You may be less negatively affected when a new editor at your publisher doesn't care for your work, or when the venue that hosts your readings closes, if you can return to one of the other projects you have on the back burner. Keeping your options open can provide a sense of control.

The idea of the poet as troubadour, traveller, teacher and entrepreneur is close to my heart. This is probably because it resembles my life to date more than the idea of working for a single academic institution or publisher. Like a lot of poets, I give lectures, teach workshops in schools and colleges, and edit manuscripts covering all genres from romance novels to business reports. I have run literary salons and been paid by hundreds of different festivals, colleges and organisations. For a decade, performing and hosting literary events made up at least 50% of my income from poetry. Historically, selling copies of my books at events has made up roughly a tenth of my yearly income from poetry. I have taken on commissions to create and run large poetry events in venues such as theatres, galleries and museums. I have given private poetry lessons and made radio shows and podcasts, some of which are funded by arts organisations. It would be hard to say what I enjoy doing the most, but there are hundreds of ways a poet can make a living and supplement the money they make from their writing.

Running writing groups or poetry classes

If you're thinking about running a comprehensive series of classes, it's best to be an experienced poet with a couple of published books to your name and a working knowledge of 20th- and 21st-century poetry. If you are not quite there yet, you can easily arrange to teach a few one-off classes as part of a bigger event taking place near you, either in a physical space or online. Literary festivals, other programmes serving the community (such as local LGBTQ+ Pride or Black History events), libraries and arts venues (such as galleries and theatres), offer plenty of possibilities for an enthusiastic would-be educator to run an event over a weekend or during a quiet evening. These venues or their funders can pay you a modest fee, and one-off events of this kind can develop over time into a poetry course.

Once you have the outline of a poetry course, you can start running writing and feedback sessions in a library, café or pub, or online. If you feel you've created something unique, you can approach an organisation with an established reputation for teaching poetry. If they see the value of what you offer, they can give you space, help you monetise the course, and give it legitimacy by hosting it on their campus or in another venue connected to theirs. If you have an area of expertise, either in a particular style of poetry, another art form you can combine with poetry, or a theme or hobby that genuinely fascinates you, it is worth leaning into that and creating at least one spectacular workshop or short course that you feel can be best taught by you alone. It does not have to be unique, but ask yourself what you can offer that few others can.

The teaching route suits patient, tactful, well-read and confident people who communicate well and are prepared to engage with a vastly different range of abilities and personalities. Some of your students will be opinionated, some will be shy, and some will go on to create impressive projects that outdo your own poetic CV. A skilful teacher will have to address these very different sets of needs and personalities, and what each student hopes to get out of the class.

Running events for young writers

Some poets might find it especially rewarding to teach young people as part of youth groups, school activities and after-school clubs, which may be eligible for community or national arts funding. The focus of such a group may be on developing young people's performance skills and helping them to express themselves in writing. The teacher's literary knowledge would not need to be as high-level as someone wishing to teach intermediate or advanced adult poets, but they *would* need other skills suited to working with young people. Anyone thinking about working with children will need to arrange a DBS check (a background check of your criminal records); this is a requirement for going into schools, even if you're only planning on doing so now and then.

Editing a poetry magazine

Editing a poetry magazine can be a source of relatively steady income as well as prestige, but it is a full-time job, even if the hours may technically be part-time. As well as a strong artistic vision, this role requires business sense, people skills and experience of filling out funding applications. Jobs on established magazines are competitive and, because a lead editor or poetry editor is often in place for years, turnover is quite low. I am delighted to see new magazines spring up and succeed, even in today's challenging climate, but it's not for nothing that people say if you want to make a small fortune in publishing, you need a large one first. If you have a strong urge to launch a new publication but you are not sure about committing to something on this scale, try running a webzine online first. This will give you the flexibility to produce one-off print publications which can be paper zines, chapbooks or pamphlets with short selections from a poet you've discovered. This allows you to create a tailored publishing business on your own terms, without the non-negotiable publishing and proofreading schedule that a print magazine requires. Established poets can also work with magazines and literary organisations to provide funded mentorships to emerging, early-career poets whose work shows promise, and these mentorships will be funded by the magazine or organization, who in turn are likely to be funded by the Arts Council or other charitable foundations.

Giving readings and performances

If your style has something in common with performance poetry or you're an established name, you can supplement your writing with performances. Some poets use it as their primary source of income or at least aspire to increase the percentage of the money they make from performing. One way of making a full-time career out of poetry is to make 50-minute (or longer) shows and tour your work, but this requires being as consummate a show-person as you are a writer, and eager to embrace the highs and lows of life on the road. This route requires focus, resilience and self-belief. I'd suggest you need 'thick skin' too; hardly any poets have that, so performance poets would be advised to invest in developing other forms of toughness, self-care and coping strategies for days on the road and nights in front of an audience. Writers, actors and comedians must maintain the difficult balance of remaining sensitive enough to make art and respond to the world around them, and tough enough to manage late nights on railway station platforms, solitary hotel breakfasts, poor reviews and the occasional social media pile-on. Performers do not have to be extroverts but, to fully enjoy the unprecedented options for self-expression provided by performance, they must firmly believe in what they are doing.

Commissions from local literary festivals

Many cities have their own literary or cultural festivals, and the organisers are likely to pass on part of their funding from the Arts Council or city council to a writer for a project that speaks to a place or theme relevant to that city. Mills, mines, markets, historical battles, theatre districts, Huguenot, Bangladeshi or Irish neighbourhoods can all be a source of inspiration. When putting together a pitch for an event like this, poets might theme their offering around an upcoming anniversary of an important day for the town or community. This approach suits the rigorous and organised, as these commissions are time-sensitive and require research. Local festival organisers will be looking for poets with a taste for combining their writing with visual and aural elements (video, film, audio soundscapes or dance). The poet might work on their own, with a group, or in partnership with another local artist or musician to create an immersive experience for the public to enjoy. Open-minded organisers will be looking for both types of event – the large-scale, multimedia type that's location-specific and might require music, projectors and lighting, and the small, flexible type that only requires a microphone and some willing participants and can be run anywhere from a library to a village green.

Events at local literary or community festivals

It is worth getting to know the organisers of your local festivals, as there is often funding for a poet to run a couple of hours of readings with their friends, an open mic or a poetry Slam. These smaller events are also attractive to hard-working festival organisers because they can be arranged at the last minute, aren't dependent on big-name artists and can work well to get audience members into a venue or fill an awkward-length slot between

Poetry

programmed events. Local literary festivals may also commission a writer to create a new poem or series of poems, or a printed pamphlet or anthology about the city or the festival's theme. If you are already inspired by the place where you live, look out for opportunities to share your location-specific writing with the community. Audiences enjoy hearing about the places they know, and that familiarity can be a powerful way to get them on your side.

Writing articles and editing manuscripts

Writing articles and editing manuscripts are much more than nice-to-have options for an aspiring writer. Journalism and editing are full-time careers, or should be, and they require a great deal of professional knowledge. However, most freelance copy-editors and journalists are already used to working with different newspapers and magazines, taking on various types of work, ghostwriting and generally adopting a portfolio approach to their careers, either out of choice or necessity. Experienced poets can also pick up reviewing work for poetry magazines, as these are keen to find appropriate reviewers for new books and to develop the next generation of poetry critics. Reviews editors generally want to diversify the voices in their reviews section, in terms of backgrounds, identities and geography. For example, reviewers from outside London or reviewers with a disability might fit the brief that a reviews editor is looking for, provided that the would-be reviewer can also write well and has a compelling understanding of the book or poet they are writing about. Look online for 'Ledbury Poetry Critics' (https://ledburypoetry.org.uk/home/ledbury-poetry-critics), a national mentorship programme for poetry reviewers, which is aimed at encouraging new and diverse voices.

Writing in another genre alongside your poetry

Whole books and careers have been devoted to the other things you might write, not least the other titles in the *Writers' & Artists'* series. Most writers do try out more than one genre in their lifetime. There is significant overlap between poets and the following categories (though you might just as easily come across a romance author or graphic novelist who also writes poems):

• **Children's and young adult (YA) writers.** Poets often write books for young children, sometimes in verse and sometimes not. Fantasy and mythical themes are popular and reasonably paid options. Established prose writers for young adults, such as Sharon Creech, as well as poets who started out in spoken word and Slam, like Mahogany L. Browne, often turn their hands to young adult novels in verse.

• **Non-fiction authors.** Poets often have specialist interests and a way with words that makes them ideal candidates to write non-fiction books.

• **Playwrights.** The rhythm of page poetry, the staged nature of performance poetry, and the desire to create something ambitious and long-form from similar raw materials have led to interesting creations and collaborations over time. Full plays in verse have waxed and waned in popularity throughout the 20th century, but now performance poets are doubling back by creating extensive works of poetry-based theatre. Like poets, playwrights are aware of the measure, beat and timings of certain words. Poetry and playwriting have shared a long relationship, from T.S. Eliot's verse plays to the contemporary works of Mike Bartlett – who, as well as writing one play, *King Charles III*, in blank verse, writes his other playscripts in a singular way that indicates exactly how the lines should be paused and punctuated by the actors.

Even if the portfolio model of career is not for you, here are some ways of broadening your skill set that you may not have considered. There are plenty of online and in-person opportunities to help you master those that pique your interest:

• **Video, radio and podcasting.** This is ideal for creating live or recorded readings and reaching new and international audiences through digital channels.

• **Visual art.** If you have skills in this area, you can combine your poetry and artistic abilities. You might design and illustrate your own chapbook, or curate an exhibition that includes poetry and painting, photography or sculpture.

• **Comedy and/or acting.** Many comedians offer classes and sometimes private tutoring. Even if you don't see yourself as the next Edinburgh award-winner, cracking a couple of jokes before a reading can be a real icebreaker.

Taking on projects for a variety of different clients can be seductive for a creative person, and it can be a positive thing in terms of your growth as a writer and strengthening different parts of your portfolio.

Sophia Blackwell is a performance poet with three published collections. Her poetry has been anthologised by Bloodaxe, Nine Arches and the Emma Press among others, and her most recent collection of poetry was longlisted for the Polari Prize. She is also the author of a novel and of the *Writers' & Artists' Poetry Writers' Handbook* (Bloomsbury 2022). Sophia has lectured at the Oxford University Faculty of Continuing Education and at Falmouth University. Notable gigs include four times at Glastonbury on the Poetry&Words Stage, Women of the World (WOW) Festival at the South Bank and headlining a national tour with Hammer and Tongue. For more information see www.sophiablackwell.co.uk. Follow her on Twitter @sophiablackwell.

This article is an extract from Chapter 7 in the *Poetry Writers' Handbook* by Sophia Blackwell (Bloomsbury 2022 © Sophia Blackwell 2022).

See also...
- *Getting your poetry out there*, page 316
- *Poems for the page and on stage*, page 307
- *Guerilla podcasting*, page 348

Poetry

Being a poet and a publisher

Aaron Kent urges writers to build and engage in a supportive, collaborative, nurturing community in which to grow creatively, with the many opportunities, challenges and encouragement this will provide. As both poet and publisher, he explains that finding the right places to share your work but, above all, enjoying the act of creating are key.

I grew up unaware that the arts were a career option – I assumed that was just something rich people did in their spare time rather than a viable ambition. It was a field where the gates had been securely shut and not one where individuals of low socioeconomic status stood a chance of entering, particularly as allowing us in threatened the system they had created to benefit themselves. Eventually I learnt that you *could* have a career in the arts, but you had to have either connections or money – both things that weren't prevalent outside of the middle and upper classes. This sounds frustrating because it is, because gentrification works for those people, and disseminating the arts more widely threatens the boundaries already set. Fortunately, there is a pathway that degentrifies the industry, one that dismantles gates and offers solutions: it's called community.

'Community', as a word, can be looked down upon by artists who already find themselves with a readership and a practice, but it's important to remember that community can exist as an idea that holds inclusion at its core. What those who already sit beyond the gated walls tend to ignore is that they reside in a community – a community that boasts exclusion at its heart; one that is defined by who it keeps out, and the hierarchies it presents. I cling, firmly, to the working-class motto: It's not about rising above your community, it's about rising with it. And that is a sentiment the gatekeepers don't like, because they lose control over who can access the arts. So, first and foremost, my advice is to build a community or engage as part of one. When you're involved this way, you'll find people keen to celebrate your successes and console you in your struggles, and you can offer the same. You'll find artistic growth in the collaboration of admiring others' work, and your work will grow from active and passive engagement with the work of others.

Now that technology is so prevalent, this collaboration doesn't have to be something that happens purely in person – you can create these gatherings and connections anywhere. There are artists I talk to in time zones across the world whose friendship has helped me to become a better author. Charlie Baylis, for example, has been my assistant editor at Broken Sleep Books (www.brokensleepbooks.com) since the day I started it, but we've never met and he spends most of the year in Spain, only coming back to the UK occasionally to visit family. But he's an important part of my artistic growth, as are the multitude of poets and artists I connect with over WhatsApp, social media and email. These are people who see opportunities to share with each other, who cast an eye over each other's work, who boost each other when we need it. This is a connection that money can't buy, because it is built and grounded in selflessness, and it doesn't shut the gates to people on the basis of pre-existing capabilities.

I was 16 when I first wrote a poem. I was 27 before I wrote a poem I liked. Between 16 and 24 I didn't really read any poetry; I was raised in the second most deprived area of Northern Europe, Redruth in Cornwall, and my English teacher was just happy if a dozen or so students actually did any work in class – so there was no inspirational 'Dead Poets Society' education. My parents didn't have an education beyond secondary school, and education wasn't an aspirational thing, it was just a chore to complete as part of the journey to adulthood. So, when I dropped out of my A levels and worked full-time as a barista maestro, I had no literary platform to work from, and no real desire to engage with one. But I continued to write, and write poorly, because I had no community; there was nobody whose work I read, and therefore I felt no ambition to improve, as I now do when reading poetry by Stuart McPherson. There was nobody pushing me beyond my boundaries and encouraging me to grow artistically, the way Azad Ashim Sharma now does ... nobody, like Andre Bagoo, Martha Sprackland, Andrew McMillan, whose encouragement helped me to believe in myself. And so, writing by myself, with no readers, no ambition, no drive, I stagnated into work that existed as just another chore. If you're writing because you're purely interested in the response – whether that's a review, publication or money – then the act of creation becomes no more than a task designed to achieve something else. The fundamental part of art, for me at least, is to enjoy the creating of art – to get a boost from putting ink to paper or fingers to a keyboard or paint to a canvas. If creating something has lifted your morale and made you proud, or happy, or understand yourself at a deeper level, then the work is a success, regardless of how it is received later.

Through Broken Sleep Books we get over 6,000 submissions a year, so I read a lot of cover letters and bios, and I see a noticeable difference between somebody who has sent their work to every possible magazine and journal hoping for publication, and somebody who has a clear idea of the type of journal they want to be published by. For many people, there's a perception that collecting acceptances is more valuable than it actually is. The key, instead, is to ensure proper research with regards to submissions, to find places that fit with your work and who publish writers and writing you want to be positioned alongside. This is all part of that community I've spoken of – remember, it's harder to feel a part of anything if you're trying to be a part of *everything*. Art that situates itself with intention and care is more likely to benefit from the work it resides with than art that exists purely to attain a name to put in a covering letter.

Finally, one of the most important parts of my practice has been to engage in what I call 'creative sorbet'. This means that when I hit a wall and think I can no longer create or write, I move to a different artistic form – whether that's painting, or playing my bass guitar, or learning a difficult recipe. By engaging your creative practice elsewhere, you take your mind off that artistic block and stimulate different artistic muscles. It doesn't matter, to me, if my painting is good or not; what matters is that I created something using a different skillset and then, when I return to writing, those things I learnt about myself and my practice are brought back with me. It also means you immerse yourself in different creative practitioners. The US painter Barnett Newman is currently more important to my writing than many writers are, because his art makes me reconsider how I write.

These reasons, and more, matter because if you've enjoyed the act of creating and got something out of it, if you've got people around you to share in the highs and lows, who challenge you, and you've achieved something before the art has entered the world, then you've won the battle – regardless of the result. If you've got *this* in place, then the rejections matter less and the successes taste sweeter.

Aaron Kent is a poet and publisher from Cornwall, now living in Wales. He runs the poetry press Broken Sleep Books (www.brokensleepbooks.com) and his debut poetry collection, *Angels the Size of Houses*, was published by Shearsman Books in 2021. Aaron has had work published in *Poetry London, Poetry Wales, The Rialto, Prototype, The North, The Scores, Wild Court, Blackbox Manifold, Butchers Dog, BAX (2020)* and *Prelude*, among others. He has recently finished his first novel. Aaron was awarded the Awen Medal in 2020. Follow him on Twitter @GodzillaKent and @brokensleep.

Poetry

Getting your poetry out there

Neil Astley knows that you need talent, passion, patience and dedication to become a published poet. He gives valuable advice on the possibilities, pitfalls and rewards that any budding poet might encounter.

Are you a poet – yet?

This article assumes that you have a potential readership or audience for your poetry, and that where you need guidance is in how to reach all those readers. But most poets just starting out believe that. There is, however, *no* readership for poets who *think* they are ready to publish but whose work isn't really *there* yet. If you've *not* immersed yourself in poetry for years – which involves intensive reading and absorbing poetry from all periods – to think of yourself as a poet is self-delusion. No one will want to read you, and your attempts to get your work out there will be met with rejection, frustration and disappointment – and self-righteous indignation if you're one of those would-be writers who think they're geniuses waiting to be discovered. People either have talent or they don't, and no amount of self-promotion and/or even education in the way of poetry workshops or MA courses will make you a poet if you don't have an insatiable passion for *reading* poetry (not just your own) and an original way of writing it. But if you've been drawn to poetry, and have *read* as much poetry as you can get hold of, I'd say you're halfway there.

A poet's reading list

One of the poets I publish, Hannah Lowe, was an English teacher who'd always loved poetry but wasn't familiar with the full range of contemporary poetry until her mother gave her a copy of the Bloodaxe anthology *Staying Alive* as a birthday present. That book made her think that *she* could write poetry. With other younger poets writing now, the process has often been the other way round; maybe they've read Simon Armitage, Carol Ann Duffy, Seamus Heaney and Philip Larkin, but they haven't read their Shakespeare, Donne, Keats, Wordsworth, Coleridge, Browning, Dickinson, Frost, Yeats, Auden and Eliot, all essential reading for anyone who wants to write poetry.

Without that groundwork reading, your own work will go nowhere. But all is not lost. If you really do have a gift for poetry, but life circumstances have been such as to make your reading patchy, stop thinking of getting your work out there now, and for the next year, just read and reread judiciously without thinking of writing. Start with the *Norton Anthology of Poetry* (W.W. Norton, 6th edn 2018) and the *Penguin Book of English Verse* (Penguin, new edn 2004), and get hold of books by the major figures they include; then *The Rattle Bag* (Faber & Faber 1982, 2005), *Emergency Kit* (Faber & Faber 2004) and the *Staying Alive* anthology series (Bloodaxe Books 2002, 2004, 2011 and 2020) and read more by the poets who most appeal to you. When you come back to writing, a year or more later, both you and your poetry will have changed. The poems you had wanted to get out there earlier will go in the bin, and you'll be writing poetry that should interest other readers.

Getting critical feedback

Next you need feedback. If you can find a good writing group or workshop in your area, that can be helpful. Even if you disagree with other people's comments on your work, their feedback should still show what aspects of your poems don't work for other readers. Later, once you've been working on your poetry for at least a year or two, it would be helpful to go on one of the writing courses (which are more week-long workshops than taught courses as such) run by the Arvon Foundation at three centres in England, or by Tŷ Newydd in Wales or Moniack Mhor in Scotland. Or contact the Poetry School in London (https://poetryschool.com) which offers online tuition, downloads, workshops and summer schools. There are also part-time MA courses run by numerous universities and colleges throughout Britain, but I don't think those are right for relative beginners; to gain full benefit from such courses (which cost thousands of pounds in fees) I think you need to have been writing seriously for at least five years. (See page 683 for a list.)

You can also start sending out poems to magazines; their websites will say whether you should submit online or if you need to send half a dozen poems with a stamped addressed envelope for their possible return. It won't be hard to get poems taken by the smallest of the magazines. The real challenge will be in sending work to the long-standing, leading poetry or literary magazines edited by significant poets or critics. These might include *Acumen, Agenda, The Dark Horse, Granta, Iota, The London Magazine, Magma Poetry, The North, Orbis, PN Review, Poetry London, The Poetry Review, Poetry Wales* or *The Rialto*. There are also literary and cultural journals that publish poems, but these are much harder for new writers to break into, such as the *London Review of Books* and the *Times Literary Supplement*; somewhat perversely, you may find you have more luck with the political press: the *Morning Star, New Statesman* and the *Spectator* all publish newcomers as well as established poets.

Just as important as getting poems accepted is getting them rejected, especially if that includes getting a note back from an editor with a comment on your submission that makes something click. You may think that what you're writing now is great, but there will be flaws. There are always improvements that can be made that make all the difference between a half good poem and a really good one. Poets judging poetry competitions talk

Poetry magazines

Acumen	**PN Review**
See page 39	See page 78
Agenda	**Poetry London**
See page 40	See page 78
The Dark Horse	**The Poetry Review**
www.thedarkhorsemagazine.com	See page 78
The London Magazine	**Poetry Wales**
See page 70	See page 78
Magma Poetry	**The Rialto**
See page 71	See page 83
The North	
https://poetrybusiness.co.uk/the-north-magazine/	

For a fuller list see www.bloodaxebooks.com/links. See also *Magazines UK and Ireland* starting on page 39 and *Poetry organisations* on page 322.

Poetry

about 'the wrong note', a line or phrase in a poem that sticks out as not belonging there or needing to be changed even with just one word added or a phrase taken out, and they can't give the prize to that poem because readers will see it too, but the poet is too close to the work and isn't aware of it.

To submit or not to submit?

So the first lesson in how to get your poetry out there is *not* to send it out, or not yet. Put it in a drawer for six months and come back to it; with that amount of distance from the work, you should be able to fix that 'wrong note' and also make the whole poem read more smoothly. Also – and this is absolutely essential – read the poem aloud. As you're writing it, and when you think you've finished it, and when you come back to it months later. Again, poets who haven't done this all talk about only realising what doesn't work in a poem when they were reading it aloud to an audience; trying not to let their expression show that they've just read a bum line at the live event, but rushing home afterwards to correct it. And if you do all your writing on a computer, print out your poems, and read through and edit them on paper. What may look right on a computer screen will often not *feel* right on paper, and then you'll see what needs to be edited. This is also where magazine rejections are helpful: six months later, going back to the poem you thought was your best but which kept being returned, you see the 'wrong note', fix the problem, send it out, and the poem is taken right away.

Don't submit to magazines unless you're familiar with the kind of work each one publishes. They are all different, and you will not be able to publish much unless you research the field and send to those whose output you like and respect. If you live in or can get to London, Edinburgh or Manchester, spend a day in the National Poetry Library (formerly the Saison Poetry Library) at the Southbank Centre, the Scottish Poetry Library or the Manchester Poetry Library and read the latest issues of the current magazines, and afterwards take out subscriptions to those you like most. Familiarity with the work of other poets is an important part of that process: if you're expecting others to read your work, you should read theirs too and learn from it; and support the magazines which support you. Join the Poetry Society and you'll receive *The Poetry Review* and *Poetry News* every quarter; join the Poetry Book Society and you'll receive their four Choices over the course of the year with the PBS *Bulletin* (including highly illuminating pieces by the poets about their books). The National Poetry Library also has two websites: www.nationalpoetrylibrary.org.uk, which includes listings of all the current print and online magazines, and http://poetrymagazines.org.uk, which has an archive covering many of the leading journals where you can read their back issues.

You can familiarise yourself with the editorial taste of online magazines much more easily. Some magazines publish both print and online editions, while others that started out as print have gone over completely to online publication. But so much poetry is published online now – and online imprints come and go – that readers and writers alike find it hard to see the wood for the trees, an appropriate metaphor to use here given that the cost and labour involved in printing and distributing magazines used to discourage poorly edited publications from flourishing. For a list of significant webzines which currently publish poetry, see the box overleaf. These are the webzines (some quite new, not all exclusively poetry) picked out by poets I've consulted as the places where they'd most like to see their work, and where the younger poets in particular go to read their peers. It's worth adding that they also want their work to be featured or discussed in several webzines which don't take submissions, notably *The Quietus* (http://thequietus.com), *Sabotage Reviews* (http://sabotagereviews.com) and *Wild Court* (http://wildcourt.co.uk). And the ultimate accolade is getting your poems into America's *Poetry* magazine, with all the work it publishes being added to a historic online archive that goes back to 1912. The recently established reciprocal publication by *Poetry* and *The Poetry Review* of selections by US and UK poets has helped make this less of a pipe dream for British poets.

Get noticed through competitions and performance

Building up a coherent body of work can take years. As your work matures, so your confidence grows, and you start getting more and more poems taken by magazines and perhaps win prizes in poetry competitions. And some of the poetry competitions are worth trying, but as with the magazines, don't submit blindly; do your research. Just as you can almost predict which poets will win each year's poetry prizes from who the judges are, or what kind of work the combination of judges on each prize's judging panel is likely to favour, so it is with the poetry competitions. And the timing of their deadlines is such that you can't usually submit the same poems to more than one of the main poetry competitions in any one year. So check out the main competitions and submit to those judged by the poets you admire. As well as the Poetry Society's National Poetry Competition, these might include the Basil Bunting, Bridport, Bristol, Cardiff, Cheltenham,

Popular webzines

And Other Poems
http://andotherpoems.com

Atrium
https://atriumpoetry.com

Bad Lilies
www.badlilies.uk

bath magg
www.bathmagg.com

The Fortnightly Review
http://fortnightlyreview.co.uk

Ink Sweat and Tears
www.inksweatandtears.co.uk

The Lake
www.thelakepoetry.co.uk

London Grip
http://londongrip.co.uk

The Manchester Review
www.themanchesterreview.co.uk

Pulsar Poetry
www.pulsarpoetry.com

The White Review
www.thewhitereview.org

Ledbury, Manchester, *Mslexia* (women only) and *Poetry London* competitions. (See *Competitions* on page 328 under *Poetry organisations*.)

The recent growth of festivals and venues with open mic slots has given new writers opportunities to read their work in public; and you don't have to be a performance poet for your work to go down well with audiences, you just have to read strong work and read it well. Don't overrun your time slot and give a straightforward presentation of your work, which means a short introduction only, use your 'natural' voice and don't adopt the highly mannered whining delivery style favoured by poets who should know better.

Once you've published widely in magazines and are starting to do readings, you'll be at the stage of seeking out a small press willing to publish a pamphlet or chapbook (15 to 20 poems). Most pamphlets are sold at readings, and having a pamphlet to give to organisers and to sell at events can lead to more opportunities to read your work. And finally –

we're talking about years now – you might have a book-length manuscript (typescript) of around 50 poems which you think worthy of publication. But the chances of having this taken up by one of the 'big eight' leading poetry imprints (Bloodaxe, Cape, Carcanet, Chatto, Faber, Granta, Penguin and Picador) are exceedingly slim. Apart from Granta, Penguin and Picador, which don't consider unsolicited submissions except from literary

Poetry publishers

THE BIG EIGHT

Bloodaxe Books
See page 130

Jonathan Cape
See page 188

Carcanet
See page 134

Chatto & Windus
See page 188

Faber & Faber
See page 144

Granta Books
See page 61

Penguin
See page 172

Picador
See page 170

SMALLER PRESSES

Arc Publications
See page 126

Blue Diode
See page 131

Broken Sleep Books
See page 133

Burning Eye Books
See page 133

Cinnamon Press
See page 136

Dedalus Press
See page 140

The Emma Press
See page 143

Eyewear Publishing/The Black Spring Press Group
https://blackspringpressgroup.com

flipped eye publishing
See page 145

The Gallery Press
(Ireland) See page 147

Happen*Stance*
www.happenstancepress.com

Nine Arches Press
See page 166

Offord Road Books
See page 167

Out-Spoken Press
See page 169

Pavilion Poetry
See page 170

Peepal Tree Press
See page 171

Salmon Poetry
See page 177

Seren
See page 180

Shearsman Books
See page 180

Smith|Doorstop Books
www.poetrybusiness.co.uk/smith-doorstop

Smokestack Books
See page 181

Templar Poetry
See page 184

the87press
www.the87press.co.uk

Valley Press
See page 187

Verve Poetry Press
See page 187

The Waywiser Press
See page 189

For a fuller list of poetry publishers visit www.bloodaxebooks.com/links.

Poetry

agents, we all receive *thousands* of submissions every year, but the annual output of first collections from *all* eight imprints is rarely more than a dozen books *in total*. Much wiser to try the smaller poetry presses you'll find listed in this *Yearbook*, and you won't need an agent to do this. The only poets with agents are writers who are also novelists, journalists or playwrights. Don't think of ebooks as any kind of solution. Ebooks don't give poets the massive readership reached by writers of thrillers or romance, amounting to just 4% of total poetry sales.

Poets, beware!

Finally, a word of warning. There are certain firms which charge poets to publish their work or which require payment for copies of anthologies in which your work appears as a condition of publication. Poets starting out are particularly susceptible to what is known as vanity publishing. Reputable publishers or magazines of any size will pay authors for their work, usually with royalties in the case of books. If you are asked to pay for the production of your book by a publisher who sends you a flattering 'reader's report' on your work, try asking a local printer to give you an estimate for printing a few hundred copies of your book. The likelihood is that the cost will be considerably lower, and if you want your work to be read by friends, colleagues and people in your local community, the circulation you can achieve by this DIY method will be more effective. The normal arrangements for publishing also involve the author receiving complimentary copies of a book or a free contributor's copy of a magazine or anthology. If you're asked to pay to see your own work in print, you are paying to have it published. For more information see the website Vanity Publishing (www.vanitypublishing.info) and also the advice offered by the Society of Authors (www.societyofauthors.org/SOA/MediaLibrary/SOAWebsite/Guides/Vanity-Publishing.pdf).

If you're unable to get your book published but are confident of selling enough copies at readings, there are effective ways of self-publication covered by other articles in this *Yearbook*. As an alternative to local printers, a number of poets use the self-publishing website www.lulu.com, which offers a distribution channel in addition to well-produced books and ebooks.

Neil Astley is the Editor of publisher Bloodaxe Books, which he founded in 1978. His own books include novels, poetry collections and anthologies, most notably the Bloodaxe *Staying Alive* series: *Staying Alive* (2002), *Being Alive* (2004), *Being Human* (2011) and *Staying Human* (2020). He has edited three collaborations with Pamela Robertson-Pearce, *Soul Food: Nourishing Poems for Starved Minds* (2008), and the DVD-books *In Person: 30 Poets* (2008) and *In Person: World Poets* (2017). He has published two novels, *The End of My Tether* (Scribner 2002), which was shortlisted for the Whitbread First Novel Award, and *The Sheep Who Changed the World* (Flambard Press 2005).

Poetry organisations

Below are some organisations which provide budding poets with opportunities to explore, extend and share their work.

WHERE TO GET INVOLVED

A range of organisations – from local groups to larger professional bodies – exists at which emerging and established poets can access support or learn more about others' work. A concise selection appears below.

The British Haiku Society

16 Croft Gardens, Andover, Hampshire SP10 2RH
email britishhaiku@gmail.com
website www.britishhaikusociety.org.uk
Facebook www.facebook.com/thebritishhaikusociety

Pioneers the appreciation and writing of haiku and kindred forms of verse in the UK, and has links with similar organisations throughout the world. Currently there are around 400 BHS members from 27 countries. Members receive a quarterly journal, *Blithe Spirit*, an annual members' anthology and a newsletter. Runs the annual British Haiku Society Awards in three categories: haiku, tanka and haibun; publishes books concerning haiku and related matters, and is active in promoting the teaching of haiku in schools and colleges. Founded 1990.

Literature Wales

Glyn Jones Centre, Wales Millennium Centre, Bute Place, Cardiff CF10 5AL
tel 029-2047 2266
email post@literaturewales.org
website www.literaturewales.org

National company for the development of literature in Wales. Working to inspire communities, develop writers and celebrate Wales' literary culture. Activities include the Wales Book of the Year Award, the Children's Laureate Wales and Bardd Plant Cymru schemes, creative writing courses at Tŷ Newydd Writing Centre, writer's bursaries and mentoring, and the National Poet of Wales initiative. The organisation is a member of the Arts Council of Wales' Arts Portfolio Wales.

The Poetry Book Society

Milburn House, Dean Street,
Newcastle Upon Tyne NE1 1LF
tel 0191 230 8100
email enquiries@poetrybooksociety.co.uk
website www.poetrybooks.co.uk
Facebook www.facebook.com/poetrybooksoc
Twitter @poetrybooksoc

Book club for readers of poetry founded in 1953 by T.S. Eliot. Every quarter, expert poet selectors choose one outstanding publication (the PBS Choice), and recommend four other titles to deliver to PBS members. The PBS also produces the quarterly membership magazine, the *Bulletin*, which contains in-depth reviews, interviews with international poets and extensive listings. PBS members also enjoy 25% off all book orders and access to a lively poetry community with nationwide events.

The Poetry Business

Campo House, 54 Campo Lane, Sheffield S1 2EG
tel 0114 438 4074
email office@poetrybusiness.co.uk
website www.poetrybusiness.co.uk

Publishes books, pamphlets and audio under its Smith|Doorstop imprint; runs the literary magazine, *The North*. Also organises an international Book & Pamphlet competition, Writing Days, online workshops and runs an advanced writing school for published poets

Poetry Ireland

11 Parnell Square East, Dublin D01 ND60, Republic of Ireland
tel +353 (0)1 6789815
email info@poetryireland.ie
website www.poetryireland.ie

Organisation committed to achieving excellence in the reading, writing and performance of poetry throughout the island of Ireland. Poetry Ireland receives support from The Arts Council (An Chomhairle Ealaíon) and The Arts Council of Northern Ireland and enjoys partnerships with arts centres, festivals, schools, colleges and bookshops at home and abroad. Its commitment to creating performance and publication opportunities for poets at all stages of their careers helps ensure that the best work is made available to the widest possible audience. Poetry Ireland publishes the well-regarded journal, *Poetry Ireland Review*.

The Poetry Society

22 Betterton Street, London WC2H 9BX
tel 020-7420 9880
email info@poetrysociety.org.uk
website www.poetrysociety.org.uk

A leading voice for poets and poetry in Britain. Established over a century ago to promote a more general recognition and appreciation of poetry, the Society has more than 3,000 members. With education initiatives, commissioning and publishing programmes, and a calendar of performances, readings and competitions, the Society champions poetry in its many forms.

The Society offers advice and information to all, with exclusive offers and discounts available to members. Every quarter, members receive copies of *The Poetry Review* and the Society's newsletter, *Poetry News*. The Society also publishes education resources; organises events including an Annual Lecture and National Poetry Day celebrations; runs Poetry Prescription, a critical appraisal service available to members for £40 and non-members for £50; and provides an education advisory and training service, as well as school and youth memberships.

Competitions run by the Society include the annual National Poetry Competition, with a first prize of £5,000, and the Foyle Young Poets of the Year Award. Founded 1909.

The Seamus Heaney Centre at Queen's

c/o School of Arts, English and Languages, Queen's University Belfast, Belfast BT7 1NN
tel 028-9097 1077
email shc@qub.ac.uk
website www.seamusheaneycentre.com
Director Professor Glenn Patterson

Runs a prestigious Poetry Summer School and awards an annual First Collection Poetry Prize. Also hosts an array of visiting Fellows and a programme of talks, readings and performances throughout the year. The current Seamus Heaney Chair in Poetry is Nick Laird. The Centre's founding director was Ciaran Carson. Founded 2003.

Shortlands Poetry Circle

Ripley Arts Centre, 24 Sundridge Avenue, Bromley BR1 2PX
tel 020-8464 9810
email shortlands@poetrypf.co.uk
website www.poetrypf.co.uk/shortlands.html
President Anne Stewart

Meets twice a month during term time and one meeting per calendar month online. Visitors welcome. Founded 1911.

Survivors' Poetry

95 Wick Hall, Furze Hill, Hove BN3 1NG
tel (01273) 202876
email drsimonjenner@gmail.com
Director Simon Jenner

National charity and survivor-led arts group which coordinates artistic activities using poetry to make connections between creativity and mental health. The quarterly newsletter, *Poetry Express*, is free to access by emailing: bricolage92@hotmail.com

Tower Poetry

Christ Church, Oxford OX1 1DP
tel 07849 625906
email tower.poetry@chch.ox.ac.uk
website www.chch.ox.ac.uk/towerpoetry
Facebook www.facebook.com/towerpoetry
Twitter @towerpoetry

Exists to encourage and challenge everyone who reads or writes poetry. Funded by a generous bequest to Christ Church, Oxford, by the late Christopher Tower, the aims of Tower Poetry are to stimulate an enjoyment and critical appreciation of poetry, particularly among young people in education, and to challenge people to write their own poetry.

Ver Poets

tel (01582) 715817
email gregsmith480@gmail.com
website www.verpoets.co.uk
Secretary Gregory Smith
Membership £15 p.a. UK; £20 p.a. overseas; £10 p.a. students

Encourages the writing and study of poetry. Holds evening meetings and daytime workshops in the St Albans area, as well as workshops via Zoom. Holds members' competitions and the annual Open Competition. Founded 1966.

WHERE TO GET INFORMATION

Your local library is a good first port of call and should have information about the poetry scene in the area. Many libraries are actively involved in spreading the word about poetry as well as having modern poetry available for loan.

Alliance of Literary Societies (ALS)

email allianceoflitsocs@gmail.com
website www.allianceofliterarysocieties.org.uk
Facebook www.facebook.com/allianceofliterarysocieties
Twitter @alliancelitsocs
Instagram @alliancelitsocs
Chair Marty Ross

Umbrella organisation for literary societies and groups in the UK. It provides support and advice on a variety of literary subjects, as well as promoting cooperation between member societies. Its publications include a twice-yearly members' newsletter, *Not Only But…*, and an annual journal, *ALSo*. ALS holds an AGM weekend which is hosted by a different member society each year, moving around the UK, or online. Founded 1973.

Arts Council England

tel 0161 934 4317
email enquiries@artscouncil.org.uk
website www.artscouncil.org.uk

National development agency for the arts in England, providing funding for a range of arts and cultural activities. It supports creative writing including poetry, fiction, storytelling, spoken word, digital work, writing for children and literary translation. It funds a range of publishers and magazines as well as providing grants to individual writers. Contact the enquiries team for more information on funding support and advice.

Arts Council of Wales

Bute Place, Cardiff CF10 5AL
tel 0845 8734 900
email information@arts.wales
website https://arts.wales
Facebook www.facebook.com/celfyddydau
Twitter @Arts_Wales_

Independent charity, established by Royal Charter in 1994. It has three regional offices and its principal sponsor is the Welsh Government. It is the country's funding and development agency for the arts, supporting and developing high-quality arts activities. Its funding schemes offer opportunities for arts organisations and individuals in Wales to apply, through a competitive process, for funding towards a clearly defined arts-related project.

Manchester Poetry Library

Manchester Metropolitan University, Grosvenor Building, Cavendish Street, Manchester M15 6BG
email poetrylibrary@mmu.ac.uk
website www.mmu.ac.uk/poetry-library
Twitter @mcrpoetrylib
Instagram @mcrpoetrylibrary
Director Becky Swain

Public poetry library: free and open to all. Aims to expand access to poetry and to encourage the writing of it at all levels, from primary school to professional publication. Core collection includes 19th- to 21st-century poetry in English from around the world, as well as poetry in translation. Audio and print versions available. Runs events that celebrate the role of local communities and languages.

National Association of Writers' Groups

Old Vicarage, Scammonden, Huddersfield HD3 3FT
email info@nawg.co.uk
website www.nawg.co.uk

Aims to bring cohesion and fellowship to isolated writers' groups and individuals, promoting the study and art of writing in all its aspects. There are many affiliated groups and associate (individual) members across the UK.

National Poetry Library

Level 5, Royal Festival Hall, Southbank Centre, London SE1 8XX
tel 020-7921 0943
email info@poetrylibrary.org.uk
website www.nationalpoetrylibrary.org.uk
Facebook www.facebook.com/NationalPoetryLibrary

Twitter @natpoetrylib
Instagram @nationalpoetrylibrary
Membership Free with two forms of ID, one photographic and the other showing a UK address

The largest public collection of modern poetry in the world. It is open to everyone and free to join (see above stipulations and please check website for opening times). Members can borrow from the extensive loan collections, including audio items, and take advantage of the library's e-loan service through which ebooks can be loaned at distance. The extensive collection of current poetry magazines gives a window into the breadth of poetry in the UK and beyond. The library runs regular live readings, a programme of exhibitions and children's events throughout the year. Its website features publishers' information, poetry news and a list of UK-wide events.

Northern Poetry Library

The Chantry, Bridge Street, Morpeth, Northumberland NE61 1PD
tel (01670) 620391
email mylibrary@northumberland.gov.uk
website http://northernpoetrylibrary.org.uk
Twitter @nplpoetry

Largest collection of contemporary poetry outside London, housing over 15,000 titles and magazines covering poetry published since 1945. Founded 1968.

Scottish Poetry Library

5 Crichton's Close, Canongate, Edinburgh EH8 8DT
tel 0131 557 2876
email reception@spl.org.uk
website www.scottishpoetrylibrary.org.uk

Houses over 45,000 poetry-related items: books, magazines, pamphlets, recordings and the Edwin Morgan Archive (featuring rare works by Morgan and others). The core of the collection is contemporary and classic poetry written in Scotland – Scots, Gaelic and English – but classic Scottish poetry as well as contemporary works from almost every part of the world are also available. All resources, advice and information are readily accessible, free of charge. The SPL has its own shop and holds regular exhibitions and poetry events, including reading and writing groups and outreach projects throughout the nation, details of which are available on the library website. Closed Saturday and Sunday. Founded 1984.

ONLINE RESOURCES

There is a wealth of information available for poets at the click of a mouse; the suggestions below are a good starting point.

The Poetry Archive

email admin@poetryarchive.org
website www.poetryarchive.org
Facebook www.facebook.com/PoetryArchive

Twitter @PoetryArchive
Instagram @thepoetryarchive

World's premier online collection of recordings of poets reading their work. Over 700 authors featured. Features the voices of contemporary English-language poets as well as those from the past, including C. Day Lewis, Paul Farley and Dorothea Smartt. The Archive is added to regularly. Funded by donation; a membership scheme is available to help keep collections freely accessible.

The Poetry Kit
email info@poetrykit.org
website www.poetrykit.org
Twitter @thepoetrykit

Collates a wide variety of poetry-related information, including events, competitions, courses and more for an international readership.

Poetry Space
email susan@poetryspace.co.uk
website www.poetryspace.co.uk

Specialist publisher of poetry and short stories, as well as news and features, edited by Susan Jane Sims. Operates as a social enterprise with all profits being used to publish online and in print, and to hold events to widen participation in poetry. Submissions of poems, stories, novel extracts, photographs and artwork accepted all year for Young Writers' and Artists' Space (18s and under; work by under-16s particularly welcomed).

Poets and Writers
website www.pw.org
Facebook www.facebook.com/poetsandwriters/
Twitter @poetswritersinc

US-based online magazine and e-newsletter on the craft and business of writing.

Sabotage Reviews
email director@sabotagereviews.com
email poetry@sabotagereviews.com
website www.sabotagereviews.com
Contacts Charley Barnes (general enquiries), Karen Goodwin (poetry), Phil Olsen (fiction)

Small press review site. Welcomes articles and reviews of 500–1000 words on poetry, fiction and the spoken word, but check website guidelines carefully prior to submitting any work – full poetry collections or novels are rarely covered on the site.

WHERE TO CELEBRATE POETRY

Festival information should be available from Arts Council England offices (see page 507). See also *Festivals and conferences for writers, artists and readers* on page 593. As well as the list below, major poetry festivals each year include Aldeburgh and Cheltenham. Poetry also often features prominently at the Glastonbury and Latitude Festivals.

The British Council
British Council Customer Service UK, Bridgewater House, 58 Whitworth Street, Manchester M1 6BB
tel 0161 957 7755
email uk-literature@britishcouncil.org
website https://literature.britishcouncil.org
Twitter @litbritish

Information on events, authors and projects.

Canterbury Festival
Festival House, 8 Orange Street, Canterbury, Kent CT1 2JA
tel (01227) 452853
email info@canterburyfestival.co.uk
website https://canterburyfestival.co.uk
Takes place 21 October–4 November 2023

Kent's international arts festival showcases performing arts from around the world and runs year-round projects to inspire creativity in people of all ages. It commissions new work, champions emerging talent and supports those seeking careers in the cultural industries.

Ledbury Poetry Festival
The Master's House, St Katherine's, Bye Street, Ledbury HR8 1EA
tel (01531) 636232
email director@poetry-festival.co.uk
website www.poetry-festival.co.uk
Artistic Director Chloe Garner
Takes place July and throughout the year

The UK's biggest celebration of poetry and spoken word, attended by poets from all over the world. Established and upcoming talents take part in a wide variety of events, from masterclasses, walks, talks and films through to breakfasts, music, exhibitions and bike rides. International Poetry Competition launches every February.

WHERE TO PERFORM

Poetry evenings are held all over the UK and the suggestions listed below are worth checking out. Others can be found by visiting your local library or your Arts Council office, or by visiting the What's On section of the Poetry Society website (https://poetrysociety.org.uk/events/). The Poetry Library (www.nationalpoetrylibrary.org.uk/events-exhibitions) is also an excellent source for upcoming poetry events. Also look out for local groups at which members can share their work.

As we go to press, many established poetry events are now returning to live events. Please check their website or social media contacts for any status updates.

Allographic

tel 07904 488009
email openmic@allographic.co.uk
website https://allographica.blogspot.com
Facebook www.facebook.com/allographica
Twitter @allographica
Instagram @allographica
Contact Fay Roberts

Cambridge-based live or Zoom events with new and
upcoming names from the spoken word scene and a
set of workshops for aspirant poets, storytellers and
other writers and performers. Also produces a range
of publications, from anthologies to books and
pamphlets, that can be purchased online.

Apples and Snakes

The Albany, Douglas Way, London SE8 4AG
tel 07496 393793
email info@applesandsnakes.org
website www.applesandsnakes.org

Exists to support poets at all stages of their careers.
Runs regular live events and artist development
programmes across the country, working
collaboratively to ensure that unheard voices become
heard. Founded 1982.

Book Slam

email elliott@bookslam.com
website www.bookslam.com
Contact Elliott Jack

Founded with the aim of returning literature to the
heart of popular culture, Book Slam invites authors,
poets, singer-songwriters and comedians to a
thinking person's cabaret. Various venues; see website
for details.

Café Writers Norwich

Louis Marchesi, Tombland, Norwich NR3 1HF
email info@cafewriters.co.uk
website www.cafewriters.co.uk
Twitter @cafewriters
Instagram @cafe.writers
Contacts Ramona Herdman, Julia Webb, Stuart
Charlesworth, Anne Bailey

Readings of poetry and prose in a relaxed and
welcoming atmosphere, on the second Monday of
every month. Open mic slots available. Some events
on Zoom.

Coffee House Poetry

email coffpoetry@aol.com
website www.coffeehousepoetry.org

Readings, courses, classes and the annual Troubadour
International Poetry Prize.

Genesis Poetry Slam

Genesis Cinema, 93–95 Mile End Road,
London E1 4UJ

email poetry@genesis-cinema.co.uk
Facebook www.facebook.com/GenesisSlam
Contacts Laurie Eaves, Caz Teague

Three-round poetry slam. Held the first Thursday of
every month. Slots should be booked via the email
above.

Jawdance

Rich Mix, 35–47 Bethnal Green Road,
London E1 6LA
email info@applesandsnakes.org
website https://richmix.org.uk/events/jawdance
Facebook www.facebook.com/applesandsnakes
Twitter @ApplesAndSnakes
Host Yomi Sode, Kat François

Poetry, film and music night, currently every third
Wednesday of the month. Check website for details.

Kent & Sussex Poetry Society

email kentandsussexpoetry@gmail.com
website www.kentandsussexpoetry.com

Local group with national reputation. Organises
monthly poetry readings (some online), workshops
and an annual poetry competition.

Loud Poets

Scottish Storytelling Centre, 43–45 High Street,
Edinburgh EH1 1SR
email hello@iamloud.co
website www.iamloud.co
Creative Director Kevin Mclean, *Operations Director*
Mark Gallie, *Producer* Dr Katie Ailes, *Marketing
Manager and Producer* Bex Sherwood

Spoken word showcases and poetry slams. See
website for touring locations; Edinburgh shows
(often monthly) are held at the address above.

Out-Spoken

Southbank Centre, Belvedere Road, London SE1 8XX
email info@outspokenldn.com
website www.outspokenldn.com
Facebook www.facebook.com/outspokenLDN
Twitter @OutSpokenLDN
Instagram @outspokenldn

Monthly poetry and live music event. See website or
social media accounts for forthcoming dates and start
times. Also runs an annual poetry prize awarded in
three categories: Performance; Page; and Film.
Submissions open in January, with winners in each
category and a cash prize for the overall winner.
Submissions can be made via the website (see above);
a fee may be applicable.

Poets' Café

South Street Arts Centre, 21 South Street,
Reading RG1 4QU
email info@poetscafereading.co.uk
website www.poetscafereading.co.uk
Twitter @Poets_Cafe

Hosts Vic Pickup, Zannah Kearns, Rika Banerjee

Reading's longest-running poetry platform, organised and hosted by The Poetry Society's Reading Stanza. Held on the second Friday of each month, this event consists of an open mic section and a full reading by an established poet. See website for details of online events.

Polari

email paulburston@btinternet.com
website www.polarisalon.com
Twitter @polarisalon
Contact Paul Burston

Multi-award-winning LGBTQ+ literary salon, which also goes on tour: see website for forthcoming events. Focuses on established authors but has some pre-arranged spots per event for up-and-coming LGBTQ+ writers. Based at the British Library, but see website for full details of event locations.

Rainbow Poetry Recitals

2 Old Farm Court, Shoreham BN43 5FE
tel (01273) 465423
email rainbow.poetry@hotmail.co.uk
Administrator Hugh Hellicar
Membership £5 p.a.

Poetry meetings and recitals at two branches in London and four in Sussex. Poetry appreciation and members' poems. Magazine available on request. Founded 1994.

WHERE TO WRITE POETRY

Arvon

Lumb Bank – The Ted Hughes Arvon Centre, Heptonstall, Hebden Bridge, West Yorkshire HX7 6DF
tel (01422) 843714
email lumbbank@arvon.org
Totleigh Barton, Sheepwash, Beaworthy, Devon EX21 5NS
tel (01409) 231338
email totleighbarton@arvon.org
The Hurst – The John Osborne Arvon Centre, Clunton, Craven Arms, Shrops. SY7 0JA
tel (01588) 640658
email thehurst@arvon.org
website www.arvon.org

Hosts residential creative writing courses and retreats in three rural writing houses. With the opportunity to live and work with professional writers, participants transform their writing through workshops, one-to-one tutorials, time and space to write. Five-day courses and shorter courses are available in a wide range of genres, including writing for children and young adults, fiction, poetry, theatre, creative non-fiction. An online programme of writing courses, masterclasses and live readings also runs

year-round. Grants and concessions are available to help with course fees. Founded 1968.

Cannon Poets

22 Margaret Grove, Harborne, Birmingham B17 9JH
email martin@cannonpoets.org.uk
email greg@cannonpoets.co.uk
Meets at The Moseley Exchange, The Post Office Building, 149–153 Alcester Road, Moseley, Birmingham B13 8JP usually on the first Sunday of each alternate month at 2pm
website www.cannonpoets.org.uk
Facebook www.facebook.com/CannonPoetsBirmingham

Cannon Poets have met monthly since 1983. The group encourages poetry writing through:

• workshops run by members or visitors
• break-out groups where poems are subjected to scrutiny by supportive peer groups
• ten-minute slots where members read a selection of their poems to the whole group
• publication of its journal, *The Cannon's Mouth* (email poetry and poetry-related submissions to greg@cannonpoets.org.uk).

Members are encouraged to participate in poetry events and competitions. Cannon Poets' annual poetry competition, Sonnet or Not, invites poems of just fourteen lines in length. Entrants may choose any one of the traditional sonnet forms or experiment with alternative fourteen-line forms, perhaps using half rhyme, metarhyme or blank verse. The first prize is £500 and the deadline for entries is 31 December of each year. See website for details.

City Lit

1–10 Keeley Street, London WC2B 4BA
tel 020-7831 7831
email writing@citylit.ac.uk
website www.citylit.ac.uk/courses/history-culture-and-writing/writing
Twitter @citylit

Offers classes and courses (online and in-person) on poetry appreciation and writing for children, as well as a wide range of other topics.

The Poetry School

Somerset House, Strand, London WC2R 1LA
tel 020-7582 1679
website www.poetryschool.com

Teaches the art and craft of writing poetry, with courses in London and around the UK, ranging from evening classes, small seminars and individual tutorials, to one-day workshops, year-long courses and an accredited MA. Activities for beginners to advanced writers, with classes happening face-to-face and online. Three termly programmes a year, plus professional skills development projects and CAMPUS, a social network for poets.

Tŷ Newydd Writing Centre

Llanystumdwy, Cricieth, Gwynedd LL52 0LW
tel (01766) 522811
email tynewydd@literaturewales.org
website www.tynewydd.wales

Runs residential writing courses encompassing a wide variety of genres and caters for all levels, from beginners to published poets. All the courses are tutored by established writers. Writing retreats are also available; see website for full details, including prices.

Wey Poets (Surrey Poetry Centre)

Friends Meeting House, 3 Ward Street,
Guildford GU1 4LH
tel (01252) 702450 (admin)
email weypoets@gmail.com
email bb_singleton@hotmail.com
website www.weypoets.com

Small, long-standing group with quality input. New members/visitors and enquiries very welcome. Group meets 2–4:30pm for each event: third Wednesday of the month for workshops, September to June (first Wednesday in December). Additional speaker events on first Wednesday in November, March, April and May. Supportive workshops for original poetry. See website for up-to-date information on the current chair, or contact Belinda Singleton on the email address above.

COMPETITIONS

There are now hundreds of competitions to enter. As a rule, as the value of the prize increases, so does the prestige associated with winning. To decide which ones are most appropriate for your work, make sure you know who the judges are and think twice before paying large sums for an anthology of 'winning' poems which will be read only by entrants wanting to see their own work in print. The Poetry Library publishes a list of competitions online (www.nationalpoetrylibrary.org.uk/write-publish/competitions). See also *Prizes and awards* on page 543.

Literary prizes are given annually to published poets and as such are non-competitive. Information on some high-profile awards can be found on the Booktrust website (www.booktrust.org.uk/what-we-do/awards-and-prizes/).

HELP FOR YOUNG POETS AND TEACHERS

National Association of Writers in Education (NAWE)

Tower House, Mill Lane, off Askham Fields Lane,
Askham Bryan, York YO23 3FS
tel 0330 333 5909
email admin@nawe.co.uk
website www.nawe.co.uk

National membership organisation which aims to advocate for creative writing: enhancing knowledge and understanding of the subject, supporting writers and good practice in teaching and facilitation in all settings. NAWE promotes creative writing as both a distinct discipline and an essential element in education generally. Its membership is national and international and includes those working in Higher Education, freelance writers working in schools and community contexts, and the teachers and other professionals who work with them. It runs a national directory of professional members offering workshops, talks and other services, produces a weekly opportunities bulletin, publishes two journals – *Writing in Education* and *Writing in Practice* – and holds a national conference (this was online in 2023). Professional Membership includes public liability insurance cover.

Professional Graduate Membership is available for university creative writing students who have recently graduated and aims to support the move from student to working as a professional writer in education and the community, offering the benefits of Professional Membership at a discounted rate.

Poetry Society Education

The Poetry Society, 22 Betterton Street,
London WC2H 9BX
tel 020-7420 9880
email educationadmin@poetrysociety.org.uk
website www.poetrysociety.org.uk

An arm of The Poetry Society aiming to facilitate exciting and innovative education work. For over 30 years it has been introducing poets into classrooms, providing comprehensive teachers' resources and producing accessible publications for pupils. It develops projects and schemes to keep poetry flourishing in schools, libraries and workplaces, giving work to hundreds of poets and allowing thousands of children and adults to experience poetry for themselves.

Through projects such as the Foyle Young Poets of the Year Award and Young Poets Network, The Poetry Society gives valuable encouragement and exposure to young writers and performers.

Schools membership offers a range of benefits, including quarterly Poetry Society publications, books and posters, and free access to the Poets in Schools placement service. Youth membership is also available (for ages 11–18; from £25 p.a.) and offers discounts, publications, poetry books and posters.

Young Poets Network

email educationadmin@poetrysociety.org.uk
website https://ypn.poetrysociety.org.uk
Facebook www.facebook.com/YoungPoetsNetwork
Twitter @youngpoetsnet

Online resource from The Poetry Society comprising features about reading, writing and performing poetry, plus new work by young poets and regular writing challenges. Open to anyone under the age of 25.

YOUNG POETRY COMPETITIONS

Children's competitions are included in the competition list provided by the Poetry Library: this is free online at www.nationalpoetrylibrary.org.uk/write-publish/competitions. Further information on literary prizes can be found on the BookTrust website (www.booktrust.org.uk/what-we-do/awards-and-prizes).

Foyle Young Poets of the Year Award

The Poetry Society, 22 Betterton Street, London WC2H 9BX
tel 020-7420 9880
email fyp@poetrysociety.org.uk
website https://foyleyoungpoets.org/
Facebook www.facebook.com/thepoetrysociety
Twitter @PoetrySociety

Annual competition for writers aged 11–17. Prizes include publication, mentoring and a residential writing course. Deadline 31 July. Free to enter. Founded 2001.

Christopher Tower Poetry Competition

Christ Church, Oxford OX1 1DP
tel 07849 625906
email tower.poetry@chch.ox.ac.uk
website www.chch.ox.ac.uk/towerpoetry
Twitter @TowerPoetry

Annual poetry competition (open from October to February) from Christ Church, Oxford, aimed at students aged between 16 and 18 in UK schools and colleges. The poems should be no longer than 48 lines, on a different chosen theme each year. Free to enter. Prizes: £5,000 (1st), £3,000 (2nd), £1,500 (3rd). There will also be ten commended awards of £500 each.

See also...

● *Publishers of poetry*, page 765

Further reading

Addonizio, Kim, *Ordinary Genius: A Guide for the Poet Within* (W.W. Norton 2012)

Bell, Jo and Jane Commane, *How to Be a Poet: A 21st-Century Guide to Writing Well* (Nine Arches Press 2017)

Bell, Jo and guests: *52: Write a Poem a Week – Start Now, Keep Going* (Nine Arches Press 2015)

Blackwell, Sophia, *Writers' & Artists' Poetry Writers' Handbook* (Bloomsbury, 2022)

Chisholm, Alison, *A Practical Guide to Poetry Forms* (Compass Books 2014)

Fairfax, John and John Moat, *The Way to Write* (Penguin Books, 2nd edn revised 1998)

Greene, Roland et al., *Princeton Encyclopedia of Poetry and Poetics* (Princeton University Press, 4th edn 2012)

Hamilton, Ian and Jeremy Noel-Tod, *The Oxford Companion to Modern Poetry in English* (Oxford University Press, 2nd edn 2014)

Kowit, Steve, *In the Palm of Your Hand: A Poet's Portable Workshop* (Tilbury House, 2nd edn 2017)

Maxwell, Glyn, *On Poetry* (Oberon Books 2017)

Oliver, Mary, *Rules for the Dance: Handbook for Writing and Reading Metrical Verse* (Houghton Mifflin 1998)

Padel, Ruth, *52 Ways of Looking at a Poem: A Poem for Every Week of the Year* (Vintage 2004)

Padel, Ruth, *The Poem and the Journey: 60 Poems for the Journey of Life* (Vintage 2008)

Roberts, Philip Davies, *How Poetry Works* (Penguin Books, 2nd edn 2000)

Sampson, Fiona, *Poetry Writing: The Expert Guide* (Robert Hale 2009)

Sansom, Peter, *Writing Poems* (Bloodaxe 1993, repr. 1997)

Whitworth, John, *Writing Poetry* (A&C Black, 2nd edn 2006)

Poetry

Screen and audio
Successful screenwriting

Anna Symon suggests what it takes to forge a career as a screenwriter. She gives practical advice on how to develop the skills and traits needed to succeed in this creative, collaborative and competitive field.

How do you become a professional screenwriter? Unfortunately, there is no one answer, and there's certainly no recognised career path. Some writers come from fiction or the theatre. Others arrive from film and television production, having previously worked as, say, a script editor or documentarian (as I myself did). But, increasingly, plenty of screenwriters do seem to be coming straight to the medium, without any previous story-telling or writing experience. This could be because, with the proliferation of television streaming platforms, there is such a thirst for new content. So the good news is that it's a great time to start out.

Although the field will always be hugely competitive, there are definitely more opportunities than there were five or ten years ago. However, before you start, I believe you need to work out if you have a writer's soul. What do I mean by this? It's hard to sum up in a word or two but all the good writers I know care deeply and are curious about the world around them. Sometimes this curiosity is deeply buried, sometimes it's right on the surface. But it manifests as an interest in scratching below the veneer of life, a compulsion to examine widely held truths, and to express a point of view. I think it makes us a fun bunch of people to hang out with, because we like to question what we see around us, make sense of the world or simply enjoy observing its complexity and absurdity. If that rings a bell and you want to scratch that itch, the next step is to sit down (or stand up) and write. And that's when you need stamina.

There's no shortcut to a career in screenwriting. The craft of telling stories appears deceptively straightforward because we are all so story-literate. Our world is flush with narrative: not just in entertainment, but in advertising and social media, as well as in the stories we constantly tell ourselves about our own lives. So we know what stories are, and can recognise good ones, but learning how to create them successfully takes time. You need to practise as hard as you would at a piano if you wanted to be a concert pianist. They say it takes ten years to become an overnight success and I think, in screenwriting, that's true. It was certainly true for me. The good news is that the ten years honing your craft can be very rewarding. They are certainly some of the most fun times I've had in my life. It's the time when you are reading books, watching films, reading scripts, trying to absorb what everyone else is doing, while all the time writing your own stuff. Perhaps thinking about whether you have a voice and, if you do, what it is? I wouldn't worry too much about that. Write from the heart, lay down the story as you see it, and leave it to others to discover your voice. I truly believe that, with enough time and effort, the majority of screenwriting skills can be learnt. If you think in an interesting way, and have something to say, you can learn the nuts and bolts of how to put a screenplay together.

For some lucky new screenwriters, they'll get off to a flying start and get paid while they are still learning their craft – although they will then make their mistakes in public (which can test the ego). For others, at the start of their writing journey, they are penning spec scripts, unpaid and largely unnoticed, each one hopefully better than the last until, one day, they find that people ask to read their work and then pay for it. (It should be said that all professional writers will have their work reviewed, so you have to find a way to deal with public criticism, which can feel incredibly exposing.)

If 'a career' means getting paid for your writing, then in fiction that means getting published. In television and film, it means getting a project into 'development'. You may well make a healthy living as a full-time, paid screenwriter (particularly in film) for quite a long time before you get a project green lit and on screen. It can be a long haul, otherwise known as 'development hell', trying to get something made. This is a paid process, as scripts go back and forth from broadcaster to producer to writer, with a pile of notes and tweaks along the way. There's a reason for the much-quoted saying: 'Writing is re-writing.' Be prepared for more voices and stakeholders than you would expect commenting on your work – and don't become a screenwriter unless you genuinely enjoy collaboration with other creatives. Professional input from script editors, directors and producers can, and should, massively improve your work. However, at times it can feel like your insides are being scraped with a rusty blade. Get used to it.

If, given all this, you still want to write screenplays there are a few steps you can take along the way to give yourself the best chance. Firstly, I would recommend signing up for as much good quality training as you can afford. I did an MA in Screenwriting and it went a long way towards demystifying both the craft and the business. The course had links with the industry, so it was a first shot at meeting producers and agents and learning how I could turn what I had written into a commercial proposition that a broadcaster would want to finance and an audience would want to watch. More importantly, it was the first time I met a whole cohort of others on the same journey as me. I found my tribe. It was also an opportunity for us all to find people to read and critique our work, to develop that thick skin for what was coming down the road. There were a few people on the course who genuinely couldn't take criticism of their work, however constructively it was offered, and for those people it was useful to discover that screenwriting was not right for them.

The second step comes out of the first, and it is to find a smart, sensitive first reader of your work. This person doesn't have to be a writer, but it should be someone who will be honest with you and whose creative opinion you value. It does feel extremely exposing to have someone question work that took you so long to create, but having fresh eyes on it is essential. It means that when you sit down to write another draft, as you must if you're serious about it, you'll have a sense of where its strengths and weaknesses are – which parts are intriguing, which bits a little slow. Quite often the most useful feedback is to learn which scenes or sequences don't really make sense yet – even if they do to you. 'It's not on the page yet' is a common note given. This means that, despite the fact you feel you have expressed a particular storyline or character point, it is not 'landing' for the reader. If the reader doesn't 'get it', nor will an audience. It needs more work ...

In that sense your first reader is your best friend, who will protect you from harsher criticism from the outside world. Listen to them ... carefully. Try not to be too defensive or write off their notes as them just not 'getting' you. You don't have to alter anything. But you may find that what they pick up on is an area of the script that you weren't quite sure about yourself, a problem you thought you had solved but in your heart of hearts knew wasn't working. Let the criticism settle and then buoy yourself up to tackle the problem head on in your next pass. On the other hand, the reader's thoughts may be inexplicable to you – a real surprise. In that case, I'd suggest finding another reader if you can. Listen carefully to them too. If they come up with a similar point, then I'd suggest you try and do some work on that area of the script.

Try out a few readers if you can. See who you are in tune with – but by that I don't mean the person who simply says: 'Amazing, I loved it'. However evolved a script is, there is always something to talk about. Sometimes the most useful thing is simply to discuss the script with someone who has read it. It forces you to articulate what you are trying to express as your work develops. If you feel really stuck, with lots of contradictory thoughts on your work, and are not sure if something's there yet, I'd suggest sending it to a professional script editor. Make sure you have done everything you possibly can to get the script to this stage, so you don't waste your money getting notes you could have given yourself.

Finally, don't send your work out into the world too soon. If you are looking for an agent, or you have met a producer, and you have that precious email address and their invitation to send in a script, pause a moment. Think carefully. This person would not have suggested you send something in unless they intend to read it. Contrary to popular opinion, everyone is looking for new talent, new voices. There is no reason that new voice won't be yours, but the field is very competitive. You are new and therefore a risk. There are lots of talented writers out there already, with long track records. Your work has to have the potential to be as good as theirs … or better. So you need to seriously impress at this point. You almost certainly won't get another chance with this particular person. So, force yourself to look at your script again; if there is a character that you think is still rather two-dimensional or a plot point that feels coincidental, your reader will pick that up too. If, on the other hand, you read through your script one final time and you genuinely feel there is nothing more you can do to improve it, then you are ready to hit 'send'. Good luck!

Anna Symon's scriptwriting credits include the adaptation of Sarah Perry's *The Essex Serpent* for Apple TV (2022), the BBC series *Mrs Wilson* (2018), the ITV series *Deep Water* (2019) and Channel 4's *Indian Summers* (2015–16). She is a graduate of the Channel 4 Screenwriting Programme and previously worked as a producer/director in current affairs and documentaries. Follow her on Twitter @AnnaSymon.

Adapting books for stage and screen

Ana Garanito outlines the essential elements of the adaptation process, an exciting journey of deconstruction and reconstruction, and stresses the importance of seeking out, understanding and protecting the authored voice and the crucial 'pillars' of a book.

Books provide proof of concept for any commissioner. The American TV market is producing more adaptations than ever before and some of the UK film market's biggest successes of recent years have been adaptations. Adapting a book for stage or screen allows us to use the leverage of the original and create even more around it – think *Game of Thrones*, *American Gods* or *The Handmaid's Tale*.

How you adapt a novel will prompt various outcomes. Hopefully it will get commissioned after initial development. When it's made (and if it's based on a much-loved book) it could meet with a ready-made audience's approval … or not. And if you have built a relationship with the author or the estate, your approach may receive the ultimate blessing. No pressure!

This article is not an exhaustive list of what to do, but it focuses on a few key essentials for tackling an adaptation. As Head of Scripted at Green Door Pictures, I'm currently developing a number of adaptations across TV and film, but the advice below can absolutely apply to any form of adaptation, such as optioning life rights, a stage show, a documentary, radio, literature, even music.

The 'why?'

Before beginning any adaptation, we always ask: Why this novel? Why now? Why is it relevant? Why should we (the producer) make it and why should you (the writer) adapt it? We also have to make sure it is not competing with anything else already in development or production that will hamper its chances of a commission; a similar project is an excuse to reject your one.

It's also worth considering which is the best format – stage, film, TV, digital short, audio series, etc. Then it's necessary to break it down even further; for example – if you choose TV, which broadcaster? Which slot? As you do this, you will inevitably start to consider who your audience is. If you are planning to start an adaptation without a producer alongside you just yet, ask yourself all the same questions, because the answers should certainly be part of your sales pitch as you look to option it from the author, find a production company, or pitch to a commissioner.

If adapting someone else's work, before optioning the book you should meet or speak with the author if you can. Having the two of you discuss the book and any potential approach to the adaptation is invaluable, and it's even better if you have your producer by your side.

And again, when you're ready to dive in, the most important question to ask the author is 'Why?' Why did they write this book? What do they want an audience to take away from reading the book? Knowing the author's reasoning means you can understand the beating heart of the book and in turn become a genuine custodian of it. An adaptation will inevitably carry changes from the original book, but truly embracing the 'why' can help inform the decisions you make. If you need to lose anything from the original because the film or

TV series can't accommodate it, as long as the 'why' still remains within its reimagining, you're protecting the very essence of the whole book.

I have worked on adaptations where the author has been dead for a number of years and the book is out of copyright, which means that understanding the 'why' happens through research on the internet, digging deep within books around the author or novel and doing the necessary analysis and evaluation. It's important – especially if it's a classic – to understand the motivation for the book, because any reimagining will be analysed (and potentially criticised) by a long-established fanbase.

The 'how?'

How you handle the adaptation will be a key consideration for anyone commissioning you to write. Not only must you be clear about how you would tackle the adaptation so it can be translated successfully to stage or screen, but you need to articulate this with confidence to the author, producer and/or commissioner. The one thing that everyone (myself included) is looking for is an authored voice – a truly unique and singular take on a story, theme or issue. What is it about your handling of the book that makes this a must-have and yet still retains the tone of the original?

After establishing the 'Why?', we must turn to the nuts and bolts of adapting a piece of work. This largely means breaking down the whole book and rebuilding it, from the ground up, into your desired format. Narrative arc, characters, tone, timeline – the whole lot. Get under its skin. Know it inside and out, but always keep the 'Why?' close by. If and when you decide that some elements can't make their way into the adaptation or need to be reconfigured, as long as it's in service of the 'Why?', you can justify it to all those around you.

When you have all the components laid out in front of you, you can then determine 'the pillars of the novel', as I like to call them. These are the essential elements that are important to retain even when you make significant changes from the original. These could be tone, key characters, setting, story points, themes or issues that are unique to the book. I've worked on adaptations that have been difficult either because they were structurally complex or sometimes because of their rather dated handling of diversity or other themes. However, in both cases, the pillars of the original lay beneath. By simplifying the through-line of the emotional journey, it was then possible to create an alternative structure or commentary for the adaptation.

Film, TV, theatre and audio series are all completely different disciplines and you could take a single text and adapt it in different ways for each of those formats. Your take on that adaptation will be important and will inevitably change the original. That's fine and as it should be, but it can be a shock to an author – so be sure to warn people! You should always be as transparent as possible. I say all this knowing the author may not necessarily have right of approval, or any final decision may sit with someone else such as a producer, but a good relationship managed by you or your producer means you will build trust and also ensure that everyone involved understands the transformation that is about to take place.

Diversity and representation

Whatever story you're adapting, I assume you want it to be seen by the biggest and widest audience possible. Diversity may be considered a buzz word, but it's actually just good practice. Consider the diversity within your world and amongst your characters. Is it relevant to the audience you want to sell your story to? Do you understand the backgrounds you're writing about? Research them if you don't. The word that should be considered more often is 'representation'. This is about authenticity. Are you reinforcing stereotypes, or can you accurately depict a character through understanding their upbringing, religion, disabilities, cultural heritage, sexuality or gender?

Consider the language you use to describe those characters and the world. This means the terminology you use in your script to describe a disability or culture, for example. It will say a lot about how you see the world. Whether describing a character's cultural heritage, faith or disability, your words are the blueprint for how an entire crew will discuss those characters, how an actor approaches and reflects on a character (even how comfortable they will feel discussing it openly) and how an audience will finally consider the representation of that character. Are you promoting or dismantling stereotypes?

Your people

Whether you are adapting your own book, have been commissioned to adapt a book or are bringing it to a production company, it is important that the producer you're working with gets the novel and gets you, and that you are all aligned on how to tackle the adaptation. Life is short and development is long, so you don't want to spend that time feeling a disconnect with the people who are supposed to be steering you and selling your adaptation. How do they intellectually and emotionally respond to the book and your plans for it? Do you like them? Will they have your back? They need to help protect you from multiple voices, navigate the whole process efficiently and manage the expectations of the author if needed.

If you have optioned the book yourself and are looking for a producer, always consider their company ethos and back catalogue. I'm always surprised when projects have been pitched to me that are very similar to shows we have already produced and aired. Do your homework. Watch their shows.

Take a moment

Everyone is on the lookout for a good story, an authored voice and a new creative challenge. It is an exciting time to be a creator of content because there are so many more outlets to pitch to. As much as your adaptation may change the original, if you can retain the 'Why?' and honour the pillars of the book, you can create an adaptation from an honest place that is endorsed by all the stakeholders. Some of the criticism around the handling of the new *Star Wars* films or the final seasons of *Game of Thrones* is about how they failed to honour the essential pillars of the original and all the rules that were established previously.

There is always a time, just before I start any development, when I take a deep breath and appreciate that – regardless of whether we have a manuscript in front of us at that moment – we still have a blank page before us. It may seem overwhelming to consider how to deconstruct and reconstruct, but that's the good stuff! Rediscovering that work as a film, TV series, audio series or theatre piece is a glorious journey. Enjoy every minute of it because, if you do, your audience will also.

Ana Garanito has over 20 years' broadcast industry experience. Her work for Green Door Pictures includes *In the Long Run* (Sky One), *Turn Up Charlie* (Netflix), *Tree* (a theatre co-production with the Young Vic and Manchester International Festival) and *Concrete Cowboy*, a feature film based on the novel by Greg Neri.

A way with words: writing comedy

Ian Martin tells how, over time, thanks to such essentials as tenacity and serendipity, his job description widened from humble hack to writer and screenwriter. He has firm advice and encouragement for fellow writers as he shares what he has learned along the way.

Congratulations, you're a WRITER! Even when you're starting out and are nowhere close to making a living from it, identifying as 'a writer' is empowering. It's more than a job description. It's motivational. A declaration of intent, a glorious definition of *you*. And *me*. Yeah, get *us* ... we're part of a global community that includes Nobel laureates, Pulitzer Prize winners and Oscar-bagging screenwriters. Dazzling company.

Yeah, it feels great to big ourselves up. However ... let's embrace reality, put things into perspective and – counterpoint – 'ensmallen' ourselves. In the spirit of those gladiator-slaves whispering '*memento mori*' in the ears of Roman generals, let me remind you of what we actually do, physically. We type for a living, all of us. And this is no less inclusive – nearly every writer these days taps at a keyboard. Outcomes vary. At this very moment a poet is coaxing words from some plasmic thoughtfield, through her brain, along her fingers and onto the page. Simultaneously, a copywriter somewhere is knocking out 400 words about a foot spa. They're both writers, although obviously the copywriter's earning more.

I've typed for a living since 1973 when, as a gormless 20 year-old, I started work as a junior reporter for a local paper in County Durham. That newspaper, like thousands of others, is long gone – bought up as part of a job lot by freesheet publishers, then amalgamated with other papers, 'value-engineered' down to a skeleton staff, then entirely de-boned and discarded. Local journalism, once an unshakeable keystone of community life, providing essential scrutiny of local government affairs, has never recovered from the blunt trauma of the internet and its ruthless harvesting of small ads. Half a century on, though, I can still feel the thrill of my first byline in print. Oh my days ... the smell of the newsprint. The thud as a massive sheaf of fat broadsheets landed on the reception desk. And there it was – my name just above the fold, a ragged little yard-high tower of '*by Ian Martin*'. It's never left me, that narcissistic urge to shine, to see my name or hear it. 'I'm a writer', we say, which is really just shorthand for 'I'm an insufferable show-off'.

Life was so insanely different then – I sometimes marvel at my luck. In those days you could be taken on by one of the old newspaper groups, trained in journalism law, sub-editing, shorthand, all the craft skills. The three years of my indentureship taught me how to write a narrative; they don't call them news stories for nothing. Incidentally, the three big storytelling principles of soap operas are exactly those used in journalism, and indeed, in all writing: 1) HEAT – who's angry with whom, why, and what will they do now? 2) TOPSPIN – a touch of velocity just before ad breaks and credits, to keep the viewer wanting more. News stories also need snappy intros to pull the reader in; those clickbait one-liners, like 'You Won't Believe What This Once-Handsome Child Star Looks Like Now, He's Horrific!!!' are the apotheosis of topspin. Of course, you won't click on the link, you're not a monster. Nevertheless, a tiny part of you wants to see what a haunted, middle-aged 40-stone human tragedy looks like. And 3) PIPEWORK – fill the casual viewer/reader in as subtly as possible with background info. Exposition, we call it now. For we are *writers*.

What my journalism training *didn't* teach me was the First Law of Journalism. As a trainee reporter I'd assumed it was something like 'Always speak truth to power' or 'Give voice to the powerless'. Then I encountered the fearsome might of sub-editors and learned that the First Law of Journalism was FILL THE SPACE. Seems quaint now, the idea of casting off a word count to fit an outline on paper. Imagine … finite space. Little did we know that the global connectivity of science fiction – the telly somehow hooked up to a telephone so flat and small you could slip it into a pocket – would actually happen. Now, life before the internet is unthinkable. And it has proved vitally important for writing opportunities; anyone can set up a blog, or a newsletter, or a website, or a podcast. (It's proved invaluable for time-wasting too – that integral part of a writer's life. In the old days, we had to stare out of a window.)

I've been a hack all my life. I was in (massively unprofitable) bands for years, and I juggled that with magazine stints. Really not making enough to make ends meet, especially with a young family. We were permanently skint. I'd fallen into architectural journalism by accident – we had to sell the car, and I needed a job I could get the bus to. And even when I went fully freelance in the early '80s we stayed badly overdrawn, but were kept afloat, just, by a silly satirical column I wrote in an architecture magazine for 27 years. And here's the rub. I know there may be people reading this, writers who are losing faith in themselves, without the confidence to approach commissioning editors or producers or agents, and I am here to tell you that the greatest gift an aspiring writer can have is tenacity. Never, ever, ever give up. If you think you're good enough to make a living as a writer, back yourself and keep going. Keep at it, I implore you. Make yourself unignorable.

I always wanted to be a writer and I always wanted to be funny. In every steady hack job I had, I ended up writing a silly column. I'd been writing that piss-taking one about architecture for a decade before it was noticed by a features editor at a national newspaper, who invited me to write something with a similar tone about arts and culture. Oh, I was well chuffed. Every Friday it appeared. For about ten weeks, until it didn't. They decided it was a poor fit and I was dropped there and then, like lead from a shot tower. Reader, my feelings were hurt. But vengeance burned in my heart. It throbbed in my veins. They were right, by the way. The column was, in retrospect, rubbish. Overthought and over-wrought. Nevertheless, how DARE they deny me a ventilation shaft for my brilliance? How DARE they snatch away my byline? Once a hack, always a hack.

This was in 1999, when both our children had left home for university. It felt rather like early retirement. Also – stroke of luck – my brother had just been made redundant. Together we started a weekly online satirical website ('martian.fm – from the north of the heart'). I wrote the words; Paul did the artwork and everything else, including actually making it happen. Nobody was paying us, and I spent two or three days a week writing stuff for it. Still, it was the most hilarious of times – me and my bro down in the cellar with a bottle of scotch and each other as the only audience. Week in, week out for three years, congratulating ourselves on our excoriating website so niche it was cult, and so cult it was months before the readership was into three figures. There were times when it seemed utterly absurd, shrieking into the void. The feature that took the most time every week was 'Hansard Late', a fictitious record of rowdy drunken evening proceedings in the Commons, MC'd by a very sweary, very angry Scottish Speaker.

Then the email arrived. I thought it was a prank at first. It apparently came from comedy genius Armando Iannucci, who needlessly explained that he'd produced *The Day Today* and *Knowing Me, Knowing You* and who said 'I like your stuff. It makes me laugh'. Would I be interested in chucking some jokes at a Channel 4 thing he was putting together? It did seem quite an *elaborate* prank …

And so my screenwriting career began, a few days after my 50th birthday. After the Channel 4 thing (a young Olivia Colman read out my 'Controversial Swearing Rap Millionaires – Court Appearances', my first TV credit), I went on to do a bit of radio stuff before Iannucci invited me to a swearing pass on the first three *The Thick of It* scripts. I got mythologised as the show's 'swearing consultant', but – for the record – all the writers wrote swears; I didn't just do swears, I became a full member of the writing team. The first 'alt' (alteration) of mine that got through actually removed a swear: 'He's f**king useless' became 'He's as useless as a marzipan dildo'. I've been working with Iannucci pretty much every year since. But if I hadn't been writing martian.fm he'd almost certainly never have noticed me, and I wonder how my 21st century would have turned out.

Anyway, look – in screenwriting terms I'm nowhere *near* the top of my profession. League Division 3 or 4, say. I am now a 'writer', but I'll always be a hack. And, like all old hacks, I have quite a good sense of how much space I have left in this piece and had better start stuffing it with advice:

• **Keep going**. My screenwriting career started late, and only then because I couldn't bear not to keep showing off. I wasn't washed up at 50, so there's no need for anyone to be. Also, duh, you can't be a writer if you don't write. Even if it's just for your own amusement, even if you're just giggling with mates on Twitter, even if it's a terrible diary that'll never be read by anyone … **write**. Every day. You're not going to get worse, are you?

• **Welcome the criticism, love the notes**. The hardest thing about exposing your work to others for the first time is people not unconditionally loving it. Get over it. Get over yourself. In time you will *love* criticism – the more destructive the better; all writing needs to be stress-tested. Notes are your friends. People will give notes and it will make your thing better, which is what you want (unless you're deranged). You might not understand at first why other people say this or that isn't working, but – come on – if it isn't working for them, it isn't working. Fix it.

• **Get an agent**. I know, it's a conundrum. If you haven't had anything published or broadcast, you're less of a catch; you stand more chance of getting noticed if you have an agent. Find the ones who specialise in what you write; pitch yourself. How to find an agent? I dunno … maybe get some sort of writers' and artists' yearbook or whatever.

• **Join a union.** This isn't just about you, it's about us. The stronger the union, the stronger the union member.

Good luck. We all need it. However hard you work at it, you still need to catch a break. Serendipity is what we call it, for we are *writers*.

Ian Martin is an Emmy award-winning comedy writer and producer. His screen credits include *The Thick of It*, *The Death of Stalin*, *Veep* and *Avenue 5*. He has written for the *Architects' Journal*, *New Statesman*, the *Observer* and the *Guardian*. His books include *Epic Space* (Unbound 2017) and *The Coalition Chronicles* (Faber & Faber 2011). Follow him on Twitter @IanMartin.

Writing series for television

Scriptwriter Russell Lewis has tough-talking advice about making your way into the competitive and collaborative business of writing for television, and describes how, when that break comes, you can succeed if you give it your all and never stop learning.

The first rule of Write Club is: you do not talk about Write Club.

The stock reply to the question, 'What advice would you give to someone who wanted to be a television writer?' is, of course, 'Don't' Seriously. Develop another ambition. Become the fluffer for a tiger-mating program, or a teething ring for rattlesnakes. But you've invested in a copy of *Writers' & Artists' Yearbook*, so you must believe that it's something you want to do – you crazy, idealistic little fool! Let's see if I can put you off.

It's difficult to catch a break and find a way into the industry – but then, you know that, or you wouldn't be reading this. No short cuts or magic formulae lie within the body of this article, only some vestigial amount of fellow feeling. We have all been there. Every writer you like has been there, and every writer you detest. They have all been on the same journey. There is only graft, and patience, and frustration, and more patience, and anger, and even more patience, and very, very occasionally, a bit of luck. And that's just to get a foot in the door. So, why do it at all? Well – let's be honest, it beats working for a living ... Who was it said: 'Find the thing you love, and let it kill you'? Those who answered Madeleine Elster, go to the back of the class.

However, I promise you, if you have talent then somewhere, amongst all the pain and patience and frustration and anger and more patience, something will happen. You will get better at what you're doing. And 'getting better at what you're doing' is a process without end. Every day is a school day. You know that scene or line of dialogue that yesterday was a line in the sand that you scratched out with your own blood and sweat, and which you swore to defend against all comers to your last breath? Today, you will decide that you don't need it. You will find a more elegant and infinitely more economical way to make the same point, or a better one, or decide that you don't need it at all, and the piece will be improved a thousandfold by its excision. Very likely, your good colleagues will have been telling you this – or something like it – for some time. They couldn't tell you exactly what needed to be done, but they just knew they were bumping on something around that section. But – *here's the important bit* – you absolutely had to walk that lonely moonlit mile yourself to get to the moment of epiphany. That's the drug. That's what keeps us coming back for more. It's the Devil's candy – we know we shouldn't but, like the beat-up old ex-con in every heist movie, we keep coming back for one ... last ... job.

You will hear your peers (and others) talk self-mockingly about 'Writer Monkeys'. It's okay when we do it, but the 'others' aren't allowed to disparage. I'm proud to be a Writer Monkey, and you should be, too. Because it's a slight misnomer. What we actually are is the 'Problem-Solving Ape'. A script – any script – is, at its most basic level, a sequence of problems and solutions. In the first instance – be they physical, emotional or moral – those problems are intentional points of plot and narrative, the building blocks of story. Bring me the broomstick of the Wicked Witch of the West. What's a saloon bar owner to do with two letters of transit? What did he mean, 'Rosebud'? What should Sophie choose, and how can she live with that choice? How could anyone? Resolving those problems, answering those questions – while maintaining the established integrity of the imagined world in which they exist, and retaining the audience's interest in the solution – is more than half the job. I suppose it's what the late, great William Goldman called 'the spine'. Find the spine of your story, and all else follows. (Seriously, if you want to do this, read Goldman; let *Adventures in the Screen Trade* (Warner Books 1983) become your Bible.) Another way of putting it is, 'What's it about?'. When you begin, you may not have that answer down pat. You may not know. You may have a vague idea, a mood you want to catch, a feeling. Some things we wish to express are so gossamer and fragile that they're nigh on impossible to nail down straight out of the traps. In part, the process of writing is an uncovering – a chipping away at the block of marble to discover the form that lies within.

But back to the advice … Outside of the 'soaps', long-form drama series with high volume and turnover where a writer can develop their chops are few. The BBC has its writing scheme – and that's a way in for some. That route leads, typically – in the first instance – to continuing drama, a.k.a. the aforementioned 'soap'. And that's terrific. There are many fantastic talents who have come through that forcing ground – some of my favourite writers. I started with drama on a variation of the same, a show called *The Bill*, which was then a bi-weekly policier. The difference between that show and the current continuous dramas is that *The Bill* wasn't storylined; the 'episodes' were essentially 22-minute playlets. You could take it pretty much anywhere you wanted to go, provided you stuck to the one Golden Rule (and we only had one rule) – everything had to be seen from a police point of view. Otherwise, you could do what you liked.

It took me about a year to get through the door on that show. I'd been turned down, repeatedly. I'd come from a performing background – and that kind of weighed against being taken seriously – but the greatest bit of good luck that ever came my way arrived in the shape of a young woman by the name of Gina Cronk (insert Hollywood Recognition Applause here). Gina had been working in Reception, but – like your faithful correspondent – had ambition and ideas above her station. She'd just been made up from assistant script editor to script editor and consequently was looking to fill her flight roster with her own writers. If that hadn't happened, I would never have been seen and may have never got started. I don't doubt that the spec half-script I put in was pretty awful, but she saw something in there and gave me a break. I owe her pretty much everything.

The other thing the BBC's Writersroom has (at least at the time of writing) is a brilliant resource of scripts that you can download and read at your leisure, by people who really know what they're doing. Read every play, script and screenplay you can get your hands on. *That's* how you learn to know your way around a script. You watch the shows, and you read the scripts. See what was dropped; see what was added. Take note of who the script editor was. If it's a recent show, odds are that the script editor is still a script editor and hasn't ascended to the purple of Producerdom. Get in touch with them. If you're local, offer to buy them a cup of tea in a brightly lit public place and throw yourself upon their mercy. Beg, weep, grovel, offer whatever inducements you both consider legal, acceptable and, moreover, physically possible to get them to clue you in to what's going on in their department and the wider industry. They will know far better than anyone which shows are crewing up, which are looking for writers, what's in development, which of the afternoon dramas have a slot. If you are not local, try to do the same thing, initially, via email. Become pen pals, but (useful tip) – *don't be weird*. And remember – TV doesn't have to be your first port of call. A well-received fringe play or radio play can open just as many doors as the spec script. Get a rehearsed reading together. Invite agents and script editors and producers – especially agents – because representation is important. It will help get you in the room; after that you're on your own.

When that break comes, be ready to throw everything you've got at it. If you're pitching for a slot on an existing show, find the gap in the internal market. Know that show inside out. If everyone else is turning left, you turn right. Nothing to frighten the horses – you're not there to reinvent the wheel – but there will be characters who have been a bit under-served, or a coming curve that you can get ahead of. Furthermore, leave your pride and ego at the door; they're surplus to requirements. No matter how much you privately disagree, you will attend to the notes you are given diligently and with utmost dispatch, as if they were the Word of God. If that means you have to go a couple of nights without sleep to make the production deadline, then that is what you will do. This is not your great oeuvre or *meisterwerk*; this is episode 5, series 3, of whatever it might be. SERVE THE SHOW. Cut the throat of your favourite lines and characters and scenes if ordered to do so, without flinching or a moment's remorse. Stay light on your feet as production issues arise which will inevitably impact your script. Don't be precious about any of it. You've just lost the most important location? Write around it. *One of the regulars has had an accident and won't be available to shoot scenes 3, 24, 55A, 57 and 103B tomorrow … however, another character is available. Oh, and the first assistant director says the schedule is still 'over' and they won't be able to make the day; the request is to amalgamate scenes 55A and 57 while losing a page from their current page-count of three. We'll also have to cut 103B – and fold in the important information into scene 24. And, by the way, we're going to need it by close of play … today.*

Here's my modern heresy: I don't believe you can teach someone how to write. I think the snake-oil salesmen who tell you they can are exactly that. You can learn how to write – and you never stop learning – but that's a different thing. We learn by *doing*. You can no more teach someone to write than you can teach them to think or feel. You can provide them with a supportive environment, a creative soft space where they can stumble and fall frequently and safely. You can be a sounding board who offers thoughts about their work – a new angle, a different approach to a narrative problem or a way to rework the plot. But these are creative and editorial conversations you can expect to have all the time with your colleagues – commissioners, executives, producers, directors, actors – and especially, above all else, your editor. The good ones are worth their weight in diamonds and will save your arse more times than you can thank them, without it becoming an embarrass-ment – and really, you *do* need to thank them. So will many of the others on that list; because … (all together now) television – or film, radio or theatre – is a collaborative medium. This places the writer (who, you will remember, 'does not play well with others') in something of a cleft stick.

To illustrate this dichotomy, I keep two messages on my wall. The first reads, 'Television is a collaborative medium'. The second reads, 'COLLABORATORS WILL BE SHOT!' As Morgan Freeman's Detective Somerset observes at the end of the film *Se7en*: 'I agree with the second part'.

In the beginning was the word. Stay limber.

Oh, and the second rule of Write Club is …?

Russell Lewis began his career as a child actor. His earlier TV credits included episodes of *Perfect Scoundrels*, *Taggart*, *The Bill*, *Wycliffe*, *Inspector Morse*, *Kavanagh QC*, *Spooks* and *Lewis*. He wrote for *Between the Lines* (1992), winner of the Writers' Guild of Great Britain TV Original Drama Series Award, and *Murphy's Law* (2003). He also co-wrote three of the Sharpe films. Russell devised and has written every script for all nine series of *Endeavour*, the last of which transmitted in spring 2023, and he adapted five of the Peter James' books featuring DS Roy Grace for *Grace* on ITV starring John Simm. The first was transmitted in 2021 and the following four in 2022.

See also...
- *Successful screenwriting*, page 331

Getting your audiobook published

Laura Smith shares her knowledge of the audio publishing world, with options and advice on how to create a high-quality product, safeguard your rights as an author and tap into the potential of this increasingly popular format.

Over the past 15 years the audiobook market has been transformed. Audio is the fastest-growing part of the publishing industry, with new listeners, publishers and authors coming to the format each year. With things moving quickly, it can be hard to navigate what is best for you and your book. But if you get your audiobook publication right, you unlock a new pool of potential fans and another stream of revenue to reward you for the hard slog of writing your book. So here's what you need to know.

Understanding the audiobook market

The audiobook market comprises three main elements:

1. Digital audiobooks for consumers, accessed through Amazon, Audible, Apple, Kobo, Google, Spotify and a host of other large platforms. Smaller independent retailers are also innovating and establishing themselves in the market. The digital retail space is by far the biggest part of the market by revenue.

2. E-lending in public libraries. There are various platforms used in libraries across different territories, notably OverDrive (the Libby app; www.overdrive.com) and BorrowBox (www.borrowbox.com).

3. Physical CDs: bought by public libraries for loaning. This is still essential for libraries, and a good source of revenue for authors. There is also still a small market for CDs in consumer stores, but it is now small and selective, and mostly sold through online retailers such as Amazon.

Each part of the market has a broadly different demographic and, with new listeners coming to the format each year, the 'average listener' is constantly changing. But all you need to know is that the audiobook market holds a section of people who don't read books. Yes! As crazy as it sounds to us book-folk, some people just don't. But before you write them off, consider the millions of people who listen to podcasts, radio or music for hours each day. Some are migrating to long-form and discovering that they *do* have time for audiobooks. An audiobook could be their gateway drug into your back catalogue.

There is also a portion of the population who love great storytelling but are unable to read physical books, for a variety of reasons. Making your books accessible to *all* people can only be a good thing for your readership and your sales.

So how are people listening? The majority of audiobook fans listen through a smartphone or smart speaker, and they buy or borrow books through apps such as Audible (www.audible.co.uk), Audiobooks.com (www.audiobooks.co.uk), Apple Books (www.apple.com/uk/apple-books) or library lending apps. Visibility within each app is crucial to the success of your book, and we'll cover more on that later.

Know your rights

Before your work can become an audiobook you need to figure out who will publish it; so it is important that you pay attention to your audio rights. Whether you are self-published, represented by a literary agent, or work directly with a publisher – be clear on who owns your rights, for how long and in which territories. Crucially, establish *when* your audiobook will be published. For most books, the best time to publish an audiobook is at the same time as the ebook and print edition. An audiobook takes several months to plan and produce, so if your publisher doesn't have a plan for your audiobook six months ahead of the ebook release, you need to start asking questions.

If you are represented by a literary agent, they should explore the options for audio publishing when your book goes out on submission. Is it more lucrative for you to retain the rights and sell to an independent audio publisher? What plans does the publisher have creatively for your audiobook, and how will they bring it to market? If you raise and discuss these things at an early stage, you are more likely to get a clear plan for your audiobook.

If you are an indie author, you could consider recording and publishing the audiobook yourself, but this option is high risk. There is a significant financial investment needed up front; the recording needs to be high-quality or you risk poor reviews that damage sales. Without the clout of a large publisher, you may not get best terms or marketing placements needed to attract listeners to your book in a competitive marketplace. Audible's ACX scheme (www.acx.com) offers a way in for authors but, before committing to one retailer in a rapidly evolving market, look carefully at the terms, returns policy and exclusivity agreements they offer.

Many self-published authors choose to publish their ebooks and paperbacks independently but work with an audio publisher (such as W.F. Howes Ltd, who have an imprint called QUEST that caters for indie and Kindle authors) to publish their audiobook and distribute more widely across all retailer platforms and global markets.

Finding your voice

Once you have decided on your route to market, you will be faced with the most important decision for your book: who should read it – or more accurately, who is the best person to perform your work for the listener? Well, the overwhelming majority of audiobook listeners prefer to listen to a professional audiobook narrator or actor, rather than the author. So, unless you are reading your memoir and have broadcasting or acting experience, you probably aren't the right voice for the job.

For most listeners, the narrator's voice is the deciding factor in how they rate a book. The skill and nuance of the best audiobook narrators can elevate your work to a new level and create something truly special for you and your fans. Audiobook narration is extremely difficult – it takes training and preparation, and there are many successful actors who would admit they cannot do it. The most skilled narrators are able to create atmosphere, tension and comedic timing, *and* embody a full cast of characters for 12 hours with minimal mistakes.

When it comes to casting, it is important to cast authentically. For example, if your book is a first-person narrative from the perspective of a young Scottish woman, that's the voice you need to cast. If you have a dual narrative, time slip or some other narrative set-up, consider more than one voice to bring your story to life. If you have thoughts about characterisation, accents or unusual pronunciations, share these with your publisher or recording partner as soon as possible. Preparation for the audiobook recording takes time, and everyone across the recording team needs to know if you imagine your protagonist having a Yorkshire accent that you didn't mention anywhere in the text!

You may wonder whether you need a celebrity voice to get audiobook sales. In most cases the answer is no. Some narrators have a fan base among audiobook listeners, so it is worth browsing the reviews to see who is best rated in your category. But it is more important to get the right voice for your character, with a high-quality recording, a thorough edit and a proof-listen.

Visual impact

Next you will need to consider artwork. The dimensions for an audiobook cover are different to those for print, with the jacket presented as a square rather than a rectangle, owing historically to the shape of a CD cover. To potential listeners, who will see your book cover in an app on their smartphone as a digital 'stamp', only a square thumbnail will be visible. When consulting on cover artwork with your designer or publisher, ask how it will be adapted for audio and whether it is bold and simple enough to make an impact as a thumbnail.

Marketing

As your publication date approaches, you will need to bring listeners to your book. If you are working with a publisher, ask them about their marketing plan and how you can help. Do they have marketing and PR strategy specifically for audio, and how does it differ from their ebook and print campaign?

If you have an established readership, think about how you usually reach them. Perhaps you have a large mailing list or an active Facebook community. And if you have a significant social media following, what content can your publisher provide to share with them? Be open with ideas and suggestions that suit your readership. If you have a budget for advertising, make sure your ads are carefully targeted to reach potential listeners.

Once your book is published, encourage reviews. Reviews and ratings can make or break the success of your audiobook, change how visible it is within retailer algorithms and offer useful feedback. The more positive reviews you get, the more likely your audiobook will be to get selected for retailer spotlights and promotions.

Writing for audio

If you know your work has a future as an audiobook, please bear this in mind as you write. You may love using infographics or detailed lists in your books, but these won't work when read aloud. If necessary, consider adaptations or rewrites for visual sections of your book. Try reading troublesome pages out loud to yourself or have someone read them to you. It is surprising how well you can evaluate your writing by doing this, and it is a great way to hear how your book will work in audio.

Do you have an established audience and love the audio format? Then why not explore an audio-first project? A story told entirely through sound is ripe with creative possibilities. As the market changes, the lines between audiobook, audio documentary, podcast and audio drama are merging – with exciting results. If you have a compelling story to tell, it might find a home as an audio exclusive. At W.F. Howes we recently launched WFH ORIGINAL, an imprint for audio-first projects which are commissioned, developed and tailored to the audio format. As the audio market evolves, there are more opportunities for writers in this area, whether through publishers, studios or production companies.

What next?

Armed with more information about the audio publishing world, you can consider what is right for your work. Reflect on what matters to you the most, be it keeping financial risk to a minimum, having full creative control, or having a high-cost, full-cast studio production. Ask questions, get feedback and enjoy listening to the finished product.

Laura Smith is Acquisitions Manager at W.F. Howes, the UK's leading independent audiobook publisher. Over the past 12 years she has worked across commissioning, contracts, casting, marketing and sales of audiobooks. Laura has acquired and published audiobooks across fiction, non-fiction and children's categories, including books by Marian Keyes, Val McDermid, Sally Rooney, Chris Brookmyre, Gregg Hurwitz, Hilary Mantel and LJ Ross. She oversees a team acquiring audiobook rights from agents and publishers, as well as running the WFH ORIGINAL imprint, comprising works commissioned and produced exclusively for audiobook format. For more information see www.wfhowes.co.uk.

See also...
- *Audio providers and distributors*, page 221
- *Audio dramatist or novelist?*, page 352

Screen and audio

Guerilla podcasting

Writer and podcaster Sam Delaney describes his route into, and enthusiasm for, podcasting and the benefits this liberating and engaging medium offers to writers. He has advice for fledgling podcasters on keeping it simple and consistent to build an enduring bond with their audience.

Like so many people, I started a podcast during lockdown in 2020. Unlike 90% of those people, I kept mine going beyond the pandemic when life got back to normal and time was at more of a premium. I'm glad I did, because 'The Reset' (my podcast about mental health) served as the springboard for my book, *Sort Your Head Out: mental health without all the bollocks*, which was published by Constable in early 2023. The book has already outsold any of my previous three and provided me with a huge sense of satisfaction and fulfilment. But it would never have happened without the podcast laying a path for it.

My previous book, *Mad Men and Bad Men*, had been published by Faber in 2015 and the sales were pretty average. I was aware that might have been my last chance of attracting the backing of a decent publisher. It was certainly ambitious to contemplate pitching a new book, on a new topic I'd never written about before, aimed squarely at a market that was notoriously difficult to reach (i.e. men). But I knew that there were men out there who were engaged by my take on mental health – because they had been listening to my podcast consistently for two years. The audience was growing all the time. I had tangible data to prove it. I also had the interactions on social media to prove that there was a vibrant and ongoing conversation taking place around the podcast. Loaded with all this evidence, my book proposal carried serious weight and this – as far as Constable were concerned at least – managed to offset other, perfectly legitimate concerns … such as 'blokes simply don't want a book about mental health by Sam Delaney or anyone else for that matter.'

I have no doubt that it was the success of the podcast that convinced them to give me a book deal. The advance was the smallest I had ever received, but that was fine. I realised they were taking a gamble on me. This book meant a great deal more to me than any of the others. It was the book I would have needed to read ten years previously when, in my mid-thirties, I had become overwhelmed and burned out by the combined pressures of work, family and unresolved childhood issues and, in a bid to self-medicate, I'd fallen into a pretty serious drink and drug addiction. I had felt alone in my feelings of anxiety and depression and too ashamed to speak about them. I thought people who spoke out about their mental health were hippies and/or whingers. That's why I never owned up and asked for help until it was almost too late. So, once I had been clean, sober and (relatively) sane for a few years, I started talking about this stuff in a language that people like me – the sort of recovering Jack the lads who had grown up taking nothing seriously, least of all themselves – could relate to.

Anyway, that was the idea at the top of my proposal. But, as I say, without the compelling stats around the podcast that appeared underneath my creative idea, it wouldn't have come close to convincing a publisher's hard-nosed sales and marketing team. They took a chance that my podcast audience might also be convinced to read my book. And it paid off for them. And not all of my podcast audience had to actually read it; *Sort Your Head Out* has so far sold almost as many audiobooks as hardback copies.

It's not just the vulgar business of audience size and data analytics that a podcast can provide to an author. There are very real creative benefits too. Nurturing ideas in real life – putting things out there and seeing how an audience responds – is so much more effective than sitting at a desk alone and trying to conjure fully-rounded ideas out of the ether. Podcasts are easy to produce, publish and market, as long as you keep things simple. And this means you can try out ideas on a whim and constantly adjust your creative output until it feels right. By the time I sat down to write *Sort Your Head Out* I was confident in my tone of voice, and I felt comfortable about expressing some of the deepest and darkest aspects of my own mental health. I had been practising for years on the podcast and getting useful feedback from listeners all along the way.

These are just some of the ways in which a podcast can help get a book idea off the ground. But for it to work in this way, a podcast has to be lightweight, lo-fi and enjoyable to make. Too many people approach podcasting as a vast, complex and over-thought production which does more to eat up time and energy than to serve as a catalyst for broader creative endeavour. If you overreach with your podcast, it will become just another obstacle preventing you from ever sitting down to write.

If you google 'how to make a podcast' you will be bombarded with thousands of articles and tutorial videos by self-proclaimed experts telling you how to produce a piece of pitch-perfect audio magic that will capture the attention of millions and make you rich. Few of them have had much actual success with their own podcast and all of them tell you the process is difficult and full of caste-iron rules. It doesn't make much sense for them to tell you that starting a podcast is as easy as plugging a cheap microphone into your laptop, speaking into it for half an hour, and then uploading it to the internet – or that this kind of no-frills podcast has just as much chance of success as one that's been more painstakingly produced.

But I *can* tell you that, because I have done it. And not just once. 'The Reset' was actually my second successful podcast to have built an audience and led to bigger things. In 2018 I had launched 'Top Flight Time Machine' with my friend Andy Dawson. What started out as a football nostalgia pod became a weird, free-form stumble through the lives of two middle-aged dads and – in its five-year lifespan – it has been downloaded over 15 million times, completed four nationwide sell-out live tours, and generated enough dough to pay for both our mortgages. There was no plan, no elaborate format, and few production values behind our success. It was a case of making it up as we went along and responding quickly to what the audience seemed to enjoy. And then doing it again and again: as with 'The Reset', consistency was key. In fact, a commitment to making and publishing the podcast on a regular and predictable basis was perhaps our only concession to profession-alism. Through that commitment, the podcasts have cultivated audience loyalty. Listeners will keep coming back for more if they know when and where you will be there for them.

For years I worked as a host on national radio (I presented 'Drive Time' on Talk Radio and was a regular on the BBC and talkSPORT). Sound journalistic values, broadcasting expertise and technical skill are pretty essential components of that world. I found the Wild-West nature of podcasting very liberating by comparison. I didn't need to go into every topic with one eye on the clock; I wasn't held back by Ofcom regulations or so-called Reithian values; there were no advertisers to satisfy. I could explore things, try stuff out, muck about, swear, make mistakes and stumble across successes. So many podcasters try to do the opposite of all that: they try to recreate a radio show format as a podcast; so many of them devise suffocating formats that only serve as an albatross round their necks.

One of the most common podcasting tropes is the quirky, guest-driven format whereby a different person is booked each week to answer the same recurring question: 'What's your favourite sandwich?' 'What are your top five road trips?' 'Name your fantasy cricket team…' Some of these podcasts are really fantastic, but most collapse quite quickly because booking a guest every week (especially one who is funny, interesting or has the sort of profile that might actually help you reach an audience) is a massive pain – especially for a lone podcaster operating without a budget or a production team. Most new podcasts don't publish beyond the fifth episode. Only the top 1% of the world's four million plus podcasts (i.e. those with audience figures of more than 20,000 per episode) make any reasonable money from advertising. It can take years to get anywhere near those figures if you're not already a celebrity in the real world. So where's the incentive to keep going if making it is a hassle, you're not getting paid, and nobody seems to be listening?

This is why I tell people to make sure their podcast is about is something they can actually see themselves talking about for half an hour, at least once a week, for the rest of their lives. That's why it's best not to make your subject matter too narrow. On 'The Reset' I talk about mental health in the loosest possible sense; after all, everything in life impacts on your mind and your feelings one way or another. So, one week it might be a very focused look at the benefits of therapy and the next it might be an open-ended chat with my guests about the very worst jobs they've ever worked in. A narrow format based on an oddball premise might seem fun to start with, but it soon runs out of steam. And those formats are only ever as good as the guest you manage to book, so I prefer formats that are not guest-dependent. Put yourself, as the host, at the centre of the whole thing. After all, you can always rely on yourself to turn up and record the podcast when others won't. More importantly, the podcast should be an exercise in nurturing an audience – building their support and stimulating their engagement. It's hard to do that when the audience don't know who they're getting as a guest from one week to the next. It's your personality they should be engaging with, not the format. A podcast – with all it's rough edges, messy bits, mistakes and authenticity – allows for an intimacy to grow between host and listener. It's a unique relationship that can't be generated in the same way by radio or TV, with all their rigorous conceits and slightly unnatural choreography.

So make a podcast that is messy, that is explorative, that is happy to fail. Get a cheap mic from Amazon and record it in the smallest room in your home. That will make it sound better. Try to keep it no more than 35 minutes long (all the data shows most listeners don't go past this length anyway). Invite interesting guests or mates on, by all means, but not at the expense of your own voice. Put yourself and your worldview at the heart of it. Talk about stuff you find interesting and enjoyable. Keep doing it. Make it easy for yourself. Upload it on Acast (www.acast.com) or Soundcloud (https://soundcloud.com) – it's free and will be distributed automatically across all of the podcasting outlets from Spotify to Apple and beyond. Then share it far and wide on your socials. When listeners respond, interact with them. Start a conversation. Build a relationship. Your audience might grow to just a few hundred people. But size is less important than quality: if you are consistent, authentic and enthusiastic you will be able to build a bond with your audience that is priceless. They will encourage you, advise you, and help you to believe in yourself during times of doubt and insecurity. These are all the things a writer needs. And they can all be found in podcasting.

Sam Delaney is a freelance writer, broadcaster and podcaster from London, author of *Get Smashed* (Sceptre 2007), *Night of the Living Dad* (John Murray 2009), *Mad Men and Bad Men* (Faber & Faber 2015) and *Sort Your Head Out* (Constable 2023). A graduate of the University of Sussex, Sam became a journalist in magazines, including as Editor-in-Chief of *Heat* magazine, 2009–11, and of Comedy Central UK, 2013–15. He has hosted numerous shows on BBC 5 Live, BBC London and talkSPORT, and presented documentaries for BBC Three and Channel 4. Currently Sam is co-host of the *Top Flight Time Machine* podcast and writes and podcasts regularly about mental health via *The Reset*. His website is www.samdelaney.co.uk. Listen to *The Reset* at samdelaney.substack.com.

Audio dramatist or novelist?

Writer Jonathan Myerson describes what has drawn him towards audio drama, how closely this form of storytelling relates to the art of a novelist, and where it differs. He explains the freedom offered by audio drama, as well as its dangers and demands, and outlines some crucial elements for success.

I cannot leave home without a book. The thought of being stuck with spare minutes and nothing to read … it's agony. So there is always a book – usually a novel – in my coat pocket. Even the dog complains.

As a chain-reader of fiction since my teenage years, I am not quite sure how I became a dramatist. But then again, I'm not surprised that audio drama has become my chosen form – I've dabbled in TV drama (too melodramatic), film (too much second-guessing) and even animation (still can't even draw stick men), but it is audio drama that I keep coming back to. I have also written novels, which is probably the one *un*surprising element in that spectrum: there's a clear affinity between a story told on the page and a story conveyed purely in sound.

To begin with, both the novel and the audio drama take shape only in the reader's or listener's mind. The well-worn maxim that 'the pictures are better on radio' rings equally true for the novel, whose scenes exist in that netherworld between the actual and the imagined, forcing the reader-audience to add the missing elements. And audio dramas, like novels, must tread the thin line between what the character might observe and what the story demands. A novelist – any good novelist, anyway – includes only the elements which are crucial for the given scene. Anything else – as we all discover when editing our own prose – is just typing.

This is also the stricture which a good audio dramatist must obey. Back when the BBC believed that younger audiences craved an alternative soap to *The Archers*, I wrote for a drama called *Citizens*. And it taught me one glorious lesson: very sporadically would you be reminded that one character (it was the landlord of the pub, I think) was in a wheelchair. For most scenes it was wholly irrelevant and therefore not mentioned (not even as a sound effect). A novelist would do the same. But in any other storytelling form, it would be inescapable in every frame, and would inevitably misdirect the audience's attention constantly.

Perhaps this is why so many of our great novelists have turned simultaneously to audio drama – William Trevor, Rose Tremain and Hilary Mantel, for instance – and so many audio dramatists have tried their hand at novels – recently and most notably Rachel Joyce. In fact, the latter's breakout bestseller, *The Unlikely Pilgrimage of Harold Fry*, started life as a (somewhat shorter) play for BBC Radio 4. Apart from the budget-busting range of eras and locations available to audio dramas and novels, both forms crucially enable the writer to tell you only what they want you to focus on – leaving you to pour your own imaginative fuel onto the rest.

I'll admit that, when I started writing my first novel after more than a decade as a dramatist, I went through a period of shock. I was accustomed to simply typing terse scene-settings (maybe 'deck of freighter during force 8 storm' or 'the characters stroll through an autumnal forest glade') and leaving it to the crew to execute my demands. Suddenly, with no production staff, I was going to have to bring all of this to life myself, to find the precise and most convincing sequence of words to make it real. And then my second realisation: this wouldn't be simply 'Sound Effects Disc 37B' or a studio manager waltzing across crisp packets. No, here my words were free to evoke exactly what it feels like for the characters to endure that storm or breathe the leafy mist coming in on that October air. It would all be about the characters' response to these surroundings. Their perspective would be my liberation.

And perspective brings us back to that crucial element of audio drama storytelling: just as many novels are written either in the first person or in close third person, audio dramas thrive on that same intense bond between listener and central character. If asked to define the role of the modern novel, I would say it's a 300-page exploration of What It's Like to Be X (whether X is a woman of 60 who has just discovered her husband's secret love child or X is a mixed-race teen on a West London estate where it's all about to kick off). At their most successful, audio dramas perform the same function. Sure, you can choose to bounce around between different characters in different places, but any audio drama gains hugely from a central pivot - the sort of viewpoint you'd take for granted in a novel. Emile Zola defined art as 'a corner of creation seen through a temperament' and that ticks the audio drama boxes just as neatly.

As always in the writing game, though, there's no such thing as a free lunch. That central temperament will also do its best to pull you down the fatal primrose path for audio drama writers: the internal monologue. Many novels thrive on this kind of commentary, but at this point drama and prose must part ways. For me, the internal monologue is the enemy of live drama, and any play must feel *live*, must hum with the danger of *now*, with the unknowingness of its characters. And that's why the internal monologue is the dramatist's sworn enemy. For so many seemingly good reasons, voice-over will feel like the solution to all your problems: anything which you cannot convey in sound can instantly get itself described. What's more, it's your chance to speak directly and unimpeded to the audience. But characters in drama, unlike prose fiction, must always be up against a ticking clock and, as soon as a character has unlimited and unopposed time to unleash their thoughts and reflections, that clock stops ticking.

So my advice on the 'narratorly voice-over' is: Handle With Extreme Caution. That direct channel into the mind and feelings of the protagonist, that self-dissecting honesty, will erode any genuine suspense. If the central character understands himself, why does the audience need to even try? Imagine if the curtain went up on the latest production of *Hamlet* and the title character strode to the front of the stage and announced he has an issue with getting things done, is probably a bit confused about his sexuality, and let's not even talk about his mother issues. Would you bother to watch the ensuing four hours? No, you watch the five acts in order to work all this out for yourself.

Worse than self-knowledge, a voice-over becomes a safety net underlying your plot, because however bad things turn out, this character is still able to tell us about what happened, and how they have come to terms with those events. Often, when I fulminate about voice-overs, people throw something like *Sunset Boulevard* back at me (non-spoiler alert: Scene 1 reveals William Holden's corpse floating in the swimming pool and the rest of the film unravels his journey to that point), but even that trades on a Zen-like resignation in Holden's narration. In other words, he survived, he's down with it, and you don't need to worry.

So how then to ensure that the audio drama remains your protagonist's story? How to generate that solidity of POV? It's not easy, but now we come full circle back to the novelist's skill set. Any novelist writing in first or close third person takes for granted that their protagonist appears in every scene. Yes, in a shorter drama that can make the plotting tricky, but you can always contrive the setting and 'agenda' of your scenes so that everything is revealed (though beware those faux voice-overs: the Therapist's Couch, the Endlessly Patient Best Friend!). Once you have finagled your plotting to tell it all through action involving your protagonist, the coherence and focus of your play is assured. The listener is now freed to walk a single, ribbon-like journey – and we're back to Harold Fry.

Of course, in this sense, a protagonist is not always a single person. In 1998 Bruce Springsteen agreed to play a concert in East Germany, behind the Berlin Wall. My play, *Born in the GDR*, dramatises how three young people first had the crazy idea of asking him, and how they squeezed the whole scheme past the Stasi and then staged a concert in front of what is still the largest audience ever in Europe. Those three people, as a joint enterprise, are the protagonist – one or more of them is in every scene. They are the ribbon; they are the temperament through whom we view this particular corner of creation.

In fact, many of my plays – because they dramatise actual events – have demanded this approach. In my trilogy of plays about *The Clintons*, Bill and/or Hillary is in every scene; it was their show, their unfolding. We never jump to the other side's POV. What happens is happening to them. Or think sideways: Anthony Minghella's *Cigarettes and Chocolate* explores the mystery of why the pivotal character has stopped speaking. The result is a brilliant set of agonised, one-sided conversations with a woman who won't reply. The other characters can say what they want, but they are still talking to someone – it's not just narration into a convenient theatrical void. And the clock remains ticking ... until, at the last, she reveals the reason for her silence.

And why stop there? We now all carry a device engineered for self-advertisement and this hands the audio dramatist a sledgehammer with which to demolish the fourth wall entirely. My podcast serial *That Was Then* has the central character secretly recording everything – for her own safety, as much as anything – into her phone, both the events and her follow-up diary. In fact, we even recorded it on location on an iPhone in order to generate that kind of scratchy, amateurish recording (but Apple outwitted us, and the quality was barely distinguishable from the BBC's best in-house microphones). But the protagonist's need to hide the recordings from everyone, including her own family, kept that clock ticking loudly; the drama remains set firmly in the now.

So I am often asked, how do you know if your next idea is a novel or an audio drama? And the truthful answer is, I don't know. In so many respects, they're the same thing and ask the same from their audiences – but don't forget that they make slightly different demands on the writer.

A word on words: throughout this piece I have used the term 'audio drama'. Now that the world of podcasts has reinvented this particular wheel, the words 'radio drama' seem needlessly old-fashioned. Nowadays audio dramas are sometimes known as 'scripted podcasts', but I find that dull and unwieldy. Certainly, someday soon, podcast providers will be creating more hours of audio drama than the BBC – and the Corporation is the only reason still to call it 'radio' drama.

Jonathan Myerson is the author of over 50 individual dramas for the BBC (Radio 4, Radio 3 and World Service), as well as episodes of series *Westway* and *Citizens*. For TV, he has written episodes of *The Bill*, *EastEnders* and *Holby City*. His audio drama series include *The Republicans*, *Doctor Zhivago* and *Number 10* (winner of the Writers' Guild Award for Best Radio Drama). His most recent podcasts are *Nazis: The Road To Power* and *Nuremberg*, both multi-episode dramatic retellings for BBC Sounds, and *That Was Then*, a scripted 15-episode drama. Jonathan has been nominated for an Oscar and won a BAFTA in 1999 for his animated film of *The Canterbury Tales*. After ten years running the prestigious Novel Writing MA at City University London, he now consults for www.finishyournovel.org.

Writing for videogames: a guide for the curious

Chris Bateman shines a light on videogame writing, its nature and challenges, and has essential advice for anyone hoping to build a career in the rewarding and creative world of game narrative and design.

So you've played a few videogames, and marvelled at the production values and the intensity of the experience, but were perhaps a little underwhelmed by the stories you've encountered. Like any writer, you can't resist a creative challenge and you know that with the right tools you could do a better job. The question is: what do you need to create videogame narrative? How do you begin? Where do you go to make it happen?

Let's start with the bucket of cold water – you will not end up writing for videogames if it's just an idle fancy; it takes a real commitment to work in games writing and – make no mistake – this is the toughest medium to work in. But at the same time, working on a game story, helping a team bring characters into beautifully animated life and working with voice actors to give a soul to those animations, can be hugely rewarding. Working on an animated movie or TV show carries the same emotional payoff, is substantially easier, and gives more creative control to the writing team, but if you're dedicated to your dream of writing for games, or don't think anything else would quite satisfy your creative needs, videogame writing is a path you can take.

Getting started

So how do you get the opportunity? As with most jobs, you frustratingly need to have prior experience to get hired. If you've already written novels, short stories, radio plays, screenplays, stage plays or anything of the kind, you can try fishing for work with that experience but you're likely to come up against a certain resistance from game developers. One way around this, especially if you're a writer with time to invest in career-building, is to lend your support to indie games (i.e. low-budget projects) that are advertising on sites like Gamasutra (www.gamasutra.com) or via social media asking for help. They may be willing to take on a writer (typically unpaid) and in return you can get experience working in games. It's not a glamorous way to start, but gaining experience seldom is.

If you have a little money to invest in your career, consider attending one of the major industry events like Develop in Brighton or GDC in San Francisco (see box for details), where you can hear from experienced game writers and get networking. This was more or less how my company, International Hobo, built up clients in the early years, although admittedly I'd already worked on several critically acclaimed games at that point. You can also go to these events and set up meetings with developers to talk about what you can offer. There's usually a meeting app provided with the ticket, and there are also third-party options, like MeetToMatch (www.meettomatch.com), which are often worth the extra cost.

How game projects begin

Let's say you've found a developer willing to work with you. Now is the time to pitch that screenplay you wrote as a dynamite basis for a videogame, right? Sorry, no. Videogames are never made from screenplays (we don't even have a standard format for one!) and very few start as story concepts either. If you want to make your own glossy digital masterpiece for games consoles, you'd better have a few million in your back pocket to fund production. Otherwise, accept that your job as game writer is to assist a development team to get the most out of the game they're making, by helping them discover opportunities to get more out of characters or settings or theme (a subtlety many game developers tend to overlook).

Typically, a game begins as either a prototype, showing off what the game is like, or as a concept document – a short pitch for a game. Concept documents are quite similar to the proposals that a book publisher or agent expects to be submitted (and often written after the manuscript is completed). Laying out the story in broad strokes is part of the concept and so can be an element of the documentation from the very beginning – although, in practice, writers seldom get attached to projects this early. This, however, is short-sightedness on the part of developers, who actually could use your input at this stage. You can pitch your services to companies in this way – but expect scepticism if you can't show evidence that you have a handle on how stories in games work.

How do you build up your understanding of the workings of videogame? The easiest way is to play games. You can learn a lot from playing videogames, but don't just play the latest releases or you'll end up playing solely what are called AAA games (i.e. multi-million-dollar blockbusters) and, as a writer trying to break into games, you won't be working on these. Play older games, play new games made on a low budget, and play games from wildly different genres. While you're networking, you can even ask game developers which games they rate for clever use of story materials ... you'll get plenty of suggestions! Another

Networking opportunities

Develop Conference
www.developconference.com
Europe's leading convention and expo for those working in game development. Held annually in Brighton for three days in July.

Game Development Conference (GDC)
www.gdconf.com
The world's largest professional gaming industry event, incorporating The Independent Games Festival and The Game Developers Choice Awards. Takes place over five days every March in San Francisco.

Gamescom
www.gamescom.global
Europe's largest expo, and a good networking opportunity. Held in August each year in Cologne.

International Game Developers Association (IGDA)
https://igda.org
US-based with a global network of over 150 chapters and Special Interest Groups (SIGs) with individual members from all fields of game development: programmers and producers, designers and artists, writers and other experts.

WGA – Writers Guild of America
www.wga.org
Union that represents writers for film, TV and games, combining WGA West and WGA East. Like the WGGB, its UK equivalent, the WGA honours writers for games in its annual awards. See page 507.

WGGB – Writers' Guild of Great Britain
https://writersguild.org.uk
Union that supports UK-based writers, including games writers, with a useful guide *Writing for Videogames* on its site. See page 498.

option is to watch online videos of other people playing games. Some game writers will cluck their tongues at this suggestion, but you don't need to be able to play a certain kind of game to work on its story, you just have to be able to appreciate how it works; other people's player experiences can be just as useful for this (in some cases, more useful) because games are not played in the same ways by all players.

Narrative design

In the early 2000s, when I was setting up International Hobo, my colleagues and I conceived of our job as 'narrative design'. It's a term that has now crept out into the industry thanks to the International Game Developers Association, for which I set up the Game Writing Special Interest Group (you might want to check this out as a helpful community for game writers at all stages of their careers; see box). Narrative design is the intersection of game design and writing: it's about putting a player into the centre of your story or, perhaps more accurately, about turning a story inside-out so that it can work when the central character is (nearly) beyond your control. A player isn't an actor, so you'll need to provide reasons for them to take on the role provided – or alternatively give them opportunities to mess around with the world.

There are several key aspects of narrative design you'll need to consider:

1. Dialogue

You'll need to decide if your focus will just be on dialogue – in which case, expect the scenarios to be almost entirely dictated to you, and prepare to work with a low level of creative influence – or if you're going to get involved with narrative design. This means having a hand in the structuring of the game materials, which in turn means understanding game design as well as writing. Woe betide the conventional screenwriter who thinks they will 'fix' videogames by making them more like movies!

2. Cut scenes and voice actors

Almost everything you want to do to make a conventional narrative work is too expensive. You will struggle to get much budget for animated sequences (called *cut scenes*, or *FMV* – full motion videos) and if you're having to tell your story in this way you're working in the wrong medium. Talking heads (i.e. voice actors providing dialogue to animated characters in the game) is a powerful and relatively cost-effective tool, but the moment you need one of the characters to be animated in a specific way (say, banging their fist on a table for emphasis) you're draining money from the budget. As a writer, words are your greatest tool so use them to great effect. If the game has voice recording (most mid-budget or higher games do) the voice actors will be able to 'sell' your dialogue to the player without you having to specify animations for emphasis. If it doesn't, well, then you get an even greater opportunity to make every word count, because it's your text being read directly by the players. Either way, don't use more lines than you need to advance the narrative.

3. Narrative spaces

The other key element of narrative design is location: games typically flow through environments and, as a writer, you can use your grasp of locations to great effect in discussions with the developer. As always, though, every location costs money to make and, unlike for film or TV, you can't just nip out with a location crew if you need footage; everything has to be painstakingly built by the team. That means nothing should go into the game that isn't absolutely necessary, and ideally you shouldn't be creating more locations than are needed.

Theatre is a much better guide than film in this regard. The playwright has to think about how it works on stage; you don't have an entire set put up just for an actor to say two lines and walk off. In a game, every location has to earn its time. Unlike theatre sets, however, videogame environments are typically vast open spaces; that gives you the opportunity to paint in stories, without text or dialogue, by using environmental storytelling. You won't get the budget to show, say, a werewolf tearing apart a village, but you can show the aftermath and let the player piece together the back story from what they can find.

4. World-building

Some games, particularly computer role-playing games, also rely on a depth of lore – and the need for the associated texts can be a way for a writer to get added to a project. World-building is part of the writer's toolkit, and while few game developers will let you put together the world for their game single-handed, they may well be delighted for you to write short texts that fill in the substance of their setting. I won't lie to you – this may involve a great deal of writing descriptions for weaponry, but I have to say I found it very rewarding to paint a picture of a fantasy world solely from the swords, shields, jewellery and clothing players will encounter. There's a challenge here that no other medium will give you.

Part of the team

Ultimately, writing for games is about working in a team in which different professionals have a hand in making everything happen. The most important thing you can do, as a writer, when you join a developer is to acknowledge that the programmers and artists are the ones who are actually making the game – your job is to help bring out the best in what they're doing. If you can place yourself in the service of a developer, your writing can take videogames to another level. That's what keeps me going. There are always new ways to tell stories in games, and it's my pleasure and honour to work with developers to help them discover the right one for their project.

Chris Bateman a game designer, technology ethicist, and founder of the award-winning creative consultancy International Hobo. He is best known for the games *Discworld Noir* and *Ghost Master* and his book *Game Writing: Narrative Skills for Videogames* (Cengage Learning 2007, 2nd edition Bloomsbury 2021). His other books include *Imaginary Games* (2011) and *Chaos Ethics* (2014), both published by Zero Books, and *The Virtuous Cyborg* (Eyewear Publishing 2018). Chris has an MSc in Artificial Intelligence/Cognitive Science and a PhD in game aesthetics, and has worked on over 80 published games. He sits on the editorial board for the *International Journal of Play*, and the thinking group for the Digital Futures Commission. He writes three-minute reflections on contemporary problems at Stranger Worlds and How to Live in Them (https://strangerworlds.substack.com), and you can find out more about him at his company's blog (https://blog.ihobo.com).

Television and radio

The information in this section has been compiled as a general guide for writers, artists, agents and publishers to the major companies and key contacts within the broadcasting industry. As personnel, corporate structures and commissioning guidelines can change frequently, readers are encouraged to check the websites of companies for the most up-to-date information.

REGULATION

Advertising Standards Authority

Castle House, 37–45 Paul Street, London EC2A 4LS
tel 020-7492 2222
website www.asa.org.uk
Facebook www.facebook.com/adauthority
Twitter @ASA_UK
Chief Executive Guy Parker

The UK's independent regulator of advertising across all media. Its work includes acting on complaints and taking action against misleading, harmful or offensive advertisements.

Ofcom

Riverside House, 2A Southwark Bridge Road, London SE1 9HA
tel 020-7981 3000, 0300 123 3000
website www.ofcom.org.uk
Facebook www.facebook.com/ofcom
Twitter @Ofcom
Chief Executive Melanie Dawes

Accountable to Parliament and exists to further the interests of consumers by balancing choice and competition with the duty to encourage plurality, protect viewers and listeners, promote diversity in the media and ensure full and fair competition between communications providers.

TELEVISION

There are five major TV broadcasters operating in the UK: the BBC, ITV, Channel 4 (S4C in Wales), Channel 5 and Sky. In Ireland, RTÉ is the country's public service broadcaster.

The BBC

BBC Broadcasting House, Portland Place, London W1A 1AA
website www.bbc.co.uk

The BBC is the world's largest broadcasting organisation, with a remit to provide programmes that inform, educate and entertain. Established by a Royal Charter, the BBC is a public service broadcaster funded by a licence fee. Income from the licence fee is used to provide services including:

• seven national TV channels plus regional and local programming

• ten national radio stations
• 41 local radio stations
• national radio services each in Scotland, Wales and Northern Ireland
• BBC Online Services
• BBC World Service

Anyone in the UK who watches or records TV programmes (whether via TV, online, mobile phone, games console, digital box, etc), or watches or downloads any BBC programmes from BBC iPlayer, needs a TV licence. The Government sets the level of the licence fee. The annual cost is £159. For full details of which services require a TV licence, visit: www.tvlicensing.co.uk.

Governance

BBC Board

The BBC is governed by a board. Tim Davie, Director-General, sits on the board alongside other BBC executive and non-executive members. More information is available at: www.bbc.co.uk/aboutthebbc.

Ofcom

External regulation of the BBC is carried out by Ofcom.

What does the BBC do?

The following provides a selective overview of the BBC's main services and key contact information we consider most relevant to our readership.

Television

The BBC's seven national TV channels, provide entertainment, news, current affairs and arts programming for the whole of the UK: BBC One, BBC Two, BBC Three, BBC Four, CBeebies, BBC News and BBC Parliament.
    Chief Content Officer Charlotte Moore
    Controller, BBC Three Fiona Campbell
    Controller, iPlayer Dan McGolpin
    Director, Children's & Education Patricia Hidalgo Reina
    Head, BBC Sport Philip Bernie

BBC Content

BBC's online services include news, sport, weather, CBBC, CBeebies, BBC iPlayer and the school learning and revision site, BBC Bitesize. Sites are developed to provide audiences with access to content on a variety of devices including tablets, smartphones and computers. Gives access to the BBC's radio and TV programme archives, through BBC Sounds and BBC iPlayer.

News Group

BBC News incorporates network news (the newsroom, news programmes such as *Newsnight*, political programmes such as *Daily Politics*, and the weather team), English Regions and Global News.
Ceo, News & Current Affairs Deborah Turness

Nations

One of the largest divisions in the BBC, with staff working in England, Scotland, Wales and Northern Ireland. The division produces a range of content across TV, radio and online for audiences locally, across all of the UK and globally.
Director, Nations Rhodri Talfan Davies

BBC Studios

BBC Studios works with British writers, directors and programme-makers to create content every year through production bases in the UK and in partnership with countries around the world.
Ceo Tom Fussell

BBC Studioworks

A wholly owned subsidiary of the BBC, works with media companies to create and manage content across all genres for a diverse range of broadcasters and platforms, including ITV, Channel 4 and Sky, as well as the BBC.
Ceo Andrew Moultrie

BBC World Service Group

Incorporates BBC World Service and BBC Global News and includes the BBC World News Television Channel, the BBC's international-facing online news services in English, BBC Monitoring Service and BBC Media Action (the BBC's international development charity).
Director, BBC World Service Liliane Landor

Britbox

website www.britbox.com

A digital video subscription service created by the BBC and ITV Plc, serving the UK, Europe, North America, Australia and South Africa. It is focused on British television series and films, mainly featuring current and past series and films supplied from the main UK public service broadcasters.

Commissioning

For full details of editorial guidelines, commissioning, production and delivery guidelines, and how to submit a proposal, see www.bbc.co.uk/commissioning.

Developing and producing programmes is complex and requires substantial knowledge of production and broadcasting. BBC Pitch (www.bbc.co.uk/commissioning/pitch) is the BBC's commissioning tool designed for UK-based

production companies and BBC in-house production teams to submit content proposals for BBC Network Television. Individuals and members of the public cannot use BBC Pitch. If you are a member of the public with an idea, see www.bbc.co.uk/commissioning/talent.

Who's who in commissioning?

Television (genre commissioning)

Chief Content Officer Charlotte Moore

Children's

Head of Commissioning & Acquisitions Kate Morton (0–6), Sarah Muller (7–12)

Comedy

Director of BBC Comedy Jon Petrie, *Head of Comedy* Tanya Qureshi, *Head of Development* Navi Lamba, *Commissioning Editors* Ben Caudell, Seb Barwell, Gregor Sharp, Emma Lawson

Daytime and Early Peak

Head of Daytime and Early Peak Commissioning Rob Unsworth, *Commissioning Editors* Lindsay Bradbury, Alex McLeod, Neil McCallum, Rachel Platt, Julie Shaw, Muslim Alim, Helen Munson

Drama

Director of BBC Drama Lindsay Salt, *Head of Development* Sami El-Hadi, *Senior Commissioning Editor* Lucy Richer, *Commissioning Editors* Jo McClellan, Gaynor Holmes, Rebecca Ferguson, Nawful Faizullah, Danielle Scott-Haughton

Entertainment

Head of Commissioning, Entertainment Kalpna Patel-Knight, *Senior Commissioning Editor* Jo Wallace, *Commissioning editors* Ruby Kuraishe, Katie Taylor, Rachel Ashdown, Pinki Chambers, Sarah Clay, Suzanne McManus, Saul Fearnley, Clodagh O'Donoghue

Factual

Director of Unscripted Kate Phillips, *Arts and Classical Music* Suzy Klein, *Documentaries* Clare Sillery, *Specialist Factual* Jack Bootle, *Factual Entertainment and Events* Catherine Catton

BBC Nations

Director, Nations Rhodri Talfan Davies
   BBC Cymru Wales *Director* Rhuanedd Richards, *Head of Commissioning* Nick Andrews, *Commissioners* Christina Macaulay, Sian Harris, Paul Forde, Sorelle Neil
   BBC Scotland *Director* Stephen Carson, *Head of Multiplatform Commissioning* Louise Thornton, *Commissioners* Gareth Hydes, David Harron, Tony Nellany, Gavin Smith, Steve Allen, Gaynor Holmes, Muslim Alim, Ishbel Maclennan (Gaelic programming)
   BBC Northern Ireland *Senior Head of Content Comissioning* Eddie Doyle, *Comissioning executives* Fiona Keane (Ulster-Scots), Justin Binding, Karen

Kirby (Irish Language)

BBC Writersroom

email writersroom@bbc.co.uk
website www.bbc.co.uk/writersroom
Facebook www.facebook.com/BBCWriters
Twitter @bbcwritersroom

BBC Writersroom seeks to discover, develop and champion new and experienced writers across the UK. Unsolicited submissions are accepted as part of Open Call submission windows, announced on the BBC Writersroom Opportunities page. Shortlisted writers are offered a development programme through either the Voices or Drama Room groups which include expert masterclasses, craft sessions and discussions to provide participants with core tools and knowledge to write for broadcast television.

The BBC Writersroom also offers other bespoke development programmes including the Writers' Access Group for deaf, disabled and neurodivergent writers and the Pilot scheme for credited/agented writers. The BBC Writersroom blog provides a wealth of behind-the-scenes commentary from writers and producers who have worked on BBC TV and radio programmes: www.bbc.co.uk/blogs/writersroom.

Education and training

The BBC has adopted a recruitment system called the BBC Careers Hub. It allows candidates to apply for jobs, source interview tips, learn about the BBC's recruitment processes and get advice about CVs, applications and assessments: www.bbc.co.uk/careers and https://careershub.bbc.co.uk/members.

Trainee Schemes, Work Experience and Apprenticeships

website www.bbc.co.uk/careers/trainee-schemes-and-apprenticeships

For full details of the BBC's trainee and apprenticeship schemes, see website.

BBC Academy

website www.bbc.co.uk/academy

A free, online learning resource providing practical advice and information on all aspects of working in TV, radio and online.

Channel 4

124–126 Horseferry Road, London SW1P 2TX
tel 0345 076 0191
website www.channel4.com
Facebook www.facebook.com/Channel4
Twitter @Channel4

A publicly owned television network that is freely available to all in the UK. Its commercially-funded, publicly owned structure enables all profit generated to be directly reinvested back into its public service remit. As a publisher-broadcaster, Channel 4 commissions UK content from the independent production sector and currently works with over 300 creative companies across the UK every year. It provides a digital streaming service, All 4, and a network of 12 television channels, aiming to create change by representing unheard voices and reinventing entertainment.

Management team

Chief Executive Alex Mahon

Chief Content Officer Ian Katz

Chief Marketing Officer Zaid Al-Qassab

Director of People Kirstin Furber

Commissioning

Information about commissioning and related processes and guidelines can be found at www.channel4.com/info/commissioning. Email addresses for most individuals named below can be found on the relevant parts of the website under 4Producers.

Comedy

Head of Comedy Charlie Perkins, *Senior Commissioning Editor* Andy Bereton, *Commissioning Editors* Laura Riseam, Joe Hullait

Daytime and Features

Head of Daytime Jo Street, *Programme Coordinator & Genre Assistant* Cerise Carroll, *Commissioning Editors* Kate Thomas, Clemency Green, Jayne Stranger, Deborah Dunnett

Documentaries

Head of Documentaries Alisa Pomeroy, *Senior Commissioning Editors* Madonna Benjamin, Anna Miralis, *Commissioning Editors* Will Rowson, Sacha Mirzoeff, Simon Lee, Rita Daniels

Drama

Head of Drama Caroline Hollick, *Commissioning Editors* Gemma Boswell, Gwawr Lloyd, Rebecca Holdsworth

Entertainment and Events

Head of Entertainment & Events Phil Harris, *Head of Live Events& Entertainment Commissioning Editor* Tom Beck, *Commissioning Editors* Steven Handley, Cimran Shah, Genna Gibson

Factual Entertainment

Head of Factual Entertainment Alf Lawrie, *Commissioning Editors* Ian Dunkley, Lee McMurray, Daniel Fromm, Tim Hancock, Vivienne Molokwu, Luke Mcfarlane, Cal Turner

News and Current Affairs

Head of News & Current Affairs Louisa Compton, *Commissioning Editors* Adam Vandermark, Nevine Mabro, Joanne Potts, Debbie Ramsay

Sport

Screen and audio

Head of Sport Pete Andrews, *Commissioning Executive* Antonia Howard-Taylor, *Commissioning Editor* Joe Blake-Turner

4Skills

website https://careers.channel4.com/4skills

Through 4Skills, Channel 4 aims to help people who want to work in the broadcasting industry gain experience, qualifications and career development. There are a range of options including apprenticeship, graduate and scholarship programmes, work experience, training, events and workshops. For full details see website.

Channel 5

17–29 Hawley Crescent, Camden Town, London NW1 8TT
tel 020-3580 3600
website www.channel5.com
Facebook www.facebook.com/channel5uk
Twitter @channel5_tv
Director of Programming Ben Frow

Brands include Channel 5, 5Star, 5Select and 5USA, and an on-demand service, My5. Channel 5 works with independent production companies to provide its programmes.

Commissioning

Factual, News and Current Affairs

Commissioning Editors Guy Davies, Lucy Willis, Daniel Pearl

Factual Entertainment, Features and Entertainment

Commissioning Editors Adrian Padmore, Dan Louw, Denise Seneviratne, Emma Westcott, Kit Morey, Greg Barnett

Acquisitions

Acquisitions Managers Cherry Yeandle, Anna-Belen Dunlop

Children's Programming: Milkshake!

General Manager Kids & Family Louise Bucknole

ITV Plc

2 Waterhouse Square, 138–142 Holborn, London EC1N 2AE
website www.itv.com
website www.itvplc.com
Facebook www.facebook.com/itv
Twitter @ITV
Chief Executive Carolyn McCall
Chairman Andrew Cosslett
Managing Director of Media & Entertainment Kevin Lygo
Managing Director of Commercial Kelly Williams
Managing Director of ITV Studios Julian Bellamy
Director of Group Strategy Samir Ahmad
Group Communications and Corporate Affairs Director Paul Moore

General Counsel and Company Secretary Kyla Mullins
Chief People Officer David Osborn

The ITV network is responsible for the commissioning, scheduling and marketing of network programmes on ITV and its digital channel portfolio including ITV2, ITV3, ITV4 and ITVBe. It is the UK's largest commercial TV network. In addition to TV broadcasting services, ITV also delivers programming via a number of platforms, including ITV Hub which is the home for children's channel CITV.

ITV Studios is the UK's largest production company and produces over 7,000 hours of original content annually. ITV Studios (UK) produces programming for the ITV network's own channels as well as other UK broadcasters including the BBC, Channel 4, Channel 5 and Sky. ITV also has an international production business which produces for broadcasters around the world.

Commissioning

ITV's commissioning areas include current affairs, daytime, digital, drama, entertainment, factual entertainment and sport. Information, FAQs and guidelines for commissioning can be found at www.itv.com/commissioning.

Current Affairs

Controller of Current Affairs Tom Giles

Daytime

Commissioning Editors Lara Akeju, Leanne Clarke

Digital

Controller Paul Mortimer

Drama

Head of Drama Polly Hill, *Senior Commissioning Editor* Helen Ziegler, *Commissioner* Huw Kennair Jones

Entertainment

Head of Entertainment Katie Rawcliffe, *Commissioners* Natalie Rose, David Smyth, *Commissioning Editors* Louise Major, Lily Wilson, Kevin O'Brien, Joe Mace, Paula Thomas

Factual Entertainment

Head of Factual Entertainment Sue Murphy, *Controller* Jo Clinton-Davis, *Commissioner* Kate Teckman, Satmohan Panesar, *Commissioning Editor* Nicola Lloyd

Sport

Director of Sport Niall Sloane, *Assistant Commissioner* Richard Botchway

Recruitment, training and work experience

Information about training schemes, work experience and recruitment at ITV can be found at www.itvjobs.com, including details of ITV Academy, a traineeship scheme which enables people seeking experience in the TV industry to gain hands-on knowledge.

ITV Network regions

The ITV Network is made up of the following regions:

ITV Anglia www.itv.com/news/anglia

ITV Border www.itv.com/news/border

ITV Calendar www.itv.com/calendar

ITV Central www.itv.com/news/central

ITV Granada www.itv.com/news/granada

ITV London www.itv.com/news/london

ITV Meridian www.itv.com/news/meridian

ITV TyneTees www.itv.com/news/tyne-tees

ITV Wales www.itv.com/news/wales

ITV West Country www.itv.com/news/westcountry

STV Group www.stv.tv (Scotland)

UTV www.itv.com/news/utv (Northern Ireland)

Channel TV www.itv.com/news/channel

RTÉ

Donnybrook, Dublin 4, Republic of Ireland
tel +353 (0)20 83434
email info@rte.ie
website www.rte.ie
Facebook www.facebook.com/ExploreRTE
Twitter @rte
Director General Dee Forbes

RTÉ (Raidio Teilifis Éireann) is Ireland's national public service broadcaster. A leader in Irish media, it provides comprehensive, free-to-air multimedia services.

Commissioning

RTÉ works in partnership with independent producers to create many of Ireland's favourite TV programmes. It commissions content in seven groups: drama, entertainment, music and comedy, factual, arts and culture, Cláracha Gaeilge, sport, and young people's programmes. Full details of commissioning guidelines, specifications and submissions can be found at www.rte.ie/commissioning.

Director of Content Jim Jenning

Deputy Director of Content Niamh O'Connor

Group Head of Arts & Culture Ann-Marie Power

Group Head of Cláracha Gaeilge (Irish Programs) Niamh Ní Churnáin

Acting Head of Drama David Crean

Group Head of Entertainment & Music Alan Tyler

Group Head of Factual Sean MacGiollaPhadraig

Group Head of Sport Declan McBennett

Head of Children's & Young People's Content Suzanne Kelley

Executive Producer Eimear O'Mahony

S4C

Canolfan S4C Yr Egin, Carmarthen SA31 3EQ
tel 0370 600 4141
website www.s4c.cymru/en
Facebook www.facebook.com/S4C
Twitter @S4C
Ceo Sian Doyle
Chief Operating Officer Elin Morris
Director of Content Geraint Evans
Chief Content Officer Llinos Griffin-Williams

S4C is a Welsh-language television channel which transmits live from 6 a.m. and late at night, and features news, drama, documentaries, music, entertainment and children's programmes. Shows are available to stream 24 hours a day on the S4C app. An online service called Hansh is aimed mainly at the 16–34 audience. Independent production companies produce most of the programmes; the BBC also produces around 520 hours a year for the channel. See website for full details of commissioning and production guidelines and personnel.

DIGITAL TV PROVIDERS

Amazon Prime/Amazon Studios

website https://press.amazonstudios.com
Twitter @AmazonStudios
Head of Amazon Studios Jennifer Salke, *UK Country Manager* John Boumphrey

Amazon Prime streams to over 200 territories. Its original content includes film, television shows and live coverage of events and sport. All Amazon Prime original content is acquired and created by Amazon Studios. Amazon Studios does not accept submissions but their IMDbPro service gives subscribers access to industry contacts, in-development projects looking for creatives, casting notices, and box office trends and insights. More information can be found at: https://pro.imdb.com/company/co0319272.

Apple TV+

website www.apple.com/uk/apple-tv-plus
Facebook www.facebook.com/appletv
Twitter @AppleTV
Creative Director, Europe Worldwide Video Jay Hunt

Original content is added monthly and focuses primarily on scripted content across a range of genres, including children's, as well as documentaries and talk shows.

BT

81 Newgate Street, London EC1A 7AJ
tel 020-7356 5000 (switchboard)

Customer postal address BT Correspondence Centre, Providence Row, Durham DH98 1BT
website www.player.bt.com/#/home
Ceo Philip Jansen

BT offers subscription television services in the UK, through BT TV, which provides on-demand content, entertainment channels and live sports channels including BT Sport and Sky Sports.

Disney+
website www.disneyplus.com/en-gb
Facebook www.facebook.com/DisneyPlusUK
Twitter @DisneyPlusUK
President of Disney Streaming Alisa Bowen

Disney's digital streaming service primarily distributes original films and television series produced by Walt Disney Studios and Walt Disney Television, with dedicated hubs for Disney, Pixar, Marvel, Star Wars, National Geographic and Star. Star also streams films and television shows produced by Disney-owned production companies.

Facebook Watch
website www.facebook.com/watch
Twitter @FacebookWatch
Head of Global Creative Strategy Ricky van Veen

Facebook's digital streaming service is available to its two billion users and focuses on scripted, reality and talk shows which are available live and on demand. Aims to share content which will spark discussion and engagement across the social media site.

Freesat
23–24 Newman Street, London W1T 1PJ
tel 0345 313 0051
website www.freesat.co.uk
Facebook www.facebook.com/freesat
Ceo Jonathan Thompson
Freesat is a British free-to-air satellite television service, made up over 170 channels and online streaming platforms. A joint venture between the BBC, ITV, Channel 4 and Channel 5.

Hulu
website https://press.hulu.com/corporate
Facebook https://en-gb.facebook.com/hulu
Twitter @hulu
President Joe Earley

An American-only streaming service that incorporates both live channels and on-demand television and film, and has over 48 million subscribers. Original content is streamed first on Hulu and then screened around the world through partnerships with national companies such as the BBC and Channel 4.

Netflix
website https://media.netflix.com/en
Facebook www.facebook.com/NetflixUK

Twitter @NetflixUK
Co-Ceos Ted Sarandos, Greg Peters

Netflix was the world's first digital streaming service and now has over 231 million members from over 190 countries. Netflix's original film and television shows cover all genres, including children's and YA, and is available in a range of languages.

Sky
Grant Way, Isleworth TW7 5QD
tel 0330 100 0333
website www.skygroup.sky
Facebook www.facebook.com/sky
Twitter @skytv
Ceo UK and Europe Stephen van Rooyen

Sky is a British telecommunications company which provides a range of television and internet services in the UK, including entertainment, news and sport. It owns a number of subsidiaries including NOW TV. Through Sky Studios they produce original films and television shows throughout Europe. Full details of commissioning guidelines and contacts can be found at www.skygroup.sky/skystudios/commissioning.

Virgin Media
Griffin House, 161 Hammersmith Road, London W6 8BS
tel 0345 454 1111
website www.virginmedia.com
Facebook www.facebook.com/virginmedia
Twitter @virginmedia
Ceo Lutz Schüler
Virgin Media provides a range of television and internet services throughout the UK. Virgin TV is the largest cable television provider in the country.

YouView
2nd Floor, Aldgate Tower, 2 Leman Street, London E1 8FA
email info@youview.com
website www.youview.com
Ceo Riccardo Balestiero

YouView is a hybrid television platform in the UK, developed by a partnership of telecommunications operators including BT and TalkTalk, and broadcasters including the BBC, ITV, Channel 4 and Channel 5.

ORGANISATIONS CONNECTED TO TELEVISION BROADCASTING

BARB
20 Orange Street, London WC2H 7EF
email enquiries@barb.co.uk
website www.barb.co.uk
Twitter @BARBtelevision
Chief Executive Justin Sampson

The Broadcasters Audience Research Board is the official source of viewing figures in the UK.

Ipsos MORI

3 Thomas More Square, London E1W 1YW
tel 020-3059 5000
website www.ipsos.com/en-uk
Twitter @IpsosUK
Ceo Ben Page

One of the UK's leading research companies: conducts surveys for a wide range of major organisations (such as BARB and RAJAR), as well as for other market research agencies.

Pact – see page 531

Public Media Alliance

Room 02.101, Lawrence Stenhouse Building, University of East Anglia, Norwich NR4 7TJ
tel (01603) 592335
email info@publicmediaalliance.org
website www.publicmediaalliance.org
Twitter @PublicMediaPMA
Ceo Kristian Porter

World's largest association of public broadcasters. Provides advocacy, support, knowledge exchange, research and training opportunities for public media worldwide.

Royal Television Society

3 Dorset Rise, London EC4Y 8EN
tel 020-7822 2810
email info@rts.org.uk
website www.rts.org.uk
Facebook www.facebook.com/RoyalTelevisionSociety
Twitter @RTS_media
Ceo Theresa Wise

An educational charity promoting the art and science of television and the leading forum for discussion and debate on all aspects of the TV community.

RADIO

UK domestic radio services are broadcast across three wavebands: FM, medium wave and long wave. A number of radio stations are broadcast in both analogue and digital and there are growing numbers of stations broadcasting in digital alone. Digital radio (DAB – digital audio broadcasting) is available through digital radio sets, car radios, online, and on games consoles and mobile devices such as smartphones and tablets. Radio provision in the UK comprises of public service radio programming provided by the BBC and programming provided by independent, commercial stations.

BBC Radio

The BBC operates 10 national radio stations offering music and speech programming for the whole of the UK: Radio 1, Radio 1 Xtra, Radio 2, Radio 3, Radio 4, Radio 4 Extra, Radio 5 Live, Radio 5 Live Sports Extra, Radio 6 Music and Asian Network. In addition, there are 40 regional/local radio stations. The BBC Sounds website and app host all of the BBC's live radio stations alongside a catalogue of BBC programmes, interviews, podcasts and playlists available to stream.

Commissioning

For full details of commissioning and delivery guidelines, see www.bbc.co.uk/commissioning/radio.
Radio 1/1Xtra/Asian Network *Head of Radio 1* Aled Haydn Jones, *Head of Radio 1 Xtra* Faron McKenzie, *Head of Asian Network* Ahmed Hussai
Radio 2 *Head* Helen Thomas, *Commissions Executive* Laura Busson
Radio 3 *Controller* Sam Jackson, *Schedules Manager* David Ireland
Radio 4/4 Extra *Controller* Mohit Bakaya, *Commissioning Editors* Rhian Roberts (Digital), Alison Hindell (Drama), Julia McKenzie (Comedy and Entertainment), Hugh Levinson (Factual), Daniel Clarke (Factual), Matthew Dodd (Arts)
Radio 5 Live/5 Live Sports Extra *Controller* Heidi Dawson, *Commissioning Editor* Richard Maddock
Radio 6 Music *Head of Station* Samantha Moy
World Service *Controller* Jon Zilkha, *Commissioning Editors* Gwenan Roberts, Simon Pitts, *Podcast Commissioning Editor* Jon Manel

Commercial radio

There are over 250 commercial radio stations operating in the UK, most of which serve a local area or region. A number of commercial radio stations operate nationally, including Classic FM, Absolute Radio, talkSport and LBC. The majority of commercial radio stations are owned by one of three groups:

Bauer Media

website www.bauermedia.co.uk

Global Radio

website https://global.com/radio

Wireless Group

website www.wirelessgroup.co.uk

ORGANISATIONS CONNECTED TO RADIO BROADCASTING

Media.info

email info@media.info
website https://media.info/uk

This website provides detailed listings of UK radio stations alongside information about TV, newspapers, magazines and media ownership in the UK.

The Radio Academy

Suite 303, Pill Box Studios, 115 Coventry Road,
London E2 6GH
tel 0800 044 3811
email info@radioacademy.org
website www.radioacademy.org
Facebook www.facebook.com/radioacademy
Twitter @radioacademy
Chair Helen Thomas

The Radio Academy is a registered charity with
branches across the UK dedicated to the promotion
of excellence in radio broadcasting and production.
For over 30 years the Radio Academy has run the
annual Audio and Radio Industry Awards (ARIAS),
which celebrate content and creativity in the industry.

Radiocentre

15 Alfred Place, London WC1E 7EB
tel 020-7010 0600
website www.radiocentre.org
Twitter @Radiocentre
Chief Executive Matt Payton

Radiocentre is the voice of UK commercial radio.
Works with government, policy makers and
regulators, and provides a forum for industry-wide
debate and discussion.

RAJAR

15 Alfred Place, London WC1E 7EB
tel 020-7395 0630
website www.rajar.co.uk
Twitter @RAJARLtd
Chief Executive Jerry Hill

RAJAR – Radio Joint Audience Research – is the
official body in charge of measuring radio audiences
in the UK. It is jointly owned by the BBC and the
RadioCentre on behalf of the commercial sector.

Screen and audio

Theatre
Getting your script noticed

James McDermott describes how an aspiring new playwright can grow into their craft and find their own unique writing voice. He has advice on how to develop valuable skills, techniques, passion and perseverance and to make full use of beneficial resources, opportunities and connections to bring your work onto the stage.

The world of writing and of theatre can seem intimidating to the new playwright. As an early-career writer based outside of London, here is my advice on how to get started, how to make regional work and how to write your 'calling card' script: that script that will get you noticed.

Growing up queer in rural Norfolk, I didn't feel engaged with the dramas played out at the local cinemas and theatres; LGBTQ stories based in the East of England were rarely staged or screened. So, aged 18, I started writing the plays I needed to see in the world, which asserted and celebrated experiences like mine. In all your work, and especially in the first script you create and submit, I'd advise you to write what you love and what you feel impelled to write. If *you* don't feel a deep connection to your work, then a producer-director and ultimately your audience might not either. Writing something that audiences will get excited about is your goal.

I realised pretty quickly that, if I wanted to be a dramatist, I couldn't simply sit down at a laptop and write a great script – just as an aspiring musician can't sit down at a piano and crack out a symphony overnight. If you want to be a musician, you have to study music, learn and practise chords. If you want to be a scriptwriter, you have to watch, read and study other scripts, talk to writers, learn and practise dramaturgy – the dramatist's equivalent of chords. So, between 2012 and 2016, I studied for a BA then an MA in Scriptwriting at the University of East Anglia under playwrights Steve Waters and Timberlake Wertenbaker. Among many other things, they taught me that drama derives from the Greek word 'draein' which means 'to do' or 'to take action': drama is about a hero taking action to try and do something. If a hero could just do what they wanted, there would be no story – the story is in the struggle – and so the hero encounters internal and external obstacles they have to overcome in order to achieve their goal. In trying to overcome these obstacles, the hero is changed. Ensure your protagonist is in action, overcoming internal and external obstacles, in pursuit of achieving their objective.

At that time I was also introduced to the fundamentals of **five-act dramatic structure**, which now underpins my writing and teaching. In short, most Western dramatic stories can be broken down into five acts. In Act One, we meet heroes in trouble who want something to make life better: three little pigs are homeless, so they want to build houses and live happily ever after. In Act Two, things initially go well for the heroes as they pursue their want: three little pigs go their separate ways, gather different materials and build their own houses. It's important for things to go well, so that there's something for the heroes to lose in Act Three when things go badly as obstacles gather strength: the wolf arrives and blows down one of the houses. In Act Four, things get worse, and it looks like the heroes will never overcome the obstacles to get what they want unless they can change: the wolf blows down a second house, and the three little pigs look set to be killed unless they can work together to defeat the wolf. In Act Five, the heroes do or don't change, do or don't overcome the obstacles, and do or don't get what they want: the three little pigs learn to work together, defeat the wolf and live happily ever after in one house. This model acts as a torch for me when I'm trying to find my way in and out of planning, writing and rewriting drama.

It's important to stress – you don't have to study scriptwriting at university. That academic approach to creative training isn't for everyone and courses in tertiary education can be incredibly expensive; I had a student loan to support me during my BA and was lucky enough to receive a bursary from UEA to fund my MA. Instead, there are several great books on scriptwriting craft you could study: John Yorke's *Into The Woods: How Stories Work and Why We Tell Them* (Penguin 2014) and Russell T. Davies' *Doctor Who: The Writer's Tale* (BBC Books 2008) have proved invaluable to me. I also participated in several free scriptwriting groups run by theatres across the country: in London, I attended the Royal Court Writers Group, Soho Theatre's Writers Lab and Hampstead Theatre's Inspire Programme; in the East of England, I attended Menagerie Theatre's Young Writer's Programme and Mercury Theatre's Playwrights Group. Taking part in these groups gave me the space and time to learn how to craft, write and **workshop** new scripts under the tutelage of professional playwrights, create new connections and begin collaborations with theatres and artists across the country. This was invaluable for me as a theatre-maker based in East Anglia.

During my time at UEA, I wrote my **'calling card' script**. It was a solo play called *Rubber Ring* about a sexually confused Norfolk teenager desperate to get to London to find his hero Morrissey and to find himself. That play was a real declaration of who I am as a person and as a writer; it was queer, camp, sassy, vulnerable, East Anglian and full of both low- and highbrow pop cultural references. In short, my voice on the page sounded like my speaking voice and the voice in my head. In my own practice, I see my 'voice' as a writer as mapping the movement of my mind on the page, as well as documenting all those things that are manifest in my speaking voice: my accent, dialect, rhythm, insecurities, obsessions and sense of humour. Don't worry about making your writing just smart, serious or funny: try and put all of the beautiful mess of yourself onto the page. Many people are clever, sincere and humorous in similar ways, but only *your* mind moves in the distinct way it does, only *your* speaking voice sounds as it does. Mapping both of those things on the page feels like a good step towards ensuring your writing voice is uniquely yours.

Writing a script and not hearing it is like writing a song and not playing it. So, having written your script, try it out in front of an audience. Look out for the annual Open Call on the BBC Writersroom website (www.bbc.co.uk/writersroom). It was there I saw a call out for ten-minute extracts from comedy plays to be produced by Velvet Trumpet theatre company at a **scratch night**, an evening where several writers try out new work in front of an audience. I submitted the first ten pages of *Rubber Ring* and it was selected for performance at the Southwark Playhouse. Seeing and hearing the work in front of a live audience taught me how and where the play was and wasn't working. Before sending out your script in its entirety, I recommend trying out extracts in front of an audience to see if it's 'singing'; keep an eye out for the numerous scratch nights and script development opportunities listed on BBC Writersroom and on the London Playwrights Blog (https://londonplaywrights-blog.com). These are both great sources of information and support for the emerging playwright. Taking part in these scratch nights also allows you to connect with and potentially collaborate with the many new writers, actors, directors, producers and agents who attend.

> **Definitions**
>
> • The **calling card script** is the one that gets you noticed within the industry. It's the sample that you hope will entice agents, production and theatre companies and lead to commissions.
>
> • A **scratch night** is a chance to test your script-in-progress to see what works and what doesn't in order to help you rewrite and refine it.
>
> • **Workshopping** a script typically involves actors performing the latest version of your script at a table read or staged read-through.

The short extract of *Rubber Ring* went down well and Velvet Trumpet asked to read the rest of the play. They went on to produce the show at the Pleasance Islington before touring it nationwide. A month or two before the show was scheduled to be staged, I emailed lots of people I wanted to work with or learn from and invited them to see the show. These included agents I'd like to represent my work, literary managers of theatres I'd love to write for, and actors, writers and directors whose practice I admired. Many ignored my emails, several politely declined my invitation, but some said yes and came along to see the play, including Micheline Steinberg Associates who became my first agent and several artistic directors in East Anglia who went on to commission new work from me.

When you have that initial calling card script staged, or even scratched or workshopped, don't be shy about emailing those people you want to work with and learn from and inviting them along. Make sure you don't send a generic email to everybody; write an authentic honest email explaining why you'd like that particular person to give up their time and engage with your work. Emailing people you admire can feel daunting but, as an anxious queer working-class writer, I remember a piece of advice I was once given: The straight middle-class people who dominate the industry might not think twice about emailing anybody. So, if you aren't from that background, the only way you change your life and the industry is by stepping up and reaching out.

With a produced play and an MA under my belt, I then approached several of my local theatres to ask if I could set up a scriptwriting course in their buildings (… the swagger of being in your early twenties!). Several said yes, including the ever-supportive Norwich Theatre Royal where I have now taught scriptwriting for six years. This gave me a creative part-time day job to support my writing. It also allowed me to create, for other local writers, an inexpensive course I wish had existed when I was starting out. Reading, thinking and talking about writing all day also helped me to understand my craft better. If you want to learn how to do something, teach it. Leading writing groups in my local theatres also meant that, as a kind of writer in residence, I was a first port of call if one of those venues needed a new play written.

If you're a scriptwriter outside London, connect with your local theatres. Offer to teach there or send them your plays. For so many venues, funding depends on engaging with local talent – so they want and need you. Like a business card, that calling card script leads to other work: 'Rubber Ring' helped me secure an agent, a play text publisher (Samuel

Theatre

French), and several other productions including *Time and Tide* (Park Theatre), *Robin Good: The Politico-Panto* (Norwich Playhouse) and *Ghosted* (Out There Festival).

I wish you the very best of luck with your scriptwriting. Write the work you love and need to see. The harder you work, the luckier you'll get. Never give up.

James McDermott is a scriptwriter, poet and creative writing teacher based in East Anglia. His publications include *Rubber Ring* and *Time and Tide* (Samuel French 2020) and the poetry collections *Manatomy* (Burning Eye Books 2020) and *Wild Life* (Nine Arches Press 2023). James has written episodes of *EastEnders* and plays for BBC Radio 4. He is a lecturer in scriptwriting at the University of East Anglia and an Arvon writing tutor. For more information see https://jamesmcdermottwriter.weebly.com.

See also...

- *How to get your play published and performed,* page 373
- *Theatre producers,* page 381
- *Writers' retreats and creative writing courses,* page 683

How to get your play published and performed

Playwright Temi Wilkey offers her experience and practical steps for the writer who is ready to discover, share and develop their own dramatic voice, to fulfil the dream of seeing their work performed on stage.

Getting your play published and performed is a long road – and people have taken many different routes. I don't think there's any one way to achieve it, and I'm by no means an expert but I was fortunate enough to have my first play, *The High Table*, programmed in a co-production with Birmingham Rep and the Bush Theatre in 2019 and staged in 2020.

How on earth did a first-time writer get her debut play programmed at these two prestigious theatres? you may ask. Reader, that's a question I've asked myself a lot. I'm not entirely sure I have all the answers but, if you keep reading, we'll explore the process in detail.

First things first ...

Write a play

Okay, so this seems an obvious first step – but it's crucial and is the only bit you have any real control over. Putting pen to paper is sometimes the hardest thing to do. How do you wrestle with all the ideas in your head and get them down into one comprehensible narrative? How do you structure it? What if ... it is really bad?

I can't answer those questions for you, but I'm sure you can resolve them yourself if you sit down and write. Some would-be playwrights seek help in getting creative answers to these questions through creative writing courses where they are taught how to write for the theatre. Others are brave enough to get started on their own, without external support. I knew that I couldn't afford another course or degree after my undergraduate study, but I didn't feel confident enough to try writing a play on my own, so I applied to be in a writers' group.

Writers' groups are brilliant if you need some guidance or encouragement to write your play. I applied for the Royal Court's 'Introduction to Playwriting' group, as I only needed to send in ten pages for my application. I'd highly recommend doing this if you think a writers' group could be helpful for you (see https://royalcourttheatre.com/playwriting/writers-groups for more information). Even if you can't write a full-length play, you can definitely have a go at writing ten pages; if you're accepted into the group, you get much closer to answering the questions we're all asking at the start. For those who live outside London, this is also a brilliant group to apply to because the Royal Court covers your travel to attend sessions.

I was accepted into the group and each week, over a ten-week period, I met with a teacher and ten other aspiring playwrights. We read plays and talked about character, plot and structure. The guidance from our group leader was incredible, but the most helpful thing for me was having a group of peers who were also trying to write a play. I learnt so much from them about how other people write; sometimes it confirmed that the way I was doing things was okay, but far more often it challenged me to try and approach things in different ways.

Theatre

One of the greatest things that a writers' group can give you is a deadline. Usually at the end of a group's duration you're expected to hand in a draft of an original play. External deadlines can be a really motivating force to get you to finish your play. If you're not in a writers' group, I'd recommend finding other external deadlines, whether they're play-writing awards or theatre submissions windows. Whatever it is, find a deadline (with a realistic timeframe) so that there is somewhere you *have* to send a finished play to (no matter what state it's in).

Apart from seeking out the external impetus provided by award deadlines and writers' groups run by theatres, the biggest advice I'd give to any writer is to write the play that *you* need to write. Remember, those external forces are helpful on a purely pragmatic basis; use them for the time pressure they exert, but not as an artistic goalpost. When I was in the Royal Court writers' group, they made it very clear that we should not try to write whatever it is we thought a 'Royal Court play' was. Of course, there's always a part of you that hopes they'll read the first draft of the play you've written after the group finishes and say, 'Wow. This is perfect! We have to stage this immediately.' And that may just happen! Being a writer is about developing your own voice and creating work that speaks to what *you* care about.

So write the play that you need to write, the play that you've always wanted to see – whether you do it on your own, by taking a course, or by attending a writers' group. And when it's ready, the right theatre will find it.

Which brings us neatly onto our next step ...

Share the play

Once you've written your play, it's time to share it. Send it in for submissions windows, to literary departments, to 'scratch nights'. Send it far and wide. We writers – especially women – can be notoriously shy about sharing our work. Lisa Spirling (Artistic Director of Theatre 503) said, when I was on a panel with her, that men are much more likely to share their work with her, even when it's not very good, whereas women and non-binary writers are more likely to wait until they think their play is as close to perfect as possible before they do. News flash: your work is never going to be perfect, even in performance. The point of a new writing theatre is to find new writers – that's literally their job! And lots of them are very good at it. They might see some potential in your work, even if the draft you send in isn't perfect. So don't get in your own way, and do share your work.

That being said, I didn't send my play, *The High Table*, straight out to all the new writing theatres immediately on completion of my first draft. I sent it to lots of friends first. I sent

Scratch

Scratch is about sharing an idea with the public at an early stage of its development. When you scratch an idea, you can ask people questions and consider their feedback. This helps you work out how to take your idea on to the next stage. It's an iterative process that can be used again and again. Over time, ideas become stronger because they are informed by a wide-range of responses.

The feedback is an important part of the process but scratch is not about doing everything that people's feedback suggests; it is about using the responses to help you understand how people currently receive it and to help you shape your idea. The feedback doesn't have to be a Q&A, you can simply share your idea 'live' and, by doing this, you can often tell what works and what doesn't. Scratch recognises that when an idea does not fully succeed, or even when it crashes and burns, that there is great learning to be gathered.

© Battersea Arts Centre

it to people I trusted in the industry, whom I knew would give me their honest opinion. I also sent it into theatre companies with windows of submission that were just for feedback and got some thoughts back from them. However, nothing can compare to the dramaturgical support you get from someone who is interested in staging your text. I'd really recommend sharing your work with any directors you know, or can get an introduction to through your other contacts, and trying to organise a rehearsed reading.

A friend shared a call-out for LGBTQ+ plays and I sent my play to established playwright Tom Wright, who was organising some rehearsed readings alongside the opening of his play *My Dad's Gap Year* at the Park Theatre. When I met him, his approach to giving notes was so different from everyone else's. His feedback was bold, honest and practical. I often use the image of 'getting under the hood' when I talk about writing; well, Tom got under the hood of my play with me. And this was because he had a stake in it. Because it was a rehearsed reading, he was directly considering how the play would work in front of an audience. It gave the writing a new lease of life.

You learn so much about what needs to change in your play when you're collaborating and when you hear it read by actors. The redrafting carried out on *The High Table* during the rehearsed reading process was an instrumental step towards it eventually being staged. It was important not only for its creative development, but also because Tom championed the play to the Bush Theatre before I met their directorial team.

If you're planning to invite theatres to a rehearsed reading, make sure you give them lots of notice (at least a month) and then remind them again a week beforehand. A rehearsed reading is a great way of sharing your work because it's something to invite people to that brings your work off the page. Literary departments in theatres read a lot of plays, but they're in this industry because they love live theatre, and a rehearsed reading comes as close to that experience as possible.

On my podcast, *Making It with Temi Wilkey* (www.bushtheatre.co.uk/artists/podcast-making-it-with-temi-wilkey), I interview emerging playwrights about how they write and make a living. Ella Road's experience was very similar to mine. When we discussed the process of programming her play, *The Phlebotomist*, Ella told me that, although many theatre managers she invited to her rehearsed reading didn't end up coming, the literary manager of The Hampstead did – and that's how it came to be programmed and performed there in 2018.

The important thing about sharing your work is it increases your chances of it getting staged. Someone *might* bite. Here's what to do if they do.

Work with a theatre

If you're lucky enough to have a theatre interested in staging your work, my advice is: be open to their notes and work fast. When you meet them they're trying to suss out what it would be like to work with you. So be nice . . . but not too nice! If they're the right theatre for your play, they'll understand your work and their suggestions will illuminate the inconsistencies within your play and, hopefully, make you feel inspired and excited to write the next draft. But you know your text better than anyone. If their notes are wrong, disregard them; but listen with an open heart and, if their notes feel right, take them on board.

After the Bush Theatre read *The High Table*, I went in to speak to them and they gave me some great notes, most of which I agreed with, and then they said they'd be really

Theatre

interested in reading the next draft. They didn't give me any timelines, but Lynette Linton, the artistic director, said she was 'interested in it being quite quick'. Assuming they couldn't give me any firm deadlines without giving me a fee, I took the hint. Who knows what their actual programming timelines were?! This was my shot so, I turned the next draft around in a matter of days. Not everyone needs to do this, but it felt important for me to seem reliable. It was my first play and I knew that it might need more work in the run-up to it being staged, so I wanted to show them that I could take notes and come back on things if necessary, but ultimately be easy to work with and reliable in submitting drafts.

They liked the next draft and organised an internal reading of the play. After that, there was a lot of waiting around, a lot of anxiety, doubt. But eventually they said they wanted to programme it. Elation, happy screams and tears of joy ensued … and the rest is history. Ultimately, I think *The High Table* was staged because it found a home at the right theatre at the right time. They were interested in it because it fitted the artistic vision of the theatre and they were willing to invest their creative energy into making it happen.

It feels like it had a lot to do with luck. But, looking back, I realise that you can certainly help to create your luck by: 1) writing a play that's true to your artistic voice; 2) sharing it far and wide and getting feedback to develop it; and if a theatre shows interest in it, 3) doing your very best to prove that you can deliver.

Temi Wilkey is an actor and playwright. She studied English at Cambridge University before training with the National Youth Theatre REP company in 2014. She was a member of the Royal Court's Young Writers' Group in 2017. Her debut play, *The High Table*, was produced at the Bush Theatre, London, in Lynette Linton's debut season and won the Stage Debut Award for Best Writer in 2020. She co-founded and co-directed the Drag King company, Pecs, performing in the sell-out runs of their shows at venues including Soho Theatre, The Yard and Tate Britain. She was a writer on season three of *Sex Education* for Netflix which won her a nomination for the NAACP award for Outstanding Writing in a Comedy Series. She has written two episodes for Disney+'s *Wedding Season*. Temi is currently adapting Bernardine Evaristo's Booker Prize-winning novel, *Girl, Woman, Other*. She is currently on the BFI Flare x BAFTA Crew programme mentored by Russell T. Davies.

How to write for the theatre

Gill Kirk shares her tried-and-tested formula for anyone drawn to writing for stage and screen, with advice on developing valuable connections, knowledge and skills, and embracing the challenge without losing the fun.

Writing for theatre – how is it done? Like anything else, there's a trick. There are five things you need. Keep those in mind, and you can't go far wrong.

The five essentials

The first: a passion for human connection.

The second: acceptance that to do anything well, you must commit to constantly improving your craft; art is no exception.

Third: heck – just goddamned playfulness.

Fourth: 'abundance' in self-help lingo, i.e. a furious refusal to be stingy and an embarrassing belief in creative incontinence.

Fifth: *dahlings*, it's theatre! You must understand a little (or even better, a lot) of our industry's economics.

You've already sussed that they're all equally important. Connect, build your craft, be playful, be abundant, be economically realistic. Interdependent, these five essentials nourish each other. Take care of them all and at the very least you'll enjoy yourself in the wonderful world of writing for theatre. (Worst? You might become a millionaire. Be careful …).

1. Passion for connection

What's that all about? In common with its cousins (circus, live music, stand-up and magic), theatre's where artifice, effort and creativity meet to go wild. Here, we surrender to the moment: anything could happen. You – the audience – are part of it. Because that's who theatre is for. If you want to see creations of yours on stage (oh, yes, you do!), with people paying to watch, you must take – and keep – people with you. Great connection-making is smart.

The best playwrights are passionate about connecting with other humans . They won't tell you what to feel, but will present a human in a predicament, so that you snag your heart on the jagged nails of their character. They won't bore, but *lure* you through their maze, 'til your Werther's Originals are forgotten loot, and you're unrecognisable from the 'you' of 7pm.

When you think 'I have this play I want to write …', first put yourself in the audience's seat. Imagine how you would love this story to unfold. Remember what delights you in theatre, what frustrates and even bores you. If your imagination's rusty, just loiter outside when an audience comes out – it's horribly educational. Or learn how to review plays (*don't* ever abuse this position; think carefully when you praise a show or warn an audience).

You need maximum audience contact, but that's not the only connection you need. Actors, directors, stage managers, venue teams and other writers will all fuel you through this exciting experience. Playwrights are questioning souls, and we're hard on ourselves. We need others to learn from and make our work better, to share the downs and the ups.

If you have these connections when you write, you will also improve your connection with yourself. And that will make you a better writer, too.

How can you make theatre connections?

Find online and real-life communities – writers' groups (especially those doing readings with actors). Use this book: see *Film, theatre and television* (page 530) and *Writers' organisations* (page 534). Don't assume small theatres can't work with writers; many offer incredible opportunities you won't get in larger spaces. Build connections through social media, if you're that way inclined. And above all, *meet* people. I'm a long-term single parent, free-lancing outside London – I know this can be hard. But the theatre connections I've made have been life-changing .

I've a photo on my phone of a gang of my mates at night, laughing and pointing at an illuminated poster, and it's my name on the poster they're pointing at – because it's in lights. And behind that picture sprawls a criss-cross of connections made over the last 12 years. In 2011, I met a director at a 24 Hour Play (https://24hourplays.com) show. In 2019, I ran a workshop for her theatre company, because my day job is in strategic communications, and we agreed they should stop looking so hard for stories – it was exhausting and the fun had leaked a little, all over the floor. Almost too late, I realised this was advice I should take myself, and headed off on holiday to Pitlochry. I promised myself I would not write. Nor would I go to the lovely theatre there – instead, I would just *live*.

But what normal human being can do a day-long walk and NOT invent a story? I didn't write it down, I just recorded it on my phone … every minute or so. On the last night of the holidays, I caved in and visited the theatre, and, incredibly, the actor from a 2010 one-man short play of mine was in the cast. A chatty front of house staffer noticed that I appeared to know someone in the show and persuaded me to buy a ticket, stay after and say hello (what a salesman!). So I did, and the actor said nice things about my writing, and told me that there were great writers' opportunities there; why didn't I drop the new work team a wee line…? I sent them the bonkers collection of ideas from that day-long walk – and they offered me a residency.

I applied for grants to cover the costs (Society of Authors, Peggy Ramsay Trust – see page 495 and page 585) and had ten amazing days in Pitlochry to develop the show. A few months later, my small local theatre gave me space for a day and a night to run a workshop and 'script in hand'. A kindly West End producer I'd met through two local writers, as well as an actor-director from a writers' group, gathered together a cast and crew. We would pay them through £5 tickets and what was left of the grant funding. The producer then spotted an opportunity to show the play at the New Wimbledon Theatre; we applied and won the slot. But then Covid arrived … I lost my team, and assumed I'd lost the New Wimbledon. I asked everyone for help; they helped, but I couldn't find a new director or producer. Then I asked a woman I'd only ever met on Twitter: Maybe she knew people who'd want this great opportunity – a theatre, a script? And yes, she knew someone: herself. With incredible energy, she found a team and got the show on the road.

A week before our London show, I was working for a friend at a posh event he was running. There, I met the editor of a local culture mag. She ran a piece on me and the play. Months later, an old copy of that mag lay on a cafe table, when this *Yearbook*'s editor came to my town. And here we are – you couldn't (I didn't) make it up. Of course, at times I've hidden away, and said no to stuff. But look where the yeses can get you. This is why connection matters.

2. Improving your craft

Before my work got on stage, I'd done no formal learning about scripts or stories. It was writers, directors and actors who taught me so much, by having me in rehearsals, doing readings, sharing work and feedback. Then, thanks to script development with Bath's Theatre Royal and a run at Bath's Rondo Theatre, my second script won me a place on the incredible 4Screenwriting programme run by Channel 4 (they select 12 writers from thousands of entrants). Here I realised that, to write an hour of TV, I needed solid craft guidelines and I taught myself story structure. I use this every day, beyond scriptwriting, as a professional communicator and non-professional parent. There are a billion books on story structure, but you can see my 'easy-to-remember' guide (using 1970s kids' TV icon *Mr Benn*) on my blog at https://gillkirk.com/2014/01/20/and-as-if-by-magic-the-story-structure-appeared.

I rework every single script with other people. If it's not a commissioned work, I pay a dramaturg and/or gather a group of actors I've met through small readings and scratch nights (again, promising sources of crowdfunder cash or copious offers of new connections, cake and coffee). You cannot do this alone.

3. Playfulness

Why are we here … to bore? Who are we here for … us?

'Of course not, Gill!', I hear you roar. 'We want to transport people. Challenge, tease, excite, soothe, calm, provoke.' Excellent news.

This doesn't need much explaining. Just don't take yourself too seriously, even when writing the most gothic grimness. This is play. What you make and present is a gift. Keep a place inside yourself that's light. It will make everything else (craft, connection, abundance and economics) much more fun. If you haven't already, check out Elizabeth Gilbert's *Big Magic* (Riverhead Books 2015), *Impro* (Methuen Drama 2007) by Keith Johnstone and *The Games People Play* (Penguin Life 2016) by Eric Berne. And if you can't do that, as Nina says in Anthony Minghella's *Truly, Madly, Deeply*, 'Say "bum" and "Trotsky" twice a day before meals.'

4. Abundance

Abundance? Why? Answer: so you can kill your darlings. What?! How horrible. No, how wonderful! As you see with connection and play and craft, a good playwright has to be generous and know when to give things away. Don't hold back. Get it out. Share so you can improve, then write another one.

I often found (especially at the start) that collaborators would ask, 'Why's this character even here?' 'What does this line mean?' Then I'd realise: we were looking at 'legacy text' – cold leftovers from the first draft that I couldn't bear to bin. But a play isn't for the writer. After a few years, you realise there's a whole universe of people, places and circumstances inside you who've never yet met a stage and that's OK. They're still useful – they have opinions about people and stuff; they might help you grow new worlds. But if you are 'mean' (afraid) with your writing, if you hold too tight, and find it too hard to take feedback (or to give it well), you harm your craft. It's a paradox, but, in short, don't worry about getting it right. Just get it written. Lots of it. Then expose it to air. This will improve your craft.

5. Economics

If you think theatre tickets are expensive, try actually making theatre. Now that's expensive – and ticket sales rarely cover the costs. It means everyone is underpaid and people give too much of their time for free. Don't exploit them. This thing we do is a huge privilege. That means working-class writers – especially women – are rare; it's hard to write, unpaid, when your priorities are caring, clothing, housing. So, no matter your personal circumstances, when you build connections with commissioners who can pay for scripts (companies, venues, producers) talk to them about money. Ask about their writing budgets and funds for everything else; ask what grants are available. Check the WGGB (Writers' Guild of Great Britain; see page 498) writers' fee levels and Equity's rates cards (www.equity.org.uk) and work out how much your five-person show will cost to rehearse and put on before you write it (don't forget director, stage manager, crew, insurance, space …). And don't let money get you down. Theatre economics are always tough, yet we make magic all the time. We crowdfund. We cry at Arts Councils. And do amazing things on the cheap. But it's part of your job to understand how it works – you're creating employment for others.

Alongside this, know that playwriting isn't likely to be your only career. The myth of the full-time, well-fed playwright comes from an age when the curse of inherited wealth meant a chap just had to find something to do. Remember, doing other paid work feeds your imagination and connection, so that you can be the writer that you're going to be. Yes, a playwright is a many-splendoured thing.

How to work in theatre? Connect, play, be abundant, build craft, know the economics. From your first five-minute creation, you are a playwright, joining a very wonderful fellowship. In the last week, I've workshopped with 70 year-old and 20 year-old first-timers, seen a friend's new show, gloom-Zoomed with the new and 'famous', and – best of all – a mate of mine from a HighTide (https://hightide.org.uk) workshop a decade ago just won the Women's Prize. Welcome to the fold.

Gill Kirk is a scriptwriter and playwright whose work includes *Skin in the Game*, at New Wimbledon Theatre. She worked as a political lobbyist before setting up her own strategic communications consultancy in 2005. For more information see https://gillkirk.com, with links to her blog. Follow her on Twitter @gill_kirk.

See also...
- *How to get your play published and performed*, page 373
- *Prizes and awards*, page 543

Theatre producers

This list is divided into metropolitan theatres (below), regional theatres (page 384) and touring companies (page 390). See also *Literary agents for television, film, radio and theatre* on page 767.

There are various types of theatre companies and it is helpful to know their respective remits. Many of those that specialise in new writing are based in London (for example, Hampstead Theatre, Royal Court, Bush Theatre, Soho Theatre), but also include the Royal Exchange Manchester, Everyman Theatre Liverpool, Leeds Playhouse, etc. Regional repertory theatre companies are based in towns and cities across the country and may produce new plays as part of their repertoire. Commercial production companies and independent producers typically are unsubsidised profit-making theatre producers who may occasionally be interested in new plays to take on tour or to present in the West End. Small- or middle-scale touring companies explore or promote specific themes or may be geared towards specific kinds of audiences.

You may also be able to find independent theatre producers who could be keen to collaborate, especially at the start of their careers, or consider drama schools or amateur companies, both of which sometimes develop and produce new work. See the *Actors' & Performers' Yearbook* (Bloomsbury; published annually in October) for further information.

LONDON

Almeida Theatre
Almeida Street, London N1 1TA
email info@almeida.co.uk
website https://almeida.co.uk
Twitter @AlmeidaTheatre
Instagram @almeida_theatre
Artistic Director Rupert Goold, *Executive Director* Denise Wood, *Literary Manager* Stephanie Bain, *Director of Participation and Work for Young People* Dani Parr

Stages approximately six shows per year, both new work (such as *The Secret Life of Bees*) and reimagined classics. Does not accept unsolicited scripts.

Offers a range of opportunities for young people, including the Young Creatives group (for those interested in creating musical theatre), the Young Company (for aspiring actors), Young Producers, Young Designers and Technicians, and a Youth Advisory Board. Also works with schools in a variety of ways, including free tickets, bespoke workshops, career tasters and teacher training.

The Bridge Theatre
3 Potters Fields Park, London SE1 2SG
tel 0333 320 0052
email info@bridgetheatre.co.uk
website www.bridgetheatre.co.uk
Twitter @bridgetheatre
Co-directors Nicholas Hytner, Nick Starr

Home of the London Theatre Company. Focuses on the commissioning and production of new shows, as well as staging the occasional classic. Founded 2017.

Bush Theatre
7 Uxbridge Road, London W12 8LJ
tel (admin) 020-8743 3584
email info@bushtheatre.co.uk
website www.bushtheatre.co.uk/artists/get-involved/submissions
Twitter @bushtheatre
Artistic Director Lynette Linton

Home to hundreds of groundbreaking premieres since its inception in 1972 – many of them Bush commissions – and has hosted guest productions by leading companies and artists from around the world. Check the website for submissions windows and full guidelines, including information on unsolicited submissions.

Donmar Warehouse
41 Earlham Street, Seven Dials, London WC2H 9LX UK
email office@donmarwarehouse.com
website www.donmarwarehouse.com
Twitter @DonmarWarehouse
Instagram @donmarwarehouse
Artistic Director Michael Longhurst, *Executive Director* Henny Finch, *Literary Manager* Craig Gilbert

Independent producing house. Recent productions include *The Band's Visit*, *Watch on the Rhine* and *Trouble in Butetown*.

Works with new writers through training programmes but does not accept unsolicited scripts. Authors may invite Donmar staff to see their plays by contacting them on the above email, at least four weeks before the production opens. Also works with young audiences via its LOCAL programme, schools partnerships and school performances.

Finborough Theatre

118 Finborough Road, London SW10 9ED
tel 020-7244 7439
email literaryteam@finboroughtheatre.co.uk
website https://finboroughtheatre.co.uk/literary/
Facebook www.facebook.com/FinboroughTheatre
Twitter @finborough
Instagram @finboroughtheatre
Artistic Director Neil McPherson

Presents new writing, revivals of neglected plays from 1800 onwards, music theatre and UK premieres of foreign work. All productions are on a box office split. There are no rental fees. Unsolicited scripts are accepted, but see literary policy on website before sending. Also runs writers' development programme. Founded 1980.

Hampstead Theatre

Eton Avenue, London NW3 3EU
tel 020-7449 4200
email info@hampsteadtheatre.com
website www.hampsteadtheatre.com
Twitter @Hamps_Theatre

Designed with writers in mind, allowing for flexible staging within an intimate main house auditorium and a second studio space. Accepts full-length plays from agented and unagented UK-based writers throughout the year.

Jermyn Street Theatre

16B Jermyn Street, London SW1Y 6ST
email info@jermynstreettheatre.co.uk
website www.jermynstreettheatre.co.uk/work-with-us/
Facebook www.facebook.com/JSTheatre
Instagram @jermynstreettheatre
Artistic Director Stella Powell-Jones, *Executive Director and Co-founder* Penny Horner, *Executive Producer* David Doyle

Programmed and receiving house in central London. Stages new plays (by writers such as Esther Freud and Stephen Berkoff), revivals (Ibsen, Coward and Sondheim, for example), new versions of European classics and high-quality musicals, as well as one-off musical and literary events. Collaborates with theatres around the world, and over recent years has expanded into online work and theatre-on-film.
Does not accept unsolicited scripts; production proposals preferred. Works mostly with mid-career or established authors, but open to emerging voices. Synopses should be emailed in the first instance. Winner of Fringe Theatre of the Year 2021 at *The Stage* Awards. Founded 1994.

Bill Kenwright Ltd

BKL House, 1 Venice Walk, London W2 1RR
tel 020 7446 6200
email info@kenwright.com
website www.kenwright.com
Twitter @BKL_Productions
Managing Director Bill Kenwright

Award-winning prolific commercial theatre and film production company, presenting revivals and new works for the West End, international and regional theatres. Productions include *Blood Brothers*, *Heathers*, and *The Shawshank Redemption*.

Kiln Theatre

269 Kilburn High Road, London NW6 7JR
tel 020-7372 6611
email info@kilntheatre.com
website https://kilntheatre.com
Twitter @KilnTheatre
Artistic Director Indhu Rubasingham, *New Work Associate* Tom Wright

Presents at least six productions per year, aiming to provoke debate and engage the audience. Many of these are commissioned and written specifically for the theatre, or are programmed in collaboration with national or international companies. Unable to accept unsolicited submissions. Formerly the Tricycle Theatre.

King's Head Theatre

115 Upper Street, London N1 1QN
tel 020-7226 8561
email info@kingsheadtheatre.com
website www.kingsheadtheatre.com
Twitter @KingsHeadThtr
Artistic Director Mark Ravenhill, *Associate Director* Hannah Price

Off-West End theatre producing opera, LGBTQI+ plays and revivals.

Lyric Hammersmith

Lyric Square, King Street, London W6 0QL
tel 020-8741 6850
email enquiries@lyric.co.uk
website www.lyric.co.uk
Twitter @LyricHammer
Artistic Director Rachel O'Riordan

West London's largest producing and receiving theatre. Unsolicited scripts for in-house productions not accepted.

Neal Street Productions Ltd

1st Floor, 26–28 Neal Street, London WC2H 9QQ
tel 020-7240 8890
email post@nealstreetproductions.com
website www.nealstreetproductions.com
Twitter @NealStProds
Founders Sam Mendes, Pippa Harris, Caro Newling

Film, TV and theatre producer of new work and revivals. No unsolicited scripts or treatments; work accepted only via an agent. Founded 2003.

The Old Red Lion Theatre

418 St John Street, London EC1V 4NJ
tel 020-7837 7816
email info@oldredliontheatre.co.uk
website www.oldredliontheatre.co.uk
Facebook www.facebook.com/oldredliontheatre/
Twitter @ORLTheatre
Executive Director Damien Devine

Interested in contemporary pieces, especially from unproduced writers. No funding: incoming production company pays to rent the theatre. All submissions should be sent via email. Founded 1977.

Orange Tree Theatre

1 Clarence Street, Richmond, Surrey TW9 2SA
tel 020-8940 0141
email literary@orangetreetheatre.co.uk
website www.orangetreetheatre.co.uk
Facebook www.facebook.com/OrangeTreeTheatre
Twitter @OrangeTreeThtr
Artistic Director Tom Littler, *Literary Associate* Guy Jones

Producing theatre presenting a mixture of new work, contemporary revivals and rediscoveries in an intimate in-the-round space. Unsolicited work is not accepted but writers should visit the website for up-to-date information about opportunities. Enquiries can be addressed to the Literary Associate at the email address above.

The Questors Theatre

12 Mattock Lane, London W5 5BQ
email enquiries@questors.org.uk
website www.questors.org.uk
Facebook www.facebook.com/questorstheatre/
Twitter @questorstheatre
Executive Director Doug King

Largest independent community theatre in Europe. Produces 15–20 shows a year, specialising in modern and classical world drama. Visiting productions hosted too. No unsolicited scripts. Also runs a youth theatre for young people aged between 6–18, as well as summer workshops.

Royal Court Theatre

(English Stage Company Ltd)
Sloane Square, London SW1W 8AS
tel 020-7565 5050
email literary@royalcourttheatre.com
website https://royalcourttheatre.com/script-submissions
Twitter @royalcourt
Interim Executive Director Erica Campayne, *Literary Manager* Jane Fallowfield

Programmes new plays that ask bold questions about today's world: these should be original in form or theme and unlikely to be produced elsewhere. Submissions accepted all year round using online submissions portal only. Authors with access should contact the theatre via the email address above.

Royal National Theatre

South Bank, London SE1 9PX
tel 020-7452 3333
email scripts@nationaltheatre.org.uk
website www.nationaltheatre.org.uk
Twitter @NationalTheatre
Artistic Director Rufus Norris

New Work Department considers submissions from the UK and Ireland. No synopses, treatments or hard copy submissions; full-length scripts (minimum playing time one hour) can be sent in as pdfs or Word documents to the email address above.

@sohoplace

4 Soho Place, Charing Cross Road, London W1D 3BG
email info@sohoplace.org
website https://sohoplace.org/
Twitter @sohoplacelondon
Instagram @sohoplace
Founder and Producer Nica Burns

Flexible 602-seat in-the-round auditorium with programming that aims to push theatre boundaries. The first new-build West End Theatre for fifty years. Founded 2022.

Soho Theatre

21 Dean Street, London W1D 3NE
tel 020-7478 0117
email submissions@sohotheatre.com
website https://sohotheatre.com/project/writers-lab
Twitter @sohotheatre
Executive Director Mark Godfrey, *Creative Director* David Luff

Aims to discover and develop new playwrights, produce a year-round programme of new plays and attract new audiences. Producing venue of new plays, cabaret and comedy. The Writers' Lab offers support for new writers over a nine-month drafting process. Founded 1972.

Theatre Royal, Stratford East

Gerry Raffles Square, London E15 1BN
tel 020-8534 7374
website www.stratfordeast.com
Twitter @stratfordeast
Artistic Director Nadia Fall, *Executive Director* Eleanor Lang

Middle-scale producing theatre. Specialises in new writing, including developing contemporary British musicals. Welcomes new plays that are unproduced, full in length, and which relate to its diverse multicultural, Black and Asian audience.

Unicorn Theatre

147 Tooley Street, London SE1 2HZ
tel 020-7645 0560
email hello@unicorntheatre.com
website www.unicorntheatre.com
Facebook www.facebook.com/unicorntheatre
Twitter @unicorn_theatre
Artistic Director Justin Audibert, *Co-Executive Directors* Bailey Lock, Helen Tovey

Produces a year-round programme of theatre for children and young people under 21. In-house productions of full-length plays with professional casts are staged across two auditoria, alongside visiting companies and education work. Rarely commissions plays from writers who are new to it, but it is keen to hear from writers who are interested in working with the theatre in the future. Do not send unsolicited MSS, but submit a short statement describing why you would like to write for the Unicorn along with a CV or a summary of your relevant experience.

White Bear Theatre Club

138 Kennington Park Road, London SE11 4DJ
tel 07496 442747
email info@whitebeartheatre.co.uk
website https://whitebeartheatre.co.uk
Twitter @WhiteBearTheatr
Artistic Director Michael Kingsbury

Metropolitan new writing theatre company. Welcomes scripts from new writers: send queries to whitebearliterary@gmail.com. Founded 1988.

Young Vic Theatre Company

66 The Cut, London SE1 8LZ
tel 020-7922 2922
email programming@youngvic.org
website www.youngvic.org
Facebook www.facebook.com/youngvictheatre
Twitter @youngvictheatre
Artistic Director Kwame Kwei-Armah, *Executive Director* Lucy Davies

Leading London producing theatre. Unsolicited scripts are not accepted, but proposals and outlines can be submitted via Dropbox on the Young Vic website. Artists can also invite members of the artistic team to see their work via the email above; invitations should give at least four weeks' notice. Founded 1969.

REGIONAL

Abbey Theatre Amharclann na Mainistreach

26 Lower Abbey Street, Dublin D01 K0F1, Republic of Ireland
tel +353 (0)1 8872200
email info@abbeytheatre.ie
website www.abbeytheatre.ie
Twitter @AbbeyTheatre
Artistic Director Caitríona McLaughlin, *Executive Director* Mark O'Brien, *Literary and New Work Director* Ruth McGowan

Ireland's national theatre. The Abbey Theatre commissions and produces new Irish writing and contemporary productions from the canon, alongside hosting and presenting work by other Irish and international artists and companies

Yvonne Arnaud Theatre Management Ltd

Millbrook, Guildford, Surrey GU1 3UX
tel (01483) 440077
email yat@yvonne-arnaud.co.uk
website www.yvonne-arnaud.co.uk
Twitter @YvonneArnaud
Director and Chief Executive Joanna Read

Producing theatre which also receives productions. Runs activities for education providers throughout the year.

The Belgrade Theatre

Belgrade Square, Coventry CV1 1GS
tel 024-7625 6431
email admin@belgrade.co.uk
website www.belgrade.co.uk
Twitter @BelgradeTheatre
Creative Director Corey Campbell

Repertory theatre producing drama, comedy and musicals. Does not accept unsolicited scripts; email short synopses first to the address above. Runs a series of training development opportunities, including its Springboard initiative.

Birmingham Repertory Theatre Ltd

Broad Street, Birmingham B1 2EP
tel 0121 245 2000
email stage.door@birmingham-rep.co.uk
website www.birmingham-rep.co.uk/take-part/talent-development/foundry
Twitter @BirminghamRep
Artistic Director Sean Foley

Oldest building-based theatre company in the UK. Aims to create artistically ambitious popular theatre for a wide audience. Presents over 60 productions on its three stages every year, as well as touring its productions nationally and internationally.

Well-established, diverse learning and outreach programme continues today with a youth theatre, and the Rep Foundry theatre-makers programme. Commissioning and production of new work is a key plank of the theatre's mission: over the last 15 years, the company has produced more than 130 new plays. See website for forthcoming opportunities. Founded 1913.

The Bootleg Theatre Company

23 Burgess Green, Bishopdown, Salisbury,
Wilts. SP1 3EL
tel (01722) 421476
email colinburden281@gmail.com
website www.bootlegtheatre.com/tearawayfilms
Contact Colin Burden

New writing theatre company whose recent
productions include *Girls Allowed* by Trevor Suthers,
A Rainy Night in Soho by Stephen Giles, and *The
Squeaky Clean* by Roger Goldsmith. Also produces
compilation productions of monologues/duologues:
these have included *15 Minutes of Fame*, *Tales from
The Street* and *Parting Shots*. Founded 1985.

Bristol Old Vic

King Street, Bristol BS1 4ED
tel 0117 949 3993
email admin@bristololdvic.org.uk
website https://bristololdvic.org.uk/for-artists/writers/
open-session
Twitter @BristolOldVic
Artistic Director Nancy Medina, *Executive Director*
Charlotte Geeves

Oldest theatre auditorium in UK (opened in 1766).
See website for more details on submission windows
and related requirements. The Bristol Old Vic
company was founded 1946.

Chichester Festival Theatre

Oaklands Park, Chichester, West Sussex PO19 6AP
tel (01243) 784437
email literary@cft.org.uk
website www.cft.org.uk
Twitter @chichesterFT
Executive Director Kate Bourne

Stages annual Summer Festival Season April–October
in the Festival and Minerva Theatres together with a
year-round education programme, winter touring
programme and youth theatre Christmas show. Does
not accept unsolicited scripts. The Learning,
Education and Participation (LEAP) department runs
a programme of events for all ages, including
workshops, performances, talks and tours.

Contact Theatre Company

Oxford Road, Manchester M15 6JA
tel 0161 274 0600
website https://contactmcr.com/
Twitter @ContactMcr
Artistic Director and Chief Executive Keisha
Thompson, *Head of Creative Development* Laura
Whitehurst

Multidisciplinary arts organisation focused on
working with and for young people aged 13 and
above. Offers a range of free projects, from writing to
music and drama, including the Contact Young
Company ensemble.

Creation Theatre Company

tel (01865) 766266
email boxoffice@creationtheatre.co.uk
website www.creationtheatre.co.uk
Facebook https://en-gb.facebook.com/
CreationTheatre
Twitter @creationtheatre
Instagram @creationtheatre
Chief Executive and Creative Producer Lucy Askew

Award-winning producing theatre company,
specialising in digital and site-specific inventive
theatre in extraordinary locations. Creators of
Creation Home Delivery, live & interactive online
drama classes for ages 5–16, designed to inspire a lifelong love of stories and storytelling. Also delivers
theatre and creativity classes for children during both
term time and the school holidays. Does not accept
unsolicited manuscripts.

Curve

Rutland Street, Leicester LE1 1SB
tel 0116 242 3560
email contactus@curvetheatre.co.uk
website www.curveonline.co.uk/artists/artist-
development
Twitter @CurveLeicester
Chief Executive Chris Stafford, *Artistic Director*
Nikolai Foster

Regional producing theatre company. Artist-
development opportunities include Curve Connect
and Writerslab programmes: the latter offers a
writer's course and twice-yearly script submission
window.

Derby Theatre

15 Theatre Walk, St Peter's Quarter, Derby DE1 2NF
email creatives@derbyplayhouse.co.uk
website www.derbytheatre.co.uk/about-us/in-good-
company
Facebook www.facebook.com/DerbyTheatre
Twitter @DerbyTheatre
Artistic Director and Chief Executive Sarah Brigham,
Creative Learning Director Caroline Barth

Regional producing and receiving theatre. The In
Good Company programme offers opportunities for
theatre-makers and companies in the region.

Druid

The Druid Building, Flood Street,
Galway H91 PWX5, Republic of Ireland
tel +353 (0)91 568660
email info@druid.ie
website www.druid.ie
Twitter @DruidTheatre
Artistic Director Garry Hynes

Producing theatre company presenting a wide range
of plays, with an emphasis on new Irish writing.
Submission window for scripts: July–September (see

website for details). Tours nationally and internationally.

The Dukes

Moor Lane, Lancaster LA1 1QE
tel (01524) 598500
email ask@dukes-lancaster.org
website https://dukes-lancaster.org
Twitter @TheDukesTheatre
Chief Executive Karen O'Neill

Producing theatre and cultural centre. Its Young Writers scheme was launched in January 2017. See website for up-to-date information about the theatre's productions and programming approach.

Dundee Rep and Scottish Dance Theatre Limited

Tay Square, Dundee DD1 1PB
tel (01382) 227684
email info@dundeereptheatre.co.uk
website www.dundeereptheatre.co.uk
Twitter @DundeeRep
Artistic Director (Dundee Rep)/Joint Chief Executive Andrew Panton, *Executive Director/Joint Chief Executive* Liam Sinclair

Regional repertory theatre company with resident ensemble. Mix of classics, musicals and new commissions.

Everyman Theatre Cheltenham

7 Regent Street, Cheltenham, Glos. GL50 1HQ
tel (01242) 512515
email admin@everymantheatre.org.uk
website www.everymantheatre.org.uk
Twitter @Everymanchelt
Creative Director Paul Milton

Regional presenting and producing theatre promoting a wide range of plays. Small-scale experimental, youth and educational work encouraged in The Studio Theatre. Contact the Creative Director before submitting material.

Exeter Northcott Theatre

Stocker Road, Exeter, Devon EX4 4QB
tel (01392) 722417
email info@exeternorthcott.co.uk
website www.exeternorthcott.co.uk
website www.exeternorthcott.co.uk/get-creative
Twitter @ExeterNorthcott
Interim Joint Ceos Emma Stephenson, Kelly Johnson

460-seat producing and receiving venue offering a varied programme of shows and touring productions. The Young Creatives programme offers a range of development and extension opportunities for theatre-makers from the age of 11.

Harrogate Theatre

Oxford Street, Harrogate, North Yorkshire HG1 1QF
tel (01423) 502710

email info@harrogatetheatre.co.uk
website www.harrogatetheatre.co.uk
Twitter @HGtheatre
Chief Executive David Bown, *Head of Education* Hannah Draper

Predominantly a receiving house; rarely produces productions in-house. Unsolicited scripts not accepted.

HOME: Theatre

2 Tony Wilson Place, First Street, Manchester M15 4FN
tel 0161 200 1500
email info@homemcr.org
website www.homemcr.org
Twitter @HOME_mcr
Director & Ceo Dave Moutrey

Purpose-built centre for international contemporary art, theatre and film. Hosts drama, dance, film and contemporary visual art with a strong focus on international work, new commissions and talent development. Founded 2015.

Leeds Playhouse

Playhouse Square, Quarry Hill, Leeds LS2 7UP
tel 0113 213 7700
website https://leedsplayhouse.org.uk
Twitter @LeedsPlayhouse
Artistic Director and Ceo James Brining

Seeks out the best companies and artists to create theatre in the heart of Yorkshire. Its artistic development programme, Furnace, discovers and supports new voices, while developing work with established practitioners. It provides a creative space for writers, directors, companies and individual theatre-makers to refine their practice at all stages of their career. The Creative Engagement team works with more than 12,000 people every year reaching out to refugee communities, young people, students, older people and people with learning challenges.

Live Theatre

Broad Chare, Quayside, Newcastle upon Tyne NE1 3DQ
tel 0191 232 1232
email info@live.org.uk
website www.live.org.uk
website www.live.org.uk/index.php/creative-opportunities/children-young-people/schools-teachers
Twitter @LiveTheatre
Executive Director & Joint Ceo Jacqui Kell, *Artistic Director & Joint Ceo* Jack McNamara

New writing theatre company and venue. Stages 3–6 productions per year of new writing, plus touring plays from other new writing companies. The Live Youth Theatre programme is free and open to young people between the ages of 10 and 25. CPD and Inset support for teachers is also available.

Troubador
Publishing Limited

The home of **Matador**

ABOUT US...

We help authors get published with bespoke, market-leading self-publishing services – taking authors and their books from manuscript to market.

WITH AUTHORS AT THE HEART OF ALL WE DO

We work in partnership with authors to design, create, publish, market, distribute and sell quality books across print and digital formats, putting customers at the heart of what we do. We use our 30 years' experience and expertise to give the best self-publishing experience – working with our authors to publish and sell beautiful books, making publishing dreams come true.

PRODUCTION, MARKETING, SALES AND DISTRIBUTION

We have unparalleled experience in book production. But far more, we have a retail trade and PR marketing department that can actively promote your work; and we have real bookshop distribution.

Our aim is to publish a book that you are proud of and then to get it sold.

OUR SERVICES...

BOOK PRODUCTION

From manuscript through editing, typesetting, design and print, we produce high-quality books using our market-leading services.

MARKETING

Our marketing experts use their experience to make retail buyers aware of your book and to get the media talking about it.

SALES AND RETAIL DISTRIBUTION

Our own warehousing, bookshop distribution and sales teams ensure seamless fulfilment of bookshop orders.

EBOOKS AND AUDIOBOOKS

Publishing your ebooks and audiobooks to the highest standard and distributing them worldwide.

NEXT STEPS?

Get started with a no-obligation conversation with one of our publishing team about what you want to achieve and how we can help you. What you'll get:

- The opportunity to ask a publishing professional anything about self-publishing
- Helpful advice from the best in the business on the options available to you
- Honest advice based on 30 years in the self-publishing business
- No obligation, commitment or hard sell.

Troubador Publishing
Unit E2, Airfield Business Park, Harrison Rd, Market Harborough

5.0 ★★★★★ 10 reviews

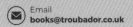

Troubador Publishing
Reviews 9 • Excellent
★★★★½

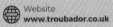
Phone
0116 279 2299

Email
books@troubador.co.uk

Website
www.troubador.co.uk

CREATIVE WRITING COURSES & EVENTS

In-person and Online Writing Weeks, Masterclasses, Writing Days and Weekly Readings

"My new notebook was soon overflowing with advice that changed my whole perspective on writing"

Grants and concessions available

Book now at arvon.org

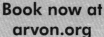

faber *academy*

Manuscript *Assessment*

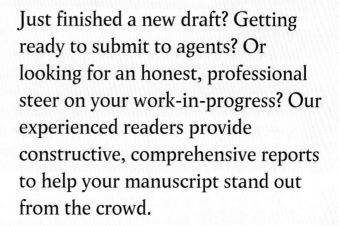

Just finished a new draft? Getting ready to submit to agents? Or looking for an honest, professional steer on your work-in-progress? Our experienced readers provide constructive, comprehensive reports to help your manuscript stand out from the crowd.

Book now with the code WAYB24 to receive a 10% discount

Visit faberacademy.com or call 0207 927 3827

We are a creative team of writers, authors, scriptwriters, academics, editors and journalists who adopt a team development approach to literary projects.

londonghostwriting.com

Who are we?

About Us

We are ghosts. We work on your behalf, unseen and confidential.

Established in 2016, The London Ghostwriting Company is a leading service in the production of submission and print ready ghostwritten manuscripts.

Editorials: CIEP Advanced Professionals providing developmental edits, line-edits and assessments with the support and supervision of a wider team.

Ghostwriting: Represented professionals providing story solutions in all forms, all managed in-house. Our team of pros write novels, memoirs, screenplays and non-fiction books as co-authors and ghostwriters.

londonghostwriting.com

info@londonghostwriting.com

@LGC_ghost

Your story, your book.

londonghostwriting.com

THE LONDON GHOSTWRITING COMPANY

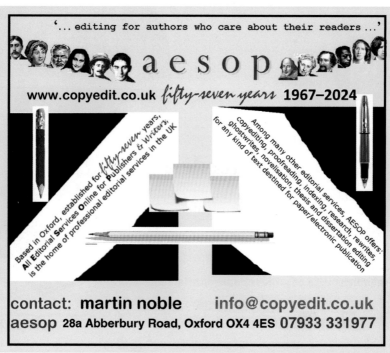

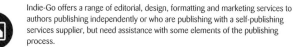

Inspired Authors,
Inspiring Readers

Mainstream & Partnership Publishing

The Book Guild Ltd has a solid reputation in publishing quality books for over 35 years. Authors are invited to submit manuscripts with commercial sales potential in all genres for consideration, particularly in non-fiction. All submissions are first considered for traditional publishing; if we do not feel a manuscript is suitable for traditional publishing, we then consider it for our partnership (co-funded) publishing option. We only make any sort of publishing offer on around 10% of submissions.

Traditional Publishing

Under our traditional publishing model, we bear all the costs of publishing, and we may also pay an advance on royalties to the author. Around 70% of our non-fiction and 30% of our fiction is published under our traditional publishing route.

Partnership (co-funded) Publishing

If we can't offer a traditional publishing arrangement for a manuscript, we may make a partnership publishing offer, but only if we believe the manuscript has commercial potential. Our co-funded option enables us to publish more risky commercial titles in partnership with the author, sharing the risk and (hopefully) rewards.

The Book Guild will always fund some of the costs of publishing under our Partnership Publishing arrangement, ranging from 25% to 75% of the cost. We do not offer a wholly author-financed option for publishing (i.e. self-publishing).

For further details and submission information, visit our website; or give us a call.

bookguild.co.uk

0800 999 2982   enquiries@bookguild.co.uk

The Book Guild Ltd is a subsidiary of Troubador Publishing Ltd

THE WRITERS' & ARTISTS' GUIDES

The bestselling Writers & Artists brand provides up-to-date, impartial and practical advice on how to write and get published.

Writers' & Artists' Guide to Writing for Children and YA
by Linda Strachan
978-1-4729-7005-3

Writers' & Artists' Guide to Getting Published
by Alysoun Owen
978-1-4729-5021-5

Writers' & Artists' Guide to Self-Publishing
978-1-4729-7029-9

Writers' & Artists' Guide to How to Hook an Agent
by James Rennoldson
978-1-4729-7007-7

Writers' & Artists' Guide to How to Write
by William Ryan
978-1-4729-7874-5

£16.99 each. Available from your local bookshop or online at
www.writersandartists.co.uk/shop

Writers&Artists

The essential toolkit on how to publish like a pro

www.writersandartists.co.uk

BLOOMSBURY PUBLISHING
LONDON · NEW DELHI · NEW YORK · SYDNEY

Liverpool Everyman and Playhouse

Liverpool and Merseyside Theatres Trust Ltd,
5–11 Hope Street, Liverpool L1 9BH
tel 0151 708 3700
email newworks@everymanplayhouse.com
website www.everymanplayhouse.com/script-submissions
Facebook www.facebook.com/everymanplayhouse
Twitter @LivEveryPlay
Chief Executive Mark Da Vanzo

Produces and presents theatre. Looks for original work from writers based within the Liverpool city region up to twice a year: email pdfs or Word documents along with a completed submission form during the regular submission windows (see website for this and further details of submission specifications).

Mercury Theatre Colchester

Balkerne Gate, Colchester, Essex CO1 1PT
tel (01206) 577006
email info@mercurytheatre.co.uk
website www.mercurytheatre.co.uk
Twitter @mercurytheatre
Executive Producer Tracey Childs, *Executive Director* Steve Mannix, *Creative Director* Ryan McBryde

Active producing theatre in East Anglia, aiming to put theatre at the heart of the community it serves and to make work in Colchester that reaches audiences regionally and nationally. Runs a comprehensive Creative Learning & Talent programme to support artists and theatre-makers at all stages of their development.

The New Theatre: Dublin

The New Theatre, Temple Bar, 43 East Essex Street, Dublin D02 XH92, Republic of Ireland
tel +353 (0)1 6703361
email thenewtheatre1997@gmail.com
website www.thenewtheatre.com
Artistic Director Anthony Fox, *Dramaturgs* Stephen Murray, Dee Burke, Jessica Traynor

Innovative theatre supporting plays by new Irish writers and others whose work deals with issues pertaining to contemporary Irish society. Welcomes scripts from new writers. Seats 66 people. Founded 1997.

New Vic Theatre

Etruria Road, Newcastle under Lyme ST5 0JG
tel (01782) 717954
email admin@newvictheatre.org.uk
website www.newvictheatre.org.uk
Twitter @NewVicTheatre
Artistic Director Theresa Heskins, *Managing Director* Fiona Wallace

Europe's first purpose-built theatre-in-the-round, presenting drama, contemporary and new plays, comedy and a range of one-night concerts. Also runs the award-winning Borderlines community programme and creative learning opportunities for ages 4 to adults.

The New Wolsey Theatre

Civic Drive, Ipswich, Suffolk IP1 2AS
tel (01473) 295900
email info@wolseytheatre.co.uk
website www.wolseytheatre.co.uk
Facebook www.facebook.com/NewWolsey
Twitter @NewWolsey
Instagram @newwolsey
Chief Executive/Artistic Director Douglas Rintoul

Mix of producing and presenting in 400-seater main house, studio and community building. Founded 2000.

Northern Stage (Theatrical Productions) Ltd

Barras Bridge, Newcastle upon Tyne NE1 7RH
tel 0191 242 7210
email info@northernstage.co.uk
website www.northernstage.co.uk
Twitter @northernstage
Artistic Director Natalie Ibu, *Executive Director* Kate Denby

The largest producing theatre company in the North-East of England. Presents local, national and international theatre across three stages and runs an extensive participation programme.

Nottingham Playhouse

Nottingham Playhouse Trust Ltd, Wellington Circus, Nottingham NG1 5AF
tel 0115 941 9419
website https://nottinghamplayhouse.co.uk/get-involved/young-people/
Twitter @NottmPlayhouse
Artistic Director Adam Penford, *Chief Executive* Stephanie Sirr

Seeks to nurture new writers from the East Midlands primarily through its Artist Development programme, Amplify. Also offers a range of groups and youth theatres for young people aged 2 and above; see website above for full details.

Octagon Theatre

Howell Croft South, Bolton BL1 1SB
tel (01204) 520661
email literary@octagonbolton.co.uk
website www.octagonbolton.co.uk
Twitter @octagontheatre
Chief Executive Roddy Gauld, *Artistic Director* Lotte Wakeham

Fully flexible professional theatre, which reopened in summer 2021 following extensive refurbishment. Year-round programme of own productions and visiting companies, including a studio theatre for creative engagement, family theatre, new work and emerging artists.

Queen's Theatre, Hornchurch

Billet Lane, Hornchurch, Essex RM11 1QT
tel (01708) 443333
email info@queens-theatre.co.uk
website www.queens-theatre.co.uk
website www.queens-theatre.co.uk/get-involved/
youth-theatre
Twitter @QueensTheatreH
Executive Director Mathew Russell

Regional theatre working in outer East London, Essex
and beyond. Each annual programme includes home-
grown theatre, visiting live entertainment and
learning and participation projects.

Royal Exchange Theatre Company Ltd

St Ann's Square, Manchester M2 7DH
tel 0161 833 9833
email suzanne.bell@royalexchange.co.uk
website www.royalexchange.co.uk/literary-new-
writing
website www.writeaplay.co.uk
Facebook www.facebook.com/rx
Twitter @rxtheatre
Executive Director Steve Freeman, *Artistic Directors*
Bryony Shanahan and Roy Alexander Weise, *New
Writing Associate* Suzanne Bell

Varied programme of major classics, new plays,
musicals, contemporary British and European drama.
Focus on new writing, writer development, creative
collaborations and community participation. (See
website for forthcoming script submission windows
for writers based in the North West. Facilitates and
delivers the Bruntwood Prize for Playwriting
biennially (see second website listed above).

Royal Lyceum Theatre Company

30B Grindlay Street, Edinburgh EH3 9AX
tel 0131 248 4800
email info@lyceum.org.uk
website www.lyceum.org.uk
Twitter @lyceumtheatre
Artistic Director David Greig

Producing theatre with a diverse year-round
programme of classic, contemporary and new drama.
Interested in the work of Scottish writers.

Royal Shakespeare Company

The Royal Shakespeare Theatre, Waterside,
Stratford-upon-Avon, Warks. CV37 6BB
tel (01789) 296655
email newwork@rsc.org.uk
website www.rsc.org.uk
website https://37plays.co.uk
Facebook www.facebook.com/thersc
Twitter @TheRSC
Co-artistic Directors Daniel Evans, Tamara Harvey,
Head of New Work Pippa Hill

Produces Shakespeare's plays alongside new work by
contemporary writers and the work of Shakespeare's

contemporaries on its two main stages, the Royal
Shakespeare Theatre and the Swan Theatre. In
addition, its studio theatre, The Other Place,
produces cutting-edge new work. For all its stages,
the Company commissions new plays, new
translations and new adaptations that illuminate the
themes and concerns of Shakespeare and his
contemporaries for a modern audience. The Literary
department does not accept unsolicited work but
rather seeks out writers it wishes to work with or
commission, and monitors the work of writers in
production in the UK and internationally. Writers are
welcome to invite the Literary department to
readings, showcases or productions by emailing the
address above.

Salisbury Playhouse

Malthouse Lane, Salisbury, Wilts. SP2 7RA
tel (01722) 320117; box office (01722) 320333
email info@wiltshirecreative.co.uk
website www.wiltshirecreative.co.uk
Facebook www.facebook.com/wiltscreative
Twitter @wiltscreative
Artistic Director Gareth Machin, *Executive Director*
Sebastian Warrack

Regional producing and presenting theatre with a
broad programme of classical and contemporary
plays in two auditoria. Does not accept unsolicited
scripts. The Playhouse is committed to a programme
of original drama with a particular focus on South-
West writers. Please check website for current
information on script submission.

Shakespeare North Playhouse

Prospero Place, Prescot L34 3AB
tel 0151 433 7156
email artists@shakespearenorthplayhouse.co.uk
website https://shakespearenorthplayhouse.co.uk/
create-participate/artists/#artists-4
Twitter @ShakespeareNP
Instagram @shakespearenorthplayhouse
Chief Executive Melanie Lewis, *Creative Director and
Programmer* Laura Collier

Performances (theatre, music, comedy), workshops,
events and activities inspired by Shakespeare but
relevant to modern audiences. The venue's
seventeenth-century-style Cockpit Theatre seats 450
spectators, and can be configured into two
formations: end-on and in-the-round. The venue is
also home to a fully-accessible outdoor performance
garden funded by the Ken Dodd Charitable
Foundation, exhibition gallery, 60-seater studio
theatre, learning centre, events spaces, and a cafe and
bar with outdoor piazza.
    Committed to working with local artists in order
to develop innovative, diverse work: contact the
Culture and Learning team via the email above with
information in the first instance (see website for
guidance). Unsolicited scripts not accepted. Named

Theatre Building of the Year at *The Stage* Awards 2023. Founded 2022.

Sheffield Theatres

(Crucible, Tanya Moiseiwitsch Playhouse & Lyceum)
55 Norfolk Street, Sheffield S1 1DA
tel 0114 249 5999
website www.sheffieldtheatres.co.uk
Chief Executive Tom Bird

Large-scale producing house with distinctive thrust stage; mid-scale flexible space; Victorian proscenium arch theatre used mainly for touring productions.

Sherman Theatre

Senghennydd Road, Cardiff CF24 4YE
tel 029-2064 6900
website www.shermantheatre.co.uk/theatre-makers
Twitter @shermantheatre
Chief Executive Julia Barry, *Artistic Director* Joe Murphy

Produces new work and revivals. Seeks to stage high-quality and innovative drama with a local, national or international perspective. Develops work by Welsh and Wales-based writers, both in English and Welsh. Participatory work with youth theatres, community engagement, and mentorship of new artists. Check website for information on forthcoming submission windows for unsolicited scripts (typically 2 per year). Founded 2007.

Show of Strength Theatre Company Ltd

74 Chessel Street, Bedminster, Bristol BS3 3DN
tel 0117 953 5976
email info@showofstrength.org.uk
website www.showofstrength.org.uk
Facebook www.facebook.com/showofstrength
Twitter @Showofstrength
Creative Producer Sheila Hannon

Small-scale company committed to producing new and unperformed work. Unsolicited scripts not accepted. Founded 1986.

Stephen Joseph Theatre

Westborough, Scarborough,
North Yorkshire YO11 1JW
tel (01723) 370540
email scripts@sjt.uk.com
website www.sjt.uk.com/aboutus/new_writing
Twitter @thesjt

Regional repertory theatre company presenting approx. 5 productions a year, many of which are premieres. Unsolicited scripts accepted from represented and unrepresented writers; see website for details.

Swansea Grand Theatre

Singleton Street, Swansea SA1 3QJ
tel (01792) 475715
email swansea.grandmarketing@swansea.gov.uk
website www.swanseagrand.co.uk
Facebook www.facebook.com/swanseagrandtheatre
Twitter @swanseagrand
Theatre Manager Paul Hopkins

Regional receiving theatre.

Theatr Clwyd

Mold, Flintshire CH7 1YA
tel (01352) 344101
email writers@theatrclwyd.com
website www.theatrclwyd.com
Twitter @ClwydTweets

Largest producing theatre in Wales, creating up to 14 productions each year in English, Welsh and bilingually. Productions are a mix of classic plays, contemporary revivals, musicals and new writing. Will consider plays by writers, particularly Welsh, Wales-based or with Welsh themes, and usually offers 6 writing residencies each year. No literary department, so authors should expect to wait for a response to unsolicited scripts.

Theatre Royal Bath

Sawclose, Bath BA1 1ET
tel (01225) 448815
website www.theatreroyal.org.uk
Twitter @TheatreRBath
Director Danny Moar

One of the oldest theatres in Britain. Comprising three auditoria – the Main House, the Ustinov Studio Theatre and the Egg Theatre for children and young people – the Theatre Royal offers a varied programme of entertainment all year round.

Theatre Royal Plymouth

Royal Parade, Plymouth PL1 2TR
tel (01752) 668282
email literary@theatreroyal.com
website www.theatreroyal.com
Twitter @TRPlymouth
Chief Executive Officer and Executive Producer James Mackenzie-Blackman

Specialises in the production of new plays. Its engagement and learning work engages young people and communities in Plymouth and beyond. The award-winning waterfront production and learning centre, TR2, offers set, costume, prop-making and rehearsal facilities.

Theatre Royal Windsor

32 Thames Street, Windsor, Berks. SL4 1PS
tel (01753) 863444
email info@theatreroyalwindsor.co.uk
website www.theatreroyalwindsor.co.uk
Facebook www.facebook.com/TheatreWindsor/
Twitter @TheatreWindsor
Executive Producer Bill Kenwright, *Co-Directors* Anne-Marie Woodley, Jon Woodley

Theatre

Regional producing theatre presenting a wide range of productions, from classics to new plays.

Traverse Theatre

10 Cambridge Street, Edinburgh EH1 2ED
tel 0131 228 3223
website www.traverse.co.uk
Twitter @traversetheatre
Artistic Director Gareth Nicholls

Annual programme of creative writing and talent development opportunities, including workshops, casting calls and networking events – see website for further details.

Visible Fictions

Suite 325/327, 4th Floor, 11 Bothwell Street, Glasgow G2 6LY
email laura@visiblefictions.co.uk
website https://visiblefictions.co.uk
Twitter @visiblefictions
Artistic Director Dougie Irvine, *Producer* Laura Penny

Specialises in professional productions for young audiences and their families across a range of artforms, from theatre to film, puppetry to immersive experiences. Also works in creative learning settings – community, educational, institutional, and professional – to make bespoke projects to accompany and enhance artistic experiences of young audiences.

Watford Palace Theatre

20 Clarendon Road, Watford, Herts. WD17 1JZ
tel (01923) 225671
website www.watfordpalacetheatre.co.uk
Twitter @watfordpalace

Regional theatre. Produces and co-produces seasonally, both classic and contemporary drama and new writing. Accepts unsolicited scripts from Hertfordshire-based writers.

York Theatre Royal

St Leonard's Place, York YO1 7HD
tel (01904) 658162
website www.yorktheatreroyal.co.uk
Facebook www.facebook.com/yorktheatreroyal
Twitter @yorktheatre
Instagram @yorktheatreroyal
Creative Director Juliet Forster

Repertory productions, tours.

TOURING COMPANIES

Actors Touring Company

email atc@atctheatre.com
website www.atctheatre.com
Facebook www.facebook.com/actorstouringcompany
Twitter @ATCLondon
Instagram @actorstouringcompanyatc
Artistic Director Matthew Xia

Small- to medium-scale touring company producing international new writing and new plays by global and global majority writers, for audiences in the UK and internationally. Does not accept unsolicited scripts.

Boundless Theatre

Big Local Works, 4 Market Place, South Bermondsey, London SE16 3UQ
tel 020 7072 0140
email hello@boundlesstheatre.org.uk
website www.boundlesstheatre.org.uk
website https://boundlesstheatre.org.uk/projects/accelerator
Instagram @boundlessabound
Artistic Director and Ceo Rob Drummer

Creates new plays with and for audiences aged 15 to 25. Tours the UK and internationally. Its Accelerator programme helps new voices develop their work; there is a cash bursary of £2,500, alongside other sources of support. Founded 2001 (as Company of Angels).

Eastern Angles

Eastern Angles Centre, Gatacre Road, Ipswich IP1 2LQ
tel (01473) 218202
email admin@easternangles.co.uk
website www.easternangles.co.uk
Twitter @easternangles
General Manager Jess Baker

Touring company producing new work with a regional theme. Stages 3–4 productions per year. Also runs a community, arts and heritage hub in Ipswich with satellite a venue in Peterborough. Welcomes scripts from new writers in the East of England region. Founded 1982.

Graeae Theatre Company

Bradbury Studios, 138 Kingsland Road, London E2 8DY
tel 020-7613 6900
email josh@graeae.org
website www.graeae.org
Facebook www.facebook.com/graeae
Twitter @graeae
Instagram @graeaetheatrecompany
Artistic Director Jenny Sealey OBE, *Executive Director* Kevin Walsh, *Literary Coordinator* Josh Elliott

Small- to mid-scale touring company placing Deaf and disabled artists centre stage. Welcomes scripts from Deaf and disabled writers. Founded 1980.

Headlong Theatre

3rd Floor, 207 Waterloo Road, London SE1 8XD
tel 020-7633 2090
email info@headlong.co.uk
website https://headlong.co.uk
Twitter @HeadlongTheatre

Artistic Director Holly Race Roughan, *Executive Director* Lisa Maguire

Mid- to large-scale touring company presenting a provocative mix of new writing, reimagined classics and influential twentieth-century plays.

Hull Truck Theatre Co. Ltd
50 Ferensway, Hull HU2 8LB
tel (01482) 224800
email admin@hulltruck.co.uk
website www.hulltruck.co.uk
Twitter @HullTruck
Artistic Director Mark Babych, *Executive Director* Janthi Mills-Ward

Producing and receiving theatre with a national reputation for new writing. Premieres of new plays, including own commissions, have included works by Tanika Gupta, Amanda Whittington, Bryony Lavery, James Graham and Richard Bean.

The London Bubble
(Bubble Theatre Company)
5 Elephant Lane, London SE16 4JD
tel 020-7237 4434
email admin@londonbubble.org.uk
website www.londonbubble.org.uk
Twitter @LBubble
Instagram @bubbletheatre
Co-Ceos Lucy Bradshaw, Marie Vickers

Aims to provide the artistic direction, skills, environment and resources to create inspirational, inclusive and involving theatre for the local community and beyond. Also runs a number of groups for children and young people as well as an adult drama group.

M6 Theatre Company
Studio Theatre, Hamer C.P. School,
Albert Royds Street, Rochdale, Lancs. OL16 2SU
tel (01706) 355898
email admin@m6theatre.co.uk
website https://m6theatre.co.uk
Facebook https://en-gb.facebook.com/M6Theatre
Twitter @M6Theatre
Artistic Director Gilly Baskeyfield

Touring theatre company specialising in creating and delivering innovative theatre for young audiences.

New Perspectives Theatre Company
Park Lane Business Centre, Park Lane, Basford,
Nottingham NG6 0DW
tel 0115 927 2334
email info@newperspectives.co.uk
website www.newperspectives.co.uk
Facebook www.facebook.com/
newperspectivestheatrecompany
Twitter @NPtheatre
Artistic Director Angharad Jones

Touring theatre company, staging a minimum of 2 productions. The company tours new writing to theatres, arts centres, festivals and rural village halls around the country. Founded 1973.

Paines Plough
Stockroom, 38 Mayton Street, London N7 6QR
tel 020-7240 4533
email office@painesplough.com
website https://painesplough.com/get-involved/invite-us
Facebook www.facebook.com/painesploughHQ
Twitter @painesplough
Instagram @painesplough
Joint Artistic Directors Katie Posner, Charlotte Bennett

Commissions and produces new plays by British and Irish playwrights. Tours at least 6 plays per year nationally for small- and mid-scale theatres. Seeks original plays that engage with the contemporary world and are written in a distinctive voice.

Proteus Theatre Company
Proteus Creation Space, Council Road, Basingstoke,
Hants RG21 3DH
tel (01256) 354541
email info@proteustheatre.com
website www.proteustheatre.com
Twitter @proteustheatre
Artistic Director and Chief Executive Mary Swan

Small-scale touring company particularly committed to new writing and new work, education and community collaborations. Produces up to 3 touring shows per year plus community projects. Founded 1981.

Red Ladder Theatre Company
3 St Peter's Buildings, York Street, Leeds LS9 8AJ
tel 0113 245 5311
email rod@redladder.co.uk
website www.redladder.co.uk
Twitter @redladder
Artistic Director Rod Dixon

Theatre performances with a radical and dissenting voice. National touring of theatre venues and community spaces. Commissions one or 2 new plays each year. Runs the Red Grit Project, a free theatre-training programme for over-18s.

Sphinx Theatre Company
email info@sphinxtheatre.co.uk
website www.sphinxtheatre.co.uk
Twitter @Sphinxtheatre
Artistic Director Sue Parrish

Specialises in writing, directing and developing roles for women. Accepts unsolicited scripts via the email address above.

Stockroom
38 Mayton Street, London N7 6QR
email martin@stockroom.co.uk

website www.@stockroom.co.uk
Twitter @wearestockroom
Executive Producer Martin Derbyshire

Touring company producing 'plays for the nation' for audiences across the UK. Founded 1993; formerly Out of Joint. Renamed 2021.

Talawa Theatre Company

Fairfield Halls, Park Lane, Croydon CR9 1DG
tel 020-7251 6644
email contact@talawa.com
website www.talawa.com
Facebook www.facebook.com/
TalawaTheatreCompany
Twitter @TalawaTheatreCo
Instagram @talawatc
Artistic Director Michael Buffong

Welcomes submissions from Black writers in the UK. Script-reading service available twice a year. See website (FAQs page) for details of submission windows. Also runs TYPT, a programme for emerging theatre-makers aged between 18 and 25.

Theatre Absolute

c/o 59 Oldfield Road, Coventry CV5 8FU
tel 07799 292957

email info@theatreabsolute.co.uk
website www.theatreabsolute.co.uk
Facebook www.facebook.com/TheatreAbsolute
Twitter @theatreabsolute
Contact Julia Negus

Independent producer of contemporary theatre work, script development, and other live art events. The company is funded project to project and not able to receive unsolicited scripts. Founded 1992.

Theatre Centre

The Albany, Douglas Way, Deptford,
London SE8 4AG
tel 020-7729 3066
email admin@theatre-centre.co.uk
website www.theatre-centre.co.uk
Facebook www.facebook.com/TheatreCentreUK
Twitter @TClive
Artistic Director Rob Watt, *Executive Director and Ceo* Emma Rees

Young people's theatre company producing plays and workshops which tour nationally across the UK. Productions are staged in schools, arts centres and other venues. Keen to nurture new and established talent, encouraging all writers to consider writing for young audiences. Also runs creative projects and manages writing awards: see website for details. Founded 1953.

Literary agents
What does a literary agent do?

An agent has three main roles. James Rennoldson briefly encapsulates what these are.

The job of a literary agent is to sell your manuscript to publishers and secure terms beneficial in both the short- and long-term life of your book. They understand you creatively and look to support and develop your career as a writer. Agents act on your behalf by championing your book, brokering the best deal possible for it and acting as a buffer between you and your publisher. They do the worrying so you can do the writing.

Broadly speaking, an agent's job can be broken down into three areas: **creative, business** and **people-related**.

In a **creative** sense, an agent has to be in sync with what their writers are working towards and hone manuscripts so that they reach their potential. In being offered representation, you will have gained a passionate, influential supporter of your book and creative outlook in general. Agents may work through several versions of your manuscript with you ahead of sending it out to commissioning editors they have identified as potentially interested in bidding for the rights. If the process of rewriting means tightening up character arcs, concentrating on giving your book more 'heart' or restructuring to create a pacier plot, then your agent will support you in that. This means you need to trust them and be willing to let go of your book enough to be guided by someone with your best interests at heart and an eye on what they know editors are looking for. Before approaching an agent, you should have a reasonable idea where your book would sit within a bookstore; an agent will be an expert on the market, with knowledge as to how books are categorised and in which genre they are likely to sit.

This overarching appreciation of publishing as a commercial enterprise is where an agent's creative support meets their eye for **business**. Agents constantly have their ear to the ground for deals being done; the sorts of books editors are buying and where rights are being sold for particular titles. This informs their strategy when it comes to approaching potential buyers of a manuscript, and also how much to push for during financial negotiations. All of which, of course, needs to be tied up contractually, and an agent's keen eye for small print is something that benefits their authors. It's the meat and potatoes of an agent's job to look into any sort of contractual query (financial or otherwise) and find solutions so that their authors are rewarded for their writing.

The third attribute of a literary agent complements both the creative and commercial elements of their role. Like most jobs in the Arts (and beyond!) being able to **relate to people** counts for a great deal. The business side of their job, for example, comes down to having good contacts. This requires acquiring an understanding of what commissioning editors have on their wish lists and is built up over time through chance conversations or more formal meetings. These are the moments when they can put forward manuscripts, either by planting a seed and mentioning how excited they are by a book one of their unpublished clients is putting finishing touches to, or by proclaiming a book to be ready and one an editor must read. As a yet-to-be published writer, this, as far as you're concerned, is the primary role of the agent – to champion your book and pitch it with such passion that an editor feels compelled to put everything else aside and read it. Whether it be in person over a coffee or by email, an agent's ability to transfer their enthusiasm for your project is integral to their job.

Being able to relate to people is more than an agent being a good salesperson for their authors, though. There's a huge difference in approach between chasing royalty payments or interrogating the terms of a publishing agreement, for example, to that needed to support an overwhelmed debut author suddenly stifled by imposter syndrome. Perhaps the greatest test of an agent's emotional dexterity is how they handle their authors in order to bring out the best in them and their work. Do they need 'tough love' and hard deadlines, or will they respond more to a sympathetic ear that coaxes them through a crisis of confidence?

Extracted from the *Writers' & Artists' Guide to How to Hook an Agent* (Bloomsbury 2020) by **James Rennoldson**, Product Owner, Writers & Artists.

What a debut novelist should expect from an agent

Sallyanne Sweeney explains what a literary agent's job entails, and the range of roles that may include as they work closely with, and for, an author to ensure the best possible outcome for a debut novel.

Congratulations! You've beaten the slush pile. You have a literary agent. Dream realised, job done, right?

Signing to an agency is an exciting time both for authors and agents. One of the best parts of my job is taking on a new client – that fizz of anticipation mixed with a slight trepidation, as now the work really begins. You may well be wondering what happens next, and it's okay not to know what to expect at this stage; your agent is there to guide you through everything that lies ahead. You may have been in the position of choosing between multiple offers of representation or you may have found 'the one' on your first try. Either way, it's a good idea to meet your new agent or at least have a phone conversation before accepting their offer. This is your chance to ask about their process and discuss expectations – and if you don't feel comfortable asking these questions, are they the right agent for you?

The debut

When I started working in publishing, the submissions pile tended to tower precariously in the office corner, gathering dust. Since then, the attitude towards debuts has completely shifted (and, thankfully for everyone, electronic submissions have become the norm). Publishers have proven they can launch debuts into the world as major brands, with marketing campaigns to match. The competition between agents to sign talented new authors is fierce, and for good reason: Nielsen BookScan recorded more debut novels in the top 150 fiction titles published in 2020 than in 2019, with sales of the top 10 debutants up 151%.

No two paths to publication are the same and my relationship with clients differs according to their individual needs and styles. Last year, I sold five debut novelists across children's and adult fiction. With one of these authors, the period from their joining the agency to agreeing a publication deal was a matter of weeks, after a contracted round of edits and a swift auction. With another, we had been working together for five years by the time I sold her manuscript, so her 'debut' was actually the second novel I'd 'gone on submission' with. Many debut novels are anything but. Sometimes that first book will be published later; more often than not, it remains in a drawer.

Below are the key elements the agent will bring to your new partnership.

1. The edit

By the time of securing an agent, you will have already revised and honed your manuscript, sometimes over multiple drafts. The bad news: you need to be prepared for several more. The good news: this time, you're not working alone.

An agent will work with you to get the manuscript into as polished a state as possible for submission. This creative back-and-forth is one of the most rewarding (and time-consuming) aspects of my job. It's a vital investment from your agent and one that will hopefully pay off – remember, you have one chance to make a winning first impression on publishers. I start with the 'big picture' or structural edits, homing in on how to get the best out of the story and characters, and identifying what might not be working as well as it could be. The final stage focuses on a line edit and looking for anything that might have been missed in previous drafts. How many rounds come in between completely depends on the individual manuscript.

Your agent should share your vision and ambition for your book and want to work with you to make it the best it can be. You don't have to agree with, or implement, all these edits, but they should serve as a useful guide through your revisions. I'm always happy for an author to find their own solutions to my editorial concerns; the magic is often in the unexpected and I love when an author thinks around the issue and elevates their work in a way I could never have anticipated.

2. The sale

While my client is working on their edits, I'll be progressing things behind the scenes, discussing the manuscript with editors and finessing both the pitch and the submission list.

Passion sells and, in the same way you might rush to tell all your friends and family about a wonderful book you've just read, I want to be 'going on submission' feeling excited about pressing a manuscript into the hands of editors I think will love it. This entails knowing editors' tastes, keeping in constant touch about what publishers are buying and looking for, researching the market, looking at trends, and reading recently published titles. You won't necessarily be aware of all of this going on as you're working on edits, but it's a good idea to keep your agent informed of your progress so that they can plan their timing for submission. Once you've both signed off on the final manuscript, you're ready to go.

Most authors find being on submission tough. You've now done everything you can, and your manuscript is out of your hands. I'd advise trying to keep yourself occupied while waiting on news, whether that's throwing yourself into your next book or scrubbing your skirting boards, as is one client's habit – whatever it takes! It can be a nerve-wracking time for agents, too. At Mulcahy Sweeney Associates we are extremely selective about new authors we take on because we want to maintain our high success rate in sales. An agent's reputation is on the line with each submission and we want editors to respond quickly and positively to every manuscript from our agency, ideally to immediately call and tell us they love it as much as we do (and make us a compelling offer at the same time).

3. The deal

Hopefully, you'll have one or multiple publishers wishing to acquire your debut novel and your agent will guide you through this process. My job is to get the best deal for my author, thinking strategically beyond this first book to look ahead at the author's career as a whole. This means not only orchestrating a competitive auction to secure the optimal advance, royalties and rights, but also matchmaking the author with the right editor and ensuring the commitment of the full publishing team for the book.

When you have accepted a publisher offer, your agent will cast a forensic eye over the finer detail of the contract. This is the less glamorous side of agenting, but no less important – examining the small print (for example, negotiating favourable high discount, reversion and option clauses) and worrying about the minutiae of the deal – so that the author doesn't have to.

4. Rights

All along the way, an agent will be thinking about subsidiary rights – in particular, US, translation and dramatic rights – ensuring that they build momentum after that primary deal. This initial energy surrounding a title can create ripples around the world that lead to a wave of international offers, which in turn maintains that buzz at home. To try to achieve this, I'll regularly discuss forthcoming projects with literary scouts (employed by international publishers to flag up the 'hot' titles in the English language markets) and our co-agents, and pitch to international publishers or production companies myself at the London, Bologna and Frankfurt book fairs.

5. Advocacy

An agent's job doesn't end once you have a publisher on board (or indeed, many publishers around the world). As my clients' foremost champion, I stay involved throughout the whole publication process and beyond, bringing my own ideas and experience and making sure things flow as smoothly as possible. As a debut author, you may not know which concerns are worth raising and which are standard practice. What do you do if you hate your cover or the publisher's proposed title, if no copies have shown up at a scheduled event, or if your signature advance is nowhere to be seen? Your agent can tell you what's acceptable – or not – and advocate on your behalf so that your relationship with the publisher stays purely creative.

6. The long game

What happens when (… whisper it …) things go wrong? If your debut novel doesn't sell, or it does but isn't the success you'd hoped for? Your agent should be there in bad times as well as good, as your creative and business partner throughout your whole career and not just your debut. As great as it is to get immediate offers on a book, I find immense satisfaction in securing a harder-fought deal for an author. Agents get rejected too (and it hurts!), but when I believe in a book I will persist in fighting for it. Sometimes, if I think we just haven't found the right match yet and there hasn't been a common editorial concern flagged in the responses, I'll start a second submission round; one such novel on my list ended up selling at auction and winning awards, after being rejected across the board in its first publisher outing. In some instances, this might first entail a further round of edits with the author, after going through the publisher feedback together. Or, in what's a tougher call, you and your agent might decide that it's time to move on to your next novel … which might be the one that sets the world alight.

What can an author do throughout this whole journey? Keep the faith and keep writing. Most authors with long careers will work with different publishers and editors along the way but usually with the same agent. Your debut should be only the very beginning of this long and successful partnership.

Sallyanne Sweeney started her career at Watson, Little Ltd, where she became a director in 2011. In 2013 she joined Mulcahy Associates, part of the MMBcreative group, and since 2021 has been a director of the renamed Mulcahy Sweeney Associates. Sallyanne was Chair of the Children's Agents' Circle 2014–18. See https://mmbcreative.com/agents/sallyanne-sweeney for more information and follow her on Twitter @sallyanne_s.

Literary agents

Putting together your submission

Hellie Ogden spells out what the time-pressed agent is looking for in a book submission and provides advice and examples of what *is*, and what *is not*, likely to help a new author secure an agent.

Any agent will tell you they get huge numbers of submissions sent to them daily – perhaps up to 100 or so each week. And it's true, we do, but that fact shouldn't be unduly intimidating. It always amazes me, despite the amount of information available on agents' sites and from resources such as this *Yearbook* and the Writers & Artists website (www.writersandartists.co.uk), how many of these submission emails are hastily and sloppily written – full of spelling, punctuation and, in some cases, factual errors. These I will reject straightaway. The number of smart, professional cover letters that I receive is much smaller (approximately 25% of all those I see) and these will be bumped up my submission pile.

The cover letter

There are some key points to remember when putting your submission together: personalise your covering letter/email, addressing it to a specific, correctly named agent, and send it in line with each agent's guidelines on their site. Include a brief introduction about yourself and your book and what material you are attaching as specified by each agency. This would typically include three sample chapters and a synopsis, which should be in documents attached to your cover letter email and not added to the body of the email itself.

Knowing the market

What will elevate your submission package comes down to two things. Firstly, know where your book sits in the market or which genre it falls within. It may sound obvious, but having market awareness is really smart. It shows that you have done your research and, because of that, you have an idea of what other published titles it might sit alongside on the booksellers' shelves or in online stores. On top of falling in love with your writing, agents themselves will be strategising and formulating a pitch around how your book will be positioned. Is your book YA, upmarket commercial, narrative non-fiction, literary, psychological suspense? Your agent will have a good idea of what 'type' of book you have written, but it's encouraging to see an author considering these questions too, showing an awareness of the commercial side of publishing and some understanding of the market.

The elevator pitch

The second crucial element of your submission is the 'elevator pitch'. This need only be a paragraph long, around 100–150 words, but contains the most important lines you will write in your cover email. This is your opportunity to be creative and to stand out positively. The elevator pitch is your chance to sell your hook – an agent's eyes will flip to that part of the letter first. Take inspiration from blurbs on the back of published books in your genre; don't rush it and don't overcomplicate it; focus on one key plot point and one unique angle.

A good and a not-so-good example

Overleaf is an example of a submission letter I received a few years ago. I subsequently took on the author. I was instantly drawn to her letter: in her opening lines, she provides a clear sense of the book's genre and highlights her relevant writing experience. She has an understanding of my client list and her elevator pitch is really strong and compelling. The book's title isn't perfect, but it does feel relevant to the genre. She finishes by including a brief biography and (what I always appreciate) her telephone number, so I can be in touch quickly! It's always useful, too, to mention when you have submitted to other agents and to remain honest and transparent throughout the submission process.

As an extreme example of a bad cover letter, overleaf is one that I've cobbled together to highlight the errors a surprising number of authors make:

• It's not directed at an individual agent, it's arrogant in tone, and it's packed full of spelling mistakes.

• The writer has sent in a random selection of chapters – the ones that they think are the best. *All* your chapters should be the best examples of your writing and equally strong; send the first three chapters, not a random selection.

• Although I'm a big fan of comparison titles to highlight where your book might sit, the ones included here are contradictory and confusing.

Synopsis

The synopsis can challenge even the most confident of writers, and it shouldn't take precious time away from perfecting the manuscript itself. I would never turn down a manuscript if I loved the book but the synopsis didn't stylistically blow me away. In fact, I won't even open the synopsis until I've had a look at the manuscript itself. It's a simple map of the book, ideally a page long, detailing the beginning, middle and end of your story. Concentrate on the key points and don't overload it with detail.

It's an extremely exciting stage getting your manuscript ready to go out to agents, but I can't stress enough the importance of spending a good chunk of time on your approach. Do your research; read widely so you are aware of the market; spend time in bookshops looking at the backs of books and at titles too. Write, rewrite and write that pitch again! Keep it tight and compelling. Spend time on your synopsis but don't fret over it and, more importantly, try to make those opening three chapters of your work as wonderful as possible.

I often recommend to new writers that they read *The Bookseller* online – the publishing trade magazine (www.thebookseller.com). It's a great resource not only for researching an agent, but also for understanding a little about the market. Remember that agents are reading constantly, so don't nag if you don't hear back from them immediately; do check individual agency guidelines for response times. It's worth noting, too, that around the time of the three major book fairs each year – Bologna (usually March/April, children's and YA only, www.bolognachildrensbookfair.com), London (usually March, www.londonbookfair.co.uk) and Frankfurt (usually October, www.buchmesse.de/en) – agents are extremely busy, so I would suggest not submitting during the weeks running up to, during and just after the fairs.

From: Heidi Hopeful

14/02/2018

Subject: Submission of Bones by Heidi Hopeful

To: agent@literaryagency.com

Dear Hellie,

I hope you don't mind me contacting you directly. You have been highly recommended to me by an editor at Faber, who I worked with on the Faber Writing-a-Novel course a few years ago.

I would love you to be one of the first people to look at my upmarket thriller. I have thought long and hard about agents and I would absolutely love to work with you if you felt *Bones* was right for you. You have a wonderful, eclectic list and I hope that I might fit in well alongside your existing clients. I particularly love M.J. Arlidge's *Eeny Meeny*, which is just unputdownable, and the character of Helen Grace is fascinating - a detective who struggles with her demons so differently from other crime novel detectives.

My novel, *Bones*, tells the story of how Beth Chase's life is shattered when her 17-year-old son goes missing. When a body is pulled from the Thames outside her riverside home, Beth is convinced it is her missing son. Although it is soon evident the bones have been in the water far longer, she becomes fixated on them, her search for Louis becoming ever more frantic. As strange things begin to happen in the river house, the life of a former inhabitant emerges and Beth grows obsessed by events that unfolded there centuries ago.
But are these things really happening, or are they all in Beth's mind? Can the house on the river and its secrets lead Beth to her son, or is it spinning her away from him?

In my day job I write for a number of national parenting magazines and websites, on everything from how to travel across a continent with a potty-training toddler, to persuading your monsters that Haribo Sours are not one of the major food groups. Recent titles include *Families Magazine* and *Families Online*. I also write the blog *21stCenturyMum*.

I hope you don't mind but I have taken the liberty of attaching my novel, as well as a brief synopsis.

Thank you so much, and apologies for the excruciating length of this email! I look forward to hearing from you. My telephone number is *XXX* and I have submitted to a small number of agents.

Best wishes,

Heidi Hopeful

Literary agents

An example of a good submission email

From: Neil Chance   01/04/2018

Subject: HEY, LOOK AT THIS!!!!

To: agent@literaryagency.com

Dear Sir/Madam/Miss/Mz (that should cover you all),

I am writing to give you an exclusive first look at the future of publishing. A book that will literally change our society.

'The Face of God is an ugly one my son' is a fast-paced but literary thriller that follows the adventures of an innocent postie who gets sucked into the world of forensic archaeology and the dark underbelly of the Christian church, and must race across the world to stop a terrifying prophecy from coming true.

Dan Brown sold buckets of 'The DaVinci Code' and I plan to do the same. But where his book was based on cheap and easy hearsay, the myths and truths exposed in my book are the result of years of my own painstaking research into Christian conspiracies which I undertook during my twenty-five year career as a post office manager. I thin the book will hopefully steal away some of Mr Brown's fans but also appeal to readers of the likes of Graham Greene and John Updike.

If you're interested then read on – I've included the opening, closing and middle chapter to give you a flavour of the novel at its best places! I've already mapped out four possible sequals to this book – each more death defyingly thrilling than the last. I also have a backlist of more historical adventures – very Indiana Jones-esque, when men were men and women were in distress – which I'm sure you'll love as much as 'The Face of God is an ugly one my son.'

I look forward to a long and fruitful career with you,

Best,

N.O. Chance

An example of a poor submission email

Good luck! It's the best feeling in the world discovering new talent and nurturing debut writers.

Hellie Ogden is a literary agent and co-head of the London books department at WME. She featured in *The Bookseller* Rising Stars list and was shortlisted for the Kim Scott Walwyn Prize. She looks for novels with bold storytelling, moving prose and vivid, thought-provoking characters. In non-fiction she is looking for unique personal stories and work that has a social following with cross-media potential, as well as cookery, nature writing and lifestyle. As an editorially focused agent, she has a keen interest in helping to develop and nurture debut writers and build international careers. Follow her on Twitter @hellieogden

Your non-fiction proposal for agents and publishers

Literary agent Rebecca Carter describes the potential impact of a well-crafted book proposal for turning your non-fiction idea into a published book. She explains the essential components and qualities of a book proposal, what agents and publishers are looking for, and the guiding role an agent plays in this key step towards publication.

Dreams and reality

Before getting down to the practicalities, let's start with some dreams ... because all writing, and therefore publishing, begins with the imagination. As a literary agent, I dream of submitting a non-fiction proposal to a publisher in which my short pitch (over the phone or in a covering letter) is so compelling that the editor drops everything to read the proposal as soon as it reaches their inbox. They skip lunch; they cancel meetings; the proposal is so unputdownable, so thrillingly original, so in tune with the zeitgeist that the editor tells their colleagues they simply must read it immediately. The colleagues share the editor's enthusiasm, the acquisitions process is fast-tracked and, by the end of the day (okay, maybe by the next morning), the publisher has put in an offer. Within 24 hours I have a ten-way auction up and running, and by the end of the week the author has the book deal of their dreams.

Such dream-like events do occasionally happen. This is because the majority of non-fiction is sold on short, easy-to-read proposals.[1] The advantage of a proposal is that it can be read in a lunch break and shared rapidly with others. Editors can't read 300-page novels over lunch, and it's easier to persuade their colleagues to prioritise reading 30 pages over 300 pages that will entail giving up more of their evening or weekend (publishers have little time to read submissions during working hours). However, the advantageous brevity of a proposal is also its disadvantage, as it has to achieve a great deal in a few pages. The best proposals make you feel you have already read the future book in miniature, without diminishing your desire to read the whole book itself as soon as it can be delivered. Many times I have seen a proposal set not just the UK publishing scene alight, but the international one too, securing deals in America and in translation in a matter of days.

Submitting a non-fiction proposal to a literary agent

Writing such a document will inevitably seem daunting. As a literary agent, a crucial part of my time is spent helping the writers I represent find the best structure and voice for their proposals. It is rare for me to submit a proposal to a publisher without carefully workshopping it with the writer, sometimes over a number of weeks or months. By making the process collaborative, and breaking it down into manageable chunks, I try to dispel the fear. I roleplay the reader, stress-testing the proposal both as a potential publisher and a potential book buyer. But if you're not lucky enough to be contacted out of the blue by a literary agent offering proposal-writing help, due to the up-front strength of your particular story or expertise, how do you persuade an agent to take on your non-fiction idea in the first place?

[1] My use of the word 'majority' here is pretty unscientific; I have consulted no statistics but have simply gone by experience. Also, I'm referring to a very specific type of non-fiction proposal, i.e. the narrative kind submitted to general trade rather than to academic or specialist publishers.

As I'm sure every agent contributing to this *Yearbook* will tell you, always consult the *submission criteria* on the agency's website and try to obey these as closely as possible. Most agencies ask for a complete non-fiction proposal, and possibly even a sample chapter or two. Although it's likely the proposal you submit to an agent will change substantially before it is submitted to a publisher, it still needs to be the best you can make it, without the agent's input. There are many (free and not-so-free) resources and courses on proposal-writing out there for you to find. It's worth researching them until you discover the common threads that are most useful to you personally. Even if you've already written all or a substantial part of your book, you might think of reverse-engineering it into a proposal so that it's quicker for the agent to grasp.

After that, spend lots of energy thinking up a great title and subtitle, and writing a *short pitch letter* that describes succinctly and arrestingly: 1) what the book is about; 2) why you are the best person to write it; 3) why it is timely and different from other books in the field; and 4) why you have chosen to approach this particular agent (perhaps because of the other authors they represent, or the type of book they say they are looking for). It may sound harsh, but I tend to know within three or four sentences of a pitch letter whether I'm interested enough in the author to take their email seriously and read their proposal. That's because I can immediately imagine myself pitching the book to publishers. The pitch letter does not need to be flashy and make big claims (it's probably better not to), but it needs to have a compelling confidence, and clarity of tone and purpose. I have taken on some authors who have simply written me a really good letter describing a proposal they would like to write, and asking if they can have a conversation with me about it. But I'm not recommending this strategy; these were mainly authors who had written books before and therefore had a track record. However, this illustrates how important your short pitch letter is. The proposal effectively confirms that you are capable of writing a long work of prose to realise your idea – or at least that you have the ambition and skills to become capable of it.

Why is your idea a book, and what kind of book is it?

There are some questions I ask myself when I'm considering whether to offer representation to a non-fiction writer (and if the proposal indicates that the writer already has a firm grasp of the answers to these, it always inspires confidence):

• Most importantly – will the subject matter sustain a book-length treatment, or would it work better as a long-form essay?
• If it passes the above 'Is it a book?' test, what *kind* of book is it?
• Does the writer understand the type of non-fiction they are trying to write, and the strategies they might use to engage their reader?
• Are the chapters separate, self-contained essays, or does the whole book have a strong narrative propulsion?
• Is it a book that a reader would dip into – or one they would devour from cover to cover?
• If the latter, how does the writer demonstrate that the narrative arc will be exciting?

I often like proposals which start with an extended piece of writing presenting an introductory story that relates to the book. This allows the writer to showcase both their storytelling abilities and the voice in which the book will be written. It immediately draws a reader into the world of the book, and signals to a potential publisher what 'genre' of non-fiction the book aspires to. It is harder to demonstrate these qualities with a more abstract description of what the book will be about. This is not to say that a proposal shouldn't have a more explanatory section that describes the author's vision for it, both in terms of its contents and its place in the bookshop. But you don't necessarily need to put that first. There are no absolute rules for ordering your proposal – you can be creative about it, allowing your material to guide you, whilst also making sure you say everything you need to.

How long should the proposal be? Again, allow the material to guide you – I've submitted proposals of 8,000 words and of 40,000. The *chapter summaries* are really important as they show if you have a strong sense of that crucial narrative arc: too short and they are boring and uninformative; too long and there's a danger the reader feels they are reading the chapter itself, but in a duller form than in the actual book.

Can you *afford* to write the book?

When I look at my non-fiction submissions, I am of course asking myself whether I think I can sell the proposal to a publisher – but I'm also wondering whether the author can realistically afford to write the book. This might seem counterintuitive: surely the agent's role is to get the author an advance that finances them to turn the proposal into a finished manuscript? But there are many factors to be considered here. The advance offered may not end up being that big, and even big advances are paid out in tranches on signature, delivery and publication. The book might require expensive research and illustration permissions, or travel to distant places. Even if the author can do the research from the comfort of their own home, it will require lots of time. Will the author be able to take enough time off from their day job not only to write the book but to promote it? Is their day job one that is complementary to the book project (perhaps giving them a ready-made platform from which to promote the book) or is it one that will impede it? If they don't have a day job, and the book advance isn't large, how are they going to live?

Books are costly to write – in time, money and emotion. Does the author understand this? Agents can only smooth the path so far; authorial doggedness and determination are a prerequisite. The delivery date given in a proposal needs to be realistic. There is nothing more stressful for a non-fiction author than the fear that the contract might be cancelled because of late delivery. After securing a deal for an author, I consider it part of my role to cheer them on and offer regular hydration as they steadily run the marathon of finishing the book.

Reality and dreams – full circle

For an author eager to get on and write a book, proposals can seem a bore. Why do you have to spend time describing your book when you just want to start researching and writing it? I sympathise! Why, I lament to myself, do I have to spend time persuading publishers to publish something when they should be able to see my author's native genius immediately? The truth is that proposals are more than just sales documents. They are the book in microcosm and, as such, they accomplish a lot of the book-writing work in advance. Authors often tell me they are grateful for time spent workshopping a proposal because it means that, when they start writing the book, they are not facing a blank page: they have the scaffolding in place to cling to as they climb. By the way, that doesn't mean writers can't redesign bits of the building if perhaps they discover, in the process of writing, that Chapter Two would be better as Chapter Four. A proposal should never be a prison.

I've mixed a lot of metaphors in this piece, so let's return to the dreams. Yes, I dream of ten-way auctions – but I also dream of the great satisfaction of simply finding a publisher for a book. Maybe the proposal is excellent but only one publisher wants it; that's all it takes for a book to exist and make an impact in the world, and for its ideas to enter someone else's imagination. It is thrilling for an agent to help a writer take their book idea from dream to reality. First, though, you have to write the proposal …

Rebecca Carter has worked in publishing for 30 years, first as a book scout, then as an editor and publisher, and since 2012 as a literary agent. In January 2023 she set up independently as Rebecca Carter Literary. She represents fiction and non-fiction. In non-fiction she is looking for original thinkers and writers in the areas of history, politics, culture, science, nature and the environment, and for memoirists and authors who aren't afraid to blend and cross genres. See www.rebeccacarterliterary.com for more information. Follow her on Twitter @RebeccasBooks.

Advice from an 'accidental' agent

Clare Grist Taylor, experienced publisher turned literary agent, highlights the importance of building trust between agent and author. She believes that a big part of her role is to provide editorial and emotional support for her authors; here she considers what a budding non-fiction author should take into account when preparing to publish.

I founded The Accidental Agency after a long career on the other side of the publishing fence and with a deep and enduring love of being a non-fiction editor and publisher. The words 'poacher' and 'gamekeeper' have been used. But I'm sure that my experience of working with all types of authors writing so many different types of books for all sorts of readers could have provided no better starting point for my work as an agent.

For me, the best editors have always combined market and commercial nous and judgement with the interpersonal skills needed to encourage and enable their authors. It is a relationship based on trust and respect, requiring the editor to act variously as counsellor, challenger, confidante and sounding board. As an agent, while market knowledge and judgement remain essential, I find that these 'soft' communication skills loom even larger. Writing is inherently exposing, and it's important that I provide a safe haven for my authors to explore and test new ideas, suffer crises of confidence, moan and rage, exult and despair. It's about being a true critical friend who is, usefully, at one remove from their publishers.

It is not a relationship to be taken lightly either, which is why it's so important that authors understand what an agent can (and can't) do for them and that both parties are prepared for the journey ahead. Writing is hard, even for the most natural and accomplished of writers. Convincing a publisher that your book should be published can be even harder. All of this takes hard work, resilience, persistence and often (whisper it) a healthy dose of being in the right place at the right time. It also means being realistic – taking a good, hard look at what you want to achieve and why.

Does a non-fiction author really need an agent?

Be honest with yourself. You need to understand your motivations for writing, and the true size and scope of the audiences you're writing for; both of these will have implications on how your book might be published.

Many non-fiction authors will not be giving up the day job any time soon. There's nothing wrong with writing a book to reflect, reinforce or support your professional or personal credentials, or for a more defined market – which is the basis, after all, of much academic, professional and, increasingly, self-publishing. But, given that the immediate monetary rewards are likely to be minimal, you're unlikely to secure the services of an agent to help you ... and you might not need to. Many academic or professional publishers actively invite submissions and provide lists of their editors on their websites. So, find an in-house editor sympathetic to your work or, if self-publishing, a freelance editor to coach and inspire you, and to help you marshal and communicate your ideas. Partnership publishing – where you make an up-front investment to support publication – can be a good halfway house; do check any contracts carefully though, and be aware of potential vanity publishing scams (see *Paid-for publishing services: Is it a steal?* on page 605).

If you have different ambitions for your book, aiming for a more general audience or a more traditional publishing deal, then the world becomes trickier, the rewards potentially greater but often more elusive. That's when an agent can really add value, and not simply in terms of helping you to find the right editor and publisher, negotiating the best deals and maximising what you'll earn as a result, crucial though that is. Because, before that, there's plenty of editorial work and thinking to do. The right agent will help you to marshal your ideas into book form, whether that's creating a book proposal that will also act as a blueprint and guide when it comes to writing or reviewing, or helping to craft draft chapters. It's a competitive world out there, so you need to think carefully about what your book offers, why it should be published, and how to anticipate and meet the objections you'll face. A properly persuasive book proposal, accompanied by well-constructed and compellingly written sample chapters, can make all the difference.

Before I wrote this piece, I talked to some of my authors about this process, what they'd learnt and what they wanted to pass on to others embarking on their own journeys. Below are some of the points they wanted to share.

1. Have a vision for what you want to achieve

Although most authors won't have in-depth knowledge of the world of publishing or the latest publishing trends, you can start to create a vision for yourself of the book you want to write. What will it look like? Where will it sit in a bookshop? Who can you imagine reading it? What other books will it be like? Visit the largest bookshop you can and spend time with comparable books. Think about things you might not have considered before, such as the relationship between the type of content and the book format and price. Consider titles and subtitles. Look at which publisher is publishing which types of books. Read author acknowledgements to identify likely agents and editors.

2. Stop and think before you write

Bear in mind Abraham Lincoln's famous advice that, if he were given six hours to cut down a tree, he would spend the first four sharpening the axe. Starting to write non-fiction without a very clear idea about what you want to say, and how, is a very bad idea indeed. I have lost track of the number of manuscripts that have crossed my desk with an appeal for help to sort them out; this is never, I can assure you, a task to be taken on lightly. In my experience, there are two main culprits:

• Blog as would-be book

This is my shorthand for a book that may start with a convincing argument or story but can't sustain the narrative in book-length form. If it's meant to be a blog, let it be a blog.

• If I were to start again, I wouldn't start from here ...

Diving straight into writing without a proper sense of structure, focus, key messages or narrative arc will only make the (already difficult) task of writing a book even harder. Don't be tempted to make it up as you go along. Although plans will inevitably morph and change as the writing progresses, doing the serious thinking up front is essential.

Creating a convincing and compelling case for your book is not just about making it attractive for publishers. It's also about challenging yourself to hone your argument, sharpen your structure and write the best book you can. This is harder to do in retrospect than at the outset.

3. Non-fiction is about telling stories

Telling stories is about creating a connection with the reader. This is as true for even the most hard-nosed, how-to non-fiction as it is for the latest Booker Prize winner. Think about the narrative arc for your book: How can you communicate your story/information to create maximum resonance with readers? What's going to grab and hold their attention? Look at books you admire and ask yourself why. The chances are that they created a powerful connection that has stayed with you. This is also true when creating book proposals. A proposal is a mini book in its own right; it needs the right elements in a logical order, in order to be compelling and to engage the reader's attention. You need to tell your story.

4. Trust, collaboration and iteration

Whether you're working with an agent or an editor, that relationship must be based on trust. Publishing is a collaborative business, and, for me, that starts with the content. We all like to think that the best books emerge fully formed, with little intervention along the way. Some do – but, in my experience, that's rare. Even the most talented authors benefit from well-delivered and insightful feedback and input from someone whose opinion they value.

Being open to this collaboration and a healthy dose of iteration (write; review; edit; repeat) will undoubtedly result in a better book – but make sure the trust is there. You need a sounding board that works for you.

What goes in a good non-fiction book proposal?

- A compelling title, often with a more descriptive subtitle.
- An overview of the book's purpose and vision, showing clearly what the book will do and why it should be published; its key themes; what's special or unique about it; what does it offer?
- The markets/audiences for the book: who will buy it and why; how will you reach them?
- Positioning statement: how your book compares with similar and competing titles.
- Proposed overall length and schedule for writing.
- An outline of chapters, with clear synopses and notes on sources, as relevant.
- Thoughts on illustrations and where they can be sourced, where relevant.
- Author profile and credentials.
- Publicity contacts and links; access to marketing channels; how you can help to support publication.
- Ideas for potential endorsers and reviewers.
- Sample chapters.

5. Content is king – but positioning matters too

No publisher is going to take on a book with uninteresting, flawed or badly written content, but even the best content in the world often needs a helping hand to get noticed. That's why you need to consider and identify how your book can be positioned in its markets. Some authors find this difficult or distasteful but, if you want to be published, it's simply part of the deal.

Positioning involves everything from the right attention-grabbing title and subtitle through to a strong sense of how you, as author, can help to publicise and promote the book. It's strongly related to that vision of your work I mentioned earlier, and it requires you to think carefully about how your book will compare and contrast with other, similar titles in the market. There may be a tricky balancing act between taking a sensible decision to look and feel a bit like the other fish in the sea – for familiarity's sake – and offering something genuinely new or different. Comparisons with other writers and titles can work – but be careful not to overuse shorthand descriptions of the 'Malcolm Gladwell meets Daniel Pink' type, unless they're spot on. And don't try to shoehorn your work into a genre or type that is currently in vogue just to make it sound more marketable.

That's because you need to …

Literary agents

6. Write the book *you* want to write

Way back in my career, a wise colleague warned me off pairing a recalcitrant author with a more reliable co-author with the phrase: 'Publisher marriages don't work'. In some areas of non-fiction, using an author's expertise to write to a brief can work, but, in general, I firmly believe that authors should write the books they want to write. That doesn't mean you should not accept guidance and support along the way, or that you should write books that have no potential or market. But the best books come from an author's passion, and passion is hard to manufacture.

Good luck! Non-fiction is a buoyant, stimulating and deeply satisfying area of publishing. It'll be good to have you on board.

Clare Grist Taylor is founder of The Accidental Agency, specialising in intelligent and inspiring non-fiction. She has worked in publishing for over 35 years, with experience across trade, professional and academic sectors. She still gets a buzz when talking to potential authors, from matching authors with publishers and seeing books well published. Clare is a trustee of the Montgomeryshire Literary Festival and an advisory board member at the University of Wales Press. See www.accidentalagency.co.uk for more information.

What a literary agent can do for you

Literary agent Sarah Such explains her role and the reasons why it's worth engaging an agent to represent you as an author in our multimedia world.

I founded Sarah Such Literary Agency in 2007. My list of authors is wide-ranging and varied, and includes award-winners and bestsellers, such as Jeffrey Boakye, Anne Charnock, Antony Johnston and Vina Jackson, as well as debut writers like Sabrina Pace-Humphreys. They are representative of my own broad reading tastes and publishing experience (I was previously editorial director at Duckworth and publicity director at Penguin Books) in both literary and commercial publishing.

I specifically look for distinct and original voices, and writers who are outstanding in their field. And I help shape the long-term careers of authors who are often writing across genre and format. Some writers prefer to represent themselves; others may not see the need for a literary agent, since some publishers now offer authors the chance of submitting their work un-agented. The offer of a publishing deal direct from an enthusiastic editor following a publisher's open submission can look enticing to a new author excited to be published for the first time, while the prospect of paying a literary agent commission for the whole lifetime of a work can be daunting. Typically, however, a good literary agent will negotiate considerably better financial terms for the author.

How a literary agent earns their commission

The reality is that a good literary agent should always earn their commission by adding value to every publishing deal they negotiate; as often as not, that means not only increasing an author's financial terms through bettering advances, nuanced negotiation and deals in numerous territories, but also by ceding far fewer rights.

1. Finding the right publisher for your work

Because reputable literary agents work solely by commission, to justify their time they can only take on authors when they feel strongly enough about a work, and when they think there is a good chance of placing a work with a publisher. It's quite possible that I will spend several months working editorially with an author prior to submission, and if the author's book is not placed, there is no payment due to me as agent.

So, from the outset, a literary agent will give serious thought not only to the traditional publishing potential for the work (what revisions are necessary, how to pitch the work, where it lies in the market place and submission to the right editor and publisher) but also to the work's potential in some, if not all, of the following areas: newspaper serial extracts, foreign rights, film, TV, theatre and radio (dramatic, documentary or serialisation), audiobook (one of the fastest growing areas of publishing, served by specialist audiobook publishers, such as W.F. Howes, as well as by traditional publishers), picturisation or graphic novel rights, as well as electronic versions rights and merchandising rights. Whereas ebook rights, i.e. the verbatim text of the work (mirroring the print title) for the sole purpose of reading, are usually part of a traditional publishing contract, electronic version rights – or multimedia rights, as they are sometimes known – allow adaptations that include images, sounds and graphics.

I'll give some examples of what this means in practice. Over and above traditional publishing agreements, I have recently been in discussions about licensing the electronic adaptation rights to a graphic novel, which will allow for an interactive experience with both text and pictures. These are separate from ebook rights or film and television rights. Even in manuscript, some books are clearly filmic or have potential to tell a story in a different format. The film rights to Matthew De Abaitua's seminal artificial intelligence novel *The Red Men* (Snowbooks 2007; shortlisted for the Arthur C. Clarke Award) were acquired by Shynola Films before it was even published, as were virtual reality rights to another author's work before it was submitted. By contrast, the TV rights to cyber-thriller *The Exphoria Code* by Antony Johnston, the first in the Brigitte Sharp series, were acquired in 2020 by Red Planet Pictures three years after publication and are currently in development. The popularity of podcasts and the listening experience, in addition to the increased global market for audiobooks, has led to publishers such as Audible commissioning Audible Originals (books commissioned specifically for audiobook listeners, that will only appear in print later). An example is the 2022 title *Secrets: What We Hide and Why* by Kit Caless, which was acquired exclusively as an Audible Original in five languages. The print and ebook editions will be published traditionally supported by an existing platform. Another of my authors, Jeffrey Boakye, co-presents the Prix Italia 2022 and Prix Europa 2022-winning BBC Radio 4 series *Add to Playlist* as well as having published both a children's book, Yoto Carnegie Greenaway Medal-longlisted, *Musical Truth* (Faber Children's 2021) and his adult non-fiction book about racism in the education system, *I Heard What You Said* (Picador 2022), an Amazon non-fiction Book of the Year 2022, with the TV rights in negotiation to be optioned. His debut middle-grade fiction debut, *Kofi and the Rap Battle Summer* and *Musical World* (a sequel to *Musical Truth*) are published this year (Faber Children's 2023). Others are writing original film scripts, videogames and developing podcasts, a large growing area including rights that authors need to be sure not only of safeguarding but agreeing competitive deals. The writing life of an author can be a varied one over the course of a career, and part of the challenge is making good choices to sustain a long career in ever-altering landscapes and markets.

The starting point for any writer, therefore, should be to ensure that they value and take their own work seriously, either by finding a literary agent to advise them or, if unagented, by understanding exactly what they are signing up to, as well as the long-term implications of any publishing contract they enter into. Publishing contracts (in all their many varied forms) have become more complicated in a global market place, and choosing the right publisher for your work – crucially which rights are granted to a publisher – is one of the fundamental reasons why a writer needs an experienced literary agent to navigate increasingly complex waters. A poor publishing deal is frequently a lost opportunity, because it results in valuable rights that could be exploited separately (i.e. earn an author greater remuneration) being tied up as part of the publishing agreement.

An unagented author should think carefully before signing a publishing contract without either seeking advice from the Society of Authors (SoA; see page 495), who have an excellent contract vetting service for members where an author has a publishing contract in-hand, or from publishing industry contract experts such as Contracts People (www.contractspeople.co.uk) who are not literary agents but rather offer a contract service to review, advise and negotiate publishing contracts on a professional fee basis.

2. Negotiating deals

Most successful writers appoint a literary agent because a strong author/literary agent relationship plays a pivotal role for any writer serious about their work and long-term future in an ever-fluctuating industry where there are few guarantees. It is also done because a writer does not have time – nor often the inclination – to negotiate their own publishing deals, never mind numerous publishing deals in foreign languages throughout the world (when a book has a global market).

The impact that the Covid-19 pandemic (as well as Brexit) had on the global print publishing industry should not be underestimated, with rapid growth in online book sales and an increase in ebook and audiobook sales, particularly once VAT was removed from the price of ebooks, notwithstanding that post-pandemic, customer loyalty particularly to independent bookshops and buying locally has helped sustain the printed book market. This may well lead to literary agents pushing to negotiate stronger royalty positions for their authors in these areas where sales are increasing dramatically. It is now not unusual to receive high advance offers from specialist audiobook publishers for the audiobook rights alone. The demand for books to option for TV and film, both fiction and non-fiction, has seldom been stronger with the popularity of BBC iPlayer and streaming services such as Apple TV+, Disney+, Netflix and Amazon Prime. Literary agents have close relationships with literary scouts and TV scouts. An author needs to be aware of the potential value of their work in different formats. As the publishing industry readjusts, also considering the increasing influence of social media platforms such as TikTok, it may be more necessary than ever to find a good literary agent to place work in a very competitive new publishing landscape. Literary agents spend time working editorially with writers honing their work and submission, and they have close relationships with editors and publishers, know their lists and what they are looking for.

3. Championing you as an author

The literary agent plays a key role in the publishing process by working to give voice to an author's work, initially through the submission process, but then primarily with the author's publisher and to the outside world, including media and readers. A writer can go from having a six-figure publishing deal at the dizzying heights of the publishing experience, with sizeable marketing budgets, to finding their next book is not acquired if sales figures are less than expected. Or, at a more mundane level, an author can find the simplest things – such as their editor leaving before their book is published – can impact their publication and longer-term relationship with a publisher. In the long trajectory of a writer's publishing life, having a literary agent who can champion a writer, voice their concerns with the publisher on their behalf, retrench in times of difficulty and help plan and shape their publishing career is vital for professional longevity.

4. Long-term support

As a minimum, working with a literary agent should result in considerably more favourable and industry-competitive contracts, and therefore substantially more earnings over the lifetime of a work. It ensures greater accountability from UK and/or US publishers, as agents work closely with their authors and their publishers throughout the publication process, and a direct relationship with foreign publishers, for example, where foreign rights are retained – since literary agents broker separate publishing deals with publishers in each

Literary agents

separate territory. Some nine years after the original UK publication, I agreed a repeat deal for the Danish rights to Vina Jackson's *Eighty Days Trilogy* (Orion 2012). Books can have long lives in many territories. Ensuring that new deals are being brokered, new opportunities are explored (unsurprisingly there has been a recent surge in demand for romance and uplifting fiction) and that an author is issued payment promptly is all part of a literary agent's role.

More broadly, a literary agent works with their author to advise, shape and help plan their career. I first started working with Antony Johnston because at one time I was one of the few literary agents who represented graphic novelists. I negotiated mainstream publishing deals for his graphic novel adaptations of Anthony Horowitz's *Alex Rider* novels with Walker Books. Since then, his graphic novel *The Coldest City* (Oni Press 2012) was adapted into the film *Atomic Blonde*, and he has written the highly praised *Brigitte Sharp* thriller series (Lightning Books 2017–) as well as *The Organised Writer* for Bloomsbury (2020) – a non-fiction book about the writing process. His new two-book cosy crime series, *The Dog Sitter Detective*, written during lockdown, sold at auction and is published this year (Allison & Busby 2023), and needed careful positioning so that it was separate to Antony's spy thrillers.

Confidential conversations and trust between author and literary agent are crucial to steer major decisions – such as moving from one publisher to another, or advising on shaping a career that traverses different genres and formats including fiction, non-fiction and children's books. It is also telling that publishing industry insiders who are also published writers nearly always appoint literary agents, even though they are wholly familiar

What an agent provides

Authors say they value Sarah's ...

'... passion and commitment ... I am thrilled by the opportunities and feel protected and supported going forward.'

Jeffrey Boakye, author of *Hold Tight* (Influx Press 2017), *Black, Listed* (Dialogue Books 2019), *Musical Truth* (Faber Children's 2021), *I Heard What You Said* (Picador 2022), *Kofi and the Rap Battle Summer* (Faber Children's 2023) and *Musical World* (Faber Children's 2023)

'... experience, tenacity, tranquillity, charm and professionalism. She conducts her business with the utmost integrity.'

Kit Caless, author of *Spoon's Carpets: An Appreciation* (Square Peg 2016, Vintage Digital 2016), and *Secrets: What We Hide and Why* (Audible Original 2022), co-publisher of Influx Press and a *Bookseller* Rising Star 2019

'... help in shaping and developing my career. Thanks to her input I'm now in a situation where I can be a full-time writer, doing what I love, with deals in the UK, around Europe and also in the US. Over the years she has helped me make decisions that are business-smart but that also feel "right" for me.'

Louisa Leaman, author of *The Perfect Dress* (Transworld Digital 2019, Corgi 2020) and *Meant To Be* (Transworld Digital 2020, Corgi 2021)

'... rare combination of skills. Whenever I seek her opinion on my work, I know that she will always take time to give me the honest and thorough answer I need. She also applies the excellent market knowledge and broader cultural savviness, which is so essential to any writer working today.'

Caroline Sanderson, author of *A Rambling Fancy: In the footsteps of Jane Austen* (Cadogan Guides 2006) and *Someone Like Adele* (Omnibus 2012)

'... [role as] guide, philosopher, and friend. Her editorial input has been absolutely invaluable. She has managed always to tread that delicate line between being endlessly supportive and encouraging without giving false expectations, which from the perspective of the author (and authors are a needy bunch) is so vital.'

Heather Cooper, author of *Stealing Roses* (Allison & Busby 2019) and *Arresting Beauty* (Beachy Books Ltd 2023)

with industry practice and publishing contracts. At times in any writer's career there can be concerns about how their work is being promoted or published by their publisher, or whether the publication date is optimum, or when an author needs more input or information; perhaps the author needs to go in a different writing direction altogether. Quite often an author may be successful in one area of publishing but yearns to write in another genre. The ability to navigate such decisions and aspects of the publishing process astutely is something that an author needs to be able to sustain in the longer term; at these times authors can benefit immensely from having a literary agent.

In all writers' careers there will be challenges as well as celebrations. It is the literary agent's role to champion, represent and lobby for the author, to get to the bottom of issues and to help even the most successful author navigate the many troughs and peaks of their publishing career.

Sarah Such founded Sarah Such Literary Agency in 2007. Her previous roles have included Publicity and Marketing Manager at Chatto & Windus, Publicity Director at Penguin Books UK, Senior Editor at Hodder & Stoughton and Editorial Director at Duckworth. She has been shortlisted for Literary Agent of the Year at the British Book Awards three times. Sarah was a judge for Mslexia's 2017 first novel competition and the London Short Story competition 2018. She was a panellist on the Royal Society of Literature's 2023 Careers in Literature event with King's College London.

Follow her on Twitter at @sarahsuch and at https://sarahsuchliteraryagency.tumblr.com.

See also...
● *Breaking into comics*, page 472

A day in the life of a literary agent

Charlotte Seymour reveals the many different strands of an agent's day-to-day work. She explains how fulfilling the role of literary matchmaker and author's champion requires endless perseverance – and makes for a full and often unpredictable day.

One of the best things about working as a literary agent is the variety that fills each and every day and night (I often wake up in the morning surrounded by pages from manuscripts I'm looking at, a published novel I'm reading for pleasure and probably a cookbook too – always good for browsing if you can't get to sleep …). It's a common misconception that people who work in publishing spend all day reading; in fact, most of us do all our reading at home in the evenings and at weekends – otherwise, books would simply never make it onto readers' shelves or Kindles.

So exactly what do agents do in their daily work? Agents come in all shapes and sizes, and have varying interests and ways of working, but an agent is by necessity protean, acting as an author's reader, editor and mentor, their greatest champion and staunchest defender. Here are some of the key elements of my day-to-day work:

1. Discovering authors

Discovering and supporting writing is at the essence of what we do, and as with everything else about the job, we do it in a variety of ways. I always keep an eye on the unsolicited submissions coming in, for although the vast majority are blanket submissions, rather than being targeted to my personal interests, there are gems to be found from time to time. Existing clients and contacts will also often recommend writers to us.

There is an ever-growing number of creative writing courses and writers' festivals which agents are invited to attend, and while it's by no means a requirement of getting published to undertake a costly MA or similar qualification, such courses do offer writers access to industry professionals and vice versa. I make sure also to visit local writers' groups and other book-related events, from launches to readings – you just never know who you might meet.

Finally, when it comes to non-fiction, I will regularly approach someone who is an expert in their field – whether a chef or a scientist – with a view to developing a proposal. So the process of finding new authors to work with is a very proactive one; occasionally, something special will land in your inbox, but, more often than not, you have to go out and find it for yourself!

2. Developing an author's work

Once I've signed up a new author, I will do whatever it takes to get the manuscript or proposal to the stage where I feel it is ready to show to editors. Sometimes it's a case of going through multiple drafts until the work feels as polished as I know how to make it. At other times, and with non-fiction in particular, you can take an idea and working proposal to editors and offer them more input on how they would shape and publish a project.

3. Submitting to editors

When the material is ready, I make an initial round of submissions to those publishing houses I think would be the best fit for the author. In some cases, a book will sell very quickly at auction; in others, it's a question of persisting for many months, or even longer, until you find the one editor who falls for the book. If that book doesn't work, rather than giving up, you think about why it didn't sell and then get working on something new with the author.

At Strand Bookstore in New York, I saw a tote bag (every publishing girl and boy's best friend) for sale bearing the well-known feminist slogan 'Nevertheless she persisted', and I always think this sums up my job. As an agent, you need endless perseverance – and often a bit of luck.

4. Negotiating a publishing deal

When a publisher or several publishers offer for a book, I will negotiate the best possible publishing deal for the author, not just in terms of the money being offered but also the publisher's plans for how to edit, position and promote the book and the author. Sometimes, in an auction, an agent will choose a publisher who offers slightly less money than another but who is a better overall fit for the author.

5. The run-up to publication, and beyond

Getting a publishing deal for an author is a hugely exciting moment, but it's by no means the end of an agent's job. From the moment we have a signed contract, in the run-up to and following publication, I will be regularly checking in with the publisher to ensure that everything is on track, finding out how many copies are being printed, what coverage the publicist has lined up, how the book is performing, and so on. I will also be working with my colleagues and partner agents who sell foreign rights, and film and TV rights, to bring the work to as many other territories and platforms as possible.

6. Keeping up with editors and the book market

An agent is essentially a literary matchmaker, so we dedicate a lot of time to getting to know the individual editors who acquire in the genres we represent, and to understanding their tastes and interests. For those of us based in London and the UK, we can meet fairly easily at any time of year, and a week will rarely go by when I don't see an editor for coffee or visit their office to find out what they've been buying recently and tell them about the projects I have coming up.

I work with English-language publishers across the world as well, so the London Book Fair every spring is a good opportunity to meet with visiting editors; I will also spend a week in New York each year if I can. From time to time I meet with film and TV scouts and producers who are looking for content to adapt. Whoever I'm seeing and wherever we are, I am constantly championing my authors, even if the book in question won't be ready for another year.

Finally, in addition to keeping in touch with editors, I try to stay on top of the book market by reading reviews every week, making sure to read newly published books as well as those I'm working on and just spending hours in bookshops, familiarising myself with what's new on the shelves. I go into a bookshop at least once a week, ostensibly for 'research purposes', though I often leave with something to add to the ever-growing pile!

Highs and lows

One of the best moments as an agent is when you can call an author to let them know you've found them a publisher – and the right publisher for them. After that, the point when it starts to feel more real is when you see the final cover, and of course when you get to hold a print copy for the first time. There are low moments too: brilliant books that you just can't sell, ideas that never quite come to fruition, disappointing sales and dashed expectations. For every peak there's usually a trough, and as an agent you have to weather the storms with and for your authors, as well as celebrating the successes.

The very unpredictability of the job is also one of the greatest joys: some books are instant hits and others are slow burners; reviews can be amazing and sales minuscule; 30 publishers might turn down a book and it goes on to win prizes. You never know quite what's around the corner – and it's thrilling.

A typical day ...

Sometimes I'm out all day to meet with editors, and if I'm reading or editing a new manuscript, I usually work from home, but when I'm in the office, a typical day might go something like this:

Morning

• I get to work and answer any emails that have come in overnight. Two publishers have sent draft contracts for books they have acquired from me, so I will check that the contracts accurately reflect what we've agreed and mark any amendments I want to make before sending back to the publisher.
• I send a new book out on submission, calling editors first to pitch it to them if we haven't already spoken about it, or not recently.
• Then I check in with any editors who are considering other projects I have out on submission and set a deadline for offers on a book for which I've received a first offer.

Afternoon

• After lunch, I have a phone call with an author to discuss progress on their latest book, and then another call with one of our US co-agents to catch up on the authors we are representing for one another.
• Towards the end of the day, I usually look at any unsolicited submissions that have come in by email. It's very rare that I will call in a full manuscript, but I have taken on several wonderful authors from the so-called 'slush pile', one of whose work sold in my biggest deal to date.

Evening

• As I spend so much of the day looking at a computer screen, I'll often print off anything I want to read and take it home with me.

Charlotte Seymour is a literary agent at Johnson & Alcock. She previously worked as an agent at Andrew Nurnberg Associates and as a literary scout at Eccles Fisher Associates. She was Secretary of the Association of Authors' Agents 2019–21 and a *Bookseller* Rising Star 2021.

This article first appeared on the author Sarah Pearse's website, https://sarahpearse.co.uk. Sarah's debut novel, *The Sanatorium*, was published by Transworld in February 2021 and her second novel *Retreat* was published in 2022. Charlotte is her agent.

Querying an agent: top tips about submission

Catherine Cho offers valuable advice for new authors on the submission process, with five essential tips on how to prepare and submit the perfect query package for your book.

I have a lot of faith in the submissions process. It is how I've found nearly all of my authors – writers who just happened to send me a query email along with their first few chapters. But, as much as I want to read my submissions (or 'queries', as we say in the USA), it is often the last thing on my to-do list. Like most agents, my working day is focused on my clients, and so I read submissions in my free time – in the early morning hours, on the tube between meetings or in the evenings after my children have gone to bed. I know that the querying process can be incredibly frustrating and opaque. It's not a perfect process, but what I think is helpful to know is that I want to find a manuscript; I want to say yes.

It's common to hear about the sheer number of queries an agent receives, and it's true. I'm continually amazed by the number of people who write books. I receive over 100 queries a week, and there are agents who receive many more than this. I share this not to be discouraging but as a reminder that when you're preparing your query, you want to make sure that your work and query package is strong. I truly believe that if your book is compelling, then ultimately, it will find a home.

I do know what it's like to be on the other side of the screen. I'd always thought of myself as an agent first – writing was something of an accident. I wrote a memoir that was published in 2020; it was about my experience of postpartum psychosis after the birth of my son. I will never forget how vulnerable I felt putting so much of myself into a piece of work. As an agent, I try to remember that behind every submission, there is a story. I share these tips in the hope that it will give some insight into the querying (submission) process. It's a dream for me to fall in love with something I'm reading – and I feel that sense of possibility every time I open my submissions inbox.

1. Edit again ... and again

My first tip has to be about revision. The most important thing will always be the quality of the work. When you have finished your book, there is often a compulsion to send it out to agents straight away. This is completely natural; you've finished your work and you want someone to read it. However, it's important to resist this feeling and give yourself the space to read your book again, and revise. *Never* send out a first draft. A first impression is the most important one, and you'll need time and space away from your project to be able to read it with perspective. If you can, set the book away for a month or two, and then re-read it again. Edit it again.

The querying process is not the place to receive feedback. Sometimes we hear writers say that they will send out a project to see what agents will say about it, but this can be a very discouraging approach. It's a terrible feeling to send out a project that you know is probably not ready and, most of the time, agents will not give feedback. I often have writers ask me if I can give editorial advice, but I resist doing this unless I have a clear idea of what I think would improve the book. Firstly because it is subjective, but also because, if I'm not able to give a considered and thoughtful response to a manuscript, I don't think it's helpful for me to offer a quick reaction.

Remember that there will always be more edits after signing with an agent, and even more after receiving a publication offer. The best thing you can do for yourself ahead of the querying process is to make your manuscript as strong as it can be, so you feel confident that you're presenting your best work. When I finished my first draft, I was really excited to share it because I couldn't believe I'd finished. I wanted to share it with an agent, but I fought that urge and set it aside for several weeks. When I opened it again, I realised it wasn't ready, and so I redrafted. I think the version I eventually sent to my agent was my eleventh or twelfth draft. I would go on to do another three drafts with my agent, ones that completely took my book apart. Each time I felt I'd gone the furthest I could go – but we kept pushing, and the book kept getting better.

2. Make your opening page the best

The opening sentences of a book are so important in the querying process. I remember being at a conference panel and hearing an agent say that they often stopped reading at the first sentence – which is a terrifying thing to hear, but I think it illustrates how important it is. The strongest opening page or sentence is one that is immediate and distinctive.

As an agent, I remember reading the openings of my clients' books. I'm usually immediately drawn in by the first few lines, and if I don't want to stop reading, then I know that it's something for me. There are many resources about opening pages and scenes, but what is probably most helpful is to look at your favourite books and read their opening paragraphs. Imagine that you're browsing in a bookshop, you open a book that seems intriguing – what are you looking for from those first lines? What will draw you in?

I know that coming up with an opening is very difficult. As a writer, it's something I struggled with. The opening of my book changed multiple times. While I always knew how I wanted my book to be structured, I couldn't figure out the best place to *begin*. Initially I started with what I thought was the most exciting part of the memoir, as a kind of prologue, and then I changed it to something that was slower paced. Each time, it didn't feel quite right. My agent was the one who suggested moving a section from the mid-point of the book to the opening. She was right. This opening helped the book when it was on submission to editors, and it remained in place, word for word, when published.

3. Research

Research is your best friend when it comes to the querying process. Reading this *Yearbook* is already a great first step. It will put you ahead of many of the submissions we receive. It's important to research the agents you choose to submit to. There is no point in sending your picture book to an agent who doesn't represent children's books, or in sending a romantic comedy to an agent who specialises in thrillers.

An agent's taste is subjective (the entire industry is subjective) and so the goal is to find an agent who is looking for the book you've written. And these days, it's so easy to find out what an agent wants – most of us have a social media profile and manuscript wish lists that outline what we're looking for. I would also recommend looking at the acknowledgements section of your favourite authors, or of authors you feel write in the same space that you do, to see who represents them, because that can be a good indicator of someone who is on the lookout for a book like yours.

4. Perfect your query letter

Aside from the material itself, the query letter is the most important part of your submission. There are many opinions on best practices, but I would say the most important thing is that it should be clear and concise. On reading your letter I should have a clear understanding of what your book is and what it's about. That's why many agents will ask for a logline, which is a film industry term, but it's to say what your book is about in one or two sentences. People often tend to put *everything* into their first book, and so the narrative can become muddled or lacks a clear sense of narrative urgency.

So think: Do you know who your readership is? Do you know what books are similar to your own? I truly believe that a writer must also be a reader – it is a red flag for me when a writer says in a submission that they've never read anything like their own work before. There will always be some element of it you can find out there in the marketplace. If someone asks you, 'So, what's your book about?', see if you can describe it concisely: 'It's a book about X'. If you find yourself describing a lot of events that happen in the book: 'Well, this is a book where this happens, and then this happens, and it's about this …', perhaps it doesn't have the narrative drive you need to draw in a reader. This is true for non-fiction, memoir, as well as novels – a compelling book is one that is focused.

There was only one agent I had in mind to represent my book. Admittedly, I had a clear advantage because she was my colleague, so I didn't have to follow the traditional query process. However, I did have to convince her that I knew exactly what my book was about – it was one of the first things she asked me. It wasn't enough that it was a memoir about a difficult experience; I told her that, at the heart of it, my book was about identity and what happens when your identity is blown apart – how do you put yourself back together?

Read as many sample query letters as you can; many authors have generously shared theirs online as examples. When you're writing your query letter, first put as much as you can in, and then cut it down as much as possible. Give your draft letter to someone who has no idea what your book is about and then check: do they have an immediate understanding of what your book is about? I don't think any agent expects a polished sales document, but remember – the query letter is your way of presenting your work. There is a strong correlation between a well-crafted query letter and a compelling manuscript.

5. Focus on the writing process

It can sometimes feel like querying/submission is the most important thing, and that if you have an agent, that's everything. But, actually, signing with an agent is just the first step; finding an editor, finding a readership … there are many more steps in the publishing journey. I recommend that you focus on the process, focus on the writing. It is the best way to get a book published, if that is the goal, but publishing a book isn't the most effective end goal in itself. Storytelling is a craft, and the quality many successful authors share is that they write not to get published, but because they *have* to write. The writing is something that is completely in your control. And the more you write, the better you'll become.

Catherine Cho is a literary agent at Paper Literary, which she founded in 2021. She began her publishing career in New York at Folio Literary Management, before moving to London to work at Curtis Brown where she was promoted to associate agent. She became an agent at Madeleine Milburn Agency, selling six- and seven-figure deals in the US and UK. Catherine is the author of *Inferno: A Memoir of Motherhood and Madness* (Bloomsbury Circus 2020), which was shortlisted for the *Sunday Times* Young Writer of the Year Award. For more information see www.paperliterary.com. Follow her on Twitter @Catkcho.

Literary agents

Literary agents UK and Ireland

The *Writers' & Artists' Yearbook*, along with the Association of Authors' Agents and the Society of Authors, takes a dim view of any literary agent who asks potential clients for a fee prior to reading a manuscript. We advise you to treat any such request with caution and to let us know if that agent appears in the listings below. It is assumed that all agents listed do *not* charge a 'reading fee'. Agents may charge additional costs later in the process but these should only arise once a book has been accepted by a publisher and the author is earning an income. We urge authors to make the distinction between upfront and additional charges. Authors should also check agents' websites before making an enquiry and should familiarise themselves with submission guidelines, agent preferences and manuscript formatting.

*Member of the Association of Authors' Agents
sae = self-addressed envelope

The Accidental Agency

email clare.gristtaylor@accidentalagency.co.uk
website www.accidentalagency.co.uk
Contact Clare Grist Taylor

Agency specialising in non-fiction for adults. Represents memoir, nature writing, history, current affairs, popular science and psychology, lifestyle and wellbeing, smart thinking, business/personal-professional development and humour/gift. *Commission* Home 15%, overseas 20%, film/TV 20%. Submissions should be made via the website. No fiction, academic texts, poetry or children's books.
   Authors include Roger Morgan-Grenville, Simon Morley, Jessica Joelle Alexander, Sue Unerman, Kathryn Jacob, Amanda Goodall, Diane Watt, Lindsey Harrad, Clare Paterson, Mark Edwards, Heidi Ellert-McDermott, Kate Kelland, Mari Takayanagi, Oliver Lewis, Sara Ward. *Founded* 2019.

Aevitas Creative Management UK Ltd

49 Greek Street, London W1D 4EG
email ukenquiries@aevitascreative.com
website www.aevitascreative.com/acm-uk
Twitter @AevitasUK
Ceo & Agent Toby Mundy *Agents* Trevor Dolby, Max Edwards, Sara O'Keeffe, Maria Cardona Serra, Emily Sweet

A management company that represents writers, speakers and brands. Wide range of genres represented including history, science, biography, autobiography, politics and current affairs, literary fiction, crime, thrillers. *Commission* Fiction and non-fiction: Home 15%, USA/translation 20%. Submissions via website. No plays or poetry.
   Clients include Stephen Bush, Graham Farmelo, Daniel Finkelstein, Jeffrey Gedmin, David Goodhart, Charles Handy, Nicholas Humphrey, Charlie Hamilton James, Ian Leslie, Owen Matthews, Richard V. Reeves, Alex R. Holmes, Geoffrey Wheatcroft. *Founded* 2014.

The Agency (London) Ltd*

24 Pottery Lane, London W11 4LZ
tel 020-7727 1346
email childrensbookssubmissions@theagency.co.uk
website https://theagency.co.uk/childrens-books/childrens-home/
Twitter @TheAgencyBooks
Instagram @theagencybooks

Works in conjunction with overseas agents. The Agency also represents screenwriters, directors, playwrights and composers. Represents picture books, including novelty books, fiction for all ages including teenage fiction and series fiction. *Commission* Home 15%, overseas 20%. Submission guidelines on website. *Founded* 1995.

Aitken Alexander Associates Ltd*

291 Gray's Inn Road, London WC1X 8QJ
tel 020-7373 8672
email reception@aitkenalexander.co.uk
website www.aitkenalexander.co.uk
Twitter @AitkenAlexander
Instagram @AitkenAlexander
Directors & Agents Clare Alexander, Lesley Thorne, Lisa Baker, Chris Wellbelove, Emma Paterson, *Agents* Monica MacSwan, Amy St Johnston, *Film/TV/Stage Rights* Lesley Thorne, Jazz Adamson

Fiction and non-fiction. *Commission* Home 15%, USA/translation 20%, film/TV 15%. Email preliminary letter with half-page synopsis and first 30 pages to submissions@aitkenalexander.co.uk. No plays. *Founded* 1977.

AMP Literary

76 Nowell Road, London SW13 9BS
email anna@ampliterary.co.uk
website www.ampliterary.co.uk
Founder Anna Pallai

The agency is searching for unique non-fiction writers. With strong connections across various media platforms, from digital to TV, AMP develops ideas beyond print to maximise exposure. Specialises in commercial non-fiction with a focus on bold female voices. *Commission* UK 15%, USA 20%. Submissions to submissions@ampliterary.co.uk. Include a synopsis and at least three chapters.

Authors include Natasha Devon, Terri White, Anita Mangan, Annalisa Barbieri, Eleanor Ross, Nadine White, Nichi Hodgson, Maddy Anholt, Ellen Jones. *Founded* 2016.

The Ampersand Agency Ltd*

Ryman's Cottages, Little Tew, Oxon OX7 4JJ
tel (01608) 683677/683898
email submissions@theampersandagency.co.uk
website www.theampersandagency.co.uk
Contacts Peter Buckman, Jamie Cowen, Anne-Marie Doulton

Literary and commercial fiction and non-fiction. *Commission* Home 15%, USA 15–20%, translation 20%. Writers should consult the website for information on agents' preferences and submission guidelines. No poetry, books for young children or scripts.

Clients include Tariq Ashkanani, Quentin Bates, Helen Black, Sharon Bolton, Ben Crane, Cora Harrison, Mark Hill, Tendai Huchu, Adrian Selby, Vikas Swarup, and the estates of Georgette Heyer, Jin Yong, Angela Thirkell, Winifred Foley and John James. *Founded* 2003.

Darley Anderson Literary, TV and Film Agency*

Estelle House, 11 Eustace Road, London SW6 1JB
tel 020-7385 6652
website www.darleyanderson.com, www.darleyandersonchildrens.com
Twitter @DA_Agency
Instagram @darleyanderson_agency
Founder Darley Anderson, *Agents* Adult fiction: Darley Anderson, Camilla Bolton, Clare Wallace, Tanera Simons. Children's fiction: Clare Wallace, Lydia Silver, Becca Langton, Darley Anderson, Chloe Davis. *Contacts* Mary Darby (Head of Rights), Kristina Egan (Children's Rights Manager), Georgia Fuller (Rights Manager), Salma Zaragh (Rights Associate), Kira Walker (Rights Assistant)

Overseas associates APA Talent & Literary Agency (LA/Hollywood) and leading foreign agents in selected territories. All commercial fiction and non-fiction. Special interests (fiction): all types of thrillers, crime and mystery, horror; all types of American and Irish novels; comic fiction; popular women's fiction, contemporary and historical romantic fiction, rom-coms, and book club/accessible literary fiction. Special interests (non-fiction): autobiographies, memoirs, sports books, popular psychology, self-help, diet, health, animals, interior design, gardening, religious. *Commission* Home 15%, USA/translation

20%, film/TV/radio 20%. Send covering letter, one page synopsis and first three chapters. Return postage/sae essential for reply. See website for agent specialties. No poetry, novellas, academic books, scripts or screenplays.

Clients include Chris Carter, Lee Child, Martina Cole, John Connolly, Margaret Dickinson, Tana French, T.M. Logan, Stephen Spotswood, Annie Murray, Beth O'Leary, B.A. Paris, Phaedra Patrick, K.L. Slater, Catherine Steadman, Tim Weaver. *Founded* 1988.

Artellus Ltd*

30 Dorset House, Gloucester Place, London NW1 5AD
tel 020-7935 6972
email submissions@artellusltd.co.uk
website www.artellusltd.co.uk
Twitter @Artellus
Agents Leslie Gardner (Director), Gabriele Pantucci (Chairman), Darryl Samaraweera (Company Secretary), Jon Curzon

International literary agency representing writers in all fields and genres. Handles a wide range of fiction, from literary to crime, fantasy and sci-fi, and non-fiction, in areas including history, current affairs, science, economics, investigative journalism, culture and food. Also interested in fine writers in translation. *Commission* Home 15%, direct sales to USA 20%, rest of world 15%. Submissions in the form of a covering note attaching the first three chapters and synopsis. Submissions also accepted by post.

See the website for a full client list. *Founded* 1986.

ASH Literary*

email info@ashliterary.com
website www.ashliterary.com
Twitter @ashliterary
Instagram @ashliterary
Literary Agents Alice Sutherland-Hawes, Saffron Dodd

Children's and YA focused agency representing authors and illustrators covering picture books to YA titles, including graphic novels. All genres represented. *Commission* Home 15%, translation/dramatisation 20%. Send first three chapters and synopsis through QueryManager. Does not handle adult fiction or non-fiction.

Clients include Kereen Getten, Alex Falase-Koya, Radiya Hafiza, Jess McGeachin, Poonam Mistry, Úna Woods. *Founded* 2020.

Tassy Barham Associates

email tassy@tassybarham.com
Proprietor Tassy Barham

Specialises in representing European and American authors, agents and publishers in Brazil and Portugal, as well as the worldwide representation of Brazilian authors. *Founded* 1999.

Kate Barker Literary Agency*

tel 020-7688 1638
email kate@katebarker.net
website www.katebarker.net

Commercial and literary fiction for adults including crime, thriller, suspense, women's fiction, historical and reading group fiction. Non-fiction including narrative non-fiction, popular psychology and science, smart thinking, business, history, memoir, biography, lifestyle and wellbeing. *Commission* Home 15%, overseas 20%, film/TV 20%. Submissions via the website. Does not represent sci-fi, fantasy or children's picture books. *Founded* 2016.

Bath Literary Agency*

5 Gloucester Road, Bath BA1 7BH
email submissions@bathliteraryagency.com
website www.bathliteraryagency.com
Twitter @BathLitAgency
Instagram @bathlitagency
Contact Gill McLay

Specialist in fiction for children and young adults. Also accepts submissions in picture books, non-fiction and author illustrators. *Commission* UK 15%, overseas 20%, film/TV 20%. For full submission details, refer to the website.

Clients include Fox Benwell, Jake Biggin, Conor Busuttil, Philippa Forrester, Dr Jess French, Joe Haddow, Demelsa Haughton, Harry Heape, Laura James, Pippa Pixley, Dr Shini Somara, Tessa Strickland, Anna Terreros Martin, Tweedy, Chris Wakling. *Founded* 2011.

The Bell Lomax Moreton Agency*

Suite C, Victory House, 131 Queensway, Petts Wood, Kent BR5 1DG
tel 020-7930 4447
email agency@bell-lomax.co.uk
website www.belllomaxmoreton.co.uk
Twitter @BLM_Agency
Executives Paul Moreton, Lauren Gardner, Jo Bell, Katie Fulford, Justine Smith, John Baker, Lorna Hemingway, Julie Gourinchas, Rory Jeffers, Sarah McDonnell

Will consider most fiction, non-fiction and children's (including picture books, middle grade and YA) book proposals. Submission guidelines on website. Physical submissions should be accompanied by an sae for return and an email address for correspondence. Does not represent poetry, short stories or novellas, education textbooks, film scripts or stage plays. *Founded* 2000.

Lorella Belli Literary Agency Ltd (LBLA)*

Westbourne Studios, Unit 106, 242 Acklam Road, London W10 5JJ
tel 020-7727 8547
email info@lorellabelliagency.com
website www.lorellabelliagency.com
Facebook www.facebook.com/LorellaBelliLiteraryAgency
Twitter @lblaUK
Proprietor Lorella Belli

Full service literary and management agency. Works with film/TV and overseas associates; represents American literary agencies in the UK. Also sells translation, audio, film/TV and other rights on behalf of British publishers, literary agents and independent authors. Fiction and general non-fiction. Particularly interested in first-time writers and successful self-published authors, books which have international appeal, multicultural writing, books on Italy, crime, mysteries, thrillers, psychological suspense, reading group fiction, women's romance, historicals, memoirs, personal development, popular history, popular science, current affairs, soft business, investigative journalism. *Commission* Home 15%, overseas/dramatic 20%. Send a query email about your work before submitting it. Only online submissions considered. May suggest revision. No children's, sci-fi, fantasy, academic, poetry, original scripts or short stories.

Clients include Nancy Barone, Ruth Dugdall, Joy Ellis, Jemma Hatt, Lisa Hobman, Joffe Books, Angela Marsons, Holly Martin, Nicola May, Dreda Say Mitchell, Rick Mofina, Matt Potter, Layla Saad, Siddarth Shrikanth, Silvertail Books. *Founded* 2002.

The Bent Agency*

17 Kelsall Mews, Richmond TW9 4BP
email info@thebentagency.com
website www.thebentagency.com
Agents Nicola Barr, Gemma Cooper, Molly Ker Hawn, Zöe Plant

Full-service literary agency with offices in the UK and USA. Represents a diverse range of genres including history, humour, lifestyle, inspiration, memoir, literary fiction, children's and commercial fiction. Only accepts email queries. See website for detailed query and submission guidelines.

Clients include Faridah Abike-Iyimide, B.B. Alston, Gary John Bishop, Dhonielle Clayton, Stephanie Garber, Guy Gavriel Kay, Hilary McKay, Jo Spain, Robin Stevens, Angie Thomas, Jessica Townsend. *Founded* 2009.

Berlin Associates Ltd

7 Tyers Gate, London SE1 3HX
tel 020-7836 1112
email submissions@berlinassociates.com
website www.berlinassociates.com
Twitter @berlinassocs
Agents Marc Berlin, Stacy Browne, Matt Connell, Alexandra Cory, Rachel Daniels, Charlie MacVicar, Yas Lewis, Julia Mills, Maddie O'Dwyer, Laura Reeve, Fiona Williams, Emily Wraith, Julia Wyatt

A boutique agency representing writers, directors, producers, designers, composers and below-the-line talent across theatre, film, TV, radio and new media. All genres represented. The majority of new clients are taken on through recommendation or invitation; however, if you would like your work to be considered for representation, email a CV along with a brief outline of your experience and the work you would like to submit for consideration. No prose/fiction. *Founded* 2003.

The bks Agency

Pennine Place, 2A Charing Cross Road, London WC2H 0FH
website www.thebksagency.com
Contacts Jason Bartholomew, Jessica Killingley, James Spackman, Joanna Kaliszewska, Morwenna Loughman

A literary management agency representing fiction and non-fiction authors. A division of Midas. Genres represented include non-fiction: history, politics, current affairs, biography, memoir, narrative non-fiction, business, personal development, general lifestyle and wellbeing, sport, music, culture and smart thinking; fiction: crime, mystery, thriller, suspense, women's fiction, reading group fiction, literary fiction, graphic fiction/non-fiction and YA. Pitch ideas via the online form. See website for full guidelines. No poetry.
  Authors include Noor Hibbert, Eleanor Tweddell, Jo Wimble-Groves, Ellie Wallace, Timi Merriman Johnson, Melanie Blake, Pete Wharmby, Eva Mozes Kor, Kate Dramis, Emily Katy, Jane Cholmeley, Doro Globus, Jill Halfpenny, Kingston Trinder, Maike Winters. *Founded* 2018.

The Blair Partnership*

PO Box 7828, London W1A 4GE
tel 020-7504 2520
email info@theblairpartnership.com
website www.theblairpartnership.com
Twitter @TBP_agency
Instagram @theblairpartnership_agency
Founding Partner & Agent Neil Blair, *Agency Director* Rory Scarfe, *Agents* Hattie Grünewald, Rachel Petty, Jordan Lees, Bea Fitzgerald

Represents a range of people internationally from debut and established writers to broader talent across business, arts, politics, sport and lifestyle. Range of work spans fiction, non-fiction, digital, TV and film production. Considers all genres of fiction and non-fiction for adults, young readers and children. Will consider unsolicited MSS. Fiction: email the specific agent with a covering letter, a one-page synopsis and the first three chapters. Non-fiction: email a proposal document and writing sample. Not currently accepting screenplays, short stories or poetry.
  Clients include Lizzy Dent, Earthling Ed, Sue Fortin, Henry Fraser, Tyson and Paris Fury, Dr Pippa Grange, Emma Hayes MBE, Sir Chris Hoy, Louise

Jensen, Lee Lawrence, Luna McNamara, Nancy Tucker, Jon Sopel, J.K. Rowling, Stephanie Yeboah. *Founded* 2011.

Blake Friedmann Literary, TV & Film Agency Ltd*

Ground Floor, 15 Highbury Place, London N5 1QP
tel 020-7387 0842
email info@blakefriedmann.co.uk
website www.blakefriedmann.co.uk
Book Agents Isobel Dixon, Kate Burke, Juliet Pickering, Sian Ellis-Martin, *Film/TV Agents* Julian Friedmann, Conrad Williams, Anna Myrmus

Full-length MSS. Fiction: crime, thrillers, women's fiction, historical fiction, speculative fiction and literary fiction; a broad range of non-fiction. Media Department handles film and TV rights, and represents scriptwriters, playwrights and directors. *Commission* Home 15%, overseas 20%. Preliminary letter, synopsis and first three chapters via email. See website for full submission guidelines.
  Authors include Graeme Armstrong, Bolu Babalola, Graeme Macrae Burnet, Edward Carey, Will Dean, David Gilman, Kerry Hudson, Peter James, Lucy Mangan, Joseph O'Connor, Sheila O'Flanagan, Monique Roffey. *Scriptwriters* include Andy Briggs, Marteinn Thorisson, Stuart Urban. *Founded* 1977.

The Book Bureau Literary Agency

7 Duncairn Avenue, Bray, Co. Wicklow A98 R293, Republic of Ireland
tel +353 (0)1 276 4996
email thebookbureau123@gmail.com
website http://thebookbureauliteraryagency.com
Managing Director Ger Nichol

Works with agents overseas. Sub-agents: The Rights People. Full-length MSS. Fiction only: general, thrillers, crime, Irish novels, literary fiction, women's commercial novels. *Commission* Home 15%, USA 20%, translation 25%. Send preliminary letter, synopsis and three sample chapters (single line spacing); return postage required. Email preferred. No horror, sci-fi, children's or poetry.
  Clients include Ciara Geraghty, Patricia Gibney, Claire Allan, Amanda Robson, Sian O'Gorman, Dr Paula McGrath, Dr Ellen McWilliams, Dan Brotzel, Cormac O'Keeffe, Aidan Conway, Gillian Harvey, Nicola Gill, Michael O'Toole. *Founded* 1998.

Alan Brodie Representation

14 The Barbon Buildings, Red Lion Square, London WC1R 4QH
tel 020-7253 6226
email abr@alanbrodie.com
website www.alanbrodie.com
Twitter @abragency
Instagram @abragency
Managing Director Alan Brodie, *Agent* Victoria Williams

Specialises in stage plays, literary estates, radio, TV and film. Represented in all major countries. *Commission* Home 10%, overseas 15%. No unsolicited scripts; recommendation from known professional required. No prose, fiction or general MSS. *Founded* 1996.

Brotherstone Creative Management*
Mortimer House, 37–41 Mortimer Street, London W1T 3JH
email info@bcm-agency.com
website https://bcm-agency.com
Contact Charlie Brotherstone

Represents an eclectic list of authors, from academics, musicians and cookery writers through to novelists of commercial and literary fiction. The agency guides each client through every part of the publishing process and draws upon a wide contact network to develop their careers across all media. *Commission* UK 15%, USA direct 20%, dramatic 20%, translation 20%, TV 15%. Submissions by email to submissions@bcm-agency.com. For fiction, include the first three chapters or 30 pages, a one- or two-page synopsis and a short covering letter; for non-fiction, send a detailed outline with a sample chapter and a covering note. Does not represent children's and young adult fiction, sci-fi and fantasy novels or unsolicited short story and poetry collections.

Clients include Brett Anderson, Stephen Bayley, A.A. Gill, Dan Hicks, Kirstin Innes, Joanne Molinaro, George The Poet, Anna Stothard, Jessie Ware, Giles Yeo. *Founded* 2017.

Jenny Brown Associates*
31 Marchmont Road, Edinburgh EH9 1HU
email info@jennybrownassociates.com
website www.jennybrownassociates.com
Contact Jenny Brown, Lucy Juckes, Lisa Highton

Literary fiction, crime writing and narrative non-fiction including literary memoir and nature writing; writing and illustration for children, both fiction and non-fiction. Has a preference for working with writers or illustrators based in Scotland. *Commission* Home 15%, overseas/translation 20%. A small agency which only reads submissions at certain points in the year; always check website before sending work. No poetry, sci-fi, fantasy or academic.

Clients include Lin Anderson, Shaun Bythell, Christopher Edge, Gavin Francis, Alex Gray, Joanna Hickson, Ruth Hogan, Kathleen Jamie, Helen Kellock, Sally Magnusson, Sara Maitland, Jonathan Meres, Ann O'Loughlin, Chitra Ramaswamy, Malachy Tallack. *Founded* 2002.

Felicity Bryan Associates*
2A North Parade, Banbury Road, Oxford OX2 6LX
tel (01865) 513816
email agency@felicitybryan.com
website www.felicitybryan.com

Translation rights handled by Andrew Nurnberg Associates; works in conjunction with US agents. Literary and commercial upmarket fiction and general non-fiction, with emphasis on history, biography, science and nature. *Commission* Home 15%, overseas 20%. All submissions and queries through website. No sci-fi and fantasy, horror, erotica, romance, self-help, graphic novels, scripts or poetry.

Clients include Karen Armstrong, Catherine Belton, Louis de Bernières, Jonathan Coe, Edmund de Waal, Reni Eddo-Lodge, Peter Frankopan, Damon Galgut, Thomas Halliday, Tim Harford, Anna Hope, Gill Hornby, Diarmaid MacCulloch, Jon Savage, Lucy Worsley. *Founded* 1988.

C&W Agency*
(previously Conville & Walsh)
Cunard House, 15 Regent Street, London SW1Y 4LR
tel 020-7393 4200
website www.cwagency.co.uk
Twitter @CWAgencyUK
Instagram @CWAgencyUK
Agents Clare Conville, Susan Armstrong, Sophie Lambert, Alexander Cochran, Emma Finn, Lucy Luck, Richard Pike, Carrie Kania

Handles all genres of fiction, non-fiction and children's worldwide. *Commission* Home 15%, overseas 20%. Submissions welcome: first three chapters, cover letter and synopsis by email to the agent you would like to consider your work. Part of the Curtis Brown Group of Companies; simultaneous submission accepted. No picture books, poetry or dramatic works.

Fiction clients include Matt Haig, M.L. Stedman, Rachel Joyce, Kevin Barry, Andrew Michael Hurley, Joanna Cannon, Nathan Filer, S.J. Watson, D.B.C. Pierre, Jess Kidd. *Non-fiction clients* include Dolly Alderton, Misha Glenny, Tim Spector, Christie Watson, Ben Wilson. *Founded* 2000.

Georgina Capel Associates Ltd*
29 Wardour Street, London W1D 6PS
tel 020-7734 2414
email [firstname]@georginacapel.com
website www.georginacapel.com
Agents Georgina Capel, Rachel Conway, Simon Shaps, Irene Baldoni, Philippa Brewster

Literary and commercial fiction, history, biography; film and TV; also writers for children and young adults. *Commission* Home/overseas 15%. Postal submissions preferred, but do accept email. Include a covering letter, synopsis and first three chapters.

Clients include Julia Copus, Adrian Goldsworthy, Philip Hoare, Dan Jones, Tobias Jones, Adam Nicolson, Ben Okri, Chibundu Onuzo, Olivette Otele, Andrew Roberts, Ian Sansom, Simon Sebag Montefiore, Jo Shapcott, Lesley Thomson and the estate of Fay Weldon. *Founded* 1999.

Rebecca Carter Literary

tel 07717 581710
email rebecca@rebeccacarterliterary.com
website www.rebeccacarterliterary.com
Twitter @RebeccasBooks
Instagram @rebeccacarterliteraryagent
Director Rebecca Carter

Full service agency with a broad international reach across the media industry. Literary fiction, crime and thriller. Narrative non-fiction with an emphasis on books that engage with the past and the issues of our times in an imaginative way. *Commission* Home 15%, overseas 20%, film/TV 20%. Send submission to submissions@rebeccacarterliterary.com, with a synopsis and three sample chapters.

Clients include Alice Albinia, Rutger Bregman, Elly Griffiths, Xiaolu Guo, Andrew Harding, Olivia Laing, Ferdia Lennon, Gavin McCrea, Nell Stevens, Rebecca Stott. *Founded* 2022.

Robert Caskie Ltd

tel 07900 431005
email robert@robertcaskie.com
website www.robertcaskie.com
Twitter @rcaskie1

Represents a broad range of writers of fiction (particularly reading group and literary) and non-fiction (narrative, nature writing, memoir, politics and social issues). *Commission* Home 15%, overseas 20%. Email submission to submissions@robertcaskie.com. For fiction: send an introductory email and the first three chapters. For non-fiction: send an introductory email, a detailed outline and a sample chapter. Does not represent children's, crime and thriller, YA, horror or sci-fi.

Authors include Louis Theroux, Sarah Winman, Libby Page, Emma Barnett, Sir Trevor McDonald, Lord Michael Cashman, Ilana Fox, Manda Scott, Kate Spicer, Lorraine Candy. *Founded* 2020.

The Catchpole Agency

53 Cranham Street, Oxford OX2 6DD
tel 07789 588070
email james@thecatchpoleagency.co.uk
website www.thecatchpoleagency.co.uk
Instagram @thecatchpoles
Proprietor James Catchpole

Agents for authors and illustrators of children's books from picture books through to YA novels, with a specialism in editorial work. Email submissions@thecatchpoleagency.co.uk with a covering letter which includes a one- or two-sentence elevator pitch, the intended readership and a writing sample pasted directly into the body of the email. See additional submissions details on the website.

Authors include Polly Dunbar, S.F. Said, Michelle Robinson, Emer Stamp, Sean Taylor. *Founded* 1996.

Chapman & Vincent*

21 Ellis Street, London SW1X 9AL
email chapmanvincent@hotmail.co.uk
Directors Jennifer Chapman, Gilly Vincent

A specialist agency acting mainly as a packager. Works with Elaine Markson in the USA. Non-fiction agent packagers for texts suitable for major illustration in heritage, interiors, gardening and cookery. *Commission* Home 15%, overseas 20%. Not currently seeking new clients but will reply to all sensible approaches by email without attachments in this limited area. No postal submissions.

Teresa Chris Literary Agency Ltd*

43 Musard Road, London W6 8NR
tel 020-7386 0633
email teresachris@litagency.co.uk
website www.teresachrisliteraryagency.co.uk
Director Teresa Chris

All fiction, especially crime, women's commercial, general and literary fiction. Representation in all overseas territories. *Commission* Home 10%, overseas 20%. Send an email with an introductory letter, synopsis and the first three chapters. Will only respond if interested. No sci-fi, horror, fantasy, short stories, poetry or academic books.

Clients include Dilly Court, Stephen Booth, Rory Clements, Julie Cohen, Kate Rhodes, M.A. Bennett. *Founded* 1988.

Anne Clark Literary Agency*

email submissions@anneclarkliteraryagency.co.uk
website www.anneclarkliteraryagency.co.uk
Facebook www.facebook.com/anneclarkliterary
Twitter @AnneClarkLit
Contact Anne Clark

Specialist in fiction, non-fiction and picture books for children and young adults. *Commission* Home 15%, overseas 20%. Submissions by email only. See website for details.

Clients include Mike Barfield, Anne Booth, Moira Butterfield, Lou Carter, Emily-Jane Clark, Pippa Goodhart, Cath Howe, Penny Joelson, Ruth Lauren, Leah Mohammed, Rebecca Patterson, Jason Rohan, Lucy Rowland. *Founded* 2012.

Mary Clemmey Literary Agency*

6 Dunollie Road, London NW5 2XP
tel 020-7267 1290
email mcwords@googlemail.com

High-quality fiction and non-fiction with an international market. TV, film, radio and theatre scripts from existing clients only. Works in conjunction with US agent. *Commission* Home 15%, overseas 20%, performance rights 15%. No unsolicited MSS. No children's books or sci-fi. *Founded* 1992.

Jonathan Clowes Ltd*

tel 020-7722 7674
email admin@jonathanclowes.co.uk
website www.jonathanclowes.co.uk
Directors Ann Evans, Nemonie Craven Roderick

Literary and commercial fiction and non-fiction, film, TV, theatre (for existing clients) and radio. Email for general enquiries. Works in association with agents overseas. *Commission* Home 15%, overseas 20%. Send covering email with synopsis and first three chapters attached. Check agents' interests and availability before submitting.

Clients include Arthur Conan Doyle Characters Ltd, Simon Critchley, Brian Freemantle, Francesca Hornak, Gruff Rhys, and the literary estates of Doris Lessing, Elizabeth Jane Howard, Michael Baigent, Dr David Bellamy and Richard Leigh. *Founded* 1960.

Colwill & Peddle*

email submissions@colwillandpeddle.com
website www.colwillandpeddle.com
Twitter @colwillpeddle
Instagram @colwillandpeddle
Agents Charlotte Colwill, Kay Peddle

Focused on finding new voices and untold stories. Works with a number of foreign, film and TV co-agents to sell the rights to our clients' work internationally, in all formats and mediums. Charlotte is looking for adult fiction, children's fiction and non-fiction, and children's author-illustrators. Kay is looking for non-fiction: history, politics, essays, popular science, biography, memoir, travel, cookery and current affairs. *Commission* Home 15%, USA/foreign 20%. See website for detailed submission guidelines. Does not represent screenwriters or poets.

Authors include Kimberly McIntosh, Helen Graves, Joe Mulhall, It's a Continent, Kerri Andrews, Richard Smyth, Jess Morgan, Gianni Washington, Mark Illis, Kasia Delgado, Rupal Patel, Cecily Blench, Jemima Foxtrot, Samuel Blanchett. *Founded* 2022.

Coombs Moylett Maclean Literary Agency

120 New Kings Road, London SW6 4LZ
tel 020-8740 0454
website www.cmm.agency
Contacts Lisa Moylett, Jamie Maclean, Zoe Apostolides

Interested in well-written commercial fiction, particularly historical, crime/mystery/suspense, thrillers, women's fiction from chick-lit sagas to contemporary and literary fiction. Considers most non-fiction, particularly history, biography, current affairs, politics, how-to, true crime and popular science. *Commission* Home 15%, overseas 20%, film/TV 20%. Works with foreign agents. Please note that whole books and manuscript submissions via post and/or email will not be accepted. Check the website

for details on how to submit. Does not handle poetry, plays or scripts for film and TV, children's or YA.

Clients include Leye Adenle, Dr Sarah Woodhouse, Simon Brett, Ian Dunt, Jonathan Gash, John Gardner, Jonathon Green, Lisa Hall, Chris Hart, Mark McCrum, Frankie McGowan, Catriona McPherson, Malachi O'Doherty. *Founded* 1997.

Creative Authors Ltd

11A Woodlawn Street, Whitstable, Kent CT5 1HQ
email write@creativeauthors.co.uk
website www.creativeauthors.co.uk
Twitter @creativeauthors
Instagram @creativeauthors
Director Isabel Atherton

Fiction, women's fiction, literary fiction, non-fiction, humour, history, science, autobiography, biography, business, memoir, health, cookery, arts and crafts, crime, children's fiction, picture books, YA, graphic novels and illustrators. *Commission* Home 15%, overseas 20%. Only accepts email submissions.

Authors and illustrators include Guojing, Ged Adamson, Zuza Zak, Colleen Kosinski, Dr Keith Souter, E.A. Hanks, Caroline Young, Tamara Sturtz-Filby, Kristen Bateman. *Founded* 2008.

Rupert Crew Ltd*

Southgate, 7 Linden Avenue, Dorchester DT1 1EJ
tel (01305) 260335
email info@rupertcrew.co.uk
website www.rupertcrew.co.uk
Managing Director Caroline Montgomery

International representation, handling accessible literary and commercial fiction and non-fiction for adult and children's (8+) markets. *Commission* Home 15%, overseas 20%, film/TV/radio 20%. No unsolicited MSS: see website for current submission guidelines. No picture books, plays, screenplays, poetry, journalism, sci-fi and fantasy or short stories. *Founded* 1927.

Cull & Co.*

website https://cullandco.com
Twitter @CullandCoAgency
Ceo & Agent Tom J. Cull

Independent agency specialising in non-fiction for adults. Works in conjunction with overseas agents in translation and film/TV. Wide range of genres represented including history, espionage, biography, autobiography, pop culture, sport, politics and current affairs. Occasional fiction including literary fiction, crime and thrillers. *Commission* Home 15%, overseas 20%, film/TV 20%. Submissions via website. No plays or screenplays, poetry, children's books or YA.

Clients include Michael Smith, Rachel Lichtenstein, C.J. Schuler, Mary Novakovich, Seth Thevoz, Robert Sellers, Henry R. Schlesinger, Nicholas Farrell, Sarah-Louise Miller, Jeremy Black. *Founded* 2017.

Curtis Brown*

Cunard House, 15 Regent Street, London SW1Y 4LR
tel 020-7393 4400
email cb@curtisbrown.co.uk
website www.curtisbrown.co.uk,
www.curtisbrowncreative.co.uk
Twitter @CBGBooks, @cbcreative
Chair Jonny Geller, *Head of Books* Stephanie
Thwaites, *Senior Agents* Sheila Crowley, Gordon
Wise, *Agents* Felicity Blunt, Jonathan Lloyd, Alice
Lutyens, Lucy Morris, Cathryn Summerhayes,
Heritage Becky Brown, Norah Perkins, *Associates* Lisa
Babalis, Sabhbh Curran, Isobel Gahan, Viola Hayden,
Jess Molloy, *Audio & Podcasts* Sophia MacAskill,
Anna Weguelin

Represents prominent writers of fiction and non-
fiction, from winners of all major awards to
international bestsellers and from debuts to literary
estates. Also manages the international careers of
authors, with strong relationships in translation and
US markets as well as a growing European-language
business. Offers full-service representation in film,
TV, theatre, audio, events and other performance. In
fiction, works across many genres, both literary and
those aimed at a popular audience, and looks for
strong voices and outstanding storytellers in general
fiction, crime, thrillers, psychological suspense,
speculative and historical fiction, YA and children's
books. Non-fiction list includes leading
commentators and thinkers, historians, biographers,
social media influencers, lifestyle brands, scientists
and writers of quality narrative non-fiction. See
website and individual agent webpages. Simultaneous
submissions with C&W. *Founded* 1899.

Dark House Literary & Screen Agency Ltd

19 Tottenhall Road, London N13 6HY
tel 07812 004546
email submission@darkhouse.uk
website www.darkhouse.uk
Twitter @DarkHouseAgency
Managing Director Andreas Charalambous

Represents the works of authors and creatives
working within the horror and dark fantasy genres,
including adult fiction, non-fiction, graphic novels,
children's (with subtle horror themes) and YA. Also
interested in screenplays for TV and film. Email
submissions only. Fiction: attach a Word document
that includes a brief synopsis and the first three
chapters of the MS. Non-fiction: include a proposal,
short synopsis and up-to-date CV. Does not
represent works of poetry, picture books, theatrical
scripts and any other genres bar horror and dark
fantasy. *Founded* 2023.

Caroline Davidson Literary Agency*

5 Queen Anne's Gardens, London W4 1TU
tel 020-8995 5768

email enquiries@cdla.co.uk
website www.cdla.co.uk

Handles exceptional novels, memoirs and non-fiction
of originality and high quality. All submissions must
be in hard copy. Email submissions are not
considered. For non-fiction, send letter with CV and
detailed, well thoughtout book proposal, including
chapter synopsis. For fiction, send letter, CV, three-
line pitch, synopsis and the first 50 pages and last ten
pages of text. No reply without large sae with correct
return postage. CDLA dislikes fantasy, horror, sci-fi
and crime.

Authors include Emma Donoghue, Chris
Greenhalgh, Richard Hobday, Helena Whitbread.
Founded 1988.

Felix de Wolfe

20 Old Compton Street, London W1D 4TW
tel 020-7242 5066
email info@felixdewolfe.com
website https://felixdewolfe.com
Twitter @felixdewolfe
Instagram @felixdewolfe
Agents Caroline de Wolfe, Wendy Scozzaro, Rob
Hughes, Dom Scozzaro

Theatre, films, TV, sound broadcasting and fiction.
Works in conjunction with many foreign agencies.
Commission Home 10–15%, overseas 20%. For
fiction, send a CV/biography with a synopsis and the
first 15 pages of your work. Not currently accepting
unsolicated literary submissions. *Founded* 1947.

DGA Ltd

2nd Floor, 40 Rosebery Avenue, Clerkenwell,
London EC1R 4RX
tel 020-7240 9992
email rachel@davidgodwinassociates.co.uk
website www.davidgodwinassociates.com
Twitter @DGALitAgents
Instagram @DGALiterary
Directors David Godwin, Heather Godwin

Broad range of fiction and non-fiction with a strong
focus on literary. Send first 30 pages with synopsis
and cover letter to
submissions@davidgodwinassociates.co.uk.

Clients include Simon Armitage, Christina Lamb,
Richard Holmes, Claire Tomalin, Jeremy Paxman,
Norman Davies, Vikram Seth, Arundhati Roy,
William Dalrymple, Shehan Karunatilaka, Geetanjali
Shree. *Founded* 1995.

DHH Literary Agency*

23–27 Cecil Court, London WC2N 4EZ
tel 020-7836 7376
email enquiries@dhhliteraryagency.com
website www.dhhliteraryagency.com
Facebook www.facebook.com/dhhliteraryagency
Twitter @dhhlitagency

Agents David H. Headley, Broo Doherty, Hannah Sheppard, Harry Illingworth, Emily Glenister, Tom Drake-Lee

Represents fiction, women's commercial fiction, crime, thriller, literary fiction, speculative fiction, sci-fi and fantasy. Non-fiction special interests include narrative non-fiction, memoir, history, cookery and humour. Also children's and YA fiction. *Commission* UK 15%, overseas 15% (20% where a sub-agent is used). Send informative preliminary email with first three chapters and synopsis. Consult website for correct email addresses for each agent. New authors welcome. No plays or scripts, poetry or short stories.

  Authors include Stuart Turton, Femi Kayode, Micaiah Johnson, Anna Jacobs, Jules Wake, Phillipa Ashley, Amanda Jennings, Jo Thomas, Ragnar Jonasson, M.W. Craven, Anita Frank, Victoria Selman, Sarah Bonner, Abi Elphinstone. *Founded* 2008.

Diamond Kahn & Woods Literary Agency*

Top Floor, 66 Onslow Gardens, London N10 3JX
tel 020-3514 6544
email info@dkwlitagency.co.uk
email submissions.ella@dkwlitagency.co.uk
email submissions.bryony@dkwlitagency.co.uk
website www.dkwlitagency.co.uk
Twitter @DKWLitAgency
Agents Ella Diamond Kahn, Bryony Woods

Literary and commercial fiction (including all major genres) and non-fiction for adults, plus children's, YA and crossover fiction. Interested in new writers. *Commission* Home 15%, USA/translation 20%. Email submissions only. Send three chapters and synopsis to one agent only.

  Clients include Virginia Macgregor, S.E. Lister, Chris Lloyd, Nicole Burstein, David Owen, Caroline O'Donoghue, Sharon Gosling, Sylvia Bishop, Katherine Orton, Calum McSwiggan, Laura Jane Williams, Catriona Silvey, Jayne Cowie, Natalie Hart, Daisy May Johnson. *Founded* 2012.

Elise Dillsworth Agency

9 Grosvenor Road, Muswell Hill, London N10 2DR
email elise@elisedillsworthagency.com
website www.elisedillsworthagency.com
Twitter @EliseDillsworth
Owner & Literary Agent Elise Dillsworth

Represents literary and general fiction and non-fiction in the areas of memoir, biography, travel and cookery, with a keen aim to reflect writing that is international. *Commission* Home 15%, overseas 20%. Send preliminary letter, synopsis and first three chapters (or approximately 50 pages). No postal submissions accepted. See website for full submission guidelines. Does not represent sci-fi, fantasy, plays, film/TV scripts or children's books.

  Authors include Yvonne Battle-Felton, Maria Bradford, Anthony Joseph, Foday Mannah, Charlotte Morgan-Nwokenna, Irenosen Okojie, Yewande Omotoso, Hanna Randall, Noo Saro-Wiwa, Courtney Pine, Aisling Watters and the estates of Roy Heath and Diane Oliver. *Founded* 2012.

Robert Dudley Agency

135A Bridge Street, Ashford, Kent TN25 5DP
tel 07879 426574
email info@robertdudleyagency.co.uk
website www.robertdudleyagency.co.uk
Proprietor Robert Dudley

Non-fiction only. Specialises in history, biography, sport, management, politics, military history, current affairs. *Commission* Home 15%, overseas 20%, film/TV/radio 20%. Will suggest revision. Email submissions preferred. All material sent at owner's risk. No MSS returned without sae.

  Authors include Edoardo Albert, Ben Barry, Michael Broers, Elsie Burch Donald, Prit Buttar, Ambrogio Caiani, Tim Hannigan, Kit Holden, Halik Kochanski, Mungo Melvin, Adrian Phillips, Brian Holden Reid, Mary Colwell, Chris Sidwells, Martyn Whittock. *Founded* 2000.

Dunn Fogg

PO Box 78047, London N4 9LP
email info@dunnfogg.co.uk
website https://dunnfogg.co.uk/
Agents Ben Dunn, Jack Fogg

A full-service, independent literary agency. Fiction: literary, crime, book club, historical, sci-fi and fantasy. Non-fiction: memoir, narrative, sport, business, popular science, big ideas, music, food and media tie-in. *Commission* Home 15%, overseas 20%. Fiction: synopsis, brief biography and first three chapters or 50 pages of your novel. Non-fiction: pitch of the book, brief biography and sample chapter(s). No children's or YA.

  Clients include Annie MacManus, Daisy May Cooper, Dan Schreiber, Dr Richard Firth-Godbehere, Meriel Schindler, Sophia Handschuh, Paul Sexton, Andrew 'Beef' Johnston, Christian Sylt, Caroline Reid, Ania Bas, Ben Timberlake, Teo van den Broeke, Nina Pottell. *Founded* 2021.

Eddison Pearson Ltd*

West Hill House, 6 Swains Lane, London N6 6QS
tel 020-7700 7763
email enquiries@eddisonpearson.com
website www.eddisonpearson.com
Contact Clare Pearson

Small, personally run agency. Children's and YA books, fiction and non-fiction, poetry. *Commission* Home 10–15%, overseas 15–20%. Enquiries and submissions by email only; email for up-to-date submission guidelines. May suggest revision where appropriate.

  Authors include Valerie Bloom, Sue Heap, Caroline Lawrence, Robert Muchamore, Mary Murphy, Megan Rix. *Founded* 1997.

Edwards Fuglewicz Literary Agency*

49 Great Ormond Street, London WC1N 3HZ
tel 020-7405 6725
Contacts Ros Edwards, Jill McCluskey

Literary and commercial fiction; non-fiction: biography and narrative non-fiction (including animal stories). *Commission* Home 15%, USA/translation 20%. No email submissions. No children's fiction, sci-fi or horror. *Founded* 1996.

Fillingham Weston Associates

20 Mortlake, 20 Mortlake High Street, London SW14 8JN
tel 020-8748 5594
website www.fillinghamweston.com
Agent Kate Weston, *Consultant* Janet Fillingham

Film, TV and theatre only. *Commission* Home 15%, overseas 15–20%. Strictly no unsolicited MSS; professional recommendation required. No books. *Founded* 1992.

Film Rights Ltd

(In association with Laurence Fitch Ltd)
11 Pandora Road, London NW6 1TS
tel 020-8001 3040
email information@filmrights.ltd.uk
email information@laurencefitch.com
website www.filmrights.ltd.uk,
www.laurencefitch.com
Contact Brendan Davis

Incorporating The London Play Company. Represented in USA and abroad. Theatre, films, TV and sound broadcasting. *Commission* Home 10%, overseas 15%.

Clients include Carlo Ardito, John Chapman, Peter Coke, Ray Cooney OBE, Dave Freeman, John Graham, Robin Hawdon, Jeremy Lloyd (plays), Dawn Lowe-Watson, Glyn Robbins, Edward Taylor, the estates of Dodie Smith and Frank Baker, the literary estates of N.C. Hunter and Michael Pertwee. *Founded* 1935.

42*

Palladium House, 7th Floor, 1–4 Argyll Street, London W1F 7TA
email info@42mp.com
website https://www.42mp.com/books/
Agents Eugenie Furniss, Marilia Savvides, Emily MacDonald

Full-service representation, including placing books with producers for adaptation in film, television, podcasting and other types of media. Our authors are published in over 40 languages. Fiction: all types of thrillers, crime and mystery, historical fiction, speculative fiction, women's fiction, accessible literary/reading group fiction, grounded horror and grounded sci-fi. Non-fiction: biography, history, memoir, investigative, popular psychology and a wide range of narrative non-fiction. *Commission* Home 15%, USA/translation 20%, film/TV 20%. See website

for agent wish lists and contact information, as well as submission guidelines. No poetry, plays or academic books.

Authors include Catherine Bailey, Clare Balding, Julian Clary, Hanna Jameson, Emily Maitlis, Jessica Moor, Abi Morgan, Neil Oliver, Matthew Reilly, Keith Stuart, S.K. Tremayne, Adriana Trigiani. *Founded* 2019.

Fox & Howard Literary Agency*

39 Eland Road, London SW11 5JX
tel (01824) 790817
email enquiries@foxandhoward.co.uk
website www.foxandhoward.co.uk
Contact Charlotte Howard, Chelsey Fox

General non-fiction: biography and memoirs, history and current affairs, mind, body & spirit, health and personal development, popular science and maths. *Commission* Home 15%, overseas 20%. The client list is currently closed. *Founded* 1992.

FRA*

(formerly Futerman, Rose & Associates)
91 St Leonards Road, London SW14 7BL
tel 020-8255 7755
email guy@futermanrose.co.uk
website www.futermanrose.co.uk
Contacts Guy Rose

Non-fiction: biography (especially sport, music and politics), show business and current affairs; scripts for TV and film. No unsolicited MSS. Send a chapter breakdown and two or three sample chapters (non-fiction) or a sample section of the work (scripts). No children's, sci-fi or fantasy.

Clients include Larry Barker, Sir Bryan Carsberg, Rt Hon Sir Iain Duncan Smith MP, Paul Ferris, Rt Hon Mark Francois MP, Keith Gillespie, Sir Mike Gooley, Dame Sara Khan, Austen Morgan, Max Morgan-Witts, Paul Nicholas, His Hon Judge Chris Nicholson, Liz Rettig, Sir Tommy Steele, Paul Stinchcombe KC, Simon Woodham. *Founded* 1984.

Fraser Ross Associates

Larchwood, 42 Hadfast Road, Cousland, Midlothian EH22 2NZ
email agentlmfraser@gmail.com
email kjross@tiscali.co.uk
website www.fraserross.co.uk
Facebook www.facebook.com/fraserrossassociates
Twitter @FraserRossLA
Instagram @fraserrossassociates
Partners Lindsey Fraser, Kathryn Ross

Writing and illustration for children's books, fiction and non-fiction for adults. See website for submission guidelines. *Founded* 2002.

Jüri Gabriel

35 Camberwell Grove, London SE5 8JA
tel 020-7703 6186
email juri@jurigabriel.com

Quality fiction and non-fiction; radio, TV and film, but selling these rights only in existing works by existing clients. *Commission* Home 10%, overseas 20%, performance rights 10%. Submit three sample chapters plus a one- to two-page synopsis and sae (if using snail mail) in the first instance. Will suggest revision where appropriate. No short stories, articles, verse or books for children.

Authors include Jack Allen, Gbontwi Anyetei, Nick Bradbury, Prof. Christopher Day, Paul Genney, Pat Gray, Mikka Haugaard, Robert Irwin, Pat Johnson, Richard Mankiewicz, David Miller, John Outram, Philip Roberts, Roger Storey, Fiona Subotsky. *Founded* 1983.

Gleam Titles

10 Triton Street, London NW1 3BF
email gleamtitles@gleamfutures.com
website www.gleamfutures.com/gleam-titles

Looking for original, brave and exciting new voices. Particularly interested in writers who are using social media and the online space to share their content in a creative and effective way. Works with clients to help them nurture a direct connection with their audience across their channels. Part of Gleam Futures talent management company. Represents a wide range of fiction and non-fiction. The agency works with all sorts of writers and experts, including journalists, comedians, scientists, illustrators and podcasters. Email submissions only. See website for details.

Authors include Paula Sutton, ADHD_Love, James and Clair Buckley, Max Dickins, Amber Fossey, Emmanuel Asuquo, Omari McQueen, Abby Rawlinson, Grace Victory, Dr Becky Smethurst, Tiwalola Ogunlesi, Female Invest, Katie Pix, Nadia Sawalha, Kat Farmer.

The Good Literary Agency*

email info@thegoodliteraryagency.org
website www.thegoodliteraryagency.org
Twitter @thegoodagencyuk
Instagram @thegoodagencyuk

Represents authors from backgrounds under-represented in UK publishing including writers of colour, working class writers, disabled writers, LGBTQ+ writers and anyone who feels that they or their stories are under-represented. Non-fiction (including history, science, economics, politics, self-help, lifestyle, pop culture and memoir); fiction (all genres, in particular crime and thriller, contemporary love stories, family sagas, historical, sci-fi and fantasy); children's and YA (all genres in fiction and non-fiction for readers 8+). For detailed submission guidelines, visit the website.

Authors include Christian Adofo, Paula Akpan, Sharan Dhaliwal, Lizzie Huxley-Jones, Kenny Imafidon, Mikaela Loach, Wenyan Lu, Eleanor Medhurst, Saima Mir, Musa Okwonga, Penny

Pepper, Jon Ransom, Vasundra Tailor, Eva Verde, Hafsa Zayyan. *Founded* 2018.

Bill Goodall Literary Agency

26 Lower Road, Malvern, Worcs. WR14 4BX
email bill@billgoodall.co.uk
website www.billgoodall.co.uk
Twitter @BGLitAgency
Owner & Director Bill Goodall

Adult fiction, including (but not exclusively) commercial/literary crime and thriller, and general fiction. *Commission* Home 15%, overseas/translation 20%; film/TV Home 15%, overseas 20%. Send synopsis plus first three chapters or 50 pages, whichever is shorter, by email as Word attachments. No postal submissions. No sci-fi and fantasy, horror, short stories, poetry or children's books.

Clients include Ian Moore, Tom Benjamin, C.J. Farrington, Mandy Byatt, Leigh Russell, Sophie Morton-Thomas, Diana Finley, Kevin Sullivan, James Brydon, Jez Pinfold, Mark Dowd. *Founded* 2018.

Graham Maw Christie*

37 Highbury Place, London N5 1QP
email enquiries@grahammawchristie.com
website www.grahammawchristie.com
Twitter @litagencyGMC
Instagram @litagencyGMC
Contacts Jane Graham Maw, Jennifer Christie

General non-fiction: autobiography/memoir, business/smart thinking, humour and gift, food and drink, craft, health and wellness, lifestyle, parenting, self-help/how-to, popular science/history/culture/reference. Email submissions only. Will suggest revisions. See website for submission guidelines. Also represents ghostwriters. No fiction, children's or poetry.

Authors include Louise Allen, Sharon Blackie, Natalie Cawley, Sally Coulthard, Milli Hill, Vex King, Tim James, NEOM, Prof. Tom Oliver, The Black Curriculum, Veganuary, Lizzie Waterworth, Raynor Winn. *Founded* 2005.

Annette Green Authors' Agency

5 Henwoods Mount, Pembury,
Tunbridge Wells TN2 4BH
tel (01892) 263252
email annette@annettegreenagency.co.uk
website www.annettegreenagency.co.uk
Partners Annette Green, David Smith

Fiction: literary, general, women's, historical, romance and fiction for older children. Non-fiction: popular culture, history and science. *Commission* Home 15%, overseas 20–25%. Preliminary email or letter, synopsis, sample chapter and sae essential. No picture books, dramatic scripts, poetry, sci-fi or fantasy.

Authors include Andrew Baker, Louis Barfe, Tim Bradford, Bill Broady, Katherine Clements, Terry

Darlington, Elizabeth Haynes, Jane Kerr, Maria McCann, Adam Macqueen, Audrey Reimann, Trisha Sakhlecha, Katie Hutton, Rachael McGill, Elizabeth Woodcraft. *Founded* 1998.

Christine Green Authors' Agent*

email info@christinegreen.co.uk
website www.christinegreen.co.uk
Twitter @whitehorsemews
Contact Christine Green

Literary and commercial fiction, narrative (novelistic) non-fiction. General fiction welcome. *Commission* Home 15%, overseas 20%. Preliminary queries by email welcome. Email submissions only. No genre sci-fi or fantasy, travelogues, self-help, picture books, scripts or poetry.
   Clients include Maeve Binchy, Mary Beckett, Ita Daly, Sairish Hussain, Ali Lewis, Gaile Parkin, Alice Redmond. *Founded* 1984.

Louise Greenberg Books Ltd*

End House, Church Crescent, London N3 1BG
tel 020-8349 1179
email louisegreenberg@btinternet.com
website https://louisegreenbergbooks.co.uk

Literary fiction and non-fiction. *Commission* Full-length MSS: home 15%, overseas 20%. New writers by recommendation only. No telephone enquiries. *Founded* 1997.

Greene & Heaton Ltd*

T18, West Wing, Somerset House, Strand, London WC2R 1LA
tel 020-8749 0315
email submissions@greeneheaton.co.uk
email info@greeneheaton.co.uk
website www.greeneheaton.co.uk
Twitter @GreeneandHeaton
Contacts Carol Heaton, Judith Murray, Antony Topping, Claudia Young, Laura Williams, Holly Faulks, Imogen Morrell, *Translation Rights Director* Kate Rizzo

Handles translation rights directly in all major territories. Fiction and non-fiction. *Commission* Home 15%, USA/translation 20%, film/TV 20%. Email submissions accepted, but no reply guaranteed. Postal submissions not accepted. No original scripts for theatre, film or TV.
   Clients include Laura Barnett, Lucy Clarke, Sabine Durrant, Marcus du Sautoy, Hugh Fearnley-Whittingstall, Jyoti Patel, Michael Frayn, Joseph Knox, Ian McGuire, Thomasina Miers, Clare Chambers, Temi Oh, C.J. Sansom, Andrew Taylor and the estate of P.D. James. *Founded* 1963.

The Greenhouse Literary Agency

email info@greenhouseliterary.com
website www.greenhouseliterary.com
Director Chelsea Eberly, *Agent* Kristin Ostby

Children's fiction and non-fiction: illustrators who write picture books, middle-grade through to teen/YA novels, and graphic novels. Some women's fiction. Submissions via QueryManager only; see website for submission guidelines. No poetry, short stories or film scripts.
   Authors include Gavin Aung Than, Sarwat Chadda, Winifred Conkling, Andrea Contos, Alexandra Diaz, Bill Doyle, Theanne Griffith, Michelle Lam, Rebecca Mock, Kelis Rowe, Ali Standish, Emily Thiede, Ngozi Ukazu. *Founded* 2008.

Greyhound Literary Agents*

49 Greek Street, London W1D 4EG
email info@greyhoundliterary.co.uk
website www.greyhoundliterary.co.uk
Twitter @GreyhoundLitAg
Directors Charlie Campbell, Sam Edenborough *Agents* Charlotte Atyeo, Maria Brannan, Natalie Galustian, Philip Gwyn Jones, Dotti Irving, Julia Silk

Fiction and non-fiction for adults and children. Represent YA and some picture books for authors whose work is represented in other areas. *Commission* Home 15%, USA/film/TV 20%, translation 20%. Submissions via website. No plays, poetry or scripts.
   Clients include Jennifer Lucy Allan, Beach, Victoria Belim, SJ Bennett, Edward Brooke-Hitching, Jen Campbell, Rebecca Front, Julian Gough, Ed Hawkins, Maisie Hill, Will Hill, Michael Holding, Anthony McGowan, Clare Seal, the estate of Alan Rickman. *Founded* 2022.

David Grossman Literary Agency Ltd

9 Lamington Street, London W6 0HU
tel 020-8741 2860
email submissions@dglal.co.uk

Works in conjunction with agents in New York, Los Angeles, Europe, Japan and China. *Commission* Full-length MSS: home 10–15%, overseas 20% (including foreign agent's commission), performance rights 15%. No submissions by email without a preceding preliminary letter or message briefly describing the work and justifying its publication. *Founded* 1976.

Marianne Gunn O'Connor Literary, Film/TV Agency

Morrison Chambers, 32 Nassau Street, Dublin 2, Republic of Ireland
tel +353 (0)16 669100
email submissions@mariannegunnoconnor.com
website www.mariannegunnoconnor.com
Contact Marianne Gunn O'Connor

Represents literary fiction, upmarket fiction including book club and psychological suspense; children's books, middle-grade, YA, New Adult and crossover fiction; exciting new non-fiction authors with a focus on narrative non-fiction, health, some memoir and biography. No screenplays.
   Clients include Liz Nugent, Louise Nealon, Christy Lefteri, Mike McCormack, Patrick McCabe, Sheila

Armstrong, Nana Oforiatta Ayim, Catherine Prasifka, Shane Hegarty, Disha Bose, Claudia Carroll, Melatu-Uche Okorie, Kevin Power, Sinead Moriarty, Kathleen McMahon. *Founded* 1996.

Gwyn Palmer Associates (Literary Agents) Ltd

email robertgwynpalmer@gmail.com
Contact Robert Gwyn Palmer

Non-fiction only, including (but not limited to) self-help, memoir and autobiography, history, cookery, economics, popular science, graphic design, architecture and design. *Commission* Home 15%. Make initial contact via email with an outline of the proposal. No fiction, poetry or children's.

Authors include Daniel Fryer, Ben Aldridge, Tom Goodwin, Sarah Stamford, Paul Farrell, Marcus Bawdon, Dr Jason Frowley, Emma Armstrong, Adrian Waddington CBE, Alvin Carpio. *Founded* 2005.

The Hamilton Agency

12A Portland Road, London W11 4LA
email matthew@thehamiltonagency.co.uk
website https://thehamiltonagency.co.uk/
Twitter @MWHamilton
Founder & Agent Matthew Hamilton

Represents writers of non-fiction, with a particular interest in politics, music and entertainment. Submissions via the website using the form provided. No queries by post or phone. Submissions must include a covering letter, short author bio and a brief synopsis. An excerpt or the full MS can be included at submission.

Authors Nigel Biggar, Rose Boyt, John Crace, Andrew Doyle, Mary Harrington, Konstantin Kisin, Paul Mason, Douglas Murrary, Seamas O'Reilly, Paul Rees, Louise Perry, Nina Power, Will Sergeant, Mick Wall, A.N. Wilson. *Founded* 2019.

The Hanbury Agency Ltd, Literary Agents*

Suite 103, Lower Marsh, London SE1 7AB
email enquiries@hanburyagency.com
website www.hanburyagency.com

Represents general fiction and non-fiction. See website for submission guidelines.

Authors include George Alagiah, Tom Bergin, Simon Callow, Jane Glover, Oscar de Muriel, Nick Frost, Paul Gorman, Roman Krznaric, Margarette Lincoln, Judith Lennox, Kate Raworth, Simon Sharpe, Charles Saumarez Smith, Jerry White. The agency has a strong stable of ghostwriters. *Founded* 1983.

Hardman & Swainson*

S106, Somerset House, London WC2R 1LA
tel 020-3701 7449
email submissions@hardmanswainson.com
website www.hardmanswainson.com
Twitter @hardmanswainson
Directors Caroline Hardman, Joanna Swainson

Literary and commercial fiction, crime and thriller, women's and accessible literary. Non-fiction, including memoir, biography, popular science, history and philosophy. *Commission* Home 15%, USA/translation 20%, film/TV 20%. Submissions by email only; check the website for details. Will work editorially with the author where appropriate. No poetry, screenplays or picture books.

Clients include Dinah Jefferies, Liz Trenow, Ali McNamara, Giovanna Fletcher, Helen Fields, The Unmumsy Mum, Daniel M. Davies, Beth Kempton, Tracy Buchanan, Rachel Edwards, B.P. Walter. *Founded* 2012.

Antony Harwood Ltd

103 Walton Street, Oxford OX2 6EB
tel (01865) 559615
email mail@antonyharwood.com
website www.antonyharwood.com
Contacts Antony Harwood, James Macdonald Lockhart, Jo Williamson

General and genre fiction; general non-fiction. *Commission* Home 15%, overseas 20%. Will suggest revision.

Clients include Louise Doughty, Peter F. Hamilton, Alan Hollinghurst, A.L. Kennedy, Douglas Kennedy, Dorothy Koomson, Amy Liptrot, George Monbiot. *Founded* 2000.

A.M. Heath & Co. Ltd*

6 Warwick Court, London WC1R 5DJ
tel 020-7242 2811
email enquiries@amheath.com
website www.amheath.com
Twitter @amheathltd
Contacts Bill Hamilton, Victoria Hobbs, Euan Thorneycroft, Alexandra McNicoll (translation rights), Oliver Munson, Julia Churchill (children's), Rebecca Ritchie, Florence Rees, Tom Killingbeck

Literary and commercial fiction and non-fiction, children's and film/TV. *Commission* Home 15%, USA/translation 20%, film/TV 15–20% by agreement. Digital submission via website. No screenplays, poetry or short stories except for collections.

Clients include Lauren Beukes, Lindsey Davis, Katie Fforde, Michelle Harrison, Annie Lord, Conn Iggulden, Cynan Jones, Sophia Money-Coutts, the estate of Hilary Mantel, Maggie O'Farrell, Kamila Shamsie, Afua Hirsch, Zeinab Badawi, David Abulafia, the estate of George Orwell. *Founded* 1919.

HHB Agency Ltd*

62 Grafton Way, London W1T 5DW
tel 020-7405 5525
email heather@hhbagency.com
email elly@hhbagency.com
website https://hhbagency.com/
Twitter @hhbagencyltd
Contacts Heather Holden-Brown, Elly James

Non-fiction: journalism, history and politics, contemporary autobiography and biography, ideas, entertainment and TV, business, memoir, food and cookery. Fiction: women's commercial, book club, historical and thrillers. *Commission* 15%.

Authors include Nick Barratt, Lottie Bedlow, Charlotte Betts, Emma Burstall, Rory Cellan-Jones, Suzanne Goldring, Molly Green, James Hanning, Mishal Husain, Saliha Mahmood Ahmed, Louise Minchin, Pip Payne (The Slimming Foodie), Dr Max Pemberton, Rosemary Shrager, Rachel Trethewey. *Founded* 2005.

Sophie Hicks Agency*
60 Gray's Inn Road, London WC1X 8LU
email info@sophiehicksagency.com
website www.sophiehicksagency.com
Twitter @SophieHicksAg
Agents Sophie Hicks, Sarah Williams

Adult fiction and non-fiction. Also handles children's books for 9+. Represented in all foreign markets. *Commission* Home/USA 15%, translation 20%. Email submissions only, see website for guidelines. No poetry, scripts or illustrated books.

Authors include Anne Cassidy, Lucy Coats, Eoin Colfer, Dan Davies, Ruth Fitzmaurice, Tristan Gooley, Shahroo Izadi, Benedict Jacka, Signe Johansen, Emerald Fennell, Padraig Kenny, Andrew Meehan, Claire Nelson, Alex Smith, Tom Whipple. *Founded* 2014.

David Higham Associates Ltd*
6th Floor, Waverley House, 7–12 Noel Street, London W1F 8GQ
tel 020-7434 5900
email dha@davidhigham.co.uk
website www.davidhigham.co.uk
Managing Director Lizzy Kremer, *Books* Veronique Baxter, Nicola Chang, Jemima Forrester, Stephanie Glencross, Georgia Glover, Anthony Goff, Andrew Gordon, Harriet Moore, Caroline Walsh, Jessica Woollard, *Foreign Rights* Alice Howe, Giulia Bernabe, Anna Watkins, Margaux Vialleron, Ilaria Albani, Hana Grisenthwaite, Sam Norman, *Film/TV/Theatre* Nicky Lund, Clare Israel, Georgie Smith

Agents for the negotiation of all rights in literary and commercial fiction, and general non-fiction. Represented in all foreign markets either directly or through sub-agents. All genres, children's fiction and picture books, plays, film and TV scripts, offering a full service across all media. *Commission* Home 15%, USA/translation 20%, scripts 10%. See website for submissions policy.

Clients include Naomi Alderman, Belinda Bauer, J.M. Coetzee, Bernard Cornwell, Stephen Fry, Paula Hawkins, Owen Jones, Robert Macfarlane, Carole Matthews, Val McDermid, Alexander McCall Smith. The children's list features Roald Dahl, Michael Morpurgo, Cressida Cowell, Jacqueline Wilson. *Founded* 1935.

Holroyde Cartey Ltd*
email claire@holroydecartey.com
email penny@holroydecartey.com
website www.holroydecartey.com
Contacts Claire Cartey, Penny Holroyde

A literary and artistic agency representing a list of award-winning and bestselling authors and illustrators. Welcomes submissions from debut and established authors. *Commission* Headline 15%. See website for submission guidelines. *Founded* 2015.

Vanessa Holt Ltd*
59 Crescent Road, Leigh-on-Sea, Essex SS9 2PF
tel (01702) 473787
email v.holt791@btinternet.com

General fiction and non-fiction. Works in conjunction with foreign agencies and publishers in all markets. *Commission* Home 15%, overseas 20%, film/TV/radio 15%. No unsolicited MSS and submissions preferred by arrangement. No overseas submissions. *Founded* 1989.

Kate Hordern Literary Agency Ltd*
18 Mortimer Road, Clifton, Bristol BS8 4EY
tel (01179) 239368
email kate@khla.co.uk
email anne@khla.co.uk
website https://khla.co.uk
Agents Kate Hordern, Anne Williams

A small agency with an international reach representing a wide range of fiction, some non-fiction and some children's. See website for further details of what the agency is looking for and for submission guidelines. *Founded* 1999.

Valerie Hoskins Associates Ltd
20 Charlotte Street, London W1T 2NA
tel 020-7637 4490
email info@vhassociates.co.uk
website www.vhassociates.co.uk
Proprietor Valerie Hoskins, *Agent* Rebecca Watson

Film, TV and radio; specialises in animation. Works in conjunction with US agents. *Commission* Home 12.5%, overseas max. 20%. No unsolicited MSS; preliminary letter and sae essential.

Authors include Joe Alexander, Andy Amfo, Bill Armstrong, Paul Boateng, Tom Bradby, Guy Burt, Laurence Davey, Michelle Gayle, Matthew Graham, Sarah Gordon, Henrietta Hardy, Sarah Louise Hawkins, Paul Mari, Jeff Povey, E.L. James. *Founded* 1983.

Clare Hulton Literary Agency*
email info@clarehulton.co.uk
website www.clarehulton.com
Director Clare Hulton

Represents numerous bestselling and award-winning authors. Specialises in non-fiction especially cookery, health and fitness, parenting, music, self-help, commercial non-fiction and memoir. The agency also has a small but growing fiction list. Submissions consisting of a synopsis and sample chapter should be sent by email. No fantasy, poetry, screenplays, YA or children's proposals.

Authors include Kay and Kate Allinson, Jackie Kabler, Dan Toombs, James Haskell, Chloe Madeley, Amy Sheppard, Matt Roberts, Emma Rowley, Craig and Shaun McAnuff, Catherine Phipps, Kwoklyn Wan, Sarah Howells, #itsfine, Liz O'Riordan, Willow Crossley. *Founded* 2012.

IMG UK Ltd

Building Six, 566 Chiswick High Road, London W4 5HR
tel 020-8233 5000
email sarah.wooldridge@img.com
website www.img.com
Literary Agent Sarah Wooldridge

Celebrity books, sports-related books, non-fiction and how-to business books. *Commission* Home 15%, USA 20%, elsewhere 25%. No emails. No theatre, fiction, children's, academic or poetry.

Authors include Michael Johnson, Colin Montgomerie, John McEnroe, Katherine Grainger, Ken Brown, Nicole Cooke, Dave Alred, Judy Murray, Thomas Bjorn, Padraig Harrington. *Founded* 1960.

Independent Talent Group Ltd

40 Whitfield Street, London W1T 2RH
tel 020-7636 6565
website www.independenttalent.com
Twitter @ITG_Ltd

Specialises in scripts for film, theatre, TV, radio. Client base encompasses actors, directors, writers, producers and their production companies, below-the-line talent, casting directors, presenters, comedians and voice-over artists.

Intercontinental Literary Agency Ltd*

10 Waterloo Court, Theed Street, London SE1 8ST
tel 020-7379 6611
email ila@ila-agency.co.uk
website www.ila-agency.co.uk
Contacts Nicki Kennedy, Jenny Robson, Clementine Ahearne, Katherine West, Alix Shaw, Elizabeth Guess

Represents translation rights only. *Founded* 1965.

Bev James Management and Literary Agency

Gable House, 18–24 Turnham Green Terrace, Chiswick, London W4 1QP
email enquiries@bevjames.com
website www.bevjames.com
Twitter @Bev_James
Instagram @bevjamesmanagement
Founder Bev James

Works with clients from concept through to release, focusing on career strategy and building author

brands and businesses. Looks for clients with purpose-driven goals who desire to make a positive impact. Specialises in non-fiction, especially lifestyle, cooking and health and fitness.

Clients include Joe Wicks MBE, Caroline Hirons, BOSH!, Dr Rupy Aujla, Kate Silverton, Hannah Martin, Owen O'Kane, Ed Jackson, Holly Tucker MBE, Anna Mathur, Dija Ayodele, Amelia Freer, Charlotte Stirling Reed, Dr Sabrina Cohen-Hatton, James Davies.

Janklow & Nesbit (UK) Ltd*

66–67 Newman Street, Fitzrovia W1T 3EQ
tel 020-7243 2975
email submissions@janklow.co.uk
website www.janklowandnesbit.co.uk
Twitter @JanklowUK
Instagram @janklownesbituk
Agents Will Francis, Claire Paterson Conrad, Julia Eagleton, Emma Leong, *Foreign Rights* Mairi Friesen-Escandell, Nathaniel Alcaraz-Stapleton, Ellis Hazelgriove, Maimy Suleiman

Represents a bestselling, global and award-winning range of commercial and literary fiction and non-fiction, children's and YA. Handles translation rights directly or through sub-agents in all territories. US rights handled by Janklow & Nesbit Associates in New York. Send informative covering letter with full outline (non-fiction), synopsis and first three sample chapters (fiction) by email only. Include your name, the title of your work and the name of the agent you are submitting to in the email subject line. No plays or film/TV scripts.

Clients include Dr Rangan Chatterjee, Ed Yong, Rowan Coleman, Adam Rutherford, Mya-Rose Craig, Hannah Fry, Oliver Burkeman, Michel Faber, Sunjeev Sahota, Kiran Millwood Hargrave, M.J. Arlidge, Lucy Cooke, Sharna Jackson, Tsedal Neeley, Chukwuebuka Ibeh. *Founded* 2000.

JFL Agency Ltd

48 Charlotte Street, London W1T 2NS
tel 020-3137 8182
email agents@jflagency.com
website www.jflagency.com
Agents Alison Finch, Dominic Lord, Gary Wild

TV, radio, film. *Commission* 10%. Initial contact by preliminary email to representation@jflagency.com; do not send scripts in the first instance. See website for further information. No novels, short stories or poetry.

Clients include Humphrey Barclay, Adam Bostock-Smith, Bill Dare, Ed Dyson, Jan Etherington, Phil Ford, Rob Gittins, Gabby Hutchinson Crouch, Lisa McMullin, Julie Parsons, David Semple, James Serafinowicz, Pete Sinclair, Paul Smith, Fraser Steele. *Founded* 2011.

Johnson & Alcock Ltd*

West Wing, Somerset House, Strand, London WC2R 1LA

tel 020-7251 0125
website www.johnsonandalcock.co.uk
Contacts Michael Alcock, Anna Power, Ed Wilson,
Charlotte Seymour

All types of commercial and literary fiction, and
general non-fiction. YA and children's fiction (ages
9+). *Commission* Home 15%, USA/translation/film
20%. For fiction and non-fiction, send first three
chapters, full synopsis and brief covering letter with
details of writing experience. For email submission
guidelines see website. Return postage essential. No
short stories, poetry or board/picture books.
Founded 1956.

Tibor Jones & Associates

PO Box 74604, London SW2 9NH
email enquiries@tiborjones.com
website www.tiborjones.com
Contact Kevin Conroy Scott

Literary fiction and non-fiction, category fiction,
music autobiographies and biographies. Send first
five pages, synopsis and covering letter via email.
 Authors include Wilbur Smith, Guillermo Arriaga,
Deborah Curtis, Olafur Eliasson, Hala Jaber, Paul
Lake, Hans Ulrich Obrist, Bernard Sumner,
Christopher Winn. *Founded* 2007.

Robin Jones Literary Agency (RJLA)

66 High Street, Dorchester on Thames OX10 7HN
email robijones@gmail.com
Twitter @AgentRobinJones
Director Robin Jones

Adult fiction and non-fiction: literary and
commercial. Script consultancy, structural and
development editing, indexing, proofreading, self-
publishing consultancy and copy editing services.
High-concept non-fiction especially ecological,
environmental, political, radical and alternative, and
philosophical. Also Russian- and Slavic-themed
fiction and non-fiction. *Commission* Home 15%,
overseas 20%. In first instance, send synopsis, 50-
page sample, and cover letter detailing writing
experience. No theatre/plays, YA or children's.
 Clients include Sir David Madden, Ben Rowland,
Alex Flynn, Waqas Ahmed, Chrissie Hynde, Philip
Lymbery, Isabel Oakeshott, Dr Paul Jackson (Co-
founder of Unthank Books, Unthology, Unthank
School and UnLit Festival). *Founded* 2007.

Jane Judd Literary Agency*

18 Belitha Villas, London N1 1PD
tel 020-7607 0273
website www.janejudd.com
Twitter @janelitagent

General non-fiction and fiction. Works with agents in
the USA and most foreign countries. *Commission*
Home 10%, overseas 20%. No longer accepting new
clients.
 Authors include Jill Mansell, Anne O'Brien, John
Brunner, David Winner, S.W. Perry, Michelle Birkby,

Andy Dougan, Quentin Falk, Margaret Rooke,
Margret Geraghty. *Founded* 1986.

Kane Literary Agency*

2 Dukes Avenue, London N10 2PT
tel 020-8351 9680
website www.kaneliteraryagency.com
Director Yasmin Kane

Interested in discovering new writers and launching
the careers of first-time writers. Literary and
commercial fiction, children's fiction (middle grade
to YA). Non-fiction: memoirs, metaphysics.
Commission Home 15%, overseas 20%. Send
submissions by email only; no submissions by post.
For fiction, send a covering letter with the first three
chapters and a synopsis; for non-fiction, send a
covering letter and full book proposal plus two
sample chapters. See website for further information.
 Authors include Christopher Moore, Richard
Butchins, Colleen MacMahon, Sarah Harris, Ruchita
Misra, Min Day. *Founded* 2004.

Michelle Kass Associates Ltd*

85 Charing Cross Road, London WC2H 0AA
tel 020-7439 1624
website www.michellekass.co.uk
Agents Michelle Kass, Russell Franklin

Literary and commercial fiction. Scripts for film and
TV. Works with agents around the world.
Commission Home 10%, overseas 15–20%. Submit
first three chapters. No unsolicited material, phone in
first instance. *Founded* 1991.

Keane Kataria Literary Agency

email info@keanekataria.co.uk
website www.keanekataria.co.uk
Partners Sara Keane, Kiran Kataria

Boutique agency representing quality commercial
fiction and non-fiction. Women's commercial fiction
(contemporary, historical, romantic comedy, saga),
reading group fiction, historical fiction, cosy crime,
narrative non-fiction. *Commission* Home 15%, USA/
translation 20%. See website for current submission
guidelines. No children's, YA, sci-fi/fantasy, thrillers,
academic, short stories, poetry, plays or film/TV
scripts.
 Clients include Tommy Barnes, Jan Casey, Lucy
Coleman, Lynne Francis, Helen Fripp, Claire
Heywood, Jenny Kane, Fay Keenan, Judy Leigh,
Gabrielle Malcolm, Rosie Meddon, Beth Moran, Amy
Myers, Fiona Veitch Smith, Alexandra Walsh.
Founded 2014.

Ki Agency Ltd*

Studio 105, ScreenWorks, 22 Highbury Grove,
London N5 2ER
tel 020-3214 8287
email meg@ki-agency.co.uk
email roz@ki-agency.co.uk

website www.ki-agency.co.uk
Twitter @kiagency
Director Meg Davis, *Agent* Roz Kidd

Represents writers of fiction, non-fiction and screenplays for film or TV. Email synopsis and three chapters or full-length screenplay. No unsolicited MSS. No children's or poetry.

Clients include Anne Perry, M.R. Carey, Claire North, Angela Slatter, Daniel Church, John Allison, Amber Chen, Matthew Feldman, Ryan Love, Adam Roberts, Moira James-Moore, Cassie Jauffret-Lenzi, Tiarna Armstrong, Fiona Barnett and the estate of Fred Hoyle. *Founded* 2011.

Knight Features Ltd

Trident Business Centre, 89 Bickerseth Road, London SW17 9SH
tel 020-3051 5650
website www.knightfeatures.com/literary-agency-cover-pages
Twitter @KnightFeatures
Directors Andrew Knight, Sam Ferris, Gaby Martin

Business and communication, history and military history, puzzles, general interest, comics, graphic novels and literary estates management. Send letter accompanied by synopsis, three sample chapters and sae, or via website submission page. No fiction, poetry, cookery or memoirs.

Authors include David J. Bodycombe, Frank Dickens, Barbara Minto, Ralph Barker, Frederic Mullally, David Kerr Cameron, W. H. Canaway, Patrick MacGill. *Founded* 1985.

Knight Hall Agency Ltd

Lower Ground Floor, 7 Mallow Street, London EC1Y 8RQ
tel 020-3397 2901
email office@knighthallagency.com
website www.knighthallagency.com
Contacts Charlotte Knight, Samara Wash

Specialises in writers for stage, screen and radio but also deals in TV and film rights in novels and non-fiction. *Commission* Home 10%, overseas 15%.

Clients include Simon Amstell, Simon Beaufoy, Jeremy Brock, Matthew Dunster, Jemima Khan, Francis Lee, Liz Lochhead, Martin McDonagh, Simon Nye, Ol Parker, Ripley Parker, Lucy Prebble, Philip Ridley, Robert Thorogood, Laura Wade. *Founded* 1997.

Laxfield Literary Associates*

tel 07746 751820
email info@laxfieldliterary.com
website https://laxfieldliterary.com
Twitter @laxfieldlit
Founder Emma Shercliff

Represents authors from Norfolk and Suffolk and writers from under-represented backgrounds. Keen to receive work from authors based in Africa, the Middle East and Ukraine. Translation rights, screen rights and permissions are handled by Blake Friedmann Literary Agency. Looking for literary and commercial fiction and non-fiction, particularly creative non-fiction, travel writing, memoir and nature writing. Email submissions only to submissions@laxfieldliterary.com. For fiction, include a covering letter, a synopsis and the first three chapters. For non-fiction, include a covering letter with a CV, a one-page summary of the project, chapter outline and three sample chapters. Does not represent plays, screenwriting, fantasy, children's books or YA.

Clients include Kalaf Epalanga, Victoria Panton Bacon, Heather Parry, Olumide Popoola, Tom Shakespeare, Luke Wright. *Founded* 2020.

LBA Books*

91 Great Russell Street, London WC1B 3PS
tel 020-7637 1234
email info@lbabooks.com
website www.lbabooks.com
Twitter @LBA_Agency
Agents Luigi Bonomi, Amanda Preston, Louise Lamont, Hannah Schofield

Fiction and non-fiction. Keen to find new authors and help them develop their careers. Works with foreign agencies and has links with film and TV-production companies. Fiction: commercial and literary fiction, thrillers, crime, psychological suspense, YA, children's, women's fiction, fantasy. Non-fiction: history, science, memoir, parenting, lifestyle, cookery, TV tie-in. *Commission* Home 15%, overseas 20%. Send preliminary letter, synopsis and first three chapters. No postal submissions. No poetry, short stories or screenplays.

Authors include Sarah Alderson, Fern Britton, Mensun Bound, Lesley Kara, Simon Kernick, Susan Lewis, Fiona Lucas, Kavita Puri, Natali Simmonds, Jane Monckton Smith, Alice Roberts, Simon Scarrow, Heidi Swain, Karen Swan, Alan Titchmarsh. *Founded* 2005.

Susanna Lea Associates Ltd*

South Wing, Somerset House, Strand, London WC2R 1LA
tel 020-7287 7757
email london@susannalea.com
website www.susannalea.com
Twitter @SLALondon
Directors Susanna Lea, Kerry Glencorse

General fiction and non-fiction. Send query letter, brief synopsis, the first three chapters and/or proposal. No plays, screenplays or poetry.

Authors include Carole Cadwalladr, Tom Service, Ramla Ali, Susan Spindler, Tom Mustill, Marie Phillips, Alice O'Keeffe, Alice Adams, Ingrid Betancourt, Dr Mukwege, Marc Levy, Sabri Louatah, Violaine Huisman, Louisa Hall. *Founded* in Paris 2000, New York 2004 and London 2008.

Barbara Levy Literary Agency*

64 Greenhill, Hampstead High Street,
London NW3 5TZ
tel 020-7435 9046
email submissions@barbaralevyagency.com
website www.barbaralevyagency.com
Director Barbara Levy

Translation rights handled by the Buckman Agency; works in conjunction with US agents. Adult fiction and general non-fiction. Film and TV rights for existing clients only. *Commission* Full-length MSS: home 15%, overseas by arrangement. Preliminary letter with synopsis and sae essential, or by email. *Founded* 1986.

Lewinsohn Literary Agency

58 Old Compton Street, London W1D 4UF
email queries@lewinsohnliterary.com
website www.lewinsohnliterary.com
Instagram @lewinsohnliterary
Agent & Director Becky Thomas

Translation rights handled by Blake Friedmann Literary Agency. Email submissions only. For fiction, send a covering letter, a synopsis, and 50 pages as a Word document. For non-fiction, include a covering letter, an introduction to the project, a basic chapter breakdown and a sample chapter. Ideally as a Word document, pdf will be accepted if the project is highly illustrated. No poetry collections, fantasy, historical or children's including YA.

Authors include Kae Tempest, Hollie McNish, Dean Atta, Justin Myers, Sabrina Mahfouz, Gemma Cairney, Michael Pedersen, Will Burns, Carl Anka, Vanessa Kisuule, Cecilia Knapp, Richard Milward. *Founded* 2021.

Limelight Celebrity Management Ltd*

10 Filmer Mews, 75 Filmer Road, London SW6 7JF
tel 020-7384 9950
email mail@limelightmanagement.com
website www.limelightmanagement.com
Facebook www.facebook.com/
LimelightCelebrityManagement/
Twitter @Fionalimelight
Contacts Fiona Lindsay, Maclean Lindsay

General fiction, crime, thrillers, historical, suspense, mystery, women's commercial fiction. Also non-fiction in the areas of arts and crafts, cookery, biography, autobiography, popular science, business, natural history, sport, travel, health. *Commission* Full-length and short MSS: home 15%, overseas 20%, TV/radio rights 10–20%. Will suggest revision where appropriate.

Clients include James Martin, Oz Clarke, Theo Randall, Paul Gayler, Antony Worrall Thompson, Nigel Colborn, Tim Wonnacott, Pierre Koffman, Salvatore Calabrese, Lesley Waters. *Founded* 1991.

Lindsay Literary Agency*

East Worldham House, Alton, Hants GU34 3AT
tel (01420) 831430
email info@lindsayliteraryagency.co.uk
website www.lindsayliteraryagency.co.uk
Twitter @LindsayLit
Founder Becky Bagnell

Specialists in children's fiction and non-fiction, teen/YA, middle grade and picture books. *Commission* Home 15%, translation 20%. Send first three chapters, synopsis and covering letter by email. No submissions by post. Will suggest revision.

Authors include Pamela Butchart, Christina Collins, Donna David, Sam Gayton, Sital Gorasia Chapman, Ruth Hatfield, Larry Hayes, J.M. Joseph, Giles Paley-Phillips, Josh Silver, Daniel Tawse, Sharon Tregenza, Rachel Valentine, Sue Wallman, Joe Wilson. *Founded* 2008.

The Literary Office

71–75 Shelton Street, London WC2H 9JQ
tel 07910 267336
email jenny.todd@theliteraryoffice.com
website www.theliteraryoffice.com
Founder Jenny Todd

Literary agent and publishing advisor representing quality literary and commercial fiction, non-fiction, YA, film and TV. Drawn to works of originality by inventive, relevant and multi-faceted writers and artists, and committed to developing long-term strategies for their careers. *Commission* Home 15%, overseas 20%. Submissions via website. Send covering letter, synopsis and three sample chapters. *Founded* 2021.

The Liverpool Literary Agency*

tel 07742 603459 /07917 788964
email submissions@liverpool-literary.agency
website www.liverpool-literary.agency
Twitter @LiverpoolLit
Agents Clare Coombes, Matthew McKeown, Laura Bennett

Looking for adult fiction (all genres) and children's fiction, specifically chapter book (ages 5–7 and 7–9) and middle-grade fiction (ages 8–12). Only accepting submissions from writers born or currently living in the North of England. Submissions should include a synopsis and the first three chapters by email, with an author bio included in the covering email. See website for further submission guidelines. Do not accept children's picture books, scripts, non-fiction, poetry, short stories or YA.

Authors include David Beckler, Jack Byrne, Rachel Bowdler, Caron McKinlay, Ashleigh Nugent, Danielle Owen-Jones, Helen Parusel, Michael Sellars, Stephanie Sowden. *Founded* 2020.

Andrew Lownie Literary Agency

36 Great Smith Street, London SW1P 3BU
tel 020-7222 7574

email andrew@andrewlownie.co.uk
website www.andrewlownie.co.uk
Twitter @andrewlownie
Director Andrew Lownie

Handles non-fiction, working in association with a range of sub-agents around the world. Represents biography, history, reference, current affairs and packaging journalists and celebrities for the book market. Represents inspirational memoirs and ghostwriters. *Commission* Home/USA 15%, translation 20%, film 20%. Non-fiction submissions should include synopsis, author profile, chapter summaries and sample material. Will suggest revision.

Authors include Jeremy Dronfield, Juliet Barker, Roger Crowley, Tom Devine, Robert Hutchinson, Lawrence James, Sean McMeekin, Daniel Tammet, *The Oxford Classical Dictionary, The Cambridge Guide to Literature in English* and the estates of Joyce Cary and Julian Maclaren-Ross. *Founded* 1988.

Luithlen Agency

88 Holmfield Road, Leicester LE2 1SB
tel 0116 273 8863
email penny@luithlenagency.com
website www.luithlenagency.com
Agents Jennifer Luithlen, Penny Luithlen

Children's fiction, all ages up to YA. *Commission* Home 15%, overseas 20%, performance rights 15%. See website for submission information. *Founded* 1986.

Lutyens & Rubinstein*

21 Kensington Park Road, London W11 2EU
tel 020-7792 4855
email submissions@lutyensrubinstein.co.uk
website https://agency.lutyensrubinstein.co.uk
Agents Sarah Lutyens, Felicity Rubinstein, Jane Finigan, Daisy Parente, Jenny Hewson

Fiction and non-fiction, commercial and literary. *Commission* Home 15%, overseas 20%. Send material by email with a covering letter and short synopsis. Submissions not accepted by hand or by post. *Founded* 1993.

David Luxton Associates Ltd*

23 Hillcourt Avenue, London N12 8EY
website www.davidluxtonassociates.co.uk
Twitter @DLuxAssociates
Instagram @davidluxtonassociates
Agents David Luxton, Nick Walters, Rebecca Winfield

Agency specialising in non-fiction, especially sport, wellbeing, memoir, history, politics and nature writing. Also handles foreign rights for September Publishing, Judith Murdoch Literary Agency, Eve White Literary Agency Ltd, Kate Nash Literary Agency and Graham Maw Christie Literary Agency. Consult website for submission guidelines.

Submissions should be directed to Sam Rac (admin@davidluxtonassociates.co.uk). *Founded* 2011.

Eunice McMullen Ltd

Low Ibbotsholme Cottage, Off Bridge Lane, Troutbeck Bridge, Windermere, Cumbria LA23 1HU
tel (01539) 448551
email eunice@eunicemcmullen.co.uk
website www.eunicemcmullen.co.uk
Director Eunice McMullen

All types of children's fiction, particularly picture books and older fiction. *Commission* Home 15%, overseas 15%. No unsolicited scripts. Telephone or email enquiries only.

Authors include Alison Friend, Charles Fuge, Cally Johnson Isaacs, James Mayhew, Momoko Abe, Mark McKinley. *Founded* 1992.

Marjacq Scripts Ltd*

The Space, 235 High Holborn, London WC1V 7DN
tel 020-7935 9499
email [firstname]@marjacq.com
website www.marjacq.com
Twitter @MarjacqScripts
Agents Diana Beaumont, Leah Middleton, Philip Patterson, Imogen Pelham, Catherine Pellegrino, Sandra Sawicka

Full-service agency. Handles all rights. In-house legal, foreign rights, book-to-film and interactive media support. Commercial and literary fiction and non-fiction, crime, thrillers, horror, sci-fi, commercial women's fiction, romantic fiction, graphic novels, children's, history, lifestyle, contemporary issues, screenwriting. *Commission* Home 15%, overseas 20%, film 20%. Send first 50 pages with synopsis by email to appropriate agent. See website for further submission guidelines. No poetry or theatre.

Clients include Daisy Buchanan, Jimi Famurewa, Roopa Farooki, Helen FitzGerald, Finbar Hawkins, Paul Herron, Andrea Mara, Marie Le Conte, Stuart MacBride, Claire McGowan, Alex North, Bryony Pearce, Kassia St Clair, Matt Wesolowski. *Founded* 1973.

The Marsh Agency Ltd*

50 Albemarle Street, London W1S 4BD
tel 020-7493 4361
email hello@marsh-agency.co.uk
website www.marsh-agency.co.uk
Twitter @TheMarshAgency

Offers international representation to a wide range of writers, literary agents and publishing companies. No unsolicited submissions. *Founded* 1994.

MBA Literary and Script Agents Ltd*

62 Grafton Way, London W1T 5DW
tel 020-7387 2076
website www.mbalit.co.uk
Twitter @mbaagents

Book Agents Diana Tyler, David Riding, Susan Smith, Sophie Gorell Barnes, *Film/TV Agent* Susan Smith, *Radio/Theatre Agent* Sophie Gorell Barnes

Fiction, non-fiction, children's books. Foreign rights handled by Louisa Pritchard Associates. *Commission* Home 15%, overseas 20%, TV/theatre/radio 10%, film 15%. See website for submission guidelines.

Clients include Sufiya Ahmed, Anne-Marie, Sita Brahmachari, Dr Amanda Brown, Jeffrey Caine, Julian Jones, Rosanna Ley, Stef Penney, Mina Smallman, estate of Anne McCaffrey. *Founded* 1971.

Madeleine Milburn Literary, TV & Film Agency*

The Factory, 1 Park Hill, Clapham, London SW4 9NS
tel 020-7499 7550
email submissions@madeleinemilburn.com
website www.madeleinemilburn.co.uk
Facebook www.facebook.com/
MadeleineMilburnLiteraryAgency
Twitter @MMLitAgency
Instagram @madeleinemilburn
Directors Madeleine Milburn, Giles Milburn, *Dramatic Rights Agent* Hannah Ladds, *Senior Agent* Hayley Steed, *Agents* Hannah Todd, Olivia Maidment, Emma Bal, *Senior Children's & YA Agent* Chloe Seager, *Associate Agents* Rachel Yeoh, Maddy Belton

Special interest in launching the careers of debut authors. Represents a dynamic and prize-winning range of bestselling adult fiction and non-fiction, young adult and children's fiction.

Represents British, American, Canadian and international authors. Builds the international careers of authors. Handles all rights in the UK, USA and international markets including film/TV/radio and digital. Literary fiction, upmarket commercial fiction, book club, women's, crime and thrillers, psychological suspense, historical, romance, mystery, horror, comedy, sci-fi and fantasy, history, politics, biography, psychology, nature, travel, philosophy, science, narrative non-fiction, food writing, memoir, cookery, illustrated non-fiction, film/TV tie-ins. Children's fiction for all ages including 6–8 years, 9–12 years, teen, YA, New Adult and crossover. *Commission* Home 15%, USA/Canada/translation 20%, film/TV 20%. No submissions by post. See submission guidelines and agency news on website. Works editorially with all clients.

Authors include Gail Honeyman, C.L.Taylor, Nita Prose, Clare Pooley, Ashley Audrain, Matthew Blake, Charmaine Wilkerson, C.J. Tudor, Katherine May, Fiona Barton, Mark Edwards, Elizabeth Macneal, Yomi Adegoke, Emma Stonex, Jack Jordan. *Founded* 2012.

Rachel Mills Literary Ltd*

M27, South Wing, Somerset House, Strand, London WC2R 1LA

website www.rachelmillsliterary.co.uk
Twitter @rmliterary
Instagram @rachelmillsliterary
Agents Rachel Mills, Nelle Andrew

Focused on fiction and non-fiction which can effect positive change, aimed at an upmarket, mainstream audience. Non-fiction: big ideas books, popular science, popular economics, popular psychology, narrative non-fiction, memoir, health, wellbeing, lifestyle, food, the environment, feminism, nature writing. Fiction: literary, commercial, clever and upmarket female fiction, historical, suspense, thrillers, crime, high concept. *Commission* Home 15%, overseas 20%, film/TV 20%. Send synopsis and first three chapters for fiction. For non-fiction send proposal and full biography. Please check website for individual agent's email addresses. Does not represent erotica, children's, sci-fi and fantasy, short stories, business, educational or academic books.

Authors include Elizabeth Day, Bryony Gordon, Sara Collins, Heidi Perks, Catherine Gray, Alice Vincent, Hassan Akkad, David Nutt, Peter Walker, Uju Asika, Claire Ratinon, Max La Manna, Twisted. *Founded* 2019.

MMB Creative*

(Mulcahy Sweeney Associates Ltd)
The Old Truman Brewery, 91 Brick Lane, London E1 6QL
tel 020-3582 9379
email mulcahyadmin@mmbcreative.com
website https://mmbcreative.com/books/
Twitter @MulcahyLitAgent
Contacts Ivan Mulcahy, Sallyanne Sweeney, Edwina de Charnace

Fiction and non-fiction. Biography, crime, finance, historical, lifestyle, sport, thrillers, women's interests, adult, children's, youth, commercial, literary. Send query with synopsis, author bio and sample writing via website only. See website for full guidelines.

Clients include Ha-Joon Chang, Juno Dawson, Felicity Everett, Ian Kelly, Steven Lenton, Lisa McInerney, Alan McMonagle, Roisin Meaney, David Mitchell, Simon Philip, E.M. Reapy, Robert Webb, Dapo Adeola, Nathan Bryon, Brian Cox. *Founded* 2016.

Morgan Green Creatives Ltd

157 Ribblesdale Road, London SW16 6SP
email kirsty@morgangreencreatives.com
website www.morgangreencreatives.com
Founder Kirsty McLachlan

Actively looking for fresh talent and to be challenged with new ideas, inspired and moved by great writing, and to find unique and distinct voices with compelling stories to tell. Represents fiction, non-fiction and children's book writers. Submission by email which includes a covering letter within the body of the email, plus 30 pages of your work attached. *Founded* 2020.

Judith Murdoch Literary Agency*

19 Chalcot Square, London NW1 8YA
tel 020-7722 4197
website www.judithmurdoch.co.uk
Contact Judith Murdoch

Full-length fiction only. Especially interested in commercial women's fiction and crime. *Commission* Home 15%, overseas 20%. Closed to new submissions. No sci-fi and fantasy, poetry, short stories or children's.

   Clients include Diane Allen, Trisha Ashley, Frances Brody, Jill Childs, Rosie Clarke, Diney Costeloe, Kate Eastham, Leah Fleming, Faith Hogan, Emma Hornby, Lola Jaye, Ali Mercer, Elizabeth Morton, Kitty Neale. *Founded* 1993.

Mushens Entertainment*

email submissions@mushens-entertainment.com
website www.mushens-entertainment.com
Twitter @MushensEnt, @mushenska, @lizadeblock, @Rachel_Neely_, @kiyarosevans
Contact Juliet Mushens, Liza DeBlock, Rachel Neely, Kiya Evans

Fiction and non-fiction. *Commission* Home 15%, overseas 20%. For fiction: send an email addressed to a specific agent with subject line 'Fiction Submission: [Title of work]', the cover letter in the body of the email and a synopsis and the first three chapters or approximately 10–15,000 words as attachments. For non-fiction: email addressed to a specific agent with subject line 'Non-Fiction Submission: [Title of work]', the cover letter in the body of the email and a proposal or the first 10–15,000 words attached. Does not represent picture books, middle grade, children's fiction younger than teen, novellas, short stories, poetry, screenplays, comics/graphic novels or erotica.

   Authors include Jessie Burton, Claire Douglas, Stacey Halls, Ali Land, Laura Jane Clark, Taran Matharu, Kuchenga, Della Hicks-Wilson, James Oswald, Jennifer Saint, Abigail Dean, Richard Osman. *Founded* 2020.

Kate Nash Literary Agency*

email submissions@katenashlit.co.uk
website https://katenashlit.co.uk/
Facebook www.facebook.com/
KateNashLiteraryAgency
Twitter @katenashagent, @justinnashlit, @saskialeach_, @BethFerguson__
Contacts Kate Nash, Justin Nash, Saskia Leach, Bethany Ferguson

Represents commercial, general, genre fiction and popular non-fiction. Open to approaches from both new and established authors. General fiction, book club, literary fiction, crime and thriller, historical fiction, romantic fiction, women's fiction, sci-fi and fantasy, YA, popular non-fiction. *Commission* UK and Ireland 15%, USA 15% (20% sub-agented), overseas 20%, book to screen 20%. See website for full submission guidelines. No poetry, drama, comedy, erotica, short stories or children's picture books.

   Clients include P.R. Black, Alice Castle, Lesley Cookman, Lucy Cruickshanks, Helena Dixon, Lesley Eames, Paul Gitsham, Jane Lovering, Faith Martin, Andie Newton, Bella Osborne, Emma Royal, Alex Shaw, Maggie Sullivan, D.E. White. *Founded* 2009.

The North Literary Agency

The Chapel, Market Place, Corbridge, Northumberland NE45 5AW
email hello@thenorthlitagency.com
website http://thenorthlitagency.com/
Twitter @northlitagency
Instagram @northlitagency
Agents Julie Fergusson, Allan Guthrie, Lina Langlee, Kevin Pocklington, Mark Stanton

Agency based across the north of England and Scotland, doing business globally. Looking for all types of fiction and narrative non-fiction. Email a brief covering letter plus a synopsis (fiction) or proposal (non-fiction) and 15,000-word sample to submissions@thenorthlitagency.com. Check website for full submission guidelines. No academic writing, poetry, self-help, picture books or screenplays.

   Clients include Ned Boulting, Simon Conway, Gavin Extence, Simon Goddard, Cass Green, Sophie Hardach, Roger Hutchinson, John Ironmonger, Ed James, Andy Jones, Sheena Kalayil, Guy Kennaway, Craig Robertson, Adam Southward, the estate of Paul Torday. *Founded* 2017.

Northbank Talent Management*

email info@northbanktalent.com
website www.northbanktalent.com
Twitter @northbanktalent

Adult fiction and non-fiction. Fiction: women's fiction, reading group fiction, crime, thrillers, literary fiction with a strong storyline, historical fiction, speculative fiction. Non-fiction: politics, current affairs, memoir, celebrity, autobiography, biography, business, lifestyle, history, science, self-help, smart thinking. *Commission* Home 15%, overseas/rights in other media 20%. Send cover letter, synopsis and first three chapters as Word or Open Document attachments to either fiction@northbanktalent.com or nonfiction@northbanktalent.com. Aims to give initial response within two weeks. No poetry, academic books, plays, scripts or short stories. No children's without referral.

   Authors include Brian Cox, Iain Dale, Anthony Seldon, Camilla Cavendish, Damian Collins, Carla Valentine, Christopher Harding, Chris Mason, Nino Strachey, Owen Matthews, Paul Brand, Marion Todd, Catherine Mangan, Phoebe Luckhurst, Victoria Scott. *Founded* 2006.

Andrew Nurnberg Associates Ltd*

3–11 Eyre Street Hill, London EC1R 5ET
tel 020-3327 0400

email info@nurnberg.co.uk
website www.andrewnurnberg.com
Twitter @nurnberg_agency
Managing Directors Jenny Savill (ANA), Doug Wallace (ANAI)

Represents adult and children's authors, agent and publisher clients in the fields of literary and commercial fiction and general non-fiction for the sale of rights throughout the world via offices in the UK and overseas. *Founded* 1977.

Originate Literary Agency

71–75 Shelton Street, Covent Garden,
London WC2H 9JQ
email nataliejerome@originateliterary.co.uk
Twitter @OriginateLit
Instagram @originateliterary
Founder & literary agent Natalie Jerome

Actively looking to platform new voices who push boundaries and want to create change on a global stage. Represents a broad range of genres including YA, commercial fiction and non-fiction. *Commission* Home 15%, overseas 20%. Send a covering note including a brief biography and the first three chapters of your book (for illustrated titles send sample spreads with your proposal) by email to originatesubmissions@originateliterary.co.uk. Does not represent academic and educational texts.
   Clients include Sir Lenny Henry (children's publishing), David Harewood, Amir Khan, Eric Collins. *Founded* 2023.

Deborah Owen

78 Narrow Street, Limehouse, London E14 8BP
tel 020-7987 5119/5441
Contact Deborah Owen

Small agency specialising in only two authors: Delia Smith and David Owen. No new authors.
Founded 1971.

Paper Lion Ltd

13 Grayham Road, New Malden, Surrey KT3 5HR
tel 07748 786199, (01276) 61322
email katyloffman@paperlionltd.com
email lesleypollinger@paperlionltd.com
website www.paperlionltd.com
Agents Katy Loffman, Lesley Pollinger

A cross-media literary agency. The client list includes award-winning authors, literary estates and publishers. Has a strong focus on the exploration of digital opportunities and expertise in solving complex copyright, dramatic rights and literary issues from the present and past.
   Clients include Max Allen, Diane Barker, Nick Drake-Knight, Stewart Ferris, Catherine Fisher, Dave Gatward, Bill Palmer, Saviour Pirotta, HopeRoad Ltd, the estates of authors including Grantley Dick-Read, Bruce Hobson, D.H. Lawrence, Ada Lovelace and John Wyndham. *Founded* 2017.

Paper Literary*

email submissions@paperliterary.com
website www.paperliterary.com
Twitter @PaperLiterary
Agents Catherine Cho, Katie Greenstreet

An agency focused on storytelling with a vision of building author careers internationally. Represents commercial fiction, crime, reading group and literary fiction, and narrative non-fiction titles. *Commission* Home 15%, USA 20%, translation/book-to-film 20%. Send a query letter, synopsis, and the first three chapters (up to 10,000 words) by email. Does not represent children's, screenplays or dramatic works.
   Authors include Sarah Underwood, Soon Wiley, Brooke Robinson, Rae Rashad, Tasha Coryell, Karen Ball. *Founded* 2021.

PBJ Management

22 Rathbone Street, London W1T 1LG
tel 020-7287 1112
email general@pbjmanagement.co.uk
website www.pbjmanagement.co.uk
Contacts Peter Bennett-Jones, Caroline Chignell

Represents writers, performers, presenters, podcasters, composers, directors, producers and DJs. Specialises in comedy. *Commission* Theatre 15%, film/TV/radio 12.5%.
   Clients include Rowan Atkinson, Armando Iannucci, Eddie Izzard, Lenny Henry, Mawaan Rizwan, Simon Blackwell, Adam Buxton, Richard Ayoade, Tim Minchin, Tim Key, Nina Conti, Maisie Adam, John Cleese, Sally Phillips, James Acaster. *Founded* 1988.

Jonathan Pegg Literary Agency*

c/o Workshop, 47 Southgate Street,
Winchester SO23 9EH
tel (01962) 656101
email info@jonathanpegg.com
website https://jonathanpegg.com
Founder & Agent Jonathan Pegg

Specialises in full-length quality fiction and non-fiction. See website for genre categories represented. *Commission* Direct 15%, co-agented 20%. Email submission to submissions@jonathanpegg.com. For fiction, include a synopsis plus three sample chapters. For non-fiction include a synopsis and proposal which includes a chapter plan and writing sample. Does not represent children's fiction, YA or pure fantasy.
   Authors include Dr Nafeez Ahmed, Michael Blastland, Steve Bloomfield, Alex Brummer, Alex Christofi, Nick Davies, Dr Stuart Farrimond, Kaffe Fassett OBE, Zac Goldsmith, Robert Lacey, Tom McCarthy, General Sir Michael Rose, Jonathan and Angela Scott, Carolyn Steel, Prof. Sir David Spiegelhalter OBE. *Founded* 2008.

Pérez Literary & Entertainment Ltd*

49 Greek Street, London W1D 4EG
email assist@perezliterary.com
website www.perezliterary.com
Twitter @perez_literary
Instagram @perezliterary
Managing Director Kristina Pérez

A transatlantic agency working holistically throughout the English-speaking world. Represents a wide variety of fiction and non-fiction, from book club to horror to current affairs. *Commission* Home 15%, USA 15%, overseas 20%. Submission guidelines on website. *Founded* 2023.

Peters Fraser & Dunlop Ltd*

55 New Oxford Street, London WC1A 1BS
tel 020-7344 1000
email info@pfd.co.uk
website https://petersfraserdunlop.com
Facebook www.facebook.com/pfdagents
Twitter @PFDAgents
Ceo Caroline Michel, *Literary agents* Caroline Michel, Tim Bates, Samantha Brace, Kate Evans, Adam Gauntlett, Sarah Hornsley, Lucy Irvine, Cara Lee Simpson, Annabel Merullo, Silvia Molteni, Fiona Petheram, Laurie Robertson, Elizabeth Sheinkman, Lisette Verhagen, *Associate Agent* Daisy Chandley, *Estates* Dan Fenton, Agnes Watters, *Film & TV* Rosie Gurtovoy, Jonathan Sissons, *Broadcast & Live Events* Tris Payne, *Foreign Rights* Rebecca Wearmouth, Lucy Barry, Antonia Kasoulidou, Mariam Quraishi

Represents authors of fiction and non-fiction, presenters and public speakers throughout the world. PFD runs its own digital publishing imprint called Agora Books Ltd (www.agorabooks.co). Email submissions addressed to individual agents. Include covering letter, synopsis or outline and first three chapters as well as author biographies. See website for submission guidelines. Does not represent scriptwriters.
  Authors include Jeanette Winterson, Simon Schama, Edna O'Brien, Bear Grylls, Michael Caine, Onjali Q. Rauf, Lisa Thompson, Jamie Bartlett, Lesley Pearce, Chi-chi Nwanoku, Rose Tremain, Niall Williams, Jamie Susskind, Kenya Hunt, Ruby Wax. *Founded* 1924.

PEW Literary*

46 Lexington Street, London W1F 0LP
tel 020-7734 4464
email info@pewliterary.com
website www.pewliterary.com
Agents Patrick Walsh, Margaret Halton, Eleanor Birne, Doug Young

Boutique agency with a strong list of prize-winning authors. Non-fiction, fiction, graphic novels. *Commission* Home 15%, overseas 20%, film/TV 20%. Submit a covering letter with a synopsis and first three chapters (fiction) or a proposal including an outline and sample chapter (non-fiction). No poetry, children's picture books, plays or academic titles.
  Clients include Nick Harkaway, H.M. Naqvi, Luke Jennings, Keggie Carew, Laura Cumming, Jim al-Khalili, Tom Holland, Helen Castor, Andrea Wulf, Anita Anand, Gaia Vince, Simon Singh, Bill Browder, Mark Cocker. *Founded* 2016.

Portobello Literary*

email info@portobelloliterary.co.uk
website www.portobelloliterary.co.uk
Founder Caro Clarke

Looking for unique and engaging writing that disrupts the status quo. Represents fiction: commercial and literary, all genres from speculative fiction and fantasy to gripping crime; and non-fiction: narrative, memoir, popular science, big ideas, travel, food writing and cookery books, nature, culture, essays, queer culture and intersectional feminism. Email a synopsis and short bio with the first three chapters or 50 pages (fiction) or a chapter outline and first three chapters (non-fiction). No children's and YA.
  Authors include Polly Atkin, Jenny Chamarette, Rachel Charlton-Dailey, Mona Dash, Samantha Dooey-Miles, Harry Josephine Giles, C.L. Hellisen, Russell Jones, Louise Kenward, Aefa Mulholland, J.C. Niala, Andrés N. Ordorica, Wendy Pratt, Christina Riley, Elspeth Wilson. *Founded* 2022.

Shelley Power Literary Agency Ltd*

33 Dumbrells Court, North End, Ditchling, East Sussex BN6 8TG
tel (01273) 844467
email sp@shelleypower.co.uk
Contact Shelley Power

General fiction and non-fiction. Works in conjunction with agents abroad. No longer accepting submissions. *Commission* Full-length MSS: home 12.5%, USA/translation 20%. Preliminary letter essential – may be sent by email. No children's books, YA, sci-fi, fantasy, short stories, poetry, screenplays or plays. *Founded* 1976.

Redhammer Management Ltd

website https://redhammer.info
Vice President Peter Cox

A boutique literary agency providing in-depth management for a restricted number of clients. Specialises in works with international book, film and TV potential. Participates in Pop-Up Submissions every Sunday; submit a title, brief description and first 700 words of the work. No radio or theatre scripts.

The Lisa Richards Agency

108 Upper Leeson Street, Dublin D04 E3E7, Republic of Ireland
tel +353 (0)1 637 5000

email info@lisarichards.ie
website www.lisarichards.ie
Contact Faith O'Grady

Handles fiction and general non-fiction. Overseas associate: The Marsh Agency for translation rights. Commission Ireland 10%, UK 15%, USA/translation 20%, film/TV 15%. Approach with proposal and sample chapter for non-fiction and three to four chapters and synopsis for fiction (sae essential).

Clients include Prof. Marie Cassidy, Mick Clifford, Aoife Dooley, Austin Duffy, PJ Gallagher, Christine Dwyer Hickey, Paul Howard (aka Ross O'Carroll-Kelly), Michelle McDonagh, Richard Hogan, Harry McGee, Ronan McGreevy, Mary O'Donoghue, Damien Owens, Gill Perdue, Sheena Wilkinson. Founded 1998.

Richford Becklow Agency

2 Church Street, Peasenhall, Suffolk IP17 2HL
tel (01728) 660879
email lisa.eveleigh@richfordbecklow.co.uk
website www.richfordbecklow.com
Twitter @richfordbecklow
Contact Lisa Eveleigh

Literary and commercial fiction and non-fiction. Historical fiction, saga, crime, romantic comedy, biography and memoir. Commission Home 15%, overseas 20%. We are no longer accepting unsolicited submissions. Please refer to the website for editorial services. Does not represent books for children or young adults.

Authors include Amanda Austen, Mary Alexander, Hugo Barnacle, Stephen Buck, Ralph Fevre, Jane Gordon-Cumming, Catherine Haig, Carol McGrath, R.P. Marshall, Tony Slattery, Jonathan Socrates, Simon Westwood, Grace Wynne-Jones, Sophie Parkin, Adrienne Vaughan. Founded 2011.

Robertson Murray Literary Agency

3rd Floor, 37 Great Portland Street, London, W1W 8QH
tel 020-7580 0702
email info@robertsonmurray.com
website https://robertsonmurray.com/
Facebook www.facebook.com/RobertsonMurrayLiteraryAgency
Twitter @RMLitAgency
Co-founders Charlotte Robertson, Hilary Murray, Agent Jenny Heller

Fiction: commercial and literary fiction in any genre except sci-fi. Non-fiction: welcomes all non-fiction, including memoir and biography, personal development, lifestyle, cookery, history, current affairs, popular science, sport and humour. Submission via the website which includes full submission guidelines. Does not represent academic texts, poetry, or scripts for film, TV or stage. Currently closed for new children's submissions. Founded 2019.

Rocking Chair Books Literary Agency*

2 Rudgwick Terrace, St Stephens Close, London NW8 6BR
email representme@rockingchairbooks.com
website www.rockingchairbooks.com
Twitter @rockingbooks
Contact Samar Hammam

Dedicated to original and page-turning books. Currently open for submissions. Focuses on adult commercial fiction, literary fiction, graphic novels and non-fiction for publication around the world. Also works with other agencies to represent their translation or English language rights, including Mulcahy Sweeney Associates and the Raya Agency. Commission Home 15%, translation/adaptation rights 20%. Submission by email only. No children's, YA or sci-fi (unless they are crossover).

Authors include Warsan Shire, Dominique Duong, Christina Fonthes, Brian Turner, Kay Medaglia, Nydia Hetherington, Laura Coleman. As co-agent alongside The Raya Agency for Arabic Literature in Translation: Dima Wannous, Khaled Khalifa, Samar Yazbek, Hoda Barakat. Founded 2013.

Rogers, Coleridge & White Ltd*

20 Powis Mews, London W11 1JN
tel 020-7221 3717
email info@rcwlitagency.com
website www.rcwlitagency.com
Twitter @RCWLitAgency
Instagram @rcwliteraryagency
Managing Director Peter Straus, Deputy Managing Director Georgia Garrett, Directors Nelka Bell, Sam Copeland, Stephen Edwards, Natasha Fairweather, Laurence Laluyaux, Zoë Waldie, Claire Wilson, Jon Wood, Agents Cara Jones, Matthew Turner

International representation for all genres of fiction, non-fiction, children's and YA. Commission Home 15%, USA 20%, translation 20%. Note that due to the volume of unsolicited queries, it is policy to respond (usually within six weeks) only if interested in the material. See website for submissions information. Founded 1967 as Deborah Rogers Ltd, 1989 as Rogers, Coleridge & White Ltd.

The Ruppin Agency*

website www.ruppinagency.com
Twitter @ruppinagency
Directors Jonathan Ruppin, Emma Claire Sweeney

Represents both commercial and literary fiction, and serious non-fiction. Looking for writing with ambition, originality and relevance. Particularly interested in submissions from writers from under-represented communities including working class, LGBTQ+, people of colour, those with disabilities and those outside London catchment area. Also operates Writers' Studio, a nationwide mentoring scheme for writers of fiction, YA and non-fiction, directed by author Emma Claire Sweeney.

Commission Home 15%, translation 20% (rights handled by The Marsh Agency). Full details of areas of interest and submission requirements on website. No sci-fi and fantasy, horror, poetry, plays, graphic novels, children's/YA, professional or academic.

Clients include Kate Beales, Conor Glynn, Aoife Mannix, Sally J. Morgan, Jude Piesse, Devika Ponnambalam, Nicola Williams. Founded 2017.

The Sayle Literary Agency*

1 Petersfield, Cambridge CB1 1BB
email info@sayleliteraryagency.com
website www.sayleliteraryagency.com
Proprietor & Agent Rachel Calder

Uses specialist co-agents to sell books in foreign language markets, in the USA and for film/TV. Translation rights handled by The Marsh Agency Ltd. Film and TV rights handled by Sayle Screen Ltd. US rights handled by Dunow, Carlson and Lerner. Fiction: general, literary, crime. Non-fiction: current affairs, social issues, travel, biographies, history. Commission Home 15%, USA/translation 20%. List is currently closed. No plays, poetry, textbooks, children's, technical, legal or medical books. Founded 1896.

Sayle Screen Ltd

11 Jubilee Place, London SW3 3TD
tel 020-7823 3883
email info@saylescreen.com
website www.saylescreen.com
Agents Jane Villiers, Matthew Bates, Kelly Knatchbull, Eva Robinson

Specialises in scripts for film, TV, theatre and radio. Represents film, TV and theatre rights in fiction and non-fiction for The Sayle Literary Agency, JULA Ltd, Greene & Heaton Ltd and Rogers, Coleridge and White Ltd. Works in conjunction with agents in New York and Los Angeles. Unable to consider unsolicited material unless recommended by producer, development executive or course tutor. Email a CV, covering letter and details of your referee or course tutor to submissions@saylescreen.com. Every submission carefully considered, but responds only to submissions it wishes to take further; not able to return material sent in.

Linda Seifert Management Ltd

29–30 Fitzroy Square, London W1T 6LQ
tel 020-3327 1180
email contact@lindaseifert.com
website https://lindaseifert.com
Twitter @lindaseifert
Agent Edward Hughes

Represents writers, directors and producers for film, TV and radio only. Commission Home 10%, overseas 20%. No book authors. Not currently accepting unsolicited submissions.

Clients include Lee Cronin, Stephen Volk, Paul Gerstenberger, Nathan Cockerill, Gavin Scott, Mark

Bussell and Justin Sbresni, Adam Butcher, Sean Grundy, Tim Lebbon, Paul Staheli, Marco Van Belle, Keith Storrier, Nancy Netherwood. Founded 2002.

The Sharland Organisation Ltd

The Manor House, Manor Street, Raunds, Northants NN9 6JW
tel Mike: 07710 449654, Alice: 07803 009588
email tso@btconnect.com
website www.sharlandorganisation.co.uk
Directors Mike Sharland, Alice Sharland

Specialises in film, TV and stage rights throughout the world. Founded 1988.

Sheil Land Associates Ltd

LABS House, Rm 9–25, 15–19 Bloomsbury Way, London WC1A 2TH
tel 020-7405 9351
email info@sheilland.co.uk
website www.sheilland.co.uk
Twitter @sheilland
Agents UK & USA Sonia Land, Gaia Banks, Piers Blofeld, Ian Drury, Natalie Barracliffe, Film/Theatre/TV Lucy Fawcett, Rebecca Lyon, Foreign Rights Alba Arnau, Lauren Coleman

Literary and commercial fiction and non-fiction; adult and children's. Overseas associates Georges Borchardt, Inc. US film and TV representation: CAA, APA and others. Represents book club, commercial and literary fiction: thrillers, crime, romance, drama, sci-fi and fantasy and YA; and non-fiction: biography, politics, history, military history, gardening, travel, cookery, humour. Commission Home 15%, USA/translation 20%. Welcomes approaches from new clients to start or to develop their careers. Send cover letter, synopsis and first three chapters. Please send submissions to: submissions@sheilland.co.uk.

Clients include Sally Abbott, Peter Ackroyd, Pam Ayres, Steven Carroll, Nadine Dorries, Robert Fabbri, Janice Hallett, Graham Hancock, Susan Hill, Mark Lawrence, The Brothers McLeod, Gill Paul, Diane Setterfield, Amanda Duke, and the estate of Catherine Cookson. Founded 1962.

Caroline Sheldon Literary Agency Ltd*

71 Hillgate Place, London W8 7SS
tel 020-7727 9102
email email@carolinesheldon.co.uk
website www.carolinesheldon.co.uk
Twitter @CarolineAgent
Contacts Caroline Sheldon, Millie Van Grutten

Represents fiction, non-fiction, children's books and illustration. Interested in all major fiction genres – historical, romance, contemporary, humour, fantasy, crime and thriller. In non-fiction, interested in personal stories and anything involving animals. Represents children's books in every genre and age range from picture books through middle grade to YA. In illustration, the agency is looking for high-quality work in every style. Works closely with a media agent on film, TV and other opportunities. *Commission* Home 15%, USA/translation 20%, film/TV 20%. To submit work send an introductory email addressed to either Caroline Sheldon or Millie Van Grutten: in the subject line write 'Proposal and [title of the work]'; at the head of the email include a three-line synopsis; give further full information in the email about the work and yourself. Authors – send the first three chapters or equivalent length. Illustrators – attach work or include a link to your portfolio. *Founded* 1985.

Hannah Sheppard Literary Agency
email enquiries@hs-la.com
website www.hs-la.com
Twitter @HS_LA_News
Instagram @HS_LA_News
Founder & Literary agent Hannah Sheppard

Actively seeking new authors, particularly from underrepresented groups. Current wish lists can be found on the website. Represents children's fiction (primarily across middle grade, teen and YA), commercial adult fiction (with a focus on crime/thriller and women's fiction) and a very small amount of non-fiction. *Commission* Home 15%, overseas 20%, film/TV 20%. Submission via form on website. No poetry or screenplays.
  Clients include Dee Benson, Jim Beckett, Sarah Bonner, Abi Elphinstone, Gabrielle Kent, Olivia Lara, Jon Lander, Chris McGeorge, Kate Mallinder, Morgan Owen, Keris Stainton. *Founded* 2023.

Sinclair-Stevenson
3 South Terrace, London SW7 2TB
tel 020-7581 2550
Director Christopher Sinclair-Stevenson

General – no children's books. *Commission* Full-length MSS: home 15%, USA/translation 20%. Will suggest revision. *Founded* 1995.

Skylark Literary Ltd*
19 Parkway, Weybridge, Surrey KT13 9HD
tel 020-8144 7440
email info@skylark-literary.com
email submissions@skylark-literary.com
website www.skylark-literary.com
Facebook www.facebook.com/SkylarkLiteraryLtd
Twitter @skylarklit
Directors Joanna Moult, Amber Caraveo

Specialists in children's and YA fiction. Keen to support new and established authors. Agents have editorial backgrounds and will work closely with clients on their manuscripts to increase chances of publication. All genres considered. *Commission* Home 15%, overseas 20%. Will consider unsolicited submissions. Submissions by email only. Will suggest revision where appropriate. No adult fiction/non-fiction.

Clients include Amy Wilson, Simon James Green, Alyssa Hollingsworth, Rachel Burge, Nizrana Farook, Lesley Parr, Em Lynas, Lily Dyu, Sarah Todd Taylor, Naomi Gibson, Lucy Hope, Lee Newbery, Aislinn O'Louglin, Clare Harlow, Eilish Fisher. *Founded* 2014.

Robert Smith Literary Agency Ltd*
The Perie, 24 Broomhill Road,
Woodford Green IG8 9A
tel 020-8504 0024
email robert@robertsmithliteraryagency.com
website www.robertsmithliteraryagency.com
Directors Robert Smith, Anne Smith

Predominantly non-fiction. Autobiography and biography, topical subjects, history, lifestyle, inspirational, popular culture, entertainment, sport, true crime, cookery, self-help, health and nutrition. *Commission* Home 15%, overseas 20%. No unsolicited MSS. Will suggest revision.
  Authors include Peta Bee, David Berridge, Clive Driscoll, Penny Farmer, Stephen Fulcher, Steven Gallant, Angela Gallop, Chistine Handy, Julian Hayes, Roberta Kray, Carol Ann Lee, Ann Ming, Theo Paphitis, Derek and Pauline Tremain, James Reed. *Founded* 1997.

The Soho Agency Ltd*
(previously LAW/Lucas Alexander Whitley Ltd)
16–17 Wardour Mews, 2nd Floor, London W1F 8AT
tel 020-7471 7900
website www.thesohoagency.co.uk
Twitter @TheSohoAgencyUK
Managing Director Rowan Lawton, *Agents* Mark Lucas, Julian Alexander, Araminta Whitley, Rowan Lawton, Alice Saunders, Ben Clark, Sophie Laurimore, Helen Mumby, Carina Rizvi, Philippa Milnes-Smith (Children's and YA), Marina de Pass, Niamh O'Grady

Full-length commercial and literary fiction, non-fiction, fantasy, YA and children's books. Special interests (fiction): accessible literary fiction, character-led narrative, contemporary romance, crime, domestic dramas, historical, psychological suspense and thrillers, reading group fiction, romantic comedy, women's fiction. Special interests (non-fiction): big ideas, business, history, inspirational stories and people, leadership, memoir, philosophy, science. *Commission* Home 15%, USA/translation 20%. Representation in all markets. Unsolicited MSS considered. See website for further information about the clients and genres represented and essential information on submissions. No postal submissions. No plays, poetry or textbooks.
  Clients include Tom Bradby, Poorna Bell, Frank Gardner, Tim Peake, Bettany Hughes, Lindsey Kelk, Sophie Kinsella, Andy McNab, Kate Mosse, Henry Marsh, Chris Riddell, Lauren Child, Michael Robotham, Nigel Slater, Alison Weir. *Founded* 1996.

SP Literary Agency

email info@sp-agency.co.uk
website http://sp-agency.co.uk/
Facebook www.facebook.com/sp.literary.agency
Agents Philippa Perry, Abigail Sparrow

Represents authors and illustrators across children's, YA and adult fiction and non-fiction. Email submissions are preferred; attach a synopsis and the first three chapters to a covering email. Children's or YA submissions should also be clearly marked in the subject line.

Elaine Steel Writers' Agent*

49 Greek Street, London W1D 4EG
tel (01273) 739022
email es@elainesteel.com
website www.elainesteel.com
Contact Elaine Steel

Represents screen, radio, theatre and book writers. Does not read unsolicited material. Any consideration for representation must be by email and accompanied by a CV together with a short outline of the work to be submitted.

Authors include Gwyneth Hughes, Penny Woolcock, James Lovelock, Michael Eaton, Ian Kennedy Martin, Pearse Elliott, Neil Brand, Brian Keenan. *Founded* 1986.

Abner Stein*

China House, Suite 137, 100 Black Prince Road, London SE1 7SJ
tel 020-7373 0456
email info@abnerstein.co.uk
website www.abnerstein.co.uk
Contacts Caspian Dennis, Sandy Violette

Fiction, general non-fiction and children's. *Commission* Home 15%, overseas 20%. Not taking on any new clients at present.

Micheline Steinberg Associates

Studio 315, ScreenWorks, 22 Highbury Grove, London N5 2ER
email info@steinplays.com
website www.steinplays.com
Twitter @SteinbergAssocs
Agent Micheline Steinberg, *Literary Associate* Helen MacAuley

Represents writers/directors for theatre, opera, musicals, television, film, radio and animation, as well as writer-directors, translators and librettists. Media rights in fiction and non-fiction on behalf of book agents, including Watson, Little Ltd. Also works in association with agents overseas. *Commission* Home 10%, with associates 15–20%. No unsolicited submissions. Industry recommendation preferred. No poetry or prose (except for existing clients).

Authors include David K. Barnes, Julie Jones, Rob Kinsman, Jonathan Larkin, Susie McKenna, Glyn Maxwell, Robin Norton-Hale, Debbie Owen, Lisa Parry, Mark Robertson, Danny Spring, Jane Upton, Steve Waters, Sarah Woods. *Founded* 1987.

Rochelle Stevens & Co

2 Terretts Place, Upper Street, London N1 1QZ
tel 020-7359 3900
email info@rochellestevens.com
website www.rochellestevens.com
Twitter @TerrettsPlace
Directors Rochelle Stevens, Frances Arnold

Scripts for TV, theatre and radio. *Commission* Home 10%. Recommendation from industry professional required. Email to introduce yourself and include the recommendation. Will request a writing sample if interested. Does not accept book submissions. *Founded* 1984.

Sarah Such Literary Agency

38 Church Road, Barnes, London SW13 9HN
tel 020-8741 2107
email info@sarah-such.com
website https://sarahsuchliteraryagency.tumblr.com
Twitter @sarahsuch
Instagram @sarahsuch1
Director Sarah Such

High-quality literary and commercial non-fiction and fiction for adults, young adults and children. Always looking for exciting new writers with originality and verve. Translation representation: The Buckman Agency. Film/TV representation: Lesley Thorne, Aitken Alexander Associates Ltd. Particular focus on literary and commercial debut novels, thrillers, topical fiction and quality women's fiction, biography, narrative non-fiction, memoir, history, popular culture and humour. *Commission* Home 15%, overseas 20%, film/TV 20%. Will suggest revision. Submit synopsis and three sample chapters (as a Word attachment by email) and an author biography. No postal submissions unless requested. No unsolicited MSS or telephone enquiries. Film/TV scripts for established clients only. No radio or theatre scripts, poetry, fantasy, self-help or short stories (unless full collections).

Authors include Matthew De Abaitua, Jeffrey Boakye, Kit Caless, Rob Chapman, Anne Charnock, Heather Cooper, Vina Jackson, Maxim Jakubowski, Antony Johnston, Louisa Leaman, Sabrina Pace-Humphreys, Vesna Maric, Caroline Sanderson, Nikhil Singh, Mike Wendling. *Founded* 2007.

The Susijn Agency Ltd

820 Harrow Road, London NW10 5JU
tel 020-8968 7435
email info@thesusijnagency.com
website www.thesusijnagency.com
Agent Laura Susijn

Specialises in world rights in English- and non-English-language literature: literary fiction and general non-fiction. *Commission* Home 15%, overseas 20%, theatre/film/TV/radio 15%. Send synopsis and three sample chapters.

Authors include Peter Ackroyd, Saud Alsanousi, Robin Baker, Hwang Sok-yong, Radhika Jha, Uzma Aslam Khan, Christine Leunens, Mazen Maarouf, Parinoush Sainee, Darren Simpson, Sunny Singh, Paul Sussman, Alex Wheatle, David Whitehouse, Yan Lianke. *Founded* 1998.

Simon Trewin Literary and Media Rights Agency

Soho Works, 2nd Floor, 180 Strand, London WC2R 1EA
email simon@simontrewin.co.uk
website www.simontrewin.co.uk
Twitter @simontrewin
Instagram @simontrewin

Represents fiction and non-fiction. Email in first instance to introduce yourself and the book you are working on.

Authors include Patience Agbabi, Charlotte Bradman, Sam Blake, John Boyne, Dr Harry Cliff, Chloe Esposito, International Literary Properties, Claire Kilroy, Keith Lowe, Paul Lynch, Andrew Miller, Agnes Poirier, Dr Matthew Sweet, William Warr. *Founded* 2019.

Jane Turnbull Agency*

Postal address Barn Cottage, Veryan Churchtown, Truro TR2 5QA
tel (01872) 501317
email jane@janeturnbull.co.uk
website www.janeturnbull.co.uk

Specialises in high quality non-fiction. Works in conjunction with Aitken Alexander Associates Ltd for sale of translation rights. Genres: biography, history, natural history, lifestyle, memoir, humour, TV tie-ins, cookery, some literary and YA fiction. *Commission* Home 15%, USA/translation 20%, performance rights 15%. See website for submission guidelines.

Authors include Kevin McCloud, Prue Leith, Penny Junor, David Lindo, Kate Bradbury, Kate Watson-Smyth, Lucy O'Brien, Andy Mulligan, Frederick Taylor, Lynne Murphy, Miki Berenyi, Jo Bradford, Richard Van Emden. *Founded* 1986.

Nick Turner Management Ltd

tel 020-3723 8833
email nick@nickturnermanagement.com
website https://nickturnermanagement.com
Twitter @nickturnermgmt
Agents Nick Turner, Phil Adie

Represents writers and directors for film, TV and radio worldwide. Specialises in TV drama, comedy, continuing drama and children's. *Commission* Home 10%, overseas 15–20%. *Founded* 2016.

Two Piers Literary Agency

email hello@twopiersagency.com
website https://twopiersagency.com/
Facebook www.facebook.com/TwoPiersAgency
Twitter @TwoPiersAgency
Instagram @twopiersagency
Agent Rufus Purdy

Represents fiction and non-fiction, including children's (from 7+) and memoir. Submissions through form on website. For fiction, submit the first three chapters and a one-page synopsis; for non-fiction, send three chapters and proposal. Submissions must include a covering letter. *Founded* 2021.

United Agents Ltd*

12–26 Lexington Street, London W1F 0LE
tel 020-3214 0800
email info@unitedagents.co.uk
website www.unitedagents.co.uk
Agents Seren Adams, Kat Aitken, Sarah Ballard, Caroline Dawnay, Ariella Feiner, James Gill, Jodie Hodges, Millie Hoskins, Molly Jamieson, Eli Keren, Caradoc King, Robert Kirby, Laura Macdougall, Yasmin McDonald, Amy Mitchell, Zoe Ross, Sophie Scard, Rosemary Scoular, Emily Talbot, Charles Walker, Kate Walsh, Anna Webber, Jane Willis

Fiction and non-fiction. *Commission* Home 15%, USA/translation 20%. See website for submission details. *Founded* 2008.

Jo Unwin Literary Agency*

West Wing, Somerset House, London WC2R 1LA
email info@jounwin.co.uk
website www.jounwin.co.uk
Twitter @jounwin, @rachelphilippa, @MillyReilly
Agents Jo Unwin, Rachel Mann, Milly Reilly

Represents authors of literary fiction, commercial women's fiction, non-fiction, cookery, YA fiction and fiction for children aged 5+ (picture books only accepted if written by established clients).

Authors include Alexina Anatole, Richard Ayoade, Charlie Brooker, Candice Carty-Williams, Eliza Clark, Jenny Colgan, Kit de Waal, Caleb Femi, Gabriel Krauze, Siobhan McSweeney, A.J. Pearce, Georgia Pritchett, Bethany Rutter, Annabel Sowemimo, The White Pube. *Founded* 2016.

Suzann Wade Agency

9 Wimpole Mews, London W1G 8PB
email admin@suzannwade.com
website www.suzannwade.com

Represents talent and writers globally. Focuses on script development and options on novels with companies such as Channel 4, BBC, ITV and Netflix. Particularly interested in unique memoirs, comedies and crime that could be optioned for film or TV. Please submit via email and include your bio and a synopsis of your writing (one page). Responds only to those applicants that they are interested in. No academic books. *Founded* 2006.

Wade & Co. Literary Agency Ltd

33 Cormorant Lodge, Thomas More Street, London E1W 1AU
tel 020-7488 4171
email rw@rwla.com
website www.rwla.com
Director Robin Wade

General fiction and non-fiction. Most genres represented. *Commission* Home 10%, overseas 20%. See website for submission guidelines. Email submissions preferred. New authors welcome. No poetry, plays, screenplays, sci-fi and fantasy, YA, children's books, picture books or short stories. *Founded* 2001.

Watson, Little Ltd*

Suite 315, ScreenWorks, 22 Highbury Grove, London N5 2ER
tel 020-7388 7529
email office@watsonlittle.com
website www.watsonlittle.com
Twitter @watsonlittle
Managing Director James Wills, *Agents* Laetitia Rutherford, Donald Winchester, Megan Carroll, Ciara McEllin, *Rights Director* Rachel Richardson

Offers a full service to its clients across all aspects of media. Handles a wide range of fiction and non-fiction for adults and children and works in conjunction with US agents and selected film and TV associates. Adult Fiction: literary, commercial women's, historical, reading group, crime and thriller. Non-fiction: history, science, popular psychology, memoir, humour, cookery, self-help. Children's: YA and middle-grade fiction, picture books and children's non-fiction in all genres. *Commission* Home 15%, USA/translation 20%. Email submissions@watsonlittle.com with an informative preliminary letter, synopsis and sample chapters. No poetry, TV, play or film scripts.
  Authors include Luci Adams, Jenny Blackhurst, Susan Blackmore, Sophie Claire, Martin Edwards, Christopher Fowler, Sarah Gristwood, Greg Jenner, Holan Liang, Alex Marwood, Margaret Mahy, Alan Moore, Fiona O'Brien, Alex Pavesi, Colin Wilson. *Founded* 1970.

WGM Atlantic Talent and Literary Group

5 Chancery Lane, London WC2A 1LG
tel 020-3637 2064
email hello@wgmatlanticgroup.com
website www.wgmtalent.com
Facebook www.facebook.com/wgmtalent
Twitter @WGMAtlantic

Represents international and UK-based screenwriters, playwrights and authors and is recognised for developing northern talent and close relationships with industry partners.

Whispering Buffalo Literary Agency Ltd

97 Chesson Road, London W14 9QS
tel 020-7385 465
email info@whisperingbuffalo.com
website www.whisperingbuffalo.com
Director Mariam Keen

Commercial and literary fiction, non-fiction, children's and YA fiction. Special interest in book-to-screen adaptations; TV and film rights in novels and non-fiction handled in-house. *Commission* Home 15%, overseas 20%. Only accepts submissions by email. Will suggest revision. *Founded* 2008.

Eve White Literary Agency Ltd*

15 Alderney Street, London SW1V 4ES
tel 020-7630 1155
email eve@evewhite.co.uk
email ludo@evewhite.co.uk
website www.evewhite.co.uk
Twitter @EveWhiteAgency
Contacts Eve White, Ludo Cinelli

Boutique agency representing commercial and literary fiction and non-fiction, children's fiction and film/TV tie-ins. *Commission* Home 15%, overseas 20%. Will suggest revision where appropriate. See website for up-to-date submission requirements. No submissions by post.
  Clients include Ruth Ware, James Norbury, Eloise Head, Jane Shemilt, Andy Stanton, Rae Earl, Sarah J. Naughton, Saskia Sarginson, Rebecca Reid, Len Pennie, Damian Le Bas, Luan Goldie, Sarah Ockwell-Smith, James Clarke, Clare Bourne. *Founded* 2003.

Dinah Wiener Ltd*

12 Cornwall Grove, London W4 2LB
tel 020-8994 6011
email dinah@dwla.co.uk
Director Dinah Wiener

Fiction and general non-fiction, film and TV in association. *Commission* Home 15%, overseas 20%, film/TV in association 15%. Taking on no new clients. No plays, scripts, poetry, short stories or children's books. *Founded* 1985.

Alice Williams Literary*

tel 020-7385 2118
email submissions@alicewilliamsliterary.co.uk
website www.alicewilliamsliterary.co.uk
Twitter @alicelovesbooks
Contact Alice Williams

Specialist literary agency representing writers and illustrators of picture books, children's fiction, teen/YA fiction and children's non-fiction. *Commission* Home 15%, USA/translation 20%, film/TV 20%. By email only; attach full typescript and synopsis, two or three picture book texts or illustration portfolio. See website for further guidelines and submission openings.

Clients include Fiona Barker, Lauren Beard, Jo Clarke, Ruby Clyde, Rachael Davis, Rachel Delahaye, Meg McLaren, Natelle Quek, Matt Ralphs, Rose Robbins, Fabi Santiago, Suzy Senior, Ciara Smyth, Clare Helen Welsh, Pete Williamson. *Founded* 2018.

WME*

(William Morris Endeavour, UK)
100 New Oxford Street, London WC1A 1HB
tel 020-7534 6800
email ldnsubmissions@wmeagency.com
website www.wmeagency.com
Books Matilda Forbes Watson, Hellie Ogden, Fiona Baird, Suzannah Ball, *Foreign Rights* James Munro, Florence Dodd, *TV* Antonia Melville, Tom Micelli

Worldwide talent and literary agency with offices in London, New York, Beverly Hills, Nashville and Sydney. Literary and commercial fiction, crime, thrillers, YA fiction, middle-grade fiction, memoir, self-help, lifestyle, sci-fi, fantasy, women's fiction, serious non-fiction and popular culture. *Commission* UK 15%, USA/translation 20%, film/TV 10%. Please submit via email to the address above with the first three chapters, a synopsis and a covering email.

· *Clients* include Mohsin Hamid, Alice Munro, Kiley Reid, Akala, Amor Towles, Greer Hendricks, Sarah Pekkanen, Lori Gottlieb, Jhumpa Lahiri, Glennon Doyle, Soma Sara, Laura Dave, Dave Grohl, Ellie Goulding, Brené Brown. *Founded* 1898.

The Writers' Practice

tel 07940 533243
email jemima@thewriterspractice.com
website http://thewriterspractice.com
Twitter @writerspractice
Literary Agent & Editorial Consultant Jemima Hunt, *Editorial Consultants TV & Film Scripts* Jeremy Page, Henry Fitzherbert

A boutique literary agency and editorial consultancy that specialises in launching debut authors and book-to-screen deals. Interested in commercial and literary fiction and specialises in memoir and narrative non-fiction. Works closely with writers on all aspects of book development. *Commission* Home 15%, overseas 20%. For fiction, submit a synopsis and three chapters; for non-fiction, submit a pitch, book outline and sample chapter.

Clients include H.B. Lyle, Mikey Cuddihy, Emma Baxter-Wright, Turning Earth. *Founded* 2012.

The Wylie Agency (UK) Ltd

17 Bedford Square, London WC1B 3JA
tel 020-7908 5900
email mail@wylieagency.co.uk
website www.wylieagency.co.uk

Literary fiction and non-fiction. No unsolicited MSS. *Founded* 1996.

Susan Yearwood Agency*

2 Knebworth House, Londesborough Road, London N16 8RL
tel 020-7503 0954
email submissions@susanyearwoodagency.com
website https://susanyearwoodagency.com
Twitter @sya_susan
Contact Susan Yearwood

Book club fiction, commercial fiction and non-fiction; children's fiction, middle grade and YA. *Commission* Home 15%, overseas 20%. Send submission with covering letter and brief synopsis via email. Submissions not accepted by hand or post. Tends not to read sci-fi and fantasy in adult fiction, short stories or poetry.

Authors include Suzanne Snow, Fil Reid, Sarupa Shah. *Founded* 2007.

YMU Books*

180 Great Portland Street, London W1W 5QZ
tel 020-8742 4950
email YMUBooksSubmissions@ymugroup.com
website www.ymugroup.com
Twitter @YMULiterary
Instagram @YMULiterary
Managing Director Amanda Harris

A bespoke literary division within leading talent management agency, YMU Group. Represents authors who are elite in their field across fiction, non-fiction and children's. *Commission* Home 15%, USA 20%.

Clients include Ant & Dec, Francis Bourgeois, Fearne Cotton, Tom Daley, Jane Dunn, Paloma Faith, Noel Fitzpatrick, Jake Humphrey, Matt Lucas, Ant Middleton, Stacey Solomon. *Founded* 2021.

Zeno Agency Ltd*

Primrose Hill Business Centre,
110 Gloucester Avenue, London NW1 8HX
tel 020-7096 0927
email info@zenoagency.com
website www.zenoagency.com
Twitter @zenoagency
Director John Berlyne, *Agent* Stevie Finegan

Most adult fiction genres represented (commercial, crime/thriller, romance etc.) with a specialism in sci-fi, fantasy and horror. Children's fiction from picture books through YA. Non-fiction from specialists in their fields and authors with strong personal stories to tell (narrative, memoir, biography etc). Some illustrated non-fiction considered. *Commission* Home 15%, overseas 15% (via sub-agents 20%). Does not consider poetry, plays or film scripts.

Authors include Ben Aaronovitch, Aliette De Bodard, Travis Baldree, Jonathan Carroll, Charlaine Harris, Grady Hendrix, William Gibson, Brandon Sanderson, Lavie Tidhar, the estate of Roger Zelazny. *Founded* 2008.

Literary agents overseas

This list includes only a selection of agents across Australia and New Zealand (below), Canada (page 453) and the USA (page 455). Additional agency listings can be found at www.writersandartists.co.uk/resources/listings. Before submitting material, writers are advised to visit agents' websites for detailed submission guidelines and to ascertain terms.

sase = self-addressed stamped envelope

AUSTRALIA AND NEW ZEALAND

Alex Adsett Literary
PO Box 694, Tugun, QLD 4224
email agent@alexadsett.com.au
website https://alexadsett.com.au/
Literary agents Alex Adsett, Rochelle Fernandez

Full service literary agency, representing quality works of fiction and non-fiction for children, teens and adults. Fiction: literary and commercial fiction, crime, mystery, romance, sci-fi and fantasy. Children's: chapter book, middle-grade and YA fiction (chapter or genre). Non-fiction: narrative non-fiction with a hook. Submission by invitation only; no unsolicited submissions. Founded 2008.

ALM: Australian Literary Management
Suite 1, 2A Booth Street, Balmain, NSW 2041
tel +61 (0)2 9818 8557
email alphaalm8@gmail.com
website http://austlit.com
Proprietor Lyn Tranter

For full details of genres represented, see website. Unsolicited submissions welcome. Submissions should include a one- to two-page synopsis and covering letter. Writing sample on request. Does not consider TV or film scripts of any kind, poetry, self-help, sci-fi and fantasy or books for children by unpublished authors. Does not accept self-published work or previously published works, including ebooks, or writing by non-Australian authors. Founded 1980.

Cameron's Management Pty Ltd
Level 7, 61 Marlborough Street, Surry Hills, NSW 2010
tel +61 (0)2 9319 7199
email info@cameronsmanagement.com.au
website www.cameronsmanagement.com.au
Agents Anthony Blair, Needeya Islam, Lisa Fagan, James Ward, Jeanne Ryckman (book authors)

An agency representing writers, directors, actors, presenters, designers, cinematographers, editors, composers and book authors across the full range of the film, television, live performance and publishing industries. Only accepts submissions in accordance with guidelines on website. Founded 1976.

Curtis Brown (Australia) Pty Ltd
email submission@curtisbrown.com.au
website www.curtisbrown.com.au
Twitter @curtisbrownaus

Australia's oldest and largest literary agency representing a diverse range of Australian and New Zealander authors. Submissions open periodically throughout the year; check their website for current details and upcoming submission periods. Send cover email, synopsis and first three chapters. Founded 1967.

Jenny Darling & Associates
PO Box 5328, South Melbourne, VIC 3205
email office@jennydarling.com.au
website www.jennydarling.com.au
Contact Jenny Darling

Adult fiction and non-fiction. Commission Home 15%, international/translation 20%, film/TV 20%.
Authors include Garry Disher, Mem Fox, Lian Hearn, Tim Winton and Charlotte Wood. Founded 1998.

Drummond Agency
PO Box 572, Woodend, VIC 3442
tel +61 (0)3 5427 3644
email info@drummondagency.com.au
website www.drummondagency.com.au/index.htm

Considers both fiction and non-fiction for adults and YA fiction, but no fantasy or sci-fi. Query by telephone, email or letter. Do not send attachments unless requested. Represents Australian and New Zealand citizens based in Australia. Does not represent educational materials, poetry, plays, film scripts or children's picture books.
Authors include Randa Abdel-Fattah, Vikki Wakefield, Claire Zorn, Deborah Burrows, Margareta Osborn, Yvette Walker. Founded 1997.

High Spot Literary
email [firstname]@highspotlit.com
website www.highspotlit.com
Facebook www.facebook.com/highspotlit
Twitter @HighSpotLit
Founders Vicki Marsdon, Nadine Rubin Nathan, Associate Agent Catherine Wallace, Junior Agents Nina Leon, Fergus Inder

A full-service agency dedicated to guiding authors to success through working with publishing partners and providing guidance and support to manage their author profile. See website for full submissions guidelines. Does not represent erotica, poetry or visual coffee table books at this time. Considers very few short story collections.

Margaret Kennedy Agency
PO Box 1433, Toowong, Brisbane, QLD 4066
tel +61 (0)7 3870 9996
email hannah@margaretkennedyagency.com
website www.margaretkennedyagency.com
Twitter @mkliterary
Agent Hannah Douglas, *Consultant* Margaret Kennedy

A full-service literary agency representing adult fiction and literary non-fiction. Areas of special interest include non-fiction written by experts for general readers, food writing with a story, and essays and genre-defying short-form pieces. Submissions are open in January and July only. Send a brief query letter with the first 50 pages (fiction) or a letter and proposal (non-fiction). Does not consider genre fiction, self-help books, children's books or illustrations. *Founded* 1996.

Left Bank Literary
website www.leftbankliterary.com
Instagram @leftbankliteraryagency
Agents Gaby Naher, Grace Heifetz, Tom Gilliatt

A Sydney-based literary agency specialising in quality fiction and non-fiction. Works closely with clients to develop their manuscripts to their greatest potential before representing them to publishers and other media organisations. To submit your work for consideration, send a preliminary 'pitch' through the website form including book title, genre, brief synopsis and author bio. Agents will be in contact should they wish to read your manuscript. Does not represent self-help, fantasy, romance, picture books, early reader, middle grade and YA, stage/screenplays, comics or poetry.

Sarah McKenzie Literary Management
tel +61 (0)4 1603 5061
email submissions@smlm.com.au
website www.smlm.com.au
Contact Sarah McKenzie

Provides advice, advocacy and representation for Australian and New Zealander authors, helping them to shape and polish their writing projects. Actively seeks established and emerging authors of commercial and literary fiction, non-fiction and children's fiction (including picture books, middle grade, YA and graphic novels). Submissions via email only. For fiction and memoir, include a covering letter, one- to two-page synopsis and 20 consecutive pages of the MS. For non-fiction, include a covering letter, one-page summary, author bio, one or two sample chapters and a table of contents. Does not represent works that have been previously self-published in any form, speculative fiction, novellas or poetry collections.

Jane Novak Literary Agency
PO Box 774, Five Dock, Sydney, NSW 2046
tel +61 (0)2 9281 8648
email jane@janenovak.com
website www.janenovak.com

Represents writers across all genres as well as a number of literary estates. Submissions are currently closed for fiction and children's/YA. Non-fiction submissions will be considered in digital form only. You must inform the agency if you have submitted your work to a publisher or another agency.
 Authors include Helen Garner, Kate Grenville, Suzie Miller, David Malouf, Gerald Murnane, Behrouz Boochani, Patrick White.

Playmarket
PO Box 9767, Wellington 6141
email info@playmarket.org.nz
website www.playmarket.org.nz
Director Murray Lynch

Playwrights' agent, adviser and bookshop. Representation, licensing and script development of New Zealand plays and playwrights. Licenses productions of New Zealand plays nationally and around the world. *Founded* 1973.

Zeitgeist Agency
Level 1, 142 Smith Street, Summer Hill, NSW 2130
tel +61 (0)4 1035 5790
email query@zeitgeistagency.com
website www.zeitgeistagency.com
Instagram @zeitgeistwriters

International literary, screen, theatre and talent management agency representing writers (fiction, non-fiction, memoir, screen and stage) and illustrators. Submit query or submission via email with 'Query' in the subject line. Specific submission guidelines for each genre can be found on the website.
 Clients include Holly Ringland, Yumi Stynes, Kate Scott, Vivian Pham, Susan Johnson, Benjamin Law, Mawunyo Gbogbo, Megan Rogers, Murong Xuecun, Annabel Abbs, Kristen Loesch, Daria Desombre, Haska Shyyan, AJ Betts, Gabriela Larios. *Founded* 2009.

CANADA

Acacia House Publishing Services Ltd
51 Chestnut Avenue, Brantford, ON N3T 4C3
tel +1 519-752-0978
email bhanna.acacia@rogers.com
Managing Director Bill Hanna

Literary fiction/non-fiction, quality commercial fiction, most non-fiction. *Commission* English worldwide 15%, translation 25%, performance 20%. Works with overseas agents. Query first by email with sample of 50 pages max. No horror or occult. *Founded* 1985.

Rick Broadhead & Associates

47 St. Clair Avenue West, Suite 501, Toronto, ON M4V 3A5
tel +1 416-929-0516
email info@rbaliterary.com
website https://rbaliterary.com

Interested in non-fiction, especially in the following categories: history, politics, business, true crime, investigative journalism, natural history/environment, national security/intelligence, current affairs, biography, science, pop culture, self-help, health, medicine, humour. Email queries preferred to submissions@rbaliterary.com. Writing sample on request. Not currently accepting fiction novels, screenplays, poetry or children's books.

The Bukowski Agency Ltd

20 Prince Arthur Avenue, Suite 12-I, Toronto, ON M5R 1B1
tel +1 416-928-6728
email assistant@bukowskiagency.com
website www.bukowskiagency.com
Agent Denise Bukowski

Specialises in international literary fiction and up-market non-fiction for adults. See website for submission guidelines. Currently closed to unsolicited submissions. Does not represent genre fiction, children's literature, plays, poetry or screenplays. *Founded* 1986.

CookeMcDermid

320 Front Street W #1105, Toronto, ON M5V 3B6
tel +1 647-788-4010
email admin@cookemcdermid.com
website https://cookemcdermid.com
Agents Dean Cooke, Martha Webb, Suzanne Brandreth, Ron Eckel, Rachel Letofsky, Paige Sisley, Cody Caetano, Hana El Niwairi, Sally Harding

Represents authors of literary, commercial, sci-fi and fantasy fiction; a broad range of narrative non-fiction; health and wellness resources; and middle-grade and YA books. Sells Canadian and American rights directly. The in-house rights team sells UK and translation rights, in conjunction with a network of co-agents around the world. CMD also sells film and TV rights directly, in addition to working with associates in New York and LA. Submission via online form.

Clients include John Irving, Geddy Lee, Cherie Dimaline, Omar el Akkad, Maye Musk, Jody Wilson-Raybould, Billy-Ray Belcourt, Michael Crummey, Claudia Dey, Elamin Abdelmahmoud, Robyn Doolittle, Scaachi Koul, Jen Agg, Robert Munsch, Ivan Coyote. *Founded* 2017.

Donaghy Literary Group

tel +1 647-527-4353
email [firstname]@donaghyliterary.com
website www.donaghyliterary.com
Facebook www.facebook.com/DonaghyLiteraryGroup
Twitter @DonaghyLiterary
Agents Stacey Donaghy, Valerie Noble

Provides full-service literary representation to clients at all stages of their publishing career. Specialises in commercial fiction and seeking YA and adult novels. Genres represented include romance, women's fiction, thriller, mystery, suspense, sci-fi, fantasy, historical fantasy and historical fiction. Visit agent pages on the website for information on each agent and what they are currently looking for. Only accepts query submissions via QueryManager. Do not query by phone or email. Welcomes both established and new writers.

P.S. Literary Agency

2nd Floor, 2010 Winston Park Drive, Oakville, ON L6H 5R7
email info@psliterary.com
website www.psliterary.com
Twitter @PSLiterary
President & Principal Agent Curtis Russell, *Senior Literary Agents* Carly Watters (Senior Advisor), Maria Vicente (Advisor), Adria Goetz, *Literary Agents* Eric Smith, Claire Harris, *Associate Agents* Stephanie Winter, Cecilia Lyra

Represents both fiction and non-fiction works to publishers in North America, Europe and throughout the world. Categories include commercial, upmarket, literary, women's fiction, mystery, thriller, romance, sci-fi, fantasy, historical, LGBTQI+, YA, middle grade, picture books, graphic novels, memoir, history, politics, current affairs, business, wellness, cookbooks, sports, humour, popular science, popular psychology, popular culture, design and lifestyle. Send queries to query@psliterary.com. Do not send email attachments unless specifically requested. Does not accept submissions via mail or telephone. *Founded* 2005.

Seventh Avenue Literary Management

email info@seventhavenuelit.com
website www.seventhavenuelit.com

One of Canada's largest non-fiction and personal management agencies. Helps authors develop proposals and manuscripts for submission and negotiates on their behalf with publishing houses in Canada, the USA and worldwide. Authors' books are published by a range of publishers including international houses, independents and specialist presses. Send short query via email including a short description of your project and a brief bio. See the website for specific guidelines.

Beverley Slopen

131 Bloor Street West, Suite 711, Toronto,
ON M5S 1S3
tel +1 416-964-9598
email beverley@slopenagency.ca
website https://slopenagency.com
Agent Beverley Slopen

Represents a diverse list of authors in fields ranging
from literary and commercial fiction to history, non-
fiction, anthropology, biography and selected true
crime and self-help. Does not take on many new
authors and tends to concentrate on Canadian-based
writers. See website for details of authors, titles and
submission guidelines. Does not handle poetry,
horror, romance or illustrated books, and publishes
very few children's titles.

Westwood Creative Artists

386 Huron Street, Toronto, ON M5S 2G6
email wca_office@wcaltd.com
website https://wcaltd.com
Twitter @WCA_LitAgency
Instagram @westwoodcreativeartists
President Jackie Kaiser, *Agents* Chris Casuccio, Emmy
Nordstrom Higdon, Sara Harowitz, John Pearce, Meg
Wheeler

Represents Canadian authors. Interested in literary
fiction, quality commercial fiction for adults and YA,
including mysteries and thrillers, and non-fiction in
the areas of memoir, history, biography, science,
journalism and current affairs. Email submissions to
submissions@wcaltd.com. Send a covering letter and
10–20 pages of MS in body of email. See website for
full submission guidelines. Does not represent
screenwriters, playwrights or poets.

USA

**Member of the Association of American Literary
Agents*

Aevitas Creative Management*

19 West 21st Street, Suite 501, New York, NY 10010
tel +1 212-765-6900
website https://aevitascreative.com
Facebook www.facebook.com/AevitasCreative/
Twitter @AevitasCreative

A full-service literary agency with offices in New
York, Boston, Washington DC, Los Angeles and
London, representing scores of award-winning
authors, thinkers and public figures. See website for
full submission and agent details. *Founded* 2016.

The Axelrod Agency*

55 Main Street, PO Box 357, Chatham, NY 12037
tel +1 518-392-2100
email steve@axelrodagency.com
email lori@axelrodagency.com
website https://axelrodagency.com

President Steven Axelrod, *Foreign Rights Director* Lori
Antonson

Works with overseas agents. *Commission* Fiction:
home 15%, overseas 20%, film/TV rights 15%.
Submit full-length MSS. Will suggest revision where
appropriate. *Founded* 1983.

The Bent Agency*

45 Lyme Road, Suite 206, Hanover, NH 03755
email info@thebentagency.com
website www.thebentagency.com
Instagram @thebentagency
Agents Jenny Bent, Victoria Cappello, Claire Draper,
Louise Fury, James Mustelier, John Silbersack,
Desiree Wilson

Represents a diverse range of genres including
history, humour, lifestyle, inspiration, memoir,
literary fiction, children's and commercial fiction.
Only accepts email queries. See website for detailed
query and submission guidelines.

The Bindery Agency

email info@thebinderyagency.com
website www.thebinderyagency.com
Instagram @thebindery.agency
Founder Alexander Field, *Managing Director* Ingrid
Beck, *Agents* Trinity McFadden, Andrea Heinecke,
Associate Agent John Blase

In addition to literary representation, the agency also
consults with businesses and organisations on
publishing strategy and develops highly specialised
book projects offering a variety of boutique
publishing options. Currently represents authors of
general non-fiction, religion, literary fiction, sci-fi and
fantasy, biography and memoir, pop culture,
leadership, spiritual growth, Christian spirituality and
more. To query about literary representation, email
your book proposal along with a cover letter. Include
a summary of your book concept, table of contents,
author biography, at least two sample chapters,
relevant contact information and your publishing
story. Currently does not represent screenplays, plays,
or illustrators. *Founded* 2017.

David Black Agency*

335 Adams Street, Suite 2707, Brooklyn, NY 11201
tel +1 718-852-5500
email dblack@dblackagency.com
website www.davidblackagency.com
Facebook www.facebook.com/davidblackagency
Twitter @dblackagency
Contacts David Black, Rica Allannic, Jennifer Herrera,
Gary Morris, Susan Raihofer, Sarah Smith, Joy
Tutela, Anna Zinchuk, Ellen Scott

Represents an extensive list of both prescriptive and
narrative non-fiction including business, memoir,
history, politics, fitness and sport. Also represents
both commercial and literary fiction, middle grade
and YA. Queries to be addressed to specific agent and

by email, unless otherwise specified. For most up-to-date submission guidelines and agent preferences see website.

Clients include Mitch Albom, Chris Kimball, Billie Jean King, Dann McDorman, Robert Simonson, Jonathan Eig, Julia Cameron, Ian O'Connor, Deborah Lipstadt, Danny Seo, Emily Timberlake, Lindy West, Rodney Scott, Jessie Damuck, Devon Price. *Founded* 1989.

Blue Heron Literary*

email submissions@blueheronliterary.com
website www.blueheronliterary.com
Agent Amy Levenson

A Seattle-based boutique agency that places fiction and non-fiction with publishers throughout the USA and internationally. Accepts non-fiction manuscripts and proposals from both first-time and established authors. Submissions currently closed.

The Booker Albert Literary Agency

PO Box 20931, York, PA 17402
bookeralbertinfo@gmail.com
website www.thebookeralbertagency.com
Twitter @BookerAlbertLit
Agents Brittany Carter, Jordy Albert, *Junior agents* Abigail Varnado, Helen Lane

Full service agency representing adult, YA and middle-grade fiction. Submission via QueryManager only. See agents' individual profiles on website for specific guidelines and areas of interest. No picture books, non-fiction or screenplays at this time.

Georges Borchardt Inc.*

136 East 57th Street, New York, NY 10022
tel +1 212-753-5785
website www.gbagency.com
Directors Georges Borchardt, Anne Borchardt, Valerie Borchardt

Full-length and short MSS. *Commission* Home/performance 15%, UK/translations 20%. Agents in most foreign countries. No unsolicited MSS. *Founded* 1967.

Bradford Literary Agency*

5694 Mission Center Road, Suite 347, San Diego, CA 92108
email queries@bradfordlit.com
website www.bradfordlit.com

Currently looking for fiction (romance, speculative fiction, women's, sci-fi and fantasy, mystery, thrillers, historical, horror, magical realism, children's and YA) and non-fiction (relationships, biography, memoir, self-help, lifestyle, business, parenting, narrative humour, pop culture, illustrated/graphic design, parenting, food and cooking, mind, body & spirit, history and social issues). Queries accepted only via QueryManager. See website for detailed submission guidelines and for links to each agent's QueryManager form. Not currently looking for poetry, screenplays, short stories, westerns, inspirational/spiritual, horror, New Age, religion, crafts or gift books.

Brandt & Hochman Literary Agents Inc.*

1501 Broadway, Suite 2605, New York, NY 10036
tel +1 212-840-5760
website https://brandthochman.com
Agents Gail Hochman, Marianne Merola, Emily Forland, Emma Patterson, Jody Kahn, Henry Thayer, Mitchell Waters

Fiction and non-fiction for the general trade market. See website for full list of agents and the genres represented by each. *Commission* Home 15%, overseas 20%, performance rights 15%. Queries by email or post (include a sase). Send a one- to two-page query letter with a book project and writing credentials. No screenplays or textbooks. *Founded* 1913.

The Brattle Agency

PO Box 380537, Cambridge, MA 02238
tel +1 617-721-5375
email submissions@thebrattleagency.com
website https://thebrattleagency.com

A full-service agency providing assistance to clients in all areas related to their work including editorial guidance, submission and sale of works to both large and small publishers, contract negotiations, foreign language sales, film and television licences and marketing and publicity strategies. Semi-annual reading period for open submissions; see website for details. Queries should include a formal cover letter, brief synopsis and a CV (if submitting an academic manuscript).

Authors include Chris Amenta, Carlos Bauer, Martin Dubrow, Joan Chase, Paul Griffiths, Minsoo Kang, Joanna Luloff, Luke Salisbury, Gilmore Tamny, Carl Vigeland. *Founded* 2008.

Browne & Miller Literary Associates*

52 Village Place, Hinsdale, IL 60521
tel +1 312-922-3063
email mail@browneandmiller.com
website www.browneandmiller.com
Twitter @BrowneandMiller
Contact Danielle Egan-Miller

General adult fiction and non-fiction. *Commission* Home 15%, overseas 20%. Works in conjunction with foreign agents. Query by email in first instance. Will suggest revision. No children's (including YA), fantasy, short stories, poetry, memoirs, screenplays or academic work. *Founded* 1971.

Maria Carvainis Agency Inc.*

Rockefeller Center, 1270 Avenue of the Americas, Suite 2915, New York, NY 10020

tel +1 212-245-6365
email mca@mariacarvainisagency.com
website www.mariacarvainisagency.com
President & Literary Agent Maria Carvainis

Represents a wide range of fiction and non-fiction with special interest in literary and mainstream fiction, mystery and suspense, thrillers, historicals, contemporary women's fiction, YA and middle grade, memoir, biography, history, business, psychology, pop culture and popular science. *Commission* Home 15%, overseas 20%. Email and postal submissions are accepted. Send a query letter, a synopsis of the work, first 5–10 pages and a note of any writing credentials. See website for full submission guidelines. Does not represent screenplays, children's picture books, sci-fi, or poetry. *Founded* 1977.

The Chudney Agency
72 North State Road, Suite 501, Briarcliff Manor, NY 10510
tel +1 201-758-8739
email steven@thechudneyagency.com
website https://thechudneyagency.com
Contact Steven Chudney

Represents authors of children's books and adult fiction. Submissions via email. Does not accept sci-fi, non-fiction, plays, screenplays or film scripts. *Founded* 2002.

Don Congdon Associates Inc.*
88 Pine Street, Suite 730, New York, NY 10005
tel +1 212-645-1229
email dca@doncongdon.com
website www.doncongdon.com
Agents Cristina Concepcion, Michael Congdon, Katie Grimm, Katie Kotchman, Maura Kye-Casella, Susan Ramer

Full-length and short MSS. General fiction and non-fiction. *Commission* Home 15%, overseas 20%, performance rights 15%. Works with co-agents overseas. No unsolicited MSS. Query/submissions by email or QueryManager only, per agent preference; submit synopsis and first chapter. Full submission guidelines can be found on our website. *Founded* 1983.

The Doe Coover Agency*
PO Box 668, Winchester, MA 01890
tel +1 781-721-6000
email info@doecooveragency.com
website www.doecooveragency.com
Agents Doe Coover, Colleen Mohyde

Specialises in non-fiction: business, history, popular science, biography, social issues, cooking, food writing, gardening; also literary and commercial fiction. *Commission* Home 15%, overseas 10%. Email queries only. No poetry or screenplays. *Founded* 1986.

Corvisiero Literary Agency
1180 Avenue of the Americas, 8th Floor, New York, NY 10036
email info@corvisieroagency.com
website www.corvisieroagency.com
Twitter @CorvisieroLit
Instagram @corvisierolit
Contacts Marisa A. Corvisiero, Tessa Shaffer, Maggie Sadler, Kendyll Drilling

Offers international literary representation, management, and coaching services to fiction and non-fiction for all ages, in a wide spectrum of genres including screenplays. Only submit to one agent at a time via QueryManager. For fiction, send a query letter, one- to two-page synopsis and first five pages. For non-fiction, include a full proposal and sample chapter. For screenplays, include your logline, genre, and upload the first 20 pages of your script. Not currently representing collections of short stories, novellas, essays, or poetry. *Founded* 2012.

Cullen Stanley International*
745 Fifth Avenue, Suite 500, New York, NY 10151
tel +1 917-677-4074
email submissions@cullenstanleyinternational.com
website www.cullenstanleyinternational.com
Contacts Cullen Stanley

Specialises in international rights representation on behalf of authors, agencies and publishers. Represents books with international appeal that will find readers in many languages around the world. Authors seeking representation are encouraged to send a query via email. Query letters should contain your publication history, biographical information and a brief synopsis of your work; attach the first ten pages of your manuscript. Does not accept hard copy submissions. *Founded* 2017.

Richard Curtis Associates Inc.*
c/o International Literary Properties,
286 Madison Avenue, Suite 1002, New York, NY 10017
tel +1 212-772-7363
Contact Richard Curtis

Not currently accepting submissions. *Founded* 1970.

Curtis Brown, Ltd*
228 East 45th Street, Suite 310, New York, NY 10017
tel +1 212-473-5400
email info@cbltd.com
website www.curtisbrown.com
Twitter @CurtisBrownLtd
Instagram @curtisbrown.ltd
Ceo Timothy Knowlton, *President* Peter Ginsberg (at CA branch office), *Vice Presidents* Katherine Fausset, Holly Frederick, Jonathan Lyons, Laura Blake Peterson, *Contact* Kerry D'Agostino, James Farrell, Alexandra Franklin, *Film & TV Rights* Holly Frederick, *Film & TV Rights Associate* Alexandra Franklin, *Translation Rights* Sarah Perillo

Fiction and non-fiction, juvenile, film and TV rights. No unsolicited MSS. See individual agents' entries on the Agents page of the website for specific query and submission information. *Founded* 1914.

Liza Dawson Associates*

121 West 27th Street, Suite 1201, New York, NY 10001
email lwu@lizadawson.com
website www.lizadawsonassociates.com
Twitter @LizaDawsonAssoc
Ceo Liza Dawson

A full-service agency which draws on expertise as former publishers. Commercial and literary fiction and non-fiction. See website for full details of genres represented by individual agents, submission guidelines and email contacts.

Clients include Annie Barrows, Bob Brier, Pierce Brown, Zen Cho, Britt Frank, Ross Gay, R.F. Kuang, Victoria Law, Julia Lee, Victoria Christopher Murray, David Santos Donaldson, Charles Stross and the estate of Eleanor Roosevelt. *Founded* 1996.

Sandra Dijkstra & Associates*

PMB 515, 1155 Camino Del Mar, Del Mar, CA 92014
tel +1 858-755-3115
website www.dijkstraagency.com
Contacts Sandra Dijkstra, Elise Capron, Jill Marr, Thao Le, Andrea Cavallaro, Jessica Watterson, Jennifer Kim, Ariel Renner

Fiction: literary, contemporary, women's, romance, suspense, thrillers and sci-fi. Non-fiction: narrative, history, journalism, business, psychology, self-help, science and memoir/biography. *Commission* Home 15%, overseas 20%. Works in conjunction with foreign and film agents. Email submissions only. Please see website for the most up-to-date guidelines.

Clients include Amy Tan, Maxine Hong Kingston, Lisa See, Chitra Divakaruni, Jasmin Darznik, Eric Foner, Ian Morris, Walter Johnson, Erika Lee, Mae Ngai, Lillian Faderman, Roshani Chokshi, Elena Armas, Jessie Sima, Ali Hazelwood. *Founded* 1981.

Dunham Literary Inc.*

email query@dunhamlit.com
website www.dunhamlit.com
Contact Jennie Dunham, Anjanette Barr

Literary fiction and non-fiction, children's books. *Commission* Home 15%, overseas 20%. Send query by email including a synopsis and first five pages in the body of the email. *Founded* 2000.

Dunow, Carlson & Lerner*

27 West 20th Street, Suite 1107, New York, NY 10011
email mail@dclagency.com
website www.dclagency.com
Agents Henry Dunlow, Jennifer Carlson, Betsy Lerner, Arielle Datz, Stacia Decker, Erin Hosier, Eleanor Jackson, Julia Kenny, Edward Necarsulmer, Nicki Richesin, Chris Rogers, Rachel Vogel

Represents literary and commercial fiction, a wide range of non-fiction and children's literature for all ages. Query letters with first ten pages of your work preferred by email (no attachments). For query letters by post, include sase. *Founded* 2005.

Dystel, Goderich & Bourret LLC*

1 Union Square West, New York, NY 10003
tel +1 212-627-9100
website www.dystel.com
Facebook www.facebook.com/DGandB
Twitter @DGandBTweets
Contacts Jane Dystel, Miriam Goderich, Michael Bourret, Jim McCarthy, Lauren Abramo, Stacey Glick, Ann Leslie Tuttle, Jessica Papin, John Rudolph, Sharon Pelletier, Amy Bishop, Michaela Whatnall, Leslie Meredith

General fiction and non-fiction: literary and commercial fiction, narrative non-fiction, self-help, cookbooks, parenting, sci-fi and fantasy, children's and YA. *Commission* Home 15%, overseas 19%, film/TV/radio 15%. See website for submission guidelines. *Founded* 1994.

The Ethan Ellenberg Literary Agency*

155 Suffolk Street, Suite 2R, New York, NY 10002
tel +1 212-431-4554
email agent@ethanellenberg.com
website www.ethanellenberg.com
President & Agent Ethan Ellenberg, *Senior Agent* Evan Gregory, *Agent* Bibi Lewis

Fiction and non-fiction. Commercial fiction: sci-fi and fantasy, romance, thrillers, mysteries, women's and general fiction; also literary fiction with a strong narrative. Non-fiction: current affairs, history, adventure, true crime, science, health, psychology, cookbooks and spirituality. Children's fiction: interested in YA, middle grade and younger, of all types. Will consider picture books and other illustrated works. Accepts unsolicited MSS by email and seriously considers all submissions, including first-time writers. For fiction, submit synopsis and first 50 pages. For non-fiction, send a query letter and proposal (outline, sample material up to 50 pages, author CV, etc). For children's works, send complete MS. Illustrators should send 4–5 sample illustrations. Unable to return any material from overseas. No scholarly works, poetry, short stories or screenplays. *Founded* 1984.

Fairbank Literary Representation*

21 Lyman Street, Waltham MA 02452
tel +1 617-576-0030
email queries@fairbankliterary.com
website http://fairbankliterary.com
Twitter @FairbankLit
Contacts Sorche Elizabeth Fairbank

Represents more literary fiction than commercial. Interested in narrative non-fiction with an emphasis on women's voices, global perspectives and class and race issues. Seeking children's works (picture books and middle grade) by illustrator authors, as well as diverse illustrators of any type. Also represents various works of prescriptive non-fiction, such as quality lifestyle books, food, wine and design, and is currently keen on acquiring more gift books and impulse buys, especially with a humour angle. Query by email preferred but accepted by mail as well. For full submission guidelines see website. *Founded* 2002.

Diana Finch Literary Agency*

116 West 23rd Street, Suite 500, New York, NY 10011
tel +1 646-375-2081
email diana.finch@verizon.net
website https://dianafinchliteraryagency.submittable.com
Facebook www.facebook.com/DianaFinchLitAg
Twitter @DianaFinch
Owner & Agent Diana Finch

Memoirs, narrative non-fiction, science, history, environment, business, literary fiction, current affairs, health and how-to, sci-fi and fantasy, YA and middle-grade fiction. *Commission* Domestic 15%, foreign 20%. Queries through website; for fiction, include the first ten pages; for non-fiction, include full proposal and sample chapters.
   Clients include Noliwe Rooks, Azadeh Moaveni, Antonia Juhasz, Loretta Napoleoni, Owen Matthews, Greg Palast, Thaisa Frank, Eric Simons, Thomas Goltz, Mark Schapiro, Christopher Leonard, Robert Marion MD. and the estate of Joanna Russ. *Founded* 2003.

FinePrint Literary Management*

207 West 106th Street, Suite 1D, New York, NY 10025
email submissions@fineprint.com
website www.fineprintlit.com
Ceo Peter Rubie, *Agents* Laura Wood, Lauren Bieker, Zachary Honey

Represents fiction and non-fiction, adult and children. Also handles book-to-film, TV dramatic rights, and worldwide subsidiary rights for agency authors. Each agent has specific interests; these are detailed on our website. Query by email. For fiction, include a query letter, synopsis, short biography of the author and first two chapters. For non-fiction, include a query letter and a proposal. Detailed help on writing a proposal is on our website. Address the email to the appropriate agent. No longer accepting printed submissions unless specifically asked to send one. *Founded* 2007.

Folio Literary Management*

The Film Center Building, 630 9th Avenue, Suite 1101, New York, NY 10036
tel +1 212-400-1494
website www.foliolit.com
Twitter @FolioLiterary
Instagram @folioliterary

Represents both first-time and established authors. Seeks upmarket adult fiction, literary fiction, commercial fiction that features fresh voices and/or memorable characters, and narrative non-fiction. Folio Jr is devoted exclusively to representing children's book authors and artists. Consult agents' submission guidelines on the website before making contact.

The Friedrich Agency*

email mfriedrich@friedrichagency.com
email lcarson@friedrichagency.com
email hcarr@friedrichagency.com
email hbrattesani@friedrichagency.com
website www.friedrichagency.com
Agents Molly Friedrich, Lucy Carson, Heather Carr, Hannah Brattesani

Represents literary and commercial fiction for adults, plus narrative non-fiction and memoir. Accepts queries by email only. Query only one agent. No unsolicited MSS. No attachments to query emails unless invited. See website for detailed submission guidelines.
   Clients include Elizabeth Strout, Karen Joy Fowler, Ruth Ozeki, Laurie Frankel, Jane Smiley, Sy Montgomery, Terry McMillan, Esmeralda Santiago, Cathleen Schine, Eileen Garvin, Leila Mottley, Rachel Harrison, John Verdon , Florence Williams, Archer Mayor.

Gelfman Schneider Literary Agents Inc.*

850 Seventh Avenue, Suite 903, New York, NY 10019
email mail@gelfmanschneider.com
website www.gelfmanschneider.com
Agents Jane Gelfman, Deborah Schneider, Heather Mitchell, Penelope Burns

General adult fiction and non-fiction. *Commission* Home 15%, overseas 20%. Works in conjunction with ICM Partners and Curtis Brown, London. See website for detailed submission guidelines and information on which agents are accepting queries/submissions. *Founded* 1992.

Global Lion Intellectual Property Management Inc.

PO Box 669238, Pompano Beach, FL 33066
tel +1 754-222-6948
email liseanne@globallionmgt.com
website www.globallionmanagement.com
Facebook www.facebook.com/GlobalLionManagementMgt/
Twitter @globallionmgt
Instagram @globallionmgt
President & Ceo Liseanne Miller

Specialises in non-fiction and commercial fiction including thrillers and true crime, as well as books with film, TV or global publishing potential. Works in conjunction with agents worldwide. Initial submissions should include a synopsis, author biography, manuscript sample and details of personal social media and self-promotion.

Clients include Sir Ken Robinson, Deborah Kagan, Doug Mader, Rabbi Mordecai Schreiber, Anthony DeStefano, Ann Pearlman, Ivor Davis.

Barry Goldblatt Literary LLC*
594 Dean Street, Brooklyn, NY 11238
tel +1 718-832-8787
website http://bgliterary.com/
Contact Barry Goldblatt

Represents YA and middle-grade fiction, as well as adult sci-fi and fantasy. Has a preference for quirky, offbeat work. Submission via QueryManager only. No non-fiction. *Founded* 2000.

Frances Goldin Literary Agency*
214 West 29th Street, Suite 1006, New York, NY 10001
tel +1 212-777-0047
email agency@goldinlit.com
website www.goldinlit.com
Twitter @GoldinAgency
Agents Sam Stoloff, Ellen Geiger, Matt McGowan, Caroline Eisenmann, Roz Foster, Jade Wong-Baxter, Sulamita Garbuz, Ayla Zuraw-Friedland, Alison Lewis

Fiction (literary and high-quality commercial) and non-fiction. Email submissions welcome. For fiction, memoir, essays, or narrative non-fiction, send a query letter and the first 10–15 pages in the body of your email. For all other non-fiction, send a query letter. Does not handle screenplays, romance, and hardly any poetry. *Founded* 1977.

Irene Goodman Literary Agency*
27 West 24th Street, Suite 804, New York, NY 10010
email agentfirstname.queries@irenegoodman.com
website www.irenegoodman.com
Facebook www.facebook.com/IreneGoodmanAgency
Twitter @IGLAbooks
Instagram @iglabooks
Agents Irene Goodman, Miriam Kriss, Barbara Poelle, Kim Perel, Victoria Marini, Whitney Ross, Pam Gruber, Natalie Lakosil, Lee O'Brien, Margaret Danko

Principally represents commercial fiction with an emphasis on women's voices, romantic novels, historical fiction, mystery, crime and suspense novels. Also represents middle-grade and young adult books, including fantasy. Non-fiction areas of interest include narrative non-fiction of cultural, social or historical relevance, popular culture, biography, memoir, science and psychology. Works in collaboration with the foreign rights agency Baror International who deal with foreign publishers directly. Query by email and addressed to one agent only; send query letter and first ten pages of a

manuscript for fiction, and a query letter for non-fiction. Does not represent picture poetry or screenplays. *Founded* 1989.

Sanford J. Greenburger Associates Inc.*
55 Fifth Avenue, New York, NY 10003
tel +1 212-206-5600
website www.greenburger.com
Facebook www.facebook.com/GreenburgerAssociates/
Twitter @GreenburgerLit
Instagram @greenburger_associates
Agents Heide Lange, Faith Hamlin, Dan Mandel, Matt Bialer, Rachael Dillon Fried, Wendi Gu, Sarah Phair, Alexander Slater, Abigail Frank, Iwalani Kim, Bailey Tamayo, Alex Reubert

Fiction and non-fiction, film and TV rights. Only accepts queries by email. See website for submission guidelines. *Founded* 1932.

The Joy Harris Literary Agency Inc.*
1501 Broadway, Suite 2605, New York, NY 10036
tel +1 212-924-6269
email contact@joyharrisliterary.com
website www.joyharrisliterary.com
Twitter @JoyHarrisAgency
Instagram @joyharrisliterary
Agents Joy Harris, Adam Reed, Alice Fugate

Represents adult and children's literary fiction and non-fiction. Submissions should be emailed, comprising a query letter and an outline or sample letter. See website for detailed submission guidelines. No unsolicited manuscripts. Does not currently accept poetry, screenplays, genre fiction or self-help submissions. *Founded* 1990.

Hartline Agency
123 Queenton Drive, Pittsburgh, PA 15235
tel +1 412-829-2483
email [firstname]@hartlineliterary.com
website www.hartlineagency.com
Agents Joyce Hart, Jim Hart, Linda Glaz, Cyle Young, Patricia Riddle-Gaddis

Actively seeking new and established authors in a variety of genres and categories, both fiction and non-fiction. Detailed submission guidelines are available on the website and on individual agent pages. Works primarily with authors living in the USA or Canada but international authors are considered on an individual basis by each agent. Does not represent short fiction, screenplays, scripts, poetry or magazine articles.

John Hawkins & Associates Inc.*
80 Maiden Lane, Suite 1503, New York, NY 10038
tel +1 212-807-7040
email jha@jhalit.com
website www.jhalit.com
President Moses Cardona, *Agents* Warren Frazier, Anne Hawkins

Fiction and non-fiction; YA. *Founded* 1893.

The Jeff Herman Agency LLC

PO Box 1522, Stockbridge, MA 01262
tel +1 413-298-0077
email jeff@jeffherman.com
website www.jeffherman.com

Business, reference, popular psychology, technology, health, spirituality, general non-fiction. *Commission* Home/overseas 15%. Works with overseas agents. Will suggest revision where appropriate. *Founded* 1986.

HG Literary*

6 West 18th Street, Suite 7R, New York NY 10011
email [firstname]@hgliterary.com
website www.hgliterary.com
Twitter @HGLiterary
Instagram @hgliterary
Contacts Carrie Hannigan, Josh Getzler, Soumeya Bendimerad Roberts, Victoria Wells Arms, Julia Kardon, Rhea Lyons, Brianne Johnson, Jon Cobb, Ellen Goff, Hannah Popal.

Represents a variety of both commercial and literary fiction, including women's literature, crime and mystery novels, historical fiction and thrillers. Also represents children's picture books, middle-grade and young adult fiction. Non-fiction areas of interest include memoir and narrative non-fiction relating to business, current affairs, popular psychology, science, food and select works of photography. Query by email and addressed to one agent only. For full submission guidelines and agent preferences see website. *Founded* 2011.

Hill Nadell Literary Agency

6442 Santa Monica Blvd., Suite 200A, Los Angeles, CA 90038
tel +1 310-860-9605
email queries@hillnadell.com
website www.hillnadell.com
Twitter @HillNadell
Instagram @hillnadell
Agents Bonnie Nadell, Dara Hyde

Literary and commercial fiction, narrative non-fiction, current affairs, memoirs, popular culture, cookbooks, graphic novels, and select children's books. *Commission* Home 15%, overseas 20%. Works in conjunction with agents in Scandinavia, France, Germany, Holland, Japan, Spain and more. Send query electronically via the form on the website. No scripts or screenplays. *Founded* 1979.

InkWell Management

521 Fifth Avenue, Suite 2600, New York, NY 10175
tel +1 212-922-3500
email info@inkwellmanagement.com
website https://inkwellmanagement.com
Twitter @inkwellmgmt

Fiction and non-fiction. *Commission* Home/overseas 15%. Query with a cover letter and one or two chapters (authors) or link to portfolio (illustrators) to submissions@inkwellmanagement.com. *Founded* 2004.

JABberwocky Literary Agency Inc.

49 West 45th Street, 5th Floor, New York, NY 10036-4603
website www.awfulagent.com
Twitter @awfulagent
President Joshua Bilmes, *Vice President* Eddie Schneider, *Coo* Brady McReynolds, *Agents* Lisa Rodgers, Bridget Smith, *Subsidiary Rights Director* Susan Velazquez

Agency specialising in sci-fi and fantasy. There are six acquiring agents; for their individual submission and query guidelines, visit the website. *Founded* 1994.

Heather Jackson Literary Agent*

email query@hjlit.com
website www.hjlit.com

Specialises in practical and narrative commercial non-fiction and 'can't put it down, must read now' fiction. Represents novelists and authors in personal health and wellbeing, history, popular science and psychology, politics and current affairs, business, memoir and self-help. Does not accept unsolicited proposals or manuscripts. Send a query email with a brief description of your book, its uniqueness in the marketplace and why you, and only you, can write it. Do not send attachments. Can only respond to projects of interest. *Founded* 2017.

Janklow & Nesbit Associates

285 Madison, 21st Floor, New York, NY 10017
tel +1 212-421-1700
email info@janklow.com
email submissions@janklow.com
website www.janklowandnesbit.com
Twitter @JanklowNesbit
President Luke Nesbit

Commercial and literary fiction and non-fiction. Works in conjunction with Janklow & Nesbit (UK) Ltd. Submissions: send an informative cover letter, synopsis/outline and the first ten pages. For picture book submissions, include a dummy and at least one full-colour sample. For graphic novels, send ten illustrated pages with text and a synopsis. Address submissions to an individual agent, including your email address or a return envelope with sufficient postage for material to be returned. *Founded* 1989.

Keller Media Inc.

578 Washington Boulevard, Suite 745, Marina Del Rey, CA 90292
tel +1 800-278-8706
email help@kellermedia.com
website https://kellermedia.com
Facebook www.facebook.com/KellerMediaInc
Twitter @KellerMediaInc

Ceo & Senior Agent Wendy Keller, *Editorial Director* Alex Schnitzler, *Editorial Assistant* Will Reicher, *Query Manager* Elise Howard

Non-fiction for adults: business, science, self-improvement, psychology, relationships, wellness, health and non-traditional health, career, personal finance, nature, cookery, spirituality, history, and ecology/green movement. To inquire, please refer to https://kellermedia.com/query and complete the form. Does not represent fiction, poetry, memoirs, autobiographies, true crime or screenplays. *Founded* 1989.

Harvey Klinger Inc.*

300 West 55th Street, #11V, New York, NY 10019
email queries@harveyklinger.com
website www.harveyklinger.com
Twitter @HKLiterary
Agents Harvey Klinger, David Dunton, Andrea Somberg, Wendy Levinson, Rachel Ridout, Cate Hart, Jennifer Herrington, Analieze Cervantes

Commercial and literary adult and children's fiction and non-fiction – serious narrative through to self-help psychology books by authors who have already established strong credentials in their respective field. *Commission* Home 15%, overseas 25%. See website for submission guidelines and submission form. *Founded* 1977.

The Knight Agency*

email admin@knightagency.net
website https://knightagency.net
Facebook www.facebook.com/knightagency/
Twitter @KnightAgency
Instagram @the.knight.agency

Represents both first-time and established authors across a wide range of genres. For the genre interests of individual agents and detailed submission guidelines, see website. All queries should be sent via QueryManager. *Founded* 1996.

kt literary*

9249 S. Broadway 200–543, Highlands Ranch, CO 80129
tel +1 720-344-4728
email queries@ktliterary.com
website https://ktliterary.com
Twitter @ktliterary
Instagram @ktliterary
Agents Kate Testerman, Sara Megibow, Renee Nyen, Hilary Harwell, Kelly Van Sant, Jas Perry, Kari Sutherland, Savannah Brooks, Tara Gilbert, Laurel Symonds, *Associate agent* Chelsea Hensley

Primarily middle-grade and YA fiction. In adult, also seeking romance, sci-fi, fantasy and contemporary fiction. Queries are accepted via QueryManager. No postal submissions.

  Clients include Maureen Johnson, Stephanie Perkins, Matthew Cody, Ellen Booraem, Trish Doller,

Amy Spalding, Roni Loren, Casey McQuiston, Rebecca Roanhorse, Stefan Bachmann, Jason Hough. *Founded* 2008.

Susanna Lea Associates

331 West 20th Street, New York, NY 10011
tel +1 646-638-1435
email ny@susannalea.com
website www.susannalea.com
Twitter @SLANYC
Agents Susanna Lea, Stephanie Cabot, Lauren Wendelken

General fiction and non-fiction with international appeal. Send query letter, brief synopsis, the first three chapters and/or proposal via email. No plays, screenplays or poetry.

  Clients include Marc Levy, Jessie Inchauspé, Ingrid Betancourt, V.V. Ganeshananthan, Nicola Griffith, Louisa Hall, Ayaan Hirsi Ali, Tracey Lange, Margareta Magnusson, Fiona McFarlane, Mindy Mejia, Tom Mustill, Dolen Perkins-Valdez, Putsata Reang, Adam Ross. *Founded* in Paris 2000, New York 2004, London 2007.

Levine Greenberg Rostan Literary Agency*

307 Seventh Avenue, Suite 2407, New York, NY 10001
tel +1 212-337-0934
email submit@lgrliterary.com
website www.lgrliterary.com
Twitter @LGRLiterary
Instagram @lgrlit
Principals Jim Levine, Daniel Greenberg, Stephanie Rostan, *Agents* Sarah Bedingfield, Lindsay Edgecombe, Victoria Skurnick, Kerry Sparks, Danielle Svetcov, Monika Verma, Tim Wojcik, Courtney Paganelli

Represents literary and commercial fiction, non-fiction and books for young readers across a diverse range of genres. Submissions via online form.

Julia Lord Literary Management*

38 West Ninth Street, New York, NY 10011
email query@julialordliterarymgt.com
website www.julialordliterarymgt.com
Contacts Julia Lord, Ginger Curwen

Currently looking for submissions in the following genres: narrative non-fiction, reference, biography, history, lifestyle, sports, humour, science, adventure, general fiction, historical fiction, thrillers, mysteries, graphic fiction and non-fiction. Email and postal queries accepted. See website for details about the agency, its authors and submission guidelines. *Founded* 1999.

Donald Maass Literary Agency*

Suite 252, 1000 Dean Street, Brooklyn, NY 11238
tel +1 212-727-8383

email info@maassagency.com
website https://maassagency.com
Agents Donald Maass, Jennifer Jackson, Cameron McClure, Katie Shea Boutillier, Michael Curry, Caitlin McDonald, Paul Stevens, Jennifer Goloboy, Kiana Nguyen, Kat Kerr, Anne Tibbets

Specialises in fiction of all genres. *Commission* Home 15%, overseas 20%. Only submit to one agent and include a synopsis and first five pages of your MS. Does not represent poetry, picture books, or screenplays. *Founded* 1980.

Margret McBride Literary Agency*
PO Box 9128, La Jolla, CA 92038
tel +1 858-454-1550
email mmla@mcbridelit.com
website www.mcbrideliterary.com
President Margret McBride, *Associate Agent* Faye Atchison

Non-fiction including business, personal finance, health and wellness, history, psychology, true crime, politics and culture. Occasionally represents commercial and literary fiction. *Commission* Home 15%, overseas 25%. Only accepts submissions via QueryManager. No poetry or children's books.
   Clients include John David Mann, Bob Burg, Grant Sabatier, Colin Cowie, Benjamin Bikman, Marc Milstein, Brian Dovey, Tom Morris, Jim Tenuto, Annasue Wilson, Vivian Zottola, Chin Ning Chu, Spencer Johnson, Sheldon Bowles, Ken Blanchard. *Founded* 1981.

McIntosh & Otis Inc.*
207 East 37th Street, Suite BG, New York, NY 10016
tel +1 212-687-7400
email info@mcintoshandotis.com
website https://mcintoshandotis.com
Twitter @McIntoshAndOtis
Agents Elizabeth Winick Rubinstein, Christa Heschke, Daniele Hunter, Adam Muhlig

Adult and children's literary fiction and non-fiction. Electronic submission only, either by email or QueryManager. For fiction, send query letter, synopsis, author and first three chapters. For non-fiction, send query letter, proposal, outline, author bio, and three sample chapters. For children and YA submissions, query letter, synopsis, and the first three chapters and any relevant illustrations. Does not represent poetry, screenplays, and original theatrical or dramatic works of any kind. *Founded 1928.*

Carol Mann Agency*
55 Fifth Avenue, New York, NY 10003
tel +1 212-206-5635
email submissions@carolmannagency.com
website www.carolmannagency.com
Twitter @carolmannagency
Instagram @carolmannagency
Contacts Carol Mann, Gareth Esersky, Joanne Wyckoff, Dani Segelbaum

Interested in fiction and non-fiction on the following subjects: business, food, health, history and politics, humour and popular culture, memoir, relationships and parenting, science and technology, spirituality and religion. *Commission* Home 15%, overseas 20%. Works in conjunction with foreign and film agents. Submission by email only with no attachments. For fiction, send a query letter including a brief bio, and the first 25 pages of your MS. For non-fiction, send a query letter including a brief bio, a synopsis/proposal and the first 25 pages of your MS. *Founded* 1977.

The Evan Marshall Agency*
1 Pacio Court, Roseland, NJ 07068-1121
tel +1 973-287-6216
email evan@evanmarshallagency.com
website www.evanmarshallagency.com
President Evan Marshall

General fiction. Works in conjunction with overseas agents. *Commission* Home 15%, overseas 20%. Will suggest revision. Considers new clients by referral only. *Founded* 1987.

Jean V. Naggar Literary Agency Inc.*
216 East 75th Street, Suite 1E, New York, NY 10021
tel +1 212-794-1082
email jvnla@jvnla.com
website www.jvnla.com
Twitter @JVNLA
Instagram @jvnlainc
President & Agent Jennifer Weltz, *Agents* Alice Tasman, Ariana Philips, Alicia Brooks

Mainstream commercial and literary fiction, non-fiction (narrative, memoir, journalism, psychology, history, pop culture, humour and cookery books), young readers (picture, middle grade, YA). Works in conjunction with foreign agents. Submit queries via form on website. *Founded* 1978.

Alison Picard, Literary Agent
PO Box 2000, Cotuit, MA 02635
tel +1 508-477-7192
email ajpicard@aol.com

Adult fiction and non-fiction, children's and YA. *Commission* Home 15%. Please send query via email (no attachments). No short stories, poetry, plays, screenplays or sci-fi and fantasy.
   Clients include David Housewright, Caryl Rivers, Jessica Fisher, David Alan Johnson, Susan Froetschel. *Founded* 1985.

Pippin Properties Inc.
110 West 40th Street, Suite 1704, New York, NY 10018
tel +1 212-338-9310
email info@pippinproperties.com
website www.pippinproperties.com
Facebook www.facebook.com/pippinproperties
Twitter @LovethePippins

Instagram @pippinproperties
Contacts Holly McGhee, Elena Giovinazzo, Sara Crowe

Focuses on children's book authors and artists, including picture books, middle grade, graphic novels and YA novels, and adult trade books on occasion. *Commission* Home 15%, overseas 25%. Query specific agent by email. For authors, include the first chapter and short synopsis, or entire picture book. For illustrators, send a query letter detailing your background in illustration and links to website with a dummy or other examples of your work. *Founded* 1998.

Rees Literary Agency*
One Westinghouse Plaza, Suite A203, Boston, MA 02136-2075
tel +1 617-227-9014
email [firstname]@reesagency.com
website www.reesagency.com
Agents Ann Collette, Lorin Rees, Rebecca Podos, Kelly Peterson, Taj McCoy

Represents literary and commercial fiction, memoirs, history, biography, business, YA and middle grade, self-help, psychology and science. *Commission* Home 15%. See the website for individual agents' submission guidelines. *Founded* 1983.

The Angela Rinaldi Literary Agency*
email info@rinaldiliterary.com
website www.rinaldiliterary.com

Mainstream and literary fiction: women's, multicultural, mysteries, suspense, historical thrillers; non-fiction: memoir, biography, relationships, psychology, health/medical/wellness, business, parenting, cooking, lifestyle and personal finance. *Commission* Home 15%, overseas 25%. Email submissions only. For fiction, send a brief synopsis and paste the first ten pages. Non-fiction queries should include a detailed cover letter, your credentials and any publishing history. *Founded* 1994.

Root Literary*
email info@rootliterary.com
website www.rootliterary.com
Twitter @RootLiterary
Instagram @rootliterary

Identifies talent, negotiates deals and advocates for books all the way from submission to publication. Represents authors, author-illustrators, graphic novelists and illustrators. Submissions via email or QueryManager. For authors, submit the first ten pages in body of email to submissions@rootliterary.com. For author-illustrators, illustrators and graphic novelists, please send work samples to illustrators@rootliterary.com. Specific guidelines for illustrations can be found on the website. No screenplays or poetry, no authors of picture book texts only.

Jane Rotrosen Agency*
318 East 51st Street, New York, NY 10022
tel +1 212-593-4330
email info@janerotrosen.com
website www.janerotrosen.com
Twitter @Jane_Rotrosen
Instagram @jra_janerotrosenagency
Founder Jane Rotrosen Berkey, *Agents* Andrea Cirillo, Meg Ruley, Annelise Robey, Amy Tannenbaum, Christina Hogrebe, Rebecca Scherer, Kathy Schneider, Jessica Errera, Logan Harper, *Associate agent* Hannah Strouth

Represents authors of fiction and non-fiction. Genres represented include women's fiction, suspense, thrillers, mysteries, crime fiction, historical novels, YA, fantasy, psychological suspense and romantic comedy. Visit individual agent pages on the website for their specific interests and contact details. Submissions by email. For fiction, include a synopsis and first three chapters. For non-fiction, include a proposal and sample chapters. Do not currently accept plays, screenplays or children's picture books.

Clients have produced over 1,000 international and domestic bestsellers in all formats. *Founded* 1974.

Susan Schulman Literary Agency LLC*
454 West 44th Street, New York, NY 10036
tel +1 212-713-1633
email susan@schulmanagency.com
Twitter @SSchulman

Agents for negotiation in all markets (with co-agents) of fiction and general non-fiction, children's books, academic and professional works, and associated subsidiary rights including plays, television and film. *Commission* Home 15%, UK 7.5%, overseas 20%. Return postage required. Email enquiries to queries@schulmanagency.com.

Scott Meredith Literary Agency
PO Box 3090, Grand Central Post Office, New York, NY 10163-3090
email aklebanoff@scottmeredith.com
website www.scottmeredith.com
President Arthur Klebanoff

General fiction and non-fiction. *Founded* 1946.

Scovil Galen Ghosh Literary Agency, Inc.*
276 Fifth Avenue, Suite 708, New York, NY 10001
tel +1 212-679-8686
email info@sgglit.com
website www.sgglit.com
Contacts Russell Gallen, Jack Scovil, Anna Ghosh, Ann Behar

Represents a wide range of commercial and literary fiction, with an emphasis on novels with strong characters and distinct, new voices. Non-fiction tastes generally lean towards the literary scale and favour works that have something new to teach their reader. Areas of interest include biography and memoir, business and politics, contemporary culture, journalism, nature, history, science and sport. Picture books, children's, middle-grade and YA fiction also of interest. Foreign rights handled by co-agency Baror International, Inc. Query by post or email to one agent. *Founded* 1992.

Philip G. Spitzer Literary Agency Inc.*

50 Talmage Farm Lane, East Hampton, NY 11937
tel +1 631-329-3650
email annelise.spitzer@spitzeragency.com
website www.spitzeragency.com
Facebook www.facebook.com/SpitzerLit/
Twitter @SpitzerLit
Agents Anne-Lise Spitzer, Lukas Ortiz, *Office* Kim Lombardini

General fiction and non-fiction; specialises in mystery/suspense/thriller, true crime, biography and memoir. Client list currently full. *Founded* 1969.

Sterling Lord Literistic, Inc.*

594 Broadway, New York, NY 10012
tel +1 212-780-6050
email info@sll.com
website www.sll.com
Twitter @SterlingLordLit
President Philippa Brophy, *Executive Vice President* Laurie Liss, *Chair* Peter Matson, *Chief Operating Officer* Nadyne Pike, *Vice President* Doug Stewart, *Senior agents* Robert Guinsler, Neeti Madan, Jim Rutman, *Agents* Elizabeth Bewley, Danielle Bukowski, Jessica Friedman, Mary Krienke, Sarah Landis, Jenny Stephens, *Foreign rights* Szilvia Molnar, Amanda Price, *Associate agents* Maria Bell, Christopher Combemale

Works with a number of co-agents in all major foreign territories. Also has connections in TV and film development and production. Represents a range of fiction and non-fiction in a variety of subject areas. Fiction list features books for both the commercial and literary market, including thrillers, gentle fantasy and sci-fi, and novels of cultural or geographical reference. Picture books, children's, middle-grade and YA fiction are also strongly represented. Non-fiction areas of interest cover everything from biography and memoir to current affairs, journalism and science. More commercial subject areas such as food, lifestyle, self-help and travel are also covered. Query via online form. For agent preferences see website.

Clients James McBride, Chanel Miller, William Gibson, Rachel Maddow, Hannah Gadsby, Gabrielle Zevin , Jason Rekulak, Phoebe Robinson, Alejandro Varela, Jenny Lawson, Stan and Jan Berenstain, Sheila Heti, Raquel Vasquez Gilliland, Shelby Mahurin, Bryan Washington. *Founded* 1952.

3 Seas Literary Agency*

PO Box 444, Sun Prairie, WI 53590
tel +1 608-332-3430
website www.threeseasagency.com
Twitter @threeseaslit
Agents Michelle Grajkowski, Cori Deyoe, Stacey Graham, Stephanie Stevens, Kara Grajkowski

A full-service literary agency representing authors who write romance, women's fiction, sci-fi and fantasy, thrillers, YA and middle-grade fiction, as well as select non-fiction titles and picture books. Accepts submissions through QueryManager only. Genre-specific submission guidelines can be found on the website. Will only reply if interested in your work. *Founded* 2000.

Trident Media Group

355 Lexington Avenue, Floor 12, New York, NY 10017
tel +1 212-333-1511
email info@tridentmediagroup.com
website www.tridentmediagroup.com
Facebook www.facebook.com/TridentMediaGroup
Twitter @Trident_Media
Instagram @trident_media

Adult and children's fiction and non-fiction across a variety of genres. *Commission* Home 15%, overseas 20%, in conjunction with co-agents/theatre/films/TV 15%. Will suggest revision. Query one agent via online form. Writing sample on request. *Founded* 2000.

Watkins/Loomis Agency Inc.

PO Box 20925, New York, NY 10025
tel +1 212-532-0080
email assistant@watkinsloomis.com
website www.watkinsloomis.com

Specialises in literary fiction, biography, memoir and political journalism. No unsolicited MSS. Representatives Abner Stein (UK) and The Marsh Agency Ltd (foreign). No unsolicited MSS. *Founded* 1908.

WME

11 Madison Avenue, 18th Floor, New York, NY 10010
tel +1 212-586-5100
website www.wmeentertainment.com

Worldwide talent and literary agency with offices in New York, Beverly Hills, Nashville, Sydney and London. Represents bestselling authors, critically acclaimed literary writers, award-winning thought leaders and up-and-coming talent. *Founded* 1898.

Wolf Literary Services*

Suite 603, 135 West 29th Street, New York, NY 10001
email queries@wolflit.com
website www.wolflit.com
Twitter @WolfLiterary

Represents fiction, non-fiction, illustrated books. Follow the submission guidelines on the website to submit your project via email or QueryManager, as applicable. Does not accept mailed queries. Does not represent screenplays. *Founded* 2008.

WordLink Incorporated

PO Box 395, Enola, PA 17025
tel +1 631-882-3462
website www.wordlink.us
Facebook www.facebook.com/wordlink.us

Represents works of fiction and non-fiction as well as television and film internationally. Send a query letter or use online form. See website for detailed submission guidelines. *Founded* 1998.

Writers House LLC*

120 Broadway, 22nd floor, New York, NY 10271
tel +1 212-685-2400
website www.writershouse.com

Fiction and non-fiction for adults and children, including film and TV rights. Represents literary and commercial fiction, women's fiction, sci-fi/fantasy, narrative non-fiction, history, memoirs, biographies, psychology, science, parenting, cookbooks, how-to, self-help, business, finance, young adult and juvenile fiction/non-fiction and picture books. Send a query letter and a synopsis of your work addressed to one agent; email preferred. Does not represent screenplays. *Founded* 1973.

The Wylie Agency Inc.

250 West 57th Street, Suite 2114, New York, NY 10107
tel +1 212-246-0069
email mail@wylieagency.com
website www.wylieagency.com

Literary fiction and non-fiction. Offices in New York and London. No unsolicited MSS accepted.

Art and illustration
Illustrating non-fiction books

Freelance illustrator Frances Moffatt describes her route into professional non-fiction illustration and gives practical advice for aspiring illustrators on finding that first commission and the process from contract through to publication and beyond.

The world of non-fiction books provides a wealth of illustration opportunities for the freelance illustrator, but is often overlooked by illustration graduates in favour of children's middle-grade fiction and picture books. Non-fiction is an exciting, diverse sector of publishing to work in and can range from commissions for cookery books and instructional guides on exercise and fashion to adult colouring books.

My own journey to illustrating non-fiction began after I graduated from my MA in Illustration and, fittingly, consulted the *Writers' & Artists' Yearbook* to identify potential clients. I had come to the conclusion that my portfolio was suited to the 'lifestyle' market, with a predominantly female focus, and subjects such as fashion, health and beauty. I duly combed the *Yearbook* to find appropriate publishers and then sent off small promotional packs containing a bundle of postcards, a business card and a covering letter to my chosen publishers. I put all this information in a spreadsheet so I could keep track of whom I had contacted and when, and whether I had followed that up with a phone call.

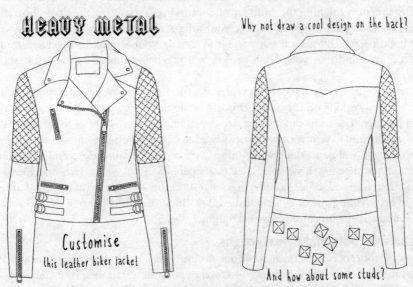

Illustrations by Frances Moffatt from *Fashion Exercise Book* (Batsford)

Around 18 months later, I received an exciting email from Pavilion Books asking me if I would like to illustrate a fashion-themed colouring and doodle book aimed at the young adult and adult markets, to which I swiftly replied a resounding 'Yes!'. It turned out that one of the designers in their art department had liked the promo package I sent and had pinned up one of my postcards on her desk to keep me in mind if any suitable projects came up. *Fashion Exercise Book* was published in 2014 by Batsford (a Pavilion imprint), and I went on to illustrate a further book, *Pick Up a Pen*, in 2018, for their Portico list.

It's a commonly held belief that if you want to work in any aspect of the creative industries it is important to have 'contacts', but I can honestly say that, in my own experience and that of many other illustrators I know, this has not been the case. If your work is good, you have a solid online portfolio, and knowledge of where your work sits in the publishing market, then you have every chance of seeing your work in print. Also keep in mind that building a sustainable career as an illustrator is a marathon, not a sprint, and not getting an immediate response from potential clients is not a failure. In my case, I had some positive and encouraging feedback from art directors at various publishing houses, but it took nearly two years to receive an actual commission.

Commission, ideas and initial meeting

So … you have been commissioned to illustrate a book, either following an approach by a publisher or your own pitch. The next step is to sign your contract. Publishing contracts are long and have many clauses, so it is essential to read them carefully and to seek advice if there are any sections you don't understand. If you are a member of the Association of Illustrators (AOI), the professional body for illustration within the UK (https://theaoi.com; see page 525), you can access free legal and contracts advice.

In a publishing contract for illustrating a book, you will generally get an advance and a percentage of royalties from any sales. Your advance will then be paid in three parts: the first instalment on signing the contract, the second on submitting the final illustrations and the third on publication. Therefore your full payment will be spread out over a long period of time, which means it's important to manage your time and budget accordingly, and to understand that your book project will inevitably run alongside other shorter projects.

After agreeing the contract, the next step is a meeting with your commissioning editor and the team working on the book. This can be done over Skype or Zoom or in person, which I prefer. The team can vary in size depending on the nature of the project. It's a great opportunity to visit your publisher's headquarters, have a face-to-face meeting with the people you will be working with and to discuss potential directions and possibilities. For the initial meeting, it's a good idea to prepare some rough sketches and ideas, any visual inspiration and some examples of similar successful titles on the market. This doesn't have to be anything elaborate or polished; for this stage I usually use a PowerPoint for images and a sketchbook for ideas and roughs.

Synopsis, layouts and pencil roughs

Your book concept may be taken to a book fair, such as London or Frankfurt, which is an opportunity for co-editions to be sold to foreign publishers. For this, your publisher will need a written synopsis of the book and around three finished spreads. This is a really helpful step for you as an illustrator, because it means you get a clear idea of the publisher's vision for the book and the feel and the tone that they, and you, are looking for.

Once the synopsis has been pinned down, it's time to do the roughs for each spread, and this can take different forms depending on the book. For example, when I was working on *Fashion Exercise Book*, a colouring book with brief slogans on each page rather than proper 'text', it was quite an organic process. We started off with a list of ideas for page content, and then I worked closely with the designer, sending work back and forth until we arrived at a consistent look and feel for the illustrations. As a result, after a couple of spreads we had established a routine of sending through the rough pencil spreads for any adjustment and approval, and then sending the inked-up finals as I completed them, until the book was finished.

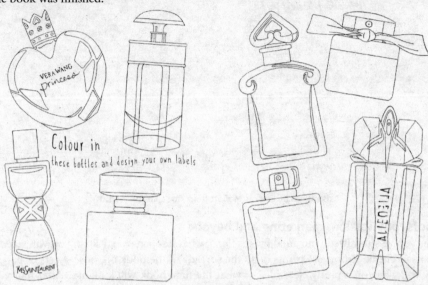

Illustrations by Frances Moffatt from *Fashion Exercise Book* (Batsford)

However, for *Pick Up a Pen*, because there was copy involved it required a bigger team, the process was slightly different and more formalised. I had input into the synopsis of the book, which was written up by a ghostwriter; I then submitted a pdf of pencil roughs of the whole book for approval, outlining what was going to be on each spread. Clearly at this point the text had not been written, but from the initial three spreads sent to book fairs I had an idea of the amount of text that would be on each page, which meant I could plan out the size and number of illustrations. As a result, my images for this book were a whole series of black-and-white 'spot' illustrations, which I submitted to the publisher in one batch at the end of the development stage; these were then sent to the book designer for page layout and the addition of limited accent colour.

So you will find that, when working on illustration for non-fiction books, there is commonality in the different stages of the project, but there is not just one set process or way of working. The main thing to remember is that clear and professional communication with the client and team at all times is paramount. It's likely that most of this communication will be conducted by email if you don't live near the publisher's offices (and they may well even be in a different time zone), so it's important to respond to all emails in a timely manner, and to just ask if you have questions or queries about any aspect of the brief or process. It's also really important to manage expectations; if you feel you are struggling with your deadline, it's best to speak up straightaway. It is much better to bring up any timing issues with as much notice as possible, and to negotiate an extension, than to struggle on and miss your deadline, as there is generally a little space in the schedule to allow for delays. And remember to *enjoy* the process! Freelance illustration can be a solitary profession at times, so illustrating a book allows you to be part of a creative team of experts in their field, which is an inspiring and rewarding experience.

Illustrations by Frances Moffatt from *Pick up a Pen* (Portico)

Proofs, publication, marketing and beyond

After you've submitted your final illustrations, what happens next? First, you will receive proofs to check. Proofs are prints of all the spreads of the book on loose sheets of paper; they will give you a pretty clear idea of what the final book will look like. After that you will receive a sample copy of the book, which for me is always a high point – the culmination of many months of hard work brought together in final form, ready to be sold.

The process of creating a book, from commission to publication, is a long one, usually around 12 months. Therefore you will have a long break between completing your illustrations and promoting the publication of your book, which involves a very different mindset and skills. You will need to work with your publisher on a marketing strategy, and you will also need to take responsibility for promoting the book yourself through social media, traditional media and in-person events.

In the weeks leading up to publication, you need to start building excitement and anticipation for your product across social media. You can start dropping 'teaser' images (small excerpts) from your book, along with a link to where people can pre-order; you can give your audience an insight into your development process, showing images of your pencil roughs or filming a short 'behind the scenes' video. In addition, you can work with your publisher to organise a book launch event – which is a great opportunity to both promote your book and to celebrate too! Venues for these can range from bookshops to restaurants to galleries.

At this stage you may also see your book published in co-editions across various countries with different publishers. In these cases, the front cover design may be amended or changed, and the book may be given a new title. For example, *Fashion Exercise Book* was published in France as *My Fashion Book – Coloriages Creatifs* (Éditions Marie Claire 2015) with a red and purple rather than an orange cover.

Once the process is over it's a great idea to keep in touch with your publishers, sending them updates on your new work, through further promotional packs or email links to your updated website, so they can keep you in mind for any future projects. When you have one book illustration project in your portfolio, you'll be in a strong position as you go back to your trusty *Writers' & Artists' Yearbook* for your next round of marketing. Potential clients will be more likely to commission you, as they have evidence you have already successfully handled illustrating a book from start to finish.

The good news is, if you're reading this, you are already on Step One of your journey towards being a published illustrator for non-fiction. If you have the passion and drive to continue to refine your illustrative practice, and have a considered and consistent marketing plan, you can move forward with confidence knowing that you are equipped with the knowledge and skills to make your publishing dreams a career reality. Good luck!

Frances Moffatt is a freelance illustrator, writer, and educator. She has worked on a range of commissions for clients across editorial, publishing, fashion, beauty, product and live event illustration and is the author/illustrator of *Fashion Exercise Book*, *Pick Up a Pen* and *Fashion Colouring and Doodling*, all published by Pavilion Books. She has many years' experience of lecturing in illustration and design at degree level, and has spoken at design events and festivals, including TEDxBloomsbury. She is a co-founder of The School of Illustration (www.theschoolofillustration.com), an industry-focused virtual school for illustrators, providing online courses, workshops and mentoring. For more information see www.francesmoffatt.com.

Breaking into comics

Antony Johnston has advice for any writer keen to build a career in comics and graphic novels on how to showcase and pitch their work in a challenging field where networking, quality and enthusiasm are essential.

Writing comics and graphic novels is challenging and fun. The medium of sequential narrative art is unique in its applications and possibilities, one that can produce a similar level of immersion and engagement to books yet is as visually striking as movies or TV. It's also littered with the bodies of writers who've taken on the form without truly understanding it.

I won't belabour the point but, suffice it to say, if you have little experience of comics, I strongly urge you to immerse yourself in them before you try to write one. Must you have been reading comics since you were a child? Not at all. There are some great writers who came to comics later in life, but those people did their homework: they fell in love with the medium and set about analysing how it works, how to achieve wondrous immersion through the combination of words and still images. If you're new to comics, you must do the same.

It also won't hurt to read up on the industry itself. Monthly comics is a strange business, punching far above its weight in cultural influence, yet conducted with almost shocking informality. Seminal works are lionised and commemorated for decades; yet, to make a living, writers must constantly generate new work, new ideas, and (with only very rare exceptions) write several different titles per month. In some ways the job is closer to being a magazine writer than a novelist. Instead of submitting a single manuscript to many publishers, you will submit many pitches to a few publishers. And 99% of the time you will be pitching, rather than submitting a finished manuscript.

'But wait!', you say, 'I don't want to write monthly comics. I want to write graphic novels.' To which I say, 'Godspeed, and don't give up the day job.' I am (to the best of my knowledge) the most prolific Anglophone graphic novelist, with 20 published 'Original Graphic Novels', aka OGNs.[1] I believe graphic novels are the future of the comics medium, and for two decades I've backed up that belief with my output. But I've also supplemented my income by writing monthly comics, videogames, film, books and more, because English-language graphic novels do not yet pay a living wage for 99% of their practitioners.

To break into monthly comics is to join a small club that, to the novice, can feel impenetrable. The old joke goes that it's like breaking out of prison; whenever someone discovers a new route, it's sealed up behind them to prevent others using it. This is partly because there's no formal path to becoming a professional comics writer – no union, no industry programs, no official mentors. Some further education institutions now teach graphic novel writing modules (see box on page 473), but there is no route from there to getting hired that doesn't require the same shoe leather as it does for everyone else.

Despite changing technology, then, the problem for aspiring writers will always be the same: How do you showcase that work to the people who can buy it from you or commission you to write other work? The good news is that the answer is also unchanged: write comics in your own time, find aspiring artists to draw them, and show them to

---

[1] The majority of books in a store's graphic novel section are actually collections of previously published monthly comics. A 'true' graphic novel is one that has never been serialised and is published as a single volume, like a prose novel. OGNs are increasingly common, but still in the minority.

editors. By necessity, such scripts should be short. Nobody will draw your 800-page epic for free. Frankly, it's unfair to expect any artist to draw more than half a dozen pages gratis, no matter how good you think it may look in their portfolio. And from your perspective, there's no need; an experienced editor can judge your work within five or six pages. So get used to writing short comic stories and finding artistic collaborators to draw them (unless you can also draw your own stories, but even in that case much of what follows will still apply).

How you show this work to editors depends on many factors, including your comfort with technology, your geographical location, your financial means, and your ease in social interactions. There's no 'One True Way' and comics is not an agent-driven industry, so it really is up to you to determine the best path.[2] The simplest method nowadays is to put your work online. Facebook, Tumblr, even Twitter and Instagram – along with gallery sites such as DeviantArt – have made it essentially free to post your comic samples where anyone with a link can see them. The real hurdle is getting editors to click that link in the first place, and this is where the importance of *networking* rears its head.

Let's clear something up: despite its bad reputation, networking does not mean getting work by charm alone. It's about building a relationship with people – editors, yes, but also other writers, artists, and publishers – so that when they see your name on a piece of work, they'll be inclined to look at it. An inclination is all it will get you; there are no guarantees. But the alternative is to build online buzz about your talent and wait for editors to come knocking on your door. That's not impossible, but it takes a rare talent, and it subjects your destiny to the whims of others. The best way to build those relationships, meanwhile, is at the whim of changing times. Some editors still prefer to meet new creators, especially writers, at conventions. The time and effort it takes to attend a comic-con shows them you're serious; this is especially true for UK creators travelling to the US, still where the biggest are held (it's a truism that some of us fly 6,000 miles every year to spend time with people who live in the next town over). But, increasingly, relationships with editors and other creators are reinforced, and sometimes entirely built, online – which is good news for anyone unable to make it to a convention.

Conventions themselves are the second way to get your work in front of editors, by giving them photocopied samples. Make sure you have many copies, and that you can afford to give them all away; editors will expect to keep them for reference. What hasn't changed, whether online or in person, are the ground rules about behaviour: be polite, be professional, and take criticism or feedback on board with decorum. Under no circum-

Graphic novel writing courses

University of Dundee
MLitt/MDes Comics & Graphic Novels
www.dundee.ac.uk/postgraduate/comics-graphic-novels-mdes

Edinburgh Napier University
MA Creative Writing
www.napier.ac.uk/courses/study-areas/english-creative-writing-and-publishing/creative-writing

University Centre Grimsby
BA (Hons) Professional and Creative Writing
https://grimsby.ac.uk/course-detail/ba-hons-professional-and-creative-writing/H1130_0/6784/

University of Worcester
Creative Writing and Illustration BA (Hons)
www.worcester.ac.uk/courses/creative-writing-and-illustration-ba-hons

[2] Very few comic creators have agents. There's rarely enough money in it, and in any case not many agents are familiar with the industry's idiosyncrasies. Comics publishers know this, however; they won't object if you have an agent, but not having one is entirely normal and won't count against you.

stances argue with an editor who criticises your portfolio – you may think that warning unnecessary, but I've seen it happen, and such people do not get hired.

Let's progress to pitching. You've cultivated a relationship, made some impressive sample comics, and an editor wants to read/hear your new pitch. This is a true achievement, and merely reaching this stage puts you well ahead of the pack. But now you're competing for a publisher's budget against other creators, many of whom will be seasoned pros. So focus on quality and on a compelling tale, well-told.

There are scant resources on writing pitches, because everyone approaches them differently. If possible, ask the editor what they prefer to see, or if they can give you a sample to use as a template; but equally, remember that they don't know exactly what you're pitching. Ultimately, it's your decision what's relevant to the pitch in question. (The Marvel/DC superhero market is an exception; new writers are expected to pitch very short takes on existing characters in just a few sentences.)

The golden rule of pitches is, paraphrasing Einstein, to make them 'as short as possible, but no shorter'. Plot and main characters, yes, of course. Tone and format, if they're important. And finally, if the editor doesn't know you, any *relevant* credentials. But no more. The only other thing required is your name and email address on the title page.

If you're pitching at a convention, you'll be expected to do so verbally. Don't panic! Nobody expects you to be a slick salesman, and the same principle applies to pitching by email. Editors understand that writers are not always the best advocates of our own work. But whether in person or in writing, they will expect to see enthusiasm. So stick to the story, to your idea, and don't be afraid of getting excited – I might even say *get over yourself*, because writers are often humble, self-effacing and modest to a literal fault. Remember, when an editor asks you to pitch, they've already decided they might want to work with you. It's up to you to convince them they're right. I'm not suggesting you become an egotist, but if your pitch is filled with hedging caveats (… 'I'm not sure about that', 'I haven't figured this part out yet', 'I don't know how many people will be interested' …) who could blame an editor for passing on it? Believe in your ideas without apology. Nobody else will do it for you.

So, finally, your pitch has been accepted. You've negotiated a contract and been commissioned to write something. What happens now? What should you expect, when you reach the promised land of being paid to write comics? Well, that's when the real work starts. From this point on your destiny is firmly in your own hands, and to give specific advice about comics scriptwriting would require a whole book. The most important things to remember are not about your script, but about your conduct. Be professional; be clear and upfront about what your editor expects from you; maintain good communication with your collaborators; and always, *always* hit your deadlines, because an artist, colourist, letterer, and even printer, are all waiting on you.

Follow those principles, create good work, and one day you'll look up from your keyboard to remind yourself you're being paid to write comics. Have fun.

Antony Johnston is a *New York Times* bestselling graphic novelist, author and screenwriter, and the creator of *Atomic Blonde*, which was adapted from his graphic novel *The Coldest City* (Oni Press 2012). His other comics work includes its sequel *The Coldest Winter* (Oni Press 2016), the epic series *Wasteland* (Oni Press 2006–14), adaptations of Antony Horowitz's *Alex Rider* novels (Walker Books 2006–), Marvel's *Daredevil* series (2010–12), *The Fuse* (Image Comics 2014–17) and many more. Antony's novels include the murder mystery *The Dog Sitter Detective* (Allison & Busby 2023) and spy thrillers *The Exphoria Code* (2017), *The Tempus Project* (2020), and *The Patrios Network* (2022) for Lightning Books, which are now in development for TV. His work for writers includes the productivity guide *The Organised Writer* (Bloomsbury 2020) and his podcast *Writing and Breathing*. Find him online at www.antonyjohnston.com and @antonyjohnston.

Comic conventions

This is a non-exhaustive list of UK events - from small zine fairs to enormous pop-culture conventions - where you can attend as an exhibitor. (The list of subject to change, so do check online for up-to-date information)
www.dundee.ac.uk/postgraduate/comics-graphic-novels-mdes

London Comic Con (February & November) - www.londoncomicconspring.com

Megacon Live Birmingham (March) - megaconlive.com/birmingham
ACME Scotland Comic Con, Glasgow (March & September) - acmecomiccon.squarespace.com

Swansea Comic & Gaming Convention (April) scgc.org.uk
Glasgow Zine Fest (April) - glasgowzinelibrary.com
Brighton illustration Fair (April/May) www.instagram.com/wearebif

Em-Con, Nottingham (May) - nottingham.em-con.co.uk
Portsmouth Comic Con (May) - portsmouthcomiccon.com
Edinburgh Zine Fest (May) - www.edinburghzinelibrary.com
Comic Con Liverpool (May) - www.comicconventionliverpool.co.uk
Lawless Comic Con, Bristol (May) - lawlesscomiccon.co.uk
MCM London (May & October) - www.mcmcomiccon.com

Glasgow Comic Con (June) www.glasgowcomiccon.com
SunnyCon, Newcastle (June) - www.sunnyconanimeexpo.com
Comics Salopia, Shrewsbury (June) - comicssalopia.com

South London Comic & Zine Fair (July) - twitter.com/slczf
East London Comics & Arts Festival (July) - elcaf.co.uk (seems to be on hiatus for 2022 fingers crossed it returns in 2023)
London Film & Comic Con (July) londonfilmandcomiccon.com
Macc-Pow, Macclesfield (July) - www.facebook.com/maccpow
Megacon Live Manchester (July) megaconlive.com/manchester

Film & Comic Con Glasgow (August) www.filmandcomicconglasgow.com
Comic Con Wales (August) - www.comicconventionwales.co.uk

Tripwire Comic Con, Bristol (September) - tripwirecomiccons.com
Hackney Comic & Zine Fair (September) - hackneycomicfair.com
Pride Comic Art Festival, Bristol (September) - pridecaf.co.uk
Comic Con Northern Ireland, Belfast (September) - www.comicconnorthernireland.co.uk
ICE Comic Con, Birmingham (September) - internationlcomicexpo.wordpress.com

ShortBox Comics Fair, online (October) - shortboxcomicsfair.com
Nottingham Comic Con (October) - nottinghamcomiccon.co.uk
Lakes International Comic Art Festival, Cumbria (October) - www.comicartfestival.com

Thought Bubble Festival, Harrogate (November) - www.thoughtbubblefestival.com
MCM Birmingham (November) - www.mcmcomiccon.com

York Zine Fest (December) - www.facebook.com/yorkzinefest

Big Glasgow Comic Page (various months) - www.bigglasgowcomicpage.com
UK Comic & Gaming Festivals (various months) - www.ukcgf.com

Art and illustration

Creating comics

Hannah Berry describes how the creative world of comics , with its range and appeal, requires enthusiasm, resourcefulness and opportunism for success. She has advice on how to find an outlet and build a following for your work, as well as tips on how to seek out funding, get due remuneration for your work and protect its ownership.

The conversation goes like this: 'What do you do?' 'I work in comics!' 'Oh wow! What kind of comics do you make?' 'Well, you know the kind that are household names and get turned into nine-figure-budget blockbuster films?' 'Yeah?' 'Not those!'

The world of comics, behind its most visible popular image, is surprisingly wide-ranging, and I've managed to work in comics for nearly 20 years without penning a single superhero (I probably wouldn't turn it down if the opportunity arose, though. Give me a shout, Marvel.) I've made self-published zines, I've made literary graphic novels, I've made weekly cartoon strips. I've had comics in publications from *2000 AD* to the *New England Journal of Medicine*, and I've contributed to any number of anthologies in between. My career is nonsensical, total chaos, and I love it. Even when I hate it, I love it.

Making comics feels like the purest form of storytelling to me, with every aspect of the visuals and the text playing off each other in a delicious narrative alchemy. People unfamiliar with comics are surprised when I use the word 'subtle', but comics often are. They can be subtle, sincere and eloquent, or they can be surreal, discordant romps, or stark and abstract, or journalistic and impassioned … They can be anything, and they can be made by anyone. And the best thing about making comics is that, even when you're making them all alone at home, you're not totally alone. The community side of the scene is thriving and, with the existence of so many local groups, national organisations and collectives, it's a very accessible and extremely welcoming scene to get involved in.

From my experience, the UK comics scene is largely run on pervasive, infectious enthusiasm, rather than (unfortunately) actual money, which may explain why one tenth of professional creators who consider comics their primary job are still only able to make them in their spare time.[1] It's not all bad, though. Alongside its unfortunate hurdles – little-to-no career-supporting infrastructure, or money, or opportunities – this uniquely scrappy and independent ecosystem has many benefits: getting started is incredibly easy, the community support is strong, and there are very few gatekeepers. Still, if you've read this far then I'm assuming you're either my mother or you're seriously interested in getting involved with comics, so let's dive into a (non-exhaustive) overview.

In the very beginning, given that your career will be largely driven by that aforementioned enthusiasm, you need to ask yourself what kind of comics you enjoy reading and making. Are you drawn to certain characters? Specific genres? Are you funny, even if you do say so yourself? Do you have issues or themes you want to explore? Do you want to write, or draw, or both? What kind of stories do you like to read and/or tell? Do you see any of that reflected in the comics out there? If so, take a close look at those creators and see what they're doing: what festivals they go to; where they sell their comics; who (if anyone) publishes them; who their audiences are. If, on the other hand, you don't see it out there, you'll be forging your own path – so shine on, you beautiful diamond.

[1] See article on page 472 Breaking into comics for more information the area of comic creation.

Webcomics

The outlet for your work depends entirely on the kind of comics you want to make, and how much time/energy/money you have to put towards it at that particular moment.

Webcomics are a financially low-stakes way of getting your work out into the world. These could be short, snappy gag cartoons or long-running sagas featuring a broad cast of characters but, in order to build up an audience, you'll need to be regular and consistent with your output. It's a real test of self-discipline, but the best and most prolific webcomic creators can amass huge followings across the entire Anglophone world, including highly comics-literate North America, and that leads to any number of opportunities. Your comics could be on your own dedicated website (which you can choose to monetise via advertising), on a dedicated webcomics platform such as Webtoon (who pay creators based on views), or simply on social media (no money, only prestige).

Self-publishing

And then there's paper. Sweet, sweet paper. Comics and graphic novels published by traditional publishers are very much in the minority; overwhelmingly the comics produced in the UK are self-published or small press comics. Publishers usually take care of the printing, packaging, shipping and promotion, but will take a bigger cut; going solo means you'll take on all the responsibility yourself but get all of the profit.

In self-publishing, the production values are entirely up to you. You can spend hundreds on a glossy full-colour print run, with spot varnish and French flaps, or you can print your own copies and staple them together. Whatever you choose, try not to go overboard with that first print run, no matter how appealing the economies of scale are; it's better to pay a little extra on a second print run after the first has sold out than to be sitting on boxes of unsold stock.

How many you print depends on where you're selling them. The best way to reach new audiences directly is to apply to be an exhibitor at a festival – essentially standing behind a table selling to passers-by. Thought Bubble (www.thoughtbubblefestival.com) and the Lakes International Comic Art Festival (www.comicartfestival.com) are two of the biggest festivals focusing solely on comics, and they attract hundreds of exhibitors and thousands of guests each year. But there are plenty of other festivals, zine fairs and conventions all over the UK – and around the world if you're feeling adventurous. There are some excellent guides online on 'tabling'; I'd recommend setting yourself up to take card payments, as cash has fallen extremely out of favour since the pandemic. And have fun – remember to leave your table occasionally so you can wander round, chat to others and look at their work. This is your best chance to explore what's out there, free from promoted content and algorithms.

You can keep the sales momentum going outside of festivals by selling your comic (physical or digital versions) through your own secured website, or through a retailing platform that gives you your own storefront, such as BigCartel (www.bigcartel.com) or Shopify (www.shopify.co.uk), or through online marketplaces like Comixology (https://support.comixology.com/hc/en-us) or Etsy (www.etsy.com). If you want your comics to be sold by professionals, you can (and should!) also take your comics to bricks-and-mortar comic shops, many of which will have a healthy small press section, and ask nicely if they'll stock them. Finally, if your comic has connections to any special interest or any particular group, don't be afraid to approach organisations who share that interest. The Wellcome

Collection (https://wellcomecollection.org) in London, for example, has an excellent health, medicine and science comics section in their bookshop.

Pricing your work is tough, as the urge to be competitive – and sometimes the feeling that your work is unworthy – can easily override making an actual profit. You'll need to calculate what you've already spent (on printing, paper, etc) and how much you *will* spend (on postage, packing, discount offered to a retailer, online payment fees, festival fees and expenses). The price you sell your work at will need to incorporate all of these *plus* make all the time you put into it worthwhile. Don't try to compete with bigger retailers or publishers; remind yourself that creative works everywhere have been devalued by outdated capitalist economic models which do not accurately reflect value. Whatever you choose, you'll still spend forever convincing yourself it was the wrong decision, so you might as well price your work up: you're worth it!

Self-publishing and webcomics both involve large amounts of self-promotion in order to get your work seen and drum up sales. For the love of God, don't sit back and wait to be 'discovered' or you'll be waiting a long time! The problem with comics in the UK is that the readership is still small; convincing the wider public that comics are for *everyone*, by *anyone*, on any subject imaginable, is a perpetual struggle. Your biggest audience as a comics creator is likely to be other creators … there's a joke about the same fiver being passed around a convention as everyone buys each other's work (and it's funny because it's true). Promoting your work to your own friends and peers doesn't have to feel grubby, and it's actually easier if you've taken the time to help others spread the word on their work too. Comics websites like Broken Frontier (www.brokenfrontier.com) provide news and reviews on indie comics, and you can always politely submit your work for review to reach a wider audience and get some nice quotes.

Remember that it's a very, very small world, and that word can spread fast. Be kind, be respectful, help others wherever you can, and treat every job and every person profession-ally, even – especially – if you don't feel like a professional yet.

Funding

Increasingly, comics creators and publishers are funding their projects through crowd-funding. This is a great option if you've already built up an audience for your comics, and it can take a lot of the guesswork out of production. It takes a gargantuan effort to crowd-fund a project, though, so this is a situation in which working as part of a collective could be advantageous – splitting the responsibilities and sharing the load. Remember to budget carefully, be realistic with the amount you need, and seek advice from other creators who have already crowdfunded their projects.

Many creators also receive regular donations from their readers, through sites like Patreon (www.patreon.com) and Ko-Fi (www.ko-fi.com), in exchange for access to exclusive content, work in progress, etc. It's a friendly but structured way to stay connected with and reward a loyal readership.

Being published by a publisher

Self-publishing isn't the only form of publishing, of course. Back in 2005 I sent a letter to Jonathan Cape, who I'd noticed were publishing graphic novels, asking if they'd be inter-ested in looking at my graphic novel-in-progress. They looked, they liked, they made an offer. Absurd? Yes. But the point is they were looking for fresh new creators at the time, and this is still largely the case. I have it on good authority that most large publishers wait for submissions from agents, but most agents don't represent comics creators, so it seems that even now the best way in is to get in touch directly. Do your research, find out who is publishing the kind of stories you want to tell, use tact and precision, and submit your best letter outlining your story. There is excellent advice on this exact process elsewhere in this book (see e.g. *Putting together your submission*, page 398), but, as an added note of optimism, I'd say that comics submissions seem to spend a lot less time waiting on that slush pile.

Work-for-hire

There are two modes of authorship when it comes to comics: the traditional author model and the work-for-hire model. In the former you're paid an advance and royalties and retain ownership of the copyright of your work. This is usually where you're doing all the writing and artwork yourself, although you can be co-author with another creator. It's worth noting that publishers using the traditional model don't usually match artists and writers in-house, so if you're an artist-only or writer-only who wants to work in this way you'll need to find someone to team up with first. (It's a good idea, if you're collaborating on something speculative with another creator, to get an agreement down in writing about who owns the copyright of the final product, and what can and can't be done with it; it may feel pre-emptively cynical, like a pre-nup, but you're protecting each other from future heartaches.)

The work-for-hire model is mostly used by publishers producing regular comic books and magazines, often involving licensed characters, in which the editor will put together a team of creators doing the writing, pencilling, inking, colouring and lettering. You're generally paid a one-off fee for the work but have no creative control over the finished product. In this situation, you might be pitching either the story as a writer or yourself as an artist. Most of these publishers will tell you how to submit work on their websites, but they do often visit festivals and conventions where they can be approached directly. This is a competitive area, so be prepared to knock on a few doors!

Sadly, in customary practice, comics creators' keenness to work in comics has too often been exploited. This is not so much the case any more, but there is still an unpleasant hangover to be aware of. Before you sign a contract with any publisher, commissioner or co-creator, be sure to run it past an organisation such as the Society of Authors (see page 495) or Association of Illustrators (page 525), an agent or legal professional. No reputable publisher, commissioner or co-creator will be upset by you seeking out an informed opinion. If they are, I'd suggest they're not so reputable after all and you'll have saved yourself a lot of trouble down the line.

The other elephant in the room is the remuneration elephant. Technically, making comics is a skilled job and can (and should) be done in exchange for money, but realistically – as with most work in the arts – it's likely to be a while before you make a significant profit. You can put the work out first and hope to build up an audience (e.g. webcomics, self-publishing) or you can look around for paid work (e.g. freelancing, work-for-hire) for which you'll first need to build up a prerequisite skill set, and possibly contact list. Either way, you're playing the long game – we all are; 87% of creators supplement their income with other work.[2] However, if you are not being paid, you should be working on what *you*

[2] *UK Comics Creators Survey* 2020. Survey funded by Arts Council England, British Council and the Scottish Centre for Comics Studies, University of Dundee, conducted by H. Berry and the Audience Agency; available on http://hannahberry.co.uk/survey.

Art and illustration

© Hannah Berry; first appeared in *Prospect* magazine November 2020

want to work on, whether your own personal projects that fulfil your creative needs, work that you know you can use to promote yourself, or goodwill projects if you're in a position to do so. If you're being asked to do free work as a favour, think carefully before taking it on, and regard anything that's being promised in the future with a skeptical eye. Your work has value; many people know this but hope that *you* don't.

With comics being such a broad, informal church, the big question is: What does 'success' look like to you? Is it critical praise? Accolades? Financial stability? Being seen? Creative expression? All of these things are possible, even if some are harder to reach than others. One of the key differences between comics and other areas of the arts in the UK is that it's a huge grassroots community with not much of an establishment. Official opportunities are quite limited and extremely competitive, so most creators end up carving out their own opportunities.

Think of yourself as ivy, slowly but persistently climbing a wall. The ascent might feel inexorably slow, but the wall is erratic and peculiar and you'll find many surprising places to anchor your aerial roots, which is key. The single biggest thing I can impress on you is the need to be vigorously, ferociously opportunistic. The more proactive you are, both inside and outside of the comics scene, the more adventurous and resourceful you are, the further you will grow (and the more of the wall you will engulf with your leafy tendrils). Enjoy the ascent, remember that you're doing your best on a difficult surface, and celebrate that ridiculous, glorious wall every chance you get.

Hannah Berry is an award-winning comics creator, writer, cartoonist and illustrator; a Fellow of the Royal Society of Literature and UK Comics Laureate 2019–21. Her first graphic novel *Britten & Brülightly* was published by Jonathan Cape in 2008, with the French edition chosen for the Official Selection of the Festival International de la Bande Dessinée d'Angoulême. Her second graphic novel *Adamtine* was published in 2012 and her third, *Livestock*, in 2017, both by Jonathan Cape. *Livestock* won Berry a Best Writer Award at the 2017 Broken Frontier Awards and was nominated in the Best Graphic Novel category. She is a founding committee member of the Society of Authors' Comics Creators Network and a Trustee of the Cartoon Museum. For more information see https://hannahberry.co.uk. Follow her on Twitter and Instagram @streakofpith.

See also...

Art agents and commercial art studios

Before submitting work, artists are advised to make preliminary enquiries and to ascertain terms of work. Commission varies but averages 25–30%. The Association of Illustrators (see page 525) provides a valuable service for illustrators, agents and clients.

sae = self-addressed envelope
*Member of the Society of Artists Agents
†Member of the Association of Illustrators

Advocate Art Ltd

Suite 7, The Sanctuary, 23 Oakhill Grove, Surbiton, Surrey KT6 6DU
tel 020-8390 6293
email mail@advocate-art.com
website www.advocate-art.com
Facebook www.facebook.com/advocateart
Twitter @advocateart01
Directors Edward Burns, Caroline Burns

Has 12 agents representing over 300 artists and illustrators. Bespoke illustration for children's books, greetings cards and fine art publishers, gift and ceramic manufacturers. For illustrators' submission guidelines see website. Animation, design and original content represented through LaB – Writers and Artists colLaBorate. Also original art gallery, stock library and website in German, Spanish and French. Founded 1996.

Allied Artists/Artistic License

tel 07971 111256
email info@allied-artists.net
website www.alliedartists-illustration.co.uk
Contact Gary Mills

Represents over 90 illustrators ranging in styles from realistic through stylised to cute, for all types of publishing but particularly children's illustration. Commission: 35%. Founded 1983.

Darley Anderson Illustration Agency

Unit 19, Matrix Studios, 91 Peterborough Road, London SW6 3BU
tel 020-7385 6652
website www.darleyandersonillustration.com
Instagram @darleyanderson_illustration
Managing director & Agent Clare Wallace, *Directors* Darley Anderson, Rosanna Bellingham, *Agents* Lydia Silver, Becca Langton (US Agent), Chloe Davis

Represents bestselling and award-winning illustrators. Works across all areas of publishing, from picture books to gift titles to graphic novels, across fiction and non-fiction, collaborating with both adult and children's publishers worldwide. Actively looking for new talent, especially illustrators from under-represented backgrounds. Commission: 20%. Submission guidelines: send an email with portfolio attached as a pdf or in the body of the email, along with information about yourself and links to social media channels used to display your work. Author-illustrators should send texts as pdf or Word attachments, along with a brief synopsis and illustration samples. Submissions should be made directly to the agent of choice. Founded 1988.

Arena Illustration Ltd*†

31 Eleanor Road, London E15 4AB
tel 020-8555 9827
website www.arenaillustration.com
Contact Tamlyn Francis

Represents 29 artists. Average commission: 25%. Founded 1970.

The Art Agency

21 Morris Street, Sheringham, Norfolk NR26 8JY
tel (01263) 823424
email artagency@me.com
website www.the-art-agency.co.uk
Facebook www.facebook.com/illustrationagency
Director Beryl Leitch

Provides non-fiction, reference and children's book illustration. Specialises in non-fiction illustrations across a wide variety of subjects and age groups. Submit up to six samples by email along with a link to your website. Founded 1990.

Artist Partners Ltd*†

22 Albion Hill, Ramsgate, Kent CT11 8HG
tel 020-7401 7904
email christine@artistpartners.com
website www.artistpartners.com
Managing Director Christine Isteed

Represents artists, including specialists, producing artwork in every genre for advertising campaigns, storyboards, children's and adult book covers, newspaper and magazine features and album covers. New artists are considered if their work is of high standard. Submission should be by email only. Commission: 30%. Founded 1951.

Artistique International

Suite 7, The Sanctuary, 23 Oakhill Grove, Surbiton KT6 6DU
tel 07532 712002
email mail@artistique-int.com
website www.artistique-int.com
Contact Alison Berson

Specialises in editorial and advertising. The mission is to bring the highest quality illustrations to their clients. Offices in London, Marbella, New York and Singapore. Founded 2016.

The Artworks*

64 Cranbourne Avenue, London E11 2BQ
email submissions@theartworksinc.com
website www.theartworksinc.com
Contacts Stephanie Alexander-Jinks, Alex Hadlow, Lucy Scherer

Represents 35 illustrators for design and advertising work as well as for non-fiction children's books, book jackets, illustrated gift books and children's picture books. Commission: 30% design and advertising, 25% publishing advances, 15% royalties, 25% book jackets. Founded 1983.

Beehive Illustration

42A Cricklade Street, Cirencester, Glos. GL7 1JH
tel (01285) 644001
email enquiries@beehiveillustration.co.uk
website www.beehiveillustration.co.uk
Contact Paul Beebee

Represents 200 artists specialising in ELT, education and general children's publishing illustration. Commission: 25%. Founded 1989.

The Big Red Illustration Agency

tel 0808 120 0996
email enquiries@bigredillustrationagency.com
website www.bigredillustrationagency.com
Facebook www.facebook.com/thebigredillustrationagency
Twitter @big_red_author
Director Adam Rushton

Represents a number of professional illustrators. Over the years has developed strong relationships with a wide range of clients including children's book publishers, design agencies, greetings card companies and toy manufacturers. Founded 2012.

The Bright Agency*

103–105 St John's Hill, London SW11 1SY
tel 020-7326 9140
US Office 50 West Street, C12, New York, NY 10006
tel +1 646-604-0992
email mail@thebrightagency.com
website www.thebrightagency.com
Ceo Vicki Willden-Lebrecht, *Director* Arabella Stein

Areas of representation include: children's illustration, greeting and gift (cards, social stationery, giftwrap), design and advertising (editorial, branding, adult publishing, packaging, web and digital, typography), animation, literary (children's fiction and non-fiction, adult fiction and non-fiction, graphic novels) and licensing (toys and games, digital gaming, fabric and apparel, and homewares). For illustration, writing and animation submissions guidelines see website. No submissions by post. Clients include: Benji Davies, David Litchfield, Yasmeen Ismail, Chris Chatterton, Diane Ewen, Laura Hughes, Galia Bernstein, Mechal Roe, Aura Lewis, Karl James Mountford, Jane Newland, Brenna Nation and Hannah Peck. Founded 2002.

Central Illustration Agency

9 Perseverance Works, 38 Kingsland Road, London E2 8DD
tel 020-3222 0007
email info@centralillustration.com
website www.centralillustration.com
Twitter @ciablog
Contact Benjamin Cox

An international resource for commercial art and motion graphics for the advertising, design and publishing industries. Commission: 30%. Founded 1983.

Collaborate Agency

Unit 7, Hove Business Centre, Fonthill Road, Hove, Brighton BN3 6HA
tel (01273) 251700
email hello@collaborate.agency
website https://collaborate.agency/
Facebook www.facebook.com/collaborate
Twitter @c0llab0rate
Instagram @collaborateagency
Directors Caroline Burns, Edward Burns

Works on books for all ages and in all genres. Artists are skilled across all creative disciplines. Illustrators, editors, photographers, designers, web developers and animators are based in Brighton, London, New York, Gibraltar, Singapore and Seville studios. Founded 2008.

Creative Coverage

49 Church Close, Locks Heath, Southampton, Hants. SO31 6LR
tel (01489) 808261
email info@creativecoverage.co.uk
website www.creativecoverage.co.uk
Facebook www.facebook.com/CreativeCoverage
Twitter @CreativeCov
Instagram @creativecov
Co-founders Tim Saunders, Caroline Saunders

Fine art book publisher and artists' agent. Marketing for selected professional artists. Founded 2013.

Dutch Uncle

Suite 156, Building 3, Chiswick Park,
566 Chiswick High Road, London W4 5YA
tel 020-7336 7696
email info@dutchuncle.co.uk
website www.dutchuncle.co.uk
Facebook www.facebook.com/dutchuncle
Twitter @AgencyDU
Instagram @agencydu

Represents and seeks out creative talent for clients
looking to commission content such as animation,
illustration, book design and data visualisations.
Offices in New York and Tokyo. Founded 2006.

Eastwing†

99 Chase Side, Enfield EN2 6NL
tel 020-8367 6760
email art@eastwing.co.uk
website www.eastwing.co.uk
Contacts Andrea Plummer, Abby Glassfield

Represents artists who work across advertising,
design, publishing and editorial. Commission:
25–30%. Founded 1985.

Eye Candy Illustration

Field Cottage, Saintbury WR12 7PX
tel 020-8291 0729
email info@eyecandyillustration.com
website www.eyecandyillustration.com
Managing Director Mark Wilson

Represents 50+ artists producing work for advertising
campaigns, packaging, publishing, editorials, greeting
cards, merchandising and a variety of design projects.
Submit printed samples with sae or email low-res jpg
files via website. Founded 2002.

Folio Illustration Agency†

10 Gate Street, London WC2A 3HP
tel 020-7242 9562
email info@folioart.co.uk
website www.folioart.co.uk

All areas of illustration. Founded 1976.

Good Illustration Ltd

118 Dumbreck Road, London SE9 1XD
tel 020-8123 0243 (UK) / +1 347-627-0243 (US)
email draw@goodillustration.com
website www.goodillustration.com
Directors Doreen Thorogood, Kate Webber, Tom
Thorogood

Represents 50+ artists for advertising, design,
publishing and animation. Send sae and samples.
Commission: 25% publishing, 30% advertising.
Founded 1977.

Graham-Cameron Illustration

59 Hertford Road, Brighton BN1 7GG
tel (01273) 385890

email enquiry@gciforillustration.com
Alternative address The Art House, Uplands Park,
Sheringham, Norfolk NR26 8NE
tel (01263) 821333
website www.gciforillustration.com
Partners Helen Graham-Cameron, Duncan
Graham-Cameron

Represents 37+ artists and undertakes illustration for
publishing and communications. Specialises in
educational, children's and information books. Phone
before sending A4 samples with sae or email samples
or link to a website. No MSS. Founded 1985.

Handsome Frank*

email hello@handsomefrank.com
website www.handsomefrank.com
Twitter @Handsome_Frank
Founders Jon Cockley, Tom Robinson

Represents 40+ creatives, across 5 continents.
Predominantly working with clients across
advertising, design, and publishing. Ranging from
global brands to bold start-ups. Artists interested in
being represented should email 9 low-res jpgs to
submissions@handsomefrank.com. Founded 2010.

Holroyde Cartey Ltd

email claire@holroydecartey.com
website www.holroydecartey.com
Directors Claire Cartey, Penelope Holroyde

Represents high-quality illustrators. Welcomes
submissions from debut and established illustrators.
Only accepts submissions via email. Aims to respond
to every submission within about 6 weeks. Please
send a portfolio of a dozen or so images in either jpg
or pdf format of up to 5MB in size. Founded 2015.

IllustrationX*†

4th Floor, Silverstream House, 45 Fitzroy Street,
London W1T 6EB
tel 020-7720 5202
email hello@illustrationx.com
website www.illustrationx.com/uk
Facebook www.facebook.com/weareillustrationx
Twitter @illustrationx

Welcomes submissions from illustrators and
animators whose work is distinctive and innovative.
Only accepts applications from artists through
submissions page: www.illustrationx.com/
applications. Founded 1929.

Image by Design Art Licensing

Suite 3, 107 Bancroft, Hitchin, Herts. SG5 1NB
tel (01462) 451190
email hello@ibd-licensing.co.uk
website www.ibd-licensing.co.uk
Contact Hugh Brenham

Art licensing agency representing talented creatives.
Artwork for greeting cards, stationery, home decor,
wall art, tableware, textiles, puzzles, giftware and

more. Choose from an extensive portfolio of designs or commissions bespoke artwork. Founded 1987.

Inky Illustration
483 Green Lanes, London N13 4BS
tel 0121 330 1312
email info@inkyillustration.com
website https://inkyillustration.com/
Facebook www.facebook.com/inkyillustration
Twitter @inkyillo

The range of illustrators have experience working with clients, on international advertising campaigns, publications and editorials, as well as commissions for smaller companies. Always happy to receive new work. New artists should fill out the application form on the website or email to: submissions@inkyillustration.com. Hard copies of work are accepted with an sae if the work is to be returned. Founded 2009.

JSR
Unit 4, 3 Lever Street, London EC1V 3QU
tel 020-7228 6667
email illustration@jsragency.com
website www.jsragency.com
Facebook www.facebook.com/jsragency
Twitter @jsragency
Founder & Director Jamie Stephen

Before submitting work for consideration artists should take a look at roster and make sure their work does not overlap with the artists currently represented. Please provide a pdf of your best work and website details in your submission: submissions@jsragency.com. Founded 2005.

B.L. Kearley Art & Antiques
Glebe House, Bakers Wood, Denham, Bucks. UB9 4LG
tel (01895) 832145
email christine.kearley@kearley.co.uk
website www.kearley.co.uk
Agent C.R. Kearley

Represents 30+ artists. Mainly specialises in children's book and educational illustration for the domestic market and overseas. Known for realistic figurative work. Specialises in the sale of original book illustration artwork. Commission: 25%. Founded 1948.

Kids Corner
1 Mailing Street, West Street, Lewes BN7 2NZ
tel 020-7593 0506
email claire@meiklejohn.co.uk
website www.kidscornerillustration.co.uk
Managing Director Claire Meiklejohn

Represents illustrators, from award-winning to emerging artists for children's publishing. Styles include fun, cute, stylised, picture book, young fiction, reference, graphic, traditional, painterly and digital. See also Meiklejohn Illustration (page 485). Founded 2015.

Lemonade Illustration Agency
167–169 Great Portland Street, 5th Floor, London W1W 5PF
tel 07891 390750
email gary@lemonadeillustration.com
US office 347 Fifth Ave, Suite 1402, New York, NY 10016
website www.lemonadeillustration.com

Represents 180+ international illustrators and character development artists working in all media from advertising brands to children's picture books. The team work with many leading children's book, children's literature, e-learning and educational publishers across the world. Any submissions from illustrators by email must contain a website link (no attachments) or hard copies of samples can be sent by post with an sae to the London office. Sadly cannot reply to all submissions received due to the volume received. Also has offices in Wakefield, Sydney and Dubai. Founded 2001.

David Lewis Illustration Agency
3 Somali Road, London NW2 3RN
tel 020-7435 7762 / 07931 824674
email info@davidlewisillustration.com
Director David Lewis, *Associate* Lisa Britton

Considers all types of illustration for a variety of applications but mostly suitable for book and magazine publishers, design groups, recording companies and corporate institutions. Also offers a comprehensive selection of images suitable for subsidiary rights purposes. Send sae with samples. Commission: 30%. Founded 1974.

Lipstick of London*
78 Clarendon Drive, London SW15 1AH
tel 07966 176989
email mc@lipstickillustration.com
website www.lipstickillustration.com
Twitter @LipstickAgency
Editor Founder Marie-Claire Westover

Agency with artists who have experience spanning advertising, design, fashion, packaging, publishing, editorial, digital and motion and live events. Founded 2012.

Frances McKay Illustration
17 Church Road, West Mersea, Essex CO5 8QH
tel 07703 344334
email frances@francesmckay.com
website www.francesmckay.com
Proprietor Frances McKay

Represents 15–20 artists for illustration mainly for children's books. For information on submissions please look at the website. Submit email with low-res scans or colour copies of recent work; sae essential for return of all unsolicited samples sent by post. Commission: 25%. Founded 1999.

Meiklejohn Illustration*†
1 Mailing Street, West Street, Lewes BN7 2NZ
tel 020-7593 0506
email claire@meiklejohn.co.uk
website www.meiklejohn.co.uk
Managing Director Claire Meiklejohn

Represents illustrators, covering a wide range of styles, from traditional, children's publishing, photorealistic, cartoon to contemporary. See also Kids Corner (page 484). Founded 1973.

The Monkey Feet Illustration Directory
email enquiries@monkeyfeetillustration.com
website www.monkeyfeetillustration.com

Presents portfolios for artists creating work for children's book publishers, design agencies, greeting cards and toy companies. Founded 2012.

NB Illustration*
Home Farm, East Horrington, Somerset BA5 3EA
tel 07720 827328
email info@nbillustration.co.uk
website www.nbillustration.co.uk
Directors Joe Najman, Charlotte Dowson

Represents 50+ artists and will consider all material for the commercial illustration market. For submission details see website. Submissions by email only. Commission: 30%. Founded 2000.

Outline Artists
90 The Avenue, London NW6 7NN
tel 07595 920113
email camilla@outlineartists.com
website www.outlineartists.com
Contacts Camilla Parsons, Ellie Phillips

An illustration and animation agency. Represents a diverse roster of talented image-makers from around the world. Founded 2015.

Phosphor Art Ltd*†
40 High West Street, Dorchester, Dorset DT1 1UR
tel 020-7064 4666
email info@phosphorart.com
website www.phosphorart.com
Director Catriona Wydmanski

Represents 46 artists and specialises in innovative graphic digital illustration with artists working in watercolour, oil and gouache as well as pen and ink, scraper, charcoal and engraving styles. Also

animation. Incorporates Ian Fleming Associates and The Black and White Line. Commission: 33.3%. Founded 1988.

The Plum Agency
Chapel House, St. Lawrences Way, Reigate, Surrey RH2 7AF
tel (01737) 244095
email letterbox@theplumagency.com
website https://theplumagency.com/
Directors Mark Mills, Hannah Whitt

Represents 200+ artists and authors, producing texts and illustrations for children's publishing, advertising, editorial, greeting cards and packaging. See website for submission procedure. Commission: 30%. Founded 2006.

Sylvie Poggio Artists Agency
62 Ainsdale Road, London W5 1JX
tel 07775 894870
email sylvie-p@sylviepoggio.com
website www.sylviepoggio.com
Facebook www.facebook.com/Sylvie-Poggio-Artists-agency-700285410097943
Twitter @sylviepoggioart
Directors Sylvie Poggio, Bruno Caurat

Represents 40 artists producing illustrations for publishing and advertising. Founded 1996.

Tallbean
tel (01728) 454921
email heather@tallbean.co.uk
website www.tallbean.co.uk
Founder Heather Richards

Provides specialist illustrators offering a range of styles. The team of well-established and creative illustrators is kept relatively small to ensure a close working relationship. Founded 1996.

Vicki Thomas Associates
195 Tollgate Road, London E6 5JY
tel 020-7511 5767
email vickithomasassociates@yahoo.co.uk
website www.vickithomasassociates.com
Twitter @VickiThomasA
Instagram @VickiThomasA
Consultant Vicki Thomas

Considers the work of illustrators and designers working in greetings/gift industries, and promotes work to gift, toy, publishing, licensing and related industries. Email sample images, covering letter and CV. Commission: 30%. Founded 1985.

Card and stationery publishers that accept illustrations and photographs

Before submitting work, artists and photographers are advised to ascertain requirements of the company they are approaching, including terms and conditions. Only high-quality material should be submitted.

sae = self-addressed envelope
*Member of the Greeting Card Association

The Almanac Gallery*
Unit 3, St. Modwen Park, Haresfield, Stonehouse, Gloucester GL10 3EZ
tel (01452) 888999
email submissions@greatbritishcards.co.uk
website www.greatbritishcards.co.uk

Specialises in contemporary art and beautiful charity Christmas cards. Part of The Great British Card Company. Founded 1980.

Card Connection Ltd*
Park House, South Street, Farnham, Surrey GU9 7QQ
tel (01252) 892300
email enquiries@cardconnection.co.uk
website www.card-connection.co.uk
Managing Director Graham, *Staff Creative Director* Kelly Courtena

Everyday and seasonal greetings card designs. Styles include cute, fun, juvenile, traditional, contemporary, humour and photographic. Humorous copy and jokes plus sentimental verse. Founded 1992.

CardsWorld Ltd t/a 4C For Charity
114 High Street, Stevenage, Herts. SG1 3DW
tel 0800 999 3553
email design@charitycards.org
website www.charitycards.org

Contemporary and traditional Christmas cards for the corporate and charity market (London, international and festive themes). Submit low-res artwork by email no larger than 5MB. No verses or cute styles. Works with over 70 charities. Founded 1966.

Dry Red Press*
Metway Studios, 55 Canning Street, Brighton BN2 0EF
tel (01273) 241210
email info@dryredpress.com
website www.dryredpress.com
Instagram @dry_red_press
Contacts Laura McDonald, Kicki Ringqvist

Publishes the work of contemporary British artists to produce high-quality greeting cards. See website for details. Founded 2009.

Simon Elvin Ltd*
Wooburn Industrial Park, Wooburn Green, Bucks. HP10 0PE
tel (01628) 526711
email studioadmin@simonelvin.com
website www.simonelvin.com
Art Director Sarah Vockins, *Studio Manager* Rachel Green

Female/male traditional and contemporary designs, female/male cute, wedding/anniversary, birth congratulations, fine art, photographic animals, flowers, traditional sympathy, juvenile ages, special occasions and gift wrap. Looking for submissions that show flair, imagination and an understanding of greetings card design. Artists should familiarise themselves with the ranges, style and content. Submit a small collection of either colour copies or prints (no original artwork) and include an sae for return of work. Submit digital portfolio or examples of work via email. Founded 1977.

The Great British Card Company
Unit 3, St Modwen Park, Haresfield, Stonehouse, Gloucester GL10 3EZ
tel (01452) 888999
email submissions@paperhouse.co.uk
website www.greatbritishcards.co.uk
Facebook www.facebook.com/GreatBritishCardCompany
Twitter @GreatBritCards

Incorporating Paper House (page 488), Medici Cards (page 487) and The Almanac Gallery. Publishers of everyday, Christmas and spring greeting cards, notecards, gift wrap and gift bags. Particularly welcomes new humorous submissions. For a full listing of brands published visit website. Founded 1980.

Green Pebble*
The Studio, Hall Farm (Behind Urban Jungle), London Road, Weston, Beccles NR34 8TT

tel (01502) 710427
email ruby@greenpebble.co.uk
website www.greenpebble.co.uk
Publisher Michael Charles

Publisher of fine art greeting cards and associated products by artists. See website for style before submitting. Send a minimum of six design thumbnails via email. Founded 2010.

Hallmark Cards Plc*

Dawson Lane, Dudley Hill, Bradford BD4 6HN
tel (01274) 252000
email creative-opportunities@hallmark-uk.com
website www.hallmark.co.uk
Facebook www.facebook.com/hallmarkukandireland
Twitter @HallmarkUK
Instagram @hallmarkuk

See website for freelance opportunities and submission details. Founded 1997.

In Ya Feelings*

website https://inyafeelings.com/
Facebook www.facebook.com/inyafeelingscards
Twitter @in_ya_feelings

Greeting cards designed for and inspired by the Black culture. Founded 2021.

Lanternfish Publishing*

tel (01263) 825280
email lanternfishpublishing@gmail.com
website www.lanternfishpublishing.co.uk
Founder Amy Christie

Based in North Norfolk, Lanternfish's art cards and prints are sold throughout the UK and overseas. Works closely with artists and designers to create beautiful greetings cards and art prints, which are suitable for art galleries, gift shops, card shops, garden centres and more. All greetings cards are printed in the UK. Founded 2011.

Leeds Postcards

4 Granby Road, Leeds LS6 3AS
email xtine@leedspostcards.com
website www.leedspostcards.com
Contact Christine Hankinson

Publisher and distributor of postcards; feminism, animal rights and socialism. Send only suitable and relevant jpg files to email above. If published, paid by advance royalty on print run. Founded 1979.

The Letter Arty*

69–71 Lever Street, Manchester M1 1FL
email matt@theletterarty.co.uk
website https://theletterarty.co.uk/
Facebook www.facebook.com/theletterarty
Founder Matt Simpson

The Letter Arty provides cards of quality design and typography produced in a sustainable way. On the lookout for new items to add to the collection. See website for details on submitting artwork. Founded 2019.

Ling Design Ltd*

Westmoreland House, Westmoreland Street, Bath BA2 3HE
tel (01225) 838574
email enquiries@lingdesign.co.uk
website www.lingdesign.co.uk
Facebook www.facebook.com/greetingsbyling
Twitter @GreetingsByLing
Head of Design Claire Twigger

Publishers of greetings cards and gift packaging. Founded 1998.

Medici Cards

Unit 3, St Modwen Park, Haresfield, Stonehouse, Gloucester GL10 3EZ
tel (01452) 888999
email submissions@greatbritishcards.co.uk
website www.greatbritishcards.co.uk

Specialises in market-leading art and photographic cards. Brands include National Geographic, English Heritage, Royal Horticultural Society and Medici Cards Blue Label. Founded 1997.

Miko Greetings

85 Landcroft Road, East Dulwich, London SE22 9JS
tel 020-8693 1011 / 07957 395739
email info@miko-greetings.com
website www.miko-greetings.com
Head Creative & Illustrator, Mik Brown aka Miko, Creative Photographer Toby Brown, Consultant Annie Horwood

Produces high-end, quality, humorous illustrated and photographic greetings cards. Cards are mainly blank for any occasion. Currently introducing some occasions cards. Also produces 'wall art' of all the company's designs, high-quality prints in sizes from A5 to A2. Founded 2014.

Moonpig

Herbal House, 10 Back Hill, London EC1R 5EN
email hellodesign@moonpig.com
Facebook www.facebook.com/Moonpig
Twitter @moonpiguk
Ceo Nickyl Raithatha

Offers designs from many of the leading card publishers in the UK, such as Paperlink, Pigment, Carte Blanche Greetings, and licensors such as Disney, Warner Brothers, Universal and Hasbro, as well as many smaller independent publishers and designers. The company is always on the lookout for new designs and inspirational talent across all key categories of cards (humour, sentiment, traditional, topical and trend). If you have created a range of cards that you think would be suitable, please send them to the email above with a short covering letter and examples of your work. Founded 2000.

Natural Partners Art*

33 Church Howle Crescent, Marske-by-Sea, Redcar,
North Yorks TS11 7EJ
tel 07714 768956
website www.naturalpartnersart.co.uk
Founders Joe Cole, Karen Cole

Publishers of fine art greetings cards. Works with a
number of artists. Founded 2011.

Paper House

Unit 3, St Modwen Park, Haresfield, Stonehouse,
Gloucester GL10 3EZ
tel (01452) 888999
email art@paperhouse.co.uk
website www.greatbritishcards.co.uk

Producers of everyday, birthday, special occasions
and family relations greeting cards; plus spring
seasons and Christmas. Specialising funny/humorous
cards and always looking for new copy/ideas. Also
interested in photographic, contemporary and trend-
driven imagery. Founded 1980.

Paperlink Ltd*

356 Kennington Road, London SE11 4LD
tel 020-7582 8244
email info@paperlink.co.uk
website www.paperlink.co.uk

Publishes a range of humorous and contemporary art
greeting cards. Produce products under licence for
charities. Always keen to hear from new artists,
cartoonists and copywriters. Please check submission
guidelines. Founded 1986.

Pineapple Park*

Unit A & B High Road, Deadmans Cross, Haynes,
Shefford, Beds. SG17 5QQ
tel (01234) 381214
email info@pineapplepark.co.uk
website www.pineapplepark.co.uk

Illustrations and photographs for publication as
greeting cards. Contemporary, cute, humour: submit
artwork or laser copies with sae. Photographic florals
always needed. Humour copy/jokes accepted without
artwork. Founded 1993.

Nigel Quiney Publications Ltd*

Cloudesley House, Shire Hill, Saffron Walden,
Essex CB11 3FB
tel (01799) 520200
email carl.pledger@nigelquiney.com
website www.nigelquiney.com
Contact Carl Pledger

Everyday and seasonal greeting cards including
traditional, photographic, humour, contemporary
and cute. Submit by email or colour copies and
photographs by post, no original artwork.
Founded 1987.

Raspberry Blossom*

Unit 12, Trident Park, Poseidon Way,
Royal Leamington Spa, Warwick CV34 6SW
email hello@raspberryblossom.com
website www.raspberryblossom.com
Facebook www.facebook.com/loveraspberryblossom
Twitter @loveraspberryb
Founders Rebecca Green, Mark Green

Family-run greetings card company with everything
designed and printed in the UK. See website for
collaborative opportunities with artists.
Founded 2014.

Felix Rosenstiels Widow & Son Ltd

Fine Art Publishers, 33–35 Markham Street,
London SW3 3NR
tel 020-7352 3551
email artists@rosentiels.com
website www.rosenstiels.com

Invites offers of artwork of a professional standard for
reproduction as picture prints for the picture framing
trade. Any type of subject considered. See website for
submission details. Founded 1880.

Santoro London*

Rotunda Point, 11 Hartfield Crescent,
London SW19 3RL
tel 020-8781 1100
email submissions@santoro-london.com
website www.santoro-london.com
Directors Lucio Santoro, Meera Santoro

Publishers of innovative and International award-
winning designs for 3D pop-up cards, greeting cards,
gift wrap and gift stationery. Bold, contemporary
images with an international appeal. Subjects
covered: contemporary, humour, photography, pop-
up, cute, kawaii, quirky, fashion, retro. Submit
samples in digital format (jpg or pdf files).
Founded 1985.

Second Nature Ltd*

10 Malton Road, London W10 5UP
tel (01983) 209590
email design@secondnature.co.uk
website www.secondnature.co.uk
Facebook www.facebook.com/SecondNatureLtd

Contemporary artwork for greeting cards and
handmade cards; jokes for humorous range; short
modern sentiment; verses. Founded 1981.

James Ellis Stevens Ltd

Unit 5.12 Paintworks, Bath Road, Bristol BS4 3EH
tel 0117 927 7667
email info@jamesellis.com
website www.jamesellis.com
Instagram @jamesellisco
Director Anna Stevens

Publishers of design-led sustainable and plastic-free
greetings cards and stationery from a wide range of

artists and illustrators. Members of 1% for the Planet. Founded 2003.

Noel Tatt Group/Impress Publishing*

Appledown House, Barton Business Park,
Appledown Way, New Dover Road, Canterbury,
Kent CT1 3TE
tel (01227) 811600
email mail@noeltatt.co.uk
website www.noeltatt.co.uk

General everyday cards including Christmas. Will consider verses. Founded 1964.

Tomcat Cards*

Overdene, 27 Orchard Road,
Rowlands Gill NE39 1DN
tel (01207) 775987
email info@tomcat.cards
website www.tomcat.cards
Founder Lynne Thomas

Works with artists who like drawing cats. Founded 2010.

UK Greetings Ltd*

Mill Street East, Dewsbury, West Yorks. WF12 9AW
tel (01924) 465200

website www.ukgreetings.co.uk
Ceo James Conn

For submissions, please visit website. Founded 1997.

Wishing Well Studios*

Chichester Business Park, City Fields Way,
Tangmere PO20 2FT
tel (01243) 792600
email creative.recruitment@cbg.co.uk
website www.carteblanchegreetings.com
Studio Manager Jude Williams

Part of Carte Blanche Group. Rhyming and prose verse 4–24 lines; also jokes. All styles considered. Don't send originals. Email attachments less than 3MB. Founded 1996.

Woodmansterne Publications Ltd*

1 The Boulevard, Blackmoor Lane, Watford,
Herts. WD18 8UW
tel (01923) 200600
website www.woodmansterne.co.uk

Publisher of greeting cards and social stationery featuring fine and contemporary art and photography (colour and b&w). Submit colour copies, photographs or jpg files by email. Founded 1968.

Societies, prizes and festivals

Festival fun: your guide to why, how and what

Author and screenwriter Adam Hamdy, co-founder of crime and thriller festival Capital Crime, sings the praises of literary festivals. He has tips on how to find, prepare for, enjoy, and reap rewards from the festival experience and all it has to offer both authors and readers.

Why go to a literary festival?

Whether you're an aspiring or established author, or reader, if you've never been to a literary festival I'd highly recommend going. I went to my first literary festival in 2016, shortly before my debut novel, *Pendulum* (Headline 2016), hit the shelves. My publisher sent me to the Theakston Old Peculier Crime Writing Festival (see page 603) to promote the book and build relationships with bloggers, journalists and other authors. Unsure of what to expect, I was nervous on the drive up, but within an hour of arriving my only regret was that I hadn't been to a festival sooner.

I've been to the Cannes Film Festival, but I can't imagine walking up to Martin Scorsese or Steven Spielberg and managing to say anything more than, 'It's lovely to meet …' before suited bouncers whisked me away. Literary festivals are nothing like that. I soon found myself chatting to new, established and downright legendary authors. Perhaps it's because we spend so much time alone, with nothing but our imaginations and the tyranny of a daily word count, but most writers are a gregarious bunch, always up for a chat and a laugh. And, because every writer you ever meet has their own horror story of rejections and knockbacks, you will find that, as a group, we're very accessible and happy to share our thoughts and experiences of the industry. If you want to learn about publishing a book, finding an agent, or the craft of writing, hang out at a festival bar.

In addition to informal opportunities to forge new relationships and learn from the pros, most festivals offer a structured programme of events designed to interest everyone from the general reader to the most established author. In our first year at Capital Crime, we had Ian Rankin and Don Winslow in conversation, an industry panel on how to become published, a creative masterclass with Anthony Horowitz, an interview with Kate Atkinson and so much more. There were heavyweight discussions about true-life crime and fun sessions; the role-play and banter of the Capital Crime debut novelists quiz – 'Whose Crime Is It Anyway?' - had the audience in stitches. After a pandemic hiatus, Capital Crime 2022 was an even bigger event.

While they're fun and entertaining experiences for readers, I would advise aspiring authors to go to festivals as soon as they can. Most festivals feature discussion about the craft and business of writing, so authors can learn a lot. I wish I'd gone to festivals when I was starting out as a writer because I think I could have saved myself a lot of heartache.

They're great places to meet agents, hear what the industry is looking for and learn what life as an author is really like. A number of aspiring authors who attended Capital Crime went on to be signed with agents; it really can be a springboard for your career.

How to prepare for your first festival

If the idea of going to a festival has piqued your interest, you might want to start with a local event. Most UK towns and cities host a literary event, and if it's local it's likely to be a less costly experience than a distant, travel-and-hotel festival. If you belong to a writers' group, book club or have bookish friends, you might be able to convince others to attend with you, reducing potential angst. You might also want to check your local bookshops, as many run regular events that are good warm-ups for the full-blown festival experience. Even in deepest, darkest Shropshire, I have been to some amazing events run by independent bookshops – Booka in Oswestry is brilliant at attracting big-name authors as well as showcasing debut writers – which can give you a taste of the live experience.

When you're ready for one of the big festivals – Cheltenham, Hay, Harrogate, Capital Crime – make sure you plan ahead to get the most from the experience. Research the travel and accommodation available and ask around on social media for hints and tips on where to stay and how to reduce costs. Most festivals offer an 'early bird' discount for people who buy their tickets well in advance so, if you're sure you're going, save money by booking early.

Some festivals offer tickets to individual events, others sell 'rover' passes. Check the programme and make sure your ticket allows you to get into the events you're keen to attend. Capital Crime and a few other festivals offer concession prices for people on low incomes or specific groups, such as librarians. Make sure you check to see what discounts might be available before booking.

Once you've booked and sorted out travel and accommodation, take time to plan your schedule. When you're there, it's all too easy to get drawn into conversation at the bar, lose track of time and miss events. Allow yourself enough time to rest and grab tea, coffee or a bite to eat. If you're planning to go to author signings, make sure you know when they are and don't dawdle! Some big-name authors limit how many books they'll sign and will rarely be seen in the bar, so their signing appearance is the only time you'll be able to grab them.

Dress code is whatever you feel comfortable in. It helps to know a bit about the festival you're attending. At the Theakston Old Peculier Crime Writing Festival in Harrogate, for example, a lot of time is spent outside socialising in the beer tent and on the lawns of the famous Old Swan Hotel – so take clothes that reflect the vagaries of the British summer! Many festival sessions are held in large conference venues, and some can be chilly if the air-conditioning is too high or overwarm if there's no AC at all, which means layers are a good idea – so you can cool down or wrap up, depending on your internal climate control.

Most festivals provide tote bags and goodies. These are much sought-after and hugely helpful to stow all the books you may end up buying at the festival bookshop. You may not go *intending* to add to your reading pile but, believe me, you will. We had to buy another bookcase to accommodate all the books purchased at Capital Crime last year!

Every festival is different

Do your research. Find out which festivals fit your personality and interests. Bloggers and journalists review festivals and talk about their experiences, which means you can get a good sense of a festival's ethos and atmosphere by reading what's been written about them online.

Some festivals run competitions or host special events. Capital Crime runs its New Voices Award, which is designed to give unsigned authors the opportunity to win a cash prize and garner some industry attention. Harrogate hosts an author dinner, where guests are able to spend a couple of hours with published authors over a meal. ThrillerFest in New York runs a best first-line competition in addition to its more widely publicised awards. Scour the festival's website and check on social media to ensure you know exactly what your chosen festival offers.

Attending as a panellist

As an author, you might be eligible to appear at the festival as a panellist. The right time to introduce yourself to a festival organiser is when you have a debut novel heading towards publication. If your book is going to be traditionally published, your publisher will usually make the festival organiser aware of the debut, but it doesn't hurt to connect with them directly as well. Check the festival website for information on being a panellist and how to get in touch.

If you are fortunate enough to be invited to appear at a festival, have a think about the panel topic the organisers give you and prepare some thoughts on interesting angles or subjects for discussion. Festivals are a live event, and you're there to entertain and engage the audience, not to sell your book. Selling your book is a happy by-product of an appreciative audience. If the audience feels you're an interesting or entertaining person, they will expect those qualities to be found in your work.

Perhaps you're nervous about speaking in public – I think most people are – but remember the audience is there because they're interested in what you have to say. Booklovers tend to be a friendly crowd and will be sympathetic to the fact that you're out of your comfort zone. Take some deep breaths (it really does help) and speak a little slower and a little louder than normal, so your audience can hear you.

Although this may not sound very 'artist-in-a-garret', do think about your author brand. Hopefully, you've taken time to find your author voice and to discover who you are as a storyteller. Do the same with your public persona. What makes you stand out as a person? What do you bring to an event that no one else can? Once you've understood who you are, practise – take the opportunity to appear at as many events as possible, large or small.

Societies, prizes and festivals

Festival dos and don'ts

- Do network with authors and other readers. Festival-goers are a friendly bunch and are generally happy to chat and provide advice.
- Dress code is whatever you feel comfortable in.
- Do have fun. Festivals are supposed to engage and entertain. Make the most of your time.
- Do read as many books by attending authors as possible. This will help you get more out of their events and to ask informed questions. Which brings us to the next point...
- Do ask questions. Authors love to be challenged and engaged. But...
- Don't hog the microphone. Keep your question short and to the point. If you have something you'd like to discuss with an author in more detail, save it for the signing.
- Don't be rude. Publishing is a polite world and rudeness doesn't generally get results.
- Don't be afraid to ask for help. Festivals employ staff and volunteers who are there to help you. Don't be afraid to approach them with any issue, no matter how big or small.

Hone your public speaking. It's like anything else in life – practice makes perfect, and the more preparation you do, the better the experience should be for you and your audience.

Also, given the times we live in, be sure to promote your appearance on social media. Sometimes, amid the buzz and busyness of the festival, it can be easy to forget to take photos and the obligatory selfie. Do try to record these moments – it's not only a useful tool for connecting with other authors and promoting your book, but it's also a lovely way to remember the experience. Writing brings plenty of lows, so it's always important to celebrate the highs; I certainly count all my festival experiences as among the highs. In fact, it was while I was in New York, buzzing with the excitement of ThrillerFest (https://thrillerfest.com), that I joined forces with bookseller and agent extraordinaire David Headley to set up Capital Crime.

Adam Hamdy is an author and screenwriter, and co-founder of the crime and thriller festival Capital Crime (www.capitalcrime.org). Adam has a law degree from Oxford University and worked as a strategy consultant before taking up his writing career. He is the author of *The Other Side of Night* (Pan Macmillan 2022), and the Scott Pearce series (Pan Macmillan) – *Black 13* (2020) and *Red Wolves* (2021). He has co-written *Private Moscow* (Arrow 2020), *Private Rogue* (Arrow 2021) and *Private Beijing* (Penguin 2022) with James Patterson. For more information see www.adamhamdy.com.

See also...
• *Festivals and conferences for writers, artists and readers*, page 593

Society of Authors

The SoA is the UK trade union for all types of writers, illustrators and literary translators at every stage of their careers.

Founded in 1884, the Society of Authors now has over 10,000 members. Members receive unlimited free advice on all aspects of the profession, including confidential clause-by-clause contract vetting, access to professional and geographic author communities, and a wide range of exclusive offers. It campaigns and lobbies on the issues that affect authors and holds hundreds of events online and across the UK each year, offering opportunities for authors to network and learn from each other. It manages more than 58 literary estates, the income from which helps to fund the organisation's work.

Members

SoA members include household names, such as Malorie Blackman, Neil Gaiman, Lemn Sissay and Joanne Harris, but they also include authors right at the start of their careers. Amongst the SoA membership are academic writers, biographers, broadcasters, children's writers, crime writers, dramatists, educational writers, ELT writers, health writers, ghostwriters, graphic novelists, historians, illustrators, journalists, medical writers, non-fiction writers, novelists, poets, playwrights, radio writers, scriptwriters, short story writers, translators, spoken word artists, YA writers and more.

The benefits available to all SoA members include:
• assistance with contracts, from negotiation and assessment of terms to clause-by-clause, confidential vetting;
• unlimited advice on queries, covering any aspect of the business of authorship;
• taking up complaints on behalf of members on any issue concerned with the business of authorship;

Membership

The Society of Authors
24 Bedford Row, London WC1R 4EH
tel 020-3880 2230
email info@societyofauthors.org
website www2.societyofauthors.org
Chief Executive Nicola Solomon

There are two membership bands: Full and Associate membership.

Full membership is available to professional writers, poets, translators and illustrators working in any genre or medium. This includes those who have: had a full-length work traditionally published, broadcast or performed commercially; self-published or been published on a print-on-demand or ebook-only basis and who meet sales criteria; published or had broadcast or performed an equivalent body of professional work; or administrators of a deceased author's estate.

Authors at the start of their careers are invited to join as Associates.

Associate membership is available to anyone actively working to launch a career as an author. This includes: authors who are starting out in self-publishing but who are not yet making a profit; authors who have been offered a contract for publication or agent representation but who are not yet published; students engaged on a course of at least one academic year's duration that will help them develop a career as an author, as well as other activities that mark the early stages of an author's career. Associate members enjoy all the same services and benefits as Full members.

Membership is subject to election and payment of subscription fees.

The subscription fee (tax deductible) starts at £29.25 per quarter, or £20.50 for those aged 35 or under. A concessionary rate for over 65s is available on request. Joint membership also available.

Societies, prizes and festivals

• pursuing legal actions for breach of contract, copyright infringement and the non-payment of royalties and fees, when the risk and cost preclude individual action by a member and issues of general concern to the profession are at stake;

• conferences, seminars, meetings and other opportunities to network and learn from other authors;

• regular communications and a comprehensive range of publications, including the SoA's quarterly journal, *The Author*;

• discounts on books, exclusive rates on specialist insurance, special offers on products and services and free membership of the Authors' Licensing and Collecting Society (ALCS; see page 718);

• Authors with Disabilities and Chronic Illnesses – a peer support network for authors living and working with health challenges;

• Comics Creators Network – a professional support network for all types of comics creators;

• Children's Writers and Illustrators Group – a professional community of writers and illustrators who create content for the children's publishing market;

• Educational Writers Group – protecting the interests of educational authors in professional matters, especially contracts, rates of pay, digitalisation and copyright;

• Poetry and Spoken Word Group – a new, increasingly active group to which all new member poets are subscribed on joining SoA;

• Scriptwriters Group – representing members working in radio, TV, film and games development;

• Society of Authors in Scotland – organises a varied and busy calendar of activities in Scotland through a committee of volunteers;

• Translators Association – a source of expert advice for individual literary translators and a collective voice representing the profession (see page 532);

• Carers Network – a new group designed to help keep writers writing when they take on caring responsibilities for someone with an illness or disability.

The SoA also coordinates a growing network of over 37 local author communities across the UK.

Campaigning and lobbying

The SoA is a voice for authors and works at a national and international level to improve terms and treatment of authors, negotiating with all parties including publishers, broadcasters, agents and governments. Current areas of campaigning include contract terms, copyright, freedom of expression, tax and benefits arrangements and Public Lending Right (PLR; see page 655) – which the SoA played a key role in establishing. With the ongoing impacts of the Covid-19 pandemic and Brexit, the SoA continues to lobby for better terms, benefits and rights for authors and other creative professionals.

In the UK the SoA lobbies parliament, ministers and departments and makes submissions on relevant issues, working closely with the Department for Culture, Media and Sport and the All Party Parliamentary Writers Group. The SoA is a member of the British Copyright Council and was instrumental in setting up ALCS. They chair the Creators for Rights Alliance (CRA), a partnership of unions and member organisations from across the creative industries, working together on common interests such as copyright, payment and credit, and in 2022 launched the cross-industry 'Pay the Creator' campaign. It is recognised by the BBC in the negotiation of rates for authors' contributions to radio drama, as well as for the broadcasting of published material.

The SoA is a member of the European Writers' Council and applies pressure globally, working with sister organisations as part of the international Authors' Foundation.

The SoA also works closely with other professional bodies, including the Association of Authors' Agents, the Booksellers Association, the Publishers Association, the Independent Publishers Guild, the British Council, the National Union of Journalists and the Writers' Guild of Great Britain. (See the societies listings that start on page 503.)

Awards and grants

The SoA supports authors through a wide range of awards and grants. Over £120,000 is given in prizes each year and more than £250,000 is distributed in grants.

The SoA administers:

• the annual SoA Awards – ten prizes for poetry, fiction and non-fiction, and illustration, awarding authors at the beginning of their careers as well as those well established;

• two audio drama prizes: the Imison Award for a writer new to radio drama and the Tinniswood Award;

• awards for translations from Arabic, Dutch/Flemish, French, German, Greek, Italian, Spanish and Swedish into English;

• the Authors' Foundation and K Blundell Trust, which give grants to assist authors working on their next book;

• the Francis Head Bequest and the Authors' Contingency Fund, which assist authors who, through physical mishap, are temporarily unable to maintain themselves or their families;

• the *Sunday Times* Charlotte Aitken Young Writer of the Year Award;

• the ALCS Educational Writers' Awards.

Societies, prizes and festivals

WGGB (Writers' Guild of Great Britain)

The WGGB is the TUC-affiliated trade union for writers.

WGGB represents writers working in film, television, radio, theatre, books, poetry, animation, comedy and videogames. Formed in 1959 as the Screenwriters' Guild, the union gradually extended into all areas of freelance writing activity and copyright protection. It comprises professional writers in all media, united in common concern for one another and regulating the conditions under which they work.

Apart from necessary dealings with Government and policies on legislative matters affecting writers, the WGGB is, by constitution, non-political, has no involvement with any political party and members pay no political levy.

WGGB employs a permanent general secretary and other permanent staff and is administered by an Executive Council of around 20 members.

WGGB agreements

WGGB's core function is to negotiate minimum terms in those areas in which its members work. Those agreements form the basis of the individual contracts signed by members. It also gives individual advice to its members on contracts and other matters and maintains a welfare fund to help writers in financial trouble.

Membership

The Writers' Guild of Great Britain
First Floor, 134 Tooley Street, London SE1 2TU
tel 020-7833 0777
email admin@writersguild.org.uk
website www.writersguild.org.uk
Facebook www.facebook.com/thewritersguild
Twitter @The WritersGuild
General Secretary Ellie Peers

Full membership: Members pay approximately 1.2% of earnings from professional writing using a banding system (min. £198, max. £2,000 p.a.).

Candidate membership: £108 p.a. restricted to writers who have not had work published or produced at WGGB-approved rates.

Student membership: £30 p.a. for student writers aged 18 or over, studying at BA level or below.

Affiliate membership: £300 p.a. for people who work professionally with writers, e.g. agents, technical advisers.

Members receive a weekly email newsletter. The WGGB website contains full details of collective agreements and WGGB activities, plus a 'Find a Writer' service and a dedicated Members' area; information is also made available on Twitter, Facebook and other social media channels. Other benefits include: legal advice and contract vetting; free training; member events, discounts and special offers (subject to membership tier).

Television

WGGB negotiates minimum terms agreements with the BBC, ITV, Pact (Producers' Alliance for Cinema and Television; see page 531) and TAC (representing Welsh-language television producers).

WGGB TV agreements regulate minimum fees, residuals and royalties, copyright, credits and general conditions for television plays, series and serials, dramatisations and adaptations, soaps, sitcoms and sketch shows. One of the WGGB's most important achievements has been the establishment of pension rights for members. The BBC, ITV and independent producers pay a pension contribution on top of the standard writer's fee on the understanding that the WGGB member also pays a contribution.

The switch to digital television, video-on-demand and download-to-own services, mobile phone technology and the expansion of the BBC's commercial arm have seen WGGB in constant negotiation over the past decade. WGGB now has agreements for all of the BBC's digital channels and for its joint venture channels. In May 2012 it signed new agreements with the BBC extending minimum terms over online services such as iPlayer. From April 2015 the first payments under the Writers Digital Payments scheme (a not-for-profit company) were paid out to writers whose work had been broadcast on BBC iPlayer and ITV Player. In 2016 WGGB negotiated a 75% fee increase for writers working under its 2003 Pact agreement, and also started work on rewriting the agreement. In 2017 it negotiated a new script agreement for television and online with the BBC.

Film

In 1985 an agreement was signed with the two producer organisations: the British Film and Television Producers' Association and the Independent Programme Producers' Association (now known as Pact). Since then there has been an industrial agreement covering UK film productions and pension fund contributions have been negotiated for WGGB members. The Agreement was renegotiated in February 1992 and consultations on an updated arrangement are in progress.

Radio

WGGB has a standard agreement for Radio Drama with the BBC, establishing a fee structure that is reviewed annually. It was comprehensively renegotiated in 2005 resulting in an agreement covering digital radio. In 1985 the BBC agreed to extend the pension scheme already established for television writers to include radio writers. WGGB has special agreements for Radio 4's *The Archers* and for BBC iPlayer. A separate agreement covers the reuse of old comedy and drama material on digital BBC Radio 4 Extra. It has also negotiated rates for podcasts.

Books

WGGB fought for the loans-based Public Lending Right (PLR, see page 655) to reimburse authors for books lent in libraries. The scheme is now administered by the British Library; WGGB is represented on its advisory committee. WGGB has a Books Committee, which works on behalf of book writers and poets. Issues affecting members include authors' earnings, self-publishing, print-on-demand services and ebooks, and in 2022 the union launched the 'Is It A Steal?' joint campaign with the Society of Authors to tackle bad practice in the hybrid/paid-for publishing sector.

Theatre

In 1979 WGGB, together with the Theatre Writers' Union, negotiated the first industrial agreement for theatre writers. The Theatres National Committee Agreement (TNC) covers the Royal Shakespeare Company, the Royal National Theatre Company and the English Stage Company at the Royal Court. When their agreement was renegotiated in 2007, WGGB achieved a long-standing ambition of a minimum fee of £10,000 for a new play; this has since risen to £13,257.

In June 1986, a new agreement was signed with the Theatrical Management Association (now UK Theatre), which covers 95 provincial theatres. In 1993, this agreement was comprehensively revised and included a provision for a year-on-year increase in fees in line with the Retail Price Index. The agreement was renegotiated in 2015.

After many years of negotiation, an agreement was concluded in 1991 between WGGB and the Independent Theatre Council (ITC), which represents 200 of the smaller and fringe theatres as well as educational and touring companies. This agreement was revised in 2002 and the minimum fees are reviewed annually. WGGB is currently talking to the ITC about updating the agreement. The WGGB Theatre Committee holds an annual forum for Literary Managers and runs the Olwen Wymark Theatre Encouragement Award scheme. In 2022 the union launched a landmark New Play Commission Scheme to address the severe impact Covid-19 had on playwrights and new writing in the theatre sector, resulting in commissions for 18 new plays.

Videogames
WGGB counts games writers amongst its members and holds regular networking events for them, as well as celebrating their achievements at the annual Writers' Guild Awards. The union publishes guidelines for games writers and those who work with them, outlining best practice in this growing area.

Other activities
WGGB is in touch with Government and national institutions wherever and whenever the interests of writers are in question or are being discussed, for example, submitting evidence to a Parliamentary Inquiry on the lack of working-class writers. It holds cross-party Parliamentary lobbies with Equity and the Musicians' Union to ensure that the various artforms they represent are properly cared for, and writers' voices are heard during, for example, the Brexit transition and the Covid-19 pandemic. Working with the Federation of Entertainment Unions, WGGB makes its views known to bodies, such as Arts Council England and Ofcom on a broader basis.

WGGB is an active affiliate of the British Copyright Council, Creators' Rights Alliance and other organisations whose activities are relevant to professional writers.

Internationally, WGGB plays a leading role in the International Affiliation of Writers Guilds, which includes the American Guilds East and West, the Canadian Guilds (French and English) and the Irish, Mexican, French, Israeli, South African and New Zealand Guilds. When it is possible to make common cause, the Guilds act accordingly. WGGB takes a leading role in the Fédération des Scénaristes d'Europe.

On a day-to-day basis, WGGB gives advice on contracts, and takes up issues that affect the lives of its members as professional writers. Other benefits include access to free and discounted training, exclusive events and discounts and a dedicated online members' area. Full members are entitled to submit a profile for inclusion in the WGGB online *Find A Writer* directory; pay no joining fee for membership to Writers Guild of America East or West; and are eligible for Cannes accreditation. Regular committee meetings are held by specialist WGGB Craft Committees and its active branches across the UK organise panel discussions, talks and social events. WGGB also has an Equality & Diversity Committee where activists have been involved in many initiatives, including an access rider to reduce access barriers for freelance writers.

Recent campaigns include Equality Writes, following an independent report commissioned by WGGB which revealed the shocking lack of gender equality in the UK screen industries. The union has also campaigned against the privatisation of Channel 4, and to tackle bullying and harassment in the creative industries. In 2019 it declared a 'climate emergency' and pledged to put the climate crisis at the heart of everything it does. It has also taken a stand against proposed Government anti-strike legislation.

Each year WGGB presents the Writers' Guild Awards, covering all the areas in which its members work. These are the only cross-media awards in which writers are honoured by their peers.

Alliance of Independent Authors

ALLi is the professional association for self-publishing writers and advisors.

The Alliance of Independent Authors (ALLi) is a global organisation with a mission of fostering ethics and excellence in self-publishing and advocating for author-publishers.

Founded in 2012 at the London Book Fair by author, poet and creative mentor, Orna Ross, ALLi is headquartered in London but with members all over the world. In addition to its member services, the organisation offers outreach education to the self-publishing community through its popular online Self-Publishing Advice Center, which features a blog, podcast, bi-annual online conference and series of guidebooks, and supports Ross's annual Self-Publishing Advice Conference.

ALLi has an Advisory Board of author-publishers, educators and service providers, and an active Watchdog desk which rates self-publishing services and provides community alerts. It also publishes a Directory of vetted services, ranging from large global players like Amazon KDP and Ingram Spark to local freelancers. Many of these services offer discounted services to ALLi authors.

ALLi advocates for the interests of independent authors within and outside the literary, publishing and bookselling sectors, and works with ambassadors, other authors associations and grassroots organisations to promote diversity and accessibility, through a 'Self-Publishing for All' campaign.

Other campaigns include 'Open Up To Indie Authors', which urges the inclusion of author–publishers in literary programmes and events; 'AskALLi', which pledges to answer any self-publishing question anyone might have; and 'Self-Publishing 3.0', a campaign to raise the average income for authors and poets through use of technology and creative business practice.

Membership

The Alliance of Independent Authors
7 Bell Yard, City of Westminster,
London WC2A 2JR
email info@allianceindependentauthors.org
website www.allianceindependentauthors.org,
https://selfpublishingadvice.org
Twitter @IndieAuthorALLi

ALLi offers three grades of membership for authors:

Associate membership (£69 p.a.) is open to writing/publishing students with an interest in self-publishing and non-published writers (or translators) preparing a book for self-publication.

Author membership (£89 p.a.) is open to writers or translators of books for adults who have self-published a full-length title (55,000+ words) or series of shorter books; writers of children's/young adult books who have self-published one or more titles.

Authorpreneur membership (£119 p.a.) is open to full-time self-publishing authors who earn their living from their author business and can show evidence of 50,000 book sales in the last two years; applications are assessed.

Benefits include self-publishing advice, guidance and community; vetted services, service ratings and watchdog desk; legal and contract appraisal; discounts and deals; professional and business development; campaigns and advocacy.

ALLi also has two partner memberships: for self-publishing services; and for other authors' organizations that align with ALLi's ethos.

Societies, associations and clubs

This list is divided into the following sections: Representation and publishing; Arts councils, Royal Societies and funding; Copyright and licensing; Editorial, journalism and broadcasting; Literacy; Libraries and information; Literary; Art, illustration and photography; Film, theatre and television; Translation; Bibliographical and academic; Members' clubs; Writers' organisations; and Music. Some also offer prizes and awards (see page 543).

REPRESENTATION AND PUBLISHING

American Booksellers Association
333 Westchester Avenue, Suite S202, White Plains, NY 10604, USA
tel +1 800-637-0037
email info@bookweb.org
website www.bookweb.org

A national non-profit trade organisation that works with booksellers and industry partners to ensure the success and profitability of independently owned book retailers and to assist in expanding the book community. Provides education and information dissemination, offers business products and services, creates relevant awareness programmes and engages in public policy. Founded 1900.

Association of American Literary Agents
302A West 12th Street, Suite 122, New York, NY 10014, USA
email assistant@aalitagents.org
website https://aalitagents.org

A professional organisation of over 415 agents who work with authors and illustrators. Founded 1991.

Association of American Publishers
455 Massachusetts Avenue, NW Suite 700, Washington, DC 20001, USA
tel +1 202-347-3375
email info@publishers.org
website https://publishers.org
Twitter @AmericanPublish

AAP is the largest trade association for US books, journals and education publishers, providing advocacy and communications on behalf of the industry and its priorities nationally and worldwide. Founded 1970.

The Association of Authors' Agents
c/o The Society of Authors, 24 Bedford Row, London WC1R 4EH
tel 020-3880 2230
website www.agentsassoc.co.uk
President Catherine Clarke, *Secretary* Camille Burns
The AAA exists to provide a forum which allows member agencies to discuss issues arising in the profession; a collective voice for UK literary agencies in public affairs and the media; and a code of conduct to which all members commit themselves. Please note that the AAA is not able to offer advice on finding representation by an agent or getting published. Founded 1974.

Association of Canadian Publishers
401 Richmond Street W, Studio 257A, Toronto, ON M5V 3A8, Canada
tel +1 416-487-6116
email admin@canbook.org
website https://publishers.ca
Executive Director Kate Edwards

Represents approximately 115 Canadian-owned and controlled book publishers from across the country. Activities include government and public relations, marketing initiatives, research and communications, and professional development. Founded 1976.

Australian Publishers Association
60/89 Jones Street, Ultimo, NSW 2007
tel +61 (0)2 9281 9788
website www.publishers.asn.au
Twitter @AusPublish

The APA is the industry body for Australian book, journal and electronic publishers. Founded 1948.

The Australian Society of Authors
Suite C1.06, 22–36 Mountain Street, Ultimo, NSW 2007
tel +61 (0)2 9211 1004
email asa@asauthors.org
website www.asauthors.org

The ASA is the professional association for Australia's authors and illustrators. Provides advocacy, support and advice for authors and illustrators in matters relating to their professional practice. Founded 1963.

Australian Writers' Guild
Level 4, 70 Pitt Street, Sydney, NSW 2000
tel +61 (0)2 9319 0339
email admin@awg.com.au
website www.awg.com.au

The professional association representing writers for stage, screen, radio and online. Has protected and promoted their creative and professional interests for 60 years. Founded 1962.

The Booksellers Association

6 Bell Yard, London WC2A 2JR
tel 020-7421 4640
email mail@booksellers.org.uk
website www.booksellers.org.uk
Twitter @BAbooksellers
President Hazel Broadfoot

A membership organisation for all booksellers in the UK and Ireland, representing over 95% of bookshops. Key services include National Book Tokens, Batch Payment Services and BatchLine. Founded 1895.

Canadian Authors Association

19 Machell Avenue, Aurora, ON L4G 2R6
tel +1 877-905-1921 ext. 800
email office@canadianauthors.org
website www.canadianauthors.org
Facebook www.facebook.com/
canadianauthorsassociation
Twitter @canauthors
Administrative Director Brandi Tanner

A membership-based organisation for writers in all areas of the profession. Has branches across Canada that provide writers with a wide variety of programmes, services and resources to help them develop their skills in the craft and business of writing. Founded 1921.

Canadian Publishers' Council

Suite 6060, 3080 Yonge Street, Toronto,
ON M4N 3N1
tel +1 647-255-8880
email dswail@pubcouncil.ca
website https://pubcouncil.ca
Twitter @pubcouncil_ca
President David Swail

Represents the interests of Canadian publishing companies that publish books and other media for schools, colleges and universities, professional and reference markets, the retail and library sectors. Founded 1910.

Canadian Society of Children's Authors, Illustrators & Performers

720 Bathurst Street, Suite 412, Toronto, ON M5S 2R4
tel +1 416-515-1559
email office@canscaip.org
website www.canscaip.org
Twitter @CANSCAIP
Administrative Director Helena Aalto
Membership $85 p.a. member; $45 p.a. friend

CANSCAIP is a membership-based non-profit organisation that supports the professional development of Canada's community of authors, illustrators and performers for children and teens. Founded 1977.

Creative UK

Tomorrow Building, 130 Broadway, 2nd Floor, Suite 7, MediaCityUK, Salford M50 2UW
tel 0333 023 5240
email info@wearecreative.uk
website www.wearecreative.uk
Facebook www.facebook.com/WeAreCreativeUK
Twitter @WeAreCreativeUK
Instagram @wearecreativeuk

The national network for the creative industries. Champions the social and economic value of the creative industries by connecting and supporting talent, businesses and organisations, providing development opportunities at a local and national level through their network of partners, offering tailor-made resources and financial expertise.

Federation of European Publishers

Chaussee d'Ixelles, 29/35 Box 4, 1050 Brussels, Belgium
tel +32 2770 1110
email info@fep-fee.eu
website www.fep-fee.eu
Twitter @FEP_EU

Represents the interests of European publishers on EU affairs and informs members on the development of EU policies which could affect the publishing industry. Founded 1967.

Independent Publishers Guild

PO Box 12, Llain, Login SA34 0WU
tel (01437) 563335
email info@independentpublishersguild.com
website www.independentpublishersguild.com
Chief Executive Bridget Shine
Membership Open to new and established publishers from all sectors and of all sizes, plus suppliers and service providers.

The IPG is the UK's largest network of publishers and has served, supported and represented independents for over 60 years. It delivers two popular annual conferences featuring speakers from across publishing and beyond, a range of other events and numerous resources to help members do better business. Coordinates the Independent Publishing Awards, a mentoring programme, collective stands at book fairs and training via the IPG Skills Hub; and provides members with weekly ebulletins and special deals on publishing products and services. Founded 1962.

International Authors Forum

6th Floor, International House,
1 St Katherine's Way, London E1W 1UN
tel 020-7264 5707
email luke.alcott@internationalauthors.org
website www.internationalauthors.org
Twitter @IntAuthors
Executive Administrator Luke Alcott

Represents authors around the world and has a membership made up of authors' organisations from every continent. Campaigns for authors' rights at the UN and national levels. Organises events, publications and opportunities for knowledge sharing to promote the importance of creative work financially, socially and culturally. Keeps members up to date with international developments in copyright law.

International Publishers Association

23 Avenue de France, 1202 Geneva, Switzerland
tel +41 22-704 1820
email info@internationalpublishers.org
website www.internationalpublishers.org
Facebook www.facebook.com/
InternationalPublishersAssociation
Twitter @IntPublishers
President Karine Pansa, *Secretary-General* José Borghino

The IPA is a federation of national, regional and international publishers' associations. It promotes and protects publishing worldwide, with a focus on copyright and freedom to publish. Its membership comprises 92 organisations from 76 countries worldwide. Founded 1896.

Irish Writers Centre

19 Parnell Square, Dublin D01 E102, Republic of Ireland
tel +353 (0)1 872 1302
email info@writerscentre.ie
website https://irishwriterscentre.ie
Facebook www.facebook.com/irishwritersctr
Twitter @IrishWritersCtr
Director Valerie Bistany

National support and development centre and membership organisation for Irish writers, carrying out its work online and in-person. The IWC works with writers of all types and talents, and actively encourages writers from all communities to engage in creative writing. Provides opportunities for skill development, gaining industry knowledge and networking with other writers. Founded 1991.

Irish Writers' Union/Comhar na Scríbhneoirí

Irish Writers Centre, 19 Parnell Square, Dublin 1, Republic of Ireland
email info@irishwritersunion.org
website https://irishwritersunion.org
Facebook www.facebook.com/IrishWritersUnion
Twitter @WritersUnion_ie

The Union advances the cause of writing as a profession, to achieve better remuneration and more favourable conditions for writers and to provide a means for the expression of the collective opinion of writers on matters affecting their profession. Offers free contract advice and negotiation for members. Founded 1986.

Literature Alliance Scotland

email admin@literaturealliancescotland.co.uk
website https://literaturealliancescotland.co.uk/membership/
Twitter @LitScotland

LAS is the membership organisation dedicated to advancing the interests of Scotland's literature and languages locally, nationally and internationally. Brings together a network of writers, publishers, educators, librarians and literature organisations to achieve its aims.

The Munster Literature Centre

Frank O'Connor House, 84 Douglas Street, Cork T12 X70A
email info@munsterlit.ie
website www.munsterlit.ie
Facebook www.facebook.com/munsterliteraturecentre
Twitter @MunLitCentre

Promotes and celebrates literature and writers, especially within Munster. As well as organising The Cork International Poetry Festival and The Cork International Short Story Festival each year, the centre runs workshops, readings and competitions to support new and established writers. Founded 1993.

New Zealand Writers Guild

525 Rosebank Road, Avondale, Auckland 1026
tel +64 (0)9 360 1408
email guildhq@nzwg.org.nz
website www.nzwg.org.nz

Represents the interests of New Zealand writers (TV, film, radio and theatre); to establish and improve minimum conditions of work and rates of compensation for writers; to provide professional services for members. Founded 1975.

Out on the Page

email contact@outonthepage.co.uk
website www.outonthepage.co.uk
Facebook www.facebook.com/outonthepage/
Twitter @outonthepage
Instagram @outonthepage

Connects, develops and promotes LGBTQ+ writers and writing. Aims to create a world in which LGBTQ+ writing is more visible and where writers feel less isolated and more able to define their own measures of success, develop their writing, engage with the publishing business and reach their desired audiences. Encourages publishers and other organisations to be more vocal in their support of LGBTQ+ writing and to create safe and supportive spaces for writers, and establishes networks, courses, workshops, retreats and other events. Founded 2018.

The Personal Managers' Association Ltd

email info@thepma.com
website www.thepma.com

Professional body for talent agencies in the UK. Membership comprises agencies who represent artists, writers, directors and creatives, working in screen, theatre and radio. Founded 1950.

Professional Publishers Association

White Collar Factory, 1 Old Street Yard, London EC1Y 8AF
tel 020-7404 4166
email info@ppa.co.uk
website www.ppa.co.uk
Twitter @PPA_Live

The association for publishers and media businesses in the UK. PPA's role is to promote and protect the interests of the industry in general, and member companies in particular. The association's membership consists of the UK's largest publishing companies and 150 smaller independent publishers. Founded 2013.

Publishers Association

First Floor, 50 Southwark Street, London SE1 1UN
email mail@publishers.org.uk
website www.publishers.org.uk
Twitter @PublishersAssoc
President Antonia Seymour, *Ceo* Dan Conway, Perminder Mann

A member organisation for UK publishing, representing companies of all sizes and specialisms. Their members produce digital and print books, research journals and educational resources across genres and subjects. Exists to champion publishing to the wider world and to provide their members with everything they need to thrive. They have helped change laws, improved business conditions and inspired people to become publishers. Founded 1896.

Publishers Association of New Zealand

Level 6, 19 Como Street, Takapuna, Auckland 0622, New Zealand
tel +64 (0)9 280 3213
email admin@publishers.org.nz
website www.publishers.org.nz
Twitter @Publishers_NZ

PANZ represents book, educational and digital publishers in New Zealand. Members include both the largest international publishers and companies in the independent publishing community.

Publishers' Association of South Africa

House Vincent, Wynberg Mews, 1st Floor, Unit 104, Brodie Road, Wynberg 7800
tel +27 (0)21 762 9083
email pasa@publishsa.co.za
website www.publishsa.co.za

PASA is the largest publishing industry body in South Africa and is committed to creativity, literacy, the free flow of ideas and encouraging a culture of reading. It aims to promote and protect the rights and responsibilities of the publishing sector in South Africa.

Publishers' Publicity Circle

email publisherspublicitycircle@gmail.com
website www.publisherspublicitycircle.co.uk
Twitter @publicitycircle
Secretary/Treasurer Madeline Toy

Enables all book publicists to meet and share information regularly. Monthly meetings provide a forum for press journalists, TV and radio researchers and producers to meet publicists collectively. Awards are presented for the best PR campaigns. Monthly newsletter includes recruitment advertising.

Publishing Ireland/Foilsiú Éireann

63 Patrick Street, Dun Laoghaire, Dublin A96 WF25, Republic of Ireland
website www.publishingireland.com
Facebook www.facebook.com/PublishingIreland
Twitter @PublishingIRL
General Manager Orla McLoughlin

Enables publishers to share expertise and resources in order to benefit from opportunities and solve problems that are of common concern to all. It comprises most of the major publishing houses in Ireland with a mixture of trade, general and academic publishers as members. Founded 1970.

Publishing Scotland

Scott House, 10 South St Andrew Street, Edinburgh EH2 2AZ
tel 0131 228 6866
email enquiries@publishingscotland.org
website www.publishingscotland.org
Chief Executive Marion Sinclair

A network for trade, training and development in the Scottish publishing industry. Runs events throughout the year, including workshops and courses, spotlights opportunities and supports the Scottish publishing industry and those who work within it. Founded 1973.

Scottish BPOC Writers Network (SBWN)

email scottishbpocwriters@gmail.com
website https://scottishbpocwritersnetwork.org/
Facebook www.facebook.com/groups/ScottishBAMEWritersNetwork/
Twitter @scotbpocwriters
Instagram @scotbpocwriters

SBWN highlights diverse literary voices and connects Scottish BPOC writers with the wider literary sector in Scotland. Prioritises BPOC-led opportunities, partners with literary organisations to facilitate conversations around inclusive programming and overcoming systemic barriers, and offers professional development programming for members. Membership is free and open to any MPOC writer or literary professional who is Scottish or based in Scotland and participates in the groups activities.

Society of Artists Agents

website https://saahub.com
Twitter @SaaAgents

Formed to promote professionalism in the illustration industry and to forge closer links between clients and artists through proper terms and conditions that protect the interests of both. Actively campaigns to protect copyright and intellectual property. Founded 1992.

The Society of Authors

– see page 495

Society of Young Publishers

c/o The Publishers Association, First Floor, 50 Southwark Street, London SE1 1UN
email sypchair@thesyp.org.uk
website www.thesyp.org.uk
Twitter @SYP_UK, @SYPIreland, @SYP_LDN, @SYPNorth, @SYP_Oxford, @SYPScotland, @SYP_SouthWest
Instagram @syp_uk, @syp_london, @syp.north, @oxford_syp, @sypscotland, @syp_southwest
Membership £30 p.a. employed standard; £24 p.a. student/unemployed; £18 p.a. digital membership

The SYP supports those of any age looking to get into publishing, or those within the first ten years of their career who are looking to get ahead. It is made up of six regional committees (Ireland, London, North, Oxford, Scotland and South West), and a UK team responsible for the organisation's oversight. These committees organise mentorship schemes for current and aspiring publishers based in the UK and Ireland. Two annual conferences are held, as well as numerous in-person and digital events each month – including socials, career panels and more. Founded 1949.

Theatre Writers' Union – see page 498

Writers Guild of America, East Inc.

250 Hudson Street, Suite 700, New York, NY 10013
tel +1 212-767-7800
website www.wgaeast.org
Facebook www.facebook.com/WGAEast
Twitter @WGAEast

WGAE represents writers in screen, TV and new media for collective bargaining. It provides member services including pension and health, as well as educational and professional activities. Founded 1954.

Writers Guild of America, West Inc.

7000 West 3rd Street, Los Angeles, CA 90048
tel +1 323-951-4000
website www.wga.org

WGAW represents and services writers in film, broadcast, cable and multimedia industries for purposes of collective bargaining, contract administration and other services, and functions to protect and advance the economic, professional and creative interests of writers. Founded 1933.

Writers Guild of Canada

366 Adelaide Street West, Suite 401, Toronto, ON M5V 1R9
tel +1 416-979-7907; toll free +1-800-567-9974
email info@wgc.ca
website www.writersguildofcanada.com
Facebook www.facebook.com/writers.guild.12
Twitter @WGCtweet

Represents professional screenwriters. Negotiates and administers collective agreements with independent producers and broadcasters.

WGGB (Writers' Guild of Great Britain) – see page 498

Writers Guild of Ireland

Art House, Curved Street, Temple Bar, Dublin 2, Republic of Ireland
tel +353 (0)1 670 9970
email info@script.ie
website http://script.ie/
Ceo Hugh Farley, *Chairperson* Jennifer Davidson

Represents writers' interests in theatre, radio and screen. Founded 1969.

The Writers' Union of Canada

600–460 Richmond Street West, Suite 600, Toronto, ON M5V 1Y1, Canada
tel +1 416-703-8982
email info@writersunion.ca
website www.writersunion.ca

National arts service organisation for professionally published book authors. Founded 1973.

ARTS COUNCILS, ROYAL SOCIETIES AND FUNDING

Arts Council/An Chomhairle Ealaíon

70 Merrion Square, Dublin D02 NY52, Republic of Ireland
tel +353 (0)1 618 0200
website www.artscouncil.ie/home
Facebook www.facebook.com/artscouncilireland
Twitter @artscouncil_ie
Instagram @artscouncilireland

The national development agency for the arts in Ireland. Promotes the arts through funding, research, information sharing, setting standards and encouraging appreciation. Founded 1951.

Arts Council England

tel 0161 934 4317
website www.artscouncil.org.uk
Facebook www.facebook.com/artscouncilofengland
Twitter @ace_national
Instagram @aceagrams

The national development agency for arts and culture in England, distributing public money from the government and the National Lottery. Organisations, artists, events and initiatives can receive funding to help achieve the Council's mission of providing art and culture for everyone. There are nine regional offices: Newcastle, Leeds, Manchester, Nottingham, Birmingham, Cambridge, Brighton, Bristol and London. Visit the website for information on funding support and advice, an online funding finder and funding FAQs. Founded 1946.

Arts Council of Northern Ireland

Linen Hill House, 23 Linenhall Street,
Lisburn BT28 1FJ
tel 028-9262 3555
email info@artscouncil-ni.org
website www.artscouncil-ni.org
Chief Executive Roisín McDonough

Promotes and encourages the arts throughout Northern Ireland. Artists in drama, dance, music and jazz, literature, the visual arts, traditional arts and community arts can apply for support for specific schemes and projects. The value of the grant will be set according to the aims of the programme. Artists of all disciplines and in all types of working practice, who have made a contribution to artistic activities in Northern Ireland for a minimum period of one year within the last five years, are eligible.

Australia Council

PO Box 576, Pyrmont, NSW 2009, Australia
tel +61 (0)2 9215 9000
website www.australiacouncil.gov.au
Ceo Adrian Collette

Provides a broad range of support for the arts in Australia, embracing music, theatre, literature, visual arts and crafts, dance, First Nations arts, community and experimental arts.

Books Council of Wales/Cyngor Llyfrau Cymru

Castell Brychan, Aberystwyth, Ceredigion SY23 2JB
tel (01970) 624151
email castellbrychan@books.wales
website https://llyfrau.cymru/en
website www.gwales.com
Ceo Helgard Krause

A national charity which supports and develops the publishing industry in Wales. It promotes literacy and reading for pleasure through a range of public campaigns, activities and events across Wales, often working in partnership with schools, libraries and other literary organisations. The Council works with publishers to nurture new talent and content in Welsh and English as well as offering specialist editing, design, marketing and distribution services. It administers grants to publishers and independent booksellers. Partly funded by the Welsh Government through Creative Wales and from the commercial operations of its wholesale book distribution centre. Founded 1961.

British Academy

10–11 Carlton House Terrace, London SW1Y 5AH
tel 020-7969 5200
website www.thebritishacademy.ac.uk
Facebook www.facebook.com/TheBritishAcademy
Twitter @BritishAcademy_
Ceo Hetan Shah

The UK's national academy for humanities and social sciences. The Academy is an independent fellowship of world-leading scholars and researchers; a funding body for research, nationally and internationally; and a forum for debate and engagement. It produces a wide range of publications, for academic and more general readerships.

The British Council

Bridgewater House, 58 Whitworth Street,
Manchester M1 6BB
tel 0161 957 7755
website www.britishcouncil.org
Facebook www.facebook.com/britishcouncil
Twitter @BritishCouncil
Chief Executive Scott McDonald, *Director of Cultural Engagement* Mark Stephens

The UK's international organisation for cultural relations and educational opportunities. Builds connections, understanding and trust between people in the UK and other countries through arts and culture, education and the English language. Working in close collaboration with book trade associations, the Literature team participates in major international book fairs.

Collaborates with offices overseas to broker relationships and create activities which link artists and cultural institutions around the world. Works with writers, publishers, producers, translators and other sector professionals across literature, publishing and education. The Visual Arts team shares UK visual arts around the world, connecting professionals internationally through collaborative exhibition programmes, digital networking, training and development and delegations. Manages and develops the British Council Collection and the British Pavilion at the Venice Biennale.

Creative Scotland

Waverley Gate, 2–4 Waterloo Gate,
Edinburgh EH1 3EG

email enquiries@creativescotland.com
website www.creativescotland.com
Twitter @CreativeScots

The public body that supports the arts, screen and creative industries across all parts of Scotland on behalf of everyone who lives, works or visits there. Through distributing funding from the Scottish Government and the National Lottery, Creative Scotland enables people and organisations to work in and experience the arts, screen and creative industries in Scotland by helping others to develop great ideas and bring them to life. Creative Scotland supports writers and publishers based in Scotland through a range of funds and initiatives.

The Gaelic Books Council/Comhairle nan Leabhraichean

32 Mansfield Street, Glasgow G11 5QP
tel 0141 337 6211
email alison@gaelicbooks.org
website www.gaelicbooks.org
Director Alison Lang

Stimulates Scottish Gaelic publishing by awarding publication grants for new books, commissioning new works from established and emerging authors and providing editorial advice and guidance to Gaelic writers and publishers. Has a bookshop in Glasgow that stocks all Gaelic and Gaelic-related books in print. All stock is listed on the website. Founded 1968.

Guernsey Arts Commission

Candie Museum, Candie Road, St Peter Port, Guernsey GY1 2UG
tel (01481) 220711
email info@arts.gg

Helps promote, develop and support the arts in Guernsey through exhibitions, a community arts programme and public events.

Literature Wales

Glyn Jones Centre, Wales Millennium Centre, Bute Place, Cardiff CF10 5AL
tel 029-2047 2266
email post@literaturewales.org
website www.literaturewales.org
Facebook www.facebook.com/LlenCymruLitWales
Twitter @LitWales
Instagram @llencymru_litwales

The national company for the development of literature in Wales. Works to inspire communities, develop writers and celebrate Wales' literary culture. Activities include the Wales Book of the Year Award; the Children's Laureate Wales and Bardd Plant Cymru schemes; creative writing courses at Tŷ Newydd Writing Centre; the professional development scheme Representing Wales; writer's bursaries and mentoring; the National Poet of Wales

initiative and more. The organisation is a member of the Arts Council of Wales' Arts Portfolio Wales.

Literature Works

c/o The Arts Institute Office,
Roland Levinsky Building, Plymouth University,
Drake Circus, Plymouth PL4 8AA
email info@literatureworks.org.uk
website www.literatureworks.org.uk
website www.quaywords.org.uk
Twitter @LitWorks

Literature Works is the regional literature development agency for South West England, a registered charity and an Arts Council England National Portfolio organisation. Its aim is to open up the flexible literature artform of poetry and story, creative writing and reading as widely as they can to the benefit of all in the South West of England. They host a thriving online community of emerging and established writers, nurture talent and provide resources for writers in the region.

Royal Academy of Arts

Burlington House, Piccadilly, London W1J 0BD
tel 020-7300 8090
website www.royalacademy.org.uk
President Rebecca Salter

An independent institution led by eminent artists and architects whose purpose is to be a clear, strong voice for art and artists. Its public programme promotes the creation, enjoyment and appreciation of the visual arts through exhibitions, education and debate. It holds major loan exhibitions throughout the year, as well as the annual Summer Exhibition, and runs Royal Academy Schools, a free fine art postgraduate programme for early career artists. Founded 1768.

Royal Birmingham Society of Artists

RBSA Gallery, 4 Brook Street, St Paul's Square, Birmingham B3 1SA
tel 0121 236 4353
email rbsagallery@rbsa.org.uk
website www.rbsa.org.uk
Facebook www.facebook.com/rbsagallery
Twitter @rbsagallery
Instagram @rbsagallery
Membership Friends £40 p.a.

RBSA is an artist-led charity, which supports artists and promotes engagement with the visual arts through a range of exhibitions, events and workshops. It runs its own exhibition venue, the RBSA Gallery, in Birmingham's historic Jewellery Quarter, a short walk from the city centre. The gallery is open five days a week and admission to all exhibitions is free.

Royal Institute of Oil Painters

17 Carlton House Terrace, London SW1Y 5BD
tel 020-7930 6844

website https://theroi.org.uk
Twitter @InstituteRoi

Promotes and encourages the art of painting in oils. Open Annual Exhibition at the Mall Galleries, The Mall, London SW1.

Royal Institute of Painters in Water Colours

17 Carlton House Terrace, London SW1Y 5BD
tel 020-7930 6844
email info@mallgalleries.com
website www.royalinstituteofpaintersinwatercolours.org
Facebook www.facebook.com/RIwatercolours
Twitter @RIwatercolours
Instagram @royal_institute_watercolours
President Chris Myers
Membership Elected from approved candidates' list

Promotes the appreciation of watercolour painting in its traditional and contemporary forms, primarily by means of an annual exhibition, at the Mall Galleries, The Mall, London SW1, of members' and non-members' work and also through members' exhibitions at selected venues in Britain and abroad. It is one of the oldest watercolour societies in the world. Founded 1831.

The Royal Musical Association

9 Patterson Avenue, Chorlton-cum-Hardy, Manchester M21 9NB
tel 07817 974004
email exec@rma.ac.uk
website www.rma.ac.uk
Twitter @RoyalMusical
President Prof. Barbara Kelly, *Contact* Dr Amanda Babington

Promotes the investigation and discussion of subjects connected with the art and science of music. Sponsors conferences, study days and research/training events. Publishes the *Journal of the Royal Musical Association, Royal Musical Association Research Chronicle*, and the RMA Monographs series. Founded 1874.

The Royal Photographic Society

RPS House, 337 Paintworks, Arnos Vale, Bristol BS4 3AR
tel 0117 316 4450
email info@rps.org
website www.rps.org
Facebook www.facebook.com/royalphotographicsociety
Twitter @The_RPS
Instagram @royalphotographicsociety
Membership £122 p.a. UK; £110 p.a. overseas; £92 p.a. over-65s; £56 p.a. under-25s, students and concessions

A world-leading photographic community with a membership of over 10,000 photographers worldwide. It aims to connect people with photography and inspire people through exhibitions, an award-winning journal, awards and events; to help photographers create images through its educational programmes and public initiatives; to recognise skill and creativity and connect photographers. Membership is open to anyone with an interest in photography. Founded 1853.

The Royal Scottish Academy of Art and Architecture

The Mound, Edinburgh EH2 2EL
tel 0131 624 6110
website www.royalscottishacademy.org
Director Colin Greenslade

Led by eminent artists and architects, the Royal Scottish Academy (RSA) is an independent voice for cultural advocacy and one of the largest supporters of artists in Scotland. It administers a number of scholarships, awards and residencies and has a historic collection of Scottish artworks and an archive, recognised by the Scottish Government as being of national significance. The Academy cherishes its independence from local or national government funding, relying instead on bequests, legacies, sponsorship and earned income. For information on open submission exhibitions, artist scholarships and residencies, or to discuss making a bequest to the Academy, visit the website. Founded 1826.

The Royal Society

6–9 Carlton House Terrace, London SW1Y 5AG
tel 020-7451 2500
email library@royalsociety.org
website https://royalsociety.org
Facebook www.facebook.com/theroyalsociety
Twitter @royalsociety
President Sir Adrian Smith PRS, *Treasurer* Prof. Jonathan Keating FRS, *Biological Secretary* Dame Linda Partridge FRS, *Physical Secretary* Sir Peter Bruce FRS, *Foreign Secretary* Sir Robin Grimes FRS, *Executive Director* Dame Julie Maxton

The independent scientific academy of the UK and the Commonwealth, dedicated to promoting excellence in science and science writing.

Royal Society of Arts

8 John Adam Street, London WC2N 6EZ
tel 020-7930 5115
email general@rsa.org.uk
website www.thersa.org
Facebook www.facebook.com/theRSAorg
Twitter @theRSAorg
Instagram @thersaorg

The RSA works to remove barriers to social progress, driving ideas, innovation and social change through an ambitious programme of projects, events and lectures. Supported by Fellows, an international network of influencers and innovators from every field and background across the UK and overseas. Welcomes people of any nationality and background who will support the organisation's aims. Founded 1754.

Royal Society of British Artists

email info@royalsocietyofbritishartists.org.uk
website www.royalsocietyofbritishartists.org.uk
Facebook www.facebook.com/
RoyalSocietyBritishArtists
Twitter @RoyalSocBritArt
Instagram @royal_society_british_artists
Honorary Secretary Brenda Davies

Incorporated by Royal Charter for the purpose of encouraging the study and practice of the arts of painting, sculpture, drawing and printmaking. The RBA Annual Exhibition at the Mall Galleries, The Mall, London SW1 is open to non-member artists, with many awards offered to both members and non-members. In partnership with The Arts Society, work from younger artists is also encouraged, and the work of 20 A-level students, the RBA Star Students, is included in the exhibition. Also offers a month-long Rome Scholarship, as well as other awards and the possibility of exhibiting work in the RBA Rising Stars exhibition in central London for artists aged 35 or under.

Royal Society of Literature

Somerset House, Strand, London WC2R 1LA
tel 020-7845 4679
email info@rsliterature.org
website www.rsliterature.org
Facebook www.facebook.com/RoyalSocietyLiterature
Twitter @RSLiterature
Instagram @royalsocietyofliterature
President Bernardine Evaristo
Membership £60 p.a. or £40 for those aged 18–30 (fees decrease by £10 after the first year)

The RSL is the UK's charity for the advancement of literature. It acts as a voice for the value of literature, engages people in appreciating literature, and encourages and honours writers through its events programme, awards and prizes and outreach programme. The Benson medal and title Companion of Literature are awarded to recognise excellence in writing. Founded 1820.

Royal Society of Marine Artists

17 Carlton House Terrace, London SW1Y 5BD
tel 020-7930 6844
email rsma.contact@gmail.com
website www.rsma.org

The aim of the society is to promote and encourage the highest standards of marine art. Welcomes submissions for their Annual Open Exhibition at the Mall Galleries, The Mall, London SW1, which is usually held from late September (more information at www.mallgalleries.org.uk). Membership is achieved by a consistent record of success in having work selected and hung at this event and ultimately by election by the members.

The Royal Society of Miniature Painters, Sculptors and Gravers

email info@royal-miniature-society.org.uk
website www.royal-miniature-society.org.uk
Facebook www.facebook.com/RoyalMiniatureSociety
Twitter @royalminiature
Instagram @royalminiature
Executive Secretary Claire Hucker
Membership By selection and standard of work over a period of years (ARMS associate, RMS full member)

An open Exhibition is held annually at the Bankside Gallery, Thames Riverside, 48 Hopton Street, London SE1 9JH. For online submission details see the website. Applications and enquiries to the Executive Secretary. Granted Royal Charter in 1905. Founded 1896.

Royal Society of Painter-Printmakers (RE)

Bankside Gallery, 48 Hopton Street, London SE1 9JH
tel 020-7928 7521
email info@re-printmakers.com
website www.re-printmakers.com
President Prof. David Ferry

Promotes all forms of printmaking. Election of Associates is held annually; for details check the website. New members are elected by the council based on the quality of their work alone, in a tradition reaching back over 100 years. Three members' exhibitions per year are held at Bankside Gallery, plus open submission printmaking exhibitions. Founded 1880.

Royal Society of Portrait Painters

17 Carlton House Terrace, London SW1Y 5BD
tel 020-7930 6844
email info@mallgalleries.com
website www.therp.co.uk
website www.mallgalleries.org.uk

Upholds the values and practices of the discipline, and seeks to explore and develop new artistic models and perspectives. Annual Exhibition at Mall Galleries, The Mall, London SW1, of members' work and work drawn from an open selection. Runs a programme of annual awards. Provides consultancy to those wishing to commission a portrait. Founded 1891.

Royal Society of Sculptors

Dora House, 108 Old Brompton Road, London SW7 3RA
tel 020-7373 8615
email info@sculptors.org.uk
website www.sculptors.org.uk

An artist-led membership organisation which supports and connects sculptors throughout their careers and offers exhibitions, artists' talks, creative workshops and events.

Royal Watercolour Society

Bankside Gallery, 48 Hopton Street, London SE1 9JH
tel 020-7928 7521
email info@royalwatercoloursociety.com
website www.royalwatercoloursociety.co.uk
Facebook www.facebook.com/
RoyalWatercolourSociety
Twitter @RWS_Art

An artist-led society whose members work in a variety of media including gouache, acrylic, pen and ink, pigment, collage and mixed media as well as traditional watercolour. Promotes, by example and education, the understanding, appreciation and enjoyment of these media. The RWS Open invites submissions from artists at all stages of their careers, winners receive the Young Artists Award which allows them to exhibit and promote their work through the society for two years. Membership by election. Founded 1804.

Royal West of England Academy

Queens Road, Clifton, Bristol BS8 1PX
tel 0117 973 5129
email info@rwa.org.uk
website www.rwa.org.uk
Director Alison Bevan

The RWA, Bristol's first art gallery, brings world-class visual art from across the globe to the South West. Its vision is to be the region's leading centre for the exhibition, exploration and practice of the visual arts, recognised as a place that enriches the lives of people from all communities and backgrounds.
Founded 1844.

COPYRIGHT AND LICENSING

Australian Copyright Council

PO Box 1986, Strawberry Hills, NSW 2012, Australia
tel +61 (0)2 9101 2377
email info@copyright.org.au
website www.copyright.org.au
Facebook www.facebook.com/AusCopyrightCouncil
Twitter @AusCopyright
Instagram @AusCopyrightCouncil
Chief Executive Officer Eileen Camilleri

Provides easily accessible and affordable practical information, legal advice, education and forums on Australian copyright law for content creators and consumers. It represents the peak bodies for professional artists and content creators working in Australia's creative industries and Australia's major copyright collecting societies, including the Australian Society of Authors, the Australian Writers' Guild and the Australian Publishers Association.

The Council advocates for the contribution of creators to Australia's culture and economy and the importance of copyright for the common good. It works to promote understanding of copyright law and its application, advocate for appropriate law reform and foster collaboration between content creators and consumers. Founded 1968.

Authors' Licensing and Collecting Society Ltd – see page 718

British Copyright Council

1st Floor, Goldings House, 2 Hayes Lane,
London SE1 2BH
email info@britishcopyright.org
website www.britishcopyright.org
Twitter @BritCopyright
Vice-President Geoffrey Adams, *President of Honour* Maureen Duffy, *Chairman* Trevor Cook

Defends and fosters the true principles of copyright and its acceptance throughout the world; brings together bodies representing all who are interested in the protection of such copyright; and keeps watch on any legal or other changes which may require an amendment of the law.

Copyright Clearance Center Inc.

222 Rosewood Drive, Danvers, MA 01923, USA
email info@copyright.com
website www.copyright.com
Facebook www.facebook.com/CopyrightClear
Twitter @copyrightclear

Aims to remove the complexity from copyright issues and make it easy for businesses and academic institutions to use copyright-protected materials while compensating publishers and content creators for their work.

The Copyright Licensing Agency Ltd – see page 716

DACS (Design and Artists Copyright Society) – see page 720

FACT

Regal House, 70 London Road, Twickenham,
Middlesex TW1 3QS
tel 020-8891 1217
email contact@fact-uk.org.uk
website www.fact-uk.org.uk
Twitter @factuk

The Federation Against Copyright Theft protects the content, product and interests of the film and television broadcasting industries and is regarded as the leader in intellectual property protection.
Founded 1983.

The Irish Copyright Licensing Agency

63 Patrick Street, Dun Laoghaire, Dublin A96 WF25,
Republic of Ireland

tel +353 (0)1 662 4211
email info@icla.ie
website www.icla.ie
Executive Director Samantha Holman

Licenses schools, higher education institutions and other users of copyright material to copy, reuse and share extracts of such material, and distributes the monies collected to the authors and publishers whose works have been copied. Founded 1992.

PICSEL (Picture Industry Collecting Society for Effective Licensing)

112 Western Road, Brighton, East Sussex BN1 2AB
tel 07377 535095
email info@picsel.org.uk
website www.picsel.org.uk

A not-for-profit collecting society that ensures that all visual artists, creators and representative rights holders of images receive fair payment for various secondary uses of their works, following the initial publication, such as copying pages from books and magazines for use in schools and universities. It works to ensure that all licence fees collected are distributed equitably, efficiently and in a transparent manner. Founded 2016.

EDITORIAL, JOURNALISM AND BROADCASTING

American Society for Indexing

1628 E. Southern Ave. 9–223, Tempe, AZ 85282, USA
tel +1 480-245-6750
email info@asindexing.org
website www.asindexing.org
Facebook www.facebook.com/asindexing
Twitter @ASIndexing
Executive Director Gwen Henson

Increases awareness of the value of high-quality indexes and indexing; offers members access to educational resources that enable them to strengthen their indexing performance; keeps members up to date on indexing technology; advocates for the professional interests of indexers.

Association of Freelance Editors, Proofreaders and Indexers of Ireland

email info@afepi-ireland.com
website www.afepi-ireland.com
Facebook www.facebook.com/AFEPI.Ireland
Twitter @AFEPI_Ireland

AFEPI Ireland is a professional organisation for publishing and editorial freelancers in Ireland. It fosters high standards in editing, proofreading and indexing; protects the interests of its members; and helps to match authors, indie writers, publishers, businesses, public bodies and charitable organisations with suitable editorial freelancers. Membership is available to experienced professional editors, proofreaders and indexers. For services for publishers and authors, see the online directory of freelance professional editors, proofreaders and indexers based in Ireland and Northern Ireland. Founded 1985.

British Association of Journalists

PO Box 742, Winchester SO23 3QB
email office@bajunion.org.uk
website www.bajunion.org.uk
General Secretary Matthew Myatt

Non-political trade union for professional journalists. Aims to protect and promote the industrial and professional interests of journalists. Founded 1992.

British Guild of Agricultural Journalists

444 Westwood Heath Road, Coventry CV4 8AA
tel 07584 022909
email secretary@gaj.org.uk
website www.gaj.org.uk
Twitter @gajinfo
President Baroness Boycott, *Chairman* Catherine Linch, *General Secretary* Nikki Robertson
Membership £78 p.a. (full membership); £39 (retired/student membership)

Promotes high standards among journalists, photographers and communicators who specialise in agriculture, horticulture, food production and other rural affairs, and contributes towards a better understanding of agriculture. Founded 1944.

British Society of Magazine Editors

4 Conway Road, London N14 7BA
tel 020-8906 4664
email admin@bsme.com
website www.bsme.com
Twitter @bsmeinfo
Instagram @_bsme

The only society in the UK exclusively for magazine and digital editors. Represents the needs and views of editors and acts as a voice for the industry.

The Chartered Institute of Journalists

PO Box 765, Waltham Abbey EN8 1NT
tel 020-7252 1187
email memberservices@cioj.org
website https://cioj.org
Twitter @CIoJournalist

The senior organisation of the profession, the Chartered Institute is an independent organisation that promotes standards and ethics. There are three parts to the work carried out on behalf of members: professional, charitable and trade union. Founded 1884.

CIEP (Chartered Institute of Editing and Proofreading)

8 Devonshire Square, London EC2M 4YJ
tel 020-8785 6155

email office@ciep.uk
website www.ciep.uk
Facebook www.facebook.com/EditProof
Twitter @The_CIEP

A membership organisation promoting excellence in English language editing, and setting and demonstrating editorial standards. It is a community, training hub and support network for editorial professionals – the people who work to make text accurate, clear and fit for purpose. The CIEP runs online courses and workshops in copy-editing, proofreading and related skills, for people starting an editorial career and those wishing to broaden their competence. Its also maintains an online directory of experienced editorial professionals. In addition to providing professional training, the CIEP publishes factsheets and guides on various aspects of editing and business skills for the self-employed. The CIEP was known as the Society for Editors and Proofreaders before being awarded its Royal Charter in 2019.

Editors' and Proofreaders' Alliance of Northern Ireland

email info@epani.org.uk
website www.epani.org.uk
Twitter @epa_ni
Coordinator Averill Buchanan

Establishes and maintains high professional standards in editorial skills in Northern Ireland. For services for authors, see the directory of freelance professional editors, proofreaders and indexers.

European Broadcasting Union

L'Ancienne Route 17A, Postal Box 45,
CH–1218 Grand-Saconnex, Geneva, Switzerland
tel +41 (0)22-717 2111
email info@ebu.ch
website www.ebu.ch
Twitter @EBU_HQ
Director General Noel Curran

EBU is the world's foremost alliance of public service media (PSM). Its mission is to make PSM indispensable. It has 112 members in 56 countries, and an additional 30 associates in Asia, Africa, Australasia and the Americas. Members operate nearly 2,000 television, radio and online channels and services, broadcasting in more than 160 different languages. Together they reach audiences of more than one billion people around the world. EBU's television and radio services operate under the trademarks of Eurovision and Euroradio.

Foreign Press Association in London

Overseas House, Royal Overseas League, Park Place,
St James's Street, London SW1A 1NN
tel 020-7792 4565
email accreditation@fpalondon.org
website www.fpalondon.org
Facebook www.facebook.com/foreignpressassociation
Twitter @FPALondon
Director Deborah Bonetti

The oldest and largest association of foreign journalists in the world. All major international news outlets are represented. Provides access and accreditation to a wide variety of events in the UK, and provides access to Parliament, N10 and the Royal Palaces. Organises press trips and briefings with ministers and leading figures in all departments. The FPA is one of the gatekeepers of the UK Press Card Authority (PCA) and provides UK Press Cards to bona fide international journalists. Founded 1888.

Independent Press Standards Organisation

Gate House, 1 Farringdon Street, London EC4M 7LG
tel 0300 123 2220
email inquiries@ipso.co.uk
website www.ipso.co.uk
Facebook www.facebook.com/ipsonews
Twitter @IpsoNews

IPSO is the independent regulator of the newspaper and magazine industry. It exists to promote and uphold the highest professional standards of journalism in the UK and to support members of the public in seeking redress where they believe that the Editors' Code of Practice has been breached.

Journalists' Charity

11 Ribblesdale, Roman Road, Dorking,
Surrey RH4 3EX
tel (01306) 887511
email enquiries@journalistscharity.org.uk
website https://journalistscharity.org.uk
Facebook www.facebook.com/journalistscharity
Twitter @JournoCharity
Ceo James Brindle

For the relief of hardship amongst journalists, their widows/widowers and dependants. Financial assistance and retirement housing are provided. Founded 1864.

The Media Society

Broadgate Tower, 3rd Floor, 20 Primrose Street,
London EC2A 2RS
email admin@themediasociety.com
website www.themediasociety.com/index.php
Honorary President Peter York
Membership £45 p.a., £10 p.a. students

Exists to promote and encourage collective and independent research into the standards, performance, organisation and economics of the media and to hold regular discussions and debates on subjects of topical or special interest and concern to print and broadcast journalists and others working in or with the media. Up to 22 evening debates and events organised throughout the year. From 2023, a return to physical venues has been interspersed with online events, which are subsequently made available in video format online. Also publishes up to six newsletters each year. Founded 1973.

National Council for the Training of Journalists

The New Granary, Station Road, Newport, Essex CB11 3PL
tel (01799) 544014
email info@nctj.com
website www.nctj.com
Facebook www.facebook.com/nctjpage
Twitter @NCTJ_news

The NCTJ is a registered charity and awarding body which provides multimedia journalism training. Full-time accredited courses run at various colleges, universities and independent providers in the UK. Distance learning programmes and short courses are also available. Founded 1951.

National Union of Journalists

72 Acton Street, London WC1X 9NB
tel 020-7843 3700
email info@nuj.org.uk
website www.nuj.org.uk
Facebook www.facebook.com/groups/nujournalists
Twitter @NUJofficial

Trade union for journalists and photographers, including freelances, in the UK, Republic of Ireland, Paris, Brussels and the Netherlands. It covers the newspaper press, news agencies, magazines, broadcasting, periodical and book publishing, public relations departments and consultancies, information services and new media. The NUJ mediates disputes, organises campaigns, provides training and general and legal advice. Official publications: *The Journalist* (bi-monthly), e-newsletters *NUJ Branch* and *NUJ Informed*, the online *Freelance Directory* and *Freelance Fees Guide*, the *NUJ Ethical Code of Conduct* and policy pamphlets and submissions.

News Media Association

c/o 2nd Floor, 55 Ludgate Hill, London EC4M 7JW
tel 020-3848 9620
email nma@newsmediauk.org
website www.newsmediauk.org
Twitter @newsmediaorg

Promotes the interests of news media publishers to government, regulatory authorities, industry bodies and other organisations whose work affects the industry.

Reporters Without Borders

CS 90247, 75083 Paris Cedex 02, France
tel +33 (0)1 4483 8484
email secretariat@rsf.org
website https://rsf.org/en
Facebook www.facebook.com/Reporterssansfrontieres
Twitter @RSF_en

Provides information on the media freedom situation worldwide and issues regular press releases about abuses against journalists and about different kinds of censorship. It also protects journalists and bloggers in danger, acts as a pressure group and publishes the World Press Freedom Index. Its main activities are advocacy, awareness campaigns, assistance and legal aid and cyber-security. Founded 2014.

Scottish Newspaper Society

17 Polwarth Grove, Edinburgh EH11 1LY
email info@scotns.org.uk
website www.scotns.org.uk
Represents and safeguards the interests of the Scottish newspaper industry, to maintain press freedom and improve the industry's profile. Founded 2009.

Society of Editors

Stationers Hall, Ave Maria Lane, London EC4M 7DD
tel 07599 954636
email office@societyofeditors.org
website www.societyofeditors.org
President Kamal Ahmed

Formed from the merger of the Guild of Editors and the Association of British Editors, it has members in national, regional and local newspapers, magazines, broadcasting and digital media, journalism, education and media law. It campaigns for media freedom, self regulation, the public's right to know and the maintenance of standards in journalism.

Society of Indexers – see page 650

Society of Women Writers & Journalists

42 Brookside Avenue, Polegate, Eastbourne, East Sussex BN26 6DH
email ourswwj@gmail.com
website www.swwj.co.uk
Facebook www.facebook.com/societyofwomenwriters
Twitter @SWWJ

The SWWJ aims to encourage literary achievement, to uphold professional standards, to promote social contact with fellow writers and to defend the dignity and prestige of the writing profession in all its aspects. Advocates for equal opportunities, recognition and remuneration for women. Full and Associate members can now use the appropriate post-nominals (e.g., MSWWJ and FSWWJ) after their name and receive a press card. See website for a full list of benefits and information. Founded 1894.

Sports Journalists' Association

tel 020-8916 2234
email info@sportjournalists.co.uk
website www.sportsjournalists.co.uk
Facebook www.facebook.com/sportsjournalistsGB/
Twitter @SportSJA

The SJA represents sports journalists across the country and is Britain's voice in international sporting affairs. Offers advice to members covering major events and acts as a consultant to organisers of major sporting events on media requirements. Member of the BOA Press Advisory Committee. Founded 1948.

Voice of the Listener & Viewer

The Old Rectory Business Centre, Springhead Road, Northfleet DA11 8HN
tel (01474) 338716
email info@vlv.org.uk
website www.vlv.org.uk
Facebook www.facebook.com/VLVUK
Twitter @vlvuk
Administrator Lucy Regan
Membership From £30 p.a.; academic, corporate and student rates available

VLV's mission is to campaign for accountability, diversity and excellence in UK broadcasting, seeking to sustain and strengthen public service broadcasting to the benefit of civil society and democracy in the UK. It holds regular conferences and seminars and publishes a bulletin and an e-newsletter. Founded 1983.

Yachting Journalists' Association

website www.yja.world
Honorary President Chris English, *Chairman* Clifford Webb
Membership £50 p.a. (£45 p.a. if paid by Standing Order)

Promotes greater awareness of all aspects of leisure boating through the professional services offered by its members. Represents hundreds of specialist marine journalists, photographers, TV and radio presenters, and web editors across all major sailing and boating regions in the world. Members vote annually for the Yachtsman of the Year and the Young Sailor of the Year Award and host several important functions annually on both the British and international maritime calendar. Founded 1955.

LITERACY

BookTrust

G8 Battersea Studios, 80 Silverthorne Road, London SW8 3HE
tel 020-7801 8800
email query@booktrust.org.uk
website www.booktrust.org.uk
Twitter @Booktrust
Ceo Diana Gerald, *Chair of Trustees* John Coughlan

The UK's largest children's reading charity, dedicated to getting children reading because children who read are happier, healthier, more empathetic and more creative; they also do better at school. BookTrust reviews at least one children's book each day and runs the Waterstones Children's Laureate, BookTrust Storytime Prize and BookTrust Lifetime Achievement Award.

Children's Books Ireland

17 North Great George's Street, Dublin D01 R2F1, Republic of Ireland
tel +353 (0)1 872 7475
email info@childrensbooksireland.com
website www.childrensbooksireland.ie
Ceo Elaina Ryan, *Deputy Ceo* Jenny Murray, *Programme & Events Manager* Aoife Murray

Champions every child's right to develop a love of reading. They aim to engage young people in reading, foster a greater understanding of books for young people and act as a core resource for those with an interest in books for children in Ireland. Celebrates the importance of authors and illustrators and work in partnership with the people and organisations who enhance children's lives through books.

Forward Arts Foundation

tel 020-8187 9861
email info@forwardartsfoundation.org
website www.forwardartsfoundation.org

Promotes appreciation and engagement with poetry through programmes and initiatives that run throughout the year. As well as advocating for the positive social impact of poetry and growing poetry audiences, the Foundation supports and celebrates poets, works closely with schools and libraries, organises National Poetry Day each year and runs the Forward Prizes for Poetry.

LoveReading4Kids

157 Shooters Hill, London SE18 3HP
tel 020-3004 7204
website www.lovereading4kids.co.uk
Facebook www.facebook.com/lovereading4kids
Twitter @lovereadingkids

A book recommendation site for children's books ranging from toddlers to teens. Ensures that whatever their age or interest, there is a steady stream of book recommendations available. Offers a variety of free services for parents and anyone who is interested in buying the best books for children. Supports parents, teachers and school librarians in helping engender a lifelong love of reading in children. The website features Kids' Zone, an area designed specifically for children, with competitions, quizzes and book-related material.

National Literacy Trust

68 South Lambeth Road, London SW8 1RL
tel 020-7587 1842
email contact@literacytrust.org.uk
website https://literacytrust.org.uk
Facebook www.facebook.com/nationalliteracytrust
Twitter @Literacy_Trust
Instagram @literacy_trust

An independent charity that helps change lives through literacy. It campaigns to improve public understanding of the importance of literacy, as well as delivering projects and working in partnership to reach those most in need of support.

Read for Good

26 Nailsworth Mills, Avening Road, Nailsworth, Glos. GL6 0BS
tel (01453) 839005
email reading@readforgood.org
website www.readforgood.org
Facebook www.facebook.com/readforgood
Twitter @ReadforGoodUK
Instagram @readforgood

The charity wants all children and young people in the UK to be able to develop a life-long love of reading, positively shaping their futures and creating a more equal society. The charity runs Readathon and Track My Read programmes in thousands of schools, motivating children to read for pleasure. The Read for Good in Hospitals programme provides a regular supply of books and storyteller visits to children in the UK's major children's hospitals.

The Reading Agency

24 Bedford Row, London WC1R 4EH
tel 07933 181889
email info@readingagency.org.uk
website www.readingagency.org.uk
Facebook www.facebook.com/readingagency
Twitter @readingagency
Instagram @readingagency

A charity whose mission is to tackle life's big challenges through the proven power of reading. Works closely with public libraries, publishers, health partners and volunteers to bring reading programmes to adults and young people across the UK. Funded by Arts Council England, it supports a wide range of reading initiatives for adults and young people including Reading Ahead, designed to build people's reading confidence and motivation, and World Book Night, an annual celebration of books and reading which takes place on 23 April. The Reading Friends programme tackles loneliness and isolation among older people by starting conversations through reading.

Scottish Book Trust

Sandeman House, Trunk's Close, 55 High Street, Edinburgh EH1 1SR
tel 0131 524 0160
email info@scottishbooktrust.com
website www.scottishbooktrust.com
Facebook www.facebook.com/scottishbktrust
Twitter @ScottishBkTrust

Scotland's national agency for the promotion of reading, writing and literature. Programmes include: Bookbug, a free universal book-gifting programme which encourages families to read with their children from birth; an ambitious schools programme including national tours; the virtual events programme Authors Live; the Live Literature funding programme, a national initiative enabling Scottish citizens to engage with authors, playwrights, poets, storytellers and illustrators; a writer development programme, offering mentoring and professional development for emerging and established writers; and a readership development programme featuring a national writing campaign, as well as Book Week Scotland, during the last week in November. Founded 1998.

Seven Stories – The National Centre for Children's Books

30 Lime Street, Ouseburn Valley, Newcastle upon Tyne NE1 2PQ
tel 0300 330 1095
email info@sevenstories.org.uk
website www.sevenstories.org.uk
Facebook www.facebook.com/7stories
Twitter @7stories
Instagram @7stories

Champions the art of children's books to ensure its place as an integral part of childhood and national cultural life. The world of children's books is celebrated through unique exhibitions, events for all ages and a national archive. The work of over 200 British authors and illustrators, including Judith Kerr, Enid Blyton, Michael Morpurgo and David Almond is cared for in the archive collection – and it is still growing. Seven Stories is a charity – all the money earned and raised is used to save, celebrate and share children's books so that future generations can enjoy Britain's rich literary heritage. Arts Council England and Newcastle Culture Investment Fund regularly fund Seven Stories' work, giving children's literature status and establishing new ways of engaging young audiences. Founded 1996.

Story Therapy

1 Sugworth Lane, Radley, Abingdon-on-Thames, Oxon OX14 2HZ
email admin@storytherapyresources.co.uk
website www.storytherapyresources.co.uk
Facebook www.facebook.com/storytherapy
Twitter @StoryTherapy
Contact Hilary Hawkes

A non-profit social enterprise creating stories and resources, especially story-themed resources, that support children's emotional health and mental wellbeing. Founded 2016.

LIBRARIES AND INFORMATION

Campaign for Freedom of Information

email admin@cfoi.org.uk
website www.cfoi.org.uk
Facebook www.facebook.com/CampaignFOI
Twitter @CampaignFOI

A non-profit organisation working to defend and improve public access to official information and to ensure that the Freedom of Information Act is implemented effectively. Advises members of the public about their rights to information under FOI and related laws, helps people challenge unreasonable refusals to disclose information, encourages good practice by public authorities and provides FOI training.

CILIP (The Library and Information Association)

Room 150 British Library, 96 Euston Road, London NW1 2DB
tel 020-8159 4925
website www.cilip.org.uk
Facebook www.facebook.com/CILIPinfo
Twitter @CILIPinfo
Membership Varies according to level and income

The leading professional body open to librarians, information specialists, knowledge managers and non-practitioner supporters, with members in the UK and internationally. CILIP's objective is to put library and information skills at the heart of a democratic, equal and prosperous information society.

English Association

University Road, Leicester LE1 7RH
email hello@englishassociation.ac.uk
website www.englishassociation.ac.uk
President Rob Penman

Both a membership association and a learned society for people passionate about English language, literature and creative writing. Brings together individuals and organisations with a wealth of expertise from all sectors of education and all areas of English studies, and has a long history of engagement with national and international bodies. The elective Fellowship recognises outstanding achievement in English studies, and Officers and Committee members are leaders in their field. Through a large portfolio of publications, an events programme, networking and campaigning, the Association has shaped the discipline, and continues to connect English teachers in schools, colleges and universities. Founded 1906.

English Speaking Board (International)

tel (01695) 573439
email customer@esbuk.org
website https://esbuk.org/web/
Facebook www.facebook.com/
EnglishSpeakingBoardUK/
Twitter @ESBUK

An internationally accredited awarding organisation with a mission to promote clear, effective communication at all levels by providing high-quality speech and language qualifications. ESB

International's range of assessments support learners to possess the oracy and English language skills they need in order to achieve their aspirations. The 70/70 campaign aims to close the disadvantage gap in accessing qualifications.

Offers an extensive portfolio of speech qualifications including a new speech pathways qualification which gives greater flexibility to learners. These qualifications are designed for schools who wish to use spoken language to raise pupil achievement and develop enrichment programmes. ESOL Skills for Life and ESOL international qualifications are also accessible for individuals for whom English is not a first language. Centres may be eligible for financial support through its Christabel Burniston Fund.

The English-Speaking Union

Dartmouth House, 37 Charles Street, London W1J 5ED
tel 020-7529 1550
email esu@esu.org
website www.esu.org

An educational charity and membership organisation that promotes international understanding and tolerance through widening the use of the English language throughout the world. Runs programmes, competitions and exchanges to give young people the speaking and listening skills and the cross-cultural understanding they need to thrive. Members contribute to its work across the world. Founded 1918.

Institute of Internal Communication

Scorpio House, Rockingham Drive, Linford Wood, Milton Keynes MK14 6LY
tel (01908) 232168
email enquiries@ioic.org.uk
website www.ioic.org.uk

As the only professional body dedicated to internal communication in the UK, it exists to help organisations and people succeed through promoting internal communication of the highest standard. Founded 1949.

Private Libraries Association

29 Eden Drive, Hull HU8 8JQ
email maslen@maslen.karoo.co.uk
website www.plabooks.org
President Matthew Haley, *Honorary Secretary* Jim Maslen, *Honorary Journal Editors* David Chambers, David Butcher, James Freemantle
Membership £30 p.a.

International society of book collectors and lovers of books. Publications include *The Private Library* (quarterly), *Private Press Books* (annual), and other books on book collecting. Founded 1956.

LITERARY

Alliance of Literary Societies

email allianceoflitsocs@gmail.com
website www.allianceofliterarysocieties.wordpress.com
President James Naughtie

An umbrella organisation of about 100 literary societies which aims to act as a valuable liaison body between member societies to share knowledge, skills and expertise, and also acts as a pressure group when necessary. The Alliance can assist in the preservation of buildings, places and objects which have literary associations. Its publications include a twice-yearly newsletter and an annual journal, *ALSo*. The ALS holds an annual literary weekend hosted by a different member society each year.

Association for Scottish Literature

c/o Dept of Scottish Literature,
University of Glasgow, 7 University Gardens,
Glasgow G12 8QH
tel 0141 330 5309
email office@asls.org.uk
website www.asls.org.uk
President David Goldie, *Secretary* Moira Hansen,
Director Duncan Jones
Membership £65 p.a. individuals; £18 p.a. UK students; £100 p.a. corporate

Promotes the study, teaching and writing of Scottish literature and furthers the study of the languages of Scotland. Publishes annually *New Writing Scotland*, an anthology of new Scottish writing; an edited text of Scottish literature; a series of academic journals; and the eZine *The Bottle Imp*. Also publishes *Scotnotes* (comprehensive study guides for major Scottish writers), literary texts and commentaries designed to assist the classroom teacher, and a series of occasional papers. Organises two conferences a year. Founded 1970.

The Jane Austen Society

20 Parsonage Road, Henfield, West Sussex BN5 9JG
email hq@jasoc.org.uk
website https://.janeaustensociety.org.uk
Membership £28 p.a.; £33 p.a. joint; £12 p.a. student (UK); £38 p.a. overseas; £43 p.a joint overseas; £50 p.a. corporate

The Society fosters the appreciation and study of the work, life and times of Jane Austen (1775–1817), and the Austen family. Regular publications, meetings and conferences; ten branches and groups in UK. Founded 1940.

The Beckford Society

The Timber Cottage, Crockerton,
Warminster BA12 8AX
tel (01985) 213195
email sidney.blackmore@btinternet.com
website www.beckfordsociety.org
Membership from £30 p.a.

Promotes an interest in the life and works of William Beckford of Fonthill (1760–1844) and his circle. Encourages Beckford studies and scholarship through exhibitions, lectures and publications, including *The Beckford Journal* (annual) and occasional newsletters. Founded 1995.

Arnold Bennett Society

4 Field End Close, Trentham,
Stoke-on-Trent ST4 8DA
email arnoldbennettscty@btinternet.com
website www.arnoldbennettsociety.org.uk
Facebook www.facebook.com/arnoldbennettsociety
Twitter @BennettSoc
Chairman Professor Ray Johnson MBE
Membership £17.50 p.a. individuals; £20 p.a. family

Promotes the study and appreciation of the life, works and times not only of Arnold Bennett (1867–1931), but also of other provincial writers with a particular relationship to north Staffordshire.

The E.F. Benson Society

The Old Coach House, High Street, Rye,
East Sussex TN31 7JF
tel (01797) 223114
email info@efbensonsociety.org
website www.efbensonsociety.org
Secretary Allan Downend
Membership £12 p.a. single; £15 p.a. joint; £20 p.a. overseas

Promotes interest in the author E.F. Benson (1867–1940) and the Benson family. Arranges an annual literary evening, annual outing to Rye (July) and other places of Benson interest, talks on the Bensons and exhibitions. Archive includes the Austin Seckersen Collection, transcriptions of the Benson diaries and letters. Publishes postcards, anthologies of Benson's works, a Mary Benson biography, books on Benson and an annual journal, *The Dodo*. Also sells out-of-print Bensons to members. Founded 1984.

The Brontë Society

Brontë Parsonage Museum, Church Street, Haworth,
Keighley, West Yorkshire BD22 8DR
tel (01535) 642323
email bronte@bronte.org.uk
website www.bronte.org.uk
Twitter @bronteparsonage

The Society cares for and promotes the accredited collections and literary legacy of the Brontë family. It is an Arts Council National Portfolio Organisation and presents an exciting contemporary arts programme, alongside changing exhibitions and learning and engagement programmes. *Brontë Studies* and the *Brontë Gazette* are published three times a year. The museum is open Wednesday to Sunday all year round.

The Browning Society

64 Blythe Vale, London SE6 4NW
email browningsociety@hotmail.co.uk
website www.browningsociety.org
Honorary Secretary Jim Smith
Membership £20 p.a.

Aims to widen the appreciation and understanding of the lives and poetry of Robert Browning (1812–89) and Elizabeth Barrett Browning (1806–61), as well as other Victorian writers and poets. Founded 1881; refounded 1969.

The John Buchan Society

72 Ravensdowne, Berwick-upon-Tweed,
Northumberland TD15 1DQ
tel (01289) 302913
website www.johnbuchansociety.co.uk
Membership Secretary Alison Gallico
Membership £20 p.a. full; overseas and other rates on application

Promotes a wider understanding of the life and works of John Buchan (1875–1940). Encourages publication of Buchan's works and supports the John Buchan Story Museum in Peebles. Also holds regular meetings and social gatherings; produces a newsletter and a journal. Founded 1979.

Byron Society (Newstead Abbey)

Acushla, Halam Road, Southwell NG25 0AD
website www.newsteadabbeybyronsociety.org
Twitter @byron_society
Chairman Ken Purslow
Membership £30 p.a.

Promotes research into the life and works of Lord Byron (1788–1824) through seminars, discussions, lectures and readings. Publishes *The Newstead Review* (annual). Founded 1988.

The Lewis Carroll Society

email secretary@lewiscarrollsociety.org.uk
email membership@lewiscarrollsociety.org.uk
website https://lewiscarrollsociety.org.uk
Facebook www.facebook.com/groups/68678994062
Twitter @LewisCarrollSoc
Membership £25 p.a. UK; £30 p.a. Europe; £35 p.a. elsewhere; special rates for students and institutions

Promotes interest in the life and works of Lewis Carroll (Revd Charles Lutwidge Dodgson, 1832–98) and encourages research. Activities include regular meetings, exhibitions and a publishing programme that includes the first annotated, unexpurgated edition of his diaries in nine volumes, the society's journal *The Carrollian*, a newsletter, *Bandersnatch*, and the *Lewis Carroll Review*. An archive hosting 50 years of scholarly journals is available to members through an online portal. Founded 1969.

The John Clare Society

email sueholgate@hotmail.co.uk
website https://johnclaresociety.wordpress.com/

Membership UK: £15 p.a. individual; £20 p.a. joint; £5 p.a. student; Overseas: £20 p.a.

Promotes a wider appreciation of the life and works of the poet John Clare (1793–1864). Founded 1981.

The Wilkie Collins Society

email paul@paullewis.co.uk
website https://wilkiecollinssociety.org
Secretary Paul Lewis
Membership £16 p.a. EU; £28 p.a. international

Promotes interest in the life and works of Wilkie Collins (1824–89). Publishes a newsletter, an annual scholarly journal and reprints of Collins's lesser known works. Founded 1981.

The Joseph Conrad Society (UK)

c/o The Polish Social and Cultural Association,
238–246 King Street, London W6 0RF
email theconradian@aol.com
email hughepstein@hotmail.co.uk
website www.josephconradsociety.org
Chairman Robert Hampson, *Honorary Secretary* Hugh Epstein, *Advisory Editor* of *The Conradian* Allan H. Simmons

Activities include an annual international conference; publication of *The Conradian* and a series of pamphlets; administering the Juliet McLauchlan Prize, a £200 annual award for the winner of an essay competition; and offering resources and support to scholars. Founded 1973.

Dickens Fellowship

The Charles Dickens Museum, 48 Doughty Street,
London WC1N 2LX
email postbox@dickensfellowship.org
website www.dickensfellowship.org
Honorary Secretary Paul Graham
Membership £17 p.a.

Based in the house occupied by Charles Dickens (1812–70) during the period 1837–9. Publishes *The Dickensian* (three each year). Founded 1902.

The George Eliot Fellowship

website www.georgeeliot.org
Facebook www.facebook.com/TheGeorgeEliotFellowship
Twitter @GeorgeEliotLove
Chairman John Burton
Membership £18 p.a. (£15 p.a. concessions) individuals; £23 p.a. (£20 p.a. concessions) couples; £15 p.a. students (under 25)

Promotes an interest in the life and work of George Eliot (1819–80) and helps to extend her influence; arranges meetings, study days and conferences; produces an annual journal (*The George Eliot Review*), newsletters and other publications. Back numbers of all editions of the *George Eliot Review* are now online, via the website. Works closely with educational establishments in the Nuneaton area.

The Fellowship, with its sister charity, Griff Preservation Trust, intend to open a George Eliot Visitor Centre in the near future. Awards the annual George Eliot Fellowship Prize (£500) for an essay on Eliot's life or work, which must be previously unpublished and not exceed 4,000 words. Founded 1930.

The Folklore Society

50 Fitzroy Street, London W1T 5BT
tel 020-3915 3034
email thefolkloresociety@gmail.com
website www.folklore-society.com

Collection, recording and study of folklore. Founded 1878.

The Gaskell Society

37 Buckingham Drive, Knutsford, Cheshire WA16 8LH
tel (01565) 651761
email gaskellsociety@gmail.com
website www.gaskellsociety.co.uk
Facebook www.facebook.com/TheGaskellSociety
Twitter @GaskellSociety
Membership Secretary Jackie Tucker
Membership £23 p.a. UK; £28 p.a. joint/European/institution; £15 p.a. student in full-time education; £30 p.a. non-European

Promotes and encourages the study and appreciation of the work and life of Elizabeth Cleghorn Gaskell (1810–65). Holds regular meetings in Knutsford, London and Manchester; organises visits and residential conferences; produces an annual journal and bi-annual newsletters. Founded 1985.

Graham Greene Birthplace Trust

email secretary@grahamgreenebt.org
website https://grahamgreenebt.org
Facebook www.facebook.com/Graham-Greene-International-Festival-55327438605
Twitter @FestivalGreene
Membership £14, £19 and £22 p.a. for the UK, Europe and rest of world respectively; £38, £52 and £60 respectively for three years, all including the quarterly newsletter

Exists to study the life and the wide-ranging works (novels, stories, plays, films, non-fiction and journalism) of Graham Greene (1904–91). For over 20 years, the Trust has presented the popular and engaging Graham Greene International Festival. It publishes a quarterly newsletter, *A Sort of Newsletter*, available to Friends of the Trust, and organises the Graham Greene audio trails in Berkhamsted. It has a very active website and a presence on social media.

The Thomas Hardy Society

c/o Kingston Maurward College, Dorchester, Dorset DT2 8PY
tel 07867 666737
email info@hardysociety.org
website www.hardysociety.org
Membership £28 p.a. UK or £40 p.a. overseas for print and online journals; £20 p.a. UK and overseas for online only; £15 p.a. students for print and online journals; £10 p.a. students for online only

Promotes and celebrates the life and work of Thomas Hardy (1840–1928). Publishes *The Thomas Hardy Journal* (annual) and *The Hardy Society Journal* (two p.a.). Biennial conference and festival held in July and annual Study Day conference held every April, both in Dorchester. Regular events throughout the year, including the London Lecture, the Hardy Birthday Weekend and the Westminster Abbey wreath laying. Founded 1967.

The James Hilton Society

22 Well House, Woodmansterne Lane, Banstead, Surrey SM7 3AA
email info@jameshiltonsociety.co.uk
website www.jameshiltonsociety.co.uk
Chairman Richard Hughes
Membership £13 p.a.; £10 p.a. concessions; £18 p.a. overseas

Promotes interest in the life and work of novelist and scriptwriter James Hilton (1900–54). Publishes a newsletter three times a year and a bi-annual scholarly journal, and organises conferences. Founded 2000.

The Sherlock Holmes Society of London

email sherlockjournal@yahoo.com
website www.sherlock-holmes.org.uk
Press & Publicity Officer Roger Johnson

The Society is open to anyone with an interest in Sherlock Holmes, Dr John H. Watson and their world. A literary and social society, publishing a bi-annual scholarly journal and occasional papers, and holding meetings, dinners and excursions. Founded 1951.

Housman Society

Abberley Cottage, 7 Dowles Road, Bewdley DY12 2EJ
email info@housman-society.co.uk
website www.housman-society.co.uk
Twitter @housmansoc
Membership £15 p.a. UK; £20 p.a. overseas

Aims to foster interest in and promote knowledge of A.E. Housman (1859–1936) and his family. Sponsors various events at English literary festivals. Publishes an annual journal and bi-annual newsletter. Founded 1973.

Richard Jefferies Society

email richardjefferiessociety@btinternet.com
website www.richardjefferiessociety.org
Facebook www.facebook.com/groups/10150129529455538

Promotes interest in the works of Richard Jefferies, including encouraging reading and studying of his works. Hosts meetings, lectures and events; research is published in an annual journal alongside articles and book reviews; runs the Richard Jefferies Award and provides bursaries for related research projects. Founded 1950.

The Johnson Society

Johnson Birthplace Museum, Breadmarket Street, Lichfield, Staffs. WS13 6LG
email info@thejohnsonsociety.org.uk
website www.johnsonnew.wordpress.com
Twitter @SamJohnsonSoc
General Secretary Marilyn Davies

Aims to encourage interest in, and study of, the writings, life and times of Dr Samuel Johnson (1709–84); support the Samuel Johnson Birthplace Museum, by helping to maintain and enhance its contents; assist in preserving other physical memorials of Johnson and his contemporaries, including books, manuscripts, artefacts, buildings, statues, plaques and Johnson's Willow. Publishes *Transactions* annually. Founded 1910.

Johnson Society of London

email memsec@johnsonsocietyoflondon.org
website www.johnsonsocietyoflondon.org
Membership £25 p.a. individual; £30 p.a. joint; £20 p.a. student

Promotes the study of the life and works of Dr Johnson (1709–84) and perpetuates his memory in the city of his adoption. Founded 1928.

Keats–Shelley Memorial Association

KSMA Registered Office, 11 Staple Inn, London WC1V 7QH
email hello@keats-shelley.org
website www.keats-shelley.org
Facebook www.facebook.com/keatsshelleyhouse
Twitter @Keats_Shelley

Owns and supports the house in Rome where John Keats died in 1821. Since 1909, a museum open to the public celebrates the poets Keats (1795–1821), Shelley (1792–1822), Lord Byron (1788–1824) and the novelist Mary Shelley (1797–1851). Regular events, bursaries for young scholars, bi-annual *Keats–Shelley Review* and online resources. The Keats–Shelley Memorial Association runs the annual Keats–Shelley Prize and the Young Romantics Prize, open to young writers aged 16–18. Founded 1903.

The Kipling Society

Bay Tree House, Doomsday Garden, Horsham, West Sussex RH13 6LB
email michaelrkipling@gmail.com
website www.kiplingsociety.co.uk
Chairman Dr Alex Bubb
Membership £29 p.a. UK; £31 p.a. Europe; £35 p.a. R.O.W; £10 p.a. student

Encourages discussion and study of the work and life of Rudyard Kipling (1865–1936) by assisting in the study of his writings, holding discussion meetings, publishing a quarterly journal and website (with a Readers' Guide to Kipling's work), maintaining a Kipling Library at Haileybury School in Hertfordshire and running an annual writing competition.

The Charles Lamb Society

BM-ELIA, London WC1N 3XX
email h.goodman@bathspa.ac.uk
website www.charleslambsociety.com
Chair Felicity James, *Membership Secretary* Helen Goodman
Membership £24/$45 p.a. individual; £32 p.a. couple; £5/$10 student/early career; £32/$60 p.a. corporate

Publishes the academic journal *The Charles Lamb Bulletin* (twice a year). The Society's extensive library of books and MSS by and about Charles Lamb (1775–1834) is housed at the Guildhall Library, Aldermanbury, London EC2P 2EJ. Founded 1935.

The D.H. Lawrence Society

tel (01530) 270367
email brenda.sumner@gmail.com
website www.dhlawrencesociety.com
Facebook www.facebook.com/dhlawrencesociety/
Twitter @DHLawrenceSoc
Chairman Alan Wilson, *Treasurer* Sheila Bamford, *Secretary* Brenda Sumner
Membership £20 p.a. standard; £22 p.a. overseas; £18 p.a. concessions/students

Aims to bring together people interested in D.H. Lawrence (1885–1930), to encourage study of his work, and to provide information and guides for people visiting Eastwood. Founded 1974.

The T.E. Lawrence Society

PO Box 728, Oxford OX2 9ZJ
email chairman@telsociety.org.uk
website www.telsociety.org.uk
Membership £24 p.a. UK; £32 p.a. overseas

Promotes the memory of T.E. Lawrence (1888–1935) and furthers education and knowledge by research into his life; publishes a journal (bi-annual) and newsletter (three p.a.). Founded 1985.

The Marlowe Society

email marlowe.society.uk.chair@gmail.com
website www.marlowe-society.org
Facebook www.facebook.com/marlowesociety/
Twitter @MarloweSociety_

Aims to extend appreciation and widen recognition of Christopher Marlowe (1564–93) as the foremost poet and dramatist preceding Shakespeare, whose development he influenced. Founded 1955.

The John Masefield Society

email thejohnmasefieldsociety@hotmail.com
website www.johnmasefieldsociety.org
Membership £5 p.a.; £10 p.a. overseas; £8 p.a. family/institution

Societies, prizes and festivals

Promotes the life and works of the poet John Masefield (1878–1967). Maintains an archive and library located in Ledbury; holds an annual lecture and other, less formal, readings and gatherings; publishes an annual journal and frequent newsletters. Founded 1992.

William Morris Society
Kelmscott House, 26 Upper Mall, London W6 9TA
tel 020-8741 3735
website www.williammorrissociety.org
Twitter @WmMorrisSocUK
Honorary Secretary Frances Graupner

Spreads knowledge of the life, work and ideas of William Morris (1834–96); publishes a magazine (three each year) and an academic journal (two each year). Visit the website for details of how to join the society or access the library, archive and collections. Founded 1955.

The Edith Nesbit Society
21 Churchfields, West Malling, Kent ME19 6RJ
email edithnesbit@gmail.com
website www.edithnesbit.co.uk
Membership £10 p.a. individual; £12 p.a. joint; £15 p.a. organisations

Promotes an interest in the life and works of Edith Nesbit (1858–1924) by means of talks, a regular newsletter and other publications, and visits to places associated with her. Founded 1996.

Wilfred Owen Association
email woa@1914-18.co.uk
website www.wilfredowen.org.uk
Twitter @WilfredOwenAssn
Membership £15 p.a. UK; £15 p.a. overseas (digital journal) and £35 p.a. overseas (print journal); £12 p.a. concession (under 25, over 70)

Commemorates the life and work of Wilfred Owen (1893–1918); encourages and enhances appreciation of his work through visits, public events and a bi-annual journal. Founded 1989.

The Beatrix Potter Society
email info@beatrixpottersociety.org.uk
website www.beatrixpottersociety.org.uk
Facebook https://en-gb.facebook.com/beatrixpottersociety
Twitter @BeatrixPotterSo
Instagram @beatrixpottersociety

Promotes the study and appreciation of the life and works of Beatrix Potter (1866–1943) as author, artist, diarist, farmer and conservationist. Regular lectures, meetings, conferences and events in the UK and USA. Distributes a journal and newsletter three times a year. Small publishing programme. Founded 1980.

The Powys Society
Flat D, 87 Ledbury Road, London W11 2AG
tel 020-7243 0168
email chris.d.thomas@hotmail.co.uk
website www.powys-society.org
Honorary Secretary Chris Thomas
Membership £22 p.a. UK; £26 p.a. overseas

Promotes the greater public recognition and enjoyment of the writings, thought and contribution to the arts of the Powys family, particularly John Cowper (1872–1963), Theodore Powys (1875–1953) and Llewelyn Powys (1884–1939), and the many other family members and their close friends. Publishes an annual scholarly journal (*The Powys Journal*) and three newsletters per year, as well as books by and about the Powys family, and holds an annual weekend conference in August, as well as organising other activities throughout the year. Founded 1967.

The J.B. Priestley Society
website www.jbpriestleysociety.com
General Secretary Rod Slater, *Information Officer* Michael Nelson, *Membership Secretary* Tony Reavill
Membership £15 p.a. single (UK); £18 p.a. single (overseas); £20 p.a. family; £10 p.a. concessions

Promotes the knowledge, understanding and appreciation of the published works of J.B. Priestley (1894–1984) and the study of his life and career. Holds lectures and discussions and social events. Publishes a newsletter and journal. Founded 1997.

The Ruskin Society
email secretary.of.the.ruskin.society@gmail.com
website https://ruskinsociety.uk/
Twitter @ruskinsociety
Membership £20 p.a. general, £5 p.a. student

Celebrates the life, work and legacy of John Ruskin (1819–1900). Organises lectures and events exploring Ruskin's ideas and placing them in a modern context. Organises a regular programme of events including talks, visits and study days in the UK. Founded 1997.

The Malcolm Saville Society
27 Whitehills Way, Kingsthorpe, Northampton, Northamptonshire NN2 8EW
email mystery@witchend.com
website www.witchend.com
Membership £15 p.a. UK; £17.50 p.a. Europe; £21 p.a. elsewhere

Promotes interest in the work of children's author Malcolm Saville (1901–82). Regular social activities, library, book and merchandise sales and a magazine (up to four each year). Founded 1994.

The Dorothy L. Sayers Society
30 Greenfield, Witham, Essex CM8 2FA
tel (01376) 515626
email info@sayers.org.uk
website www.sayers.org.uk
Chair Seona Ford, *Bulletin Secretary* Jasmine Simeone, *Membership* Margaret Hunt

Membership e-version of *Bulletin*: £20 p.a. UK and R.O.W; £10 p.a. under-25s. Printed version (mailed): £27 p.a. UK, £33 p.a. Europe, £36.50 p.a R.O.W

Aims to promote and encourage the study of the works of Dorothy L. Sayers (1893–1957); to collect archive materials and reminiscences about her and make them available to students and biographers; to hold an annual conference and other meetings; to publish *Proceedings*, pamphlets and a bi-monthly *Bulletin*; to make grants and awards. Founded 1976.

The Shaw Society
tel 020-7435 6497
email contact@shawsociety.org.uk
website www.shawsociety.org.uk
Twitter @ShawSoc
Chair Maureen Clark-Darby
Membership £25 p.a., £35 p.a. family membership

Works towards the improvement and diffusion of knowledge of the life and works of Bernard Shaw (1856–1950) and his circle. Publishes *The Shavian*. Meets regularly for script-in-hand performances and discussion. SHAW2020, one of the theatre companies supported by The Shaw Society, is dedicated to promoting Shaw's plays and writing, bringing them to wider, diverse audiences, especially now that Shaw's works are out of copyright.

The Robert Louis Stevenson Club
website https://robert-louis-stevenson.org/rls-club

Fosters interest in Robert Louis Stevenson's life (1850–94) and writings through various events and a quarterly newsletter. Founded 1920.

The Edward Thomas Fellowship
The Edward Thomas Study Centre,
Petersfield Museum and Art Gallery, St Peters Road,
Petersfield, Hampshire GU32 3PF
email etsc.petersfield@outlook.com
website www.edward-thomas-fellowship.org.uk
Chairman Jeremy Mitchell
Membership £15 p.a. UK; rates vary overseas

Celebrates and fosters interest in the life and work of Edward Thomas (1878–1917), poet and writer, and assists in the preservation of places and things associated with him. Holds Edward Thomas related walks and talks throughout the year and a biennial Literary Festival. In partnership with Petersfield Museum and Art Gallery, the Fellowship has established the Edward Thomas Study Centre based around the Tim Wilton-Steer collection of books by and about Edward Thomas. There are over 2,500 books and artefacts in the collection, which are available to researchers, readers and general visitors. Open Wednesdays and Thursdays, or contact for access arrangements. Founded 1980.

Dylan Thomas Society
5 Cwmdonkin Drive, Uplands, Swansea SA2 0RA
tel (01792) 472555

email info@dylanthomassociety.com
website www.dylanthomassociety.com
website www.dylanthomasbirthplace.com
Chairman Geoff Haden
Membership £15 p.a. single; £20 p.a. couple;
£10 p.a. student

Based at the Dylan Thomas Birthplace and Family Home. The society promotes an interest in the works of Dylan Thomas (1914–53) and other writers. Founded 1977.

The Tolkien Society
website www.tolkiensociety.org
Facebook www.facebook.com/TolkienSociety
Twitter @TolkienSociety
Instagram @tolksoc
Membership Postal: £35 p.a. UK; £40 p.a. EU; £50 p.a. ROW; add £15 p.a. for family membership; Online: £30 p.a.; £10 p.a. students

An educational charity and literary society devoted to the study and promotion of the life and works of J.R.R. Tolkien.

The Trollope Society
PO Box 505, Tunbridge Wells, Kent TN2 9RW
tel (01747) 839799
email info@trollopesociety.org
website www.trollopesociety.org
Chairman Dominic Edwardes
Membership £26 p.a. UK; £36 p.a. international

Has produced the first ever complete edition of the novels of Anthony Trollope (1815–82). Founded 1987.

The Walmsley Society
18 Pinfold Close, Barkisland, Halifax,
West Yorkshire HX4 0EY
website www.walmsleysoc.org
President Dr Sean Walmsley
Membership £13 p.a. single, £15 p.a. family, £12 p.a. concession (UK); £20 p.a. (overseas)

Promotes and encourages an appreciation of the literary and artistic heritage left to us by Leo Walmsley (1892–1966) and J. Ulric Walmsley (1860–1954). Founded 1985.

The Hugh Walpole Society
10 Parkleigh Road, London SW19 3BU
email egerton.mark@gmail.com
website www.hughwalpole.org
Chairman Nicholas Redman, *Administration* Mark Egerton
Membership Individual membership £17.50 p.a. (UK), £22.50 p.a (EU), £27.50 (R.O.W); Institutional membership £27.50 p.a. (UK), £32.50 p.a. (EU), £37.50 p.a. (R.O.W)

The society's goal is to bring the work of this long-neglected author back into the limelight and to get more people reading and enjoying his stories again.

Walpole enjoyed enormous popularity in the 1920s and 1930s and his books once sold thousands of copies. Publishes *The Hugh Walpole Review* bi-annually. Founded 2020.

Mary Webb Society

c/o Anne Williams, Concord College, Acton Burnell,
Shrewsbury SY5 7PF
tel (01694) 731631
website www.marywebbsociety.co.uk
Secretary Anne Williams

For devotees of the literature and works of Mary Webb (1881–1927) and of the Shropshire countryside of her novels. Publishes two newsletters p.a., organises four events p.a. including a two-day Summer School in various locations related to Webb's life and works. Lectures and tours arranged for individuals and groups. The Society archive is continually being added to. Founded 1972.

The H.G. Wells Society

153 Kenilworth Crescent, Enfield,
Middlesex EN1 3RG
email secretaryhgwellssociety@hotmail.com
website https://hgwellssociety.com
Chairman Mark Egerton, *Secretary* Brian Jukes
Membership £22 p.a. UK (£15 retired/student/unwaged); £27 p.a. EU (£20); £30 ROW (£23); Institutions: £35 p.a. UK, £40 p.a. EU, £45 p.a. ROW

Promotes an active interest in and an appreciation of the life, work and thought of H.G. Wells (1866–1946). Publishes *The Wellsian* (annual) and *The Newsletter* (bi-annual). Founded 1960.

The Oscar Wilde Society

website https://oscarwildesociety.co.uk
Membership Secretary Veronika Binoeder, *Honorary Secretary* Vanessa Heron

Promotes knowledge, appreciation and study of the life, personality and works of the writer and wit Oscar Wilde (1854–1900). Activities include meetings, lectures, readings and exhibitions, and visits to associated locations. Members receive a journal, *The Wildean* (two each year), a newsletter/journal, *Intentions* (four each year) and regular e-newsletters. Founded 1990.

The Henry Williamson Society

website www.henrywilliamson.co.uk
President Robert Williamson

Encourages a wider readership and greater understanding of the literary heritage left by Henry Williamson (1895–1977). Publishes a newsletter and hosts regular events. Founded 1980.

The P.G. Wodehouse Society (UK)

email info@pgwodehousesociety.org.uk
website www.pgwodehousesociety.org.uk
Membership £22 p.a.

Promotes the enjoyment of P.G. Wodehouse (1881–1975). Publishes *Wooster Sauce* (quarterly) and *By The Way* papers (four each year) which cover diverse subjects of Wodehousean interest. Holds events, entertainments and meetings throughout Britain. Founded 1997.

Virginia Woolf Society of Great Britain

12 Elm Park Road, Winchmore Hill,
London N21 2HN
tel 020-8245 3580
email lindsay.martin@cantab.net
website www.virginiawoolfsociety.org.uk
Facebook www.facebook.com/VWSGB
Twitter @VirginiaWoolfGB
Instagram @virginiawoolfsociety
Membership Secretary Lindsay Martin
Membership £20 p.a.; £26 p.a. Europe; £30 p.a. outside Europe

Acts as a forum for British admirers of Virginia Woolf (1882–1941) to meet, correspond and share their enjoyment of her work. Publishes the *Virginia Woolf Bulletin*. Founded 1998.

Francis Brett Young Society

82 Lodgefield Road, Halesowen,
West Midlands B62 8BA
tel 07800 601371
website www.fbysociety.co.uk
Chairman Dr Michael Hall, *Secretary* Mrs Catherine Grimmitt
Membership £7 p.a., £70 life for individual; £10 p.a., £100 life joint; £5 p.a. full-time students; £7 p.a. societies and institutions

Provides opportunities for members to meet, correspond, and to share the enjoyment of the works of Francis Brett Young (1884–1954). Publishes a journal (two each year). Founded 1979.

ART, ILLUSTRATION AND PHOTOGRAPHY

The Association of Illustrators

Somerset House, Strand, London WC2R 1LA
tel 020-7759 1010
email info@theaoi.com
website www.theaoi.com
Facebook www.facebook.com/theaoi
Twitter @theaoi

Trade association which supports illustrators with licensing and contract advice, promotes illustration and encourages professional standards in the industry. Presents an annual programme of events and holds an annual competition, the World Illustration Awards, in partnership with the *Directory of Illustration*. Founded 1973.

The Association of Photographers

2nd Floor, 201 Haverstock Hill, London NW3 4QG
tel 020-7739 6669
website www.the-aop.org
Facebook www.facebook.com/
AssociationOfPhotographers
Twitter @AssocPhoto
Instagram @assocphoto

Exists to protect and promote the worth and standing of its members, to vigorously defend, educate and lobby for the interests and rights of all photographers, especially in the commercial photographic industry. Founded 1968.

Axis

The Art House, Drury Lane, Wakefield WF1 2TE
email hello@axisweb.org
website www.axisweb.org
website https://community.axisweb.org
Facebook www.facebook.com/axisweb.org
Twitter @axisweb
Instagram @axisweb

Axis is an independent UK charity, which aims to share the art experience to create a healthier society. They foster knowledge and the appreciation of the visual arts through showcasing visual arts practice; offering opportunities to engage with and experience visual arts via events, artists talks, writing and films; and supporting artists' needs through membership that offers access to spaces, opportunities, commissions, bursaries, networking, workshops, mentoring, legal help and £10 million public liability insurance.

BAPLA (British Association of Picture Libraries and Agencies)

52 High Street, Pinner, Middlesex HA5 5PW
tel 020-8297 1198
email sohalia@bapla.org.uk
website https://bapla.org.uk
Twitter @baplaUK

BAPLA is the trade association for picture libraries in the UK. Members include the major news, stock and production agencies as well as sole traders and cultural heritage institutions. Founded 1975.

The Blackpool Art Society

The Studio, Wilkinson Avenue,
Off Woodland Grove, Blackpool FY3 9HB
tel (01253) 768297
email sec@blackpoolartsociety.co.uk
website www.blackpoolartsociety.co.uk/index.html

Hosts various exhibitions (members' work only). Studio meetings, demonstrations, workshops and lectures. Founded 1884.

British Institute of Professional Photography

The Artistry House, 16 Winckley Square,
Preston PR1 3JJ
tel (01772) 367968
email admin@bipp.com
website www.bipp.com
Facebook www.facebook.com/theBIPP
Twitter @thebipp
Instagram @thebipp

An internationally recognised qualifying organisation with over 100 years' experience in supporting and networking photographers. Delivers education, qualifications and professional development to photographers through a challenging qualifications structure alongside a full programme of training courses and events. Founded 1901.

British Interactive Media Association

tel 020-3538 6607
email web@bima.co.uk
website https://bima.co.uk
Membership Open to any organisation or individual with an interest in multimedia

BIMA is Britain's digital community which connects, develops and champions the industry. It facilitates professional networks, career development, business growth and the establishment of best practice standards. It also gives members a voice on issues affecting the industry. Founded 1985.

Cartoonists Club of Great Britain

website www.ccgb.org.uk
Facebook www.facebook.com/TheCartoonistsClub
Twitter @CartoonistsGB
Instagram @Cartoonistsclub

The UK's largest cartoonists' organisation, started by Fleet Street cartoonists and providing a social base for cartoonists wherever they may live or work. It has grown to include many different types of cartoonist. Social gatherings are held several times a year at different places around the country, and occasionally members also attend events abroad. It has a thriving online presence, forums for members and non-members, and a members' portfolio allowing them to promote their work. Publishes the monthly magazine *The Jester*. Founded 1960.

The Chartered Society of Designers

1 Cedar Court, Royal Oak Yard, Bermondsey Street, London SE1 3GA
tel 020-7357 8088
email info@csd.org.uk
website www.csd.org.uk
Facebook www.facebook.com/
charteredsocietyofdesigners
Twitter @csdminerva
Instagram @csdminerva

The internationally recognised body for the design profession, providing support and guidance for designers at every stage of their career. Works to promote and regulate standards of competence, professional conduct and integrity, including representation on government and official bodies, design education and awards. The services to members include general information, publications and guidance on copyright and other professional issues.

Event & Visual Communication Association

tel 020-3771 5642
email info@evcom.org.uk
website www.evcom.org.uk
Facebook www.facebook.com/EVCOMUK1/
Twitter @EVCOMUK

EVCOM is the only membership association that represents the corporate events and corporate film industries. Champions and supports the industry, hosting events, facilitating knowledge sharing and setting standards.

Federation of British Artists

17 Carlton House Terrace, London SW1Y 5BD
tel 020-7930 6844
email info@mallgalleries.com
website www.mallgalleries.org.uk
Facebook www.facebook.com/mallgalleries
Twitter @mallgalleries

Administers nine major National Art Societies at Mall Galleries, The Mall, London SW1. Founded 1961.

Fine Art Trade Guild

2 Wye House, 6 Enterprise Way, London SW18 1FZ
tel 020-7381 6616
email info@fineart.co.uk
website www.fineart.co.uk
Facebook www.facebook.com/FineArtTradeGuild

Promotes the sale of fine art prints and picture framing in the UK and overseas markets; establishes and raises standards amongst members and communicates these to the buying public. The Guild publishes *Art + Framing Today*, the trade's longest established magazine, and various specialist books. Founded 1910.

FOCAL (Federation of Commercial AudioVisual Libraries International Ltd)

27 Mortimer Street, London W1T 3BL
tel 020-3948 1999
email info@focalint.org
website www.focalint.org
Facebook www.facebook.com/focalinternational
Twitter @FOCALint

A not-for-profit trade association for the commercial audio-visual library industry, with members in over 30 countries. Founded 1985.

Free Painters & Sculptors London

email info@freepaintersandsculptors.co.uk
website www.freepaintersandsculptors.co.uk
Facebook www.facebook.com/fpsartistgroup/

FPS is an established, artist-led organisation that promotes and exhibits a talented membership of painters, sculptors, printmakers and photographers at renowned central London galleries twice a year. With over 65 years of experience, FPS helps artists build long-term networks that develop artistic sustainability, exposure and sales, while also encouraging artists to create work on their own terms and therefore be 'free'. FPS was originally associated with the ICA (Institute of Contemporary Arts) and founding members included Roy Rasmussen, Lyall Watson and Maurice Jadot, who all feature in the permanent Tate Collection. FPS welcomes applications from talented artists at all stages of their career. Founded 1952.

Greeting Card Association

PO Box, Teddington TW11 1EL
tel 020-7619 9266
email hello@gca.cards
website www.gca.cards
Facebook www.facebook.com/GreetingCardAssociation
Twitter @GCAUK
Instagram @GCA_UK
Chief Executive Amanda Fergusson

The GCA is an independent not-for-profit trade organisation operating for the benefit of members, who include greeting card publishers, retailers and suppliers and individuals working in the card industry. Supports members by providing a forum for them to promote their businesses, specialist information, access to specialist suppliers and organising events and networking opportunities. Founded 1919.

The Guild of Aviation Artists

Studio 100, 161 High Street, Ruislip HA4 8JY
tel 0333 130 2223
email admin@gava.org.uk
website www.gava.org.uk
President Michael Turner
Membership £70 p.a. full; £55 p.a. associates; £35 p.a. friends; £15 p.a. young friends (aged under 25 years and in continuing education)

Formed to promote aviation art through the organisation of exhibitions and meetings. Holds an annual open exhibition and £1,000 prize for 'Aviation Painting of the Year'. Quarterly members' newsletter. Founded 1971.

Guild of Railway Artists

website www.railart.co.uk
Facebook www.facebook.com/The-Guild-of-Railway-Artists-520306528057416

Aims to forge a link between artists depicting railway subjects and to give members a corporate identity. Stages railway art exhibitions and members' meetings and produces books of members' works. Founded 1979.

Hesketh Hubbard Art Society

17 Carlton House Terrace, London SW1Y 5BD
tel 020-7930 6844
email info@mallgalleries.com
website www.mallgalleries.org.uk/whats-on/events/
hesketh-hubbard-art-society
Membership £330 p.a.

Offers both amateur and professional artists the
opportunity to work from life models in untutored
sessions. Membership includes 44 drawing sessions
and no cover charge. Prospective members are
invited to attend one session free before deciding if
they wish to apply for membership. Founded 1930.

The Hilliard Society of Miniaturists

tel 07582 019359
email info@hilliardsociety.org
website www.hilliardsociety.org
President Rosalind Pierson
Membership £60 p.a. artist member; £25 p.a. friend
member

Aims to increase knowledge and promote the art of
miniature painting. Annual exhibition held in June at
Wells; showcases members work and produces a
newsletter. Founded 1982.

Imaginative Book Illustration Society

email ibissec@martinsteenson.co.uk
website www.bookillustration.org
Membership enquiries Martin Steenson

IBIS was established to encourage research into, and
to facilitate, the exchange of information on book
and periodical illustrations, the artists and their
publishers. The Society has a worldwide membership
including artists, collectors, bibliographers, writers
and general enthusiasts. Whilst IBIS embraces all
aspects of illustrative art, the main emphasis is on the
illustration of texts in English since the 1830s.
Founded 1995.

Institute of Designers in Ireland

WeWork, 2 Dublin Landings, North Dock,
Dublin D01 V4A3
email info@idi-design.ie
website www.idi-design.ie
Facebook www.facebook.com/idiireland
Twitter @IDIIreland

Irish design profession's representative body,
covering every field of design. Founded 1972.

International Society of Typographic Designers

email info@istd.org.uk
website www.istd.org.uk

Working closely with graphic design educationalists
and the professional community, it establishes,
maintains and promotes typographic standards
through the forum of debate and design practice.

Membership is awarded to practising designers,
educators, writers, critics, theorists of design and
students who demonstrate, through the quality of
their work, their commitment to achieving the
highest possible quality of visual communication. It
publishes a journal, *Typographic*. Students of
typography and graphic design are encouraged to
gain membership of the society by entering the
annual student assessment scheme. Membership is
also available to anyone who has an interest in
typography and graphic design. Founded 1928.

Master Photographers Association

140 Coniscliffe Road, Darlington DL3 7RT
tel (01325) 356555
email membership@thempa.com
website www.thempa.com

Promotes and protects professional photographers.
With over 60 years in the professional photography
industry, the MPA prides itself in developing some of
the industry's leading photographers.

National Acrylic Painters' Association

28 Polmennor Drive, Carbis Bay, Cornwall TR26 2SQ
email contact@napauk.com
website www.napauk.com
Membership £45 p.a.

Promotes interest in, and encourages excellence and
innovation in, the work of painters in acrylic. Holds
an annual exhibition and regional shows and
administers awards. Founded 1985.

National Society for Education in Art and Design

3 Masons Wharf, Potley Lane, Corsham,
Wilts. SN13 9FY
tel (01225) 810134
email info@nsead.org
website www.nsead.org
Twitter @NSEAD1
General Secretary Michele Gregson

The leading national authority concerned with art,
craft and design across all phases of education in the
UK. Offers the benefits of membership of a
professional association, a learned society and a trade
union. Has representatives on national and regional
committees concerned with art and design education.
Publishes *International Journal of Art and Design
Education* online (three each; Wiley Blackwell) and
AD magazine for teachers. Founded 1888.

The Pastel Society

email info.thepastelsociety@gmail.com
website www.thepastelsociety.org.uk
Facebook www.facebook.com/thepastelsociety
Twitter @PastelSociety
Instagram @pastelsociety.uk

Pastel and drawings in all dry media. Annual
Exhibition open to all artists working in dry media

held at Mall Galleries, The Mall, London SW1. Members elected from a list of approved candidates. See website for submission and membership fees. Founded 1898.

The Picture Research Association

website www.picture-research.org.uk
Twitter @PRA_Association

The PRA is a professional organisation of picture researchers and picture editors specifically involved in the research, management and supply of visual material to the media industry. Registered members are listed on the website and can be located through the Find Researchers page, along with lots of useful information about the picture industry. Founded 1977.

Printmakers Council

Ground Floor Unit, 23 Blue Anchor Lane,
London SE16 3UL
tel 07531 883250
email admin@printmakerscouncil.com
website www.printmakerscouncil.com
Facebook www.facebook.com/PrintmakersCouncil
Twitter @PMCouncil
Instagram @printmakerscouncil
Membership £75 p.a.; £30 students, join online

Artist-led group which aims to promote the use of both traditional and innovative printmaking techniques by holding exhibitions of prints, providing information on prints and printmaking to both its membership and the public, and encouraging cooperation and exchanges between members, other associations and interested individuals. Archives held by the V&A and Scarborough Museums Trust. Founded 1965.

Professional Cartoonists' Organisation

email info@procartoonists.org
website www.procartoonists.org
Facebook www.facebook.com/UKProfessionalCartoonists
Twitter @procartoonists
Instagram @procartoonists
YouTube @pcotv1578
Membership £80 p.a.

The organisation showcases UK cartoonists through its portfolio pages, a cartoon news blog and public events such as The Herne Bay Cartoon Festival. Founded 2006.

SAA

Millenium House, Brunel Drive, Newark,
Notts. NG24 2DE
tel 0800 980 1123
email help@saa.co.uk
website www.saa.co.uk

Facebook www.facebook.com/SupportingAllArtists
Instagram @supportingallartists
Membership from £45 p.a.

Supporting all artists, from complete beginners and enthusiasts to professionals. SAA is the largest art community with 30,000 members, and welcomes new members. Membership includes access to hundreds of member-only inspirational videos, *Paint & Create* magazine (delivered bi-monthly), exclusive discounts and offers on materials, paintings insurance for exhibitions and third-party public liability. Founded 1992.

The Society of Botanical Artists

c/o WMT, Verulam Point, Station Way,
St Albans AL1 5HE
email info@soc-botanical-artists.org
website www.soc-botanical-artists.org
Presidents Diane Marshall, Shevaun Doherty, Claire Ward
Membership By election, £145 p.a.

Aims to encourage the art of botanical painting. Entry details for the open exhibitions are available on the website. Founded 1985.

Society of Graphic Fine Art

email enquiries@sgfa.org.uk
website www.sgfa.org.uk
Facebook www.facebook.com/SocietyofGraphicFineArt
Twitter @SGFADrawing
President Les Williams

With over 160 elected members across the UK, the Society of Graphic Fine Art (The Drawing Society) exists to promote and exhibit works of high quality in colour or black and white, with the emphasis on good drawing and draughtsmanship, in pencil, pen, brush, charcoal or any of the forms of original printmaking. The Society holds an annual Open Exhibition with prizes and awards in many categories. Founded 1919.

Society of Heraldic Arts

Chairman of the Appointments Board,
8 Abbot Close, Ottery St Mary, Devon EX11 1FH
email k.arkinstall@tiscali.co.uk
website www.heraldic-arts.com
President Anthony Wood, *Chairman of the Appointments Board* Kevin Arkinstall

Serves the interests of heraldic artists, craftsmen, designers and writers, to provide a 'shop window' for their work, to obtain commissions on their behalf and to act as a forum for the exchange of information and ideas. Also offers an information service to the public. Candidates for admission as craft members should be artists or craftsmen whose work comprises a substantial element of heraldry and is of a sufficiently high standard to satisfy the requirements of the society's advisory council. Founded 1987.

Societies, prizes and festivals

Society of Scribes and Illuminators

6 Queen Square, London WC1N 3AT
email honsec@calligraphyonline.org
website www.calligraphyonline.org
Membership £46 fellows; £37 lay members; £30 friends

Aims to promote and preserve the art of calligraphy, bringing the beauty of handwritten letters to the modern world, moving with the times to embrace contemporary lettering whilst upholding the traditions of the craft. Education programme includes a correspondence course, an advanced training scheme, mentorship towards fellowship, a programme of study days, a series of masterclasses and recommendations for local learning opportunities. A specialist sales shop, an archive/library and a bi-annual journal, *The Scribe*, are available to members. Founded 1921.

Society of Wildlife Artists

17 Carlton House Terrace, London SW1Y 5BD
tel 020-7930 6844
email info@mallgalleries.com
website www.swla.co.uk
President Harriet Mead
Membership £75 p.a. full; £220 p.a. associate

Aims to promote and encourage the art of wildlife painting and sculpture. Open Annual Exhibition at Mall Galleries, The Mall, London SW1, for any artist whose work depicts wildlife subjects (botanical and domestic animals are not admissible). Runs a bursary scheme for young artists to cover the costs of education, travel and materials.

The Society of Women Artists

email rebeccacottonswa@gmail.com
website www.society-women-artists.org.uk
President Helen Sinclair, *Executive Secretary* Rebecca Cotton
Membership Membership by election, based on 6 works submitted to the exhibition.

A registered UK charity dedicated to promoting women artists and the art they create. Exhibits annually at the Mall Galleries. Successfully selected work should be handed in to Mall Galleries, The Mall, London SW1 (check website for date). Founded 1855.

The Turner Society

BCM Box Turner, London WC1N 3XX
email jmwturnersociety@gmail.com
website www.turnersociety.com
Membership £30 p.a. individuals; £30 p.a. overseas surface mail; £45 p.a. overseas airmail; £600 life member

Promotes the study and appreciation of the life and works of J.M.W. Turner (1775–1851). Publishes *Turner Society News* (two each year). Founded 1975.

FILM, THEATRE AND TELEVISION

AITA/IATA asbl International Amateur Theatre Association

email secretariat@aitaiata.net
website www.aitaiata.net
Facebook www.facebook.com/aitaiata
Twitter @aita_iata
President Aled Rhys-Jones, *Vice Presidents and Councillors* Sofia Wegelius, Tim Jebsen, *Treasurer and Councillor* Anna-Karin Waldemarson

Encourages, fosters and promotes the exchanges of non-professional theatre organisations and individuals and of student, educational and adult theatre activities at international level. Organises international seminars, workshops, courses and conferences, and collates information of all types for national and international dissemination. Holds a programme of festivals celebrating theatre and children's theatre.

BAFTA

195 Piccadilly, London W1J 9LN
tel 020-7734 0022
email reception@bafta.org
website www.bafta.org
Facebook www.facebook.com/bafta
Twitter @BAFTA
Chief Executive Jane Millichip

The British Academy of Film and Television is a world-leading independent arts charity that brings the very best work in film, games and television to public attention and supports the growth of creative talent in the UK and internationally. Through its Awards ceremonies and year-round programme of learning events and initiatives (which includes workshops, masterclasses, scholarships, lectures and mentoring schemes in the UK, USA and Asia) BAFTA identifies and celebrates excellence, inspires and nurtures new talent, and enables learning and creative collaboration. Founded 1947.

BECTU (Broadcasting Entertainment Communications and Theatre Union)

New Prospect House, 8 Leake Street, London SE1 7NN
email info@bectu.org.uk
website https://bectu.org.uk/
General Secretary Mike Clancy

BECTU (a sector of the trade union Prospect) aims to defend the interests of writers in film, TV and radio. By virtue of its industrial strength, the union is able to help its writer members to secure favourable terms and conditions. In cases of disputes with employers, the union can intervene in order to ensure an equitable settlement. Its production agreement with Pact lays down minimum terms for writers working in the documentary area. Founded 1991.

BFI (British Film Institute)

21 Stephen Street, London W1T 1LN
tel 020-7255 1444
website www.bfi.org.uk
Facebook www.facebook.com/BritishFilmInstitute
Twitter @BFI
Instagram @britishfilminstitute

The BFI supports, nurtures and promotes the arts of film, television and the moving image. A registered charity, funded by government and earned income, and a distributor of National Lottery funds, the BFI is at the heart of the UK's fast-growing screen industries, protecting the past and shaping their future across the UK. It works in partnership with cultural organisations, government and industry to make this happen. Founded 1933.

Independent Theatre Council

The Albany, Douglas Way, London SE8 4AG
tel 020-7403 1727
email admin@itc-arts.org
website www.itc-arts.org
Facebook www.facebook.com/
independenttheatrecouncil
Twitter @itc_arts
Membership £190 p.a.

Enables the creation of high-quality professional performing arts by supporting, representing and developing the people who manage and produce it. It has over 450 members from a wide range of companies, venues and individuals in the fields of drama, dance, opera, musical theatre, puppetry, mixed media, mime, physical theatre and circus. Founded 1974.

Little Theatre Guild of Great Britain

tel 07971 474721
email secretary@littletheatreguild.org
website www.littletheatreguild.org
Secretary Anne Gilmour

Promotes closer cooperation amongst the little theatres constituting its membership, acts as a coordinating and representative body on behalf of the little theatres, maintains and advances the highest standards in the art of theatre, and assists in encouraging the establishment of other little theatres.

Pact (Producers Alliance for Cinema and Television)

3rd Floor Fitzrovia House, 153-157 Cleveland Street, London W1T 6QW
tel 020 7380 8230
website www.pact.co.uk
Twitter @PactUK
Chief Executive John McVay

The UK trade association that represents and promotes the commercial interests of independent feature film, television, animation and interactive media companies. Headquartered in London, it has regional representation throughout the UK in order to support its members, including an office in Leeds. An effective lobbying organisation, it has regular and constructive dialogues with government, regulators, public agencies and opinion-formers on all issues affecting its members, and contributes to key public policy debates on the media industry, both in the UK and in Europe. It negotiates terms of trade with all public service broadcasters in the UK and supports members in their business dealings with cable and satellite channels and streaming services. It also lobbies for a properly structured and funded UK film industry and maintains close contact with other relevant film organisations and government departments.

Player-Playwrights

email pplaywrights@gmail.com
website www.playerplaywrights.co.uk
Facebook www.facebook.com/groups/
playerplaywrights
Secretary Lynne O'Sullivan
Membership £15 in first year and £10 thereafter (plus £3 per attendance); guests and audience welcome (non-members £4 entrance)

The society reads, performs and discusses plays and scripts submitted by members, with a view to assisting the writers in improving and marketing their work and enabling actors to showcase their talents. New writers and new acting members are always welcome. Check website for details of group meets. Founded 1948.

The Society for Theatre Research

Savile House, 4 Mansfield Road, Oxford OX1 3TA
email contact@str.org.uk
website www.str.org.uk
Twitter @TheSTR
Honorary Secretary Brianna Robertson-Kirkland

Supports and promotes theatre research. Publishes the journal *Theatre Notebook* along with at least one major book per year, holds public lectures, and makes annual research grants. Also awards an annual prize for best book published in English on British Theatre. Founded 1948.

TRANSLATION

American Literary Translators Association

email info@literarytranslators.org
website www.literarytranslators.org
Executive Director Elisabeth Jaquette

ALTA is a broad-based professional association dedicated to the promotion of literary translation through services to literary translators, forums on the theory and practice of translation, and collaboration

532 Societies, prizes and festivals

with the international literary community. Hosts an annual conference, offers fellowships and mentorship for emerging translators and bestows five translation awards. Founded 1978.

British Centre for Literary Translation
School of Literature, Drama and Creative Writing, University of East Anglia, Norwich Research Park, Norwich NR4 7TJ
tel (01603) 592785
email bclt@uea.ac.uk
website www.bclt.org.uk
Facebook www.facebook.com/bcltuea
Twitter @bcltuea

A research centre within the School of Literature at the University of East Anglia in Norwich. It supports an MA in Literary Translation at the University of East Anglia, an increasing variety of undergraduate modules in the subject, and an extensive programme of PhD research. BCLT works in close partnership with the National Centre for Writing and a wide range of other national and international organisations to deliver a programme of activities which support the professional development of literary translators and promote the recognition of literary translation as a profession. These include the annual Sebald Lecture, held in the spring at the British Library in London, and the International Literary Translation and Creative Writing Summer School, held in July at UEA in Norwich. Founded 1989.

Chartered Institute of Linguists
7th Floor, 167 Fleet Street, London EC4A 2EA
tel 020-7940 3100
website www.ciol.org.uk
Facebook www.facebook.com/charteredinstituteoflinguists
Twitter @CIOL_Linguists
Instagram @ciollinguists

CIOL is the foremost international membership organisation for all language professionals and is the only one offering a pathway to Chartership. Its diverse membership includes translators and interpreters, language teachers, university lecturers and linguists who use their foreign language skills in business, the professions and government.

CIOL's associated charity, CIOL Qualifications, is an Ofqual-accredited awarding body offering professional qualifications in translation and public service interpreting. CIOL publishes a quarterly magazine, *The Linguist*, free to members and available to non-members by subscription. *The Linguist* offers its readers a wide range of articles that are of interest to anyone working with languages. Founded 1910.

The Institute of Translation and Interpreting
Milton Keynes Business Centre, Foxhunter Drive, Linford Wood, Milton Keynes MK14 6GD
tel (01908) 325250
website www.iti.org.uk
Facebook www.facebook.com/ITIofficial
Twitter @ITIUK
Instagram @iti.uk
Membership From £110 p.a.

The ITI is the independent professional association of practising translators and interpreters. With the aim of promoting the highest standards in the profession, ITI serves as a focal point for all those who understand the importance of translation and interpreting to the economy and community. It offers guidance to those entering the profession and advice to both people offering their language services and their potential customers. Founded 1986.

Translators Association
24 Bedford Row, London WC1R 4EH
tel 020-3880 2230
email info@societyofauthors.org
website www.societyofauthors.org/Groups/Translators

Specialist group within the membership of the Society of Authors (see page 495), the Translator's Association advocates for the rights and interests of emerging and established literary translators in all genres. Offers unlimited contract vetting and industry advice to members, co-programmes the Literary Translation Centre at the London Book Fair and actively engages with the sector through campaigns and events.

BIBLIOGRAPHICAL AND ACADEMIC

The Association of Learned and Professional Society Publishers
Egale 1, 80 St Albans Road, Watford, Herts. WD17 1DL
email admin@alpsp.org
website www.alpsp.org
Twitter @alpsp

ALPSP is the international membership trade body which supports and represents not-for-profit organisations that publish scholarly and professional content and those that partner with and provide services to not-for-profit publishers. ALPSP has nearly 300 members in 30 countries. Its mission is to connect, inform, develop and represent the international scholarly and professional publishing community.

Bibliographical Society
c/o Institute of English Studies, University of London, Senate House, Malet Street, London WC1E 7HU
email admin@bibsoc.org.uk
website www.bibsoc.org.uk
Facebook www.facebook.com/BibSoc
Twitter @BibSoc

The senior learned society dealing with the study of books and their history. Promotes and encourages study and research in the fields of historical, analytical, descriptive and textual bibliography as well as the history of printing, publishing, bookselling, bookbinding and collecting. Publishes the journal *The Library*. Founded 1892.

Cambridge Bibliographical Society

University Library, West Road, Cambridge CB3 9DR
email cbs@lib.cam.ac.uk
website www.lib.cam.ac.uk/collections/cambridge-bibliographical-society

Encourages the study of bibliography, including book and MS production, book collecting and the history of libraries. It publishes *Transactions* (annual) and a series of monographs, and arranges a programme of lectures and visits. Founded 1949.

Classical Association

email office@classicalassociation.org
website www.classicalassociation.org
Honorary Secretary Dr A. McAuley

Exists to support the study and teaching of the Greek and Roman world in all its inspiring forms. This includes its history, civilisations and languages, plus its interaction with other cultures, both ancient and modern. The Association sponsors the UK's largest annual classics conference and works to promote access to the classical world in schools, universities and beyond.

Early English Text Society

Faculty of English, St Cross Building, Manor Road, Oxford OX1 3UL
email eets@ell.ox.ac.uk
website www.eets.org.uk
Twitter @EEngTextSoc
Honorary Director Prof. V. Gillespie, *Executive Secretary* Prof. D. Wakelin, *Treasurer & Membership Secretary* Dr Daniel Orton
Membership £30 p.a.

Aims to bring unprinted early English literature within the reach of students in sound texts. Founded 1864.

Edinburgh Bibliographical Society

c/o 27 Heatherfields Glade, Adambrae Parks, Livingston, West London EH54 9JE
email secretary@edbibsoc.org
website www.edbibsoc.org
Secretary Heather Holmes
Membership £18 p.a.; £25 p.a. corporate; £12 p.a. full-time students

Encourages bibliographical activity through organising talks for members, particularly on bibliographical topics relating to Scotland, and visits to libraries. See website for submission guidelines and prizes. Publishes a journal (annual, free to members) and other occasional publications. Founded 1890.

Oxford Bibliographical Society

Bodleian Library, Broad Street, Oxford OX1 3BG
email secretary@oxbibsoc.org.uk
website www.oxbibsoc.org.uk
Membership £30 p.a. UK; £40 p.a. Europe; £45 p.a R.O.W

Exists to encourage bibliographical research. Publishes monographs. Founded 1922.

MEMBERS' CLUBS

The Arts Club

40 Dover Street, London W1S 4NP
tel 020-7499 8581
email membership@theartsclub.co.uk
website www.theartsclub.co.uk
Instagram @the_arts_club

A private members' club for all those connected with or interested in the arts, literature and science. Founded 1863.

Authors' Club

Whitehall Place, London SW1A 2HE
email info@authorsclub.co.uk
website www.authorsclub.co.uk
Facebook www.facebook.com/authorsclub1891
Twitter @AuthorsClub
President John Walsh, *Chairperson* Lucy Popescu
Membership Associate £150 p.a.

A club for all those professionally engaged with literature, the Authors' Club welcomes as members writers, publishers, critics, journalists and academics. Administers the Authors' Club Best First Novel Award, the Art Book Prize and the Stanford Dolman Travel Book of the Year Award. Founded 1891.

New English Art Club (NEAC)

email info@neac.co.uk
website www.newenglishartclub.co.uk

The New English Art Club (NEAC) is an elected society of contemporary painters whose ethos resides in art informed by the visual world and personal interpretation. Its Annual Exhibition held at London's Mall Galleries showcases work by its members and aspiring artists selected from an open submission.

Scottish Arts Club

24 Rutland Square, Edinburgh EH1 2BW
email admin@scottishartsclub.com
website www.scottishartsclub.com
Facebook www.facebook.com/scottishartsclub
Twitter @ScottishArtsCL
Instagram @thescottishartsclub

The Scottish Arts Club is a social hub for artists and those interested in the arts. Professional members include painters, sculptors, filmmakers, actors, musicians, playwrights, poets, novelists, journalists, architects, designers, dancers and diplomats. The Club also welcomes lay members and anyone who is interested in the arts. Runs a programme of awards for art, literature and performance. Founded 1873.

WRITERS' ORGANISATIONS

All Party Parliamentary Writers Group
tel 020-7264 5700
email allpartywritersgroup@alcs.co.uk
website www.allpartywritersgroup.co.uk
Chair Giles Watling MP, *Administrator* Barbara Hayes

The Group has some 60 Members from both Houses and seeks to represent the interests of all writers; to safeguard their intellectual property rights and ensure they receive a fair level of recognition and remuneration for their contribution to the economy and society as a whole. Founded 2007.

Alliance of Independent Authors – see page 502

Association of British Science Writers
email info@absw.org.uk
website www.absw.org.uk
Facebook www.facebook.com/BritishScienceWriters
Twitter @absw
Chair Andy Extance, *Honorary President* Roger Highfield

A membership organisation for media professionals who cover science, medicine, environment, mathematics, engineering and technology. Champions independence and excellence in the reporting of science, medicine, engineering and technology. Trains and supports journalists and writers at all stages of their careers through conferences, summer schools and awards, in addition to a range of networking, training and debating events. Membership details/application through website only.

Association of Christian Writers
email admin@christianwriters.co.uk
website www.christianwriters.co.uk
Facebook www.facebook.com/groups/24831838019
Twitter @ACW1971
Membership From £26 p.a. Membership year runs from 1 April to 31 March and includes quarterly issues of *Christian Writer* magazine sent by post.

ACW aims to inspire excellence in writing from a Christian world view. Equips Christian writers through writers' days around the UK, workshops and writing competitions. Members encourage each other online and in affiliated local groups. Publishes a daily blog, *More Than Writers*. Please note that ACW is not a publisher. Founded 1971.

Authors Aloud UK
72 Castle Road, St Albans, Herts. AL1 5DG
tel (01727) 893992
email info@authorsalouduk.co.uk
website www.authorsalouduk.co.uk
Facebook www.facebook.com/Authors-Aloud-UK-497942623573822
Twitter @AuthorsAloudUK
Instagram @AuthorsAloudUK
Directors Naomi Cooper, Annie Everall

An author booking agency which brings together authors, illustrators, poets, storytellers and trainers with schools, libraries and festivals in the UK and internationally, to promote enthusiasm for reading, both for enjoyment and information. Works with children's authors who wish to visit schools and libraries, in person and virtually, and who are published by mainstream children's publishers. Also arranges author tours and book related events for publishers and other organisations.

Book Aid International
39–41 Coldharbour Lane, London SE5 9NR
tel 020-7733 3577
email info@bookaid.org
website www.bookaid.org
Twitter @Book_Aid

Book Aid International is a UK registered charity which facilitates international book donation and library development. Every year they provide over one-million books to thousands of communities who have limited opportunities to read, and works with partners to support and establish libraries. The charities vision is a world where everyone has access to books that will enrich, improve and change their lives.

Book Marketing Society
email admin@bookmarketingsociety.co.uk
website www.bookmarketingsociety.co.uk
Twitter @BMSoc

Launched with the objective of becoming the representative body of marketing within the book industry. It provides a forum for sharing best practice, inspiration and creativity across the sector through regular awards and a lively programme of member meetings, development workshops, masterclasses and social events. Anyone who works for a book publisher, book retailer or book wholesaler is eligible for membership, including those working in associated areas of the publishing and book retailing industry.

BookTrust Represents
G8 Battersea Studios, 80 Silverthorne Road, London SW8 3HE
tel 020-7801 8826
email booktrust.represents@booktrust.org.uk
website www.booktrust.org.uk/booktrustrepresents
Twitter @Booktrust

A project to support and promote authors and illustrators of colour and to reach more readers through school visits, special events and festivals. The project also supports aspiring and new authors and illustrators of colour with training, mentoring, events and an online community. Find out more about the project and the associated research into the ethnicity of authors and illustrators in the UK on the website. Founded 2019.

The British Fantasy Society

email secretary@britishfantasysociety.org
website www.britishfantasysociety.org
Membership Digital: £30 p.a. Print: £45 p.a. single, £50 p.a. joint (UK); £55 p.a. single, £60 p.a joint (Europe); £70 p.a. single, £75 p.a. joint (R.O.W)

For readers, writers and publishers of fantasy, horror and related fields, in literature, art and the cinema. There is an annual convention, FantasyCon, and the British Fantasy Awards are sponsored by the society. Publications are the *BFS Journal* and *BFS Horizons*. Founded 1971.

British Guild of Beer Writers

c/o Cask Marque, B10 Seedbed Centre, Wyncolls Road, Severalls Business Park, Colchester CO4 9HT
email secretary@beerguild.co.uk
website www.beerguild.co.uk
Facebook www.facebook.com/BritBeerWriters/
Twitter @Britbeerwriters
Secretary Mike Hampshire
Membership £55 p.a.

Aims to improve standards in beer and cider writing and at the same time extend public knowledge of beer, cider and breweries. Awards are given annually to writers, broadcasters and other communicators judged to have made the most valuable contribution to this end. Publishes an online directory of members with details of their publications and their particular areas of interest. Founded 1988.

The British Guild of Travel Writers

Larking Gowen, 1 Clayton Business Park, Great Blakenham, Ipswich IP6 0NL
tel 020-8144 8713
email hello@bgtw.org
website www.bgtw.org
Facebook www.facebook.com/TravWriters
Twitter @TravWriters
Instagram @travwriters

Arranges meetings, discussions and visits for its members (who are all professional travel journalists) to promote and encourage the public's interest in travel. Annual awards for journalism (members only) and the travel trade. Founded 1960.

The British Haiku Society

16 Croft Gardens, Andover, Hampshire SP10 2RH
email britishhaiku@gmail.com
website www.britishhaikusociety.org.uk
Facebook www.facebook.com/thebritishhaikusociety

Pioneers the appreciation and writing of haiku and kindred forms of verse in the UK, and has links with similar organisations throughout the world. Currently there are around 400 BHS members from 27 countries. Members receive a quarterly journal, *Blithe Spirit*, an annual members' anthology and a newsletter. Runs the annual British Haiku Society Awards in three categories: haiku, tanka and haibun; publishes books concerning haiku and related matters, and is active in promoting the teaching of haiku in schools and colleges. Founded 1990.

British Science Fiction Association Ltd

The Hollies, 67 James Street, Stoke on Trent ST4 5HR
email membership@bsfa.co.uk
website www.bsfa.co.uk
Twitter @BSFA
Membership £31 standard; £20 concession; £33 joint; £20 digital

A membership organisation for authors, publishers, booksellers and readers of science fiction, fantasy and allied genres. Currently publishes *The BSFA Review*, a free digital magazine reviewing recent science fiction and fantasy releases across all media, and runs regular events with authors which are free and open to the public. Exclusively for members, BSFA publishes *Focus*, aimed at writers of all levels, as well as *Vector*, a critical journal featuring interviews, essays, reviews and other features, including peer-reviewed academic articles. Members can also participate in Orbiters, BSFA's network of online writers' workshops.

The BSFA has historically had strong ties with Eastercon, the UK's largest annual science fiction convention; Eastercon is home to the annual BSFA Awards, where awards are given in four categories: best novel, best short story, best artwork, and best non-fiction. Founded 1958.

Circle of Wine Writers

tel (01753) 882320
email administrator@circleofwinewriters.org
website www.circleofwinewriters.org
Membership by election

An association for those engaged in communicating about wines and spirits. Produces *The Circular* (monthly online newsletter), organises tasting sessions as well as a programme of meetings, talks and trips. Founded 1960.

Crime Readers' Association

email hello@thecra.co.uk
website www.thecra.co.uk
Facebook www.facebook.com/groups/CRAbookchat
Contact Vicki Goldie

Offers readers an insight into the novels and non-fiction of the largest community of crime writers in the world: the Crime Writers' Association (CWA). Subscribers to the Crime Readers' Association receive multiple benefits free of charge: Case Files, a bi-monthly eZine focusing on new books and containing fascinating features and articles from members of the CWA; CRA News, a monthly newsletter containing insider news of books and their authors; crime-writing events; and crime-writing opportunities such as competitions and courses as well as exclusive discounts and giveaways

Crime Writers' Association

email secretary@thecwa.co.uk
website www.thecwa.co.uk
Facebook www.facebook.com/CrimeWritersAssociation
Twitter @The_CWA
Secretary Vickie Goldie

The CWA represents writers of all kinds of crime fiction and non-fiction and at all stages of their careers. Membership is open to crime writers of both fiction and non-fiction, both traditionally published and self-published who can prove their professionalism, from anywhere in the world, plus anyone whose business is closely connected with crime writing. Membership benefits include book promotional platforms, monthly members' magazine *Red Herrings*, local chapters for social events, annual conference, free tax helpline from H.W. Fisher, and links with organisations such as the Society of Authors and HWA. Also runs the Debut Dagger and Margery Allingham Short Mystery competitions, as well as the world-renowned Dagger awards for published titles. Founded 1953.

The Critics' Circle

c/o Rick Jones, 17 Rosenthal Road, Catford, London SE6 2BX
email criticscircleallsections@gmail.com
website https://criticscircle.org.uk
President Robert Thicknesse, *Honorary Treasurer* Peter Cargin, *Honorary Secretary* Rick Jones

The Critics' Circle was established to promote the art of criticism, uphold its integrity, foster and safeguard the professional interests of its members, provide opportunities for socialising and networking, and support the advancement of the arts. Membership is by invitation only and granted only to persons engaged regularly and substantially in the writing or broadcasting of criticism of dance, drama, film, literature, music and the visual arts. Founded 1913.

TheFED – A Network of Writing and Community Publishers

email FWWCParchive@gmail.com
website www.thefed.btck.co.uk
website www.thefedarchive.wordpress.com
Facebook www.facebook.com/groups/TheFEDfriends
Twitter @FWWCP_Archive
Membership £25 p.a. funded groups; £15 unfunded; £10 waged/higher income individuals; £5 unwaged/low income

A not-for-profit organisation run by volunteers which continues the work started by the Federation of Worker Writers and Community Publishers. Details of former and current activities associated with TheFED, are advertised on the website. TheFED allows writers to submit their work through its websites and hosts TheFED archive in collaboration with TUC Library Collections, London Metropolitan University and Syracuse University, New York; it has associations with other local and national events and encourages networking between member groups.

The Garden Media Guild

Katepwa House, Ashfield Park Avenue, Ross-on-Wye, Herefordshire HR9 5AX
tel (01989) 567393
email admin@gardenmediaguild.co.uk
website www.gardenmediaguild.co.uk
Facebook www.facebook.com/gdnmediaguild
Twitter @GdnMediaGuild
Honorary Secretary Geoff Hodge
Membership £80 p.a.; associate membership £120 p.a.; probationary membership £60 p.a. Full membership is open to those who earn a significant part of their income from communicating information on the subject of gardening and horticulture.

Aims to raise the quality of garden writing, photography and broadcasting, to help members operate efficiently and profitably, to improve communication between members and to promote liaison between members and the broader horticultural industry. The Guild administers annual awards to encourage excellence in garden writing, photography, trade and consumer press journalism, TV and radio broadcasting, online media and blogging. Founded 1991.

Guild of Food Writers

51 High Street, Welford, Northampton NN6 6HT
tel 07565 192477
email admin@gfw.co.uk
website www.gfw.co.uk
Twitter @GuildFoodWriter
Instagram @thegfw
Secretary Ruth Watson
Membership £92 p.a.

Aims to bring together professional food writers including journalists, broadcasters and authors, to compile a comprehensive and detailed directory of members, to extend the range of members' knowledge and experience by arranging discussions, tastings and visits, and to encourage the development of new writers by every means, including competitions, awards, bursaries and mentorship. Awards entry is not restricted to members of the Guild. Founded 1984.

Guild of Health Writers

Dale Lodge, 88 Wensleydale Road, Hampton, Middlesex TW12 2LX

tel 020-8941 2977
email admin@healthwriters.com
website www.healthwriters.com
Twitter @HealthWritersUK
Membership £50 p.a.

A national, independent membership organisation representing Britain's leading health journalists and writers. It was founded to encourage the provision of readable and accurate health information to the public. Members write on every aspect of health and wellbeing, from innovative medical science to complementary therapies and lifestyle issues. They value the training and networking opportunities that the Guild provides. Founded 1994.

The Guild of Motoring Writers
General Secretary: Melissa Chadderton,
Argyll House, 1 River Road, Littlehampton,
West Sussex BN17 5BN
tel (01903) 386423
email generalsec@gomw.co.uk
website www.gomw.co.uk
Facebook www.facebook.com/gomwuk
Twitter @gomw_uk

The largest organisation of its kind in the world representing automotive journalists, photographers, broadcasters and artists. Based in the UK, it represents more than 500 members. It aims to raise the standard of motoring journalism, to encourage motoring, motorsport and road safety, and to promote professional training of journalists. Works closely with the motor industry and provides a link between fellow members around the world. Also aims to safeguard the interests of members in relation to the aims of the Guild. Founded 1944.

Hakluyt Society
c/o The Map Library, The British Library,
96 Euston Road, London NW1 2DB
tel 07568 468066
email office@hakluyt.com
website www.hakluyt.com

Publication of original narratives of voyages, travels, naval expeditions and other geographical records. Founded 1846.

Harleian Society
College of Arms, 130 Queen Victoria Street,
London EC4V 4BT
tel 020-7236 7728
email thsduke@gmail.com
website http://harleian.org.uk
Chairman Sir Thomas Woodcock KCVO DL, FSA,
Honorary Secretary T.H.S. Duke FSA, Clarenceux King of Arms

Instituted for transcribing, printing and publishing the heraldic visitations of Counties, Parish Registers and any manuscripts relating to genealogy, family history and heraldry. Founded 1869.

Historical Novel Society
website http://historicalnovelsociety.org/
Facebook www.facebook.com/historicalnovelsociety
Twitter @histnovsoc
Chairman Richard Lee
Membership £40 p.a.

Promotes the enjoyment of historical fiction. Based in the US and UK but welcomes members (who can be readers or writers) from all over the world. Publishes print magazines, organises conferences and local chapters. Founded 1997.

Historical Writers' Association
The Union Building, 51– 59 Rose Lane,
Norwich NR1 1BY
email admin@historicalwriters.org
website https://historicalwriters.org
Facebook www.facebook.com/HistoriaHWA
Twitter @HistoriaHWA
Membership £65 p.a. full, £40 p.a. associate (UK); £50 p.a. (overseas)

Association created by authors, publishers and agents of historical writing, both fiction and non-fiction, which provides professional and social support to members and creates opportunities online and in person for members to meet with fellow writers and enthusiasts of all things historical. Organises a range of regional events.

Horror Writers Association
PO BOX 56687, Sherman Oaks, CA 91413, USA
email hwa@horror.org
website https://horror.org
Facebook www.facebook.com/groups/Horrorwritersassoc
Twitter @HorrorWriters
President John Edward Lawson
Membership From $59 p.a.

The HWA is a worldwide organisation of around 1,400 writers and publishing professionals dedicated to promoting the interests of writers of horror and dark fantasy. There are various levels of membership including new writers, established writers, professionals, academics and non-writing horror professionals. The HWA gives the iconic Bram Stoker Awards® on an annual basis, as well as hosting horror conventions, and provides a range of services to its horror writer, editor and publisher membership base. Founded 1987.

International Thriller Writers
PO Box 311, Eureka CA 95502, USA
email KimberleyHowe@thrillerwriters.org
website https://thrillerwriters.org/
Facebook www.facebook.com/ThrillerWritersOrganization
Twitter @thrillerwriters
Instagram @internationalthrillerwriters

An honorary society of authors who write thrillers, which covers subjects such as murder mystery, detective, suspense, horror, supernatural, action, espionage, true crime, war and adventure. The organisation facilitates events and programmes for successful authors to help debut authors develop their careers, as well as promoting literacy, supporting libraries and other organisations, and furthering the interests of the genre. Hosts an annual conference with publishers, editors and agents, ThrillerFest; a writing workshop programme, CraftFest; and an event which allows aspiring authors to meet and pitch to literary agents, AgentFest.

The Munster Literature Centre

Frank O'Connor House, 84 Douglas Street, Cork T12 X70A
email info@munsterlit.ie
website www.munsterlit.ie
Facebook www.facebook.com/munsterliteraturecentre
Twitter @MunLitCentre

Promotes and celebrates literature and writers, especially within Munster. As well as organising The Cork International Poetry Festival and The Cork International Short Story Festival each year, the centre runs workshops, readings and competitions to support new and established writers. Founded 1993.

The Mythopoeic Society

website www.mythsoc.org

A non-profit international literary and educational organisation for the study, discussion and enjoyment of fantastic and mythic literature, especially the works of Tolkien, C.S. Lewis and Charles Williams. 'Mythopoeic' (myth-oh-PAY-ik or myth-oh-PEE-ik) means 'mythmaking' or 'productive of myth' and aptly describes much of the fictional work of the three authors who were also prominent members of an informal Oxford literary circle (1930s–50s) known as the Inklings. Membership is open to all scholars, writers and readers of these literatures. The Society sponsors three periodicals: *Mythprint* (a bulletin of book reviews, articles and events), *Mythlore* (scholarly articles on mythic and fantastic literature), and *Mythic Circle* (a literary annual of original poetry and short stories). Each summer the society holds an annual conference, Mythcon. Founded 1967.

National Association of Writers and Groups

Old Vicarage, Scammonden, Huddersfield HD3 3FT
email info@nawg.co.uk
website www.nawg.co.uk
Facebook www.facebook.com/NAWGNews
Twitter @NAWGnews
Secretary Chris Huck
Membership £50 p.a. per group; £25 p.a. individuals

Advances the education of the general public throughout the UK, including the Channel Islands, by promoting the study and art of writing in all its aspects. Publishes *LINK*, a bi-monthly magazine, and a bi-monthly newsletter; holds the Festival of Writing annually in August/September; runs competitions with cash prizes (open to all and some free for members); and facilitates online workshops and writing weekends. New members always welcome. Founded 1995.

National Centre for Writing

Dragon Hall, 115–123 King Street, Norwich NR1 1QE
email info@nationalcentreforwriting.org.uk
website https://nationalcentreforwriting.org.uk
Facebook www.facebook.com/NationalCentreforWriting
Twitter @WritersCentre
Instagram @writerscentre

Celebrates and explores the artistic and social power of creative writing and literary translation. An ongoing programme of innovative collaborations engages writers, literary translators and readers in projects that support new voices and new stories and respond to the rapidly changing world of writing. Based at the historic Dragon Hall in Norwich, where workshops and mentoring are regularly available for writers at all levels, both face-to-face and online. Projects range from the Desmond Elliott Prize to vibrant festivals such as the City of Literature strand of Norfolk & Norwich Festival. Founded 2018.

New Writing North

Northumbria University, Newcastle upon Tyne NE1 8ST
email office@newwritingnorth.com
website https://newwritingnorth.com
Facebook www.facebook.com/newwritingnorth
Twitter @NewWritingNorth

Supports writing and reading in the North of England. Commissions new work, creates development opportunities and nurtures talent. Founded 1996.

New Writing South

email hello@newwritingsouth.com
website www.newwritingsouth.com
Facebook www.facebook.com/newwritingsouth
Twitter @newwritingsouth
Instagram @newwritingsouth

New Writing South champions all kinds of new creative writing in the South East and beyond. It develops writers' careers and helps fresh talent to flourish by providing development opportunities and commissioning new work. NWS is committed to nurturing an inclusive community of writers, regardless of background or previous experience.

Nothing in the Rulebook

email nothingintherulebook@gmail.com
website www.nothingintherulebook.com
Facebook www.facebook.com/nitrb/

Twitter @NITRB_Tweets
Co-founders Samuel Dodson, Daniel Sutherland,
Editor Ellen Lavelle

A collective of creative writers dedicated to creative expression and celebrating and supporting artists and ideas. Contributors include both new and aspiring artists alongside established and award-winning voices. Publishes new writing (non-fiction, fiction and poetry), as well as feature pieces, reviews and interviews with artists and writers. Nothing in the Rulebook also seeks to bring people together through collective projects and events. Founded 2015.

Owned Voices
website https://ownedvoices.com/
Facebook www.facebook.com/OwnedVoices
Twitter @OwnedVoices
Instagram @ownedvoices

Creative writing and publishing workshop created specifically for writers from backgrounds traditionally under-represented in publishing including BAME, working class, LGBTQ+, or writers with disabilities. Workshops cost £35 but some free spaces are available for writers on low incomes. Check the website for future dates. Also collaborates on events, panel discussions and other opportunities to support under-represented writers.

PEN International
email info@pen-international.org
website https://pen-international.org
Facebook www.facebook.com/peninternational/
Twitter @pen_int

A world association of writers. PEN was founded to promote friendship and understanding between writers and to defend freedom of expression within and between all nations. The initials PEN stand for Poets, Playwrights, Editors, Essayists, Novelists – but membership is open to all writers of standing (including translators), without distinction of gender, creed or race, who subscribe to these fundamental principles. PEN takes no part in state or party politics. Founded 1921.

English PEN Centre
24 Bedford Row, London WC1R 4EH
tel 020-7046 7046
email enquiries@englishpen.org
website https://englishpen.org

Scottish PEN Centre
The Writers' Museum, Lady Stair's Close,
Lawnmarket, Edinburgh EH1 2PA
tel 0131 226 5590
email info@scottishpen.org
website https://scottishpen.org

Irish PEN Centre
Irish Writer's Centre, 19 Parnell Square, Dublin D01 E102
email irishpen20@gmail.com
website https://irishpen.com

Pen to Print
tel 020-8227 2267
email pentoprint@lbbd.gov.uk
website https://pentoprint.org
Facebook www.facebook.com/OfficialPentoPrint
Twitter @Pen_to_Print
Instagram @officialpentoprint

A free writer development programme based in libraries. As an Arts Council-funded library, it provides a safe, collaborative environment to develop writers' authentic voices. Aspiring writers, especially those from backgrounds that are under-represented in publishing, are encouraged to reach communities with their stories and inspire potential in others. Free activities include writing classes and workshops; competitions including The Book Challenge; author talks; ReadFest literary festival; *Write On!* magazine (print); *Write On! Extra* magazine (online); and *Write On! Audio* podcast.

The Poetry Book Society – see page 322

The Poetry Society – see page 322

The Romantic Novelists' Association
email info@romanticnovelistsassociation.org
website https://romanticnovelistsassociation.org

Promotes romantic fiction and encourages good writing within the genre. Inclusive of all forms of romantic fiction and welcomes authors from all backgrounds. Represents around 1,000 writers, agents, editors and other publishing professionals.

Unpublished writers are able to join through the New Writers' Scheme which includes full membership and the opportunity to submit one book-length MS for critique each year. Any MS which is subsequently published is eligible for the Joan Hessayon Award. The Katie Fforde Bursary is intended for unpublished writers who would not otherwise be able to afford membership, it provides membership for one year and a place at the annual conference.

See also The Romantic Novel of the Year Awards page 572. Founded 1960.

Scattered Authors' Society
email scatteredauthorssociety@gmail.com
website www.scatteredauthors.org

Provides a forum for informal discussion, contact and support for professional writers in children's fiction. Founded 1998.

Scottish Association of Writers
Brackenbank, Crosshands, Mauchline,
East Ayrshire KA5 5TP
email secretary@scottishassociationofwriters.com
website www.scottishassociationofwriters.com
Facebook www.facebook.com/groups/Sawriters
Secretary Susan McVey

Promotes writing in Scotland. Organises an annual conference attended by writers who are members of affiliated clubs which features workshops and talks. Website features group and writer resources. The Council organises outreach visits to writing clubs to promote good practice, offer workshops and advise on the current writing market. Founded 1969.

Scottish Fellowship of Christian Writers

website www.sfcw.info
Facebook www.facebook.com/Scottish-Fellowship-of-Christian-Writers-393556520670479
Membership £12 p.a.

To inspire, encourage and support Christians living in Scotland to make use of their creative writing talents. It publishes *Showcase*, a magazine comprising members' own writing, and *FNU* (Fellowship News and Updates), a regular e-newsletter. The group also runs day conferences in May and November each year. Over 100 members. Founded 1980.

SCBWI (Society of Children's Book Writers and Illustrators)

email ra@britishscbwi.org
website https://britishisles.scbwi.org
Facebook www.facebook.com/groups/SCBWI
Twitter @scbwi
Instagram @scbwi_british_isles
Co-Regional Advisers, SCBWI-British Isles Natascha Biebow and Alison Gardiner

An international organisation for professional writers, illustrators, editors, publishers, agents, librarians, educators, booksellers and others involved with literature for young people. Ensures young people have access to high-quality and inclusive reading material. Hosts in-person and online guest speakers; networking or professional development events; publishing conferences; opportunities to meet industry professionals; marketing and publicity training; and writing and illustrating masterclasses. Also publishes a quarterly newsletter, *The Bulletin*, and administers awards and grants. Founded 1971.

The Society of Civil and Public Service Writers

website www.scpsw.org

Welcomes serving and retired members of the civil service, armed forces, police, local government, NHS and other public servants. Members can be aspiring or published writers. Holds monthly competitions for short stories, articles and poetry, mostly with a cash prize. In 2020, the society published a major Anthology, *Dancing with Words*, with 40 contributors, 200 pieces and 490 pages of stories, anecdotes and poetry. A quarterly publication, *The Author*, is free to members. Founded 1935.

The Society of Medical Writers

SoMW, Acre-Rise Cottage, Upper Ludstone, Claverley, Wolverhampton WV5 7DH
email moldywarp@doctors.org.uk
website https://somw.org.uk

Recruits members from all branches of the medical profession, together with all professions allied to medicine, to foster interest in literature and in writing – not solely about medicine but also about art, history, music, theatre, etc. Members are encouraged to write fiction, poetry, plays, book reviews and non-fiction articles. Prizes are awarded for short story, poetry, unpublished article or essay, best non-fiction and best written clinical paper. Publishes *The Writer* (two p.a.) and holds annual conferences and workshops. Founded 1989.

Speaking Volumes

email sharmilla.beezmohun@speaking-volumes.org.uk
website https://speaking-volumes.org.uk/
Facebook www.facebook.com/SpeakingVolumesLiveLiteratureProductions/
Twitter @Speak_Volumes

A live literature organisation which brings together diverse audiences and under-represented writers. Projects include live events, tours, workshops, festival appearances, readings and talks. They also publish anthologies and resources, and are a source of information about Britain's diverse literary scene past and present. Founded 2010.

Spread the Word

The Albany, Douglas Way, London SE8 4AG
email hello@spreadtheword.org.uk
website www.spreadtheword.org.uk
Facebook www.facebook.com/spreadthewordwriters
Twitter @STWevents
Instagram @spreadthewordwriters

London's literature development agency, a charity and a National Portfolio client of Arts Council England. Develops the careers and creative talents of London's under-represented writers. Initiates change-making research and developmental programmes that prioritise equity and access. Partners with people and organisations to diversify storytelling and enrich the UK's literature ecology. Founded by Bernardine Evaristo and Ruth Borthwick.

The Worshipful Company of Stationers and Newspaper Makers

Stationers' Hall, Ave Maria Lane, London EC4M 7DD
tel 020-7248 2934
email admin@stationers.org
website www.stationers.org
Master Anthony Mash, *Clerk* Giles Fagan
One of the Livery Companies of the City of London. Connected with the printing, publishing, bookselling, newspaper and allied trades. Founded 1403.

Writers Advice Centre for Children's Books

Riverbank House, 1 Putney Bridge Approach, London SW6 3JD
tel 020-7801 6300
email info@writersadvice.co.uk
website www.writersadvice.co.uk
Facebook www.facebook.com/writersadvice
Twitter @writersadvice
Managing Editor Louise Jordan

Dedicated to helping new and published children's writers by offering both editorial advice and tips on how to get published. The Centre also runs workshops, an online children's writing correspondence course and publishes a small list of its own under the name of Wacky Bee Books. Founded 1994.

Writing East Midlands

The Garage Studios, Unit 4, 41-43 St Mary's Gate, Notts. NG1 1PU
tel (01157) 934110
email info@writingeastmidlands.co.uk
website https://writingeastmidlands.co.uk
Facebook www.facebook.com/WritingEM
Twitter @WritingEM
Instagram @writingeastmidlands

Removes barriers and encourages equal access to writing and publishing by supporting writers throughout their careers. Services include workshops and writing courses, mentorships and career development, MS appraisals, organising festivals, conferences and events, and facilitating residencies for writers in schools, libraries and museums. Also works with specific groups of under-represented people such as refugees, migrants, domestic abuse survivors, offenders and the elderly.

Writing West Midlands

Studio 130, Zellig, Gibb Street, Birmingham B9 4AT
tel (01212) 462770
website https://writingwestmidlands.org/
Facebook www.facebook.com/writingwestmidlands/
Twitter @writingwestmidlands

A literature development agency which aims to improve access to creative opportunities for both readers and writers through support, resources and events. The Room 204 development programme provides mentoring, networking, workshops and other opportunities: applications must be submitted via the website. Also runs the Birmingham Literature Festival and the West Midlands Readers' Network. Founded 1999.

MUSIC

American Society of Composers, Authors and Publishers

250 West 57th Street, New York, NY 10107, USA
tel 020-7439 0909
website www.ascap.com
Facebook www.facebook.com/ascap
Twitter @ascap
Instagram @ascap

An organisation founded and governed by its members, it is the leading performance rights organisation representing more than 850,000 songwriters, composers and music publishers.

The Guild of International Songwriters & Composers

30 Brantwood, Chester Le Street, Co Durham DH2 2UL
tel 0330 202 0760
email gisc@songwriters-guild.co.uk
website www.songwriters-guild.co.uk
Membership £65 p.a.

Gives advice to members on contractual and copyright matters; assists with protection of members' rights; online copyright service and international collaboration register free to members; outlines requirements of record companies, publishers and artists.

Independent Society of Musicians

4–5 Inverness Mews, London W2 3JQ
tel 020-7221 3499
email membership@ism.org
website www.ism.org
Facebook www.facebook.com/ISMusicians
Twitter @ISM_music
Chief Executive Deborah Annetts
Membership £183 p.a. standard; £52 p.a. early career rate; £17 p.a. students

Professional body for musicians. Promotes and supports the art of music and protect the interests of those working as professionals within the music profession. Provides expert advice for its members. Publishes a quarterly magazine, *Music Journal*, and an annual Handbook. Founded 1882.

The Ivors Academy

1 Upper James Street, London W1F 9DE
tel 020-7636 2929
email contact@ivorsacademy.com
website www.ivorsacademy.com
Membership £92 p.a. standard; £50 p.a. for under-25s

The trade association for songwriters and composers of all genres in the UK. As champions of music creators, it has three pillars of activity: celebrating, cultivating and campaigning. Flagship awards – The Ivors and The Ivors Composer Awards – recognise the power and brilliance of music creators. A programme of educational and inspirational events runs throughout the year, where members can share their insights and expertise, develop their craft and collaborate with one another. The Ivors Academy exists to research, consult and lobby to ensure that the rights of members are protected. To become a member, you must be a member of PRS for Music or another performance rights organisation.

Music Publishers Association

2nd Floor, Synergy House,
114–118 Southampton Row, London WC1B 5AA
tel 0333 077 2350
email mpainfo@mpagroup.com
website https://mpaonline.org.uk
Facebook www.facebook.com/
MusicPublishersAssociation
Twitter @the_MPA
Instagram @thempaonline

Trade organisation representing over 200 UK music publishers: promotes and safeguards its members' interests in copyright, trade and related matters. Sub-committees and groups deal with particular interests. Founded 1881.

PRS for Music

1st Floor Goldings House, 2 Hay's Lane,
London SE1 2HB
tel 020-7580 5544
website www.prsformusic.com
Twitter @PRSforMusic

Represents the rights of songwriters, composers and music publishers around the globe. Headquartered in the UK, it works on behalf of its members to grow and protect the value of their rights. With a focus on innovation and integrity, PRS for music lobbies for a global standard for music royalties to ensure creators are paid whenever their musical compositions and songs are streamed, downloaded, broadcast, performed and played in public. Founded 1914.

Prizes and awards

This section has two parts: an alphabetical listing of prizes, competitions and awards; and an alphabetical list of grants, bursaries and fellowships, and the organisations that award them. Check individual websites for entry guidelines and deadlines. See page 768 for details of prizes and awards by genre.

PRIZES, COMPETITIONS AND AWARDS

ABSW Awards
email info@absw.org.uk
website www.absw.org.uk/pages/major-programmes
Facebook www.facebook.com/BritishScienceWriters
Twitter @absw

Administered by the Association of British Science Writers and recognise excellence in science journalism across 15 categories including Journalist, Feature, Podcast, News Analysis, and Newcomer. 1st prize in each category: £500. Entry: free for members; £55 per category for non-members. Submissions open in January and winners announced in July.

Academy of British Cover Design: Annual Cover Design Competition
Underbelly, 11 Hoxton Square, London N1 6NU
website https://abcoverd.co.uk
Twitter @ABCoverD

Recognises covers produced for any book published between 1 January and 31 December each year, by any designer in the UK, for a UK or overseas publisher. Designers may enter their own work or the work of other designers. There are ten categories: Children's (0–5) and (6–12), Young Adult, Mass Market, Literary Fiction, Crime/Thriller, Sci-Fi/Fantasy, Non-Fiction, Series Design, and Classic/Reissue. A cover can only be submitted in one category unless it is entered as an individual cover and again as part of a series design. Entry is free. Voting opens to the public for two hours before the award ceremony.

The Ackerley Prize for Autobiography and Memoir
website www.englishpen.org/prizes/pen-ackerley-prize

An annual prize of £3,000 is given for an outstanding work of literary autobiography or memoir written in English and published during the previous year by an author of British nationality. No submissions: books are nominated by the judges only. Founded 1982.

Aesthetica Art Prize
21 New Street, York YO1 8RA
email art-prize@aestheticamagazine.com
website https://aestheticamagazine.com/artprize/
Facebook www.facebook.com/aestheticamagazine
Twitter @AestheticaMag
Instagram @aestheticamag

Administered by *Aesthetica* Magazine, it recognises established and emerging visual media talent. Work submitted can be on any theme, but the prize is especially interested in work that addresses our changing world. Entries can be in any visual medium, including painting, drawing, video, installation, performance, photography and film. There are two prize categories: the Main Prize open to all creatives including students and graduates (£10,000) and the Emerging Prize open to students and recent graduates only (£1,000). An exhibition of the finalists is held at a major public gallery; the finalists and a selected longlist are published in an anthology. Previous winners have exhibited across the UK and around the world. Founded 2007.

Aesthetica Creative Writing Award
21 New Street, York YO1 8RA
email writing@aestheticamagazine.com
website https://aestheticamagazine.com/creative-writing-award/
Facebook www.facebook.com/aestheticamagazine
Twitter @AestheticaMag
Instagram @aestheticamag

Administered by *Aesthetica* magazine, it celebrates innovative poetry and short fiction. Entries can be on any subject, but the prize is particularly interested in work that explores our changing world. There are two categories: Poetry and Short Fiction. Poetry submissions must be 40lines or less and short fictions can be up to 2,000 words. Entry fee: £12 (poetry); £18 (short fiction). The winner of each category receives £2,500 and a package of other prizes and benefits. A shortlist of 20 short fiction and 40 poetry entries are also published in an annual anthology.

ALCS Educational Writers' Award
The Society of Authors, 24 Bedford Row, London WC1R 4EH
tel 020-3880 2230
email prizes@societyofauthors.org
website www.societyofauthors.org/ALCS-award

Alternates each year between books in the 5–11 and 11–18 age groups. It is given to an outstanding example of traditionally published non-fiction (with or without illustrations) that stimulates and enhances learning. The work must have been first published in the UK, in the English language, within the previous two calendar years. The total value of the prizes is £2,000.

The ALCS Tom-Gallon Trust Award

The Society of Authors, 24 Bedford Row, London WC1R 4EH
tel 020-3880 2230
email prizes@societyofauthors.org
website www.societyofauthors.org/tom-gallon
Twitter @Soc_of_Authors

An annual award of £1,000, with £500 for a runner-up, for a submitted short story, open to writers who have had at least one short story accepted for publication and are ordinarily resident in the United Kingdom, Commonwealth or the Republic of Ireland. The submission should not exceed 5,000 words.

Dinesh Allirajah Prize for Short Fiction

email info@commapress.co.uk
website https://commapress.co.uk/resources/prizes

Hosted by Comma Press and the University of Central Lancashire, it is open to anyone 18 years or over who is a UK resident. The submitted story must not have been published anywhere previously in print or online. One entry per author. 1st prize: £500.

ALTA Awards

email rachaeldaum@literarytranslators.org
website https://literarytranslators.org/awards

The American Literary Translators Association awards prizes in five categories at their annual conference: The National Translation Award for prose and poetry (and the only translation prize to take the quality of the source language text into consideration); The Lucien Stryk Asian Translation Prize ($6,000) for a translation of an Asian work in any Asian language into English; The Italian Prose in Translation Award (IPTA) ($5,000) for a translation of fiction or literary non-fiction from Italian into English; The Spain-USA Foundation Translation Award (SUFTA) ($5,000) for literary prose by authors of Spanish nationality in Spanish, Catalan, Basque or Galician into English; ALTA Travel Fellowships ($1,000) are awarded to between four and six emerging translators to fund their attendance at the ALTA conference.

The Hans Christian Andersen Awards

International Board on Books for Young People, Nonnenweg 12, CH–4055, Basel Switzerland
tel +41 61 272 2917
email ibby@ibby.org
website www.ibby.org
Facebook www.facebook.com/ibby.international
Twitter @IBBYINT
Instagram @ibby.international

Given every other year by IBBY, they recognise lifelong achievement and are presented to an author and an illustrator whose complete works have made an important, lasting contribution to children's literature. The selection criteria include the aesthetic and literary qualities of writing and illustrating, as well as the ability to see things from the child's point of view and the ability to stretch the child's curiosity and imagination. The complete works of the author and of the illustrator are taken into consideration. The Author's Award has been given since 1956 and the Illustrator's Award since 1966.

Arablit Story Prize

email info@arablit.org
website https://arablit.org/
Facebook www.facebook.com/arablit/
Twitter @arablit
Instagram @arablitorg

Recognises short stories translated from Arabic into English. Stories can be in any genre and must not have been previously published in translation. Submit a cover letter, the translated story (maximum 3,000 words), the original story and proof of the right to publish a translation. The winning story is awarded $500 to be split between the author and translator.

ARIAS (Audio & Radio Industry Awards)

website www.radioacademy.org
Twitter @radioacademy

Run by The Radio Academy, they recognise the best in the UK audio and radio industry and celebrate outstanding achievement. The awards offer stations, podcasters, publishers, presenters and production companies an annual opportunity to enter work in a range of categories reflecting today's UK audio and radio landscape. Founded 1982.

The Australian/Vogel's Literary Award

email vogel@allenandunwin.com
website www.allenandunwin.com/being-a-writer/the-australian-vogel-s-literary-award

An annual award of $20,000 for a chosen unpublished work of fiction, Australian history or biography. Entrants must be under 35 years of age on the closing date and must normally be residents of Australia. The MS must be between 50,000–80,000 words and must be an original work entirely by the entrant written in English. It cannot be under consideration by any publisher or award. Closing date: 31 May. Founded 1980.

Authors' Club Awards

Whitehall Place, London SW1A 2HE
email info@authorsclub.co.uk
website www.authorsclub.co.uk
Twitter @AuthorsClub

The Authors' Club supports the best in contemporary writing through its four annual literary awards. The Richard Schlagman Art Book Awards, in association with the Whitechapel Gallery, for the best book on art or architecture published in English, anywhere in the world, in the previous year. Awards are given in eight categories, including an overall Book of the Year. The Best First Novel Award, for the most promising debut novel first published in the UK in the previous year. Open to British, Irish or UK-based authors; there is no age limit. The Jhalak Prize, in association with Media Diversified, for black, Asian and minority ethnic writing across all genres in the UK (see page 561). The Stanford Dolman Award, in partnership with Stanfords, for the most outstanding work of literary travel writing of the past year. For full details of each prize and links to individual submission guidelines, see the website.

The Baillie Gifford Prize for Non-Fiction

website www.thebailliegiffordprize.co.uk
Twitter @BGPrize

Rewards the best of non-fiction and is open to authors of any nationality. It covers all non-fiction in the areas of current affairs, history, politics, science, sport, travel, biography, autobiography and the arts. Formerly known as The Samuel Johnson Prize (1999–2015), it is the most prestigious non-fiction prize in the UK, worth £50,000 to the winner.

Bardd Plant Cymru (Welsh-Language Children's Poet Laureate)

Books Council of Wales, Castell Brychan, Aberystwyth, Ceredigion SY23 2JB
tel (01970) 624151
email castellbrychan@books.wales
website https://llyfrau.cymru/en

Raises the profile of poetry amongst children and to encourage them to compose and enjoy poetry. During their term of office the bard will visit schools as well as help children to create poetry through electronic workshops. The scheme's partner organisations are: S4C, the Welsh Government, the Books Council of Wales, Urdd Gobaith Cymru and Literature Wales.

Bath Flash Fiction Awards

email helpdesk@bathflashfictionaward.com
website https://bathflashfictionaward.com/enter/
Facebook www.facebook.com/bathflashaward
Twitter @BathFlashAward

Host to two international flash fiction writing competitions: the Bath Flash Fiction Award and the Bath Novella-in-Flash Award. Entrants have the opportunity to appear in print and digital anthology collections, published by Ad Hoc Fiction, with overall winners receiving cash prizes.

Bath Flash Fiction Award

Has three rounds per year: March to June, July to October, and November to February. Entries should not exceed 300 words. 1st prize £1,000; 2nd prize

£300; 3rd prize £100; 50 longlisted entrants will be offered publication in the end of year print and digital anthology. Entry fee: from £7.50.

Bath Novella-in-Flash Award

Runs once per year, with a 6,000–18,000 word limit; each flash that makes up the novella should not be more than 1,000 words. Entries can be on any theme or subject but must be original, written in English and for adult or young adult readers; non-fiction and fiction written for children are not permitted. 1st prize: £300; 2 runners-up receive £100 each; all three winners are published individually. Entry fee: £18.

The Bath Novel Award

PO Box 5223, Bath BA1 0UR
email info@bathnovelaward.co.uk
website www.bathnovelaward.co.uk
Twitter @bathnovelaward

Celebrates unpublished or independently published writers of novels for adults or young adults. Submissions: first 5,000 words plus one-page synopsis. Prize: £3,000. Entries open December until May. Entry fee: £29 per novel; sponsored places available for low-income writers.

BBC National Short Story Award

email bbcnssa@bbc.co.uk
website www.bbc.co.uk/programmes/b0079gw3

In partnership with Cambridge University, it is one of the most prestigious awards for a single short story (maximum 8,000 words); it expands opportunities for British writers, readers and publishers of the short story, and honours the UK's finest exponents of the form. The winner receives £15,000 and their story will be broadcast on Radio 4; 4 runners-up receive £600. Visit the website to meet the judges and find out how to enter. Founded 2005.

British Guild of Travel Writers Members' Excellence Awards

Larking Garden, 1 Clayton Business Park, Great Blakenham, Ipswich IP6 0NL
tel 020-8144 8713
email hello@bgtw.org
website https://bgtw.org/awards/
Facebook www.facebook.com/TravWriters
Twitter @TravWriters

Celebrates the best travel writing, photography, blogging and broadcasting. The 14 categories include: Feature, Book, Blogger and Photographer. Awards are presented at an annual gala.

Binsted Prize

email info@SDPF.org.uk
website http://www.sdpf.org.uk/competition/
Twitter @SDPFestival

The South Downs Poetry Festival welcomes poems on any theme. Poems should be no longer than 50 lines and should not have been published. Prizes: 1st: £300; 2nd: £150; 3rd: £50. An anthology of the winning and commended poems will be published, the winning poems will also appear in the South Downs Poetry Festival magazine, *Poetry & All That Jazz*. Prize winners and commended poets will be invited to read their entry at the festival. Entry fee: £5 for the first poem, £4 for subsequent poems; poets aged 16–25 can enter for £3 per poem.

The Biographers' Club Slightly Foxed Best First Biography Prize

Ariane Bankes, E6 Albany, Piccadilly,
London W1J 0AR
tel 07985 920341
email ariane.bankes@gmail.com
website www.biographersclub.co.uk
Prize Administrator Ariane Bankes

Awarded to the best book written by a first-time biographer. The Prize, worth £2,500, is sponsored by *Slightly Foxed, The Real Reader's Quarterly*. Only entries submitted by publishers will be accepted for consideration. Literary memoirs are also eligible but celebrity autobiographies and ghostwritten books are not.

To qualify, books must have a publication date between 1 January and 31 December in the preceeding year (proofs are acceptable). Three copies of each book should be submitted no later than 31 October (enclose a press release to confirm publication date) along with an entry form (downloadable from the website). Entry fee: £25 per title.

The Biographers' Club Tony Lothian Prize

c/o Ariane Bankes, E6 Albany, Piccadilly,
London W1J 0AR
tel 07985 920341
email ariane.bankes@gmail.com
website www.biographersclub.co.uk
Prize Administrator Ariane Bankes

Sponsored by her daughter, Elizabeth, Duchess of Buccleuch, it supports uncommissioned first-time writers working on a biography. Applicants should submit a proposal of no more than 20 pages including a synopsis and ten-page sample chapter (double-spaced, numbered pages), CV and a note on the market for the book and competing literature (all unbound), to the prize administrator. 1st prize: £2,000. Entry fee: £15.

Blogger's Book Prize

Studio 10, Glove Factory Studios, Brook Lane, Holt, Wilts. BA14 6RL
email editor@nbmagazine.co.uk
website www.nbmagazine.co.uk/bloggers-book-prize

Celebrates the passion, knowledge and support that book bloggers bring to publishing, writing and

reading communities. Publishers submit titles which are both inclusive and popular among book clubs; all submissions are reviewed by book bloggers who choose titles for the award shortlist. Each shortlisted book is represented by an individual book blogger who champions their book on social media. As well as a public vote, both the book and the social media campaign are presented to a judging panel of book bloggers and industry professionals. The winning book receives a cash prize split between author and blogger.

Blue Pencil Agency First Novel Award

email info@bluepencilagency.com
website https://bluepencilagency.com/

Open to unrepresented authors for a novel in any adult fiction genre. Cash prizes and agent introductions for winner and runners up. Entry fee: £24. Founded 2017.

Blue Pencil Agency Pitch Prize

email info@bluepencilagency.com
website https://bluepencilagency.com/

Open to unrepresented authors for a novel opening in any adult fiction genre. Up to ten winners will have the opportunity to pitch their novel to the literary agent judge. Entrants should submit the first 500 words of their opening chapter and a 300-word synopsis. Entries open in August and close in November. Entry fee: £12. Founded 2019.

The Boardman Tasker Award for Mountain Literature

8 Bank View Road, Darley Abbey, Derby DE22 1EJ
tel (01332) 342246
website www.boardmantasker.com
Twitter @BoardmanTasker

Given for a work of fiction, non-fiction, drama or poetry, the central theme of which is concerned with the mountain environment. The prize of £3,000 commemorates the lives of mountaineers Peter Boardman and Joe Tasker. Authors of any nationality are eligible but the work must be published or distributed in the UK. Entries from publishers only. Founded 1983.

OCM Bocas Prize for Caribbean Literature

email info@bocaslitfest.com
website www.bocaslitfest.com
Twitter @bocaslitfest

Recognises literary books by Caribbean writers (writers must have been born in the Caribbean or hold Caribbean citizenship). Books published in the calendar year 2023 will be eligible for the 2024 prize. There are two deadline dates for entries: books published before November 2023 (to be received by the prize administrators by mid-November) and books published between 1 November and 31 December 2023 (which should be received by the prize administrators by the first week of January 2024). Books are judged in three categories: Poetry; Fiction (including novels and short stories); and literary Non-Fiction (including books of essays, biography, autobiography, history, current affairs, travel and other genres which demonstrate literary qualities and use literary techniques, regardless of subject matter). Textbooks, technical books, coffee-table books, specialist publications and reference works are not eligible. There is an entry fee of US$35. The overall winner will receive an award of US$10,000. Prize guidelines and entry forms available via the website.

The Bollinger Everyman Wodehouse Prize for Comic Fiction

website www.everymanslibrary.co.uk
Twitter @Everymanslib

The UK's leading prize dedicated to comic fiction. Awarded to the most original comic novel of the previous 12 months. The winner receives a case of Bollinger Special Cuvée, a jeroboam of Bollinger, a complete set of the Everyman Wodehouse collection and a rare-breed pig is named after the winning novel for a year. Eligible novels are published in the UK between 1 June and 31 May. The winner is announced in the Autumn. Closing date: February; shortlist announced in April. Launched in 2000 on the 25th anniversary of the death of P.G. Wodehouse.

Book Edit Writers' Prize

email writersprize@thebookedit.co.uk
website www.thebookedit.co.uk/writers-prize

Supports unpublished novelists who are from backgrounds and communities under-represented in publishing. Eight winners will be selected to read their work at an Agent Showcase in front of industry professionals, including literary agents. The selected writers will receive training and an opportunity to practise reading their work aloud, and an anthology of the readings will be published online. All entrants receive advice on mentoring, courses and editing. Entrants should submit the first 1,000 words of a novel, a synopsis of the novel and details of their writing experience to date. Founded 2021.

The Booker Prize

1st Floor, 10 Queen Street Place, London EC4R 1BE
email contactus@bookerprizefoundation.org
website www.thebookerprizes.com

Awarded by the Booker Prize Foundation to the author of the best (in the opinion of the judges) eligible novel. Any novel in print or electronic format, written originally in English and published in the UK and Ireland by an imprint formally established in the UK or Ireland is eligible. Entries are accepted only from UK and Irish publishers. 1st

prize: £50,000; six shortlisted authors: £2,500. Founded 1969.

The International Booker Prize

1st Floor, 10 Queen Street Place, London EC4R 1BE
email contactus@bookerprizefoundation.org
website www.thebookerprizes.com

Awarded annually for a single work of fiction, translated into English and published in the UK and Ireland. Both novels and collections of short stories are eligible. As an acknowledgement of the importance of translation, the £50,000 prize is divided equally between the author and the translator. Each shortlisted author and translator receives £2,500. Entries only from UK and Irish publishers.

Books Are My Bag Readers Awards

website www.nationalbooktokens.com/vote

Curated by bookshops and chosen by readers, categories include: Fiction, Non-Fiction, Poetry, Young Adult Fiction, Children's Fiction, Breakthrough Author, and Readers' Choice, which is nominated exclusively by readers.

BookTrust Storytime Prize

BookTrust, G8 Battersea Studios,
80 Silverthorne Road, London SW8 3HE
tel 020-7801 8826
email StoryTimePrize@booktrust.org.uk
website www.booktrust.org.uk/what-we-do/awards-and-prizes

Celebrates the best books for sharing with young children aged 0–5 with a particular focus on books that have a wide appeal to parents and carers across our diverse nation, and for stories which can be read and enjoyed over and over again. The prize is run in collaboration with public libraries and librarians and the shortlisted titles are shared with families. Publishers are invited to enter up to five books per imprint.

The Branford Boase Award

30 Winton Avenue, London N11 2AT
tel 023-8899 3369
email anne.marley@tiscali.co.uk
website www.branfordboaseaward.org.uk
Facebook www.facebook.com/branfordboaseaward
Twitter @BranfordBoase

An annual award of £1,000 is made to a first-time writer of a full-length children's novel (age 7+) published in the preceding year; the editor is also recognised. Encourages new writers for children and recognises the role of perceptive editors in developing new talent. The Award was set up in memory of the outstanding children's writer Henrietta Branford and the gifted editor and publisher Wendy Boase who both died in 1999. Closing date for nominations: end of December. Founded 2000.

Breakthrough x Black Ballad Mentoring Programme

email help@curtisbrowncreative.co.uk
website www.curtisbrowncreative.co.uk/course/
breakthrough-black-ballad-mentoring-programme-
0523

A mentoring programme for Black women writers, run in collaboration between Curtis Brown Creative and Black Ballad. Four writers will receive guidance from a published mentor over nine months and a tutorial with a literary agent. Entrants can apply with a writing project at any stage, from just starting to redrafting, in one of the following categories: Children's or YA Novel, Adult Novel, Short Stories, Memoir, or Narrative Non-Fiction. Applicants should submit 3,000 words of their project, a one-page synopsis and a completed entry form. Three of the mentorships are reserved for Black Ballad members (including new members) and one place is available for a low-income writer who cannot afford membership. Founded 2023.

Brick Lane Bookshop Short Story Prize

Brick Lane Bookshop, 166 Brick Lane,
London E1 6RU
tel 020-7247 0216
email enquiries@bricklanebookshop.org
website https://bricklanebookshop.org/2023-short-
story-prize/
Facebook www.facebook.com/bricklanebookshop
Twitter @BrickLaneBooks
Instagram @bricklanebookshop

A competition for short fiction between 1,000 and 5,000 words, sponsored by Mushens Entertainments and in partnership with Spread the Word. 1st prize: £1,000; 2nd prize: £250; 3rd prize: £100. All winners receive feedback and a development meeting, membership to the London Writers Network, and four free places to attend workshops and courses. Entry fee: £10.

The Bridport Prize

Bridport Arts Centre, South Street, Bridport,
Dorset DT6 3NR
email kate@bridportprize.org.uk
website www.bridportprize.org.uk

Annual prizes are awarded in five categories: poetry and short stories (1st prize: £5,000; 2nd prize: £1,000; 3rd prize: £500); flash fiction (under 250 words; prize: £1,000); memoir and Peggy Chapman-Andrews First Novel Award (1st prize: £1,500 and a mentoring package). Entry fees: £12 poems; £14 short stories; £11 flash fiction; £24 memoir; £24 novel. A Young Writer Award of £500 is given to the writer aged 16–25 who places highest in the competition each year.

Closing date each year: 31 May for poetry, short story, flash fiction and novel; 30 September for memoir. Entries should be in English, original work, typed or clearly written, and never published or read on radio/TV/stage. Winning stories are read by a leading London literary agent, without obligation, and two anthologies of winning entries are published each autumn. Top three poems are submitted to the Forward Poetry Prizes and top 13 eligible stories are submitted to the BBC National Short Story Award. Send sae for entry form or enter online.

The Bridport Prize Memoir Award

Bridport Arts Centre, South Street, Bridport,
Dorset DT8 3NR
email kate@bridportprize.org.uk
website https://bridportprize.org.uk/the-competition/
memoir-award/

Offers support to new memoir writers. Entrants must not have traditionally published a memoir before or have a contract with a publisher and must not be represented by a literary agent. Entrants should submit the first chapters of a memoir (maximum 8,000 words) and a 300-word overview. 1st prize: £1,500 plus mentoring from the Literary Consultancy; 2nd prize: £750 plus a full manuscript appraisal; three highly commended entries: £150 plus a 50-page appraisal. Entry fee: £24. Closing date: 30 September. Founded 2022.

British Academy Medals and Prizes

The British Academy, 10–11 Carlton House Terrace,
London SW1Y 5AH
tel 020-7969 5200
email prizes@thebritishacademy.ac.uk
website www.thebritishacademy.ac.uk/prizes-medals

Prizes and medals are awarded by the British Academy for outstanding work in various fields of the humanities and social sciences on the recommendation of specialist committees: Brian Barry Prize in Political Science; Burkitt Medal for Biblical Studies; Derek Allen Prize (made annually in turn for Musicology, Numismatics and Celtic studies); Edward Ullendorff Medal (Semitic languages and Ethiopian studies); Grahame Clark Medal (Prehistoric Archaeology); Sir Israel Gollancz Prize (English studies); Kenyon Medal (Classical Studies and Archaeology); British Academy Book Prize for Global Understanding; Peter Townsend Prize (Social Policy); Rose Mary Crawshay Prize (English Literature); Serena Medal (Italian studies); Leverhulme Medal and Prize (Humanities and Social Sciences); and The Landscape Archaeology Medal. Presentations are made in Autumn.

The British Academy Book Prize for Global Cultural Understanding

The annual £25,000 British Academy Book Prize for Global Cultural Understanding is awarded to a non-fiction book that has made an outstanding contribution to global cultural understanding for a wider public audience. The British Academy is the UK's national academy for humanities and social sciences, and eligible books come from the subjects that fall within those disciplines, from archaeology, history and psychology to philosophy, languages and cultural studies. The award recognises books that demonstrate rigorous original and high-quality research, and which are engaging and accessible to read. Nominations for the 2024 prize will open January; judges will select a shortlist of up to six books, announced in September; the winner will be announced in November. Previous winners include: Alia Trabucco Zeran, Sujit Sivasundaram, Hazel V. Carby, Toby Green and Kapka Kassabova.

The British Book Awards

The Bookseller, The Stage Media Company Ltd., 47 Bermondsey Street, London SE1 3XT
email polly.smith@thebookseller.com
website www.thebookseller.com/awards

Also known as The Nibbies, these awards showcase and honour the books that have had the biggest impact on readers, and the publishers and booksellers who supported them; celebrating the connection between books, their makers and their audience. For full entry criteria and details for all award categories, see the website.

British Czech and Slovak Association Writing Competition

24 Ferndale, Tunbridge Wells, Kent TN2 3NS
tel (01892) 543206
email prize@bcsa.co.uk
website www.bcsa.co.uk

Recognises fiction or non-fiction on the links between Britain and the Czech and Slovak Republics, at any time in their history, or society in those republics since the Velvet Revolution in 1989. There is an optional theme each year. 1st prize: £400; 2nd prize: £150. Winning entries published in *British Czech & Slovak Review*. Length: 2,000 words. Entry is free. Closing date: end of July each year. Founded 2002.

British Fantasy Awards

The Apex, 2 Sheriffs Orchards, Coventry CV1 3PP
email awards@britishfantasysociety.org
website www.britishfantasysociety.org/british-fantasy-awards
Facebook www.facebook.com/britishfantasysociety
Twitter @BritFantasySoc

Awarded in up to 15 categories including novels, novellas and short stories, and presented each autumn at FantasyCon to works published in the previous year. Past winners include Neil Gaiman, Angela Slatter, Lavie Tidhar and Tanith Lee. Publishers, writers, editors and readers are able to contribute to a list of eligible works. The shortlist is currently decided by a vote of British Fantasy Society members, and the winners decided by a jury. Founded 1972.

British Fantasy Society Short Story Competition

email shortstorycomp@britishfantasysociety.org
website https://britishfantasysociety.org/short-story-competition/

Celebrates short stories from any fantasy or horror sub-genre. Stories must be unpublished and in English. 1st prize: £100; 2nd prize: £50; 3rd prize: £20. All winners receive one year's membership and publication in *BFS Horizons* magazine.

British Haiku Society Awards

email bhsawardsadmin@fastmail.co.uk
website http://britishhaikusociety.org.uk/bhsawards/
Facebook www.facebook.com/thebritishhaikusociety

Awards prizes in three categories: haiku, tanka and haibun. Submissions must be in English, unpublished and not under consideration for any other prizes. Prizes in each category: 1st: £125; runner-up: £50. All winners will be published in the BHS journal, *Blithe Spirit*.

British Science Fiction Association Awards

email info@bsfa.co.uk
website https://bsfa.co.uk/
Twitter @bsfa

Honours sci-fi writing and promotes the genre. Awards are made for novels, short fiction, children's fiction, non-fiction, and artwork. There are three rounds: longlist (September to December), shortlist (January) and final vote (opens February and closes at noon on the day of the awards ceremony). Founded 1970.

Anne Brown Essay Prize

Number 11, Wigtown,
Dumfries and Galloway DG8 9HN
email annebrownessayprize@wigtownbookfestival.com
website www.wigtownbookfestival.com.blog/anne-brown-essay-prize
Facebook www.facebook.com/WigtownBookFestival
Twitter @WigtownBookFest

Awarded by Wigtown Book Festival which promotes intelligent and thought-provoking literary essays. Established in memory of former festival trustee and radio journalist, Anne Brown. Essays can be published or unpublished, must not exceed 4,000 words and can be on any subject, but entrants are encouraged to explore 'aspects of our shared social, cultural or emotional lives'. Writers must be from or living in Scotland. 1st prize: £1,500. Entry: free.

Bruntwood Prize for Playwriting

email bruntwood.prize@royalexchange.co.uk
website www.writeaplay.co.uk
Twitter @bruntwoodprize

Recognises playwriters regardless of background or experience. Unperformed plays are judged anonymously and read by a team of over 100 directors, producers, actors, managers, critics, agents and other industry professionals. There are four prize categories: The Bruntwood Prize (£16,000), The Judges Award (£8,000), The Bruntwood Prize International Award (£8,000) and The North West Original New Voice Award and Residency (£8,000). Each winner will enter into a development process with the Royal Exchange Theatre in an endeavour to bring their work to production. Founded 2006.

Gordon Burn Prize

email office@newwritingnorth.com
website https://newwritingnorth.com/gordon-burn-prize/

Run by New Writing North, in partnership with the Gordon Burn Trust, Faber & Faber and Newcastle University. Celebrates fiction and non-fiction in the style of Gordon Burns. Founded 2012.

The John Byrne Award

email share@johnbyrneaward.org.uk
website www.johnbyrneaward.org.uk
Facebook www.facebook.com/TheJohnByrneAward/
Twitter @johnbyrneaward
Instagram @thejohnbyrneaward

Seeks submissions which examine societal or personal values, ideals or beliefs and have the potential to create interesting real-life debate or discussion. The online exhibition invites applicants every month and there is also an overall winner each year. Work is accepted across all creative disciplines and entries are free; artists should submit their work with an accompanying rationale which clearly articulates how the work is relevant to the award's aims. Monthly winners receive £250 each; the annual winner receives £7,500.

The AKO Caine Prize for African Writing

Canopi, 7-14 Great Dover Street, London SE1 4YR
email info@caineprize.com
website www.caineprize.com
Twitter @caineprize

Awarded to an African writer of a short story published in English. The prize, worth £10,000, was launched to encourage and highlight the richness and diversity of African writing by bringing it to a wider audience internationally. The focus on the short story form reflects the contemporary development of the African storytelling tradition. See the website for eligibility and submission guidelines. Founded 1999.

Caledonia Novel Award

email caledoniaaward@gmail.com
website https://thecaledonianovelaward.com

Award for unpublished and self-published novelists. Novels can be of any genre for adults or young adults. The award is open to writers of any nationality who are over 18. Entries cost £25, with the winner receiving £1,500, and the writer of the best novel from the UK and Ireland winning a free place on a writing course at Moniack Mhor Creative Writing Centre. The Award provides a number of sponsored places to low-income writers who are unable to afford the fee. For more information, see the competition rules on the website.

Canterbury Festival Poet of the Year

Festival House, 8 Orange Street, Canterbury, Kent CT1 2JA
tel (01227) 452853
email tina@canterburyfestival.co.uk
website https://canterburyfestival.co.uk

Managed by the Festival Friends, the competition attracts entries locally, nationally and internationally. Open from March to June. Entries that make the longlist will be published in an anthology. The overall winner, announced on National Poetry Day, receives a £200 cash prize. Submission costs £5. Founded 2007.

Carnegie Medal – see The Yoto Carnegies

The Paul Cave Prize for Literature

49 Church Close, Locks Heath, Southampton, Hampshire SO31 6LR
tel (01489) 808621
email tsaunderspubs@gmail.com
website https://tsaunderspubs.weebly.com/the-paul-cave-prize-for-literature.html
Twitter @TimJourno

Open to all forms of poetry (haiku, free verse, sonnet, acrostic, villanelle, ballad, limerick, ode, elegy), flash fiction, short stories and novellas. Entries must be new and published; open to international writers. Poems should not exceed 30 lines; flash fiction 300 words; short stories 1,000 words; and novellas 10,000 words. Prizes: poem: £25; flash fiction: £25; short story: £50; novella: £100. Submissions open in March and close in September. Entry fee: poems and flash fiction from £8; short stories from £12; novellas from £35.

The Lucy Cavendish Fiction Prize

Lucy Cavendish College, University of Cambridge, Lady Margaret Road, Cambridge CB3 0BU
email comms@lucy.cam.ac.uk
website www.fictionprize.co.uk
Facebook www.facebook.com/lucycavcollege
Twitter @LucyCavColl
Instagram @LucyCavendishCollege
Founder Prof Janey Todd OBE

Helps undiscovered female writers launch their literary careers. The Prize has developed a formidable reputation for attracting first-class writing talent; many shortlisted and winning authors have secured publishing deals. Judges are seeking entries that combine literary merit with 'unputdownability'.

All shortlisted entrants receive a half-hour one-to-one consultation with the competition sponsors Peters, Fraser and Dunlop (a literary and talent agency). The 2024 winner will also receive a cash prize of £1,500.

Submissions must be unpublished and anyone who has previously had a full-length novel accepted for publication is not eligible to enter. Entrants must be resident in the UK or Ireland. Founded 2010.

Peggy Chapman-Andrews First Novel Award

The Bridport Prize, Bridport Arts Centre, South Street, Bridport, Dorset DT6 3NR
email kate@bridportprize.org.uk
website https://bridportprize.org.uk/the-competition/novel-award/

Enter first chapter(s) of a novel, up to 8,000 words, plus 300-word synopsis. 1st prize: £1,500 plus consultation with literary agents A.M. Heath and publisher Headline; 2nd prize: £750; three runners-up receive £150 each. All winners also receive support from the Literacy Consultancy. Extracts from the longlisted novels are published in an annual anthology in October. Closing date 31 May each year. Enter by post or online. Entry fees £24 per novel. Founded 2014.

The Sunday Times Charlotte Aitken Young Writer of the Year Award

email Rlaw@societyofauthors.org
website www.youngwriteraward.com
Facebook www.facebook.com/YoungWriterAward
Twitter @YoungWriterYear

A prize of £10,000 is awarded for a full-length published or self-published (in book or ebook format) work of fiction, non-fiction or poetry, by a British or Irish author aged 18–35. Runners-up receive £1,000 each. The winning book will be a work of outstanding literary merit. For submission information, see the website.

Cheltenham Illustration Awards

email pittvillepress@gmail.com
website www.cheltenham-illustration-awards.com

The awards are divided into two sections: Student (aged 18 and over) and Emerging and Established Illustrators. Entries must relate to that year's theme. The selected work will be showcased in an exhibition and published in the *Cheltenham Illustration Awards Annual*, which will be distributed to education institutions and publishers.

The Cheshire Novel Prize

website https://cheshirenovelprize.com
Facebook www.facebook.com/cheshirenovelprize
Twitter @prize_novel
Instagram @cheshirenovelprize

Only accepts entries from unagented writers; self-published writers may apply. Every unsuccessful entrant will receive at least one paragraph of feedback explaining why they were not longlisted. Submit a one-page synopsis and the first 5,000 words of a novel for adults or young adults (not children). Entry fee £25; sponsored entries are available for writers who are under-represented in publishing. 1st prize: £1,500; 2nd prize: £500.

The Children of the Night Award

The Dracula Society, 213 Wulfstan Street, East Acton, London W12 0AB
email info@thedraculasociety.org.uk
website www.thedraculasociety.org.uk/the-children-of-the-night-award.html

Administered by The Dracula Society to recognise the best gothic fiction (including horror and supernatural) in the previous year. Nominations are made by members of the society and judged by a committee. Previous winners include Terry Pratchett, Michelle Paver and Frances Hardinge. Founded 198͡

The Children's Book Award

email childrensbookaward@fcbg.org.uk
website https://fcbg.org.uk/childrens-book-award-2023
Twitter @FCBGNews

Awarded annually to authors and illustrators of children's fiction published in the UK. Children participate in the judging of the award and their votes are the deciding factor. Awards are made in the following categories: Books for Younger Children, Books for Younger Readers, and Books for Older Readers. Founded 1980.

The KPMG Children's Books Ireland Awards

Children's Books Ireland,
17 North Great George's Street, Dublin 1 D01 R2F1, Republic of Ireland
tel +353 (0)1 872 7475
email info@childrensbooksireland.ie
website www.childrensbooksireland.ie

Leading annual children's book awards in Ireland. The awards are: the Book of the Year, the Eilís Dillon Award (for a first children's book), the Honour Award for Fiction, the Honour Award for Illustration, the Judges' Special Award and the Junior Juries Award. Schools and reading groups nationwide take part in the Junior Juries programme: participating groups make their own selection of suitable titles from the books shortlisted for the awards in March, using a specially devised activity pack to guide them in their reading; each group then votes for their favourite book. Closing date: November for work published between 1 January and 31 December of an awards year. Shortlist announced in February; winners announced in May. Founded 1990.

Societies, prizes and festivals

The Children's Laureate

BookTrust, Studio G8, Battersea Studios,
80 Silverthorne Road, London SW8 3HE
tel 020-7801 8800
email childrenslaureate@booktrust.org.uk
website www.childrenslaureate.org.uk
Twitter @UKLaureate

The idea for the Children's Laureate originated from
a conversation between (the then) Poet Laureate Ted
Hughes and children's writer Michael Morpurgo. The
post was established to celebrate exceptional
children's authors and illustrators and to
acknowledge their importance in creating the readers
of tomorrow. Quentin Blake was the first Children's
Laureate (1999–2001), followed by Anne Fine
(2001–03), Michael Morpurgo (2003–05), Jacqueline
Wilson (2005–07), Michael Rosen (2007–09),
Anthony Browne (2009–11), Julia Donaldson
(2011–13), Malorie Blackman (2013–15), Chris
Riddell (2015–17), Lauren Child (2017–19), Cressida
Cowell (2019–22) and Joseph Coelho (2022-24).
Founded 1999.

Cholmondeley Awards

The Society of Authors, 24 Bedford Row,
London WC1R 4EH
tel 020-3880 2230
email prizes@societyofauthors.org
website www.societyofauthors.org/prizes/Society-of-
Authors-Awards/Cholmondeley
Twitter @Soc_of_Authors

These honorary awards recognise the achievement
and distinction of individual poets. Submissions
cannot be accepted.

CLA Intellectual Property Award

1 St Katherine's Way, London E1W 1UN
email CLAcompetitions@cla.co.uk
website https://cla.co.uk/essayprize

Open to 16–19 year olds based in UK schools and
colleges who are asked to submit an essay, podcast or
video around subjects concerning copyright and
intellectual property. 1st prize: £300; 2nd prize: £200;
3rd prize: £100. Each year the CLA will set a specific
question that the students must respond to.
Founded 2020.

Arthur C. Clarke Award

website www.clarkeaward.com

An annual prize of a number of pounds sterling equal
to the current year (e.g. £2,024 in 2024) plus an
engraved bookend is given for the best sci-fi novel
with first UK publication during the previous
calendar year. Titles are submitted by publishers.
Founded 1985.

The David Cohen Prize for Literature

PO Box 1277, Newcastle upon Tyne NE99 5BP
tel 0191 204 8850
email office@newwritingnorth.com
website www.newwritingnorth.com
website www.davidcohenprize.com

Recognises writers who use the English language and
are citizens of the UK or the Republic of Ireland,
encompassing dramatists as well as novelists, poets
and essayists. The biennial prize, of £40,000, is for a
lifetime's achievement and is donated by the John S.
Cohen Foundation. Arts Council England funds an
additional prize of £10,000 (The Clarissa Luard
Award) which is given by the winner to a fellow
author or literary organisation. The David Cohen
Prize for Literature is not open to applications but is
awarded by an independent judging panel.
Founded 1993.

Comedy Women in Print Awards

email hello@comedywomeninprint.co.uk
website www.comedywomeninprint.co.uk
Twitter @CWIPprize
Instagram @cwipprize

The first UK and Ireland comedy literary prize to
shine a light on witty women authors. Awards
include Published Comedy Novel and Unpublished
Comedy Novel, plus innovative rotating categories.
The unpublished winner receives a publishing deal;
two runners-up receive a place on a masters writing
course. Entry forms, terms and conditions and
submission guidelines can be found on the website.
Founded 2019.

The Comma Press Emerging Translators Award

email info@commapress.co.uk
website https://commapress.co.uk/resources

Gives participants of Bristol Translates Summer
School their first publishing opportunity. Entrants
should submit a sample translation from any
language into English. The winner will receive
feedback and editorial support, and a commission to
translate a single story for a Comma Press anthology.

Commonwealth Short Story Prize

Commonwealth Foundation, Marlborough House,
Pall Mall, London SW1Y 5HY
email creative@commonwealthfoundation.com
website www.commonwealthwriters.org/
shortstoryprize/info/
Facebook www.facebook.com/cwfcreative
Twitter @cwfcreatives
Instagram @cwfcreatives

Administered by the Commonwealth Foundation, it
is awarded for the best piece of unpublished short
fiction (2,000–5,000 words) in English. Regional
winners receive £2,500 and the overall winner
receives £5,000. Translated entries are also eligible, as
are stories written in selected languages other than
English. The competition is free to enter and open to

any citizen of a Commonwealth country who is aged 18 and over.

The Pol Roger Duff Cooper Prize

email DuffCooperPrize@gmail.com
website www.duffcooperprize.org

An annual prize for a literary work in the field of biography, history, politics or poetry published in English and submitted by a recognised publisher during the previous 12 months. The prize of £5,000 comes from a trust fund established by the friends and admirers of Duff Cooper, 1st Viscount Norwich (1890–1954) after his death, with a £1,000 contribution from Pol Roger Champagne.

The Rose Mary Crawshay Prize

The British Academy, 10–11 Carlton House Terrace, London SW1Y 5AH
tel 020-7969 5200
email prizes@thebritshacademy.ac.uk
website www.thebritishacademy.ac.uk

Awarded each year for an historical or critical book by a woman, on any subject connected with literature. Eligible nominations must be for books published within the last three years. Nominations open in December and close in January, and are invited from Fellows of the British Academy. Prize: £500. Founded 1888.

Creative Future Writers' Award

Community Base, 113 Queens Road, Brighton BN1 3XG
tel (01273) 234780
email info@creativefuture.org.uk
website www.creativefuture.org.uk

An annual development programme for talented writers who lack opportunities due to mental health, disability, health or social circumstances. Includes the UK's only national writing competition for all under-represented writers, alongside a series of workshops in hubs throughout the UK. Prizes, including cash and professional writing development opportunities, are awarded for both poetry and short fiction. Winning submissions are also published in an anthology alongside work by guest authors. Founded 2013.

Cundill History Prize

840 Dr Penfield Avenue, Room 233, Montreal, QC H3A 1A4
tel +1 514-398-4400
email admin.cundillprize@mcgill.ca
website www.cundillprize.com
Facebook www.facebook.com/cundillprizemcgill
Twitter @CundillPrize

Awarded each year to an individual who has published a book in English determined to have had, or likely to have, a profound literary, social and intellectual impact. Administered by Montreal's

McGill University, the Cundill Prize recognises outstanding works of non-fiction that are grounded in scholarly research while retaining wide appeal and interest to the general public. The Prize is the largest non-fiction history prize in the world and welcomes submissions on any historical period or subject, regardless of the nationality or place of residence of the author. 1st prize: $75,000; 2 runners-up receive $10,000 each.

CWA Dagger Awards

c/o CJAM, Peershaws, Berewyk Hall Court, White Colne, Colchester CO2 6QB
email secretary@thecwa.co.uk
website www.thecwa.co.uk/the-daggers
Contacts Vicki Goldie (CWA Secretary), Mike Stotter (Daggers Liaison)

Administered by the Crime Writers' Association. Winners of the Diamond Dagger and the Publishers' Dagger are nominated by CWA members. The Gold Dagger, the Ian Fleming Steel Dagger, the John Creasey Dagger, the Dagger for Crime Fiction in Translation, the ALCS Gold Dagger for Non-Fiction, the Short Story Dagger and the Historical Dagger are nominated by publishers via the CWA website (email dagger.liaison@thecwa.co.uk). Authors can also nominate their own titles via the CWA website. The Dagger in the Library winner is nominated by library staff via the CWA website.

The ProWritingAid CWA Debut Dagger

email secretary@thecwa.co.uk
website www.thecwa.co.uk/debuts/debut-dagger
Facebook www.facebook.com/groups/thedebuts

Sponsored by ProWritingAid, the Debut Dagger is the UK's prestigious, international crime-writing competition. Entrants should be unpublished and unagented.

Shortlisted writers get feedback from the panel of judges – comprising top crime agents, editors and a bestselling crime author – and have their work shown to agents and publishers who specialise in crime. Every year, shortlisted authors secure representation and/or a contract this way. The winner receives £500. Entrants should submit the opening of a crime novel (3,000 words maximum) and a 1,500-word synopsis via the website portal. The novel does not need to be completed. Entry fee: £36. The competition opens 1 October and closes at 6pm on the last working day of February.

CWA Margery Allingham Short Mystery Prize

email secretary@thecwa.co.uk
website www.thecwa.co.uk/ma

A prestigious annual competition for a short story of up to 3,500 words that follows Margery Allingham's definition of a mystery (see website). The international competition is open to all writers, published or unpublished. The story itself must not previously have been published in any form.

1st prize: £500 plus two tickets to CrimeFest the following year. Entry fee: £12. The competition opens on 1 October and closes at 6pm on the last working day of February.

CYMERA Prize for Speculative Short Fiction

email info@cymerafestival.co.uk
website www.shorelineofinfinity.com/cymera-shoreline-of-infinity-prize-for-speculative-short-fiction-2023

Recognises the best Scottish writers of sci-fi, fantasy and horror writing. Entry is open to anyone living in Scotland or who identifies as Scottish either by birth or inclination. Entries should be unpublished stories containing elements of speculative writing, must be written in English, Scots, Gaelic or another Scottish language (with translation in English), and should not exceed 2,500 words. Prizes: 1st: £150, one ticket to a CYMERA writing workshop of their choice and publication in *Shoreline of Infinity* Magazine (CYMERA Special); all shortlisted stories will be published on the CYMERA website.

The Rhys Davies Short Story Competition

Swansea University, Singleton Park,
Swansea SA2 8PP
email rdshortstory@swansea.ac.uk
website www.swansea.ac.uk/cultural-institute/rhys-davies-short-story-competition/

Established to celebrate the prose writer Rhys Davies, the competition recognises excellent short stories written by Welsh writers. Applicants are invited to submit a short story on any subject and in any style. Entries must not exceed 5,000 words and should not have been published or previously entered into a competition, the author must be a citizen or resident of Wales. Entry fee: £8; free entries are available for low-income writers. 1st prize: £1,000; 11 runners-up will receive £100 each; all 12 winners are published in an anthology. Founded 1991.

Derwent Art Prize

tel 020-3653 0896
email info@parkerharris.co.uk
website www.derwent-artprize.com
Facebook www.facebook.com/derwentartprize
Twitter @DerwentArt
Instagram @derwentartprize

Rewards excellence by showcasing the very best 2D and 3D artworks created in pencil or coloured pencil as well as water soluble, pastel, graphite and charcoal by British and international artists. Prizes totalling over £12,500 are awarded. Since the Derwent Art Prize began, the competition has attracted more than 7,000 entries from over 67 countries. For detailed submission guidelines and entry fees, see the website. Founded 2012.

Desperate Literature Short Fiction Prize

tel +34 911-88-80-89
email prize@desperateliterature.com
website https://desperateliterature.com/prize/
Twitter @DesperateLit

Celebrates the best new short fiction. Run in partnership with 14 foundations and associations, offers not only a cash prize and writing retreats but the opportunity to be published in multiple print and online journals, have your work put in front of literary agents and performed in multiple countries. The overall winner receives €1,500 cash prize, a week's residency at the Civitella Ranieri Foundation and a manuscript assessment and follow-up meeting with a literary editor from The Literary Consultancy. Runners up receive cash prizes and a meeting with a literary agent. Founded 2018.

Deutsche Börse Photography Foundation Prize

email foundation@deutsche-boerse.com
email info@tpg.org.uk
website www.deutscheboersephotographyfoundation.org/en/support/photography-prize.php
website https://thephotographersgallery.org.uk/
Instagram @dboersphotographyfoundation, @thephotographersgallery

Rewards a living photographer, of any nationality, who has made the most significant contribution to the medium of photography in Europe during the previous year (1st prize £30,000). Founded by the Photographers' Gallery and awarded together with the Deutsche Börse Photography Foundation, a non-profit organisation dedicated to the collection, exhibition and promotion of contemporary photography. Founded 1996.

DUBLIN Literary Award

Dublin City Library and Archive,
138–144 Pearse Street, Dublin 2, Republic of Ireland
tel +353 (0)1 6744802
email literaryaward@dublincity.ie
website https://dublinliteraryaward.ie
Facebook www.facebook.com/DubLitAward
Twitter @DublinLitAward
Instagram @dublincityoflit

Sponsored by Dublin City Council and managed by Dublin City Libraries, nominations are made by libraries in capital and major cities throughout the world. Novels are nominated solely on the basis of 'high literary merit', may be written in any language, but must be translated into English. 1st prize: €100,000; if translated, the author receives €75,000 and the translator €25,000. Founded 1996.

East Anglian Book Awards

email competitions@nationalcentreforwriting.org.uk
website www.nationalcentreforwriting.org.uk/

Comprised of six categories: fiction, general non-fiction, poetry, children's, history and tradition, and biography and memoir, with the £1,000 prize money going to the East Anglian Book of the Year. The Exceptional Contribution Award is given to a key figure in the world of literature, publishing, writing and editing, etc. Books must be largely set in East Anglia or be written by an author living in the region.

Closing date for entries: July. Books must have been published within the calendar year of the previous award's closing date and the one for the current year. Once entries are open (June), two copies of the book should be sent to: East Anglian Book Awards, National Centre for Writing, Dragon Hall, 115–123 King Street, Norwich NR1 1QE. Alternatively, ebook formats can be sent via email.

Edge Hill Short Story Prize
Edge Hill University,
Department of English and Creative Arts,
St Helens Road, Ormskirk, Lancs. L39 4QP
tel (01695) 584133
email cowanb@edgehill.ac.uk
website www.edgehill.ac.uk/shortstory
Twitter @EHUShortStory
Contact Billy Cowan

Awarded annually by Edge Hill University for excellence in a published single-authored short story collection. The winner will receive £10,000. There is also a Readers' Choice prize of £1,000. Publishers are entitled to submit collections published during the preceding year. Authors must be normally resident in the UK or Ireland.

Edinburgh International Flash Fiction Award
email admin@scottishartsclub.com
website www.scottishartsclub.com/awards
Facebook www.facebook.com/scottishartsclub
Twitter @ScottishArtsCL
Instagram @thescottishartsclub

A prize for short stories which must not exceed 250 words. Submissions are open February to April. 1st prize: £500.

The T.S. Eliot Prize
c/o T.S. Eliot Foundation,
3 Kensington Court Gardens,
Kensington Court Place, London W8 5QE
website https://tseliot.com/prize/
Director Michael Sims

An annual prize of £25,000, with £1,500 for each of the ten shortlisted poets, is awarded by the T.S. Eliot Foundation to the best collection of new poetry published in the UK or the Republic of Ireland during the year. Submissions are invited from publishers in June with a closing date of early August. The shortlist is announced in October and the winner in January, the day after the T.S. Eliot Prize Readings in the Royal Festival Hall.

Encore Award
Royal Society of Literature, Somerset House,
London WC2R 1LA
tel 020-7845 4679
email martha.stenhouse@rsliterature.org
website https://rsliterature.org/award/encore-award/

Celebrates the best second novel of the year. The award fills a niche in the catalogue of literary prizes by celebrating the achievement of outstanding second novels. 1st prize: £1,000.

English Association English 4–11 Children's Picture Book Awards
The English Association, Leicester LE1 7RH
email awards@englishassociation.ac.uk
website https://englishassociation.ac.uk/english-4-11-picture-book-awards

Presented by the English Association to the best children's picture books of the year, both fiction and non-fiction, in the age ranges 4-7 years and 7-11 years. The winning books are chosen by the editorial board of *English 4-11*, the journal for primary teachers published by the English Association, from a shortlist selected by a panel of teachers and Primary specialists. Each year, one of the books submitted is selected as the recipient of the Margaret Mallett Prize for Children's Non-Fiction. Founded 1995.

European Union Prize for Literature
email info@euprizeliterature.eu
website www.euprizeliterature.eu
Twitter @EUPLPrize

Supported by the Creative Europe programme of the European Union, this award is an annual initiative to recognise the best emerging fiction writers in Europe. An overall winner and 5 special mentions are collectively announced and later celebrated at an EUPL award ceremony. To encourage translation and circulation of literature, an anthology of the winning books is published, featuring excerpts both in original language and in an English or French translation. Founded 2008.

FAB Prize for Undiscovered Talent
email prize@fabfaber.co.uk
website www.fabprize.org
Twitter @FaberChildrens

Set up by Faber Children's and Andlyn Literary Agency, this is an annual competition for unagented and unpublished writers and illustrators from Black, Asian and/or non-white minority ethnic backgrounds. Now with the additional backing of BookTrust and the Association of Illustrators, the competition winners and runners up are not only offered mentoring, but also exposure to literary agents and editors alongside access to training and shadowing schemes. The prize offers a unique opportunity to kick-start a writing or illustrating career and get a foot in the door. Entries must be text or artwork for children aged 1–18 years. 1st prize: £1,500 each for text and illustration plus a bundle of support; 2nd prize: £500 each; one commended writer: a place on a five-part programme, Insights into the Publishing Process. Founded 2017.

The Alfred Fagon Award

email info@alfredfagonaward.co.uk
website www.alfredfagonaward.co.uk
Facebook www.facebook.com/alfredfagonaward
Twitter @AlfredFagonAwrd
Administrator Pauline Walker

An annual award of £6,000 for the Best New Play of the Year (which need not have been produced) for the theatre in English. TV and radio plays and film scripts will not be considered. Only writers of Caribbean and African descent resident in the UK are eligible. Applicants should apply online. Closing date: end July. Founded 1997.

FeedARead.com Book Awards

tel 07948 392634
email edward@youwriteon.com
website www.youwriteon.com

Arts Council-funded publishing site which facilitates awards for new fiction and non-fiction writers. Random House and Orion provide free professional critiques for the highest rated new writers' opening chapters and short stories on FeedaRead.com each month. The three adult fiction or non-fiction books judged to be the best books each year are published by FeedaRead.com as Award Winner Editions. The publishing awards are worth £1,000, including publishing, advertising and online sales. Writers can enter at any time throughout the year: closing date is 31 December each year. Founded 2010.

Financial Times and McKinsey Business Book of the Year Award

email bookaward@ft.com
website www.ft.com/bookaward

Identifies the book that provides the most compelling and enjoyable insight into modern business issues including management, finance and economics. Submissions should be made via a publisher. The winner receives £30,000 and runners up each receive £10,000. Founded 2005.

First Novel Prize

c/o Daniel Goldsmith Associates Ltd,
Gridiron Building, One Pancras Square,
London N1C 4AG
email hello@danielgoldsmith.co.uk
website www.firstnovel.co.uk

Organised by the literary consultancy Daniel Goldsmith Associates, it is open to previously unpublished and independently published novelists. Open to extracts of up to 5,000 words from novels of

any adult genre. Judges include a leading literary agent and an adult fiction commissioning editor. 1st prize £1,000; shortlist prize £500. For full entry guidelines and entry fees, see the website. Entries are open February to May every year.

Fish Publishing Writing Prizes

Fish Publishing, Durrus, Bantry, Co. Cork,
Republic of Ireland
email info@fishpublishing.com
website www.fishpublishing.com/writing-contests
Facebook www.facebook.com/FishPublishingIreland
Twitter @fishpublishing

International writing prizes set up to publish and encourage new writers. There are four prizes available: the Fish Short Story Prize, the Fish Short Memoir Prize, the Fish Flash Fiction Prize and the Fish Poetry Prize. Ten winners from each prize are published in the annual Fish Anthology and each competition has cash and other prizes including residencies and courses. Founded 1994.

Fitzcarraldo Edition/Mahler & Lewitt Studios Essay Prize

email essayprize@fitzcarraldoeditions.com
website https://fitzcarraldoeditions.com/prizes/essay-prize

Gives the best emerging essay writers a chance to develop their talent. The winner receives £3,000, a residency at the Mahler & LeWitt Studios in Spoleto, Italy, and their book is published by Fitzcarraldo Editions. It provides the winner with their first experience of publishing a book, from planning, research and writing through to editing, production and publicity. Entrants should be unpublished and resident in Great Britain and Ireland. Entrants should submit a 5,000-word proposal for a book-length essay (minimum 25,000 words) and a 5,000-word writing sample. Essay proposals should explore and expand the possibilities of the essay form, there is no restriction on theme or subject matter; the proposal should outline the subject matter, scope, style and structure of the proposed essay, include a word count, delivery date and biographical note, and must not have previously been submitted to a publisher.

Rathbones Folio Prize

email info@rathbonesfolioprize.com
website www.rathbonesfolioprize.com
Twitter @RathbonesFolio
Instagram @rathbones_folio
Executive Director Minna Fry

Open to all works of literature written in English and published in the UK. All genres and all forms of literature are eligible, except work written primarily for children. The format of first publication may be print or digital. Books are nominated and judged by members of the Rathbones Folio Academy; there is no public submissions process. The Prize will be awarded in March for books published in the previous calendar year. The prize is worth £30,000. See the website for submission details and dates.

Fool for Poetry Chapbook Competition
The Munster Literature Centre,
Frank O'Connor House, 84 Douglas Street,
Cork T12 X704
email foolforpoetry@munsterlit.ie
website https://www.munsterlit.ie/fool-for-poetry/

Run by the Munster Literature Centre, it is open to new, emerging and established poets from any country, but at least one of the winners will be previously unpublished. Entry fee: €25. 1st prize: €1,000; 2nd prize: €500. Both winners will receive a chapbook publication and 25 complimentary copies. The winning poets are also offered a reading and three nights' accommodation at the Cork International Poetry Festival.

Forward Prizes for Poetry
Forward Arts Foundation, Somerset House, Strand,
London WC2R 1LA
tel 020-8187 9861
email info@forwardartsfoundation.org
website www.forwardartsfoundation.org

Four prizes are awarded annually: the Best Collection published in the UK and Republic of Ireland (£10,000); the Felix Dennis Prize for Best First Collection (£5,000); the Best Single Poem: Written, published but not as part of a collection, pamphlet or anthology (£1,000); and the Best Single Poem: Performed or Produced (£1,000).

All poems entered are also considered for inclusion in the *Forward Book of Poetry*, an annual anthology. Entries for the Best Collection and Best First Collection must be submitted by book publishers and, for Best Single Poem: Written, by editors of newspapers, periodicals, magazines or online journals, or by competition organisers, in the UK and Ireland. Best Single Poem: Performed or produced, is the only category which allows self-submission. Founded 1992.

The Franco-British Society's Literary Prize
c/o The British Library, 96 Euston Road,
London NW1 2DB
email info@franco-british-society.org
website www.franco-british-society.org
Contact David Mackintosh

Recognises a full-length work of literature which contributes most to Franco–British understanding. It must be first published in the UK between 1 January and 31 December, and written in English by a citizen of the UK, British Commonwealth or the Republic of Ireland. Closing date: 31 December.

Garden Media Guild Awards
Katepwa House, Ashfield Park Avenue,
Ross-on-Wye, Herefordshire HR9 5AX
tel (01989) 567393
email admin@gardenmediaguild.co.uk
website www.gardenmediaguild.co.uk/awards
Facebook www.facebook.com/gdnmediaguild
Twitter @GdnMediaGuild

Celebrate gardening communication across seventeen categories, including books, journalism, radio, TV, blogs and social media, and an additional Lifetime Achievement Award. Awards are presented at a ceremony each year.

The Ginkgo Prize for Ecopoetry
email jaz@poetryschool.com
website https://ginkgoprize.com/
Twitter @ginkgoprize
Instagram @ginkgo.prize

In association with the Poetry School, it highlights the role poetry can play in raising awareness, gaining insight, and provoking concern for the ecological imperatives of our time. Awarded to a single poem, the overall winner receives £5,000. Applicants must be 18 or over. Poems can be be of any length or form but must, in some way, explore ecology. Entry fee: first poem £7; subsequent poems £4 each. Founded 2015.

Gladstone History Book Prize
Administrative Secretary, Royal Historical Society,
University College London, Gower Street,
London WC1E 6BT
tel 020-7387 7532
email membership@royalhistsoc.org
website https://royalhistsoc.org/prizes/gladstone-history-book-prize/

An annual award (value £1,000) for a history book. The book must be on any historical subject which is not primarily related to British history; be its author's first solely written history book; have been published in English during the previous calendar year; be an original and scholarly work of historical research.

One non-returnable copy of an eligible book should be submitted by the publisher before 31 December. Should the book be shortlisted, two further copies will be required.

The Goethe-Institut Award for New Translation
The Society of Authors, 24 Bedford Row,
London WC1R 4EH
tel 020-3380 2230
email prizes@societyofauthors.org
website www.societyofauthors.org/prizes/translation-prizes/Goethe-Institut

Open to British translators, including those who have been resident in the UK for the past 3 years, who translate literature from German into English. The winner will be awarded prize money of €1,000 and a place at the International Translator's meeting, including a visit to the Leipzig Book Fair.

Goldsboro Books Glass Bell Award

23-27 Cecil St, London WC2N 4EZ
tel 020-7497 9230, 020-7836 7376
email enquiries@goldsborobooks.com
website www.goldsborobooks.com/
Facebook www.facebook.com/GoldsboroBooks
Twitter @GoldsboroBooks
Instagram @GoldsboroBooks
Directors David Headley, Daniel Gedeon, *Manager* Rebecca McDonnell, *Events Manager* Jake Beechey

Awarded annually to an outstanding work of contemporary fiction, rewarding quality storytelling in any genre. The winner of the Glass Bell will receive £2,000 in prize money, and a handmade glass bell. The jury of ten consists of team members from Goldsboro Books. There is no fee, or limit to the number of books that a publisher may submit, allowing both established and debut authors a chance to win. Previous winners include Claire Whitfield, Chris Cleave, John Boyne, Christina Dalcher and Taylor Jenkins Reid. *Founded* 2017.

The Goldsmiths Prize

c/o Department of English & Creative Writing, Goldsmiths University of London, New Cross, London SE14 6NW
email goldsmithsprize@gold.ac.uk
website www.gold.ac.uk/goldsmiths-prize/
Twitter @GoldsmithsPrize
Prize Coordinator Livia Franchini *Literary Director* Tim Parnell

Celebrates the qualities of creative daring and rewards fiction that breaks the mould or extends the possibilities of the novel form. Prize open for submissions late January; closing date for submission of entry forms late March; closing date for submission of books early July; shortlist announced late September/early October; winner announced November. 1st prize: £10,000. Founded 2013.

The Gourmand World Cookbook Awards

Paseo Pintor Rosales, 50–28008, Madrid, Spain
email pilar@gourmandbooks.com
email edouard@gourmandbooks.com
website www.cookbookfair.com
President Edouard Cointreau

Recognises the best food and drink books published around the world. Entries are free and any book published within the year can be entered by sending one copy of the book to the Gourmand Library at the address above. The library was created in 2013 to house the reference collection of cookbook and wine book titles of the awards. For further details about past winners, see the website. Founded 1995.

The Faber/Observer/Comica Graphic Short Story Prize

website www.faber.co.uk/about-faber/graphic-short-story-prize/

Offers a £1,000 cash prize and publication in the *Observer New Review*. One runner-up recieves £250 and publication on theguardian.co.uk. Entries must be in English and unpublished; the layout should be four pages across a double-page spread and be able to be scaled up and down as necessary. Founded 2007.

The Griffin Poetry Prize

The Griffin Trust for Excellence in Poetry, 363 Parkridge Crescent, Oakville, ON L6M 1A8
tel +1 905-618-0420
email info@griffinpoetryprize.com
website www.griffinpoetryprize.com
Facebook www.facebook.com/GriffinPoetryPrize
Twitter @griffinpoetry

Awarded annually for the best collection of poetry written in, or translated into, English. The winner will receive C$130,000 and shortlisted poets will each receive C$10,000. Submissions are accepted from publishers only. Founded 2000.

Jane Grigson Trust Award

email award@janegrigsontrust.org.uk
website https://janegrigsontrust.org.uk/the-award/

Award for first-time food and drink writers who have been commissioned but not yet published. The Award is open to non-fiction books on food and drink including cookbooks, memoir, travel and history so long as the primary subject is food and/or drink. 1st prize: £2,000. Founded 2016.

The Guild of Beer Writers Awards

c/o Cask Marque, B10 Seedbed Centre, Wyncolls Road, Severalls Business Park, Colchester CO4 9HT
email secretary@beerguild.co.uk
website www.beerguild.co.uk/awards/
Facebook www.facebook.com/BritBeerWriters/
Twitter @Britbeerwriters

Open to anyone who makes content related to or communicates about beer, including journalists, authors, bloggers, poets, illustrators, filmmakers, broadcasters and photographers. Categories vary each year but focus on writing, audio and video on beer-related subjects. Prizes in each category: 1st: £1,000; 2nd: £500.

Guild of Food Writers Awards

51 High Street, Welford, Northampton NN6 6HT
tel 07565 192477
email awards@gfw.co.uk
website www.gfw.co.uk/latest-awards
Twitter @GuildFoodWriter
Instagram @thegfw

Recognises achievements in food writing and broadcasting. There are 16 categories across books, magazines and self-published content, on subjects including food, drinks, restaurants, recipes and investigative journalism. Entries open in January and winners are announced in June. Founded 1996.

Hay Book of the Year

The Drill Hall, 25 Lion Street,
Hay-on-Wye HR3 5AD
tel (01497) 822620
email admin@hayfestival.org
website www.hayfestival.com/projects
Facebook www.facebook.com/hayfestival
Twitter @hayfestival
Instagram @hayfestival

Nominations for the award can be made by publishers, authors and members of the public; the latter are asked to vote on the shortlisted titles. The winner is publicised during the festival and on the festival website and social media.

The Eccles Centre & Hay Festival Writer's Award

The Drill Hall, 25 Lion Street,
Hay-on-Wye HR3 5AD
tel (01497) 822 620
email admin@hayfestival.org
website www.hayfestival.com/eccles-centre-hay-festival-writers-award
Facebook www.facebook.com/hayfestival
Twitter @hayfestival
Instagram @hayfestival

Supports writers in the creative stage of a new fiction or non-fiction project on a theme central to the Eccles Centre's Americas collection. Celebrated globally through a series of events profiling winners at Hay Festival editions in Colombia, Peru, Mexico and Wales. Two winners will receive £20,000 in four quarterly grants, access to the expertise of the British Library's curatorial staff and the opportunity to work with the Eccles Centre and Hay festival.

Henshaw Press Short Story Competition

c/o Hobeck Books, 4 Norbury Manor Barns, Manor Drive, Norbury, Staffs. ST20 0RL
email hobeckbooks@gmail.com
website www.henshawpress.co.uk
website www.hobeck.net/henshaw-press-competition

Runs four times a year: March, June, September and December. Open world-wide to writers over 16 years. Entries should be unpublished short stories, can be on any subject and should be no more than 2,000 words. Judging panel consists of academic and professional writers. Winning stories published biannually in an anthology by Hobeck Books. Also offers free critique service for short stories written by

people under 16. 1st prize: £200; 2nd prize: £100; 3rd prize: £50. Entry fee: £6; all profits donated to charity.

The PEN Hessell-Tiltman Prize

English PEN, 24 Bedford Row, London WC1R 4EH
tel 020-7250 8382
email events@englishpen.org
website www.englishpen.org/prizes/pen-hessell-tiltman-prize

An annual prize of £2,000 awarded to a non-fiction work of high literary merit covering any historical period and published during the previous year. Biography, autobiography and books written primarily for the academic market are excluded. Submissions must come through publishers. Full details can be found on the English PEN website. Founded 2002.

William Hill Sports Book of the Year Award

website https://news.williamhill.com/sports/sports-book-of-the-year/
Twitter @BookiePrize
Instagram @BookiePrize

The world's most valuable and longest-established literary sports-writing prize. Previous winners include Jeremy Wilson and three-time-winner, Duncan Hamilton. The winner receives £30,000 and a trophy. Shortlisted authors receive a leather-bound copy of their book and £3,000. Founded 1989.

The Calvin and Rose G. Hoffman Memorial Prize

The King's School, 25 The Precincts, Canterbury, Kent CT1 2ES
email bursar@kings-school.co.uk
Contact The Hoffman Administrator

This annual prize is awarded to the writer of the best distinguished scholarly essay on Christopher Marlowe and his relationship to William Shakespeare. Entries should be 5,000 words or longer.
Closing date: 1 September.

I AM Writing Competitions

email competitions@iaminprint.co.uk
website www.iaminprint.co.uk/competition/
Facebook www.facebook.com/WritersWkend
Twitter @WritersWkend

I AM Writing Festival administer an awards programme across eight categories: crime/thriller, historical, romance, sci-fi/fantasy, poetry, flash fiction, middle grade/YA and picture books. Winners are announced at the festival. Prizes include cash prizes, feedback from literary agents and online meetings with publishing professionals.
Entry fee: £11.

The Imison Award

The Broadcasting Committee,
The Society of Authors, 24 Bedford Row,
London WC1R 4EH
tel 020-3880 2230
email info@societyofauthors.org
website www.societyofauthors.org/prizes/audio-drama/imison

Sponsored by the Peggy Ramsay Foundation and the Authors Awards and Advancement charity, it is awarded to an audio drama script by a writer new to the medium. Submissions are accepted from any party, e.g., producer, broadcasting organisation, writer, agent. 1st prize: £1,000. Founded 1994.

Indie Book Awards

6 Bell Yard, London WC2A 2JR
tel 020-7421 4656
email emma.bradshaw@booksellers.org.uk
website www.booksaremybag.com/IndieBookAwards/About
Facebook www.facebook.com/booksaremybag
Twitter @booksaremybag
Instagram @booksaremybag

The only awards given to an author or illustrator on behalf of independent bookshops. The awards showcase the best paperback reads for the summer. Awards are given in four categories: Fiction, Non-Fiction, Children's Fiction, and Picture Book. For entry guidelines and shortlist details see the website.

Indie Champions Awards

website https://uk.bookshop.org/lists/annual-indie-champions-awards
Facebook www.facebook.com/BookshopOrgUK
Twitter @bookshop_org_uk

Recognises authors, publishers and associated organisations that have supported independent bookshops through Bookshop.org and used the platform in innovative ways. The Author categories – Fiction, Non-Fiction, Children's, Lifestyle and Culture – celebrate authors who have made the greatest efforts, including through linking to and promoting the platform, providing additional or exclusive content, and taking part in events. The Indie Champions Title of the Year is awarded to the single title that has generated the most income for independent bookshops in the preceding year.

The K&IM Information Resources Awards

CILIP, 7 Ridgmount Street, London WC1E 7AE
tel 020-7255 0500
email jdburntoak@virginmedia.com
website www.cilip.org.uk

Information Resources Award

Awarded annually for outstanding information resources that are available and relevant to the knowledge, information management and library sector. Awards are made to both print and electronic resources. Recommendations are invited from Members of CILIP (the Chartered Institute of Library and Information Professionals), publishers and others, who are asked to submit nominations via the website. Winners receive a certificate.

The Walford Award

Awarded annually to an individual for an outstanding contribution to the knowledge and information management services.

The International Poetry Business Book & Pamphlet Competition

The Poetry Business, Campo House,
54 Campo Lane, Sheffield S1 2EG
tel 0114 438 4074
email office@poetrybusiness.co.uk
website www.poetrybusiness.co.uk
Directors Peter Sansom, Ann Sansom

Entrants are invited to submit a collection of 20 pages of poetry. Two winners will be selected by the judges to be published by award winning imprint, Smith|Doorstop books. There is also an opportunity to submit a full-length manuscript, which, where the judges feel it is appropriate, will be published as a book in the following year. Full-price entry: £29; free entries available for those who cannot afford the entry fee. Poets over the age of 18 writing in English from anywhere in the world are eligible. Founded 1986.

International Prize for Arabic Fiction

Mailbox V100, Hill House,
210 Upper Richmond Road, London SW15 6NP
email fleurmontanaro@yahoo.co.uk
website https://arabicfiction.org
Facebook www.facebook.com/InternationalPrizeArabicFiction
Twitter @Arabic_Fiction
Prize Administrator Fleur Montanaro

Rewards excellence in contemporary Arabic creative writing and increase the international reach of Arabic fiction through the English translation of its winners. The six shortlisted finalists receive USD$10,000, with a further USD$50,000 going to the winner.

An Post Irish Book Awards

137 Hillside, Dalkey, County Dublin A96 DP86, Republic of Ireland
tel +353 (0)85 1449574
email bert@agile-ideas.com
website www.irishbookawards.irish/
Administrator Bert Wright

A set of industry-recognition awards set up by a coalition of Irish booksellers to celebrate the extraordinary quality of Irish writing, to help bring the best books to a wider readership annually, and to promote an industry under severe competitive pressures. The awards include 18 categories spanning the entire spectrum of literary genres. Thousands of ordinary readers vote to select the winners every year and the awards are presented at a Gala Dinner and Awards Ceremony in late November each year.

The current headline sponsor is An Post, the state-owned provider of postal services in the Republic of Ireland. Submissions open 1 June; shortlist announced late October. Founded 2007.

Kerry Group Irish Novel of the Year Award

Listowel Writers' Week, 24 The Square, Listowel, Co. Kerry V31 RD93, Republic of Ireland
tel +353 (0)68 21074
email info@writersweek.ie
website https://writersweek.ie/competitions/

An annual award for a work of literary fiction by an Irish author. Novels must have been published in the previous year; six copies of each book must be submitted. There is no entry fee. 1st prize €20,000; 4 runners-up receive €500. Founded 1971.

Richard Jefferies Award

email award@richardjefferiessociety.org
website www.richardjefferiesaward.org/

Recognises the best nature writing of the year which reflects the heritage and spirit of Richard Jefferies' countryside books. Nominations can be made by anyone; there are no fees. To qualify for the entry, the book must be published (not re-published) within the calendar year and not contain previously published elements. First English translations of recent work are eligible. Ebooks are excluded from the award. Sponsored by the White Horse Bookshop, the winner receives £1,000. Founded 2015.

Jhalak Prize

email info@jhalakprize.com
website www.jhalakprize.com
Twitter @jhalakprize
Instagram @jhalakprize

Seeks out the best books by British/British resident BAME writers and awards one winner £1,000 along with a unique work of art created by artists of colour as part of the annual Jhalak Art Residency. All winners and shortlisted authors receive membership to The London Library. Entries can be in any genre of fiction, non-fiction, short story, graphic novel or poetry. The prize exists to celebrate the achievements of writers of colour. For submission guidelines and details of key dates see the website. Founded 2016.

Joffe Books Prize

email prize@joffebooks.com
website www.joffebooks.com/prize
Facebook www.facebook.com/joffebooks
Twitter @joffebooks
Instagram @joffebooks

Established to find new crime fiction writers of colour. Entrants must be from Black, Asian, Indigenous and minority ethnic backgrounds writing in any crime fiction genre, including psychological thrillers, cosy mysteries, police procedurals, suspense mysteries, and domestic noirs. Entrants must be UK residents or British citizens and must be writing in English. 1st prize: a two-book publishing deal with Joffe Books and a £25,000 audiobook offer from Audible for the first book. Entrants should submit a full-length manuscript, a synopsis of the book and a biography. Founded 2021.

Keats–Shelley Prize

KSMA Registered Office, 11 Staple Inn, London WC1V 7QH
email hello@keats-shelley.org
website www.keats-shelley.org
Facebook www.facebook.com/keatsshelleyhouse
Twitter @Keats_Shelley

Invites writers of all ages to submit essays or poems which respond to the work or lives of the Romantics. Essays may be on any related subject and should not exceed 3,000 words. Poems can be serious or comic, traditional or avant-garde and elegies or elegiac, but must respond to that year's theme. The value of the prizes is £5,000. Entry fee: free (essays), £10 (poems). Founded 1988.

Kent and Sussex Poetry Society Open Poetry Competition

email kentandsussexpoetry@gmail.com
website www.kentandsussexpoetry.com
Facebook www.facebook.com/kentandsussexpoetrysoc
Twitter @KentSusXPoetry

Open to all unpublished poems, no longer than 40 lines. 1st prize: £1,000; 2nd prize: £300; 3rd prize: £100, 4th: four at £50. Closing date: 31 January. Entry fee £5 per poem (£4 per poem if submitting 3+ poems). Founded 1985.

Kindle Storyteller Award

website www.amazon.co.uk/b?ie=UTF8&node=12061299031

Open to submissions of new English-language books in any genre. Titles must be previously unpublished and be available as an ebook and in print via Kindle Direct Publishing. The award shortlist is decided by reader feedback and a panel of industry judges.

The winning author will receive £20,000. Competition entry period runs from 1 May to 31 August.

Kipling Society John McGivering Poetry Competition

email kswritingprize@gmail.com
website www.kiplingsociety.co.uk/readers-guide/prize-2023-2023.htm

Administered by the Kipling Society and funded by the late John McGivering, it invites poems on the subjects of Rudyard Kipling and war. Poems should not exceed 30 lines, can address any aspect of war from any angle and must be connected, either directly or indirectly, with Kipling's life or works. Entries cost £5 each and should be submitted by May 1st. 1st prize: £350; 2nd prize: £100; 3rd prize: £50. There is also a Younger Poets' Competition on the same subject. 1st prize: £75; 2nd prize: £25. All winning entries from both prizes will be published in the Kipling Journal. Founded 2022.

The Kitschies

email submissions@thekitschies.com
website https://thekitschies.com
Twitter @TheKitschies

Awards the year's most progressive, intelligent and entertaining works that contain elements of the speculative or fantastic. Four awards: Red Tentacle (Novel), Golden Tentacle (Debut) and Inky Tentacle (Cover art). Open for submissions in late spring/early summer and closed in late autumn/early winter, with awards presented in late winter each year. Prizes total £2,500. There is no fee to enter. Founded 2009.

Kraszna–Krausz Book Awards

email info@kraszna-krausz.org.uk
website www.kraszna-krausz.org.uk
Twitter @kraszna_krausz

Awards which recognise individuals or groups of individuals who, in the opinion of the judges, have made an outstanding original or lasting contribution to the literature of, or concerning the art and practice of, photography or the moving image. Two winning titles are selected; one in the field of photography and one in the field of the moving image (including film, television and digital media). From the total submissions, a longlist of ten books is selected in both categories by the judges. This is then reduced to shortlists of three, from which two final winning publications will be chosen. Each winning book receives a £5,000 cash prize. Founded 1985.

Lambda Literary Awards

P.O. Box 20186, New York, NY 10014
tel +1 213-277-5755
email admin@lambdaliterary.org
website https://lambdaliterary.org/awards/
Facebook www.facebook.com/LambdaLiterary
Twitter @LambdaLiterary
Instagram @lambdaliterary

Established to increase the visibility of LGBTQIA+ storytelling in all of its forms, they are divided into 25 categories including Fiction, Non-Fiction, Poetry, Memoir/Biography, Romance, Anthology, Children's, YA, Comics, Drama, Erotica, Mystery, Speculative Fiction and LGBTQIA+ Studies. Special awards are also given to individual writers for their contribution to LGBTQIA+ storytelling. Winners are announced at an award show in New York each year. Founded 1989.

Laurel Prize for Ecopoetry

Poetrty School, Somerset House Exchange, Strand, London WC2R 1LA
website https://laurelprize.com/
Twitter @laurelprize
Instagram @thelaurelprize

Established by Simon Armitage and in association with the Poetry School, it is awarded to the best collection of nature or environmental poetry that highlights the challenges and potential solutions to the climate crisis. The overall winner receive £5,000, donated by Poet Laureate's Honorarium and is open to published poetry collections of over 40 pages written in English. 2nd prize: £2,000; 3rd prize: £1,000; Best First Collection receives £500. Founded 2020.

Leapfrog Global Fiction Prize

Can of Worms Press, 7 Peacock Yard, Iliffe Street, London SE17 3LH
email info@canofworms.net
website www.canofworms.net/prize
website www.leapfrogprize.org

Aimed at writers of literary and commercial fiction. It has two categories: the adult fiction category includes novels, novellas and short story collections; the YA and middle-grade fiction category includes novels only. For both categories the minimum word count is 22,000 and work must be unpublished (individual stories in a collection may have already been published and self-published work which sold less than 200 copies is considered unpublished). Submissions open from November through to April. Submissions are judged blind by a panel of readers before a shortlist is submitted to the final judge; last year's judge was National Book Award winner Nancy Pearl. The 1st prize is publication with Leapfrog Press in the USA and Can of Worms Press outside the USA. Finalists receive $150 and a manuscript critique from one or more of the judges.

Ledbury Poetry Competition

Ledbury Poetry House,
Elizabeth Barrett Browning Institute, Homend, Ledbury HR8 2AA
email director@ledburypoetry.org.uk
website https://ledburypoetry.org.uk
Twitter @ledburyfest
Instagram @ledburyfest
Director Chloe Garner

Supports the work of emerging poets. Entries should not have been previously published and must be forty lines or less. 1st prize: £1,000 and a place on a week-long poetry course. All winners are invited to perform their winning poem at the Ledbury Poetry Festival.

The Lindisfarne Prize for Crime Fiction

email admin@darkskiespublishing.co.uk
website www.ljrossauthor.com/philanthropy/lindisfarne-prize
Publishing Director James Ross

Recognises outstanding writing in the genre of crime or thriller fiction. It is open to all new, emerging and established writers who are from, or whose work celebrates, the North East of England and who have not previously had their submission published in any form (though they might have had other stories published before). Entrants must submit a short story of no more than 10,000 words or the first two chapters and a synopsis of their work in progress, to be considered.

The winning entry will be awarded a prize of £2,500 to support the completion of their work and funding towards a year's membership of industry associations. Entries are open from 31 January – 30th June. For full terms and conditions, see the website.

Listening Books Members Choice Award

tel 020-7407 9417
email info@listeningbooks.org.uk
website www.listeningbooks.org.uk/extra/members-choice-award
Facebook www.facebook.com/ListeningBooks12/
Twitter @ListeningBooks
Instagram @listeningbooks

Recognises readers' favourite audiobooks. Audiobooks with the highest number or listens amongst Listening Books members form the shortlist; the winner is decided by a member's vote and recognised in an online presentation hosted by patron Stephen Fry.

Listowel Writers' Week Poetry Competitions

Listowel Writers' Week, 24 The Square, Listowel, Co. Kerry V31 RD93, Republic of Ireland
tel +353 (0)68 21074
email info@writersweek.ie
website www.writersweek.ie/competitions

Holds two poetry competitions: the Piggott Poetry Prize for the best collection of new poetry (€12,000 prize) and the Poetry Collection Award for a collection of 6-12 poems or one long poem of comparable length (€2,500 prize). Full details and submission guidelines are on the website. No entry form required. Founded 1971.

Litfest Wildlife Photography Competition

The Storey, Meeting House Lane, Lancaster LA1 1TH
tel (01524) 509005
email info@litfest.org
website https://litfest.org/wildlifephotography2023/
Facebook www.facebook.com/litfestlancaster
Twitter @Litfest
Instagram @LitfestLancaster

An award specifically for wildlife photographers in the Nothwest of England. 30 photographers are selected and their work is shown in The Gallery at The Storey. Judges select the three best photographs from adults and the three best from under 18s, each receives a copy of a book on the subject of wildlife photography. Free to enter.

Little, Brown Award for Crime Fiction (University of East Anglia)

School of Literature, Drama and Creative Writing, University of East Anglia, Norwich Research Park, Norwich NR4 7TJ
email ldc.schooloffice@uea.ac.uk

This prize of £3,000 is awarded annually for the best writer of crime fiction on the University of East Anglia MA in Creative Writing (Crime Fiction). The prize is open to all students enrolled on the MA in Crime Fiction in a given year and will be based on the material submitted by students for their final assignment of a full-length crime fiction manuscript. The winner will be chosen by a panel of Little, Brown editors. For further information, contact the School of Literature, Drama and Creative Writing.

Nilsson Local Heritage Writing Award

Listowel Writers' Week, 24 The Square, Listowel, Co. Kerry V31 RD93
tel +353 0682 1074
email info@writersweek.ie
website https://writersweek.ie/competitions/

Awarded to the best book on local heritage and history by an Irish author. The work must have been published in the previous year. Two hard copies must be submitted; there is no entry fee. 1st prize: €1,000; 2nd prize: €400.

The London Hellenic Prize

The Hellenic Centre, 16–18 Paddington Street, London W1U 5AS
email msm@londonhellenicprize.org
website www.londonhellenicprize.eu
Twitter @LHellenicPrize

Established by the London Hellenic Society, it is worth £10,000. It is awarded to authors of original works written in (or translated into) English and inspired by Greece or Greek exploits, culture or history at any time from the ancient past to the present day. Although it will always strive to recognise works of excellence, any winner must be accessible to a broad readership. Founded 1996.

London Independent Story Prize

email entry@londonindependentstoryprize.co.uk
website www.londonindependentstoryprize.co.uk
Facebook www.facebook.com/LIStoryPrize
Twitter @LIStoryPrize

Creates a networking opportunity for writers and a community that embraces multicultural differences and unique approaches to story writing. Competition categories include poetry, flash fiction, short story, screenplay and stageplay, and now accepts short and feature films. All creative writing submissions are considered for the LISP anthology. Submission via the website.

The London Magazine Poetry Prize

11 Queen's Gate, London SW7 5EL
tel 020-7584 5977
email info@thelondonmagazine.org
website www.thelondonmagazine.org/category/tlm-competition
Twitter @TheLondonMag

A chance to be published in the UK's oldest literary magazine, established in 1732. Poems submitted must be previously unpublished and no longer than 40 lines. Entry fee: first entry £10; subsequent entries cost £5 each; low-income writers can submit up to three poems for £5. 1st prize: £500, 2nd prize: £300, 3rd prize: £200, plus publication in the magazine.

London Press Club Awards

Stationer's Hall, Ave Maria Lane,
London EC4M 7DD
tel 020-7520 9082
email info@londonpressclub.co.uk
website https://londonpressclub.co.uk/
Twitter @londonpressclub

Take place each Autumn, honouring categories which include: Print Journalist, Broadcaster, Scoop, Young Journalist, Daily Newspaper and Sunday Newspaper. Judges are invited to put forward suggestions for each category, and editors are invited to make submissions to the judges.

The Elizabeth Longford Prize for Historical Biography

32 Brunswick Gardens, London W8 4AL
tel 07875 088371
email katie.hambly1@btinternet.com
website www.elhb.uk
Twitter @katiehamblypr

A prize of £5,000 is awarded annually for a biography published in the year preceding the prize in memory of acclaimed biographer Elizabeth Longford, and sponsored by Flora Fraser and Peter Soros. It is judged by a panel of distinguished biographers and historians. No unsolicited submissions are accepted

and works in translation are not eligible. Founded 2003.

The Sir William Lyons Award

Argyll House, 1 River Road, Littlehampton,
West Sussex BN17 5BN
email generalsec@gomw.co.uk
website www.gomw.co.uk
Facebook www.facebook.com/gomwuk
Twitter @gomw_uk

Established in memory of Sir William Lyons, founder and president of Jaguar Cars, and set up to encourage young people to foster interest in motoring and the motor industry through automotive journalism. Open to any person of British nationality resident in the UK aged 17–23 years at the closing date of 1 October. Full details are available on the website.

Macavity Awards

email janet@mysteryreaders.org
website https://mysteryreaders.org/macavity-awards/
Facebook www.facebook.com/Mystery-Readers-Journal-106038129436981

Named after T.S. Eliot's Macavity the mystery cat, the awards recognise the best mystery books of the year as nominated and voted by Mystery Readers International Members. There are five categories: Mystery Novel, First Mystery, Mystery Short Story, Non-Fiction/Critical and the Sue Feder Memorial Award for Best Historical Mystery. Founded 1987.

The McKitterick Prize

The Society of Authors, 24 Bedford Row,
London WC1R 4EH
tel 020-3880 2230
email prizes@societyofauthors.org
website www.societyofauthors.org/prizes/fiction/mckitterick
Twitter @Soc_of_Authors

Open to debut novels published in the UK and unpublished submissions (excluding works for children) by authors over the age of 40. The work must be in English and published within the previous year or unpublished.

Bryan MacMahon Short Story Award

Listowel Writers' Week, 24 The Square, Listowel,
Co. Kerry V31 RD93, Republic of Ireland
tel +353 (0)68 21074
email info@writersweek.ie
website https://writersweek.ie/competitions/
Facebook www.facebook.com/writersweek

Awarded to the best short story (up to 3,000 words) on any subject. Prize: €1,000. Entry fee: €13. No entry form required, enter online.

The Macmillan Prize for Illustration

Macmillan Children's Books, 6 Briset Street,
London EC1M 5NR

email macmillanprize@macmillan.co.uk
website www.panmacmillan.com/mac-prize-entry-page

Three prizes are awarded annually for unpublished children's book illustrations by art students in higher education institutions in the UK. The books should be between 24–32 pages, the text can be fiction or non-fiction and the artwork must meet the specifications given on the website. 1st prize: £1,000; 2nd prize: £500; 3rd prize: £250. Founded 1985.

The Sarah Maguire Prize

Poetry Translation Centre, The Albany,
Douglas Way, Deptford SE8 4AG
email prizes@poetrytranslation.org
website www.poetrytranslation.org/sarah-maguire-prize

Biennial prize in the memory of Sarah Maguire (1957–2017), the founder of the Poetry Translation Centre and champion of international poetry. Awarded to the best book of poetry from a living poet from beyond Europe in English translation, published anywhere in the world. Winning poets and translators will divide a prize of £3,000. Founded 2019.

The Manchester Writing Competition

The Manchester Writing School at Manchester Metropolitan University, Grosvenor East Building, Cavendish Street, Manchester M15 6BG
tel 0161 247 2000
email writingschool@mmu.ac.uk
website www.mmu.ac.uk/writingcompetition/
Twitter @McrWritingSchl
Chair of Judges Adam O'Riordan (fiction), Malika Booker (Poetry)

The Manchester Writing School, the home of creative writing within the Department of English at Manchester Metropolitan University, hosts this competition which was created by UK Poet Laureate (2009–19) Carol Ann Duffy and is designed to celebrate Manchester as an international city of writers, find diverse new voices, and create opportunities for writer development.

The Manchester Fiction Prize

Entrants are asked to submit a short story of up to 2,500 words. An award of £10,000 is made to the overall winner or winners. Entry fee £18 (100 subsidised entries are available for £8).

The Manchester Poetry Prize

Entrants are asked to submit a portfolio of three to five poems totalling up to 120 lines. An award of £10,000 is made to the overall winner or winners. Entry fee £18 (100 subsidised entries are available for £8).

The Michael Marks Awards for Poetry Pamphlets

email admin@michaelmarksawards.org
website www.michaelmarksawards.org
Facebook www.facebook.com/MichaelMarksAwards
Twitter @MarksAwards
Instagram @MichaelMarksAwards

Supported by the Michael Marks Charitable Trust, and in partnership with the British Library, Wordsworth Grasmere, The *TLS* and Harvard University's Center for Hellenic Studies, the awards raise the profile of poetry pamphlets. Include prizes for pamphlet, illustrations and publisher. Pamphlets must have been published in the year preceding the submission deadline in September and can be submitted by poets and illustrators themselves or by publishers on their behalf. A separate award, The Environmental Poet of the Year prize, is awarded for a portfolio of new poetry, which is then published as a pamphlet as part of the prize. The submission deadline is late August/early September each year. Prizes range from £1,000 to £5,000, and include a writer-in-residence cultural tour of Greece with the Harvard Center for Hellenic Studies. Winners are announced at an Awards Night at the British Library. Founded 2009.

The Somerset Maugham Awards

The Society of Authors, 24 Bedford Row,
London WC1R 4EH
tel 020-3880 2230
email prizes@societyofauthors.org
website www.societyofauthors.org/somerset-maugham
Twitter @Soc_of_Authors

Awards are for writers under the age of 30. Candidates must be a British national, or resident in Great Britain and Northern Ireland for three years prior to the date of submission. Poetry, fiction, non-fiction, *belles lettres* or philosophy, but not dramatic works, are eligible. Entries should be full length and submitted by the publisher. The prize money should be used for foreign travel that will enrich their work.

McIlvanney Prize for the Scottish Crime Novel of the Year

Bloody Scotland, c/o The Mitchell Library,
North Street, Glasgow G3 7DN
website https://bloodyscotland.com/prizes/
Twitter @BloodyScotland

A crime book is eligible if the author was born or raised in Scotland, is a permanent resident of Scotland or has a strong and enduring connection to Scotland. The winner of The McIlvanney Prize will receive £1,000 and a prize of £500 will be awarded to the Debut of the Year.

The Bloody Scotland Crime Debut of the Year

The award recognises new talent in crime writing, with the same criteria as the McIlvanney Prize. 1st prize: £500. Founded 2019.

The Juliet McLauchlan Prize

c/o The Polish Social and Cultural Association,
238–246 King Street, London WC1V 7QH

email hughepstein@hotmail.co.uk
website www.josephconradsociety.org/
prizes_study_grants.htm

Awarded by the Joseph Conrad Society for an essay on any aspect of the work and life of Joseph Conrad. The Prize aims to foster new interest in and study of the the writer. The prize is dedicated to the memory of the society's first Chair, Juliet McLauchlan. Essays must be between 5,000–7,000 words, written in English and cannot previously have been published. 1st prize: £200.

The Media Freedom Awards

Stationers Hall, Ave Maria Lane, London EC4M 7DD
tel 07599 954636
email office@societyofeditors.org
website www.societyofeditors.org
Twitter @PressAwardsuk

Annual awards celebrating excellence in campaigning and investigative journalism.

Moore Prize for Human Rights Writing

email submissions@cgmoorefoundation.org
website www.cgmoorefoundation.org/prize
Facebook www.facebook.com/cgmoorefoundation.org
Twitter @cgmoorefoundat1
Instagram @cgmooreprize

Awarded to a work of non-fiction which promotes values consistent with the advancement of human rights and dignity. Submitted works must achieve this through narratives which incorporate one of the following: illustrates abuses and violations of human rights; contributes to a greater understanding of the way human rights are administered; focuses on monitoring and enforcement of human rights legislation; generates awareness of human rights issues related to privacy, freedom of expression and dissemination of information. 1st prize: £1,000. Authors and publishers can submit work, readers can nominate work through the website. Submissions must be at least 80,000 words long, published in the previous year, in English and if co-authored there must not be more that three authors. Entry is free and open to authors worldwide.

The Moth Nature Writing Prize

email enquiries@themothmagazine.com
website www.themothmagazine.com
Twitter @themothmagazine
Instagram @themothmagazine

Awarded to an unpublished piece of prose or poetry which best combines exceptional literary merit with an exploration of the writer's relationship with the natural world. The winner is chosen by a different judge each year. Previous judges include Richard Mabey, Helen Macdonald and Max Porter. 1st prize: €1,000 plus a week-long retreat at Circle of Misse in France; 2nd prize: €500; 3rd prize: €250. The word limit is 4,000 and there is a fee of €15 per story or

poem. The winning pieces are published in the *Irish Times* online. Closes 15 September. For full entry details and guidelines, see the website. *Founded* 2020

The Moth Poetry Prize

email enquiries@themothmagazine.com
website www.themothmagazine.com

Awarded annually to twelve unpublished poems, chosen by a different judge each year. Previous judges include Billy Collins, Nick Laird and Nobel prizewinner Louise Gluck. 1st prize: €6,000, three runner-up prizes of €1,000 and eight prizes of €250 for commended poems. Anyone over 16 can enter. There is a fee of €15 per poem. All four poems appear in the *Irish Times* online. Closes 31 December. For full entry details and guidelines, see the website.

The Moth Short Story Prize

email enquiries@themothmagazine.com
website www.themothmagazine.com

Awarded annually to three unpublished stories, chosen by a different judge each year. Previous judges include Sarah Hall, Ali Smith and Mark Haddon. 1st prize: €3,000; 2nd prize: a week-long retreat at Circle of Misse in France plus a travel stipend; 3rd prize: €1,000. Anyone over 16 can enter. The word limit is 3,000 and there is a fee of €15 per story. The winning story will appear in the *Irish Times* summer reading series. Closes 30 June. For full entry details and guidelines, see the website.

Mslexia Awards

PO Box 656, Newcastle upon Tyne NE99 1PZ
tel 0191 204 8860
email competitions@mslexia.co.uk
website https://mslexia.co.uk/competitions/
Facebook www.facebook.com/Mslexia/
Twitter @mslexia
Instagram @mslexia

The awards programme includes two annual poetry competitions (single poem and poetry pamphlet), two annual short fiction competitions (short story and flash fiction), two biennial novel competitions (novels for adults and novels for children and young adults), and one biennial memoir competition. Prizes include cheques, publication, mentoring, manuscript feedback, pitching workshops and introductions to agents and editors. Submission details vary by prize.

Michael Murphy Memorial Poetry Prize

The English Association, Leicester LE1 7RH
email hello@englishassociation.ac.uk
website https://englishassociation.ac.uk/michael-murphy-memorial-prize-poetry-competition/

A biennial prize celebrating a distinctive first book of poetry in honour of the eponymous poet. The winner receives £1,000 and a review of their collection appears in a selection of the English Association's publications. See the website for more information and to enter.

Mustapha Matura Award and Mentoring Programme
email info.mustaphamatura@gmail.com
website www.alfredfagonaward.co.uk/mustapha-matura-award
Twitter @MustaphaMatura
Administrator Pauline Walker

An annual award of £3,000 for newly emerging playwrights aged 25 and younger. Winners also receive nine months of mentoring. Only writers of Caribbean and African descent resident in the UK are eligible. Submitted plays must be new and original; plays do not need to have been produced but if they have been, they must have been produced in the period since the previous August. Television, radio and film scripts are not eligible. Founded 2021.

The Mythopoeic Fantasy Award for Adult Literature
email awards@mythsoc.org
website www.mythsoc.org

Given to the fantasy novel, multi-volume novel or single-author story collection for adults published during the previous year that best exemplifies the spirit of the Inklings.

The Mythopoeic Awards are chosen from books nominated by individual members of the Mythopoeic Society and selected by a committee of Society members. Authors, publishers and their representatives may not nominate their own books for any of the awards, nor are books published by the Mythopoeic Press eligible for the awards. The Mythopoeic Society does not accept or review unsolicited manuscripts.

The Mythopoeic Scholarship Award in Myth and Fantasy Studies
email awards@mythsoc.org
website www.mythsoc.org

Given to scholarly books on specific authors in the Inklings tradition, or to more general works on the genres of myth and fantasy.

The Mythopoeic Scholarship Award in Inklings Studies

Given to books on J.R.R. Tolkien, C.S. Lewis and/or Charles Williams that make significant contributions to Inklings studies.

National Poetry Competition
The Poetry Society, 22 Betterton Street, London WC2H 9BX
tel 020-7420 9880
email info@poetrysociety.org.uk
website https://poetrysociety.org.uk/competitions/national-poetry-competition/
Facebook www.facebook.com/thepoetrysociety
Twitter @PoetrySociety
Instagram @thepoetrysociety

Accepts poems up to 40 lines long on any theme (previously unpublished and written in English). Judged by a panel of three leading poets. 1st prize: £5,000. For entry guidelines visit the website. Entry costs £7 for the first poem submitted and £5 for each subsequent poem in the same submission. Free entries available for writers on low income. Entrants to the National Poetry Competition can opt in to be considered for the Peggy Poole Award which awards a year of mentorship. Founded 1978.

Nature Chronicles Prize
email emma@naturechroniclesprize.com
website https://naturechroniclesprize.com
Facebook www.facebook.com/naturechroniclesprize
Twitter @NaturePrize

A biennial literary award for unique, essay-length (2,000–8,000 words) non-fiction that responds to the times we are in and the world as it is, challenging established notions of nature writing where necessary. The winner will receive £10,000 and five runners up £1,000 each. All six winning entries will be published in an anthology.

New Angle Prize for East Anglian Literature
Ipswich Institute, Reading Room and Library, 15 Tavern Street, Ipswich IP1 3AA
tel (01473) 253992
email library@ipswichinstitute.org.uk
website www.ipswichinstitute.org.uk/NAP.html
Twitter @PrizeNewAngle
Prize Coordinator Jo Rooks

A biennial award for a recently published book of literary merit, associated with or influenced by the UK region of East Anglia (defined here as Norfolk, Suffolk, north Essex, Cambridgeshire and the Fens).

The 2025 award will be open to works of fiction or poetry, first published between 1 January 2023 and 31 December 2024. Past winners include Mark Cocker (*Crow Country*), Jim Kelly (*Death Watch*), Jules Pretty (*This Luminous Coast*), Kate Worsley (*She Rises*), Julia Blackburn (*Threads, the Delicate Life of John Craske*) and Anna Mackmin (*Devoured*). 1st prize: £2,000; £500 for one runner-up.

New Anglia Manuscript Prize
email newangliaprize@laxfieldliterary.com
website https://laxfieldliterary.com/new-anglia-manuscript-prize

Sponsored by the National Centre for Writing in Norwich, it is open to unpublished writers from Suffolk and Norfolk. Applicants must submit a completed manuscript of at least 30,000 words. Winning entries are awarded £500 and receive representation from Laxfield Literary Associates. There is no fee to enter. Founded 2020.

Societies, prizes and festivals

New Media Writing Prize

website http://newmediawritingprize.co.uk
Facebook www.facebook.com/newmediawritingprize
Twitter @NMWPrize

Showcases exciting and inventive stories that integrate a variety of formats, platforms and digital media. Encourages and promotes the best in new media writing and seeks to lead the way towards the future of the 'written' word and storytelling. There are three prizes: Chris Meade Memorial Main Prize, Digital Journalism Award and Student Prize. Founded 2010.

The New Poets Prize

The Poetry Business, Campo House,
54 Campo Lane, Sheffield S1 2EG
tel 0114 346 3037
email office@poetrybusiness.co.uk
website www.poetrybusiness.co.uk
Directors Peter Sansom, Ann Sansom

A pamphlet competition for writers between the ages of 17 and 24. Entrants are invited to submit short poetry collections of 12 pages. Two outstanding collections will be selected to receive a year of support from The Poetry Business: a publisher and writer development agency with a strong reputation for discovering, developing and publishing outstanding new poets. The two New Poets Prize winners will also have their winning collection published under The New Poets List, an imprint dedicated to discovering, mentoring, and publishing young and emerging poets. Poets, writing in English, from anywhere in the world are eligible. Entry fee: £10. A number of free entries are available for those who cannot afford the entry fee. Entries can be submitted by post (with a cheque and completed entry form) or online via the website.

New Welsh Writing Awards: Rheidol Prize for Prose with a Welsh Theme or Setting

PO Box/Blwch Post 170, Aberystwyth,
Ceredigion SY23 1WZ
tel (01970) 628410
website https://newwelshreview.com/awards

Recognises the best writing in short form (5,000–30,000 words) with the winner receiving £1,000 cash as an advance against publication and a critique by a leading literary agent. Other prizes include writing retreats, publication in the magazine and subscription to the magazine. Entries cost £12 with some free entries available for low-income writers. Founded 2015.

New Writers Award

Scottish Book Trust, Sandeman House,
Trunk's Close, 55 High Street, Edinburgh EH1 1SR
tel 0131 524 0160
email applications@scottishbooktrust.com
website www.scottishbooktrust.com/writing-and-authors/new-writers-awards/
Facebook www.facebook.com/ScottishBookTrust/
Twitter @scottishbktrust

An annual awards programme supporting individuals committed to developing their writing. There are three categories: Fiction and Narrative Non-Fiction, Poetry, and Children's and YA. In association with Gaelic Books Council there are awards available specifically for writers working in Gaelic; The Callan Gordon Award is an additional award given every two years for a writer of poetry or short stories. Applicants should supply a personal statement, details of their writing experience, a description of the project they plan to work on and a sample of their writing: for Fiction and Narrative Non-Fiction and Children's and YA: a short story, several stories or an extract from a longer work, maximum 3,500 words; for Poetry: 12 pages of poetry. Award winners receive a package of support tailored to their project, including £2,000 to allow them to focus on their work; mentoring from writers and industry professionals; performance and presentation training; the opportunity to showcase work to publishers and agents; and a week-long writing retreat. See the website for full application details; applications close July.

New Zealand Book Awards for Children and Young Adults

c/o NZ Book Awards Trust,
72 Te Wharepōuri Street, Wellington 6023
tel +64 (0)27 773 9855
email childrensawards@nzbookawards.org.nz
website www.nzbookawards.nz/new-zealand-book-awards-for-children-and-young-adults

Celebrates excellence in, and provide recognition for, the best children's books published in New Zealand. Awards are presented in six categories: Picture Book, Junior Fiction (the Wright Family Foundation Esther Glen Award), Young Adult Fiction, Non-Fiction (the Elsie Locke Award), Illustration (the Russell Clark Award) and te reo Māori (the Wright Family Foundation Te Kura Pounamu Award). Each of these awards carries prize money of $7,500. The overall prize, the Margaret Mahy Book of the Year award, carries a further prize of $7,500. A $2,500 prize (The NZSA Best First Book Award) is also awarded to a previously unpublished author or illustrator. Eligible books must have been published in New Zealand between April and March in the period preceding the awards' August ceremony date.

Nielsen Bestseller Awards in association with Coutts

c/o Agile Ideas, Studio 10, Glove Factory Studios,
Brook Lane, Holt BA14 6RL
tel (01225) 302266

email hazel.kenyon@agile-ideas.com
website https://nielsenbestsellerawards.com
Twitter @BestsellerAwards

Presented to publishers and authors of books that achieve outstanding sales through the UK retail book trade. Any title that had sold more than 250,000 copies (Silver), 500,000 copies (Gold) or 1,000,000 copies (Platinum) is recognised.

Both print and ebook sales are counted and all sales from publication (or from when Nielsen BookScan UK TCM records began: 1998 for print books and January 2014 for ebooks) are included. Continual award scheme with an annual review ceremony held every January when multiple awards are given out to various successful authors. Founded 2001.

Nine Dots Prize
email questions@ninedotsprize.org
website https://ninedotsprize.org/
Twitter @NineDotsPrize

Recognises innovative thinking in response to contemporary social issues. Entrants are asked to submit a 3,000-word response to a question posed about the problems facing the modern world. The author can agree or disagree, critique or reject, but must address the question fully and insightfully. The winner will receive $100,000 to fund a short book on the same subject. Runs every 2 years. Founded 2016.

The Seán Ó Faoláin International Short Story Competition
The Munster Literature Centre,
Frank O'Connor House, 84 Douglas Street,
Cork T12 X704
email info@munsterlit.ie
website www.munsterlit.ie/ofaolain-competition
Facebook www.facebook.com/OFaolainCompetition
Twitter @MunLitCentre

Sponsored by the Munster Literature Festival and dedicated to the Irish writer and theorist, Seán Ó Faoláin. The winner receives €2,000 and a featured reading at the Cork International Short Story Festival (including four-night hotel stay and full board).

Ockham New Zealand Book Awards
c/o Auckland Writers Festival, Suite 9A,
44–52 Wellesley Street West, Auckland 1010
tel +64 (0)9 376 8074
email awards@nzbookawards.org.nz
website www.nzbookawards.nz

Celebrates excellence in, and provide recognition for, the best books published annually in New Zealand. Awards are presented in four categories: Fiction, Poetry, Illustrated Non-Fiction and General Non-Fiction. The winner of the fiction category, the Jann Medlicott Acorn Prize for Fiction, wins more than $62,000. Winners of the other three categories each receive $12,000. Other awards include a Best First

Book Award for each of the four categories, and Te Murau o te Tuhi, a special Māori Language Award presented at the judges' discretion. Eligible books must have been published in New Zealand in the calendar year preceding the awards ceremony date.

The Orwell Prizes
The Institute of Advanced Studies,
University College London, Gower Street,
London WC1E 6BT
tel 020-3108 1618
email alice.adonis@theorwellprize.co.uk
website www.orwellfoundation.com
Contact Alice Adonis

Awarded annually for books and journalism that come closest to George Orwell's ambition to 'make political writing into art'. Five prizes are awarded annually: the Orwell Prize for Political Fiction, the Orwell Prize for Political Writing, the Orwell Prize for Journalism, the Orwell Prize for Exposing Britain's Social Evils and the Orwell Prize for Reporting Homelessness. Each prize is worth £3,000 to the winner; shortlists are published on the website and widely publicised, with the winner announced in June/July. Deadline for entry is January. Work published between June and May of the subsequent year is eligible; books must be first published in the UK or Ireland. Founded 1994.

Out Spoken Poetry Press Prize
email info@outspokenldn.com
website www.outspokenldn.com/prize-for-poetry-tc
Facebook www.facebook.com/outspokenldn
Twitter @OutSpokenLDN
Instagram @outspokenldn

Recognises unpublished poets in three categories: page poetry, performance poetry and poetry in film. Page poems can be in any style but must be written primarily in English by one author; performance poetry must be submitted as high-quality video footage and longlisted entrants must be able to perform at a slam; film entrants should include poetry as narration or subtitles. Entry fee: £5 per entry; maximum of 5 entrees per person. One overall winner will receive £700.

Page Turner Awards
tel 020-8133 6375
email paula@pageturnerawards.com
website https://pageturnerawards.com/
Facebook www.facebook.com/PageTurnerAwards
Twitter @PageTurnerAward
Founders Ken Sheridan, Paula Sheridan

An inclusive series of awards designed for writers from any background, age, race or interest. The awards open each year in January and close at the end of May. Following the judging, longlists, shortlists and finalists are announced across August/September followed by an award winners' and prize winners' online ceremony in October. The awards are made up of five literary awards: one each for published books, unpublished books, and screenplays, an award for young writers, and a mentorship programme. Founded 2020.

Parliamentary Book Awards

6 Bell Yard, London WC2A 2JR
email mail@booksellers.org.uk
website www.booksellers.org.uk/industryinfo/
eventsandawards/ParliamentaryBookAwards
Twitter @BAbooksellers

Administered each year by the Publishers Association and the Booksellers' Association, they champion the best political writing in the UK and to recognise the important link between the worlds of politics and publishing. They are the only political book awards curated by bookshops and voted for by parliamentarians. Each year publishers nominate books in three categories: Best Biography, Memoir or Autobiography by a Parliamentarian; Best Non-Biographical Book by a Parliamentarian; and Best Political Book by a Non-Parliamentarian. Founded 2016.

The People's Book Prize

website www.peoplesbookprize.com
Facebook www.facebook.com/pages/The-Peoples-Book-Prize/200637717319384
Twitter @PeoplesBkPrize
Founder & Prize Administrator Tatiana Wilson,
Patron Emeritus Frederick Forsyth, *Founding Patron* Dame Beryl Bainbridge

Awards are given in three categories: Fiction, Non-Fiction, and Children's. Titles must be submitted by publishers, with a limit of three titles per category.

The Samuel Pepys Award

Paul Gray, Haremoor House, Faringdon, Oxon SN7 8PN
tel 07802 301297
email plgray@btinternet.com
website www.pepys-club.org.uk

A biennial prize is given to a book published in English making the greatest contribution to the understanding of Samuel Pepys, his times or his contemporaries. The winner receives £2,000 and the Robert Latham Medal. Closing date: 30 June 2025 (for publication between 1 July 2023 and 30 June 2025). Founded by the Samuel Pepys Award Trust in 2003 on the tercentenary of the death of Pepys.

Pitch Perfect at Bloody Scotland

Bloody Scotland, c/o The Mitchell Library, North Street, Glasgow G3 7DN
email info@bloodyscotland.com
website https://bloodyscotland.com/announcements/
bloody-scotland-pitch-perfect-session-seeks-aspiring-crime-writers/

Facebook www.facebook.com/bloodyscotland
Twitter @bloodyscotland

An opportunity for eight aspiring authors to pitch their novel in front of literary agents and other industry professionals. All participants will receive constructive feedback; all previous winners have received representation from a literary agent and most have been published.

The Plough Prize

The Plough Arts Centre, 9–11 Fore Street, Great Torrington, Devon EX38 8HQ
tel (01805) 622552
website www.theploughartscentre.org.uk/poetry-prize
Twitter @PloughArts

Poetry competition; poems should not exceed 40 lines. 1st prize: £1,000; 2nd prize: £500; 3rd prize: £250. Visit website for full entry criteria, submission guidelines and a downloadable entry form.

Poets & Players Competition

email poetsandplayerscomp@gmail.com
website https://poetsandplayers.co/competition
Twitter @PoetsandPlayers

Invites poems on any subject and in any style or form. Poems should not have been published, online or in print, must not be under consideration for any other prizes and should not exceed 40 lines; translations are excluded. 1st prize: £600; 2nd prize: £200; 3rd prize: £100. Entry fee: £4 per poem or £10 for three poems.

Polari Book Prize

email paulburston@btinternet.com
website www.polarisalon.com
Facebook www.facebook.com/groups/36989183143
Twitter @polarisalon

Recognises emerging and established LGBTQIA+ literary talent in three categories: the Book Prize, the First Book Prize, and the Children's and YA Prize. Any full length novel, novella, short story collection, memoir, book of poetry or published play text written in English by a writer born or based in the UK or Ireland is eligible. Writers must identify as LGBTQIA+ or explore LGBTQIA+ characters in the work submitted. The winners of the First Book Prize and the Children's and YA Prize receive £1,000 each and the winner of the Book Prize receives £2,000. Full eligibility and submission guidelines can be found on the website.

The Popcorn Writing Award

email development@popcorngroup.co.uk
website https://popcorngroup.co.uk/awards/popcorn-writing-award-in-edinburgh/
Twitter @ThePopcornGroup
Instagram @thepopcorngroup

Recognises imaginative playwriting being performed at the Edinburgh Festival Fringe. Submitted plays must not have had a significant run before the festival and must be performed at one of the festival's partnering venues. Applicants should submit their play and a summary of no more than 50 words to their venue. The winning writers share a £6,000 prize fund. Founded 2019.

The Portico Prize
Portico Library, 57 Mosley Street,
Manchester M2 3HY
tel 0161 236 6785
email prize@theportico.org.uk
website www.theportico.org.uk
Facebook www.facebook.com/ThePorticoLibrary
Twitter @ThePortico
Instagram @porticolibrary

A biennial prize is awarded for a published or self-published work of fiction, non-fiction or poetry which best evokes the spirit of the North of England. The winning prize is £10,000. There is a standard £50 fee per entry, with discounted fees available to non-profit publishers and self-published entries. Founded 1985.

Primadonna Prize
Primadonna Festival CIC, Laffitts Hall, Pettaugh,
Suffolk IP14 6DT
email primadonnafestival.prize@gmail.com
website https://primadonnafestival.com/prize
Facebook www.facebook.com/primadonnafestival/
Twitter @PrimadonnaFest
Instagram @primadonnafestival

Established to widen access to the publishing industry; it is the first literary prize to judge without regard to spelling and grammar. Entrants must be unagented and unpublished, and their work must be of a high quality and have the potential to become a full-length book. Prizes: 1st: a book contract with HQ with an advance of £7,500 and assistance from Curtis Brown agent, Alice Lutyens, to turn their shortlisted piece into a publishable book; 2nd: a cash prize and mentoring. Entrants should submit 500 words of fiction on that year's subject; shortlisted entrants will be required to submit another 3,000–5,000 words. Entry fee: £8; free entries are available for writers on a low income.

V.S. Pritchett Short Story Prize
Royal Society of Literature, Somerset House, Strand,
London WC2R 1LA
tel 020-7845 4679
email info@rsliterature.org
website https://rsliterature.org/award/v-s-pritchett-short-story-prize/

An annual prize of £1,000 is awarded for a previously unpublished short story of between 2,000–4,000 words. Closing date for entries: September. Founded 1999.

Queen Mary Wasafiri New Writing Prize
c/o School of English and Drama, Queen Mary, University of London, Mile End Road,
London E1 4NS
tel 020-7882 2686
email wasafirinewwritingprize@qmul.ac.uk
website www.wasafiri.org/new-writing-prize

Awarded in three categories: Fiction, Life Writing, and Poetry and is open to anyone worldwide who has not published a complete book in the category they wish to enter. The three category winners will be published by *Wasafiri* magazine and receive a cash prize of £1,000 each. They will also be offered mentoring (depending on eligibility). The prize was launched to support new writers, with no limits on age, gender, nationality or background; some subsidised entry fees are available.

QuietManDave
email writingschool@mmu.ac.uk
website www.mmu.ac.uk/qmdprize/

Named in honour of the writer Dave Murray, the prize is awarded to exciting examples of flash fiction and flash non-fiction, which can include anything from creative non-fiction to blog posts and reviews. Writers must be aged 16 or over; the award is eager to celebrate older writers who found writing later in life. Submissions should not exceed 500 words. Prizes in each category: 1st: £1,000; 2nd: £200; 3rd: £50. Entry fee: £5; sponsored entry is available for those on a low income.

Reedsy Short Story Contest
email prompts@reedsy.com
website https://blog.reedsy.com/creative-writing-prompts/contests/

A weekly short story competition. Each week a new batch of prompts are released around a common theme. Stories should be between 1,000–3,000 awards. 1st prize: $250 and online publication. Entry fee: $5.

Republic of Consciousness Prize for Small Presses
email rofcprize@gmail.com
website www.republicofconsciousness.com/prize

Supports, promotes and celebrates small presses in the UK and Ireland. Rewards the best fiction published by small presses publishing fewer than 12 books a year. In the last five years over £80,000 has been awarded to publishers and authors. Money is split between shortlistees, rather than focussed entirely on the winner. Recent winners: Fitzcarraldo Editions for *Animalia* by Jean-Baptiste Del Amo, trans. Frank Wynne (2020); Jacaranda Press for *Lote* by Shola von Reinhold (2021); Tilted Axis for *Happy Stories, Mostly* by Norman Erikson, trans. Tiffany

Taso. The RofC also runs a monthly small press book subscription service and a book club. Founded 2017.

The Rialto Nature and Place Poetry Competition

The Rialto, PO Box 309, Aylsham NR11 6LN
email matt.howard@therialto.co.uk
website www.therialto.co.uk/pages/nature-poetry-competition-2022

The Rialto, working in association with the RSPB, Birdlife International, The University of Leeds Poetry Centre and the Cambridge Conservation Initiative, invites poems that deal with any aspect of nature and place. Poems must be unpublished, written in English and not exceed 40 lines. 1st prize: £1,000; 2nd prize: £500; 3rd prize: £250. 1st entry costs £7, subsequent entries cost £4 each.

BAFTA Rocliffe New Writing Competition

email office@rocliffe.com
website www.rocliffe.com
Facebook www.facebook.com/BAFTARocliffe
Twitter @rocliffeforum
Instagram @rocliffeproductions

Rocliffe was set up in 2000 by producer Farah Abushwesha to champion emerging writing and directing talent and develop diverse stories with an international outlook. Run in partnership with BAFTA, there are two categories for 2023: TV Drama and Children and YA. The categories SitCom and Film will return in 2024. All categories are judged by readers, a script selection panel and an industry jury, selected for their proven expertise in that medium. Three winners will receive access to an industry showcase with professional actors and directors, industry introductions, bespoke masterclasses and a tailored career planning and profile building session to provide support navigating the industry. Bursaries are available for applicants who cannot afford the admission fee.

Deborah Rogers Foundation Writers Award and David Miller Bursary

email info@deborahrogersfoundation.org
website www.deborahrogersfoundation.org/writers-award
website www.deborahrogersfoundation.org/bursary

Set up in memory of Deborah Rogers, a literary agent, who died in 2014. The Foundation supports emerging talent by means of two biennial awards: the Writers Award, which gives £10,000 to an unpublished author to enable them to complete a first book; and the DRF David Miller Internships, in partnership with Creative Access, which offer six-week paid internships in rights and agenting to candidates from under-represented backgrounds.

The Romantic Novel of the Year Awards

email rnaawards@romanticwriters.co.uk
website www.romanticnovelistsassociation.org
Awards Organiser Sharon Ibbotson

The reader-judged awards are presented in early March in the following categories: Debut, Contemporary, Popular, Romantic Comedy, Historical, Fantasy, Shorter Novel, Saga, Christmas/Festive and Thriller. In addition, the Joan Hessayon Award is only open to members of the Romantic Novelists' Association's New Writers' Scheme who submit a MS for critique from January until the end of August and whose MS is subsequently accepted for publication.

Awards are open to both members and non-members of the RNA. Novels must be first published between 1 January and 31 December of the year of entry.

Royal Photographic Society Awards

RPS House, 337 Paintworks, Arnos Vale, Bristol BS4 3AR
tel 0117 316 4450
email info@rps.org
website https://rps.org/opportunities/
Facebook www.facebook.com/royalphotographicsociety
Twitter @The_RPS
Instagram @royalphotographicsociety

A year round programme of competitions, awards and bursaries for photographers and filmmakers in a range of mediums and genres. The TPA/RPS Environmental Bursary provides £3,000 of funding to support a project which raises awareness of environmental concerns. The RPS International Photography Exhibition (IPE) is the world's longest-running photography exhibition and invites submissions from photographers at all stages of their careers.

RSL Christopher Bland Prize

Royal Society of Literature, Somerset House, Strand, London WC2R 1LA
tel 020-7845 4679
email info@rsliterature.org
website www.rsliterature.org

Encourages and celebrates older writers. The prize is given annually to a debut novelist or popular non-fiction writer, first published at the age of 50 or over. The writer must be a citizen of, or resident in, the UK or Republic of Ireland. 1st prize: £10,000. Founded 2019.

RSL Giles St Aubyn Awards for Non-Fiction

Royal Society of Literature, Somerset House, Strand, London WC2R 1LA

tel 020-7845 4679
email info@rsliterature.org
website www.rsliterature.org

Awards offering financial assistance to authors engaged in writing their first major commissioned works of non-fiction. There are three awards valued at £10,000, £5,000 and £2,500. Founded 2017.

RSL Ondaatje Prize

Royal Society of Literature, Somerset House, Strand, London WC2R 1LA
tel 020-7845 4679
email info@rsliterature.org
website www.rsliterature.org

Endowed by Sir Christopher Ondaatje, it is awarded to a book of literary merit: fiction, poetry or non-fiction, best evoking the spirit of a place. 1st prize: £10,000. Founded 2004.

Royal Society of Portrait Painters Awards

17 Carlton House Terrace, London SW1Y 5BD
tel 020-7930 6844
email info@mallgalleries.com
website www.therp.co.uk
website www.mallgalleries.org.uk

Runs an annual programme of awards, including: the Ondaatje Prize for Portraiture (£10,000), the De Laszlo Award (£3,000), the Prince of Wales's Award for Portrait Drawing (£2,000), the Burke's Peerage Foundation Award (£2,000), Smallwood Architect's Prize (£1,000), the William Lock Portrait Prize (£20,000), The RP Award (£2,000), and the RP Prize for the Best Small Portrait (£2,000).

The Royal Society Science Book Prize

The Royal Society, 6–9 Carlton House Terrace, London SW1Y 5AG
tel 020-7451 2500
email sciencebooks@royalsociety.org
website https://royalsociety.org/awards/science-books/
Facebook www.facebook.com/theroyalsociety
Twitter @royalsociety

Sponsored by the Trivedi Family Foundation, it is open to authors of science books written for a non-specialist audience. The winner will receive £25,000 and each shortlisted author will receive £2,500. Publishers may submit any number of books. Entries may cover any aspect of science and technology but educational textbooks published for professional or specialist audiences are not eligible. Founded 1988.

The Royal Society Young People's Book Prize

The Royal Society, 6–9 Carlton House Terrace, London SW1Y 5AG
tel 020-7451 2500

email education@royalsociety.org
website https://royalsociety.org/grants-schemes-awards/book-prizes/young-peoples-book-prize
Facebook www.facebook.com/theroyalsociety
Twitter @royalsociety

Open to books for under-14s that have science as a substantial part of their content, narrative or theme. An expert adult panel choose the shortlist, but the winner is chosen by groups of young people in judging panels across the UK. The winning entry receives £10,000 and shortlisted entries receive £2,500. Entries open in December each year. Pure reference works including encyclopedias, educational textbooks and descriptive books are not eligible. The Prize is offered thanks to the generosity of an anonymous donor. Founded 1988.

RSL Literature Matters

Royal Society of Literature, Somerset House, London WC2R 1LA
tel 020-7845 4679
email info@rsliterature.org
website https://rsliterature.org/award/rsl-literature-matters/

Recognises literary excellence and past achievements. Awards are presented each year to provide financial assistance for a new piece of writing or project. Seven awards are presented each year, valued between £2,000 and £5,000 each.

RTÉ Radio, Drama On One, P.J. O'Connor Awards for Radio Drama

RTÉ Radio, Drama on One, Radio Centre, Donnybrook, Dublin 4, Republic of Ireland
email dramaonone@rte.ie
website www.rte.ie/dramaonone

For over 40 years the annual P.J. O'Connor Awards for Radio Drama have celebrated the best in new Irish writing. Candidates should submit radio plays of 40 minutes in duration. 1st prize: €5,000.

RTÉ Radio 1 Short Story Competition in Honour of Francis MacManus

RTÉ Radio 1 Short Story Competition, RTÉ Radio Centre, Donnybrook, Dublin 4, Republic of Ireland
website www.rte.ie/writing

Open to writers who hold an Irish passport or are resident on the island of Ireland. Short stories in Irish or English, should not have been previously published or broadcast. Winning entries are broadcast on RTÉ Radio.

Rubery Book Award

PO Box 15821, Birmingham B31 9EA
email enquiries@ruberybookaward.com
website www.ruberybookaward.com

An annual award for published books on any subject, including children's books, with prizes totalling

£2,800 (Book of the Year receives £2,000 and category winners £200 each). Books published by independent presses and self-published books are eligible.

Runciman Award

email runciman@anglohellenicleague.org
website https://runcimanaward.org/

An annual award, given by the Anglo-Hellenic League, to promote Anglo-Greek understanding and friendship. Entries span history, archaeology, antiquity, biography, literature, philosophy, myth, novels, travel writing and literary translations. The value of the award is £10,000. Founded 1986.

Ruth Rendell Award

68 South Lambeth Road, London SW8 1RL
tel 020-7587 1842
email contact@literacytrust.org.uk
website https://literacytrust.org.uk/about-us/ruth-rendell-award/
Facebook www.facebook.com/nationalliteracytrust/
Twitter @Literacy_Trust
Instagram @literacy_trust

Named after the author Ruth Rendell who championed literacy throughout her life, it recognises authors who exert special effort to promote literacy development. Authors can be traditionally or self-published but must have demonstrated a commitment to furthering literacy through working with charities, schools, adult education settings, or communities; using their platform to highlight literacy issues; and participating in events, workshops, awards, festivals and initiatives dedicated to reading and writing. Nominations can be made by publishers, libraries, booksellers, schools, charities and individuals through the website. Founded 2016.

The Saltire Society Literary Awards

The Saltire Society, 9 Fountain Close, 22 High Street, Edinburgh EH1 1TF
tel 0131 556 1836
email saltire@saltiresociety.org.uk
website www.saltiresociety.org.uk
Facebook www.facebook.com/saltiresociety/
Twitter @saltire_society

The Scottish Book of the Year is an annual award selected from the Saltire Society Book Award categories: First Book, Fiction Book, Non-Fiction Book, Poetry Book, Research Book, and Book Cover. The awards have a value of £2,000 each, and the Book of the Year winner receives an additional £4,000. Authors from or living in Scotland or any book which deals with the work or life of a Scot or with a Scottish problem, event or situation is eligible. The Saltire Society also celebrates the wider publishing landscape of Scotland with its Scottish Publisher of the Year Award (company) and Emerging Publisher of the Year Award (individual). Both of these recognise the work of publishers in creating and nurturing readership and writing in Scotland.

Saveas Writers' International Writing Competition

c/o Save As Writers, 35 Spillett Close, Faversham, Kent ME13 8QP
email saveas@hotmail.co.uk
website https://saveaswriters.co.uk/competitions/horizons.html

Given in two categories: Poetry (The Canterbury Christchurch Poetry Prize) and Prose (The University of Kent Fiction Prize). Entries must be unpublished and should respond or relate to that year's theme; poems should be 60 lines or less, short stories should be 3,500 words or less. Entry fee: £3 for one poem or £8 for three; £4 for one short story or £10 for three. 1st prize: £200; 2nd prize: £100; 3rd prize: £50.

Walter Scott Prize for Historical Fiction

10 Brewery Park Business Centre, Haddington EH41 3HA
tel (01620) 829800
email rebecca@stonehillsalt.co.uk
website www.walterscottprize.co.uk
Facebook www.facebook.com/walterscottprize
Twitter @waltscottprize
Administration, Publicity and Marketing Rebecca Salt

Founded by the Duke and Duchess of Buccleuch. Awarded annually, it rewards fiction of exceptional quality which is set in the past (according to Walter Scott's subtitle for Waverley, at least 60 years ago). The Prize is among the richest UK fiction prizes; the winner receives £25,000, and shortlisted authors receive £1,500 each. The Prize is usually awarded at the Borders Book Festival in Melrose each June, with a longlist announced in February and a shortlist announced in March or April.

The rules governing submission are on the website. Books must be written in English and have been published in the UK, Eire or the Commonwealth during the previous calendar year. Books must be submitted by publishers, and self-published authors are not eligible. Founded 2009.

Scottish Arts Club Short Story Competition

email admin@scottishartsclub.com
website www.scottishartsclub.com/awards
Facebook www.facebook.com/scottishartsclub
Twitter @ScottishArtsCL
Instagram @thescottishartsclub

Open to writers worldwide, both published and unpublished. Stories should not exceed 2,000 words and can be on any topic, they do not have to be related to Scotland. The winners are selected by Alexander McCall Smith.

The Isobel Lodge Award for New Scottish Writing is a special award, given as part of the competition, for unpublished writers born, living or studying in Scotland. It is named in memory of the writer and storyteller.

The Nan Shepherd Prize
14 High Street, Edinburgh EH1 1TE
email contact@nanshepherdprize.com
website www.nanshepherdprize.com
Facebook www.facebook.com/LambdaLiterary
Twitter @NanPrize
Instagram @NanPrize

The only nature writing prize for writers from under-represented backgrounds. The Prize runs every two years, seeks works of narrative non-fiction that explore nature or the environment, and invites entrants who are under-represented due to ethnicity, gender, sexuality, disability or class. Submission for the 2023 prize close in October and will reopen for the 2025 awards in August 2025. Entrants should not have published a full-length work of adult fiction or non-fiction (self-published authors are eligible). Submit a sample, a synopsis, chapter outline and biography. The winner receives a publishing deal with Canongate and a £10,000 advance. Founded 2019.

Mo Siewcharran Prize
email mosiewcharranprize@hachette.co.uk
website www.littlebrown.co.uk/landing-page/the-mo-siewcharran-prize-2023
Twitter @MoPrize

Nurtures unpublished writers from Black, Asian, mixed heritage and minority ethnic backgrounds, writing in English. Entrants to the 2023 prize must be picture book writers, but previous categories have included literary fiction, crime and thrillers; criteria for the 2024 prize are not yet available. The winner will receive £2,500 prize money and consideration for publication with Hachette Children's Group, as well as feedback on their submission, introduction to at least two literary agents, a meeting with Hachette's rights, marketing and publicity teams, and a ticket to London Book Fair. A package of prizes is also available for one runner-up and six shortlisted writers. Entrants should submit 500–700 words of text and may also submit three pieces of four-colour artwork. Founded 2019.

The André Simon Memorial Fund Book Awards
tel 07801 310973
email katie@andresimon.co.uk
website www.andresimon.co.uk
Twitter @AndreSimonAward

Celebrates excellent new writing in the fields of food and drink. Two awards of £2,000 are given annually, one each for the best new books on food and on drink. There is also a Special Commendation of £1,500 in either category. All works first published in the calendar year of the award are eligible (publisher entry only). Founded 1978.

Wilbur Smith Adventure Writing Prize
The Wilbur & Niso Smith Foundation, Unit 9, 5-7 Wells Terrace, London N4 3JU
email submissions@wilbur-niso-smithfoundation.org
website www.wilbur-niso-smithfoundation.org/awards/intro
Facebook www.facebook.com/WNSmithFoundation
Twitter @Wilbur_Niso_Fdn

Supports and celebrates today's best adventure writing. Open to writers of any nationality, writing in English. Awards are presented for fiction in three categories. The Best Published Novel (prize: £10,000) and New Voices Award (prize: one year of editorial support and one-to-one mentoring) are for full-length novels for adults or young adults. The Author of Tomorrow award (prizes: £150–£1,000 depending on age category, plus book tokens and digital publication) seeks to find the adventure writers of the future and is open to young people across the world (in age categories 16–21 years, 12–15 years and age 11 and under) who have completed a short piece of adventure writing in English. Submission guidelines, eligibility criteria, entry fees, shortlist dates and details of the previous winners for each category can be found on the website.

The Jill Smythies Award
The Linnean Society of London, Burlington House, Piccadilly, London W1J 0BF
tel 020-7434 4479
email nominations@linnean.org
website www.linnean.org

A prize of £1,000 for a botanical artist for outstanding illustrations. Established in honour of Jill Smythies whose career as a botanical artist was cut short by an accident to her right hand. The rubric states that 'the award, to be made by Council usually annually consisting of a silver medal and a purse … is for published illustrations, such as drawings and paintings, in aid of plant identification, with the emphasis on botanical accuracy and the accurate portrayal of diagnostic characteristics. Illustrations of cultivars of garden origin are not eligible.' Closing date for nominations: 30 November. Founded 1988.

Society of Medical Writers Competitions
SoMW, Acre-Rise Cottage, Upper Ludstone Claverley, Wolverhampton WV5 7DH
email moldywarp@doctors.org.uk
website http://somw.org.uk/competitions-and-awards/

Biannual awards in three categories: Fiction (2,500 words), Non-Fiction (2,500 words) and Poetry (40 lines). Entries must not have been previously published. Results are published in the society magazine, *The Writer*. All winning entries are eligible for the Wilfred Hopkins Award, given for the best piece across all categories over the entire year.

The Stephen Spender Prize

41 Wellington Square, Oxford OX4 2JF
email prize@stephen-spender.org
website www.stephen-spender.org/stephen-spender-prize

Celebrates poetry in translation, with categories for adults and young people, as well as an annually rotating spotlight highlighting a language spoken widely in the UK and a prize for schools. Entrants should translate into English any poem from any language. Overall winner will receive a £1,000 cash prize. Open to adults from all over the world; youth entrants must be UK or Irish citizens or residents, or pupils at a British School overseas. Founded 2004.

The Telegraph Sports Book Awards

email danielle@agile-ideas.com
website https://sportsbookawards.com
Twitter @sportsbookaward

Highlight the most outstanding sports books of the previous calendar year, to showcase their merits and to enhance their reputation and profile. Sponsored by *The Telegraph*, winners are announced at an annual awards ceremony. There are over ten categories to reflect every sport and genre sub-category in sports writing, including children's sports writing.

The Edward Stanford Travel Writing Awards

Stanfords, 7 Mercer Walk, Covent Garden, London WC2H 9FA
tel 020-7836 1321
website https://www.stanfords.co.uk/edward-stanford-travel-writing-awards

Administered by Stanfords, a specialist retailer of maps, travel books and other travel accessories, they recognise exceptional travel writing published in the previous year. The categories include: Travel Book of the Year, Children's Travel Book of the Year, New Travel Writer of the Year, and Outstanding Contribution to Travel Writing. The winner in each category receives a personalised hand made globe trophy.

Bram Stoker Awards

P.O. Box 56687, Sherman Oaks, CA 91413
tel +1 818-220-3965
email stokechair@horror.org
website https://horror.org/

Administered by the Horror Writers Association, they recognise superior achievement in horror writing. There are 13 categories: Novel, First Novel, Short Fiction, Long Fiction, Middle Grade, YA, Fiction Collection, Poetry Collection, Anthology, Screenplay, Graphic Novel, Non-Fiction and Short Non-Fiction. Longlisted works are nominated by society members and the jury; authors can submit their own work to the jury. Awards are presented each year as part of an association banquet. Founded 1988.

Stories Festival Competition

email storiescompetition@standard.co.uk
website https://stories.standard.co.uk/competition
Twitter @EveningStandard

Not limited to short stories, it is open to short content in a variety of forms, including spoken word, monologues, scripts and narrative podcast episodes. Entries can be fiction or memoir, must not be part of a larger work and should respond to that year's theme. Judges are looking for work that is original, relevant and showcases a distinctive voice. Entries can be: written (up to 1,000 words); video (maximum two minutes for spoken word); or audio (maximum two minutes for spoken word). BSL entries should be recorded as a video and accompanied by a transcript of no more than 1,000 words. Prizes include mentorship, masterclasses, publication and festival tickets.

STR Theatre Book Prize

email theatrebookprize@str.org.uk
website www.str.org.uk/grants-prizes/theatre-book-prize/

Given to the best book on the subject of British theatre. All new works of original research first published in English are eligible except for play text and studies of drama as literature. The Society for Theatre Research also awards research grants and administers the New Scholars Prize. Founded 1997.

Swansea University Dylan Thomas Prize

c/o Dr Elaine Canning, Executive Officer, Keir Hardie Building, Swansea University, Singleton Park, Swansea SA2 8PP
tel (01792) 513025
email DTPrize@swansea.ac.uk
website www.swansea.ac.uk/dylan-thomas-prize

The £20,000 Swansea University Dylan Thomas Prize is awarded to the best published literary work in the English language, written by an author aged 39 or under. Launched in 2006.

TA First Translation Prize

Prizes Department, The Society of Authors, 24 Bedford Row, London WC1R 4EH
email prizes@societyofauthors.org
website https://www2.societyofauthors.org/prizes/translation-prizes/ta-first-translation-prize/

Given to debut literary translation into English published in the UK and Ireland. The work must be the first solo book-length project by the entrant, co-translators are not accepted, self-published, ebook only and poetry titles are not accepted. The winner is awarded £3,000 and a runner-up is awarded £1,000; the prize is shared between the translator and their editor.

The James Tait Black Memorial Prizes
English Literature, School of Literatures,
Languages and Cultures,
The University of Edinburgh, George Square,
Edinburgh EH8 9JX
tel 0131 650 3619
email s.strathdee@ed.ac.uk
website www.ed.ac.uk/events/james-tait-black
Contact Sheila Strathdee

The James Tait Black Fiction and Biography Prizes
Fiction prize submissions: English Literature, c/o
Room 2.24, School of Literatures, Languages, and
Cultures, The University of Edinburgh, 50 George
Square, Edinburgh EH8 9LH
Biography prize submissions: English Literature, c/o
Room 3.07, School of Literatures, Languages, and
Cultures, The University of Edinburgh, 50 George
Square, Edinburgh EH8 9LH

Two prizes of £10,000 are awarded annually: one for
the best biography or work of that nature, the other
for the best work of fiction, published during the
calendar year 1 January to 31 December. The
adjudicators are lecturers in English Literature at the
University of Edinburgh, with the assistance of teams
of postgraduate readers. Entries should be in English
and published in the year of the award. Works in
translation will be considered. Both prizes may go to
the same author.

Publishers should submit two copies of any
appropriate biography, or work of fiction, as early as
possible with a note of the date of publication,
marked 'James Tait Black Prize'. Closing date for
submissions: 15 December. Founded 1918.

The James Tait Black Prize for Drama: University of Edinburgh in association with Playwright Studio Scotland
email jtbdrama@ed.ac.uk
Contact Nicola McCartney

A prize of £10,000 for a professionally produced play
which displays an original voice in theatre and one
that has made a significant and unique contribution
to the art form. The prize is open to any new work
originally written in English, Scots or Gaelic, by
playwrights from any country at any stage in their
career. The judges will be students and staff of the
University's School of Literatures, Languages and
Cultures and representatives from the wider
European theatre industry.

Plays must be formally commissioned and have
had a full professional production. Eligible plays will
have been produced between 1 January and 31
December in the year preceding the year of the
award, and run for a minimum of six performances.
The submissions must come from the producing
company or the agent of the playwright.

The Prize was suspended as a result of Covid19.
Submissions may reopen in January 2024. Please
consult the website from November 2023.

Reginald Taylor and Lord Fletcher Essay Competition
British Archaeological Association, 18 Stanley Road,
Oxford OX4 1QZ
email jsmcneill@btinternet.com
Honorary Secretary John McNeill

A prize of a medal and £500 is awarded biennially for
the best unpublished essay of high scholarly standard,
which shows original research on a subject of
archaeological, art-historical or antiquarian interest
within the period from the Roman era to AD1830.
The successful competitor will be invited to read the
essay before the Association and the essay may be
published in the Association's journal. Competitors
should notify the Honorary Editor of the intended
subject of their work in advance. Next awards:
Winter 2023 and Winter 2025. The essay should be
submitted not later than 1 November in the year of
the award and should not exceed 8,000 words.
Founded in memory of E. Reginald Taylor FSA and
Lord Fletcher FSA.

Templar Medal Book Prize
email templarmedal@sahr.org.uk
website www.sahr.org.uk

Awarded annually to the book that has made the
most significant contribution to the history of the
British Army. The winner is announced at an award's
ceremony every April and receives a cash prize. An
additional prize for Best First Book is awarded to
encourage new military writers. Founded 1981.

Theakston Old Peculier Crime Novel of the Year Award
Old Swan Hotel, Swan Road, Harrogate HG1 2SR
tel (01423) 562303
email info@harrogate-festival.org.uk
website https://harrogatetheakstoncrimeaward.com/
Facebook www.facebook.com/
HarrogateInternationalFestivals/
Twitter @HarrogateFest
Instagram @harrogatefestivals

Voted for by members of the public and a jury-panel,
celebrating excellence and originality in British and
Irish crime fiction. The winner is announced at
Harrogate International Festivals' Theakston Old
Peculier Crime Writing Festival and receives £3,000.
Previous winners include Denise Mina, Steve
Cavanagh, Val McDermid and Chris Brookmyre. An
award recognising an Outstanding Contribution to
Crime Fiction is also delivered.

Thriller Awards
PO Box 311, Eureka CA 95502, USA
email AwardsVP@thrillerwriters.org
website https://thrillerwriters.org/2023-thriller-
awards/
Facebook www.facebook.com/
ThrillerWritersOrganization

Societies, prizes and festivals

Twitter @thrillerwriters
Instagram @internationalthrillerwriters

Recognises the best thrillers of the year in six categories: Hardcover Novel, First Novel, Short Story, Paperback Original, Young Adult Novel, E-Book Original, and Audiobook. Submissions must have been written in English and published in the preceeding year.

The Times/Chicken House Children's Fiction Competition

Chicken House, 2 Palmer Street, Frome, Somerset BA11 1DS
tel (01373) 454488
email competitions@chickenhousebooks.com
website www.chickenhousebooks.com
Twitter @chickenhsebooks
Contact Jazz Bartlett Love

Open to unpublished writers of a full-length children's novel (age 7–18). Entrants must be over 18 and novels must not exceed 80,000 words in length. There are two winners, both of whom are announced in *The Times* and receive a worldwide publishing contract with Chicken House with a royalty advance of £10,000 and £7,500 respectively. The winner is selected by a panel of judges which includes children's authors, journalists, publishers, librarians and other key figures from the world of children's literature. For competition opening and closing dates, consult the Chicken House website.

The Tinniswood Award

Society of Authors, 24 Bedford Row, London WC1R 4EH
tel 020-3880 2230
email info@societyofauthors.org
website www.societyofauthors.org/prizes/audio-drama/the-tinniswood-award

Presented annually for the best original audio drama script of the year. The Society of Authors perpetuate the memory of radio and TV comedy scriptwriter Peter Tinniswood through the award, which celebrates and encourages high standards in radio drama. Submissions will be accepted from any party (producer, broadcasting organisation, writer, agent, etc). The award is sponsored by the ALCS.

Tir na n-Og Awards

Books Council of Wales, Castell Brychan, Aberystwyth, Ceredigion SY23 2JB
tel (01970) 624151
email wbc.children@books.wales
website https://llyfrau.cymru/en/gwobrau/tir-na-nog
Facebook www.facebook.com/LlyfrDaFabBooks
Twitter @LlyfrDaFabBooks

Established to promote and raise the standard of children's and young people's books in Wales. Three awards (prize: £1,000 each) are presented annually by the Welsh Books Council and are sponsored by the

Chartered Institute of Library and Information Professionals Cymru/Wales: The best English-language book of the year with an authentic Welsh background: fiction and factual books originally in English are eligible, translations from Welsh or any other language are not eligible; the best original Welsh-language book aimed at the primary school sector; the best original Welsh-language book aimed at the secondary school sector. Founded 1976.

The Paul Torday Memorial Prize

The Society of Authors, 24 Bedford Row, London WC1R 4EH
tel 020-3880 2230
email prizes@societyofauthors.org
website www.societyofauthors.org/prizes/authors-awards/fiction/the-paul-torday-prize
Twitter @Soc_of_Authors

A prize for debut novelists aged 60 or over, set up in honour of Paul Torday, who published his first novel *Salmon Fishing in the Yemen* aged 60. The winner receives £1,000 and a set of Paul Torday's collected works. Runners-up receive one specially selected Paul Torday novel with a commemorative book plate. Novels must have been published in English in the UK, and submissions can only be made by the publisher.

The Translation Prizes

The Society of Authors, 24 Bedford Row, London WC1R 4EH
tel 020-3880 2230
email prizes@societyofauthors.org
website www.societyofauthors.org/prizes/translation-prizes
Twitter @Soc_of_Authors

The Society of Authors offers a number of prizes for published translations into English from Arabic, Dutch, French, German, Hebrew, Italian, Spanish, Swedish and Japanese. The Society also administers the TA First Translation Prize, which is an annual prize of £2,000 for a debut literary translation from any language published in the UK.

The Betty Trask Prize

The Society of Authors, 24 Bedford Row, London WC1R 4EH
tel 020-3880 2230
email prizes@societyofauthors.org
website www.societyofauthors.org/betty-trask
Twitter @Soc_of_Authors

Celebrates debut novels in English (published or unpublished), of a traditional or romantic nature. Authors must be under the age of 35, a resident in Great Britain and Northern Ireland or the Commonwealth for three years prior to the date of submission for the prize, or a British national.

Trocaire Poetry Ireland Poetry Prize

Maynooth, Co. Kildare W23 NX63
tel +353 (1) 629 3333

email info@trocaire.org
website www.trocaire.org/poetry-competition
Facebook www.facebook.com/trocaireireland
Twitter @trocaire

Supports poets at all stages of their careers through two categories: published and unpublished. Entrants are asked to submit up to three poems. Page poems should be submitted in one document and spoken word poetry as mp3 audio files accompanied by a transcript. 1st prize: two week retreat or €300 worth of time in a recording studio, and publication in a booklet; runners-up: tickets to a literary festival to the value of €250. Winners and runners-up are invited to read at an online awards ceremony and receive either a subscription to Poetry Ireland Review or an assessment of their work through Poetry Ireland's Critical Assessment service.

The V&A Illustration Awards

Victoria & Albert Museum, London SW7 2RL
email villa@vam.ac.uk
website www.vam.ac.uk/info/va-illustration-awards

Biennial awards open to illustrators living or publishing in the UK and students who have attended a course in the UK over the last two years. Previous awards included the following categories: Book Illustration, Book Cover Design, and Illustrated Journalism; the categories are currently being reviewed for the next awards. Winners each receive £3,000, with the overall winner receiving £8,000. Founded 1972.

Ver Poets Open Competition

website www.verpoets.co.uk
Competition Secretary Terry Jones

Open to those aged 16 and over for poems of up to 30 lines of any genre or subject matter, which must be an unpublished work in English. 1st prize: £600; 2nd prize: £300; 3rd prize: £100. Entry by email or post. Closing date: 30 April. Entry fee: £4 per poem, three poems for £10 (£3 per poem thereafter). Anthology of winning and selected poems with Adjudicator's Report usually available from mid-June, free to those included.

James Cropper Wainwright Prize

email danielle@agile-ideas.com
website https://wainwrightprize.com/
Facebook www.facebook.com/WainwrightPrize
Twitter @wainwrightprize

Awarded annually to the books which most successfully encourage their readers to explore the outdoors and nurture a respect for the natural world. There are three categories: Nature Writing, Writing on Conservation and Children's Writing on Nature and Conservation. A prize fund of £7,500 is shared between three winners. Founded 2014.

Wales Book of the Year Award

Glyn Jones Centre, Wales Millennium Centre, Bute Place, Cardiff CF10 5AL
tel 029-2047 2266
email post@literaturewales.org
website www.literaturewales.org/our-projects/wales-book-year
Facebook www.facebook.com/LlenCymruLitWales
Twitter @LitWales
Instagram @llencymru_litwales
Literature Wales Executive Director Claire Furlong

Administered by Literature Wales, it is presented to the best Welsh and English-language works first published in the year preceding the ceremony in the fields of creative writing and literary criticism in four categories: Poetry, Fiction, Creative Non-Fiction, and Children and Young People. Annual highlights include the shortlist announcement in June and the awards ceremony in July.

The Warwick Prize for Women in Translation

email womenintranslation@warwick.ac.uk
website https://warwick.ac.uk/fac/cross_fac/womenintranslation
Coordinator Holly Langstaff

Addresses the gender imbalance in translated literature and increase the number of international women's voices accessible to a British and Irish readership. Awarded annually to the best eligible work of fiction, poetry, literary non-fiction, work of fiction for children or young adults, graphic novel or play text, written by a woman, translated into English by a translator (or translators) of any gender, and published by a UK or Irish publisher. The £1,000 prize is divided between writer and translator/s. Founded 2017.

Wasafiri Essay Prize

c/o School of English and Drama, Queen Mary, University of London, Mile End Road, London E1 4NS
tel 020-7882 2686
email wasafiri@qmul.ac.uk
website www.wasafiri.org/wasafiri-essay-prize/

Established to recognise and support contemporary literature researchers and academics who are at the start of their career. The judging panel are looking for critical essays which are innovative, engaging, nuanced and pay close attention to both style and content. Entrants must have received a PhD in the previous eight years; essays must be between 6,000–9,000 words and on the subject of international contemporary literature. The winner receives £250, publication in *Wasafiri* and a mentoring session.

Waterstones Debut Fiction Prize

203–206 Piccadilly, London W1J 9HD
website www.waterstones.com

Societies, prizes and festivals

Recognises the support that bookseller recommendations give to authors and books. All debut fiction is eligible regardless of genre and including translated fiction. The winner receives £5,000 and promotion in Waterstones shops throughout the country.

Wells Festival of Literature Competitions

email competitions@wellsfestivalofliterature.org.uk
website www.wellsfestivalofliterature.org.uk/2023-international-competitions/
Facebook www.facebook.com/Wellslitfest
Twitter @wellslitfest
Instagram @wellsfestivalofliterature

Administers awards throughout the year in three categories. Poetry: Poems may be on any subject but must not exceed 35 lines; 1st prize: £1,000; 2nd prize: £500; 3rd prize: £250. Short story: Stories may be on any subject and should be between 1,000–2,000 words; 1st prize: £700; 2nd prize: £300; 3rd prize: £200. Books for children: Writing should be for children aged 7+, including young adults; entrants should submit the first two chapters or first 20 pages, whichever is the shortest, and a synopsis; 1st prize: £700; 2nd prize: £300; 3rd prize: £200. There is an additional prize of £100 for a local writer in each category. Entry fee: £6 per category.

The White Review Short Story and Poet's Prize

email prizes@thewhitereview.org
website www.thewhitereview.org/prize/
Twitter @TheWhiteReview

Supports emerging writers, who experiment with the form in which they write. The prize awards £2,500 each to the best piece of short fiction and the best poetry portfolio by a writer resident in the UK or Ireland who has yet to secure a publishing deal. Entry fee: £12.50; free entries are available for writers on low income. For submission and eligibility guidelines and entry terms and conditions, see the website. Founded 2013.

The Whitfield Prize

Administrative Secretary, Royal Historical Society, University College London, Gower Street, London WC1E 6BT
tel 020-7387 7532
email administration@royalhistsoc.org
website https://royalhistsoc.org/prizes/whitfield-book-prize/

Awarded for the best work on a subject within a field of British or Irish history. It must be its author's first solely written history book, an original and scholarly work of historical research and published in English. 1st prize: £1,000. Founded 1976.

Wigtown Poetry Prize

Number 11, Wigtown,
Dumfries and Galloway DG8 8HN
email mail@wigtownbookfestival.com
website www.wigtownpoetryprize.com/poetry-competition
Facebook www.facebook.com/WigtownBookFestival
Twitter @WigtownBookFest

Scotland's International Poetry Prize recognises poetry across three categories.

The Wigtown Prize: A main prize, plus two prizes for poetry in Scots and Gaelic. Wigtown Prize: 1st prize: £1,500; runner-up: £200. Wigtown Scots Prize and Scottish Gaelic Prize: 1st: £500; runner-up: £200.

Alastair Reid Pamphlet Prize: 1st prize: pamphlet production from Gerry Cambridge.

Fresh Voice Award: Exclusively for poets who have not published a full-length collection and live in the Dumfries and Galloway region. 1st prize: professional support, mentoring and a retreat at Moniack Mhor Creative Writing Centre.

Poems should not exceed 40 lines and pamphlets should not exceed 12 pages. Entry fee: £6.50 for first entry, discounts available for subsequent entries. Founded 2005.

Wildlife Photographer of the Year

The Natural History Museum, Cromwell Road, London SW7 5BD
website www.nhm.ac.uk/visit/wpy/competition.html

Open to photographers of all experience levels, aged 18 and over. There are 16 categories, ranging from Animal Portraits to Photojournalism and Urban Wildlife to Underwater Photography. The Grand Title award is given to the photographer whose individual image is judged to be the most striking and memorable. Prizes range in value depending on the category. The Young Wildlife Photographer of the Year recognises photographers aged 17 and under.

Winchester Poetry Prize

c/o University of Winchester, Sparkford Road, Winchester, Hampshire SO22 4NR
email hello@winchesterpoetryfestival.org
website www.winchesterpoetryfestival.org/prize

Awarded to poetry of up to 40 lines. Entries should be in English, typed and never before published. 1st prize: £1,000; 2nd prize: £500; 3rd prize: £250. An anthology of longlisted entries is published annually. Entry fee: £5 for first poem, £4 for subsequent poems. Enter online or by post. Closing date: 31 July each year. The judge for the 2023 prize was Zaffar Kunial. Founded 2016.

Windham-Campbell Prizes

Beinecke Rare Book & Manuscript Library, 121 Wall Street, New Haven, CT 06510-1242
website https://windhamcampbell.org/

Administered by the University of Yale, each year 8 writers are awarded $175,000 each to support their writing. Writers are recognised for their merit or potential and can come from anywhere in the world; since its inception writers from twenty-one countries have been represented. Nominations and judging are anonymous, publishers or authors can nominate themselves. Founded 2013.

Wingate Literary Prize
email admin@wingate.org.uk
website www.wingatefoundation.org.uk/literary_prize
Twitter @Wingateprize

An annual prize of £4,000 is awarded, in association with JW3, for a work of fiction or non-fiction which best translates the idea of Jewishness to the general reader. Founded 1977.

The Wolfson History Prize
email wolfsonhistoryprize@wolfson.org.uk
website www.wolfsonhistoryprize.org.uk
Twitter @wolfsonhistory

Awarded annually for over 50 years to promote and recognise outstanding history written for a general audience, the Wolfson History Prize is the most valuable history writing prize in the UK. Books are judged on the extent to which they are carefully researched, well-written and accessible to the non-specialist reader. Books must be published in the UK in the calendar year preceding the year of the prize. The subject matter of the book may cover any aspect of history, including historical biography. The author must be normally resident in the UK during the year of publication and not be a previous winner of the prize. Previously shortlisted authors are eligible. The winning author will be awarded £50,000. The five remaining shortlisted authors will be awarded £5,000 each. All submissions must come via the publisher. Full details on the process are available online.

Women Poets' Prize from the Rebecca Swift Foundation
email info@rebeccaswiftfoundation.org
website www.rebeccaswiftfoundation.org/women-poets-prize/

Biennial award given to three women poets who are resident in the UK. The Prize is free to enter and the winners each receive a cash bursary plus two years pastoral coaching and professional mentorship with partners such as The Literary Consultancy, Apples and Snakes, Poetry School and Verve Festival. Founded 2018.

Women's Prize for Fiction
email submissions@womensprizeforfiction.co.uk
website www.womensprizeforfiction.co.uk
Twitter @WomensPrize

Celebrates excellence, originality and accessibility in writing by women in English from throughout the world. It is the UK's most prestigious annual book award for fiction written by a woman and also provides a range of educational, literacy and research initiatives to support aspiring or emerging writers and readers.

The Women's Prize for Fiction is awarded annually for the best full novel of the year written by a woman and published in the UK. Any woman writing in English – whatever her nationality, country of residence, age or subject matter – is eligible, submitted by a publisher. The winner receives £30,000 and a limited edition bronze figurine donated by the artist Grizel Niven.

Women's Prize for Non-Fiction
email submissions@womensprizeforfiction.co.uk
website https://womensprizeforfiction.co.uk/
Facebook www.facebook.com/womensprize
Twitter @womensprize
Instagram @womensprize

Celebrates excellence in writing and research and strong and original narrative voices. Entry is open to all works of narrative non-fiction, including history, memoir, biography, nature writing, science, and philosophy, and all writers who identify as female, from across the globe, who are published in the UK. The winner will receive £30,000 and a statuette given by the Charlotte Aiken Trust. Founded 2023.

World Illustration Awards
Association of Illustrators, Somerset House, Strand, London WC2R 1LA
tel 020-7759 1010
email awards@theaoi.com
website www.theaoi.com/world-illustration-awards
Facebook www.facebook.com/theaoi
Twitter @theaoi
Instagram @WorldIllustrationAwards

Presented in partnership with the *Directory of Illustration*, the awards programme celebrates contemporary illustration across the globe. A panel of international judges create a 500 strong longlist and shortlists 200 projects, which are celebrated in an online showcase, a catalogue and with an online industry events programme. For submission guidelines, categories and prizes, see the website.

Writers' & Artists' Yearbook 2024 Short Story Competition
website www.writersandartists.co.uk/competitions

See information panel on page vi of this edition or visit the website for details.

Writing Magazine: 750 words
website www.writers-online.co.uk/writing-competitions/750-words-competition/
Facebook www.facebook.com/Writingmagazine
Twitter @WritingMagazine

A monthly competition run by Writing Magazine for a piece of writing that does not exceed 750 words.

The winner receives £200 and publication in the magazine, the runner-up receives £50 and publication in the competition showcase. Entry fee: £7.50 for non-members, £5 for members.

Writing Magazine: Grand Prize

website www.writers-online.co.uk/writing-competitions/writers-grand-prize-2023/
Facebook www.facebook.com/WritingMagazine
Twitter @WritingMagazine

Open to short stories in any form and on any topic. Stories must not exceed 2,000 words. Prizes: 1st: £1,000 and publication in Writing Magazine; 2nd: £250; 3rd: £100; 4th: a mini-critique of the work; 5th: twelve-month Writers Online membership. Entry fee: £15 for non-members, £10 for members.

Writing Magazine: Swanwick Competition

website www.writers-online.co.uk/writing-competitions/open-competitions/
Facebook www.facebook.com/Writingmagazine
Twitter @WritingMagazine

Offers writers a fully inclusive stay at Swanwick Writers' Summer School, a week-long programme for writers of all ages, abilities and genres. There are three categories and one shared theme each year: short stories of up to 1,000 words, poems of up to 40 lines, pieces of writing for children of up to 1,000 words. 1st prize: Swanwick Writers' Summer School; 2nd prize: twelve-month Writers Online membership; 3rd prize: a copy of the *Writers' & Artists' Yearbook*. Entry fee: £7.50 for non-members, £5 for members.

The Yoto Carnegies

Room 150 British Library, 96 Euston Road, London NW1 2DB
email carnegies@cilip.org.uk
website www.yotocarnegies.org.uk

Nominations for the following two awards are invited from members of CILIP (the library and information association), who are asked to submit one title per Medal, accompanied by an explanation of how the book they have selected meets the Medal criteria. The awards are selected by librarian judges from the Youth Libraries Group of CILIP. One title from each shortlist will receive a prize awarded by children vote for their favourites as part of the awards' shadowing scheme.

Yoto Carnegie Medal for Writing

Awarded annually for an outstanding book for children (fiction or non-fiction) written in English and first published in the UK during the preceding year or co-published elsewhere within a three-month time lapse. The Yoto Carnegie Medal for Writing winner is awarded £5,000 prize money from the Colin Mears Award annually.

Yoto Carnegie Medal for Illustration

Awarded annually for an outstanding illustrated book for children first published in the UK during the preceding year or co-published elsewhere within a three-month time lapse. Books intended for older as well as younger children are included, and reproduction will be taken into account. The Yoto Carnegie Medal for Illustration winner is awarded £5,000 from the Colin Mears Award fund each year.

Zooker Award

Arkbound, Backfields House, Upper York Street, Bristol BS2 8QJ
email editorial@arkbound.com
website http://arkbound.com/zooker-award/

Encourages first-time authors from disadvantaged backgrounds and to reward works of social value; principally those that touch upon the themes of environmental sustainability and social inclusion, encouraging positive changes in behaviour or attitude for readers. Submitted work must have been published (not self-published) in the last two years. The prize is £500 and in the event that there is insufficient sponsorship or entry fees, the award will be carried over to the next year. Entry fee: £4.50. For full details, visit the website.

GRANTS, BURSARIES AND FELLOWSHIPS

Arts Council England

tel 0161 934 4317
email enquiries@artscouncil.org.uk
website www.artscouncil.org.uk
Facebook www.facebook.com/artscouncilofengland
Twitter @ace_national

The national development agency for the arts in England, providing funding for a range of arts and cultural activities. Through its funding schemes it provides organisations, artists, events and initiatives funding to help them achieve the Council's mission of providing art and culture for everyone. Visit the website for information on funding support and advice, an online funding finder and funding FAQs.

The Arts Council/An Chomhairle Ealaíon

70 Merrion Square, Dublin D02 NY52, Republic of Ireland
tel +353 (0)1 618 0200
website www.artscouncil.ie/home
Facebook www.facebook.com/artscouncilireland
Twitter @artscouncil_ie

Outlines all of its funding opportunities for individuals, groups and organisations on website. Covers writing, art, theatre, film, music and more. Also publishes regular information on grants and awards, news and events, and arts policy.

The Authors' Contingency Fund

Grants Department, The Society of Authors,
24 Bedford Row, London WC1R 4EH
tel 020-3880 2230
email grants@societyofauthors.org
website www.societyofauthors.org

Makes modest grants to established, published authors who find themselves in sudden financial difficulty. Guidelines and application form available via the website.

The Authors' Foundation

The Society of Authors, 24 Bedford Row,
London WC1R 4EH
tel 020-3880 2230
email grants@societyofauthors.org
website www.societyofauthors.org/grants/grants-for-works-in-progress
Twitter @Soc_of_Authors

Provides grants for professional writers to help develop a work-in-progress. Applications are open on a rolling basis, awarding funding (in addition to a proper advance) for research, travel or other necessary expenditure.

Open to applications from authors commissioned by a commercial British publisher to write a full-length work of fiction, poetry or non-fiction, or those without a publishing contract, who have had one previous book published commercially and where there is a strong likelihood that a further book will be published in the UK. Please visit the website for an application and guidelines. Founded 1984.

Carole Blake Open Doors Project

Blake Friedmann Literary Agency, Ground Floor,
15 Highbury Place, London N5 1QP
email sian@blakefriedmann.co.uk
website http://blakefriedmann.co.uk/carole-blake-open-doors-project
Twitter @BlakeFriedmann

A programme which encourages candidates from a diverse range of backgrounds to enter the publishing industry, it includes one internship and one mentorship. The internship can be in-person, remote or hybrid and includes working closely with Blake Friedmann agents, the opportunity to attend meetings with editors and clients, and the chance to be involved in the day-to-day life of a literary agent. The mentorship was established to support candidates who have commitments which would prevent them from completing an internship or who would not be able to travel to London. It is fully online and allows the successful candidate to gain insight into literary agencies and publishing, and advice on career development. Applications close in May each year.

The K. Blundell Trust

The Society of Authors, 24 Bedford Row,
London WC1R 4EH
tel 020-3380 2230
email funding@societyofauthors.org
website www.societyofauthors.org/grants/grants-for-works-in-progress
Twitter @Soc_of_Authors

Grants are given to published writers under the age of 40 to assist with the development of their next book. This work must 'contribute to the greater understanding of existing social and economic organisation' and may be fiction or non-fiction. The fund is open for applications on a rolling basis. See the website for application form and guidelines; apply by email.

Stern Bryan Fellowship

c/o Dr Glenda Cooper, Department of Journalism,
City, University of London, Northampton Square,
London EC1V 0HB
email Stern.fellowship@gmail.com
website www.city.ac.uk/prospective-students/finance/funding/stern-bryan-fellowship

Established in memory of *Washington Post* editor Laurence Stern, it offers a three-month residency at the *Washington Post* for a British journalist working in print, digital, radio or television. Previous winners have gone on to work for Channel 4, the *Guardian* and the *Daily Mail*. Applicants should submit a CV, two references and three samples of recent work.

Creative Scotland

Waverley Gate, 2–4 Waterloo Place,
Edinburgh EH1 3EG
email enquiries@creativescotland.com
website www.creativescotland.com/funding
Twitter @CreativeScots

The public body that supports the arts, screen and creative industries across all parts of Scotland on behalf of everyone who lives, works or visits there. Through distributing funding from the Scottish Government and the National Lottery, Creative Scotland enables people and organisations to work in and experience the arts, screen and creative industries in Scotland by helping others to develop great ideas and bring them to life. Creative Scotland supports writers and publishers based in Scotland through a range of funds and initiatives.

Discoveries

email discoveriesprize@curtisbrown.co.uk
website www.curtisbrowncreative.co.uk/discoveries-2023

A writers' development programme for aspiring female writers of all ages and backgrounds, supported by Audible and Curtis Brown. The winner will be offered representation by Curtis Brown Literary Agency, the opportunity to workshop their MS with an Audible editor and a cash prize of £5,000. One shortlisted writer will receive a scholarship to attend a Write Your Novel course (worth £1,800) and a mentoring session. All longlisted authors are invited to take part in a Writing Development Course. Entry is free; writers are required to submit the first 10,000 words of a novel (that does not need to be complete) and a synopsis of up to 1,000 words via the website.

Emerging Poets Development Scheme
email info@outspokenldn.com
website www.outspokenldn.com/epds

Provides access to the world of poetry by offering one year of support and resources to emerging poets. The mentorship will include one-to-one sessions, feedback, workshops and professional development sessions. Four places are available, two of which will be given to writers living in the North of England. Applicants should provide a sample of their work, either five poems or four A4 pages, whichever is longer.

The Eric Gregory Awards
The Society of Authors, 24 Bedford Row,
London WC1R 4EH
tel 020-3380 2230
email prizes@societyofauthors.org
website www.societyofauthors.org/eric-gregory
Twitter @Soc_of_Authors

Recognises a collection of poetry by authors under the age of 30. Founded by the late Dr Eric Gregory, it encourages young poets to devote more time to writing. Candidates must be a British National or resident in Great Britain and Northern Ireland or the Commonwealth for three years prior to the date of submission. Submissions must be in English. Candidates must be under the age of 30 on 31 March in the year of the award (i.e. the year following submission). The work submitted may be a published or unpublished volume of poetry, drama-poems or *belles lettres*; and no more than 30 poems should be submitted.

Hawthornden Fellowships
The Administrator, Hawthornden Literary Retreat,
Hawthornden Castle, Lasswade,
Midlothian EH18 1EG
tel 0131 440 2180
website www.hawthorndenliteraryretreat.org

Applications are invited from novelists, poets, dramatists and other creative writers whose work has already been published. The Retreat provides four-week fellowships in a peaceful setting. Application forms are available from January for Fellowships awarded in the following year. Deadline for applications 30 June.

Francis Head Bequest
Grants Department, Society of Authors,
24 Bedford Row, London WC1R 4EH
tel 020-3880 2230
email grants@societyofauthors.org
website www.societyofauthors.org

Provides grants to published British authors over the age of 35 who need financial help during a period of illness, disablement or temporary financial crisis.

Ignite Fellowship
Scottish Book Trust, Sandeman House,
Trunk's Close, 55 High Street, Edinburgh EH1 1SR
tel 0131 524 0160
email applications@scottishbooktrust.com
website www.scottishbooktrust.com/writing-and-authors/ignite-fellowship
Facebook www.facebook.com/ScottishBookTrust/
Twitter @scottishbktrust

Supports established writers who are embarking on or working through a significant project. Writers can apply whether the project is in the early stages or already a work-in-progress. There are three awards available. In partnership with the Gaelic Books council one of the awards will be given to a writer working in Gaelic; writers working in Scots are also encouraged. All fellows receive support tailored to their project, including £2,000 to allow them to focus on their work; press and PR training; support in marketing and promoting their project; and a week-long writing retreat.

The P.D. James Memorial Fund
Society of Authors, 24 Bedford Row,
London WC1R 4EH
tel 020-3380 2230
email funding@societyofauthors.org
website www.societyofauthors.org/grants/P-D-James-memorial-fund

Offers regular payments to a small number of Society of Authors members who find themselves in financial hardship. To be eligible, applicants must have been a SoA member for at least ten years (this does not have to be continuous). Awards are given by committee to long-term members who are either over the age of 60 or who are completely incapacitated for work. The fund currently distributes £2,200 per annum to each recipient. For more information, see the website.

Northern Writers' Awards
email awards@newwritingnorth.com
website http://northernwritersawards.com/
Facebook www.facebook.com/newwritingnorth
Twitter @NewWritingNorth

Established by New Writing North, the Northern Writers' Awards support work-in-progress by new, emerging and established writers across the North of England. The Awards support writers creatively as they develop their work through publication, as well as helping them to progress professionally and to navigate their way through the publishing industry. Categories include Poetry, Fiction, Hachette Children's Novel, Channel 4 Writing for Television, and Debut. Founded 2000.

The Peggy Ramsay Foundation
7 Savoy Court, London WC2R 0EX
email prf@harbottle.com
website www.peggyramsayfoundation.org

Grants are made to writers of stage plays in accordance with the criteria on the Foundation's website. Awards are made at intervals during each year. A total of approx. £200,000 is expended annually. Founded 1992.

The Royal Literary Fund
3 Johnson's Court, off Fleet Street,
London EC4A 3EA
tel 020-7353 7150
email help@rlf.org.uk
website www.rlf.org.uk
Facebook www.facebook.com/royalliteraryfund
Twitter @rlfwriters
Twitter @writersmosaic
Instagram @writersmosaic

A UK charity that supports writers in financial need through grants and education and community based-projects. The Fellowship scheme provides funding for writers to work one-to-one with university students; the Fund also provides writing development workshops in schools and community initiatives designed to increase engagement and empowerment. Writers who have benefitted from support include novelists, poets, playwrights, screenwriters and translators, such as James Joyce, D.H. Lawrence, Dylan Thomas, Edith Nesbit, Bram Stoker, Anna Burns, Monique Roffey and Ali Smith. Also publishes an online magazine, *Writers Mosaic. Founded* 1790.

The Travelling Scholarships
The Society of Authors, 24 Bedford Row,
London WC1R 4EH
tel 020-3880 2230
email prizes@societyofauthors.org
website www.societyofauthors.org/prizes/fiction/travelling-scholarships
Twitter @Soc_of_Authors

Established by an anonymous benefactor to enable British creative writers to keep in touch with their colleagues abroad. Scholarships are nominated by assessors; applications are not accepted. Founded 1944.

David T.K. Wong Fellowship
School of Literature, Drama and Creative Writing, University of East Anglia, Norwich Research Park, Norwich NR4 7TJ
email davidtkwongfellowship@uea.ac.uk
website www.uea.ac.uk/about/school-of-literature-drama-and-creative-writing/creative-writing/writing-fellowships

The David T.K. Wong Fellowship is an annual award of £26,000 to enable a fiction writer who wants to write in English about East and Southeast Asia to spend a year in the UK, at the University of East Anglia in Norwich. The Fellowship is named after its sponsor David T.K. Wong, a retired Hong Kong businessman, who has also been a teacher, journalist and senior civil servant, and is a writer of short stories. The Fellowship will be awarded to a writer planning to produce a work of prose fiction in English which deals seriously with some aspect of life in East and Southeast Asia (Brunei, Cambodia, Hong Kong, Indonesia, Japan, Korea, Laos, Macau, Malaysia, Mongolia, Myanmar, People's Republic of China, Philippines, Singapore, Taiwan, Thailand and Vietnam). The 2022/23 Fellow is Mishi Saran.

Opportunities for under-represented writers

There has been an acknowledgement across the publishing industry that many voices have not found it easy to be heard and promoted amongst the many hundreds and thousands of books published every year. Publishers, agents, authors and prize-awarding organisations have started to actively encourage and nurture a more diverse range of writers who have new stories to tell. There has been an increase in open submissions, prizes, bursaries and other schemes aimed at previously less represented groups. Some of the more established awards have full entries in this *Yearbook* (as indicated below) and some of the newer ones are listed in full here.

PRIZES AND AWARDS

Creative Future Writers' Award
See page 553

Disabled Poets Prize
email hello@disabledpoetsprize.org.uk
website https://disabledpoetsprize.org.uk
Twitter @DisabledPoets

The UK's first poetry prize specifically for disabled poets, launched in collaboration with Spread the Word, Verve Poetry Press and CRIPtic Arts. Prize rewards the best poetry created by deaf and disabled poets across three categories: Single Poem, Unpublished Pamphlet, and Poem Performed in British Sign Language. Prizes in each category: 1st: £500; 2nd: £250; 3rd: £100; three highly commended entries: £50. The winning entry in the unpublished pamphlet category also receives a publication deal with Verve Poetry Press. All winning writers receive career development opportunities with The Literary Consultancy and the Arvon Foundation. Founded 2023.

The Diverse Book Awards
email hello@thediversebookawards.co.uk
website www.thediversebookawards.co.uk

Administered by author Abiola Bello and publicist Helen Lewis to celebrate diversity in book publishing in the UK and Ireland. There are four fiction award categories: Adult, YA, Children's, and, new from 2023, Picture Books. Entries can be traditionally or self-published but must have been published in the preceding year. The winner in each category receives a trophy as well as access to a range of opportunities including marketing workshops, inclusion in Pen&Inc magazine, panel spots and more. 2022 winners: Kia Abdullah, *Next of Kin* (Adult); Natasha Bowen, *Skin of the Sea* (YA); Benjamin Dean, *Me, My Dad and the End of the Rainbow* (Children's). Founded 2020.

FAB Prize for Undiscovered Talent
See page 555

Future Worlds Prize for Fantasy & Science Fiction Writers of Colour
email info@futureworldsprize.co.uk
website www.futureworldsprize.co.uk
Twitter @FutureWorldsPrz
Instagram @futureworldsprize

Uncovers unpublished fantasy and sci-fi writers of colour. Entrants must not be published, under contract with a publisher or have won another writing competition. Entrants should submit an extract from a short story or the opening chapters of a novel (5,000–10,000 words), a synopsis of their work (1,000 words) and a covering letter. Prizes: 1st: £4,000; 2nd: £2,000; up to six runners-up: £800. All shortlisted writers will receive four mentoring sessions over a one-year period. Founded 2018.

The JBA Over 50 Debut Award
31 Marchmount Road, Edinburgh EH9 1HU
email debut@jennybrownassociates.com
website https://jennybrownassociates.com/news
Facebook www.facebook.com/JennyBrownAssociates/
Twitter @JennyBrownBooks
Instagram @JennyBrownBooks

The Award from Jenny Brown Associates recognises debut authors aged 50 or older, who are both unpublished and unrepresented. Entrants should submit the first 5,000 words of a novel, a one-page synopsis and a personal statement including date of birth and the inspiration for the work. Winners will be chosen by a panel of judges. 1st prize: £1,000 and a place on a residential writing course at Moniack Mhor Creative Writing Centre; runners-up will receive mentoring sessions tailored to their work. Founded 2023.

Jhalak Prize

See page 561

The JKP Writing Prize

email writingprize@jkp.com
website https://uk.jkp.com/
Facebook www.facebook.com/
jessicakingsleypublishers
Twitter @JKPBooks
Instagram @jkpbooks

Established to give new and unagented writers who are under-represented within publishing the opportunity to put their work in front of a panel of published authors and professional editors. The winning writers receive a cash prize and are published in an anthology. Submissions must be original and unpublished. Future prize dates and entrant guidelines will be announced on social media. The 2019 awards invited submissions from transgender and non-binary writers on the theme of trans every day, and the 2022 awards invited Stories of Resistance from writers from Black, Asian, mixed heritage and minority ethnic groups. Founded 2019.

Joffe Books Prize

email prize@joffebooks.com
website www.joffebooks.com/prize
Facebook www.facebook.com/joffebooks
Twitter @joffebooks
Instagram @joffebooks

Established to find new crime fiction writers of colour. Entrants must be from Black, Asian, Indigenous and minority ethnic backgrounds writing in any crime fiction genre, including psychological thrillers, cosy mysteries, police procedurals, suspense mysteries, and domestic noirs. Entrants must be UK residents or British citizens and must be writing in English. 1st prize: a two-book publishing deal with Joffe Books and a £25,000 audiobook offer from Audible for the first book. Entrants should submit a full-length manuscript, a synopsis of the book and a biography. Founded 2021.

The London Writers' Awards

The Albany Centre, Douglas Way, London SE8 4AG
email bobby@spreadtheword.org.uk
website www.spreadtheword.org.uk/projects/london-writers-awards

Awards programme set up by Spread the Word for London-based prose writers who identify as being from a background currently under-represented in publishing: disabled, LGBTQIA+, working class or writers of colour. The awards are given across four genres: literary fiction (including short stories), commercial fiction, narrative non-fiction, and children's (including middle-grade and YA fiction, excluding picture books). Founded 2018.

#Merky Books New Writers' Prize

email merkybooks@penguinrandomhouse.co.uk
website www.penguin.co.uk/merky-new-writers-prize
Twitter @MerkyBooks
Instagram @MerkyBooks

A prize for unpublished and unagented writers of fiction, non-fiction or poetry, aged between 16 and 30. One winner will receive a publishing contract; all longlisted authors are invited to a writing camp which includes workshops, panel talks and editorial review. Entrants should submit a 200-word synopsis and 1,500-word extract for works of fiction and non-fiction or a 200-word synopsis and 500-word extract for works of poetry. Previous winners featured in the line-up of the #Merky Books Literature Festival, which took place in April 2023 as part of In the Round Festival. Founded 2021.

Morley Prize for Unpublished Writers of Colour

61 Westminster Bridge Road, London SE1 7HT
tel 020-7450 1969
email morleylitprize@morleycollege.ac.uk
website www.morleygallery.com/morley-lit-prize-applicants
Facebook www.facebook.com/MorleyGallery/
Twitter @MorleyGallery
Instagram @morleygallery

Celebrates Britain's history of diverse literature and supports new voices within it. Open to all unpublished writers of colour regardless of genre or subject matter. Submissions: Fiction: the first 30 pages of a novel, a three-page outline and a 3,000-word personal statement; Non-fiction: 30-page summary, including a table of contents and writing sample. All shortlisted writers will attend a digital advice session with a literary agent and the winner will receive £500, a manuscript review and a one-hour meeting with a literary agent. Founded 2021.

The Nature Writing Prize for Working Class Writers

email workingclassnatureprize@gmail.com
Twitter @CLASSNATURE

Established to support writers who self-identify as working class and have never been published. Submit 1,000 words of nature writing (fiction, non-fiction and poetry all accepted). Prizes include paid commissions, writing courses, mentoring sessions and book bundles. Founded 2020.

Polari Book Prize

See page 570

RSL Christopher Bland Prize

See page 572

RSL Sky Arts Writers Award

Royal Society of Literature, Somerset House,
London WC2R 1LA
tel 020-7845 4679
email info@rsliterature.org
website https://rsliterature.org/award/sky-arts-rsl-writers-award/

The awards were set up to nurture British writers of colour at the start of their career across five categories: Fiction, Non-Fiction, Poetry, Playwriting, and Screenwriting. One winner in each category receives ten mentoring sessions, spread out over 12 months, with a Royal Society of Literature (RSL) Fellow and two sessions with Booker-prize winner Bernardine Evaristo. Founded 2021.

The Nan Shepherd Prize

14 High Street, Edinburgh EH1 1TE
email contact@nanshepherdprize.com
website www.nanshepherdprize.com
Facebook www.facebook.com/LambdaLiterary
Twitter @NanPrize
Instagram @NanPrize

The only nature writing prize for writers from under-represented backgrounds. The Prize runs every two years, seeks works of narrative non-fiction that explore nature or the environment, and invites entrants who are under-represented due to ethnicity, gender, sexuality, disability or class. Submission for the 2023 prize close in October and will reopen for the 2025 awards in August 2025. Entrants should not have published a full-length work of adult fiction or non-fiction (self-published authors are eligible). Submit a sample, a synopsis, chapter outline and biography. The winner receives a publishing deal with Canongate and a £10,000 advance. Founded 2019.

Mo Siewcharran Prize

See page 575

Watson, Little x Indie Novella Prize

email info@indienovella.co.uk
website www.indienovella.co.uk/writing-prize-page
Facebook www.facebook.com/IndieNovella
Twitter @indienovella
Instagram @indienovellapublishing

The prize is for unpublished or self-published writers of novels, novellas and short stories who are resident in the UK. Each year the prize focuses on a different set of themes; the 2023 themes were characters and community, climate, and crime fiction. Entrants should submit the opening 5,000 words of a longer piece of writing along with a 300-word synopsis. Longlisted entrants will be asked to submit their full manuscript. The winners will receive feedback and a session with an agent at Watson, Little, who will represent the finished novel if it is suitable. Commended entries will also receive feedback, reviews from judges and will have an extract of their work published in an anthology. Founded 2021.

Writers' & Artists' Working-Class Writers' Prize

Bloomsbury Publishing plc, 50 Bedford Square, London WC1B 3DP
tel 020-7631 5985
email waybcompetitions@bloomsbury.com
website www.writersandartists.co.uk/competitions

Open to unpublished writers who consider themselves to be from a working-class background. The winner will receive mentoring support, a £200 cash prize, one year's subscription to the Society of Authors, free admission to any Writers & Artists (W&A) event and a writing guide bundle including the latest edition of the *Writers' & Artists' Yearbook* or the *Children's Writers' & Artists' Yearbook*.

EVENTS, BURSARIES AND OTHER SCHEMES

The Malorie Blackman Scholarships for Unheard Voices

website www.citylit.ac.uk/malorie-blackman-scholarships

Three annual awards worth up to £1,000 each, to fund one year's study within the Creative Writing department at City Lit. Writers are welcome from under-represented groups, including (but not exclusive to) people with disabilities, who are members of the LGBTQIA+ community, who are from lower socioeconomic backgrounds or who are from BAME backgrounds. Founded 2020.

Book Edit Writers' Prize

email writersprize@thebookedit.co.uk
website www.thebookedit.co.uk/writers-prize

Supports unpublished novelists who are from backgrounds and communities under-represented in publishing. Eight winners will be selected to read their work at an Agent Showcase in front of industry professionals, including literary agents. The selected writers will receive training and an opportunity to practise reading their work aloud, and an anthology of the readings will be published online. All entrants receive advice on mentoring, courses and editing. Entrants should submit the first 1,000 words of a novel, a synopsis of the novel and details of their writing experience to date. Founded 2021.

BookTrust Represents

See page 534

Breakthrough x Black Ballad Mentoring Programme

email help@curtisbrowncreative.co.uk
website www.curtisbrowncreative.co.uk/course/
breakthrough-black-ballad-mentoring-programme-0523

A mentoring programme for Black women writers, run in collaboration between Curtis Brown Creative and Black Ballad. Four writers will receive guidance from a published mentor over nine months and a tutorial with a literary agent. Entrants can apply with a writing project at any stage, from just starting to redrafting, in one of the following categories: Children's or YA Novel, Adult Novel, Short Stories, Memoir, or Narrative Non-Fiction. Applicants should submit 3,000 words of their project, a one-page synopsis and a completed entry form. Three of the mentorships are reserved for Black Ballad members (including new members) and one place is available for a low-income writer who cannot afford membership. Founded 2023.

Carole Blake Open Doors Project

See page 583

Creative Access

c/o ITV, Westworks, 195 Wood Lane,
London W12 7FQ
email info@creativeaccess.org.uk
website www.creativeaccess.org.uk
Facebook www.facebook.com/CreativeAccessUK
Twitter @_CreativeAccess
Instagram @_CreativeAccess

One of the UK's leading diversity, equity and inclusion organisations which provides career support and fosters development for those from under-represented communities. Working with leading creative organisations across the UK, Creative Access provides a range of services to help support employer partners create inclusive workplaces; including recruitment programmes, research-driven consultancy and training. Founded 2012.

Curtis Brown Creative

See page 684

Design. Publishing. Inclusivity.

email contact@dpi.org.uk
website www.dpi.org.uk
Twitter @dpi_org
Instagram @dpi_org

The mentorship scheme runs twice a year and offers ten applicants an opportunity to develop skills to pursue a career in book design. No prior education or experience is required, but existing designers are eligible to apply. Each successful applicant is matched with a mentor for six months. Applicants must be from an under-represented background, including Black, Asian or minority ethnicity, disabled, neurodivergent, LGBTQIA+ or working class. Founded 2022.

Early Career Bursaries for London Writers

The Albany, Douglas Way, London SE8 4AG
email emily@spreadtheword.org.uk
website www.spreadtheword.org.uk/projects/early-career-bursaries/
Facebook www.facebook.com/spreadthewordwriters
Twitter @STWevents
Instagram @spreadthewordwriters

Each year the bursaries provide three writers with funds to help the development of their craft and career progression. They are intended to support writers of commercial and literary fiction and narrative non-fiction, whose work is at any stage, from early development to close to completion. Writers must be living in London, on low income or in receipt of benefits, and from communities which are under-represented in publishing, including those who are Black, Asian or of the Global Majority, from a working-class background, LGBTQIA+, refugees, carers, deaf or disabled. The bursaries are worth £15,000, £10,000 and £5,000, and each recipient also receives a package of support including mentoring, writing retreats, writer networks and meetings with publishing professionals. Submissions should include a 3,000-word extract, 300 words explaining how the applicant is under-represented and another 300 words explaining what the applicant hopes to achieve through the scheme. Founded 2022.

Emerging Writers Programme

tel 020-7766 4765
email emergingwriters@londonlibrary.co.uk
website www.londonlibrary.co.uk/about-us/ll-emerging-writers

Open to all writers above the age of 16, the programme offers writers, in all genres, one year's free membership to The London Library and includes writing development masterclasses, and literary networking opportunities. The Virago Participation Bursary (funded by Virago Books) is awarded to black women and black non-binary writers to assist with any financial issues that might prevent them from accessing the full programme. Founded 2019.

Escalator Development Scheme

Dragon Hall, 115–123 King Street,
Norwich NR1 1QE
email info@nationalcentreforwriting.org.uk
website https://nationalcentreforwriting.org.uk/escalator
Facebook www.facebook.com/
NationalCentreforWriting
Twitter @WritersCentre
Instagram @writerscentre

A scheme for unpublished fiction writers based in the East of England who do not yet have an agent, in particular those who identify as LGBTQIA+ or whose ethnicity is under-represented in publishing. Successful participants receive eight months of mentoring which includes feedback, discussion and goal-setting; networking with fellow participants; an opportunity to showcase work to agents, publishers and other industry professionals; subsidised places on workshops, courses and masterclasses; and resources to help promote their writing in the future. Founded 2004.

The Greene Door Project

T18, West Wing, Somerset House, Strand, London WC2R 1LA
tel 020-7759 1186
website http://greeneheaton.co.uk/the-greene-door/the-greene-door-project/
Twitter @greeneandheaton

Greene & Heaton Literary Agency offers mentoring and manuscript feedback sessions to writers who are under-represented in publishing in terms of ethnicity, gender, disability or socioeconomic background. Applicants should submit a cover letter, a synopsis of their work and no more than the first 5,000 words of a novel. Founded 2018.

HarperCollins Author and Design Academy

Westerhill Road, Bishopsbriggs, Glasgow G64 2QT
email enquiries@harpercollins.co.uk
website www.harpercollinsacademy.co.uk
Facebook www.facebook.com/HarperCollinsPublishersUK
Twitter @harpercollinsuk
Instagram @harpercollinsuk

A training programme for writers from BAME backgrounds who are under-represented in publishing. Courses run twice a year for six weeks and are available in three genres: fiction, non-fiction and writing for children. A Design course runs once a year. All successful applicants also receive publishing masterclasses and support from a mentor. Applicants must not be represented by a literary agent and should apply online to one of the three courses. Founded 2021.

Inscribe

email contact@peepaltreepress.com
website www.peepaltreepress.com/inscribe
Twitter @INSCRIBEwriters

Supports writers of colour in England to professionally advance their creative work and their careers through coaching, mentoring, workshops, residentials, training, newsletters, publications and general advice. Founded 2009.

Megaphone Writer Development Scheme

email megaphone.write@gmail.com
website https://megaphonewrite.com
Twitter @MegaphoneWrite

An Arts Council England funded project which offers a year of one-to-one mentoring and masterclasses for writers of colour based in England who are writing a novel for children or teenagers. Bursaries are available for writers who cannot afford the fees.

Middle Way Mentoring

email f.shaikh@dahliapublishing.co.uk
website http://middlewaymentoring.co.uk/

A two-year professional development scheme for Black, Asian and minority ethnic writers based in the Midlands. Successful applicants will receive mentoring and career coaching, participate in writing masterclasses and workshops led by industry experts, and complete a portfolio of work to showcase at festivals and submit to prizes, literary journals and the prizes' anthology. Applicants should submit a covering letter, a writing sample, a biography and a writing CV. Founded 2023.

The Octopus Scheme

email hello@thenovelry.com
website www.thenovelry.com/scholarships

Established by The Novelry to offer fully funded scholarships for places on their Ninety Day Novel course for under-represented writers. Applicants can include writers from a low-income background, primary carers, ex-offenders, writers with a disability, writers of colour and writers from the LGBTQIA+ community. Successful applicants will also receive The Ninety Day Novel Course including one-to-one coaching. Applicants should follow the instructions on the website to apply. Scholarships are sponsored by authors including Sophie Kinsella, Rachel Joyce and Ajay Chowdhury. Founded 2022.

TLC/Arts Council England Free Reads Scheme

East Side, Platform 1, Kings Cross Station, London N1C 4AX
tel 020-3751 0757 ext. 800
email info@literaryconsultancy.co.uk
website www.literaryconsultancy.co.uk/editorial/ace-free-reads-scheme
Director Aki Schilz

In 2001, TLC received funding from Arts Council England to enable the provision of bursaried manuscript assessments for writers from low-income households. The scheme is known as the Free Reads Scheme and offers access to TLC's core services to writers who might not be able to afford them. Free Reads are selected by a range of literature development bodies from across the UK, and there

are currently 17 organisations benefitting from the scheme. For detailed submission guidelines and eligibility information, see the website.
Founded 2001.

WriteNow Programme

WriteNow - The Penguin Random House Group, 20 Vauxhall Bridge Road, London SW1V 2SA
email writenow@penguinrandomhouse.co.uk
website www.penguin.co.uk/company/creative-responsibility/writenow/whats-on-offer.html
Twitter @PenguinUKBooks

A programme by PRH which nurtures and publishes new, unpublished writers from under-represeneted communities. All applicants attend workshops that provide the aspiring writer with tools, contacts, information and access to the publishing and TV industries. Shortlisted applicants receive feedback from an editor and their submission is shared with BBC Studios for consideration. Successful applicants receive one year of mentoring with a Penguin editor to develop their writing and career and a £1,000 writing grant. All applicants should submit 1,000 words from a book they are working on and shortlisted writers will be required to submit a further 5,000 words.

Writers & Artists

Bloomsbury Publishing plc, 50 Bedford Square, London WC1B 3DP

tel 020-7631 5985
email AccessWA@bloomsbury.com
website www.writersandartists.co.uk/accessible-to-all
website www.writersandartists.co.uk/bursary-opportunities

Financial assistance to a combined value of £4,000 has been made available to help ensure that everything W&A offers – events, writing courses and editing services – is accessible to all. See the website for more details and eligibility.

OPEN SUBMISSIONS

Ayebia Clarke Publishing Ltd

See page 127

Hashtag BLAK

See page 152

Lantana Publishing

See page 159

Out-Spoken Press

See page 169

Peepal Tree Press

See page 171

Societies, prizes and festivals

Prize winners

This is a selection of high-profile literary prize winners from 2022–23 presented chronologically. Details of these prizes are included in the *Yearbook*, starting on page 543.

May 2022

International Booker Prize
Tomb of Sand by Geetanjali Shree, translated by Daisy Rockwell

International Dylan Thomas Prize
No One is Talking About This by Patricia Lockwood

Jhalak Prize
The Roles We Play by Sabba Khan

June

The Yoto Carnegie Medal
October, October by Katya Balen, illustrated by Angela Harding

The Yoto Kate Greenaway Medal
Long Way Down by Jason Reynolds, illustrated by Danica Novgorodoff

Walter Scott Prize for Historical Fiction
News of the Dead by James Robertson

Women's Prize for Fiction
The Book of Form and Emptiness by Ruth Ozeki

Commonwealth Writers' Short Story Award
and the earth drank deep by Ntsika Kota

July

The Orwell Prizes
My Fourth Time, We Drowned by Sally Hayden (Political Writing Book Prize); *Small Things Like These* by Claire Keegan (Political Fiction Book Prize); George Monbiot for the *Guardian* (Journalism Prize)

August

James Tait Black Memorial Prizes
A Shock by Keith Ridgway (Fiction); *Finding the Raga: An Improvisation on Indian Music* by Amit Chaudhuri (Biography)

October

BBC National Short Story Award
Blue 4eva by Saba Sams

BBC Young Writers' Award
Little Acorns by Elena Barham

The Booker Prize
The Seven Moons of Maali Almeida by Shehan Karunatilaka

The Bridport Prize
My Father and I Drive Back to St. Louis for his Mother's Funeral by Chaun Ballard and *After You Self-Medicate with Roethke's The Waking Read by Text-to-Speech App* by Roberta Beary (Poetry); *Some Creatures Trapped in Ice* by Hilary Taylor (Flash Fiction); *This is Going to be Huge* by Trent England (Short Story); *I Want* by Zad El Bacha (The Peggy Chapman-Andrews Award for a First Novel)

Crime Writers' Association Gold Dagger Award
Sunset Swing by Ray Celestin

Forward Prizes for Poetry
All the Men I Never Married by Kim Moore (Best Poetry Collection); *Amnion* by Stephanie Sy-Quia (Best First Collection); *Up Late* by Nick Laird (Best Single Poem)

Nobel Prize for Literature
Annie Ernaux

November

The Baillie Gifford Prize for Non-Fiction
Super-Infinite by Katherine Rundell

National Book Awards (USA)
The Rabbit Hutch by Tess Gunty (Fiction); *South to America: A Journey Below the Mason-Dixon to Understand the Soul of a Nation* by Imani Perry (Non-Fiction); *Ally My Rage* by Sabaa Tahir (Young People's Literature); *Punks: New & Selected Poems* by John Keene (Poetry); *Seven Empty Houses* by Samantha Schweblin, translated by Megan McDowell (Translated Literature)

Waterstones Book of the Year
The Story of Art Without Men by Katy Hessel

January 2023

T.S. Eliot Prize for Poetry
Sonnets for Albert by Anthony Joseph

March

Rathbones Folio Prize
Constructing a Nervous System: A Memoir by Margo Jefferson

Festivals and conferences for writers, artists and readers

There are hundreds of arts festivals in the UK each year. We list a selection of literature, writing, and general arts festivals which include literary events. Space constraints and the nature of an annual publication together determine that only brief details are given; see websites for a full programme 2023–24.

The Aldeburgh Literary Festival
42 High Street, Aldeburgh IP15 5AB
tel (01728) 452587
email johnandmary@aldeburghbookshop.co.uk
website www.aldeburghbookshop.co.uk/aldelitfest
Takes place March

Organised by John and Mary James of The Aldeburgh Bookshop, the festival aims to unite the local with the global. Speakers have included two Nobel Prize winners, two Chancellors of the Exchequer and one Pulitzer Prize winner. Tickets can be obtained by returning a physical booking form to the bookshop either in person or by mail. Founded 2002.

Aldeburgh Poetry Festival
website www.poetryinaldeburgh.org
Facebook www.facebook.com/AldeburghPoetry
Twitter @PoetryAldeburgh
Takes place November

A volunteer-led annual festival of contemporary poetry. In-person events take place over one weekend, and online events take place in the preceding week. Founded 1989.

Appledore Book Festival
Festival Office, Docton Court Gallery,
2 Myrtle Street, Appledore, Bideford,
Devon EX39 1PH
email director@appledorebookfestival.co.uk
website www.appledorebookfestival.co.uk
Facebook www.facebook.com/appledorebookfestival
Twitter @AppledoreBkFest
Instagram @appledorebookfestival
Festival Director Jane Beaton
Takes place 15–23 September 2023

Founded by children's author Nick Arnold, this annual festival aims to entertain, inform and inspire a love of reading and creative writing with events on a diverse range of subjects. Features both fiction and non-fiction authors as part of their extensive school programme and a range of public events for all ages. Founded 2006.

Aspects Irish Literature Festival
Town Hall, The Castle, Bangor BT20 4BT
website www.aspectsfestival.com
Twitter @aspectsfestival

Takes place September–October

An annual celebration of contemporary Irish writing, based in Bangor, with novelists, poets and playwrights. Includes readings, children's events and exhibitions.

Aye Write! Glasgow's Book Festival
Glasgow Life, Commonwealth House,
38 Albion Street, Glasgow G1 1LH
tel 0141 287 4350
email ayewrite@glasgowlife.org.uk
Facebook www.facebook.com/AyeWrite/
Twitter @AyeWrite
Takes place May

Brings together the best undiscovered local talent with a wealth of established writers from the city and nationwide. A free children's festival, Wee Write, runs in tandem with the main festival. Creative writing workshops and masterclasses are on offer. Founded 2005.

The Bath Festival
Bath Festivals, 1A Forum Buildings, Bath BA1 1UG
tel (01225) 463362
email info@bathfestivals.org.uk
website https://bathfestivals.org.uk/the-bath-festival
Twitter @TheBathFestival
Takes place May

An annual festival with leading guest writers. Includes readings, debates, discussions, workshops and events.

Bay Tales Live
website https://baytales.com
Facebook www.facebook.com/BayTales
Twitter @bay_tales
Instagram @bay_tales
Takes place March

A crime fiction festival based in the north east of England. The Festival takes place over one day at the Whitley Bay Playhouse, and fringe events take place over one weekend. Includes panel discussions, author readings, interviews and signings and an onsite bookshop. The Festival has received support from publishers including Simon & Schuster, Penguin Michael Joseph, Pan Macmillan, Quercus, Transworld and HarperNorth. Previous speakers include patron Ann Cleeves, Abir Mukherjee, Ruth Ware, Sarah Vaughan and Louise Candlish. Founded 2020.

Birmingham Literature Festival

Studio 130, Zellig, Gibb Street, Birmingham B9 4AT
tel 0121 246 2770
email programming@writingwestmidlands.org
website www.birminghamliteraturefestival.org
Twitter @BhamLitFest
Programmes Director Antonia Beck
Takes place 5-8 October 2023

The annual Birmingham Literature Festival, a project of Writing East Midlands, gathers household names and rising stars to celebrate the power of words. Showcases the very best writers, speakers, thinkers, activists and artists from the UK and across the world.

Bloody Scotland Festival

Caledonia Exchange, 19ᴀ Canning Street, Edinburgh EH3 8HE
email info@bloodyscotland.com
website www.bloodyscotland.com
Twitter @BloodyScotland
Takes place 15-17 September 2023

Based in Stirling, this international crime writing festival has brought hundreds of crime writers, both new and established, to the stage. Festival events cover a range of criminal subjects from fictional forensics, psychological thrillers, tartan noir, cosy crime and many more. With an international focus at the heart of Bloody Scotland, crime writing talent from outside of Scotland is always welcome. Founded 2012.

Baillie Gifford Borders Book Festival

Harmony House, St Mary's Road, Melrose TD6 9LJ
email info@bordersbookfestival.org
website www.bordersbookfestival.org
Facebook www.facebook.com/bordersbookfestival
Twitter @BordersBookFest
Instagram @bordersbookfest
Takes place June

An annual festival with a programme of events featuring high-profile and bestselling writers, including a Family Festival programme. Winner of the Walter Scott Prize for Historical Fiction is announced during the festival. Founded 2004.

Borris House Festival of Writing and Ideas

email info@festivalofwritingandideas.com
website https://festivalofwritingandideas.com
Facebook www.facebook.com/writingandideas
Twitter @Writingandideas
Instagram @writingandideas
Takes place June

Brings together speakers, including international novelists, poets, musicians, academics and journalists, for a weekend of stimulating conversation. Events are spread across the grounds of Borris House and the small village of Carlow. Recordings are also shared online as part of the festival's podcast. Founded 2011.

Boswell Book Festival

website www.boswellbookfestival.co.uk
Facebook www.facebook.com/boswellbookfestival
Twitter @bozzyfest
Instagram @boswellbookfest

The world's only festival of biography and memoir, named after Ayrshire biographer James Boswell. The festival is programmed around stories taken from the inspirational lives of people past and present, shared through writing, drama, art and music. Events include discussions with authors and personalities and writing workshops.

Bradford Literature Festival

Horton Building, University of Bradford, Richmond Road, Bradford BD7 1DP
tel (01274) 044140
email info@bradfordlitfest.co.uk
website www.bradfordlitfest.co.uk
Facebook www.facebook.com/bradfordlitfest
Twitter @BradfordLitFest
Founder & Director Syima Aslam
Takes place June–July

An annual arts event and year-round cultural outreach programme that hosts a diverse range of authors, poets, speakers, musicians and artists from Bradford, the UK and around the world. Taking place over ten days, the programme includes over 400 events and performances. Founded 2014.

Black British Book Festival

Izabella House, 24–26 Regents Place, Jewellery Quarter, Birmingham B1 3NJ
email info@blackbritishbookfestival.com
website https://blackbritishbookfestival.com
Twitter @BBBookFestival
Instagram @BBBookFestival
Takes place October

Dedicated to celebrating Black writers across all genres and at all stages of their career. Increases accessibility by demystifying the publishing process and providing opportunities. Also promotes literacy and a love of reading. Founded 2021.

Brighton Festival

Church Street, Brighton BN1 1UE
tel (01273) 709709
email info@brightonfestival.org
website www.brightonfestival.org
Facebook www.facebook.com/brightonfestival
Twitter @brightfest
Takes place May

An annual arts festival with an extensive national and international programme featuring theatre, dance, music, opera, literature, outdoor and family events. Founded 1967.

Budleigh Salterton Literary Festival
10 Fairfield Close, Exmouth EX8 2BN
tel (01395) 262635
email festival@budlitfest.org.uk
website https://budlitfest.org.uk
Facebook www.facebook.com/BudleighSaltertonLiteraryFestival
Twitter @BudleighLitFest
Director Annie Ashworth, *Chair* Sue Briggs
Takes place 20-24 September 2023

Held beside the sea on the Jurassic Coast, the festival features leading writers and celebrities, events for families and workshops for writers. Includes an outreach programme in schools and is one of the biggest literary festivals in the South West. Founded 2009.

Buxton International Festival
3 The Square, Buxton, Derbyshire SK17 6AZ
tel (01298) 72190
website https://buxtonfestival.co.uk
Facebook www.facebook.com/buxtonfestival
Twitter @BuxtonFestival
Takes place 6-23 July 2023

The renowned opera and music programme is complemented by a Books Series, featuring distinguished authors mainly, but not exclusively, in the sphere of history, biography, music and politics. Founded 1979.

Cambridge Literary Festival
tel (01223) 515335
email hello@cambridgeliteraryfestival.com
website https://cambridgeliteraryfestival.com
Facebook www.facebook.com/CamLitFest
Twitter @camlitfest
Takes place April and November

Brings together an eclectic mix of writers, thinkers and speakers, covering poetry, politics, fiction, finance, history, hip-hop, comedy and current affairs. Founded 2003.

Canterbury Festival
Festival House, 8 Orange Street, Canterbury, Kent CT1 2JA
tel (01227) 452853
email info@canterburyfestival.co.uk
website https://canterburyfestival.co.uk
Takes place 21 October-4 November 2023

Kent's international arts festival showcases performing arts from around the world and runs year-round projects to inspire creativity in people of all ages. It commissions new work, champions emerging talent and supports those seeking careers in the cultural industries.

Capital Crime Festival
23-25 Cecil Court, London WC2N 4EZ
email info@capitalcrime.org
website www.capitalcrime.org
Twitter @CapitalCrime1
Takes place 31 August-2 September 2023

One of the largest celebrations of crime and thriller fiction featuring leading crime and thriller creatives. It welcomes international authors and filmmakers to London and brings the best of everything crime and thriller-related to fans through entertaining and thought-provoking events. Founded 2019.

Charleston Festival
Charleston, Firle, Lewes, East Sussex BN8 6LL
tel (01323) 811626
email info@charleston.org.uk
website www.charleston.org.uk/festival
Twitter @CharlestonTrust
Takes place May

Charleston, the modernist home and studio of painters Vanessa Bell and Duncan Grant, hosts an annual literary festival which attracts artists, writers, performers and changemakers, and celebrates the best in art, literature, ideas and politics.

The Times and Sunday Times Cheltenham Literature Festival
Hub8, The Brewery Quarter, Cheltenham GL50 3FF
tel (01242) 850270
email boxoffice@cheltenhamfestivals.com
website www.cheltenhamfestivals.com/literature
Facebook www.facebook.com/cheltenhamfestivals
Twitter @cheltlitfest
Takes place 6-15 October 2023

The annual festival is one of the oldest literary events in the world and is one of the largest of its kind in Europe. Events include debates, talks and lectures, poetry readings, novelists in conversation, exhibitions, discussions, workshops and a Lit Crawl. Has both an adult and family programme, with events for toddlers to teenagers. Founded 1949.

Chiswick Book Festival
St Michael & All Angels Parish Hall, Priory Avenue, Chiswick, London W4 1TX
email admin@chiswickbookfestival.net
website www.chiswickbookfestival.net
Facebook www.facebook.com/chiswickbookfestival
Twitter @W4BookFest
Instagram @chiswickbookfest
Takes place 6-13 September 2023

Brings writers and readers together to support reading-related charities. Since its inception it has raised over £120,000. Hosts a range of literary events, covering history, poetry, biography, fiction, thrillers, gardens, food, wine, politics, creative writing and self-help. Children's book events are also central to the festival, encouraging a love of both reading and writing. Founded 2009.

Cliveden Literary Festival

tel 020-3488 3401
email info@clivedenliteraryfestival.org
website www.clivedenliteraryfestival.org
Facebook www.facebook.com/clivedenlitfest
Twitter @clivedenlitfest
Instagram @clivedenlitfest
Takes place 30 September–1 October 2023

Set in Cliveden, the English country house with a unique history of politics and intrigue, the festival continues the tradition of the house as a sanctuary for literature lovers. Since 1666 its literary salon, helped inspire writers such as Alexander Pope and George Bernard Shaw, Jonathan Swift and Alfred Lord Tennyson to Sir Winston Churchill. The programme of events, including talks and panel discussions, is announced each summer. Founded 2017.

Cork International Short Story Festival and Poetry Festival

Frank O'Connor House, 84 Douglas Street, Cork T12 X70A
tel +353 (0)21 4322396
email info@munsterlit.ie
website www.munsterlit.ie
website www.corkshortstory.net
website www.corkpoetryfest.net
Twitter @MunLitCentre
Takes place May (Poetry Festival), October (Short Story Festival)

Run by the Munster Literature Centre, these festivals include readings, workshops, seminars and public interviews involving some of the world's best writers and poets. Founded 2000.

Creative Folkestone Book Festival

Quarterhouse, Mill Bay, Folkestone, Kent CT20 1BN
tel (01303) 760740
email info@creativefolkestone.org.uk
website www.creativefolkestone.org.uk/folkestone-book-festival
Facebook www.facebook.com/FolkestoneBookFestival
Twitter @CreativeFstone
Instagram @creativefstone

An opportunity to gather, tell stories, exchange ideas and encourage debate on a wide range of topics. Founded 2002.

CrimeFest

email info@crimefest.com
website www.crimefest.com
Facebook www.facebook.com/crimefest.bristol
Twitter @CrimeFest
Takes place May

An annual, Bristol-based convention for both those who like to read an occasional crime novel and die-hard fanatics. Drawing top crime novelists, readers, editors, publishers and reviewers from around the world, it gives all delegates the opportunity to celebrate the genre in a friendly, informal and inclusive atmosphere. The CrimeFest programme consists of interviews with its featured and highlighted guest authors; over 60 events with more than 150 participating authors; and a gala awards dinner. Founded 2008.

Cuckfield Book Festival

email info@cuckfieldbookfest.co.uk
website https://cuckfieldbookfest.co.uk
Facebook www.facebook.com/cuckfieldbookfest
Twitter @CuckfieldBF
Instagram @cuckfieldbookfest
Takes place 5-8 October 2023

Includes talks and workshops featuring authors from a wide range of genres across fiction, non-fiction and poetry. Also a programme of events for young people. Founded 2016.

Cúirt International Festival of Literature

Galway Arts Centre, 47 Dominick Street, Galway H91 X0AP, Republic of Ireland
tel +353 (0)91 565886
email info@cuirt.ie
website www.cuirt.ie
Twitter @CuirtFestival
Instagram @cuirtfestival
Takes place April

One of Europe's oldest book festivals, and a leading voice for literature both internationally and across Ireland. The festival began as a celebration of poetry and has since grown to a week-long celebration of all forms of writing. Through a festival every April and a year-round programme of engagement, Cúirt brings readers and writers together to tell stories, share new perspectives, and celebrate writing, books and reading in all forms. Founded 1985.

CYMERA

email programme@cymerafestival.co.uk
website www.cymerafestival.co.uk
Facebook www.facebook.com/cymerafest
Twitter @CymeraF
Instagram @cymerafestival
Takes place June

Scotland's festival of sci-fi, fantasy and horror writing, provides a blend of in-person and online events, featuring writer panels, workshops, quizzes and games. Also runs a year-round programme of events. The Brave New Words scheme offers a platform for emerging and newly published writers to read their work in front of an audience, just before some of the main events. A limited number of tickets are available for those who are on low income or unemployed.

The Daunt Books Festival

83–84 Marylebone High Street, London W1U 4QW
tel 020-7224 2295
email enquries@dauntbooks.co.uk
website https://dauntbooks.co.uk/festival
Twitter @dauntbooks
Takes place Spring

This annual celebration of literature goes to show that a bookshop is not just a place to buy books but a space to bring readers together, to foster a literary community and to have a great deal of fun in the process. Key speakers over the years have included Michael Palin, Antonia Fraser, Katherine Rundell, Claire Tomalin, Owen Jones, George Saunders, Sebastian Barry, Sarah Perry, Peter Frankopan and Michael Morpurgo.

Deptford Literature Festival

email festival@spreadtheword.org.uk
website http://deptfordlitfest.com
Takes place March

Celebrates the diversity and creativity of Deptford and Lewisham through words, stories and performance. Run by Spread the Word, each year the festival is curated around a different theme. The Festival features writers, artists and arts organisations based in the area, and hosts creative writing workshops and a programme of events for children and families.

Derby Book Festival

13 Lavender Row, Darley Abbey, Derby DE22 1DF
email hello@derbybookfestival.co.uk
website www.derbybookfestival.co.uk
Facebook www.facebook.com/DerbyBookFestival
Twitter @DerbyBookFest
Instagram @derby_book_festival
Takes place Spring and Autumn

Celebrates the joy of books and reading for all ages and interests, with a programme featuring great writers, poets, historians, politicians, illustrators, storytellers and musicians. Each year the festival welcomes internationally celebrated bestselling authors as well as a broad range of local writing talent. In addition to its core programme of events, the organisers operate community-focused projects across Derby and in schools. Founded 2015.

Dublin Book Festival

email info@dublinbookfestival.com
website www.dublinbookfestival.com
Twitter @DublinBookFest
Instagram @dublinbookfest
Takes place 8–12 November 2023

Brings together the best of Irish publishing, offering a chance for the voices of both established and up-and-coming authors to be heard. Held in The Printworks, Dublin Castle, the festival's events include book launches, interviews, workshops, a children's and schools programme and lots more. Founded 2006.

Durham Book Festival

New Writing North, PO Box 1277,
Newcastle upon Tyne NE99 5PB
email rebecca@newwritingnorth.com
website https://durhambookfestival.com
Twitter @durhambookfest
Takes place October

A book festival for new and established writers, taking place in the historic city of Durham in a variety of historic venues including the Gala Theatre. Founded 1990.

East Riding Festival of Words

website www.festivalofwords.co.uk
Facebook www.facebook.com/erwordfest/
Twitter @erwordfest
Takes place October

One of the UK's leading literature festivals. The festival includes authors' events, readings, panel events, workshops, children's activities and performances. Founded 2000.

Edinburgh Comic Art Fair

Facebook www.facebook.com/comicartfestival
Twitter @edinburghcomic
Takes place November

ECAF is a gathering of artists, comic authors, fans and readers that expands the reach and creativity of the genre and offers unique events, from writing poetry graphic novels to illustrating folk tales. Comic creators take part in panels, talks, workshops and portfolio reviews.

Edinburgh International Book Festival

Edinburgh College of Arts, 74 Lauriston Place,
Edinburgh EH3 9DF
tel 0131 718 5666
email admin@edbookfest.co.uk
website www.edbookfest.co.uk
Twitter @edbookfest
Takes place 12-28 August 2023

A key event in Edinburgh's annual August festival season and one of the largest public celebrations of words and ideas in the world. Around 600 UK and international writers appear in over 500 events for adults, children and schools. Programme details available in June. Founded 1983.

Ennis Book Club Festival

email info@ennisbookclubfestival.com
website www.ennisbookclubfestival.com
Takes place First weekend in March

An annual literary weekend which brings together book club members, book lovers, writers and other artists. Includes lectures, readings, discussions, theatre, music and more. Founded 2007.

Societies, prizes and festivals

Falmouth Book Festival

email colin@falmouthbookfestival.com
website www.falmouthbookfestival.com
Facebook www.facebook.com/FalmouthBookFestival
Twitter @BookFalmouth
Takes place 16-22 October 2023

Brings people together to engage with and share a love of literature in all its forms. Includes author talks, poetry readings and free workshops for children and families, as well as events which celebrate the local area and natural landscape. In association with Falmouth University. Founded 2021.

Foxes' Retreat Festival of Writing

The Old Kennels, Birdsgrove Lane,
Ashbourne DE6 2BP
tel (07734) 328762
email myszka@foxesretreat.com
website www.foxesretreat.com
Facebook www.facebook.com/retreatfoxes
Twitter @RetreatFoxes
Takes place 6–13 August 2023

A week-long festival in the Peak District focused on creativity and wellbeing. Catered accommodation available includes private rooms, campervans and tents. Workshops, led by experienced writers and editors, cover character building, poetry, flash fiction, short stories, drama and memoir. Optional activities include yoga, river swimming, reiki, drumming, sound bath, holotropic breathwork and spoken word.

Granite Noir

His Majesty's Theatre, Rosemount Viaduct,
Aberdeen AB25 1GL
tel (01224) 641122
website www.aberdeenperformingarts.com/granite-noir/
Twitter @GraniteNoirFest
Takes place February

Inspired by the contribution that Scottish writers make to crime fiction and the city of Aberdeen, the line-up each year features authors and publishing representatives. Events include talks, workshops, walking tours and exhibitions. Some events are live-streamed online.

Guildford Book Festival

c/o Tourist Information Office, 155 High Street,
Guildford GU1 3AJ
tel (01483) 444334
email alexandrews@guildfordbookfestival.co.uk
website www.guildfordbookfestival.co.uk
Twitter @gfordbookfest
Director Alex Andrews
Takes place 1–18 October 2023

An annual festival with a diverse programme of outstanding conversation and lively debate to further an interest and love of literature through involvement and entertainment. Hosts author events, workshops

and a schools programme, plus selected online events. Founded 1989.

Raworths Harrogate Literature Festival

tel (01423) 562303
email info@harrogate-festival.org.uk
website https://harrogateinternationalfestivals.com/raworths-literature-festival
Facebook www.facebook.com/HarrogateInternationalFestivals
Twitter @HarrogateFest
Instagram @harrogatefestivals
Takes place October

Four days of literary events featuring bestselling authors, designed to entertain, inspire, educate, challenge and amuse audiences. Founded 2013.

Hay Festival

The Drill Hall, 25 Lion Street,
Hay-on-Wye HR3 5AD
tel (01497) 822620
email submissions@hayfestival.org
website www.hayfestival.com
Facebook www.facebook.com/hayfestival
Twitter @hayfestival
Instagram @hayfestival
Takes place May; Hay Festival Winter Weekend takes place 23–26 November

Brings together writers, musicians, filmmakers, historians, politicians, environmentalists and scientists from around the world to communicate challenging ideas. The 2023 festival featured Margaret Atwood, Caleb Azumah Nelson, Alexander McCall Smith and Marina Hyde. Hundreds of events over ten days. Within the annual festival is a festival for families and children, HAYDAYS, which introduces children, from toddlers to teenagers, to their favourite authors and holds workshops. Programme published April. Founded 1987.

Huddersfield Literature Festival

email info@huddlitfest.org.uk
website www.huddlitfest.org.uk
Festival Director Michelle Hodgson
Takes place March

Showcasing new, emerging and established writers and artists, the blended programme includes venue-based, hybrid and online author talks, writing and performance workshops, multi-arts performances, innovative special projects, spoken word events and family-friendly events. Includes many free and low-cost events, and several with subtitling by Stagetext. Founded 2006.

I Am Writing Festival

email iamwriting@iaminprint.co.uk
website https://iaminprint.co.uk
Twitter @iaminprint
Instagram @iaminprint

Directors Sarah Post, Elane Retford
Takes place May

A festival for writers working towards publication based in Bristol; all abilities are welcome, from beginners to those ready to approach agents and publishers. The festival hosts a variety of workshops, talks and panels featuring debut and bestselling authors, agents and publishers across all book genres. Includes creative writing classes, competition announcements, the opportunity for manuscript feedback. A pitch party takes place on the Friday. Founded 2022.

Ilkley Literature Festival

9 The Grove, Ilkley LS29 9LW
tel (01943) 601210
email info@ilkleylitfest.org.uk
website www.ilkleyliteraturefestival.org.uk
Facebook www.facebook.com/ilkleylitfest
Twitter @ilkleylitfest
Director Erica Morris, *Programme Manager* Becky Wholley
Takes place 7–23 October

One of the UK's longest-running and widest-ranging literature festivals with over 100 events, from author discussions to workshops, readings, literary walks, children's events and a festival fringe. Founded 1973.

Independent Bookshop Week

website www.booksaremybag.com/IndependentBookshopWeek
Facebook www.facebook.com/booksaremybag
Twitter @booksaremybag
Instagram @booksaremybag
Takes place June

An annual celebration of independent bookshops, part of the Books Are My Bag campaign to promote high street bookshops and shopping locally and sustainably. Founded 2006.

International Literature Festival Dublin

13 Adelaide Road, Dublin D02 P950, Ireland
email info@ilfdublin.com
website https://ilfdublin.com
Twitter @ILFDublin
Takes place May

Ireland's premier literary event gathers the finest writers to debate, provoke and delight in Merrion Square Park, Dublin. The Festival continues to champion Dublin's position as a UNESCO City of Literature, celebrating the local alongside the global and the power of words to change the world. With readings, discussions, debates, workshops, performances and screenings. Founded 1998.

Jewish Book Week

Raymond Burton House, 129–131 Albert Street, London NW1
email info@jewishbookweek.com
website https://jewishbookweek.com
Twitter @JewishBookWeek
Festival Director Claudia Rubenstein
Takes place February/March

A ten day festival of writing, arts and culture, with contributors from around the world and sessions in London and nationwide. Includes events for children and teenagers. Founded 1952.

King's Lynn Festival

Fermoy Gallery, 7–9 St George's Courtyard, King Street, King's Lynn, Norfolk PE30 1EU
tel (01553) 767557
email info@kingslynnfestival.org.uk
website www.kingslynnfestival.org.uk
Facebook www.facebook.com/kingslynnfestival
Twitter @KLFestival
Instagram @kingslynnfestival
Artistic Director Ambrose Miller
Takes place 16–19 July plus year round events

An annual arts festival with a music focus, including literature events featuring leading guest writers. Founded 1951.

King's Lynn Literature Festivals

email enquiries@lynnlitfests.com
website www.lynnlitfests.com
Twitter @lynnlitfests
Chairman Tony Ellis
Takes place September/March

Poetry Festival (22–24 September): An annual festival which brings 12 worldwide-published poets to King's Lynn for a weekend of readings and discussions.

Fiction Festival (March): An annual festival which brings ten published novelists to King's Lynn for a weekend of readings and discussions.

Ledbury Poetry Festival

Ledbury Poetry House, Barrett Browning Institute, Homend, Ledbury HR8 2AA
tel (01531) 634156
email director@ledburypoetry.org.uk
website www.poetry-festival.co.uk
Facebook www.facebook.com/ledburyfest/
Twitter @ledburyfest
Instagram @ledburyfest
Artistic Director Chloe Garner
Takes place 30 June–9 July 2023

Features nationally and internationally renowned poets, together with a poet-in-residence programme, slams, competitions, workshops, community events and exhibitions. It also runs poetry events for children. Hosts an annual Poetry Competition, with £1,000 prize money.

Leeds Lit Fest

email enquiries@leedslitfest.co.uk
website www.leedslitfest.co.uk
Facebook www.facebook.com/LeedsLitFest

Twitter @LeedsLit
Instagram @leeds_lit_fest
Takes place February/March

Celebrates the vibrant and thriving literature scene in Leeds with local writers and performers showcasing their talents along with national and international artists. Hosts an exciting programme of author talks, workshops, panels, performance, digital, poetry and spoken word events. Founded 2019.

Listowel Writers' Week

24 The Square, Listowel, Co. Kerry V31 RD93, Republic of Ireland
tel +353 (0)68 21074
email info@writersweek.ie
website https://writersweek.ie
Facebook www.facebook.com/writersweek
Twitter @WritersWeek
Takes place June

Brings together writers and audiences at unique and innovative events in the historic and intimate surroundings of Listowel, County Kerry. At its heart is a commitment to developing and promoting writing talent, underpinned by the values of partnership, inclusivity and civic responsibility. Events include workshops, readings, seminars, lectures, book launches, art exhibitions and a comprehensive children's and teenagers' programme. Founded 1971.

Litfest

The Storey, Meeting House Lane, Lancaster LA1 1TH
tel (01524) 509005
email marketing@litfest.org
website www.litfest.org
Facebook www.facebook.com/LitfestLancaster
Twitter @Litfest
Takes place March

Features local, national and international writers, poets and performers. Litfest is the literature development agency for Lancashire with a year-round programme of readings, performances and workshops. Founded 1978.

London Literature Festival

email literatureandspokenword@southbankcentre.co.uk
website www.southbankcentre.co.uk
Facebook www.facebook.com/southbankcentre
Twitter @southbankcentre
Takes place 19–29 October 2023

Combines the best of the year-round literature events with an engaging festival programme, encompassing free public programming, thematically focused talks and debates, newly commissioned performances and a family offer to coincide with the half-term school holiday. Founded 1967.

Manchester Children's Book Festival

Manchester Metropolitan University, All Saints Building, Manchester M15 6BH
email mcbf@mmu.ac.uk
website www.mmu.ac.uk/mcbf
Facebook www.facebook.com/MCBFestival
Twitter @MCBFestival
Instagram @mcbfestival

Year-round activities celebrating the very best writing for children, inspiring young people to engage with literature and creativity across the curriculum and offering extended projects and training to ensure the events have an impact and legacy in classrooms. Founded 2009.

Manchester Literature Festival

The Department Store, 5 Oak Street, Manchester M4 5JD
email office@manchesterliteraturefestival.co.uk
website www.manchesterliteraturefestival.co.uk
Twitter @McrLitFest
Co-Directors Cathy Bolton and Sarah-Jane Roberts
Takes place October

An annual two-week festival showcasing new commissions and celebrating the best literature and imaginative writing from around the world. Note that MLF only accepts a small number of submissions each year, with the majority of the festival being curated by the team.

Marlborough Literature Festival

email general@marlboroughlitfest.org
website www.marlboroughlitfest.org
Facebook www.facebook.com/MarlboroughLitFest
Twitter @MarlbLitFest
Festival Patron Sir Simon Russell Beale
Takes place 28 September–1 October 2023

An annual literary festival in the market town of Marlborough, celebrating the best in writing and reflecting the legacy of writers linked to the town such as Siegfried Sassoon, John Betjeman and William Golding. Champions new and upcoming writers as well as established names and offers a varied programme of events for all ages, including fiction, non-fiction, poetry, children's events and creative writing workshops in local venues in and around Marlborough. Has a strong outreach programme, delivering free author talks to local schools. Founded 2010.

Monty Lit Fest

Montgomery Town Hall, Broad Street, Montgomery, Powys SY15 6PH
email enquiries@montylitfest.com
website https://montylitfest.com
Facebook www.facebook.com/montylitfest
Twitter @montylitfest
Instagram @montylitfest
Takes place June

A diverse programme of events brings together a wide range of audiences to celebrate writers who live in or write about Wales. Founded 2016.

National Eisteddfod of Wales
40 Parc Ty Glas, Llanishen, Cardiff CF14 5DU
tel 0845 409 0300
email gwyb@eisteddfod.cymru
website https://eisteddfod.wales
Facebook www.facebook.com/eisteddfod
Twitter @eisteddfod
Takes place 5–12 August 2023

Wales's largest cultural festival. Activities include competitions in all aspects of the arts, fringe performances and majestic ceremonies. In addition to activities held in the main pavilion, it houses trade stands along with a literary pavilion, arts exhibition, an outdoor performance stage and a purpose-built theatre. The event is held in a different part of Wales every year. Founded 1861.

National Poetry Day
email info@forwardartsfoundation.org
website https://nationalpoetryday.co.uk
Facebook www.facebook.com/PoetryDayUK
Twitter @PoetryDayUK
Instagram @nationalpoetryday
Takes place 6 October 2023

Organised by the Forward Arts Foundation to encourage poetry reading and writing. Combines poetry recommendations and teaching resources with nationwide events to highlight the artistic and social value of poetry. Each year it takes place on the first Thursday in October and explores a different theme. Founded 1999.

Newcastle Noir
website www.newcastlenoir.co.uk
Facebook www.facebook.com/NewcastleNoir
Twitter @NewcastleNoir

An annual crime fiction festival established to promote top-class crime writing in the region and to celebrate an intriguing and increasingly diverse genre. Founded 2014.

*Noir*wich Crime Writing Festival
tel (01603) 593412
email noirwich@uea.ac.uk
website www.noirwich.co.uk
Facebook www.facebook.com/noirwich
Twitter @NOIRwichFEST
Takes place 8–9 September 2023

Celebrates the sharpest noir and crime writing over two days of author events and writing masterclasses in the historic city of Norwich, UNESCO City of Literature. *Noir*wich is presented by the University of East Anglia. Founded 2015.

Norfolk & Norwich Festival
Norwich Guildhall, Gaol Hill, Norwich NR2 1JS
tel (01603) 877750
email info@nnfestival.org.uk
website https://nnfestival.org.uk
Facebook www.facebook.com/NNFestival
Twitter @NNFest
Takes place May

For 17 days each year the festival transforms public spaces, city streets, performance venues, parks, forests and beaches, bringing people together to experience a variety of events spanning music, theatre, literature, visual arts, circus, dance and free outdoor events. Founded 1988.

Northern Short Story Festival
website www.bigbookend.co.uk/nssf
Facebook www.facebook.com/NoShoStoFest
Twitter @NoShoSto
Instagram @noshosto

Aims to bring the best in short story writing to Leeds to celebrate the many writers in the region and to support independent presses working nationwide. Provides regular pop-up events, networking opportunities and workshops, and runs The Academy scheme to help short story writers with their creative development. Founded 2016.

Off the Shelf Festival of Words Sheffield
Cathedral Court, 46 Church Street, Sheffield S1 2GN
tel 0114 222 3895
email offtheshelf@sheffield.ac.uk
website www.offtheshelf.org.uk
Takes place 13–29 October 2023

Join writers, historians, poets, artists, scientists, journalists and musicians at this diverse and innovative festival, celebrating books, words and ideas. Events for all ages in Sheffield and South Yorkshire.

Oundle Festival of Literature
email oundlelitfestival@hotmail.co.uk
website www.oundlelitfest.org.uk
Facebook www.facebook.com/OundleFestivalOfLiterature
Twitter @OundleLitEvents
Festival Director Helen Shair

Runs a programme of year-round events aimed at exciting, informing, entertaining and educating a wide variety of people through talks, discussions and workshops by award-winning and local authors and poets. Held in a variety of venues in the beautiful market town of Oundle. Founded 2002.

FT Weekend Oxford Literary Festival
c/o Critchleys, Beaver House,
23–28 Hythe Bridge Street, Oxford OX1 2EP

Societies, prizes and festivals

email info@oxfordliteraryfestival.org
website https://oxfordliteraryfestival.org
Takes place March/April

An annual festival for both adults and children held in venues across the city and university. Presents topical debates, fiction and non-fiction discussion panels, and adult and children's authors who have recently published books. Topics range from contemporary fiction to discussions on politics, history, science, gardening, food, poetry, philosophy, art and crime fiction. Founded 1998.

Paisley Book Fest

email bookfest@renfrewshire.gov.uk
website https://paisleybookfest.com
Facebook www.facebook.com/BookPaisley
Twitter @bookpaisley
Instagram @paisleybookfest
Takes place February

Celebrates Scottish arts and culture. Events include author talks, writing workshops and publishing advice, covering a range of genres including poetry, flash fiction and memoir. Also runs a Writer in Residence scheme and a schools programme. Facilitates the Janet Coats Memorial Prize.

Primadonna Festival

Laffitts Hall, Framsden Road, Pettaugh, Stowmarket, Suffolk IP14 6DT
tel 07764 752731
email primadonnafestival@gmail.com
website https://primadonnafestival.com
Facebook www.facebook.com/primadonnafest
Twitter @primadonnafest
Director Catherine Riley
Takes place 28–30 July 2023

A festival of books and ideas, and the first in the UK to specifically give prominence to (cis and trans) women writers, BIPOC authors, members of the LGBTQI+ community, working-class authors, those with disabilities and groups who have traditionally been disadvantaged in the arts by their background or circumstance. All ideas, and all kinds of people, are welcome: most especially those that might not think a literary festival is 'for them'. Founded 2019.

Rye Arts Festival

tel 07850 877647
email andy.stuart@ryeartsfestival.org.uk
website https://ryeartsfestival.org.uk
Facebook www.facebook.com/Ryeartsfestival
Twitter @Ryearts
Takes place 15–30 September 2023

Set in the historic town of Rye, The Festival is the largest multi-arts festival in East Sussex. It presents a programme of literary events, talks, panel discussions and workshops featuring leading writers of fiction, non-fiction, poetry, music and drama. Founded 1971.

Salisbury International Arts Festival

Wiltshire Creative, Salisbury Playhouse, Malthouse Lane, Salisbury SP2 7RA
tel (01722) 320333
email info@wiltshirecreative.co.uk
website www.wiltshirecreative.co.uk
Facebook www.facebook.com/wiltscreative
Twitter @WiltsCreative
Instagram @WiltsCreative
Takes place May–June

A thriving, annual multi-arts festival that delivers over 150 arts events each year, including concerts, comedy, poetry, dance, exhibitions, outdoor spectacles and commissioned works. Founded 1974.

The Self-Publishing Conference

tel 0116 279 2299
email books@troubador.co.uk
website www.selfpublishingconference.org.uk
Twitter @Selfpubconf

The UK's longest established self-publishing conference. This annual event covers all aspects of self-publishing from production through to marketing and distribution. The conference offers plenty of networking opportunities and access to over 16 presentations. Founded 2013.

Shetland Noir

Mareel, Lerwick, Shetland ZE1 0WQ
tel (01595) 745500
email admin@shetlandarts.org
website www.shetlandarts.org/festivals/shetland-noir
Facebook www.facebook.com/shetlandnoir/
Twitter @shetlandnoir
Takes place June

Dedicated to crime fiction, events include author talks, panel discussions, workshops and outings around Shetland. The 2023 festival was run in collaboration with Shetland Arts literary festival, Wordplay, and featured writers Richard Osman, Val McDermid and Elly Griffiths.

The South Downs Poetry Festival

email info@SDPF.org.uk
website http://www.sdpf.org.uk/
Twitter @SDPFestival

An annual pop-up festival which spans the length and breadth of the South Downs National Park and the surrounding area. Poets, actors, musicians and publishers take part in readings, performances, screenings, discussions and walks, celebrating new, established and beloved writers. Organised by Focus Arts and facilitates the Binsted Prize. Founded 2016.

The Stanfords Travel Writers Festival

website www.stanfords.co.uk/stanfords-travel-writers-festival
Takes place January/February

Held at Destinations: The Holiday & Travel Show in London's Olympia, it hosts book launches and live author events. Founded 2014.

StAnza: Scotland's International Poetry Festival

tel (01334) 475000 (box office)
email stanza@stanzapoetry.org
website www.stanzapoetry.org
Facebook www.facebook.com/stanzapoetry
Twitter @StAnzaPoetry
Instagram @stanzapoetry
Operations Manger Suzie Kirk Dumitru
Takes place March

Dedicated to programming a wide diversity of poetries and poets, alongside other art forms such as music and visual art. It is international in focus and has a hybrid format, including both live and digital events. Founded 1997.

States of Independence

website http://
leicestercentreforcreativewriting.our.dmu.ac.uk/
Facebook www.facebook.com/StatesOfIndependence/
Twitter @StatesofIndie
Takes place March

An annual one-day festival celebrating independent publishing. Hosted by the Leicester Centre for Creative Writing at DMU, the 2023 festival was online. Involves independent publishers from the region and beyond. A free event with a varied programme of sessions and a book fair. Founded 2010.

Stories Festival

email eventsteam@standard.co.uk
website https://stories.standard.co.uk/

Run by the London *Evening Standard* newspaper, it celebrates the way that stories connect with people and bring people together. Features authors, poets, screenwriters, comedians, actors and producers across interviews, panels, screenings and other events.

Stratford-upon-Avon Literary Festival

email info@stratfordliteraryfestival.co.uk
website www.stratlitfest.co.uk
Facebook www.facebook.com/stratfordlitfest
Twitter @StratLitFest
Instagram @stratfordlitfest
Takes place May with events in Autumn

A feast of workshops, panel discussions, celebrity and author events. The festival also runs a programme of educational events and projects for families and regional schools aimed at entertaining and inspiring children and encouraging literacy, as well as events in the community and writing workshops in prisons. Founded 2008.

The Summer Festival of Writing

4 Acer Walk, Oxford OX2 6EX
tel 0345 459 9560
email info@jerichowriters.com
website https://jerichowriters.com/events/summer-festival-of-writing
Takes place June–August

A three-month online festival for all writers to connect with others from across the world. Writers have the opportunity to hear from literary agents, publishers and professional authors. This includes pitching work to literary agents; receiving live feedback from industry professionals; and entering writing competitions.

Swindon Festival of Literature

Lower Shaw Farm, Shaw, Swindon, Wilts. SN5 5PJ
tel (01793) 771080
email swindonlitfest@lowershawfarm.co.uk
website www.swindonfestivalofliterature.co.uk
Festival Director Matt Holland
Takes place May

An annual celebration of live literature and the arts through prose, poetry, drama, dance, music, circus skills and storytelling, with readings, discussions, performances and talks in theatres, arts centres, parks and pubs. A festival of ideas and entertainment with leading authors, speakers and performers. Founded 1984.

Theakston Old Peculier Crime Writing Festival

Old Swan Hotel, Swan Road, Harrogate HG1 2SR
tel (01423) 562303
email info@harrogate-festival.org.uk
website www.harrogateinternationalfestivals.com/crime-writing-festival
Facebook www.facebook.com/HarrogateInternationalFestivals
Twitter @HarrogateFest
Instagram @harrogatefestivals
Takes place 20–23 July 2023

The world's largest and most prestigious celebration of crime fiction, featuring over 100 authors. Founded 2003.

Two Rivers Book Fest

Field House, Thrandeston, Diss, Norfolk IP21 4BU
email info@waveneyandblytharts.com
website https://waveneyandblytharts.com/book-fest

Shines a light on the people who create books and get them into the hands of readers. Guest speakers include authors, publishers, bookshop owners, librarians and creative writing teachers. Local history and writers are also explored and celebrated. Founded 2019.

UEA Live

Arts and Humanities Events,
University of East Anglia, Norwich NR4 7TJ
tel (01603) 592286
email uealive@uea.ac.uk
website www.uealive.com
Facebook www.facebook.com/uealitfest
Twitter @UEALitfest
Takes place February to May

Based at the University of East Anglia, where some of the greatest writers of today have studied and worked, including Kazuo Ishiguro, Ian McEwan and Anne Enright. Previously known as the UEA Literary Festival. Founded 1991.

Warwick Words History Festival

The Court House, Jury Street, Warwick CV34 4EW
tel 07944 768607
email info@warwickwords.co.uk
website https://warwickwords.co.uk
Twitter @WarwickWords
Takes place 2–8 October 2023

Celebrates historical writing, both fact and fiction. Provides an opportunity to meet authors and discuss their work. Founded 1999.

WayWORD Festival

website www.waywordfestival.com
Facebook www.facebook.com/waywordabdn
Twitter @waywordabdn
Instagram @waywordabdn
Takes place 19–24 September 2023

A student and youth-led cross-arts festival exploring unconventional forms of expression in collaboration with the University of Aberdeen and the WORD Centre for Creative Writing. Events take place in-person and online, feature a diverse line-up and include conversations with authors, panel discussions, book launches, workshops and performances.

Wells Festival of Literature

email admin@wellsfestivaloflliterature.org.uk
website www.wellsfestivaloflliterature.org.uk
Facebook www.facebook.com/Wellslitfest
Twitter @wellslitfest
Instagram @wellsfestivaloflliterature
Takes place 27 October–4 November 2023

Features leading writers of fiction and non-fiction, poets, politicians, performers and more. All events take place in Cedars Hall in the heart of Wells, England's smallest city. Administers four competitions. Festival run entirely by volunteers with all profits going to help fund educational projects in local schools and colleges to encourage young people to love literature and to celebrate the written word. Founded 1992.

Wigtown Book Festival

11 North Main Street, Wigtown,
Dumfries and Galloway DG8 9HN
email mail@wigtownbookfestival.com
website https://wigtownbookfestival.com
Facebook www.facebook.com/WigtownBookFestival
Twitter @WigtwonBookFest
Takes place 22 September–1 October 2023

Ten-day annual festival in Scotland's National Book Town, bringing readers, aspiring writers and published authors together across 200 events. In addition to the festival, runs events throughout the year, facilitates a mentorship programme for writers and administers two prizes. Also runs Hooked Festival for Young Readers and Writers. Founded 1999.

Wimbledon Book Fest

35 Wimbledon Hill Road, London SW19 7NB
email info@wimbledonbookfest.org
website www.wimbledonbookfest.org
Twitter @Wimbookfest
Takes place 12–22 October 2023

Fosters a space for art and culture within the community. Guest speakers include writers from all genres, with a focus on inspiring stories, diversity and inclusion. Runs educational workshops and projects for young people during the festival and throughout the year. Founded 2006.

Winchester Poetry Festival

c/o University of Winchester, Sparkford Road, Winchester, Hampshire SO22 4NR
email hello@winchesterpoetryfestival.org
website www.winchesterpoetryfestival.org
Twitter @WinPoetryFest
Instagram @winchesterpoetry
Contact Amy Juliet Brown
Takes place October

A biennial festival dedicated to poetry. See website for confirmed dates and activities for the 2023 festival. Founded 2013.

WOW London Festival

The HKX Building, 3 Pancras Square, London N1C 4AG
website https://thewowfoundation.com
Facebook www.facebook.com/womenoftheworldfestival
Twitter @WOWisglobal
Instagram @wowisglobal
Takes place March

Established by the Women of the World (WOW) Foundation to celebrate women, girls and non-binary people and facilitate conversations around gender discrimination. Includes authors across a range of genres discussing the potential for literature and other forms of media to combat discrimination and promote positive representation. Other events take place across the UK all year round. Founded 2010.

YALC (Young Adult Literature Convention)

email yalc@showmastersevents.com
website https://londoncomicconwinter.com/YALC
Facebook www.facebook.com/ukYALC
Twitter @yalc_uk

YALC is a celebration of the best YA books and authors. It is an interactive event where YA fiction fans can meet their favourite authors, listen to panel discussions and take part in workshops. Founded 2014.

Self-publishing and indie authors

Paid-for publishing services: *Is it a steal?*

The UK writers' unions, the Society of Authors (SoA) and the Writers' Guild of Great Britain (WGGB), investigated the practices of companies that charge writers to publish their work while taking rights. The findings were published in their 2022 report *Is it a steal?* Their investigation into 'hybrid'/paid-for publishing services raises awareness and works for change in what is a growing section of the writer services sector. Authors are advised to read the report and heed its advice.

Below are key extracts from this report. The full version can be found at: https://writersguild.org.uk/wp-content/uploads/2022/05/REPORT-Is-it-a-steal.pdf

As part of an investigation into practices in the sector, the SoA and the WGGB carried out a survey of authors who had used 'hybrid'/paid-for publishing services. 240 writers responded to the survey which ran online between 28 February and 25 April 2021.

The findings of that survey have informed our in-depth assessment of the relationship between writers and companies who often refer to themselves as 'hybrid', 'partnership' or 'contributory' publishers (among other terms) but which have much in common with what have historically been described as 'vanity' publishers.

Summary findings:
- 94% of respondents lost money, typically in the thousands.
- The average loss was £1,861 with some writers reporting losses as high as £9,900.
- The median cost of publication was £2,000.
- A median of only 67 books were sold per deal, resulting in royalties of only £68.
- 59% of writers said their book was not available to buy in retail outlets.

We received reports of aggressive marketing tactics by 'hybrid'/paid-for publishers in their approaches to writers, their manipulative sales approaches, unclear contracts, obscure publishing processes and services that fell far short of expectations and value.

Recommendations

1. We have identified an urgent need to educate writers about all models of publishing and to support them through any publishing process they choose. We have made five recommendations for writers to follow.

2. We strongly urge all publishers to commit to 15 key publishing principles, including offering clarity about their business models, production and book-marketing capacity, as well as notifying people who enter into 'hybrid'/paid-for agreements about their Consumer Rights.

3. We are working with third parties – including the Publishers Association, the Independent Publishers Guild, and various advertising platforms – who in various ways give these 'hybrid'/paid-for companies credibility, to ensure that they are not helping to

promote or validate companies whose operations are based on poor practice and the exploitation of writers.

What is 'hybrid'/paid-for publishing?

In a traditional or conventional trade publishing contract, a publisher provides everything from editing and printing to marketing, publicity and distribution. It takes a licence of rights and pays writers a fee or an advance, and royalties. It does not ask for payments from a writer. It funds its operation by sales of books and is therefore investing cash and resources, and taking a risk on the book's success.

'Hybrid'/paid-for publishing deals should also not be confused with self-publishing. Writers can self-publish at very little cost to themselves, but even if they pay a **self-publishing service provider** to edit, design, produce and market their book, the rights will remain with the writer. The writer receives all profits after the sales platform or distributor takes its cut and can extract themselves from the agreement at any time. Such service providers are funded by payments agreed, and preferably negotiated, with the author.

Defining 'hybrid'/paid-for publishing services

If a writer pays money for publication and grants the company a licence of rights or if the company takes a share of any profits, the writer is dealing with a 'hybrid'/paid-for publishing service.

The companies in question sometimes describe themselves as 'contributory', 'subsidy' or 'partnership' publishers, but they have much in common with what used to be called 'vanity' publishers. In their marketing approaches to writers, they often suggest that they operate as traditional publishing houses. In fact, some are run as imprints of major publishers, gaining legitimacy from their parent brands.

At first glance, 'hybrid'/paid-for publishing deals can look much like traditional publishing agreements, but they are very different. There is rarely any sign of expenditure by the 'hybrid'/paid-for publisher except what is funded by the author. As such, terms like 'hybrid', 'contributory' and 'partnership' can appear deliberately misleading. Writers pay the publisher. They are offered no advance, and there is usually no undertaking or intention by the 'hybrid'/paid-for publisher to publish the work other than as an ebook and/or as Print on demand ('POD'), or in an ultra-short print run. The writer does not own any of the books produced except for limited initial copies.

Anyone can set themselves up as such a publisher, regardless of their financial stability, publishing knowledge and experience, or commercial expertise. Start-up and overhead costs are minimal, and expenses are funded by writers, not by income from book sales.

At the point of submitting a work for publication, writers are vulnerable. They have invested a great deal of time, work, energy and creativity in their manuscript. Now they want to be read, and for their work to be legitimised.

'Hybrid'/paid-for publishing services often exploit this desire, sending excessive praise about manuscripts and telling writers what they want to hear. They might claim their approach is better than traditional publishing or self-publishing, without ever explaining what that means. They will stress how excited they are to be working with the writer. Of course, at the point of hearing a 'publisher' express interest in their work like this, it can be difficult for a writer to step back and see it for what it is: a sales approach, designed to take advantage of writers' hopes, their passion for their work and their desire for validation – not to mention their lack of knowledge about the complexities of the publishing industry.

In our view, of all the publishing approaches available, a 'hybrid'/paid-for deal is the worst option a writer can take. In our direct experience of working with SoA and WGGB members, and as our research bears out, 'hybrid'/paid-for publishing deals do not result in enough sales or exposure to justify the payment by the author. For many years, even before researching for this report, we have seen how such services fall short of expectations, with writers unnecessarily handing over rights and control over their manuscripts, along with large sums of money. We have seen the impact this has on writers' careers and confidence in their work, and on their finances. We have seen too many cases where the 'hybrid'/paid-for model amounts to a counterfeit approach to publishing. We invariably advise writers against it.

If you are a writer considering a 'hybrid'/paid-for deal, we recommend taking the following five steps before you commit:

1. Educate yourself.
The publishing industry is complex. Do your research to get a broad understanding of how it works and the options available before you commit to any publishing deal. For starters, download the free SoA guide What type of deal is that? for a no-nonsense introduction to the pros, cons and gotchas of five publishing approaches.

2. Consider carefully what you want from publication and whether a 'hybrid'/paid-for deal is the best way to achieve it.
Is a 'hybrid'/paid-for publishing deal a better option than self-publishing, with its substantial investment from you as well as surrendering rights in your work? To commission self-publishing services will probably cost you less and you will retain all rights in your work.

3. Look closely at the detail of the deal.
How much will you have to pay? What is covered for that payment? Are there guarantees on the number of books to be printed? And will you own any of them, or will you have to pay more to get hold of copies yourself ('author copies')? What rights are you giving away? Will you have to make further payments later? Can you terminate the deal, when and how?

4. Research the company offering the deal.
Ask the SoA and WGGB what we know about them. Ask others who have used the company. Look for online reviews (though be mindful of paid-for positive reviews) and check their history at Companies House. Check the Watchdog Advisory Ratings on the Alliance of Independent Authors' (ALLi) website. In short, don't sign with a company unless you are confident about what you can expect if you work with them.

5. Have your contract vetted.
Remember that all contracts are negotiable. If you are an SoA or WGGB member, get your contract vetted as part of your membership. We recommend that you always do this regardless of the type of deal or contract you are being offered.

Is it a steal? is supported by the Authors' Licensing and Collecting Society (ALCS). © The Society of Authors and Writers' Guild of Great Britain – April 2022.

See also...
- *Society of Authors*, page 495
- *WGGB (Writers' Guild of Great Britain)*, page 498

Understanding book design

Freelance designer Catherine Lutman guides you through the purpose and process of book design, and the numerous elements that must work together to suit a book's specific requirements, with the useful terminology and details you need to know about typography and layout, briefing a designer, and the use of imagery and illustrations.

The cover of a book typically draws a consumer to pick it up, glance at the back cover, and then scan a few pages at random from inside. And then it's essential to make sure the pages are legible, professionally designed, and appropriate for the genre. No matter how strong the cover or the content, if the *internal* pages are poorly laid out the reader will be put off. Many design decisions influence how a reader experiences your content – and the more complex the content, the more involved is the work of the designer.

Typography and layout

The design of the internal pages is a delicate balancing act between many factors:

• **Typography** – the art and technique of arranging type. The designer will decide the style and organisation of all the words in the book, including titles, headings, sub-headings, body text, quotes, featured text, tables, captions, indents, footnotes, running heads and/or footers and page numbers.

• **Hierarchy** – the organisation of elements on the page according to their importance or the order in which they should be read. Hierarchy helps us navigate the book and process the content. It can be achieved through the use of scale, weight, colour and spacing.

• **Margins** – these perform several functions in the book. Margins provide space for the reader to hold the book; they keep the text block or content away from the gutter (thee inner margin of a book); they make the book visually appealing and reserve space for running heads, footers and page numbers. A larger margin is usually found at the inner edge than at the outer, as the binding means the book does not lay completely flat.

• **Grid** – a structure of lines that aid the designer in organising and aligning the page elements.

• **Baseline grid** – designers can choose to align some or all of the text to a baseline grid (see the diagram overleaf). When text is aligned in this way, subconsciously readers perceive pages as neater and more harmonious.

• **Leading (line spacing)** – the vertical space between lines of text. It should feel comfortable to the eye.

• **White space** – a well-balanced page layout will include generous white space. Resist the temptation to overcrowd the page in order to keep the extent down.

• **Measure (line width)** – the designer takes care that the width of the text blocks, and therefore number of words on a line, is comfortable for the reader to scan. Where a single block would be too wide, columns of text can be used.

• **Imagery** – the scale, position and type of imagery is fundamental to how the content is experienced. If an image is placed across a double-page spread, care must be taken that important details (such as one or more people in the image) are not lost in the gutter.

• **Tables, charts and graphs** – these need to display information effectively and accurately and can add interest to the layout.

• **Colour scheme** – the choice of colours in two- and four-colour books is integral to the design. Choosing to publish a book in colour has cost implications but, in a children's picture book for example, it is usually a matter of necessity.

• **Extent** – the total number of pages in the book. The extent is made up of *signatures* or *sections*; each of these is a sheet of paper folded into eight, 16 or 32 pages. Therefore, the extent of the book will jump up in these increments. Designers bear this in mind as they work with the layouts to make sure the layout fills the sections.

• **Paper** – the choice of coated or uncoated paper and the weight and colour of the paper are all design decisions. A bulky, non-reflective, uncoated paper may be preferable for a novel, whereas a full-colour photography book may print best on a bright white, coated paper.

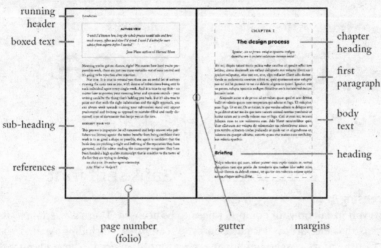

Layout and hierarchy

Grid and baseline grid

Choice of fonts

There are hundreds of fonts with many classifications, but for the purposes of book layout design the two main types are *serif* and *sans serif*. A serif is a small stroke at the end of the larger stroke in a letter; a sans serif font does not have these. Broadly speaking, sans serif fonts are considered more modern and serif fonts more traditional. However, it is generally accepted that serif fonts are easier and more comfortable to read for long passages of text; this is why the majority of novels are set in serif fonts, whether they are historical or contemporary. In a text-based book, sans serif fonts can be useful for headings, subheadings and extra material that you may want to give more emphasis to, as they can provide contrast to the body copy and help distinguish the page hierarchy or create interest in the layout.

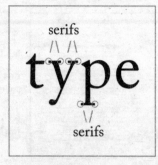

Serif font   Sans serif font

Font licensing

Any fonts you install on your computer need to be licensed. There are certain fonts called *system fonts* that are already installed on every computer (including Arial, Times New Roman, Courier and Georgia) but, for any other fonts, you need to have a licence for each machine they are used on. An experienced designer will have built up a library of licensed fonts and, if they have a Creative Cloud (www.adobe.com/uk/creativecloud.html) subscription for design applications such as InDesign and Photoshop, they will have a licence to use any fonts from the Adobe Typekit library. Some fonts are only available from particular type foundries and can be expensive; some companies even commission fonts and hold their exclusive licence. Free font sites such as Dafont (www.dafont.com) are popular, but always check the licence as some 'free' fonts are only free for personal use, which means that you cannot use them in any material you intend to sell or distribute commercially.

Typesetters

For certain types of publication, it is common practice for the designer to design a sample chapter and pages from the prelims and endmatter; after these are approved, they then hand the layout of the complete book over to a typesetter. This approach is appropriate for a lengthy book in which each chapter or section is similar or is very text-heavy in content, such as a novel or reference book. A heavily illustrated book, such as a children's book, cookery book or an art book, or one that is not lengthy would be laid out entirely by a designer. Your designer can advise you on what is appropriate for your book and may be able to find a typesetter for you if needed.

Briefing the 'internals'

Depending on the type of book and the skill set of the designer, you may wish to treat the design of the cover and internals (internal content) separately and brief different designers to do each part. Obviously, a cover design is often highly creative whereas a page layout may require a very precise and detailed mindset, but many book designers are experienced in working in either discipline. Fees for the design of the internals can vary widely depending on complexity and extent: some designers quote per page and others quote for a sample chapter, expecting the layout of the whole book to be undertaken by a typesetter. The brief for the internals may include the following elements:

• **Sample** – a representative sample of the content.
• **Summary of content** – chapter titles, content of prelims and endmatter.
• **Imagery** – description of any imagery to be sourced.
• **Page plan** – may be a requirement for certain types of book.
• **Trimmed page size** – if the cover is hardback, this will be slightly smaller than the cover size.
• **Number of colours** – a novel would typically be one colour (black), whereas a children's book would be four-colour. Some books have colour sections with plates of photographs and other images.

NB If you are briefing the internals to a different designer than the cover, you will need to add the description, genre, look and feel, target market and competition to the brief.

Design process for internals

The designer commonly works up several double-page spreads for each initial design option, based on the sample you provided, giving fewer options than for a cover. The layouts try to include all the key elements from the content: chapter headings, introduction, body text, imagery, any text features, running heads or footers and page numbers. The designer may suggest additional elements to add interest, such as ornaments (small decorative symbols that separate sections) or boxed text.

The aim of the first round is to pick the option that will be carried forward and perfected. Once the sample chapter has been designed, the prelims and endmatter can be designed and, if the services of a typesetter are being used, the book can be handed over to be typeset. If the designer is laying out the book from beginning to end, there can be a lengthy process of building up the layouts as the content is finalised, culminating in rounds of proofing.

Imagery and illustration

If you intend to use graphic elements in your book, there are some important technical and legal aspects to bear in mind, particularly if you plan to source the images yourself. Design, illustration and photography are seen as distinct disciplines. Although some creatives provide some or all of these services, you may need to engage a different person as designer, illustrator or photographer. Your designer may be able to suggest illustrators or photographers, or they may suggest sourcing images from an image library.

Copyright

It is vital that you have permission to use any imagery in your book: you cannot simply pull an image from the internet and use it. Firstly, an image dragged from a website is unlikely to be of print quality and, secondly, it is illegal to use intellectual property in your book without acquiring the explicit right to do so. You could commission an illustrator or photographer to create original work for your publication or purchase a licence to use an image.

Commissioning an illustrator or photographer

If you have decided to commission original imagery, the process of selecting an illustrator or photographer is much the same as finding a designer. Ask to see their portfolio to get an idea of their style and experience. As with design, some areas of photography or illustration are highly specialised, and some people may work in a specific area such as technical illustrations or food photography. Most illustrators or photographers do not automatically grant you a licence to own the artwork outright; instead, they retain the copyright and would expect a further fee for a reprint or repurpose. Clarify this point when you commission them to do the work.

When briefing the illustrator or photographer, you can make good use of mood boards. Some illustrations need to be extremely specific and briefed individually; you may need them to fit a designated space in the layout and supply requested dimensions for each one. A photographer might require the collaboration of additional people for the shoot: an art director, stylist and assistant commonly form the team. The book designer often takes the role of art director. Post-production work such as retouching and colour correction might be needed, although some photographers undertake these tasks themselves.

Royalty-free images

A royalty-free image is one you can buy a simple licence to use right away, without negotiating the fee and usage with an agent. Libraries such as Shutterstock (www.shutterstock.com), iStock (www.istockphoto.com) or Adobe Stock (https://stock.adobe.com/uk) have many hundreds of thousands of royalty-free photographs, illustrations and graphics you can purchase. You need to make sure the licence you purchase covers the usage you need; for example, some licences have a restriction on the number of times the image can be printed (and in which territories) and where they can be reproduced. Generally, though, a standard licence will suffice for use in your book.

Rights-managed images

Rights-managed images, found on sites like Getty Images (www.gettyimages.co.uk), are sold on a one-time-use basis for reproduction in a specific way. These can be of a very high quality by a well-known artist or photographer, or they may cover a specialised subject. A rights-managed image is usually considerably more expensive than a royalty-free image.

Summary

Many elements come together to make up the design of your book and determine its success. At every stage, effective communication and collaboration with experienced professionals will give you the best chance of achieving your goal – to create a memorable and appropriate design that showcases your work and puts it in the hands of your intended audience.

Catherine Lutman is an award-winning freelance designer, art director and design manager based in London. She has 20 years' experience in the publishing industry and has worked with many of the world's leading publishers. Catherine specialises in the design of non-fiction, reference and illustrated books on a wide range of subjects from artist's monographs to children's reference. A selection of her work can be seen at www.catherinelutman.com.

This article is an extract from Chapter 3 'Design: from manuscript to finished book' by Catherine Lutman in the *Writers' & Artists' Guide to Self-Publishing* (Bloomsbury 2020), © Bloomsbury Publishing Plc 2020.

Building your author brand

What is an 'author brand' and why does it matter? Sam Missingham shares her tips and techniques on how self-published authors can develop their profile to attract readers to their work.

Most people I meet hate the idea that authors are brands; they seem to assume that this means the publishing industry is treating them like tins of baked beans, sports clothing or chocolate bars. I think there is a fear that this is part of a dehumanising process treating an author like a product with a logo to be packaged and sold. This reveals a lack of understanding of what is involved in building an author brand and why it is so important. The aim of a strong author brand – to put it into much more positive terms – is to build an authentic relationship with readers and, further, to encourage readers to think and feel certain emotions. It is also about establishing your uniqueness.

Most of us already have connections with the authors of our favourite books. Think for a second about, say, Ian Rankin. If you enjoy his books, you might be interested in Edinburgh, the character of Rebus, and the type of crime novels Ian writes. If you are more of a fan, you may have heard him speak at an event, you might follow him on social media, you might know that Ian likes a pint and visiting record shops, and that he loves taking photos of his walks around his home city. You can probably recognise that he has a unique voice. How have Ian and his publishers (Hachette UK) built his brand? Ian has done the most important part, which is to write consistently great books for over 20 years, and this is undoubtedly the best way to build an authentic relationship with readers and establish an author brand. His publishers have amplified his unique voice through publicity, marketing and events. They ran a week-long Rebus event in Edinburgh and reinforced Ian's brand across the city and beyond.

To help you establish your own unique brand in practical ways, here are three important elements of author branding you can focus on.

1. Design

The design elements of your author brand involve the creative choices you make for your book covers, your website, your social media and anything else that is seen by the market and potential readers (which is considered 'outward-facing'). I think it is always useful to think in terms of 'genre signposting', which in simple terms means the colours, imagery and fonts or typography that are typically used. The use of styles that follow existing publishing standards will immediately identify the genre your book fits into – if it is sci-fi, a young adult novel, Regency romance, or a cookery book. Some people think all crime or romance books look the same, but actually they have been designed with similar elements so that readers immediately recognise them.

Here's how to establish the design elements of your author brand.

• Ask a professional designer to help you. This is always my first piece of advice. Designers who have experience working in publishing have a deep understanding of genres, of what readers expect, and of wider design trends and how they can make you look like a professional writer. A lot of self-published authors are still designing their own covers and many of them just aren't good enough. Don't forget – the aim is to attract readers of your genre; your cover will set their expectations of your book.

• Identify three or four authors who are successful in your genre; take a good, critical look at their covers and their websites, sign up to their newsletters, check out their social media accounts and do a Google image search on their names. You should see some similarities in the design elements they have used. Then pick out elements that you like and which you think could work for you and your books. Ask yourself how you can express your *uniqueness* within this established aesthetic.

• If you are designing your own covers, ads, website and social media assets, keep things simple: within the bounds of the genre aesthetic that you've identified above. Choose a very small number of colours, fonts and images and use them across your promotion and marketing. Consistency and repetition play a part in building your brand. Canva, www.canva.com, is an excellent design tool and can take you a long way towards looking like a professional author.

• Get feedback from readers, industry insiders, bloggers and booksellers on what you are currently doing. What do they think when they look at your book cover? And at your website? What could you do better? You will probably be quite surprised by their answers. Listen to them. Try to avoid asking partners or friends, because they will rarely give you honest, informed feedback.

These design elements should be used consistently across your website, social media, ads, point of sale, merchandise and any other touchpoints you have with your readers.

2. Voice

Your author voice refers to how and what you communicate, the tone you take, and what you make your readers think and feel. Looking at existing, successful examples is always useful, such as Marian Keyes, who has a fantastic author voice: she is incredibly funny, kind and open; she is an absolute master of social media – brilliant on Twitter, makes great videos on Instagram, and her newsletter is hilarious. Take a look at www.mariankeyes.com, Twitter @MarianKeyes, www.facebook.com/MarianKeyes and www.instagram.com/marian_keyes. You will notice that Marian talks regularly about her mum, her love of makeup, her nieces and nephews, Ireland, her travels, and occasionally her ailments. Her openness, authenticity and humour, along with her brilliant books, make her an incredibly popular and successful author. Her voice plays an important part in this. Navigate the sites and social media of authors you admire or in the genre in which your own books sit: what inspires you, what can you emulate?

A little side-note about authenticity: some authors I have worked with think that this involves revealing everything about themselves, and this is not the case. Think carefully about what you are happy to talk about – whether that is your hobbies, family or social life. We all need boundaries and privacy, so think this through. If you are working with a publicist, they will ask you about this, to find hooks to pitch your story to journalists. Be clear about how much of yourself you are willing to reveal. Once you have established these topics, make sure you talk honestly about them; maintaining an inauthentic author persona might be possible for a while, but is not sustainable long term.

Back to author voice. What you say and how you say it will influence how your readers, agents, booksellers and publishers feel about you. What would you like them to think? That you are fun, inspiring, knowledgeable, supportive? Find a way to convey your values through your voice. LJ Ross is a very successful author, whose bestselling *DCI Ryan* mysteries are set in the north east of England. She shares her love of the region, supports local people and businesses, and runs several philanthropic initiatives. Her readers are incredibly engaged with her books and they know that she, in turn, is incredibly committed to them.

Your voice should be within keeping of your genre and appropriate for your audience. Never lose sight of who your readers and wider audience are; so if you write children's books, don't forget that your voice must appeal to parents, teachers and school librarians, as well as being suitable for children.

3. Consistency and repetition

Once you have established the elements of your author brand, you should use them everywhere and consistently. You want your audience to become familiar with you. Your imagery, colours, voice and covers will all help them to do that. Consider using the same author photo across all of your social media; people will recognise you and, if they enjoy you on Twitter, will probably follow you elsewhere. Add the same photo somewhere prominent on your website too.

Here are a few other tips to help you establish your author brand:

• If you already have some readers, ask for their feedback: What do they like? What do they enjoy about what you share? What do they think about your covers? Run some polls on Twitter or on your Facebook page.

• Engage with a group of your hardcore fans and use them as a sounding board. Treat them like your VIP readers. You can provide them with unique and pre-publication access to some of your content in return for their input.

• Read some of the reader or blogger reviews of your books in case these are useful to suggest how to improve what you do. If you don't want to do this yourself, consider asking someone you trust to pull out any positive points – and any constructive criticism in the negative ones (it *is* there sometimes!).

• Go into a bookshop and have a good look at where your book sits on the shelf (or where you hope it will sit, if it's not published yet); see which authors are being highlighted in your genre; take photos. If you feel confident enough, talk to a bookseller – they really are the fount of all knowledge and will probably give you insights that you simply can't get elsewhere.

Go through a similar process on Amazon (and other online booksellers) in the categories and subcategories where your book will sit. Look at the bestsellers in each category; go to their websites and look at their ads, their blurbs, and consider the tone they are using.

There is always so much to learn from other more established authors. Learn from the best – and adapt ideas to work for you. In addition to Ian Rankin, LJ Ross and Marian Keyes, I would highly recommend the following authors.

• Rob Biddulph (www.robbiddulph.com) is a children's author who has absolutely nailed his brand. Take a look at #DrawWithRob to see how he engaged with his readers during the Covid-19 pandemic and built on all of the positive elements of his approach.

• Salena Godden (www.salenagodden.co.uk) is a brilliant author and poet; take a look at how she uses social media, videos and live performances to create a very strong author identity.

• Simon Alexander Ong (www.simonalexanderong.com) is a business book author and life coach; his author brand is spot-on for the professional audience he is trying to attract. He is particularly good on Instagram (www.instagram.com/simonalexandero).

• Joanne Harris (www.joanne-harris.co.uk) is brilliant at everything; there are all kinds of ideas and tips you could pick up from her use of social media.

I hope this advice will help you nail *your* author brand and convince you just how important it is to an author's publishing strategy.

Sam Missingham is founder of The Empowered Author, a book marketing service for authors. Find out more at https://theempoweredauthor.com and follow her on Twitter @samatlounge.

See also...
• *Getting your book stocked in a high-street bookshop*, page 617

Getting your book stocked in a high-street bookshop

So you've written your book. It's finally finished, you have it printed, and you're ready to share it with readers. But how do you get your self-published novel onto the shelves of a high-street bookshop? Independent bookseller Sheila O'Reilly guides you on your way.

How to contact booksellers

Ideally booksellers like to be emailed. It gives us time to think about your proposal; it gives us time to chat to our colleagues, and it gives us the opportunity to deal with the request within our normal day. If you do decide to show us the book in person, please don't visit unannounced. It's beneficial instead to email ahead so we can arrange a quick appointment for you with the appropriate buyer, at a time that works with the shop diary.

What booksellers need to know

To help us make our decision, you should include the following information on your proposal:
• A quick synopsis of the book – two or three sentences is perfect.
• A couple of lines about who you are.
• The sales details:
  - How much your book retails for.
  - How much you are selling it to bookshops for. (Trade terms vary between publishers.) The market research agency Nielsen reports that the average discount received by bookshops from publishers is just over 40% off the recommended retail price. In the UK, the publisher almost always pays for the carriage charge in getting the books to the bookshop.
  - A professional invoice outlining your terms of business.
  - The format (paperback/hardback). We would always recommend that the book has a spine; that the title is printed on the spine; and that there is a 13-digit EAN bar code (based on the ISBN) printed on the book.
  - Returns information. The most usual trade practice for independently published titles would be for the books to be supplied on 'consignment terms' (which means that the bookshop will pay for the stock once it has sold and can return unsold stock when it chooses). An alternative is 'sale or return', where the bookshop pays for the stock according to the payment terms of your invoice, but has the right to return unsold stock for a full refund.
  - Payment terms and the length of time the bookshop should have the stock for sale. If after this agreed length of time the books have not sold it is your responsibility to collect unsold stock. If the books are not collected after three months, the bookseller can dispose of the stock as they deem fit.
  - A few sample pages for us to read.
  - Why you think the book will sell in our bookshop.
  - Who the competitors – or comparable authors – are in your eyes.
  - In which section we should display the book.
  - A jpg image of the book cover or jacket.

- If the book has any local ties; is it set in our area? Did you go to school around the corner?

- Any local publicity lined up or in the pipeline (e.g. features, interviews or extracts in local news media). This can have real value in improving local sales.

Tips

• Be competitive regarding the pricing of your book. A standard paperback is around £8.99.

• Look at the production quality; a well-presented finished product speaks volumes. Look at books in similar genres to your own on bookshop shelves and note the current design styles/finishes/fonts being used.

• Give important consideration to the cover or jacket design. Review the competition, check out the award-winning designs from the latest British Book Design & Production Awards (www.britishbookawards.org). If you want your book to take up space on a shelf face out (the most popular display method) the jacket must be of stunning design and quality. Book cover design is a specialist discipline, so commissioning an experienced designer is often the best way to give your book an edge alongside other publications.

• Pick your time of year carefully. The majority of new writers are launched in the beginning of the year. If you release too close to Christmas, your book will get lost on the shelves. If you come in February or March, we often have the space to display your book where it has a better chance of selling.

• Booksellers would not welcome being sent an Amazon link in your proposal. Whilst, of course, Amazon is likely to be another outlet for your book, most high-street bookshops choose to have no commercial dealings with Amazon because of the perceived negative impact they have had on Britain's high streets and physical bookshops.

• Think about how you might promote your book and direct people to the bookshop for sales. We send our sales information to Nielsen/BookScan, so if we sell a lot of copies your book will get noticed around the book industry.

• Outline what will be your marketing and publicity plan to generate interest for the book.

• Supply: make sure your book can be distributed via the national trade wholesalers Gardners (www.gardners.com), at a standard trade discount, with returns. If in the Republic of Ireland, use either Easons (www.easons.com) or Argosy (www.argosybooks.ie).

• Ask your printer how they can help to distribute your book via the wholesalers mentioned above. Many will take care of this on your behalf. For instance, a traditional book printer like Clays will warehouse copies of your books then distribute them when wholesale orders come in, while IngramSpark/Lightning Source will print each copy to order and distribute them to retailers via the main wholesale routes.

• Fix a realistic wholesale discount when you set up your book for distribution, whether you do this directly via the wholesalers or via your printer. It might be tempting to keep the discount as low as possible to increase your royalties, but the lower you make it the less realistic it will be for a bookshop to stock it. Do your research – find out how much of a cut the wholesaler will take (as a very general guide, it could be in the area of 15%), and remember that the average discount bookshops receive is in the region of 40% of the cover price.

• Thinking through and planning for these elements of distribution will simplify our ordering/reordering of your book and increases your chance of being stocked by us tenfold. Whilst bookshops might from time to time agree to being supplied directly by an author, each time a separate supplier is set up for an individual book it adds greatly to the bookshop's paperwork and accounting burden and, more importantly, means that it takes longer to reorder the book once it sells. Most bookshops order every day from Gardners, Easons or Agrosy at the click of a button, and so ensuring those wholesalers have stock of your book is the best way to make it easily accessible to every bookshop in the country.

• Months before the book is due to be published, begin the social media campaign and include your local bookshops.

• Gather the email addresses of friends and contacts, and once the book is published tell them that they can order it through such-and-such a bookshop. This will show the local bookshop that there is interest and they, in turn, are more likely to say 'yes' to stocking your book.

• If you sell copies direct to all your friends and family, it is unlikely that the local bookshop will have a market to sell to. If you persist in taking this step, don't be surprised if after a month or so you get an email from them announcing they have sold none and want to return the books.

• If you have a website, please direct potential customers to any bookshops that have agreed to stock your book.

• If a bookshop does order copies of your book and agrees to be supplied by you directly, then don't forget to deliver the books along with an invoice. It is very important the latter has your contact details (for future orders) and bank details (for payment).

• Do not constantly call the bookshop to check on sales (tempting as that might be).

How a typical high-street bookshop decides on the books to stock

Every bookshop has a finite amount of space and budget to spend each month. The book buyers will go through a series of decisions before saying 'yes' or 'no' to any particular book.

For many bookshops the decision is helped by the representatives from publishers, who will brief them on the new books, why they believe it will sell in the bookshop and what promotion the publisher is putting behind the book.

Here is an outline of some of the decisions taken by a bookseller before deciding to stock a book:

Our market: we understand what our customers like to read and what genres sell well. We tailor our stock around that (we also try and find the books customers didn't know they liked).

Our tastes: if we read and love a book, you can be sure we're going to be telling our customers about it.

The subject: if a book is on a topic that we feel will be of interest to our customers, then that is a huge swaying factor for us.

The author: if we know their work and their track record, we can make a judgement on how well we think the book will sell for us. Also, if the author is local and is likely to have a local following and/or supportive friends and family, then this will influence us.

Marketing: we look at what sort of promotion the book will be getting locally, further afield and on social media (is there already a buzz around it?).

Format and price: this is a major selling point for us; it's not unusual to wait for a paperback to come out before taking a chance on a title.

Self-publishing and indie authors

Design: as with the format, we look at the jacket. Sometimes a stunning cover can be the swaying point between us taking a book or not.

After all this, the bookseller may decline to stock your book. Don't take that personally or expect an explanation; time does not allow that for every book we decline to stock.

One thing to remember is, please don't be disheartened if we say 'no' to your book. What works for some bookshops doesn't work for others. What sells huge numbers in, say, the Edinburgh Bookshop might not sell in Bath and what sells in Bath may not sell in Oswestry. That's the beauty of high-street bookshops – they are all different. You can find lists of Britain's bookshops at www.booksellers.org.uk/bookshopsearch.aspx.

What can you expect from a bookshop?

Despite the many one-way tips above, getting a book into a reader's hands is very much a team effort between an author, a publisher and a bookseller. Here's what you can expect from a bookshop when you approach them with your book:
• In all circumstances, to be treated with the respect and consideration you'd expect any business to give to a potential business partner.
• Once the bookseller has had a chance to consider the book properly, a clear and prompt answer as to whether or not the bookshop is willing to accept the book into its stock.
• If the bookshop does take the book and the book sells, to pay you promptly in accordance with the payment terms you have specified and to give quick consideration to reordering more stock.
• If the bookshop is included in any social media campaign around a book it has agreed to stock, to participate actively in that campaign.

Extracted from the Booksellers Association *Want to Get Your Book Stocked in a High Street Bookshop?* written by **Sheila O'Reilly**, an experienced independent bookseller, who previously owned Dulwich Books, London. For the complete guide see www.booksellers.org.uk/Industry-Info/Industry-Info/Getting-your-book-stocked-in-a-high-street-bookshop.

See also...
• *Getting books to market: how books are sold*, see page 110

In praise of fanfic

Hari Patience-Davies uncovers the rich field of fanfiction, a world full of creative opportunities and possibilities, where prequels, sequels, crossovers, alternate universes and viewpoints, 'fix-its' and 'what ifs' provide fertile ground for writers to practise and enjoy their craft.

Recently I read an amazing reimagining of Jane Austen's *Pride and Prejudice* (1813). Unlike other versions that have appeared over the years, this one featured no zombies and no murders in need of solving at Pemberley Hall – instead it was an exquisitely plotted alternative life of Elizabeth Bennet that unfurled over about 500,000 words (the original novel is only around 120,000 words long), wherein our heroine followed the drum to the Peninsula War with her first husband. Such was the scope of the story that it had several alternate endings and an impressive cameo from the Duke of Wellington.

I'd love to recommend it to everyone I've ever met, but I suspect that more than a few of them would turn their noses up at it. You see, it wasn't a published novel but a story written by a fan, something generally referred to as fanfic or fanfiction.

What is fanfic?

There are many ways of describing fanfiction – some call it theft, others 'unoriginal drivel', still more have mocked it for being full of badly spelled porn written by teenagers. But if we're looking for a basic description, a fanfic is a story (or comic or video edit) that is based on an original work by someone else. That work could be a novel, a comic book, a television show or film – it could even be based on a podcast or cartoon strip. A particularly 'Marmite' (you love it or you hate it) area of fanfic is Real Person Fiction or RPF, in which the author conjures a story where their favourite pop star is in love with them, or possibly in love with their bandmate, or maybe just running a coffee shop somewhere in the Lower East Side. You would be hard-pressed to describe RPF as being based on an original work by another creative though. Some could possibly be claimed by the public relations experts who feed stories to the tabloids.

It might be easier to say what fanfic is not. It is not profitable. It is not sellable. It is not something that any fan can claim is entirely theirs, even if the particular creative interpretation is their own, as it is grown from the seed of someone else's idea. Fanfiction is written without authorisation or permission. Sometimes an author may be approached by a copyright owner (the original author, their estate or publisher) to write an official prequel or sequel, such as Geraldine McCaughrean's *Peter Pan in Scarlet* (OUP 2006). Commissioned work is not fanfiction; it may have been written by a fan but, because that fan had permission, it doesn't meet the criteria.

So why, in this *Yearbook* designed to help struggling writers and artists find their way into paid creative work, are we talking about fanfic? Because, while we may all dream of *Sunday Times* bestseller lists, Hollywood three-picture-deals, or writing the Great British Novel, we shouldn't lose sight of what brought us here in the first place – the sheer joy of creation. Historically fanfiction has fallen into something of a grey area. In the early days of the internet author and publishers pushed back hard, sending 'cease and desist' letters, in some cases to children. Entire fanfiction archive websites disappeared overnight when faced with the wrath of a major studio or publisher. It was standard operating practice for years for fanfiction writers to include a disclaimer at the top of every chapter saying something like: 'I do not own these characters and am writing this story for my own amusement and not for any profit'.

In 2014, UK copyright law was amended to include: 'Fair dealing with a work for the purposes of caricature, parody or pastiche does not infringe copyright in the work'.[1] Many have taken this to mean that fanfiction – so long as it is not generating any money – is legal. As with many questions of legality, the enforcement of this depends upon the creativity of your legal counsel and the flexibility of the judge hearing the case. We are not legal experts here at the *Yearbook* and, should you wish to write something that could be classed as fanfiction for the purposes of profitable publication, we would advise speaking to a lawyer with expertise in copyright law first.

Fanfiction websites

The website Archive of Our Own (AO3; https://archiveofourown.org) looks to US copyright law for protection. On their website AO3 state: '… fanworks are creative and transformative, core fair uses, and [we] will therefore be proactive in protecting and defending fanworks from commercial exploitation and legal challenge.' AO3 is an entirely non-profit, non-commercial endeavour, funded by regular donation drives that ensure the servers stay on and the site stays live; they also maintain a legal support service for fans who may need it.

Now, instead of cracking down on fanfic writers, authors are advised by publishers and lawyers not to read any of the fanfiction associated with their works. The fear is that, if an author is known to read fanfic, and if an idea first explored by a fan should surface in a future novel by the original author, then the author could be sued by the fan-writer. I've seen several tweets and blogs by content creators asking people not to send them character musings or sequel ideas, as even reading someone else's take could prevent them from writing a potential sequel.

So, the legal threat to fanfiction is gone but the social stigma remains. Fanfiction is regarded as derivative, lesser, a juvenile pursuit – a reputation that I feel is entirely undeserved. It's time for us to re-evaluate the worth of fanfiction, both as readers and writers.

Why write fanfic?

Do you remember when you were a child? If your toy box was anything like mine,

Fanfiction websites

Archive of Our Own (AO3)
https://archiveofourown.org

The largest fanfiction website in the world, which hosts over 8.9 million fanworks across over 48,570 fandoms. Established in 2007, this is the main home for fanfic online – especially as it has its own lawyers who work to ensure that fanfic authors are protected from legal threats. Perhaps as a result of this legal protection, AO3 has no formal restrictions on content for publication, though it does ask that all users tag any sexually explicit or potentially problematic work. Any story published with no warning tags in place is automatically placed behind a disclaimer, to prevent people from stumbling across it accidentally. In 2019 AO3 won the Hugo Award for Best Related Work.

Fanfiction.net (FF.net)
www.fanfiction.net

The second largest fanfiction website, started in 1998, has over 12 million registered users and hosts stories in over 40 languages. In comparison to AO3, FF.net has stricter publishing guidelines in terms of what is allowed to be published; no explicit adult fiction is permitted (though some can still be found that has yet to be removed) and anything related to works published by Anne Rice, Laurel K. Hamilton, Robin Hobb and several other authors are also banned at each author's request.

---

[1] The Copyright and Rights in Performances (Quotation and Parody) Regulations 2014; www.legislation.gov.uk/uksi/2014/2356/regulation/5/made.

you never had a full set of everything … a few My Little Ponies, a He-Man, some Barbies and one random Care Bear. Short of the full cast needed to recreate a favourite movie or story, I was forced to create crossover mash-ups: a My Little Pony might rescue Barbie from a kidnapping to thwart the evil plans of He-Man; the next day He-Man might need rescuing from the nefarious clutches of the Care Bear. Fanfic can be like that – take all your favourite characters, throw them into a scenario, and munch some popcorn while they figure it out.

There's a huge amount of freedom in not writing for publication. You get to experiment – to try out new genres or new styles. If you're someone who over-writes, you could hone your short-form writing by taking on the challenge of writing 100-word 'drabbles' or three-sentence stories. If you want to work on your dialogue, you could attempt to tell a story using only speech and see if you can still make it clear who is saying what.

Fanfiction offers many opportunities for writing and style exercises. When you're writing a story set in an established universe some of the heavy lifting is already done – you don't need to describe characters or establish the rules of the world, as your audience already knows them. That leaves you the freedom to focus in on the type of story you want to write. Author Neil Gaiman has said that fanfiction is 'a good place to write while you've still got training wheels on',[2] and it is certainly true that being able to write in someone else's universe – where your audience already knows the rules and you don't have to explain them – is a comforting place to start.

What could I write?

Have you ever wondered what Irene Adler's internal narrative might have been in *Sherlock*? Or Darth Vader's thoughts at the end of *The Empire Strikes Back*? Considering how certain events might have been seen from someone else's point of view is a standard fanfiction trope. Twisting the narrative like this can reveal hidden motivations and may even make sense of some of the apparent plot holes. This is not an approach unique to fanfiction, as many authors have revisited the stories of out-of-copyright characters, as in the reimagining of Mrs Rochester from Charlotte Brontë's *Jane Eyre* (1847) in *Wide Sargasso Sea* (André Deutsch 1966) by Jean Rhys.

Rather than a different point of view, you could try a different universe – or rather an alternate universe (AU). Again, this is a wide-ranging trope, found in well-known creative works such as the film *Apocalypse Now*, an alternate universe re-telling of Joseph Conrad's *Heart of Darkness*, or *10 Things I Hate About You*, which brings Shakespeare's *The Taming of the Shrew* into an American high school. In an AU you might find superheroes teaming up as food truck chefs in Manhattan or facing off as coaches of rival sports teams. AUs cover a wide array of possibilities; popular recurring themes include placing all the characters in high school or running a coffee shop together. It's well known now that *Fifty Shades of Grey* (Vintage Books 2011) started life as an AU fanfic of Stephanie Meyer's *Twilight* series (Little, Brown 2005–08).

Another approach to alternate universes is to take a 'what if' approach to a canon moment … What if Sam and Dean Winchester of *Supernatural* were African American? What if Aragorn was female? What if Veronica Mars became an FBI agent? … What changes would this make to the existing canon? Would the Winchesters have had a different reaction from the law-enforcement officers they worked with to kill monsters? Would Aragorn have

[2] Neil Gaiman Journal, Monday, April 08, 2002; http://journal.neilgaiman.com/2002/04/in-relation-to-current-burning-topic.asp

still been well received as the returning king? Would Veronica have found happiness solving federal crimes? Fanfic gives the writer, and their audience, a way of exploring these possibilities. It's something that Marvel comics have done for years with their *What If ...?* special issues and short runs like *1602* and *Powerless*, so it's not too surprising to find their fans exploring similar ideas in 'fic'.

A type of story which fits within alternate universes but is so common as to have its own label is the crossover. What if Buffy Summers was a Jaeger pilot (*Pacific Rim*) – who would her co-pilot be? Or what would Bilbo Baggins' daemon be? Was Eliot Spencer from *Leverage* ever a member of a Stargate team (the showrunners say he was, but they couldn't get permission to mention it on screen)? It's fun to see fictional universes collide, and the copyright owners have used this to great effect with team-up games such as *Super Smash Bros* or *Kingdom Hearts*, the occasional visit by Mulder and Scully to *The Simpsons*' Springfield, and the massive multi-show crossovers run each year for *Arrow*, *The Flash*, *Legends of Tomorrow* and more.

It's not unusual for fans to be dissatisfied with the twists and turns that the official narrative has taken. Marvel Cinematic Universe fans rebelled en masse, with the #CoulsonLives hashtag, after Coulson's apparent death in *The Avengers*. In time, he was resurrected to lead *Marvel's Agents of SHIELD* television show, but before that happened fanfiction writers had provided myriad examples of how Agent Coulson miraculously survived or mysteriously came back to life, as 'fix-it fics'. Sometimes fix-its are also crossovers, in which characters from one show or book turn up to help solve a problem in another. *Leverage*, featuring Robin-Hood-like criminals, is so popular as a fix-it crossover partner that its characters have helped fix fandoms from *The Avengers* to *The Walking Dead*.

These five tropes barely scratch the surface of the ocean of possibilities there are in fanfiction – it's a very open field and all contributions are welcome.

A final thought

Some people might ask why they should waste their time writing fanfiction when they could be working on an original work for publication. To that I offer three responses:

1. Any form of regular writing practice can make you a better writer.

2. Even if you never get published, writing and sharing fanfic online can connect you to a community of readers, who will generally offer incredibly positive commentary on your work (in 20 years of writing fanfic I have received a grand total of two negative comments out of thousands). That audience can help you feel pride and delight in your writing on even the most difficult day.

3. Creative hobbies are proven to make people happier[3] – and even better at their day jobs – with a 15–30% increase in positive performance reviews tracked in one study.[4] Happy people are also 12% more productive at work.[5]

---

[3] 'New research published by the Society for Personality and Social Psychology (and not the Institute of the Completely Obvious, as you may have expected), says that valuing your time more than the pursuit of money leads to feelings of greater wellbeing. And by valuing your time, they mean spending it wisely on hobbies, exercising or being with your family.'Hobbies make us happier –so ignore the mockery, and enjoy,' Fay Schopen; www.theguardian.com/commentisfree/2016/jan/11/hobbies-happier-gardening-bird-watching-stroking-cat

[4] 'One study from San Francisco State University found that people who often engaged in a creative activity scored 15–30% higher on performance rankings. They were also more likely to come up with creative solutions to on-the-job problems." How hobbies can improve your happiness and productivity at work,' Aytekin Tank; https://www.fastcompany.com/90389174/how-hobbies-benefit-your-productivity

[5] 'Economists carried out a number of experiments to test the idea that happy employees work harder. In the laboratory, they found happiness made people around 12% more productive.' https://warwick.ac.uk/newsandevents/pressreleases/new_study_shows

Nobody writes fanfiction to get famous; though some people have made it through the glass ceiling between fan-writer and professional author due to their fanfiction works, they are the exception, not the rule. No, we write fanfiction because it's a creative outlet, and because as fanfic writers we may even develop fans of our own who leave positive feedback on our work and increase our kudos. We write for the joy of creation, the excitement of receiving glowing comments and the accomplishment of finishing a story. We write because we have to, and we write because – although not all of us get to be published – with fanfiction we can all get to be read.

Hari Patience-Davies has been finding joy and fulfilment writing fanfiction for over 20 years, but she won't tell you her AO3 username. Hari is co-founder and Storytelling Coach for Patience Davies Consulting, www.patiencedavies.com.

Publishing services for independent authors

This is a selection of the expanding list of companies that offer editorial, production, marketing and distribution support predominantly (but not exclusively) for authors who want to publish independently. As with all the organisations mentioned in the *Yearbook*, we recommend that you check carefully what companies offer and their fees; also be aware of any minimum commitment requirements. A longer list of companies and individuals who provide similar services is included in our subscription service: www.writersandartists.co.uk/shop/subscriptions.

POD = print on demand.

AESOP (All Editorial Services Online for Publishers & Writers)

28A Abberbury Road, Iffley, Oxford OX4 4ES
tel 07933 331977
email aesop@copyedit.co.uk
website www.copyedit.co.uk
Contact Martin Noble

Services include copy-editing, rewriting, proofreading, indexing and editorial reports and reviews. Advice to publishers, authors and literary agents also available, as is support with ghostwriting, novelisation, research and fact-checking. Extensive range of topics and genres covered. Established 1979.

Amolibros

Loundshay Manor Cottage, Preston Bowyer, Milverton, Somerset TA4 1QF
tel (01823) 401527
email amolibros@aol.com
website www.amolibros.com
Director Jane Tatam

Services include print and ebook design, production, copy-editing and distribution through online retailers. Sales and marketing services include design and production of adverts, leaflets, author websites, distribution of press releases and direct mail campaigns.

A1 Book Publishing UK

Room 1, 48 Park Road, Birmingham B18 5JH
tel 0800 002 911
email a1booksuk@gmail.com
website https://a1proofreading.co.uk/a1-book-publishing-uk
Facebook www.facebook.com/A1-Book-Publishing-UK-240624720597580/
Contact Ian Melling

Editorial services for self-publishing authors, including proofreading manuscripts (£9.99 per 1,000 words), book covers, book design and eBook conversion. KDP/Amazon publishing service

available for £245. Distribution and marketing support also available. Founded 2012.

arima publishing

ASK House, Northgate Avenue, Bury St Edmunds, Suffolk IP32 6BB
tel (01284) 717885
email info@arimapublishing.com
website www.arimapublishing.co.uk

Offers POD options in hardback and paperback formats. Distributes print books through wholesalers, and to online retailers. Proofreading and image scanning also available. Also provides a typing service for handwritten manuscripts. Authors receive a royalty rate of 30% of full cover price for direct sales from the arima online bookshop, and 20% for general sales.

Suzanne Arnold

email suzanne@suzannearnold.com
website www.suzannearnold.com
Facebook www.facebook.com/suzannearnoldeditor
Twitter @SArnold_editor

Advanced Professional Member of the Chartered Institute of Editing with over 20 years' experience working for publishers and businesses. Focuses on copy-editing (spelling, grammar and consistency) and proofreading non-fiction for adults.

Art Circus Books

132 Frankwell, Shrewsbury SY3 8JX
email info@artcircusbooks.co.uk
website www.artcircusbooks.co.uk

Produces books for artists, whether for general publication or in support of artist exhibitions, concerts and events. Provides advice and support to artists wishing to self-publish across all aspects of the publishing process as well as print-management. Also works in collaboration with UKGiclee (Fine Art Printers). Founded 2013.

Betterwrite

107A Maas Road, Birmingham B31 2PP
tel 0121 475 5876

email robertmatthews_edit@yahoo.co.uk
website https://betterwrite.com
Contact Rob Matthews

Experienced team of twelve editors, all members of the Chartered Institute of Editing and Proofreading, working across multiple fiction genres: crime/thriller/mystery, adventure/fantasy/romance, sci-fi, historical, children's books, YA fiction and commercial women's fiction. Non-fiction projects also undertaken. Authors are matched with the most appropriate editor for their work and the text is prepared for publication or self-publication. Structural, developmental and line editing services all available; see website for full details.

Blue Elephant Storyshaping

email hello@blueelephantstoryshaping.com
website www.blueelephantstoryshaping.com
Director Natascha Biebow MBE

Offers professional, bespoke editorial and project management services for picture book creators (authors and author/illustrator teams) who wish to self-publish. Includes storyshaping from idea to finished, print-ready PDF, including text shaping and editing, development of roughs to final artwork cover concept and copy, marketing pitch and final proofread. Authors can collaborate with an experienced picture book expert to create their envisaged book. See website for full details of services available.

BookPrinting UK

Remus House, Coltsfoot Drive, Woodston, Peterborough PE2 9BF
tel (01733) 898102
email info@bookprintinguk.com
website www.bookprintinguk.com
Twitter @BookPrintingUK

Colour and b&w printing and POD books in a range of bindings. Can provide custom illustration and interior layout options, as well as typesetting. Supplies templates for formatting manuscript files before sending. Can also distribute print books direct to customers. Prints bookmarks, posters and flyers.

Cameron Publicity and Marketing Ltd

180 Piccadilly, London W1J 9HF
tel 020-7917 9812
email info@cameronpm.co.uk
website www.cameronpm.co.uk
Facebook www.facebook.com/CameronPublicity
Twitter @CameronPMtweets
Director Ben Cameron

Publicity and marketing campaigns for publishers and independent authors including media awareness, websites and social media. Founded 2006.

The Choir Press

132 Bristol Road, Gloucester GL1 5SR
tel (01452) 500016

email enquiries@thechoirpress.co.uk
website www.selfpublishingbooks.co.uk
Contact Rachel Woodman

Publishing services. Copy-editing and print-ready file preparation. Print-on-demand distribution. Founded 1982

The Conrad Press Ltd

43 Nunnery Fields, Canterbury, Kent CT1 3JT
tel (01227) 472874
email jamesessinger@theconradpress.com
website www.theconradpress.com
Facebook www.facebook.com/theconradpress
Twitter @theconradpress
Instagram @theconradpressltd_
Managing Director James Essinger, *Deputy Managing Director* Zoe Verner

Subsidy publisher: authors make a contribution to the publishing costs but these are refunded from book sales revenue. Titles range across all genres including novels, children's books (no picture books), YA fiction and non-fiction, memoirs, short stories and collections of poetry. Founded 2015.

Consulting Cops for Writers

1 Keeper Lodges, Epping, Essex CM16 5HP
tel 07968 582423
email enquiries@consultingcops.com
website www.consultingcops.com
Twitter @ConsultingCops
Instagram @consultingcops
Ceo & Founder Lyndon Smith

Experienced team of serving and former police officers/staff, offering to match writers' crime-related work with the relevant expert and supply them with the information needed to ensure projects read authentically. Services include: scene/chapter/whole project review; research; consultation. Website includes a variety of useful author aids, including police ranks, acronyms, phonetic alphabet and websites to assist further research.

Cornerstones

2 Green Barton, Swyre, Dorchester, Dorset DT2 9DN
tel (01308) 897374
email helen@cornerstones.co.uk
website https://cornerstones.co.uk
Facebook www.facebook.com/CornerstonesUK
Twitter @CornerstonesLit
Founder Helen Bryant

Transatlantic literary consultancy. Editorial packages include industry-style reader's reports, one-to-one mentoring, final-stage copy-editing and proofreading, as well as the intensive Edit Your Novel online course. Founded 1998.

Ingrid Cranfield

16 Myddelton Gardens, London N21 2PA
tel 020-8360 2433 , *tel* 07708 60878

Self-publishing and indie authors

email ingrid_cranfield@hotmail.com
website http://ingridcranfield.co.uk

Advisory and editorial services for authors, publishers and media, including critical assessment and appraisal, copy-editing, rewriting, proofreading, research, interviews; also training in editing and proofreading, creation of guidelines for authors. Special interests: geography, travel, exploration, adventure; language and literacy; government and politics; education; art and architecture (including Japanese); family histories. Translations from German and French. Founded 1972.

Andrew Crofts
email croftsa@aol.com
website https://andrewcrofts.com

Experienced and bestselling ghostwriter and author; more than 80 books published. Also guides clients through independent publishing processes.

Dissect Designs
2 Hamilton Place, Aldershot GU11 3HT
email tim@dissectdesigns.com
website www.dissectdesigns.com
Twitter @dissectdesigns
Contact Tim Barber

Bespoke book cover design for hardbacks, paperbacks, ebooks or audiobooks by an experienced cover designer. All genres covered.

eBookPartnership.com
7 Bell Yard, London WC2A 2JR
email helpdesk@ebookpartnership.com
website www.ebookpartnership.com
Twitter @ebookpartners

Technical services for authors, publishers, and content owners, including converting documents into eBook files, suitable for upload to all retailers, subscription services, and e-libraries. All types of content handled, as is audio/visual integration. Robust distribution service, featuring daily reports and fast update capabilities for all clients. Customers receive 100% of royalties. Founded 2010.

eBook Versions
27 Old Gloucester Street, London WC1N 3AX
website www.ebookversions.com
Proprietor John Ransley

Offers ebook, paperback, hardback and audiobook self-publishing and distribution through Amazon Kindle Direct Publishing, Barnes & Noble, Google Play Book Store, IngramSpark, iTunes and Kobo Books. Fees begin at £95 for ebook conversion of a manuscript of up to 100,000 words. POD paperback and hardback pre-press production is available from £295, and audiobook production from £195. OCR scanning of hardbacks, paperbacks and typescripts is also offered

The Empowered Author
email sam@theempoweredauthor.com
website https://theempoweredauthor.com/
Facebook www.facebook.com/groups/
EmpoweredAuthor

Supportive online group helping authors market their books effectively, with experienced marketers Sam Missingham and Katie Sadler. Membership: £10 per month. A directory of publishing professionals and organisations offering a range of services to writers is also available.

Exprimez
email matthew@exprimez.com
website https://exprimez.com
Founder Matthew Smith

Publishing consultancy offering an extensive range of representative and bespoke support services for authors and organisations, including book coaching, writing and publishing tools, manuscript consulting, developmental book editing, ghostwriting, social media training, content development, rights, contracts and marketing.

Frank Fahy Publishing Services
5 Barna Village Centre, Barna, Co. Galway, H91 DF24, Republic of Ireland
tel +353 (0)86 2269330
email frank.fahy0@gmail.com
website https://frankfahypublishing.wordpress.com/

Specialises in preparing manuscripts for book production, either as printed books or digital ebooks. This can include, as required, copy-editing and/or proofreading, or preparing presentations for submission to publishers. Estimates are free of charge and authors' individual requirements discussed. Publishing projects of all kinds considered, from individuals, institutions or businesses. Founded 2007.

Finish Your Novel
email info@finishyournovel.org
website www.finishyournovel.org
Mentors Clare Allan, Alexandra Benedict, Jonathan Myerson

Bespoke mentoring service from the former directors of the Novel Writing MA at City University London, all of whom have extensive experience in guiding writers from first idea to finished manuscript. Taster sessions available. Also offered: full draft readings; specialist webinars; and a range of support tailored to specific needs. See website for pricing information.

Firsty Group
Oxford House, 12–20 Oxford Street, Newbury RG14 1JB
tel (01635) 581185
email info@firstygroup.com
website http://firstygroup.com
Twitter @firstygroup
Instagram @firstygroup

Provides web development and e-commerce solutions for the publishing industry, from bespoke projects to bolt-on software as a service. Founders of Glassboxx, a digital fulfilment solution which enables publishers, authors and retailers to sell and deliver ebooks and audiobooks directly to the end customer with secure DRM.

Gecko Edit

email kath@geckoedit.com
website www.geckoedit.com
Facebook www.facebook.com/GeckoEdit/
Contact Katherine Kirk

Offers professional proofreading, copy-editing and line-editing services for self-published and traditionally published authors of all genres, including adult and young adult science fiction, fantasy, speculative fiction, romance, women's fiction and historical fiction. Specializes in US English (CMOS). Professional member of the Chartered Institute of Editing and Proofreading and rated Excellent as a partner member of the Alliance of Independent Authors.

Grammar Factory Publishing

3906-25 Telegram Mews, Toronto, ON M5V 3Z1, Canada
email info@grammarfactory.com
website https://grammarfactory.com
Executive Publisher Scott MacMillan

Professional service publisher offering ghostwriting, editing and publishing services; customers include speakers, business leaders and entrepreneurs.

Grosvenor House Publishing

Link House, 140 The Broadway, Tolworth, Surrey KT6 7HT
tel 020-8339 6060
website www.grosvenorhousepublishing.co.uk
Facebook www.facebook.com/GrosvenorHousePublishing
Founder Kim Cross

Publishes across a range of genres including children's and non-fiction in colour, b&w, POD, paperback, hardback and ebook formats. Offers a £795 publishing package which includes typesetting and five free print copies as well as an ISBN, and print and ebook distribution via online retailers. Marketing services include producing posters and postcards, and website set-up from template with two years' hosting. Ebook publishing costs £195 if the print edition of the book has been produced by the company and £495 otherwise. Print costs and royalties depend on book specification. A proofreading service is offered at a rate of £5 per 1,000 words. See website for full list of costs.

HelpMePublish Consultancy

61A Great Titchfield St, London W1W 7PP
tel 07710 523591
email info@helpmepublish.co.uk
website www.helpmepublish.co.uk
Contacts Brian Jarman, Annabel Hughes

Offers proofreading and editing services, as well as advice for authors on how to get their work published, from finding an agent to self-publishing. See website for information on rates and how to book an initial consultation.

Indexing Specialists (UK) Ltd

29 Norway Street, Portslade BN41 1GN
email indexers@indexing.co.uk
website www.indexing.co.uk
Contact Milla Hills

Experienced indexers for all types of books and encyclopedias, on professional, scientific and general subjects. Large projects involving multiple indexers can be arranged. Founded 1965.

The Inkwell Group

The Old Post Office, Kilmacanogue, Co. Wicklow A98 V215, Republic of Ireland
tel +353 (0)1 2765921, +353 (0)87 2835382
website www.inkwellwriters.ie
Facebook www.facebook.com/writing.ie
Twitter @writing_IE
Contact Vanessa Fox O'Loughlin

Literary consultancy providing industry-led critique, readers reports and editing services, plus career-strategy consultancy. Also offers a full range of 'Getting Published' events and workshops for festivals and organisations. Founded 2006.

Jelly Bean Self-Publishing

Candy Jar Ltd, Mackintosh House, 136 Newport Road, Cardiff CF24 1DJ
tel 029-211 57202
email submissions@jellybeanselfpublishing.co.uk
website www.jellybeanselfpublishing.co.uk
Twitter @Jelly_BeanUK
Director Shaun Russell

Self-publishing imprint of Candy Jar Books. Services include editing, typesetting, illustration, cover design, website design, audiobook production and marketing support. Can accommodate authors of various genres, budgets and timetables. Welsh Self-Publisher of the Year 2020. Founded 2012.

Journey Books

Bradt Guides, 31A High Street, Chesham, Bucks. HP5 1BW
tel (01753) 893444
email journeybooks@bradtguides.com
website www.bradtguides.com/journeybooks/

Contract publishing imprint from travel publisher, Bradt Guides. Offers a range of publishing services, from an initial editorial report to full trade publication with professional editing, typesetting, design and worldwide distribution for print and ebooks. A particular expertise in travel-related books but will consider all proposals. Suitable for both first-timers and previously published authors looking to publish independently. See website for full range of packages and pricing.

Kindle Direct Publishing

website https://kdp.amazon.com
Facebook www.facebook.com/KindleDirectPublishing
Twitter @AmazonKDP

Ebook self-publishing and distribution platform for Kindle and Kindle Apps. Its business model offers up to a 70% royalty (on certain retail prices between $2.99–$9.99) in many countries and availability in Amazon stores worldwide. POD options are also available. Note that KDP Select makes books exclusive to Amazon (which means they cannot be sold through an author's personal website, for example), but authors can share in the Global Fund amount every time the book is borrowed from the Kindle Owners' Lending Library.

Kobo Writing Life

email writinglife@kobo.com
website www.kobo.com/p/writinglife
Facebook www.facebook.com/KoboWritingLife
Twitter @kobowritinglife
Instagram @kobo.writing.life

Ebook self-publishing platform where authors can upload manuscripts and cover images. These files are then converted into ebooks before being distributed through the Kobo Store. Authors are able to set pricing and DRM territories, as well as track sales. Royalty rates vary depending on price or territory; enquire directly. Free to join. Owned by Rakuten.

Lavender and White Publishing

Snipe Lodge, Moycullen, Co. Galway, Republic of Ireland
email info@lavenderandwhite.co.uk
website www.lavenderandwhite.co.uk
Facebook www.facebook.com/Lavender-and-White-Publishing-201996279902790/
Twitter @LavenderandW
Editorial Director Jacqueline Broderick, *Editor* Sarah Lewis

Services for self-publishing include editing, proofreading, cover design, typesetting, ebook conversion and POD. Marketing and sell-through support also available, alongside mentoring and ghostwriting. Costs vary depending on services required; email for a quote. Easy payment options available.

Liminal Pages

PO Box 12923, Bishop's Stortford CM23 9NL
email sophie@liminalpages.com
website https://liminalpages.com
Facebook www.facebook.com/liminalpages
Twitter @liminal_pages
Contact Sophie Playle

Development editing, manuscript critiques, line and copy-editing. Specialises in speculative and literary fiction; also offers courses. Founded 2013.

The Literary Consultancy (TLC)

East Side, Kings Cross Station, London N1C 4AX
tel 020-3751 0757, ext. 800
email info@literaryconsultancy.co.uk
website https://literaryconsultancy.co.uk
Director Aki Schilz, *Head of Writing Services* Joe Sedgwick

Supports writers of fiction, non-fiction, poetry, scripts and children's books. Offers a range of services for writers at all levels, including manuscript assessment, developental editing, and editor one-to-ones. Also online and in-person mentoring, and a membership programme, 'Being A Writer'. Fees vary depending on service. Industry links with agents and publishers. Approved by Arts Council England. Founded 1996.

Nicky Lovick

35 Brondesbury Road, London NW6 6BA
tel 07971 829252
email nickylovick@gmail.com
website https://nickylovick.com
Twitter @LovickNicky

Book editor with more than 20 years' experience in structural editing, copy-editing and proofreading. Specialises in women's commercial fiction, crime and thrillers. Works for both top five and independent publishers.

Manuscripts & Mentoring

25 Corinne Road, London N19 5EZ
tel 07973 300276
email manuscriptmentoring@gmail.com
website www.genevievefox.com
Twitter @genevievefox21
Contact Genevieve Fox

Helps both fledgling and experienced writers of fiction, non-fiction, memoir and YA fiction get from first draft to finished manuscript. Primary services include editing, manuscript overviews as well as advice on structure, plot, themes and characterisation. One-to-one tutoring, mentoring and coaching, writing plans, ghostwriting; and creative writing courses also available. Genevieve Fox is a published author and holds a doctorate in Creative Writing.

Matador

Troubador Publishing Ltd, Unit E2, Airfield Business Park, Harrison Road, Market Harborough, Leics. LE16 7UL
tel 0116 279 2299

email books@troubador.co.uk
website www.troubador.co.uk/matador
Facebook www.facebook.com/matadorbooks
Twitter @matadorbooks
Managing Director Jeremy Thompson, *Operations Director* Jane Rowland

Self-publishing imprint of Troubador Publishing. Offers POD, short-run digital- and litho-printed books as well as audiobooks and ebook production, with distribution through high-street bookshops and online retailers. Also worldwide ebook distribution. Author services include all book, ebook and audiobook production, trade and retail marketing, plus bookshop distribution and sales representation by Star Book Sales. Founded 1999.

Mereo Books

2nd Floor, 6–8 Dyer Street, Cirencester, Glos. GL7 2PF
tel 020-3286 8686
email info@mereobooks.co.uk
website www.mereobooks.com
Twitter @MereoBooks
Director Antonia Tingle, *Editor-in-Chief* Chris Newton

Publishes in hardback, paperback, audio and ebook formats. Also offers ghostwriting services. Allocates ISBNs and distributes to online retailers including Amazon and Barnes & Noble, as ebooks or POD and from stock through Orca Book Services trade distribution or through their international sales network of agents. Additional services include editing, typesetting, interior layout design, cover design, ebook production, book promotion and book marketing for both fiction and non-fiction titles, all using in-house expertise.

MiblArt

email team@miblart.com
website https://miblart.com/
Twitter @miblart
Instagram @miblart
Cover design company for self-published authors. Services offered include ebook and print cover design, illustrated book cover design, and ebook and print formatting. Also creates marketing materials for authors (banners for social media, logos, bookmarks, brochures, websites). Author benefits include unlimited number of revisions and quick turnround times. No upfront payment required. Authors retain all copyrights. Founded 2015.

MJV Literary Author Services

71–75 Shelton Street, London WC2H 9JQ
email authors@mjvliterary.com
website www.mjvliterary.com
Contact Matt McAvoy

Offers professional proofreading, copy-editing and beta-reading services for self-published and traditionally published authors of all genres, including fiction, non-fiction and children's books, as well as a popular ebook and KDP-ready Kindle-book creation service, at $49. As part of the company's #ReturnToRealBooks campaign, KDP-formatted print-ready typesetting is offered free with all proofreading and copy-editing instructions. Other services include translation into English with full copy-editing, for non-English language authors. Editing services start from $6.95 per 1,000 words, and all instructions include two human editor passes and software checks as standard. Trees planted with every job.

New Generation Publishing

51 Gower Street, London WC1E 6HJ
tel (01234) 711956
email info@newgeneration-publishing.com
website www.newgeneration-publishing.com
Facebook www.facebook.com/NewGenerationPublishing
Twitter @NGPublishing

Provides publication in paperback, hardback, ebook and audiobook with global print and retail distribution. Publishing packages range from Standard Paperback to the Bestseller options; bespoke packages are also available. Services include layout, cover design, ISBN allocation, editing, proofreading, bookselling, bookstore placement, website design and manuscript critique. Distribution provided via online retailers, high-street shops, libraries and wholesalers. Promotional materials available including distributed press releases and social media. Free marketing and promotional support service also offered. Offices in London and Buckinghamshire; author visits can be arranged. Free guide to publishing available on request.

Peter Nickol

tel (01392) 255512
email pnickol@phonecoop.coop

Music editing and music typesetting for book publishers. All types and genres of music covered. Founded 1987.

Paragon Publishing

4 North Street, Rothersthorpe, Northants NN7 3JB
tel (01604) 832149
email intoprint@live.com
website www.intoprint.net
Proprietor Mark Webb

Packagers of non-fiction and fiction books for independent authors, working regularly with novelists, poets, academics, businesses, associations and writers' groups. Provides a range of editorial services, alongside design, cover design and typesetting services, to create print-ready PDFs in b&w or colour as well as print-on-demand options. Publishes Kindle, and ePub on Play and Kobo, and multilingual editions. Experienced at working with new writers to help them to publish, providing ISBN, marketing consultancy and distribution to booksellers worldwide. Ghostwriting and illustration services also available. Founded 1992.

Pomegranate PA

Clavering House, Clavering Place,
Newcastle upon Tyne NE1 3NG
tel 07443 490752
email karen@pomegranatepa.co.uk
website www.pomegranatepa.co.uk
Twitter @pomegranatepa
Freelance Proofreader Karen Stubbs

Proofreading and editorial services. All subjects considered. Founded 2013.

Prepare to Publish Ltd

tel (01865) 922923
email mail@preparetopublish.com
website www.preparetopublish.com
Editor Andrew Chapman

Editorial and typesetting agency for book production. Services include copy-editing and proofreading services (non-fiction, with particular specialism in history), plus print and digital formatting. Free advice on self-publishing. Clients typically include publishers looking to outsource the editorial process, businesses planning publications and authors who have completed a first draft.

Publishing Services

Woofferton Grange, Brimfield, Ludlow,
Shrops. SY8 4NP
tel 07984 585861
email susanne@susannelumsden.co.uk
website www.susannelumsden.co.uk
Twitter @SusanneLumsden
Contact Susanne Lumsden

Experienced non-fiction editor (former editorial director) offering publishing services to charities and organisations. Services are best suited to those with existing sales and/or marketing platforms who wish to publish books to mainstream standards. Initial project appraisal covers publishing requirements such as format/s, pricing if applicable, editorial work, design and printing and sales and marketing (including online).

PublishNation

Suite 544, Kemp House, 152 City Road,
London EC1V 2NX
email david@publishnation.co.uk
website www.publishnation.co.uk
Publisher David Morrison

Offers POD paperback and Kindle format ebooks, available through Amazon. Publication in both print and digital formats costs £325 or £175 for Kindle format. Images may be included from £3.95 each. A range of book sizes is available, as are free template book covers. Enhanced cover design costs £40. Marketing services include creation of a press release, social media accounts and author website. Standard proofreading is £8 per 1,000 words, while an 'express' option from £125 focuses on the beginning of the manuscript. Editorial critique reports range in price from £99 for manuscripts of up to 15,000 words to £219 for manuscripts of up to 120,000 words.

The Joey Quince Editorial and Ghostwriting Agency

17 Carlton House Terrace, London SW1Y 5AH
tel 07396 344505
email joey@jq-agency.co.uk
website www.jq-agency.co.uk
Editor Joey Quince

Provides a range of services, taking authors from initial idea to final product across multiple genres including fiction, business and academic books, children's writing, memoir and sport. Founded 2019.

Reedsy

email service@reedsy.com
website https://reedsy.com
Twitter @ReedsyHQ
Founders Emmanuel Nataf, Matt Cobb, Ricardo Fayet, Vincent Durand

Established community that helps authors connect freelance publishing professionals, including editors, designers and marketers. Other services include Reedsy Learning, a free online publishing school, as well as Reedsy Discovery, a book review service. Founded 2014.

Rethink Press

Ivy House, Beccles Road, Fritton, Norfolk NR31 9HB
email info@rethinkpress.com
website www.rethinkpress.com
Facebook www.facebook.com/RethinkPress
Twitter @RethinkPress
Instagram @rethinkpress
Founders Lucy McCarraher, Joe Gregory

Independent hybrid publisher of business and self-development books, offering professional writing, coaching and publishing packages for print, ebook and audiobook titles. Specialises in books by entrepreneurs, experts and business leaders.

The Right Book Company

c/o SRA Books, Studio 6, 9 Marsh Street,
Bristol BS1 4AA
tel 0117 422 5540
email info@therightbookcompany.com
website http://therightbookcompany.com
Facebook www.facebook.com/therightbookcompany
Twitter @therightbookco
Founder, Director and Publisher Sue Richardson

Brings business and personal development books to local and international markets, working with experts, thought leaders and business owners. Aims to help authors to build their authority and brand, leverage opportunity and have their message heard by their target audience.

Rowanvale Books Ltd

The Gate, Keppoch Street, Roath, Cardiff CF24 3JW
tel 029-2128 0895
email info@rowanvalebooks.com
website www.rowanvalebooks.com
Twitter @RowanvaleBooks
Managing Director Cat Charlton

Largest self-publishing company in Wales. Provider of services such as proofreading and copy-editing, cover design and illustration, ebook conversion, paperback and hardback printing, marketing and PR support. Distribution to over 40,000 online and print retailers and libraries worldwide. Works in partnership with the British Council. Founded 2012.

The Self-Publishing Partnership Ltd

10B Greenway Farm, Bath Road, Wick,
nr. Bath BS30 5RL
tel (01225) 478444
email enquiries@selfpublishingpartnership.co.uk
website www.selfpublishingpartnership.co.uk
Twitter @SelfPublishBath
Contacts Douglas Walker, Garry Manning

Offers a range of services for self-publishing authors, including proofreading and copy-editing, page design and typesetting and cover design (bespoke or standard). Assistance with ebooks, ISBNs, trade and legal cataloguing, promotion and marketing, and order fulfilment (invoicing & distribution) also available.

Self-Publishing Review

email editor@selfpublishingreview.com
website www.selfpublishingreview.com
Facebook www.facebook.com/selfpublishingreview
Twitter @selfpubreview
Instagram @selfpubreview

Professional editorial reviews, Amazon ebook promotions, marketing services and book editing for independent titles. US based. Founded 2008.

SilverWood Books

14 Small Street, Bristol BS1 1DE
tel 0117 910 5829
email enquiries@silverwoodbooks.co.uk
website www.silverwoodbooks.co.uk
Twitter @SilverWoodBooks
Publishing Director Helen Hart

Complete self-publishing service for adult and children's books (including picture books), from manuscript feedback to editing and proofreading, professional cover and page design, typesetting, ebook hand-formatting and conversion, b&w and colour POD, short-run and lithographic printing,

one-to-one support and coaching. Distributes to bookshops via wholesalers and to online retailers including Amazon. See website for price information.

Smart Quill Editorial & Scouting

email info@smartquilleditorial.co.uk
website http://smartquilleditorial.co.uk
Literary Consultant, Editor and Scout Philippa Donovan

Structural edits and line edits, with prices from £1,200. Scouts for literary agents and film/tv producers. Fiction (all genres), narrative non-fiction, YA, middle grade and picture books. Judge for the London Book Fair Cameo Book to Screen Awards 2019 and 2020.

Softwood Self-Publishing

email swspublishing@gmail.com
website www.swspublishing.com
Facebook www.facebook.com/swspublishing
Twitter @swspublishing
Instagram @swspublishing
Director Maddy Glenn, *Creative Director* Nathan James

Bespoke editing, formatting, cover design, illustration, and printing services. Writers' coaching and free Zoom publishing consultations also available. Book marketing services include social media strategies and management, alongside book distribution guidance and free online book listing service for all self-published authors. Provider of creative writing and self-publishing workshops; see website for details of future events. Founded 2017.

Spiffing Covers

6 Jolliffe's Court, 51–57 High Street, Wivenhoe, Colchester, Essex CO7 9AZ
tel (01206) 585200
email enquiries@spiffingcovers.com
website www.spiffingcovers.com
Facebook www.facebook.com/spiffingcovers
Twitter @spiffingcovers
Managing Director Stefan Proudfoot

Independent publishing agency specialising in fully bespoke services and one-to-one consultation with clients. Offers a range of services, from cover design to editing and proofreading and international multi-channel distribution. Also assists authors with brand-building for their own independent publishing. Authors retain their own copyright and all royalties. Founded 2013.

Tantamount

Coventry University Technology Park, Puma Way, Coventry CV1 2TT
tel 024-7722 0299
email hello@tantamount.com
website www.tantamount.com
Twitter @TantamountBooks

Specialists in print, standard reflowable, and enhanced rich-media digital publications, as well as branding for authors. Offers a range of editorial, design and publishing services to individual authors and publishing houses. Integrated online presence and self-publishing services allow writers to deal with a single supplier for all digital, design and publishing requirements and to achieve a coherent brand image for their work. Specialist support for first-time professional writers through 'From Authority to Authorship' mentoring programme. Founded 2002.

Michael Terence Publishing

Two Brewers House, 2A Wellington Street,
Thame OX9 3BN
tel 020-3582 2002
email admin@mtp.agency
website www.mtp.agency/submissions
Founders Karolina Robinson, Keith Abbott

Supports self-publishing authors across a range of genres: fiction (including crime, science fiction, historical, children's, poetry) and non-fiction (including biography, true stories). Special consideration given to new and little-published authors. Open for submissions from authors worldwide: see website for full details, including costs. Founded 2016.

Try Writing

tel 07773 797817
email traceyiceton@hotmail.co.uk
website www.trywriting.co.uk
Contact Tracey Iceton

Provides a full range of manuscript appraisal/critiquing services, editorial guidance and one-to-one mentoring programmes for emerging creative writers across all genres/forms of writing but specialises in fiction (short stories and novels). Services are tailored to authors' individual needs and offer constructive advice designed to help manuscripts achieve publishable standard. Try Writing is run by Tracey Iceton PhD, author of the *Celtic Colours Trilogy* (Cinnamon Press) and creative writing tutor.

Tucann Books

Unit 9, Blackthorn Way,
Five Mile Lane Business Park, Five Mile Lane,
Washingborough, Lincoln LN4 1BF
tel (01522) 790009
email studio@tucann.co.uk
website https://tucann.co.uk
Managing Director Tom Cann

Offers a fully integrated book production service, from original MSS assessment to finished product using in-house printing and binding. Founded 1986.

2QT Publishing Services

tel (01729) 821046
website www.2qt.co.uk
Facebook www.facebook.com/2QTPublishing
Director Catherine Cousins

Services include editing and proofreading, manuscript critique, cover design and typesetting. Also offers ebook conversion and access to distribution, POD and other printing options.

User Design, Illustration and Typesetting

tel 07790 924159
email info@userdesignillustrationandtypesetting.com
website www.userdesignillustrationandtypesetting.com
Director Thomas Bohm

Book design, book cover design, graphic communication design, illustration, proofreading and typesetting service. Other services include information design, website design, accessibility and usability. Founded 2003.

White Magic Studios

Fairbourne Drive, Atterbury,
Milton Keynes MK10 9RG
tel 020-3475 0507
email info@whitemagicstudios.co.uk
website www.whitemagicstudios.co.uk
Facebook www.facebook.com/whitemagicstudiosuk

Offers a range of services to authors, including book cover design, text layout and formatting, illustrations for children's books, author website set-up, book trailers and ebook conversion. Editorial support also available: see website for full range of options.

whitefox

25 Horsell Road, London N5 1XL
email info@wearewhitefox.com
website www.wearewhitefox.com
Facebook www.facebook.com/wearewhitefox
Twitter @wearewhitefox
Instagram @whitefox_publishing
Partners Annabel Wright, John Bond

Full-service publishing solutions for writers, industry specialists and brands. Tailored advice from an experienced team guides authors through the entire process from editorial and design through to print, sales and distribution. Founded 2012.

Claire Wingfield Editorial & Literary Services

email contact@clairewingfield.co.uk
website www.clairewingfield.co.uk
Contact Claire Wingfield

Full range of editing and proofreading services, plus a made-to-measure literary consultancy service for writers of fiction and non-fiction. The consultancy service includes a detailed report that identifies the strengths and weaknesses of a MS/proposal, giving plenty of suggestions for improvement. Full book-production services now available. Founded 2006.

The Word Tank
2 Springfield Cottages, Bletchinglye Lane,
Rotherfield TN6 3NN
email enquiries@thewordtank.com
website www.thewordtank.com
Twitter @thewordtank
Contacts Chris Brock, Victoria Brock

Professional editing and publishing services from an experienced team, including proofreading, copy-editing, copywriting, cover design and interior formatting. Also independent publishing and marketing support. Partner members of Alliance of Independent Authors; professional members of Chartered Institute of Editors and Proofreaders.

Wrate's Editing Services
14C Woodland Road, London SE19 1NT
tel 020-8670 0660
email danielle@wrateseditingservices.co.uk
website http://wrateseditingservices.co.uk
Twitter @WratesEditing
Instagram @wrates_editing
Contact Danielle Wrate

Helps authors with all aspects of the self-publishing process, from draft manuscript to publication. Primary services include proofreading, copy-editing, manuscript assessment, cover design, interior layout, ebook conversion, printing, ISBN registration and marketing. Works with both novelists and non-fiction authors; free, no-obligation sample edit and publishing guide available. Founded 2013.

WRITERSWORLD
2 Bear Close Flats, Bear Close, Woodstock,
Oxon OX20 1JX
tel 0800 121 4960
email enquiries@writersworld.co.uk
website www.writersworld.co.uk
Founder & Owner Graham Cook

Specialises in self-publishing, POD books and book reprints. Also issues ISBNs on behalf of authors, pays them 90% of the royalties and supplies them with copies of their books at print cost. Worldwide book distribution. Founded 2000.

The Writing Hall
33 Mount Pleasant, Ackworth, Pontefract,
West Yorkshire, WF7 7HU
tel 07983 089621
email diane@thewritinghall.co.uk
website www.thewritinghall.co.uk
Facebook www.facebook.com/thewritinghall
Twitter @thewritinghall
Contact Diane Hall

Services include developmental editing and copy-editing, proofreading, typesetting, cover design, small run printing, ebook formatting, writing workshops, book launches and literary events, and marketing and social media coaching. Also available: writing coaching/mentoring, manuscript critique, ghostwriting and literary consultancy and advice. Submissions are welcome in most genres, particularly contemporary fiction, business titles, romance, comedy. Founded 2007.

@YouCaxton
23 High Street, Bishops Castle, Shrops. SY9 5BE
email newbooks@youcaxton.co.uk
website www.youcaxton.co.uk
Facebook www.facebook.com/pages/YouCaxton-Publishing/133150206770479
Twitter @YouCaxton
Partners Robert Fowke, Robert Branton and Steven Edwards

Specialises in memoir and general non-fiction, selected fiction and full-colour productions and art books. Support for self-publishers includes structural editing, copy-editing, proofreading, cover design and interior layout, print and ebook production and a full distribution service. Additional services comprise a range of marketing tools for self-publishing, author websites and web pages, a book packaging and design service for publishers and a publication project-management service for academic and corporate clients. Also provides a fine-art printing service for photographers and artists.

Resources for writers
Editing: what the professional writer needs to know

Editor Dea Parkin describes which different types of 'editing' an aspiring novelist can expect their work to undergo.

I started out as a copywriter before wandering into journalism, and I've edited novels for the last 15 years, so I'm familiar with the various different types of editing. Although editing is a word that every writer knows, the term means different things to journalists, commercial writers and novelists. What all editing has in common is an outsider's professional view on your work; an outsider, moreover, who is more experienced than one writer can ever be and who brings all their expertise to bear. For all writers, that's invaluable.

Editing for novels
Developmental editing (also known as structural, content or substantive editing)
This is the kind of editing most people envisage in connection with fiction. Developmental editing looks at the narrative arc or plot of a novel, characterisation, storyline, structure, voice, and also at the quality of the writing. Some editors prefer to make annotations to the actual manuscript with margin comments or inline coloured text; others are more 'hands-on' and will actually change words, move sections around, delete sentences and perhaps make suggestions for elements to be expanded upon.

Both styles of developmental editing should be sent to the author with an editor's report, although it's likely to be shorter from the hands-on editor. The editing report highlights the strengths of the work, identifies its weaknesses, proposes any changes, and explains in depth the reasons for them. Editors vary in how much detail they delve into in their report; one might say, for example: 'The protagonist lacks agency in the crucial midsection; find a way in which the outcome can depend on her actions rather than those of the other characters,' whereas another editor might go on to make several suggestions as to how this could be achieved.

This illustrates how individual editing can be; the way one editor works might suit one writer but not another. And each editor has their own individual strengths: one might excel at spotting holes in a plot or identifying where something isn't particularly well explained or is too ambiguous; another might be hot on viewpoint and voice; a third may be adept at character arcs. Of course, an editor should be good at all three – and much more besides – but, as with writers, each has their own special forte. The best editors find ways to maximise the writer's strengths and reduce the impact of any weaknesses. Once you begin to understand what an editor can do for a writer you realise how valuable it is to have one – and, as a reader, you understand how different that final book now in your hands might have looked in its raw state.

When writing a contracted work for a publisher, you're more likely to encounter the 'hands-on' kind of developmental editor who will make changes to your manuscript, but that's not a given. Similarly, when using a freelance, there's no guarantee you'll get the 'comments-only' kind. When looking for a freelance editor, though, whether you ask other writers for recommendations or use organisations such as ALLi, the CIEP or the Crime Writers' Association for pointers, you can ask for an example of how they work to ascertain whether their style of editing is what you prefer. And it's not just the level of editorial input that should concern you. Over the years, I've been surprised at the differing tones used in manuscript comments by editors working for me: some are very gentle and every comment is prefaced with 'You might like to consider…' or 'Maybe you could think about…'; others are more brusque: 'Waffles. Condense.' This is something else to think about if you are free to choose your editor: are you a delicate flower who responds well to a subtle hint that something could be improved, but who wilts at anything smacking of criticism, or do you respond best to direct instruction and find anything else irritatingly unnecessary? Most writers – and editors – probably fall between the two, but it's worth looking at a trial sample to check that its tone suits you.

Many writers nowadays invest in freelance editing not only if they intend to publish independently but also as a precursor to securing a traditional publishing contract; they recognise that an agent or commissioning editor is more likely to choose a manuscript for a new novel which is in a near-finished state than one that needs more work. Finding an editor whose skillset is the best match for your own is not always easy. Recommendations are a good place to start, and it's also worth approaching editors who work with authors in the same genre as you, in order to narrow it down. Check out author testimonials on editors' websites and, if you're seriously considering their services, ask to be put in touch with one or two authors they quote, as well as studying that sample edit.

Copy-editing

This is the other main type of editing novelists will encounter. It is the final editing process their writing undergoes once developmental editing is concluded. (There is another element called line-editing. It looks closely at your use of language and your writing style, its clarity and expressiveness, and your choice of words. It's now more or less amalgamated with copy-editing, although it sometimes overlaps with developmental editing instead.)

Sensitivity readers are increasingly employed by publishers and an author might find their editor recommends one. The reader might read the novel during the developmental editing stage or later, depending on the publisher. If you're publishing independently, it's sensible to have it done prior to the copy-edit, in case significant changes are called for.

Sometimes people confuse copy-editing with proofreading (see below) and think copy-editing is only about spelling or punctuation or grammar. It is indeed about all those things, but much more; it's about how you use words best to convey your story. For instance, a copy-editor will be looking out for:

• Repetition of words or phrases (except if deliberate, for effect);
• Use of adverbs instead of strong, evocative verbs;
• Use of a bland or everyday expression instead of a more creative term;
• Sticking with the same syntax pattern rather than varying sentence construction;
• Forgetting to shorten sentences when you want to increase pace;
• Incorrect facts, anachronisms, and continuity errors;

• Not adhering to the chosen tense (except where it's varied deliberately to good effect);
• Confusion of viewpoint and the dreaded head-hopping, where points of view switch from one character to another within one scene;
• Inconsistency in use of the subjunctive;
• Inconsistency in general; including the formatting of dates, times and numbers.

Just as with developmental editors, copy-editors vary in their approach: some make visible changes wherever they see a need (using Word's 'Track Changes' or similar); others use comments to ask the writer to make revisions. But most copy-editors will employ both of these methods, meaning that inconsistencies and errors are weeded out while, for more significant revisions, the author has options to choose from or suggestions to inspire their own ideas. The best copy-editors strike a perfect balance between amending prose so that it is 'correct' and allowing the author's own voice and style to shine through.

After this, consistency is their most important aim. This makes for ease of reading. Discrepancies or inconsistent styling, even if they're not consciously noticed by the reader, tend to affect the reading experience and make it uncomfortable, reducing the book's credibility. If the inconsistencies are spotted, then just as with typos, the reader is pulled right out of the story. So for example, copy-editors would look at whether the ending for irregular verbs in the past tense consistently either '-ed' or '-t' (e.g. *learned* or *learnt*, *spoiled* or *spoilt*)? Is the serial or Oxford comma (which comes before *and* after the last object in a list and is now hugely fashionable in British English where only a few years ago it was only used in cases of ambiguity) used throughout – or not? Is *while* used consistently (recommended) rather than *whilst*? Are vocative commas used throughout as they should be? (These are the commas that should always be used in direct address before a character's name, or before any word that's used instead of a name such as *dear* or *sir* or *Your Majesty*. The classic example that explains why we need them is: 'Let's eat, Grandma.' Remove the vocative comma and the meaning is entirely changed!) If italics are used for thoughts without speech tags in one chapter, is this applied throughout the book? Are inverted commas used unnecessarily? Are capital initials used erroneously for generic nouns instead of only for proper names?

To achieve this consistency, copy-editors should all have a **style guide** (either provided by the publisher, setting out its 'house style', or their own if they are working for an independent author) and should create a **style sheet** (see *Glossary of publishing terms* on page 665) for each individual manuscript they work on. This style sheet not only enables them to keep track of decisions made and to implement them consistently but, importantly, it acts as a blueprint for the author for revisions to this novel and the next, as well as being crucial for the proofreader at the next stage in the editing process.

Proofreading

Proofreading is there as a safety net to pick up inconsistencies and errors – but only when the pages are 'set' or laid out ready for publication, in whatever form. If you have a traditional contract, you might not even be involved in this stage. If you're publishing independently, proofreading is the last process your novel should undergo. But it's not really editing – it's double-checking that no errors remain or have crept in as the text has been changed, for example from a Word document to a pdf or epub. It can be disconcerting how many errors, that should have been picked up in copy-editing, scream for attention once the text is in a different format and laid out in its final form, with chapter headings, pagination, indentation, justification and so on. (Useful knowledge: when you're self-editing, printing the work out or reformatting it in a different font and type size can be a very big help in reading the work with fresh eyes.) Creating and applying these layout rules consistently are sometimes the copy-editor's remit, but otherwise will be implemented and always checked again at proofing stage. This is where mistakes, such as Chapter Eight appearing twice, should be picked up! In advance of this, and to make the proofreader's work easier, authors might find it helpful to get to grips with the styles facility in Word which helps when preparing novels and non-fiction alike.

Multiple edits

A single developmental edit isn't usually the only one that's required. Once a novel has been edited and passed back to the author, it's their turn to make changes (necessary even if they've received a hands-on edit, as the author needs to approve the changes the editor made and perhaps react to requests for additional material); then those revisions need to be looked at in turn. Sometimes the process is complete after two edits, but occasionally a novel will go to a third edit or more, and authors need to be prepared for that. The same is true for copy-edits; if you've made any revision after the copy-editor returned the manuscript to you (and almost certainly you will have done so, because you've been asked to), then it should revert to the copy-editor for a final or penultimate pass.

Where a writer is paying for the editing themselves, that has cost implications. Many writers forget to budget for this. Very often an editor won't charge as much for subsequent revisions (editing is often charged at a rate per 1,000 words) but, even so, cost is going to be a major consideration. Which brings us to reasons why it's good to self-edit.

Self-editing

If you're going to submit your work to a publisher or commission a freelance editor, why should you spend much time and effort on your own editing? Here are some points to consider:

• **The more professional your work, the more likely it is that a literary agent or publisher's commissioning editor will want it.**

'Professional' means a lot of things, but a cohesive narrative arc, effective writing style, 'showing not telling' in all the right places (for hints, see the self-editing tips at the end of this section) and finding the best characters to tell a gripping story are significant. Sometimes the character who

Editing software

Writing and editing software packages can be very useful (see *Software for writers* on page 670). These packages examine the strength of your writing and their suggestions are extremely helpful. They're also pretty easy to use. However, they don't claim to be a substitute for a developmental editor, and nor for a skilled copy-editor, who looks at much more than spelling, grammar and punctuation. But they are useful. I'd definitely consider using one, either if you're new to creative writing or if you know that, while you have great ideas, your language itself isn't a strength. Such software may benefit more experienced or proficient writers too, as it can point out ways to improve your writing that you might not have come across, but it lends a significant advantage to those less confident. Ask around and get testimonials before committing yourself, and take advantage of any free trial.

starts off telling the story is too tangential, and you might decide someone who makes more decisions that propel the plot forward is a better choice. Or sometimes the personality who is close to the main character is able to lend greater depth and perspective to their story – think of Dr Watson rather than Sherlock Holmes, or Hastings in the Agatha Christie novels rather than Poirot. Equally important is near-perfect presentation, with consistent formatting, use of vocative commas (a clear flag that you know what you're doing) and smooth yet illuminating prose. Not only does such professionalism make the manuscript better, it demonstrates to your intended recipient that you take your writing seriously – which is Number Two on their Wanted list, after the quality of the book.

• **If you're publishing independently, everything depends on you.**

Make sure every element you can control is as good as it can be. Using a professional editor for your book is essential and, just as with a commissioning editor, they too will respond well to a manuscript that bears the hallmarks of self-editing and will be motivated to do a superior job for you. Editors sigh when they receive a manuscript where the author has obviously just dashed off a first draft and hit Send. And if they're having to spend time pointing out basic problems, they're not focusing on areas where some input might make your novel really shine. This is particularly the case with critiques, where there is only space to explore the most obvious drawbacks to a work. The more work you've invested yourself, the less editors will need to do, and this should affect both the original rate you're charged, especially with copy-editing, and the number of edits of each kind. If you are an independent author wishing to self-publish, editing will be one of your major outlays – so everything you can do to reduce the cost makes sense.

• **Self-editing pays off when entering competitions.**

Writers don't always reach out to an editor if they're entering their work in writing competitions, although the rules rarely prohibit this and it can make a big difference; even a critique really helps, as authors can get too close to their work. Yet if you're developing

Self-editing: what to look out for and amend

• Reporting (telling) instead of *showing* us live action as it happens to your characters.

• Protagonists not having agency, so things happen to them because of others or because of chance; it's their *own* decisions and actions that should drive the plot.

• Starting too early in a story and showing too much 'status quo' before we get to the inciting event.

• Chunks of exposition that would be better removed or distributed through the text more subtly.

• Spending too long on elements that don't contribute to the storyline or characterisation.

• Telling the story too distantly and therefore not sufficiently investing your reader in the characters.

• Trying to show the story from too many different viewpoints ... Whose story is this? Whose chapter or scene is this? Why? Work it out, and then stick to your decision.

• Words such as *just, really, rather, quite, slightly, actually,* and especially *then* and *now,* cut these as much as possible. *Then* is often redundant because the chronology is implied by describing one action followed by another.

• Remove filter words: identify instances where you can delete *she knew ..., he felt ..., it seemed ...* to write more directly and powerfully in a character's head.

• Repetition of the subject in a sentence with multiple clauses, unless for emphasis. It is best to use as few words as necessary.

• Confusion between *they're, there* and *their,* and words such as *wave/waive, rein/reign.*

• Spelling compound words like *postcard* or *goodbye* inconsistently – as two words here and one word there. Check the dictionary for which words are open compounds (two words, such as *no one*), closed (one word) and which are hyphenated words. For the rules on hyphenation, see *New Hart's Rules* (OUP).

• If in doubt whether a word takes an initial capital, the rule is only to capitalise it if it's an actual (proper) name. Seasons, for example, don't take a capital: spring is not the same as Paul.

• Ensure there's a hard page break at the end of each chapter. Use a header with your name and the title. Number your pages.

your self-editing skills, then this can be where hard work really pays off. I'm a keen advocate of entering writing competitions; it's hugely motivating to submit a piece of writing you've worked on, whatever the outcome. It helps develop your professionalism too, making you pay attention to presentation requirements, word counts and deadlines. As the facilitator of both the Margery Allingham Short Mystery Prize (www.thecwa.co.uk/ma) and the CWA's Debut Dagger competition (see page 553), every year I notice that it's the work which has been polished till it blazes out in glory that makes the longlists. While the plots, characters and settings of those longlisted entries vary infinitely, the quality of the writing and the presentation are what consistently shout 'professional'.

• **Self-editing helps you learn your craft.**

The biggest incentive to self-editing is that, by so doing, you learn your craft. This is an ongoing process; the more you wield your editing pen, the sharper your writing becomes. Through editing and honing your work you'll come to understand your own strengths and weaknesses and discover how to highlight the one and minimise the other.

Resources

Bell, James Scott, *Revision and Self-Editing for Publication*, 2nd edn (Writer's Digest Books 2013)

Brody, Jessica, *Save the Cat! Writes a Novel* Jessica Brody (Ten Speed Press 2018)

Browne, Renni and King, Dave, *Self-editing for Fiction Writers*, 2nd edn (William Morrow & Co. 2004)

Hardy, Janice, *Understanding Show, Don't Tell (And Really Getting It)* (Fiction University 2016)

Ryan, William, *Writers' & Artists' Guide to How to Write* (Bloomsbury 2021)

Vogler, Christopher, *The Writer's Journey: Mythic Structure for Writers* (Pan Books 1999)

Ward, Lesley and Woods, Geraldine, *English Grammar for Dummies* (John Wiley 2009)

New Hart's Rules: The Oxford Style Guide (OUP 2014)

The Chicago Manual of Style, 17th edn (University of Chicago Press 2017)

Dea Parkin is founder and Editor-in-Chief at editorial consultancy Fiction Feedback. She works with freelance editors to provide a service encompassing developmental editing and copy-editing, as well as critiques, to writers who want to get published. Dea is also coordinator at the Crime Writers' Association and oversees the CWA Debut Dagger and Margery Allingham Short Mystery Prize. She is a published poet and writer of fiction. For more information see www.fictionfeedback.co.uk and follow her on Twitter @DeaWriter.

See also...

• *Who's who in publishing*, page 663
• *Glossary of publishing terms*, page 665

Writing an award-winning blog

Successful book blogger Julia Mitchell tells how she found a creative and fulfilling outlet as well as an inspiring, supportive and productive community through blogging, and urges others to take the leap and get started.

'Hello, my name's Julia and the internet is my life.' Does that sound sad? Well, how about this: 'Hi there, my name's Julia and I'm an award-winning book blogger with thousands of followers on Instagram, and I'm making an income from being creative online'. Now that's more like it!

So how did this all begin? Back in 2016 I started my book-themed Instagram account, Julia's Bookcase, when I was fresh out of university and in need of something productive to do with my time. While lolling about in bed in the middle of the night, I spontaneously created a new Instagram account and uploaded a photo of the book that I was reading, *A Darker Shade of Magic* (Tor Books 2015) by Victoria Schwab, and an obsession was born. As my skills improved, I found myself submerged in a community of avid readers.

Fast forward to 2019 and along came my second 'child', my blog – Julia's Bookcase. As much as I loved Instagram, I'd been craving a place where I could create long-form content that was evergreen and would be discovered again and again by bookish internet wanderers. I've since filled that space with a varied mix of book recommendations, Instagram tips and details of my literary travels. To date I've written about boutique hotels, a national book-shop town, a residential library, a real-life Hobbit Hole and more. The web is where I've carved out a little space just for myself – a place to open up and pour my heart out, and where I can connect with others like me. There's no one to edit me or tell me no; I never have to ask permission or persuade others to see my point of view. It's my own little rabbit hole to escape into every evening and weekend.

So my blog was born and to my delight I found, waiting for me on the internet, a huge community of amazing, creative entrepreneurs. There were writers, photographers, artists, designers and crafters, bookworms, travellers, fashionistas, beauty experts and minimalists, all sharing their creations with the world and inspiring me to continue contributing my own. The web is a place where the playing field has been levelled, and softer, more cautious creatives (like myself!) have an equal chance of being heard. It's where the quiet people thrive. To date, I've worked with a number of high-profile brands, from National Express and Visit Scotland to Universal Pictures and *Stylist* magazine. I've created sponsored Instagram posts on both my grid and my stories, and written advertorial pieces on my blog for Bookatable.com and Fora, a wonderful flexible working space in East London. This isn't a full-time gig for me (I spend my days working in book publishing), but by night my creative projects have blossomed into a successful and fulfilling side hustle. I'm just an ordinary person who's worked hard … and if I can do it, then you can do it too.

Time to get started

So take a moment to think about a project you've always wanted to launch but never quite had the courage to begin. If you're reading this, then you're probably a writer, so perhaps you've always liked the idea of running your own blog - a place where you can write the words of your choosing and make money doing it. Or maybe you relish the idea of pairing words with images and sharing your love of sustainable fashion on a dedicated Instagram account of your own. This is the seed of an idea, and my first advice for you is simply to *begin*. Forget about producing a perfect, complete work of art and just get started, learning as you go. One of the great things about the internet is that, when you start a creative project like this, no one's going to be watching. You can experiment without consequence.

Setting up a basic blog is easy, and you won't need even a smidge of coding knowledge. There are a number of sites such as WordPress, Squarespace and Wix, which will guide you through the process of setting up your first fully functioning website, and all for free. It's a quick process, and you can easily get it up and running within the space of a Sunday afternoon. If you have the budget, then I would recommend purchasing your own URL as it looks more professional (for example, juliasbookcase.com instead of juliasbookcase.squarespace.com), although this isn't compulsory. How frequently you post is up to you, but I'd encourage you to find a schedule that you can realistically and consistently stick to. When it comes to finding and retaining readers, social media is your friend. I share all of my blog posts with my followers on Instagram, which is where the majority of my website traffic comes from, but I also regularly share my writing on Twitter, and always make the most of SEO. Pinterest is another blogger favourite for increasing traffic, although don't feel like you need to try all of these channels at once. I suggest you start by setting up an adjacent Instagram account – all you need to do is download the app and sign up.

Find your community

When you're creating something online, it's vital to embrace community – both fitting into one and moulding one of your own. It can be so easy to get bogged down in the technicalities of a project when you're first starting out … like whether you should host your blog on WordPress or Squarespace (I use Squarespace) or what colour scheme you should follow on your Instagram account. But unless you find your tribe, that is, the people

A blogger's jargon buster

Instagram 'post'

Nowadays there are a variety of ways of sharing content on Instagram, and the first one is as a simple feed **post**, i.e. a traditional static post of the kind you'll find on your home screen when opening Instagram. Once you've got the basics down, I'd highly recommend adding music, which can make your photo much more likely to be seen.

Instagram 'story'

Alternatively, content can be shared on your Instagram **story**: stories are found at the top of the homepage and expire after 24 hours.

Instagram 'carousel'

Similar to an Instagram post, a **carousel** allows a creator to share two or more photos for viewers to scroll through. It's a nice way to share multiple shots relating to a shared topic.

Instagram 'reel'

One of the newer ways to create content on Instagram, a **reel** allows you to share photos or video with music and is a great way to get yourself seen by people who don't already follow you.

SEO

Also known as **search engine optimisation**: this is the process of optimising your content so that it can be found through search engines such as Google.

who are interested in what you're creating, then it's unlikely that many people will see it at all, regardless of its quality.

If you're launching a blog, I urge you to start a Twitter or Instagram account to run alongside it. That's where you will find like-minded people and create friendships with those who will read your blog posts. On Instagram, try scrolling down the 'bookstagram' hashtag, liking and commenting on the photos that catch your eye. Don't produce spam but leave meaningful comments and follow accounts that you would like to see again. Whatever project you're starting, this is how to get found on a web that is saturated with the voices of others. My favourite Instagram guru, Sara Tasker, likes to say 'there's always room at the top' and I wholeheartedly agree.

So here you are – this is your permission slip to take the leap and start something magical.

Julia Mitchell is a book editor by day and an award-winning blogger, Instagrammer and freelance writer by night. In 2020, she was named The London Book Fair UK's Book Blogger of the Year. She's obsessed with all things bookish, owns a colour-coordinated bookshelf and has a penchant for strong cups of tea.

How creative writing courses benefit a writer

Martin Ouvry explains the value and range of courses for writers of all levels and experience. He describes the practical and motivational power of learning together, whether online or offline, to boost a writer's personal confidence and creativity.

I'm sitting at my desk (a farmhouse-kitchen table – scrubbed pine planks with all manner of knots and whorls in the grain: thermals, dunes, the contours of maps) in front of a window with a view of gardens, the backs of other houses. On my screen, my students start to join me, arriving first in their ones and twos, then a flurry – the feeling is almost no different from that of people drifting purposefully into a room with a hinged door and only four walls. A few moments' attention to their tech, then they look up and return my greetings. Some are thoughtful, intent; most are all smiles.

'How has everyone been getting on?' I ask. 'Anyone feel you've made progress since we saw each other last?'

And off we go. It's clear that everyone is keen to be here at our virtual table together, and I know that each member of the group has come both for the shared experience and for a particular reason, or reasons, of their own.

***

I've devised courses in various contexts over a number of years and have seen how writers can grow by taking part. (Can writing be taught? Further details below ...) I've taught all sorts, from nervous beginners to breakthrough talents with gleaming new publishing deals (who are far from immune to nerves themselves). The novel, the short story, the memoir, I can teach all these forms because I'm lucky enough to have studied under some brilliant teachers and, equally important, I've done a lot of writing in my time and have had the good fortune to have benefited from the occasional prize or award.

There's a vast range of courses on offer these days, for every stage in a writer's life. To the new writer, the prospect of sharing one's work (which always feels intimate, whatever form it takes) can be daunting. The task of completing a book-length project, meanwhile, can seem as immense as building a cathedral ... (Can I actually finish something as colossal and intricately fashioned as a novel? Others can, so why have I always faltered in the past?)

For the new or would-be writer, then, short courses, usually of ten weeks, are a great way to find out what might be done. Many universities offer term-length courses (starting at as little as £200), and many independent courses, including my own, also run along those lines. Away from the ambience of the university scene, entities such as the 'online writing club' Jericho Writers (page 686), Writers & Artists (page 689) and other literary consultancies now run short courses alongside their editing and manuscript assessment services. (See *Writers' retreats and creative writing courses* section, beginning on page 683.)

While more experienced writers can also benefit greatly from short courses (and I'll give some examples of how), they might instead – or afterwards – choose to apply for one of the many MAs in Creative Writing (around £9,000) or a programme linked to a publishing house or literary agency (£350–£4,000). Of these, the Faber Academy (see page 684) and Curtis Brown Creative (see page 684) come immediately to mind. These options tend to have an element of selectivity, and thus the aspiring writer envisages not only the opportunity to spend time with other passionate practitioners, but also an instantly recognisable notch on their CV, with, perhaps, a faster track to getting noticed by agents and editors.

Very short courses – from just three days – also abound, such as the famous Arvon residential writing retreats (around £400-£800; see page 683 and page vii), while the *Guardian* and others run a variety of 'masterclasses' pitched at different levels of experience/accomplishment. And finally, a plethora of online-only courses can be found on platforms such as Udemy (www.udemy.com) and Skillshare (www.skillshare.com).

So, prevailing opinion has it that writing can be taught, but we must qualify that truth. A writer's voice contains at least something of everything we have read; along with paper and a pencil, or a laptop, this is what we bring into the classroom with us when we start out. True, there are other ingredients, but the fact remains that one cannot easily teach those who have grown up on a strict diet of airport novels to imbue their sentences with Elizabethan elegance or 18th-century panache. But one can certainly point them in the direction of those sources, should they wish to experiment in that way. Whether it's through a greater appreciation of Angela Carter's magic touch or Kazuo Ishiguro's flawless ventriloquism, many of my newcomers remark that they're beginning to read – and therefore to approach their own writing – in a whole new way.

One can also introduce the apprentice writer to a range of techniques, devices, concepts and insights that might percolate into their craft. Practical advice is highly valued, too: ideas on how to organise your emerging pages – how to handle this wayward young beast; how to open up the time to write – the *licence* to immerse yourself, even when the prospect of being paid to do so is still a distant dream.

The learning for the more experienced writer often involves reminders – of wise and unwise habits, fruitful techniques, the fundamentals on which excellent writing is built – and, say, exercises designed to address specific aspects of their emerging draft. And we can all be introduced to authors we haven't come across before. The curriculum itself is small, but its elements can be viewed from many different angles, time and time again. Plus, crucially, everyone who signs up for a writing course can expect to reap the benefits of that gentle (technical term alert) kick up the arse to produce and share new pages. Feedback on work in progress is vital to us all, from the novice to the Nobel laureate.

One member of my independent writing group sums up her feelings like this:
'To me, it's kind of like having a personal trainer. Sure, I could exercise at home without any help. But will I? If I exercise alone, I'll keep doing the same things and probably won't change up my routine. I probably won't challenge myself anywhere near as much. And because no one with expertise is watching, I'll keep making the same mistakes without realizing it. The other writers in the class are very important to learning. Seeing how they write, and what they see in my writing. It goes without saying that the quality of the teacher is key. In the field of medicine, people (well, doctors) tend to think that being knowledgeable makes them good teachers. Not so. The right teacher gives a balanced mix of encouragement and challenge.'

The important thing is not to be didactic. Guide, yes – lead the group to examples of great writing and explore together the decisions that great writers have made. Set exercises that are not simply prompts but can feed directly into work in progress. Offer examples of what you have found most helpful to your own writing process. Give feedback that's based on long, hard experience. But don't lay down the law – individual writing talent doesn't thrive on following supposed dos and don'ts ('show, don't tell' being the most obvious and most ossified example – the best writers do both). Seedling talent is a delicate thing; if you scatter rules in the soil around personal creativity it can harm it at the root.

I have learnt to teach my courses as if I were writing a novel: planned, of course, but with a high degree of flexibility week by week in terms of how the narrative arc will play out. Just as, in the writing of many of the best novels, it's the characters, the people, who will determine key aspects of the plot, so the characters around our table will, to a greater or lesser extent, show me where our story needs to go in order to bring the greatest benefit to the greatest number. My groups navigate the road or river without always knowing what lies around the next bend.

One of my newcomers tells me this:

'Not only has it given me the tools to structure a plot and think about character/ dialogue/point of view, it has given me the motivation, and belief in myself, I was severely lacking … The biggest gain is that I am now in a community of people with the same interest in creative writing as myself.'

To feel that one is not alone in one's endeavours, and the social dimension more broadly, is a key consideration for many, and it warms the heart to know how communal and convivial sessions can still feel in the age of hybrid and online. In my experience, the atmosphere around the virtual table can be just like being in that room with four walls, behind that hinged door – with the added dimension that writers in, say, London can easily meet and spend time with writers in Lisbon, San Francisco, Mumbai.

Others sign up with a very specific plan: 'Martin, I'm 50,000 words into the draft of my first novel and I think your course could be just the thing to get me to the end.' That novel, *The Moon Is Backwards* (Luar Livros 2022) by Justine Strand de Oliveira, revolves around the creation of modern Brazil and enjoyed a timely and important (given the political landscape in Brazil at that moment) release.

Yet others choose to return to structured courses with a publishing contract already in their hands. Ayesha Manazir Siddiqi, whose novel, *The Centre*, was published by Picador in 2023, first joined my independent course while she was working on that book and came back to me with a view to aiding her work on her follow-up. Ayesha outlined her reasons for being with us while she wrote *The Centre*:

'The class has truly become a joy, and opened up a massive window for me, giving me the encouragement and space to embark upon this precious project.'

Clearly, then, new and experienced writers alike see the benefits of sitting down together, both as members of groups and as one-to-one mentees. The 'massive window' Ayesha describes can be filled with many things: support and encouragement; invigorating ideas; technical know-how and practical advice; guidance on contacting agents and publishers; hitherto undiscovered literary treasures; a community of like-minded souls; that gentle kick up the arse … And whether you come with a solid plan in mind or just to see what you can do, there's no doubt that courses can help you write more, write better and get your writing noticed in the wider world of books. To see a piece of work to publication takes luck as well as hard work, and courses can make you luckier.

***

The two-hour session has passed in a trice and we say our farewells until next time. (It's interesting how much psychology and philosophy comes into the room amid the discussion of writing per se – psychology, philosophy, medicine, health, education, poetry, art, science, mathematics, music, politics, the family … Whether novels, short stories, memoirs, it's all very much about people in the end.) So, we wave goodbye and my writers melt away; this is not the week for us to meander (purposefully) down to the pub on the corner, but there will be plenty of time for all that.

Martin Ouvry is a writer, teacher, editor and musician. He recently completed his novel *The Cost of Loving* with the generous support of Arts Council England. His short fiction has appeared in publications such as *Esquire*, *New Writing* (Picador) and the *London Magazine*. He has been a Hawthornden Fellow and is a Wingate Scholar. Martin has taught creative writing for the British Council, Arts Council England, at City, University of London, UEA, Imperial College London and elsewhere. He delivers independent writing courses and mentoring programmes, and volunteers at the Chelsea Community Hospital School, bringing creative writing workshops to young people with mental health issues. For more information and to contact him, see martinouvry.com.

See also...
- *Reading as a writer*, page 234
- *Writers' retreats and creative writing courses*, page 683

Indexing

A good index is essential to the user of a non-fiction book; a bad index will let down an otherwise excellent book. The functions of indexes, and the skills needed to compile them, are explained here by the Society of Indexers.

An index is a detailed key to the contents of a document, unlike a contents list, which shows only the sections into which the document is divided (e.g. chapters). An index guides readers to information by providing a systematic arrangement of entries (single words, phrases, acronyms, names and so on) in a suitably organised list (usually alphabetical) that refers them to specific locations using page, column, section, frame, figure, table, paragraph, line or other appropriate numbers or hyperlinks.

Professional indexing

A well-crafted index produced by a skilled professional with appropriate subject expertise is an essential feature of almost every non-fiction book. A professional indexer has subject knowledge and considers the text from the readers' perspective, anticipating how they will approach the subject and what language they will use. The indexer analyses the content of the text and provides a carefully structured index to guide readers efficiently into the main text of the book.

A detailed, comprehensive and regularly updated Directory of Professional Indexers is on the Society of Indexers' website. Professional competence is recognised in three stages by the Society. Professional Members (MSocInd) have successfully completed initial training (see below) or have many years' continuous experience. Advanced Professional Members (MSocInd(Adv)) have demonstrated skills and experience gained since their initial training, while Fellows of the Society of Indexers (FSocInd) have undergone a rigorous Fellowship pathway, revised in 2022, to demonstrate both continuing professional development and evaluation of their index quality.

Indexing fees depend on many factors, particularly the complexity of the text, but for a straightforward text the Society recommends £29.75 an hour, £3.35 per page, or £9.00 per 1,000 words. Indexing should normally be organised by the publisher, but may be left to the author to do or to arrange. It is rarely a popular task with authors, and they are often not well suited to the task, which takes objectivity, perspective, speed, patience, attention to detail and, above all, training, experience and specialist software. Moreover, authors are generally too close to the text by this stage.

Ebooks and other electronic material

An index is necessary for ebooks and other electronic material. It is a complete myth that users of ebooks can rely solely on keyword-based retrieval systems; these pick out far too much information to be usable and far too little to be reliable. Only careful analysis by the human brain creates suitable index terms for non-fiction ebooks. There are no shortcuts for judging relevance, for extracting meaning and significance from the text, for identifying complex concepts, or for recognising different ways of expressing similar ideas. Index entries must also be properly linked to the text when a printed book is converted into an ebook. Linked indexes can be achieved via the technique of embedded indexing, where index entries are anchored within the text at their precise location.

The Society of Indexers

The Society of Indexers was founded in 1957 and is the only autonomous professional body for indexers in the UK. The main objectives of the Society are to promote high standards in all types of indexing and highlight the role of indexers in the organisation of knowledge; to provide, promote and recognise facilities for both the initial and the further training of indexers; to establish criteria for assessing conformity to indexing standards; and to conduct research and publish guidance, ideas and information about indexing.

Further information

Society of Indexers
Woodbourn Business Centre, 10 Jessell Street,
Sheffield S9 3HY
tel 0114 453 4928
email admin@indexers.org.uk
website www.indexers.org.uk
Twitter @indexers
Membership (2023) new member £120 p.a. (including 25% discount valid for first year of membership); standard membership £160 p.a.

The Society holds an annual conference and publishes *The Indexer* journal, the *SIdelights* member newsletter and other occasional publications, with further resources on its website. It runs several local groups and ongoing CPD sessions, both in person and online, to foster member-to-member communications, professional development and mutual support. The Society also instigated a National Indexing Day (#indexday), which takes place each March, to commemorate its founding date, to celebrate indexes and indexers and to provide events for publishers to learn more about indexing.

Indexing as a career

Indexing is often taken up as a second career, frequently drawing on expertise developed in some other field. Both intellectually demanding and creative, it requires considerable and sustained mental effort. Indexers need to be well-organised, flexible, disciplined and self-motivated, and resilient enough to cope with the uncertainties of freelance work. The Society of Indexers' long-established training course, which has received the CILIP Seal of Recognition (see CILIP page 518), gives a thorough grounding in indexing principles and practice on real documents. Based on the principle of open learning, it enables students to learn in their own way and at their own pace. There is access to study materials, practice exercises and quizzes, and links to a wide range of useful resources. Online tutorials are undertaken at various stages during the course. After completing the four assessed modules, which cover the core indexing skills, students undertake a book-length practical indexing assignment. Successful completion of the course leads to Accreditation, designation as a Professional Indexer (MSocInd), and entry in the Society's online *Directory of Professional Indexers*.

Further reading

Booth, P.F., *Indexing: The Manual of Good Practice* (K.G. Saur 2001)
British Standards Institution, *British Standard Recommendations for Examining Documents, Determining their Subjects and Selecting Indexing Terms* (BS6529:1984)
'Indexes' (chapter from *The Chicago Manual of Style*, 17th edn; University of Chicago Press 2017)
International Standards Organisation, *Information and Documentation – Guidelines for the Content, Organization and Presentation of Indexes* (ISO 999:1996)
Mulvany, N.C., *Indexing Books* (University of Chicago Press, 2nd edn 2005)
Stauber, D.M., *Facing the Text: Content and Structure in Book Indexing* (Cedar Row Press 2004)

ISBNs: what you need to know

The Nielsen BookData ISBN Agency for UK & Ireland receives a large number of enquiries about the ISBN system. The most frequently asked questions are answered here; for more information visit www.nielsenisbnstore.com.

What is an ISBN?

An ISBN is an International Standard Book Number and is 13 digits long.

What is the purpose of an ISBN?

An ISBN is a product number, used by publishers, booksellers and libraries for ordering, listing and stock control purposes. It enables them to identify a particular publisher and allows the publisher to identify a specific edition of a specific title in a specific format within their output.

Contact details

Nielsen BookData ISBN Agency for UK and Ireland
3rd Floor, Midas House, 62 Goldsworth Road, Woking GU21 6LQ
tel (01483) 712215
email isbn.agency@nielseniq.com
website www.nielsenisbnstore.com

Does an ISBN protect copyright?

A widely held belief is that an ISBN protects copyright. It doesn't, it is an identifier, a product code. The copyright belongs to the author. In general, publishers don't tend to buy copyrights for books. They license the copyrights, which the author retains.

What is a publisher?

The publisher is generally the person or organisation taking the financial and other risks in making a product available. For example, if a product goes on sale and sells no copies at all, the publisher loses money. If you get paid anyway, you are likely to be a designer, printer, author or consultant of some kind.

What is the format of an ISBN?

The ISBN is 13 digits long and is divided into five parts separated by spaces or hyphens.
• Prefix element: for the foreseeable future this will be 978 or 979
• Registration group element: identifies a geographic or national grouping. It shows where the publisher is based
• Registrant element: identifies a specific publisher or imprint
• Publication element: identifies a specific edition of a specific title in a specific format
• Check digit: the final digit which mathematically validates the rest of the number
The four parts following the prefix element can be of varying length.
Prior to 1 January 2007 ISBNs were ten digits long; any existing ten-digit ISBNs must be converted by prefixing them with '978' and the check digit must be recalculated using a Modulus 10 system with alternate weights of 1 and 3. The ISBN Agency can help you with this.

Do I *have* to have an ISBN?

There is no legal requirement in the UK and Ireland for an ISBN and it conveys no form of legal or copyright protection. It is simply a product identification number.

Why should I use an ISBN?

If you wish to sell your publication through major bookselling chains, independent book-shops or internet retailers, they will require you to have an ISBN to assist their internal processing and ordering systems.

The ISBN also provides access to bibliographic databases, such as the Nielsen BookData Database, which use ISBNs as references. These databases help booksellers and libraries to provide information for customers. Nielsen BookData has a range of bibliographic meta-data and retail sales monitoring services which use ISBNs and are vital for the dissemi-nation, trading and monitoring of books in the supply chain. The ISBN therefore provides access to additional marketing opportunities which could help sales of your product.

Where can I get an ISBN?

ISBNs are assigned to publishers in the country where the publisher's main office is based. This is irrespective of the language of the publication or the intended market for the book.

The ISBN Agency is the national agency for the UK and Republic of Ireland and British Overseas Territories. A publisher based elsewhere will not be able to get numbers from the UK Agency (even if you are a British Citizen) but can contact the Nielsen BookData ISBN Agency for details of the relevant national Agency.

If you are based in the UK and Ireland you can purchase ISBNs online from the Nielsen BookData ISBN Store: www.nielsenisbnstore.com.

How long does it take to get an ISBN?

If you purchase your ISBNs online from the Nielsen BookData ISBN Store you will receive your ISBN allocation within minutes. If you are purchasing ISBNs direct from the ISBN Agency via an off-line application, it can take up to five days. The processing period begins when a correctly completed application is received in the ISBN Agency and payment is received.

How much does it cost to get an ISBN?

ISBNs can be bought individually or in blocks of ten or more; visit the ISBN Store to find out more. Refer to www.nielsenisbnstore.com or email the ISBN Agency: isbn.agency@nielseniq.com.

Who is eligible for ISBNs?

Any individual or organisation who is publishing a qualifying product for general sale or distribution to the market. By publishing we mean making a work available to the public.

Which products do NOT qualify for ISBNs?

Any publication that is without a defined end should not be assigned an ISBN. For example, publications that are regularly updated and intended to continue indefinitely are not eli-gible for an ISBN.

Some examples of products that do not qualify for an ISBN are:
• Journals, periodicals, serials, newspapers in their entirety (single issues or articles, where these are made available separately, may qualify for ISBN);
• Abstract entities such as textual works and other abstract creations of intellectual or artistic content;
• Ephemeral printed materials such as advertising matter and the like;
• Customised print-on-demand publications (Publications that are available only on a limited basis, such as customised print-on-demand publications with content specifically

tailored to a user's request shall not be assigned an ISBN. If a customised publication is being made available for wider sale, e.g. as a college course pack available through a college book store, then an ISBN may be assigned);

• Printed music;
• Art prints and art folders without title page and text;
• Personal documents (such as a curriculum vitae or personal profile);
• Greetings cards;
• Music sound recordings;
• Software that is intended for any purpose other than educational or instructional;
• Electronic bulletin boards;
• Emails and other digital correspondence;
• Updating websites;
• Games.

Following a review of the UK market, it is now permissible for ISBNs to be assigned to calendars and diaries, provided that they are not intended for purely time-management purposes and that a substantial proportion of their content is textual or graphic.

What is an ISSN?

An International Standard Serial Number. This is the numbering system for journals, magazines, periodicals, newspapers and newsletters. It is administered by the British Library, *tel* (01937) 546959; *email* issn-uk@bl.uk; *website* www.bl.uk/help/Get-an-ISBN-or-ISSN-for-your-publication#

Where do I put the ISBN?

The ISBN should appear on the reverse of the title page, sometimes called the copyright page or the imprint page, and on the outside back cover of the book. If the book has a dust jacket, the ISBN should also appear on the back of this. If the publication is not a book, the ISBN should appear on the product, and on the packaging or inlay card. If the publication is a map, the ISBN should be visible when the map is folded and should also appear near the publisher statement if this is elsewhere.

I am reprinting a book with no changes – do I need a new ISBN?

No.

I am reprinting a book but adding a new chapter – do I need a new ISBN?

Yes. You are adding a significant amount of additional material, altering the content of the book.

I am reprinting a book with a new cover design – should I change the ISBN?

No. A change of cover design with no changes to the content of the book should not have a new ISBN.

I am changing the binding on the book to paperback rather than hardback. Do I need a new ISBN?

Yes. Changes in binding always require new ISBNs even if there are no changes to the content of the book.

I am changing the price – do I need a new ISBN?

No. Price changes with no other changes do not require new ISBNs and in fact must not change the ISBN.

Public Lending Right

Under the PLR system, payment is made from public funds to authors and other contributors (writers, illustrators/photographers, translators, adapters/retellers, ghostwriters, editors/compilers/abridgers/revisers, narrators and producers) whose books (print, audiobook and ebook) are lent from public libraries. Payment is annual; the amount authors receive is proportionate to the number of times that their books were borrowed during the previous year (July to June).

How the system works

From the applications received, the PLR office compiles a database of authors and books (the PLR Register). A representative sample of book issues is recorded, consisting of all loans from selected public libraries. This is then multiplied in proportion to total library lending to produce, for each book, an estimate of its total annual loans throughout the country. The estimated loans are matched against the database of registered authors and titles to discover how many loans are credited to each registered book for the calculation of PLR payments, using the ISBN printed in the book (see below).

Parliament allocates a sum each year (£6.6 million for 2021/22) for PLR. This fund pays the administrative costs of PLR and reimburses local authorities for recording loans in the sample libraries (see below). The remaining money is divided by the total estimated national loan figure for all registered books in order to work out how much can be paid for each estimated loan of every registered ISBN.

Further information

Public Lending Right – British Library
Boston Spa, Wetherby, West Yorkshire LS23 7BQ
tel (01937) 546030
website www.bl.uk/plr
website www.plrinternational.com
Contact Head of PLR Operations

The UK PLR scheme is administered by the British Library from its offices in Boston Spa. The UK PLR office also provides registration for the Irish PLR scheme on behalf of the Irish Public Lending Remuneration office.

Application forms, information and publications are all obtainable from the PLR Office. See website for further information on eligibility for PLR, loans statistics and forthcoming developments.

British Library Advisory Committee for Public Lending Right

Advises the British Library Board, the PLR Head of Policy and Engagement and Head of PLR Operations on the operation and future development of the PLR scheme.

Limits on payments

If all the registered interests in an author's books score so few loans that they would earn less than £1 in a year, no payment is due. However, if the books of one registered author score so high that the author's PLR earnings for the year would exceed £6,600, then only £6,600 is paid. (No author can earn more than £6,600 in PLR in any one year.) Money that is not paid out because of these limits belongs to the fund and increases the amounts paid that year to other authors.

The sample

Because it would be expensive and impracticable to attempt to collect loans data from every library authority in the UK, a statistical sampling method is employed instead. The sample represents only public lending libraries – academic, school, private and commercial libraries are not included. Only books which are loaned from public libraries can earn PLR; consultations of books on library premises are excluded.

The sample consists of the entire loans records for a year from libraries in more than 41 public library authorities spread through England, Scotland and Wales, and whole data is collected from Northern Ireland. Sample loans represent around 20% of the national total. All the computerised sampling points in an authority contribute loans data ('multi-site' sampling). The aim is to increase the sample without any significant increase in costs. In order to ensure representative sampling, at least seven libraries are replaced every year and a library cannot stay in the sample for more than four years. Loans are totalled every 12 months for the period 1 July–30 June.

An author's entitlement to PLR depends on the loans accrued by his or her books in the sample. This figure is averaged up to produce first regional and then finally national estimated loans.

ISBNs

The PLR system uses ISBNs (International Standard Book Numbers) to identify books lent and correlate loans with entries on the PLR Register so that payments can be made. ISBNs are required for all registrations. Different editions (e.g. 1st, 2nd, hardback, paperback, large print) of the same book have different ISBNs. See *ISBNs: what you need to know* on page 652.

Authorship

In the PLR system the author of a printed book or ebook is any contributor such as the writer, illustrator, translator, compiler, editor or reviser. Authors must be named on the book's title page, or be able to prove authorship by some other means (e.g. receipt of royalties). The ownership of copyright has no bearing on PLR eligibility. Narrators, producers and abridgers are also eligible to apply for PLR shares in audiobooks and e-audiobooks.

Co-authorship/illustrators. In the PLR system the authors of a book are those writers, translators, editors, compilers and illustrators as defined above. Authors must apply for

---

Summary of the 40th year's results

Registration: authors. When registration closed for the 40th year (30 June 2022) there were 60,104 authors and assignees.

Eligible loans. The loans from UK libraries credited to registered books – approximately 33% of all library borrowings – qualify for payment. The remaining loans relate to books that are ineligible for various reasons, to books written by dead or foreign authors, and to books that have simply not been applied for.

Money and payments. PLR's administrative costs are deducted from the fund allocated to the British Library Board annually by Parliament. Total government funding for 2021/22 was £6.6 million. The amount distributed to authors was just over £6 million. The Rate per Loan for 2021/22 was 30.53 pence.

The numbers of authors in various payment categories are as follows:

*303	payments at	£5,000–6,600
372	payments between	£2,500–4,999.99
828	payments between	£1,000–2,499.99
898	payments between	£500–999.99
3,034	payments between	£100–499.99
15,592	payments between	£1–99.99
21,034	TOTAL	

* Includes 205 authors whose book loans reached the maximum threshold

registration before their books can earn PLR and this can be done via the PLR website. There is no restriction on the number of authors who can register shares in any one book as long as they satisfy the eligibility criteria.

Writers and/or illustrators. At least one contributor must be eligible and they must jointly agree what share of PLR each will take based on contribution. This agreement is necessary even if one or two are ineligible or do not wish to register for PLR. The eligible authors will receive the share(s) specified in the application.

Translators. Translators may apply for a 30% fixed share (to be shared equally between joint translators).

Editors and compilers. An editor or compiler may apply to register a 20% share if they have written at least 10% of the book's content or more than ten pages of text in addition to normal editorial work and are named on the title page. Alternatively, editors may register 20% if they have a royalty agreement with the publisher. In the case of joint editors/compilers, the total editor's share should be divided equally.

Audiobooks. PLR shares in audiobooks are fixed by the UK scheme and may not be varied. *Writers* may register a fixed 60% share in an audiobook, providing that it has not been abridged or translated. In cases where the writer has made an additional contribution (e.g. as narrator), she/he may claim both shares. *Narrators* may register a fixed 20% PLR share in an audiobook. *Producers* may register a fixed 20% share in an audiobook. *Abridgers* (in cases where the writer's original text has been abridged prior to recording as an audiobook) qualify for 12% (20% of the writer's share). *Translators* (in cases where the writer's original text has been translated from another language) qualify for 18% (30% of the writer's share). If there is more than one writer, narrator, etc the appropriate shares should be divided equally.

Dead or missing co-authors. Where it is impossible to agree shares with a co-author because that person is dead or untraceable, then the surviving co-author or co-authors may submit an application to register a share which reflects their individual contribution to the book.

Transferring PLR after death. First applications may not be made by the estate of a deceased author. However, if an author registers during their lifetime the PLR in their books can be transferred to a new owner and continues for up to 70 years after the date of their death. The new owner can apply to register new titles if first published one year before, or up to ten years after, the date of the author's death. New editions of existing registered titles can also be registered posthumously.

Residential qualifications. To register for the UK PLR scheme, at the time of application authors must have their only home or principal home in the UK or in any of the other countries within the European Economic Area (i.e. EC member states plus Iceland, Norway and Liechtenstein).

Eligible books

In the PLR system each edition of a book is registered and treated as a separate book. A book is eligible for PLR registration provided that:
- it has an eligible author (or co-author);
- it is printed and bound (paperbacks count as bound);
- it has already been published;
- copies of it have been put on sale, i.e. it is not a free handout;

• the authorship is personal, i.e. not a company or association, and the book is not crown copyright;
• it has an ISBN;
• it is not wholly or mainly a musical score;
• it is not a newspaper, magazine, journal or periodical.

Audiobooks. An audiobook is defined as an 'authored text' or 'a work recorded as a sound recording and consisting mainly of spoken words'. Applications can therefore only be accepted to register audiobooks which meet these requirements and are the equivalent of a printed book. Music, dramatisations and live recordings do not qualify for registration. To qualify for UK PLR in an audiobook contributors should be named on the case in which the audiobook is held; or be able to refer to a contract with the publisher; or be named within the audiobook recording.

Ebooks. Previously only ebooks downloaded to fixed terminals in library premises and then taken away on loan on portable devices to be read elsewhere qualified for PLR payment. Information provided by libraries suggested that the vast majority of ebook and digital audio lending was carried out 'remotely' to home PCs and mobile devices, which meant the loan did not qualify for PLR.

On 27 April 2017 the Digital Economy Bill, which included provision to extend the UK PLR legislation to include remote loans of ebooks from public libraries, received Royal Assent. The new arrangements took effect officially from 1 July 2018, and remote ebook loans data is now collected, and the first payments arising from the newly eligible loans were made in February 2020. The PLR website provides updated information on this legislation.

Statements and payment

Authors with an online account may view their statement online. Only registered authors with an offline account and no registered email address receive a statement posted to their address if a payment is due.

Most popular authors and titles for PLR year 2021/22

Top 10 authors	Top 10 titles
1 Julia Donaldson	1 *The Thursday Murder Club* – Richard Osman
2 James Patterson	2 *The Man Who Died Twice* – Richard Osman
3 Daisy Meadows	3 *The Midnight Library* – Matt Haig
4 David Walliams	4 *The Sentinel* – Lee Child
5 Lee Child	5 *The Darkest Evening* – Ann Cleeves
6 Jeff Kinney	6 *The Long Call* – Ann Cleeves
7 Ann Cleeves	7 *Harry Potter and the Philosopher's Stone* – J.K. Rowling
8 Roald Dahl	8 *The Heron's Cry* – Ann Cleeves
9 David Baldacci	9 *Shuggie Bain* – Douglas Stuart
10 Adam Blade	10 *Trust Me* – T.M. Logan

These two lists are based on loans data collected from a sample of UK public libraries between 1 July and 30 June each year. A grossing-up calculation is then applied at the end of the reporting year to provide a national estimate. They are based on PLR sample loans in the period July 2021–June 2022. They include all writers, both registered and unregistered, but not illustrators where the book has a separate writer. Writing names are used; pseudonyms have not been combined.

PLR's 'most borrowed' lists are based on loans data collected from a sample of UK public libraries between 1 July and 30 June each year. A grossing-up calculation is then applied at the end of the reporting year to provide a national estimate. See www.bl.uk/plr/popular-loans for more information.

Sampling arrangements

To help minimise the unfairness that arises inevitably from a sampling system, the scheme specifies the eight regions within which authorities and sampling points have to be designated and includes libraries of varying size. Part of the sample drops out by rotation each year to allow fresh libraries to be included. The following library authorities were designated for the year 1 July 2022–30 June 2023 (all are multi-site authorities). This list is based on the nine government regions for England plus Northern Ireland, Scotland and Wales. The composition of the PLR library authority sample changes annually and not all regions have to be represented each year.

• East – Peterborough, Suffolk
• East Midlands – Leicester, Leicestershire, Nottinghamshire
• London – Bromley, Camden, Croydon, Harrow, The Royal Borough of Kensington and Chelsea (RBKC)
• North East – Newcastle, Northumberland, Stockton-on-Tees
• North West & Merseyside – Bury, St Helens, Wirral
• South East – Bracknell Forest, Medway, Oxfordshire, Southampton, West Sussex
• South West – Cornwall, Gloucestershire, Isle of Wight, Wiltshire
• West Midlands – Dudley, Shropshire, Wolverhampton
• Yorkshire & The Humber – Calderdale, Kingston Upon Hull, Leeds, North Lincolnshire
• Northern Ireland – The Northern Ireland Library Authority
• Scotland – Glasgow, Highland, Stirling
• Wales – Bridgend, Carmarthenshire, Newport, Pembrokeshire, Powys, Swansea.

Participating local authorities are reimbursed on an actual cost basis for additional expenditure incurred in providing loans data to the PLR Office. The extra PLR work mostly consists of modifications to computer programs to accumulate loans data in the local authority computer and to transmit the data to the PLR Office.

Reciprocal arrangements

Reciprocal PLR arrangements now exist with the German, Dutch, Austrian and other European PLR schemes. Authors can apply for overseas PLR for most of these countries through the ALCS (Authors' Licensing and Collecting Society; see page 718). The exception to this rule is Ireland. Authors should now register for Irish PLR through the UK PLR Office. Further information on PLR schemes internationally and recent developments within the EC towards wider recognition of PLR is available from the PLR Office or on the international PLR website.

A matter of style: A mini A–Z of literary terms

Literary terms are linguistic and stylistic features that writers can employ to enhance their writing.

adage
A popular saying or expression which conveys a shared and often repeated belief. It might be a proverb or an **aphorism** or a maxim, but has a sense of universal truth about it.

alliteration
The repeated use of the same vowel or consonant, especially at the beginning of a series of words, to create a distinct rhythm.

allusion
A reference which is (often) subtly implied, but which assumes the reader will comprehend, based on a shared understanding or knowledge of what is being alluded to. Reference might be to a person, an event or a book.

amplification
Expanding a sentence to draw attention to or to exaggerate or intensify an aspect of a story or argument.

analogy
A comparison between two similar things used to illustrate an argument or explanation. These things might not be in any obvious sense similar, but figuratively might be drawn together to highlight a specific characteristic or sentiment.

anaphora
One or more words repeated sequentially or consecutively, especially at the beginning of a series of statements, to attract the reader's attention.

anecdote
The retelling or recounting of a personal story or experience, often to reference a specific event from which to extrapolate a broader point.

anthimeria
Swapping one part of speech in a way that is not grammatically correct, for example replacing a verb with a noun for metaphorical effect.

anthropomorphism
Animals, objects or other non-human beings given human characteristics and portrayed as though they were human.

antimetabole
When words or phrases in one part of a sentence are inverted and used in the second part.

antiphrasis
Where a word is used opposite to its actual meaning and thus is a form of irony.

aphorism
A short statement which is intended to summarise an accepted truth in a distinctively clever or witty way.

apologue
A fable or short story which is intended to teach a moral lesson, often using animals as characters.

apophasis
Asserting or emphasising something by denying it or stating that it will not be mentioned. This is also known as paralipsis.

archetype
A universal idea, image or person which serves as a common example or representation and is recognisable because of its frequent use.

assonance
The repeated use of the same vowel sounds to create a distinct rhythmic pattern, set a mood or reiterate the meaning of words.

asyndeton
Writing stripped down to its crucial meaning and essentials, where, for example, conjunctions or pronouns are omitted.

auxesis
The listing of concepts or things in their ascending order of importance.

cacophony
A series of conflicting sounds used together to create an inharmonious rhythm.

chiasmus
Where the grammatical structure of one phrase or sentence is repeated in a second phrase or sentence where a related concept appears in reverse order.

cliché

A common phrase which has been repeated so often that it has lost any sincere or impactful meaning.

diacope

The repetition of a word or words in a sentence, with other words dropped in between; used for emphasis or to enhance a description.

dissonance

An arrangement of **cacophonous** or discordant sounds to create a harsh and jarring effect.

epigram

A short, often witty statement to praise, commemorate or mock, often used as an inscription at the start of a book or chapter.

epistrophe

Successive phrases or sentences where the final word is repeated.

epithet

An adjective or description used to qualify a specifically named person or thing, that captures their most admired or despised qualities and is universally the way they are referred to.

eponym

A name (usually of a title) that is derived from a protagonist or character.

euphemism

A seemingly harmless word or phrase with a second meaning which is considered impolite or inappropriate or might wish to convey a less literal meaning in a subtle way.

euphony

A series of complementary sounds, usually vowels or soft consonants, which flow together and create a smooth rhythm.

extended metaphor

A **metaphor** which is sustained throughout a piece of writing and is returned to several times in order to extend or add depth to the comparison or meaning.

hamartia

A flaw or failure in a character, that they themselves are not usually able to see, that leads to his or her downfall.

homophone

Two or more words which sound the same but are spelt differently and have different meanings, for example 'would' and 'wood', 'flower' and 'flour'.

hyperbaton

Where words are arranged in an unexpected way that upends the usual grammatical order.

hyperbole

Exaggeration intended to emphasise and highlight, and which strays into the realm of untruth, something not to be understood literally.

idiom

A common phrase whose meaning is not literal and is specific to the language it originates from, for example 'as fit as a fiddle'.

juxtaposition

Where two things are placed together to create a contrast or invite comparison.

litotes

An understated or ironic figure of speech in which an idea or thing is emphasised by rejecting its opposite, for example, 'You won't be sorry' to convey satisfaction or pleasure.

malapropism

The misuse of words for humorous effect, named after Mrs Malaprop in R. B. Sheridan's *The Rivals* (1775).

metanoia

An exaggerated or extreme statement lessened or undermined by a successive statement which suggests a changed mind or a calmed emotion.

metaphor

Where one thing is said to be another to invite comparison or emphasise a similarity.

metonymy

A figure of speech where a word strongly associated with a thing or idea is used to represent the thing itself, for example the monarchy being referred to as 'the Crown.'

nemesis

The embodiment of a punishment often presented as an antagonist or enemy.

onomatopoeia

Words which imitate the sounds they represent, for example 'click' and 'clack', or the use of consonant sounds to mimic the sound they are describing, for example to create the rhythm of high heels on a wooden floor.

oxymoron

A phrase which joins contradictory words to create a paradox, for example 'pretty ugly'.

personification

An idea or event presented as a human operation; adopting human attributes.

pleonasm

The redundant use of extra words which repeat rather than expand meaning, such as 'burning fire' or 'a really new innovation'.

polyptoton

The repetition of a word, or its root, with a different grammatical application each time.

rhetorical question

A question which is not intended to be answered but is instead used to emphasise a point.

simile

Where one thing is said to be like another to invite comparison and emphasise a similarity.

spoonerism

When the first consonant sounds of two or more words are swapped to create a new phrase for humorous effect.

syllogism

A form of logical reasoning where two propositions or ideas, which share a common element, together confirm a given conclusion.

synecdoche

A figure of speech where the word for a part of a thing is used to refer to the whole thing, for example 'hands' to mean 'workers'.

transferred epithet

When an adjectival word or phrase is attached to a noun which it doesn't strictly describe (thus transferred), for example 'sleepless nights'.

zeugma

Where one word is used to describe two others in different contexts, for example 'she lost her keys and her temper'.

Who's who in publishing

agent

See **literary agent**.

aggregator

A company or website that gathers together related content from a range of other sources and provides various different services and resources, such as formatting and distribution, to ebook authors.

art editor

A person in charge of the layout and design of a magazine, who commissions the photographs and illustrations and is responsible for its overall appearance and style.

audio editor

A person who edits the raw audio from the recording into the final, retail-ready audiobook.

audio producer

A person who supervises the entire production process of the audiobook.

author

A person who has written a book, article, or other piece of original writing.

book packager

See **packager**.

columnist

A person who regularly writes an article for publication in a newspaper or magazine.

commissioning editor

A person who asks authors to write books for the part of the publisher's list for which he or she is responsible or who takes on an author who approaches them direct or via an agent with a proposal. Also called **acquisitions editor** or **acquiring editor** (more commonly in the USA). A person who signs up writers (commissions them) to write an article for a magazine or newspaper.

contributor

A person who writes an article that is included in a magazine or paper, or who writes a chapter or section that is included in a book.

copy-editor

A person whose job is to check material ready for publication for accuracy, clarity of message, writing style and consistency of spelling, punctuation and grammar.

desk editor

Manages a list of titles, seeing them through the editorial and production processes, and works closely with authors.

distributor

Acts as a link between the publisher and retailer. The distributor can receive orders from retailers, ship books, invoice, collect revenue and deal with returns. Distributors often handle books from several publishers. **Digital distributors** handle ebook distribution.

editor

A person in charge of publishing a newspaper or magazine who makes the final decisions about the content and format. A person in book publishing who has responsibility for the content of a book and can be variously a senior person (**editor-in-chief**) or day-to-day contact for authors (**copy-editor**, **development editor**, **commissioning editor**, etc).

editorial assistant

A person who assists senior editorial staff at a publishing company, newspaper, or similar business with various administrative duties, as well as editorial tasks in preparing copy for publication.

illustrator

A person who designs and draws a visual rendering of the source material, such as characters or settings, in a 2D media. Using traditional or digital methods, an illustrator creates artwork manually rather than photographically.

journalist

A person who prepares and writes material for a newspaper or magazine, news website, television or radio programme, or any similar medium.

literary agent

Somebody whose job is to negotiate publishing contracts, involving royalties, advances and rights sales on behalf of an author and who earns commission on the proceeds of the sales they negotiate.

literary scout

A person who looks for unpublished manuscripts to recommend to clients for publication as books, or adaptation into film scripts, etc.

marketing department

The department that originates the sales material – catalogues, order forms, blads, samplers, posters, book proofs and advertisements – to promote published titles.

narrator

A person who reads a text aloud into a recording device to create an audiobook. This may be the author of the text or a professional voice artist.

packager

A company that creates a finished book for a publisher.

picture researcher

A person who looks for pictures relevant to a particular topic, so that they can be used as illustrations in, for example, a book, newspaper or TV programme.

printer

A person or company whose job is to produce printed books, magazines, newspapers or similar material. The many stages in this process include establishing the product specifications, preparing the pages for print, operating the printing presses, and binding and finishing the final product.

production controller

A person in the production department of a publishing company who deals with printers and paper suppliers.

production department

The department responsible for the technical aspects of planning and producing material for publication to a schedule and as specified by the client. Their work involves liaising with editors, designers, typesetters, printers and binders.

proofreader

A person whose job is to check typeset pages and text for layout, design, spelling and grammatical errors missed at copy-editing, prior to publication.

publicity department

The department that works with the author and the media on 'free' publicity when a book is published – e.g. reviews, features, author interviews, bookshop readings and signings, festival appearances, book tours, and radio and TV interviews.

publisher

A person or company that publishes books, magazines or newspapers.

rights manager

A person who negotiates and coordinates rights sales (e.g. for subsidiary, translation or foreign rights). Often travels to book fairs to negotiate rights sales.

sales department

The department responsible for selling and marketing the publications produced by a publishing company, to bring about maximum sales and profit. Its tasks include identifying physical and digital outlets, ensuring orders and supplies of stock.

self-publishing services provider

Company that provides (for a fee) the complete range of activities to support a self-publishing author get their book into print or ebook. These include editorial, design, production, marketing and selling (i.e. all tasks carried out by a traditional publisher for their authors).

sensitivity reader

A person who assesses a manuscript with a particular issue of representation in mind, usually one that they have personal experience of.

sub-editor

A person who corrects and checks articles in a newspaper before they are printed.

translator

A person who translates copy, such as a manuscript, from one language into another.

typesetter

A person or company that 'sets' text and prepares the final layout of the page for printing. It can also now involve XML tagging for ebook creation.

vanity publisher

A publisher who charges an author a fee in order to publish his or her work for them and is not responsible for selling the product.

web content manager

A person who controls the type and quality of material shown on a website or blog and is responsible for how it is produced, organised, presented and updated.

wholesaler

A person or company that buys large quantities of books, magazines, etc from publishers, transports and stores them, and then sells them in smaller quantities to a range of retailers.

Glossary of publishing terms

advance

Money paid by a publisher to an author before a book is published which will be covered by future royalties. A publishing contract often allows an author an advance payment against future royalties; the author will not receive any further royalties until the amount paid in advance has been earned by sales of the book.

AI (advance information sheet)

A document that is put together by a publishing company to provide sales and marketing information about a book before publication and can be sent several months before publication to sales representatives. It typically includes details of the format and contents of the book, key selling points and information about intended readership, as well as information about promotions and reviews.

auction

An auction, usually arranged by a literary agent, takes place when multiple publishing houses are interested in acquiring a manuscript and bid against one another to secure the domestic or territorial rights.

B format

See **trade paperback**.

backlist

The range of books already published by a publisher, or indie author, that are still in print.

backmatter

See **endmatter**.

beta reader

A person who reads a book before it is published in order to mark errors and suggest improvements, typically without receiving payment.

BIC

A group of categories and subcategories that can be applied to a book to accurately describe it and to help place it in the market.

BISAC

Subject heading codes that categorise a book into topics and subtopics. Used by sellers to place your book in the correct section of their store or online listings.

blad (book layout and design)

A pre-publication sales and marketing tool. It is often a printed booklet that contains sample pages, images and front and back covers, which acts as a preview for promotional use or for sales and rights teams to show to potential retailers, customers or reviewers.

blurb

A short piece of writing or a paragraph that praises and promotes a book, which usually appears on the back or inside cover and may be used in sales and marketing material.

book club edition

An edition of a book specially printed and bound for a book club for sale to its members.

book proof

A bound set of uncorrected reading proofs. Traditionally publisher sales teams send pre-publication copies to reviewers.

brief

A set of instructions given to a designer about a project, such as a cover or internal design.

C format

A term most often used to describe a paperback edition published simultaneously with, and in the same format as, the hardback original.

co-edition

The publication of a book by two publishing companies in different countries, where the first company has originated the work and then sells sheets to the second publisher (or licenses the second publisher to reprint the book locally).

copy-editing

The editorial stage where an editor looks for spelling mistakes, grammatical errors and factual errors. They may rework sentences or paragraphs to add clarity to the work.

copyright

The legal right, which the creator of an original work has, to only allow copying of the work with permission and sometimes on payment of royalties or a copyright fee. An amendment to the Copyright, Designs and Patents Act (1988) states that in the UK most works are protected for 70 years from the creator's death. The copyright page (or imprint page) at the start of a book asserts copyright ownership and author identification.

crowdfunding

A publishing model that requires a book to surpass a financial goal before it can go into production. This money comes from pledges made by readers who back the project. In return, each backer usually receives a different level of acknowledgement (based on the amount pledged) from the author within the published book.

developmental edit

See **structural edit**.

double-page spread (DPS)

Two facing pages of an illustrated book.

edition

A quantity of books printed without changes to the content. A 'new edition' is a reprint of an existing title that incorporates substantial textual alterations. Originally one edition meant a single print run, though today an edition may consist of several separate printings, or impressions.

endmatter

Material at the end of the main body of a book which may be useful to the reader, including references, appendices, indexes and bibliography. Also called back matter.

ePub files

Digital book format compatible with all electronic devices and e-readers.

extent

The number of pages in a book.

first edition

The first print run of a book. It can occasionally gain secondhand value if either the book or its author become collectable.

folio

A large sheet of paper folded twice across the middle and trimmed to make four pages of a book. Also a page number.

frontlist

New books just published (generally in their first year of publication) or about to be published by a publisher. Promotion of the frontlist is heavy, and the frontlist carries most of a publisher's investment. On the other hand, a **backlist** which continues to sell is usually the most profitable part of a publisher's list.

frontmatter

The pages before the main chapters of a book with information about the publication and contents. This may include a copyright page, reviews, table of contents, etc.

HTML markup

Instructing the text that will appear on a webpage to look a certain way, such as bold (<b></b>) or italic (<i></i>). These markup indicators are often called tags.

imagery

The use of pictures, photographs, illustrations and other type of images within a book.

impression

A single print run of a book; all books in an impression are manufactured at the same time and are identical. A 'second impression' would be the second batch of copies to be printed and bound. The impression number is usually marked on the copyright/imprint page. There can be several impressions in an edition, all sharing the same **ISBN**.

imprint

The publisher's or printer's name which appears on the title page of a book or in the bibliographical details; a brand name under which a book is published within a larger publishing company, usually representing a specialised subject area.

inspection copy

A copy of a publication sent or given with time allowed for a decision to purchase or return it. In academic publishing, lecturers can request inspection copies to decide whether to make a book/textbook recommended reading or adopt it as a core textbook for their course.

internal(s)

Refers to the actual page design and layout of the pages that make up a book.

ISBN

International Standard Book Number. The ISBN is formed of 13 digits and is unique to a published title.

ISSN

International Standard Serial Number. An international system used on periodicals, magazines, learned journals, etc. The ISSN is formed of eight digits, which refer to the country in which the magazine is published and the title of the publication.

kill fee

A fee paid to a freelance writer for material written on assignment but not used, typically a percentage of the total payment.

manuscript

The pre-published version of an author's work, now usually submitted in electronic form.

metadata

Data that describes the content of a book to aid online discoverability – typically title, author, ISBN, key terms, description and other bibliographic information.

moral right

The right of people such as editors or illustrators to have some say in the publication of a work to which they have contributed, even if they do not own the copyright.

MS (*pl* MSS)

The abbreviation commonly used for 'manuscript'.

nom de plume

A pseudonym or 'pen-name' under which a writer may choose to publish their work instead of their real name.

out of print or o.p.

Relating to a book of which the publisher has no copies left and which is not going to be reprinted. Print-on-demand technology, however, means that a book can be kept 'in print' indefinitely.

page proofs

A set of designed and typeset pages in a book used to check the accuracy of typesetting and page layout before publication, and also as an advance promotional tool. These are provided in electronic form, such as a pdf.

paper engineering

The mechanics of creating novelty books and pop-ups.

pdf

Portable Document Format. A data file generated from PostScript that is platform-independent, application-independent and font-independent. Acrobat is Adobe's suite of software used to generate, edit and view pdf files.

point of sale (POS)

Merchandising display material provided by publishers to bookshops in order to promote particular titles.

prelims

The initial pages of a book, including the title page and table of contents, which precede the main text. Also called front matter.

pre-press

Before going to press, to be printed.

print on demand (POD)

The facility to print and bind a small number of books at short notice, without the need for a large print run, using digital technology. When an order comes through, a digital file of the book can be printed individually and automatically.

print run

The quantity of a book printed at one time in an **impression**.

public lending right

An author's right to receive from the public purse a payment for the loan of works from public libraries in the UK.

publisher's agreement

A contract between a publisher and the copyright holder, author, agent or another publisher which lays down the terms under which the publisher will publish the book for the copyright holder.

publishing contract

An agreement between a publisher and an author by which the author grants the publisher the right to publish the work against payment of a fee, usually in the form of a royalty.

query letter

A letter from an author to an agent pitching their book.

reading fee

Money paid to an editor for reading a manuscript and commenting on it. Reputable literary agents should never charge such a fee.

recto

Relating to the right-hand page of a book, usually given an odd number.

reprint

Copies of a book made from the original, but with a note in the publication details of the date of reprinting and possibly a new title page and cover design.

review copy

An advance copy of a book sent to magazines, newspapers or other media outlets (such as social media channels) for the purposes of review. A 'book proof' may be sent out before the final book is printed or published.

revises

If any corrections are made to your typeset proofs by the proofreader, a new round of proofs will be produced which are known as revises or revised proofs.

rights

The legal right to publish something such as a book, picture or extract from a text.

royalty

Money paid to a writer for the right to use their property, usually a percentage of sales or an agreed amount per sale.

royalty split

The way in which a royalty is divided between several authors or between author and illustrator.

royalty statement

A printed statement from a publisher showing how much royalty is due to an author.

sale or return

An arrangement between a retailer and publisher where any unwanted or unsold books can be returned to the publisher and the purchase costs reimbursed to the retailer. If no arrangement is in place, retailers cannot return unwanted or unsold stock to the publisher.

sans serif

A style of printing letters with all lines of equal thickness and no **serifs**. Sans faces are less easy to read in print than seriffed faces and they are rarely used for continuous text, although some magazines use them for text matter.

SEO (Search Engine Optimisation)

The process of using keywords in your content so that it can be found through search engines such as Google. Keyword can be used in metadata, titles or website URLs.

serialisation

Publication of a book in parts in a magazine or newspaper.

serif

A small decorative line added to letters in some fonts; a font that uses serifs, such as Times. The addition of serifs (1) keeps the letters apart while at the same time making it possible to link one letter to the next, and (2) makes the letters distinct, in particular the top parts which the reader recognises when reading.

slush pile

Unsolicited manuscripts which are sent to publishers or agents.

STM

The accepted abbreviation for the scientific, technical and medical publishing sector.

structural edit

Also known as **developmental edit**. This type of editing looks at the overall structure and content of your book. It should address story structure alongside plot, characters, and themes.

style sheet

A guide listing all the rules of house style for a publishing company which has to be followed by authors and editors.

submission guidelines

Instructions given by agents or publishers on how they wish to receive submissions from authors.

subscription sale or 'sub'

Sales of a title to booksellers in advance of publication, and orders taken from wholesalers and retailers to be supplied by the publisher shortly before the publication date.

subsidiary rights

Rights other than the right to publish a book in its first form, e.g. paperback rights; rights to adapt the book; rights to serialise it in a magazine; film and TV rights; audio, ebook, foreign and translation rights.

sub-title

A secondary or subordinate title of a published work providing additional information about its content. More commonly found in works of non-fiction.

synopsis

A concise plot summary of a manuscript (usually one side of A4) that covers the major plot points, narrative arcs and characters.

territory

Areas of the world where the publisher has the rights to publish or can make foreign rights deals.

Thema

A globally applicable subject classification system for books to aid the merchandising and discoverability of the title. This type of classification can be used alongside **BIC**.

trade discount

A reduction in price given to a customer in the same trade, as by a publisher to another publisher or to a bookseller.

trade paperback (B format)

A paperback edition of a book that is superior in production quality to, and larger than, a mass-market paperback edition.

trim size or trimmed size

The measurements of a page of a book after it has been cut, or of a sheet of paper after it has been cut to size.

type specification (spec)

A brief created by the design department of a publishing house for how a book should be typeset.

typeface

A set of characters that share a distinctive and consistent design. Typefaces come in families of different weights, e.g. Helvetica Roman, Helvetica Italic, Bold, Bold Italic, etc. Hundreds of typefaces exist and new ones are still being designed. Today, 'font' is often used synonymously with 'typeface' though originally font meant the characters were all the same size, e.g. Helvetica Italic 11 point.

typescript

The final draft of a book. This unedited text is usually an electronic Word file. The term 'typescript' (abbreviated TS or ts) is synonymous with 'manuscript' (abbreviated MS or ms; plural is MSS or mss).

See also...

- *Who's who in publishing*, page 663

typographic error (typo)

A mistake made when keying text or typesetting.

typography

The art and technique of arranging type.

unsolicited manuscript

An unpublished manuscript sent to a publisher without having been commissioned or requested.

USP

Unique selling point. A distinctive quality or feature of a book that distinguishes it within the market.

verso

The left-hand page of a book, usually given an even number.

voice casting

The process of finding a suitable voice artist to narrate audiobooks.

volume rights

The right to publish the work in hardback, paperback or ebook.

XML tagging

Inserting tags into the text that can allow it to be converted for ebooks or for use in electronic formats.

YA

A term used within children's publishing to refer to books written to appeal to an audience of teenagers or young adults.

Software for writers

This is a selection of software programmes and applications designed to enhance your writing experience and aid productivity. Each product has its own selection of features; we recommend you check the cost carefully, as many involve a fixed-term subscription or licence fee but do also offer free trials.

WRITING SOFTWARE

Aeon Timeline
website https://timeline.app
£47.99 one-off fee

Includes tools and features to help you understand characters, avoid plot holes and inconsistencies, and visualise your story in new ways.

Atticus
website www.atticus.io
$147 one-off fee (exc. tax)

Allows authors to use the same platform for writing and formatting; writing can also be imported. A word counter and goal tracker allow you to monitor your progress.

Bear
website https://bear.app
Free; pro $1.49 monthly; $14.99 p.a.

A note-taking tool that allows you to link notes to create an outline and apply hashtags to organise notes, and provides a focus feature to aid concentration.

Bibisco
website https://bibisco.com
Community edition: free; supporters edition: pay what you want

Designed to allow a writer to focus on their characters and develop rounded and complex narratives, with particular emphasis on the manuscript's geographical, temporal and social context.

Dabble
website www.dabblewriter.com
From $10 monthly; from $72 p.a.

Gives writers the freedom to plot, write and edit on a desktop, in a browser or offline, and automatically syncs all versions across your devices. Features include plot grids, progress tracking and goal setting.

Evernote
website https://evernote.com
Free; tiered from £5.75 monthly

Note-taking tool which allows you to sync notes across devices, identify tasks and assign schedules, and mark-up webpages and add them to your notes along with documents, images, videos and audio files.

FocusWriter
website https://gottcode.org/focuswriter
Free

Provides a simple and distraction-free writing environment with a hide-away interface, so you can focus solely on your writing.

MasterWriter
website https://masterwriter.com
$9.95 monthly; $99.95 p.a.

An extensive catalogue of words and phrases that can help improve and enrich the vocabulary in your writing. The search function will return synonyms, words used in similar contexts, common phrases, rhymes and figures of speech.

Novel Factory
website www.novel-software.com
From $75 p.a.

Plan your book with confidence by using the Roadmap feature which provides tools and structures to suit your needs. Includes detailed character overviews including biographies and images, as well as scene tabs and writing statistics about your work.

Novel Suite
website www.novelsuite.com/novel-writing-software
$12 monthly; $99 p.a.

An all-in-one novel writing application that can be used across all devices. Manage multiple books using character profiles, scene outlines and writing template tools.

Novelize
website www.getnovelize.com
$9 monthly; $65 p.a.

Developed for fiction writers, this web-based writing app means you can work on your book anywhere on any device. Keep your research in one place in the notebook displayed on the writing screen and track your progress.

NovelPad
website https://novelpad.co
$15 monthly; $120 p.a.

A writing and editing application that provides plot boards, scene cards and a consistency checker which filters your writing for specific characters and plot lines.

Obsidian

website https://obsidian.md
Free

A mapping structure which helps writers to make new connections and identify relationships between ideas and key terms in order to create a coherent narrative.

Plottr

website https://plottr.com
$25 p.a.; $99 one-off fee

Created to aid book planning and story mapping. Tracks characters and plots for easy reference, provides templates for plot outlining and visualisation, and creates an automated outline of your writing.

Scrivener

website www.literatureandlatte.com/scrivener/overview
From £42.49 one-off fee

Tailored for long writing projects with everything you need housed in one place; it is a typewriter, ring binder and scrapbook, allowing you to optimise your digital workspace.

SmartEdit Writer

website www.smart-edit.com/Writer
Free

Organically build your book one scene or one chapter at a time, then drag and drop to arrange these on your document tree. Store your research images, URLs and notes alongside work for easy access, then export your manuscript into a single Word document when ready.

Ulysses

website https://ulysses.app
$5.99 monthly; $39.99 p.a.

Document management for all writing projects, with flexible export options including pdf, Word, ebook and HTML which are appropriately formatted and styled.

WriteItNow

website www.ravensheadservices.com
From $59.95 one-off fee

Includes sophisticated world-building features to create detailed and complex settings and characters. Recommends suitable names for your characters based on the historical period and geographical setting of your story.

EDITING SOFTWARE

After the Deadline

website www.afterthedeadline.com
Free

A context-driven grammar and spelling checker, it underlines potential issues and gives a suggestion with an explanation of how you can rectify the error.

AutoCrit

website www.autocrit.com
Free; pro from $30 monthly

Analyses your entire manuscript and suggests insightful improvements in the form of an individual summary report, showing where your strengths and weaknesses lie.

Ginger

website www.gingersoftware.com
$13.99 monthly; $84 p.a.

Combines a grammar checker with tools to improve your writing, including a synonym suggester and text rephrasing.

Grammarly

website www.grammarly.com
Free; premium from £10 monthly

Provides accurate and context-specific suggestions when the application detects grammar, spelling, punctuation, word choice and style mistakes in your writing.

Hemingway Editor

website https:/hemingwayapp.com
$19.99 one-off fee

Helps you write with clarity and confidence. This application is like a spellchecker but for style. It will highlight any areas that need tightening up by identifying adverbs, passive voice, and uninspiring or over-complicated words.

iA Writer

website https://ia.net/writer
From $29.99 one-off fee

Provides tools to help you improve your writing: syntax colour-coding identifies repetitive and extraneous text, text blocking allowing moving whole sections of text, and a style checker highlights cliches and weak phrases.

Linguix

website https://linguix.com
Free; pro $60 p.a.; $85 one-off fee

Combines a range of editing tools: checks your grammar, suggests ways to paraphrase your writing to make it more succinct and aids with style and flow for non-native English writers.

PerfectIt

website https://intelligentediting.com
From £76 p.a.

Proofreading software which checks consistency, for example by applying style rules and highlighting undefined abbreviations.

ProWritingAid

website https://prowritingaid.com
Free; pro from £30 monthly; £120 p.a.; £399 one-off fee

For use via the web, or as an add-on to word processing software, it analyses your work for a multitude of potential issues such as passive voice, clichés, missing dialogue tags and pace, and suggests how you can rectify any errors or make style improvements.

SmartEdit

website www.smart-edit.com
$77 one-off fee; pro $139 one-off fee

Sits inside Microsoft Word and runs 25 individual checks whilst you work, flagging areas that need attention, including highlighting repeated words, listing adverbs and foreign phrases used and identifying possible misused words.

Vellum

website https://vellum.pub
£169.99 (ebook only); £209.99 (ebook and print)

Print and ebook formatting package that provides templates for front and endmatter, styles pages and generates versions for different platforms. Allows the user to update ebooks after they have been published. Only available for Mac.

WordRake

website www.wordrake.com
$17 monthly; $129 p.a.

When you click the 'rake' button in Microsoft Word, the text editor will read your document and suggest edits to tighten and add clarity to your work.

Wordtune

website www.wordtune.com
Free; premium from $9.99 monthly

An extension which can be added to browsers, email providers, social media and Microsoft Word. Provides a rephrasing and rewriting tool and suggests ways to shorten sentences, expand your ideas and alter your tone.

Libraries

Libraries are not just repositories for books and a source of reference. They provide an increasing range of different services, using a multitude of media to reach more diverse audiences. Countless writers attest to the importance of libraries in shaping and helping develop their creative ambitions. Local libraries are a good source of information about the writing process and how to get published. They often run or host author events, reading groups and creative writing classes.

TYPES OF LIBRARIES

• **Public libraries** are accessible to the general population and are usually funded by a local or district council. They typically offer a mix of lending and reference facilities. Public libraries are distinct from research libraries, subscription libraries and other specialist libraries in terms of their funding and access, but may offer some of the same facilities to visitors. Public library services are facing financial challenges and cuts to funding, so many library authorities are looking for new approaches to working with communities in order to build sustainable library services for the future.
• A list of **community libraries** in the UK can be found at www.publiclibrariesnews.com.
• An **academic library** is usually affiliated to an educational institution and primarily serves the students and faculty of that institution. Many are accessible to the public.
• A **subscription library** is one that is funded via membership or endowments. Access is often restricted to members but membership is sometimes extended to groups who are non-members, such as students.
• Many libraries belong to the Association of Independent Libraries and a list of members can be found on the Association's website (see below).
• Consult this website to find your nearest and local UK public libraries: www.gov.uk/local-library-services.

SOME OF THE BEST

Britain has such a wealth of comprehensive and historic libraries that a full list of them is not possible in this publication. Here is just a small selection of public libraries with outstanding collections in the UK.

Barbican Library

Barbican Centre, Silk Street, London EC2Y 8DS
tel 020-7638 0569
email barbicanlib@cityoflondon.gov.uk
website www.barbican.org.uk/your-visit/during-your-visit/library
Facebook www.facebook.com/Barbicanlibrary
Twitter @barbicanlib

The largest of London's lending libraries with a strong arts and music section, a London collection, literature events programme and reading groups.

Belfast Central Library

Royal Avenue, Belfast BT1 1EA
tel 028-9050 9150
email belfast.central@librariesni.org.uk
website www.librariesni.org.uk/libraries/greater-belfast/belfast-central-library
Facebook www.facebook.com/BelfastCentralLibrary
Twitter @BelfastCentLib

The library's reference library holds the greatest number of titles in Northern Ireland. The library houses a number of special collections including a digital film archive and the Northern Ireland Music Archive.

Library of Birmingham

Centenary Square, Broad Street, Birmingham B1 2ND
tel 0121 242 4242
email enquiries@libraryofbirmingham.com
website www.birmingham.gov.uk/info/50132/visiting_the_library_of_birmingham
Facebook www.facebook.com/libraryofbirmingham
Twitter @LibraryofBham
Instagram @the_library_of_birmingham

The largest public library in the UK and the largest regional library in Europe. Houses locally relevant collections of archives, photography and rare books. Facilities include an art gallery space. It is also home to the BFI Mediatheque, providing free access to the National Film Archive.

Bristol Central Library

Deanery Road, City Centre, Bristol BS1 5TL
tel 0117 903 7250
email bristol.library.service@bristol.gov.uk
website www.bristol.gov.uk/libraries-archives/central-library

Includes collections related to Bristol's slave trade, 19th-century travel and art. An appointment must be made by email or phone five working days in advance to view rare items.

Canterbury Library

18 High Street, Canterbury, Kent CT1 2RA
tel 03000 413131
email canterburylibrary@kent.gov.uk
website www.kent.gov.uk/libs

The main library for the city of Canterbury. Canterbury Library was the first publicly funded library in Great Britain, through innovative interpretation of the Museums Act 1845 for provision of a museum of arts and science. It is now part of a large network of public libraries managed by Kent County Council. For services see website.

Cardiff Central Library

The Hayes, Cardiff CF10 1FL
tel 029-2038 2166
email centrallibrary@cardiff.gov.uk
website https://cardiffhubs.co.uk/hub/central-library-hub/

The largest public library in Wales, opened in 2009, houses 90,000 books, 10,000 of which are in Welsh.

Leeds Library

18 Commercial Street, Leeds LS1 6AL
tel 0113 245 3071
email enquiries@theleedslibrary.org.uk
website www.theleedslibrary.org.uk
Facebook www.facebook.com/leedslibrary
Twitter @theleedslibrary

Founded in 1768 as a proprietary subscription library, it is now the oldest surviving example of this sort of library in the UK. It includes specialist collections in travel, topography, biography, history and literature. There are long runs of periodicals, popular novels, children's books, and Civil War pamphlets and Reformation Tracts. About 1,500 new books and audio/visual items are added every year.

Liverpool Central Library

William Brown Street, Liverpool L3 8EW
tel 0151 233 3069
email refbt.central.library@liverpool.gov.uk
website https://liverpool.gov.uk/libraries/find-a-library/central-library/

The collection includes 15,000 rare books, some of which date back to the 13th century.

London Library

14 St James's Square, London SW1Y 4LG
tel 020-7766 4700
email reception@londonlibrary.co.uk
website www.londonlibrary.co.uk
Facebook www.facebook.com/thelondonlibrary
Twitter @thelondonlib

A subscription lending library containing more than one million books and periodicals in over 50 languages, the collection includes works from the 16th century to the latest publications in print and electronic form. Over 6,000 new books are added each year. Membership is open to all. The library's emerging writers' programme offers writers, in all genres, one year's free membership of The London Library and includes writing development masterclasses, literary networking opportunities, peer support and guidance in use of the Library's resources. For details: www.londonlibrary.co.uk/about-us/ll-emerging-writers.

Manchester Central Library

St Peter's Square, Manchester M2 5PD
tel 0161 234 1983
email libraries@manchester.gov.uk
website www.manchester.gov.uk/centrallibrary

Manchester's main library, the second biggest public lending library in the UK, houses a number of specialist collections such as Elizabeth Gaskell, Bellot Chinese and Thomas Penson De Quincey collections.

Mitchell Library

North Street, Glasgow G3 7DN
tel 0141 287 2999
email libraries@glasgowlife.org.uk
website www.glasgowlife.org.uk/libraries/venues/the-mitchell-library
Facebook www.facebook.com/GlasgowLibraries
Twitter @GlasgowLib

One of the largest public reference library in Europe housing almost two million volumes. Holds an unrivalled collection of material relating to the city of Glasgow. The archives are open Tuesday, Wednesday and Thursday. To contact the special collections team, email specialcollections@glasgowlife.org.uk or phone 0141 287 2988.

Newcastle City Library

Charles Avison Building, 33 Newbridge Street West, Newcastle upon Tyne NE1 8AX
tel 0191 277 4100
email information@newcastle.gov.uk
website www.newcastle.gov.uk/services/libraries-culture/your-libraries/city-library-community-hub
Facebook www.facebook.com/NewcastleLibraries
Twitter @ToonLibraries

Newcastle's main public library includes a café, exhibition spaces, a rare books and watercolours collection, a viewing deck and six floors of books.

Norfolk and Norwich Millennium Library

The Forum, Millennium Plain, Norwich NR2 1AW
email libraries@norfolk.gov.uk
website www.norfolk.gov.uk/libraries-local-history-and-archives/libraries
Twitter @MillenniumLib

As well as holding tens of thousands of books, the Norfolk and Norwich Millennium Library hosts regular events with the aim of engaging the local community, including board game afternoons and expert advice sessions.

Westminster Reference Library

35 St Martin's Street, London WC2H 7HP
tel 020-7641 6200 (press 2)
email referencelibrarywc2@westminster.gov.uk
website www.westminster.gov.uk/westminster-reference-library

Twitter @WCClibraries

Specialist public reference library with collections in performing arts and art and design. Hosts regular and varied events, includes an exhibition space and a Business Information Point. Also has a range of business resources including market research, company and legal databases. Includes collection from Westminster Music Library.

LIBRARIES OF LEGAL DEPOSIT IN THE UK AND IRELAND

A library of legal deposit is a library that has the power to request (at no charge) a copy of anything published in the UK. There are six legal deposit libraries in the UK and Ireland. To obtain a copy of a book, five out of the six legal deposit libraries must make a request in writing to a publisher within one year of publication of a book, newspaper or journal. Different rules apply to the British Library in that all UK libraries and Republic of Ireland publishers have a legal responsibility to send a copy of each of their publications to the library, without a written request being made. The British Library is the only legal deposit library with its own Legal Deposit Office. Since April 2013, legal deposit also covers material published digitally and online, so that the legal deposit libraries can provide a national archive of the UK's non-print published material, such as websites, blogs, e-journals and CDs.

Agency for the Legal Deposit Libraries (ALDL)

Unit 21 Marnin Way, Edinburgh EH12 9GD
tel 0131 334 2833
email publisher.enquiries@legaldeposit.org.uk
website www.legaldeposit.org.uk

The ALDL requests and receives copies of publications for distribution to five major libraries (not the British Library). It is maintained by five legal deposit libraries and ensures that they receive legal deposit copies of British and Irish publications. The agency must request copies on behalf of the libraries within 12 months of the date of publication. On receiving such a request, a publisher must supply a copy for each of the requesting libraries under the terms of the Legal Deposit Libraries Act 2003 (UK) and the Copyright and Related Rights Act 2000 (Ireland).

Bodleian Libraries of the University of Oxford

Broad Street, Oxford OX1 3BG
tel (01865) 277162
email reader.services@bodleian.ox.ac.uk
website www.bodleian.ox.ac.uk
Facebook www.facebook.com/bodleianlibraries
Twitter @bodleianlibs

With over 13 million items and including 80,000 e-journals and vast quantities of materials in many other formats, the Bodleian Libraries together form the second-largest library in the UK after the British Library, and is the main reference library of Oxford University. It is one of the oldest libraries in Europe. It holds special collections in classics and ancient history, English, history, history of science, local history, philosophy, reference, theology and patristics.

The British Library

St Pancras Building, 96 Euston Road,
London NW1 2DB
tel 0330 333 1144 (switchboard)
Legal Deposit Office: The British Library, Boston Spa,
Wetherby, West Yorkshire LS23 7BQ
tel (01937) 546268
email legal-deposit-books@bl.uk
website www.bl.uk
Facebook www.facebook.com/britishlibrary
Twitter @britishlibrary

The British Library holds books, journals, newspapers, sound recordings, patents, original manuscripts, maps, online images and texts, plays, digital books, and poet and author recordings. The collection holds over 200 million published items from across the globe. The special collections and rare items include Shakespeare's first folio, the Magna Carta dated 1215, Lindisfarne Gospels from circa 700 and Charles Darwin's Natural Selection letter.

Cambridge University Library

West Road, Cambridge CB3 9DR
tel (01223) 333000
email library@lib.cam.ac.uk
website www.lib.cam.ac.uk

Cambridge University Library houses its own collection and also comprises four other libraries within the university. The library dates back to the 15th century and now has a collection of over eight million books and other items. It is the only legal deposit library that keeps a large percentage of its books on open access. To visit the rare books collection email: rarebooks@lib.cam.ac.uk.

National Library of Scotland

George IV Bridge, Edinburgh EH1 1EW
tel 0131 623 3700
email enquiries@nls.uk
website www.nls.uk
Facebook www.facebook.com/
NationalLibraryOfScotland
Twitter @natlibscot

The National Library of Scotland holds over 24 million items. It is the world's central source for research relating to Scotland and the Scots. The library also holds a copy of the Gutenberg Bible, a First Folio of Shakespeare, and the last letter written by Mary Queen of Scots. It contains important items relating to Jane Austen, Lord Byron and Sir Arthur Conan Doyle.

National Library of Wales

Aberystwyth, Ceredigion SY23 3BU
tel (01970) 632800
email gofyn@llgc.org.uk
website www.library.wales
Facebook www.facebook.com/llgcymranlwales/
Twitter @nlwales

The National Library of Wales was established in 1907 and holds 6.5 million books and newspapers, including many important works such as the first book printed in Welsh and the first Welsh translation of the Bible.

Trinity College Library Dublin

College Green, Dublin 2, Republic of Ireland
tel +353 (0)1 896 1127
email library@tcd.ie
website www.tcd.ie/library
Facebook www.facebook.com/tcdlibrary
Twitter @tcdlibrary

Trinity College Library is the largest library in Ireland and is home to the *Book of Kells* – two of the four volumes are on permanent public display. The library houses sound recordings, maps, databases, and a digital collection. Currently it has over seven million printed volumes with extensive collections of journals, manuscripts, maps and music reflecting over 400 years of academic development.

DESIGNATED OUTSTANDING COLLECTIONS

The Designated Outstanding Collections scheme was established in 1997 by the Museums and Galleries Commission to identify collections of national and international importance in non-national museums and galleries. In 2005 the scheme was extended to include libraries and archives. The scheme is now administered by Arts Council England and there are currently 154 Designated Outstanding Collections in England. To find out if there is a Designated Outstanding Collection library near you, visit the Designation section of the Arts Council website (www.artscouncil.org.uk/designated-collections).

SPECIALIST LIBRARIES IN THE UK

Writers often need access to specialised information sources in order to research their work. The following are a sample of specialist libraries in the UK. In addition to the libraries listed below, many university libraries hold special collections which are accessible to the public, usually by appointment. Check individual university library websites for details.

BBC Written Archives Centre

Peppard Road, Caversham Park, Reading RG4 8TS
tel 020-8008 5661
email heritage@bbc.co.uk
website www.bbc.co.uk/archive/written-archives-centre-visiting-the-archive/zfqpwty

Home of the BBC's written records. Holds thousands of files, scripts and working papers, dating from the BBC's formation in 1922, together with information about past programmes and the history of broadcasting. Does not have recordings or information about current programmes. Accredited students or staff members at a higher education institution, writers commissioned for a publication or those working towards commercial projects can arrange a visit for research purposes. By appointment only, between 10am to 5.00pm, Wednesday to Friday.

BFI National Archive and Reuben Library

Belvedere Road, South Bank, London SE1 8XT
tel 020-7255 1444
email library@bfi.org.uk
website www.bfi.org.uk/archive-collections
Facebook www.facebook.com/BritishFilmInstitute
Twitter @BFI

Established in 1933, the BFI National Archive is one of the largest film and television collections anywhere. Dating from the earliest days of film to the 21st century, it contains nearly a million titles. The archive holds over 800,000 items of film – including television programmes, documentaries, newsreels, as well as educational and training films – and is updated daily. The majority of the collection is British material but it also features internationally significant holdings. The Archive also collects films which feature key British actors and the work of British directors. Using the latest preservation methods, the BFI cares for a variety of often obsolete formats. The BFI Reuben Library at BFI Southbank is home to a huge collection of books, journals, documents and audio recordings about the world of film and television.

British Library for Development Studies (BLDS)

Institute of Development Studies at the University of Sussex, Brighton BN1 9RE
tel (01273) 678163
email blds@ids.ac.uk
website https://guides.lib.sussex.ac.uk/

Europe's largest research collection on economic and social change in developing countries.

British Newspaper Archive

tel (01382) 210100
website www.britishnewspaperarchive.co.uk
Facebook www.facebook.com/
TheBritishNewspaperArchive

Twitter @BNArchive

The British Newspaper Archive gives access to over three million historical local, national and regional newspaper pages from across the UK and Ireland. The Archive is currently in partnership with the British Library and findmypast.co.uk to digitise up to nearly 63 million newspaper pages from the British Library's vast collection.

Caird Library and Archive

Greenwich, London SE10 9NF
tel 020-8312 6516
email library@rmg.co.uk
website www.rmg.co.uk/collections/caird-library

Specialist maritime research library at the National Maritime Museum in Greenwich.

Catholic National Library

Centre for Catholic Studies,
Department of Theology and Religion,
University of Durham, Abbey House, Palace Green,
Durham DH1 3RS
tel 0191 334 1656
email ccs.admin@durham.ac.uk
website www.dur.ac.uk/theology.religion/ccs

Holds over 70,000 books, pamphlets and periodicals on theology, spirituality and related subjects, biography and history.

Chained Library

Hereford Cathedral Library and Archives,
Hereford Cathedral, 5 College Cloisters,
Cathedral Close, Hereford HR1 2NG
tel (01432) 374200
email library@herefordcathedral.org
website www.herefordcathedral.org/chained-library

Hereford Cathedral has housed a collection of books accessible to the public from the 12th century. The chaining of books was a widespread security system in European libraries from the Middle Ages to the 18th century; this is the largest to survive with all its chains, rods and locks intact. The library is open Tuesday, Wednesday and Thursday 10am to 4pm and the first Saturday in each month 10am until 1pm.

Chawton House Library

Chawton, Alton, Hants. GU34 1SJ
tel (01420) 541010
email info@chawton.net
website https://chawtonhouse.org/the-library/using-the-library/
Facebook www.facebook.com/ChawtonHouse
Twitter @ChawtonHouse

The collection focuses on women's writing in English from 1600 to 1830 and includes some manuscripts. The library also houses the Knight Collection, which is the private library belonging to the Knight family, the owners of Chawton House for over 400 years.

Chetham's Library

Long Milgate, Manchester M3 1SB
tel 0161 834 7961
email fwilde@chethams.org.uk
website https://library.chethams.com
Facebook www.facebook.com/chethamslibrary
Twitter @chelthamslibrary

Founded in 1653, this is the oldest public library in the English-speaking world. In addition to a collection of early printed books, it includes manuscript diaries, letters and deeds, prints, paintings and glass lantern slides. Use of the library is free, no membership or reader's ticket is required. Researchers need a prior appointment by phone or email (above) at least one working day in advance to consult library material.

Commonwealth Library and Archives

Commonwealth Secretariat, Marlborough House,
Pall Mall, London SW1Y 5HX
tel 020-7747 6164 (librarian) / 020-7747 6167
(archivist)
email library@commonwealth.int
website https://thecommonwealth.org/library-and-archives
Facebook www.facebook.com/commonwealthsec
Twitter @commonwealthsec

Collection covers politics and international relations, economics, education, health, gender, environment and management. Holds a comprehensive collection of Commonwealth Secretariat publications and its archives. Opening hours are Monday to Friday from 10am to 4.45pm.

Crafts Council Research Library

Crafts Council, 44A Pentonville Road,
London N1 9BY
tel 020-7806 2500
email reception@craftscouncil.org.uk
website www.craftscouncil.org.uk
Facebook www.facebook.com/CraftsCouncilUK/
Twitter @CraftsCouncilUK

This is a reference library which normally opens to the public two days a week by appointment. Houses a large collection of contemporary craft books and catalogues as well as journals. Covers ceramics, textiles, jewellery, fashion accessories and paper.

The Dana Research Centre and Library

165 Queens Gate, London SW7 5HD
tel 020-7942 4242
email smlinfo@sciencemuseum.ac.uk
website www.sciencemuseum.org.uk/researchers/dana-research-centre-and-library
Facebook www.facebook.com/sciencemuseumlondon
Twitter @sciencemuseum

Allows access to around 500,000 items covering museum studies, the history and biography of science technology and medicine and the philosophical and

Resources for writers

social aspects of these subjects. Open Thursdays and Fridays 11am until 5pm.

University of Exeter Library, Special Collections
Old Library, Prince of Wales Road, Exeter EX4 4SB
tel (01392) 263867
email libspc@exeter.ac.uk
website www.exeter.ac.uk/departments/library/special-collections

Bill Douglas Cinema Museum is home to one of the largest collections of material relating to the moving image in Britain. It is both an accredited public museum and an academic research facility and we hold a collection of over 85,000 items. Special collections include the Agatha Christie archive, which houses correspondence between Agatha Christie and Edmund Cork, between Cork and American literary agent, Harold Ober, and other interested parties. There are between 5,000-6,000 letters in the collection.

Feminist Library
The Sojourner Truth Community Centre,
161 Sumner Rd, Peckham, London SE15 6JL
tel 020-7261 0879
email admin@feministlibrary.co.uk
website www.feministlibrary.co.uk
Facebook www.facebook.co/feministlibrary
Twitter @feministlibrary

The Feminist Library holds a large archive collection of women's liberation movement literature, particularly second-wave materials dating from the late 1960s to the 1990s.

Gladstone's Library
Church Lane, Hawarden, Flintshire CH5 3DF
tel (01244) 532350
email enquiries@gladlib.org
website www.gladstoneslibrary.org

Britain's first residential library, the building houses 20,000 of Gladstone's books. Since the library opened in 1902, it has continued to acquire books specialising in those subjects that were of most interest to Gladstone: theology, history, philosophy, classics, art and literature. Researchers seeking an extended period of quiet study can stay in one of 26 rooms in the Gothic stone building.

Goethe-Institut London Library
50 Princes Gate, Exhibition Road, London SW7 2PH
tel 020-7596 4040
email library@london.goethe.org
email info-london@goethe.org
website https://www.goethe.de/ins/gb/en/sta/lon/bi2.html
Facebook www.facebook.com/goethe.institut.london
Twitter @GI_London1

Specialises in German literature, especially contemporary fiction and drama, film DVDs and books/audiovisual material on German culture and recent history. The e-library gives access to Goethe Institut libraries in the UK, Ireland and the Netherlands and allows electronic downloading of ebooks, e-audiobooks and electronic newspapers for a predetermined period of time.

Guildhall Library
Aldermanbury, London EC2V 7HH
tel 020-7332 1868/1870
email guildhall.library@cityoflondon.gov.uk
website https://www.cityoflondon.gov.uk/things-to-do/history-and-heritage/guildhall-library
Twitter @GuildhallLib

Books collection comprises over 200,000 titles dating from the 15th century to the 21st century and includes books, pamphlets, periodicals, trade directories and poll books. Covers all aspects of life in London, past and present.

Imperial War Museum Archive and Reading Room
IWM London, Lambeth Road, London SE1 6HZ
researchroom@iwm.org.uk
website www.iwm.org.uk/research/research-facilities
Facebook www.facebook.com/iwm.london
Twitter @I_W_M

Responsible for a unique national reference library with over 150,000 items on 20th- and 21st-century conflict involving British and Commonwealth countries. Along with material on military units and campaign histories, contains biographies, manuals, items relating to the economic, social and cultural aspects of war, journals, newspapers, ephemera, propaganda and digital resources. The Archive and Research Room is open three days a week (Wednesdays, Thursdays and Fridays 10am until 3pm) to nine researchers who can order up to ten items at a time per day.

Lambeth Palace Library
15 Lambeth Palace Road, London SE1 7JT
tel 020-7898 1400
email archives@churchofengland.org
website www.lambethpalacelibrary.org
Facebook www.facebook.com/LambethPalaceLibrary
Twitter @lampallib

The historic library of the Archbishops of Canterbury and the principal library and record office for the Church of England. The library opens one Saturday every month, 10am to 5pm. Check website for details. To book a spot in the reading room please fill out the contact form on the website.

The Library of the Society of Friends
Friends House, 173–177 Euston Road,
London NW1 2BJ
tel 020-7663 1135

email library@quaker.org.uk
website www.quaker.org.uk/resources/library/visit-
the-library

The library has over 80,000 books and pamphlets, including a unique collection of 17th-century Quaker and anti-Quaker material. Open to researchers Tuesdays, Wednesdays and Thursdays 10am to 5pm (with a lunchbreak 1pm to 2pm). To be able to use a desk space and work with collection material you need to register and book an appointment. Please email library@quaker.org.uk.

Linen Hall Library

17 Donegall Square North, Belfast BT1 5GB
tel 028-9032 1707
email info@linenhall.com
website www.linenhall.com
Facebook www.facebook.com/LinenHallLibraryBelfast
Twitter @thelinenhall

Renowned for its Irish and Local Studies Collection, including early Belfast and Ulster printed books and 350,000 items in the Northern Ireland Political Collection (NIPC). Also large General Lending Collection. Open Monday to Friday, 9.30am to 5.30pm.

National Art Library

Victoria & Albert Museum, Cromwell Road, London SW7 2RL
tel 020-7942 2000
email hello@vam.ac.uk
website www.vam.ac.uk/info/national-art-library
Facebook www.facebook.com/
victoriaandalbertmuseum
Twitter @V_and_A

Houses around one million books but also holds prints, drawings, paintings, photographs, ceramics and glass, textiles and fashion, furniture, design, metalwork and sculpture. The collections range from medieval manuscripts to contemporary artists' books and armorial bindings to comics and graphic novels. Anyone can register to visit its collection, which focuses on the decorative arts in the museum's collection. Currently open Tuesdays, Wednesdays and Thursdays from 11am until 5pm.

Natural History Museum Library and Information Services

Cromwell Road, London SW7 5BD
tel 020-7942 5000 (switchboard)/ 020-7942 5460 (archives/general library) / 020-7942 6156 (ornithology library, Tring)
email library@nhm.ac.uk
website www.nhm.ac.uk/research-curation/science-facilities/library
Facebook www.facebook.com/naturalhistorymuseum
Twitter @NHM_Library

Online catalogue contains all library material acquired since 1989 and about 80% of earlier items. The library collection contains more than one million items. For contact and opening times see website.

RNIB National Library Service

PO Box 173, Peterborough PE2 6WS
tel 0303 123 9999 (library); 0300 303 8313 (bookshare)
email library@rnib.org.uk
website https://readingservices.rnib.org.uk;
www.rnibbookshare.org/cms
Facebook www.facebook.com/rnibuk
Twitter @RNIB

The largest specialist library for readers with sight loss in the UK. It offers a comprehensive range of books and accessible information for children and adults in braille and Talking Books. Audio books are also available for download. RNIB Bookshare opens up the world of reading in education for learners with a print-disability, including those with dyslexia or who are blind or partially sighted.

John Rylands Research Institute and Library

150 Deansgate, Manchester M3 3EH
tel 0161 306 0555
email uml.special-collections@manchester.ac.uk
website www.library.manchester.ac.uk/rylands/
Facebook www.facebook.com/JohnRylandsLibrary
Twitter @UoMLibrary

The library is part of the University of Manchester but is open to the public. Home to 1.4 million items, including books, manuscripts, maps, artworks and objects.

Tate Library & Archive

Tate Britain, Millbank, London SW1P 4RG
tel 020-7887 8838
email reading.rooms@tate.org.uk
website www.tate.org.uk/visit/tate-britain/library-archive-reading-rooms/library

Located at Tate Britain, broadly covers those areas in which the Tate collects. The library include over 115,000 books and monographs, 175,000 recent and historic exhibition catalogues, over 10,000 artists' books, zines and serials, 3,000 print and e-journals, printed ephemera, audio and video recordings, as well as microfilm and microfiche collections and half a million press cuttings.

Wales Broadcast Library

The National Library of Wales, Aberystwyth, Ceredigion SY23 3BU
tel (01970) 6329333
email enquiry@llgc.org.uk
website www.library.wales/national-broadcast-archive

The National Library of Wales is home to the Wales Broadcast Library. There are currently 160,000 broadcasts available, and this number is expected to increase by 2026 to more than half a million. To use the Wales Broadcast Library, visitors must register first and then they will be able to view or listen to the broadcasts at the Library's Broadcast Archive Centre.

Wellcome Library

Wellcome Collection, 183 Euston Road, London NW1 2BE
tel 020-7611 8722
email library@wellcome.ac.uk
website http://wellcomelibrary.org/
Facebook www.facebook.com/Wellcomelibrary/
Twitter @WellcomeLibrary

One of the world's major resources for the study of medical history. Also houses an expanding collection of material relating to contemporary medicine and biomedical science in society.

Moving Image and Sound Collections
tel 020-7611 8899
email collections@wellcome.ac.uk

Physical materials in the collection are held in closed stores, and can be requested through the catalogue to view or listen to in the Library.

Wellcome Images
tel 020-7611 8348
email images@wellcome.ac.uk
Facebook www.facebook.com/WellcomeImages
Twitter @wellcomeimages

Collection of images, including artworks and photographs, from the library of the Wellcome Collection which have been collected over several decades.

Westminster Music Library and Archives

35 St Martin's Street, Westminster, London WC2H 7HP
tel 020-7641 6200
email musiclibrary@westminster.gov.uk
website www.westminster.gov.uk/leisure-libraries-and-community/library-opening-times-and-contact-details/westminster-music-library

Holds a wide range of scores, orchestral sets, books on music, music journals and a collection of Mozart sound recordings, formerly the GLASS collection.

Women's Library @ LSE

Lionel Robbins Building,
The London School of Economics and Political Science, 10 Portugal Street, Westminster, London WC2A 2HD
tel 020-7955 7229
email library.enquiries@lse.ac.uk

website www.lse.ac.uk/library/collection-highlights/the-womens-library
Twitter @LSELibrary

Houses the most extensive collection of women's history in the UK. Part of the London School of Economics. Open Monday to Friday, 10am to 4pm.

Wordsworth Library

Dove Cottage, Grasmere, Cumbria LA22 9SH
tel (01539) 435544
email enquiries@wordsworth.org.uk
website https://wordsworth.org.uk/
Facebook www.facebook.com/WordsworthTrust/

William Wordsworth's home, Dove Cottage, houses a small library which is situated in a two-storey converted coach house adjacent to the cottage museum. It contains treasures of all kinds related to the Romantic movement, from books to paintings and Wordsworth's manuscripts.

Working Class Movement Library

Jubilee House, 51 The Crescent, Salford M5 4WX
tel 0161 736 3601
email enquiries@wcml.org.uk
website www.wcml.org.uk
Facebook www.facebook.com/wcmlibrary
Twitter @wcmlibrary

Records over 200 years of organising and campaigning by ordinary men and women. The collection provides an insight into working people's daily lives. Collection contains: books, pamphlets, archives, photographs, plays, poetry, songs, banners, posters, badges, cartoons, journals, biographies, reports.

Wren Library

Trinity College Cambridge, Cambridge CB2 1TQ
email wren.library@trin.cam.ac.uk
email archives@trin.cam.ac.uk
website www.trin.cam.ac.uk/library/wren-library

This library houses the manuscript of Winnie-the-Pooh and the papers of philosopher Ludwig Wittgenstein. As an academic library it's only open to the public for two hours each day during term time. To view rare books and manuscripts use the first email above. To view the college archive and modern manuscripts use the second email above.

Zoological Society of London Library

Outer Circle, Regent's Park, London NW1 4RY
tel 020-7449 6293
email library@zsl.org
website www.zsl.org/about-us/library
Facebook www.facebook.com/officialzsl
Twitter @officialzsl

Contains a unique collection of journals and books on zoology and animal conservation.

ORGANISATIONS THAT SUPPORT LIBRARIES

There are many organisations which are affiliated to, and champion the use of libraries in the UK. These include:

APPG for Libraries Information & Knowledge in Parliament

website www.cilip.org.uk/page/APPGLInK

The goal of the APPG for Libraries Information & Knowledge in Parliament is to provide information and opportunities for debate about the important role libraries play in society and their future; to highlight the contribution that a wide variety of library and information services make, including those in public, school, government, health sector, colleges, private companies and university libraries; and to promote and discuss themes in the wider information and knowledge sector including the impact of technology, skills and training, professional standards and broader issues.

Arts Council England

website www.artscouncil.org.uk

Arts Council England is the developmental agency for libraries in England and has responsibility for supporting and developing libraries. See also page 323.

Association of Independent Libraries

Church Lane, Doncaster DN5 7AU
email emma.marigliano@gmail.com
website http://independentlibraries.co.uk

Developes the conservation, restoration and public awareness of independent libraries in the UK. Together, its members possess over two million books and have many listed buildings in their care. Founded 1989.

Association of Senior and Children's Education Librarians (ASCEL)

website www.ascel.org.uk

A national membership network of Senior Children's and Education Librarians. It aims to stimulate innovation and share initiatives relating to children and young people using public libraries and educational services.

BookTrust

website www.booktrust.org.uk

Aims to give everyone access to books and the chance to benefit from reading. See also page 516.

Chartered Institute of Library and Information Professionals (CILIP)

7 Ridgmount Street, London WC1E 7AE
tel 020-7255 0500

email info@cilip.org.uk
website www.cilip.org.uk

The leading professional body for librarians, information specialists and knowledge managers. Aims for a fair and economically prosperous society underpinned by literacy, access to information and the transfer of knowledge. A registered charity. Offices in London, Wales, Scotland and Northern Ireland.

The Community Knowledge Hub for Libraries

website https://libraries.communityknowledgehub. org.uk/content/community-knowledge-hub

Unites expert guidance and resources with an interactive community of organisations and local authorities involved with community-managed and supported libraries.

Friends of Libraries

Many libraries in the UK have Friends of Libraries organisations affiliated to them which support library use through charitable means. Sometimes Friends groups are set up to campaign against a potential council closures of libraries or reductions in budgets. They have been known to set up their own community libraries.

Friends of National Libraries

website www.friendsofnationallibraries.org.uk

A registered charity. Founded in 1931. Helps libraries in the UK acquire books, manuscripts and archives, in particular those that might otherwise leave the UK.

Internet Library for Librarians

email info@itcompany.com
website www.itcompany.com/inforetriever/index.htm

Internet Library for Librarians has been one of the most popular information resource sites for librarians since 1994. It is an information portal specifically designed for librarians to locate internet resources related to their profession.

Libraries Connected

email info@librariesconnected.org.uk
website www.librariesconnected.org.uk

A charity, previously known as the Society of Chief Librarians (SCL). Partly funded by Arts Council England as the Sector Support Organisation for libraries. This funding provides increased capacity with a new team of staff and trustees to work alongside members. Remains a membership organisation, made up of every library service in England, Wales and Northern Ireland.

Libraries Week

website www.librariesweek.org.uk

The first Libraries Day took place in February 2012 and is now a week-long annual event in the UK dedicated to the celebration of libraries and librarians. Author talks and competitions are arranged by local authorities, universities, library services and local community groups.

The Library Campaign
website www.librarycampaign.com

Aims to advance the lifelong education of the public by the promotion, support, assistance and improvement of libraries through the activities of friends and user groups.

Library Planet
website https://libraryplanet.net/

A crowdsourced travel guide for the libraries of the world. The intention is to inspire library travellers.

National Literacy Trust
website www.literacytrust.org.uk

Aims to improve reading, writing, speaking and listening skills in disadvantaged communities, in part through access to libraries. See also page 516.

Private Libraries Association
email info@plabooks.org
website www.plabooks.org

An international society of book collectors and lovers of books. Membership: £30 p.a. Publications include *The Private Library* (quarterly), annual *Private Press Books*, and other books on book collecting. Founded 1956.

Public Library News
website www.publiclibrariesnews.com

Promotes knowledge about libraries in the UK.

The Reading Agency
website https://readingagency.org.uk

Aims to give everyone an equal chance in life by helping people become confident and enthusiastic readers, and that includes supporting library use.

School Library Association (SLA)
1 Pine Court, Kembrey Park, Swindon SN2 8AD
tel (01793) 530166
email info@sla.org.uk
website www.sla.org.uk

The main goal of the SLA is to support people involved with school libraries, promoting high-quality reading and learning opportunities for all. Founded 1937.

Writers' retreats and creative writing courses

The following list of creative writing courses and writers' retreats is not exhaustive but is intended to give readers a flavour of the many options available. Some offer bursaries. Details of postgraduate courses are on page 689.

Anam Cara

Eyeries, Beara, Bantry, Co. Cork, P75 DP66, Republic of Ireland
tel +353 277 4441
email anamcararetreat@gmail.com
website www.anamcararetreat.com
Facebook www.facebook.com/anamcararetreat
Contact Sue Booth-Forbes

All-inclusive residential retreat offering private and common working rooms for writers and artists, who can work by themselves or with others as part of a workshop or special interest group.

Arvon

Postal address Lumb Bank – The Ted Hughes Arvon Centre, Heptonstall, Hebden Bridge, West Yorkshire HX7 6DF
tel (01422) 843714
email national@arvon.org
website www.arvon.org
Facebook www.facebook.com/arvonfoundation
Twitter @arvonfoundation
Instagram @arvon__
Chief Executive Andrew Kidd

See individual entries for Arvon's writing houses: The Hurst – The John Osborne Arvon Centre (see page 685), Lumb Bank – The Ted Hughes Arvon Centre (see page 686), Totleigh Barton (see page 688) and Writers Retreat at The Clockhouse (below).

Leading creative writing charity, known for its diverse creative writing courses and author-led events. An online programme, 'Arvon at Home', offers virtual writing weeks, masterclasses and readings. Residential five-day courses are set in historic writing houses in rural locations. Week-long courses, both in-person and at-home, include workshops and one-to-one tutorials. Courses cover a range of genres including fiction, poetry, theatre, creative non-fiction and writing for children. Grants and concessions are available. Founded 1968.

Arvon Writers Retreat at the Clockhouse

Clunton, Craven Arms, Shrops. SY7 0JA
tel (01588) 640658
email thehurst@arvon.org
website www.arvon.org/centres/clockhouse/

Co-Directors Natasha Carlish and Jo King, *Senior Administrator* Dan Pavitt, *House Manager* Ali Ford

Four apartments, each with a bedroom, study and en suite bathroom, and all food provided, for six-day and four-day writing retreats.

Anne Aylor Creative Writing Courses

46 Beversbrook Road, London N19 4QH
tel 020-7263 0669
email enquiries@anneaylor.co.uk
website www.anneaylor.co.uk
Contact Anne Aylor

Short, weekend and overseas courses, as well as customised courses for all levels of ability.

Casa Ana Creative Writing Retreats

Calle Artesa 7, Ferreirola, 18414 La Taha, Granada, Spain
tel +34 678 298 497
email info@casa-ana.com
website www.casa-ana.com/creative-writing-retreats
Contact Anne Hunt

Mentored writing retreats and courses in a 400-year-old house in Andalusia. Offers four residential writers' retreats each year in spring, summer and autumn. Nine places available in each retreat, which lasts for two weeks and includes a one-to-one mentoring service and optional reading/critiquing sessions. Also hosts week-long novel writing retreat. All retreats and courses conducted in English.

Château de Lavigny International Writers' Residence

Route d'Etoy 10, 1175 Lavigny, Switzerland
tel +41 21 808 6143
email chlavigny@hotmail.com
website www.chateaudelavigny.ch

International residence for writers in the Swiss canton of Vaud, which hosts 20 or more writers from around the world. Writers come for four weeks, in groups of up to six, from May to October. They are housed in an 18th-century manor house overlooking Lake Geneva. There is a fee for full board during four weeks; lodging for the duration is free. Sessions are in English or French and writers must be published. A small number of full-grant fellowships, including full bed and board, are offered each year.

City Lit

1–10 Keeley Street, London WC2B 4BA
tel 020-7831 7831
email writing@citylit.ac.uk
website www.citylit.ac.uk/courses/history-culture-and-writing/writing

Affordable courses on approaching agents, impressing publishers and writing fiction, poetry, short stories, memoir, non-fiction and writing for children. Courses are also available in stage and screenwriting.

The Complete Creative Writing Course

Groucho Club, 45 Dean Street, London W1D 4QB
email jamie@writingcourses.org.uk
website www.writingcourses.org.uk
Contact Jamie Winter

Friendly creative writing courses held in person (including at The Art Workers' Guild, Queen Square) and online, with a solid focus on authors developing their own work. Tutor Alice Adams is a published author and experienced teacher. Suitable for both fiction and memoir writers; topics covered include creating complex characters, dialogue, writer psychology, procrastination and goal-setting, and getting published. Costs range from £125 to £450.

Cove Park

Peaton Hill, Cove, Argyll and Bute G84 0PE
tel (01436) 850500
email information@covepark.org
website www.covepark.org
Senior Director of Programmes Alexia Holt

International artist residency centre. Offers a year-round programme of residencies for writers, translators and artists from all disciplines. See website for details of the funded residency programme and to subscribe to newsletter.

The Creative Writer's Workshop

Kinvara, Co. Galway, Republic of Ireland
tel +353 (0)86 2523428
email office@thecreativewritersworkshop.com
website www.thecreativewritersworkshop.com
Facebook www.facebook.com/IreneGrahamWritingCourses
Founder Irene Graham

Fiction and memoir-writing retreats in the West of Ireland; six-month Memoir Masterclass; 16-week memoir-writing course with workbook. The workshops are accredited by George Mason University in the USA as part of its undergraduate and graduate degree programmes

Curtis Brown Creative

Cunard House, 15 Regent Street, London SW1Y 4L
tel 020-7393 4201
email help@curtisbrowncreative.co.uk
website www.curtisbrowncreative.co.uk
Facebook www.facebook.com/CurtisBrownCreative
Twitter @cbcreative
Instagram @curtisbrowncreative

Creative writing school offering courses in London and online. Over 200 students to date have subsequently signed publishing deals; alumni include Bonnie Garmus, Kirsty Capes, Alex Hay and Julia Armfield. Subjects covered include fiction, memoirs, short stories, screenwriting and children's picture books. Curtis Brown Creative also runs the Breakthrough Writers' Programme, which offers free courses, mentoring and scholarships for under-represented writers.

Emerson College

Forest Row, East Sussex RH18 5JX
tel (01342) 822238
email bookings@emerson.org.uk
website www.emerson.org.uk
Facebook www.facebook.com/LearningatEmerson
Twitter @Emerson_Colleg

Adult education centre based on the works of Rudolf Steiner, offering space for personal, professional and artistic growth. Visual and performing arts courses, as well as training in caring professions and regenerative cultivation, take place throughout the year; full-time and modular programmes available. Founded 1962.

Faber Academy

The Bindery, 51–53 Hatton Garden, London EC1N 8HN
tel 020-7927 3827
email academy@faber.co.uk
website www.faberacademy.com
Facebook www.facebook.com/faberacademy
Twitter @faberacademy
Instagram @faber_academy
Director Joey Connolly

Expert guidance from first line to final draft. Online and in-person writing courses, as well as mentoring programmes and manuscript assessments from industry experts.

Fictionfire Literary Consultancy

110 Oxford Road, Old Marston, Oxford OX3 0RD
tel 07827 455723
email info@fictionfire.co.uk
website www.fictionfire.co.uk
Facebook www.facebook.com/FictionfireLiteraryConsultancy
Twitter @LornaFergusson
Contact Lorna Fergusson

In-person and online creative writing courses, retreats and workshops. Guest talks and workshops can be arranged for writers' groups, libraries, educational establishments, conferences and festivals. Manuscript appraisal, editing, mentoring and consultation services also available. Founded 2009.

Foxes' Retreat

The Old Kennels, Birdsgrove Lane,
Ashbourne DE6 2BP
tel 07734 328762
email myszka@foxesretreat.com
website www.foxesretreat.com
Facebook www.facebook.com/retreatfoxes
Twitter @RetreatFoxes
Director, Writer and Therapist Myszka Fox

Festival of Writing, 6–13 August 2023; extensive
programme of workshops plus full catering and
activities. Writing retreats: five-day and weekend
retreats for independent writers or those seeking one-
to-one or small-group tuition on themes. Coaching
for Writing and Writing for Wellbeing workshops
available in person and online.

Courses range from online afternoon workshops to
full novel-writing programmes.

Maria Frankland Creative Writing Courses

email maria@mariafrankland.co.uk
website www.mariafrankland.co.uk
Contact Maria Frankland

Write a Novel, Write a Collection of Poetry, Write
your Life Story and Write a Collection of Short
Stories courses. All stages of writing are supported,
from planning to publication, and follow a
progressive 26-session online programme over a year.
Visit the website to receive a free booklet: *The 7
S.E.C.R.E.T.S. to Achieving your Writing Dreams.*

The French House Party, Carcassonne

Domaine St Raymond, 11150 Pexiora, France
tel (01299) 896819 (admin)
email hello@frenchhouseparty.eu
website www.frenchhouseparty.eu
Twitter @FrenchHousePart
Director Moira Martingale

Creative courses in south-west France, covering
literature, drama, song-writing, performance, film-
making and art and mixed media.

Gale & Co

144 Liverpool Rd, London N1 1LA
tel 07944 137248
email kathy.gale@galeandco.co.uk
website www.galeandco.co.uk
Facebook www.facebook.com/kathygaleandco
Twitter @KathyGaleAndCo

Professional coaching consultancy for authors.
Experienced team of writing coaches with decades of
senior publishing experience focuses on supporting
writers to achieve success. Many of those authors
have gone on to be signed by publishers such as
Bloomsbury, Canongate and Nosy Crow, and are
represented by agencies including Curtis Brown and
David Higham.

Garsdale Retreat

Clough View, Garsdale Head, Sedbergh,
Cumbria LA10 5PW
tel (01539) 234184
email garsdaleretreat@gmail.com
website www.thegarsdaleretreat.co.uk
Contact Rebecca Nouchette

Creative writing centre in the Yorkshire Dales
National Park. Provides untutored retreats and
residential courses tutored by professional writers,
enabling participants to develop their individual
creativity. All levels of ability welcomed and a high
level of individual tuition is offered in classes with a
maximum number of eight students. All courses and
retreats are fully catered, allowing participants to
focus on their writing.

The Grange

9 Eastcliff Road, Shanklin, Isle of Wight PO37 6AA
tel (01983) 867644
email stay@thegrangebythesea.com
website www.thegrangebythesea.com

Hosts weekend residential creative writing
workshops. Secluded but close to local amenities and
the beach.

Green Ink Writers' Gym

tel 07870 630788
email info@rachelknightley.com
website http://www.rachelknightley.com/visit-the-
writers-gym/
Twitter @GIWritersGym
Instagram @greeninkwritersgym
Contact Dr Rachel Knightley

Creative writing courses, coaching and editorial
support. Sessions provide the skills, motivation and
sense of fun to guide new and experienced writers
and authors from work-in-progress to 'the end': the
motto is 'take your wordcount for a work-out'.

Hawthornden Castle

Hawthornden Literary Retreat, Lasswade,
Midlothian EH18 1EG
tel 0131 440 2180
email office@hawthornden.org
website www.hawthorndenliteraryretreat.org/about-us
Executive Director Ellyn Toscano

Peaceful retreat for published writers. Houses up to
six writers at a time, who are known as Hawthornden
Fellows. Writers from any part of the world may
apply for the fellowships. No monetary assistance is
given, nor any contribution to travelling expenses,
but Fellows board as guests of the retreat. Requests
for application forms should be made to the above
postal address. Deadline: 30 June.

The Hurst – The John Osborne Arvon Centre

Clunton, Craven Arms, Shrops. SY7 0JA
tel (01588) 640658

email thehurst@arvon.org
website www.arvon.org
Co-Director Natasha Carlish, *Senior Administrator*
Dan Pavitt

Offers residential writing courses from April to
December. Grants available. The Hurst is situated in
the beautiful Clun Valley in Shropshire, 12 miles
from Ludlow, and is set in 30 acres of woodland, with
gardens and a lake.

Irish Writers Centre – Áras Scríbhneoirí na hÉireann

19 Parnell Square, Dublin D01 E102,
Republic of Ireland
tel +353 (0)1 872 1302
email info@writerscentre.ie
website https://irishwriterscentre.ie
Facebook www.facebook.com/IrishWritersCtr
Twitter @IrishWritersCtr
Instagram @irishwriterscentre
Director Valerie Bistany

Support and development organisation for Irish
writers. Carries out its work online and in person on
an all island basis. Works with writers of all types and
talents, and actively encourages writers from all
communities to engage in creative writing. Also a
membership organisation that looks for new
opportunities for members to grow as writers and to
connect with each other through IWC programmes
and support. Founded 1991.

Isle of Wight Writing Courses and Workshops

F&F Productions, 39 Ranelagh Road, Sandown,
Isle of Wight PO36 8NT
tel (01983) 407772
email felicity@writeplot.co.uk
website www.felicityfairthompson.co.uk
website www.wightdiamondpress.com
Contact Felicity Fair Thompson

Email and postal MS critiques and editing, and one-
to-one advice on film scripts, travel writing, and
fiction. In-person options also available for beginners
and for experienced writers, including weekend
workshops, detailed discussion and individual advice.
The Writers' Weekend Conference 2023 with
authors, agents, film makers and publishers is due to
take place 3–5 November; see website for details.

Jericho Writers

Box 321, 266 Banbury Road, Oxford OX2 7DL
tel 0345 459 9560 / +1 646-974-9060 (US)
email info@jerichowriters.com
website https://jerichowriters.com
Twitter @JerichoWriters
Instagram @JerichoWriters
Founder Harry Bingham

Inclusive online writing organisation offering
editorial services and events for all genres, including

writing for children, and tutored courses. Also
available: guidance for self-publishers, masterclasses,
AgentMatch (a database of over 1,000 literary agents),
a free community for writers to connect, and expert
guides to writing and publishing. See website for
information on Festival of Writing.

Le Verger

Savignac-Lédrier, Dordogne 24270, France
tel (01223) 316539 (UK)
email info@retreatfrance.co.uk
website www.retreatfrance.co.uk
Contact David Lambert

Residential writers' retreats or tutored courses
(poetry, fiction, screenwriting, writing for the stage
and life writing) from May to October with
experienced tutors. Shared or individual
accommodation in the main house, the Piggery or a
writer's cabin; full board (with local wines) for up to
ten writers. Welcomes creative and academic writers,
artists, photographers and anyone working on a
creative project. Also offers French at all levels.
Transfers to/from Limoges airport or train station.

Limnisa Centre for Writers

Agios Georgios, Methana 18030, Greece
tel +31 681 027701, 07906 730450
email mariel@limnisa.com
website www.limnisa.com

International retreats and workshops for writers.
Offers single rooms, studios or tents and all-
vegetarian meals. Check website for details and dates.

Lumb Bank – The Ted Hughes Arvon Centre

Heptonstall, Hebden Bridge,
West Yorkshire HX7 6DF
tel (01422) 843714
email lumbbank@arvon.org
website www.arvon.org
Directors Rosie Scott, Helen Meller, *Senior
Administrator* Becky Liddell

Offers online and residential writing courses. Grants
available. Lumb Bank is an 18th-century former mill-
owner's house set in 20 acres of steep pasture land.

Marlborough College Summer School

Marlborough, Wilts. SN8 1PA
tel (01672) 892388
email admin@summerschool.co.uk
website https://summerschool.co.uk
Facebook www.facebook.com/
MarlboroughCollegeSummerSchool
Twitter @MCol_Summer
Instagram @marlboroughsummerschool

Runs from early July to early August each year.
Multi-generational event that plays host to over 500
courses, many of which specialise in creative writing,
including poetry, journalism, the novel and memoir.
Residential options available. Founded 1974.

Missenden School of Creative Arts

Missenden School of Creative Arts, Jessamine House, King Street, Tring HP23 6BE
tel 07955 484605
email info@missendenschoolofcreativearts.co.uk
website www.missendenschoolofcreativearts.co.uk
Facebook: www.facebook.com/
missendenschoolofcreativearts
Twitter: @MissendenArts
Instagram @missendenschoolofcreativearts

Weekend and summer school art, craft and general interest courses for all abilities.

Moniack Mhor

Teavarran, Kiltarlity, Beauly,
Inverness-shire IV4 7HT
tel (01463) 741675
email info@moniackmhor.org.uk
website www.moniackmhor.org.uk
Facebook: www.facebook.com//moniackmhor
Twitter: @moniackmhor
Instagram: @moniackmhor
Centre Director Rachel Humphries

Year-round residential creative writing courses, retreats and residencies. Also offers online courses, a programme of awards, residencies and retreats for writing groups and organisations. Tuition is by established writers, and the range of courses designed to suit writers at all stages. Grants available on all courses. Founded 1993.

Morley College

61 Westminster Bridge Road, London SE1 7HT
tel 020-7450 1889
email enquiries@morleycollege.ac.uk
website www.morleycollege.ac.uk
Facebook www.facebook.com/morleycollegelondon
Twitter @morleycollege
Instagram @morley_college

Offers a number of creative writing courses throughout the year, including a memoir-writing course.

The Novelry

The Gallery, The Street, Sissinghurst, Kent TN17 2JH
tel 07469 202530
email hello@thenovelry.com
website www.thenovelry.com
Facebook www.facebook.com/thenovelry
Twitter @thenovelry
Founder Louise Dean

Online writing school aimed at writers seeking to complete a novel or memoir to publishing standard. Submits graduates' work directly to literary agency partners in the UK and USA. Also offers writing courses for novelists as well as one-to-one coaching from a team of published authors and professional editors. Prospective students can book a free online chat for more information. Founded 2017.

Open College of the Arts

The Michael Young Arts Centre, Room 201, DMC02, County Way, Barnsley S70 2JW
email enquiries@oca.ac.uk
website www.oca.ac.uk
Facebook www.facebook.com/openartscollege

Distance learning arts courses. Students can undertake part-time foundation, degree or master's courses from home, at their own pace, on a variety of topics, including creative writing.

Oxford University Summer Schools

Department for Continuing Education,
1 Wellington Square, Oxford OX1 2JA
tel (01865) 270360
website www.conted.ox.ac.uk/summer-schools

Offers a range of options, including:
  Creative Writing Summer School: intensive three-week summer school in July/August at Exeter College. *Email:* writingsummer@conted.ox.ac.uk
  Write Now! Creative Writing Summer School: a one-week summer course set in the beautiful grounds of New College, with seminars and one-to-one tutorials. *Email:* summercourses@conted.ox.ac.uk
  Summer School for Adults (OUSSA): a choice of more than 60 one-week accredited courses in a variety of subjects, including creative writing. *Email:* oussa@conted.ox.ac.uk
  Also short online courses and virtual classes in creative writing and literature – multiple intakes per year. *Email:* onlinecourses@conted.ox.ac.uk

SCBWI-BI Writers' Events

email araevents@britishscbwi.org
website https://britishisles.scbwi.org/events
Twitter @scbwi
Instagram @scbwi_british_isles

Online listings of retreats and other writing and literary events across the UK organised by the Society of Children's Book Writers and Illustrators.

Scottish Universities' International Summer School

21 Buccleuch Place, Edinburgh EH8 9LN
tel 0131 650 4369
email suiss@ed.ac.uk
website www.suiss.ed.ac.uk
Facebook www.facebook.com/
ScottishUniversitiesInternationalSummerSchool/
Twitter @suiss_EDI
Administrative Manager Lauren Pope

Creative writing, theatre and performance programmes offered as part of a broader range of summer activities. The four-week Creative Writing course is aimed at developing writers; the two-week Theatre and Performance course offers an introduction to British and Irish theatre.

Skyros Writers' Lab

9 Eastcliff Road, Shanklin,
Isle of Wight PO37 6AA (admin)
tel (01983) 865566
email holidays@skyros.com
website www.skyros.com
Facebook www.facebook.com/skyroshols
Twitter @SkyrosHolidays

Support and guidance for writers at all stages of the creative process. Visiting authors have included Sophie Hannah, Sue Townsend, Marina Warner and Hilary Mantel. Courses are held on the Greek island of Skyros.

Stiwdio Maelor

Maelor, Corris, Machynlleth SY20 9SP
tel 07480 231003
email stiwdiomaelor@gmail.com
website https://stiwdiomaelor.com
Contact Veronica Calarco

Residencies with three individual studios and accommodation and communal spaces for writers and artists in the Snowdonia National Park, providing time and space to find new inspiration or continue with an ongoing project. Founded 2014.

Swanwick, The Writers' Summer School

Hayes Conference Centre, Swanwick,
Derbyshire DE55 1AU
tel (01290) 552248
email secretary@swanwickwritersschool.org.uk
website www.swanwickwritersschool.org.uk
Facebook www.facebook.com/SwanwickWriters
Twitter @swanwickwriters

Extensive choice of courses, talks and workshops. Offers several highly subsidised places for writers aged between 18 and 30, and assistance for writers unable to afford the full course fee. Full details of the programme and information on how to apply for the TopWrite Programme and Assisted Places Scheme are available on the website.

TLC Literary Adventures

East Side, Platform 1, Kings Cross Station,
London N1C 4AX
tel 020-7324 2563
email info@literaryconsultancy.co.uk
website www.literaryconsultancy.co.uk
website https://literaryconsultancy.co.uk/literary-adventures
Facebook www.facebook.com/pages/The-Literary-Consultancy/331088000235106
Twitter @TLCUK
Director Aki Schilz

Annual writing retreat led by an experienced writing tutor at Casa Ana in Andalusia, Spain. Open to writers of fiction, memoir and general non-fiction. Groups are limited to a maximum of 12.

Totleigh Barton

Sheepwash, Beaworthy, Devon EX21 5NS
tel (01409) 231338
email totleighbarton@arvon.org
website www.arvon.org
Twitter @TotleighBarton
Director Mary Morris, *Deputy Director* Beth Emery,
Administrator Kerensa Wilton

Offers residential writing courses all year round in a rural setting. Grants available. An Arvon writing house.

Travellers' Tales

58 Summerlee Avenue, London N2 9QH
email info@travellerstales.org
website www.travellerstales.org
Director Jonathan Lorie

Training agency for travel writers at all levels. Offers vocational courses with top travel photographers and travel writers in London, including beginners' weekends, masterclasses and creative retreats. Online tuition also available. Founded 2004.

Tŷ Newydd Writing Centre

Tŷ Newydd, Llanystumdwy, Cricieth,
Gwynedd LL52 0LW
tel (01766) 522811
email tynewydd@literaturewales.org
website www.tynewydd.wales
Twitter @ty_newydd

Residential creative writing courses for writers of all abilities over the age of 16. Courses cover everything from poetry and popular fiction to writing for the theatre and developing a novel for young adults. No qualifications are necessary; staff can advise on the suitability of courses. Also offers courses for schools, corporate courses and awaydays for companies. Tŷ Newydd is home to Nant, the writers' retreat cottage located on site. Run by Literature Wales, the national organisation for the development of literature in Wales.

UAL (University of the Arts, London) Short Course Office

Granary Square, 1 Granary Building, King's Cross,
London N1C 4AA
email ualshortcourses@arts.ac.uk
website www.arts.ac.uk/colleges/central-saint-martins/courses/short-courses
Facebook www.facebook.com/UALShortCourses/
Twitter @CSMShortCourses

Annual programme of courses in a variety of subjects taught by expert practitioners.

Upton Cressett Foundation

Upton Cressett Hall, Upton Cressett, Nr Bridgnorth, Shrops. WV16 6UH
tel (01746) 714373
email laura@uptoncressett.co.uk
website https://uptoncressetthall.co.uk/halls-garden/upton-cresett-foundation/

Offers retreats of up to three weeks (off season) for established authors to make progress with a literary project. Since 2019, one of the stays awarded is the Philip Kerr Fellowship, open to a writer of commercial or crime fiction. Previous fellows include artist Adam Dant, biographer Lara Feigel, historian Juliet Gardiner and the playwright Ella Hickson.

Urban Writers' Retreat

email hello@urbanwritersretreat.co.uk
website www.urbanwritersretreat.co.uk
Facebook www.facebook.com/UrbanWritersRetreat
Twitter @urbanwriters
Contact Charlie Haynes

Courses and residential retreats for writers, giving them the time and space they need to concentrate on their work. Retreats are held in Newton Abbot, Devon; all food included. Each writer has their own private room.

Writers & Artists

Bloomsbury Publishing plc, 50 Bedford Square, London WC1B 3DP
tel 020-7631 5985
email writersandartists@bloomsbury.com
website www.writersandartists.co.uk
Facebook www.facebook.com/WritersArtistsYearbook
Twitter @Writers_Artists
Contacts James Rennoldson, Clare Povey, Amelia Brown

Hosts online and offline masterclasses, conferences and writing courses throughout the year. Masterclasses and conferences are run independently or in collaboration with literary festivals, universities and charities such as Book Aid International, Literature Works and the Open University. A series of events dedicated to writing and illustrating books for children and young adults is held in March each year. Online writing courses – which cover a variety of genres – take place on weekday evenings.

Also offers a range of editing services, and works regularly with literary agents to provide guidance on the submission process. The W&A platform is free to join, contains hundreds of writing and publishing advice articles, and offers a lively community area and personalisation features.

The Writers Bureau

tel 0161 819 9922
email studentservices@writersbureau.com
website www.writersbureaucourse.com
Facebook www.facebook.com/thewritersbureau
Twitter @writersbureau

Wide range of writing-related distance-learning courses including creative writing, proofreading and copy-editing, writing for children, copywriting and poetry. Suitable for both beginners and writers wanting to brush up on their skills. Also runs Zoom writing workshops and bootcamps; see website for details.

POSTGRADUATE COURSES

Aberystwyth University

Department of English and Creative Writing, Hugh Owen Building, Penglais Campus, Aberystwyth, Ceredigion SY23 3DY
tel (01970) 621537
email english@aber.ac.uk
website www.aber.ac.uk/en/english

Courses offered include MA Creative Writing, MA Literary Studies, PhD Creative Writing and PhD English.

Anglia Ruskin University

East Road, Cambridge CB1 1PT
email answers@anglia.ac.uk
website https://aru.ac.uk/study/postgraduate/creative-writing
Facebook www.facebook.com/angliaruskin
Twitter @ARUWriting
Course Leader MA Creative Writing Jon Stone

Offers a range of postgraduate creative writing course options, as well as a further research programme in the form of a PhD. Alumni scholarships (£400) are available for the latter.

Bangor University

Bangor, Gwynedd LL57 2DG
tel (01248) 351151
email postgraduate@bangor.ac.uk
website www.bangor.ac.uk/study/postgraduate/creative-writing
Facebook www.facebook.com/BangorUniversity
Twitter @BangorUni
Instagram @bangor_university/

Offers MA Creative Writing in English and Welsh medium.

Bath Spa University

Newton Park, Newton St Loe, Bath BA2 9BN
tel (01225) 875875
email admissions@bathspa.ac.uk
website www.bathspa.ac.uk/schools/school-of-creative-industries

Offers a variety of postgraduate courses on subjects including Creative Writing, Writing for Young People, Travel and Nature Writing, Scriptwriting, and Children's Publishing.

Birkbeck College, University of London
Malet Street, London WC1E 7HX
tel 020-7631 6000
website www.bbk.ac.uk/schools/arts
Facebook www.facebook.com/
BirkbeckUniversityofLondon
Twitter @BirkbeckUoL

Courses offered include MA Creative Writing, MFA
Creative Writing, MA Creative Industries, MA
Creative and Critical Writing, MSc Management with
Creative Industries, MA Journalism and MA
Screenwriting.

Bournemouth University
Fern Barrow, Poole, Dorset BH12 5BB
tel (01202) 961916
email futurestudents@bournemouth.ac.uk
website www.bournemouth.ac.uk/study/courses/ma-
creative-writing-publishing
Facebook www.facebook.com/JoinBournemouthUni/
Twitter @bournemouthuni
Programme Leader Dr Brad Gyori

Offers MA Creative Writing and Publishing, which
combines creative support with industry-relevant
knowledge. Students can work on publishing projects
with the university's own press, Fresher Publishing.
Also runs two annual writing prizes: New Media
Writing Prize; and The Bournemouth Writing Prize.

University of Brighton
School of Humanities, Village Way, Falmer,
Brighton BN1 9PH
tel (01273) 643359
email jsm@brighton.ac.uk
website www.brighton.ac.uk/courses/study/Creative-
Writing-MA-PGCert-PGDip.aspx
Contact Dr Jess Moriarty

Offers MA Creative Writing (PGCert PGDip).
Working with professional writers, students develop
skills to produce and share stories in a variety of
genres. Provides links with local publishers, writers
and creative companies and offers a unique artist in
residency module where students work with
organisations on a specific creative brief that is linked
to their individual writing practice. Students have the
opportunity to share their work through established
student-led anthologies and open mic nights.

Brunel University London
Uxbridge, Middlesex UB8 3PH
tel (01895) 274000
website www.brunel.ac.uk/creative-writing
Twitter @Bruneluni

Offers MA Creative Writing: can be completed in one
year full-time or over two years part-time.

University of Cambridge Institute of Continuing Education
Madingley Hall, Madingley, Cambridge CB23 8AQ
tel (01223) 746222

email enquiries@ice.cam.ac.uk
website www.ice.cam.ac.uk
Facebook www.facebook.com/CambridgeICE
Twitter @litandcw_ice

Home to the University of Cambridge Centre for
Creative Writing. A wide range of short and part-
time courses at introductory and advanced levels on
creative writing, literature, and art history.

Cardiff University
Cardiff School of English,
Communication and Philosophy,
John Percival Building, Colum Drive,
Cardiff CF10 3EU
tel 029-2087 6049
email encap@cardiff.ac.uk
website www.cardiff.ac.uk/study/postgraduate

Courses offered include MA Creative Writing, MA
News Journalism, and PhD Creative and Critical
Writing (English and Welsh).

University of Central Lancashire
Preston, Lancs. PR1 2HE
tel (01772) 201201
email pgapplications@uclan.ac.uk
website www.uclan.ac.uk/postgraduate/courses/
publishing-ma
Facebook www.facebook.com/OfficialUCLan/
Twitter @UCLan
Instagram @uclanuni
Lecturer in Publishing Alexa Gregson-Kenmuir,
Digital Publishing Lecturer Dr Wayne Noble

Offers MA Publishing affiliated with the in-house
press, UCLan Publishing. This close link offers
students the opportunity to draw on the press's
resources and to gain valuable experience.

University of Chester
Parkgate Road, Chester CH1 4BJ
email pgradmissions@chester.ac.uk
website www1.chester.ac.uk/study/postgraduate/
creative-writing-and-publishing-fiction
Course Leader Dr Ashley Chantler

Offers an MA in Creative Writing: Writing and
Publishing Fiction. The course has four key modules:
Writing Short Fiction for Publication; Writing Novels
for Publication; Getting Published; and The Writing
Project.

University of Chichester
Bishop Otter Campus, College Lane, Chichester,
West Sussex PO19 6PE
tel (01243) 816000
email h.frey@chi.ac.uk
email h.dunkerley@chi.ac.uk
website www.chi.ac.uk
Contacts Professor Hugo Frey (Head of Department),
Professor Hugh Dunkerley (MA Creative Writing
Programme Coordinator)

Offers BA, MA and PhD Creative Writing. Students work with practising writers. Specialisms include: novels, short stories, creative non-fiction, writing for children, screenwriting and poetry. Hosts regular visits by high-profile writers, editors and agents. Visiting Professors: Kate Mosse and Alison MacLeod. Many students go on to publish and win prizes.

City University of London

School of Arts and Social Sciences,
Northampton Square, London EC1V 0HB
email SASS-Enquiries@city.ac.uk
website www.city.ac.uk
Facebook www.facebook.com/cityuniversitylondon
Twitter @CityUniLondon

Postgraduate courses in creative writing, English, various branches of journalism, and publishing.

University of Cumbria

Fusehill Street, Carlisle CA1 2HH
tel 0808 291 6578
email enquirycentre@cumbria.ac.uk
website www.cumbria.ac.uk
Facebook www.facebook.com/universityofcumbria
Twitter @CumbriaUni

Courses offered include MA Literature, Romanticism and the English Lake District.

De Montfort University

The Gateway, Leicester LE1 9BH
tel 0116 255 1551
email enquiry@dmu.ac.uk
website www.dmu.ac.uk

Courses offered include MA Creative Writing and MA English Language Teaching.

University of Derby

email askadmissions@derby.ac.uk
website www.derby.ac.uk/postgraduate/english-creative-writing-publishing-courses/creative-writing-ma/
Facebook www.facebook.com/derbyuni
Twitter @DerbyUni
Instagram @derbyuni
Course Leader Dr Christos Callow, Jr

Offers a practice-taught MA Creative Writing for full- and part-time students. Covers a wide range of genres, including fiction, poetry, script-writing and creative non-fiction. Alongside the creative and critical main programme, two specific career pathways have been developed to help students find future employment: Creative Writing with Publishing is centred around book production; and Creative Writing for Gaming focuses on digital and tabletop games.

University of East Anglia

Admissions Office, School of Literature, Drama and Creative Writing,
Faculty of Arts and Humanities,
Norwich Research Park, Norwich NR4 7TJ
tel (01603) 591515
email admissions@uea.ac.uk
website www.uea.ac.uk/about/school-of-literature-drama-and-creative-writing
Course Director Professor Steven Waters

Offers a well-regarded MA Creative Writing. Students may specialise in prose, poetry, scriptwriting, biography and creative non-fiction or crime fiction, and have the opportunity to learn from published writers and peers in workshops and one-to-one supervisions; and benefit from industry links. Other options include studying literature of interest as a critic, or creative critic, focusing on the modern and contemporary or medieval and early modern periods.

Edge Hill University

Department of English,
History and Creative Writing, St Helens Road,
Ormskirk L39 4QP
tel (01695) 579997
email cowanb@edgehill.ac.uk
website www.edgehill.ac.uk/course/creative-writing-ma/
Senior Lecturer Billy Cowan

Courses offered include MA Creative Writing (full- and part-time), as well as MRes and PhD programmes in creative writing.

University of Edinburgh

Old College, South Bridge, Edinburgh EH8 9YL
tel 0131 650 1000
website www.ed.ac.uk
website www.eca.ed.ac.uk
Twitter @UniofEdinburgh

Postgraduate courses include Creative Writing, Film Studies, Film Directing and Illustration.

Edinburgh Napier University

Sighthill Campus, Sighthill Court,
Edinburgh EH11 4BN
tel 0333 900 6040
email studentrecruitment@napier.ac.uk
website www.napier.ac.uk/courses/study-areas/english-creative-writing-and-publishing/creative-writing
Facebook www.facebook.com/EdinburghNapierUniversity/
Twitter @EdinburghNapier
Instagram @edinburghnapier/
Tutors David Bishop, Laura Lam, Daniel Shand

Full- and part-time MA Creative Writing. Strong focus on genre fiction. Also offers modules on graphic novels and young adult (YA).

University of Essex

Wivenhoe Park, Colchester CO4 3SQ
tel (01206) 872626

email pgadmit@essex.ac.uk
website www.essex.ac.uk/literature-film-and-theatre-studies
Facebook www.facebook.com/LiFTS.UoE/
Twitter @LiFTS_at_essex

Postgraduate courses include Creative Writing, English Language, Film Studies, Theatre Practice and Scriptwriting.

University of Exeter

Stocker Road, Exeter EX4 4PY
website www.exeter.ac.uk/postgraduate/courses/english/creative-ma/
Facebook www.facebook.com/exeteruni
Twitter @UniofExeter
Instagram @uniofexeter
Course Leader Professor Sam North

Offers MA Creative Writing, delivered by a team of internationally recognised writers. Also regularly hosts visiting speakers: writers, agents and publishers. Students publish their work in two journals, *Riptide* and *Exclamation*.

Falmouth University

Falmouth Campus, Woodlane, Falmouth, Cornwall TR11 4RH
tel (01326) 211077
website www.falmouth.ac.uk/study/postgraduate

Courses offered include MA Film & Television, MA Fine Art (online), MA Comedy Writing (online) MA Game Art, MA Illustration (online), MA Illustration: Authorial Practice, MA Professional Writing, MA Writing for Script and Screen (online) and MA Journalism (online).

University of Glasgow

Creative Writing, School of Critical Studies, 5 Lilybank Gardens, Glasgow G12 8QQ
tel 0141 330 8372
email critstudies-pgenquiries@glasglow.ac.uk
website www.gla.ac.uk/subjects/creativewriting
Twitter @UoGWriting

Courses include MLitt, MFA and DFA in Creative Writing, and MLitt by distance learning.

University of Hull

Cottingham Road, Hull HU6 7RX
tel (01482) 346311
website www.hull.ac.uk/faculties/subjects/english
Facebook www.facebook.com/UniversityOfHull
Twitter @UniOfHull

Postgraduate courses include MA Creative Writing (online), MA English (Creative Writing and English Literature) and MA Theatre Making.

Kingston University

Penrhyn Road, Kingston upon Thames, Surrey KT1 2EE
tel 020-3510 0106

website www.kingston.ac.uk
Facebook www.facebook.com/kingstonuni
Twitter @KingstonUni

Postgraduate courses in Creative Writing (MA), Journalism (MA/PgDip) and Publishing (MA). The MA Creative Writing can be completed in one year (full-time), two years (part-time) or two years full-time including a professional placement.

Lancaster University

Department of English Literature and Creative Writing, County College, Lancaster University, Lancaster LA1 4YD
tel (01524) 593089
email elcwteaching@lancaster.ac.uk
website www.lancaster.ac.uk/english-literature-and-creative-writing
Contact The Teaching Office

Courses offered include MA Creative Writing by Distance Learning, MA Creative Writing (Modular), MA Creative Writing with English Literary Studies, MA English Literary Studies with Creative Writing, MA English Literary Studies, MA English Literary Research, PhD Creative Writing, PhD English Literature and Creative Writing, PhD English Literature.

University of Leeds

Faculty of Arts, Humanities and Cultures, University of Leeds, Leeds LS2 9JJ
website https://ahc.leeds.ac.uk/
Facebook www.facebook.com/universityofleeds
Twitter @UniversityLeeds

Postgraduate courses include MA Writing for Performance and Digital Media, Creative Writing, Media Industries, and Film, Photography and Media.

University of Lincoln

Brayford Pool, Lincoln LN6 7TS
tel (01522) 882000
email enquiries@lincoln.ac.uk
website www.lincoln.ac.uk/course/crtvwtma
Facebook www.facebook.com/universityoflincoln/
Twitter @unilincoln
Instagram @unilincoln
Programme Leader Daniele Pantano

Offers MA Creative Writing. The course has a strong focus on employability and aims to prepare student writers for a professional writing or publishing career. Students also gain practical experience working on *The Lincoln Review*, an international literary journal. A wide range of professional authors, editors, producers and directors regularly visit Lincoln to speak to students: Carol Ann Duffy, Poet Laureate between 2009 and 2019, is among them.

Liverpool John Moores University

Tithebarn Street, Liverpool L2 2QP
tel 0151 231 2121

email APSadmissions@ljmu.ac.uk
website www.ljmu.ac.uk/study/courses/postgraduates/screenwriting
Programme Leader Screenwriting Richard Monks,
Programme Leader MA Writing Professor Catherine Cole

Offers MA Screenwriting (based at Liverpool Screen School) and MA Writing courses.

University of London, Goldsmiths

Goldsmiths, University of London,
London SE14 6NW
tel 020-7919 7171
website www.gold.ac.uk
Facebook www.facebook.com/GoldsmithsUoL
Twitter @GoldsmithsUoL
Instagram @goldsmithsuol

Postgraduate courses include Artists' Film and Moving Image, Art Psychotherapy, Art and Ecology, Arts and Learning, Black British Literature, Children's Literature, Children's Book Illustration, Computational Arts, Computer Games Art and Design, Creative and Life Writing, Creative Writing and Education, Curating, Digital Media, Dramaturgy and Writing for Performance, Film and Screen Studies, Filmmaking, Fine Art, Journalism, Performance Making, Radio, Script Writing and Translation.

University of London, Royal Holloway

Egham, Surrey TW20 0EX
tel (01784) 434455
website www.royalholloway.ac.uk
Facebook www.facebook.com/royalholloway
Twitter @RoyalHolloway

Postgraduate courses include Creative Writing, Screenwriting for Television and Film, Producing Film and Television.

London College of Communication

277 High Holborn, London WC1V 7EY
tel 020-7514 6500
website www.arts.ac.uk/colleges/london-college-of-communication
Facebook www.facebook.com/londoncollegeofcommunication
Twitter @LCCLondon

Postgraduate courses include Publishing, Screenwriting, Television, Photography, Games Design, Virtual Reality, Illustration, Film.

The London Film School

24 Shelton Street, London WC2H 9UB
tel 020-7836 9642
email info@lfs.org.uk
website https://lfs.org.uk

Offers an intensive one-year MA Screenwriting, and a two-year MA Filmmaking.

University of Manchester

University of Manchester, Oxford Road,
Manchester M13 9PL
tel 0161 275 3107
website www.alc.manchester.ac.uk/centrefornewwriting
Twitter @ECW_UoM

Courses offered include MA Creative Writing, MA Playwriting and MA Screenwriting.

The Manchester Writing School at Manchester Metropolitan University

Grosvenor East Building, Cavendish Street,
Manchester M15 6BG
tel 0161 247 2000
email writingschool@mmu.ac.uk
website www.mmu.ac.uk/english/mcr-writing-school
Twitter @McrWritingSchl
Creative Director Professor Carol Ann Duffy, *Contact (admission and general enquiries)* James Draper

Courses offered include Master of Fine Arts (MFA) and Master of Arts (MA) in Creative Writing with specialist routes in Novel, Poetry, Writing for Children & Young Adults, Scriptwriting and Creative Non-Fiction. Campus-based and international online distance learning, available to study full-time (MA: one year, MFA: two years) or part-time (MA: two years; MFA: three years). September and January enrolment. Scholarships available (including Joyce Nield Fund for non-UK Commonwealth students). Evening taught, with strong industry links. MFA students complete a full-length book/script. MA in Publishing presented in collaboration with the iSchool at Manchester Met and industry partners. PhD in Creative Writing, including PhD by practice.

Middlesex University

The Burroughs, Hendon, London NW4 4BT
tel 020-8411 5555
website www.mdx.ac.uk/courses/creative-media-and-writing
Facebook www.facebook.com/MiddlesexUniversity
Twitter @MiddlesexUni

Courses offered include MA Novel Writing (online distance learning) and MA Scriptwriting (Stage, Screen and Audio).

National Film and Television School

Beaconsfield Studios, Station Road, Beaconsfield,
Bucks. HP9 1LG
tel (01494) 671234
email info@nfts.co.uk
website https://nfts.co.uk
Facebook www.facebook.comNFTSFilmTV
Twitter @NFTSFilmTV

MA, diploma, certificate and short courses covering a wide range of disciplines relating to television and film.

Newcastle University

Newcastle upon Tyne NE1 7RU
tel 0191 208 6000
website www.ncl.ac.uk
Facebook www.facebook.com/newcastleuniversity
Twitter @UniofNewcastle

Courses include MPhil and PhD in Creative Writing; students benefit from close links to local partners such as Bloodaxe Books and Northern Stage. MA International Multimedia Journalism also available.

Northumbria University

Faculty of Arts, Design and Social Sciences, Lipman Building, Newcastle upon Tyne NE1 8ST
tel 0191 227 4444
email laura.fish@northumbria.ac.uk
website www.northumbria.ac.uk
Programme Leader Dr Laura Fish

Offers one- or two-year MA Creative Writing. Good links to regional literary organisations, such as New Writing North. Course leader Laura Fish is an award-winning writer of Caribbean heritage. Author of three novels, she is a Fellow of the Iowa International Writers Programme.

Nottingham Trent University

School of Arts and Humanities, Clifton Lane, Nottingham NG11 8NS
tel 0115 848 4200
email rory.waterman@ntu.ac.uk
email hum.enquiries@ntu.ac.uk
website www.ntu.ac.uk/course/english-linguistics-creative-writing
Twitter @ntuhum
Programme Leader Dr Rory Waterman

Offers a long-established and practice-based MA Creative Writing. Close links to the writing industry, an annual anthology, a programme of guest talks and workshops and many successful graduate writers. Diverse module options include: Fiction, Poetry, Writing for Stage, Radio and Screen, and Children's and Young Adult Fiction.

Oxford Brookes University

Headington Campus, Oxford OX3 0BP
email query@brookes.ac.uk
website www.brookes.ac.uk/courses/postgraduate/creative-writing/
Facebook www.facebook.com/oxfordbrookes
Twitter @oxford_brookes
Instagram @oxfordbrookes

Offers three courses in creative writing: MA, PGDip or PGCert. Tutors are themselves published writers. Creative Writing Fellows and visiting lecturers also meet students, who will eventually have the opportunity to meet literary agents from Felicity Bryan Associates, and to pitch their work to the publisher Philip Gwyn. Applications for the MA must be accompanied by a portfolio of recent creative

work: this should be either five poems, 2,000 words of prose or a proportional mixture of the two.

Oxford University

Department for Continuing Education, Rewley House, 1 Wellington Square, Oxford OX1 2JA
tel (01865) 270360
website www.conted.ox.ac.uk

MSt in Creative Writing: a two-year part-time master's degree covering prose fiction, narrative non-fiction, poetry, radio and TV drama, stage drama and screenwriting. Offers high contact hours, genre specialization and critical and creative breadth. *Email*: mstcreativewriting@conted.ox.ac.uk.

Short online courses and virtual classes in creative writing and literature; multiple intakes per year. *Email*: onlinecourses@conted.ox.ac.uk.

University of Plymouth

Drake Circus, Plymouth PL4 8AA
tel (01752) 600600
email admissions@plymouth.ac.uk
website www.plymouth.ac.uk
Facebook www.facebook.com/plymouthuni
Twitter @PlymUni

MA courses include Creative Writing and English Literature.

Queen's University, Belfast

University Road, Belfast BT7 1NN
tel 028-9024 5133
website www.qub.ac.uk
Facebook www.facebook.com/QueensUniversityBelfast
Twitter @QueensUBelfast

Offers MA/Postgraduate Diploma Creative Writing.

University of Roehampton

Grove House, Roehampton Lane, London SW15 5PJ
tel 020-8392 3000
website www.roehampton.ac.uk
Facebook www.facebook.com/roehamptonuni
Twitter @RoehamptonUni
Instagram @uni_roehampton

Postgraduate courses include Children's Literature.

The Royal Central School of Speech and Drama

Embassy Theatre, Eton Avenue, London NW3 3HY
tel 020-7722 8183
email sarah.grochala@cssd.ac.uk
website www.cssd.ac.uk
Twitter @CSSDLondon

Offers MA/MFA Writing for Stage and Broadcast Media. MA can be done in one year full-time or part-time over two years; MFA is two years, full-time.

University of St Andrews

School of English, St Andrews, Fife KY16 9AR
tel (01334) 462668
email pgeng@st-andrews.ac.uk
website www.st-andrews.ac.uk/english/postgraduate

Courses offered include PhD, MFA or MLitt Creative
Writing: Poetry or Prose; MFA or MLitt Playwriting
and Screenwriting.

University of Salford

The Crescent, Salford M5 4WT
tel 0161 295 5000
website www.salford.ac.uk
Facebook www.facebook.com/salforduni
Twitter @SalfordUni

Postgraduate courses include MA/PgDip Journalism,
MA Literature and Culture and MA Creative Writing:
Innovation and Experiment.

Sheffield Hallam University

City Campus, Howard Street, Sheffield S1 1WB
tel 0114 225 5555
email enquiries@shu.ac.uk
website www.shu.ac.uk
Facebook www.facebook.com/
sheffieldhallamuniversity
Twitter @sheffhallumuni

Postgraduate courses include Creative Writing, Sports
Journalism and Multimedia Journalism.

University of South Wales

Treforest, Pontypridd CF37 1DL
tel (01443) 760101
website www.southwales.ac.uk/courses/mphil-in-
writing
website www.southwales.ac.uk/courses/
Twitter @UniSouthWales

Offers MPhil Writing. The course has two core
elements: a writing project and a critical study based
on the published work of other authors. Also offers
MA English by Research.

University of Stirling

Stirling, FK9 4LA
tel (01786) 473171
email liam.bell@stir.ac.uk
website www.stir.ac.uk/courses/pg-taught/creative-
writing/
Facebook www.facebook.com/universityofstirling/
Twitter @StirUni
Instagram @universityofstirling
Course Director Dr Liam Murray Bell, *Associate
Professor* Dr Lorna Gibb, *Senior Lecturer* Kevin
MacNeil, *Teaching Fellow* Dr Chris Powici

Offers MLitt Creative Writing, focusing on creative
non-fiction, fiction and poetry. A sample of creative
work is required to support all applications.
Workshops, seminars and talks from visiting lecturers
are available, as is one-to-one tuition.

University of Wales Trinity Saint David

Lampeter Campus, Ceredigion SA48 7ED
tel (01570) 422351
email fhpadmissions@uwtsd.ac.uk
website www.uwtsd.ac.uk/ma-creative-writing
Facebook www.facebook.com/trinitysaintdavid
Twitter @UWTSD

Offers MA Creative Writing; can be completed in
person or through blended (mixed online and on
campus) delivery.

Warwick Writing Programme

School of Creative Arts,
Performance and Visual Cultures,
Faculty of Arts Building, University of Warwick,
Coventry CV4 7EQ
tel 024-7652 3665
email SCAPVCenquiries@warwick.ac.uk
website https://warwick.ac.uk/fac/arts/scapvc/wwp/

Postgraduate courses offered include MA Writing,
MA Writing for Media, MA Literary Translation
Studies, PhD Literary Practice and MPhil/PhD
Literary Translation Studies.

Book sites, blogs and podcasts

This is a small selection of the best book sites, blogs and podcasts recommended by the editors of the *Yearbook*. They share advice on writing, traditional publishing and self-publishing, as well as author interviews, book reviews and publishing news.

BOOK SITES AND BLOGS

Amazon Book Review

website www.amazon.com/amazonbookreview

Amazon's round-up of bestsellers and reading lists, featuring author interviews and recommendations.

The Artist's Road

website http://artistsroad.wordpress.com
Founder Patrick Ross

Blog created to record the cross-USA road trip that the author Patrick Ross took in the summer of 2010. During his trip he interviewed over 40 artists with the aim of discussing the motivations, challenges and rewards of their lifestyles, and passing on their creative wisdom. It now details his insights into living an 'art-committed life' through writing and creativity.

Book Page

website www.bookpage.com
Editor-in-Chief Trisha Ping

A book recommendation site. Editors share reviews and rate the best new releases by genre, from literary fiction and memoir to romance and crime.

Book Riot

website https://bookriot.com
Ceo & Co-founder Jeff O'Neal, *Executive Director of Content* S. Zainab Williams

A site dedicated to discussing and sharing books, as well as exploring writing and publishing. Recommendations and reviews are organised according to format and genre, and cover children's, YA and adult. Diversity and inclusion underpin the site's content and aims.

Books & Such

website www.booksandsuch.com/blog
Founder Janel Kobobel Grant

Blog from a literary agent's perspective, advising on writing query letters and improving MSS before submitting them to agents. Also addresses how to find an agent and get published. Highlights the importance of the editing process in adding to writing quality. Discusses the various aspects of traditional publishing and self-promotion.

The Bookseller

website www.thebookseller.com/comment
Editor Philip Jones

The online website of *The Bookseller*, a magazine which covers publishing industry news. Includes insights into trends and influences, interviews and articles from publishers and lists of bestsellers across a variety of genres.

Nathan Bransford

website http://blog.nathanbransford.com
Founder Nathan Bransford

This author and former literary agent blogs about the writing, editing and publishing process and includes tips on improving plots, dialogue and characters, writing a query letter and synopsis and finding a literary agent. Analyses and debates a range of topics including ebooks and their pricing, social media options, marketing, cover design and plot themes.

Collected

website www.rlf.org.uk/showcase-home
Editor Katherine Clements

Weekly articles published by writers on topics related to literature and writing. Includes discussions on genre, form, research, inspiration and the perfect place to write.

Cornflower Books

website www.cornflowerbooks.co.uk
Founder Karen Howlett

Reviews a wide range of books and has a monthly online book club. Debates cover designs and includes a 'writing and publishing' section, interviews with well-known authors about their books, writing process and routine. Selects 'books of the year' in different genres, and discusses literary festivals and prizes.

The Creative Penn

website www.thecreativepenn.com
Founder Joanna Penn

Focuses on the writing process and how to market and sell your book. Offers advice on dealing with criticism, finding an agent and writing query letters, POD and ebook publishing, as well as online and social media marketing. Debates traditional publishing, 'hybrid' and self-publishing options and includes audio/video interviews with self-published authors.

Daily Writing Tips

website www.dailywritingtips.com
Founder Maeve Maddox

Publishes new content every week with articles covering the whole writing spectrum: from grammar and punctuation to usage and vocabulary.

Dear Author

website www.dearauthor.com
Founder Jane Litte

Focuses primarily on romantic novels. All reviews are written in the form of a letter to the author. Includes interviews with authors, reading lists and an open discussion thread.

Electric Literature

website https://electricliterature.com

A hub for literary essays, criticism and news with a particular focus on the relationship between literature, society and culture. Includes conversations with authors offering advice on writing, as well as reading recommendations which encourage reading like a writer.

Fiction Notes

website www.darcypattison.com
Founder Darcy Pattison

Darcy Pattison is a published non-fiction writer and children's author, as well as an experienced speaker. Her website archives eight years of blog posts on children's writing, reviews of her work, resources for writers and information on her speaking engagements where she specialises in novel revision.

Five Books

website https://fivebooks.com
Editor Sophie Roell

A book site that asks experts to recommend the five best books in their subject and explain their selection in an interview. Recommendations range from broad introductions to specific and niche topics.

Jane Friedman

website http://janefriedman.com
Founder Jane Friedman

Focuses on digital publishing, provides tips for writers on how to beat writers' block, DIY ebook publishing, marketing your writing and publicising it online through blogs, social media and websites to create your 'author platform'. Includes guidance on copyright and securing permissions.

Jeff Goins

website http://goinswriter.com
Founder Jeff Goins

Focuses on advising authors about their writing journey, the business of writing and how to maximise productivity and profits. Highlights how authors can build a core fanbase 'tribe' through a focused approach and by adding value to social media and blogs.

Goodreads

website www.goodreads.com
Co-founder Otis Chandler

Users can see what their friends and favourite authors are reading, rate books they've read, write reviews, and customise bookshelves full of books 'Read' and books 'To Read'. A regular newsletter provides book news and author interviews. Owned by Amazon.

Helping Writers Become Authors

website www.helpingwritersbecomeauthors.com
Founder K.M. Weiland

Tips on story structure, creating memorable characters and plot development. Advice about finding writing inspiration and the writing process, story revision and MS editing stages. Includes an extensive list of books for aspiring authors.

Literary Hub

website https://lithub.com
Editor-in-Chief Jonny Diamond

Publishes original pieces and serves as a hub for online literary content from 300 partners. Includes reviews, literary criticism, excerpts and recommendations, as well as author interviews and writing advice within the 'Craft and Criticism' section. Crime Reads (https://crimereads.com) is their website dedicated to crime and thrillers.

Live Write Thrive

website www.livewritethrive.com
Founder C.S. Lakin

Set up by a writer, editor and writing coach who specialises in fiction, fantasy and YA, this blog focuses on helping writers discover what kind of copy-editing and critiquing services their work will need once it is finished. Includes articles by guest bloggers and tips on grammar.

Lovereading

website www.lovereading.co.uk
Managing Director Deborah Maclaren

Independent book recommendation site designed to inspire and inform readers, with the aim of helping them choose their next read. Features include: categories broken down by interest; downloadable opening extracts of featured books; like-for-like recommendations for discovering new authors; expert reviews and reader review panels.

The Millions

website https://themillions.com
Editor Sophia Stewart

A literary criticism and review site which includes interviews with authors on their writing process, lists of recommended books and annual 'Year in Reading' summaries from authors and editors.

The *New Yorker*: Books

website www.newyorker.com/tag/books
Editor David Remnick

The books section of the *New Yorker* dedicated to in-depth exploration and discussion of literature and literary trends. Includes author readings and interviews.

The *New York Times*: Books

website www.nytimes.com/section/books
Executive Editor Joe Kahn

The books section of the the New York Times which shares reviews, features and a bestseller list. Includes contributions from authors who share reflections on readings and insights into their writing.

A Newbie's Guide to Publishing

website http://jakonrath.blogspot.co.uk
Founder Joe Konrath

Blog by a self-published author which discusses the writing and publishing process and focuses on self-publishing ebooks, and looks at developments and trends in this area. Includes interviews with self-published authors about their books.

The Organised Writer

website http://organised-writer.com
Founder Antony Johnston

Houses a host of resources designed to make getting organised as a writer easier, including accounting spreadsheets.

Positive Writer

website http://positivewriter.com
Founder Bryan Hutchinson

A motivational blog for creatives, particularly writers, focusing on how to overcome doubt and negativity to unlock your inner creativity. It includes handy tips on marketing and interviews with other authors.

Publishers Weekly

website www.publishersweekly.com
Editorial Director Jim Milliot

A news platform that covers the international book publishing industry and is read by publishers, literary agents, booksellers, authors and readers. As well as industry news and trends, it shares reviews, bestseller lists and interviews.

Reading Matters

website http://readingmattersblog.com
Founder Kim Forrester

The site's focus is modern and contemporary fiction; reviews are personable and informative and include contributions from guest bloggers.

Lauren Sapala

website http://laurensapala.com
Founder Lauren Sapala

This blog gives pep talks to writers in moments of self-doubt. With posts about how to get inspired and stay focused, its aim is to nurture and empower your creative flame.

Savidge Reads

website https://savidgereads.wordpress.com
Founder Simon Savidge

Entertaining and chatty reviews of literary novels, from modern classics to contemporary fiction from a self-proclaimed bookaholic.

Soapbox

website www.publishersweekly.com/pw/by-topic/columns-and-blogs/soapbox/index.html
Founder Publishers Weekly

Discussions and interviews on all aspects of the literary world: writing, publishing and bookselling. Includes advice and insights as well as big topic debates including censorship, diversity and defunding libraries.

Terribleminds

website http://terribleminds.com/ramble/blog
Founder Chuck Wendig

Comical, easy-to-read blog about author Chuck Wendig's trials and tribulations whilst writing.

This Itch of Writing

website http://emmadarwin.typepad.com/thisitchofwriting
Founder Emma Darwin

An author's advice on the craft of authoring successful books both fiction and creative non-fiction.

Well-Storied

website www.well-storied.com
Founder Kristen Kieffer

A now archived blog containing many articles, resources and podcasts, focusing on the craft of writing, finding motivation and building a routine.

The Write Life

website http://thewritelife.com
Founder Alexis Grant

This blog is designed to encourage individuals to connect and share experiences with fellow writers during the different writing stages. Posts include advice on blogging, freelancing, finding an agent, publicity and self-publishing amongst other topics.

The Write Practice

website http://thewritepractice.com
Founder Joe Bunting

Focuses on the craft of writing, building a routine and how to get published; includes advice for writers on different stages of the writing process and submitting MSS to agents.

Writer Unboxed
website http://writerunboxed.com
Editor-in-Chief Therese Walsh

Comical tips on the art and craft of writing fiction, the writing process, and marketing your work. Includes interviews with established authors also offering advice.

Writers & Artists
website www.writersandartists.co.uk

Up-to-date news, views and advice on all aspects of writing and publishing on the site brought to you by the creators of this *Yearbook*. As well as guest blogs, videos and articles from established and debut writers across all genres, there are sections on self-publishing, a community area for sharing work, details of competitions and book-related events, including those hosted by Writers & Artists. Users can sign-up to receive special discounts on editorial services and books and to a regular newsletter.

PODCASTS

Always Take Notes
website www.alwaystakenotes.com
Hosts Simon Akam, Rachel Lloyd

A bi-weekly podcast interviewing a diverse range of writers and publishing industry experts on a variety of topics, from the mysteries of slush piles and per-word rates, to how to pitch a book and how data are changing the ways newspapers do business.

Backlisted
website www.backlisted.fm
Hosts John Mitchinson, Andy Miller

Created to shine a light on books that stand the test of time, each episode a writer is invited to discuss a book that they believe deserves a wider audience. Sponsored by Unbound.

Begin Self-Publishing Podcast
website https://beginselfpublishing.com
Host Tim Lewis

Promotes self-publishing by demystifying the whole process and gives advice on how to safely navigate all services available to self-published writers.

Bookclub
website https://www.bbc.co.uk/programmes/b006s5sf/episodes/downloads
Host James Naughtie

A monthly podcast which invites authors to discuss their most popular books and how they wrote them with a group of readers.

Book Riot
website https://bookriot.com/listen/shows/thepodcast
Hosts Jeff O'Neal, Rebecca Schinsky

A weekly podcast which discusses the latest news in the world of books and reading, brought to you by the editors of Book Riot.

Books and Authors
website www.bbc.co.uk/programmes/p02nrsfl/episodes/downloads
Hosts Elizabeth Day, Johny Pitts, Harriett Gilbert

A weekly podcast with highlights from BBC Radio 4 programmes Open Book, in which hosts Elizabeth Day and Johny Pitts interview bestselling authors about their work; and *A Good Read*, in which Harriett Gilbert hosts a lively discussion with her guests about their favourite books.

The Creative Penn Podcast
website www.thecreativepenn.com/podcasts
Host Joanna Penn

Published on Mondays, this weekly podcast informs aspiring authors about available publishing options and book marketing through informative discussions and interviews.

The Creative Process
website www.creativeprocess.info/interviews-page-1
Host Mia Funk

A conversation with writers, artists and creative thinkers across the Arts and STEM. Interviewees are invited to discuss their creative process and how it relates to their engagement with their work and the world around them.

Creative Writing Career
website https://creativewritingcareer.wordpress.com/podcast
Hosts Stephan Bugaj, Justin Sloan, Kevin Tumlinson

Hosted by leading industry professionals whose credits include writing for Pixar, FOX and HBO, this US podcast provides practical advice to writers on all forms of multimedia writing. Topics covered include books and comics, video games and e-publishing, and writing screenplays for television and film.

Dead Robots' Society
website http://deadrobotssociety.com
Hosts Justin Macumber, Terry Mixon, Paul E. Cooley

Created for aspiring writers by aspiring writers, this fun podcast offers advice and support by sharing anecdotes and discussing current topics of interest.

The Drunken Odyssey
website https://thedrunkenodyssey.com
Host John King

Started to create a community hub for writers, this podcast is a forum to discuss all aspects of creative writing and literature.

Fiction Writing Made Easy
website www.savannahgilbo.com/podcast
Host Savannah Gilbo

Created by an editor and book coach to share writing advice that is easy to follow. Episodes cover every stage of the writing process, from planning and writing opening pages to keeping your reader's interest to the very end.

Grammar Girl

website www.quickanddirtytips.com/grammar-girl
Host Mignon Fogarty

This award-winning weekly podcast provides a bitesize guide to the English language. Each week tackles a specific feature from style and usage, to grammar and punctuation, all in the hope of providing friendly tips on how to become a better writer.

The *Guardian* Books Podcast

website www.theguardian.com/books/series/books
Hosts Claire Armitstead, Richard Lea, Sian Cain

A weekly podcast that looks at the world of books, poetry and great writing, including interviews with prominent authors; recordings of *Guardian* live events; panel discussions examining current themes in contemporary writing; and readings of selected literary works.

Helping Writers Become Authors

website www.helpingwritersbecomeauthors.com/podcasts
Host K.M. Weiland

Published author, K.M. Weiland produces podcasts to help guide aspiring authors on how to craft and edit a manuscript ready to be sent to a literary agent.

How Do You Write

website www.howdoyouwrite.net/episodes
Host Rachel Herron

A bestselling author explores every aspect of the writing and publishing world, addressing the questions that all aspiring writers have. Subjects include how to keep writing, when you need beta readers, whether writing goals matter and what to do if your book doesn't sell.

In Writing with Hattie Crisell

website www.hattiecrisell.com/in-writing-with-hattie-crisell-podcast
Host Hattie Crisell

A journalist sits down with writers from every field (novelists, poets, screenwriters, fellow journalists) to discuss their writing process, sources of inspiration and motivation, and the advice they would pass on to aspiring writers.

I Should Be Writing

website http://murverse.com/subscribe-to-podcasts
Host Mur Lafferty

This award-winning podcast is about the process science fiction writer Mur Lafferty went through to

go from a wannabe writer to a professional, published author. It documents the highs and lows of a writing career and provides comprehensive how-to tips and interviews.

Literary Friction

website www.nts.live/shows/literaryfriction
Hosts Carrie Plitt, Octavia Bright

Hosted by two friends (one a literary agent, the other a writer). Each monthly episode centres around a theme which an author is invited to discuss. Together they share insights into the world of books and reading recommendations.

London Review Bookshop Podcast

website www.londonreviewbookshop.co.uk/podcasts-video

A weekly podcast which shares literary events held and recorded at the London Review Bookshop. Authors are invited to discuss their latest publications, covering fiction, non-fiction, poetry and essays.

The LRB Podcast

website www.lrb.co.uk
Hosts Thomas Jones, Adam Shatz, Malin Hay

Weekly episodes cover subjects taken from the most recent issue of the *London Review of Books*. Discussions range from current events to recent publications, exploring the relationship between literature and the societies in which it is published.

The *New Yorker*: Fiction

website www.newyorker.com/podcast/fiction
Host Deborah Treisman

New Yorker fiction editor, Deborah Treisman, invites an author whose work is being published by the magazine that month to join her in this monthly podcast. Each author selects a piece of short fiction from the magazine's archive to read and analyse.

The Graham Norton Book Club

website www.audible.co.uk
Host Graham Norton, *Co-hosts* Alex Clark, Sara Collins

TV star and writer, Graham Norton, hosts a series of podcasts in conversation with well-known audiobook narrators and authors on all subjects to do with books.

The Penguin Podcast

website www.penguin.co.uk/podcasts.html

This series, published fortnightly, gives intimate access to bestselling authors through interviews where they discuss their work and give examples of five things that have inspired and shaped their writing.

Reading and Writing Podcast

website http://readingandwritingpodcast.com
Host Jeff Rutherford

This interview-style podcast encourages readers to call in and leave voicemail messages and questions ready for the host to ask the guest writer, who discusses their work and writing practices.

The Self-Publishing Show
website https://selfpublishingformula.com/spf-podcast
Host Mark Dawson

Created by a bestselling self-published author to share insights into the publishing world and writing process. Advice ranges from how to craft a story to how to get in into the hands of readers around the world.

Simon Mayo's Book of the Year
website https://www.globalplayer.com/podcasts/42KedV
Hosts Simon Mayo, Matt Williams

This conversational-style podcast invites writers to discuss their favourite books and the stories that shaped their writing. Writers also share the inspiration and writing process behind their latest novel.

Six Figure Authors
website https://6figureauthors.com
Hosts Lindsay Buroker, Jo Lallo, Andrea Pearson

Created to help authors grow their careers and maximise the potential of their books. Topics covered include networking, marketing for introverts, keeping your backlist in print, taking advantage of rights sales and connecting with readers.

The *Slightly Foxed* Podcast
website https://foxedquarterly.com/category/podcast

The magazine's podcast invites author, and occasionally publishers and booksellers, to discuss literature past and present. Conversations focus on literary traditions and inspirations, writers' relationships with their contemporaries and their environment, and personal stories of lives dedicated to writing.

So I'm Writing a Novel...
website https://soimwritinganovel.com/
Host Oliver Brackenbury

Hosted by an author in the process of writing their third novel, this podcast shares his writing journey. Fellow authors are also invited onto the show to share advice and insights. Topics covered include planning, plotting, research and making progress.

Story Grid
website https://storygrid.simplecast.fm
Hosts Shawn Coyne, Tim Grahl

Hosted by a book editor with more than 25 years' experience in publishing and a struggling writer, the duo discuss what features bestselling novels have in common and how authors can utilise these to write a great story that works.

Write Now With Sarah Werner
website www.sarahwerner.com/episodes
Host Sarah Werner

A podcast produced with aspiring writers in mind; provides advice, inspiration, and encouragement to writers to find a suitable work-life balance.

Writers Aloud
website www.rlf.org.uk/showcase-home

This podcast invites published authors to discuss life as a writer and the influences and circumstances which have shaped their writing. Books, poetry, radio, television and theatre are all covered across a range of genres. The Royal Literary Fund also produce short films (In Focus) and bite-size podcasts only a few minutes long (Vox) covering similar topics.

Writer's Routine
website https://writersroutinedotcom.wordpress.com
Host Dan Simpson

Each episode interviews an author to discuss their writing routine and identify any habits that can be shared with aspiring writers to inspire creativity and increase productivity.

Writing Coach
website https://annkroeker.com/podcasts
Host Ann Kroeker

This podcast offers practical writing advice alongside tips and tricks to find inspiration and motivation. Episodes are short and concise for writers on the go. Guest authors share their experiences and insights on writing and publishing.

Writing Excuses
website www.writingexcuses.com

Produced by writers, this weekly podcast offers sensible and strategic advice to all who write, whether for pleasure or profit, on how they can revise and edit their work to create a better story. Each week there is a homework assignment and suggested reading.

You're Booked
website https://play.acast.com/s/booked
Host Daisy Buchanan

Each week a new author is invited to discuss their favourite books, the influence they had and how they made the leap from readers to writers.

Law and copyright
UK copyright law and publishing rights

Publisher Lynette Owen outlines the basic principles of copyright and how UK copyright law provides a framework for the protection of creative works, with particular reference to publishing.

Creators including writers and artists are dependent on copyright to protect their works and to underpin the arrangements they make with the publishers who bring their works to market. The United Kingdom has the oldest tradition of copyright legislation, starting with the Statute of Anne which came into force in 1710. The last full revision of UK copyright law resulted in the Copyright, Designs and Patents Act 1988 (CPDA); this replaced the 1956 Copyright Act, which in turn replaced the 1911 Copyright Act. Since the 1988 Act, there have been a number of revisions, usually undertaken via Statutory Instrument.

What is copyright?

Copyright is one aspect of intellectual property rights (IPR), which are often defined as relating to 'works of the mind'. Other aspects include design and patent rights. Copyright has both positive and negative aspects – it enables rightsholders to authorise the use of their work in a variety of ways and also to take action against unauthorised use. It is worth flagging here that there are different philosophies of copyright; the UK, in common with other Anglophone countries, operates under common law, based on factual case law, and views copyright works as property which can be traded and transferred. By contrast, countries which operate under civil law, based on civil codes, (e.g. the countries of mainland Europe) view copyright (referred to as *droit d'auteur*) more as a human right belonging to the creator, with far more restrictive regulations on how it can be exploited.

How does it work?

Each country has its own national copyright legislation which normally covers works created by citizens of that country, creators normally resident in that country and works first published in that country. There is also normally an obligation to respect the creative works originating in other countries which belong to the same international copyright conventions; this is normally undertaken in the form of 'national treatment', i.e. each member country provides to the creative works from other member states the same standard of protection it would grant to the works of its own citizens. This means that there may be varying standards of protection from country to country, for example in terms of the duration of copyright protection; there may also be differing exceptions to copyright from country to country. Most countries in the world now belong to one or more of the international copyright conventions: the Berne Convention (1886), the Universal Copyright Convention (1952) and the World Intellectual Property Organization (WIPO) Copyright Treaty (1996, but in force from 2002 – this convention reinforces the concept of copyright in the digital age). Membership of a convention requires member states to observe certain minimum standards of copyright protection.

What types of work are protected by copyright?

The CDPA (Copyright, Designs and Patents Act 1988) provides copyright protection to three main categories of creative works:

1. Original literary, dramatic, musical and artistic works

'Literary works' includes any work which is written, including tables, graphs, compilations and computer programs. It also includes databases which involve creativity in terms of selection by the compiler. Dramatic and musical works include performable works such as plays and dances, with the lyrics of musical works protected separately. Artistic works include graphic works (paintings, drawings, maps, engravings or similar works), sculptures, collages, works of architecture and works of artistic craftsmanship (although these can also be protected under design rights). All works must be original and in written or other fixed form.

2. Sound recordings, films and broadcasts

These are also protected and may involve the many different copyrights of performers, producers and broadcasters. Broadcasts traditionally covered transmission by radio and television, but now include satellite broadcasts and transmissions via the internet.

3. Copyright in typographical arrangements

This is a specific right under UK copyright law which does not appear in the legislation of many other countries. This right covers the design and layout of text and, as such, is a right quite separate from that of the creative content of the text; it belongs to the publisher in recognition of their skill and investment in the layout of a work and lasts for 25 years from the date of first publication of that version of the text.

Who owns the copyright?

The first owner of copyright is normally the creator, e.g. the writer, artist, composer, etc. The major exception to this, in UK copyright law, is if a work is created as part of the creator's regular employment, in which case copyright belongs to the employer. A good example of this would be when a publisher employs a team of lexicographers in-house to compile dictionary entries. US copyright law has a provision for 'works for hire' where content (text, illustrations, etc) may be commissioned by a publisher, usually on the basis of an outright fee, with copyright then belonging to the commissioning entity.

In the case of copyright controlled by the creator, he or she will then have a choice on how to deal with the question of copyright when dealing with a publisher. For an author or illustrator seeking a contract with a publisher, there are two possibilities:

i) They may retain ownership of the copyright and grant an exclusive licence or licences to one or more publishers for publication of the work in an agreed language, in agreed format/s, within agreed sales territories and for an agreed period of time. For example, an author could grant an exclusive licence to a UK publisher for the UK and Commonwealth markets, and a separate licence to a US publisher for the American market. This is a common scenario in trade (general) publishing.

ii) In educational, academic and professional publishing, the scenario may be different. The author may be asked to assign copyright to the publishing house – this is often a requirement for academic journal articles but may also be requested for books, even when the author is receiving an advance and ongoing royalties; it is particularly logical for multi-author works where individual contributors may each be paid an outright fee. There is often much misunderstanding of copyright assignment and publishers should always be prepared to explain to authors and illustrators their reasons for requesting it. One particularly powerful reason is that it is often much simpler to take action against piracy if copyright is in the name of the publishing house.

With the rise of the internet, there is a need for protection of internet transmissions and for user-generated works; these are covered under provisions for 'communication to the public' and 'making available to the public'. However, the question of copyright ownership in user-generated works is complex, given the scale of material which is uploaded to social media sites such as YouTube, Facebook, Twitter, Instagram, TikTok and others. If the material uploaded is original to the person undertaking the uploading, then copyright will belong to them, but a lot of such material may belong to other parties and may have been uploaded without their knowledge or consent.

What are moral rights?

Moral rights are personal to the creator and were introduced into UK copyright legislation for the first time in the CDPA 1988; they had long been a feature of civil law. They are quite separate from the economic rights of the creator and in the UK they last for the same period as copyright protection; in some other legislations they are inalienable and perpetual. They include the right of paternity (the right to be recognised as the creator), the right of integrity (the right to object to derogatory or damaging treatment of the work) and the right to object to false attribution of a work. UK legislation is unusual in that it requires the creator to assert his or her right of paternity (this is often done via a notice on the title verso page of a book); it also allows for the creator to waive his or her moral rights, something which may be necessary for certain forms of publication or when a book is used as the basis for film or television exploitation.

How long does copyright last?

In the case of the UK, the period of protection is now 70 years from the end of the year in which the creator dies – in the case of works of collaborative authorship, from the end of the year in which the last author dies. The term of protection was extended from 50 to 70 years for all works still in copyright as at 1 July 1995, as a result of an EU directive to harmonise the term of copyright within the European Union. Works published in the USA since 1 January 1978 also now have a similar period of protection. However, many countries in the world still have a shorter period of protection (e.g. China has a period of 50 years *post mortem auctoris*).

What does copyright enable the owner to do?

It enables the owner to undertake or authorise reproduction and distribution of the work to the public, as well as a range of other methods of exploiting the work, including performance, broadcasting and adaptations (which would include translations). It is normally an infringement of copyright for anyone to undertake any of these activities without authorisation from the copyright holder.

What action can be taken against copyright infringement?

UK copyright legislation permits action to be taken under civil or criminal law, depending on the nature of the infringement; penalties are decided by the courts. By contrast, the legislation of some countries defines the penalties in terms of maximum financial fines or terms of imprisonment. There are many possible categories of infringement – these could include unauthorised reproduction, unauthorised adaptation, plagiarism and passing off. In the internet age, unauthorised use of copyright content has increased; some is undertaken for commercial purposes via torrent sites, whilst other cases may be file sharing (e.g. of textbooks amongst students). The Publishers Association has a website which enables its members to issue 'notice and takedown' to infringing sites (see www.copyrightinfringementportal.com).

Are there exceptions to copyright?

Most national copyright laws list a number of uses of copyright material which can be undertaken without permission from or payment to the copyright owner, subject to certain conditions. The CDPA 1988 provides for a number of these:
• Fair dealing with a literary, dramatic, musical or artistic work for the purposes of research or study;
• Fair dealing for the purposes of criticism or review;
• Fair dealing with a work (other than a photograph) for the purpose or reporting current events.

These uses are permitted subject to due acknowledgement to the creator and the source, provided they do not adversely affect the normal interests of the copyright holder. There is no statutory definition of *fair dealing*, but most publishers would consider that fair dealing does not apply to use in the context of a commercial publication, so an author wishing to include copyright text or illustrations from outside sources in his or her own book should not assume that this is covered by fair dealing, however short the material may be.

The CDPA also provides for the copying of material for educational purposes, provided this is not undertaken by a reprographic process; thus, for example, displaying a passage of text on an interactive whiteboard is permitted. Large-scale copying of limited amounts of copyright material via photocopying or scanning (e.g. for course-packs for schools or universities, or on a company intranet) is covered under collective licences issued by the Copyright Licensing Agency (CLA) which negotiates licences to schools, colleges, universities, government departments and private businesses for such use; a share of licence revenue is paid to authors via the Authors Licensing and Collecting Society (ALCS), to visual artists via the

Useful websites

Authors Licensing and Collecting Society (ALCS): www.alcs.co.uk

Copyright Licensing Agency (CLA): www.cla.co.uk

Design and Artists Copyright Society (DACS): www.dacs.org.uk

Intellectual Property Office (IPO): www.gov.uk/government/organisations/intellectual-property-office

Picture Industry Collecting Society for Effective Licensing (PICSEL): www.picsel.org.uk

Publishers' Licensing Services (PLS): www.pls.org.uk

Publishers Association: www.publishers.org.uk

Society of Authors: www.societyofauthors.org

World Intellectual Property Organisation (WIPO): www.wipo.int/portal/en/index.html

Design and Artists Collecting Society (DACS) or the Picture Industry Collecting Society for Effective Licensing (PICSEL), and to publishers via Publishers' Licensing Services

(PLS).Organisations similar to CLA exist in many overseas countries and revenue from the copying of extracts from UK copyright works abroad is channelled to CLA via bilateral agreements with those organisations.

There are also provisions for the inclusion of short passages of published literary and dramatic works in educational anthologies, provided this does not affect the interests of the copyright holders and that such material does not represent the majority of the anthology.

The CDPA 1988 permits the making of a single copy of a copyright work by a library on behalf of a person undertaking research or private study, and it also permits libraries to make copies for the purposes of preservation or replacement of a damaged item.

There has been a copyright exception for visually impaired people since the Copyright (Visually Impaired Persons) Act 2002, giving them the right to accessible versions of copyright content (e.g. in Braille, audio or text-to-speech versions).

2014 saw the introduction of a number of amendments to existing copyright exceptions and some new exceptions, introduced via statutory instruments. Among them was an exception for copying for private use; fair dealing for non-commercial research or private study; a fair dealing exception for criticism or review or otherwise (the latter term undefined); a new exception for caricature, parody or pastiche; a new exception for text and data analysis for non-commercial research; and an extension of the exception for visually impaired persons to cover persons whose ability to read is affected by their disability (either physical or e.g. dyslexia). It remains the case that any fair dealing use must acknowledge the source and must not affect the normal interests of the rightsholder.

Copyright acts

- Copyright, Designs and Patents Act 1988 (but it is vital to use an up-to-date amended version). See www.gov.uk/government/organisations/intellectual-property-office.
- Duration of Copyright and Rights in Performances Regulations 1995 (SI 1995 No. 3297)
- Copyright and Rights in Database Regulations 1997 (SI 1997/3032) amended by the Copyright and Rights in Databases (Amendment) Regulations 2003 (SI 2003/2501)
- Copyright and Related Rights Regulations 2003 (SI 2003 No. 2498)
- Intellectual Property (Enforcement, etc) Regulations 2006 (SI 2006 No. 1028)
- Performances (Moral Rights, etc) Regulations 2006 (SI 2006 No. 18)
- Copyright and Rights in Performances (Quotation and Parody) Regulations 2014
- Copyright and Rights in Performances (Personal Copies for Private Use) Regulations 2014

How has UK copyright law changed?

In particular, UK copyright law has been influenced by a number of EU directives over the years, which have normally been implemented via statutory instruments. The most significant have been: the 1993 Directive on the Duration of Copyright and Authors' Rights (93/98/EEC), implemented via the Duration of Copyright and Rights in Performance Regulations 1995 (SI 1995 No 3297); the EC Database Directive 96/9 EC which was implemented via the Copyright and Rights in Databases Regulations 1997; and the EU Directive 2001/29/EC on the Harmonisation of Certain Aspects of Copyright and Related Rights in the Information Society, which included a transmission right and the right for copyright holders to use encryption and identifier systems to protect their works (implemented by SI 2003 No. 2498, the Copyright and Related Rights Regulations).

After two and a half years of high-profile negotiations and public debate, the European Union undertook a major copyright review. This led to the Directive on Copyright in the Digital Single Market, adopted in 2019 and to be implemented by EU member states by June 2021. In the meantime, following the outcome of the Brexit referendum of 23 June 2016, the UK left the EU on 31 January 2020, with a transition period running until 31 December 2020. From 1 January 2021 the UK was therefore free to set its own copyright agenda. The majority of the provisions of EU copyright legislation have been retained for the time being, but the UK has not implemented the 2019 DSM/Copyright Directive; it may however choose to implement similar provisions. Some key elements of the Directive (Article 17, the liability regime and monitoring/filtering obligations for online content sharing platforms, and Articles 19–21, the so-called "bestseller" provisions for remuneration for authors and performers) will not be included in UK law.

In 2021 the UK Intellectual Property Office (IPO) undertook a consultation on a possible change to the current regime on exhaustion of intellectual property rights. A move from the regional exhaustion regime which applied whilst the UK was a member of the EU to an international exhaustion regime would open up the UK market to parallel importation of competing editions of books, in particular from the USA and from developing countries where publishers have been granted licences for local low-price editions. Following strong lobbying from the creative industries, and in particular from the book trade and authors, on 18 January 2022 the UK government announced that no changes would be made at the moment, but that the matter may be subject to future review. At the time of writing, no formal decision has been reached.

Copyright under the microscope?

The last 25 years have seen a plethora of reviews of copyright – at international, multinational and national level – raising the question of the balance of interest between rightsholders and users, and questioning whether copyright remains fit for purpose. The rise of the internet has raised expectations amongst many users that content should be instantly available and preferably free of charge. The dangers of this have been seen all too clearly, in particular with the adverse impact on the music, film and computer software industries and their creators. On the other hand, some creators have been happy to make their work available under a range of Creative Commons licences, some more restrictive than others (see www.creativecommons.org/licences). There is an ongoing move towards Open Access in the academic sector, with its impact being felt particularly in the area of academic journals, but more recently extended to academic monographs.

Copyright has had a long history of adapting to developments in technology and to changing market needs; hence it remains fit for purpose and is a necessary framework that enables creators to receive a just reward for the use of their work and to recognise the skills and investment of those who, like publishers, bring their works to market. *At Risk: Our Creative Future*, a report from the House of Lords Communications Committee published on 17 January 2023, voiced concern about any government moves which would weaken copyright law and impact negatively on UK creative industries. In the same month, publishers welcomed the UK government's decision not to broaden the copyright exception for text and data mining (TDM) to include commercial use.

Further reading

Cornish, William et al., *Intellectual Property, Patents, Copyrights, Trademarks and Allied Rights* (Sweet & Maxwell, 9th edn 2019)

Bently, Lionel and Sherman, Brad, *Intellectual Property Law* (OUP, 6th edn 2022)

Caddick, Nicholas et al., *Copinger and Skone James on Copyright* (Sweet & Maxwell, 18th edn and Second Supplement 2022)

Jones, Hugh and Benson, Christopher, *Publishing Law* (Routledge, 5th edn 2016)

Owen, Lynette (Gen. Ed.), *Clark's Publishing Agreements: A Book of Precedents* (Bloomsbury Professional, 11th edn 2022)

For a view of copyright from the US perspective:

Netanel, Neil Weinstock, *Copyright: What Everyone Needs to Know* (OUP New York 2018)

Lynette Owen OBE has worked at Cambridge University Press, Pitman Publishing, Marshall Cavendish and Pearson Education, and is now a freelance copyright and rights consultant at Lynette Owen Consulting. Her book, *Selling Rights*, is published by Routledge (8th edition 2019; 9th edition due 2024). She is the General Editor of *Clark's Publishing Agreements: A Book of Precedents* (Bloomsbury Professional, 11th edition 2022).

See also...
- *Copyright Licensing Agency*, page 716

Law and copyright

A legal lexicon

data protection

The duty to protect the privacy of individuals if they share their personal information with a company (name, date of birth, gender, email or home address, etc.). This might be through a newsletter sign up, survey or book order on a website. The Data Protection Act 2018 insists that recipients of this kind of personal information must store it safely, use it only for the purpose communicated to the individual and only store data for as long as is necessary.

defamation

To defame someone is to damage their reputation and can result in legal action taken against the author or publisher if the case is serious enough. Defamatory content might include mocking and ridicule or making a false statement about a person or company. In fiction a character could be considered defamatory if they bear resemblance to a real person or body of people. Defamation court cases can be extremely expensive, meaning that publishers will often cease publication if there is even a possibility of being sued and will include clauses in their contracts stating the author is responsible (legally and financially) for any defamatory content found in their work.

intellectual property (IP)

An idea or creation which is not tangible or material but is sellable and ownable. This includes trademarks, copyrights and patents of character names, plot devices and fictional places; text, photographs and illustrations; databases and software.

libel

Defamatory statements which are written or published. This can now include social media posts and comments – the authors of which have been successfully sued in court.

moral rights

There are two key moral rights which an author should be aware of and they apply even after an author has assigned their copyright to another party. The right to paternity gives an author the right to assert themselves as the creator of a work and prevents false attribution. The right to integrity prevents a work being edited or changed without the author's permission.

permissions

If someone wants to use part or the whole of another writer's work, they must first receive their permission to do so (or the permission of the copyright or licence holder). An author must do the same if they want to use someone else's work, for example an illustration or quotation. Permissions are granted in a contract and usually in return for payment. Permissions must be cleared before publication to avoid contravening copyright.

privacy and confidentiality

A breach of privacy occurs when confidential information is shared beyond the person or people for whom it was intended and can be met with legal action. A duty of confidence exists between an author and their publisher which prevents confidential information, such as ideas and manuscripts as well as commercial information about the publisher, from being shared. An author must also respect the right to privacy – in both fiction and non-fiction – if their work is inspired by real people or events. For example, if writing about a former line of work, avoid sharing confidential or sensitive information, or if writing a romance novel, avoid basing the lead character on an ex.

slander

Defamatory statements which are spoken aloud. For an author this could include statements made during a book tour or promotional interview.

subsidiary rights

Also known as ancillary rights, i.e. secondary to **volume rights** (see below), these are rights which are licensed to a publisher which then licenses them to a third party. These might be a foreign publisher with whom a translation is negotiated or a newspaper or magazine that wishes to print an extract from a book. A literary agent will often not assign copyright in some subsidiary rights to a publisher and will manage them for an author. These include those rights that might be exploited in areas beyond the page, such as film or TV and merchandising rights.

trademark

A sign, design or expression that is legally protected which identifies the individuality of these symbols and their distinction from those used by others in a similar business and protects them from copying. For example, J.K. Rowling has copyrighted various character names and features of her *Harry Potter* series, such as Hogwarts School of Witchcraft and Wizardry and Gryffindor House.

volume rights

The rights for a publisher to publish a book in its main editions: print, audio and ebook.

Author–Publisher contracts

Publishing contracts can be lengthy; it's helpful to know what types of clauses they are likely to include and why they are there.

If you have an agent, they will negotiate your publishing contract on your behalf. Organisations such as the of the Society of Authors (see page 495) and WGGB (see page 498) offer contract review services. A contract is a legal agreement between two parties and exists to protect both author and publisher. It includes clauses on rights and obligations to avoid ambiguity as to the responsibilities of both parties. The clauses in your publishing contract are likely to include those listed below.

Definitions used throughout the contract will often be included at the beginning or in an appendix, and might include terms such as 'Net Receipts', 'Hybrid Product', 'First Serial', 'Territory' and 'Electronic Book'.

Legal operation and enforcement of the contract is covered by a few standard clauses, such as those relating to 'Interpretation', 'Arbitration', 'Confidentiality', 'Notices' and 'Entire Agreement'.

Free to publish

The author confirms that they are able to enter into the agreement and that the book they are writing is a unique, new property, their own work and will not contain any legally compromising material. Note that the first example below indicates the style of legalese in which your contract is likely to be couched:

Exclusivity 'The Author hereby grants to the Publishers during the legal term of copyright the sole and exclusive licence to publish the said work in volume form.'

Warranty and indemnity are confirmed, meaning the author states that they are freely able to enter into the agreement, is the sole author, owns the rights in the 'work' and that it is unique, i.e. has not been published elsewhere previously. It also confirms the work does not contain any libellous or defamatory material or content that isn't the author's to include, i.e. that is someone else's copyright and that the author has cleared permissions with the copyright holder for any part of somebody else's work being reproduced in the book. The author agrees to cover any legal costs, other fees or losses if they are in any way in breach of the warranty.

Territory

This is the geographical areas where the book can be sold, for example UK and Europe, or North American, or World territories.

Rights

Legal Term is the period that the contract covers, from date of signature of the contract by both parties or until rights are reverted to the author.

Granting and Reversion is when an author agrees that the publisher is allowed to publish their Work during the legal term. Rights might revert (back to the author) automatically when sales dip below a minimum annual level, of say, 50 copies. An author may negotiate to have rights in their book reverted and will be able to purchase any remaining stock. At that stage the contract is also formally terminated.

Termination might also occur if either party breaches any of the terms of the contract, for example if the author fails to deliver a manuscript of the quality expected on time and if it is found to be plagiarised. Late delivery alone would not usually be grounds for termination, but an author should always inform the agent or publisher if a contracted delivery date cannot be fulfilled.

Copyright Notice and Infringement This covers how the author's name will appear in the book, i.e. © [name of author], 202X. These clauses confirm that copyright in the Work is the property of the author. They will also make it clear that, if the publisher decides to protect the copyright of a book insofar as it threatens the value of the rights sold to a publisher, the author will assist the publisher (at the publisher's expense).

Subsidiary rights include:
• Anthology and quotation rights
• Broadcast reading and audiobook rights
• Digital and electronic rights
• Dramatisation, film, documentary, television sound broadcasting video or other mechanical reproduction rights
• English language rights (royalty exclusive)
• First serial rights (e.g. in a magazine where an extract from an original Work is serialised or published)
• Large print, educational, reprint or paperback rights licensed to a book club or to another publisher
• Micrography reprography, merchandising and manufacturing rights
• Second serial rights (rights sold subsequent to the first serial rights, see above)
• Single-extract or digest or book condensation rights
• Translation rights (royalty exclusive)
• US rights (royalty exclusive)

Each set of rights will be subject to a royalty percentage, payable to the author when these rights have been exercised. Some rights are held back or retained by an agent or author, so they might be exploited at another time and be subject to negotiation with a third party after publication. These tend to be the potentially more lucrative rights if exploited, such as dramatisation and film, translation or audio. Some 'hybrid' authors will license print rights to a publisher but retain digital book rights to allow them to self-publish in that format; a contract would make clear in which territories each edition might be sold.

Practicalities

Delivery includes a realistic delivery date and the specifications as to what will be delivered in what format (e.g. complete digital manuscript), to what extent (70,000 words including any endmatter) and accompanied by any material (extracts, quotations) for which copyright might need to be cleared.

Payments

Advances are an example of financial goodwill, a pact that author and editor have cemented through the contract to agree to work together and to make money from the activity. It is usually paid in two or three equal tranches, payable on signature of the contract, on delivery and approval of the final manuscript, and on first publication. The advance against royalties means a payment made before any actual revenue from sales of a book have been received.

Royalties are the fees paid to an author on the sale of copies of their book and are subject to sliding scales, so that as a book becomes more successful an author benefits more. As more and more copies are sold the investment the publisher made in producing the first print run will be recouped; subsequent runs might become very profitable for the publisher and rightly an agent will argue for an author to profit from this success too. Such rising royalty rates for a published price contract might look something like this:

• **on home sales**: 7.5% of the published price on the first ten thousand (10,000) copies sold; 10% of the published price up to twenty thousand (20,000) copies sold and 12.5% of the published price on all copies sold thereafter, such royalty not to be deemed a precedent between the publishers and author or agent;

• **on home sales where the discount is 52.5% or more**: four-fifths (4/5ths) of the prevailing royalty; on home sales where the discount is 60% or more: three-fifths (3/5ths) of the prevailing rate.

Free and presentation copies will be provided to the author (anywhere between six and 15 free copies) on publication and to potential reviewers as part of a promotional campaign; royalty payments are not made against these gratis copies. Authors may purchase copies of their own book at discount.

Payment process, accounting periods and other details about how and when the publisher will remunerate the author (or their agent on the author's behalf) will be included.

Publishing process

Author corrections and their proofreading responsibilities might be clearly laid out, covering what checking tasks an author will be expected to undertake and when and which might be carried out and paid for by the publisher, such as having an index prepared or clearing permissions for images or quotations. It might also include a clause in which the publisher 'reserves the right to charge the Author' for the cost of author corrections to page proofs if these are over and above the usual level of alterations. Such costs might be debited against the author's royalty account.

Promotion clauses advise that a publisher shall advertise, promote and market the Work as they deem appropriate 'in their sole discretion'. If an author feels strongly that they wish to be consulted about any aspect of promotion or cover design they could ask for such clauses to be modified. The most an author is likely to get is an amendment that agrees they will be 'consulted' and asked to 'agree' to the publisher's plan and that their agreement 'will not be unreasonably withheld'.

Publication date might not be firmly set when the contract is signed but the publisher's commissioning editor should have a clear idea of what quarter they would like the book to appear in. An agreement would usually stipulate that the book should be published within twelve months of date of delivery and acceptance 'unless prevented by circumstances over which they have no control or unless mutually agreed'.

New and updated editions for non-fiction titles might be referred to, defining what would constitute a 'new' rather than a 'revised' edition and how much new content it might include, say at least 10% new material. The author would be offered first refusal on preparing a new edition, but the publisher would want to include a clause to allow them to ask another writer to complete such a project if they perceived there was a market for it, but the original author was unable or unwilling to take on the commission.

The contract should not daunt an author. It is supposed to be a joint declaration and not biased in favour of one party or the other.

Alysoun Owen is Editor of the *Writers' & Artists' Yearbook* and author of the *Writers' & Artists' Guide to Getting Published* (Bloomsbury 2019).

Law and copyright

Protecting your content: piracy and IP

Given the marked increase in piracy in the publishing industry since the introduction of digital technology, what steps can authors take to combat IP theft and protect their work, to avoid significant financial and reputational loss? Content protection solutions provider MUSO explains the threat and provides valuable advice for self-published and ebook authors.

Protecting your intellectual property: combating piracy in the world of self-publishing

For self-published authors, intellectual property (IP) protection is a crucial aspect of success in the digital age. With the rise of digital technologies, book publishing has undergone a significant transformation. While this has made books easier to publish and more accessible, it has also exposed them to rampant piracy. The ease of sharing and distributing digital content has led to a rise in IP theft. The consequences of piracy can be severe, causing financial loss, damaging reputations, and undermining the value of an author's work. However, there are steps that self-published authors and authors of ebooks can take to protect their IP and prevent piracy.

Understanding the threat

Piracy is the unauthorised use or reproduction of someone else's work. In the context of self-publishing, piracy can occur when someone illegally downloads and distributes an author's ebook without their permission. Piracy is a widespread problem, and it can be challenging to detect and prevent.

The impact of piracy

The cost of piracy to the publishing industry is immense. According to a study by the International Intellectual Property Alliance (IIPA), the global book-publishing industry loses over $20 billion annually to piracy. Moreover, the increase in piracy is likely to continue. Piracy in the publishing industry has seen a marked rise in the last three years, with a notable uptick following the first lockdowns of the pandemic. Significantly, in May 2020 publishing overtook film as the second most in-demand media sector for digital piracy, behind TV. And publishing continues to over-index in total piracy demand. MUSO's own data showed 215 billion visits to piracy websites across all media industries in 2022, an 18% increase compared with 2021. However, looking at publishing specifically, there were 59.2 billion visits to publishing piracy sites in 2022 … a *37.1% increase* on the 2021 figure.

Piracy can have severe consequences for self-published authors. Financial loss is a significant concern. Piracy can cause authors to lose out on royalties and revenue from sales. Moreover, the proliferation of pirated copies can result in a decrease in demand for an author's work, reducing the value of their intellectual property. Piracy can also harm an author's reputation. Illegally distributed copies can be of poor quality, damaging the author's reputation as a writer. Additionally, pirated copies may be accompanied by negative reviews or comments, further undermining an author's reputation.

Steps to protect your IP

Fortunately, there are steps that self-published authors can take to protect their intellectual property and combat piracy.

1. Protect all of your content as early as possible

Don't just protect your most popular titles – ensure that *all* your books are protected. And don't wait until you find pirated copies of your content – be proactive and protect your content *before* you experience piracy. As unlicensed content is often well hidden, they are likely to have been on the internet for some time before you discover pirated copies. It's important that you get ahead of the issue.

2. Register your work with the appropriate authorities.

Registering your work with the appropriate authorities can help protect your IP rights. In the US, the Copyright Office offers copyright registration for authors (www.copyright.gov/registration). Similar services are offered by national government bodies including the Intellectual Property Office in the UK (www.gov.uk/government/organisations/intellectual-property-office). Registration can help establish evidence of ownership, making it easier to enforce IP rights in the event of piracy.

3. Monitor your work online.

Monitoring your work online can help you detect and respond to piracy. There are several tools available that can help you track your ebooks' distribution, such as the Digital Millennium Copyright Act (DMCA) Takedown Notice process. These tools can help you identify and respond to pirated copies of your work. For details, see some useful information on the Copyright Alliance's site: https://copyrightalliance.org/faqs/what-is-dmca-takedown-notice-process.

4. Understanding the nature of piracy.

Piracy in publishing is a complex and multi-faceted issue. There are many reasons for pirating content, many types of piracy, and a huge number of channels dedicated to distributing illegal ebook copies. The better you understand the contributing factors and the main sources of your pirated content, the more equipped you will be to tackle them.

5. Take legal action if necessary.

In the event of piracy, taking legal action may be necessary. This can involve sending cease-and-desist letters, filing copyright infringement lawsuits, or working with law enforcement to investigate and prosecute offenders. It is essential to seek legal advice before taking any legal action.

All of the above measures can help to reduce the piracy of your content. However, for a self-published or debut author, this can be quite daunting and take up a huge amount of time and carry a huge admin and cost burden. Anti-piracy vendors do exist that can help reduce this burden and can automate this process of trawling the internet, issuing takedown notices and getting infringing content removed at scale. Vendors should also be able to remove content from eBay, Amazon, Google and other 'grey' market sites.

Who are MUSO?

MUSO are a leading content protection solutions provider for the publishing industry. We work with all sizes of businesses across the publishing sector, from enterprise-size global publishers to thousands of independent and self-published authors. Our founding vision was to empower creative people to be more creative by taking away the time-consuming problem of piracy with best-in-class technology.

Our automated anti-piracy services are designed specifically for independent publishers and authors. Our affordable and flexible pricing enables the protection of an entire catalogue or a single book. We automatically monitor for illegal links and infringements and issues takedown notices, which remove piracy at scale across a wide range of piracy websites and search listings.

Law and copyright

Copyright Licensing Agency

The Copyright Licensing Agency (CLA) is a non-profit body established to help organisations to legally copy and share extracts from published works.

It is recognised by the government (www.gov.uk/copyright-licensing-agency-licence) as the collective licensing body for the reuse of text and images from books, journals and magazines. More information on collective licensing bodies can be found at: www.gov.uk/guidance/licensing-bodies-and-collective-management-organisations.

It licenses on behalf of its four members: ALCS (the Authors' Licensing and Collecting Society), PLS (Publishers' Licensing Services), DACS (The Design and Artists Copyright Society) and PICSEL (Picture Industry Collecting Society for Effective Licensing).

CLA's licences permit limited copying, including photocopying, scanning and emailing of articles and extracts from books, journals and magazines, as well as digital copying from electronic publications, online titles and websites. CLA issues its licences to schools, further and higher education, businesses and government bodies. The money collected is distributed to the copyright owners to ensure that they are fairly rewarded for the use of their intellectual property. It gives licensees protection against the risk of copyright infringement and includes an indemnity against legal action, offering a simple solution to copyright compliance.

Why was CLA established?

CLA was set up in 1983 by its founding members, the ALCS (see page 718) and PLS (see page 721). CLA represents creators and publishers by licensing the copying of their work and promoting the role and value of copyright. It also collects money for visual artists and has two other collective management organisation members who represent visual artists; DACS (Design and Artists Copyright Society; page 720) and PICSEL (Picture Industry Collecting Society for Effective Licensing) distribute money from CLA licence fees to visual artists such as illustrators and photographers. By championing copyright it is helping to sustain creativity and maintain the incentive to produce new work.

Further information

Copyright Licensing Agency Ltd
1 St Katharine's Way, London E1W 1UN
tel 020-7400 3100
email cla@cla.co.uk
website www.cla.co.uk

How CLA helps creators and users of copyright work

CLA provides content users with access to millions of titles worldwide. In return, CLA ensures that creators, artists, photographers and writers, along with publishers, are paid royalties for the copying, sharing and re-use of limited extracts of their published work.

Through this collective licensing system CLA provides users with the simplest and most cost-effective means of obtaining authorisation for the use of their work.

CLA has licences which enable digitisation of existing print material, enabling users to scan and electronically send extracts from print copyright works as well as copy digital electronic and online publications, including websites.

Who is licensed?

CLA offers licences to three principal sectors:
• education (schools, further and higher education);
• government (central departments, local authorities, public bodies); and
• business (businesses, industry and the professions).

The licences meet the specific needs of each sector and user groups within each sector. Depending upon the requirement, there are both blanket and transactional licences available. Every licence allows copying from most print and digital books, journals, magazines and periodicals published in the UK.

The international dimension

Many countries have established equivalents to CLA and the number of such agencies is set to grow. Nearly all these agencies, including CLA, are members of the International Federation of Reproduction Rights Organisations (IFRRO).

Through reciprocal arrangements covering 38 overseas territories, including the USA, Canada and most EU countries, CLA's licences allow copying from an expanding list of international publications. CLA receives monies from these territories for the copying of UK material abroad, passing it on to UK rights holders.

Distribution of licence fees

The fees collected from licensees are forwarded to ALCS, PLS, DACS and PISCEL for distribution to publishers, writers and visual artists. The allocation of fees is based on subscriptions, library holdings and detailed surveys of copying activity (see www.cla.co.uk/who-we-represent and read the 'Distribution Model Report'). CLA has collected and distributed over £1.5 billion as royalties to over 200,000 authors, publishers, and visual artists since 1983.

Copyright made simple

The CLA exists to simplify copyright for content users and copyright owners. They help their customers to legally access, copy and share published content while making sure copyright owners are paid royalties for the use of their work.

Their rights, licences and innovative digital services (including the Digital Content Store for Higher Education; and the Education Platform for UK schools (www.educationplatform.co.uk)) make it easy for content users to use and manage digitalised content and digital versions of books. By doing so they simplify access to the work of 117,000 authors, 25,000 visual artists and 3,500 publishers and play an important part in supporting the creative industries.

Law and copyright

Authors' Licensing and Collecting Society

ALCS is the rights management society for UK writers.

ALCS is the largest writers' organisation in the UK with a membership of over 117,000. Between September 2022 and March 2023, ALCS paid their eligible members over £39.8 million (net) in royalties. Once you've paid your £36 lifetime membership fee, whatever you've earned in secondary royalties is paid into your bank account during twice yearly distributions. You can be part of this organisation which is committed to ensuring that writers' intellectual and moral rights are fully respected and fairly rewarded. ALCS represents all types of writers and includes educational, research and academic authors drawn from the professions, scriptwriters, adapters, playwrights, poets, editors and freelance journalists, across the print and broadcast media.

Established in 1977, ALCS (a non-profit company) was set up in the wake of the campaign to establish a Public Lending Right (see page 655) to help writers protect and exploit their collective rights. The organisation now represents the interests of all UK writers and aims to ensure that they are fairly compensated for any works that are copied, broadcast or recorded.

Internationally recognised as a leading authority on copyright matters and authors' interests, ALCS is committed to fostering an awareness of intellectual property issues among the writing community. It maintains a close watching brief on all matters affecting copyright, both in the UK and internationally, and makes regular representations to the UK government and the European Union.

ALCS collects fees that are difficult, time-consuming or legally impossible for writers and their representatives to claim on an individual basis, money that is nonetheless due to them. To date, it has distributed over £600 million in secondary royalties to writers. Over the years, ALCS has developed highly specialised knowledge and sophisticated systems that can track writers and their works against any secondary use for which they are due payment. A network of international contacts and reciprocal agreements with foreign collecting societies also ensures that UK writers are compensated for any similar use overseas.

The primary sources of fees due to writers are secondary royalties from the following:

Membership

Authors' Licensing and Collecting Society Ltd
6th Floor, International House,
1 St Katharine's Way, London E1W 1UN
tel 020-7264 5700
email alcs@alcs.co.uk
website www.alcs.co.uk
Twitter @ALCS_UK
Chief Executive Barbara Hayes

Membership is open to all writers and successors to their estates at a one-off fee of £36. Members of the Society of Authors, the Writers' Guild of Great Britain, National Union of Journalists, Chartered Institute of Journalists and British Association of Journalists have free membership of ALCS. Operations are primarily funded through a commission levied on distributions and membership fees. The commission on funds generated for Ordinary members is currently 10%. Most writers will find that this, together with a number of other membership benefits, provides good value.

Photocopying and scanning

The single largest source of income, this is administered by the Copyright Licensing Agency (CLA; see page 716). Created in 1982 by ALCS and the Publishers' Licensing Services (PLS), CLA grants licences to users for copying books and serials. This includes schools, colleges, universities, central and local government departments, as well as the British Library, businesses and other institutions. Licence fees are based on the number of people who benefit and the number of copies made. The revenue from this is then split between the rights holders: authors, publishers and artists. Money due to authors is transferred to ALCS for distribution. ALCS also receives photocopying payments from foreign sources.

Foreign Public Lending Right

The Public Lending Right (PLR) system pays authors whose books are borrowed from public libraries. Through reciprocal agreements, ALCS members receive payment through a number of overseas Public Lending Right (PLR) schemes, currently from Germany, Belgium, the Netherlands, France, Austria, Estonia and Ireland. Please note that ALCS does not administer the UK Public Lending Right; this is managed directly by the UK PLR Office (see page 655).

Simultaneous cable retransmission

This involves the simultaneous showing of one country's television signals in another country, via a cable network. Cable companies pay a central collecting organisation a percentage of their subscription fees, which must be collectively administered. This sum is then divided by the rights holders. ALCS receives the writers' share for British programmes containing literary and dramatic material and distributes it to them.

Educational recording

ALCS, together with the main broadcasters and rights holders, set up the Educational Recording Agency (ERA) in 1989 to offer licences to educational establishments. ERA collects fees from the licensees and pays ALCS the amount due to writers for their literary works.

Other sources of income include a blank tape levy and small, miscellaneous literary rights.

Tracing authors

ALCS is dedicated to protecting and promoting authors' rights and enabling writers to maximise their income. It is committed to ensuring that royalties due to writers are efficiently collected and speedily distributed to them. One of its greatest challenges is finding some of the writers for whom it holds funds and ensuring that they claim their money.

Any published author or broadcast writer could have some funds held by ALCS for them. It may be a nominal sum or it could run into several thousand pounds. Either call or visit the ALCS website – see **Membership** box for contact details.

Law and copyright

DACS (Design and Artists Copyright Society)

Established by artists for artists, DACS is the UK's leading visual artists' rights management organisation.

Established by artists for artists, DACS is the flagship rights management organisation for visual artists in the UK. Passionate about transforming the financial landscape for visual artists, DACS acts as a trusted broker for 180,000 artists worldwide.

DACS is a leading voice in campaigning for artists' rights, championing their sustained and vital contribution to the creative economy. Through its services, DACS collects and distributes royalties to visual artists and their estates through Payback, Artist's Resale Right, Copyright Licensing and Artimage.

> **Contact details**
>
> **DACS**
> 33 Old Bethnal Green Road, London E2 6AA
> *tel* 020-7336 8811
> *email* info@dacs.org.uk
> *website* www.dacs.org.uk
> *Membership* Free to join

Payback

Every year, DACS pays artists for the use of artworks that are published in UK books, magazines and shown on TV. If their artwork has been published or broadcast on television, artists could be entitled to a share of millions in royalties. DACS' latest distribution saw the annual Payback scheme pay thousands of artists and their representatives a share of over £4.6 million.

Artist's Resale Right

The Artist's Resale Right is a royalty that is due when a work is resold by an art market professional for over €1,000 or the equivalent in pound sterling. DACS collects resale royalties and provide a quick, efficient payment service trusted by thousands of UK artists and estates. Artists can sign up as a member and DACS will monitor sales of artwork by auction houses, galleries and dealers and collect royalties on their behalf.

Copyright Licensing and Artimage

DACS has over 35 years of experience helping artists generate income through the licensed use of their work. Its dedicated team collaborate with artists and leading brands to facilitate partnerships that both parties can be proud of, while making sure artists' rights are always protected.

Artimage is DACS' curated image platform, which makes available over 30,000 hi-res, artist or estate-approved images to a wide range of clients. Through Artimage DACS offers a wraparound service: putting licences in place, collecting royalty fees, and releasing quality image file.

Additional Benefits for Members

DACS' Artist's Resale Right, Copyright licensing and Artimage members can all access DACS' Copyright Advice Service free of charge. This service includes advice and guidance about copyright matters and reviews of relevant sections in agreements. DACS also have a copyright enforcement service for licensing members which aims to protect artists' rights and artistic integrity by pursuing action when work is misused.

Publishers' Licensing Services

Publishers' Licensing Services' (PLS) mission is to provide efficient and effective copyright and licensing services to support publishers in providing access to their content.

PLS manages the interests of publishers in licensing the copying of extracts from books, journals, magazines and websites. PLS provides various other services, including PLSclear, which streamlines the process of seeking and managing permissions, and Access to Research, which enables free access in public libraries to academic journal articles.

A not-for-profit organisation, PLS has been serving the collective interests of publishers since 1981. It is owned and governed by four publisher trade associations.

Key activities
• Collective licensing

Collective licensing offers a simple and cost-effective solution for those who wish to copy from published materials without breaking the law, and for rights-holders where direct licensing is inefficient and not cost-effective.

PLS licenses the rights granted to it by publishers through two licensing organisations. Copyright Licensing Agency (CLA) licenses organisations in the education, public and business sectors, allowing them to copy extracts from a broad range of titles in return for a licence fee. CLA also has reciprocal agreements with equivalent organisations around the world. CLA is able, therefore, to collect licensing revenue for the use of UK publications abroad. PLS licenses some magazine publishers' rights to businesses and government through NLA media access. PLS distributes the resulting licensing revenue to publishers according to the usage data collected from users. PLS distributed over £38m of collective licensing revenue to publishers in 2022/23.

• Permissions

PLSclear is a free service that makes it quick and easy to request permission to reuse content from books, journals, magazines and websites. With hundreds of publishers using PLSclear to manage their permissions, increasing numbers of permissions-seekers are bookmarking PLSclear as their first port of call to reuse published content.

Find out more at PLSclear.com.

• Rights and Licensing Hub

The Rights and Licensing Hub is an initiative supported by PLS to share knowledge and encourage best practice in rights and licensing in all areas of the publishing industry and to raise awareness of the importance of good rights management. The resource offers publisher case studies, free online training courses, and careers advice for rights professionals.

Find out more at https://rightsandlicensing.co.uk.

Law and copyright

• Access to research

The Access to Research service provides free access to millions of academic articles in public libraries across the UK. 99% of UK local authorities are currently signed up, with approximately 3000 libraries using the service. Articles are provided directly from publishers' websites and are accessed from library computers via a discovery service called Summon, generously provided by ProQuest.

Access to Research is a unique collaboration between Publishers' Licensing Services, who administer the service, publishers, and UK public libraries.

Access to Research was launched in response to a key recommendation of the Finch Group, namely that major journal publishers should grant public libraries a licence to provide free access to their academic articles.

Find out more at www.accesstoresearch.org.uk

See also...
- *Authors' Licensing and Collecting Society*, page 718
- *Copyright Licensing Agency*, page 716
- *UK copyright law and publishing rights*, page 703

Money, tax and benefits
Managing your finances: a guide for writers

Chartered accountants Jonathan and Louise Ford of Writers Tax Limited set out a clear view of the various financial issues that a writer needs to understand and consider at each stage of their writing career, with helpful links and valuable advice.

In some ways the financial issues of being a writer are no different to pursuing any other occupation. You earn money for your skill, you deduct the costs you have incurred earning your money, and you pay tax on what's left. However, there are several factors that, in combination, make the situation of a writer unique; many writers have income from multiple sources, as well as overseas tax issues and matters concerning copyright.

We'll look at the different stages of a writer's career and the financial aspects you may need to consider as your career develops: 1) getting started – unpaid writing done for love not money; 2) paid writing often running alongside traditional employed income; 3) paid writing as main source of income; and 4) lifelong considerations.

Stage 1: getting started

When you're at an early stage of your writing career and not earning any money from it, there is little you need to do to stay compliant. However, there are still some important things you can consider.

Setting up a dormant limited company

If you are planning to write a book and you would like the royalty income of that book to be held in a limited company, then consider setting up a company even before you start writing. This will allow you to write the book on behalf of your company. If you wait to set the company up until the book is complete, and publishers are interested, then you would have to transfer the copyright of the book to the company at market value; this could cause issues in terms of valuing the copyright and can create a tax problem that could have been avoided. To decide whether this is right for you, you need to weigh up the cost and hassle of having a dormant limited company against the possible future advantages.

Creative averaging

There are a number of conditions you need to satisfy to be eligible for creative averaging; more details are available on HMRC Helpsheet HS234. One such condition is that you cannot use your first year of trading as part of any creative averaging calculation. Using the example given in the box, Theo would need to be submitting information to HMRC about his writing business from the 2019/20 tax year to be able to claim Creative averaging in 2021/22.

Loss relief against other income

It is possible for a sole trader to make a loss and to set that loss against other income. This can be beneficial for tax reasons. For example, if an author makes a loss of £5,000 and they also have *employed income* of £30,000, they could offset the £5,000 loss against their employed income so that they only have to pay tax on £25,000. To be able to offset losses against other income, you need to be able to show HMRC that the loss has been incurred on a commercial basis with a view to making

Creative averaging example

Theo earns nothing in the tax year 2020/21 while he is writing his novel.

In 2021/22 his book is published and he makes a profit of £30,000. Without creative averaging his tax bill in 2020/21 would be nothing, but in 2021/22 he would owe £3,486 income tax and £1,997.48 in National Insurance – a total of £5,483.48.

If he elects to use creative averaging, his £30,000 profit would be split across both tax years, giving him a total tax bill of £1,153.60 in 2020/21 and of £1,133.48 in 2021/22. By choosing to use creative averaging, Theo would have saved £3,194.40 over the two tax years.

a profit. A vague idea that one day you might write a book on Greece would not be sufficient evidence to get a tax deduction on the costs of your holiday.

Pre-trading expenses

If you haven't been reporting expenditure to HMRC as losses, then it is still possible to get tax relief for 'pre-trading expenditure'. The relief allows you to claim for expenditure incurred within seven years of starting to trade and, in effect, gives tax relief as if it was incurred on the first day of trading. The 'wholly and exclusive' rule will still apply, so it is important to be able to link the expenditure you are claiming to the income you are receiving. The stronger the link, the more likely HMRC are to accept it. In order to maximise any possible pre-trading expenditure claim, it is important to try and keep records and receipts *just in case* you might need them in the future.

Stage 2: paid writing as additional income

Most writers at this stage will still be running their writing business as a sole trader (or freelancer – there is no difference in terms of tax). Legally you don't need to do anything to set up as a sole trader. As soon as you start writing with a view to making a profit, you've become a sole trader. The tax system is very flexible. You can have a part-time employed job, be a partner in a bookshop and be a published author, all at the same time. Important things to consider at this stage are:

Registering with HMRC

If you earn more than £1,000 from self-employment you need to register as a sole trader with HMRC. You can do this at www.gov.uk/register-for-self-assessment/self-employed. You need to register by 5 October in your second tax year (tax years run from 6 April to 5 April).

For example, if you started on 20 November 2022 (tax year 2022/23) then you would need to register with HMRC by 5 October 2023 (tax year 2023/24). You would then get sent a tax return to complete by 31 January 2024 if filing online or 31 October 2023 if filing by paper.

Two or more writers working together may also need to consider if they are in partnership with each other. A partnership has to be registered in its own right with HMRC and submit a tax return each year.

Submitting a tax return

The tax system is called Self Assessment and this means that it is necessary for you to assess what rules and regulations apply to your tax position. There are a range of penalties that HMRC levy and, although it is possible in certain circumstances to appeal the penalties, it is well worth doing all you can to avoid them in the first place.

Keeping records

A self-employed person needs to keep records for at least 5 years from 31 January following the tax year they relate to. For example, if you have transactions in the tax year to 5 April 2023, you need to keep your records until 31 January 2029. You can keep records digitally or on paper. You should keep copies of bank statements, contracts, receipts for expenditure you are claiming for and any invoices you have raised. It is also worth keeping a note of any unusual non-business transactions. If you win £1,000 at the races or get a generous gift from Aunt Ethel, you want to be able to prove this wasn't undeclared income from writing.

It is usually a good idea to have a separate business bank account that you use just for your writing income. This will help to keep things organised and could give you a little more privacy, as your accountant – and possibly HMRC – don't have to look through all your private outgoings.

HMRC Self Assessment penalties

Late filing
Up to 3 months late £100, plus

after 3 months £10 per day for 90 days, plus

after 3 months penalties accrue at regular intervals based on 5% of the tax due or £300 – whichever is the greater.

You can estimate your penalty at www.gov.uk/estimate-self-assessment-penalties.

Late payment of tax
5% of tax due if not paid within 30 days with further 5% penalties every 6 months. Interest is also charged (currently 3%).

Incorrect returns
Penalties are charged for tax returns that HMRC consider to be incorrect. There is an appeals process. The penalties are all behaviour based and are as follows:
• Careless errors – 0% to 30% of the additional tax due.
• Deliberate errors – 20% to 70% of the additional tax due.
• Deliberate and concealed errors – 30% to 100% of the additional tax due.

Money, tax and benefits

Claiming expenses

A writer pays tax on their profit. Profit is income less allowable costs, often referred to as 'expenses'. Sometimes people talk about things being 'tax deductible', which means they can be deducted from your profit before calculating the tax bill, rather than being deducted from your tax bill. For example, if a higher-rate tax payer spends £100 on stationery, this is tax deductible and so it will reduce her profits by £100 and save income tax at 40%, i.e. £40.

Trading allowance

You can claim a £1,000 trading allowance against your self-employed income instead of claiming for expenses you have incurred. You cannot claim the trading allowance and expenses at the same time. Claiming the trading allowance would be suitable when the trading allowance is more than the expenses incurred. However, you can't use the trading allowance to turn your profit into a loss. There are also restrictions to prevent you from using the trading allowance if the income is received from a business controlled by you, or by someone connected to you.

What can you claim for?

The rule is that an expense must be 'wholly and exclusively' for the purpose of your business. Typical costs are:
• Accountancy
• Advertising
• Agent commission
• Bank charges
• Computing and IT
• Printing, postage and stationery
• Professional subscriptions
• Internet and telephone
• Software subscriptions
• Research
• Travel

Some costs may have an element of private use. In this case, HMRC will allow the cost to be apportioned provided you can justify the calculation. For example:
• Motor expenses – may be apportioned according to business use.
• Home as office – apportioned according to rooms and time spent in use.
Alternatively, you may be able to use HMRC Simplified Expenses. You can find more details at www.gov.uk/simpler-income-tax-simplified-expenses.

Cloud bookkeeping

Recent years have seen the development of relatively cheap, simple bookkeeping packages like Xero and Quickbooks. These allow you to link up your business bank account to your accounting records, so you can quickly and accurately keep track of your income and expenditure. They have the advantage of being regularly backed up, less prone to error, and easy to use. You can also store your receipts and paperwork digitally. As the UK moves towards a new system of reporting called Making Tax Digital from April 2026 (delayed from the original date of April 2023), it will become more important to be able to easily record and report your income.

Prizes and bursaries

There are many prizes and awards open to authors and other creatives, and entering competitions or seeking awards is a normal part of these professions and a good way for them to obtain extra income from their work. Such prizes are usually taxable. However, there are exceptions. When a prize is unsolicited, and awarded as a mark of honour, distinction or public esteem in recognition of outstanding achievement in a particular field, it won't be taxable. For example, if your publisher or agent enters you for a competition without your knowledge or consent, any prize money received should not be taxable.

Payments on account

For self-employed people the tax system can require payments on account of tax to be made every six months. Each payment on account is half of the previous year's tax bill.

For example: Jo's first year of trading is the tax year 2022/23; she owes tax of £4,000 for the 2022/23 tax year which is due for payment by 31 January 2024. Also, on 31 January 2024 she'll need to pay a payment on account of £2,000 towards her 2023/24 tax bill. She'll have to make a further payment of £2,000 in July 2024. Her actual tax bill for 2023/24 is £5,000. In January 2025 her payments will be:

	£
Tax due for tax year 2023/24	5,000
Less:	
Payment on account - paid 31 January 2024	2,000
Payment on account - paid 31 July 2024	2,000
Balance for 2023/24	1,000
Add:	
Payment on account for 2024/25 (50% of £5,000)	2,500
Total due 31 January 2025	3,500

When income is rising, payments on account can catch out the unwary, as each January there is both a shortfall of tax and a new, higher payment on account to pay. A sensible approach is to save for your tax throughout the year and to complete your tax return early in the tax year, so you have plenty of notice if the bill is higher than expected.

When income is falling (or ceasing) then it is possible to make a claim to HMRC to reduce payments on account so that you don't pay tax in advance that is more than necessary. If the payments on account you make are more than your tax bill, these will be offset against your next payments on account or refunded to you.

Setting up a limited company as a 'money box'

If you already have a paid job, then it's possible that your additional income from writing may take your total income into a higher tax band. If you don't need the money now, setting up a limited company could mean that the company pays corporation tax at a lower rate.

For example, Jamie earns £50,000 through his employment; he also receives £1,820 in Child Benefit in respect of his two children. He earns a further £10,000 in profit as a writer. He doesn't need to access the additional money now and is happy to leave it in his company. His tax liability as a sole trader can be compared with that of the limited company as follows:

Money, tax and benefits

Sole trader	£
Income tax on £10,000 @ 40%	4,000
High Income Child Benefit Tax Charge	1,820
Total due	5,820

Limited company	£
Corporation tax on £10,000 @ 19%	1,900
Total due	1,900

Although this is an extreme example, it shows that through using a limited company Jamie has saved £3,920 of tax on £10,000 of income. Once Jamie wants to take the money out of the company, it will be taxable on him personally, but he can control the amount paid so that it is covered by his personal allowance entirely or subject to a lower rate of tax than he is paying now. If Jamie's plans are to build up a savings buffer, so that one day he can take the plunge and become a full-time writer, then this could be of real benefit.

From 1 April 2023 the rate of corporation tax has increased. The first £50,000 of profit will continue to be taxed at 19%. Profits between £50,000 and £250,000 are taxed at a marginal rate of 26.5% and profits over £250,000 at 25%. There are also special rules that reduce the tax bands where more than one company is controlled by the same people.

Stage 3: writing as main source of income

Typically, a writer at this stage will either be self-employed or trade through a limited company. A limited company has to be 'incorporated' at Companies House and, once it is set up, it exists as a legal entity. It can enter into contracts, have a bank account, and exist without you. It is possible to trade both as a sole trader and through a limited company. It may even be the case that an author has some of their books taxed as a sole trader and other titles taxed within a limited company.

Issues on incorporation

If you do trade through a limited company, it is important to ensure that the underlying paperwork is correct. Here are some issues to bear in mind:

• For a company to receive copyright income, it must be legally entitled to the income. This can be achieved by ensuring the company exists before the book has been written and a service contract is in place between the director (i.e. the author) and the company.

IR35

IR35 was introduced in April 2000 to stop the practice of employees setting up a limited company (a 'personal service company') and invoicing their employer for their work rather than being paid as an employee. This practice led to a large tax saving for both the employer and the employee.

IR35 only applies to limited companies, so a writer who is trading as a sole trader can ignore it. From April 2021 both public entities and larger private companies will have to look at the status of people working through personal service companies and, if necessary, deduct tax and National Insurance.

For most writers operating through a personal service company, it will be clear that they are not working for anyone as disguised employment. For other writers the situation may be more uncertain. For example, a copywriter with their own company providing weekly content for a client who describes them as their 'Content Manager', pays them a regular salary, expects them to attend meetings on site and doesn't allow a substitute, may be caught by the IR35 rules.

The IR35 rules are complex and, if caught by the rules, your limited company has to pay out most of the money it receives as a salary to the employee – together with Employers National Insurance.

Specialist help should be sought if you think your company may be affected by IR35.

• It isn't sufficient to simply 'bank' any proceeds into your company. All contracts need to be properly drawn up in the company's name.

• If you simply give your copyright to your company, it can create a tax issue; HMRC will expect you to pay income tax on the market value of the gift and will also expect the company to pay tax on the income it receives. In effect, the same income could be taxed twice.

• It is possible to sell the copyright to the company. This results in a better tax position, as the company would be able to get some tax relief for the cost of the copyright, but it will require a valuation of the copyright which brings with it costs and some uncertainty.

• Once your company owns the copyright, royalty income is 'locked' into being paid to the company. If you wished to own the copyright personally, it would need to be transferred out of the company at a fair value. You may find you have a company for a much longer time than you first anticipate, because it may not be practical to close it down until the copyright has a negligible value.

VAT

VAT (Value Added Tax) is a tax that businesses are required to charge their customers for goods or services. A writer is no different from any other business and therefore must charge VAT when supplying writing services. The standard UK rate of VAT is currently 20%. VAT is a complicated subject and much of it is beyond the scope of this book. However, there are some key things a writer should be aware of.

A VAT-registered business usually submits a quarterly VAT return within one month and seven days of the end of the VAT quarter. Any VAT due is then paid by the same deadline. Being VAT-registered is not entirely bad news; a VAT-registered business has to charge VAT on their relevant services, but they can also claim back VAT on things they buy for their business. For example, in the VAT quarter ending 31 December 2022 a writer gets a publishing deal for £10,000 plus £2,000 of VAT. Their agent charges them £1,500 plus £300 VAT, and they buy a computer for writing for £500 plus £100 VAT. They would submit a VAT return to HMRC by 7 February 2023 and pay over £1,600, as follows:

	£
VAT charged	2,000
Less:	
VAT on agent's fees	300
VAT on computer	100
Paid to HMRC	1,600

Although this may make you feel worse off, especially when you are paying £1,600 to HMRC, you are in fact better off by £400 – this being the difference between the VAT you have been paid and the VAT you have paid out.

VAT registration threshold

A business needs to register for VAT when the level of sales exceeds the VAT threshold. The VAT threshold is currently £85,000 and it applies to the last 12 months. To know whether you need to register or not, you have to look back at your cumulative sales over the last 12 months and, if these exceed the VAT threshold, you must register. You are also required to register if you believe your sales in the next 30 days alone will be more than the VAT threshold – for example if you bag a big publishing deal.

Money, tax and benefits

Sole trader or limited company – the key differences

Sole trader	Limited company
Starting up	
Nothing legal required	Must be incorporated at Companies House
Closing down	
Nothing legal required	Must be formally struck off at Companies House
Legal protection	
None – you and the business are one and the same	Limited liability (but watch out for contracts that pass on liabilities to directors)
If you are sued, then all your assets are at stake	If the company is sued, then only the assets of the company are at stake
Tax on profits	
Income tax paid depending on total earnings from all sources in the year; rates may be 0%, 20%, 40% or 45% depending on income	Corporation tax paid; rates are between 19% and 26.5%
Tax on profits extracted	
Not applicable – you pay tax on profit whether extracted or not	Dividend tax due at rates of 0%, 8.75%, 33.75% or 39.35% depending on income
National Insurance	
Pay Class 2 National Insurance and Class 4 National Insurance earn over the limit	Only pay National Insurance on salaries paid to employees if they earn over the limit
Reporting	
Must complete an individual Self Assessment tax return each year	Must file accounts each year with Companies House
	Must submit a Confirmation Statement each year to Companies House
	Must file a corporation tax return each year with HMRC
	May have to run a payroll and report to HMRC
	Likely that director/shareholder will have to complete an individual Self Assessment tax return each year
Separate business bank account	
Advisable	Essential
VAT	
Can be VAT registered; it is a person that is VAT registered, not a business, which may have unintended consequences	Can be VAT registered
Creative averaging	
Can be used	Cannot be used
Why choose this one?	
Simple; cheap; you want to take all the money out of business when it's earned, not concerned about legal liability; provides legal liability protection	Possible to save tax if you don't require all the money or are able to take advantage of splitting income

Some writers will make an early 'protective' VAT registration, so that they know they are registered and don't have to worry about tripping over the VAT threshold. It is important to remember that the turnover figure is not necessarily the amount you receive. For example, a writer gets an advance of £10,000; their agent deducts 15% plus their VAT and so the writer only receives £8,200. The figure that counts towards the VAT threshold is £10,000. You do not need to include employment income in your turnover calculation or non-UK income (such as royalties from Amazon).

Finally, you need to include services you buy that are subject to the 'reverse charge' rules in your turnover calculation. For example, a writer who uses Facebook and Amazon advertising and spends, on average, more than £7,083 per month on this type of service would be required to register for VAT even if they are not making any sales themselves that are subject to VAT.

Voluntary registration
You can voluntarily register for VAT even if your sales are under the VAT registration threshold. The reason you may want to do this is to recover the VAT you are being charged – typically by your agent. For example, a writer gets a publishing deal for £25,000; their agent charges 15% commission plus VAT. If they are not VAT-registered, they'll lose the agent VAT of £750 but, if they are VAT-registered, they'd be able to recover this.

Being in the 'VAT club' will allow you to recover VAT on all your other business expenditure, such as computer costs and accountancy fees. Whether it is a good idea to register early depends on your circumstances. If you're not incurring much VAT, then it may not be worth the hassle.

What to include in your sales for VAT
You need to include all your UK sales and any foreign sales collected by your UK publisher. You can exclude any direct foreign sales (such as Amazon self-publishing or sales you or your agent have agreed with a foreign publisher). If you're a sole trader, you can exclude any employed income. But, if you are self-employed as something else too (e.g. you're both a plumber and a writer), you need to aggregate both sets of income. The VAT registration belongs to the *person*, not the *business*.

Claiming back VAT
When you first register for VAT, you can reclaim VAT on goods purchased up to four years prior to registration provided those goods are still held when registration takes place. VAT on services supplied in the six months prior to registration may also be reclaimed. To claim VAT you'll need a valid VAT receipt; a credit card receipt isn't enough, and a VAT inspector will disallow any expenditure that you can't produce a valid VAT receipt for – even if it's obvious that you would have paid VAT.

Not all expenditure has VAT charged on it:

Usually has VAT	Usually has no VAT
Agent commission	Trains, planes and taxis
Accountancy fees	Software subscriptions from overseas
Stationery	Postage
Computers and UK software	Entertainment
Internet and mobile phone	Insurance

Withholding tax and double taxation relief

Writers will often receive some or, in the case of an author selling via Amazon Kindle Direct Publishing (KDP), most of their income from an overseas source. Many foreign countries will charge a 'withholding tax' on such royalty payments, for example 30% in the case of the USA. Once withholding tax is paid, it is often not cost effective to try to recover it from the country in question, as doing so may require local professional advice and tax returns to be submitted to the country in question.

It is often possible to avoid any withholding tax being deducted in the first instance by completing the information required by the overseas publisher, so they don't have to apply withholding tax. Amazon KDP has an online tax interview to make it as easy as possible for you to comply. Other publishers in other countries will have to follow their own rules and will often ask for a Certificate of Residence to prove you are a UK tax payer. There are more details on applying for a Certificate of Residence at www.gov.uk/guidance/get-a-certificate-of-residence.

If you do suffer withholding tax, then it may be possible to use the foreign tax you have paid to offset against your tax liability on the same income when you complete your tax return. A word of warning though: you may not get back the full amount of foreign tax paid and relief is restricted to the amount of UK tax you would have to pay on the same income or the amount of foreign tax you would have paid had you complied with the requirements to avoid withholding tax.

Stage 4: Lifelong considerations

As a writer's career becomes more established, there are other financial considerations.

Pensions

State Pension

To qualify for the new State Pension, you need a minimum of 10 qualifying years and at least 35 qualifying years to receive the maximum payments. You can check your pension entitlement online at www.gov.uk/check-state-pension. If you have gaps in your pension contribution history, then you can consider making voluntary contributions.

Writers' Guild Pension Fund

For their members writing for TV, radio and film, WGGB (Writers' Guild of Great Britain) have negotiated agreements with the BBC, ITV and PACT so that pension contributions are made to the Writers' Guild Pension Fund. In return for the writer making a contribution to the fund, the production company will also make a contribution, in addition to the writer's fee. More details are available from WGGB (see page 498 for contact details).

Private pensions

If you have been employed, you may have an occupational pension from your employment in place. Most writers who have been self-employed will depend upon their own pension arrangements using 'defined contribution' schemes. Contributions to a private pension by an individual are made net of basic rate income tax. This means that a contribution of £80 actually means the amount invested is £100, with £20 being claimed by the pension company from the government. A higher-rate tax payer would save another £20 in income tax, making the cost of putting £100 into a pension just £60. There are rules regarding how much you can invest each year and many people will need professional advice as to what scheme they invest in.

Insurances

Being a self-employed writer does mean that you don't have the same safety net that many employees may have. It is sensible to think about how you and your family would manage if you died or, through injury or illness, were unable to continue to earn a living. There are insurance policies that are available to help.

- **Life insurance** can provide a lump sum or a monthly income for a period of time if you die.
- **Critical illness insurance** can provide a lump sum or a monthly income for a period of time if you are diagnosed with a critical illness.
- **Income protection insurance** can provide a monthly income if you are unable to work due to ill health.

Wills

Making a will is important for a number of reasons. Amongst other things, you can specify who inherits your assets, make tax efficient choices and provide instructions as to who looks after your minor children. A writer also needs to consider what happens with any copyright they hold as part of their estate. Copyright can last up to 70 years after death, so it may represent a valuable asset. You may also have particular instructions as to what happens to your personal papers and unpublished works. It is also worth thinking about what happens with digital assets such as blogs, social media accounts, online videos, and access to cloud storage services like Dropbox. A bit of forward planning may save a lot of trouble for the people dealing with your estate.

Jonathan Ford BSC FCA MSWW and **Louise Ford** BA FCA are the directors of Writers Tax Ltd, a firm of chartered accountants that specialises in helping authors, scriptwriters and other professional writers with their tax and accountancy needs, which they established in 2020. They both qualified as chartered accountants with Price Waterhouse in Liverpool. Jonathan worked at Grant Thornton and later as Financial Controller at Mersey TV before setting up his own company. See their website https://writers.tax for more information.

Further advice: useful websites

HMRC
www.gov.uk/government/organisations/hm-revenue-customs

Institute of Chartered Accountants in England and Wales
www.icaew.com

Institute of Chartered Accountants of Scotland
www.icas.com

These author associations offer support and advice on financial matters to their members.

National Union of Journalists
www.nuj.org.uk (see page 515)

Society of Authors
www2.societyofauthors.org (see page 495)

WGGB (Writers' Guild of Great Britain)
https://writersguild.org.uk (see page 498)

Accountancy and business software tools include:

Sage
www.sage.com/en-gb/cp/accounting

Quickbooks
https://quickbooks.intuit.com/uk

Xero
www.xero.com/uk

Money, tax and benefits

National Insurance contributions

Sarah Bradford sets out the facts about National Insurance, explaining the contributory principle that underlies it, the various classes of contribution payable by workers (both employed and self-employed), the related benefit entitlements and information on current rates and earnings thresholds.

Nature of National Insurance contributions

The payment of National Insurance contributions secures access to the state pension and to contributory benefits. This is the contributory principle of National Insurance. National Insurance contributions are payable by employed earners and their employers and also by self-employed earners. People who do not have any earnings or whose earnings are not sufficient to trigger a liability to pay National Insurance contributions can choose to pay National Insurance contributions voluntarily to maintain their contribution record.

If sufficient National Insurance contributions of the right type are paid or credited for a tax year, the year will be a qualifying year for National Insurance purposes. A person needs 35 qualifying years in order to receive the full state pension when they reach state pension age. Where a person has at least ten qualifying years, they will receive a reduced state pension.

Classes of National Insurance

There are various different classes of National Insurance contribution. The class (or classes) that you pay will depend on whether you are an employed earner, a self-employed earner, an employer or a voluntary contributor. Contributions may be earnings-related, payable on profits or payable at a flat rate, depending on the class.

The different classes of contribution are shown in the box below. Class 1, 2 and 4 contributions are only payable once earnings exceed certain thresholds and limits. The rates and thresholds applying to 2023/24 are set out in the box on page 740.

Classes of National Insurance

Nature of contribution	Payable by
Class 1 Earnings-related	Employed earners (primary Class 1 contributions)
	Employer (secondary Class 1 contributions)
Class 1A Earnings-related	Employer on taxable benefits in kind and taxable termination payments and sporting testimonials
Class 1B Earnings-related	Employer on items included within a PAYE Settlement Agreement and on the tax due under that agreement
Class 2 Flat rate	Self-employed earners
Class 3 Flat rate	Voluntary contributions
Class 3A Variable amount	Payable between 12 October 2015 and 5 April 2017 voluntarily by those who reached state pension age before 6 April 2016 to boost their state pension
Class 4 Profits-related	Self-employed earners

Contributions payable by writers and artists

As for other earners, the class of National Insurance payable by writers and artists depends on whether they are a self-employed earner or an employed earner. This is not something that they can choose – it will depend on the facts of the engagement. It is important that the employment status of the writer or artist is categorised correctly as this will affect not only what class (and therefore how) they pay, but also what benefits they are entitled to.

Categorisation – employed earner v self-employed earner

To ensure that writers and artists pay the correct class of National Insurance contributions, it is important they are correctly categorised. Employed earners will pay Class 1 National Insurance contributions, whereas self-employed earners will pay Class 2 and Class 4 contributions.

A worker's categorisation depends on the characteristics of the engagement. In many cases, it will be clear whether a worker is an employed earner or a self-employed earner. For example, a writer who is employed by a publishing firm and has a contract of employment will be an employed earner and will pay Class 1 National Insurance contributions on their earnings, whereas a freelance writer who undertakes commissions for a variety of people and is paid a fee for each commission will be a self-employed earner and will pay Class 2 and Class 4 contributions.

Characteristics of employment

The following characteristics apply to an engagement where the worker is an employed earner:
• they are required to work regularly unless they are unwell or on leave;
• they are expected to work a minimum number of hours a week and expect to be paid for the time that they work;
• a manager or supervisor is responsible for their workload and will say when a job should be finished or how it should be done;
• they must do the work themselves – they can't send someone else to do it instead;
• the business deducts tax and National Insurance from their pay;
• they are entitled to paid holiday;
• they are entitled to statutory payments;
• they can join the business's pensions scheme;
• they are subject to grievance and disciplinary procedures;
• the contract sets out the procedure applying in the event of redundancy;
• they work at the business premises or at a location specified by the business;
• they work for only that business or, if they have another job, it is completely separate;
• the offer letter and contract refer to the 'employee' and the 'employer'.

For example, a staff writer who is paid a salary and contracted to work 35 hours a week would be an employed earner.

Characteristics of self-employment

The following characteristics indicate that the writer or artist is a self-employed earner:
• they are in business for themselves and are responsible for the success or failure of the business and can make a profit or a loss;
• they decide what work they take on and where and how they do it;
• they can hire someone else to do the work;

• they are responsible for fixing unsatisfactory work in their own time;

• they agree a fixed price for a job – the fee is the same regardless of how long it takes them to do the work;

• they use their own money to buy any equipment needed and to cover the running costs of the business;

• they work for more than one client.

A writer who is commissioned to write specific articles for different publications and who works for a number of publishers, being paid a fee for each article, would be a self-employed earner.

Marginal cases

It will not always be clear whether a writer or artist is an employed earner or a self-employed earner. In this situation, it is necessary to look at the overall picture and see whether, on balance, the writer or artist is employed or self-employed. It should be noted that there is not one single definitive test, rather a question of seeing what characteristics of employment and what characteristics of self-employment are present.

In reaching a decision, the following factors need to be considered:

• The nature of the contract and the written terms – a contract for *services* indicates employment and a contract of *service* indicates self-employment.

• The nature of the engager's business and the nature of the job.

• Right of substitution – a right to send a substitute indicates self-employment.

• Mutuality of obligation – for a contract for services there must be minimum mutual obligations; the employer is obliged to offer work and the employee is obliged to do that work.

• Right of control – a high degree of control (on the part of the employer) over how and where the worker performs the work suggests employment.

• Provision of equipment – the provision by the worker of their own equipment suggests self-employment.

• Financial risk – a person who is self-employed bears a higher degree of financial risk than an employee.

• Opportunity to profit – a person who is self-employed has the opportunity to profit if they do the job quicker or under-budget.

• Length of engagement – while this is not a decisive factor, an open-ended contract is more likely to indicate employment.

• Part and parcel of the organisation – a worker who is seen as 'part and parcel' of the organisation is likely to be an employee.

• Entitlement to benefits – a worker who is entitled to employee-type benefits, such as a pension, is more likely to be an employee.

• Personal factors – a highly skilled worker may not need supervising but may still be an employee.

• Intention – while intention alone cannot determine status, it can be useful in forming an opinion on whether the worker is employed or self-employed.

Check Employment Status for Tax (CEST) tool

HMRC have produced a tool – the Check Employment Status for Tax (CEST) tool – which can be used to reach a decision on whether a writer or artist is employed or self-employed.

The tool asks a series of questions on the engagement, which must be answered honestly, in order to reach a decision. As long as the information provided is accurate and represents the reality of the engagement, HMRC will stand by the decision that is reached. The CEST tool is available on the government website at www.gov.uk/guidance/check-employment-status-for-tax.

Workers providing their services through a personal service company

Anti-avoidance rules apply where services are provided through a personal limited company or another intermediary to an end client. There are two sets of rules to consider – the off-payroll working rules and the IR35 rules. The rules that apply depend on the nature of the end client.

• Off-payroll working rules

The off-payroll working rules were introduced from 6 April 2017. They apply from the date when services were provided through an intermediary to a private sector body. The rules were extended from 6 April 2021, and from that date they also apply when the end client is a medium or large private sector organisation.

The end client must carry out a status determination to ascertain whether the worker would be an employee of the end client if they provided their services to them directly. Where this is the case, the end client must deduct tax and National Insurance from payments made to the worker's personal company (after adjusting the bill for VAT and the cost of any materials), and report this to HMRC. The worker receives credit for the tax and National Insurance on payment made to them by their personal limited company. They do not need to consider the IR35 rules because the off-payroll working rules apply instead.

• IR35

From 6 April 2021 onwards, the IR35 rules only apply where a worker provides their services to a small private sector organisation through an intermediary, such as a personal service company. The worker's personal service company must determine whether the worker would be an employee of the small private sector organisation if they provided their services directly. If the answer is 'yes' the IR35 rules apply. The intermediary must calculate the deemed employment payment at the end of the tax year, and account for tax and National Insurance on that payment to HMRC.

Employed earners – Class 1 National Insurance

Class 1 National Insurance is payable on the earnings of an employed earner. The employed earner pays primary contributions and the secondary contributor (which is generally the employer) pays secondary contributions. The payment of primary Class 1 National Insurance contributions by the employed earner is the mechanism by which the employed earner earns the right to the state pension and contributory benefits. Secondary Class 1 contributions, payable by the employer, do not earn benefit entitlement – they are akin to a tax on the employee's earnings.

Contributions are calculated by reference to earnings for the earnings period on a non-cumulative basis; no account is taken of earnings previously in the tax year, only those for the earnings period. The earnings period will normally correspond to the pay interval. However, directors have an annual earnings period, regardless of their actual pay frequency. The employer must deduct primary contributions from the employee's pay and pay them over to HMRC together with tax deducted under PAYE and the employer's secondary contributions.

• Primary Class 1 National Insurance

Primary Class 1 National Insurance contributions are payable by employees aged 16 and over until they reach state pension age (which depends on their date of birth). No contributions are payable until earnings reach the *lower earnings limit* (set at £123 per week, £533 per month, £6,396 per year for 2023/24). They are then payable at a notional zero rate until earnings reach the primary threshold. This is important as it secures the year as a qualifying year for National Insurance purposes (as long as earnings are paid above the lower earnings limit for each earnings period in the tax year). Where earnings are below the lower earnings limit, the year is not a qualifying year (although may become one if the worker receives National Insurance credits or pays voluntary contributions).

Contributions are payable on earnings above the *primary threshold* at the main primary rate of 12% until earnings reach the *upper earnings limit*. The primary threshold is set at £242 per week (£1,048 per month, £12,570 per year) for 2023/24 and is aligned with the personal allowance applying for tax purposes. The upper earnings limit is set at £967 per week, £4,189 per month and £50,270 per year for 2023/24. Contributions are payable at the additional primary rate of 2% on earnings above the upper earnings limit. For 2023/24 only, the main primary rate is set at 12% and the additional primary rate is set at 1%.

• Secondary Class 1 contributions

Secondary contributions are payable by the secondary contributor, which in most cases is the employed earner's employer. They are payable on the earnings of an employee aged 16 and above; unlike primary contributions, the secondary liability does not stop when the employed earner reaches state pension age.

Contributions are payable at the secondary rate of 13.8% on earnings in excess of the *secondary threshold* (set at £175 per week, £758 per month, £9,100 per year for 2023/24).

A higher secondary threshold applies to the earnings of employees under the age of 21 (the upper secondary threshold for under 21s), to those of apprentices under the age of 25 (the apprentice upper secondary threshold) and to armed forces veterans in the first year of their first civilian employment since leaving the armed forces. Each of these thresholds are aligned with the upper earnings limit for primary Class 1 purposes (set at £967 per week, £4,189 per month and £50,270 per year for 2023/24). A separate secondary threshold applies to the earnings of a new Freeport employee in the first 36 months of their employment with an employer with physical premises in a Freeport tax zone. This threshold is set at £481 per week, £2,083 per month and £25,000 per year. These thresholds only apply for secondary Class 1 purposes; the employee or apprentice pays the usual primary contributions.

Eligible employers can claim the Employment Allowance which is offset against their secondary Class 1 National Insurance liability. To qualify, their secondary Class 1 National Insurance liability must be less than £100,000 for 2022/23. Companies where the sole employee is also a director do not qualify for the allowance. The Employment Allowance is set at £5,000 for 2023/24 (capped at the employer's secondary Class 1 liability where this is lower).

• Earnings for Class 1 purposes

Class 1 contributions are calculated on the earnings for the earnings period. The definition of 'earnings' includes any remuneration or profits derived from the employment. This will include payments of wages and salary, but will also include other items such as statutory sick pay, statutory payments, and certain share-based remuneration. Comprehensive guidance on what to include in earnings for National Insurance purposes can be found in the HMRC guidance CWG2 *Employer further guide to PAYE and National Insurance contributions*. The 2023/24 edition is available on the government website at www.gov.uk/government/publications/cwg2-further-guide-to-paye-and-national-insurance-contributions.

• Class 1A National Insurance contributions

Class 1A National Insurance contributions are employer-only contributions payable on taxable benefits in kind and also on taxable termination payments in excess of the £30,000 tax-free threshold and taxable sporting testimonials in excess of the £100,000 tax-free threshold. They are payable at the Class 1A rate, which for 2023/24 is set at 13.8%.

• Class 1B National Insurance

Class 1B National Insurance contributions are employer-only contributions payable in place of the Class 1 or Class 1A liability that would otherwise arise on items included within a PAYE Settlement Agreement (PSA), and also on the tax due under the PSA. The Class 1B rate is aligned with the secondary Class 1 rate and is set at 13.8% for 2023/24.

Self-employed earners – Class 2 and Class 4 National Insurance contributions

Where a writer or artist is a self-employed earner, if their profits are high enough, they will pay Class 2 contributions, and also Class 4 contributions on their profits. Class 2 and Class 4 National Insurance contributions are payable via the Self Assessment system and must be paid by 31 January after the end of the tax year to which they relate (i.e. by 31 January 2025 for 2023/24 contributions).

• Class 2 National Insurance contributions

Self-employed earners are able to build up entitlement to the state pension and to certain contributory benefits through the payment of Class 2 National Insurance contributions. Contributions must be paid for the full year for the year to be a qualifying year.

Class 2 National Insurance contributions are flat-rate contributions payable by self-employed earners whose profits exceed the *lower profits threshold*, set at £12,570 for 2023/24. Class 2 National Insurance contributions are payable at the rate of £3.45 per week for 2023/24. Where a self-employed earner has profits between the small profits threshold (set at £6,725 for 2023/24) and the lower profits threshold, from 2022/23 onwards, they are treated as if they have paid Class 2 contributions at a zero rate. This provides them with a qualifying year for state pension purposes without actually having to pay Class 2 National Insurance contributions. A self-employed individual whose profits from self-employment are below the small profits threshold can pay Class 2 National Insurance contributions voluntarily. This is a cheap way to build up pension entitlement.

• Class 4 National Insurance contributions

Class 4 National Insurance contributions are payable by self-employed earners on their profits. They do not provide any benefit entitlement, and in effect are a tax on profits. No

National Insurance rates and thresholds 2023/24

National Insurance class	Rate or threshold
Class 1	
Lower earnings limit	£123 per week
	£533 per month
	£6,396 per year
Primary threshold	£242 per week
	£1,048 per week
	£12,570 per year
Secondary threshold	£175 per week
	£758 per month
	£9,100 per year
Upper earnings limit	£967 per week
	£4,189 per month
	£50,270 per year
Upper secondary threshold for under 21s	£967 per week
	£4,189 per month
	£50,270 per year
Apprentice upper secondary threshold	£967 per week
	£4,189 per month
	£50,270 per year
Veterans upper secondary threshold	£967 per week
	£4,189 per month
	£50,270 per year
Freeport upper secondary threshold	£481 per week
	£2,083 per month
	£25,000 per year
Primary (employee) contributions	
On earnings between the primary threshold and the upper earnings limit	12%
On earnings above the upper earnings limit	2%
Secondary (employer) contributions	
On earnings above the relevant secondary threshold	13.8%
Class 1A and Class 1B	
Contribution rate (employer only)	13.8%
Class 2	
Flat rate contribution	£3.45 per week
Small profits threshold	£6,725 a year
Lower profits threshold	£12,570 per year
Class 3	
Flat rate contribution	£17.45 per week
Class 4	
Lower profits limit	£12,570 a year
Upper profits limit	£50,270 a year
Main rate on earnings between the lower profits limit and the upper profits limit	9%
Additional rate on profits in excess of the upper profits limit	2%

contributions are payable on profits below the *lower profits threshold*, set at £12,570 for 2023/24. For 2023/24, Class 4 contributions are payable at the rate of 9% on profits between the lower profits limit and the *upper profits limit*, set at £50,270 for 2023/24, and on profits in excess of the upper profits limit, at the additional Class 4 rate of 2%.

Voluntary contributions – Class 3

A person can pay voluntary Class 3 contributions to plug gaps in their contributions record. Class 3 contributions are payable at the rate of £17.45 per week. Where a person has profits from self-employment below the *small profits threshold* (set at £6,725 for 2023/24), they can instead pay Class 2 contributions voluntarily; at £3.45 per week for 2023/24 this is a much cheaper option.

Maximum contributions

Where a person has more than one job, or is both employed and self-employed, there is a cap on the contributions that are payable for the year. The calculations are complex.

National Insurance credits

National Insurance credits are available in certain circumstances where people are unable to work or because they are ill. There are two types of credit. Class 1 credits count towards state pension and contributory benefits, while Class 3 credits only count towards the state pension. Further detail on National Insurance credits can be found on the government website at www.gov.uk/national-insurance-credits.

Benefit entitlement

The payment of National Insurance contributions (and the award of National Insurance credits) earns entitlement to the state pension and certain contributory benefits. Only the payment of primary Class 1, Class 2 and Class 3 contributions confer benefit entitlement. Benefit entitlement depends on the class of contribution paid.

Benefit entitlement	
Class of contributions	**Benefit entitlement**
Primary Class 1 (employed earner)	State Pension, contribution-based Jobseeker's Allowance, contribution-based Employment and Support Allowance, Maternity Allowance and Bereavement Payment, Bereavement Allowance, Widowed Parent's Allowance, Bereavement Support Payment.
Class 2 (self-employed earners)	State Pension, contribution-based Employment and Support Allowance, Maternity Allowance and Bereavement Allowance.
Class 3 (voluntary contributions)	State Pension and Bereavement Payment, Bereavement Allowance, Widowed Parent's Allowance.

Sarah Bradford BA (Hons), FCA CTA (Fellow) is the director of WriteTax Ltd and the author of *National Insurance Contributions 2022/23* (and earlier editions) published by Bloomsbury Professional. She writes widely on tax and National Insurance contributions.

Money, tax and benefits

Subject indexes
Magazines by subject area

These lists provide a broad classification and pointer to possible markets. Contacts for *Magazines UK and Ireland* start on page 39.

Magazines aimed at men

Marketing and retailing

Medicine and nursing

Military

Motor transport and cycling

Music and recording

Natural history

Publishers of fiction (UK)

Contacts for *Book publishers UK and Ireland* start on page 124.

Graphic/cartoons

Historical

Horror

LGBTQI+

Subject indexes

Short stories

Teen/YA

Translation/international

War

Publishers of non-fiction (UK)

Contacts for *Book publishers UK and Ireland* start on page 124.

Contacts for *Book publishers UK and Ireland* start on page 124.

Children's book publishers (UK)

Listings for *Book publishers UK and Ireland* start on page 124.

Publishers of plays (UK)

Playwrights are reminded that it is unusual for a publisher of trade editions of plays to publish plays which have not had at least reasonably successful, usually professional, productions on stage first. See listings starting on page 124 for contacts.

Publishers of poetry (UK)

See listings starting on page 124 for contacts.

Literary agents for children's books

The following literary agents will consider work suitable for children's books, from authors and/or illustrators of children's books. Listings start on page 422. See also *Art agents and commercial art studios* on page 481.

Literary agents for television, film, radio and theatre

Listings for these and other literary agents start on page 422.

Subject indexes

Prizes and awards by subject area

This index gives the major subject area of each entry in the main listing which begins on page 543.

BAME

Biography

Children

Drama – theatre, TV and radio

Essays

Fiction

Grants, bursaries and fellowships

Illustration

Journalism

General index

Key topics and terms that appear in the articles within this *Yearbook* are listed here.

Listings index

All companies, public and commercial organisations, societies, festivals and prize-giving bodies, that have a listing in the *Yearbook* are included in this index.